Derivatives Law
and Regulation

Derivatives Law and Regulation

THIRD EDITION

Gary E. Kalbaugh
SPECIAL PROFESSOR OF LAW
MAURICE A. DEANE SCHOOL OF LAW
HOFSTRA UNIVERSITY

CAROLINA ACADEMIC PRESS
Durham, North Carolina

ISBN   978-1-5310-2110-8
eISBN   978-1-5310-2111-5
LCCN   2021943370

Carolina Academic Press
700 Kent Street
Durham, NC 27701
(919) 489-7486
www.cap-press.com

Printed in the United States of America

To George Edward Kalbaugh
for teaching me anything is possible

Contents

Table of Principal Cases

Preface to the Third Edition

In 2010, the Dodd-Frank Act initiated an era of frenzied implementation of an immense and comprehensive swap and security-based swap regulatory regime. The last rules required by this statute were finalized in 2020. The Securities and Exchange Commission's regulatory regime for security-based swaps is slated to be operative in November 2021. After ten long years, the era of implementing the Dodd-Frank Act has passed. What fruit it bears may well be determined by the students of this generation.

Much has changed in the years following the last edition, requiring most chapters to be significantly overhauled. The finalization of the Dodd-Frank regulations means a new capital regime for swap dealers and a wholistic rule framework for security-based swaps. The Commodity Futures Trading Commission worked feverishly on efforts to simplify elements of its regulatory framework. This resulted in changes to longstanding rules and new rules to replace assortments of no-action letters and interpretations. Meanwhile, in 2020, a record number of enforcement actions were initiated, often involving novel questions such as those arising in the nascent virtual currency market.

The author during this time has only grown more indebted to his students. Their insights, perspectives, and participation in the world of ideas has been a joy. He also remains indebted to his friend, Richard A. Miller, for Richard's unflagging confidence in him.

A tradition is developing where this author recognizes the immense sacrifices of his wife, Kristin P. Kalbaugh, who weeks ago delivered their sixth child. There is no way to adequately acknowledge her sacrifices; there is no day that passes without gratitude for her. Sacrifice also has fallen on the author's children whose patience is more than anyone is entitled to expect from such little ones.

Preface to the Second Edition

Derivatives Law and Regulation was first published in 2014. Since then, the Commodity Futures Trading Commission has finalized most of the swaps regulatory framework required by the Dodd-Frank Act and a meaningful corpus of swaps regulatory caselaw has developed. Both of these occurrences are reflected in substantial updates to chapters 7 through 10.

Whereas, in 2014 the Securities and Exchange Commission's regulatory regime for security-based swaps had not begun to take shape, many of the rules are now finalized. A new chapter, chapter 16, has been added. It exclusively focuses on the regulatory framework for security-based swaps.

Had the author heeded his students' recommendation to buy virtual currency in 2011, this edition may not have been written. Due to the rapid growth of virtual currency markets, chapter 12 now includes a section on virtual currency, along with new sections on retail foreign exchange dealers and leverage transaction merchants.

Major legal developments have impacted nearly every facet of derivatives law, spanning from bankruptcy to enforcement to the extent to which commodities and securities laws have extraterritorial effect. These developments have been faithfully included.

Once more, the author is indebted to the generosity and friendship of Richard A. Miller. He has been the recipient of a collection of Richard's materials that Richard carefully accumulated and curated during the decades of his influential derivatives law practice. Many are no longer available through ordinary channels. Their availability has been a boon to the author.

Gratitude is also due to Rita M. Molesworth with whom the author has the pleasure of teaching a class at Columbia Law School. Rita's input and comments on chapter 6 have proven invaluable. Dennis A. Klejna was generous enough to comment on much of the book and Professor Lawrence A. Baxter kindly provided helpful general comments.

In the first edition of *Derivatives Law and Regulation*, the author thanked his wife, Kristin P. Kalbaugh, for her support, especially through the birth of their son. The author now has four children and, to be able to accomplish this edition in such a busy environment, testifies to Kristin's sacrifices, capabilities, and grace.

Preface to the First Edition

In keeping with common practice in the field of derivatives law, all references herein to the Commodity Exchange Act are to the named statute, not to the United States Code. The sole exception is for cases and materials which cite to the United States Code. These citations have been retained. For the reader's convenience, a Commodity Exchange Act to United States Code conversion table is appended.

Throughout, some footnotes and citations have been omitted from cases and materials.

Part of the regulatory framework for derivatives is the regulation of security-based swaps by the Securities and Exchange Commission. Though the jurisdiction of the Securities and Exchange Commission over these products is discussed in Chapter 3, at the time of writing the implementation of this regulatory framework by the SEC had still not occurred and, therefore, it is not otherwise covered herein.

Though there are many rewards for writing this book (thanking those who contributed to its production is just one), my friendship with Richard A. Miller counts foremost among them. Richard, both through his establishment of the Futures and Derivatives Law Report and his continuing encouragement and contributions to the derivatives bar, has selflessly inspired and driven the academic study of derivatives law like no other practitioner.

Richard offered his insight into every chapter, dedicating innumerable weekends to reviewing manuscript chapters (as he termed it "Coffee with Kalbaugh"). His influence on this work through both his detailed comments on drafts and the intellectual companionship he provided cannot be overstated. The author offers his warmest gratitude to Richard, without whom this work would not be possible.

The research and comments of Ariel Hazzard were superb. The foreign exchange chapter simply would not have come into being without the research and insight of Alexander F. L. Sand. Kristen Palermo has been an asset with every facet of the production of this work.

The author would also like to thank Professor Amy R. Stein for her efforts to teach him how to teach the law, Frederic M. Mauhs for his early encouragement and Marcy S. Cohen for her ongoing enthusiastic support. The chapter on manipulation owes a great debt to David Yeres. William T. Bagley and Robert G. Pickel, in addition to being preeminent contributors to the field of derivatives law in their own right, each showed great generosity with their time in relation to this book.

Thanks are also due to the author's parents, G. Edward Kalbaugh and Maria Christine Kalbaugh for their understanding and encouragement.

For well more than a year the author's wife, Kristin Kalbaugh, has patiently supported this project, even through the birth of their son. It has tested the boundaries of tolerance and the author thanks Kristin for being such a supremely dedicated spouse and mother.

Acknowledgments

The author wishes to thank the following who kindly granted permission to reprint excerpts from the following materials:

Sean M. Flanagan, *The Rise of a Trade Association: Group Interactions Within the International Swaps and Derivatives Association*, 6 Harvard Negotiation Law Review 211 (Spring 2001). Reprinted with permission of the Harvard Negotiation Law Review via Copyright Clearance Center. The copyright in the Harvard Negotiation Law Review is held by the President and Fellows of Harvard College and the copyright in the article is held by the author.

Gary E. Kalbaugh, *The Erratic Journey of U.S. Commodity Options Regulation*, 33 no. 10, Futures and Derivatives Law Report 1 (Nov. 2013). Reprinted with permission of Thomson Reuters.

Gary E. Kalbaugh, *FERC v. Barclays Bank PLC Shines a Light on CFTC and FERC Jurisdiction*, 36 no. 11 Futures and Derivatives Law Report 1 (Dec. 2016). Reprinted with permission of Thomson Reuters.

Gary E. Kalbaugh and Alexander F. L. Sand, *Cutting Back: Revisions to Dodd-Frank Derivatives Rules*, 35 no. 5 Futures and Derivatives Law Report 1 (June 2015). Reprinted with permission of Thomson Reuters.

Gary E. Kalbaugh and Richard A. Miller, *Master Agreements for OTC Derivatives* in Commercial Contracts: Strategies for Drafting and Negotiation (Vladimir R. Rossman & Morton Moskin, eds., 2d ed., Aspen Publishers 2014). Reprinted with permission of Aspen Publishers.

Lynn A. Stout, *Uncertainty, Dangerous Optimism, and Speculation: An Inquiry Into Some Limits of Democratic Governance*, 97 Cornell Law Review 1177 (2012). Reprinted with permission of Cornell University.

Derivatives Law
and Regulation

Chapter 1

An Introduction to Derivatives

A. Introduction and Scope

1. Why Study Derivatives Law?

a. Massive Size of the Market

The derivatives market is one of the largest in the world. To give a sense of how large, we can benchmark it to a familiar financial market, the equities market.

The market value of all the world's outstanding equity securities has been estimated at year-end 2020 to equal $95 trillion.[1] This is, of course, in the context of an especially volatile year — at the onset of the COVID-19 pandemic, the global equity market value dropped below $65 trillion.

The global derivatives market is comprised of derivatives traded on exchanges and derivatives traded by private agreement off of exchanges. The derivatives traded off exchanges are commonly known as "off-exchange" or "over-the-counter" derivatives. When we evaluate the size of the global derivatives market, we need to account for both methods of trading derivatives.

The estimated market value of the global off-exchange derivatives market is more than $15 trillion.[2] This reduces to gross credit exposures — amounts that parties owe one another in the over-the-counter derivatives market — of $3.2 trillion. The so-called notional value, a term we discuss in section B.3.e below, was $607 trillion — multiples of the size of the world's equity securities market. However, as will be seen, derivatives notional is not a good proxy for market value.

If we added exchange-traded derivatives into the mix, the total market value of derivatives would be much higher. Unfortunately, we run into a problem of comparing like with like because the market value of exchange-traded derivatives is not tracked. It is a massive market, though. To give a sense of how massive, more than 30 billion trades occur on exchange-traded derivatives markets in a typical year.[3]

---

1. Mark DeCambre, *Value of the World-Wide Stock Market Soars to Record $95 Trillion, Despite Resurgence of Coronavirus*, https://www.marketwatch.com/story/value-of-the-world-wide-stock-market-soars-to-record-95-trillion-despite-resurgence-of-coronavirus-11605196894 (Nov. 12, 2020).

2. Bank for International Settlements, *OTC Derivatives Statistics at End-June 2020*, https://www.bis.org/publ/otc_hy2011.htm (Nov. 9, 2020).

3. Will Acworth, *2019 Market Data — Derivatives Volume Grows BRIC by BRIC*, https://www.fia.org/marketvoice/articles/2019-market-data-derivatives-volume-grows-bric-bric (March 3, 2020).

For more discussion on the challenges of comparing the derivatives markets to other financial markets, see the inset titled "Apples and Oranges?" at the end of subsection b below.

b. The Regulatory Regime

The sheer size of the derivatives market is reason enough to study derivatives law and regulation. Another reason is the existence of a legal and regulatory framework that is comprehensive, complex, and unique to derivatives. Background in the law and regulation applying to other financial markets, such as securities markets, may be helpful in comparing regulatory approaches. The regimes, however, are completely distinct in both underlying theory and application. A foundational understanding of derivatives law is necessary for any lawyer with a financial practice.

A century ago, a portion of the exchange-traded futures market was federally regulated, and the exchange-traded options market and the remainder of the exchange-traded futures market were federally regulated just under fifty years ago. The off-exchange derivatives market, on the other hand, only began to be comprehensively regulated a decade ago. This new regulatory regime surpasses any federal financial regulatory initiative since the 1930s. The newness of this regime means that today's derivatives lawyers will have a special opportunity to shape this field of law.

Apples and Oranges?

Comparing the derivatives market and other financial markets, such as the equities market, by size is difficult. With the equities market, we use total market capital to indicate the size of the market. This represents the value of all the equity shares currently available for trading on all relevant exchanges.

Derivatives cannot usefully be quantified this way. With equities markets, outright ownership of a share is bought or sold and, therefore, calculating the value is as easy as knowing the price of the share. The value of derivatives, on the other hand, comes indirectly from the value of an underlying asset. Also, derivatives are inherently "leveraged." We discuss both concepts below.

The best approximation to market capitalization is "gross market value" which can be defined as "the sum of the absolute replacement value of all outstanding [derivatives] contracts."[a] Currently, this is only available for over-the-counter derivatives.

The notional is nearly $100 trillion. Bank for International Settlements, *Exchange-Traded Derivatives Statistics*, Table D1, http://www.bis.org/statistics/extderiv.htm (updated March 1, 2021).

As if this comparative exercise were not complicated enough already, comparing over-the-counter derivatives to exchange-traded derivatives poses its own challenges. Whereas, in the former, offsetting positions are cancelled, in the latter, they frequently are maintained.[b]

[a] Rangarajan K. Sundaram, *Derivatives in Financial Markets Development* 5 n. 3 (International Growth Center Working Paper Sept. 2012).

[b] Lori Aldinger and John W. Labuszewski, *Derivatives Market Landscape* 2 (CME Group, Fall 2013), available at https://www.cmegroup.com/education/files/derivatives-market-landscape.pdf.

2. Scope of This Chapter

Already we have introduced some key concepts. This chapter will provide the foundation needed to understand these key concepts, particularly:

- What is a derivative?
- The difference between an "off-exchange" and "exchange-traded" derivative
- Types of derivatives
- Key terminology
- Who uses or trades derivatives and why?

For those of you with finance backgrounds, this chapter will be a review of concepts of which you are likely already familiar. For everyone else, this will provide the economic foundation needed to understand the application of the related laws and regulations discussed in the following chapters.

3. Scope of This Book

The topic of this book is the law and regulation applicable to participants in the derivatives market. Throughout this book, the terms "exchange-traded derivatives" and "off-exchange derivatives," also known as "over-the-counter derivatives" or "OTC derivatives," are used. They refer to the method of trading the same fundamental instrument, a derivative.

You probably are already familiar with two terms associated with exchange-traded derivatives: futures and options. The exchange-traded derivatives market is the market on which futures and options (other than security options which are traded on securities markets and are outside the scope of this book) are traded. The venue on which these futures and options are traded is commonly referred to as a futures exchange. Prominent historical examples are the Chicago Board of Trade, Chicago Mercantile Exchange, and New York Mercantile Exchange. As it happens, after a decade of consolidation at the start of the millennium, all three have been consolidated under a single Chicago Mercantile Exchange umbrella. Exchange-traded derivatives have historically been subject to a comprehensive federal regulatory regime. The historical development of this regime is the subject of chapter 2 and the actual regulatory regime is the exclusive focus of chapters 5 and 6.

Chapter 3 outlines the statutory basis for jurisdictional and regulatory authority over derivatives. Chapter 4 focuses on the applicable regulators, especially the primary derivatives regulator, the Commodity Futures Trading Commission.

Chapter 7 examines the regulatory regime applicable to derivatives investment and trading vehicles. For example, the regulations applying to a hedge fund trading derivatives. Chapter 8 focuses on the regulatory regime for advisors on derivatives trading.

As we saw in section A.1.a above, the market for off-exchange derivatives — i.e., derivatives traded by private bilateral contractual arrangement without use of an exchange or other centralized facility — is estimated to be multiples larger than the exchange-traded market. Calculated by notional amount, it is about six times larger.[4] It is also commonly referred to as the uncleared "swaps" market.

This book examines the law and regulation of both "exchange-traded" and "off-exchange" swaps. Each are big markets in themselves. It is important to be mindful that the regulatory scheme for the off-exchange swap market, although different in some respects, has been heavily influenced by the longstanding regulatory regime for exchange-traded futures. This relatively new regulatory regime is the exclusive focus of chapters 9 through 12.

In this vein, it is important throughout this book to keep in mind the concept of "regulatory convergence." One way to define "regulatory convergence" is "the process by which the rules, regulations, or political institutions governing economic activity . . . become more similar."[5] The regulation of off-exchange derivatives represents regulatory convergence in that the manner of regulation is influenced by the existing regulatory regime applying to exchange-traded derivatives. Because on-exchange and off-exchange derivatives markets engage in similar economic activities, we should ask ourselves, was regulatory convergence inevitable? And to what extent will regulatory convergence continue? Relatedly, some believe that prevailing regulation incentivizes an ever-greater proportion of derivatives activity in the exchange-traded markets rather than the off-exchange markets. This is known as "futurization" and is discussed in chapter 10, section D.1.

For a subset of swaps known as "security-based swaps," there is a distinct regulatory regime. It is extraordinarily new — formally, it is only expected to be fully operative in November 2021. This regulatory regime is the responsibility of the Securities

---

4. *See* Bank for International Settlements, *Exchange-Traded Derivatives Statistics*, Table D1, http://www.bis.org/statistics/extderiv.htm (updated March 1, 2021); Bank for International Settlements, *OTC Derivatives Statistics at End-June 2020*, https://www.bis.org/publ/otc_hy2011.htm (November 9, 2020).

5. *See* Henry Laurence, *Symposium: The Rule of Law in the Era of Globalization, Spawning the SEC*, 6 Ind. J. Global Leg. Stud. 647, 649 (1999).

and Exchange Commission. In many ways, its regulation is similar to that of the off-exchange swaps market described in chapters 9 through 12. Chapter 13 evaluates the security-based swaps regulatory regime in the context of the swaps regulatory regime.

Much of the foreign currency market is not a derivatives market. Yet, the Commodity Futures Trading Commission has regulatory authority over large swaths of it. We examine this, and the Commodity Futures Trading Commission's similar authority over some types of leveraged, margined, or financed retail commodities in chapter 14. In this chapter, we also explore the Commodity Futures Trading Commission's authority with respect to a distinct type of agreement known as a "leverage contract." Finally, we assess the regulatory status of the growing virtual currency market.

Chapters 15 and 16 have similar focuses from different perspectives, enforcement of derivatives laws and regulations. Chapter 15 looks at the enforcement by the Department of Justice and Commodity Futures Trading Commission of the relevant anti-fraud and anti-manipulation laws and regulations. Private parties also have limited authority to bring causes of actions for violation of derivatives law and regulations. These private means of enforcing breaches of the relevant laws and regulations are the subject of chapter 16.

The derivatives market is a global one. There has been much global coordination to ensure similar national off-exchange derivatives regulatory frameworks. Moreover, with all derivatives, in international contexts, the question arises as to the cross-border application of U.S. derivatives law and regulation. These are the subjects of chapter 17.

The subject of chapter 18 is bankruptcy. As a practical matter, the federal bankruptcy regime applies differently in the context of derivatives. Additionally, several provisions of the Bankruptcy Code are specific to derivatives.

B. What Are Derivatives?

1. Definitions

There are three ways we can define and categorize derivatives. First, as we do in this chapter, we can use their economic definition, i.e., define and categorize derivatives by their economic characteristics and function.

Second, it is possible to define derivatives by the usage of industry vernacular. In other words, the terminology that a trader in the instruments or other market participant would use. This usage, of more practical benefit to a market participant, is outside of the scope of this book.[6]

---

6. However, *see, inter alia*, CME Group, *A Trader's Guide to Futures*, https://www.cmegroup .com/education/files/a-traders-guide-to-futures.pdf; Jack D. Schwager and Mark Etzkorn, A

Third, we can use the legal definition. In chapter 3, we will see how, through the definitions of "swap" and "security-based swap," derivatives have been defined for regulatory purposes.[7] It is important to remember that how derivatives are legally defined in many cases differs from the economic definition we will now examine.

2. Basic Economic Definition

Economically, a derivative is defined as an instrument the value of which is derived from the value of an underlying asset. What is meant by that? Let us suppose that I buy an apple from you. The price I pay for the apple should, in ordinary circumstances, be consistent with the market value of an apple at that moment. Let us suppose that is $1. The value of the apple is not derived from the value of something else. Since the value of a derivative is derived from the value of an underlying asset, this is not a derivative. In technical terms, it is known as a "spot" market transaction because it is a market transaction in a physical commodity, the apple.

On the other hand, suppose you and I agree that I will buy an apple from you in three months' time for the $1 market price of an apple today. If at three months' time the price of an apple skyrockets to $3, how would we value your obligation to sell me an apple for $1? Since the apple is worth $3, but I only must pay $1 for it, the agreement we have is worth $2 to me. Theoretically, when you deliver me the apple for the agreed upon $1, I could sell it to someone else for $3, netting me $2. Or, if I were going to buy and eat an apple anyway, I have saved $2 since I only need to pay $1 for something for which I would otherwise have to pay $3. The $2 value of the contract is not the value of an apple, it is *derived from* the value of an apple. Therefore, economically, this is a derivative transaction. In technical terms, the agreement today to buy an apple in two months' time is known as a "forward" contract.

In this example, where the contract has $2 of positive value to me, I am known as "in-the-money." Your position, unfortunately, would the "out-of-the-money" position. If a contract has no positive or negative value to either party, it is known as "at-the-money." Using the example of the apple transaction once more, suppose the price of an apple, instead of increasing to $3 in three months' time, had remained at $1. Then neither party would stand to gain or lose from the transaction.[8] I would be required to pay you $1 for an apple, not more or less than I could buy an apple on the spot market, and you would be paid $1 for an apple, the same amount that you could sell the apple on the spot market. Both of us are "at-the-money" in that scenario.

Complete Guide to the Futures Market (2d ed., Wiley Trading 2017); or Howard Corb, *Interest Rate Swaps and Other Derivatives* (Columbia Business School 2012).

　7. *See also* Commodity Exchange Act § 1a(47) and Securities Exchange Act § 3(a)(68).

　8. Technically, inflation would make the $1 paid in two months' time worth less than $1 paid today. For the sake of simplicity, we are ignoring that for now.

What if instead of agreeing that I will buy the apple from you in three months' time, I pay you 25 cents for the right to buy the apple from you for $1? (In the previous example, I had the obligation to buy the apple from you.) Perhaps I want to be sure that there will be an apple available for me in three months' time in case I find myself desiring an apple or perhaps I do not want to risk the price of the apple skyrocketing in the spot market? If the price of an apple in the spot market in three months' time has increased to $3, then the contract is similarly worth $2 (because I could buy the apple from you for $1 and either resell it for $3 or buy and eat the apple and save the two extra dollars I would have spent) minus the 25 cents I paid you for the right. The $1.75 value of this contract is not the value of an apple. It is *derived from* the value of an apple. This, then, also is a derivative. In technical terms, this right, but not obligation, to buy the apple at a pre-agree price in two months' time is known as an "option" contract.

Based on similar reasoning, transactions such as a stock option, commodity futures contract, or a foreign exchange swap each fall within the economic definition of derivative. What we will find is that all derivatives can be formed from three basic building blocks: options, futures/forwards,[9] and swaps. Once you understand the economic profile of these three building blocks you will be equipped with a means to understand the economic fundamentals of any derivatives transaction.

For each of these subcategories, an illustrative hypothetical will be provided, using the facts of the Ocean Waves Baking Company. The examples used all involve the acquisition of wheat, a commodity fundamental to making the Ocean Waves Baking Company's products. Though we will be using wheat, an agricultural commodity, as an example, later in this chapter we will examine derivatives that reference interest rates, foreign exchange, credit defaults, and equity prices. The sky is literally the limit with respect to what can be the subject of a derivative transaction.

Building Blocks

Without exception, every derivative in existence, no matter how seemingly complicated, is ultimately comprised of one or more of three economic building blocks: (1) options; (2) futures/forwards; and (3) swaps. And, as we will see below in subsection 3.e, swaps are effectively a series of futures/forwards. Knowing every derivative is ultimately reducible to these building blocks makes it much easier to understand derivatives. When newly encountering a derivative product, an excellent starting point is evaluating it in light of these building blocks.

---

9. While economically the distinction between futures and forwards is similar, in chapter 3, section B we look at the critical legal distinction.

3. Futures, Options, and Swaps Defined

a. Future or Forward Contract: An Example

A futures contract is a contract to buy or sell an asset at a pre-agreed price and future date. Typically, when traded off-exchange in relation to a physical, tangible good such as the apple we used in subsection 2 above, a future is termed a "forward." For the regulatory distinction between futures and forwards, see chapter 3, section B. For the purposes of this section, both futures and forwards will be referred to as futures since their fundamental economic profiles are identical.

> *Futures Example*: The Ocean Waves Baking Company's management is certain that it will need a specified amount of wheat by year's end. It could wait a year to make its purchase but, of course, the price of wheat could be a lot higher. (It could be a lot lower, too.) A possible strategy using a derivative would be for the Ocean Waves Baking Company to agree now to buy in a year's time a specified amount of wheat from a counterparty at a fixed price.
>
> *Pro*: In a year's time, if it finds out it does need wheat and the market price of wheat has gone higher, it will have locked in a lower price than the available market price.
>
> *Con*: If, in a year's time, it finds out it does not need wheat or the price of wheat is lower than the price it locked-in, it still is required to perform on the contract and buy the specified amount of wheat for the agreed price.

Let us add numbers to the above facts. Suppose that the Ocean Waves Baking Company has agreed to purchase 1,000 bushels[10] of wheat for $10,000 (the market value of 1,000 bushels of wheat at the time the contract is entered into) in one year's time. At the time the contract is entered into it is, therefore, "at-the-money."

Should wheat increase in price in the interim, the Ocean Waves Baking Company will be "in-the-money" because it will be able to purchase the wheat for $10,000 in one year's time instead of the prevailing higher market price. On the other hand, should the price of wheat decrease in the interim, the Ocean Waves Baking Company will be "out-of-the-money" because it will be locked in to purchase the wheat for $10,000 in one year's time even though it could buy the same amount of wheat for less at the prevailing market price.

---

10. A "bushel" is the main unit of measurement used to calculate grain. Originally, bushel was a volume measurement representing eight gallons. Now, for each grain market, there is a standardized weight reflecting an assumption as to the amount of grain that would fill an eight-gallon vessel. In the case of wheat, it is equal to sixty pounds.

To summarize:

Commodity	Today's Price/1,000 Bushels	Contract Settlement Date	Value of Contract at Settlement Date
Wheat	$10,000	1 Year	Unknown, depends on spot price at the time

The value of the wheat futures contract to the Ocean Waves Baking Company is illustrated graphically in figure 1.1.

If the spot price were, a year later, to have dropped to $8,000 for 1,000 bushels of wheat, the Ocean Waves Baking Company will still be locked in by the futures contract to purchase 1,000 bushels of wheat for $10,000 ("Point A" in figure 1.1).

On the other hand, if the spot price for 1,000 bushels of wheat, a year later, had increased to $12,000, the Ocean Waves Baking Company will benefit because the futures contract will require that it pay only $10,000 for 1,000 bushels of wheat that would otherwise cost $12,000 in the spot market ("Point B" in figure 1.1).

Figure 1.1 Value of Wheat Futures Contract

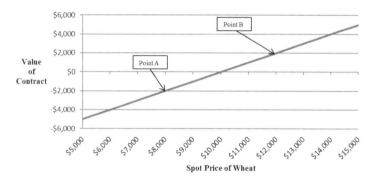

b. Future or Forward Contract: How It Trades

We go through the mechanics of how trades are executed in greater detail in chapters 5 and 6. In the meantime, it will be of benefit to offer a preliminary overview of how a trade like this would operate.

A common practice might be for the Ocean Waves Baking Company to seek access to a futures exchange. It would normally do so through an intermediary, a commodities broker.[11]

Futures exchanges have contracts available for trading in a variety of assets. This is what the parties actually trade — a contract obligating one party to buy and the

---

11. As we will see in chapter 6, the technical name for a commodities broker is, depending on its exact role, either an introducing broker or a futures commission merchant.

other party to sell an asset or its cash value. As we learned in the apple example in section B.2 above the parties do not buy or sell the asset itself.

These contracts specify: (1) the asset (including, if applicable, the minimum quality of the asset); (2) the quantity of the asset; (3) the price to be paid for the asset; and (4) the settlement date when the contract is to be performed. At this point, we have assumed that the wheat will be required to be physically delivered. That is true of most agricultural futures contracts but later we will find that futures contracts can be "cash-settled," a term discussed in detail in subsection c below. For now, since this wheat contract will be physically delivered, the contract will also specify where it must be delivered.

It is important to note that these contract terms are not negotiated. They are all pre-defined in the futures contract traded on the exchange.

There is one term that fluctuates: the price of the contract itself. The price to buy or sell a futures contract may go up and down. For example, if a futures contract obligates the purchaser to buy 1,000 bushels of wheat for $10/bushel and the spot market price is $12/bushel, the futures contract will likely have positive value since it requires the purchase of 1,000 bushels of wheat in the future for $10/bushel when it is currently worth $12/bushel. Yes, the value of wheat could drop below $10/bushel and then the obligation to buy the wheat for $10/bushel will likely have negative value.

The commodities broker places a "bid" on the futures exchange, to buy the relevant wheat contract at a specific price to any seller willing to sell at the bid price. Parties wishing to sell the same contract place an "offer" (sometimes the term "ask" is used) on the futures exchange, usually also through a commodities broker, to sell the relevant wheat contract at a specific price to any buyer willing to buy at the offer price. If the commodities broker's bid price is matched by a seller's offer price, the parties have entered into a trade.

Instead of having direct obligations to each other, though, the buyer and the seller each have a direct obligation to the clearinghouse of the futures exchange. We discuss clearinghouses in detail in chapter 5, section D.

Of course, the actual practice of trading futures and other derivatives involves complexities reflecting the uncertainties in the world. Political events, natural disasters, and societal changes all can impact derivatives markets. An example of this was in April 2020 when a build-up of oil in Cushing, Oklahoma due to reduced global oil demand resulted in scarcity of storage. This was a problem because the West Texas Intermediate Light Sweet Crude Oil futures contract traded on the New York Mercantile Exchange required buyers to accept physical delivery at Cushing, Oklahoma. Due to the storage scarcity and lack of global demand, any oil delivered to that location would have to pay high storage costs for a potentially long time. This made it economically optimal to *pay* parties to receive delivery of the oil. The Commodity Futures Trading Commission issued a report seeking to explain why this event occurred.

CFTC, *Interim Staff Report: Trading in NYMEX WTI Crude Oil Futures Contract Leading up to, on, and Around April 20, 2020*

https://www.cftc.gov/media/5296/InterimStaffReportNYMEX_WTICrudeOil
/download (Nov. 23, 2020)

[S]taff of the U.S. Commodity Futures Trading Commission . . . issue this interim report (the "Report")[12] to provide background, context, and observations regarding the trading activity leading up to, on, and around April 20, 2020 ("April 20"), for the West Texas Intermediate ("WTI") Light Sweet Crude Oil futures contract (the "WTI Contract"), traded on the New York Mercantile Exchange ("NYMEX").[13]

This Report focuses on the WTI Contract's May 2020 expiration (the "May Contract"), which settled on April 20 at a price of – $37.63 per barrel. The May Contract's April 20 negative settlement price was the first time the WTI Contract traded at a negative price since being listed for trading 37 years ago. . . .

The negative settlement price of the WTI Contract occurred on the penultimate day of trading for the May Contract, which expired on April 21. For the WTI Contract May expiry, market participants who were not intending to make or take delivery of the crude oil underlying the futures contract were expected to close out of their positions by April 21 (the May Contract's expiration date and last day of trading). As described in detail below, the process of reducing the amount of the total number of futures contracts that remain open without an offsetting position or fulfilled by delivery, or "open interest" ("OI"),[14] through trading or netting is known as "compression." The level of compression for the May Contract on April 20, and the level of trading to achieve compression, was historically high, resulting in OI in the May Contract reducing markedly throughout the day. . . .

Fundamental factors that coincided in and around the May Contract's trading and settlement at negative prices on April 20 . . . include the following:

---

12. [N. 1] . . . [T]his Report is based upon the information available to such staff at the time this Report was written, and any different, changed, or omitted facts or circumstances may require additional analysis and result in different observations. This report is interim as a result of the above and the proximity to the events. "Interim" does not suggest that any further reports will or will not be forthcoming. . . .

13. [N. 2] . . . The trading day for WTI Contracts (and many other CME contracts) is nearly 24 hours, Sunday through Friday. The April 20 trading session actually began at 6:00 p.m. Eastern Time ("ET") on Sunday, April 19. Unless otherwise indicated, reference herein to trading on April 20 refers to the trading session beginning at 6:00 p.m. ET Sunday, April 19, ending at 2:30 p.m. ET Monday, April 20. . . .

14. [N. 5] OI refers to the total number of futures contracts long or short in a delivery month or market that has been entered into and not yet liquidated by an offsetting transaction or fulfilled by delivery. OI is also referred to as "open contracts" or "open commitments." See CFTC Futures Glossary, https://www.cftc.gov/LearnAndProtect/AdvisoriesAndArticles/CFTCGlossary/index.htm#O.

- An already oversupplied global crude oil market was hit with an unprecedented reduction in demand caused by the novel coronavirus pandemic ("COVID-19"). Uncertainty over both the magnitude and duration of that loss of demand increased volatility to historic levels. . . . [C]ertain actions in response to the decline in demand by the Organization of Petroleum Exporting Countries ("OPEC"), along with 10 non-OPEC oil-exporting nations, colloquially referred to as "OPEC Plus," impacted market volatility.

- Concerns were growing in the marketplace about whether OPEC Plus or other global producers could respond quickly to the reduction in demand. These concerns raised questions about the availability of storage for excess production, and were particularly pressing at the Cushing, Oklahoma, oil terminal, which serves as the delivery point for the physically-settled WTI Contract.

- By March 2020, the working storage available at the Cushing facility was near capacity. The scarcity in capacity raised procedural concerns related to the mechanics of pipeline transportation and storage at the Cushing terminal, both of which are required to support the physical delivery process for the WTI Contract. Procedural concerns about the physical delivery process included questions about whether the WTI Contract would trade at negative prices. In or about late March and early April, NYMEX and some industry participants began preparing for the prospect of negative WTI crude oil prices, changing technology and pricing models to account for this contingency. . . . [W]hile prices in futures contracts of other commodities (such as natural gas and interest rates) traded at negative levels at various points during the last decade, the WTI Contract had not.

In addition to the fundamental factors summarized above, a number of technical factors related to market structure coincided with, and may have influenced, the April 20 negative settlement price. . . .

- Generally, in the weeks prior to the expiration of the May Contract, and specifically at the start of the April 20 trading session, OI in the May Contract was much higher than usual.

- The majority of traders holding positions in the May Contract had traded out of their positions prior to April 20. OI fell from 634,727 contracts at the start of the month of April to 108,593 contracts at the start of the April 20 trading session.

- OI was high entering the April 20 trading session, but the number of reportable traders holding positions at expiry on April 21 was consistent with prior contract months.

- Limit order book activity related to multiple products show a decrease in liquidity in the May Contract starting well before April 20.

- During the April 20 trading session, exchange-based control mechanisms (such as dynamic circuit breakers ("DCBs") designed to impose pauses in the event of rapid or large price moves) were triggered. Nevertheless, the speed and magnitude of the price moves observed on April 20 in the May Contract (particularly between 1:00 p.m. ET and the end-of-day settlement at 2:30 p.m. ET) were exceptional.

In summary, a variety of factors coincided leading up to, on, and around April 20, when WTI Contract prices fell from $17.73 per barrel at the beginning of the trading session to finally settle at −$37.63 per barrel. An oversupplied global oil market faced an unprecedented reduction in demand due to COVID-19 slowdowns and shutdowns, and the uncertainty over supply, demand, and storage capacity coincided with price volatility in the WTI Contract observed at historic levels that day. . . .

Why did this specifically affect the West Texas Intermediate Light Sweet Crude Oil futures contract and not other oil futures contracts? One reason is because the contract required physical delivery at one location. Not only did that location already have a scarcity of storage space, it also is landlocked and had no efficient alternative means of offloading oil quickly and in large amounts.

c. Options Contract: An Example

An option is a contract whereby one party grants to the other a right, but not an obligation, to take a course of action. To put it another way, in what is known as a "call" option, one of the parties agrees to sell an asset *if* the other party exercises (i.e., uses) its "option" to buy the asset. This is known as a "call" option because the party with the option to buy the asset has the right to "call" the asset to itself.

Or, in what is known as a "put" option, one of the parties agrees to buy an asset *if* the other party exercises its "option" to sell the asset. This is known as a "put" option because the party with the option to sell the asset has the right to "put" the asset to the other party.

Option contracts are distinct from futures contract because, in a futures contract, both the buyer and the seller of the asset are bound to perform. An option only binds one of the parties, leaving the other party with the *option* of requiring performance of the purchase and sale.

> *Option Example*: The Ocean Waves Baking Company is unsure of how much wheat will be needed in a year's time. It could wait a year and then see what its needs are, but its management is concerned that the price of wheat could be a lot higher. A viable alternative strategy using a derivative would be for the Ocean Waves Baking Company to buy a call option giving them the right, but not the obligation, to purchase a specified amount of wheat in a year's time. In other words, to buy the right to "call" the specified amount of wheat to it if it has the need, at a price specified by the option today.
>
> In this example, we will assume that the option is "cash-settled" meaning that, instead of physically delivering the commodity upon exercise of the option by the Ocean Waves Baking Company, the option seller will provide the Ocean Waves Baking Company the difference between the market price

of the wheat at the time the option is exercised and the price for the wheat locked in by the option.

Pro: In a year's time, if the Ocean Waves Baking Company finds out it does need wheat and the price of wheat is high, it will have locked in a lower price for that wheat than the market price. It can exercise the option. Were it a physically-settled option, the Ocean Waves Baking Company would "call" the wheat to it and, in return, pay the agreed upon price to the seller (this is known as the "strike" price). Since, in this example, the option is cash-settled, the Ocean Waves Baking Company gets paid the difference between the market value of the specified amount of wheat and the price for that wheat that was agreed in the option.

Con: If, in a year's time, the Ocean Waves Baking Company finds out that it does not need wheat, or the price of wheat is lower than the price locked-in by the option, it paid for an option it will not use.

To add numbers to the above facts, suppose that the Ocean Waves Baking Company has purchased a call option, i.e., an option to buy, 1,000 bushels of wheat for $10,000 in one year's time and has paid $1,000 for the option, an amount known as the "premium." Assuming that, at the time the Ocean Waves Baking Company purchases the option, the market or "spot price" of wheat is $10 a bushel and the option provides the Ocean Waves Baking Company the right to "purchase" the wheat for $10 a bushel (known as the "strike price") in a year's time, the option can be said to have been purchased "at-the-money," i.e., with the spot price equal to the strike price. It still would be a loss to the Ocean Waves Baking Company because of the $1,000 premium paid for the unused option.

If the strike price were less than the spot price, it would be said to be "out-of-the-money" and, if it were more than the spot price, it would be said to be "in-the-money."

To summarize:

Commodity	Today's Price/1,000 Bushels	Price for Option on 1,000 Bushels	Maturity of Option	Option Strike Price/1,000 Bushels
Wheat	*$10,000*	*$1,000*	*1 Year*	*$10,000*

The value of the wheat option to the Ocean Waves Baking Company is illustrated graphically in figure 1.2.

If the spot price of 1,000 bushels of wheat is below $10,000 in a year's time, the option will expire worthless and the Ocean Waves Baking Company will have wasted the $1,000 premium paid for the option. A spot price between $10,000 and $11,000 will result in the option having value, but not value in excess of the $1,000 premium paid by the Ocean Waves Baking Company for the option.

For example, if the spot price were $10,500 ("Point A" in figure 1.2), the Ocean Waves Baking Company would exercise its option. Since it is "cash-settled," its counterparty would not deliver the wheat. Instead, its counterparty would pay the Ocean Waves Baking Company the current market price for the wheat, $10,500, minus the strike price fixed in the option, $10,000. The $500 paid to the Ocean Waves Baking Company is still less than the premium of $1,000 which the Ocean Waves Baking Company paid for the option.

Should the spot price for 1,000 bushels of wheat exceed $11,000, the option will have value in excess of the $1,000 premium paid by the Ocean Waves Baking Company. In other words, the Ocean Waves Baking Company will be glad it purchased the option. For example, if the spot price for 1,000 bushels of wheat is $13,000 ("Point B" in figure 1.2), the Ocean Waves Baking Company's counterparty, upon exercise of the option by the Ocean Waves Baking Company, will be required to pay the current market price for 1,000 bushels of wheat, $13,000, minus the $10,000 strike price locked in by the option. The $3,000 paid to the Ocean Waves Baking Company is well in excess of the $1,000 premium it paid for the option.

We need to add one more concept. Every option has an expiration date reflecting the last day on which the option can be exercised. With "European" options that is also the *only* date on which the option can be exercised. "American" options permit exercise on any day from the trade date until the expiration date. "Bermudan" options allow exercise on specified days during the period from the trade date until the expiration date.

Why Bermudan? Because Bermuda is geographically between the United States and Europe and the option style is a hybrid of the "American" and "European" styles of options.

Figure 1.2 Value of Wheat Option

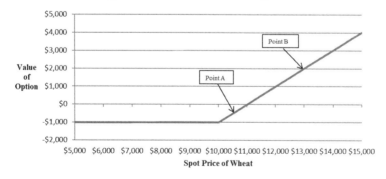

Spot Price of Wheat

Options Vocabulary

The world of options has its own vocabulary. Some of the main terms are defined below. For additional terms, see the glossary.

American Option: An option that can be exercised by the holder of the option at any time during the term of the option.

Bermudan Option: An option that can only be exercised by the holder at specified points during the term of the option.

Call Option: An option agreement where the holder of the option has the right, but not the obligation, to buy an asset in the future from a seller for a pre-agreed amount.

European Option: An option that can be exercised only by the holder at the maturity of the option.

Exercise: To use the option to require that an asset be sold to the option holder (for a call option) or bought from an option holder (for a put option).

Expiration: The last date on which an option can be exercised.

Option: An agreement whereby one party grants to the other a right, but not an obligation, to take a course of action.

Premium: The amount paid for the option by the buyer of the option to the seller of the option.

Put Option: An option agreement where the holder of the option has the right, but not the obligation, to sell an asset in the future to a buyer for a pre-agreed amount.

Strike Price: The price, if an option is exercised, that will be paid for the underlying asset.

d. Option Contract: How It Trades

Many futures exchanges trade options and at least one exclusively trades options.[15] As with the futures trade in subsections a and b above, a common practice might be for the Ocean Waves Baking Company to seek access to a futures exchange. It would normally do so through an intermediary, a commodities broker.

The options contract it would trade would specify: (1) the asset (including, if applicable for physical assets, the minimum quality of the asset); (2) whether it is to be physically-settled or cash-settled; (3) whether the option is a call option giving the holder the right to buy an asset or a put option giving the holder a right to sell an asset; (4) the quantity of the asset; (5) the "strike" price for the asset if the option is exercised; (6) the date on which the right to exercise the option expires (i.e., the expiration date); and (7) whether the option is "American," "European," or "Bermudan."

As with futures contracts, it is important to note that none of these contract terms are negotiated. They are all pre-defined in the options contract traded on the exchange.

---

15. The North American Derivatives Exchange.

There is one term that fluctuates: the premium to be paid for the option. The price to buy or sell an option contract may go up and down. For example, if an options contract is a call option providing the holder of the option the right to buy 1,000 bushels of wheat for $10/bushel and the spot market price of wheat is $12/bushel, the call option contract will clearly have positive value to the owner since it provides the owner a right to call 1,000 bushels of wheat at a price of $10/bushel when it is currently actually worth $12/bushel. However, even if wheat drops below $10/bushel the now "out-of-the-money" call option still has value unless and until it expires. It has value because there is always the possibility that, before the option expires, the price of wheat will go up again above the $10/bushel strike price.

As with futures, the commodities broker places a "bid" on the exchange, to buy the relevant wheat option for a specific premium. Parties wishing to sell the same option place an "offer" on the exchange (usually also through a commodities broker) to sell the relevant wheat contract for a specific premium. If the commodities broker's bid premium is matched by a seller's offer premium, the parties have entered into a trade.

Because the option in this example is traded on an exchange, just as with futures, the buyer and the seller each have a direct obligation to the clearinghouse of the futures exchange instead of having direct obligations to each other. We discuss clearinghouses in detail in chapter 5, section D.

The Pricing of Options

How to value an option has been historically challenging with the most significant advances only occurring relative recently in the 1970s. There are two primary mathematical models for pricing options. A derivatives lawyer is not expected to know how either of these models operate. If the below does not make sense to you — do not worry, just skip this!

The first model is the Black-Scholes or Black-Scholes-Merton model.[a] It is based on assuming that the price of the asset underlying the option will take a "random walk" which can be described mathematically as a "lognormal distribution." In practice, this model is very complicated for anyone without a mathematical background to understand.

The other model, which we will look at here is known as the "binomial model."[b] Understanding the basics of this model will help with understanding the parameters influencing the Black-Scholes model.

The binomial model assumes the price of the asset underlying the option is, in the future, as likely to increase as it is to decrease. This is known as "risk neutral" valuation. The size of its potential increases or decreases over, for example, a day, are forecast based on its "volatility." Volatility is a statistically regularized percentage likelihood of a price decrease or increase of an asset, usually based on historical data.

The binomial model creates a "tree" with, at the first time increment, one branch assuming an increase in price at the applicable volatility and one assuming a decrease in price at the applicable volatility. At the next time increment two more branches are created from each of the original two again assuming a price increase and a price decrease equal to the volatility percentage. The illustration below assumes a 20% volatility over each period and a strike price for a call option of $45.

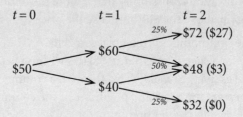

t here means "time" — it is whatever increment our model is calculating. It could be one day, one month, one hour, etc. We have assumed 20% volatility, i.e., 20% expected price increase or decrease in the asset over our selected time increment just because it makes the math easy. In real life, at least daily time increments would be used and 20% would be a very high rate of expected daily volatility.

Our model assumes that, at $t = 0$, if the price of the underlying asset is $50, the option is worth $8.25. That is because at $t = 2$ there is a 25% chance it will be worth $27 ($72 asset value – $45 strike price of option), a 50% chance it will be worth $3, and a 25% change it will be worth nothing (it would be irrational to exercise the option to buy something for $45 that is worth only $32). To put it another way: $27 × 25% + $3 × 50% + $0 + 25% = $8.25.[c]

[a] *See* Fischer Black & Myron Scholes, *The Pricing of Options and Corporate Liabilities*, 81 J. of Political Economy 637-659 (May-June 1973) and Robert C. Merton, *Theory of Rational Option Pricing*, 4 Bell Journal of Management Science 141-183 (Spring 1973). Merton and Scholes received the 1997 Nobel Prize in Economic Sciences for this work (Black had died in 1995). *See* Royal Swedish Academy of Sciences, *Press Release*, https://www.nobelprize.org /prizes/economic-sciences/1997/press-release/ (Oct. 14, 1997).

[b] Its modern incarnation stems from a 1979 paper. *See* John C. Cox, Stephen A. Ross & Mark Rubinstein, *Option Pricing: A Simplified Approach*, 7 J. of Financial Economics 229 (1979).

[c] In reality, it would be a little less than $8.25, because we would typically use a model that discounts this amount to account for inflation.

e. Swaps Contract: An Example

A swap is a contract to exchange assets periodically using predetermined pricing mechanisms. In other words, with a swap two parties agree to periodically (usually monthly) exchange the economic equivalent of one asset for the economic equivalent of another asset. They decide on the initiation of the swap how each asset will be valued on each of the periodic exchange dates.

Historically, swaps have not traded on exchanges. Instead, parties have entered into swaps by negotiating the terms directly. Since 2000, however, some swaps have traded on trading platforms or exchanges and we will see, in chapter 10, sections B.2 and C.3, that, since the passage of the Dodd-Frank Wall Street Reform and Consumer Protection Act (the "Dodd-Frank Act"),[16] some swaps are required to be traded on a trading facility or exchange and to be cleared by a clearinghouse. The examples below will assume that the swap in question is traded off-exchange, also known as being traded "over-the-counter."

Swaps are typically (though not exclusively) cash-settled, which means that, even if the swap references a physical asset, instead of delivering that physical asset the cash equivalent of the physical asset is delivered.

Swap Example: The Ocean Waves Baking Company anticipates needing 1,000 bushels of wheat each month for the next twenty-four months. It could make its purchase in the spot market each month as needed but, of course, the price of wheat is likely to vary monthly. If the price of wheat goes down, it would be a windfall to the Ocean Waves Baking Company. If, on the other hand, the price of wheat increases significantly in a particular month, it could result in financial trouble for the Ocean Waves Baking Company. To have certainty, therefore, it might agree with a counterparty to, each month for twenty-four months, pay the counterparty an agreed price (let us assume $10/bushel) multiplied by 1,000 bushels (this multiplier, 1,000 bushels in this case, is known as the "notional amount"). In return, the counterparty will pay the Ocean Waves Baking Company whatever the current market price is for wheat (agreeing beforehand on a publicly available reference for use in determining the market price of wheat on a given day) multiplied by the "notional amount" of 1,000 bushels. The amount paid by the Ocean Waves Baking Company to the counterparty is known as the "fixed" amount since the amount paid is fixed at $10/bushel multiplied by the 1,000 bushel notional amount. The amount paid by the counterparty to the Ocean Waves Baking Company is known as the "floating" amount since the amount, calculated by multiplying the current market price of wheat by the notional amount of 1,000 bushels, fluctuates each month. The Ocean Waves Baking Company can use this amount to buy 1,000 bushels of wheat in the spot market each month.

Pro: It will be possible to anticipate and plan for wheat costs over the next twenty-four months and, if wheat increases in cost at any time within this

---

16. Dodd-Frank Act, Pub. L. No. 111-20, 3124 Stat. 1376 (2010).

time period, the Ocean Waves Baking Company will have locked-in a lower price.

Con: If the Ocean Waves Baking Company finds out it does not need wheat or the price of wheat is lower than the price locked-in by the swap, it still is required to perform on the contract and pay its counterparty the fixed price agreed multiplied by the specified "notional amount" of wheat.

To add numbers to the above facts, the Ocean Waves Baking Company has entered into a swap whereby on the first business day of each month (the "payment date") for twenty-four months (the day on which the twenty-four-month period ends is the "maturity date") it will pay a fixed price of $10/bushel multiplied by a notional amount of 1,000 bushels of wheat, i.e., $10,000. In return, the counterparty agrees to pay the Ocean Waves Baking Company on the first business day of each month for twenty-four months a floating price calculated by multiplying the current market price of wheat by the notional amount of 1,000 bushels of wheat.

Suppose the first payment date is June 1 and the market price on that date for wheat is $9.80/bushel. The Ocean Waves Baking Company would be required to pay $10,000. (Since it is paying the "fixed" amount, it will be paying $10,000 on each monthly payment date). The counterparty will pay the Ocean Waves Baking Company the $9.80/bushel current market price multiplied by the notional amount of 1,000 bushels of wheat, i.e., $9,800. To make things easier, instead of the Ocean Waves Baking Company paying the counterparty $10,000 and the counterparty paying the Ocean Waves Baking Company $9,800, the Ocean Waves Baking Company just pays the difference between the two, $200, to the counterparty.[17]

If on the next payment date on July 1 the market price of wheat is now $10.50/bushel, the Ocean Waves Baking Company's fixed payment amount will still equal $10,000 while its counterparty's "floating" payment amount will now equal $10.50/bushel multiplied by the notional amount of 1,000 bushels, i.e., $10,500. Just as with the June 1 payment, instead of the Ocean Waves Baking Company paying the counterparty $10,000 and the counterparty paying the Ocean Waves Baking Company $10,500 it is easier for one payment of $500 to be made by the counterparty to the Ocean Waves Baking Company.[18] On each succeeding payment date, this same calculation will be made of the difference between the "fixed" amount agreed in the contract multiplied by the notional amount (paid by the Ocean Waves Baking Company to the counterparty) and the "floating" amount calculated by reference to the current market price multiplied by the notional amount (paid by the counterparty to the Ocean Waves Baking Company).

---

17. Or often slightly more, since the Ocean Waves Baking Company's counterparty may embed a fee in the price as a profit margin and to account for the credit risk it is exposed to due to potential non-performance by the Ocean Waves Baking Company.

18. Or often slightly less, since as noted in the preceding note, the Ocean Waves Baking Company's counterparty may embed a fee in the price to account for a profit margin and the credit risk it is exposed to, due to potential non-performance by the Ocean Waves Baking Company.

To summarize:

Commodity	Payment Dates	Maturity Date	Notional	Fixed Price	Floating Price
Wheat	First Business Day of Each Month	24 Months	1,000 Bushels of Wheat	$10 Multiplied by Notional Amount of 1,000 Bushels of Wheat	Market Price of Wheat Multiplied by Notional Amount of 1,000 Bushels of Wheat

Notice that each monthly payment date is, economically, the same as a futures contract. Therefore, each monthly payment can be illustrated graphically as in figure 1.1. Due to the twenty-four payment dates, to graph the wheat swap using the same method we did for the wheat future would require twenty-four graphs, something that is not practical. Instead, we can use the table in figure 1.3 that shows the cash flows that would occur on each payment date in a hypothetical scenario.

Figure 1.3 Hypothetical Swap Payments

Payment Date (*for each month listed below, payment is due on the first business day*)	Market Price of Wheat per Bushel (*determined by an agreed-upon public reference*)	Floating Rate (*i.e., market value of 1,000 bushels of wheat on each payment date*)	Fixed Rate (*i.e., price per 1,000 bushels of wheat agreed by the parties at the inception of the swap*)	Net Amount Payable (*a positive number represents an amount payable to the Ocean Waves Baking Company and a negative amount represents an amount payable from the Ocean Waves Baking Company*)
June	$9.80	$9,800	$10,000	−$200
July	$10.50	$10,500	$10,000	$500
August	$10.70	$10,700	$10,000	$700
September	$11.20	$11,200	$10,000	$1,200
October	$10.40	$10,400	$10,000	$400
November	$9.50	$9,500	$10,000	−$500
December	$8.80	$8,800	$10,000	−$1,200
January	$9.50	$9,500	$10,000	−$500
February	$9.40	$9,400	$10,000	−$600
March	$9.20	$9,200	$10,000	−$800

Figure 1.3 Hypothetical Swap Payments (*continued*)

Payment Date (*for each month listed below, payment is due on the first business day*)	Market Price of Wheat per Bushel (*determined by an agreed-upon public reference*)	Floating Rate (*i.e., market value of 1,000 bushels of wheat on each payment date*)	Fixed Rate (*i.e., price per 1,000 bushels of wheat agreed by the parties at the inception of the swap*)	Net Amount Payable (*a positive number represents an amount payable to the Ocean Waves Baking Company and a negative amount represents an amount payable from the Ocean Waves Baking Company*)
April	$9.60	$9,600	$10,000	−$400
May	$9.70	$9,700	$10,000	−$300
June	$10.00	$10,000	$10,000	$0
July	$10.15	$10,150	$10,000	$150
August	$10.00	$10,000	$10,000	$0
September	$9.80	$9,800	$10,000	−$200
October	$10.05	$10,050	$10,000	$50
November	$11.00	$11,000	$10,000	$1,000
December	$11.20	$11,200	$10,000	$1,200
January	$12.10	$12,100	$10,000	$2,100
February	$12.20	$12,200	$10,000	$2,200
March	$11.70	$11,700	$10,000	$1,700
April	$10.80	$10,800	$10,000	$800
May	$10.60	$10,600	$10,000	$600
Total:[1]				$7,900

[1] This does not account for the time value of money, i.e., that money received later is worth less than money received earlier due to the fact that money received earlier could have been invested for a higher return. *See* Stephen A. Ross, Randolph W. Westerfield, and Jeffrey Jaffe, Corporate Finance 64-75, (5th Ed., McGraw-Hill Higher Education 1999) for a description of this concept and associated formulae.

f. Swaps Contract: How It Trades

As noted above, swaps historically have been traded "over-the-counter," i.e., by private contract directly between parties without use of an exchange, trading facility, or intermediary, except sometimes a broker. A common practice would be for the Ocean Waves Baking Company to telephone a large financial institution specializing in swaps trading (known as a swap dealer) and ask a swaps trader working for the swap dealer to provide it a quote for the swap into which it wishes to enter.

The parties would typically already have in place a legal framework agreement specifying most of the legal terms that will apply to any trades. This framework agreement is typically documented by a standardized documentation known as the ISDA Master Agreement. The form of ISDA Master Agreement is produced by the industry association for the swaps industry, the International Swaps and Derivatives Association, commonly known as "ISDA."

The ISDA Master Agreement is comprised of a form ISDA Master Agreement, which is never directly modified by the parties, and a supplementary Schedule containing the parties' customized terms. We discuss these framework agreements in chapter 12, section E.1.

With the framework agreement in place, the parties will negotiate all the economic terms of the trade via telephone, instant messenger, or e-mail. Once they agree on the economic terms they will confirm their agreement in writing with a document known as a "confirmation" that is incorporated as part of the framework agreement.

Unlike with futures or exchange-traded options, there will be no clearinghouse to which each party to the agreement will perform and ultimately look to for performance unless they agree to have a clearinghouse perform that role. (As discussed in chapter 10, sections B.2 and C.3, some swaps are required to be traded on a facility and cleared.) Instead, each party will look to the other for performance of the bargain. In other words, they take each other's credit risk, i.e., the risk of non-performance due to a deterioration in creditworthiness. Often, there will be exchanges of collateral to mitigate the risk of non-performance.

Swaps Vocabulary

As with options, the world of swaps has its own vocabulary. Some of the main terms are defined below. For additional terms, see the glossary.

Fixed Amount: An amount required to be paid by a party to a swap and calculated by reference to a constant value.

Floating Amount: An amount required to be paid by a party to a swap and calculated by reference to a value that can change on each payment date.

Maturity Date: The last payment date on a swap.

Notional Amount: An amount used in swap transactions as a multiplier to calculate swap payments.

Payment Date: A date on which parties pre-agree to exchange swap payments.

Spread: In exchange-traded derivatives, the difference between the current bid price and the current offer price. In swaps, an amount added to swap payments

> as the swap dealer's profit and compensation for its exposure to the credit risk of its counterparty.
>
> *Swap*: An agreement to exchange payments periodically using predetermined pricing mechanisms.

C. Who Trades Derivatives?

The market participants in the derivatives markets can be broadly classified into three categories: hedgers, dealers or marketmakers, and speculators. Though their motivations for participating in the derivatives markets differ, they have a symbiotic relationship. For example, without speculators or marketmakers, a hedger may not find a party to take the other side of a trade. Without hedgers, a swap dealer will not have counterparties to which to provide a service. And, without other market participants, from whom could a speculator profit?

1. Hedgers

Hedgers are those who seek a derivative as a means to offset either a market risk, e.g., the risk of financial exposure due to fluctuations in something like interest rates or foreign exchange rates, or a credit risk, i.e., the risk of financial exposure due to a deterioration in creditworthiness.

Who are hedgers then? Hedgers represent the broadest swath of derivatives market participants. They include non-financial entities, such as the Ocean Waves Baking Company, who manufacture a good and do not want to be exposed to the risk of a cost increase of their primary supplies. They include producers of goods, such as farmers, who wish to lock in a price for their produce, or natural gas producers locking in the price they will obtain for the natural gas they extract. Many industries are exposed to oil or electricity prices and will seek to reduce exposure to an increase in those prices through hedging.

Some entities may wish to reduce their exposure to financial market risks. For example, a United States-based business with significant operations in Canada may want to use a derivative to reduce the risk of fluctuations of value between the U.S. dollar and the Canadian dollar. Most large commercial loans have "floating" interest rates. An entity may wish to hedge against the risk of these interest rates. Derivatives products for both circumstances are discussed below in sections D.2.a and b.

Even financial entities that are dealers or marketmakers also participate in the derivatives marketplace as hedgers. If a swap dealer agrees to trade a wheat swap with the Ocean Waves Baking Company, it will typically seek to neutralize its exposure to wheat so that it is "flat," i.e., whether wheat goes up or down has no net economic effect on it. It does this by entering into an offsetting swap with another swap dealer or by assessing all of its wheat exposures in the aggregate and then entering into swaps that largely offset the wheat exposure.

2. Dealers or Marketmakers

Dealer is a term predominantly used in the swaps market and marketmaker is occasionally used in the futures and options markets.

A dealer is a party who enters into trades based on counterparty demand. If an entity such as the Ocean Waves Baking Company seeks to protect against the risk of wheat prices increases, a swap dealer would be willing to quote pricing for a swap in which the Ocean Waves Baking Company could, for example, pay a fixed monthly amount for a specified number of months in return for the swap dealer paying a floating monthly amount for a specified number of months tied to the actual price of wheat in the marketplace. This would effectively lock in the current price of wheat for the Ocean Waves Baking Company. That way, if wheat prices increase, the Ocean Waves Baking Company is protected. A dealer will be equally willing to enter into a swap with a party who produces wheat and may want to pay the swap dealer the monthly market value of the wheat it produces in return for a fixed amount so that it can lock-in a fixed sale price for wheat each month.

The dealer usually profits by charging a "spread," i.e., a charge built into the swap by increasing the monthly payment made by the swap counterparty to the swap dealer. This charge reflects the risk of credit default by its swap counterparty and a fee for being willing to take the other side of the trade.

In some exchanges, a marketmaker is a defined role where, with respect to some products, the marketmaker agrees to quote both a bid price for which it is willing to buy a contract and an offer price for which it is offering to sell a contract. In this context, though, it is used more commonly to refer to a trader in the futures or options market that seeks to profit by quoting both a bid and an offer price. A marketmaker will usually be willing to buy or sell a contract since, instead of profiting from correctly anticipating a directional price trend of an asset, it is seeking to profit from the difference between the bid and offer price, known as the "spread."

3. Speculators

It could be said that dealers and marketmakers are just one type of speculator. We are using the term "speculator" to more specifically refer to a party seeking to profit from correctly anticipating a directional price trend of an asset as opposed to a dealer or marketmaker who is willing to transact on both sides of a marketplace.

Speculators sometimes evoke controversy. They are alternately condemned or praised for their role in the marketplace. The Supreme Court has taken notice that:

> The advent of speculation in futures markets produced well-recognized benefits for producers and processors of agricultural commodities. A farmer

who takes a "short" position in the futures market is protected against a price decline; a processor who takes a "long" position is protected against a price increase. Such "hedging" is facilitated by the availability of speculators willing to assume the market risk that the hedging farmer or processor wants to avoid. The speculators' participation in the market substantially enlarges the number of potential buyers and sellers of executory contracts, and therefore makes it easier for farmers and processors to make firm commitments for future delivery at a fixed price. The liquidity of a futures contract, upon which hedging depends, is directly related to the amount of speculation that takes place.[19]

On the other hand, when there is a perception that prices on derivatives markets might be "artificial" due to the activities of speculators, speculators are treated critically. When California had an energy crisis in the 2000s, numerous enforcement actions were brought against purported market manipulators. Congress passed the Energy Policy Act of 2005, the ramifications of which are discussed in chapter 4, section C.3. Trading platforms subject to a special low regulation regime and used primarily for energy products were abolished by the Dodd-Frank Act,[20] further discussed in chapter 2, section E.1.b. And a successful manipulation of the onion futures market in 1955 led to the prohibition of onion futures in 1958[21] — a prohibition still in place today.

D. Derivatives Product Categories

The primary and, in many cases, exclusive regulator of derivatives is the Commodity Futures Trading Commission ("CFTC"). The CFTC has, by regulation, classified derivatives into categories largely reflective of their historic treatment in the market.

1. Futures and Options

We have already evaluated the differences between futures and options. Futures and options can be subdivided by the product categories with which they are associated. In this way, the CFTC broadly subdivides them into: (1) futures and options on agricultural commodities; (2) futures and options on exempted commodities; and (3) futures and options on excluded commodities. Today, these subdivisions have significantly less regulatory relevance than they once did. Nonetheless, they provide a useful analytical framework.

It is important to note now that, as we discuss in much greater detail in chapter 2, sections B.2 and 3, in the context of derivatives the term "commodity" is defined

---

19. *Merrill Lynch v. Curran*, 456 U.S. 353, 358 (1982).
20. Dodd-Frank Act §§ 723 and 734.
21. Onion Futures Act, Pub. L. No. 85-839 (Aug. 28, 1958).

by law to, arguably, include nearly everything in existence. Therefore, the CFTC's tripartite subdivision is an effort to categorize every possible thing in existence that can be the subject of a futures or option trade.

a. Futures or Options on Agricultural Commodities

Agricultural commodities are defined by CFTC regulation to include a series of specifically enumerated commodities such as wheat, cotton, corn, butter, eggs, livestock, and tobacco. Also included are "products of horticulture" and a catch-all provision of all "other commodities that are, or once were, or are derived from, living organisms, including plant, animal and aquatic life, which are generally fungible, within their respective classes, and are used primarily for human food, shelter, animal feed or natural fiber."[22]

Many of these products have a long history of futures trading (as we will see in chapter 12, organized options trading is a more recent development). The first exchanges were organized exclusively to trade agricultural futures.

By custom, exchanges and traders consider the agricultural commodities to have six additional sub-categories: (1) grains and oilseeds, (2) livestock, (3) dairy, (4) lumber, (5) softs (these are commodities such as coffee, sugar, and cocoa), and (6) some biofuels.[23]

At first biofuels may seem an odd inclusion in the agricultural commodities. Indeed, most futures and options contracts in the biofuels category are more properly defined as futures and options on "exempt commodities," described in subsection c below, than agricultural commodities. Pure ethanol, since it is an additive to consumable alcoholic beverages derived from plant matter, is deemed an agricultural commodity. Denatured ethanol, a type of fuel which, although derived from plant matter, is not consumable as human food, is deemed an exempt commodity.[24]

Fertilizer is not included in the above list of agricultural commodities. Even though some exchanges group it as an "agricultural" and it is used exclusively in agriculture, it is not legally an agricultural commodity since it is not "food, shelter, animal feed or natural fiber."[25] Like biofuels other than pure ethanol, we will see that fertilizer is technically an "exempt commodity."

b. Futures or Options on Excluded Commodities

Whereas agricultural commodities are tangible, excluded commodities are all intangible. These are the financial commodities. Futures and options on excluded commodities include those referencing interest rates, foreign exchange rates, any

---

22. 17 C.F.R. §1.3 (definition of agricultural commodity).
23. *See, e.g.*, http://www.cmegroup.com/trading/agricultural.
24. CFTC, *Agricultural Commodity Definition*, 76 Fed. Reg. 41048, 41054 (July 13, 2011).
25. 17 C.F.R. §1.3 (definition of agricultural commodity, §(2)).

security, or credit risk.[26] They also include financial indices, economic or commercial indices, and any occurrence or contingency associated with a financial, commercial, or economic consequence outside of the control of the trading parties.[27]

Commonly traded futures and options on excluded commodities include futures and options referencing interest rates, such as Treasury Notes and Treasury Bonds with different maturities, futures and options referencing foreign currencies, and futures on some equity securities. Even though economically securities options are derivatives, it is important to note that legally they are not.[28]

c. Futures or Options on Exempt Commodities

The last category is defined as anything "that is not an excluded commodity or an agricultural commodity."[29] Even though this is, literally, a catch-all category, in practice it is relatively narrow. Once agricultural commodities and excluded commodities are removed, the main categories of trading products left are futures and options referencing: (1) energy products such as oil, natural gas, electricity, and coal; and (2) metals. Some metals are industrial in use and others, such as gold and silver, are categorized as precious metals.

Standard Contract Sizes for Selected Commodities on CME Group Exchanges

Commodity	Exchange	Contract Size
Cash-Settled Butter	Chicago Mercantile Exchange	20,000 Pounds
Cash-Settled Cheese	Chicago Mercantile Exchange	20,000 Pounds
Cocoa	New York Mercantile Exchange	10 Metric Tons
Coffee	New York Mercantile Exchange	37,500 Pounds
Corn	Chicago Board of Trade	5,000 Bushels
Cotton	New York Mercantile Exchange	50,000 Pounds
KC Hard Red Winter Wheat	Chicago Board of Trade	5,000 Bushels
Lean Hogs	Chicago Mercantile Exchange	40,000 Pounds
Live Cattle	Chicago Mercantile Exchange	40,000 Pounds
Nonfat Dry Milk	Chicago Mercantile Exchange	44,000 Pounds
Oats	Chicago Board of Trade	5,000 Bushels
Random Length Lumber	Chicago Mercantile Exchange	110,000 Nominal Board Feet
Rough Rice	Chicago Board of Trade	2,000 Hundredweights

---

26. Commodity Exchange Act § 1a(19).

27. *Id.*

28. Commodity Exchange Act § 1a(47)(B)(iii).

29. Commodity Exchange Act § 1a(19).

2. Swaps

As with futures, it is instructive in categorizing swaps to use the CFTC's existing framework. The CFTC divides swaps into four categories outlined in the below CFTC regulation.

CFTC Rule 1.3 (Definition of Category of Swaps)
17 C.F.R. §1.3

. . . category of swaps and any similar terms mean any of the categories of swaps listed below. . . .

(1) Rate swaps. Any swap which is primarily based on one or more reference rates, including but not limited to any swap of payments determined by fixed and floating interest rates, currency exchange rates, inflation rates or other monetary rates, any foreign exchange swap . . . and any foreign exchange option other than an option to deliver currency.

(2) Credit swaps. Any swap that is primarily based on instruments of indebtedness, including but not limited to any swap primarily based on one or more broad-based indices related to debt instruments or loans, and any swap that is an index credit default swap or total return swap on one or more indices of debt instruments.

(3) Equity swaps. Any swap that is primarily based on equity securities, including but not limited to any swap based on one or more broad-based indices of equity securities and any total return swap on one or more equity indices.

(4) Other commodity swaps. Any swap that is not included in the rate swap, credit swap or equity swap categories.

———————

Excluded from the above categories are securities options which, for regulatory purposes, are securities not derivatives, and credit or equity derivatives which reference a single security or loan or a "narrow-based security index."[30] The primary regulator of these products is the Securities and Exchange Commission ("SEC"). We discuss the SEC's role in derivatives markets in chapter 16.

The definition of "narrow-based security index" is complicated. A composite of eight or fewer securities (excluding government securities) is a "narrow-based security index." A composite of more than eight securities requires application of a complicated test to determine whether it is a "narrow-based security index" and subject to the SEC's jurisdiction or a swap on other than a "narrow-based security index" subject to the CFTC's jurisdiction.[31]

———————

30. Commodity Exchange Act §1a(47)(B)(iii) and (x).

31. *See* Commodity Exchange Act §1a(35), 17 C.F.R. §1.3(yyy), 17 C.F.R. §1.3(aaaa), 12 U.S.C. §78C(a)(55), and 17 C.F.R. §§240.3a68-1a and 240.3a68-1b.

The CFTC's category of "rate swaps" includes interest rate swaps and foreign exchange swaps. We will treat these as separate categories. Otherwise, we will use the CFTC's categories as we examine each more closely.

a. Interest Rate Swaps

Around seventy-five percent of all off-exchange derivatives by market value are interest rate derivatives.[32] Interest rate swaps, the most common interest rate derivative, are used to fix exposure to interest rates. Because of its ubiquity and relative simplicity, the interest rate swap that serves to exchange a fixed rate of interest on a pre-agreed "notional amount" for a floating rate of interest on a pre-agreed "notional amount" is called a "plain vanilla" interest rate swap.

The plain vanilla interest rate swap operates similarly to the hypothetical wheat swap in section B.3.e above. Just as in that example, one party pays the other a fixed amount on each payment date in return for payment of a floating amount on each payment date. The only difference is how the fixed and floating amounts are calculated. Instead of being calculated by reference to wheat prices, they are calculated by reference to publicly reported interest rates.

For example, the fixed rate might be 6% per annum. The notional amount, instead of being a quantity of wheat, will be a dollar amount, suppose $100,000. If the payment dates are monthly for twelve successive months, then the party paying the fixed amount would be required to pay 0.5% (6%, being an annual rate, needs to be converted to a monthly rate since the payments are monthly) multiplied by $100,000 on each of those payment dates. The fixed amount is, therefore, $500 on each payment date.

The floating rate would be determined on each monthly payment date by reference to a publicly available interest rate reference usually with an agreed upon spread added. Historically, the most used reference was the London Interbank Offered Rate, known as "LIBOR." LIBOR is an average of interest rates that select banks estimate they would have to pay if they borrowed from other banks in the London market. It is available in various tenors (i.e., length of time to maturity) and currencies, including the U.S. dollar. The least common two LIBOR tenors, those based on a one week or two month loan, are expected to be phased out by December 31, 2021, and the remaining, more commonly used tenors, are expected to be phased out by June 30, 2023. In the United States, most of the institutional marketplace is expected to transition from LIBOR to Secured Overnight Financing Rate ("SOFR") as the most common interest rate reference.

SOFR is produced by the Federal Reserve Bank of New York each day based on overnight borrowings of U.S. dollars collateralized by U.S. Treasuries in a type of

---

32. Bank for International Settlements, *Semiannual OTC Derivatives Statistics*, Table D5, http://www.bis.org/statistics/derstats.html (updated March 1, 2021).

transaction known as a repurchase agreement. In other words, it reflects the prevailing rate of interest being charged for a risk-free overnight loan in U.S. dollars.

Returning to our hypothetical swap, let us suppose the spread is 2%. If, on a particular payment date, the reference floating rate, e.g., SOFR, is 7%, the total floating rate is then 7% plus the 2% spread for a total of 9%. To convert this annualized number into a monthly rate, we would divide by 12 to get 0.75%. To calculate the floating amount payable on this payment date to the fixed amount payer we multiply 0.75% by the $100,000 notional. The floating amount payable on this payment date is, therefore, $750. As with the wheat swap, instead of having the fixed amount payer pay $500 and the floating amount payer pay $750, it is simpler to have the floating amount payer pay the $250 difference between the $500 and $750 payments to the fixed amount payer.

Most large commercial lenders historically calculated the monthly interest to be paid by the borrower by reference to LIBOR plus a spread. This also is expected to transition from LIBOR to SOFR. Interest rate swaps provide a means by which borrowers can hedge the risk of loan interest increasing. Hence the size and importance of the rate swaps market.

In the following case, a "plain vanilla" interest rate swap is described in greater detail. Note some of the benefits to this product enunciated by the court and the special role of the ISDA Master Agreement.

Thrifty Oil Co. v. Bank of America National Trust and Savings Association

322 F.3d 1039 (9th Cir. 2002)

Cynthia Holcomb Hall, Circuit Judge. . . .

To more thoroughly understand the facts of this case and the legal issues presented, the Court will provide a brief overview of derivative swap agreements. A "swap" is a contract between two parties ("counterparties") to exchange ("swap") cash flows at specified intervals, calculated by reference to an index. Parties can swap payments based on a number of indices including interest rates, currency rates and security or commodity prices.

The "plain-vanilla" interest rate swap, the simplest and most common type of swap contract, obligates one counterparty to make payments equal to the interest which would accrue on an agreed hypothetical principal amount ("notional amount"), during a given period, at a specified fixed interest rate. The other counterparty must pay an amount equal to the interest which would accrue on the same notional amount, during the same period, but at a floating interest rate. If the fixed rate paid by the first counterparty exceeds the floating rate paid by the second counterparty, then the first counterparty must pay an amount equal to the difference between the two rates multiplied by the notional amount, for the specified interval.

Conversely, if the floating rate paid by the second counterparty exceeds the fixed rate paid by the first counterparty, the fixed-rate payor receives payment. The agreed hypothetical or "notional" amount provides the basis for calculating payment obligations, but does not change hands.

For example, suppose Counterparties A and B enter into a five-year interest rate swap with the following characteristics: (1) Counterparty A agrees to pay a floating interest rate equal to LIBOR, the London Interbank Offered Rate; (2) Counterparty B agrees to pay a 10% fixed interest rate; (3) both counterparties base their payments on a $1 million notional amount and agree to make payments semiannually. If LIBOR is 9% upon commencement of the first payment period, Counterparty B must pay A: (10% — 9%) * $1 million * (.5) = $5,000. These net payments vary as LIBOR fluctuates and continue every six months for the term of the swap. If interest rates rise, the position of Counterparty B, the fixed-rate payor, improves because the payments it receives increase. For example, if LIBOR rises to 11% at the beginning of the next payment period, Counterparty B receives a net payment of $5,000 from A. Conversely, the position of Counterparty A, the floating-rate payor, improves when interest rates fall. The party whose position retains positive value under the swap is considered "in-the-money" while a party with negative value is considered "out-of-the-money." As discussed previously, the $1 million notional amount never changes hands.

Almost all interest rate swaps are documented with (1) a confirmation and (2) master agreement. Typically, master agreements are standard form agreements prepared by the International Swaps and Derivatives Association ("ISDA"). The master agreement governs all interest swap transactions between the counterparties. It includes provisions generally applicable to all swap transactions including: payment netting, events of default, cross-default provisions, early termination events and closeout netting.

Most master agreements provide that, in the event of an early termination or default, the party in-the-money is entitled to collect "termination damages." Termination damages represent the replacement cost of the terminated swap contract and are generally determined by obtaining market quotations for the cost of replacing the swap at the time of termination. . . .

Interest rate swap agreements provide a powerful tool for altering the character of assets and liabilities, fine tuning risk exposure, lowering the cost of financing or speculating on interest rate fluctuations. Borrowers can rely on interest rate swaps to reduce exposure to adverse changes in interest rates or to obtain financing characteristics unavailable through conventional lending. Interest rate swaps can modify a borrower's all-in funding costs from fixed-to-floating, floating-to-fixed or a combination of both.

Interest rate swaps have become an important part of international and domestic commerce, and the market for these instruments has experienced explosive growth. . . .

Thrifty refers to a fixed amount and a floating amount. As we have seen with respect to the Ocean Waves Baking Company's wheat swap, this terminology is also applicable to other categories of swaps. Occasionally, this fixed amount is also referred to as the "fixed leg" of a swap and the floating amount is referred to as the "floating leg" of the swap.

b. Foreign Exchange Swaps

Foreign exchange forwards are off-exchange transactions in which two parties agree to exchange a specified amount of one currency for a specified amount of another currency at an agreed-upon future date. If traded on-exchange they operate the same economically and are referred to as foreign exchange futures instead of forwards. A foreign exchange swap is a series of foreign exchange forwards, i.e., the parties agree to exchanges of currency at pre-agreed dates, often on a periodic basis, such as monthly. In a non-deliverable forward, commonly known as an "NDF," the parties net payments due on each payment date into a common currency instead of exchanging one currency for the other.

A typical cross-currency swap or cross-currency interest rate swap operates like an interest rate swap between two currencies. At the onset of the swap, one party ("Party A") provides a principal amount of a currency ("X") in exchange for a principal amount of another currency ("Y") from the other party ("Party B"). On a periodic basis, Party A pays Party B interest on Y in exchange for the receipt of interest on X from Party B. The interest could be fixed, based on floating references, or one could be fixed and the other floating. At maturity, the parties return to each other the principal exchanged at the onset of the swap.

c. Credit Swaps

The most common credit swap is a credit default swap. A credit default swap, although not an insurance product (why it is not an insurance product is the subject of discussion in chapter 4, section C.2), is economically akin to insurance. In a credit default swap, one party, a "protection buyer," pays a fee to the other party, known as the "protection seller."

In return for payment of this fee, the protection seller agrees to provide credit protection to the protection buyer with respect to a specified amount (the notional amount) of a "reference asset," usually a security such as a bond. If a specified "credit event" occurs, i.e., a bankruptcy of the issuer of the security, a payment default on the security, or specified related circumstances, the protection buyer has the right to deliver a face amount of the reference asset equal to the notional amount to the protection seller. The seller, in return, is required pay the protection buyer the full face amount of the security.

For example, assume a hypothetical credit default swap names as a reference asset Acme Bank 6.2% Bonds maturing on June 1, 2024 and specifies a $10 million notional amount. If a credit event occurs, such as a payment default on the bonds, the protection buyer can deliver to the protection seller $10 million in face value of these bonds and receive a $10 million payment for them. This is significant because a default such as a payment default almost always results in a significant impairment of the market value of an asset. The bonds are, in reality, likely to be worth significantly less than their $10 million face value. Since the credit default swap in this scenario gives the protection buyer the ability to receive $10 million for an asset unlikely to be worth $10 million, it is valuable to the protection buyer.

Credit default swaps can also be cash-settled. In these credit default swaps, an equivalent cash value is subtracted from the full face amount of the reference asset payable by the protection seller to the protection buyer in lieu of physical delivery of the actual reference asset to the protection seller.

In the case below, Deutsche Bank lost the protection of a credit default swap when it did not strictly comply with its terms. A problem faced in the early years of credit default swap trading is that available physical bonds tended to be difficult to get if a credit event occurred on a bond named as a reference asset in a large number of credit default swaps. This problem has largely resolved due to a combination of industry conventions, increasing use of cash-settled credit default swaps, and a decline from June 2006 to December 2016 of off-exchange trading in credit default swaps from 2.9% of all off-exchange derivatives trading to 1.3% of all off-exchange derivatives trading.[33]

Deutsche Bank AG v. AMBAC Credit Products, LLC

2006 WL 1867497 (S.D.N.Y. July 6, 2006)

Denis Cote, District Judge.

This is a dispute over a complex transaction between two sophisticated financial institutions. . . . [T]he central issue can be boiled down to a relatively straightforward question of contract interpretation: When was plaintiff Deutsche Bank AG ("DB") required to deliver a group of bonds to defendant Ambac Credit Products, LLC ("ACP")? DB claims that although the documents governing the disputed transaction set out a detailed timeline for delivery of the bonds, industry practice and other contractual provisions allowed for delivery well past the nominal deadline. Therefore, according to DB, ACP breached the contract when it refused to pay for the bonds DB tendered one month after the putative delivery date. . . .

The disputed transaction here is a species of credit derivative called a credit default swap ("CDS"). Credit derivatives are akin to insurance policies for holders of corporate bonds or other securities against downgrades in the credit of the issuing companies. They do this by transferring credit risk from a "protection buyer" to a

---

33. Bank for International Settlements, *Semiannual OTC Derivatives Statistics*, Table D5, http://www.bis.org/statistics/derstats.html (updated March 1, 2021) and Bank for International Settlements, *OTC Derivatives Market Activity in the First Half of 2006*, Table 1, http://www.bis.org/publ/otc_hy0611.pdf (Nov. 2006).

"protection seller."[34] A CDS is a common type of credit derivative in which the protection buyer makes a fixed payment to the protection seller in return for a payment that is contingent upon a "credit event" — such as a bankruptcy — occurring to the company that issued the security (the "reference entity") or the security itself (the "reference obligation"). The contingent payment is often made against delivery of a "deliverable obligation" — usually the reference obligation or other security issued by the reference entity — by the protection buyer to the protection seller. This delivery is known as the "physical settlement."[35] Some CDS transactions, such as the one at issue here, are known as "portfolio" transactions, meaning they cover multiple reference entities and reference obligations.

CDS transactions are of relatively recent origin, having been developed in the mid-1990s. They are highly negotiated and are customarily based on standard terms published by the International Swaps and Derivatives Association, Inc. ("ISDA"). These terms may be modified for a particular transaction. At the time the transaction at issue here was executed, the 1999 ISDA Credit Derivatives Definitions ("1999 Definitions") provided the foundation for most CDS agreements[36]. . . .

Thus, once a credit event occurs, the parties have a strictly controlled timeframe in which to act. A buyer of protection must first deliver a [notice] and then the securities within the timeframes allowed, or lose the right to obtain payment from the protection seller. Similarly, assuming the buyer has performed its obligations, the seller of protection must be prepared to make the required payment associated with the credit event within a defined and relatively short period of time following a credit event. . . .

Here, DB has utterly failed to show the existence of a market practice for credit default instruments that would have justified an expectation that it had an unlimited delivery window absent an express provision to that effect in the Confirmation. Its sole retained expert candidly admitted that she has no expertise whatsoever in the field of credit default obligations and did not disagree with any of the statements or analysis by ACP's expert, whose expertise within the field of credit default transactions was well established and unchallenged. At most, its own employees pointed to a handful of isolated CDS transactions in which late delivery of a physical settlement obligation was accepted. In none of these transactions was a non-dealer a party, and their relevance is therefore marginal at best. ACP, on the other hand, has shown through compelling evidence that the firm practice in the CDS marketplace was to require that delivery occur according to the timetable to which the parties had agreed. Under these circumstances, DB could not reasonably have expected that ACP would accept [late] delivery . . . and should have expected just the opposite.

---

34. [N. 2] A credit derivative is a synthetic instrument, however, and not all purchasers of such "protection" actually own the security covered by the transaction.

35. [N. 3] The parties can sometimes settle transactions without a transfer of securities. This is known as a "cash settlement" and is not at issue here.

36. The 1999 definitions have been supplanted by 2003 Definitions.

Indeed, the evidence shows that DB itself understood . . . that it had a firm obligation to deliver the [bonds] by the date it identified in the [notice] it sent to ACP, or within the five-business-day window that followed. In March, April, and May, as executives in the companies discussed ACP's refusal to accept DB's late-tendered bonds, DB never took the position that ACP was contractually bound to accept them. In fact, in a candid internal communication, it conceded it had "no leverage . . . at all" in the negotiations. . . .

For the foregoing reasons, each of DB's claims is denied in its entirety. The Clerk of Court shall enter judgment for the defendants and close the case. . . .

As noted in relation to swaps generally in section D.2 above, credit default swaps that reference eight or fewer securities (excluding government securities) or loans are security-based swaps, subject to SEC jurisdiction, examined in chapter 13. A credit default swap referencing nine or more securities or loans is usually subject to CFTC jurisdiction. However, it is subject to a complicated test involving evaluation of relative concentration of each security and the depth of the markets in which the securities trade.

d. Equity Swaps

An equity swap provides a means for a party to obtain an exposure to an equity without owning the equity. It also provides a means for an owner of an equity to hedge its exposure to an equity it holds. In some circumstances it can have tax benefits and, as demonstrated in the *Caiola* case below, it has been used to obtain exposure to an equity without leaving "footprints" in the marketplace that may affect the price of the equity.

The most common type of equity swap has, in effect, two floating amounts. On each payment date, one party pays a floating rate reference, such as LIBOR or SOFR plus a spread, to the other multiplied by a notional amount. In return, the other party pays percentage gains in price of a specific equity or equities multiplied by the notional amount.

Caiola v. Citibank, N.A., New York
295 F.3d 312 (2d Cir. 2002)

B.D. Parker Jr., Circuit Judge. . . .

Caiola, an entrepreneur and sophisticated investor, was a major client of Citibank Private Bank, a division of Citibank, from the mid-1980s to September 1999. During this relationship, Citibank assisted Caiola with a wide range of business and personal financial services. As a result of these transactions, which involved hundreds of millions of dollars, Caiola became one of Citibank's largest customers.

Beginning in the mid-1980s, Caiola undertook high volume equity trading, entrusting funds to Citibank who in turn engaged various outside brokerage firms.

Caiola specialized in the stock of Philip Morris Companies, Inc. ("Philip Morris") and regularly traded hundreds of thousands of shares valued at many millions of dollars. To hedge the risks associated with these trades, Caiola established option positions corresponding to his stock positions.

As Caiola's trades increased in size, he and Citibank grew increasingly concerned about the efficacy of his trading and hedging strategies. Caiola's positions required margin postings of tens of millions of dollars and were sufficiently large that the risks to him were unacceptable unless hedged. But the volume of options necessary to hedge effectively could impact prices and disclose his positions—effects known as "footprints" on the market. In early 1994, Citibank proposed synthetic trading. A synthetic transaction is typically a contractual agreement between two counterparties, usually an investor and a bank, that seeks to economically replicate the ownership and physical trading of shares and options. The counterparties establish synthetic positions in shares or options, the values of which are pegged to the market prices of the related physical shares or options. The aggregate market values of the shares or options that underlie the synthetic trades are referred to as "notional" values and are treated as interest-bearing loans to the investor. As Citibank explained to Caiola, synthetic trading offers significant advantages to investors who heavily concentrate on large positions of a single stock by reducing the risks associated with large-volume trading. Synthetic trading alleviates the necessity of posting large amounts of margin capital and ensures that positions can be established and unwound quickly. Synthetic trading also offers a solution to the "footprint" problem by permitting the purchase of large volumes of options in stocks without affecting their price.

Taking Citibank's advice, Caiola began to engage in two types of synthetic transactions focusing on Philip Morris stock and options: equity swaps and cash-settled over-the-counter options. In a typical equity swap, one party (Caiola) makes periodic interest payments on the notional value of a stock position and also payments equal to any decrease in value of the shares upon which the notional value is based. The other party (Citibank) pays any increase in the value of the shares and any dividends, also based on the same notional value.

For example, if Caiola synthetically purchased 1,000 shares of Philip Morris at $50 per share, the notional value of that transaction would be $50,000. Because this notional value would resemble a loan from Citibank, Caiola would pay interest at a predetermined rate on the $50,000. If Philip Morris's stock price fell $10, Caiola would pay Citibank $10,000. If the stock price rose $10, Citibank would pay Caiola $10,000. Citibank also would pay Caiola the value of any dividends that Caiola would have received had he actually owned 1,000 physical shares.

Caiola also acquired synthetic options, which were cash-settled over-the-counter options. Because these options were not listed and traded on physical exchanges, their existence and size did not impact market prices. Caiola and Citibank agreed to terms regarding the various attributes of the option in a particular transaction (such as the strike price, expiration date, option type, and premium). They agreed to settle these option transactions in cash when the option was exercised or expired, based on the then-current market price of the underlying security.

Caiola and Citibank documented their equity swaps and synthetic options through an International Swap Dealers Association Master Agreement ("ISDA Agreement") dated March 25, 1994. The ISDA Agreement established specific terms for the synthetic trading. After entering into the ISDA Agreement, Caiola, on Citibank's advice, began to enter into "coupled" synthetic transactions with Citibank. Specifically, Caiola's over-the-counter option positions were established in connection with a paired equity swap, ensuring that his synthetic options would always hedge his equity swaps. This strategy limited the amount he could lose and ensured that his risks would be both controllable and quantifiable. . . .

———————

Without Caiola's knowledge, Citibank, after its merger with Solomon Smith Barney, stopped entering into synthetic positions on Caiola's behalf and, instead, entered into physical positions. These ended up exposing Caiola to losses he would not have suffered if the synthetic positions were retained. The court concluded that the swap positions were covered under SEC Rule 10b-5,[37] an SEC rule prohibiting fraud in relation to securities transactions.

In addition to being subject to the SEC's anti-fraud jurisdiction, equity derivatives can trigger reporting requirements under securities and antitrust laws since they reference securities and can be a synthetic substitute for direct ownership of a security.

e. Other Swaps

The CFTC defines "other commodity swaps" as "Any swap that is not included in the rate swap, credit swap or equity swap categories." As a practical matter, the primary remaining category is commodity swaps.

We examined a commodity swap in detail in the wheat swap example in section B.3.e above. In a commodity swap the fixed amount is usually based on the current market price of a commodity and the floating amount is calculated by reference to the market price of the commodity on each subsequent payment date.

Also included in this category are swaps that are exotic in nature and, therefore, not easily categorized as a rate, credit, equity, or commodity swap. One example of such a derivative would be a weather derivative in which payment exchanges between the parties are correlated to specified weather events.

———————

37. 17 C.F.R. § 240.10b-5.

E. Practical Application of Derivatives

During the financial crisis that began in 2007 and referred to herein as the "Financial Crisis," derivatives were the subject of significant criticism. This criticism is evaluated in chapter 9, section B.

However, as apt as these critiques may sometimes be, it is important to keep in mind that derivatives also offer societal benefits. Some practical applications of derivatives were illustrated by our above examples with the Ocean Waves Baking Company. Indeed, many companies — and even governments — use derivatives to manage risk, ranging from price volatility of commodities such as oil or cattle to interest rate volatility. For a company engaged in cross-border transactions requiring multiple currencies, foreign exchange derivatives may be an essential element for reducing the risk of currency fluctuations.

Many of the perceived benefits and shortcomings of derivatives were outlined before the Financial Crisis by the General Accounting Office. The prescience of the report is remarkable in anticipating many of the challenges faced in the Financial Crisis that would strike more than a decade later.

United States General Accounting Office, *Financial Derivatives — Actions Needed to Protect the Financial System*
GAO/GGD 94-133 (May 18, 1994)

. . . The risks posed by derivatives use include (1) credit risk . . . ; (2) market risk (adverse movements in the price of a financial asset or commodity); (3) legal risk (an action by a court or by a regulatory or legislative body that could invalidate a financial contract); and (4) operations risk (inadequate controls, deficient procedures, human error, system failure, or fraud). These general types of risk exist for many financial activities, but the specific risks in derivatives activities are relatively difficult to manage, in part, because of the complexity of some of these products and the difficulties in measuring these risks. For example, because derivatives might be used in conjunction with other assets and liabilities, measuring the extent of market risks of derivative products alone is not sufficient to understand firms' total market risk. . . .

Derivatives are globally used financial products that have evolved to meet the demand for cost-effective protection against risks associated with rate and price movements. Derivatives essentially unbundle and transfer those risks from entities less willing or able to manage them to those more willing or able to do so. The values of derivatives are based on, or derived from, the value of an underlying asset, reference rate, or index — called the underlying. Common types of underlying assets are stocks, bonds, and physical commodities, such as wheat, oil, and lumber. An example of an underlying reference rate is the interest rate on the 3-month U.S. Treasury bill. An example of an underlying index is the Standard & Poor's 500 Index, which measures the performance of 500 common stocks.

Derivatives include customized and standardized contracts. Some derivatives are customized contracts between parties (also called counterparties) that include one or more negotiated terms in addition to price. These terms can include the quality and quantity of the underlying, time and place of delivery, and method of payment. Other derivatives are standardized contracts whose terms are fixed — except for price, which the market determines. Derivatives can be privately negotiated by the parties; these are called over-the-counter (OTC) derivatives. Derivatives also can be traded through central locations, called organized exchanges, where buyers and sellers or their representatives meet to determine derivatives prices; these are called exchange-traded derivatives. . . .

Market participants use derivatives (1) to hedge, or to protect against adverse changes in the values of assets or liabilities; (2) to speculate, or to assume risk in attempting to profit from anticipating changes in market rates or prices; and (3) to obtain more desirable financing terms.

Hedgers protect themselves from market risk, which is the exposure to the possibility of financial loss caused by adverse changes in the values of assets or liabilities. They protect themselves by entering into derivatives transactions whose values are expected to change in the opposite direction as the values of their assets or liabilities. For example, a hedger can protect asset values through derivatives transactions that increase in value as the asset values decline. The increases in values of the derivatives contracts (profits) will offset, or hedge, the decrease in values of the assets (losses).

In contrast, speculators take on risk in an attempt to profit from changes in the values of derivatives or their underlyings. Rather than owning the underlying, speculators can use derivatives as a more affordable way to attempt to profit from anticipating movements in market rates and prices. As speculators enter into transactions with hedgers and other speculators, they provide liquidity to the derivatives markets, thereby helping to ensure that high volumes of trading can occur without significantly affecting prices.

Some derivatives enable market participants to obtain more desirable financing in two ways. First, as we discuss later in this chapter, market participants can work together to take advantage of differences in the rates at which they borrow money. Second, an important by-product of hedging is the enhanced creditworthiness of the hedger. Banks will extend more favorable financing terms to firms that have reduced their market risk through hedging activities.

In achieving these purposes, derivatives can be more cost-effective than transactions in the underlying cash markets because of the reduced transaction costs and the leverage that derivatives provide. For example, instead of buying or selling $100,000 worth of U.S. Treasury bonds, a market participant can realize the benefits of buying or selling the same amount of bonds by using a derivatives contract and posting a deposit, called a margin, of only about $1,500, or 1.5 percent of the face amount of the bonds. Likewise, a market participant can achieve a result similar to buying or selling all of the stocks in the Standard & Poor's 500 Index by buying or selling a derivatives contract on this index for as little as 5 to 10 percent of the cost of the underlying stocks. . . .

Although derivatives can provide economic benefits, dealers and end-users can experience extensive unanticipated losses if they do not carefully manage the risks associated with the use of derivatives. Several large U.S. and international firms have reported extensive losses from derivatives transactions as a result of unanticipated market movements and weaknesses in their risk management systems. The Group of Thirty and bank regulators have also reported weaknesses in risk management systems of derivatives dealers and end-users. Although strong corporate governance is critical to the success of any risk management system, it is particularly crucial for managing the risks of complex and potentially volatile derivatives. Boards of directors, senior management, audit committees, and internal and external auditors all have key roles within the corporate governance system to manage the risks associated with derivatives.

The general types of risk associated with derivatives — credit, market, legal, and operations — exist for many financial activities. Therefore, risk-management policies and controls over such activities are also generally applicable to derivatives. However, the specific risks associated with derivatives activities are relatively difficult to manage, in part, because of the complexity of some of these products and the difficulties in measuring their risks. . . .

Derivatives serve an important function in the global financial marketplace, providing end-users opportunities to better manage financial risks associated with their business transactions. The rapid growth and increasing complexity of derivatives reflects the increased demand from end-users for better ways to manage their financial risks and from speculators for lower cost ways to potentially profit from market volatility. They also reflect the innovative capacity of the financial services industry to respond to market demands. However, the combination of global involvement, concentration, and linkages among large derivatives dealers means that the sudden failure or complete withdrawal from trading of any of these dealers could heighten the risk of liquidity problems in the markets and pose risk to the others, including federally insured banks and the financial system. In cases of severe financial stress, the federal government is likely to intervene to keep the financial system functioning. . . .

Improving U.S. derivatives regulation without coordinating and harmonizing such actions with foreign regulators has at least two risks. First, U.S. financial institutions will remain vulnerable to a crisis that begins abroad and spreads to the United States as a result of the global linkages among financial institutions and markets. Second, regulation that market participants view as too severe could cause firms to move their derivatives activities outside of the United States. However, coordinating and harmonizing regulation worldwide has been difficult to achieve because countries have different legal requirements and different approaches to regulation.

Innovation and creativity are strengths of the U.S. financial services industry, and these strengths should not be eroded by excessive regulation. However, U.S. regulatory gaps and weaknesses must be addressed, especially considering the rapid growth in derivatives activity. Policymakers and regulators must strike a proper balance between (1) allowing the financial services industry to grow and innovate and (2) protecting the safety and soundness of the nation's financial system. Achieving this balance will require unprecedented cooperation among U.S. and foreign regulators, market participants, and members of the accounting profession. . . .

Given the weaknesses and gaps that impede regulatory preparedness for dealing with a crisis associated with derivatives, GAO recommends that Congress require federal regulation of the safety and soundness of all major U.S. OTC derivatives dealers. Regulators should attempt to prevent financial disruptions from turning into crises and resolve crises to minimize risks to the financial system. Thus, firms that become insolvent should be allowed to fail but to do so in an orderly fashion. . . .

————————

As will be seen in the following chapter, only a few years after the 1994 General Accounting Office report, swaps were exempted from most regulation. The questions the General Accounting Office report raises, about the balance between having an innovative marketplace and risk-reducing regulation, remains as important today as in 1994, despite the adoption in 2010 of some of the General Accounting Office's recommendations.

Questions and Comments

1. Consider what risk the Ocean Waves Baking Company might be exposed to if there were no derivative products available to hedge its wheat exposure. Would there be other ways to mitigate its risk?

2. What if, in addition to having wheat needs, the Ocean Waves Baking Company had a major maple syrup supplier in Canada that required payment in Canadian dollars? What are some derivatives strategies that might be available to the Ocean Waves Baking Company?

3. Can the typical swap transaction be replicated by a series of futures transactions? If so, why would parties choose to enter into a swap instead of a future? In what circumstances might futures be most beneficial to an entity hedging its risks and in what circumstances might swaps be most beneficial to an entity hedging its risks?

4. On April 20, 2020, the West Texas Intermediate Light Sweet Crude Oil futures contract settled at a price of − $37.63 per barrel. It is believed to have been caused by a sudden drop in oil demand and limited storage in Cushing, Oklahoma, the location where physical delivery was required under the contract. As a result, indefinite and expensive storage costs would likely be incurred by any purchaser of this contract. What are some ways to reduce the possibility of this circumstance occurring in the future? What would be the consequences of not addressing it at all?

5. What are some transactions that you enter into in daily life that might be considered forward contracts? What about options?

6. As discussed in greater detail in chapter 3, the term "swap" is defined broadly in section 1a(47) of the Commodity Exchange Act to include some products that are not, strictly speaking, swaps. Why might that be the case? Does it matter whether the legal definition corresponds to its ordinary meaning?

7. Considering the important functions derivatives perform, why might a successful financier such as Warren Buffet have referred to swap as "financial weapons of mass destruction"?[38]

8. Are speculators a positive market force, a negative one, or both? In what contexts might speculators benefit the markets? In what contexts might speculators harm the markets? What constitutes "harm" to the market?

---

38. Berkshire Hathaway Inc., *2002 Annual Report* 15 (2003), available at http://www .berkshirehathaway.com/2002ar/2002ar.pdf.

Chapter 2

A Regulatory History of Derivatives

A. Origins

1. Antiquity

There is evidence of forward contracts in antiquity. There is little evidence of options and none of swaps.

Forward contracts, where observed, developed as a complement to pre-existing spot markets. Once there is a market in grain, for example, it does not seem to be a great leap to have a grain producer and a grain user transact an advanced purchase of the next grain harvest.

A famous example of a forward transaction in antiquity is shared by Aristotle.

Aristotle, *Politics*
Bk. 1, Ch. 11

. . . Enough has been said about the theory of wealth-getting; we will now proceed to the practical part. . . .

It would be well also to collect the scattered stories of the ways in which individuals have succeeded in amassing a fortune; for all this is useful to persons who value the art of getting wealth. There is the anecdote of Thales the Milesian and his financial device, which involves a principle of universal application, but is attributed to him on account of his reputation for wisdom. He was reproached for his poverty, which was supposed to show that philosophy was of no use. According to the story, he knew by his skill in the stars while it was yet winter that there would be a great harvest of olives in the coming year; so, having a little money, he gave deposits for the use of all the olive-presses in Chios and Miletus, which he hired at a low price because no one bid against him. When the harvest-time came, and many were wanted all at once and of a sudden, he let them out at any rate which he pleased, and made a quantity of money. Thus he showed the world that philosophers can easily be rich if they like, but that their ambition is of another sort. . . .

———————

Thales entered into a derivative, a forward transaction, when he paid for the use of the olive presses in advance.

2. Development of Forward Markets

Although there are other historical examples of forward transactions going back to antiquity, it is not until the 1600s that there is evidence of organized markets for the trading of forwards, i.e., a developed marketplace of buyers and sellers with common customs and practices. Organized exchanges for the trading of derivatives with what is known as central clearing, i.e., where each party, instead of having performance obligations to each other, commonly face a central clearinghouse, were to wait another two centuries before being established.

The most prominent early example was the Dutch tulip market in the mid-1600s. The Dutch tulip market is of additional interest to us and economic historians as an early example of an economic bubble fueled by maniacal, irrational speculation. Upon first reading the below passage on the Dutch tulip market it may appear to be referring to spot market transactions when the author describes the transactions. Today, we define it as a forward in nature because a typical transaction had one party agreeing to a purchase in six weeks' time at a price pre-agreed at the time of the transaction.

Charles Mackay, *Memoirs of Extraordinary Popular Delusions and the Madness of Crowds*

Ch. 3 The Tulipomania (2d ed., London:
Office of the National Illustrated Library 1852)

... [Tulips were] introduced into western Europe about the middle of the sixteenth century.... Rich people at Amsterdam sent for the bulbs direct to Constantinople, and paid the most extravagant prices for them. The first roots planted in England were brought from Vienna in 1600. Until the year 1634 the tulip annually increased in reputation, until it was deemed a proof of bad taste in any man of fortune to be without a collection of them.... The rage for possessing them soon caught the middle classes of society, and merchants and shopkeepers, even of moderate means, began to vie with each other in the rarity of these flowers and the preposterous prices they paid for them....

In 1634, the rage among the Dutch to possess them was so great that the ordinary industry of the country was neglected, and the population, even to its lowest dregs, embarked in the tulip trade....

The demand for tulips of a rare species increased so much in the year 1636, that regular marts for their sale were established on the Stock Exchange of Amsterdam, in Rotterdam, Harlaem, Leyden, Alkmar, Hoorn, and other towns. Symptoms of gambling now became, for the first time, apparent.... At first, as in all these gambling mania, confidence was at its height, and every body gained.... Many individuals grew suddenly rich. A golden bait hung temptingly out before the people, and, one after the other, they rushed to the tulip marts, like flies around a honey-pot.... Nobles, citizens, farmers, mechanics, seamen, footmen, maidservants, even chimneysweeps and old clotheswomen, dabbled in tulips. People of all grades converted their property into cash, and invested it in flowers.... The operations of the trade became so extensive and so intricate, that it was found necessary to draw up a code of laws for the guidance of the dealers. . . . In the smaller towns, where there was no exchange, the principal tavern was usually selected as the "show-place," where high and low traded in tulips, and confirmed their bargains. . . .

At last, however, the more prudent began to see that this folly could not last for ever. . . . It was seen that somebody must lose fearfully in the end. As this conviction spread, prices fell, and never rose again. Confidence was destroyed, and a universal panic seized upon the dealers. A had agreed to purchase ten Sempers Augustines from B, at four thousand florins each, at six weeks after the signing of the contract. B was ready with the flowers at the appointed time; but the price had fallen to three or four hundred florins, and A refused either to pay the difference or receive the tulips. Defaulters were announced day after day in all the towns of Holland. Hundreds who, a few months previously, had begun to doubt that there was such a thing as poverty in the land, suddenly found themselves the possessors of a few bulbs, which nobody would buy, even though they offered them at one quarter of the sums they had paid for them. The cry of distress resounded everywhere, and each man accused his neighbour. . . .

When the first alarm subsided, the tulip-holders in the several towns held public meetings to devise what measures were best to be taken to restore public credit. It was generally agreed, that deputies should be sent from all parts to Amsterdam, to consult with the government upon some remedy for the evil. The government at first refused to interfere, but advised the tulip-holders to agree to some plan among themselves. Several meetings were held for this purpose; but no measure could be devised likely to give satisfaction to the deluded people, or repair even a slight portion of the mischief that had been done. The language of complaint and reproach was in every body's mouth, and all the meetings were of the most stormy character. At last, however, after much bickering and ill-will, it was agreed, at Amsterdam, by the assembled deputies, that all contracts made in the height of the mania, or prior to the month of November 1636, should be declared null and void, and that, in those made after that date, purchasers should be freed from their engagements, on paying ten per cent to the vendor. This decision gave no satisfaction. The vendors who had their tulips on hand were, of course, discontented, and those who had pledged themselves to purchase, thought themselves hardly treated. Tulips which had, at one time, been worth six thousand florins, were now to be procured for five hundred; so that the composition of ten per cent was one hundred florins more than the actual value. Actions for breach of contract were threatened in all the courts of the country; but the latter refused to take cognizance of gambling transactions. . . .

There was no court in Holland which would enforce payment. The question was raised in Amsterdam, but the judges unanimously refused to interfere, on the ground that debts contracted in gambling were no debts in law. . . .

The example of the Dutch was imitated to some extent in England. In the year 1636 tulips were publicly sold in the Exchange of London, and the jobbers exerted themselves to the utmost to raise them to the fictitious value they had acquired in

Amsterdam. In Paris also the jobbers strove to create a tulipomania. In both cities they only partially succeeded. . . .

Other Early Derivatives Markets

There are other competitors for the moniker of "first derivatives market." Even preceding Holland's tulip market, Dutch forward markets in grain and herring are cited as early as the 1550s.[a]

The precursors of a forward rice market in Japan — begun as a way for noble landowners to sell their future rice production to satisfy short term cash needs — was organized in 1650.[b]

Ancient Rome used forwards so that traders could be assured supply and farmers could obtain cash in advance of harvest.[c]

Even thirteenth century mediaeval fairs are cited as precursor futures markets due to the use of bills of exchange to record transactional rights and the ability to trade and discount these bills.[d]

[a] Christian C. Day, *Is there a Tulip in Your Future?*, Journal des Economistes et des Etudes Humaines 151, 155 (Dec. 2004).

[b] J. Duncan LaPlante, *Growth and Organization of Commodity Markets*, in *Handbook of Futures Markets* 1–5 to 1–8 (Perry J. Kaufmann ed., John Wiley & Sons Inc.1984).

[c] Edward J. Swan, *Building the Global Market: A 4,000 Year History of Derivatives* 83 (Springer Netherlands 2000)

[d] H.R. Rep. 93-975 at 36 (Apr. 4, 1974).

3. Development of Futures Exchanges

Note the treatment granted by the Dutch courts to the tulip forwards. The treatment of derivatives as unenforceable gambling contracts was, until the last century, an impediment to the development of derivatives markets in the United States as well. The following article describes the treatment of a precursor to exchange-traded futures in the United States, the "contract for difference," and how the development of exchanges was a solution to the problem of legally enforcing contracts for difference.

Lynn A. Stout, *Uncertainty, Dangerous Optimism, and Speculation: An Inquiry into Some Limits of Democratic Governance*
97 Cornell L. Rev. 1177 (2012)

. . . An early American example [of a derivative] was a type of derivative known as a "difference contract." Difference contracts were agreements between two parties that one would make a payment of money to the other determined by future changes in some market phenomenon, usually the market price for an agricultural commodity like wheat or corn. They were often formally structured like modern futures contracts, with one party promising to buy wheat at today's price and the other promising to purchase it, but with the contract to be performed at some future time. However, the parties further agreed that the contract would not be performed by actually delivering the wheat. Rather, the wheat "buyer" would pay the "seller" the difference between the contract price and the market price of wheat at the time of performance.

Not surprisingly, difference contract trading proved highly appealing to speculators.... Moreover, because difference contracts were essentially wagers, they could be used to bet on price declines and to take speculative positions virtually without cost — at least, until the bet came due....

[The author notes that these "contracts for difference" were ultimately deemed unenforceable.]

[T]he common law did not try to stop those who wanted to use difference contracts to wager on the markets from doing so. It simply declined to subsidize speculators by allowing them to employ public courts to enforce their bets.[1] As a result, would-be speculators had to worry that their counterparties might not perform. A private solution to this enforcement problem soon emerged: privately organized futures exchanges....

U.S. agricultural exchanges came to be dominated not by producers and consumers dealing in physical corn or cotton, but by traders exchanging "elevator receipts" representing a quantity of a commodity stored elsewhere (e.g., in a grain elevator). Soon elevator receipts morphed into "futures contracts" that called for delivery of the commodity in the future, at today's market price. However, most exchange-traded futures were not performed by actually delivering the corn or cotton. Rather, traders employed a "set off" process, purchasing a second, offsetting futures contract for delivery of the same quantity of the same goods on the same date. Futures contracts performed by set-off were just difference contracts by another name.

Nevertheless, traders who wanted to use exchange-traded futures for speculation rather than hedging generally did not worry their counterparties might use the common-law rule against difference contracts as an excuse not to perform. This is not because public courts enforced speculative futures contracts, but because anyone who wanted to trade on a futures exchange had to use the brokerage services of an exchange member who would guarantee the traders' performance....

––––––––––

In chapter 3 the legal distinction between a forward contract and a futures contract is addressed. For the moment, it is important to note that, in a forward contract, the trading is in the asset that is the subject of the forward contract. For example, in a

––––––––––

1. [N. 88] *See Irwin v. Williar*, 110 U.S. 499, 508–09 (1884).

grain forward, the parties contract to a negotiated sale of grain. The obligations of the parties are typically directly to each other for the life of the contract, i.e., there is no central clearing.

In a futures contract, the trading is in a standardized contract for future delivery with the contract itself (and its rights and obligations) being what is bought and sold in the marketplace. A party is not negotiating and buying grain for future delivery from another party. Instead, a party is buying a standardized contract requiring the buyer to pay for the future delivery of grain and the seller to make the future delivery of grain. To have such standardized terms, there needs to be a developed and sophisticated underlying market.

In the United States, forward markets are documented as existing as early as the 1840s.[2] Around this time there is also evidence of parties trading options.[3] The formalization of contracts necessary for the development of a futures market occurred in Chicago in the 1860s.[4] The Chicago Board of Trade began centralized clearing in 1882.[5] With centralized clearing, the era of modern futures exchanges begun.

4. Bucket Shops

Meanwhile, outside of the confines of organized exchanges, "bucket shops" flourished. Bucket shops have been variously described. Justice Holmes described them as "places wherein is permitted the pretended buying and selling of grain, etc., without any intention of receiving and paying for the property so bought, or of delivering the property so sold."[6] A year later the Supreme Court again defined a bucket shop, this time as "an establishment, nominally for the transaction of . . . exchange business, or business of similar character, but really for the registration of bets, or wagers, usually for small accounts, on the rise or fall of the prices of stock, grain, oil, etc."[7] The Oxford English Dictionary cites the origin of the term "bucket shop" as a reference to low-end liquor shops.[8]

However, perhaps the best explanation for the term cites the origin of the term "bucket shop" as deriving from the practice of "bucketing" orders:

> The bucketing of grain-futures orders by their nonexecution in the pit was by no means confined to bucket shops prior to the enactment of laws against such practices. . . . Even after the Chicago Board of Trade sought

---

2. Jeffrey C. Williams, *The Origin of Futures Markets*, 56 Agricultural History No. 1 306, 308 (Jan. 1982) (symposium issue).

3. *Id.* at 309.

4. J. Duncan LaPlante, *Growth and Organization of Commodity Markets*, in *Handbook of Futures Markets* 1–11 (Perry J. Kaufmann ed., John Wiley & Sons Inc. 1984).

5. *Id.*

6. *Board of Trade of City of Chicago v. Christie Grain & Stock Co.*, 198 U.S. 236, 246 (1905).

7. *Gatewood v. North Carolina*, 203 U.S. 531, 536 (1906).

8. *Oxford English Dictionary* vol. 2, 613 (Oxford U. Press 1989).

Figure 2.1 The Evolution of Commodity Markets

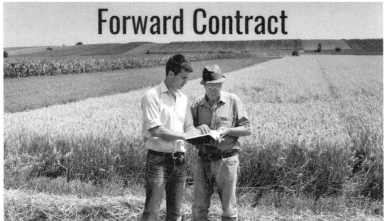

Source: Photographs used with permission of Shutterstock.com. Top photograph by Paul Prescott, middle photograph by Budimir Jevtic, and bottom illustration by Sampien.

to extirpate the bucket shops, members of the Board were in the habit of matching the orders of customers against each other instead of executing them in the pit.[9]

In other words, a bucket shop was a place where an order to buy or sell a future traded on an exchange could be made without the order being transmitted to the exchange. Instead of transmitting the order to the relevant exchange, the owner of the bucket shop would take the opposite side of the customer's order and the parties would value the contract based on the exchange's reported prices as they came in via telegram. When the bucket shop made money on a trade, the owner made sure to collect. Where it lost money, the owner frequently packed up and moved to the next town.

As a result, many of these bucket shops were deemed to be illegal gaming venues and there were various efforts to police them combining state law prohibitions and exchange-initiated investigations. For example, the Chicago Board of Trade engaged in a crackdown on bucket shops by hiring private investigators to see which of its members had telegraphic connections with bucket shops.[10] This resulted in the expulsion of members and, ultimately, the Chicago Board of Trade's efforts resulted in 281 indictments and 188 bucket shops being closed.[11]

These acts, and a Supreme Court decision in 1905 allowing for the organized exchanges to enjoin transmission of price quotations to bucket shops, led to the demise of bucket shops by 1916.[12] The legacy of bucket shops, however, was one of the motivations for the forthcoming federal regulation of futures trading.

B. The First Era of Federal Regulation, 1922–1991

1. Grain Futures Act of 1922

The first large-scale federal effort to regulate futures was the Future Trading Act of 1921.[13] The Future Trading Act taxed grain futures traded on anything but a board of trade meeting statutory criteria and designated as such by the secretary of

---

9. Federal Trade Commission, *Report on the Grain Trade* vol. V, 330 (Govt. Printing Off. 1920).

10. David Hochfelder, *Where the Common People Could Speculate: The Ticker, Bucket Shops, and the Origins of Popular Participation in Financial Markets, 1880–1920*, 93 J. of Amer. History vol. 2, 335, 354 (2006).

11. *Id.*

12. Federal Trade Commission, *Report on the Grain Trade* vol. II, 128 (Govt. Printing Off. 1920) and David Hochfelder, *Where the Common People Could Speculate: The Ticker, Bucket Shops, and the Origins of Popular Participation in Financial Markets, 1880–1920*, 93 J. of Amer. History vol. 2, 335, 355 (2006).

13. Pub. L. No. 67-66, 42 Stat. 187 (1921). A federal tax on futures transactions was intermittently imposed beginning in 1898. Cotton futures were also federally regulated beginning in 1914. In 1915, similarly to, as will be seen below, the Future Trading Act, the underlying act was declared unconstitutional. A new statute was passed in 1916. *See* CFTC, *History of the CFTC: US Futures Trading*

agriculture. In *Hill v. Wallace*, a Supreme Court opinion authored by Chief Justice Taft ruled that this was an unconstitutional assertion of the tax power since its real objective was regulatory and denied that it was a regulation of interstate commerce because "interstate commerce" was never referenced in the statute:

> It is impossible to escape the conviction, from a full reading of this law, that it was enacted for the purpose of regulating the conduct of business of Boards of Trade through supervision of the Secretary of Agriculture. . . . When this purpose is declared in the title to the bill, and is so clear from the effect of the provisions of the bill itself, it leaves no ground upon which the provisions we have been considering can be sustained as a valid exercise of the taxing power. . . . There is not a word in the act from which it can be gathered that it is confined in its operation to interstate commerce. The words 'interstate commerce' are not to be found in any part of the act from the title to the closing section.[14]

Heeding the chief justice's ruling, Congress passed the Grain Futures Act of 1922, the long title of which declared its grounding in Congress's constitutional authority to regulate interstate commerce: "An Act for the prevention and removal of obstructions and burdens upon interstate commerce in grain, by regulating transactions on grain future exchanges. . . ."[15] It was upheld by the Supreme Court in *Board of Trade of City of Chicago v. Olsen*.[16] It was limited to regulation of futures on "grain," defined as "wheat, corn, oats, barley, rye, flax and sorghum."[17]

The Act cites futures as being "affected with a national public interest" with the "transactions and prices of grain on such boards of trade . . . susceptible to speculation, manipulation, and control, and sudden or unreasonable fluctuations in . . . [price] as a result of such speculation, manipulation, or control . . . detrimental to the producer or the consumer. . . ."[18] The core of the Act was the section making it illegal for "any person to . . . make or execute . . . any contract of sale of grain for future delivery on or subject to the rules of any board of trade in the United States . . ." with exceptions for where "the seller is at the time of the making of such contract the owner of the actual physical property covered thereby, or is the grower thereof" or if the contract is "made by or through a member of a board of trade which has been designated by the Secretary of Agriculture as a 'contract market.' . . ."[19]

In other words, grain futures that were available for trading on a board of trade, i.e., an organized exchange, could only be traded on a federally-regulated organized

---

and Regulation Before the Creation of the CFTC, http://www.cftc.gov/About/HistoryoftheCFTC/history_precftc.html.

14. *Hill v. Wallace*, 259 U.S. 44, 66–67 (1922).
15. Pub. L. No. 67-331, 42 Stat. 998 (1922) [Hereinafter, "Grain Futures Act"].
16. 262 U.S. 1 (1923).
17. Grain Futures Act § 2(a).
18. Grain Futures Act § 3.
19. Grain Futures Act § 4.

exchange, known at the time as a board of trade designated as a contract market (today, the similar term "designated contract market" is in general use to formally refer to a futures exchange). The only exception was for an owner or grower of the grain in question.

Section 5 of the statute outlined specific criteria for the secretary of agriculture to apply in determining whether to designate a board of trade as a contract market, i.e., permit it to operate as a futures exchange for grain. A designated contract market failing to meet section 5's criteria could find its status as a designated contract market suspended or revoked by a Grain Futures Commission comprised of the secretary of agriculture, secretary of commerce, and attorney general.[20] A Grain Futures Administration was established under the authority of the secretary of agriculture, operating within the Department of Agriculture.[21]

2. Commodity Exchange Act of 1936

The Commodity Exchange Act, nominally an amendment to the Grain Futures Act, renamed the Grain Futures Commission as the Commodity Exchange Commission and formalized in statute the former Grain Futures Administration as the Commodity Exchange Authority.[22] As with the Grain Futures Commission, the Commodity Exchange Commission was comprised of the secretary of agriculture, secretary of commerce, and the attorney general. (We will see immediately below in subsection 3 that the Commodity Exchange Commission and Commodity Exchange Authority themselves were succeeded by the CFTC in 1974.)[23]

The commodity futures regulated by the Commodity Exchange Commission and Commodity Exchange Authority, limited in the Grain Futures Act to specified grain products, were expanded to include futures on cotton, rice, mill feeds,[24] butter, eggs, and Irish potatoes.[25] In addition to the existing requirement that boards of trade be designated as contract markets to trade futures in the enumerated commodities, two new categories of registrant were established, both in existence today. One, known as a futures commission merchant, was for entities "engaged in soliciting or in accepting orders for the purchase or sale of any commodity for future delivery on or subject to the rules of any contract market and that, in or in connection . . ." accepts money, securities or property to margin guarantee or secure such trades

---

20. Grain Futures Act § 6(a).

21. Jerry W. Markham, *The History of Commodity Futures Trading and its Regulation* 15 (Praeger Publishers 1987).

22. Pub. L. No. 74-675, 49 Stat. 1491 (1936) [hereinafter "Commodity Exchange Act"], § 3(b).

23. Commodity Futures Trading Commission Act of 1974, Pub. L. 93-463, 88 Stat. 1389 (1974).

24. Mill feeds are "by-products from the manufacture of flour, namely, bran, middlings, shorts, reddog flour, etc." Purdue University Agricultural Experiment Station, *Commercial Feeding Stuffs Quarterly Report October 2, 1919–December 31, 1919*, Bull. No. 242 at 8 (May 1920).

25. Commodity Exchange Act § 3(a) amending Grain Futures Act § 2(a).

or contracts.[26] The other, "floor broker," was for persons receiving commissions or other compensation for trading on the floor of a contract market.[27]

Over subsequent years, twelve amendments were made to the Commodity Exchange Act, further expanding its regulatory scope and including wool tops, fats and oils, cottonseed meal, cotton seed, peanuts, soybeans, soybean meal, wool, onions, livestock, livestock products, and frozen concentrated orange juice as commodities that, if traded for future delivery, were required to be traded on a board of trade designated as a contract market.

The table in figure 2.2 summarizes the amendments made to the Commodity Exchange Act between its enactment and 1970. As can be seen from figure 2.2, save for a significant broadening of the Commodity Exchange Act's enforcement provisions in February 1968, the primary thrust of most of the amendments was an expansion of the definition of commodity and, therefore, the contracts of sale for future delivery required to be traded on a designated contract market.

Figure 2.2 Amendments to Commodity Exchange Act, 1936–1970

Date of Amendment	Effect of Amendment	Citation
Apr. 7, 1938	Added wool tops to definition of commodities.	75 Pub. L. No. 471
Oct. 9, 1940	Added fats and oils, cottonseed meal, cottonseed, peanuts, soybeans, and soybean meal to definition of commodities.	76 Pub. L. No. 818
Dec. 19, 1947	Provides for publication of names, addresses, and commodities purchased and sold of traders on Boards of Trade.	80 Pub. L. No. 392
Aug. 28, 1954	Added wool to definition of commodities.	83 Pub. L. No. 690
June 16, 1955	Augmented investigatory powers of the secretary of agriculture and the Commodity Exchange Commission.	84 Pub. L. No. 82
July 26, 1955	Added onions to definition of commodities.	84 Pub. L. No. 174
July 24, 1956	Expanded hedging exemption from trading limits established by the Commodity Exchange Commission.	84 Pub. L. No. 778
Aug. 28, 1958	Amendment of multiple statutes, including Commodity Exchange Act, regarding appeals procedures.	85 Pub. L. No. 791
Aug. 28, 1958	Prohibited futures trading in onions.	85 Pub. L. No. 839
June 11, 1960	Amendment of multiple statutes, including Commodity Exchange Act, to account for use of certified mail in the same way as mail.	86 Pub. L. No. 507

---

26. Commodity Exchange Act § 3(b).

27. *Id.* This category of registrant only nominally exists today due to the decline of open outcry trading floors on exchanges.

Figure 2.2 Amendments to Commodity Exchange Act, 1936–1970 (*continued*)

Date of Amendment	Effect of Amendment	Citation
Feb. 19, 1968	Among other changes: • Added livestock and livestock products to definition of commodities; • Expanded definition of floor broker to include uncompensated individuals; • Expanded trading limits to broader "position limits" with entities acting in concert deemed to be one entity; • Inserted anti-manipulation provisions; and • Added penalties for violations.	90 Pub. L. No. 258
July 23, 1968	Added frozen concentrated orange juice to definition of commodities.	90 Pub. L. No. 418
Jan. 19, 1970	Amendment of multiple statutes by Organized Crime Control Act of 1970 (including Commodity Exchange Act) to provide for procedural changes regarding testimony and witnesses.	90 Pub. L. No. 452

3. Commodity Futures Trading Commission Act of 1974

Outside of a significant expansion in 1968, no major amendment to the Commodity Exchange Act had occurred since its passage in 1936. The Commodity Futures Trading Commission Act of 1974 overhauled the Commodity Exchange Act. Some of the reasons cited by legislators for this revision included:

• A cash market shortage of the commodities for which futures trading was subject to regulation.

• Concerns about recent frauds in the trading on markets outside the scope of regulation.

• A doubling of trading since 1969 in regulated markets and a quadrupling in the same period in unregulated markets.

• Protection of customers in unregulated markets since, among other things, there was no requirement in such markets to segregate customer funds.

• Perceived shortcomings in the designated contract markets' self-regulation particularly after 1968 amendments to the Commodity Exchange Act holding contract markets responsible for enforcement of their rules resulted in fewer rules.

• Perennial concerns about offsetting sales with no *bona fide* economic purpose, i.e., wash sales and bucketing of orders.[28]

---

28. H.R. Rep. No. 93-975, 40–52. *See also* Roberta Romano, *The Political Dynamics of Derivatives Securities Regulation*, 14 Yale J. on Reg. 279, 335, 337 (1997).

The changes wrought by the Commodity Futures Trading Commission Act were dramatic. The Commodity Exchange Authority and Commodity Exchange Commission were replaced with an independent agency known as the Commodity Futures Trading Commission (we have been referring to it herein as the "CFTC"), governed by five commissioners appointed by the president with the advice and consent of the Senate. Its powers were greatly expanded including plenary authority over futures in every commodity in existence other than foreign exchange. In addition to the existing registrant categories of designated contract market, futures commission merchant, and floor broker, two new categories of registrant were created, commodity pool operator and commodity trading advisor. (These two registration categories are the subject of chapters 7 and 8.)

Shortly before enactment of the Act, a House of Representatives report summarized the expansive authority of the CFTC.

House of Representatives Committee on Agriculture, *Commodity Futures Trading Commission Act of 1974 Report*

H.R. Rpt. 93-975 (Apr. 4, 1974)

[Title I provides that all] existing authority under the Commodity Exchange Act presently delegated to the Secretary of Agriculture and the Commodity Exchange Commission will be transferred to the new CFTC. All existing personnel of the . . . [Commodity Exchange Authority] will be transferred to and become employees of the CFTC. . . . In addition, the Commission will have its own General Counsel and legal staff as well as independent budgeting capability and its own Administrative Law Judges. . . .

A customer reparation proceeding before the Commission will be authorized . . . for handling customer complaints which arise from violations of the Act, particularly those which result in monetary damages to the customer. The Commission will have original jurisdiction to consider all such complaints which have not been resolved through the informal settlement procedure required of the contract markets and registered futures associations under the bill. . . . Initially, complaints would be considered by an Administrative Law Judge and then reviewed by the Commission before a final order is entered. A special judicial review of Commission decisions will be established for these proceedings which will allow either party adversely affected to appeal to the U.S. District Court. . . .

Title II provides broad new authority to the new Commission over futures trading in a number of areas. All commodities trading in futures will be brought within federal regulation under the aegis of the new Commission, however, provision is made for preservation of Securities Exchange Commission [*sic*] jurisdiction in those areas traditionally regulated by it. "Commodity Trading Advisors" and "Commodity Pool Operators" will be brought within the purview of the Act and will be required to register with the Commission annually. Whether trading by floor brokers and futures commission merchants for their own accounts and at the same time trading for their customers will be allowed will be determined by the Commission after a hearing within six months after enactment and if allowed, the circumstances under which it shall be conducted will be determined by the Commission.[29] The existing registration and examination for fitness requirement will be expanded to include all individuals handling customer accounts. . . . Contract markets will be required to establish their own customer claims settlement procedures complementing the Commission's procedures for the handling of customer complaints . . . and which will result in a voluntary informal settlement between the parties. Contract markets will be required to submit their bylaws, rules, regulations or resolutions which relate to the terms and conditions of futures contracts or other trading requirements to the Commission for its approval or disapproval.

The Commission will be given authority through the Attorney General to seek injunctions to stop any person from violating the Act or regulations thereunder and to stop any trader from controlling a commodity futures contract to the extent that he is effectively restraining trading in such contract but no injunction or mandamus will be issued *ex parte*. The Commission will have authority to impose monetary penalties . . . in both administrative and criminal proceedings for violations of the Act. The Commission will be authorized to require a contract market, after notice and hearings, to effectuate changes in its rules and practices which the Commission determines to be necessary for the protection of the public interest. The Commission will have authority to promulgate special rules and regulations for persons registered under the Act but who are not members of a contract market which may reasonably be required to protect the public interest. The Commission will have special emergency authority to direct contract markets to take such actions as it may deem necessary in "market emergency" situations, such as war, price controls, export embargoes, or significant intervention of a foreign government in the futures market, in order to facilitate the orderly training in or liquidation of any futures contract.

Title III provides enabling authority at the discretion of the Commission for persons registered under the Act and in the commodity trading business to establish a voluntary futures association or associations which would have authority to regulate the practices of its members in the public interest.[30] Such an association would register with the Commission and establish a uniform code of professional conduct for those in the commodities business and have disciplinary authority over its members. It would also be required to establish a procedure for the settlement

---

29. Such trading subsequently was allowed by the CFTC. *See* 41 Fed. Reg. 3192, 3203–3204 (Jan. 21, 1976) establishing 17 C.F.R. § 1.39.

30. Ultimately, after additional amendments via the Futures Trading Act of 1982, this resulted in the formation of the National Futures Association, discussed further in chapter 6, section A.2.

of claims and complaints against its members similar to that required of contract markets.

Association rules and actions would be subject to review by the new Commission. Association activity would serve solely as a complement rather than a displacement to the authority of the new Commission. . . .

———————

One substantial difference between H.R. 13113, the predecessor bill to the Commodity Futures Trading Commission Act and the version enacted into law was a modification to the scope of the CFTC's jurisdiction. The predecessor bill, H.R. 13113, conferred jurisdictional authority on the CFTC for, literally, commodity futures over everything save for onions, a commodity in which futures trading is prohibited.[31]

Although largely retained in the Act, this broad scope was objected to by the Department of the Treasury. In a resulting compromise shortly before enactment, a new carve-out from the CFTC's jurisdiction was included with the above-quoted language, known as the "Treasury Amendment." (Note that it was an amendment to the bill before enactment, not to the enacted statute.)

The Treasury Amendment added the caveat that "Nothing . . . shall be deemed to govern or in any way be applicable to transactions in foreign currency, security warrants, security rights, resales of installment loan contracts, repurchase options, government securities, or mortgages and mortgage purchase commitments, unless such transactions involve the sale thereof for future delivery conducted on a Board of Trade."[32] In effect, so long as not traded on a board of trade, i.e., an organized market for futures contracts, the CFTC had no jurisdiction over, among others, foreign currency transactions. Arguably, this language resulted in CFTC efforts to aggressively assert that markets not registered with the CFTC were, nonetheless, boards of trade, triggering CFTC jurisdiction over foreign currency forwards over such markets.[33] It also led to numerous subsequent expansions of CFTC jurisdiction over retail foreign currency transactions and foreign currency forwards discussed below in section E.1.a and in chapter 14.

The reasoning behind the original Treasury Amendment is enunciated below by the former chairman of the Federal Reserve, Alan Greenspan.

———————

31. Onion Futures Act, Pub. L. No. 85-839 (Aug. 28, 1958).

32. Pub. L. No. 93-463, 88 Stat. 1389 (1974), § 201.

33. Jerrold E. Salzman, *The Cost of Refusing to Define: Jurisdictional Turmoil and Litigation*, 18 No. 1 Futures & Derivatives L. Rep. 1, 3 (Mar. 1998): "For purposes of avoiding a political fight while retaining jurisdiction over fraudulent bucket shops, the CFTC expediently defines 'board of trade' to include the operations that it wishes to prosecute. The problem is that there is no principled argument to support the categorization of a crooked operation as a board of trade while refusing to apply that same characterization to a bank . . . dealing with the same class of customers."

Alan Greenspan, *Testimony of Federal Reserve Board Chairman Alan Greenspan on the Regulation of OTC Derivatives*

Testimony before the House Committee on Banking and Financial Services, available at http://www.federalreserve.gov/boarddocs/testimony/1998/19980724.htm

The Commodity Futures Trading Commission Act of 1974 did not make any fundamental changes in the objectives of derivatives regulation. However, it expanded the scope of the [Commodity Exchange Act ("CEA")] . . . quite significantly. In addition to creating the CFTC as an independent agency and giving the CFTC exclusive jurisdiction over commodity futures and options, the 1974 Act expanded the CEA's definition of a "commodity" beyond a specific list of agricultural commodities to include "all other goods and articles, except onions, . . . and all services, rights, and interests in which contracts for future delivery are presently or in the future dealt in."

Given this broadened definition of a commodity and an equally broad interpretation of what constitutes a futures contract, a wide range of off-exchange transactions would have been brought potentially within the scope of the CEA. The Treasury Department was particularly concerned about the prospect that the foreign exchange markets might be found to fall within the Act's scope. Aside from the difficulty of manipulating these markets, Treasury argued that participants in OTC markets, primarily banks and other financial institutions, and large corporations, did not need the consumer protections of the Commodity Exchange Act. Consequently, Treasury proposed and Congress included a provision in the 1974 Act, the "Treasury Amendment," which excluded off-exchange derivative transactions in foreign currency (as well as government securities, and certain other financial instruments) from the newly expanded CEA. . . .

---

4. The Shad-Johnson Accord

a. Jurisdictional Backdrop

The broad jurisdiction granted to the CFTC under the Commodity Futures Trading Commission Act soon brought the SEC and the CFTC into conflict. The dispute originated over whether the CFTC or the SEC had jurisdiction over options and futures on securities. The CFTC argued that it was granted exclusive jurisdiction over options and futures on all commodities, including securities and the SEC argued that it had jurisdiction over options or futures involving securities.

Three changes to the Commodity Exchange Act lay the basis for this conflict.

First, the definition of "commodity" in the Commodity Exchange Act had expanded from a handful of specified agricultural commodities to "[all] goods and articles, except onions . . . and all services, rights, and interests."[34] This definition included just about everything in existence, including securities.

Second, the CFTC was granted exclusive jurisdiction over:

> accounts, agreements (including any transaction which is of the character of, or is commonly known to the trade as, an "option" . . .) and transactions involving contracts of sale of a commodity for future delivery, traded or executed on a [designated] contract market . . . or any other board of trade, exchange, or market.[35]

Parsing this language, the CFTC was granted jurisdiction over options and futures. Since "commodity" was defined as nearly everything in existence, that the CFTC's jurisdiction was over the sale of a *commodity* for future delivery was no longer as limiting as it was when "commodity" was defined as being confined to specified agricultural products, such as corn or livestock.[36]

Third, there was a carve-out specifying that:

> [N]othing contained in this section shall (i) supersede or limit the juris-diction at any time conferred on the Securities and Exchange Commis-sion or other regulatory authorities under the laws of the United States or of any State, or (ii) restrict the Securities and Exchange Commission and such other authorities from carrying out their duties and responsibilities in accordance with such laws.[37]

In other words, to the extent that the SEC already had jurisdiction over options on securities or futures on securities, that jurisdiction would be preserved.

b. The Dispute Arises

Within a year, the first ripples of the dispute formed. In 1975, the Chicago Board of Trade, a CFTC-regulated futures exchange (i.e., a designated contract market), listed for trading futures on securities collateralized by mortgages guaranteed by a government agency, the Government National Mortgage Association. Although these securities, known as "GNMA securities," are guaranteed by a government agency, the Government National Mortgage Association, they are privately issued by mortgage lenders. The SEC formally objected to the listing of these futures.

When, in 1981, the Chicago Board of Options Exchange, an SEC-regulated secu-rities exchange, listed *options* on GNMA securities, the Chicago Board of Trade

---

34. Commodity Futures Trading Commission Act of 1974, Pub. L. No. 93-463, 88 Stat. 1389 (1974), § 201 amending Commodity Exchange Act § 2(a) (1974).

35. *Id.*

36. Additional uncertainty occurred on the question of whether "traded or executed on a [des-ignated] contract market . . . or any other board of trade, exchange, or market" applied to both options and futures or just futures.

37. Commodity Futures Trading Commission Act of 1974, Pub. L. No. 93-463, 88 Stat. 1389 (1974), § 201 amending Commodity Exchange Act § 2(a) (1974).

sued the SEC. They argued that the SEC did not have the jurisdictional authority to permit such an option to be listed by one of its registrants.

c. The Accord

While the case was pending in the Seventh Circuit,[38] the agencies came to an agreement known, based on the names of the SEC and CFTC chairmen at the time, as the Shad-Johnson Accord. The Shad-Johnson Accord:

- Granted the SEC jurisdiction over all securities options, including on indexes.
- Explicitly precluded the CFTC from exercising jurisdiction over securities options.
- Granted the CFTC jurisdiction over futures and options on futures referencing security indices other than narrow-based security indices.
- Outlawed single stock futures and options on single stock futures.

This understanding was largely enshrined in law by the Futures Trading Act of 1982.[39] One difference was that, in the statute, the SEC obtained a right of review before a futures contract on a security index other than a narrow-based security index or option on such a futures contract was listed by a CFTC-regulated exchange.[40]

d. Discord Remains

However, the Shad-Johnson Accord did not provide a lasting resolution of questions on the extent of the SEC's and CFTC's relative jurisdictions. Interpretative questions remained. These ultimately led to a reevaluation of the Shad-Johnson Accord.

Chicago Mercantile Exchange v. SEC
883 F.2d 537 (7th Cir. 1989)

Easterbrook, Circuit Judge. . . .

The CFTC regulates futures and options on futures; the SEC regulates securities and options on securities; jurisdiction never overlaps. Problem: The statute does not define either "contracts . . . for future delivery" or "option" — although it says that "'future delivery' . . . shall not include any sale of any cash commodity for deferred shipment or delivery." . . . [N]ewfangled instruments may have aspects of each of the prototypes. . . .

A futures contract, roughly speaking, is a fungible promise to buy or sell a particular commodity at a fixed date in the future. Futures contracts are fungible because

---

38. The Seventh Circuit ultimately ruled in favor of the CFTC. *See Board of Trade of the City of Chicago v. SEC*, 677 F.2d 1137 (7th Cir. 1982).

39. Futures Trading Act of 1982, Pub. L. No. 97-444, 96. Stat. 2294 (1983), § 101.

40. *Id.*

they have standard terms and each side's obligations are guaranteed by a clearing house. . . . Trading occurs in "the contract," not in the commodity. Most futures contracts may be performed by delivery of the commodity (wheat, silver, oil, etc.) Some (those based on financial instruments such as . . . the value of an index of stocks) do not allow delivery. . . .

A security, roughly speaking, is an undivided interest in a common venture the value of which is subject to uncertainty. Usually this means a claim to the assets and profits of an "issuer." . . .

Securities usually arise out of capital formation and aggregation (entrusting funds to an entrepreneur), while futures are means of hedging, speculation, and price revelation without transfer of capital. So one could think of the distinction between the jurisdiction of the SEC and that of the CFTC as the difference between regulating capital formation and regulating hedging. Congress conceived the role of the CFTC in that way when it created the agency in 1974 to assume functions that had been performed by the Department of Agriculture but which were no longer thought appropriate for that Department as futures markets expanded beyond commodities into financial instruments. . . .

Unfortunately, the distinction between capital formation and hedging falls apart when it comes time to allocate the regulation of options. . . .

The SEC consistently has taken the position that options on securities should be regulated as securities. For some years the CFTC maintained that options on securities should be regulated as futures because options are extrinsic to capital formation and because it is almost always possible to devise an option with the same economic attributes as a futures contract (and the reverse). Matters came to a head in 1980, when both agencies asserted jurisdiction over options on securities based on pools of notes. . . .

While the case was pending, the agencies reached a pact, which the SEC calls the Shad-Johnson Agreement and the CFTC calls the Johnson-Shad Agreement. (John Shad was the SEC's Chairman at the time, and Phillip Johnson the CFTC's.) This Accord (as we shall call it to avoid offending either agency) provided that jurisdiction over options follows jurisdiction over the things on which the options are written. So the SEC received jurisdiction of options on securities, while the CFTC got jurisdiction of options on futures contracts. . . .

Congress then enacted the Accord almost verbatim. . . . The legislature thought that this Accord would resolve things and restore a regime in which the SEC supervises capital formation and the CFTC hedging.

The legislation implementing the Accord left in place the premise [that] . . . if an instrument is both a security and a futures contract, then the CFTC's jurisdiction is exclusive. . . . Like many an agreement resolving a spat, the Accord addressed a symptom rather than the problem. Options are only one among many instruments that can have attributes of futures contracts as well as securities. . . .

Which means that the dispute of 1980–82 about options will be played out — is being played out — about each new instrument. . . .

Unless Congress changes the allocation of jurisdiction between the agencies, the question a court must resolve is the same as in [the] GNMA Options [case that triggered the Shad-Johnson Accord in the first place]: is the instrument a futures contract? If yes, then the CFTC's jurisdiction is exclusive, unless it is also an option on a security, in which case the SEC's jurisdiction is exclusive. So long as an instrument is a futures contract (and not an option), whether it is also a "security" is neither here nor there.

———————

The court then engaged in a complicated analysis as to whether the instrument in the case was a security or a future. It ultimately determined it was both. However, whereas the SEC had jurisdiction over securities, the CFTC had "exclusive" jurisdiction over futures. In that "jump ball" circumstance, the CFTC's "exclusive" jurisdiction over futures was deemed to win the day.[41]

Dissatisfaction with this continuing uncertainty and the prohibition on trading single stock futures led to reevaluation of the Shad-Johnson Accord.

United States General Accounting Office, *CFTC and SEC Issues Related to the Shad-Johnson Jurisdictional Accord*
GAO/GGD-00-89 (Apr. 6, 2000)

In the United States, SEC has authority over securities trading and the securities markets, and CFTC has authority over futures trading and the futures markets. According to SEC and CFTC, three amendments to the [Commodity Exchange Act (the "CEA")] . . . in 1974 led to jurisdictional disputes over securities-based futures. First, the act was amended to expand the definition of a commodity to include virtually anything — tangible or intangible.

Consequently, a security fell within the definition of a commodity. Second, the act was amended to provide CFTC with exclusive jurisdiction over all commodity futures transactions, including options on futures. Third, the act was amended to preserve SEC's preexisting authority over securities trading and the securities markets.

These three CEA amendments led to a dispute between SEC and CFTC that was eventually resolved through the Shad-Johnson Jurisdictional Accord. . . .

The accord allocated jurisdiction between SEC and CFTC for, among other things, securities-based options and securities-based futures and options on futures.[42] First, it provided SEC with jurisdiction over securities-based options, including stocks and stock indexes. Second, the accord prohibited futures (and options thereon) on

———————

41. *Chicago Mercantile Exchange v. SEC*, 883 F.2d 537, 548–549 (7th Cir. 1989).

42. [N. 12] The accord also clarified SEC and CFTC jurisdiction over options and futures on, among other things, certificates of deposit and foreign currencies.

single corporate and municipal securities. According to SEC and CFTC, the ban was intended to be temporary. . . .

Finally, the accord provided CFTC with jurisdiction over futures (and options thereon) on exempted securities[43] (other than municipal securities) and stock indexes. . . .

SEC and U.S. securities exchange officials have expressed concerns about repealing the accord trading prohibitions without first resolving the differences between the securities and commodities laws and regulations. They are concerned that, as a result of the differences, the prohibited futures could be used as substitutes for single stocks to circumvent compliance with federal securities laws and regulations. The most significant legal and regulatory differences that they identified include the lack of comparable insider trading prohibitions, margin levels, and customer protection requirements. . . .

Pivotal to addressing the legal and regulatory concerns related to repealing the current trading prohibitions is resolving the jurisdictional question of whether SEC, CFTC, or both agencies should regulate single stock and certain stock index futures. The answer to this question would determine whether such futures are regulated under the securities and/or commodities laws. In turn, the answer would affect the types of legal and regulatory changes that would be needed. According to securities exchange officials, futures on single stocks and certain stock indexes could be allowed to trade, if such futures were regulated as securities.

According to futures exchange officials, if the prohibited futures were allowed to trade, CFTC could effectively regulate them under the CEA. . . .

Repealing the accord trading prohibitions on single stock and certain stock-based index futures raises challenging legal and regulatory issues because of (1) the potential to use the prohibited futures as stock substitutes and (2) differences between securities and commodities laws and regulations. SEC, CFTC, and others have identified approaches for addressing such issues, with each approach pivoting on the jurisdictional question of whether SEC, CFTC, or both should regulate single stock and certain stock index futures. These approaches indicate that the legal and regulatory issues are resolvable. To that end, SEC and CFTC have begun working together to address these issues. However, uncertainty remains about the outcome of such efforts. Differences in SEC and CFTC perspectives, as well as in the securities and commodities laws, could continue to impede efforts aimed at reaching the compromises necessary to repeal the accord prohibitions.

The existence of active securities option and OTC equity derivatives markets, coupled with a very small but growing foreign market in single stock futures, indicates that the prohibited futures might serve a useful economic purpose. At the same time, the experience of these markets indicates that demand for the prohibited

---

43. [N. 13] Exempted securities include securities issued or guaranteed by the United States, the District of Columbia, or any U.S. state.

futures might be limited. Nonetheless, repealing the trading prohibitions could enhance the ability of the U.S. financial markets to compete and to develop innovative contracts. First, such action would allow U.S. exchanges to introduce additional stock-based futures and, in turn, let the marketplace determine their economic utility. Second, such action could allow U.S. futures exchanges to compete against other derivatives markets. Third, by eliminating the accord prohibition on certain stock index futures, U.S. firms could offer customers in the United States foreign stock index futures that could be used to hedge foreign stock investments. . . .

Recognizing that the resolution of the legal and regulatory issues pivots on the jurisdictional question of which agency or agencies should regulate single stock and certain stock index futures, continued congressional attention may be a key factor in the ultimate resolution of issues related to the repeal of the accord prohibitions.

Given the potential benefits of repealing the accord trading prohibitions and the potential for jurisdictional differences to continue to impede such efforts, we recommend that the Chairmen of SEC and CFTC (1) work together and with Congress to develop and implement an appropriate legal and regulatory framework for allowing the trading of futures on single stocks and all stock indexes, and (2) submit to Congress legislative proposals for repealing the accord trading prohibitions. . . .

———————

As noted below in section D.5, the General Accounting Office's recommendations were shortly followed by congressional action in the form of the Commodity Futures Modernization Act of 2000. The Commodity Futures Modernization Act also provided a sweeping liberalization of off-exchange derivatives trading. The off-exchange derivatives market (interchangeably referred to as "over-the-counter" or "OTC" derivatives market) had, in the interim, become sophisticated and extraordinarily large.

C. Growth in the Off-Exchange Derivatives Market

The modern swaps market is generally viewed as having begun in 1981 with a cross-currency interest rate swap brokered by Salomon Brothers between the World Bank and IBM.[44] Jon Rotenstreich, the partner at Salomon Brothers responsible for the

———————

44. *See Bank One Corp. v. C.I.R.*, 120 T.C. 174, 186 (2003) and Christian Johnson, *The Enigma of Clearing Buy-Side OTC Derivatives*, 29 Futures and Derivatives Law Report 11, no. 19 (2009), *citing World Bank: The IBM Deal That Opens a Cash Source*, Business Week, Sept. 7, 1981, 48. There are some arguments for an earlier date for the first modern swap going back as far as the 1960s. *See* Charles R. P. Pouncy, *Contemporary Financial Innovation: Orthodoxy and Alternatives*, 51 SMU L. Rev. 505, 529–531 (1998). Regardless, the IBM-World Bank swap appears to be the first to attract significant publicity.

IBM-World Bank swap noted that, at the time, "Nobody understood what the hell we were doing. . . . We were just trying to hammer it out to get the . . . thing done. . . ."[45]

From such inauspicious beginnings, a substantial market developed with the first interest rate swap generally held as being transacted in 1982, the first commodity swap in 1986, and the first equity swap in 1989.[46] By the end of 1994, more than $10 billion in notional of off-exchange interest rate derivatives and cross-currency swaps was estimated to be outstanding.[47] By 2008, that number exceeded $400 billion.[48]

An essential bridge between the IBM swap and a $400 billion marketplace (in just off-exchange interest rate derivatives and cross-currency swaps alone), was the development of standardized documentation for off-exchange derivatives under the auspices of a newly formed trade association, the International Swap Dealers Association, today known as the International Swaps and Derivatives Association or "ISDA."

The below provides an internal perspective on the incremental negotiation process used to achieve consensus in developing standardized documentation. The dividends of painstakingly building such a consensus are clear — for thirty years now this documentation is nearly universally used for the documentation of off-exchange derivatives.

Sean M. Flanagan, Student Author, *The Rise of a Trade Association: Group Interactions within the International Swaps and Derivatives Association*

6 Harv. Negot. L. Rev. 211 (Spring 2001)

The International Swaps and Derivatives Association, Inc. ["ISDA"], is a trade association for OTC derivatives dealers and other market-participants. The majority of ISDA's activities focuses on the market for privately negotiated swaps contracts. . . .

ISDA began as an informal swap documentation project undertaken by eleven financial institutions in 1984. In the early 1980s, swaps were still a novelty. Banks received large fees and substantial spreads for arranging interest-rate and currency swaps between large corporations, banks, and government entities. As swap mechanics were improved and swap volume increased, the major financial institutions that handled swaps each developed their own standard form agreements. . . . Each swap dealer's standard contract, including the definitions of the terms used in the contract, was unique.

---

45. *See* Bloomberg, *J.P. Morgan's Debt Swapping Passes Lending as Top Money-Maker* (Jan. 20, 2004) (copy on file with author).

46. *See Bank One Corp. v. C.I.R.*, 120 T.C. 174, 186 (2003) and Charles R. P. Pouncy, *Contemporary Financial Innovation: Orthodoxy and Alternatives*, 51 SMU L. Rev. 505, 530–532 (1998).

47. International Swaps and Derivatives Association, *ISDA Market Survey, 1987–Present*, available at https://www.isda.org/a/6tiDE/isda-market-survey-results1987-june-2010.pdf.

48. *Id.*

The result was that swaps with ostensibly identical terms differed depending on the individual who had negotiated the swap and the dealer from which they came. In addition, when dealers traded with one another, substantial effort was required to bridge the gaps between the two parties' forms and definitions. Negotiation over these contract terms consumed large amounts of time and effort. . . .

In 1984, Salomon Brothers contacted ten other institutions involved in the swaps market and arranged a meeting. The agenda was to discuss the development of documentation standards that would settle some of the issues that currently had to be negotiated — often at great expense — for each swap deal. An initial attempt to draft a standard form contract failed when parties involved in the process felt that the contract that was being developed too much resembled one participant's own standard form master agreement (most noticeably in typeface and layout). At this point, the group pooled its resources and retained the law firm Cravath, Swaine & Moore ("Cravath") to assist in drafting. Lawyers from Cravath attended the earliest meetings of the group. . . .

After the initial experience of failure, the parties generally assumed that the differences between the participants were too great for a consensus to be reached about what an actual standard form contract should look like. Instead, the group decided to focus on developing standard definitions for terms commonly used in swap agreements. These definitions included terms typically used in contracts and fallback provisions dictating actions in unforeseen circumstances.[49] Initially, this goal was intended to be the full extent of the group's activities. . . .

A committee of about 25 representatives from the eleven institutions was formed to work on developing . . . [standardized] definitions [for use in over-the-counter derivatives documentation]. These representatives included bankers, traders, in-house counsel, and outside counsel. The mix of participants provided the diversity of financial, legal, and practical expertise essential to developing robust documentation that would withstand the scrutiny of courts and the market. At documentation committee meetings, generally held in the offices of member institutions or outside counsel, the members discussed each definition as a group, sharing their personal and institutional opinions regarding appropriate standards and their experience with the issues involved.

Generally, each point was discussed by the group until a consensus was reached. The Cravath lawyers would try to capture the consensus in a draft definition, which then would be circulated among the group members for comment and discussion before being redrafted. The discussion, draft, comment, and redraft processes often were repeated several times for each definition. This openness was one of the keys to the success of the process. . . .

---

49. [N. 124] An example of this type of term is the "fallback rate" for LIBOR, which dictates what rates, if any, should be used to calculate payments on an interest rate swap if the interest rate index chosen as the measure of LIBOR by the parties is unavailable on the day a payment is to be calculated. . . .

When significant differences of opinion existed on the committee and consensus was not readily reached, the issue would be left to "float" without a push for an immediate resolution. Rick Grove, the Executive Director of ISDA from 1997 to January 2001, notes that policy disagreements have always been common in the organization. Successful resolution of such disagreements has been one of ISDA's key functions. . . .

Issues that remained contentious often could be resolved at the drafting stage. The outside counsel facilitating the drafting process prepared a compromise definition that met each party's interests. Alternatively, the definition was structured such that it included a menu of alternate standard definitions from which the contracting parties could choose, thereby avoiding resolution of the issue but allowing contracting parties to select for themselves.

The process of negotiating and drafting standard documentation that the documentation committee developed as it created these definitions has become the standard documentation process for ISDA projects. . . .

As the definitions project neared completion, the members of the group decided that they wanted to copyright the definitions and needed some sort of official entity to release the document and hold the copyright. The result was ISDA, the International Swaps Dealers Association,[50] which was formally created as a nonprofit corporation in 1985.

ISDA released the final definitions in 1985. While not technically a contract, the . . . [definitions, known as the "SWAPS Code,"] provided most of the key building blocks for a contract and ensured that swap dealers using it would be speaking the same language. For instance, parties could incorporate representations and warranties from the SWAPS Code wholesale by stipulating that they were incorporating them "as defined in the SWAPS Code" rather than negotiating and drafting them. The SWAPS Code was thus a great leap forward in standardization of the swaps market. . . .

The initial membership of ISDA consisted of the eleven participants in the development of the SWAPS Code. The board comprised ten representatives from those institutions with the board chairman functioning as the chief executive officer of the organization.[51] . . .

In the year following its formal creation, ISDA remained focused on standardizing terms and vocabulary, and it released an update of the SWAPS Code in 1986.

---

50. [N. 136] This name was changed in 1993 to the International Swaps and Derivatives Association to reflect the development of the industry and the expanding scope of ISDA's activities. . . . [T]he new name reflected a belief at the board level that ISDA's role was to represent the interests of the entire OTC derivatives industry, not just those of dealers.

51. [N. 139] . . . The initial directors were drawn from Shearson Lehman, Citibank, Bankers Trust, Morgan Guaranty, Salomon Brothers, Kleinworth Benson Cross Finance, Morgan Stanley, Merrill Lynch, First Boston and Goldman, Sachs.

In 1987, ISDA also published interest-rate and currency definitions. Like the original SWAPS Code, the development of these definitions was primarily done by ISDA members based in New York. During this period, some ISDA members in London, particularly Morgan Stanley's London office, began to push for the creation of a full, standardized master agreement.

Unlike the New York membership, which remained reluctant to attempt to develop a standard form contract for the industry, the London members saw a standardized master agreement as the logical next step. ISDA's board of directors agreed, and the London membership . . . took the lead role in the new documentation project. The end result was a pair of standard form master agreements, one for U.S.-dollar interest-rate swaps, and another for multicurrency interest-rate and currency swaps. Collectively, these two . . . agreements are referred to as the 1987 ISDA Master Agreement.

Major documentation accomplishments of ISDA during the early nineties included the re-drafting of the 1987 ISDA Master Agreement (resulting in the 1992 ISDA Master Agreement),[52] . . . the development of credit support and collateral documentation, and the development of definition booklets tailored to specific types of transactions. . . .

Starting in the late 1980s, the scope of ISDA's activities began to expand beyond just documentation. ISDA became involved in discussions with regulators on behalf of the OTC derivatives industry. ISDA board members and representatives now regularly testify before congressional committees. It coordinated industry opposition to CFTC and SEC regulation, acting both as an advocate for the industry and as an instrument for its self-regulation. ISDA has also lobbied successfully to get legislation passed in the U.S. explicitly recognizing the validity of netting agreements for derivatives contracts in bankruptcy contexts. . . .

In 2002, ISDA developed a successor to the 1992 ISDA Master Agreement, known as the 2002 ISDA Master Agreement. Both the 1992 and the 2002 ISDA Master Agreement are commonly used by market participants. The documentation of off-exchange derivatives is discussed in more detail in chapter 12, section E.1.

---

52. [N. 178] The re-draft . . . of the 1987 ISDA Master Agreement was motivated by several factors. First, the market had developed new financial products. . . . [I]t became desirable to design a master agreement with maximum flexibility, adding provisions, for instance, for physical settlement. The earlier agreement only provided for cash payments. . . . In addition, regulators were putting pressure on the industry to modify the close-out netting provisions in the agreement. In the 1987 Master Agreement close-out netting provisions (referred to in the industry as the "first method"), if the net value of transactions terminated upon default were calculated to be in favor of the defaulting party, no payment needed to be made by the non-defaulting party. . . . U.S. regulators preferred a system in which both parties, not just the defaulting party, were obligated to pay any net obligation to their counterparty. The 1992 ISDA Master Agreement was drafted so as to provide for this "second method" of close-out netting as an option. . . .

The growth in the off-exchange derivatives market was not without its setbacks. First, there was uncertainty in the marketplace as to whether these off-exchange derivatives might, more specifically, be deemed off-exchange commodity futures or commodity options contracts in violation of the Commodity Exchange Act. Second, it also spurred litigation. We turn to both these issues in the following section.

D. An Era of Deregulation and Growth, 1992–2007

1. Futures Trading Practices Act of 1992

Prior to 1992, the CFTC had the authority to exempt commodity option contracts from regulation under the Commodity Exchange Act.[53] However, the CFTC lacked analogous authority to exempt commodity futures contracts from regulation under the Commodity Exchange Act. This was problematic because the Commodity Exchange Act prohibits commodity futures from trading off-exchange, something discussed in detail in chapter 5, section A.1. Since swaps, at least economically, have many similarities to futures, the threat that off-exchange swaps could be deemed illegal off-exchange futures could not be addressed by the CFTC, even if the CFTC viewed a product as not necessitating regulation under the Commodity Exchange Act or the imposition of the Commodity Exchange Act's prohibition on off-exchange commodity futures. The only assistance the CFTC provided was to issue an interpretation defining the scope of "contract for the sale of a commodity for future delivery" to exclude some categories of swaps.[54]

The inadequacy of this approach was further illustrated by *Transnor (Bermuda) Limited v. BP North America Petroleum*.[55] In *Transnor*, the parties had entered into Brent crude oil contracts that had indicia of both a cash forward, in that physical delivery could be required, and a future, in that physical delivery was often not elected and there was a deep speculative market. The distinction was extremely important since off-exchange cash forward transactions were permissible and

---

53. *See* CFTC, *Regulation of Hybrid Instruments*, 54 Fed. Reg. 306984 (July 21, 1989) in which the CFTC exempted certain hybridized commodity options from regulation under the Commodity Exchange Act. *See also* CFTC, *Policy Statement Concerning Swap Transactions*, 54 Fed. Reg. 30694-01 (July 21, 1989), n. 1 citing to exemptive authority in Commodity Exchange Act §§ 4c(b) and 4c(d).

54. *See* CFTC, *Statutory Interpretation Concerning Certain Hybrid Instruments*, 54 Fed. Reg. 1139 (Jan. 11, 1989) that, unlike the exemptive relief related solely to commodity options in *Regulation of Hybrid Instruments* cited *supra* n. 53, is an interpretation presumably because the subject matter involved futures, for which the CFTC did not at the time have statutory exemptive authority. As one commentator put it, "The difference between an exclusion and an exemption is that an exempt product may be a futures contract, while an excluded product may not." Rebecca Leon, *The Regulation of Derivatives and the Effect of the Futures Trading Practices Act of 1992*, 3 Journal of Law & Policy 321, 336–337 (1994) (footnotes omitted).

55. 738 F. Supp. 1472 (S.D.N.Y. 1990).

off-exchange futures were unlawful. If they were unlawful, they were also unenforceable.

The judge ruled that the contracts were contracts "for the sale of a commodity for future delivery" under the Commodity Exchange Act and, therefore, unlawfully executed off-exchange.[56] The parties subsequently settled[57] but the uncertainty that resulted from the decision disrupted confidence in swaps markets.[58]

Without addressing its absence of statutory exemptive authority with respect to futures contracts, within six months of the *Transnor* ruling the CFTC issued an additional interpretation specifically excluding the subject transactions in *Transnor* from the scope of contracts "for the sale of a commodity for future delivery."[59] This directly contradicted the court's finding that such transactions *were* futures.

It was unknown whether in litigation to come such contracts would be ruled unenforceable off-exchange commodity futures contracts. The Department of the Treasury joined participants in the swap market in advocating for a legislative solution instead of *ad hoc*, case-by-case issuances of interpretations that may not have been given judicial deference.[60]

Largely in response to the clamor for more regulatory certainty, Congress enacted the Futures Trading Practices Act of 1992 amending the Commodity Exchange Act to grant the CFTC broad exemptive authority over futures.[61] Additionally, it created a new class of registrant, "floor trader," discussed in chapter 6, section D.

Almost immediately following passage of the Futures Trading Practices Act, the CFTC issued a broad exemption from the Commodity Exchange Act for swap agreements between "eligible swap participants" (i.e., regulated institutions or entities meeting specified asset thresholds)[62] and for the contracts that were the subject

---

56. *Transnor (Bermuda) Limited v. BP North America Petroleum*, 738 F. Supp. 1472, 1492 (S.D.N.Y. 1990).

57. *See Suit on Price of Crude Oil Is Settled*, N.Y. Times (May 23, 1990), available at http://www.nytimes.com/1990/05/23/business/company-news-suit-on-price-of-crude-oil-is-settled.html.

58. *See, e.g.,* Thomas A. Russo and Marlisa Vinciguerra, *Financial Innovation and Uncertain Regulation: Selected Issues Regarding New Product Development*, 69 Texas L. Rev. 1431, 1498 (May 1991) and C.A. "Cab" Baldwin, *Recent Changes in the Regulation of Commodity Sales and Derivatives*, 11 No. 3 ACCA Docket 76, 78 (Summer 1993) ("The parties settled the case at this point, but the multi-trillion dollar derivatives market was rocked by the implications of the court's reasoning.")

59. CFTC, *Statutory Interpretation Concerning Forward Transactions*, 55 Fed. Reg. 39188, 39189 at n. 1 (Sept. 25, 1990).

60. CFTC, *Regulation of Hybrid Instruments*, 54 Fed. Reg. 30684 (July 21, 1989).

61. Futures Trading Practices Act, Pub. L. No. 102-546, § 502.

62. CFTC, *Exemption for Certain Swap Agreement*, 58 Fed. Reg. 5587 (Jan. 22, 1993). One commentator described this at the time as a "parting gift" from Wendy Gramm, CFTC chairman and wife of then-Senator Phil Gramm, to the growing swap industry. Frank Partnoy, *The Shifting Contours of Global Derivatives Regulation*, 22 U. Pa. J. Int'l Econ. L. 421 (Fall 2001), 436–437 *citing*

of *Transnor*.[63] The swaps marketplace breathed a sigh of relief that lasted until the unsuccessful 1998 effort to bring swaps under direct CFTC supervision, discussed below in subsection 4.

2. Bankruptcy

In addition to the other statutory developments described in this chapter, during this era there were also various modifications to the Bankruptcy Code to ensure the enforceability of provisions contained in standard off-exchange derivatives transactions in the event of the bankruptcy of one of the parties. These are discussed in detail in chapter 18.

3. Bankers Trust Litigation

The market certainty intended to be provided by the Futures Trading Practices Act of 1992 did not preclude private litigation. There were open questions as to whether swaps could be construed as securities and what duty of care, if any, was owed by the seller of an off-exchange derivative to a purchaser of an off-exchange derivative.

Such was the question before the court in *Proctor & Gamble Company v. Bankers Trust Company*.[64] The backdrop was the now infamous "Bankers Trust tapes" in which employees of Bankers Trust, at the time one of the most prominent derivatives dealers, boasted of derivatives trading gains at the expense of their customers.[65] The tapes, mostly from recorded internal telephone lines that Bankers Trust later had to provide during the discovery phase of litigation,[66] contained remarks such as:

- Funny business, you know? Lure people into that calm and then totally [expletive] 'em.

Matt Rees, *Swaps Market: Farewell Gift from CFTC's Gramm for Swap Traders*, Bloomberg Business News (Jan. 14, 1993).

63. CFTC, *Exemption for Certain Contracts Involving Energy Products*, 58 Fed. Reg. 21286 (Apr. 20, 1993).

64. 925 F. Supp. 1270 (S.D. Ohio 1996).

65. These tapes were initially subject to a protective order by the trial judge in Proctor & Gamble prohibiting their disclosure. After being leaked to Business Week, they were subsequently unsealed after motions by Business Week and Proctor & Gamble. *See* Business Week, *Business Week v. The Judge*, Oct. 15, 1995, available at http://www.businessweek.com/stories/1995-10-15/business-week-vs -dot-the-judge.

66. *See* Gary E. Kalbaugh and Richard A. Miller, *Master Agreements for OTC Derivatives*, in *Commercial Contracts: Strategies for Drafting and Negotiation*, § 25.04[C][25] (Vladimir R. Rossman & Morton Moskin, eds., 2d ed., Aspen Publishers 2014).

- They would never know . . . how much money was taken out of that. . . . That's the beauty of Bankers Trust.

- [W]e set 'em up.

- I mean we told him $8.1 million when the real number was fourteen. So now if the real number is sixteen, we'll tell him that it is eleven. You know, just slowly chip away at that differential between what it really is and what we're telling him.

- [A]s soon as we quit selling dynamite, maybe we'll have a good business.

- Pad the numbers a little bit.

- [T]hese guys have done some pretty wild stuff. And you know, they probably do not understand it quite as well as they should. I think that they have a pretty good understanding of it, but not perfect. And that's like perfect for us.

- [W]hat Bankers Trust can do for Sony and IBM is get in the middle and rip them off — take a little money.[67]

Although the judge did find a potential avenue for a claim by Proctor & Gamble, the decision demonstrates the difficulty faced by a plaintiff in the absence of an explicit federal regulatory scheme. Despite Proctor & Gamble's efforts to characterize the swaps as securities or futures they were, in fact, neither. The court showed minimal deference to the fact that the SEC had claimed they were securities in parallel civil enforcement proceedings against Bankers Trust.

Proctor & Gamble Company v. Bankers Trust Company

925 F. Supp. 1270 (S.D. Ohio 1996)

Feikens, District Judge. . . .

Plaintiff, The Procter & Gamble Company ("P & G"), is a publicly traded Ohio corporation. Defendant, Bankers Trust Company ("BT"), is a wholly-owned subsidiary of Bankers Trust New York Corporation ("BTNY"). BTNY is a state-chartered banking company. BT trades currencies, securities, commodities and derivatives. Defendant BT Securities, also a wholly-owned subsidiary of BTNY, is a registered broker-dealer. The defendants are referred to collectively as "BT" in this opinion.

P & G filed its Complaint . . . alleging fraud, misrepresentation, breach of fiduciary duty, negligent misrepresentation, and negligence in connection with an interest rate swap transaction it had entered with BT. . . . This swap, explained more fully below, was a leveraged derivatives transaction whose value was based on the yield of five-year Treasury notes and the price of thirty-year Treasury bonds ("the 5s/30s swap"). . . .

---

67. Compiled from Kelley Holland and Linda Himelstein, *The Bankers Trust Tapes*, Business Week (Oct. 15, 1995), available at http://www.businessweek.com/stories/1995-10-15/the-bankers -trust-tapes, and *In the Matter of BT Securities Corporation*, CFTC Docket No. 95-3 (Dec. 22, 1994). They include dialogue regarding customers other than Proctor & Gamble.

P & G [also added] . . . claims related to a second swap. . . . This second swap was also a leveraged derivatives transaction. Its value was based on the four-year German Deutschemark rate. . . .

This motion [to dismiss P & G's claims] involves questions of first impression whether the swap agreements fall within federal securities or commodities laws. . . .

I conclude that the 5s/30s and DM swap agreements are not securities as defined by the Securities Acts of 1933 and 1934 . . . ; that these swap agreements are exempt from the Commodity Exchange Act ["CEA"]; [and] that there is no private right of action available to P & G under the antifraud provisions of that Act. . . .

I conclude that as a counterparty to swap agreements, BT owed no fiduciary duty to P & G. . . .

One leading commentator describes two "visions" of the "explosive growth of the derivatives market." Hu, *Hedging Expectations: "Derivative Reality" and the Law and Finance of the Corporate Objective*, Vol. 73 Texas L. Rev. 985 (1995). One vision, that relied upon by derivatives dealers, is that of perfect hedges found in formal gardens. This vision portrays the order — the respite from an otherwise chaotic universe — made possible by financial science.

Corporations are subject to volatile financial and commodities markets. Derivatives, by offering hedges against almost any kind of price risk, allow corporations to operate in a more ordered world.

The other vision is that of "science run amok, a financial Jurassic Park." . . .

Given the potential for a "financial Jurassic Park," the size of the derivatives market and the complexity of these financial instruments, it is not surprising that there is a demand for regulation and legislation. Several bills have been introduced in Congress to regulate derivatives.[68] BT Securities has been investigated by the Securities and Exchange Commission ("SEC") and by the Commodity Futures Trading Commission ("CFTC") regarding a swap transaction with a party other than P & G. *In re BT Securities Corp.*, Release Nos. 33-7124, 34-35136 and CFTC Docket No. 95-3 (Dec. 22, 1994). Bankers Trust has agreed with the Federal Reserve Bank to a Consent Decree on its leveraged derivatives transactions.

At present, most derivatives transactions fall in "the common-law no-man's land beyond regulations. . . ." Cohen, *The Challenge of Derivatives*, Vol. 63 Fordham L. Rev. at 2013. This is where the two highly specialized swap transactions involved in this case fall. . . .

[The P & G/BT Swap Agreements] are governed by . . . [a] standardized form, drafted by the International Swap Dealers Association, Inc. ("ISDA"). . . .

---

68. [N. 2] *See* H.R. 31, 104th Cong. 1st Sess. (1995); H.R. 20, 104th Cong. 1st Sess. (1995); H.R. 4745, 103rd Cong.2d Sess. (1994).

P & G unwound both [the DM Swap and the 5s/30s Swap early] . . . as interest rates in both the United States and Germany took a significant turn upward, thus putting P & G in a negative position *vis-a-vis* its counterparty BT. BT now claims that it is owed over $200 million on the two swaps, while P & G claims the swaps were fraudulently induced and fraudulently executed, and seeks a declaratory verdict that it owes nothing. . . .

P & G asserts that the 5s/30s and DM swaps fall within any of the following portions of [the definition of "security" in the Securities Act of 1933 and the Securities Exchange Act of 1934]: 1) investment contracts; 2) notes; 3) evidence of indebtedness; 4) options on securities; and 5) instruments commonly known as securities. . . .

Economic reality is the guide for determining whether these swaps transactions that do not squarely fit within the statutory definition are, nevertheless, securities. . . .

While the swaps may meet certain elements of the . . . investment contract [test], what is missing is the element of a "common enterprise." P & G did not pool its money with that of any other company or person in a single business venture. . . . Furthermore, BT was not managing P & G's money; BT was a counterparty to the swaps, and the value of the swaps depended on market forces, not BT's entrepreneurial efforts. The swaps are not investment contracts. . . .

As with the test whether an instrument is an investment contract, these swap agreements bear some, but not all, of the earmarks of notes. At the outset, and perhaps most basic, the payments required in the swap agreements did not involve the payment or repayment of principal. . . .

Balancing all the . . . factors, I conclude that the 5s/30s and DM swaps are not notes for purposes of the Securities Acts.

P & G argues that if the swaps are not notes, they are evidence of indebtedness because they contain bilateral promises to pay money and they evidence debts between the parties. . . .

The test whether an instrument is within the category of "evidence of indebtedness" is essentially the same as whether an instrument is a note. . . .

I do not accept P & G's definition of "evidence of indebtedness" in large part because that definition omits an essential element of debt instruments — the payment or repayment of principal. Swap agreements do not involve the payment of principal; the notional amount never changes hands.[69] . . .

The definition of a "security" in the 1933 and 1934 Acts includes the parenthetical phrase "(including any interest therein or based on the value thereof)," which could lead to a reading of the statute to mean that an option based on the value of a security is a security. Legislative history, however, makes it clear that that reading was not intended. . . .

---

69. Note that with some types of swaps, such as physically-settled foreign currency swaps, notional is exchanged by the parties.

Two Orders by the Security and Exchange Commission must be considered.

These rulings involve transactions between BT and Gibson Greetings, Inc. in swaps that have some similarities to the 5s/30s swap. *In re BT Securities Corp.,* Release Nos. 33-7124, 34-35136 (Dec. 22, 1994), and *In the Matter of Mitchell A. Vazquez,* Release Nos. 33-7269, 34-36909 (Feb. 29, 1996). In these cases, the SEC ruled that a "Treasury-Linked Swap" between BT and Gibson Greetings, Inc. was a security within the meaning of the federal securities laws. . . .

These SEC Orders were made pursuant to Offers of Settlement made by BT Securities and Vazquez. . . . They are not binding in this case . . . nor do they have collateral estoppel effect.

Even though both the Gibson Greetings, Inc. swap and the P & G 5s/30s swap derived their values from securities (Treasury notes), they were not options. . . .

Finally, P & G contends that both the 5s/30s and the DM swaps are securities simply because that is how these instruments were offered and how they have become known through a course of dealing. In support of this position, P & G points to the SEC Orders in the Gibson Greetings matter and asserts that BT labels leveraged derivatives as investments, speculative, and options; and that the financial markets and the media characterize derivatives as securities. . . .

[W]hen a party seeks to fit financial instruments into the non-specific categories of securities, those instruments must nevertheless . . . be a pooling of funds in a common enterprise. These swaps do not qualify as securities. . . .

Even if the 5s/30s and DM swaps are defined as . . . [commodity futures], swap agreements are exempt from all but the antifraud provisions of the CEA under the CFTC Swap Exemption. Title V of the Futures Trading Practices Act of 1992 granted the CFTC the authority to exempt certain swaps transactions from CEA coverage.

In response to this directive, on January 22, 1993, the CFTC . . . [provided] that swap agreements which [meet specified criteria, including that it is entered into between "eligible swap participants" are exempt from all but the anti-fraud provisions of the CEA.[70]]

The 5s/30s and DM swaps meet these criteria. . . .

P & G contends that a fiduciary relationship existed between it and BT. It argues that it agreed to the swap transactions because of a long relationship it had with BT and the trust that it had in BT, plus the assurance that BT would take on the responsibility of monitoring the transactions and that BT would look out for its interests. . . .

Even accepting these contentions as true, these contentions fail. . . .

P & G and BT were in a business relationship. They were counterparties. Even though, as I point out hereafter, BT had superior knowledge in the swaps transactions,

---

70. As noted below in subsection 5 this was superseded by the Commodity Futures Modernization Act and, as discussed in chapters 9 through 13, the Dodd-Frank Act.

that does not convert their business relationship into one in which fiduciary duties are imposed. . . .

[However,] New York caselaw establishes an implied contractual duty to disclose in business negotiations. Such a duty may arise where 1) a party has superior knowledge of certain information; 2) that information is not readily available to the other party; and 3) the first party knows that the second party is acting on the basis of mistaken knowledge. . . .

Thus, I conclude that defendants had a duty to disclose material information to plaintiff both before the parties entered into the swap transactions and in their performance, and also a duty to deal fairly and in good faith during the performance of the swap transactions. I confine these conclusions to the parameters outlined in this opinion. . . .

To summarize these rulings, I grant [BT's motions dismissing P & G's claims in which, though formally plaintiff, P & G asserted defenses to payment of $200 million which BT said was owed by P & G.]

But these rulings should not be misinterpreted. While they are required by the case management rules of civil procedure, plaintiff's case will proceed to trial [to adjudicate BT's $200 million claim against P & G.] . . .

The *Proctor & Gamble* case had several ramifications. A changing of the guard at Bankers Trust was considered to be primarily motivated by the associated scandal.[71] Bankers Trust ultimately accepted $35 million from Proctor & Gamble in lieu of the $200 million it claimed Proctor & Gamble was obligated to pay in settlement of its claims.[72] In total, due to derivatives disputes (including a prominent one with Gibson Greeting, excerpted below, in which Bankers Trust was said to have significantly understated Gibson's losses from what Bankers Trust's books showed) wrote off approximately $300 million in amounts it claimed it was otherwise owed.[73] There were allegations of improprieties with respect to nine customers in addition to Proctor & Gamble, including one based in Indonesia.[74] Bankers Trust settled related regulatory claims with the CFTC, SEC, and Federal Reserve.[75]

---

71. *See* Timothy L. O'Brien, *Bankers Trust Names Newman Chief; Passed-Over President Shanks Resigns*, Wall St. J. A4 (Oct. 20, 1995).

72. Saul Hansell, *Bankers Trust Settles Suit with P. & G.*, N.Y. Times D1 (May 10, 1996), available at http://www.nytimes.com/1996/05/10/business/bankers-trust-settles-suit-with-p-g.html.

73. *Id.*

74. Kelley Holland and Linda Himelstein, *The Bankers Trust Tapes*, Business Week (Oct. 15, 1995), available at http://www.businessweek.com/stories/1995-10-15/the-bankers-trust-tapes. For the claim of the Indonesian company, *see Bankers Trust International plc v. PT Dharmala Sakti Sejaherta and counterclaim*, [1996] C.L.C. 252 and *Bankers Trust International plc v. PT Dharmala Sakti Sejahtera & related action*, [1996] C.L.C. 518.

75. *See Proctor & Gamble*, 1276 *citing In re BT Securities Corp.*, SEC Release Nos. 33-7124 and 34-35136 (Dec. 22, 1994), CFTC Docket No. 95-3 (Dec. 22, 1994), Board of Governors of the Federal

One of these settlements, a CFTC enforcement action, related to complicated derivatives marketed to Gibson Greetings, a greeting card company. As especially highlighted in chapter 4, section B.1.b and chapter 15, the CFTC has the authority to bring civil actions for violations of the Commodity Exchange Act.

In the Matter of BT Securities Corporation

CFTC Docket No. 95-3 (Dec. 22, 1994)

... The Commodity Futures Trading Commission's ("Commission") Division of Enforcement ("Division") alleges and the Commission finds that: ...

Gibson Greetings, Inc. ("Gibson") ... primary business is manufacturing and selling greeting cards and gift wrap in the United States and abroad. . . .

This matter involves violations of the antifraud provisions of the federal commodity laws in connection with transactions in privately negotiated over-the-counter derivatives sold by BT Securities to Gibson.[76]

In May 1991, Gibson issued and privately placed ... [notes at a fixed rate of interest]. After the issuance of these notes, interest rates declined. Because the notes could not be prepaid for a number of years, Gibson began to explore the possibility of engaging in interest rate swaps to effectively reduce the interest rate paid on the notes. In connection with those efforts, Gibson sought proposals from a number of entities, and eventually decided to purchase derivatives from [BT Securities Corporation ("BT Securities")].

From November 1991 to March 1994, representatives of BT Securities proposed, and Gibson entered into, approximately 29 derivatives transactions, including amendments to existing derivatives, and terminations of derivatives or portions thereof. Over time, the derivatives sold to Gibson by BT Securities became increasingly complex, risky and intertwined. Many had leverage factors which caused Gibson's losses to increase dramatically with relatively small changes in interest rates. . . .

Gibson used the information provided by BT Securities about the value of its derivatives positions to evaluate particular transactions and to prepare its financial statements. . . .

The combination of Gibson's frequent trades on terms favorable to Bankers Trust made Gibson a particularly lucrative customer for BT Securities. During 1993 alone, the BT Securities managing director dealing with Gibson generated approximately $8 million in derivatives revenues from Gibson, out of a total of approximately $20 million from all of his derivatives customers that year. BT Securities

---

Reserve System, *Written Agreement by and Among Bankers Trust New York Corporation et al. and the Federal Reserve Bank of New York*, Docket No. 94-082-WA/RB-HC (Dec. 4, 1994).

76. [N. 3] This matter does not involve any finding or conclusion relating to the suitability of the derivative products described herein for Gibson. In addition, this Order does not affect, in any way, the legality or enforceability of swap transactions.

generated overall revenues of approximately $13 million from these transactions with Gibson. . . .

During the period from October 1992 to March 1994, BT Securities' representatives misled Gibson about the value of the company's derivatives positions by providing Gibson with values that significantly understated the magnitude of Gibson's losses. As a result, Gibson remained unaware of the actual extent of its losses from derivatives transactions and continued to purchase derivatives from BT Securities. In addition, the valuations provided by BT Securities' representatives caused Gibson to make material understatements of the company's unrealized losses from derivative transactions in the notes to its 1992 and 1993 financial statements. . . .

On two occasions when Gibson sought valuations for the specific purpose of preparing its financial statements, representatives of BT Securities provided Gibson with valuations that differed by more than 50% from the value generated by the computer model . . . recorded on Bankers Trust's books. . . .

BT Securities' managing director for the Gibson account told his supervisor in February 1994 that, "from the very beginning, [Gibson] just, you know, really put themselves in our hands like 96%. . . . And we have known that from day one." The managing director also told the Bankers Trust relationship officer responsible for the Gibson account that "these guys [Gibson] have done some pretty wild stuff. And you know, they probably do not understand it quite as well as they should. I think that they have a pretty good understanding of it, but not perfect. And that's like perfect for us." . . .

By virtue of the conduct described above, BT Securities, . . . during the period from at least October 1992, and continuing through at least March 1994, by use of the mails and the means and instrumentalities of interstate commerce, directly and indirectly has employed devices, schemes, and artifices to defraud Gibson in violation of [the Commodity Exchange Act]. . . .

The settlement resulted in a $10 million fine for Bankers Trust.[77] Separately, Bankers Trust settled with Gibson Greetings by forgiving $14 million of the $20 million it claimed was owed to it and effectively forgave $12 million owed to it by Federal Paper.[78] Bankers Trust was not the only swap provider threatened with litigation, only the most notorious. There were claims against Bear Stearns, Morgan Guaranty, and Solomon Brothers International Limited, among others.[79] In the off-exchange

---

77. *In the Matter of BT Securities Corp.*, CFTC Docket No. 95-3 at p. 6 (Dec. 22, 1994).

78. Jonathan Friedland, *Bankers Trust to Cancel Two Contracts About Derivatives with Federal Paper*, Wall St. J. A2 (Dec. 20, 1994).

79. For a survey of over-the-counter derivatives litigations in the era *see* Frank Partnoy, *The Shifting Contours of Global Derivatives Regulation*, 22 U. Pa. J. Int'l Econ. L. 421, 446–484 (Fall 2001).

derivatives market, it led to the market adoption of standardized "non-reliance" representations drafted by ISDA.[80]

The questions raised in *Proctor & Gamble* regarding the regulatory treatment for swaps — whether they should be deemed securities, commodities, or neither — were not resolved until the passage of the Commodity Futures Modernization Act of 2000 and, later, the Dodd-Frank Act.

4. Developments Leading to the Commodity Futures Modernization Act of 2000

On May 6, 1998, the CFTC, chaired by President Clinton appointee Brooksley Born, issued a "Concept Release" on over-the-counter derivatives.[81] It was cast as a reexamination of the CFTC's approach to off-exchange derivatives, triggered by market changes since 1993 and "a number of large, well-publicized, financial losses."[82] The CFTC specifically asked for public comment on seventy-five questions it posed on topics ranging from eligible products and participants to clearing, registration, capital, and reporting requirements.[83]

The Department of the Treasury, Federal Reserve Board, and SEC sent a joint letter to both houses of Congress within a month of the Concept Release condemning it and attaching proposed legislation pre-empting the CFTC from altering the *status quo ante* with respect to derivatives as of the 1993 CFTC Swap Exemption.[84]

The CFTC's claim to have "no preconceived result in mind"[85] was treated skeptically by the marketplace, particularly after the testimony of Chairman Born before the House Committee on Banking and Financial Services on July 24, 1998, in which she stated that "the OTC derivatives market is already subject to regulation by the Commission through the CEA's prohibition of OTC futures and option that are not exempted from the exchange-trading requirement . . ." and implied a looming rollback of some of the safe harbors for off-exchange derivatives established

---

80. *See* Gary E. Kalbaugh and Richard A. Miller, *Master Agreements for OTC Derivatives*, in *Commercial Contracts: Strategies for Drafting and Negotiation*, §25.04[C][24], n. 90 (Vladimir R. Rossman & Morton Moskin, eds., 2d ed., Aspen Publishers 2014).

81. CFTC, *Over-the-Counter Derivatives*, 63 Fed. Reg. 26114 (May 12, 1998).

82. *Id.* at 26114–15. The CFTC's 1998 Concept Release preceded by a few months the September bailout of hedge fund Long-Term Capital Management by a syndicate arranged by the Federal Reserve Bank of New York. *See* Gen. Accounting Off., *Report on Long-Term Capital Management*, GAO/GGD-00-3 (Oct. 1999) and President's Working Group on Financial Markets, *Leverage and the Lessons of Long-Term Capital Management* (Apr. 1999).

83. CFTC, *Over-the-Counter Derivatives*, 63 Fed. Reg. 26114, 26120–26127 (May 12, 1998).

84. *Ltr. from Robert E. Rubin, Secretary, Department of the Treasury, Alan Greenspan, Chairman, Board of Governors of the Federal Reserve System and Arthur Levitt, Chairman, Securities and Exchange Commission to The Honorable Newt Gingrich, Speaker U.S. House of Representatives* (June 5, 1998), available at http://www.treasury.gov/press-center/press-releases/Pages/cftcltr.aspx.

85. CFTC, *Over-the-Counter Derivatives*, 63 Fed. Reg. 26114, 26114, 26116 (May 12, 1998).

in 1993.[86] Largely interpreted as presaging an initiative by the CFTC to regulate off-exchange derivatives and being the cause of market uncertainty, the reaction of over-the-counter derivative market participants to the 1998 Concept Release was uniformly hostile as shown in the following comments made to the Concept Release by market participants:

- "Swap transactions have not changed in any fundamental way since the CFTC adopted its Swap Exemption in 1993. . . . The CFTC's other justifications for its review . . . divert attention from what users of these transactions truly require: a clear declaration that swaps are not futures subject to the Commodity Exchange Act. . . ."[87]

- "[The 1998 Concept Release] raises issues that may call into question the legal certainty and enforceability of OTC derivatives transactions."[88]

- "[A]ny actions taken by the Commission to implement the types of regulation contemplated by the Concept Release will serve only to foster uncertainty with respect to the enforceability and legal status of a wide variety of important financial transactions."[89]

The only (tepid) support the CFTC received on the initiative was from the two major futures exchanges.[90]

Bowing to the broad front arrayed against the CFTC, in October 1998 Congress enacted legislation substantially in the form proposed by the Treasury Department, Federal Reserve, and SEC prohibiting the CFTC from any regulatory initiatives on the matter until March 30, 1999.[91] The CFTC withdrew the Concept Release on November 17, 1999.[92] As one Commissioner noted:

> [The Concept Release] has been widely perceived, both within the derivatives industry and among other financial regulators, as indicating an intent to expand the Commission's regulatory reach with respect to OTC

---

86. *Testimony of Brooksley Born, Chairperson Commodity Futures Trading Commission Concerning the Over-the-Counter Derivatives Market Before the U.S. House of Representatives Committee on Banking and Financial Services* (July 24, 1998), available at http://www.cftc.gov/opa/speeches/opaborn-33.htm.

87. *Comments of the International Swaps and Derivatives Association to the 1998 Concept Release*, CL 34, p. 2 (Oct. 13, 1998). The comments received are available on the CFTC's website at https://www.cftc.gov/foia/comment98/foi98--019_1.htm.

88. *Comments of the Futures Industry Association to the 1998 Concept Release*, CL 41, p. 2 (Oct. 13, 1998).

89. *Comments of the New York Clearinghouse to the 1998 Concept Release*, CL 32, p. 1 (Oct. 13, 1998).

90. *Comments of the Chicago Mercantile Exchange to the 1998 Concept Release*, CL 24 (Oct. 12, 1998) and *Comments of the Chicago Board of Trade to the 1998 Concept Release*, CL 27 (Oct. 13, 1998).

91. Pub. L. No. 105-277, § 760 (Oct. 21, 1998).

92. CFTC, *Concept Release Concerning Over-the-Counter Derivatives*, 64 Fed. Reg. 65669 (Nov. 22, 1999).

derivatives. In view of that perception and any legal uncertainty it may have created, I agree to withdrawal of the Concept Release.[93]

In opposing the 1998 Concept Release, a group of industry associations had stated "We are confident that Congress, drawing upon the experience and views of all interested parties, will take appropriate action to permit continued growth in the use of these important risk management tools and to protect the reputations of the United States as a safe environment for financial innovation and a major market for these transactions."[94] Their confidence in Congress was well placed. On December 21, 2000, the Commodity Futures Modernization Act of 2000 was enacted into law.[95]

The Long-Term Capital Management Scare

In a seven-month period in 1998, Long-Term Capital Management lost ninety percent of its capital due to positions it had in the securities, futures, and swaps markets that were adversely affected by a Russian debt crisis.

At one time, it was one of the largest hedge funds in the world. The size of its positions in futures and derivatives and the secondary effects its default would have on the financial markets led the Federal Reserve to organize a private consortium to provide enough financial support for its survival.

Among the reasons cited for this scare was a lack of authority by the SEC and CFTC over affiliates of their registrants that were trading derivatives with Long-Term Capital Management. Long-Term Capital Management was cited as perhaps being the largest user in the world of interest rate swaps and had over $750 billion in swap notional amount outstanding at any one time.

Although the estimated potential losses were in the $3 billion to $5 billion range and not considered likely to cause any large financial failures, what was perceived as a close call was treated with great concern by the financial community.

Source: Gen. Accounting Off., *Report on Long-Term Capital Management*, GAO/GGD-00-3 at 1, 3, 7 (note omitted), 12 (Oct. 1999)

---

93. *Id.*

94. *Comments of ABA Securities Association, American Bankers Association, The Bankers Roundtable, The Bond Market Association, Emerging Markets Traders Association, The Energy Group, Financial Markets Lawyers Group, The Foreign Exchange Committee, Futures Industry Association, International Swaps and Derivatives Association, Securities Industry Association and U.S. Chamber of Commerce to the 1998 Concept Release*, CL 31, p. 1–2 (Oct. 13, 1998).

95. Appendix E of Pub. L. No. 106-554, 143 Stat. 2763 (2000). In addition to the clarity sought by the over-the-counter derivative marketplace, another motivation for passage of the Commodity Futures Modernization Act and, in fact an inducement for their support, was the futures exchanges' wish to offer futures based on single stocks or narrow-based securities indices, something banned by the Futures Trading Act of 1982. *See* William J. Brodsky [at the time Chairman and CEO of the Chicago Board Options Exchange], *New Legislation Permitting Stock Futures: The Long and Winding Road*, 21 Nw. J. Int'l L. & Bus. 573, 576 (Spring 2001).

5. The Commodity Futures Modernization Act of 2000

The motivation for the Commodity Futures Modernization Act was primarily regulatory certainty for the off-exchange derivatives industry and repealing the prohibition on single stock futures. The blueprint for the Act was provided over a year before its passage by a report issued by the President's Working Group on Financial Markets. In addition to the regulatory certainty for the off-exchange derivatives industry and the repeal of the prohibition on single stock futures, the report recommended establishing a statutory framework for non-retail trading facilities with a lower regulatory burden than that in place for the retail designated contract markets where futures traditionally trade (designated contract markets are the subject of chapter 5).

Note that the President's Working Group throughout uses the phrase "eligible swap participant." This was a term used to identify non-retail (i.e., high net worth institutional) counterparties by the CFTC in the 1993 CFTC Swap Exemption that granted such entities an exemption from CFTC regulation of swaps transactions so long as both parties were eligible swap participants. This is discussed above in subsection 1.

Ultimately, while adopting most of the President's Working Group's ideas, the Commodity Futures Modernization Act used a new term that captured a broader range of entities in its scope, "eligible contract participant." Therefore, when you read the following excerpt from the President's Working Group's report, references to "eligible swap participants" should be read as references to "eligible contract participants."

President's Working Group on Financial Markets,[96]
Over-the-Counter Derivatives Markets and the Commodity Exchange Act

Nov. 1999, available at www.treasury.gov/resource-center/fin-mkts /Documents/otcact.pdf

... The members of the Working Group agree that there is no compelling evidence of problems involving bilateral swap agreements that would warrant regulation under the ... [Commodities Exchange Act, hereinafter "CEA"]; accordingly, many types of swap agreements should be excluded from the CEA. The sophisticated counterparties that use OTC derivatives simply do not require the same protections under the CEA as those required by retail investors. In addition, most of the dealers in the swaps market are either affiliated with broker-dealers or FCMs that

---

96. At this time, the President's Working Group was comprised of Lawrence H. Summers, Secretary of the Treasury, Alan Greenspan, Chairman of the Board of Governors of the Federal Reserve, Arthur Levitt, Chairman of the SEC, and William J. Rainer, Chairman of the CFTC. Brooksley Born had resigned as CFTC Chairman months beforehand.

are regulated by the SEC or the CFTC or are financial institutions that are subject to supervision by bank regulatory agencies. . . .

Most OTC derivatives are not susceptible to manipulation. The vast majority of the contracts are settled in cash, based on a rate or price determined by a separate highly liquid market with a very large or virtually unlimited deliverable supply. Thus, for example, it is highly unlikely that interest rate swaps could be used to manipulate interest rates. Furthermore, prices established in OTC derivatives transactions do not serve a significant price discovery function.

Due to the characteristics of markets for non-financial commodities with finite supplies, however, the Working Group is unanimously recommending that the exclusion not be extended to agreements involving such commodities. For example, in the case of agricultural commodities, production is seasonal and volatile, and the underlying commodity is perishable, factors that make the markets for these products susceptible to supply and pricing distortions and to manipulation. . . . The CFTC should, however, retain its current authority to grant exemptions for derivatives involving non-financial commodities, as it did in 1993 for energy products, where exemptions are in the public interest and otherwise consistent with the CEA.

Accordingly, the Working Group unanimously makes the following recommendations:

- Bilateral swap agreements (including those that reference non-exempt securities) entered into by eligible swap participants, on a principal-to-principal basis, should be excluded from the CEA, provided that the transactions are not conducted on [a physical or electronic facility in which all market makers and other participants have the ability to execute transactions and bind both parties by accepting offers which are made by one member and open to all members of the facility]. . . . Certain types of electronic trading systems described below should, however, also be excluded from the CEA.

- Because the material economic terms of many swap agreements are similar, the requirement in the . . . [1993 CFTC Swap Exemption] that swap agreements not be standardized as to their material economic terms should be eliminated. Moreover, as discussed below, the Working Group is recommending that clearing of swap agreements be permitted, subject to appropriate regulatory oversight of the clearing function. Accordingly, insofar as transactions are subject to regulated clearing, the exclusion should not prohibit fungibility of contracts or require that creditworthiness be a material consideration.

- The exclusion should not extend to any swap agreement that involves a nonfinancial commodity with a finite supply.[97]

---

97. This was ultimately narrowed by the Commodity Futures Modernization Act to only agricultural commodities.

- The exclusion should only cover swaps between eligible swaps participants. . . .
- The CEA should be amended to clarify that a party to a transaction may not avoid performance of its obligations under, or recover losses incurred on, a transaction based solely on the failure of that party (or its counterparty) to comply with the terms of an exclusion or exemption under the CEA.
- To the extent that OTC derivatives transactions between eligible swap participants are excluded from the CEA, they should also be excluded from the coverage of certain state laws (such as laws designed to regulate gambling or bucket shops) that might be construed to prohibit or inappropriately regulate such transactions. . . .

The Working Group members agree that the introduction of electronic trading systems for OTC derivatives has the potential to promote efficiency and transparency, and, by enhancing liquidity and enabling firms that participate in the systems to impose more reliable internal controls on their traders, to reduce risks. Furthermore, there is not at this time a demonstrable need for regulation of systems with the characteristics described below. The method by which a transaction is executed has no obvious bearing on the need for regulation in markets. . . . Moreover, electronic trading systems for OTC derivatives have only just begun to emerge on a widespread basis, and such systems should be allowed to grow, unburdened by a new anticipatory statutory structure that could prove entirely inappropriate to their eventual evolution. . . .

Clearing of OTC derivatives has the potential to reduce counterparty risks associated with such transactions through risk management techniques that may include mutualizing risks, facilitating offset, and netting. Clearing, however, tends to concentrate risks and certain responsibilities for risk management in a central counterparty or clearinghouse. Consequently, the effectiveness of the clearinghouse's operations and risk management systems is critical for the stability of the markets that it serves. For this reason, the Working Group unanimously recommends that Congress enact legislation to provide a clear basis for the regulation of clearing systems that may develop for OTC derivatives. . . .

The Working Group's recommendations with respect to electronic trading and clearing for OTC derivatives . . . are intended to remove legal obstacles to innovations that have the potential to increase efficiency, transparency, liquidity, and competition and to reduce systemic risk. Some market participants have argued, however, that U.S. futures exchanges are at a competitive disadvantage to OTC derivatives markets as the result of CEA regulation, and that the introduction of electronic trading and clearing for derivatives outside of the CEA has the potential to exacerbate the perceived imbalance.

The Working Group acknowledges that the . . . recommended [swap] exclusion would create differences in the level of regulation between OTC derivatives that are electronically traded and cleared and products offered by futures exchanges that may have some similar characteristics.

The difference would be mitigated to some extent if the Working Group's recommendations are adopted, because futures exchanges could establish electronic trading systems and clearing systems under the same conditions as their competitors. Floor-traded futures contracts with some economic characteristics similar to the derivatives for which electronic trading systems might develop would, however, face different levels or different forms of regulation.

Where regulation exists, it should serve valid public policy goals. The justifications generally cited for regulation of the futures markets include the goals of protecting retail customers from unfair practices, protecting the price discovery function, and guarding against manipulation. With similar policy goals in mind, the Working Group has recommended limiting the proposed exclusion for swap agreements to eligible swap participants. . . .

Although the CEA gives the CFTC broad authority to grant exemptive relief if it determines it is in the public interest, the CFTC notes that the Conference Report for the . . . [Futures Trading Practices Act] specifically stated that "[t]he goal of providing the Commission with broad exemptive authority is not to prompt a wide-scale deregulation of markets falling within the ambit of the [CEA]."[98] Accordingly, the CFTC believes that further Congressional direction is necessary. . . .

––––––––––

These recommendations of the President's Working Group were substantially embodied in the Commodity Futures Modernization Act of 2000.[99]

The President's Working Group also recommended amendment of the Commodity Exchange Act to "provide that transactions in foreign currency futures and options are subject to . . . [the Commodity Exchange Act] if they are entered into between a retail customer and an entity that is neither regulated or supervised by the SEC or a federal banking regulator nor affiliated with such a regulated or supervised entity."[100] This was largely accomplished by the Commodity Futures Modernization Act's grant of jurisdiction to the CFTC over retail foreign exchange options and futures unless: (1) transacted on an SEC-regulated exchange; or (2) one of the parties is a financial institution, broker-dealer, futures commission merchant, insurance company or affiliate, financial holding company, or "investment bank holding company," a now defunct category of SEC registration.[101]

The Commodity Futures Modernization Act overturned the prohibition in the Futures Trading Act of 1982 on security futures on other than a broad-based

98. [N. 45] H.R. Rep. 102-978, 102d Cong., 2d Sess. 81 (1992).
99. Appendix E of Pub. L. No. 106-554, 143 Stat. 2763 (2000).
100. President's Working Group on Financial Markets, *Over-the-Counter Derivatives Markets and the Commodity Exchange Act* 33–34 (Nov. 1999), available at https://home.treasury.gov/system/files/236/Over-the-Counter-Derivatives-Market-Commodity-Exchange-Act.pdf.
101. Commodity Futures Modernization Act, Appendix E of Pub. L. No. 106-554, 143 Stat. 2763, §102 (2000), adding new §2(c) to the Commodity Exchange Act.

securities index and provided for the trading of a "security future," i.e., "a contract of sale for future delivery of a single security or of narrow-based security index . . ." by granting the CFTC and SEC joint jurisdiction over such products. The Act required facilities on which such products are traded to be registered with the CFTC and SEC and intermediaries to be registered as both securities broker-dealers *and* futures commission merchants.[102]

The Commodity Futures Modernization Act also blocked the SEC from "registering, or requiring, *recommending, or suggesting*" (emphasis added) registration of a security-based swap agreement traded between "eligible contract participants" as a security.[103]

This era of deregulation would prove, however, to be short-lived.

Brooksley Born, Regulatory Prophet?

In the aftermath of the 1998 CFTC Concept Release, Brooksley Born was the recipient of near universal criticism from her peer financial regulators for her effort to regulate the off-exchange derivatives industry. In the years immediately following the Financial Crisis (see section E.2 below), some have lauded her as a hero demonstrating remarkable foresight, and she was the winner of a John F. Kennedy Profile in Courage Award for her pro-regulation stance in the face of concerted opposition.[a]

[a] Justin Fox, *Brooksley Born, American Hero*, Time (Apr. 7, 2009), available at http://business.time.com/2009/04/07/brooksley-born-american-hero, and John F. Kennedy Presidential Library and Museum, *Brooksley Born*, https://www.jfklibrary.org/events-and-awards/profile-in-courage-award/award-recipients/brooksley-born-2009.

E. The Second Era of Federal Regulation

1. Fraud in the Foreign Exchange Market and the "Enron Loophole"

a. Retail Foreign Exchange

As noted above, the Commodity Futures Modernization Act granted the CFTC jurisdiction over retail foreign exchange options and futures with exceptions if traded on a securities exchange or through specified entities already subject to regulation. Disputes arose as to the extent of that jurisdiction with two circuits narrowly construing the scope of "futures" and broadly construing what were deemed to be

---

102. *See* Commodity Futures Modernization Act, Appendix E of Pub. L. No. 106-554, 143 Stat. 2763, Tit. II "Coordinated Regulation of Security Futures Products" (2000).

103. Commodity Futures Modernization Act, Appendix E of Pub. L. No. 106-554, 143 Stat. 2763, §§ 302(a) and 303(a) (2000).

foreign exchange "forwards" outside of the CFTC's jurisdiction.[104] As a result, the CFTC's acting chairman at the time stated that "a large sector of retail fraud" effectively remained "outside of the prosecutorial authority of the CFTC."[105]

Congress ultimately responded to these cases—and the CFTC's acting chairman's plea—by including in the CFTC Reauthorization Act of 2008[106] amendments to the Commodity Exchange Act expanding the CFTC's jurisdiction to include retail foreign exchange (including both spots and forwards) when "offered, or entered into, on a leveraged or margined basis, or financed" by one of the parties.[107] An exception for spot contracts remained only to the extent that such a contract was a "contract of sale that . . . results in actual delivery within 2 days; or creates an enforceable obligation to deliver. . . ."[108] In 2010, the CFTC finalized rules establishing a new category of CFTC registrant, a "retail foreign exchange dealer."[109] We discuss the CFTC's regulation of foreign exchange markets and similar regulation of retail commodity markets in chapter 14.

b. Exempt Boards of Trade and Exempt Commercial Markets

The CFTC Reauthorization Act of 2008 also sought to address what was perceived as a lax regulatory regime established by the Commodity Futures Modernization Act for derivatives trading facilities other than designated contract markets, sometimes referred to as the "Enron loophole" after the energy trading firm that filed for bankruptcy in December 2001 and was a significant trader on these markets. It also operated one such facility, EnronOnline.

The Act tightened the reporting and position limits requirements on derivatives trading facilities other than designated contract markets (which were already subject to the strictest regulatory oversight).[110] It turned out to be the opening salvo for regulation of the entire off-exchange derivatives market—one in which both exempt boards of trade and exempt commercial markets had no role. The Dodd-Frank Act provided the framework for their abolition and, by 2015, both had been formally abolished.[111]

---

104. *See CFTC v. Zelener*, 373 F.3d 861 (7th Cir. 2004) and *CFTC v. Erskine*, 512 F.3d 309 (6th Cir. 2008).

105. Walter Lukken, *Written Testimony of CFTC Acting Chairman Walter Lukken Before the Subcommittee on General Farm Commodities and Risk Management Committee on Agriculture U.S. House of Representatives* 6 (Oct. 24, 2007), available at http://www.cftc.gov/idc/groups/public/@ newsroom/documents/speechandtestimony/opalukken-29.pdf.

106. Pub. L. No. 110-234, 122 Stat. 923, Tit. XIII (2008).

107. Commodity Exchange Act § 2(c)(2)(C)(i)(I)(aa).

108. Commodity Exchange Act § 2(c)(2)(C)(i)(I)(bb).

109. CFTC, *Regulation of Off-Exchange Retail Foreign Exchange Transactions and Intermediaries*, 75 Fed. Reg. 55410 (Sept. 10, 2010).

110. CFTC Reauthorization Act of 2008, Pub. L. No. 110-234, 122 Stat. 923, §§ 13201 and 13202 (2008).

111. *See* Dodd-Frank Act §§ 723 and 734 and CFTC, *Repeal of the Exempt Commercial Market and Exempt Board of Trade Exemptions*, 80 Fed. Reg. 59575 (Oct. 2, 2015). The Dodd-Frank Act also

2. Financial Crisis of 2007–2009

The Financial Crisis has been described as the "worst since the Great Depression"[112] and as "a once-in-a-century credit tsunami."[113]

Convention places the start of the Financial Crisis in the summer of 2007,[114] though, of course, its causes lay in preceding events, particularly with respect to the structure of the market for so-called sub-prime mortgages.[115]

The Federal National Mortgage Association, better known as "Fannie Mae," is a government-sponsored entity that purchases mortgage loans meeting specified eligibility criteria from private mortgage originators. It then sponsors the issuance and sale of securities; known as mortgage-backed securities, collateralized by these mortgages. (Due to losses during the Financial Crisis, Fannie Mae was placed under the conservatorship, i.e., direct supervision, of the Federal Housing Finance Agency in 2008.[116])

Sub-prime mortgages are mortgages with mortgage eligibility criteria that are, in some respects, less strict than for the standard Fannie Mae "conventional" mortgage loan.[117] In testimony before the House of Representatives Committee of Government Oversight and Reform, former Federal Reserve Chairman Greenspan summarized the contribution to the Financial Crisis of the breakdown of the sub-prime mortgage market in the summer of 2007.

---

abolished "derivatives transaction execution facilities." Dodd-Frank Act § 734. This regulatory category never had any registrants, so the change had no direct market impact. *See* CFTC, *Adaptation of Regulations to Incorporate Swaps*, 77 Fed. Reg. 66288, 66301 (Nov. 2, 2012).

112. Gary B. Gorton, *Misunderstanding Financial Crises: Why We Don't See Them Coming* 182 (Oxford University Press 2012). *See also* Financial Crisis Inquiry Commission, *The Financial Crisis Inquiry Report* xv (Jan. 2011), available at http://fcic-static.law.stanford.edu/cdn_media/fcic-reports /fcic_final_report_full.pdf.

113. *Testimony of Alan Greenspan Before House Committee of Government Oversight and Reform* (Oct. 23, 2008), available at https://www.govinfo.gov/content/pkg/CHRG-110hhrg55764 /html/CHRG-110hhrg55764.htm.

114. Gary B. Gorton, *Misunderstanding Financial Crises: Why We Don't See Them Coming* 182 (Oxford University Press 2012) and Federal Reserve Bank of New York, *Financial Turmoil Timeline*, available at https://www.newyorkfed.org/medialibrary/media/research/global_economy/Crisis _Timeline.pdf.

115. Financial Crisis Inquiry Commission, *The Financial Crisis Inquiry Report* xxiii–xxiv (Jan. 2011), available at http://fcic-static.law.stanford.edu/cdn_media/fcic-reports/fcic_final_report _full.pdf.

116. James B. Lockhart, *Statement of FHFA Director James B. Lockhart at News Conference Announcing Conservatorship of Fannie Mae and Freddie Mac* (Sept. 7, 2008), available at https:// www.fhfa.gov/Media/PublicAffairs/Pages/Statement-of-FHFA-Director-James-B--Lockhart-at -News-Conference-Annnouncing-Conservatorship-of-Fannie-Mae-and-Freddie-Mac.aspx.

117. *See* Federal National Mortgage Association, *Eligibility Matrix*, https://singlefamily .fanniemae.com/media/20786/display.

Alan Greenspan, *Testimony of Alan Greenspan Before House Committee of Government Oversight and Reform*

Oct. 23, 2008, available at http://www.gpo.gov/fdsys/pkg/CHRG
-110hhrg55764/html/CHRG-110hhrg55764.htm

What went wrong with global economic policies that had worked so effectively for nearly four decades? The breakdown has been most apparent in the securitization of home mortgages. The evidence strongly suggests that without the excess demand from securitizers, subprime mortgage originations (undeniably the original source of crisis) would have been far smaller and defaults accordingly far fewer.

But subprime mortgages pooled and sold as securities became subject to explosive demand from investors around the world. These mortgage backed securities being "subprime" were originally offered at what appeared to be exceptionally high risk-adjusted market interest rates. But with U.S. home prices still rising, delinquency and foreclosure rates were deceptively modest. Losses were minimal. To the most sophisticated investors in the world, they were wrongly viewed as a "steal."

The consequent surge in global demand for U.S. subprime securities by banks, hedge, and pension funds supported by unrealistically positive rating designations by credit agencies was, in my judgment, the core of the problem. Demand became so aggressive that too many securitizers and lenders believed they were able to create and sell mortgage backed securities so quickly that they never put their shareholders' capital at risk and hence did not have the incentive to evaluate the credit quality of what they were selling. Pressures on lenders to supply more "paper" collapsed subprime underwriting standards from 2005 forward. Uncritical acceptance of credit ratings by purchasers of these toxic assets has led to huge losses.

The consequent surge in global demand for U.S. subprime securities by banks, hedge and pension funds, supported by unrealistically positive rating designations by credit agencies, was, in my judgment, the core of the problem. Demand became so aggressive that too many securitizers and lenders believed they were able to create and sell mortgage-backed securities so quickly, that they never put their shareholders' capital at risk, and, hence, did not have the incentive to evaluate the credit quality of what they were selling.

Pressures on lenders to supply more paper collapsed subprime underwriting standards from 2005 forward. Uncritical acceptance of credit ratings by purchasers of these toxic assets has led to huge losses.

It was the failure to properly price such risky assets that precipitated the crisis. In recent decades, a vast risk management and pricing system has evolved, combining the best insights with mathematicians and finance experts, supported by major advances in computer and communications technology.

A Nobel Prize was awarded for discovery of the pricing model that underpins much of the advance in derivatives markets. This modern risk management paradigm held sway for decades. The whole intellectual edifice, however, collapsed in the summer of last year, because the data inputted into the risk management models generally covered only the past two decades, a period of euphoria. . . .

When, in August 2007, markets eventually trashed the credit agencies rosy ratings, a blanket of uncertainty descended on the community. Doubt was indiscriminately cast on pricing of securities that had any taint of subprime. . . .

The financial landscape that will greet the end of the crisis will be far different from the one that entered it little more than a year ago. Investors, chastened, will be exceptionally cautious. Structured investment vehicles, Alt-A mortgages, and a myriad of other exotic financial instruments are not now, and are unlikely to ever find willing buyers.

Regrettably, also on that list are subprime mortgages, the market for which has virtually disappeared. Home and small business ownership are vital commitments to a community. We should thus seek ways to reestablish a more sustainable subprime mortgage market. This crisis will pass, and America will reemerge with a far sounder financial system.

Losses in the sub-prime markets and the resultant economic malaise ultimately led to, in the U.S. alone:[118]

- The bankruptcy of Lehman Brothers.
- Placement of Fannie Mae and the Federal Home Loan Mortgage Corporation, i.e., "Freddie Mac" into conservatorship.
- Bank of America's purchase of Countrywide Financial and Merrill Lynch.
- The acquisition of Wachovia by Wells Fargo.
- Washington Mutual's seizure by federal regulators and subsequent sale of its assets to JPMorgan Chase.
- The U.S. government's investment in American International Group, commonly known as "AIG," preceded by its record-making $61.7 billion quarterly loss.
- JPMorgan's purchase of Bear Stearns.
- The placement of IndyMac Bank, FSB, into receivership by the Federal Deposit Insurance Corporation.
- The bankruptcy of sub-prime lenders New Century Financial Corporation and American Home Mortgage Investment Corporation.

---

118. This list is derived from Federal Reserve Bank of New York, *Financial Turmoil Timeline*, available at https://www.newyorkfed.org/medialibrary/media/research/global_economy/Crisis_Timeline.pdf and Federal Reserve Bank of St. Louis, *The Financial Crisis: A Timeline of Events and Policy Actions*, available at https://www.stlouisfed.org/financial-crisis/full-timeline.

- Purchases by the Department of the Treasury of preferred shares in many U.S. banks as part of effort to recapitalize banks.
- The bankruptcy of General Motors.
- The bankruptcy of CIT Corporation.

To bolster market confidence and increase liquidity, various emergency programs were sponsored by the Federal Reserve and the Department of the Treasury.

In the final report of the Financial Crisis Inquiry Commission investigating the causes of the Financial Crisis, credit default swaps were described as significant contributors.[119] This led to a dissenting statement by Peter Wallison and Arthur F. Burns in which it was noted:

> Despite a diligent search, the FCIC never uncovered evidence that unregulated derivatives, and particularly credit default swaps (CDS), was a significant contributor to the financial crisis through "interconnections." The only company known to have failed because of its CDS obligations was AIG, and that firm appears to have been an outlier. Blaming CDS for the financial crisis because one company did not manage its risks properly is like blaming lending generally when a bank fails. Like everything else, derivatives can be misused, but there is no evidence that the "interconnections" among financial institutions alleged to have caused the crisis were significantly enhanced by CDS or derivatives generally. For example, Lehman Brothers was a major player in the derivatives market, but the Commission found no indication that Lehman's failure to meet its CDS and other derivatives obligations caused significant losses to any other firm, including those that had written CDS on Lehman itself.[120]

Title VII of the Dodd-Frank Act, enacted into law on July 21, 2010, imposed a new regulatory framework for off-exchange derivatives.[121]

3. The Dodd-Frank Act

The Dodd-Frank Act unwound the broad exemption from derivatives regulation provided by the Commodity Futures Modernization Act and substituted a complex regulatory framework largely inspired by the longstanding regulatory architecture for commodity futures. This framework was founded on a division of the derivatives market into "swaps" (primarily regulated by the CFTC) and "security-based swaps" (primarily regulated by the SEC). New categories of registrants were created

---

119. Financial Crisis Inquiry Commission, *The Financial Crisis Inquiry Report* xiv, 50–51 (Jan. 2011), available at http://fcic-static.law.stanford.edu/cdn_media/fcic-reports/fcic_final_report_full.pdf.

120. *Id*. at 447.

121. Pub. L. No. 11-203 (2010).

such as "swap dealers," "major swap participants," "security-based swap dealers," and "major security-based swap participants."

Prescriptive requirements were introduced regarding market operation with mandatory clearing and requirements to trade on "swap execution facilities."

These changes, and the resultant present regulatory framework, are the subject of chapters 9 through 13.

F. The Future of Derivatives Regulation

It has been a regulatory rollercoaster for derivatives, going from regulation to near total deregulation (for off-exchange derivatives) to comprehensive re-regulation. An original motivation for derivatives regulation was protection of retail customers, just as a motivation for the Commodity Futures Modernization Act's deregulation was the lesser regulatory safeguards needed for a market comprised of non-retail parties (i.e., eligible contract participants).

The Dodd-Frank Act modified this calculus. With the Financial Crisis a new perception took hold that institutions with large derivatives exposures could pose a systemic threat to the financial system. The focus, as reflected in the Dodd-Frank Act, shifted to regulating the largest market participants — the ones arguably least in need of regulatory protections — in the interest of protecting the global economy from "systemic risk."

Derivatives have been blamed for much of the Financial Crisis. Yet, they are an essential component of our financial system. The one certainty is that the effort to find the right regulatory balance will continue.

Questions and Comments

1. Why was Thales paying for the use of the olive presses in the future in the extract from Aristotle in A.1 a forward transaction and not a futures transaction? Were the facts to be repeated today, would the CFTC have regulatory jurisdiction? If not, should the CFTC have regulatory jurisdiction?

2. It has been calculated that "[i]n 1888, an estimated 25 quadrillion bushels of wheat were traded through futures contracts, even though farmers harvested only 415 million actual bushels of wheat in the United States that year."[122] What are some reasons why the amount traded as futures might be multiples larger than the amount harvested? Are the derivatives markets today different in this respect?

3. What is the difference between a derivative and a security? How do they overlap? This is a question that will continue to arise and will be further addressed in chapter 4, section C.1. It is valuable to begin considering the question now.

---

122. Lynn A. Stout, *Uncertainty, Dangerous Optimism, and Speculation: An Inquiry into some Limits of Democratic Governance*, 97 Cornell L. Rev. 1177, 1204 (2012).

4. Why were bucket shops difficult to extinguish? What might have been the public policy rationale for eliminating them? Can gambling and speculating be distinguished? If so, how?

5. Was the outcome of the Shad-Johnson Accord the best available in the circumstances? What other outcomes were possible?

6. Could the conflict triggered by Shad-Johnson have been avoided by more specific drafting of the Commodity Futures Trading Commission Act? Is "tactical ambiguity" in a statute or regulation sometimes beneficial and, if so, when and why?

7. The security futures market never blossomed. One reason cited was strict margining requirements that made trading securities options preferable. Could the SEC-CFTC dual regulatory scheme be a contributor to this market's lack of success?

8. Brooksley Born, chairman of the CFTC from 1996 until 1999, advocated that the CFTC regulate off-exchange swaps. Was she correct as a public policy matter? Has her position been vindicated by the passage of the Dodd-Frank Act in 2010 and the resulting regulation of off-exchange swaps?

9. Should the derivatives markets be regulated to protect society from the consequences of the misuse of derivatives or deregulated so the markets have the flexibility to evolve and adapt to new conditions? (This question is one that should be considered throughout this book and is a public policy question that arises in any regulatory context.)

10. Why were derivatives blamed by some for the Financial Crisis? How much did they contribute?

11. The Financial Crisis Inquiry Commission was intended to provide an authoritative, non-partisan verdict on the causes of the Financial Crisis. However, three different conclusions were reached. One was reflected in a majority report to which all six democratic members subscribed, and there were two dissenting statements authored by the four republicans. How does this impact the report's authority?

Chapter 3

The Jurisdiction Conferred by the Commodity Exchange Act

A. Introduction

The Commodity Futures Trading Commission Act of 1974 amended the Commodity Exchange Act so that, instead of having jurisdiction over futures traded on a list of agricultural commodities, the CFTC had broad — and exclusive — jurisdiction over nearly all commodity options and futures. The Dodd-Frank Act expanded this jurisdiction to grant the CFTC equally broad, albeit not exclusive, jurisdiction over most swaps. The Dodd-Frank Act also granted the CFTC the authority to police manipulation in some spot and forward commodity transactions.[1] The scope of this anti-manipulation authority is uncertain and has been the subject of litigation.

In fact, the exact extent of the CFTC's jurisdiction generally has been the subject of challenges from other regulators and private litigants. Some of these challenges have been resolved judicially or by statutory fixes. Others remain unresolved.

Legislative efforts to fine-tune the CFTC's jurisdiction historically have sought to navigate a safe passage between overly broad regulation that results in overlapping jurisdiction and overly narrow regulation that results in regulatory gaps. The process of charting this course no doubt will continue as markets evolve and experience accrues. The Dodd-Frank Act was just the most recent such effort.

Note that the CFTC's jurisdiction over foreign exchange, leveraged retail commodities, and commodity option transactions is not discussed in this chapter. The CFTC's jurisdiction over these products has always operated on an independent track, examined in chapter 14. While, in practice, the CFTC's regulation of exchange-traded options is similar to that of futures, its regimes with respect to foreign exchange and leveraged retail commodities are more distinct.

Finally, the CFTC has jurisdiction over entities it regulates. This jurisdiction is examined in the chapter related to the regulated entity.

---

1. Dodd-Frank Act § 753, amending Commodity Exchange Act § 6(c).

B. CFTC Jurisdiction Over Commodity Futures

The central pillar of the CFTC's authority is its jurisdiction over commodity futures. Its jurisdiction is plenary and exclusive. The Commodity Exchange Act states that the CFTC "shall have exclusive jurisdiction . . . with respect to accounts, agreements . . . and transactions involving . . . contracts of sale of a commodity for future delivery . . . traded or executed on" a futures exchange or similar market.[2]

On first reading, two potentially major limitations to the CFTC's authority stand out. The CFTC's jurisdiction is limited to contracts of sale of a commodity for future delivery and only when "traded or executed on" a futures exchange or similar market. However, the definition of "commodity" is arguably so broad that the limitation is almost rendered meaningless. In addition to a list of enumerated agricultural commodities, the term "commodity" includes "all other goods and articles . . . and all services, rights, and interests . . . in which contracts for future delivery are presently or in the future dealt in" with the exclusion of onions and motion picture box office receipts.[3] In other words, nearly everything in existence is potentially a commodity. See figure 3.1 for the definition in full.

Figure 3.1 Definition of Commodity in Commodity Exchange Act § 1a(9)

> Wheat, cotton, rice, corn, oats, barley, rye, flaxseed, grain sorghums, mill feeds, butter, eggs, Solanum tuberosum (Irish potatoes), wool, wool tops, fats and oils (including lard, tallow, cottonseed oil, peanut oil, soybean oil, and all other fats and oils), cottonseed meal, cottonseed, peanuts, soybeans, soybean meal, livestock, livestock products, and frozen concentrated orange juice, and all other goods and articles, except onions (as provided by section 13-1 of this title) and motion picture box office receipts (or any index, measure, value, or data related to such receipts), and all services, rights, and interests (except motion picture box office receipts, or any index, measure, value or data related to such receipts) in which contracts for future delivery are presently or in the future dealt in.

The second limitation, the requirement that the contract of sale of a commodity for future delivery be traded or executed on a futures exchange or similar market, also turns out not to be a meaningful limitation because section 4(a) of the Commodity Exchange Act requires that all contracts of sale of a commodity for future delivery be traded on futures exchanges.

We do, however, find a significant limitation on the CFTC's jurisdiction in the phrase "future delivery." The phrase is not defined by the Commodity Exchange Act other than by what it excludes: "The term 'future delivery' does not include any sale of any cash commodity for deferred shipment or delivery."[4] It is not further defined by CFTC regulation.

---

2. Commodity Exchange Act § 2(a)(1)(A).
3. Commodity Exchange Act § 1a(9).
4. Commodity Exchange Act § 1a(27).

This carve-out of any "cash commodity for deferred shipment or delivery" from what is a contract for "future delivery" is commonly known as the forward exemption. It is essential to understanding what is a contract for future delivery. Without this carve-out, something as prosaic as a magazine subscription could conceivably be a commodity future transaction since a magazine is a commodity and the subscription contemplates "future delivery" of the magazines. Due to the operation of section 4(a) of the Commodity Exchange Act, without the forward exemption, it could arguably be illegal to buy a magazine subscription other than on a futures exchange!

Although the boundary between a futures transaction and a transaction involving a "cash commodity for deferred shipment or delivery" may be obvious in the example of the magazine subscription, courts have struggled to establish a test for consistently distinguishing between the two, and the CFTC has declined to provide a further definition of these terms. By defining the terms, courts would have guidance and the CFTC could claim *Chevron* deference. On the other hand, the CFTC would have to live by its definition, potentially reducing its flexibility in asserting jurisdiction.

Due to the dearth of legislative or administrative guidance, there is a circuit split on the question of how a futures transaction is distinguished from a forward transaction, i.e., a transaction involving a cash commodity for deferred shipment or delivery. The most aggressive assertion of what is a contract for "future delivery" is the decision of the Ninth Circuit in the *Co Petro* case below.

CFTC v. Co Petro Marketing Group, Inc.

680 F.2d 573 (9th Cir. 1982)

Canby, Circuit Judge:

Co Petro Marketing Group, Inc., and individual appellants, Harold Goldstein and Michael Krivacek, (Co Petro) appeal from an order of the district court permanently enjoining them from offering, selling, or otherwise engaging in futures contracts in petroleum products, in violation of . . . the Commodity Exchange Act. . . . Co Petro contends that the contracts it sold were not subject to the Act. . . . We affirm the district court's judgment that Co Petro was offering and selling "contracts of sale of a commodity for future delivery" (futures contracts) within the meaning of . . . the Act. . . .

Co Petro is licensed by the State of California as a gasoline broker. It operated a chain of retail gasoline outlets and also acted as a broker of petroleum products, buying and reselling in the spot market several hundred thousand gallons of gasoline and diesel fuel monthly. While part of its business operations involved the direct sale of gasoline to industrial, commercial, and retail users of gasoline, Co Petro also offered and sold contracts for the future purchase of petroleum products pursuant to an "Agency Agreement for Purchase and Sale of Motor Vehicle Fuel" (Agency Agreement).

Under the Agency Agreement, the customer (1) appointed Co Petro as his agent to purchase a specified quantity and type of fuel at a fixed price for delivery at an agreed future date, and (2) paid a deposit based upon a fixed percentage of the purchase price. Co Petro, however, did not require its customer to take delivery of the fuel. Instead, at a later specified date the customer could appoint Co Petro to sell the fuel on his behalf. If the cash price had risen in the interim Co Petro was to (1) remit the difference between the original purchase price and the subsequent sale price, and (2) refund any remaining deposit. If the cash price had decreased, Co Petro was to (1) deduct from the deposit the difference between the purchase price and the subsequent sale price, and (2) remit the balance of the deposit to the customer. A liquidated damages clause provided that in no event would the customer lose more than 95% of his initial deposit.

Co Petro marketed these contracts extensively to the general public through newspaper advertisements, private seminars, commissioned telephone solicitors, and various other commissioned sales agents. The Commodity Futures Trading Commission brought this statutory injunctive action . . . seeking to enjoin Co Petro's sales of petroleum products pursuant to its Agency Agreements. . . .

Co Petro contends that the Commission lacks jurisdiction over transactions pursuant to its Agency Agreements because these agreements are "cash forward" contracts expressly excluded from regulation. . . . While [the Act] . . . provides the Commission with regulatory jurisdiction over "contracts of sale of a commodity for future delivery," it further provides that the term future delivery "shall not include any sale of any cash commodity for deferred shipment or delivery." Cash commodity contracts for deferred shipment or delivery are commonly known as "cash forward" contracts, while contracts of sale of a commodity for future delivery are called "futures contracts". See H.R.Rep.No.93-975, 93d Cong., 2d Sess. 129–30 (1974). The Act, however, sets forth no further definitions of the term "future delivery" or of the phrase "cash commodity for deferred shipment or delivery." The statutory language, therefore, provides little guidance as to the distinctions between regulated futures contracts and excluded cash forward contracts and, to our knowledge, no other court has dealt with this question. . . . Our examination of the relevant legislative history leads us to conclude that Co Petro's Agency Agreements are not cash forward contracts within the meaning of the Act.

The exclusion for cash forward contracts originated in the Future Trading Act, Pub.L.No.67-66, s 2, 42 Stat. 187 (1921). . . . There is no indication that Congress drew this exclusion otherwise than to meet a particular need such as that of a farmer to sell part of next season's harvest at a set price to a grain elevator or miller. These cash forward contracts guarantee the farmer a buyer for his crop and provide the buyer with an assured price. Most important, both parties to the contracts deal in and contemplate future delivery of the actual grain.

The exclusion was carried forward without change into the Grain Futures Act, Pub.L.No.67-331, s 2, 42 Stat. 998 (1922). In 1936, Congress enacted the Commodity Exchange Act, Pub.L.No.74-675, 49 Stat. 1491 (1936). This Act . . . reworded the exclusion to except "any cash commodity for deferred shipment or delivery." . . . Although the Act has been amended numerous times since 1936, the language excluding cash commodities for deferred shipment or delivery has remained the same. . . .

The situation for which the exclusion for cash forward contracts was designed is not present here. Co Petro's Agency Agreement customers were, for the most part, speculators from the general public. The underlying petroleum products had no inherent value to these speculators. They had neither the intention of taking delivery nor the capacity to do so. Yet it was to the general public that Co Petro made its strongest sales pitches. For example, in an advertisement in the Los Angeles Times under the headline "Invest in Gasoline," Co Petro stated: "The Sophisticated Small Investor Can Make Money Buying Gasoline. It's a high risk-high potential yield opportunity." . . .

There is nothing in the legislative history surrounding cash forward contracts to suggest that Congress intended the exclusion to encompass agreements for the future delivery of commodities sold merely for purposes of such speculation. . . .

Even though Co Petro's Agency Agreements do not fall within the exclusion for cash forward contracts, there remains the question whether they are "contracts of sale of a commodity for future delivery" (futures contracts) within the meaning of . . . the Act. Co Petro contends that its Agency Agreements cannot be futures contracts because they lack most of the common distinguishing features of futures contracts as they are known in the industry. Futures contracts traded on the designated markets have certain basic characteristics. Except for price, all the futures contracts for a specified commodity are identical in quantity and other terms. The fungible nature of these contracts facilitates offsetting transactions by which purchasers or sellers can liquidate their positions by forming opposite contracts. The price differential between the opposite contracts then determines the investor's profit or loss.

While contracts pursuant to Co Petro's Agency Agreements were not as rigidly standardized as futures contracts traded on licensed contract markets, neither were they individualized. . . .

Co Petro's customers, like customers who trade on organized futures exchanges, could deal in commodity futures without the forced burden of delivery. . . . We also reject Co Petro's final contention that, contrary to the practice in organized futures markets where price is established by public auction, it negotiated prices directly with its Agency Agreement customers. The evidence indicates that, for the most part, Co Petro unilaterally set prices for its products according to the then-prevailing market rates with the spot market determining resale prices to subsequent purchasers. Moreover, the fact that public auction did not determine Co Petro's prices is merely a result of Co Petro's failure to seek Commission licensing for organized exchange trading in petroleum futures.

In determining whether a particular contract is a contract of sale of a commodity for future delivery over which the Commission has regulatory jurisdiction . . . no bright-line definition or list of characterizing elements is determinative. The transaction must be viewed as a whole with a critical eye toward its underlying purpose.

The contracts here represent speculative ventures in commodity futures which were marketed to those for whom delivery was not an expectation.

Addressing these circumstances in the light of the legislative history of the Act, we conclude that Co Petro's contracts are "contracts of sale of a commodity for future delivery." ...

The court in *Co Petro* places great emphasis on the speculative nature of the contracts in question and on the court's determination that Co Petro's customers did not intend to take delivery of the gasoline. Other circuits have not adopted the Ninth Circuit's focus on whether the activity was speculative and on whether there was an intention to take delivery. Instead, other circuits have looked at whether the trading occurred in a fungible, easily assignable contract or directly in a commodity. As the Seventh Circuit noted (in a case we examine in chapter 14, section B.1.b), "[u]sing 'delivery' to differentiate between forward and futures contracts yields indeterminacy, because it treats as the dividing line something the two forms of contract have in common for commodities and that both forms lack for financial futures."[5] In other words, many futures contracts contemplate physical delivery and are still futures, therefore a physical delivery requirement cannot be the defining feature of what is a forward.

In the *Erskine* case below, the question of the distinction between a future and a forward was analyzed in the context of foreign exchange transactions. Although, as is discussed in chapter 14, section B.2, the particular question at issue in *Erskine* was ultimately partially resolved in the context of foreign exchange transactions by statute in 2008, the analysis of the Sixth Circuit can be applied to any analysis of whether a contract is a futures contract or a forward contract.

CFTC v. Erskine

512 F.3d 309 (6th Cir. 2008)

... We must next determine ... what constitutes a "futures contract." Generally speaking, the [Commodity Exchange Act (the "CEA")] ... vests the CFTC with regulatory jurisdiction over "futures contracts" — putatively, "transactions involving contracts of sale of a commodity for future delivery." Expressly excluded from the term "future delivery," and therefore excluded from CFTC regulation, is "any sale of any cash commodity for deferred shipment or delivery," commonly referred to as a "forward contract." Drawing a distinction between futures contracts and forward contracts has proven difficult. The district court used the Seventh Circuit's "trade in the contract" test, see [CFTC v. Zelener, 373 F.3d 861 (7th Cir. 2004)] ... at 867, but

----

5. *CFTC v. Zelener*, 373 F.3d 861, 865 (7th Cir. 2004).

the CFTC argues that it should have used a "totality of the circumstances" test, see *Andersons, Inc. v. Horton Farms, Inc.*, 166 F.3d 308, 317 (6th Cir. 1998). Based on the analysis and reasoning set forth below, we begin with the simplified distinction that a "futures contract" is a contract for a future transaction, while a "forward contract" is a contract for a present transaction with future delivery, and conclude with a specific definition for each. . . .

In 1995, the Ninth Circuit considered a claim by the CFTC that Nobel Metals was unlawfully engaging in "futures contracts," under which Nobel sold precious metals to customers who received title but directed that the actual metal be delivered to a third party. *CFTC v. Nobel Metals Int'l, Inc.*, 67 F.3d 766 (9th Cir. 1995). Relying on Co Petro, the court reasserted that the forward contract exclusion is unavailable for "contracts of sale for commodities sold merely for speculative purposes and which are not predicated upon the expectation that delivery of the actual commodity by the seller to the original contracting buyer will occur in the future." The court went on:

> To take advantage of the cash forward contract exclusion under the [CEA], the delivery requirement cannot be satisfied by the simple device of a transfer of title. As we said in Co Petro, "a cash forward contract is one in which the parties contemplate physical transfer of the actual commodity." If this were not so, the cash forward contract exception would quickly swallow the futures contract rule.

The court concluded that there was no legitimate expectation that the customers would take actual delivery of the purchased metals, and deemed the contracts futures contracts while dismissing as irrelevant the "self-serving labels" that the defendants had given the contracts.

In 1998, this Circuit considered claims by private parties, which turned on the question of whether certain grain contracts at issue were covered by the CEA and thereby subject to CFTC regulation. *Andersons*, 166 F.3d at 317. We explained:

> "Futures contracts" are governed by the CEA and concomitantly, subject to CFTC regulations. "Futures contracts" are contracts of sale of a commodity for future delivery. The term "future delivery," however, explicitly does not include any sale of any cash commodity for deferred shipment or delivery. Contracts falling under this latter definition are typically referred to as "cash forward" contracts.

> The purpose of this "cash forward" exception is to permit those parties who contemplate physical transfer of the commodity to set up contracts that (1) defer shipment but guarantee to sellers that they will have buyers and visa versa [sic], and (2) reduce the risk of price fluctuations, without subjecting the parties to burdensome regulations. These contracts are not subject to the CFTC regulations because those regulations are intended to govern only speculative markets; they are not meant to cover contracts wherein the commodity in question has an "inherent value" to the transacting parties. We hold that in determining whether a particular commodities contract

falls within the cash forward exception, courts must focus on whether there is a legitimate expectation that physical delivery of the actual commodity by the seller to the original contracting buyer will occur in the future.

. . . A "futures contract," or "future," never precisely defined by statute, nevertheless has an accepted meaning which brings it within the scope of transactions historically sought to be regulated by the CEA.

It is generally understood to be an executory, mutually binding agreement providing for the future delivery of a commodity on a date certain where the grade, quantity, and price at the time of delivery are fixed. To facilitate the development of a liquid market in these transactions, these contracts are standardized and transferrable. Trading in futures seldom results in physical delivery of the subject commodity, since the obligations are often extinguished by offsetting transactions that produce a net profit or loss. The main purpose realized by entering into futures transactions is to transfer price risks from suppliers, processors and distributors (hedgers) to those more willing to take the risk (speculators). Since the prices of futures are contingent on the vagaries of both the production of the commodity and the economics of the marketplace, they are particularly susceptible to manipulation and excessive speculation.

In contrast to the fungible quality of futures, cash forwards are generally individually negotiated sales of commodities between principals in which actual delivery of the commodity is anticipated, but is deferred for reasons of commercial convenience or necessity. These contracts are not readily transferable and therefore are usually entered into between parties able to make and receive physical delivery of the subject goods. . . .

Much has been made in the case law — and by the parties to this appeal — of Congress's failure to define a "futures contract" expressly, in either the original Commodity Exchange Act or its amendment, the Commodity Futures Modernization Act of 2000. But, this does not mean that the term "futures contract" is undefined. On the contrary, many pertinent sources have defined "futures contract," in terms that investors and traders are expected to (and do) rely upon, and it is reasonable to surmise that regulators — other than the CFTC, apparently — would rely on similar definitions, even without express codification in a federal statute. Although each differs slightly from the others, the definitions, considered altogether, exhibit a consistent theme and typically include six common elements. Based on our consideration of these numerous lay definitions, we find that, in common parlance, "futures contract" means:

> the "contract" is standardized so that it can be traded on an exchange, and is
> a fungible agreement to buy or sell
> a stated unit quantity of
> a stated commodity
> at a stated unit price
> at or before a stated future time.

See, e.g., Merriam-Webster's Dictionary of Law (contract), available at http://dictionary.reference.com/browse/contract (last accessed Jan. 3, 2008). It is important to recognize that it is the agreement or contract that is traded on an exchange. It is unremarkable (though easily enough mistaken as relevant) that the underlying commodity is also traded on a market exchange.

The alternative concept, i.e., "forward contract," is also defined by numerous sources, often with an emphasis on distinguishing it from a "futures contract." A "forward contract" is:

> neither standardized nor traded on an exchange, and is
> an individual agreement to buy or sell
> some agreed-upon quantity of
> some commodity
> at some agreed-upon price
> at some agreed-upon time in the future.

See, e.g., Merriam-Webster's Dictionary of Law (contract), available at http://dictionary.reference.com/browse/contract (last accessed Jan. 3, 2008). Thus, with a "forward contract," the underlying commodity is typically traded on a market exchange (as it typically is with a "futures contract" as well), but the agreement or contract itself is neither standardized nor traded on an exchange.

Notably, none of these definitions/distinctions makes any mention of any anticipation of actual delivery (or lack thereof). This is simply not a practical distinction. Instead, the distinction — as commonly understood — turns on the standardization and fungibility of the contract, and as the Seventh Circuit suggested, whether there is "trading in the contract," rather than trading only in the underlying commodity. . . .

A central feature in *Erskine* (and the *Zelener* decision cited in *Erskine*) is the determination that, in a futures contract, there is a fungible contract with a market for that contract and, in forwards, there is a bilateral, negotiated contract with a market for the commodity. We may ask ourselves, what is the difference between a market for a contract and a market for a commodity?

Trading in a contract requires highly standardized terms that are easily assignable to others. This is, in fact, how the futures market works with the exchange establishing a standardized contract and price the only fluctuating parameter. The trading market is specifically driven by the value of that contract (though, obviously, the fluctuating value of the underlying commodity is the predominating influence on the price of the contract).

With forwards, the contract is not standardized and is not easily assignable. It is negotiated between two parties in contemplation of the market for the commodity.

Is this distinction between the two easily observed in practice? Alternatively, is *Co Petro*'s emphasis on whether it is a speculative endeavor and physical delivery is required easier to apply? The difficulty of answering these questions is perhaps why this circuit split remains.

C. CFTC Jurisdiction Over Off-Exchange Options and Swaps

1. Off-Exchange Options

Putting aside foreign exchange options, discussed in chapter 14, section E, the CFTC's 1974 jurisdictional grant, as modified by the Futures Trading Act of 1978, conveyed broad plenary authority over commodity options.

The subsequent passage of the Commodity Futures Modernization Act of 2000 would appear to have curtailed the CFTC's off-exchange option jurisdiction solely to:

- Agricultural options;
- Retail transactions in other commodity options; and
- Fraud with respect to non-agricultural commodity options traded in the non-retail markets.

Nonetheless, though never subjected to judicial scrutiny, the CFTC maintained rules in Part 32 of the CFTC's regulations in relation to all commodity options transactions — without reference to the above limitations — and continued to explicitly claim "plenary authority" over all commodity options.[6]

The Dodd-Frank Act removed ambiguity regarding the CFTC's jurisdiction by reaffirming its jurisdiction over all commodity options, regardless of whether: (1) traded on- or off-exchange; (2) agricultural or non-agricultural; or (3) retail or non-retail. Off-exchange options are now defined as swaps and the CFTC harmonized its existing regulatory regime for off-exchange agricultural commodity options with its regime for off-exchange swaps.[7]

We discuss the regulation of commodity options in more detail in chapter 14, section E. As a general matter, off-exchange commodity options should be considered identical to swaps for regulatory purposes.

2. Swaps

Before passage of the Dodd-Frank Act, the Commodity Futures Modernization Act mostly excluded non-agricultural off-exchange swaps between "eligible contract participants," i.e., non-retail parties, from CFTC and SEC jurisdiction. The

---

6. CFTC, *Agricultural Swaps*, 75 Fed. Reg. 59666, 59668 (Sept. 28, 2010) and 76 Fed. Reg. 6095, 6098 (Feb. 3, 2011).

7. CTFC, *Commodity Options*, 77 Fed. Reg. 25320 (Apr. 27, 2012).

Dodd-Frank Act imposed a new regulatory scheme where swaps are divided into three regulatory categories: (1) swaps; (2) security-based swaps; and (3) mixed swaps.

Of these three categories, the CFTC has jurisdiction over swaps. The SEC has jurisdiction over security-based swaps, discussed in chapter 13. The CFTC and the SEC have joint responsibility with respect to mixed swaps.

The statutory definition of a "swap"—new enough that it is has not been judicially examined—is comprised of a broad economic description of options and swaps, including a laundry list of products currently traded as swaps. The definition also includes a catch-all provision for unforeseen instruments that are developed in the future and will be considered swaps.

To understand the extent of the CFTC's jurisdiction over swaps and mixed swaps, we need to closely examine the statutory definition of swap, including by noting what it excludes. Remember, the statutory definition of swaps includes options even though, as we saw in chapter 1, economically defined, options and swaps are distinct products.

There is no substitute in this context for a close review of the statute. Therefore, it is necessary to closely read figures 3.2 and 3.3. The first column in each provides the statutory language and the second seeks to explain it.

In an effort to resolve the jurisdictional battles in which the SEC and CFTC have historically engaged, the Dodd-Frank Act required the SEC and CFTC to jointly agree on a rule further defining the term "swap" and related definitions[8] or else the authority to decide between SEC and CFTC proposed definitions (or to select a compromise) would fall to the Financial Stability Oversight Council, an umbrella body of federal banking regulators.[9]

The CFTC's and SEC's joint definition largely reiterates the statutory definition outlined in figures 3.2 and 3.3 while adding a "safe harbor" exception for insurance and reinsurance transactions that might otherwise fall within the definition of "swap."

In addition to the insurance "safe harbor" exclusion and the many exclusions from the swap definition examined in figure 3.3, there is also a partial exclusion for physically-settled foreign exchange swaps and forwards, discussed in chapter 14, section B.3.

In short, the CFTC has jurisdiction over all swaps—as very broadly defined—save for: (1) security-based swaps, which are subject to SEC jurisdiction and described in chapter 4, section C.1.b and are the subject of chapter 13; (2) physically-settled foreign exchange swaps and forwards over which it has a more limited jurisdiction discussed in further detail in chapter 14, section B.3; and (3) mixed swaps over which jurisdiction is shared with the SEC, discussed in chapter 4, section C.1.c.

---

8. Dodd-Frank Act § 712(d)(1).
9. Dodd-Frank Act § 712(d)(3).

Figure 3.2 Swap Definition

Commodity Exchange Act § 1a(47)(A)	Commentary
[A]ny agreement, contract, or transaction-	
(i) that is a put, call, cap, floor, collar, or similar option of any kind that is for the purchase or sale, or based on the value, of 1 or more interest or other rates, currencies, commodities, securities, instruments of indebtedness, indices, quantitative measures, or other financial or economic interests or property of any kind; [or]	*This includes all options, including, apparently, securities options. As will be seen below, though, securities options are ultimately excluded from the definition.*
(ii) that provides for any purchase, sale, payment, or delivery (other than a dividend on an equity security) that is dependent on the occurrence, nonoccurrence, or the extent of the occurrence of an event or contingency associated with a potential financial, economic, or commercial consequence; [or]	*Note that this is so broadly worded as to potentially include insurance. Once more, just as important as seeing what is included in the definition is seeing, as we do in figure 3.3, what is excluded from the definition.*
(iii) that provides on an executory basis for the exchange, on a fixed or contingent basis, of 1 or more payments based on the value or level of 1 or more interest or other rates, currencies, commodities, securities, instruments of indebtedness, indices, quantitative measures, or other financial or economic interests or property of any kind, or any interest therein or based on the value thereof, and that transfers, as between the parties to the transaction, in whole or in part, the financial risk associated with a future change in any such value or level without also conveying a current or future direct or indirect ownership interest in an asset (including any enterprise or investment pool) or liability that incorporates the financial risk so transferred, including any agreement, contract, or transaction commonly known as-	*This describes what is traditionally within the economic definition of a swap.*
(I) an interest rate swap; (II) a rate floor; (III) a rate cap; (IV) a rate collar; (V) a cross-currency rate swap; (VI) a basis swap; (VII) a currency swap; (VIII) a foreign exchange swap; (IX) a total return swap; (X) an equity index swap; (XI) an equity swap; (XII) a debt index swap; (XIII) a debt swap; (XIV) a credit spread; (XV) a credit default swap; (XVI) a credit swap; (XVII) a weather swap; (XVIII) an energy swap; (XIX) a metal swap; (XX) an agricultural swap; (XXI) an emissions swap; and (XXII) a commodity swap; [or]	*This is a laundry list of transaction types that were in existence at the time of the definition and are deemed to be swaps.*
(iv) that is an agreement, contract, or transaction that is, or in the future becomes, commonly known to the trade as a swap; [or]	*This is a catch-all provision to incorporate future financial innovations.*
(v) including any security-based swap agreement which meets the definition of "swap agreement" as defined in section 206A of the Gramm-Leach- Bliley Act of which a material term is based on the price, yield, value, or volatility of any security or any group or index of securities, or any interest therein; or	*The Gramm-Leach-Bliley Act definition of swap agreement generally parallels the definition of swap. Note that security-based swaps are a subset of swaps. We will discuss them below.*

Commodity Exchange Act § 1a(47)(A)	Commentary
(vi) that is any combination or permutation of, or option on, any agreement, contract, or transaction described in any of clauses (i) through (v).	*This is to ensure that combinations of the foregoing fall within the definition of swap.*

Figure 3.3 Exclusions from Swap Definition

Commodity Exchange Act § 1a(47)(B)	Commentary
(i) any contract of sale of a commodity for future delivery (or option on such a contract), [certain leveraged bullion contracts], security futures product, or agreement, contract, or [leveraged, financed or margined retail foreign exchange or commodity transactions]; [and]	*(1) Commodity futures and options thereon are subject to a different CFTC regulatory regime than swaps (as discussed in section B); and (2) security futures have a distinct regime (as discussed in chapter 4, section C.1.a.)*
(ii) any sale of a nonfinancial commodity or security for deferred shipment or delivery, so long as the transaction is intended to be physically settled; [and]	*This is the so-called forward contract exemption, discussed in section B.*
(iii) any put, call, straddle, option, or privilege on any security, certificate of deposit, or group or index of securities, including any interest therein or based on the value thereof, that is subject to-(I) the Securities Act of 1933; and (II) the Securities Exchange Act of 1934; [and]	*This excludes securities options subject to SEC jurisdiction.*
(iv) any put, call, straddle, option, or privilege relating to a foreign currency entered into on a national securities exchange registered pursuant to section 6(a) of the Securities Exchange Act of 1934; [and]	*Foreign currency options entered into on a securities exchange are excluded.*
(v) any agreement, contract, or transaction providing for the purchase or sale of 1 or more securities on a fixed basis that is subject to-(I) the Securities Act of 1933; and (II) the Securities Exchange Act of 1934; [and]	*This provides a general exclusion for securities purchases.*
(vi) any agreement, contract, or transaction providing for the purchase or sale of 1 or more securities on a contingent basis that is subject to the Securities Act of 1933 and the Securities Exchange Act of 1934, unless the agreement, contract, or transaction predicates the purchase or sale on the occurrence of a bona fide contingency that might reasonably be expected to affect or be affected by the creditworthiness of a party other than a party to the agreement, contract, or transaction; [and]	*A purchase or sale subject to a contingency is not a swap unless the contingency is based on the creditworthiness of a third party, such as would be the case with a credit default swap.*
(vii) any note, bond, or evidence of indebtedness that is a security, as defined in section 2(a)(1) of the Securities Act of 1933; [and]	*Securities are not swaps even if they have economic features typically associated with swaps.*

Figure 3.3 Exclusions from Swap Definition (*continued*)

Commodity Exchange Act § 1a(47)(B)	Commentary
(viii) any agreement, contract, or transaction that is-(I) based on a security; and (II) entered into directly or through an underwriter (as defined in the Securities Act of 1933 § 2(a)(11)) by the issuer of such security for the purposes of raising capital, unless the agreement, contract, or transaction is entered into to manage a risk associated with capital raising;	*This excludes agreements between securities underwriters and the issuer of securities.*
(ix) any agreement, contract, or transaction a counterparty of which is a Federal Reserve bank, the Federal Government, or a Federal agency that is expressly backed by the full faith and credit of the United States; and	*This clarifies that acts of the U.S. government or its agencies are not to be restrained by the swap regulatory regime.*
(x) any security-based swap, other than a . . . [mixed swap, discussed in chapter 4, section C.1.c.]	*Security-based swaps are discussed in section chapter 4, section C.1.b.*

D. Anti-Manipulation Jurisdiction

The CFTC's jurisdiction with respect to manipulation is significantly broader than ordinarily is the case. This is because section 6(c) of the Commodity Exchange Act states that it is "unlawful for any person . . . to use or employ, or attempt to use or employ, in connection with any swap, or a contract of sale of any commodity in interstate commerce, or for future delivery on or subject to the rules of any registered entity, any manipulative or deceptive device or contrivance, in contravention of such rules and regulations as the Commission shall promulgate. . . ." The CFTC's associated rule expands upon the statute to prohibit "intentionally or recklessly" engaging in numerous activities that encompass fraud in addition to market manipulation.[10]

While the jurisdiction over manipulation related to a "swap" or a commodity "for future delivery" mirrors the CFTC's plenary jurisdiction over these products, the jurisdiction over "a contract of sale of any commodity in interstate commerce" is novel, added in 2010 by the Dodd-Frank Act.[11] In essence, it means that the CFTC has the authority to police manipulation in relation to any commodity sales, even those in the spot or forward market. To understand the extent of this authority, we need to look more closely at how a "commodity" is defined in the Commodity Exchange Act. The below case examines this in the context of a virtual currency fraud.

---

10. 17 C.F.R. § 180.1.

11. Section 753.

CFTC v. My Big Coin Pay, Inc.

334 F. Supp. 3d 492 (D. Mass. 2018)

Memorandum of Decision

Rya W. Zobel, Senior United States District Judge

Defendant Randall Crater and all Relief Defendants move to dismiss this case brought by plaintiff Commodity Future Trading Commission ("CFTC"). The amended complaint alleges a fraudulent "virtual currency scheme" in violation of the Commodity Exchange Act ("CEA" or "the Act") and a CFTC implementing regulation banning fraud and/or manipulation in connection with the sale of a commodity. *See* 7 U.S.C. § 9(1); 17 C.F.R. § 180.1(a). Defendants' principal argument is that CFTC fails to state a claim because My Big Coin ("MBC" or "My Big Coin"), the allegedly fraudulent virtual currency involved in the scheme, is not a "commodity" within the meaning of the Act. They also argue that the CEA provision and CFTC regulation are restricted to cases involving market manipulation and do not reach the fraud alleged here. Finally, they assert that plaintiff's amended complaint fails to support its allegations of misappropriation. The motion is denied. . . .

Mr. Crater and the non-moving codefendants "operated a virtual currency scheme in which they fraudulently offered the sale of a fully-functioning virtual currency" called "My Big Coin".[12] . . . [D]efendants enticed customers to buy My Big Coin by making various untrue and/or misleading statements and omitting material facts. The falsities included that My Big Coin was "backed by gold," could be used anywhere Mastercard was accepted, and was being "actively traded" on several currency exchanges. . . . Defendants also made up and arbitrarily changed the price of My Big Coin to mimic the fluctuations of a legitimate, actively-traded virtual currency. When victims of the fraud purchased My Big Coin, they could view their accounts on a website but "could not trade their MBC or withdraw funds." . . . Defendants obtained more than $6 million from the scheme, some of which is currently held by the several Relief Defendants.

Plaintiff brought suit on January 16, 2018, alleging violations of Section 6(c)(1) of the Commodities Exchange Act, 7 U.S.C. § 9(1), and CFTC Regulation 180.1(a), 17 C.F.R. § 180.1(a). It also moved for a temporary restraining order and a preliminary injunction. The court granted the temporary restraining order and defendants subsequently consented to a preliminary injunction. Thereafter, plaintiff amended its complaint and defendants filed the pending motion to dismiss, which both parties extensively briefed and argued. . . .

---

12. [N. 3] According to the amended complaint, a virtual currency is "a digital representation of value that functions as a medium of exchange, a unit of account, and/or a store of value, but does not have legal tender status in any jurisdiction." . . . Unlike United States dollars or other "'real' currencies," virtual currencies "use decentralized networks to track transactions between persons," and transfers are recorded in a "decentralized ledger" that functions without any "central intermediary in which both users need to trust." . . .

As an initial matter, although defendants suggest that this court does not have subject matter jurisdiction for lack of a federal question, their underlying argument that the alleged conduct did not involve a "commodity" goes to the merits of plaintiff's claim, not jurisdiction. This court has subject matter jurisdiction because the case presents a federal question, *see* 28 U.S.C. §1331, and because federal law expressly authorizes CFTC to sue and the court to grant appropriate relief, *see* 7 U.S.C. §13a-1(a); 28 U.S.C. §1345. *See, e.g.*, *CFTC v. Hunter Wise Commodities, LLC*, 749 F.3d 967, 974 (11th Cir. 2014) ("[Defendant-Appellants] argue the Commission's statutory authority, its 'jurisdiction,' does not reach the transactions at issue, but we note at the outset that this is not a matter of the court's jurisdiction to hear this case."). . . .

"The Commodity Exchange Act (CEA) has been aptly characterized as a 'comprehensive regulatory structure to oversee the volatile and esoteric futures trading complex.'" *Merrill Lynch, Pierce, Fenner & Smith, Inc. v. Curran*, 456 U.S. 353, 356, 102 S.Ct. 1825, 72 L.Ed.2d 182 (1982) (internal citation omitted) (quoting H.R. Rep. No. 93–975, at 1 (1974) (hereinafter "House Report")). Accordingly, the present Act generally grants CFTC exclusive jurisdiction over futures contracts and the exchanges where they are traded. *See* 7 U.S.C. § 2(a)(1)(A).[13] CFTC has additional powers under the statute, including the general anti-fraud and anti-manipulation authority over "any . . . contract of sale of any commodity in interstate commerce" pursuant to which it brings the claims in this case. *See* 7 U.S.C. § 9(1).

As noted above, plaintiff alleges violations of CEA Section 6(c)(1) and CFTC regulation 180.1(a). Both provisions apply to the fraud alleged in this case if the conduct involved a "commodity" under the CEA. *See* 7 U.S.C. § 9(1) (banning, *inter alia*, the use of "any manipulative or deceptive device or contrivance" "in connection with any . . . contract of sale of any commodity in interstate commerce"); 17 C.F.R. § 180.1(a) (banning, *inter alia*, the use of "any manipulative device, scheme, or artifice to defraud" "in connection with any . . . contract of sale of any commodity in interstate commerce"). Therefore, to state a viable claim, plaintiff must adequately plead that My Big Coin is a commodity.

"Commodity" is a defined term in the CEA. *See* 7 U.S.C. § 1a(9). It includes a host of specifically enumerated agricultural products as well as "all other goods and articles . . . and all services rights and interests . . . in which contracts for future delivery are presently or in the future dealt in." . . .

Defendants contend that because "contracts for future delivery" are indisputably not "dealt in" My Big Coin, it cannot be a commodity under the CEA. They take the position that in order to satisfy the CEA's "commodity" definition, the specific item in question must itself underlie a futures contract. Plaintiff responds that "a

---

13. [N. 4] Simply put, a "futures contract" is an agreement to buy or sell a certain quantity of a commodity at a certain price at a certain time in the future. *See CFTC v. Erskine*, 512 F.3d 309, 323 (6th Cir. 2008). Such contracts are standardized so they may be traded on exchanges. *See id.*

'commodity' for purposes of [the CEA definition] is broader than any particular type or brand of that commodity." Docket # 70 at 10.[14] Pointing to the existence of Bitcoin futures contracts, it argues that contracts for future delivery of virtual currencies are "dealt in" and that My Big Coin, as a virtual currency, is therefore a commodity.[15]

The text of the statute supports plaintiff's argument. The Act defines "commodity" generally and categorically, "not by type, grade, quality, brand, producer, manufacturer, or form." Docket # 70 at 11. For example, the Act classifies "livestock" as a commodity without enumerating which particular species are the subject of futures trading. Thus, as plaintiff urges, Congress' approach to defining "commodity" signals an intent that courts focus on categories — not specific items — when determining whether the "dealt in" requirement is met.

This broad approach also accords with Congress's goal of "strengthening the federal regulation of the . . . commodity futures trading industry," House Report at 1, since an expansive definition of "commodity" reasonably assures that the CEA's regulatory scheme and enforcement provisions will comprehensively protect and police the markets. That goal is particularly relevant here, given that the court is construing the term "commodity" not in a vacuum, but rather as it functions within the CEA's anti-fraud enforcement provision of Section 6(c)(1). As the Supreme Court has instructed in an analogous context, such statutes are to be "construed 'not technically and restrictively, but flexibly to effectuate [their] remedial purposes.'" *SEC v. Zandford*, 535 U.S. 813, 819, 122 S.Ct. 1899, 153 L.Ed.2d 1 (2002) (analyzing Section 10(b) of the Securities Exchange Act) (*quoting SEC v. Capital Gains Research Bureau, Inc.*, 375 U.S. 180, 195, 84 S.Ct. 275, 11 L.Ed.2d 237 (1963)).

Finally, the scant caselaw on this issue also supports plaintiff's approach. In a series of cases involving natural gas, courts have repeatedly rejected arguments that a particular type of natural gas was not a commodity because that specific type was not the subject of a futures contract. *See United States v. Brooks*, 681 F.3d 678 (5th Cir. 2012); *United States v. Futch*, 278 F. App'x 387, 395 (5th Cir. 2008); *United States v. Valencia*, No. CR.A. H-03-024, 2003 WL 23174749, at *8 (S.D. Tex. Aug. 25,

---

14. [N. 5] Plaintiff also attempts to sidestep the issue of futures contracts by arguing that My Big Coin is a "good" or an "article" and that items in these categories are commodities under the CEA even in the absence of contracts for future delivery. That argument is unavailing. The "dealt in" clause applies to both "goods and articles" as well as "services, rights, and interests." *See United States v. Brooks*, 681 F.3d 678, 694 (5th Cir. 2012) ("Natural gas is plainly a 'good' or 'article.' The question thus turns on whether it is a good 'in which contracts for future delivery are presently or in the future dealt with.'"); *Bd. of Trade of City of Chicago v. S.E.C.*, 677 F.2d 1137, 1142 (7th Cir. 1982) ("literally anything other than onions [can] become a 'commodity' and thereby subject to CFTC regulation simply by its futures being traded on some exchange"), *judgment vacated as moot SEC v. Bd. of Trade of City of Chicago*, 459 U.S. 1026, 103 S.Ct. 434, 74 L.Ed.2d 594 (1982); *CFTC v. McDonnell*, 287 F.Supp.3d 213, 228 (E.D.N.Y. 2018) ("Where a futures market exists for a good, service, right, or interest, it may be regulated by CFTC, as a commodity.") . . .

15. [N. 6] The court takes judicial notice of the undisputed facts that (a) Bitcoin futures are presently traded; and (b) no futures contracts exist for My Big Coin. . . .

2003), *order vacated in part on reconsideration*, No. CRIM.A. H-03-024, 2003 WL 23675402 (S.D. Tex. Nov. 13, 2003), *rev'd and remanded on other grounds*, 394 F.3d 352 (5th Cir. 2004). Rather, the courts held that because futures contracts in natural gas underlaid by gas at Henry Hub, Louisiana were dealt in, and because natural gas is "fungible" and may move freely throughout a national pipeline system, this was sufficient to show that natural gas, including the types at issue in these cases, was a commodity. *See Brooks*, 681 F.3d at 694-95 (observing that "it would be peculiar that natural gas at another hub is not a commodity, but suddenly becomes a commodity solely on the basis that it passes through Henry Hub, and ceases to be a commodity once it moves onto some other locale.") . . . Taken together, these decisions align with plaintiff's argument that the CEA only requires the existence of futures trading within a certain class (e.g. "natural gas") in order for all items within that class (e.g. "West Coast" natural gas) to be considered commodities.

Here, the amended complaint alleges that My Big Coin is a virtual currency and it is undisputed that there is futures trading in virtual currencies (specifically involving Bitcoin). That is sufficient, especially at the pleading stage, for plaintiff to allege that My Big Coin is a "commodity" under the Act. *See CFTC v. McDonnell*, 287 F.Supp.3d 213, 228 (E.D.N.Y. 2018) ("Virtual currencies can be regulated by CFTC as a commodity."); *In re BFXNA Inc.*, CFTC Docket 16-19, at 5–6 (June 2, 2016) ("[V]irtual currencies are encompassed in the [CEA] definition and properly defined as commodities."); *In re Coinflip, Inc.*, CFTC Docket No. 15-29, at 3 (Sept. 17, 2015) (same).[16] . . .

Defendants' motion to dismiss . . . is denied.

Commentators have identified three possible interpretations of commodity in this context.[17] The first is that only something already specifically trading on a futures exchange can be a commodity. This would mean that, in the context of the *CFTC v. My Big Coin Pay* facts, the CFTC would only have broad anti-manipulation jurisdiction if there were already a futures contract in My Big Coin in existence. The decision in the case implicitly rejected this interpretation because, at the time, only a futures contract in another virtual currency, Bitcoin, was trading.

---

16. [N. 9] While *McDonnell*, *In re Coinflip*, and *In re BFXNA* can be distinguished on their facts since each case involved the virtual currency Bitcoin, these orders are nevertheless useful data points. Each supports the court's view that the appropriate inquiry under the CEA is whether contracts for future delivery of virtual currencies are dealt in, not whether a particular type of virtual currency underlies a futures contract.

17. *See, e.g.*, ABA Derivatives and Futures Law Comm., *Digital and Digitized Assets: Federal and State Jurisdictional Issues*, https://www.americanbar.org/content/dam/aba/administrative /business_law/buslaw/committees/CL620000pub/digital_assets.pdf 69–75 (Dec. 2020), and Geoffrey F. Aronow, *What is a Commodity? Potential Limits on the CFTC's Fraud Jurisdiction*, 38 No. 11 Futures & Derivatives L. Rep. 1 (Dec. 2018).

The second interpretation is that endorsed in *CFTC v. My Big Coin Pay*, i.e., that, for the CFTC to have broad anti-manipulation jurisdiction, the general category to which the commodity belongs must at least trade on a futures exchange. In the context of *CFTC v. My Big Coin Pay*, this means that, although My Big Coins did not trade on a futures exchange, a virtual currency, Bitcoin, did. The existence of trading in the futures market of something in the same general category is sufficient for broad anti-manipulation jurisdiction.

The third interpretation is that every good, article, service, and right and interest in the world that is capable of being traded on a futures exchange is a commodity. This would mean that the CFTC would have broad anti-manipulation authority over, in effect, everything. It would also, perhaps implausibly, render superfluous the final portion of the definition of "commodity" which reads "in which contracts for future delivery are presently or in the future dealt with."[18] As a matter of practice, the CFTC has only so-far exercised its anti-manipulation jurisdiction where there is a potential nexus to derivatives markets. However, in that context, courts have been largely sympathetic to the CFTC's claims of jurisdiction over fraud in commodity cash markets.

CFTC v. McDonnell

287 F. Supp. 3d 213 (E.D.N.Y. 2018)

... The Commodity Futures Trading Commission ("CFTC") sues Patrick McDonnell and his company Coin Drop Markets. CFTC alleges defendants "operated a deceptive and fraudulent virtual currency scheme ... for purported virtual currency trading advice" and "for virtual currency purchases and trading ... and simply misappropriated [investor] funds." *See* CFTC Complaint, ECF No. 1, Jan. 18, 2018, at 1 ("CFTC Compl.").

CFTC seeks injunctive relief, monetary penalties, and restitution of funds received in violation of the Commodity Exchange Act ("CEA"). *Id.* at 11.

Until Congress clarifies the matter, the CFTC has concurrent authority, along with other state and federal administrative agencies, and civil and criminal courts, over dealings in virtual currency. An important nationally and internationally traded commodity, virtual currency is tendered for payment for debts, although, unlike United States currency, it is not legal tender that must be accepted. Title 31 U.S.C. § 5103 ("United States coins and currency ... are legal tender for all debts ...."). ....

The primary issue raised at the outset of this litigation is whether CFTC has standing to sue defendants on the theory that they have violated the CEA. Title 7 U.S.C. § 1. Presented are two questions that determine the plaintiff's standing: (1) whether virtual currency may be regulated by the CFTC as a commodity; and (2) whether the amendments to the CEA under the Dodd-Frank Act permit the CFTC

---

18. *See* figure 3.1 for a refresher on the Commodity Exchange Act's definition of "commodity."

to exercise its jurisdiction over fraud that does not directly involve the sale of futures or derivative contracts.

Both questions are answered in the affirmative. A "commodity" encompasses virtual currency both in economic function and in the language of the statute. Title 7 U.S.C. § 1(a)(9) (The CEA defines "commodity" as agricultural products and "all other goods and articles . . . and all services, rights, and interests . . . in which contracts for future delivery are presently or in the future dealt in.").

CFTC's broad authority extends to fraud or manipulation in derivatives markets and underlying spot markets. *See* Title 7 U.S.C. § 9(1). CFTC may exercise its enforcement power over fraud related to virtual currencies sold in interstate commerce. *See* Title 17 C.F.R. § 180.1. . . .

A preliminary injunction is granted in favor of the CFTC. The court finds a reasonable likelihood that without an injunction the defendants will continue to violate the CEA. . . .

Patrick McDonnell and his company CabbageTech, Corp., doing business as Coin Drop Markets ("defendants"), offered fraudulent trading and investment services related to virtual currency. . . .

Customers from the United States and abroad paid defendants for "membership" in virtual currency trading groups purported to provide exit prices and profits of up to "300%" per week. . . . Defendants advertised their services through "at least two websites, www.coindropmarkets.com and www.coindrops.club," as well as on the social media platform Twitter. . . .

"Investors" transferred virtual currency to the defendants for "day" trading. . . .

After receiving membership payment or virtual currency investments, defendants deleted their "social media accounts" and "websites and ceased communicating with . . . customers around July, 2017." . . . When customers asked for a return of their membership fee, or virtual currency investment, the defendants refused and misappropriated the funds. . . .

Virtual currencies are generally defined as "digital assets used as a medium of exchange." Skadden's Insights, *Bitcoins and Blockchain: The CFTC Takes Notice of Virtual Currencies*, Jan., 2016. They are stored electronically in "digital wallets," and exchanged over the internet through a direct peer-to-peer system. *Id.* They are often described as "cryptocurrencies" because they use "cryptographic protocols to secure transactions . . . recorded on publicly available decentralized ledgers," called "blockchains." Brief of CFTC In Support of Preliminary Injunction and Other Relief, ECF No. 21, Feb. 26, 2018, at 4 ("CFTC Brief").

The "blockchain" serves as a digital signature to verify the exchange. *See* Appendix B, *A CFTC Primer on Virtual Currencies*, Oct. 17, 2017, at 5 ("App. B, *CFTC Primer*"). "The public nature of the decentralized ledger allows people to recognize the transfer of virtual currency from one user to another without requiring any central intermediary in which both users need to trust." CFTC Brief, at 4. . . . Virtual currencies are not backed by any government, fiat currency, or commodity. Robert J. Anello, *New-Wave Legal Challenges for Bitcoin and Other CryptoCurrencies*, Law Journal Newsletters, Nov. 2017. . . .

Congress has yet to authorize a system to regulate virtual currency. T. Gorman, *Blockchain, Virtual Currencies and the Regulators*, Dorsey & Whitney LLP, Jan. 11, 2018 ("As the CFTC recently admitted, U.S. law does not provide for 'direct comprehensive U.S. regulation of virtual currencies. To the contrary a multi-regulatory approach is being used.'").

The CFTC, and other agencies, claim concurrent regulatory power over virtual currency in certain settings, but concede their jurisdiction is incomplete. . . .

Legitimization and regulation of virtual currencies has followed from the CFTC's allowance of futures trading on certified exchanges. . . . Two futures exchanges, Chicago Mercantile Exchange and the CBOE Futures Exchange, as of February 23, 2018, exceeded "$150 million in daily trading volume." . . .

Exclusive jurisdiction over "accounts, agreements . . . and *transactions involving swaps or contracts of sale of a commodity for future delivery*" has been granted to the CFTC. Title 7 U.S.C. §2 (emphasis added). Any commodity traded as a future must be traded on a commodity exchange approved by the CFTC. Title 7 U.S.C. §6. . . .

Black's Law Dictionary defines a commodity as "an article of trade or commerce." Bryan Garner, *Black's Law Dictionary*, (10th ed. 2014). Merriam Webster defines it as "[a]n economic good . . . [or] an article of commerce. . . ." Merriam Webster, https://www.merriam-webster.com/ dictionary/commodity (last visited Feb. 5, 2018).

Commentators have argued that based on common usage, virtual currency should be interpreted as a commodity.

It would make sense for regulators to treat Bitcoin as a commodity. Commodities are generally defined as "goods sold in the market with a quality and value uniform throughout the world." This categorization would be appropriate because it realistically reflects the economic behavior of Bitcoin users and squares with traditional economic conceptions of exchange. . . .

Some propose that because virtual currencies provide a "store of value" they function as commodities:

> A commodity is any item that "accommodates" our physical wants and needs. And one of these physical wants is the need for a store of value. Throughout history humans have used different commodities as a store of value — even cocoa beans — but, more persistently, gold. In contrast, a security is any instrument that is "secured" against something else. As a currency is usually secured by a commodity or a government's ability to tax and defend, it is considered to be a security. By these definitions, bitcoin with a lower case "b," is a commodity, and not a currency, while Bitcoin with a capital "B" is the technology, or network, that bitcoin moves across. The analogy would be Shale technology versus shale oil.

Jeff Currie, *Bullion Bests bitcoin, Not Bitcoin*, Goldman Sachs Global Investment Research, Mar. 11, 2014.

Others argue virtual currencies are commodities because they serve as a type of monetary exchange:

> Bitcoin should primarily be considered a commodity because it serves the function of money in its community of users. Users exchange Bitcoins to obtain property that they desire. In his seminal work, *Man, Economy, and State*, Murray Rothbard argues that all monetary exchanges are actually indirect commodity exchanges. Rothbard supports his proposition by tracing the development of money and exchange. Before the widespread adoption of a common form of money, people had to engage in bartering, or "direct exchange," in order to complete transactions. . . .

Furthermore, while Bitcoin acts as a money commodity in its community of users, from a pricing standpoint, it is valued like other commodities. The price of traditional commodities, like gold, silver, and agricultural products, vary in accordance with their demand and scarcity. When more people want a commodity that has a fixed supply, the price rises.

Similarly, the price of Bitcoin fluctuates according to the same fixed supply model. Bitcoins are scarce because the algorithm controlling how many Bitcoins are released into the market through mining [] is designed to taper the supply of bitcoins, until no more are created. Bitcoins are considered rare because there is a fixed supply of them, leading users to be willing to pay increasing prices to control them. The value of a Bitcoin is ultimately driven by supply and demand — a coin is worth whatever someone is willing to pay for it. . . .

CEA defines "commodities" as "wheat, cotton, rice, corn, oats, barley, rye, flaxseed, grain sorghums, mill feeds, butter, eggs, Solanum tuberosum (Irish potatoes), wool, wool tops, fats and oils (including lard, tallow, cottonseed oil, peanut oil, soybean oil, and all other fats and oils), cottonseed meal, cottonseed, peanuts, soybeans, soybean meal, livestock, livestock products, and frozen concentrated orange juice, *and all other goods and articles . . . and all services, rights, and interests . . . in which contracts for future delivery are presently or in the future dealt in*." Title 7 U.S.C. § 1(a)(9) (emphasis added).

The original grant of power to the CEA was designed to control trading in agricultural commodities. Other goods, as well as services, rights and interests, are now covered by the statute. *See, e.g., United States v. Brooks*, 681 F.3d 678, 694 (5th Cir. 2012) ("Natural gas is plainly a 'good' or 'article.' The questions thus turns on whether it is a good 'in which contracts for future delivery are presently or in the future dealt with.'").

The CEA covers intangible commodities. *See, e.g., In re Barclays PLC*, CFTC No. 15-25 (May 20, 2015) (regulating fixed interest rate benchmarks as commodities). . . .

After an administrative proceeding in 2015, the CFTC issued an order finding, for the first time, that virtual currencies can be classified as commodities. *In the Matter of: Coinflip, Inc.,* CFTC Docket No. 15-29 ("Bitcoin and other virtual currencies are encompassed in the definition and properly defined as commodities.").

Multiple statements defining virtual currency as a commodity have been issued by the CFTC. *See* App. B, *CFTC Primer,* at 11 ("The definition of 'commodity' in the CEA is broad. . . . It can mean physical commodity, such as an agricultural product. . . . It can mean currency or interest rate."); *CFTC Launches Virtual Currency Resource Web Page,* Press Release, Dec. 15, 2017 ("Bitcoin and other virtual currencies have been determined to be commodities under the Commodity Exchange Act (CEA). The [CFTC] primarily regulates commodity derivatives contracts that are based on underlying commodities. While its regulatory oversight authority over commodity cash markets is limited, the CFTC maintains general anti-fraud and manipulation enforcement authority over virtual currency cash markets as a commodity in interstate commerce."). . . .

Regulatory authority over commodities traded as futures and derivatives has been granted to CFTC. *Inv. Co. Inst. v. Commodity Futures Trading Comm'n,* 720 F.3d 370, 372 (D.C. Cir. 2013) ("The Commodity Exchange Act (CEA), Title 7, United States Code, Chapter 1, establishes and defines the jurisdiction of the Commodity Futures Trading Commission. Under this Act, the Commission has regulatory jurisdiction over a wide variety of markets in futures and derivatives, that is, contracts deriving their value from underlying assets.").

Title 7 U.S.C. §9(1) of the CEA makes it unlawful for any person to:

> use or employ, in connection with any swap, *or a contract of sale of any commodity in interstate commerce,* or for future delivery on or subject to the rules of any registered entity, *any manipulative or deceptive device or contrivance,* in contravention of such rules and regulations as the Commission shall promulgate by not later than 1 year after July 21, 2010 . . . (emphasis added).

17 C.F.R. §180.1 further defines the regulatory power of the CFTC:

> (a) It shall be unlawful for any person, directly or indirectly, in connection with any swap, or contract of sale of any commodity in interstate commerce, or contract for future delivery on or subject to the rules of any registered entity, to intentionally or recklessly:
>
> (1) Use or employ, or attempt to use or employ, any manipulative device, scheme, or artifice to defraud;
>
> (2) Make, or attempt to make, any untrue or misleading statement of a material fact or to omit to state a material fact necessary in order to make the statements made not untrue or misleading;
>
> (3) Engage, or attempt to engage, in any act, practice, or course of business, which operates or would operate as a fraud or deceit. . . .

The CFTC has recently expanded its enforcement to fraud related to spot markets underlying the (already regulated) derivative markets. *See, e.g.,* App. B, *CFTC Primer* (finding the CFTC has jurisdiction "if there is fraud or manipulation involving a virtual currency traded in interstate commerce"); *CFTC v. Gelfman Blueprint, Inc.,* Case No. 17-7181, 2017 WL 4228737 (S.D.N.Y. Filed Sept. 21, 2017) (suit brought by the CFTC alleging a Bitcoin Ponzi scheme, not involving future contracts).

In *Gelfman*, as in the instant case, the CFTC relied on the broad statutory authority in Section 9(1) of the CEA, and regulatory authority under 17 C.F.R. § 180.1. Specifically, the language in § 180.1 prohibiting "any person, directly or indirectly, in connection with any . . . contract of sale of any commodity in interstate commerce" from using a "manipulative device, scheme, or artifice to defraud," or making "any untrue or misleading statement of a material fact."

The portion of the statute delegating oversight authority over "*contract of sale of any commodity in interstate commerce*" allows CFTC to enforce its mandate in cases not directly involving future trades. 17 C.F.R. § 180.1 (emphasis added); *see* Gary DeWaal, *CFTC Files Charges Alleging Bitcoin Ponzi Scheme Not Involving Derivatives,* Sept. 24, 2017 ("The CFTC brought its current action [*Gelfman*] under a relatively new provision of law (enacted as part of the Dodd-Frank Wall Street Reform and Consumer Protection Act) and Commission regulation that prohibits any person from using a manipulative or deceptive device or contrivance in connection with any 'contract for sale of any commodity in interstate commerce' — not solely in connection with swaps or a commodity for future delivery.").

Where a futures market exists for a good, service, right, or interest, it may be regulated by CFTC, as a commodity, without regard to whether the dispute involves futures contracts. *See, e.g., Brooks,* 681 F.3d at 694–95 ("[F]utures contracts for natural gas are traded on NYMEX, and those futures are derivative of natural gas traded at Henry Hub. Nonetheless, the record shows that natural gas may be moved from any location to Henry Hub through the national pipeline system. Thus, it would be peculiar that natural gas at another hub is not a commodity, but suddenly becomes a commodity solely on the basis that it passes through Henry Hub, and ceases to be a commodity once it moves onto some other locale. While the price of that commodity may fluctuate with its location, and the forces of supply and demand at that location, the actual nature of the 'good' does not change.").

CFTC does not have regulatory authority over simple quick cash or spot transactions that do not involve fraud or manipulation. Title 7 U.S.C. § 2(c)(2)(C)(i)(II)(bb) (AA) (The CFTC does not have jurisdiction over "spot" transactions that "[result] in actual delivery within 2 days."). This boundary has been recognized by the CFTC. It has not attempted to regulate spot trades, unless there is evidence of manipulation or fraud. *See* App. C, CFTC Chair, Congressional Testimony ("[T]he CFTC does not have authority to conduct regulatory oversight over spot virtual currency platforms or other cash commodities, including imposing registration requirements, surveillance and monitoring, transaction reporting, compliance with personnel conduct standards, customer education, capital adequacy, trading system safeguards, cyber security examinations or other requirements.")....

Virtual currencies can be regulated by CFTC as a commodity. Virtual currencies are "goods" exchanged in a market for a uniform quality and value. Mitchell Prentis, *Digital Metal: Regulating Bitcoin As A Commodity*, 66 Case W. Res. L. Rev. 609, 626 (2015). They fall well-within the common definition of "commodity" as well as the CEA's definition of "commodities" as "all other goods and articles . . . in which contracts for future delivery are presently or in the future dealt in." Title 7 U.S.C. § 1(a)(9).

The jurisdictional authority of CFTC to regulate virtual currencies as commodities does not preclude other agencies from exercising their regulatory power when virtual currencies function differently than derivative commodities. *See, e.g.,* Jay Clayton [SEC Chair] and Christopher Giancarlo [CFTC Chair], *Regulators are Looking at Cryptocurrency,* Wall Street Journal, Jan. 24, 2018 ("The SEC does not have direct oversight of transactions in currencies or commodities. Yet some products that are labeled cryptocurrencies have characteristics that make them securities. The offer, sale and trading of such products must be carried out in compliance with securities law. The SEC will vigorously pursue those who seek to evade the registration, disclosure and antifraud requirements of our securities laws.").

CFTC has jurisdictional authority to bring suit against defendants utilizing a scheme to defraud investors through a "contract [for] sale of [a] commodity in interstate commerce." Title 7 U.S.C. § 9(1). Although the CFTC has traditionally limited its jurisdiction primarily to "future" contracts for commodities, its expansion into spot trade commodity fraud is justified by statutory and regulatory guidelines....

CFTC has made a prima facie showing that the defendants committed fraud by misappropriation of investors' funds and misrepresentation of trading advice and future profits promised to customers.... The intentional nature of the defendants' conduct, as required by 17 C.F.R. § 180.1, is evidenced by the blatant disregard of customers' complaints and their refusal to return investors' funds.....

A preliminary injunction is granted in favor of the CFTC. The court concludes that without an injunction there is a reasonable likelihood that defendants will continue to violate the CEA. A separate order outlining the terms of the relief is issued....

––––––––––

While it is clear that section 6(c) of the Commodity Exchange Act confers authority to the CFTC with respect to manipulation, the CFTC has by rule included authority to police fraud.[19] This has been the subject of recent controversy. In *CFTC v. Monex*, the defendants raised the question of how far CFTC jurisdiction extends if the CFTC has jurisdiction over ordinary fraud occurring in commodity markets

––––––––––

19. 17 C.F.R. § 180.1.

in addition to jurisdiction over market manipulation. The Ninth Circuit held that ordinary fraud is included, in a decision consistent with *McDonnell*.[20] We examine fraud and market manipulation independently in chapter 15 and we look at the *Monex* case in chapter 14, section C.3. This further highlights the importance of the definition of "commodity."

Questions and Comments

1. Evaluate the split between, on the one hand, the Ninth Circuit and, on the other hand, the Sixth and Seventh Circuits, on what constitutes a forward transaction. What are the advantages and disadvantages of each test? Is there a better alternative?

2. Is it easy to ordinarily distinguish between a forward and a future? How do we ordinarily know the difference between the two? For example, most people would not consider a magazine subscription a futures transaction. Why is it so clear that it is not?

3. Why might the definition of swap be so broad? What are the pros and cons of a broad definition compared to a more specific one?

4. Looking at some of the exclusions from the definition of "swap," are they necessary? Do the exclusions help better define what is a swap?

5. The *My Big Coin* and *McDonnell* cases involve fraud related to virtual currency. We will see that a significant amount of enforcement activity surrounds virtual currency markets. Why might that be?

6. When evaluating the CFTC's anti-manipulation jurisdiction in commodity cash markets, what interpretive lens should be used? There is an argument that the purpose of the authority was to give the CFTC jurisdiction over activities in the cash market that facilitate manipulation in the futures or swaps markets. Is *McDonnell* a step too far? Can the CFTC claim the authority to police fraud involving any commodity? What limitations apply?

---

20. *CFTC v. Monex Credit Company*, 931 F.3d 966, 976–978 (9th Cir. 2019).

Chapter 4

The Commodity Futures Trading Commission

A. Introduction

Central to the study of derivatives regulation in the United States is familiarity with the primary regulator of derivatives, the CFTC.

The CFTC is a newer regulator. The statute providing for its formation was the Commodity Futures Trading Commission Act of 1974,[1] and the Commission only convened for the first time in 1975.[2] Although the CFTC was formed as a successor to the Commodity Exchange Commission created by statute in 1936,[3] which itself was successor to the Grain Futures Commission created by statute in 1922,[4] the CFTC significantly differs from both in the broader scope of its jurisdiction. Also, unlike its predecessors, it is structured as an "independent agency" with great autonomy from the executive branch to which it formally belongs.

In this chapter, we examine the CFTC's organizational structure and its relationship with other regulators.

B. The Structure of the CFTC

1. The Commission

a. Appointment and Composition

The term "Commodity Futures Trading Commission" is used to refer to the entire agency or, dependent on context, exclusively to its five member governing body. To distinguish between the two, in this section, we will use "CFTC" when referring to the agency in its entirety and "the Commission" when referring to its governing body.

---

1. Pub. L. No. 93-463, 88 Stat. 1389 (1974).
2. *See* CFTC, History of the CFTC, https://www.cftc.gov/About/HistoryoftheCFTC/history_1970s.html.
3. Commodity Exchange Act of 1936, Pub. L. No. 74-675, 49 Stat. 1491 (1936).
4. Grain Futures Act of 1922, Pub. L. No. 67-331, 42 Stat. 998 (1922).

Each member of the Commission is referred to as a commissioner. They are appointed by the president with the advice and consent of the Senate.[5]

When its members were first appointed, the terms were staggered, with one appointee having a one-year term, another a two-year term, another a three-year term, another a four-year term, and another a five-year term. After these first appointees, every commissioner is appointed to a five-year term.[6] As a result, in each year, only one commissioner's term ends. If the office of commissioner is vacated before the end of its term, a commissioner appointed as a replacement serves for the remainder of the term.

No more than three commissioners can be from the same political party.[7] Along with the fixed terms for commissioners, this limits the control that the executive branch would be able to exercise were a new president able to replace all the commissioners with appointees from his or her own political party after assuming office.

Of the five commissioners, one is selected by the president, with the advice and consent of the Senate, to serve as chairman.[8] At any time, with the advice and consent of the Senate, the President may appoint a different commissioner as chairman, in which case, the former chairman sits for the rest of his or her term as a commissioner.

The CFTC is, based on these structural limitations, generally considered an "independent agency." Consistent with this is the CFTC's inclusion as one of nineteen "independent regulatory agencies" in the Paperwork Reduction Act of 1980.[9] However, what it means to be an "independent agency" can have different contextual meanings and, in some ways, is more a term of art than a fixed legal category.

Jennifer L. Selin and David E. Lewis, Administrative Conference of the United States

Sourcebook of United States Executive Agencies (2d ed., Oct. 2018)

What is an Independent Agency? . . .

There is no general, widely accepted definition of an independent agency across all government officials, practitioners, and scholarly disciplines, but this label or definition is consequential for both law and politics. For some scholars, primarily those in political science, public administration, and public policy, any agency established outside the [Executive Office of the President ("EOP")] or executive departments is an "independent agency."[10] Thus, under this definition, the class of independent

---

5. Commodity Exchange Act § 2(a)(2)(A).

6. *Id.*

7. *Id.*

8. Commodity Exchange Act § 2(a)(2)(B).

9. 44 U.S.C. § 3502(5).

10. [N. 156] David Epstein and Sharyn O'Halloran, Delegating Powers: A Transaction Cost Politics Approach to Policy Making Under Separate Powers (1999); [David E. Lewis, Presidents and the Politics of Agency Design: Political Insulation in the United States Government Bureaucracy,

agencies would include all administrations, commissions, and corporations outside the EOP and executive departments, such as the Environmental Protection Agency and Federal Deposit Insurance Corporation. It would not, however, include multi-member bodies inside an executive department such as the Federal Energy Regulatory Commission (within the Department of Energy) or bureaus whose heads have fixed terms such as the Federal Aviation Administration or Commissioner of the Internal Revenue Service.

For other scholars, primarily those in law, structural features, particularly fixed terms with for-cause removal protections (i.e., presidentially appointed agency leaders cannot be removed except "for-cause," "inefficiency, neglect of duty, or malfeasance in office," or similar language), and not location define independence.[11] Court jurisprudence on the issue also focuses overwhelmingly on these structural features.[12] By this definition, the class of independent agencies would include a multitude of single-headed and multi-member agencies inside and outside the executive departments. There are at least 30 agencies and subunits with administrators or directors who serve for a fixed term and are protected from removal by for-cause provisions, including multi-member agencies located within executive departments such as the National Indian Gaming Commission and agencies headed by single individuals located outside of executive departments like the Office of Special Counsel.

Statutory law and executive materials also vary in their consideration of what constitutes agency independence. For example, Title 5 defines an "independent establishment" as any establishment in the executive branch, other than the Postal Service or Postal Regulatory Commission, which is not an executive department, military department, government corporation, or part thereof.[13] The Paperwork

---

1946–1997 (2003); Harold Seidman, Politics, Position, and Power: The Dynamics of Federal Organization (1998).]

11. [N. 158] Most existing scholarship recognizes some clustering of design characteristics that together signify independence, but the most important characteristic appears to be protections against removal. . . .

12. [N. 159] E.g., Free Enter. Fund v. Pub. Co. Accounting Oversight Bd., 561 U.S. 477 (2010) (addressing the removal provisions for the Public Company Accounting Oversight Board); Buckley v. Valeo, 424 U.S. 1, 135–42 (1976) (discussing agency independence in the context of the President's removal power); Humphrey's Ex'r v. United States, 295 U.S. 602 (1935) (federal statutes may limit the removal of officials in certain types of agencies); Myers v. United States, 272 U.S. 52 (1926) (any statute by which the unrestricted power of removal is denied to the President is unconstitutional); PHH Corp. v. Consumer Financial Protection Bureau, 881 F.3d 75 (D.C. Cir. 2018) (en banc), vacating 839 F.3d 1, 14 (D.C. Cir. 2016) (addressing the constitutionality of an independent agency headed by a single director); In re Aiken County, 645 F.3d 428, 439 (D.C. Cir. 2011) (recognizing for-cause protections as a primary indicator of an independent agency); Collins v. Federal Housing Finance Agency, 254 F. Supp. 3d 841, 847–848 (S.D. Tex. 2017) (recognizing the constitutionality of an "independent agency" headed by a single individual protected from removal but for cause); Consumer Financial Protection Bureau v. Future Income Payments, 252 F. Supp. 3d 961, 971 (C.D. Cal. 2017) (providing that there is no textual basis in the Constitution for concluding independent agencies must be led by multi-member commissions).

13. [N. 162] . . . [5 U.S.C. § 1211(b)].

Reduction Act of 1980 lists 19 independent regulatory agencies and, while the majority of agencies listed are commissions [with] for-cause protections, the statute also classifies the Department of the Treasury's Offices of Financial Research and the Comptroller of the Currency as independent regulatory agencies.[14] ... Executive Order 12,866, relating to regulatory planning and review, adopts this statutory definition of independent regulatory agency.[15] ...

Interestingly, some of the traditional independent regulatory commissions have all of the ... [classical features of an independent agency] such as explicit for-cause protections, explicit staggering of terms, and party balancing limitations on appointments, but others do not. For example, while the Consumer Product Safety Commission has explicit "for-cause" protections against removal, the Commodity Futures Trading Commission and Securities and Exchange Commission do not.[16] ...

[D]iscussions of independent agencies often revolve around the set of multi-member boards and commissions ... that have for-cause protections against removal and often have quasi-judicial or quasi-legislative authority. As famously noted by the Supreme Court in *Humphrey's Executor*, these multi-member agencies are a "body of experts appointed by law and informed by experience," and the agencies' structure reduces the risk of arbitrary decision-making.[17] ...

[A]t least 61 agencies and bureaus are led by one or more individuals who serve a fixed term but are not protected by explicit for-cause removal provisions (19 are led by a single individual). Some of these agencies, like the Securities and Exchange Commission, were established at a time when legal jurisprudence cast serious doubt on the constitutionality of for-cause protections.[18] However, most of the agencies

---

14. [N. 163] 44 U.S.C. § 3502(5) (2017).

15. [N. 165] Executive Order 12,866, Regulatory Planning and Review § 3(b), 58 Fed. Reg. 51735 (Sept. 30, 1993).

16. [N. 168] However, courts have recognized implicit "for-cause" protections. *See, e.g.*, Free Enter. Fund v. Pub. Co. Accounting Oversight Bd., 561 U.S. 477 (2010); Wiener v. United States, 357 U.S. 349 (1958) (even in the absence of "for-cause" statutory provisions, the President cannot remove a member of an adjudicatory body like the War Claims Commission merely because he wants his own appointees to serve on such a commission); Humphrey's Ex'r v. United States, 295 U.S. 602 (1935) ("for-cause" provisions are constitutional in predominately quasi-legislative or quasi-judicial agencies); SEC v. Blinder, Robinson, & Co., 855 F.2d 677 (10th Cir. 1988) (recognizing implicit "for-cause" protection in the SEC because the SEC is like the FTC in that both are administrative bodies created by Congress to carry into effect legislative policies).

17. [N. 170] 295 U.S. 602, 624 (1935).

18. [N. 174] Free Enter. Fund v. Pub. Co. Accounting Oversight Bd., 561 U.S. 477, 546–57 (Breyer, J. dissenting). ... It is worth noting that, despite explicit statutory language, commissioners are largely recognized as being protected by for-cause protections. The Supreme Court has never ruled on the issue, and in the recent *Free Enterprise Fund v. Public Co. Accounting Oversight Board* decision, the parties merely stipulated that Commission members could not be removed except under the *Humphrey's Executor* standard of inefficiency, neglect of duty, or malfeasance in office. 571 U.S. 477, 487 (2010). Some question whether such a stipulation is appropriate. E.g., Free Enter. Fund v. Pub. Co. Accounting Oversight Bd., 561 U.S. 477, 545–548 (Breyer, J. dissenting); Gary Lawson, *Stipulating the Law*, 109 Mich. L. Rev. 1191 (2011). ...

and bureaus in this category were created at a time when the legal status of for-cause language was clear. When Congress creates an agency with leadership that serves for a fixed term, but that leader is not protected by explicit for-cause protections, the President legally may remove the individual from office for any reason.[19] Yet any fixed term often establishes an expected tenure of office, and that expectation may influence the susceptibility of the appointee to presidential influence. A fixed term may also mean that an individual serves for more than one presidential administration, as officials are not required to resign upon changes in administrations. Furthermore, the removal of an individual before his or her term expires may impose political costs on the President. . . .

The majority of agencies created outside the EOP and executive departments are multi-member bodies, many with fixed and staggered terms for members. In general, these agencies tend to be smaller than other federal agencies, varying from as many as 6,300 employees to just a handful. As discussed above, the most recognizable of these are the independent regulatory commissions, . . . located outside executive departments, having multi-member body, for-cause protections, staggered terms, and party balancing requirements, and exercising quasi-legislative and/or quasi-judicial power. These agencies are involved in significant ways in regulating many aspects of the economy, from antitrust to banking to labor to communications to consumer products.

There are a number of reasons why the independent commission structure was and still is appealing to policymakers. Most notably, the commission structure requires deliberation and may lead to decisions that are more moderate as commissioners compromise to reach agreement. The creation of independent agencies also helps mitigate concerns with the delegation of policymaking or adjudicatory authority to executive officials who may be tempted to use this authority for partisan benefit. Historically, most policymakers have agreed in principle to the idea of a unified executive establishment organized under the President, but justify the creation of specific independent agencies as a necessary exception to this general principle.

Beyond the allure of bipartisan or non-partisan expertise being applied to complicated national problems, creating new agencies as independent commissions also expresses the symbolic importance of specific policy areas or problems. Independent agencies can focus on a narrow task of national importance and not have to compete with other sub-department agencies for attention, budgets, or personnel.

Yet the presence of independent commissions has been controversial in the American political system, as commissions can lead to inefficiencies. The Brownlow

---

19. [N. 175] E.g., Dep't of Transp. v. Ass'n of Am. R.R., 135 S. Ct. 1225, 1232–33 (2015) (citing Office of Legal Counsel memorandum that recognized Amtrak is not an adjudicatory body and thus its Board members, who serve fixed terms, are removable by the President without cause); Shurtleff v. United States, 1829 U.S. 311, 315 (1903) (holding that only clear and explicit language can restrict the President's removal power); Parsons v. United States, 167 U.S. 324, 343 (1897) (holding that even if statutory law provides for a fixed term of office, the President still has the power of removal). . . .

Committee charged that "they do violence to the basic theory of the American Constitution that there should be three major branches of government and only three."[20] The Brownlow Committee also complained about commission performance, noting, "For purposes of management, boards and commissions have turned out to be failures."[21]

The Committee's concerns have been echoed throughout the twentieth century. While some scholars suggest that the commission structure guards against undue influence by politically powerful interests, others have argued that commissions are easily co-opted by the groups they are supposed to regulate. Inequalities in group pressure, appointment patterns that rotate industry officials into and out of agency management, and regular interaction between the agency and regulated industries ultimately can make the agency sympathetic to, or "captured" by, regulated industries. Many also claim that the promises of expertise and bipartisanship have not been realized, arguing that these agencies no longer attract the very best persons and that the increasing appointment of strong partisans or ideologues has undermined the moderate and bipartisan composition of boards.

The number of commissions of different types and the limited empirical evidence across agencies makes it difficult to generalize about the effectiveness of independent commissions except to say that there are tradeoffs associated with their political independence. Agencies designed to be insulated from political interference are going to be autonomous in ways that are useful to policymakers in some cases and frustrating in others.

When agencies are involved in adjudication or making decisions with large consequences for markets and society, most would agree that the agency should make decisions on the basis of evidence and expertise rather than on partisan considerations. The features of agency design that limit partisan influence are precisely those that characterize independent commissions. The alternative to creating independent commissions is allowing less insulated agencies to make these decisions with no particular protection from partisan influence or to use statutory details or political oversight to limit and confine the authority of executive officials. In complex areas of law and policy, however, precise statutes are difficult to craft. Detailed statutes can be counterproductive if they limit useful flexibility and prevent agencies from using expertise they have acquired. In some cases, political oversight can help correct wayward agency policymaking, but in other cases it is the source of partisan influence.

Direct accountability to elected officials through appointments, removals, and appropriations is useful for monitoring agency behavior and for correcting agency missteps. The tradeoff for Congress and the President is that the price of insulating agencies from politics is a lack of this type of direct democratic accountability because the barriers Congress and the President put in place to insulate agencies

---

20. [N. 188] President's Committee on Administrative Management, *Administrative Management in the Government of the United States* 36 (Govt. Printing Off. 1937).

21. [N. 189] *Id.* at 30.

from politics also make it harder for elected officials to monitor day-to-day agency behavior. Congress and the President still govern independent commissions through oversight and can enact new legislation, but the autonomy generated by structure can have desirable and undesirable effects. There has been much work on whether agencies of various types are more responsive to Congress or the President. While some of this work provides evidence that the commission structure makes an agency relatively more responsive to Congress, other scholarship suggests that independent commissions are removed from both congressional and presidential control. . . .

———————

At the height of the New Deal era in 1936, President Roosevelt commissioned a report on the role of administrative agencies in the government. The report was prepared by an *ad hoc* committee, the President's Committee on Administrative Management. The final report was known as the "Brownlow Report," named after its chair, Louis Brownlow. The report was adamantly critical of "independent commissions":

> These independent commissions have been given broad powers to explore, formulate, and administer policies of regulation; they have been given the task of investigating and prosecuting business misconduct; they have been given powers, similar to those exercised by courts of law, to pass in concrete cases upon the rights and liabilities of individuals under the statutes. They are in reality miniature independent governments set up to deal with the railroad problem, the banking problem, or the radio problem. They constitute a headless "fourth branch" of the Government, a haphazard deposit of irresponsible agencies and uncoordinated powers. They do violence to the basic theory of the American Constitution that there should be three major branches of the Government and only three. The Congress has found no effective way of supervising them, they cannot be controlled by the President, and they are answerable to the courts only in respect to the legality of their activities.[22]

The question of the constitutional limitations of independent agencies such as the CFTC continues to be addressed. There is some indication that the Supreme Court in recent years is applying greater scrutiny to these structures. For example, in *Seila Law LLC v. Consumer Financial Protection Bureau*, the Supreme Court ruled that the Consumer Financial Protection Bureau's structure of being headed by a single Director with removal by the President only for "inefficiency, neglect, or malfeasance" was unconstitutional. This was remedied by striking the provision of the statute limiting removal to "for cause." As the Court noted:

> The CFPB Director has no boss, peers, or voters to report to. Yet the Director wields vast rulemaking, enforcement, and adjudicatory authority over a significant portion of the U.S. economy. The question before us is whether this arrangement violates the Constitution's separation of powers.

———————

22. President's Committee on Administrative Management, *Administrative Management in the Government of the United States* 36 (Govt. Printing Off. 1937).

Under our Constitution, the "executive Power" — all of it — is "vested in a President," who must "take Care that the Laws be faithfully executed." Art. II, § 1, cl. 1; *id.*, § 3. Because no single person could fulfill that responsibility alone, the Framers expected that the President would rely on subordinate officers for assistance. . . .

The President's power to remove — and thus supervise — those who wield executive power on his behalf follows from the text of Article II, was settled by the First Congress, and was confirmed in the landmark decision *Myers v. United States*, 272 U.S. 52 (1926). Our precedents have recognized only two exceptions to the President's unrestricted removal power. In *Humphrey's Executor v. United States*, 295 U.S. 602 (1935), we held that Congress could create expert agencies led by a group of principal officers removable by the President only for good cause. And in *United States v. Perkins*, 116 U.S. 483 (1886), and *Morrison v. Olson*, 487 U.S. 654 (1988), we held that Congress could provide tenure protections to certain inferior officers with narrowly defined duties.

We are now asked to extend these precedents to a new configuration: an independent agency that wields significant executive power and is run by a single individual who cannot be removed by the President unless certain statutory criteria are met. We decline to take that step. While we need not and do not revisit our prior decisions allowing certain limitations on the President's removal power, there are compelling reasons not to extend those precedents to the novel context of an independent agency led by a single Director. . . .

We therefore hold that the structure of the CFPB violates the separation of powers. We go on to hold that the CFPB Director's removal protection is severable from the other statutory provisions bearing on the CFPB's authority. The agency may therefore continue to operate, but its Director, in light of our decision, must be removable by the President at will.[23]

b. Roles

The chairman's role is to be the presiding officer at Commission meetings and to act as the chief administrative officer of the CFTC. This is a very broad role, including hiring, supervision, and firing of staff.[24] There is an exception for appointments of heads of "major administrative units" of the CFTC. These staff members are appointed by the Commission. The chairman is also responsible for making the budget expenditures according to the budget established by the Commission.

The Commission, as noted above, is responsible for appointment of the heads of administrative divisions and offices, discussed below. The Commission also decides overall CFTC policy and establishes budgets (based on congressional

---

23. *Selia Law LLC v. Consumer Financial Protection Bureau*, 140 S. Ct. 2183, 2191–2192 (2020).
24. Commodity Exchange Act § 2(a)(6).

appropriations). Perhaps most importantly, it has the authority to promulgate rules[25] and, since 1992, provide exemptions from the Commodity Exchange Act provisions regulating futures for non-retail agreements, contracts, or transactions, or for instruments with securities or banking product characteristics.[26]

The Commission has the authority to approve civil enforcement actions for specified violations of the Commodity Exchange Act or CFTC rules.[27] It typically acts on the advice of the Division of Enforcement, discussed below in subsection 2.a.[28] Enforcement actions can be heard and decided by CFTC administrative law judges or in federal district court.[29] If brought before an administrative law judge, the judge's decisions are appealable to the Commission.[30]

As a practical matter, in recent years, the Commission brings enforcement actions in federal district court instead of before administrative law judges. In 2015, a former general counsel and current commissioner of the CFTC noted, at a time when the CFTC's head of enforcement was eyeing a resumption of use of administrative law judges:

> For more than a decade the Division [of Enforcement] has filed contested cases exclusively in federal court — the last contested enforcement case filed before a CFTC administrative law judge [was in 2001]. . . . Although the Division has never publicly explained its rationale for avoiding the administrative process during this period, it is generally believed that the Division's track record in its administrative forum as well as the higher profile of cases filed in federal court were key factors.[31]

In the meantime, federal litigation challenging the constitutionality of the SEC's appointment of administrative law judges threw into question the appointment of CFTC administrative law judges since the appointment structure and role of CFTC administrative law judges was nearly identical to the SEC's. The CFTC did not, at this time, employ any administrative law judges.[32]

The dispute over the SEC's administrative law judges related to their means of appointment. The Constitution provides parameters for the appointment of "inferior officers."[33] The Supreme Court ruled that the SEC's administrative law judges

---

25. Commodity Exchange Act § 2(a)(12).

26. Commodity Exchange Act § 4(c).

27. Namely, any time the remedies in Commodity Exchange Act §§ 6, 6b, 8a(2), 8a(3), 8a(4), or 8a(11) are being imposed. *See* 17 C.F.R. § 10.1.

28. 17 C.F.R. § 11.20(a).

29. 17 C.F.R. § 10.8.

30. 17 C.F.R. § 10.102(a)(1).

31. Dan M. Berkovitz, *The Resurrection of CFTC Administrative Enforcement Proceedings: Efficient Justice or a Biased Forum?*, 35 No. 2 Futures & Derivatives L. Rep. 1 (Mar. 2015).

32. It did employ a "judgment officer" for reparations proceedings. CFTC, *In re: Pending Administrative Proceedings* (Apr. 6, 2018), https://www.cftc.gov/sites/default/files/2018-04/ogcorder040918 .pdf. We discuss reparations proceedings in chapter 16, section B.1.

33. U.S. Const. art. 2, § 2, cl. 2.

were not appointed pursuant to these requirements because the SEC viewed them as employees not inferior officers as referenced in the Constitution. Any future administrative law judges at the CFTC will need to be appointed in accordance with the Court's decision.

Lucia v. Securities and Exchange Commission
138 S. Ct. 2044 (2018)

Justice Kagan delivered the opinion of the Court.

The Appointments Clause of the Constitution lays out the permissible methods of appointing "Officers of the United States," a class of government officials distinct from mere employees. Art. II, § 2, cl. 2. This case requires us to decide whether administrative law judges (ALJs) of the Securities and Exchange Commission (SEC or Commission) qualify as such "Officers." . . .

The SEC has statutory authority to enforce the nation's securities laws. One way it can do so is by instituting an administrative proceeding against an alleged wrongdoer. By law, the Commission may itself preside over such a proceeding. See 17 C.F.R. § 201.110 (2017). But the Commission also may, and typically does, delegate that task to an ALJ. . . . The SEC currently has five ALJs. Other staff members, rather than the Commission proper, selected them all. . . .

[A]n SEC ALJ exercises authority "comparable to" that of a federal district judge conducting a bench trial. . . .

This case began when the SEC instituted an administrative proceeding against petitioner Raymond Lucia and his investment company. Lucia marketed a retirement savings strategy called "Buckets of Money." In the SEC's view, Lucia used misleading slideshow presentations to deceive prospective clients. The SEC charged Lucia under the Investment Advisers Act, § 80b-1 *et seq.,* and assigned ALJ Cameron Elliot to adjudicate the case. After nine days of testimony and argument, Judge Elliot issued an initial decision concluding that Lucia had violated the Act and imposing sanctions, including civil penalties of $300,000 and a lifetime bar from the investment industry. . . .

On appeal to the SEC, Lucia argued that the administrative proceeding was invalid because Judge Elliot had not been constitutionally appointed. According to Lucia, the Commission's ALJs are "Officers of the United States" and thus subject to the Appointments Clause. Under that Clause, Lucia noted, only the President, "Courts of Law," or "Heads of Departments" can appoint "Officers." See Art. II, § 2, cl. 2. And none of those actors had made Judge Elliot an ALJ. To be sure, the Commission itself counts as a "Head[] of Department[]" . . . [b]ut the Commission had left the task of appointing ALJs, including Judge Elliot, to SEC staff members.

The Commission rejected Lucia's argument. It held that the SEC's ALJs are not "Officers of the United States." Instead, they are "mere employees." . . .

Lucia's claim fared no better in the Court of Appeals for the D.C. Circuit. A panel of that court seconded the Commission's view that SEC ALJs are employees rather than officers, and so are not subject to the Appointments Clause. See 832 F.3d 277, 283–289 (2016). Lucia then petitioned for rehearing en banc. The Court of Appeals granted that request and heard argument in the case. But the ten members of the en banc court divided evenly, resulting in a *per curiam* order denying Lucia's claim. See 868 F.3d 1021 (2017). That decision conflicted with one from the Court of Appeals for the Tenth Circuit. See *Bandimere v. SEC,* 844 F.3d 1168, 1179 (2016).

The sole question here is whether the Commission's ALJs are "Officers of the United States" or simply employees of the Federal Government. . . .

[The Court here explained that the administrative law judges were "Officers of the United States" because they: (1) "hold a continuing office established by law"; and (2) have "significant discretion" when carrying out important judicial functions.]

[T]he Commission's ALJs are "Officers of the United States," subject to the Appointments Clause. And as noted earlier, Judge Elliot heard and decided Lucia's case without the kind of appointment the Clause requires. . . . So what relief follows? This Court has also held that the "appropriate" remedy for an adjudication tainted with an appointments violation is a new "hearing before a properly appointed" official. . . . And we add today one thing more. That official cannot be Judge Elliot, even if he has by now received (or receives sometime in the future) a constitutional appointment. Judge Elliot has already both heard Lucia's case and issued an initial decision on the merits. He cannot be expected to consider the matter as though he had not adjudicated it before. To cure the constitutional error, another ALJ (or the Commission itself) must hold the new hearing to which Lucia is entitled.[34] . . .

We discuss much of the CFTC's enforcement authority in detail in chapter 15.

Too Many Roles?

The first chairman of the CFTC, William T. Bagley, wrote while still chairman that the "very structure is at fault when, by statute, the commission is the rule-maker, the investigator, the prosecuting attorney, the grand jury — receiving evidence of an internal action — and then the judge and jury all in the same case over the same time period."[a]

As noted in section B.1.b above, as a matter of recent practice, the CFTC does not act as "judge and jury" for enforcement actions because the actions have

---

34. [N. 6] While this case was on judicial review, the SEC issued an order "ratif[ying]" the prior appointments of its ALJs. Order (Nov. 30, 2017), online at https://www.sec.gov/litigation/opinions /2017/33-10440.pdf (as last visited June 18, 2018). . . .

> typically been brought in federal district court instead of before a CFTC admin-
> istrative law judge. But, as a general matter, is there a problem with so many
> roles vested in one agency?
>
> [a] William T. Bagley, Reign of Undue Process in Regulatory Agencies, Forum 1 (1977).

2. CFTC Staff

a. Structure and Roles

The CFTC is currently divided into seven large administrative divisions, each
with substantial staff.[35]

- The Division of Clearing and Risk oversees the clearing process in the futures
  and cleared swaps markets, whether by evaluating the applications of new registrations or investigating compliance by existing registrants and market participants. We discuss these entities in chapter 5, section D, and chapter 10, section B.

- The Division of Market Oversight has a similar function to the Division of
  Clearing and Risk with respect to trading facilities, such as exchanges. We discuss these entities in chapter 5, sections B and C, and chapter 10, section C.

- The Division of Market Participants oversees all derivatives intermediaries, off-
  exchange derivatives activities, and the activities of self-regulatory organizations.
  We discuss these entities in chapters 6 and 11. Additionally, the Office of Customer Education and Outreach is part of the Division of Market Participants.

- The Division of Data, spun off in October 2020 from the Division of Market
  Oversight, is responsible for the "analytics, visualization, and storage of data."

- The Division of Legal, formed in October 2020 from the merger of the Offices
  of General Counsel and the Executive Secretariat, is the primary provider of
  legal services to the CFTC and advice to the Commission. It has five groups:
  (1) Litigation, Enforcement & Adjudications; (2) Regulatory; (3) General Law;
  (4) Legislation & Intergovernmental Affairs; and (5) Secretariat & Information
  Management.

- The Division of Administration, successor to the Office of the Executive Director, is responsible for internal day-to-day management of the CFTC's operations.

- The Division of Enforcement is responsible for investigating and recommending
  enforcement actions to the Commission and then prosecuting the actions. We
  discuss enforcement activities in the areas of fraud and manipulation in detail
  in chapter 15. The Division of Enforcement includes the CFTC's Whistleblower

---

35. CFTC, *CFTC Organization*, https://www.cftc.gov/About/CFTCOrganization/index.htm.
The General Counsel and Executive Director roles are statutory. *See* Commodity Exchange Act
§§ 2(a)(4) and (5). The other appointments rely on the general authority in Commodity Exchange
Act § 2(a)(7)(A).

Office which, due to a potential payment of more than $100 million, may be critically depleted. By law, it can only be replenished by enforcement awards when it falls below $100 million. Legislative efforts are underway to resolve this conundrum.[36]

In addition to these large divisions, there are seven offices, Chief Economist, Inspector General, International Affairs, Legislative and Intergovernmental Affairs, Minority and Women Inclusion, Public Affairs, and LabCFTC.

The heads of the divisions and the offices are appointed by the Commission. All others are appointed by the chairman or the chairman's delegates.

The CFTC's primary office is in Washington, D.C. It also has regional offices in New York City, Chicago, and Kansas City.

LabCFTC

"Fintech" is the term for the specific technology used to support finance. The intersection between technology and finance grows ever stronger. In 2017, the CFTC took the step of creating LabCFTC as a unit in the General Counsel's office. In 2019, it was upgraded to a standalone CFTC office, reporting directly to the CFTC's Chairman.

The role of LabCFTC is to interface with fintech innovators. It provides fintech innovators with a helpful regulatory resource to streamline and facilitate interactions with the CFTC. In return, it provides the CFTC an opportunity to learn from the fintech industry about new developments.

---

b. No-Action and Other Letters

One of the most important roles of staff in the Divisions of Clearing and Risk, Market Oversight, and Market Participants is the issuance of "no-action" letters. A no-action letter is a statement by the relevant division that, provided certain facts apply, the division will not recommend enforcement action in relation to a current or proposed activity even if the activity could be construed as violating a CFTC rule. A no-action letter, since it does not bear the approval of the Commission, is not a binding statement by the CFTC — it is only binding on the division that issues it and, in theory, only the expressly referenced beneficiaries may rely on it.[37] The Commission could vote to bring an enforcement action with or without a recommendation from the Division of Enforcement even if the activity is contemplated in a no-action letter. However, despite not being enforceable against the CFTC, no-action letters are often treated by the marketplace as such and, as a practice, the CFTC makes sure to

---

36. Alexandra Berzon, *CFTC Whistleblower Program in Peril Over Potential $100 Million-Plus Payout*, https://www.wsj.com/articles/cftc-whistleblower-program-in-peril-over-potential-100-million-plus-payout-11620732600 (May 11, 2021).

37. 17 C.F.R. § 140.99(a)(2).

explicitly issue a statement withdrawing a no-action letter in advance of taking a different policy position.

Staff in the Divisions of Clearing and Risk, Market Oversight, and Market Participants may also issue interpretative letters providing advice or guidance and, when the Commission has delegated the authority to do so, exemptive letters on behalf of the CFTC providing relief from specified Commodity Exchange Act provisions or CFTC rules.[38]

The role of these staff letters—and when a formal rule is more appropriate—is an ongoing regulatory question. As seen in figure 4.1 the frequency of the use of no-action letters has fluctuated greatly during the existence of the CFTC.

Figure 4.1 Number of CFTC No-Action Letters, 1975–2020

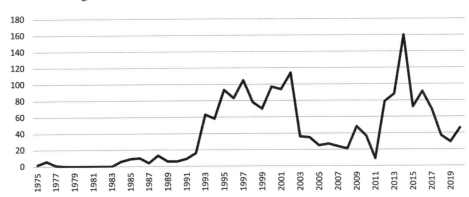

CFTC, *Directive of Chairman Heath P. Tarbert on the Use of Staff Letters and Guidance*

https://www.cftc.gov/PressRoom/SpeechesTestimony
/tarbetstatement102720 (Oct. 27, 2020)

In the regular course of administering the Commodity Exchange Act (CEA) and Commission regulations, CFTC staff often receive inquiries from the public seeking guidance or clarification on how Commission rules and regulations may apply to specific facts and circumstances.[39] Staff may respond to such inquiries through a variety of communications, including no-action, interpretive, and exemptive letters, as well as guidance and advisory statements (collectively, Staff Letters). Staff Letters vary in scope and format. For instance, a Staff Letter may simply convey an enforcement position, or it may articulate an explicit interpretation of applicable law and Commission regulations as they relate to a particular scenario. In all cases, the

---

38. 17 C.F.R. §§ 140.99(a)(1) and (3).

39. [N. 1] The procedures for requesting exemptive, no-action and interpretive letters are found in section 140.99 of the Commission's regulations at title 17, Code of Federal Regulations, 17 C.F.R. § 140.99.

views articulated in Staff Letters (with the exception of exemptive letters) are informal and advisory, and the statements are not binding on the Commission itself.[40]

Because they do not necessarily reflect the views or opinions of the Commission and are not subject to public notice-and-comment procedures, as Chairman, I direct CFTC staff to ensure that Staff Letters are limited to those circumstances that are not suitable for a general rulemaking.[41] In other words, Staff Letters should supplement, rather than replace, rulemakings.

As part of my continued commitment to providing transparency about CFTC business, I believe it is appropriate to issue this directive to CFTC staff publicly. It is important that the public understand the guidelines I am setting forth for CFTC staff to follow — and the rationale behind them — when considering whether, and the manner in which, Staff Letters should be used to address public requests for relief, interpretation, or guidance.[42]

No-Action Letters

A no-action letter is a statement issued by a division or office that it will not recommend enforcement action with respect to a proposed transaction or activity for failure to comply with a specific provision of the CEA or Commission rule, regulation, or order (together, regulations). Although it is not binding on any other division or office, or the Commission itself, a no-action letter is binding on the issuing division or office. A no-action letter may be relied upon only by the addressee of the letter. If the addressee of the letter complies with all conditions stated in the no-action letter, the issuing division or office would not recommend enforcement action based solely on the conduct described in the letter, unless the no-action letter is revoked or the division or office provides an adequate explanation of why the no-action letter is not applicable. The public at large — other than the addressee — may not rely upon the letter, but they may look to the letter as instructive of the views of the issuing division or office with regard to the particular scenario.

Generally, I believe no-action relief should be limited to the following circumstances:

- Transitional Compliance Relief. Market participants may experience operational or other difficulties that impede timely compliance with the CEA or a new or amended Commission regulation. In such cases, targeted, time-limited relief may be appropriate.

---

40. [N. 2] Depending on the type of relief, it may be binding only on the issuing division or office. Such relief would also be binding on a successor division in the event of an agency reorganization.

41. [N. 3] Rulemaking may also be appropriate for Commission exemptive action pursuant to section 4(c) of the CEA, 7 U.S.C. § 6(c). *See* 63 Fed. Reg. 3285 (Jan. 22, 1998); 63 Fed. Reg. 68,175 (Dec. 10, 1998). Exemptions under CEA section 4(c) are outside the scope of this document.

42. [N. 5] The CFTC may issue Staff Letters in response to requests from trade associations or groups that represent similarly situated persons — i.e., persons or entities that share the same or substantially the same facts and circumstances.

- "Square Peg" Relief. Market participants' transactions or activities may raise a unique issue that is not contemplated by the CEA or CFTC regulations, or the application of CFTC regulations to a transaction activity may lead to unintended consequences. No-action relief tailored to either of these narrow circumstances may be appropriate.
- Extraordinary Circumstances. Market participants may face challenges in complying with the CEA or CFTC regulations during a market crisis or another extraordinary circumstance. Time-limited no-action relief the CEA or CFTC regulations may be necessary to avoid significant market disruptions.

To be clear, a no-action letter should not establish a new policy. CFTC staff are hereby instructed to consider whether rulemaking would be a more appropriate vehicle for responding to an inquiry where a situation is encountered on a repeated basis and has industry-wide implications.

Interpretive Letters

An interpretive letter is a written statement with respect to a specific provision of a Commission regulation, provided in the context of a proposed transaction or activity.[43] It is the vehicle by which staff explains its interpretation of ambiguous terms in the regulation.

Like a no-action letter, an interpretive letter is binding on only the issuing division or office. But, unlike a no-action letter, an interpretive letter may be relied upon by the public. Notably, however, an interpretive letter it is not binding on the public. Thus, for example, if the question or situation covered by the interpretive letter arises, the public could take a different approach without necessarily being in violation of the underlying requirement(s).

It is important that an interpretive letter be derived from the specific statutory provision or regulation; it may be used to add meaning or gloss to the underlying requirement(s). As with a no-action letter, an interpretive letter should not set new policy or otherwise alter the rights and obligations of any person. Were that to be the case, rulemaking would be more appropriate than using an interpretive letter.

Staff Guidance, Advisories, and FAQs

Staff guidance, advisories, and FAQs communicate staff's expectation regarding how regulated parties may comply with a particular requirement, or inform regulated parties about staff's regulatory priorities. They represent the view of only the issuing division or office, and are not binding on any other division or office, the Commission itself, or the public. Failure to conform to guidance, an advisory, or an FAQ does not necessarily mean that the party is in violation of the applicable regulation.

Staff guidance, advisories, and FAQs should not set new policy, but rather explain how the law would apply to a unique circumstance or market event. In essence,

---

43. [N. 8] Distinctions between interpretive letters and other Staff Letters may be blurred at times. Some letters advising no-action positions may be based on staff's interpretation of the CEA or Commission regulations.

staff guidance should advise the public prospectively of the manner in which staff proposes to implement the underlying provision of the CEA or Commission regulation. As with no-action relief, CFTC staff are hereby instructed to consider whether rulemaking would be a more appropriate vehicle.

Exemptive Letters

An exemptive letter is a written grant of relief issued by a division or office when the Commission itself has exemptive authority that has been delegated to the staff. As opposed to other Staff Letters, an exemptive letter binds the Commission. Only the addressee of the letter may rely upon the relief. As is the case for other Staff Letters, an exemptive letter addresses unique facts and circumstances set forth in the letter.

Although the public may not rely upon the letter, they may look to the letter as instructive of the views of the issuing division or office with regard to the particular course of conduct, and as a basis for understanding the views of the Commission.

An exemptive letter may include conditions that are traceable to the relevant regulation. For example, an exemptive letter may be conditioned upon the addressee meeting certain criteria or complying with alternative measures to mitigate a regulatory gap. However, as this is outside the rulemaking process, the staff should take care not to set conditions that effectively amend existing regulations. CFTC staff are hereby instructed that, in the event a potential exemptive letter would provide relief that could be applicable to parties other than the requestor, or the conditions of relief are broader than existing regulations, rulemaking would be more appropriate.

Conclusion

One of the CFTC's core values is clarity: to provide transparency to market participants about our rules and processes. Staff Letters give a measure of clarity, but we generally serve our markets best when the Commission itself acts with the benefit of public input and dialogue. Public input is particularly important when novel or complex issues are involved. As a result, I believe that rulemaking should be the agency's default policymaking vehicle.

Accordingly, CFTC staff are instructed to limit Staff Letters to the relatively narrow sets of circumstances described in this directive, and to use the notice-and-comment rulemaking process for all other policymaking initiatives. These guidelines shall remain in effect until augmented, amended, or withdrawn by myself, the Commission, or any future Chairman or Commission.

The directive above, of course, did not arise in a vacuum, and staff "interpretative guidance" had, previously, been a source of controversy. In 2013, the CFTC issued "interpretative guidance"[44] that triggered litigation claiming it was a "disguised" rule. Ultimately, the interpretative guidance was upheld with the understanding

---

44. CFTC, *Interpretative Guidance and Policy Statement Regarding Compliance with Certain Swap Regulations*, 78 Fed. Reg. 45292 (July 26, 2013).

that it could not be enforced by the CFTC in the same way a rule could.[45] We discuss this event in more detail in chapter 17, section D.2.

The balance of staff authority compared to the authority of commissioners has been a perennial question. As one SEC commissioner noted in relation to the SEC:

> I believe that there is a line that can be crossed where non-public staff guidance goes from being merely helpful . . . lore to something that is more akin to secret law that, for all practical purposes, binds at least some (though perhaps not all) market participants without any opportunity for review or appeal. . . .
>
> [W]hen I hear that staff simply will not accept certain applications for entire categories of products or types of businesses for reasons not found in our rules, I wonder whether that line has been crossed. Likewise, when I hear, as I did a few months ago, that one particularly complex set of Commission rules does not matter much in practice because firms operate instead under a set of published and unpublished letters and other directives from staff, I am pretty certain that line has been crossed. Or when I hear that examiners and . . . [self-regulatory organizations] are examining firms against the terms of draft no-action letters and notes of telephone calls with Commission staff, I am confident that line has been crossed.
>
> Again, as a technical matter, none of this guidance is . . . law, and it seems unlikely that a court would readily defer to this kind of guidance. In many of these cases, however, *sub rosa* guidance by staff does, as a practical matter, bind market participants, affecting the scope of their rights and obligations and limiting the range of permissible activities. It is important for those of us working at the Commission to be honest with ourselves about this: for the affected party, this kind of guidance operates no differently from duly enacted law or regulations issued pursuant to the APA. On second thought, let me revise that: it operates no differently from duly enacted law or regulation, save for the fact that because it is . . . "secret law," it is not subject to processes to ensure that it conforms to our legislative authority; it is impossible to determine whether it applies to all similarly situated parties equally; and it is insulated from effective oversight or review, whether by the Commission or the courts.[46]

On the other hand, there are benefits to being able to obtain staff guidance. The process is typically much faster than that for a formal pronouncement, and more flexibility might be shown, than if a formal rulemaking were required.

---

45. *Securities Industry and Financial Markets Association v. CFTC*, 67 F. Supp. 3d 373 (D.D.C. 2014).

46. Hester M. Peirce, *SECret Garden: Remarks at SEC Speaks* (Apr. 8, 2019), available at https://www.sec.gov/news/speech/peirce-secret-garden-sec-speaks-040819.

C. The CFTC's Jurisdiction in Relation to Other Regulators

With the CFTC's jurisdiction outlined, in the following sections, we analyze where the CFTC's jurisdiction overlaps or conflicts with other regulators. This helps us to better understand the CFTC's jurisdictional limits. It is important to keep in mind that, whereas the Commodity Exchange Act grants the CFTC exclusive jurisdiction over futures, the CFTC does not have exclusive jurisdiction over swaps.[47]

1. The CFTC and the SEC

In chapter 2, section B.4, we examined some of the historical jurisdictional conflicts between the CFTC and SEC. Sometimes, efforts to "split the baby" led to poor outcomes, such as uncertainty over the status of securities options, only resolved in 1982 by the Futures Trading Act, and the prohibition on single stock futures, only repealed in 2000 by the Commodity Futures Modernization Act. Arguably, another such outcome is the definition of "narrow-based security index," integral to determining whether the CFTC or the SEC has jurisdiction over both a securities future and a swap referencing a security. As we will see, it is complicated and, where a quick determination is required as to whether the CFTC or SEC has jurisdiction over a trade, unwieldy.

In this section we will examine each of these, as well as "mixed swaps." Instead of requiring a firm determination by the CFTC and the SEC as to whether each swap product is a swap, subject to CFTC regulation, or a security-based swap, subject to SEC regulation, the Dodd-Frank Act permitted the CFTC and the SEC to create a "mixed swap" category for derivatives with elements of both swaps and security-based swaps.[48] Jurisdiction over these instruments is exercised by both regulators.

a. Securities Options and Securities Futures

The Shad-Johnson Accord had prohibited the listing of single stock futures on either a futures or a securities exchange. The prohibition was in place merely because the SEC and CFTC could not agree on which regulator was jurisdictionally responsible for the oversight of single stock futures, not due to any specific concerns about the nature of the product. As enshrined in the Futures Trading Act of 1982,

---

47. *See, e.g.,* the different outcomes in *Hunter v. Federal Energy Regulatory Commission,* 711 F.3d 155 (D.C. Cir. 2013), and *Federal Energy Regulatory Commission v. Barclays Bank PLC,* 105 F. Supp. 3d 1121 (E.D. Cal. 2015). In the former case, involving manipulation of futures markets, the CFTC had exclusive jurisdiction. In the latter case, involving manipulation of swaps markets, the Federal Energy Regulatory Commission was found to also have jurisdiction. *See also* Gary E. Kalbaugh, *FERC v. Barclays Bank PLC Shines a Light on CFTC and FERC Jurisdiction,* 36 No. 11 Futures & Derivatives L. Rep. NL 2 (Dec. 2016).

48. Dodd-Frank Act § 712(a)(8).

the Shad-Johnson Accord also granted the SEC jurisdiction over securities options, whether on one or multiple securities (including a securities index).

The single stock futures ban was revised in 2000 by the Commodity Futures Modernization Act and replaced by a framework in which the CFTC and SEC share jurisdiction over single stock futures and futures on a "narrow-based security index" and the CFTC has jurisdiction over everything else, i.e., securities futures on an index that is not a "narrow-based security index."

The test for a narrow-based security index is complicated. As a general matter, an index comprised of nine or fewer securities is a narrow-based security index (with some additional tests if there are exactly nine securities) and there are further exceptions based on the weighting and trading volume of the index's constituent securities.

When the Commodity Futures Modernization Act of 2000 permitted single stock futures for the first time, expectations were high. However, the market never took off as expected.[49]

One reason cited is the approach of having dual CFTC and SEC jurisdiction. CFTC-regulated exchanges trading single stock securities futures or futures on a narrow-based securities index must provide notice to the SEC and vice versa. Moreover, intermediaries must be registered as both futures commission merchants (see chapter 6) and securities broker-dealers.

The main reason cited, though, is that single stock futures have tax and margining requirements that are more punitive than apply to other futures. This is to put them on the same competitive playing field as securities options. As a result, securities options have maintained their market share.[50] In 2019 the CFTC and SEC proposed redressing this imbalance.[51] However, by the time of their final rule in November 2020 it was too late:

> Subsequent to the issuance of the 2019 Proposing Release, OneChicago, the only exchange listing security futures in the U.S., discontinued all trading operations on September 21, 2020. At this time, there are no security futures contracts listed for trading on U.S. exchanges. The final rule amendments in this release, however, would apply to customer margin requirements for security futures if an exchange were to resume operations or another exchange were to launch security futures contracts. . . .

> The CFTC believes that the final rules will, if security futures trading resumes, produce significant benefits by reducing minimum margin requirements for security futures positions to levels equal to margin levels

---

49. Daniel P. Collins, *The Future of Single Stock Futures*, Futures Magazine (July 29, 2015), available at http://www.futuresmag.com/2015/07/29/future-single-stock-futures.

50. *Id.*

51. CFTC and SEC, *Customer Margin Rules Relating to Securities Futures*, 84 Fed. Reg. 36434 (July 26, 2019).

for exchange-traded options. . . . The CFTC believes this alignment may increase competition by establishing a level playing field between security futures carried in . . . [most securities accounts] and security futures carried in a futures account . . . should OneChicago begin offering these products again or new market entrants emerge.[52]

Options on a security future,[53] including a narrow-based security index, are still banned by the Commodity Exchange Act in the absence of joint authorization by the CFTC and the SEC.[54]

It is important to remember that, although the Dodd-Frank Act made sweeping jurisdictional changes in the area of off-exchange derivatives, it did not do so with respect to exchange-traded derivatives such as single stock futures.

b. Security-Based Swaps

Security-based swaps are a subset of swaps. In other words, before a derivative can be a security-based swap, it must be a swap. In addition to having the characteristics of a swap, a security-based swap must be based on:

(1) an index that is a narrow-based security index, including any interest therein or on the value thereof;

(2) a single security or loan, including any interest therein or on the value thereof; or

(3) the occurrence, nonoccurrence, or extent of the occurrence of an event relating to a single issuer of a security or the issuers of securities in a narrow-based security index, provided that such event directly affects the financial statements, financial condition, or financial obligations of the issuer.[55]

The only categories of swaps that can come within the definition of security-based swap are those that reference securities or loans. This means that security-based swaps must be either equity swaps or credit default swaps. We discussed categories of swaps in chapter 1.

As noted above in section C.1.a, the test for a narrow-based security index was added by the Commodity Futures Modernization Act for the purpose of providing a dividing line for the listing of exchange-traded securities futures. The listing process is one in which there is the luxury of time. Accordingly, if an exchange determines that it would like to list a securities future product, it has as long as necessary to apply the layers of tests necessary to conclusively determine whether a security index is a narrow-based one or not and, therefore, whether the securities future would be subject to the SEC's or the CFTC's jurisdiction.

---

52. CFTC and SEC, *Customer Margin Rules Relating to Securities Futures*, 85 Fed. Reg. 75112, 75114, 75130 (Nov. 24, 2020).

53. This would be a derivative on a derivative.

54. Commodity Exchange Act § 2(a)(1)(D)(iii)(II).

55. Securities Exchange Act of 1934 § 3(a)(68).

The Dodd-Frank Act directly utilized this historic definition in the very different context of off-exchange trading where parties enter into individual trades, often with little time to conduct an analysis of whether the traded product meets the narrow-based security index definition or not. This has implications because the determination of whether a product is a security-based swap also determines whether the SEC's or the CFTC's regulatory requirements must be satisfied.

c. Mixed Swaps

Some swaps may be difficult to characterize as exclusively a swap or security-based swap. Accordingly, the Dodd-Frank Act provided for "mixed swaps" that contain elements of both:

> The term "[mixed swap]" includes any [security-based swap that is also] based on the value of 1 or more interest or other rates, currencies, commodities, instruments of indebtedness, indices, quantitative measures, other financial or economic interest or property of any kind (other than a single security or a narrow-based security index), or the occurrence, non-occurrence, or the extent of the occurrence of an event or contingency associated with a potential financial, economic, or commercial consequence (other than [the occurrence, nonoccurrence, or extent of the occurrence of an event relating to a single issuer of a security or the issuers of securities in a narrow-based security index, provided that such event directly affects the financial statements, financial condition, or financial obligations of the issuer]).[56]

The solution arrived at by the Dodd-Frank Act is to subject such products to regulation by both the CFTC and the SEC. Perhaps recognizing that subjecting a product to regulation by both agencies may discourage market innovation, the SEC and the CFTC have jointly stated that they "believe that the scope of mixed swaps is, and is intended to be, narrow."[57]

2. Insurance

The insurance safe harbor referenced above in chapter 3, section C.2, protects against an insurance product being regulated as a swap. Traditionally, insurance regulation is within the province of the states.

---

56. Commodity Exchange Act §1a(47)(D) and Securities Exchange Act of 1934 §3(a)(68)(D). The statutory definition appears to have minor errors. The definition provided is based on the summary in CFTC and SEC, *Further Definition of "Swap," "Security-Based Swap," and "Security-Based Swap Agreement"; Mixed Swaps; Security-Based Swap Agreement Recordkeeping*, 47 Fed. Reg. 48208, 48210 at n. 10 (Aug. 13, 2012).

57. CFTC and SEC, *Further Definition of "Swap," "Security-Based Swap," and "Security-Based Swap Agreement"; Mixed Swaps; Security-Based Swap Agreement Recordkeeping*, 47 Fed. Reg. 48208, 48291 (Aug. 13, 2012).

Credit default swaps, discussed in detail in chapter 1, section D.2.c, operate by providing "protection" to a buyer against specified "Credit Events" such as the bankruptcy of a third party. Superficially, a credit default swap bears similarities to insurance. Unlike insurance, though, there is no insurable interest requirement and, instead of operating as an indemnity against a verified loss, as is typically the case with insurance, the economic pay-off to the purchaser of a credit default swap is hard-wired into the agreement. If a Credit Event occurs, the protection buyer receives a pay-out regardless of whether the protection buyer suffered an actual economic loss.

The Dodd-Frank Act added section 12(h) to the Commodity Exchange Act that, in unequivocal form, likewise protects against a swap being regulated as insurance:

A swap —

(1) shall not be considered to be insurance; and

(2) may not be regulated as an insurance contract under the law of any State.[58]

One of the motivations for the Dodd-Frank Act's preemption of state regulation of swaps as insurance, was a September 2008 letter from the New York State Insurance Department (now part of New York State's Department of Financial Services) stating that a seller of credit default swaps, despite a previous opinion to the contrary from the Insurance Department's General Counsel, might be engaged in an act requiring an insurance license.[59] This caused a great outcry in the marketplace. Two months later, the Insurance Department withdrew its letter.[60]

Despite the revocation, the tangible possibility of state regulation of the credit default swap market as insurance was of great concern to financial market participants. The Dodd-Frank Act addressed this concern by its preemption of such regulation.

3. Federal Energy Regulatory Commission

The Federal Energy Regulatory Commission ("FERC") was formed in 1977 as the successor the Federal Power Commission.[61] Historically, FERC had jurisdiction over spot market natural gas, wholesale electricity sales, transmission of electricity in interstate commerce, and certain hydroelectric projects.[62]

---

58. Dodd-Frank Act § 722(b) adding Commodity Exchange Act § 12(h).

59. New York State Insurance Department, Circular Ltr. No. 19 (2008).

60. New York State Insurance Department, First Supplement to Circular Ltr. No. 19 (2008).

61. Department of Energy Organization Act, Pub. L. No. 95-91, 91 Stat. 565. § 402(a) (1977) and Exec. Order No. 12,009, 42 Fed. Reg. 46267 (Sept. 13, 1977). The Federal Power Commission was itself established by the Federal Water Power Act of 1920, Pub. L. No. 66-280, 41 Stat. 1063, § 1 (1920).

62. See Natural Gas Act of 1938, Pub. L. No. 75-688, 52 Stat. 821 and Federal Power Act of 1935, Pub. L. No. 74-333, 49 Stat. 847. The Federal Power Act of 1935 also renamed the statute from its previous name, Federal Water Power Act. Id.

The Energy Policy Act of 2005 expanded FERC's jurisdiction to include jurisdiction over manipulation of the spot electric energy, natural gas, transportation services, or transmission services markets.[63] After the expansion of FERC's jurisdiction to market manipulation over these products, jurisdictional disputes with the CFTC ensued.

The collision of jurisdictions came to a head when, in 2007, a trader at a large hedge fund, Amaranth, was accused by FERC and the CFTC of manipulating the natural gas market via futures positions. The trader sold natural gas futures on a futures exchange, NYMEX, in the period before the market closed. This artificially depressed the reported closing price, calculated by reference to an average of prices in the final period of trading.

Simultaneously, the trader had larger positions in natural gas swaps that benefited from lower closing prices on NYMEX. The hedge fund, Amaranth, benefited from these positions because it simultaneously had a larger quantity of short positions in natural gas swap contracts that were priced by reference to the closing prices on NYMEX.

FERC viewed its grant of authority as relating to any manipulation of the energy market, regardless of the means. FERC also believed that the Energy Policy Act of 2005 implicitly modified the Commodity Exchange Act's grant of exclusive jurisdiction over commodity futures. The CFTC, filing an amicus brief in support of the trader (note that the CFTC had already conducted its own civil enforcement proceedings against him), argued that FERC had no jurisdiction over commodity futures because of the exclusive jurisdiction over commodity futures conferred to the CFTC by the Commodity Exchange Act.

Hunter v. Federal Energy Regulatory Commission

711 F.3d 155 (D.C. Cir. 2013)

Tatel, Circuit Judge:

Pursuant to the Energy Policy Act of 2005, the Federal Energy Regulatory Commission fined petitioner $30 million for manipulating natural gas futures contracts. According to petitioner, FERC lacks authority to fine him because the Commodity Futures Trading Commission has exclusive jurisdiction over all transactions involving commodity futures contracts. Because manipulation of natural gas futures contracts falls within the CFTC's exclusive jurisdiction and because nothing in the Energy Policy Act clearly and manifestly repeals the CFTC's exclusive jurisdiction, we grant the petition for review.

According to FERC, Hunter sold a significant number of natural gas futures contracts during the February, March, and April 2006 settlement periods. During these settlement periods, Hunter's sales ranged from 14.4% to 19.4% of market volume.

---

63. 15 U.S.C. § 717c-1 and 16 U.S.C. § 824v(a).

Given their volume and timing, Hunter's sales reduced the settlement price for natural gas. Hunter's portfolio benefited from these sales because he had positioned his assets in the natural gas market to capitalize on a price decrease—that is, he shorted the price for natural gas.

Hunter's trades caught the attention of federal regulators. On July 25, 2007, the CFTC filed a civil enforcement action against Hunter, alleging that he violated section 13(a)(2) of the Commodity Exchange Act by manipulating the price of natural gas futures contracts. The next day, FERC filed an administrative enforcement action against Hunter, alleging that he violated section 4A of the Natural Gas Act, which prohibits manipulation. FERC claimed that Hunter's manipulation of the settlement price affected the price of natural gas in FERC-regulated markets. Following a lengthy administrative process, FERC ruled against Hunter and imposed a $30 million fine.

Hunter [argues] . . . that FERC lacks jurisdiction to pursue this enforcement action. The CFTC has intervened in support of Hunter on this issue. . . .

Stated simply, Congress crafted . . . [Commodity Exchange Act ("CEA")] section 2(a)(1)(A) to give the CFTC exclusive jurisdiction over transactions conducted on futures markets like the NYMEX.

In response to the California energy crisis, Congress enacted the Energy Policy Act of 2005, which significantly expanded FERC's authority to regulate manipulation in energy markets. As codified at section 4A of the Natural Gas Act, the statute makes it

> unlawful for any entity, directly or indirectly, to use or employ, in connection with the purchase or sale of natural gas or the purchase or sale of transportation services subject to the jurisdiction of the Commission, any manipulative or deceptive device or contrivance . . . in contravention of such rules and regulations as the Commission may prescribe as necessary in the public interest or for the protection of natural gas ratepayers.

FERC subsequently promulgated regulations prohibiting manipulative trading in natural gas.

The Energy Policy Act contains only two references to the CFTC. . . .

[S]ection 23 requires FERC and the CFTC to enter into a memorandum of understanding about information sharing [and] provides that it has no effect on the CFTC's exclusive jurisdiction.

As we see it, this case reduces to two questions. First, does CEA section 2(a)(1)(A) encompass manipulation of natural gas futures contracts? If yes, then we need to answer the second question: did Congress clearly and manifestly intend to impliedly repeal CEA section 2(a)(1)(A) when it enacted the Energy Policy Act of 2005?

A quick glance at the statute's text answers the first question. . . . By CEA section 2(a)(1)(A)'s plain terms, the CFTC has exclusive jurisdiction over the manipulation of natural gas futures contracts.

Against the statute's plain text, FERC marshals two counterarguments. According to FERC, although it and the CFTC "each have exclusive jurisdiction over the day-to-day regulation of their respective physical energy and financial markets, where, as here, there is manipulation in one market that directly or indirectly affects the other market, both agencies have an enforcement role." But FERC's contention that the CFTC may exclusively regulate only day-to-day trading activities — not an overarching scheme like manipulation — finds no support in CEA section 2(a)(1) (A)'s text. . . .

FERC also relies on our decision in FTC v. Ken Roberts Co., 276 F.3d 583 (D.C.Cir.2001). There, the FTC subpoenaed a company for information concerning its instructional courses about futures market trading. The company argued that the FTC had no jurisdiction to investigate instructional courses about futures markets because only the CFTC could regulate such activities. . . . Concluding that an instructional course about futures trading did not qualify as a contract, agreement, or transaction on a commodity futures market, we held that the CFTC lacked exclusive jurisdiction and the FTC's subpoena could be enforced. . . .

As we read Ken Roberts, the decision actually supports Hunter's position because it endorses a robust view of the CFTC's exclusive jurisdiction. For example, we remarked that the CFTC "was invested with exclusive jurisdiction over certain aspects of the futures trading market. The aim of [CEA section 2(a)(1)(A)], according to one of its chief sponsors, was to 'avoid unnecessary, overlapping and duplicative regulation,' especially as between the [SEC] and the new CFTC" [and] "[t]he word 'transactions,'" we further explained, "conveys a reciprocity, a mutual exchange, which seem[ed] absent from the allegedly deceptive advertising materials that the FTC [sought] to investigate." By contrast, Hunter's alleged manipulation scheme involved transacting in commodity futures contracts, thus falling on the other side of the Ken Roberts dividing line.

Because any infringement of the CFTC's exclusive jurisdiction would effectively repeal CEA section 2(a)(1)(A), we must next determine whether, as FERC insists, the Energy Policy Act constitutes a repeal by implication. On this front, FERC carries a heavy burden. . . .

"[A]bsent a clearly expressed congressional intention" to repeal CEA section 2(a) (1)(A), Morton v. Mancari, 417 U.S. 535, 551, 94 S. Ct. 2474, 41 L.Ed.2d 290 (1974), FERC cannot demonstrate that section 4A encroaches upon the CFTC's exclusive jurisdiction. Having failed to meet the high bar of showing an implied repeal, FERC lacks jurisdiction to charge Hunter with manipulation of natural gas futures contracts. . . .

For the foregoing reasons, we grant the petition for review.

The U.S. Court of Appeals for the District of Columbia interpreted the grant of "exclusive" commodity futures jurisdiction to the CFTC strictly. This has an antecedent in Chicago Board of Trade v. SEC[64] in which the Seventh Circuit ruled in favor of the CFTC in the GNMA option dispute (discussed in chapter 2, section B.4) which led to the Shad-Johnson Accord. There, although superseded by the statutory codification of the jurisdictional divide between the SEC and CFTC agreed by their respective Chairmen, Shad and Johnson, the Seventh Circuit also took a broad reading of the Commodity Exchange Act's grant of "exclusive" jurisdiction over commodity futures to the CFTC.

On the other hand, the CFTC does not have "exclusive" jurisdiction over swaps as demonstrated in *Federal Energy Regulatory Commission v. Barclays Bank PLC*.[65]

Gary E. Kalbaugh
FERC v. Barclays Bank PLC *Shines a Light on CFTC and FERC Jurisdiction*
36 No. 11 Futures and Derivatives Law Report 1 (Dec. 2016)

Introduction

The jurisdiction of the Federal Energy Regulatory Commission ("FERC") and Commodity Futures Trading Commission ("CFTC") over energy derivatives has been a source of uncertainty for over a decade. The Dodd-Frank Wall Street Reform and Consumer Protection Act[66] (hereinafter, the "Dodd-Frank Act"), though potentially clarifying FERC's and the CFTC's jurisdiction over energy derivatives, did not resolve this conflict. A recent case, *FERC v. Barclays Bank PLC*,[67] provides insight into this question, despite the facts occurring prior to passage of the Dodd-Frank Act and, therefore, its application of the pre-Dodd-Frank Act jurisdictional provisions. Namely, *FERC v. Barclays Bank PLC* clarifies that, where the CFTC is not explicitly granted exclusive jurisdiction, a court is unlike to decide that it has it by implication. . . .

Barclays traded electricity at various locations in Washington, Arizona, and California either "physically"— meaning that there is an obligation to deliver or receive electricity at a specified location and time—or "financially," discussed further below.[68] Physical pricing was determined by bilateral agreement of a "fixed" price

64. 677 F.2d 1137 (7th Cir. 1982) (*vacated as moot*, 459 U.S. 1026 (1982)).

65. 105 F. Supp. 3d 1121 (E.D. Cal. 2015), *interlocutory appeal denied, FERC v. Barclays Bank PLC*, No. 15-17251 (9th Cir. Mar. 8, 2016).

66. [N. 1] Pub. L. No. 111-203, 124 Stat. 1376 (2010).

67. [N. 2] *FERC v. Barclays Bank PLC*, 105 F. Supp. 3d 1121 (E.D. Cal. 2015), *interlocutory appeal denied, FERC v. Barclays Bank PLC*, No. 15-17251 (9th Cir. Mar. 8, 2016).

68. [N. 26] *FERC v. Barclays Bank PLC* at 1124–1125. These terms are largely akin to the common derivative market terms "physical delivery" and "cash settlement," defined respectively by the CFTC as: "A provision in a futures contract or other derivative for delivery of the actual commodity to satisfy the contract . . ." and "A method of settling futures, options and other derivatives whereby the seller (or short) pays the buyer (or long) the cash value of the underlying commodity or a cash amount based on the level of an index or price according to a procedure specified

or by reference to the volume-weighted average price of all spot (i.e., one day settlement) fixed price physical electricity transactions on a location-by-location basis.[69] This volume-weighted average price was quoted on the Intercontinental Exchange.[70]

Financially traded electricity generally occurred via swaps whereby, on each day in a month, one party, known as the fixed payer, would pay the other, known as the floating payer, a fixed rate multiplied by a specified "notional" amount of electricity.[71] In return, the floating payer, would pay the fixed payer an amount equal to the volume-weighted average price quoted for that day on the Intercontinental Exchange multiplied by the same specified "notional" amount of electricity.[72] Many of these swaps traded on the Intercontinental Exchange which, at the time, was an exempt commercial market over which the CFTC only had anti-fraud jurisdiction. Exempt commercial markets no longer exist due to operation of the Dodd-Frank Act.[73] . . .

Barclays Bank PLC was alleged to have engaged in trading on the fixed price market of "physically" traded electricity to manipulate the volume-weighted average price quoted on the Intercontinental Exchange in ways that economically benefited larger positions Barclays held in electricity traded "financially."[74] . . .

Barclays argued that the financial swaps were, in essence, futures contracts and, therefore, within the exclusive jurisdiction of the CFTC.[75] The court noted, however, that the manipulative activities alleged to have occurred were in the physical market.[76] Moreover, even if the manipulation could be said to be in the swaps market, it was unclear "how the swaps actually were futures. . . ."[77]

Since the manipulation did not occur directly on the swaps market and since, at the time, the CFTC only had anti-fraud jurisdiction over swaps, the court ruled that there was no basis to exclude FERC from jurisdiction.[78] The Energy Policy Act of 2005 had granted FERC jurisdiction over manipulation in connection with the purchase or sale of electric energy or transmission services[79] and the purchase and sale of natural gas and transportation services[80] and, at the time, the CFTC was

---

in the contract. Also called Financial Settlement." *See* CFTC, *CFTC Glossary*, http://www.cftc.gov /ConsumerProtection/EducationCenter/CFTCGlossary/index.htm (*last accessed* Nov. 26, 2016).

69. [N. 27] *FERC v. Barclays Bank PLC* at 1125–1126.

70. [N. 28] *Id.* at 1125.

71. [N. 29] *Id.* at 1126.

72. [N. 30] *Id.*

73. [N. 31] *See* Dodd-Frank Act §§ 723 & 724 and *Repeal of the Exempt Commercial Market and Exempt Board of Trade Exemptions*, 80 Fed. Reg. 59575 (Oct. 2, 2015).

74. [N. 32] *FERC v. Barclays Bank PLC* at 1128.

75. [N. 34] *FERC v. Barclays Bank PLC* at 1142.

76. [N. 35] *Id.*

77. [N. 36] *Id.*

78. [N. 37] *Id.* at 1145.

79. [N. 38] 16 U.S.C. § 824v(a).

80. [N. 39] 15 U.S.C. § 717c-1.

not granted exclusive jurisdiction with respect to any of the swaps transactions in question.[81] . . .

Subsequent to the events in *FERC v. Barclays*, two changes to the CFTC's jurisdiction occurred both of which are relevant to assessing the impact of *FERC v. Barclays*. First, a "savings clause" was added to the CFTC's jurisdiction stating, in effect, that the CFTC's exclusive jurisdiction does not limit the statutory authority of FERC over "an agreement, contract, or transaction that is entered into pursuant to a tariff or rate schedule approved by" FERC so long as it is either executed on a CFTC-regulated trading facility or clearinghouse owned or operated by a regional transmission organization or independent system operator[82] or off of such facilities entirely.[83] This change would not impact the legal analysis in *FERC v. Barclays* because the facts in the case did not involve a tariff or rate schedule approved by FERC nor were the swaps executed on a CFTC-regulated trading facility or clearinghouse owned or operated by a regional transmission organization or independent system operator.

The second change is, having been statutorily prohibited in 2000 from asserting jurisdiction over non-retail swaps other than with respect to fraud,[84] the Dodd-Frank Act granted the CFTC broad jurisdiction over swaps.[85] Unlike with respect to futures, the CFTC's jurisdiction over swaps is not exclusive unless the swaps are traded on a futures exchange[86] or a CFTC-regulated trading facility specifically for swaps known as a swap execution facility.[87] . . .

The question arises as to whether a different outcome would occur if the events in *FERC v. Barclays Bank PLC* took place after enactment of the Dodd-Frank Act since, . . . whereas at the time of the facts of *FERC v. Barclays* the CFTC did not have other than anti-fraud jurisdiction with respect to swaps, the CFTC now has broad swaps jurisdiction.

It is impossible to directly replicate the facts in *FERC v. Barclays* because the type of facility on which the swaps trading occurred, an exempt commercial market, has been statutorily abolished.[88] However, were it supposed that a manipula-

---

81. [N. 40] *FERC v. Barclays Bank PLC* at 1143–1145.

82. [N. 41] Regional transmission organizations and independent system operators are means of providing non-discriminatory access by electricity generators to transmission facilities. . . .

83. [N. 42] Dodd-Frank Act, § 722(e) (adding section 2(a)(1)(I) to the Commodity Exchange Act).

84. [N. 43] Commodity Futures Modernization Act of 2000, Appendix E of Pub. L. 106-554, 114 Stat. 2763 (2000).

85. [N. 44] *See, inter alia*, Commodity Exchange Act §§ 2(a)(1)(A), 2(c)(2)(A)(ii), 2(d), 2(e), 2(h), and 2(I).

86. [N. 46] The Commodity Exchange Act uses the technical term "designated contract market" to refer to futures exchanges. Herein, the vernacular financial term "futures exchange" is used instead.

87. [N. 47] Commodity Exchange Act § 2(a)(1)(A).

88. [N. 49] *See* Dodd-Frank Act §§ 723 & 724 and *Repeal of the Exempt Commercial Market and Exempt Board of Trade Exemptions*, 80 Fed. Reg. 59575 (Oct. 2, 2015).

tion involving swaps traded on a CFTC-regulated trading facility, such as a swap execution facility, were to occur, the better view is that, *ceteris paribus*, the CFTC has exclusive jurisdiction in light of *Hunter* and the express provisions of the Commodity Exchange Act. This is because the Commodity Exchange Act now grants the CFTC exclusive jurisdiction over "accounts, agreements (including any transaction which is of the character of, or is commonly known to the trade as, an 'option' . . .) and transactions involving swaps or contracts of sale of a commodity for future delivery . . . traded or executed on a [futures exchange] . . . or a swap execution facility. . . ."[89]

On the other hand, were the swaps not traded on a futures exchange or swap execution facility there is no basis to conclude that the CFTC has exclusive jurisdiction. Unlike futures, which are required to be traded on futures exchanges,[90] swaps can trade on futures exchanges, swap execution facilities, or "over-the-counter," i.e., by direct negotiation and bilateral agreement.[91] The Commodity Exchange Act only grants the CFTC exclusive jurisdiction over "transactions involving swaps . . . *traded or executed on a [futures exchange] . . . or a swap execution facility. . . .*"[92] Therefore, an argument that the CFTC has exclusive jurisdiction over an over-the-counter swap may not be tenable. As one court noted in a case concluding that the CFTC did not have exclusive jurisdiction over advertising related to futures trading, "a court must proceed with the utmost caution before concluding that one agency may not regulate merely because another may."[93] . . .

The CFTC's jurisdictional authority over futures, swaps, and options traded on a futures exchange or swap execution facility is exclusive. . . . Where a swap is traded other than on such a facility, the CFTC's jurisdiction is not exclusive. *FERC v. Barclays* is a reminder that, where the Commodity Exchange Act does not explicitly confer exclusive jurisdiction on the CFTC, the CFTC's jurisdiction may overlap with other regulators.

---

4. Bank Regulators

The Commodity Exchange Act is disapplied from, and the CFTC does not have jurisdiction over, "identified banking products" so long as "an appropriate banking agency certifies that the product has been commonly offered, entered into, or

---

89. [N. 50] Commodity Exchange Act § 2(a)(1)(A).

90. [N. 51] Commodity Exchange Act § 4(a).

91. [N. 52] Some categories of swaps are, however, required to be cleared by a derivatives clearing organization (i.e., a clearinghouse for futures or swaps) and on a futures exchange or swaps execution facility. . . .

92. [N. 53] Commodity Exchange Act § 2(a)(1)(A) (emphasis added).

93. [N. 54] *FTC v. Ken Roberts Co.*, 276 F. 3d 583 at 593 (D.C. Cir. 2001).

provided in the United States by any bank on or before December 5, 2000. . . ."[94] Included in "identified banking products" are deposit accounts, savings accounts, debit accounts, certificates of deposit, letters of credit, and loan participations.[95]

However, the CFTC can assert jurisdiction with respect to an identified bank product that:

(1) is a product of a bank that is not under the regulatory jurisdiction of an appropriate Federal banking agency;

(2) meets the definition of swap in section 1a(47) of the Commodity Exchange Act . . . ; and

(3) has become known to the trade as a swap . . . , or otherwise has been structured as an identified banking product for the purpose of evading the provisions of the Commodity Exchange Act (7 U.S.C. 1 et seq.) . . .[96]

In chapter 11, section D.2.a, we discuss the authority of banking regulators over the capital and margin requirements otherwise applying to swap dealers and security-based swap dealers.

5. Extraterritorial Limitations

The Commodity Exchange Act, rules promulgated by the CFTC thereunder, caselaw, and guidance issued by the CFTC together are sources that assist in determining the extent to which the CFTC's jurisdiction has extraterritorial reach. Chapter 17 examines the extraterritorial extent of the CFTC's regulation of derivatives.

6. Jurisdiction Shared with States

The Commodity Futures Trading Commission Act of 1974 preempted state regulators from enforcement where the CFTC had jurisdiction. Limited enforcement resources led to the reevaluation of this provision. As a result, the Futures Trading Act of 1978 added section 6d to the Commodity Exchange Act to provide a means for any state to enforce a Commodity Exchange Act violation. The passage of the Act was accompanied by the following Senate report summarizing the new grant of state jurisdiction.

---

94. Legal Certainty for Bank Products Act of 2000 §403 as amended by Dodd-Frank Act §725(g). Before the Dodd-Frank Act, the Legal Certainty for Bank Products Act, in §404, also provided an exclusion from the Commodity Exchange Act and CFTC jurisdiction for identified banking products developed after December 5, 2000. This section was removed by Dodd-Frank Act §725(g).

95. Legal Certainty for Bank Products Act of 2000 §402(b).

96. Legal Certainty for Bank Products Act of 2000 §403 as amended by Dodd-Frank Act §725(g).

Report of the Committee on Agriculture, Nutrition and Forestry on S. 2391
S. Rep. 95-850 (May 15, 1978)

Compounding [the problem of limited CFTC enforcement resources] was the reluctance of the states, whose regulatory authority had been preempted by the 1974 amendments, to bring parens patriae actions under the Commodity Exchange Act or actions under their general antifraud statutes. . . .

The recent experience of the Commission with commodity options transactions clearly demonstrates the need for the establishment of an effective working relationship between the commission and the states in order to ferret out and prosecute successfully commodities fraud. . . .

S.2391 adds a new Section 6d to the Commodity Exchange Act, authorizing states to institute actions seeking injunctive relief for violations of the Commodity Exchange Act, or Commission rules, regulations, or orders thereunder. The cause of action available to the states is derived directly from this Congressional enactment — not from common law principles and practice under the parens patriae doctrine. This new cause of action would not be subject to the possible limitation that the state, bringing an action parens patriae, may sue only to vindicate its quasi-sovereign interests. The Committee intends that the state may sue to enjoin acts and practices that, proceeding in violation of the Act, or rules, regulations, or orders thereunder, have injured, are injuring, or threaten to injure any resident of the state. . . .

This authority is subject to the qualification that such state actions may not be brought against a contract market [i.e., a futures exchange] or floor broker designated or registered as such with the Commission. The intent of the section is to provide states with the tools to combat fraudulent and other unlawful activity directed at their residents. Plenary authority to register, regulate, and discipline the contract markets and the "locals" whose activities are generally of the character of pit trading rather than customer contact is reserved to the Commission. . . .

The statute on which all actions brought under this section is to be based is the Commodity Exchange Act. The states would not, in these actions, be involved in enforcement of their local laws. Consistent with the Commission's exclusive jurisdiction and preemption of state regulatory activity enacted in 1974, and with the present decision to make federal law the basis for all actions brought under this section, it was also determined to make the federal courts the exclusive forum for such actions. This is consistent with the pattern established in the Securities Exchange Act of 1934, which requires private actions brought under that statute to proceed in the federal courts. The vast body of decisional law relating to SEC Rule 10b-5 securities "fraud" has developed exclusively in the federal courts. In this way, it is believed, a readily available, coherent body of law is most likely to evolve, subject to review and correction within the single, unified system of federal courts, employing common procedures throughout the United States.

It is understood that some states may desire to bring emergency actions in their own courts, and may desire to seek relief other than injunctive relief.

Notwithstanding the provisions of this section, it will remain possible, as it has been in the past, for an authorized state official to proceed in state court on the basis of an alleged violation of any general civil or criminal antifraud statute. . . .

To assure that the body of decisional law developed under this section would be coherent and consistent with national policy, new Section 6d provides that states, before instituting an action thereunder, must receive the prior approval of the Commission. State prosecutorial discretion would, therefore, be checked only to the degree that contemplated state prosecutions deviate from national policy established by the commission. . . .

The participation of the states in the enforcement of the Commodity Exchange Act is desirable. It is recognized that the widely available investigatory and prosecutorial capabilities of the states should be employed in the enforcement of the Commodity Exchange Act. Any state official who has investigative powers bestowed on his or her by state law is free, under new Section 6d, to exercise those powers in preparation for bringing any action under this section, or in determining whether such an action shall be instituted.

Each individual state remains free to allocate responsibilities internally. A state may authorize either its attorney general, or its securities administrator, or both or some other official or officials, to bring actions under this section and conduct investigations for the purpose of bringing such actions.

Questions and Comments

1. The administrative law judge system in use by the SEC and available to the CFTC has been criticized due to a perceived lack of separation of powers. Does it matter whether an administrative agency follows the constitutional process followed by federal courts if its decision is ultimately appealable to a federal court?

2. How do administrative agencies fit into our constitutional system? Can something be constitutionally part of the executive branch when the President cannot exercise direct authority over it?

3. What is the right role of staff letters? Why use a staff letter instead of a rulemaking?

4. If you were Commissioners Shad or Johnson, what accord would you have reached? Why?

5. What might have been an alternative to banning trading in single stock futures and options on single stock futures?

6. The definition of "narrow-based security index," originally used to determine whether a product could be listed on a CFTC-regulated board of trade or an

SEC-regulated exchange, was later applied to the off-exchange derivatives market to distinguish between a swap and a security-based swap. What were the consequences of doing so? What better approaches might there have been? Is there a less complicated definition that might allow for categorization to be automated?

7. Why can it sometimes be difficult to distinguish between a security and a future? What types of products are particularly hard to categorize?

8. Is the demarcation between insurance products and swaps clear? Can you think of any product that might challenge that demarcation?

9. Does subjecting a "mixed swap" to both SEC and CFTC regulation have a downside? What incentives might such regulatory treatment provide to market participants? Overall, do the jurisdictional boundaries make sense?

10. Some commentators have proposed a single "super regulator" with authority over all financial market activities. What are the pros and cons of this approach?

11. Can overlapping jurisdiction, such as between the CFTC and the states with respect to the Commodity Exchange Act, have benefits?

Chapter 5

Contract Markets

A. Background

1. Prohibition on Off-Exchange Commodity Futures

We learned in chapter 3, section B, that the CFTC has exclusive jurisdiction over commodity futures traded on an exchange or similar trading facility. At first, the limitation to commodity futures traded on an exchange or similar trading facility may seem substantial in that everything not traded on an exchange or similar trading facility is excluded.

However, another provision of the Commodity Exchange Act prohibits trading commodity futures on anything other than what it terms "a board of trade designated as a contract market." A board of trade designated as a contract market is, in essence, a futures exchange.

Therefore, when looked at together, the CFTC has exclusive jurisdiction over all commodity futures because it is illegal to trade commodity futures on anything other than an exchange or similar facility. In this chapter, we will look closely at this requirement and, in particular, at what constitutes a "board of trade designated as a contract market" on which commodity futures are required to trade. To do that, it is helpful to start by examining the actual language in the statute.

Commodity Exchange Act § 4(a)

(emphasis added)

[I]t shall be unlawful for any person to offer to enter into, *to enter into*, to execute, to confirm the execution of, or to conduct any office or business anywhere in the United States, its territories or possessions, for the purpose of soliciting or accepting any order for, or otherwise dealing in, any transaction in, or in connection with, *a contract for the purchase or sale of a commodity for future delivery* (other than a contract which is made on or subject to the rules of a board of trade, exchange, or market located outside the United States, its territories or possessions) *unless —*

(1) *such transaction is conducted on or subject to the rules of a board of trade which has been designated or registered by the Commission as a contract market . . . for such commodity;*

(2) *such contract is executed or consummated by or through a contract market; and*

(3) *such contract is evidenced by a record in writing which shows the date, the parties to such contract and their addresses, the property covered and its price, and the terms of delivery. . . .*

———————

We already known what is a "contract for the purchase or sale of a commodity for future delivery." We have been referring to it herein simply as a "futures contract" or "commodity futures contract." So we will limit our investigation in this section to determining what is a "board of trade which has been designated . . . as a contract market." There are two elements to this: (1) what is a board of trade; and (2) how is a board of trade designated as a contract market?

As we will see below in section B.1, any trading facility can be deemed to be a "board of trade." However, for a board of trade to be designated as a contract market requires the board of trade to meet statutory and CFTC regulatory standards.[1] We examine what they are in section B.2 below.

2. Market Operation

As we will see, the CFTC has broad discretion in its authority to designate a board of trade as a contract market. It is important to remember that designated contract markets, i.e., futures exchanges, are markets that are potentially accessible to retail investors, albeit through either a futures commission merchant or an introducing broker as an intermediary. We will be discussing both these categories of intermediary in chapter 6.

However, for this chapter, it is necessary to have a preliminary understanding of the general role of futures commission merchants as market intermediaries and "members" of futures exchanges. The case below summarizes the basic operation of futures exchanges, including the role of futures commission merchants.

The backdrop was the same events described in the *Hunter* case in chapter 4, section C.3. The hedge fund employing Hunter, Amaranth Advisors LLC, was alleged to have exceeded position limits and otherwise manipulated the natural gas market. Natural gas futures traders argued that the intermediating futures commission merchant that Amaranth used to clear its natural gas swaps and futures was liable for aiding and abetting Amaranth in manipulating the natural gas futures market. We revisit this case, focusing on the manipulation allegations, in chapter 15.

We are examining the case here for its excellent description of how futures markets operate, something we also looked at in chapter 1. Additionally, note the reference to "regulatory arbitrage," in this context due to the high level of regulation pertaining to a "designated contract market," i.e., futures exchange, and the lesser level of regulation applying at the time to an "exempt commercial market." Due to

———————

1. Commodity Exchange Act § 5(d)(1)(A).

concern over the potential for regulatory arbitrage, exempt commercial markets as a regulatory category were repealed by the Dodd-Frank Act along with a similar regulatory category, "exempt board of trade."[2]

In re Amaranth Natural Gas Commodities Litigation

730 F.3d 170 (2d Cir. 2013)

Debra Ann Livingston, Circuit Judge. . . .

[The New York Mercantile Exchange ("NYMEX")] is a futures and options exchange based in New York City. We have previously described the basic features of commodity futures trading:

> A commodities futures contract is an executory contract for the sale of a commodity executed at a specific point in time with delivery of the commodity postponed to a future date. Every commodities futures contract has a seller and a buyer. The seller, called a "short," agrees for a price, fixed at the time of contract, to deliver a specified quantity and grade of an identified commodity at a date in the future. The buyer, or "long," agrees to accept delivery at that future date at the price fixed in the contract. It is the rare case when buyers and sellers settle their obligations under futures contracts by actually delivering the commodity. Rather, they routinely take a short or long position in order to speculate on the future price of the commodity. Then, sometime before delivery is due, they offset or liquidate their positions by entering the market again and purchasing an equal number of opposite contracts, i.e., a short buys long, a long buys short. In this way their obligations under the original liquidating contracts offset each other. The difference in price between the original contract and the offsetting contract determines the amount of money made or lost.

Strobl v. N.Y. Mercantile Exch., 768 F.2d 22, 24 (2d Cir.1985).

One type of futures contract traded on NYMEX is for the delivery of natural gas. In its standard form, this contract obligates the buyer to purchase 10,000 MMBtu[3] of natural gas released during the contract's delivery month at the Henry Hub distribution facility in Erath, Louisiana. Trading on the future begins five years before the delivery month and ends three business days before the first calendar day of the delivery month. To determine the future's final price, NYMEX uses a weighted average of the trades executed during the final half hour of trading — 2:00 to 2:30

---

2. Dodd-Frank Act §§ 723 and 734. *See also* CFTC, *Repeal of the Exempt Commercial Market and Exempt Board of Trade Exemptions*, 80 Fed. Reg. 59575 (Oct. 2, 2015). The Dodd-Frank Act also abolished "derivatives transaction execution facilities" (Dodd-Frank Act § 734), though some stray references are still in the Commodity Exchange Act. *See, e.g.*, Commodity Exchange Act § 5(e)(2). There were never any registrants, so its abolition had no direct market impact. *See* CFTC, *Adaptation of Regulations to Incorporate Swaps*, 77 Fed. Reg. 66288, 66301 (Nov. 2, 2012).

3. [N. 2] 1 MMBtu is equal to 1 million BTU (British Thermal Unit).

P.M. — on the last trading day. This final half hour is referred to as the contract's "final settlement period," and final price as the "final settlement price."

NYMEX is a designated contract market, or "DCM." As a DCM, NYMEX may offer options and futures trading for any type of commodity, but is subject to extensive oversight from the Commodity Futures Trading Commission ("CFTC"). . . .

All trades on NYMEX must go through the exchange's clearinghouse. To finalize, or "clear," a trade, traders must transact with a NYMEX clearing member — a firm approved as a member of the clearinghouse. The seller's clearing firm will sell the contract to the clearinghouse, which then sells the contract to the buyer's clearing firm. Through this act of simultaneously buying and selling the contract, the clearinghouse guarantees both sides of the trade and ensures that neither buyer nor seller is exposed to any counterparty credit risk. The clearing firms, in turn, guarantee their clients' performance to the clearing-house.

To protect itself from risk of nonpayment, the NYMEX clearinghouse requires that its members deposit margin sufficient to cover any potential short-term losses on their clients' open positions. At the end of each trading day, the clearinghouse examines the change in value to these positions and determines whether the firm must post additional margin (generally the case if value has decreased) or receives payment on margin (generally the case if value has increased). This process is called "marking-to-market." Clearing firms engage in the same process with their customers, requiring an initial margin payment for any newly acquired position and conducting a daily recalculation of that margin requirement as the position changes in value.

In addition to clearing members, traders on NYMEX also interact with futures commissions [sic] merchants, or "FCMs." "An FCM is the commodity market's equivalent of a securities brokerage house, soliciting and accepting orders for futures contracts and accepting funds or extending credit in connection therewith." FCMs must register with the CFTC and are subject to numerous regulatory requirements. A firm may be both a clearing member and an FCM. Such dual status would enable it to both accept orders from clients and clear any resulting trades. . . .

ICE is an electronic commodity exchange based in Atlanta, Georgia. At the time of the events alleged in the amended complaint, ICE offered trading in natural gas swaps.[4] Swaps, unlike futures contracts, do not contemplate delivery of the underlying commodity. Rather, in a typical commodity swap, the buyer agrees to pay the seller a fixed amount of money and the seller agrees to pay the buyer the price of an underlying commodity at the time the swap expires. For ICE's Natural Gas Henry Hub Swap, this "floating value" paid by the seller was the final settlement value of the NYMEX natural gas future for the corresponding month. Hence, if the final settlement value of the NYMEX natural gas future was above whatever price the buyer paid for the swap, the buyer would profit; if it was below, the seller would.

---

4. [N. 3] ICE has since stopped offering natural gas swaps for trading, and instead offers trading in natural gas futures and options. . . .

Since the settlement price of an ICE Henry Hub natural gas swap was pegged to the final settlement price of the corresponding NYMEX natural gas future, the two instruments were functionally identical for risk management purposes. Indeed, arbitrageurs ensured that their prices moved in virtual lockstep with one another. Whether a trader decided to transact in ICE swaps or in NYMEX futures often depended on factors such as which market had greater liquidity.

An important difference between the two instruments, however, was that ICE did not face the same level of regulatory oversight as did NYMEX. At the time of the events alleged in the amended complaint, ICE qualified as an "exempt commercial market," or "ECM," under the CEA.[5] While this status limited both the type of instruments ICE could offer for trading and the parties that could trade them, it also exempted ICE from most of the regulatory obligations placed upon NYMEX....

The court ultimately found that the role of Amaranth's futures commission merchant in providing clearing services for its trades was insufficient on its own to support an aiding and abetting allegation under the Commodity Exchange Act. Note the court's reference to "clearing members." Clearing members are members of a futures exchange with special access privileges. A clearing member is directly responsible to the clearinghouse for the daily financial obligations in connection with its own positions and, if it is also a futures commission merchant, those of its customers. Clearing members are subject to the futures exchange's rules and discipline as a self-regulatory organization, something we discuss in section C below.

B. What Is a Designated Contract Market?

1. Board of Trade

To be "designated as a contract market," an entity first needs to meet the definition of a "board of trade." The term "board of trade" is an anachronistic one that we only commonly see today in the names of futures exchanges, such as the Chicago Board of Trade and New York Board of Trade (both wholly owned by, respectively, the Chicago Mercantile Exchange and the Intercontinental Exchange).

The Commodity Exchange Act defines a "board of trade" as "any organized exchange or other trading facility."[6] A "trading facility" (a term broader than

---

5. [N. 4] In 2008, Congress increased the CFTC's oversight of any ECM that offered trading in products the CFTC deemed to be "significant price discovery contracts." See Food, Conservation, and Energy Act of 2008, Pub.L. No. 110-246, Tit. XIII, Sub. B, 124 Stat. 1651, 2197–2204. Two years later, the Dodd-Frank Wall Street Reform and Consumer Protection Act repealed the statutory basis for ECMs....

6. Commodity Exchange Act § 1a(6).

"organized exchange" and, therefore, inclusive of an organized exchange) is, in turn, defined in the Commodity Exchange Act as:

> [A] person or group of persons that constitutes, maintains, or provides a physical or electronic facility or system in which multiple participants have the ability to execute or trade agreements, contracts, or transactions —
>
> (i) by accepting bids or offers made by other participants that are open to multiple participants in the facility or system; or
>
> (ii) through the interaction of multiple bids or multiple offers within a system with a pre-determined non-discretionary automated trade matching and execution algorithm.[7]

Described another way, a trading facility is a so-called multiple-to-multiple platform, i.e., it provides a facility (it can be electronic) for transactions between more than one offeror and more than one offeree.[8] To see what is and what is not a multiple-to-multiple platform we use three hypotheticals.

> *Example One*: User-Friendly Bank, National Association wishes to establish a web portal for the convenience of its customers. This web portal allows customers to access quotes from User-Friendly offering to buy or sell various commodity futures contracts.
>
> *Result*: This does not meet the definition of trading facility because it is a single (User-Friendly Bank) to multiple (its customers) platform. Since it is not a trading facility and, therefore, not a board of trade, contract market designation would be unavailable to User-Friendly Bank's web portal. Moreover, any offers by User-Friendly Bank to trade commodity futures contracts using the web portal (or any means other than via a designated contract market) would, as we saw in section A.1 above, violate Commodity Exchange Act section 4(a).
>
> *Example Two*: The Acme Finance Company, Inc. proposes to establish an online page where it lists requests for quotations ("RFQs") for commodity futures contracts it wishes to trade.
>
> *Result*: This is also not a trading facility and designation as a contract market would not be possible for its web page. Even though there are multiple offerors potentially responding to Acme's request for quotations, there is only one offeree, Acme. As in Hypothetical One, any RFQs by Acme Finance relating to commodity futures contracts conducted other than via a designated contract market would violate Commodity Exchange Act section 4(a).

---

7. Commodity Exchange Act § 1a(51).

8. In chapter 10, section C we discuss trading facilities for swaps, instead of commodity futures. These trading facilities are known as "Swap Execution Facilities" or "SEFs."

Example Three: The Silicon Valley MBA Co. designs a phone application that allows the listing of bids or offers for a variety of commodity futures contracts.

Result: Finally, we have a hypothetical where the definition of "trading facility" is met. Silicon Valley MBA's phone application has the potential to connect multiple offerors and multiple offerees. As a "trading facility," it would accordingly meet the definition of "board of trade" and be eligible for designation as a contract market.

Of course, since commodity futures contracts must be traded on a board of trade designated as a contract market, the Silicon Valley MBA Co. must receive CFTC designation of the phone application as a contract market before it goes live.

2. Designation of a Board of Trade as a Contract Market

a. Registration and Core Principles

An application for registration with the CFTC as a designated contract market requires much detailed information about, among others, the organizational structure of the proposed designated contract market, the business experience and qualifications of the directors and officers, its financial resources, and means of compliance with CFTC rules.[9] The CFTC is authorized by the Commodity Exchange Act to approve or deny the application within 180 days of its submission.[10] If an application is deemed by the CFTC to be "materially incomplete," the CFTC can put a stay on the running of the 180 days and notify the applicant of the specific deficiencies. Once resubmitted, the CFTC will have the greater of the remainder of the 180 days or 60 days to approve or deny the application. A designated contract market, like all CFTC registrants, is subject to CFTC rules and examinations.[11]

Designation as a contract market licenses an entity to operate a futures exchange. As we will see below in section C, futures exchanges are "self-regulatory organizations" which means that they have the authority to regulate the conduct of participants on the exchange and, in particular, those participants with special access privileges known as "members."

Partially due to this regulatory model, instead of having highly prescriptive statutory provisions for the conduct of futures exchanges, the Commodity Exchange Act enumerates high-level "core principles," leaving the exchange in its role of self-regulatory organization to supply the detail.[12]

---

9. 17 C.F.R. § 38, app. A.

10. Commodity Exchange Act § 6(a).

11. *See, e.g.*, 17 C.F.R. §§ 38 and 40.

12. The other three market categories of registrant with self-regulatory authority are also governed by statutory core principles. These are derivatives clearing organizations, commonly known

The Commodity Exchange Act provides for twenty-three core principles by which designated contract markets must abide, each of which is further expounded upon by CFTC regulation.[13] "Core principles" are intended to be less prescriptive than a laundry list of detailed rules and to provide "reasonable discretion" to the designated contract market.[14] Notice how the designated contract market is required to take further action with phrases such as "shall adopt" and "shall establish and enforce." This is the essence of "core principles": they provide a broad framework as a starting point for the designated contract market to acquit its self-regulatory role.

Core Principles for Contract Markets
Commodity Exchange Act § 5(d)

(1) Designation as contract market

> (A) ... To be designated, and maintain a designation, as a contract market, a board of trade shall comply with ... any core principle. ...

> (B) ... a board of trade ... shall have reasonable discretion in establishing the manner in which the board of trade complies with the core principles ...

(2) Compliance with rules

> (A) ... The board of trade shall establish, monitor, and enforce compliance with the rules of the contract market ...

> (B) ... The board of trade shall have the capacity to detect, investigate, and apply appropriate sanctions to any person that violates any rule of the contract market. ...

(3) ... The board of trade shall list on the contract market only contracts that are not readily susceptible to manipulation.

(4) ... The board of trade shall have the capacity and responsibility to prevent manipulation, price distortion, and disruptions of the delivery or cash-settlement process through market surveillance, compliance, and enforcement practices and procedures. ...

(5) ... [T]he board of trade shall adopt ... , as is necessary and appropriate, position limitations or position accountability for speculators.

(6) ... The board of trade ... shall adopt rules to provide for the exercise of emergency authority, as is necessary and appropriate, including the authority —

> (A) to liquidate or transfer open positions in any contract;

> (B) to suspend or curtail trading in any contract; and

---

as "DCOs," swap execution facilities, commonly known as "SEFs," and swap data repositories, commonly known as "SDRs." *See* section D below and chapter 10, section B, for discussions on derivatives clearing organizations and chapter 10, section C for swap execution facilities, and section E.2 for swap data repositories.

13. 17 C.F.R. § 38.100 et seq.
14. Commodity Exchange Act § 5(d)(1)(B).

(C) to require market participants in any contract to meet special margin requirements.

(7) . . . The board of trade shall make available to market authorities, market participants, and the public accurate information concerning . . . the terms and conditions of the contracts of the contract market [and] . . . the rules, regulations, and mechanisms for executing transactions. . . .

(8) . . . The board of trade shall make public daily information on settlement prices, volume, open interest, and opening and closing ranges for actively traded contracts on the contract market.

(9) . . . The board of trade shall provide a competitive, open, and efficient market and mechanism for executing transactions. . . .

(10) . . . The board of trade shall maintain rules and procedures to provide for the recording and safe storage of all identifying trade information. . . .

(11) . . . The board of trade shall establish and enforce . . . rules and procedures . . . ensuring the financial integrity of transactions entered into on or through the facilities of the contract market . . . and . . . the financial integrity of any . . . futures commission merchant . . . [or] introducing broker. . . .

(12) . . . The board of trade shall establish and enforce rules . . . to protect markets and market participants from abusive practices. . . . [and] to promote fair and equitable trading on the contract market.

(13) . . . The board of trade shall establish and enforce disciplinary procedures that authorize the board of trade to discipline, suspend, or expel members or market participants that violate the rules of the board of trade. . . .

(14) . . . The board of trade shall establish and enforce rules regarding, and provide facilities for alternative dispute resolution. . . .

(15) . . . The board of trade shall establish and enforce appropriate fitness standards for directors, members of any disciplinary committee, members of the contract market, and any other person with direct access to the facility. . . .

(16) . . . The board of trade shall establish and enforce rules . . . to minimize conflicts of interest. . . .

(17) . . . The governance arrangements of the board of trade shall be designed to permit consideration of the views of market participants.

(18) . . . The board of trade shall maintain records of all activities relating to the business of the contract market . . . for a period of at least 5 years.

(19) Antitrust considerations

. . . [T]he board of trade shall not —

(A) adopt any rule or taking any action that results in any unreasonable restraint of trade; or

(B) impose any material anticompetitive burden on trading on the contract market.

(20) . . . The board of trade shall . . . establish and maintain a program of risk analysis and oversight . . . [and] establish and maintain emergency procedures, backup facilities, and a plan for disaster recovery. . . .

(21) . . . The financial resources of the board of trade shall . . . [exceed] the total amount that would enable the contract market to cover the operating costs of the contract market for a 1-year period. . . .

(22) . . . The board of trade, if a publicly traded company, shall endeavor to recruit individuals to serve on the board of directors and the other decision-making bodies . . . [from] a broad and culturally diverse pool. . . .

(23) . . . The board of trade shall keep any such records relating to . . . [security-based swaps] open to inspection and examination by the Securities and Exchange Commission.

---

b. CFTC Discretion

The core principles for designated contract markets provide flexibility in implementation. Nonetheless, the CFTC retains broad authority to designate a board of trade as a contract market or, as demonstrated by the below case, decline to designate a board of trade as a contract market.

Note that the definition of "board of trade" at the time of the case below was different than the one in use since the Commodity Futures Modernization Act of 2000. It nonetheless remains as important in demonstrating the general authority of the CFTC to decide whether to approve or deny an application for designation as a contract market.

American Board of Trade, Inc. v. Bagley
402 F. Supp. 974 (S.D.N.Y. 1975)

Werker, District Judge.

Plaintiff American Board of Trade, Inc. (ABT), has brought an action against the Chairman of the Commodity Futures Trading Commission (CFTC), several of its employees and the United States Department of Agriculture by complaint filed on August 26, 1975. The complaint prays for (1) an order enjoining the defendants from interfering with his (sic) business and dealing with him (sic) in an arbitrary and capricious manner and taking his (sic) property without due process of law, (2) the designation of the plaintiff as a contract market for transactions in commodity futures, and (3) compensatory and punitive damages aggregating $1,000,000.00. (The use of the male gender is presumably a reference to Arthur W. Economou, the president of ABT.) . . .

The statute creating the CFTC was signed into law on October 23, 1974 and became effective April 21, 1975. It amended the Commodity Exchange Act, created the Commission as an independent regulatory agency and assigned broad responsibility to the Commission for the regulation of transactions involving the sale of commodities for future delivery (commodity futures).

Section 4 of the Act makes it unlawful for any person to engage in transactions in any futures contract except through members of a "board of trade" that has been designated by the Commission as a "contract market." . . .

The Commission was authorized and directed under Section 5 of the Act to grant designation "when, and only when," a board of trade has met the conditions and requirements specified in the Act. The application for contract market designation must be accompanied by a showing that the board of trade complies with . . . [Commodity Exchange Act] requirements . . .

Although the Act became effective April 21, 1975 a majority of the Commission was not appointed and confirmed until April 10, 1975. Consequently Congress determined that there would not be sufficient time for the Commission to review applications for designation before April 21, 1975 and permitted the Commission to provisionally designate boards of trade for a period not to exceed 90 days after April 21, 1975.

At the first official meeting of the Commission held on April 15, 1975 the Commission considered a regulation for provisional designation of boards of trade as contract markets.

Mr. Economou, president of ABT, along with other applicants, was notified by letter dated April 16, 1975 that the Commission was adopting a provisional designation rule which required that the applicant demonstrate to the Commission's satisfaction that it was a board of trade within the meaning of the Act and that it actually was operating as a contract market on April 15, 1975.

The object of the provisional designation rule was to prevent a disruption of the business of exchanges that were already in operation.

Applicants were instructed to file their applications by April 18, 1975, and also to file a list of their memberships, board of directors and officers and copies of their bylaws, rules, regulations and resolutions under which they operated. April 18 was the last business day before April 21, the effective date of the CFTC Act.

ABT submitted its application on April 18. The Commission considered the application on April 18 and 19 and denied provisional designation to ABT on April 19 because of the Commission's inability to determine from the information supplied whether ABT was a board of trade under the Act and the regulations.

The denial was made without prejudice to filing additional information and the decision was conveyed by telephone and telegram to Mr. Economou. ABT did not seek judicial review of that decision.

The Commission's concern was based in part on the fact that ABT did not have an exchange floor, on the uniqueness of some of the practices described in ABT's application and the uncertain impact of those practices and on the fact that the board of trade appeared to be nothing more than Mr. Economou, his wife and companies controlled by him. Seven members were listed in the application, all but one being residents of states or countries outside New York where the exchange is located.

On May 7, 1975 ABT by its attorney furnished additional information which it was informed on May 19, 1975 was inadequate. A further showing by on site inspection was requested and offered on May 20. This was resisted by Mr. Economou and his attorney. On May 22, 1975 the application of ABT again was considered by the Commission and denied. On that day Mr. Economou was again informed of the decision by letter which among other things informed ABT that it had concluded "that to be a board of trade transaction prices must be competitively determined."

The Chairman also wrote "only through a physical inspection of the trading facilities, a review of the transaction records and interviews can the Commission determine whether The American Board of Trade was a 'board of trade' and as such entitled to be considered for designation as a contract market." Further submission of written material, Mr. Economou was advised, would not significantly advance the application. . . .

On July 18, 1975 the Commission's power to grant provisional designation expired.

The Commission continued to process ABT's application as one for permanent designation after July 18, 1975. During the period April 21, 1975 through July 18, 1975 and thereafter the Commission processed in addition to ABT's application nine board of trade applications. . . . The last was granted on September 11, 1975. In addition to these applications the Commission received and processed 18,000 applications for registration by various classes of persons including futures commission merchants, persons associated with futures commission merchants, floor brokers, commodity pool operators and commodity trading advisors.

Due to the number of applications, the Commission's limited manpower and the shortness of time, the Commission had to establish priorities. The application of ABT fell in a second level of priority due to the poorly organized and less complete application and the resistance of the ABT. . . .

Considering the facts as recited above the court has reached the conclusion that plaintiff has failed to show any possibility of success on the merits . . . and its motion for a preliminary injunction is therefore denied.

With respect to defendants' motions they are granted. It appears from the factual situation here that the delays in processing plaintiff's application for permanent designation as a board of trade and as such a contract market have been due in large part to ABT's failure to comply with the requirements of the Commission and the guidelines and regulations issued under the Act. These guidelines and regulations are demonstrably reasonable considering the economic and public interest to be protected. The charge of bias made by plaintiff is frivolous. . . .

For the above reasons, I am dismissing the complaint herein. . . .

As of 2021, there were sixteen designated contract markets, some of which are under common ownership.[15] There were also a large number registered but deemed "dormant" by the CFTC.[16] By requiring commodity futures solely to be traded on designated contract markets, the Commodity Exchange Act establishes an oligopoly.[17]

As the following case illustrates, futures exchanges can be protective of this oligopoly and resistant to new entrants, especially, as was the case here, where the entrant was using a technology perceived as disruptive. However, the CFTC's discretionary authority to approve designation as a contract market is as broad as its authority to deny designation as a contract market.

Board of Trade of the City of Chicago v. CFTC

66 F. Supp. 2d 891 (N.D. Ill. 1999)

Bucklo, District Judge.

The Board of Trade of the City of Chicago, the Kansas City Board of Trade, and the Minneapolis Grain Exchange brought this action against the Commodity Futures Trading Commission (the "Commission"), seeking judicial review of the Commission's approval of the Cantor Financial Futures Exchange (the "Cantor Exchange") as a contract market. The Commission moves to dismiss for lack of subject matter jurisdiction and failure to state a claim [and] . . . has filed . . . for summary judgment. For the following reasons, the Commission's motions to dismiss are denied, and its motion for summary judgment is granted. . . .

In January 1998 the Cantor Exchange applied to the Commission for designation as a contract market for trading on certain United States Treasury futures contracts. On September 4, 1998, the Commission approved the Cantor Exchange's contract market designation application. Under 7 U.S.C. §7, the Cantor Exchange, as an applicant exchange, was required to meet numerous requirements, including showing that its operations would not be "contrary to the public interest," before being approved as a contract market. The plaintiffs argue that the Commission never made the required finding on the public interest issue and other issues, that the Commission held the Cantor Exchange to a different, lower regulatory standard than other futures exchanges, that the Commission failed to address or respond to material public comments raised by the plaintiffs, and that the Commission failed to provide notice or an opportunity to comment on the Cantor Exchange's final application. . . .

---

15. *See* CFTC, *Trading Organizations — Designated Contract Markets*, http://sirt.cftc.gov/SIRT /SIRT.aspx?Topic=TradingOrganizations&implicit=true&type=DCM&CustomColumnDisplay =TTTTTTTT.

16. *Id.*

17. However, section 5(d)(19) of the Commodity Exchange Act prohibits a designated contract market from, unless otherwise required to do so by the Commodity Exchange Act, adopting "any rule or taking any action that results in any unreasonable restraint of trade" or which imposes "any material anticompetitive burden on trading on the contract market."

Under the Commodity Exchange Act, futures contracts must be traded on exchanges, called boards of trade that have been approved by the Commission as "contract markets." 7 U.S.C. §6(a). The approval process under which a board of trade is initially designated as a contract market is governed by 7 U.S.C. §§7 and 8. Section 7 provides that the Commission is authorized to designate a board of trade as a contract market when the board of trade complies with numerous statutory requirements. . . . [Section 8] provides that if the Commission denies an application, it must state the reasons and give the board of trade an opportunity for a hearing before the Commission. . . .

The Commission's argument is essentially that, by allowing boards of trade to seek judicial review of their designation denials in the courts of appeals, Congress has precluded competing boards of trade from seeking judicial review of designation approvals in the district courts. The plaintiffs respond that the statute is merely silent on the issue of judicial review of application approvals, and that the presumption favoring review is therefore controlling. I agree. Approval for designation as a contract market is a final agency action, which is presumptively reviewable under the Administrative Procedure Act. . . . [T]he Commodity Exchange Act provides for specific procedures — including an express authorization of who may seek judicial review — for one type of agency action, denials, and no procedures for another type of agency action, approvals. This legislative scheme leaves substantial doubt as to whether Congress intended entirely to preclude judicial review of approvals, and the strong presumption in favor of review accordingly applies. . . .

The plaintiffs argue that the Cantor Exchange's provision for "exclusive time trading" [a method of providing two principals the opportunity to directly trade for a limited period] is a deviation from "open and competitive trading," which is required. . . . The Commission interpreted this regulation to include exclusive time trading as proposed by the Cantor Exchange application. . . . The interpretation is not plainly erroneous or inconsistent with the language of the regulation, which allows "other" competitive methods, and it is entitled to deference. . . .

The plaintiffs argue that the Cantor Group is a proven wrongdoer, and that it was arbitrary and capricious for the Commission not to respond to comments regarding the public interest issues raised by the Cantor Group's "control" of the Cantor Exchange.[18] In January 1997 the Commission found Cantor Fitzgerald & Co., the Cantor Group's futures commission merchant subsidiary, liable for fraud. . . . [I]ndividuals who commit disciplinary offenses [are prohibited by CFTC regulations] from serving on self-regulatory organization governing boards or committees. The Commission has interpreted this . . . to mean that only "natural persons who themselves commit disciplinary offenses" should be disqualified. . . .

---

18. [N. 3] Commentators were concerned with the Cantor Group's ability to name eight of thirteen Cantor Exchange directors.

The Commission . . . considered commentators' concerns about the Cantor Group's disciplinary history . . . and specifically addressed mechanisms that monitor the integrity of the Cantor Exchange Board. In light of this consideration, the plaintiffs have not shown that the Commission's approval order was arbitrary and capricious. . . .

The plaintiffs also have not shown that the Commission overlooked whether the Cantor Exchange will fragment treasury futures markets contrary to the public interest. The administrative record reveals that the Commission addressed concerns about market fragmentation, specifically including concerns raised by one of the plaintiffs, the Chicago Board of Trade. The plaintiffs are unsatisfied, arguing that the Commission should have spent more time addressing particular objections relating to market fragmentation. . . . The Commission addressed the major issue of policy about which the commentators expressed concerns, market fragmentation, in a reasoned manner and based on factors that are not arbitrary and capricious. . . .

For the reasons discussed above, the Commission's motions to dismiss are denied, and its motion for summary judgment is granted. . . .

By granting the CFTC's motion for summary judgement the court ruled that the CFTC's authorization of the Cantor Exchange as a designated contract market was valid, notwithstanding the plaintiff's objections.

Figure 5.1 Futures Trading Floor During the Heyday of Floor Trading

C. Designated Contract Markets as Self-Regulatory Organizations

1. Generally

As noted above in section B.2.a, designated contract markets are governed by high-level "core principles." The day-to-day regulation of each designated contract market is generally left to its own governance. The governance includes the ability to make rules, discipline members and market participants, and list new contracts for trading.

In many cases, rulemakings and new contract listings are "self-certified." This means that no CFTC pre-approval is needed so long as requirements pre-established by the Commodity Exchange Act and CFTC rules are certified by the designated contract market as having been met. Instead, notice is given to the CFTC and the rule or new contract automatically goes into effect, provided the CFTC does not issue a stay. We discuss these processes in detail in subsections 2.a and 4 below.

2. Rulemaking

a. Process

Many of the core principles require the designated contract market to issue rules. The procedure for issuing rules is, in most cases, straightforward. It merely requires a submission to the CFTC with the proposed rule, its implementation date, a certification by the designated contract market that it complies with the Commodity Exchange Act and CFTC rules, an explanation of its operation and purpose, and an explanation of any opposing views expressed in relation to the proposed rule.[19] After ten business days, the rule will automatically be deemed certified.[20]

However, there are a few exceptions to this process. The first is if the rule is a minor amendment. In lieu of applying to the CFTC for certification, a weekly summary of such rule amendments can be sent to the CFTC.[21]

The second is if the CFTC determines the rule (or proposed amendment to a rule) was inadequately explained, is potentially inconsistent with the Commodity Exchange Act or CFTC rules, or "presents novel or complex issues that require additional time to analyze."[22] In such circumstances, the CFTC has ninety additional days for review and must provide a thirty-day public comment period. If the CFTC finds that the proposed rule is inconsistent with Commodity Exchange Act or CFTC rules, it may object to implementation of the rule.[23]

The third exception is if the designated contract market voluntarily submits a proposed rule or amendment for CFTC pre-approval.[24] In such circumstances, the CFTC has forty-five days to review the proposal with an extension for an additional forty-five days if the CFTC determines that it raises novel or complex issues, is of "major economic significance," or the submission is incomplete or inadequately explained.[25]

---

19. 17 C.F.R. § 40.6(a)(7).
20. 17 C.F.R. § 40.6(b).
21. 17 C.F.R. § 40.6(d).
22. 17 C.F.R. § 40.6(c)(1).
23. 17 C.F.R. § 40.6(c)(3).
24. 17 C.F.R. §§ 40.5(a) and (c).
25. 17 C.F.R. § 40.5(d).

The fourth is if there is a material modification to a traded futures contract or option on a futures contract where the underlying commodity is one of an enumerated list of agricultural commodities.[26] Such a change must go through the same process as for voluntary submission of a rule amendment to the CFTC.

Finally, the CFTC may directly alter a designated contract market's rules if it first formally requests it and it is necessary for "the protection of persons producing, handling, processing, or consuming any commodity traded for future delivery . . . or the product or byproduct thereof, or for the protection of traders or to insure fair dealing in commodities traded for future delivery. . . ."[27] Similarly, the CFTC can direct a designated contract market to take any action necessary if the CFTC believes an emergency exists as is necessary to "maintain or restore orderly trading in or liquidation of any futures contract. . . ."[28] It is very difficult to challenge the CFTC's exercise of emergency authority since judicial review is ex post, based upon solely what information was available to the CFTC at the time, and requires the CFTC's action to have been arbitrary or capricious, an abuse of discretion, or illegal.[29]

b. Disciplinary Actions

Designated contract markets have members with direct access to trade on the exchange and, in some cases, the ability to clear trades. The members, through various committees, also are frequently responsible for much of the day-to-day operation of the exchange.

Boards of trade have a long history of requiring members to abide by internal rules and using disciplinary committees comprised of members to adjudicate infractions of rules and impose penalties. As we saw above in section B.2.a, this goes hand-in-hand with the high-level core principles that apply to designated contract markets, since they leave designated contract markets scope to develop their own more detailed and prescriptive rules. It allows for both regulatory flexibility and self-policing, freeing up CFTC enforcement resources.

In addition to applying to members, the disciplinary regime applies to anyone trading on the market. All must abide by the rules of the designated contract market and face potential sanctions for failing to do so. For example, the CME, CBOT, NYMEX, and COMEX, all part of the CME Group, have a rule in common stating that:

> Any Person initiating or executing a transaction on or subject to the Rules of the Exchange directly or through an intermediary, and any Person for whose benefit such a transaction has been initiated or executed, expressly consents to the jurisdiction of the Exchange and agrees to be bound by and comply with the Rules of the Exchange in relation to such transactions,

---

26. 17 C.F.R. § 40.4(a).
27. 7 U.S.C. § 12a(7).
28. 7 U.S.C. § 12a(9).
29. *Id.*

including, but not limited to, rules requiring cooperation and participation in investigatory and disciplinary processes.[30]

The disciplinary process, in the case of the CME Group, begins with their Market Regulation Department. The role of the Market Regulation Department is to, among others, conduct investigations. If the Market Regulation Department has "reasonable cause" to believe a violation of one of the designated contract markets' rules has occurred, it can bring its finding to the Chief Regulatory Officer. The Chief Regulatory Officer decides whether to issue charges, direct no further action be taken, or direct the Market Regulation Department to investigate further.[31] The actual hearings are held before a panel of the Business Conduct Committee.[32] There is an appeal available to a special hearing panel formed of a subset of the Board of Directors.[33] Examples of some of the possible sanctions that can be imposed by the designated contract markets in the CME Group include ordering restitution, disgorgement of monetary benefit, up to $5 million fine per violation, and suspension of trading privileges.[34] There are similar processes and sanctions with the other designated contract markets.

The Commodity Exchange Act requires contract markets to enforce their own rules.[35] This is, in part, due to the risk of members sitting on the disciplinary committee treating some members more favorably than others.

Although a failure to enforce its rules can result in liability for a designated contract market,[36] as the case below illustrates, courts have typically been deferential to their self-regulatory role. Additionally, to make a claim, a member must exhaust all procedural remedies provided for by the rules of the designated contract market and an appeal to the CFTC before seeking judicial review. This can, of course, take many years.

The below case is part of a broader series of events. The price of gold shot up overnight resulting in a $26 million margin call against a gold trader. The trader was unable to pay the $26 million, and Volume Investors, the clearing member he was trading through, went bankrupt. (We will discuss the role of clearing members in more detail, including in the context of these events, in chapter 6, section B.3.) Customers of Volume Investors who did not default were called upon to pay the shortfall in what Volume Investors owed the Commodity Exchange, Inc., a designated contract market. Multiple litigations ensued.

---

30. CME Rulebook § 418. CME Group owns CME, CBOT, NYMEX, and COMEX, and this rule is commonly adopted by each of the markets.

31. CME Rulebook § 406.

32. CME Rulebook § 408.

33. CME Rulebook § 411.

34. CME Rulebook § 402.B.

35. Commodity Exchange Act § 6b.

36. The actual standard to find the designated contract market liable is high, as it requires, generally, a finding of bad faith. We discuss this in section C.3.b below and in chapter 16, section A.2.b.

Westheimer v. Commodity Exchange, Inc.

651 F. Supp. 364 (S.D.N.Y. 1987)

Leisure, District Judge. . . .

Defendant Commodity Exchange, Inc. ("COMEX") is a duly designated contract market, pursuant to the Commodity Exchange Act, as amended (the "CEA"), and serves as a large market for the trading of precious metals futures contracts and options. COMEX is a not-for-profit corporation organized under the laws of the State of New York with its principal place of business in New York City. COMEX consists of institutional and individual members. It is a private self-regulatory organization that has been charged with law enforcement responsibilities by federal statute and regulation. . . .

Plaintiff Gerald Westheimer became a member of COMEX on June 19, 1968. Plaintiff Valerie Westheimer became a member of COMEX on July 27, 1984. The plaintiffs are married to each other.

During August 1984, an issue arose as to whether the gold option positions held by plaintiffs should be aggregated for the purposes of COMEX rules which limit the maximum number of contract positions in a particular commodity option that an individual or persons trading in common may hold. . . . COMEX's general counsel stated that plaintiffs' marital affiliation would not itself require aggregation and that COMEX did not presently intend to pursue the matter, but that "if circumstances change," COMEX might inquire further to determine whether its rules had been violated.

On March 18 and 19, 1985, plaintiffs and James R. Paruch ("Mr. Paruch") were unable to meet margin calls of approximately $26 million on gold futures options by Volume Investors Corporation ("Volume Investors"), where each of them maintained accounts for the purpose of clearing trades executed on COMEX. These and other related events resulted in the financial collapse of Volume Investors. On March 20, 1985, the COMEX Board of Governors, believing there was sufficient evidence of violations of COMEX's rules, suspended plaintiffs' membership in COMEX, pending a hearing. Specifically, the Board of Governors charged that plaintiffs failed to meet members' minimum financial requirements and failed to adhere to reporting obligations with respect to reductions in net current assets. . . .

COMEX's compliance department conducted an investigation of plaintiffs' trading activity and recommended that the COMEX Committee on Business Conduct (the "business conduct committee") issue a complaint against plaintiffs and Mr. Paruch. The business conduct committee, which is made up of COMEX members, issued a complaint on June 30, 1986, containing six counts against plaintiffs. The committee charged that plaintiffs: exceeded COMEX limits on short call gold and silver options; controlled uncovered short gold call options and uncovered short silver call options; submitted false affidavits to COMEX; and failed to notify COMEX that they were unable to fulfill trading obligations, pay debts and meet obligations to other members or member firms of COMEX.

COMEX's Supervisory Committee is scheduled to hold a disciplinary hearing based on these charges against plaintiffs. The Supervisory Committee is also scheduled to address the charges for which plaintiffs were suspended by COMEX's Board of Governors.... COMEX rules ... provide parties to the hearing with the right to review the documentary evidence compiled against them, to appear in person, to call witnesses on their behalf, to cross-examine adverse witnesses, and to retain counsel to represent them.

After receiving all of the evidence, the disciplinary hearing panel must promptly deliver a written decision ... and must set forth a summary of the evidence, a statement of findings and conclusions, and a declaration of any sanctions to be imposed. Upon an adverse decision, parties may request review by the Board of Governors, during which time the decision of the disciplinary panel may be stayed. The Board of Governors is required to issue a written decision of its findings and is empowered to order a new hearing. If a party is dissatisfied with the final determination by the Board of Governors, that party's appeal is to the CFTC.... [T]he Commission may affirm, modify, set aside or remand the action. Judicial review may be sought after the CFTC has taken action.

In addition to the action taken by COMEX with regard to the collapse of Volume Investors and plaintiffs' alleged conduct, the Commodity Futures Trading Commission (the "CFTC") has ... issued a complaint ... which names as defendants, among others, COMEX and plaintiffs. The complaint charges that COMEX violated the Commodity Exchange Act, as amended, by failing to take appropriate action to achieve compliance by plaintiffs with COMEX's rules limiting the number of contract positions in a particular commodity option that an individual or persons trading in common may hold. As to plaintiffs, the CFTC complaint charges that the Westheimers exceeded COMEX's limits on contract positions and, in turn, violated certain provisions of the CEA which refer to rules of contract markets, such as COMEX.

At the present time there is no date scheduled for the CFTC hearing. The COMEX disciplinary hearing ... [has] been adjourned ... due to ongoing settlement discussions with Mr. Paruch.

Plaintiffs state in their verified complaint (the "Complaint") that COMEX's disciplinary procedure is inherently biased against them. However, plaintiffs explain that the "primary reason" that COMEX "cannot provide plaintiffs with a fair, impartial and unbiased hearing" is the existence of the CFTC proceeding, in which COMEX is a co-defendant. Plaintiffs state that, in an attempt to "preview" plaintiffs' case before the CFTC, "COMEX has sought to force a quick trial" of its own disciplinary hearing....

The doctrine of exhaustion of administrative remedies applies to the disciplinary proceedings of a private self-regulatory organization such as COMEX, which has been charged by federal statute and regulation with law enforcement responsibilities and which serves as an integral part of an overall enforcement scheme....

The comprehensiveness of the procedure for review of a COMEX disciplinary hearing indicates a congressional intent that "self-regulation is the best 'first-line' defense against unethical or illegal" commodities practices, and application of the doctrine of exhaustion of administrative remedies prevents frustration of that intent. . . .

The charge that the COMEX hearing panel is biased or is seeking to preview plaintiffs' CFTC case provides no grounds for departure from the application of the exhaustion of remedies rule. . . .

Plaintiffs have not established the extreme circumstances necessary to justify application of an exception to the exhaustion doctrine, such as an agency's clear violation of a constitutional right or specific statutory provision, or an agency's action in gross excess of its power. Plaintiffs have also failed to demonstrate that irreparable harm will result from their exhaustion of administrative remedies. Plaintiffs' claim that defendant is seeking to preview plaintiffs' case before the CFTC rests on "too tenuous a string of possibilities" to serve as a foundation for a finding of immediate irreparable harm. . . .

Thus, the Court finds applicable the "general principle of administrative law that 'no one is entitled to judicial relief for a supposed or threatened injury until the prescribed administrative remedy has been exhausted.'" Plaintiffs' motion is denied.

——————

As a general matter, just as with an administrative process, courts hesitate to interfere with a self-regulatory proceeding while it is ongoing. Even after its resolution, courts generally show deference to the self-regulatory process so long as it does not demonstrate outright bias or similar infirmity.

3. Liability of Designated Contract Markets

a. CFTC Enforcement

The Commodity Exchange Act requires designated contract markets (and any other CFTC registrant that is a self-regulatory organization) to enforce its own rules. Accordingly, a failure by a designated contract market to enforce its rules could lead to CFTC enforcement proceedings.

Although today rules can be "self-certified" by a designated contract market, i.e., announced to the CFTC and then automatically effective after a specified time period, the Commodity Futures Trading Commission Act of 1974 initially required CFTC approval of each rule issued by a designated contract market. In the below case, during the CFTC's transition into authority after passage of the Commodity Futures Trading Commission Act, the CFTC had issued a rule requiring designated contract markets to comply with their own pre-existing rules even if the CFTC has not yet formally approved them. One aggrieved exchange challenged the CFTC's authority. As the below case demonstrates, the CFTC's authority to compel an exchange to enforce its own rules is broad and flexible.

New York Mercantile Exchange v. CFTC

443 F. Supp. 326 (S.D.N.Y. 1977)

Vincent L. Broderick, District Judge.

On June 16, 1977, the Commodity Futures Trading Commission instituted an administrative proceeding before an administrative law judge[37] to determine whether the New York Mercantile Exchange (the "Exchange") has violated the Commodity Exchange Act as amended ("the Act"), 7 U.S.C. s 1, et seq. (Supp.1977). Plaintiff Exchange thereupon commenced this action, and has moved by order to show cause for a preliminary injunction seeking, inter alia, to enjoin the Commodity Futures Trading Commission and its Commissioners (the "Commission") from pursuing the administrative proceeding. . . .

The Exchange is a board of trade which has been designated as a "contract market" for trading in futures contracts. . . .

In the proceeding sought to be enjoined, the Commission charges that the Exchange violated various provisions of the Act and the Commission regulations thereunder, in that the Exchange, with respect to futures contracts in potatoes, failed to use due diligence to secure compliance by its own members with an Exchange rule, and failed to take emergency action to prevent or eliminate market disruption. . . .

On July 18, 1975, the Exchange was designated by the Commission as a contract market. . . . The Commission expressed concern in its letter of designation that the "Exchange upgrade its rule enforcement program and maintain a staff adequate for carrying out that program." . . .

The Commission is given broad powers to make regulations under the Act, and is given specific authority to seek the court's assistance to enforce compliance with the Act and its regulations. It is also authorized to issue cease and desist orders if any contract market violates the Act or Commission regulations thereunder, and to assess civil penalties for such violations. Even where a challenge to Commission action is predicated upon alleged constitutional violation, or upon action allegedly beyond the jurisdiction of the Commission, the statute itself provides for review of that action after the administrative course has been run. Thus the Act provides for appeal by a contract market to the Court of Appeals, which can modify or set aside a Commission order if it, inter alia, infringes the Constitution or is beyond the Commission's jurisdiction. . . .

The action the Exchange seeks to enjoin will entail a trial before an administrative law judge, at which the facts and the applicable law can be fully developed. . . .

I would readily agree that . . . the Act as amended does not require the Exchange to enforce its own rules and regulations if they have not yet been approved by the Commission. I note, however, that the Act does not prohibit the Commission from

---

37. [N. 1] CFTC Docket No. 77-14, In the Matter of New York Mercantile Exchange.

requiring designated markets to enforce those of the market's rules which have not yet been approved, and I should be loath indeed to hold on the record before me, as a matter of statutory interpretation or constitutional law, that the Commission does not have residual power, grounded in the Act itself and its rule-making authority under the Act, to require the Exchange to enforce such rules. Was the existence of those rules a factor in the designation or continuance of the Exchange as a contract market? Did the Exchange explicitly or implicitly agree to enforce those rules as a condition of designation? Did the failure of the Exchange to enforce those rules frustrate the regulatory intent of the Act? These questions have not been answered before me: they undoubtedly will be fully explored before the administrative law judge, who can also consider the constitutional questions raised in this action by the Exchange. Attempts to enjoin administrative proceedings and obtain judicial relief before the prescribed administrative remedies have been exhausted are at odds with long settled rules of judicial administration. . . .

A few exceptions to the exhaustion doctrine have evolved. The Exchange correctly states that these exceptions pertain to those cases in which it is demonstrable that an agency has violated a constitutional right, has acted contrary to a specific statutory provision, or has so grossly exceeded its power as, in effect, to have flouted the will of Congress. . . .

Congress has clearly evidenced its preference for record development at the agency level. There is nothing extraordinary that is presented by this case to persuade me that the normal administrative processes should be abandoned.

In sum, the Exchange has not made a sufficient showing to take this case outside the general principle of administrative law that "no one is entitled to judicial relief for a supposed or threatened injury until the prescribed administrative remedy has been exhausted." *Myers v. Bethlehem Shipbuilding Corp.*, 303 U.S. 41, 50–51, 58 S.Ct. 459, 463, 82 L.Ed. 638 (1938). Even if [the CFTC regulation requiring the exchange to enforce its own rules pending their approval by the CFTC] . . . is invalid, a finding which I am not prepared to make, there does not appear to be a clear showing that the Commission has grossly exceeded its powers. The administrative process should be permitted to run its course. The Exchange will have ample opportunity to seek review in the Court of Appeals. . . .

––––––––––

b. Private Right of Action

An enforcement action by the CFTC is not the only means to compel a designated contract market to follow its own rules. Aggrieved individuals can, in prescribed instances, bring claims against a designated contract market if it has failed to enforce its own rules. Note that we discuss private rights of action under the Commodity Exchange Act more generally in chapter 16.

Unlike an enforcement action by the CFTC, though, in which the CFTC has broad authority to require a designated contract market to enforce its own rules, private rights of action in this context are limited solely to where the designated contract market has acted in bad faith.

Grossman v. Citrus Association of the New York Cotton Exchange, Inc.
742 F. Supp. 843 (S.D.N.Y. 1990)

Haight, District Judge. . . .

Plaintiff Gerald Grossman, d/b/a Commodity Traders Weather Service was at all times relevant to this litigation a commodities trading advisor. In short, Grossman "was at all relevant times engaged in the business of managing and investing customer funds on a discretionary basis in the commodities markets." . . .

Grossman took short positions in the [Frozen Concentrate Orange Juice, i.e. "FCOJ"] . . . market on behalf of himself and his clients . . . on which he lost money. . . .

FCOJ futures contracts are regularly traded on the Citrus Associates of the New York Cotton Exchange, Inc. ("Citrus Exchange.") . . .

In terms of the factors which influence the price of FCOJ contracts, plaintiffs identify the following "four major ongoing fundamental statistics which affect the price of FCOJ futures contracts" on "information and belief":

(i) the weather and temperatures in Florida, particularly in the months of December, January and February and especially U.S. government computer forecasts, as to whether there will be a winter "freeze" in Florida;

(ii) the first of the month, FCOJ cold storage stocks in Florida;

(iii) the average price and quantities of Brazilian imported FCOJ; and

(iv) the weekly movement of FCOJ from the processors and distributors to the wholesale grocers, supermarkets, etc. . . .

During the relevant trading period, December 12, 1985 through December 17, 1985, the trading volume in the FCOJ market was heavy and the price changes extensive. Grossman attributes that situation to certain weather reports which erroneously predicted a freeze in southern Florida. . . .

Plaintiffs contend that the weather outlook for the subject time period was artificially dire, which resulted in unduly inflated prices on FCOJ contracts. Grossman was short FCOJ contracts from December 12, 1985 through December 17, 1985 over which time the price of the contracts rose. Hearing rumors of a freeze, William Mallers, the president of First American Discount Corporation ("First American"), both former defendants in this action, called Grossman on December 16, 1985. Mallers "demanded enough margin to cover two limit days beginning Tuesday morning [the morning of December 17, 1985]." Mallers further stated that even with this additional margin he would take off half of the Joint Account's position on the opening on Tuesday if the market opened above Monday's close. The market did open up on Tuesday, December 17, 1985, and as he said he would Mallers liquidated fourteen of the twenty-eight short positions. . . .

[J]ust after the liquidation . . . Grossman put on stop limits . . . on all of his as well as his client's remaining accounts. The . . . orders were filled. . . .

As a result of covering his short positions at prices higher than that at which he sold the contracts, Grossman lost his own money as well as that invested on behalf of his clients. . . .

The Citrus Exchange is both a board of trade and a licensed contract market. . . .

The Citrus Exchange has its own by-laws to which it is clearly subject. . . . The portion of the by-laws relevant to the instant lawsuit is that covering "Emergency Action" [which permits the Citrus Exchange to take action in an "emergency" by, for example, limiting or halting trading]. . . .

In short, plaintiffs argue that the defendant Citrus Exchange improperly failed to take emergency action in the form of suspending or limiting trading in FCOJ contracts and that such failure caused them monetary loss.

The Act provides a remedy against an exchange defendant, such as the Citrus Exchange, whose actions or non-actions cause another financial loss. In addition to the causation element, plaintiffs must plead bad faith by the Citrus Exchange in order to defeat the instant motion. . . . In evaluating bad faith allegations against an exchange for improper action or non-action, the Second Circuit has said that "when self-interest or other ulterior motive unrelated to proper regulatory concerns is alleged to constitute the sole or the dominant reason for the exchange action, a complaint is sufficient even though the action was not beyond the bounds of reason." *Sam Wong & Son, Inc. v. New York Mercantile Exch.*, 735 F.2d 653, 677 (2d Cir.1984). . . .

[P]laintiffs at bar allege that "[t]he sole or dominant reason for the failure of defendant, its Board of Directors and its Executive Committee to take necessary and appropriate emergency action under the these [*sic*] circumstances was to elevate its self-interest above proper regulatory concerns, thereby constituting bad faith . . .

At the heart of plaintiffs' complaint are the weather reports for the orange belt which came out during the December 12, 1985 through December 17, 1985 time period. . . . The trading that morning was hectic and the price high, in response, plaintiffs contend, to reports of a possible weekend freeze. Plaintiffs argue that these reports were unrealistic and there was no chance of a weekend freeze. With the benefit of hindsight plaintiffs were proved right as the weekend came and went with no freeze in the orange belt. The fact remains, however, that certain reputable weather forecasters were predicting a freeze, giving traders in the market who agreed with those predictions cause to purchase FCOJ contracts, thereby driving the price of the contracts up.

In essence, plaintiffs contend that someone was intentionally driving up the price of FCOJ contracts and using a deliberately false freeze prediction as their vehicle.

However, the Citrus Exchange is not a weather forecaster and while it is charged with monitoring those factors which influence the price of the futures contracts traded on the exchange, it is not responsible for making decisions as to which of conflicting weather reports is correct and which way the market should be moving. It is precisely the fact that traders disagree over components which go into a price determination that makes the market work. . . . It is not the function of an exchange to allow the market to function only when there is no disagreement amongst traders, nor is it the function of an exchange to determine the ultimate "truth" in respect of whether prices should rise or fall. That truth is determined by the interrelationship between the buyers and sellers in the marketplace.

This is not a situation where the Citrus Exchange is alleged to have had anything to do with the publication of the allegedly false weather reports. . . . Rather, this is a case where plaintiffs argue that the Citrus Exchange should have known that someone else was engaging in the intentional publication of false weather reports and that it should then have suspended trading on December 17, 1985, which would, in the plaintiffs' view, have prevented their losses. . . .

Unless the Citrus Exchange know [sic] of a price manipulation or consciously avoided acquiring such knowledge, it was under no obligation to take any corrective action and its failure to do so cannot be said to have been in bad faith. Indeed, the Second Circuit has held that "[a] claim of bad faith must be supported by two allegations: first, that the exchange acted or failed to act with knowledge; and second, that the exchange's action or inaction was the result of an ulterior motive." *Ryder Energy Distrib. v. Merrill Lynch Commod.*, 748 F.2d 774, 780 (2d Cir.1984) (citation omitted). The complaint at bar fails in its charge of bad faith because it does not sufficiently allege that the Citrus Exchange "failed to act with knowledge." . . .

If the Citrus Exchange were itself in on a plan to elevate the price of FCOJ contracts by the publication of deliberately false weather reports, or the allowance of trading based on what it knew to be intentionally fraudulent reports, or if there was no explanation at all for the heavy market activity of December 17, 1985, plaintiffs might have a claim, but as it is they do not. . . .

In *Grossman*, the plaintiff claimed that the designated contract market's rules required emergency action to be taken and that he had a private right of action against the contract market for failing to take such action. Sometimes a designated contract market when faced with a market "emergency" may have two unpalatable choices (and face litigation either way). As the court noted in a case brought by farmers alleging harm due to an emergency resolution by the Chicago Board of Trade requiring phased reductions in large soybean positions:

> Eleanor Roosevelt once said, "[d]o what you feel in your heart to be right — for you'll be criticized anyway. You'll be damned if you do, and damned if you don't." In this case, the Chicago Board of Trade "did," and as a result

it has been "damned" with over ten years of litigation and the prospect of significant liability. However, we believed that had the Board not acted, it might have been "damned" anyway, as its inaction would have subjected it to claims. . . .[38]

In *Sam Wong & Son, Inc. v. New York Mercantile Exchange*,[39] the Second Circuit was faced with two such opposing claims: one alleging that the New York Mercantile Exchange failed to take appropriate emergency action and one related to emergency action it ultimately took:

> Wong's complaint . . . was that, once the delivery problems [in Maine potatoes] had manifested itself . . . the NYME had failed to take proper action [and the] other was that the NYME had failed in a duty to revise the Maine round white potato futures contract so that it would be a better vehicle for hedging and less susceptible to the problem that had developed. . . . [Spinale's] complaint, almost the exact opposite of Wong's, was that the Exchange should not have taken emergency action when it did, and alternatively that any action should have been less drastic. . . .[40]

The dismissal of Wong's claim was affirmed and Spinale's claim was remanded to the district court for further discovery on the question of whether the New York Mercantile Exchange acted in bad faith. It was ultimately dismissed,[41] demonstrating how difficult it is to prove that a designated contract market has acted in "bad faith."

c. Antitrust Claims

Due to the availability of treble damages with respect to antitrust claims, the complaints of plaintiffs against designated contract markets often include antitrust claims.[42] Where the designated contract market is acting in compliance with the Commodity Exchange Act or a CFTC order, the designated contract market receives qualified immunity from antitrust claims. Where a designated contract market has discretion, it is difficult to find bad faith in a case where, as was the case in *Zimmerman*, there is "close involvement and informal approval of the CFTC. . . ."[43]

---

38. *Zimmerman v. Chicago Board of Trade*, 360 F.3d 612, 630 (7th Cir. 2004).

39. 735 F.2d 653 (2d Cir. 1984).

40. *Sam Wong & Son, Inc. v. New York Mercantile Exchange*, 735 F.2d 653, 656–657 (2d Cir. 1984).

41. E-mail from Richard A. Miller, Esq. (who formerly represented Spinale) (Jan. 2, 2014).

42. *See, e.g.*, *Strobl v. New York Mercantile Exchange*, 768 F.2d 22 (2d Cir. 1985).

43. *Zimmerman v. Chicago Board of Trade*, 360 F.3d 612, 625 (7th Cir. 2004).

American Agricultural Movements, Inc. v. Board of Trade of City of Chicago

977 F.2d 1147 (7th Cir. 1992)

Flaum, Circuit Judge. . . .

The American Agriculture Movement, a national organization representing the interests of farmers . . . brought this suit against the Chicago Board of Trade and 26 of its officers and employees (collectively "CBOT") under the Commodity Exchange Act (CEA), the Sherman Anti-trust Act and state common law. . . . The [district] court . . . granted the CBOT's motion for summary judgment . . . reasoning that the CEA . . . had impliedly repealed the Sherman Act. . . . We . . . reverse the court's entry of summary judgment on the antitrust count. . . .

The CEA governs the trading of commodity futures contracts, and grants to the Commodity Futures Trading Commission (CFTC or Commission) the authority, in large measure, to implement the regulatory regime established therein. The Commission, pursuant to that authority has designated the CBOT as a "contract market" on which investors may trade various commodity futures contracts. The CBOT's status as a contract market imposes upon it a duty of self-regulation, subject to the Commission's oversight. As part of its duties, the CBOT must enact and enforce rules to ensure fair and orderly trading, including rules designed to prevent price manipulation, cornering and other market disturbances. CEA § 5(d). In performing this particular self-regulatory function, the CBOT is required to monitor "market activity for indications of possible congestion or other market situations conducive to possible price distortion."

This case involves an emergency action taken by the CBOT in response to what it claims was the threat of such a distortion. In the summer of 1989, Ferruzzi Finanziaria, S.p.A., and others (Ferruzzi Group or Ferruzzi) attempted to execute a "squeeze" in the July 1989 soybean futures market. The CBOT's Business Conduct Committee (Committee), the body charged with monitoring the soybean futures markets, determined that the Ferruzzi Group held an unusually large, and dangerous, market position; it controlled nearly 60 percent of the long open interests in the futures market, as well as over 60 percent of the cash soybeans in deliverable locations. Moreover, Ferruzzi's futures position was more than four times larger than the deliverable soybean stocks available to other cash market participants. If Ferruzzi did not substantially liquidate its position prior to the delivery date of the July 1989 contracts, the stability of the soybean futures and cash markets could have been seriously compromised.

In late June and early July, the Committee repeatedly urged the Ferruzzi Group to reduce in an orderly manner its outstanding open futures position. Ferruzzi stonewalled and declared that it would maintain its position, and in response the Committee, on July 10, recommended that the CBOT's governing board (Board) take emergency action. The following day, the Board, by a 16 to 1 vote, issued an "Emergency Resolution" (Resolution) pursuant to its self-regulatory powers. The Resolution declared a market emergency, and ordered any person or group controlling gross long or short positions in excess of three million bushels to liquidate their positions by at least 20 percent daily. In addition, it ordered that no person or group could own contracts in excess of three million bushels on July 18, or in excess of one million bushels on July 20, the last trading day for July 1989 contracts. The Board . . . immediately made the Resolution public, and . . . informed the Commission of its action.

Not surprisingly, publication of the Resolution led to a price decline in the July 1989 futures market. . . .

The Resolution no doubt restrained trade in the July 1989 soybean futures market, and for that reason would ordinarily fall within the purview of the antitrust laws. But this case is not ordinary, for here the CBOT was also subject to the dictates of the CEA and the regulatory regime established thereunder.

That regime imposes upon the CBOT a duty of self-regulation, and upon the Commission the duty to oversee the CBOT's self-regulatory activities, and grants both a certain degree of flexibility when it comes to making judgment calls regarding the efficient operation and maintenance of the futures markets. Conflicts between antitrust law and the CEA, supposed or actual, are inevitable, as exchange activities that would be considered inappropriate under the antitrust laws might arguably be justified, or even required, under the CEA. *Ricci v. Chicago Mercantile Exch.*, 409 U.S. 289, 299–300, 306, 93 S. Ct. 573, 579–80, 582–83, 34 L.Ed.2d 525 (1973). The problem, then, arises "from the need to reconcile pursuit of the antitrust aim of eliminating restraints on competition with the effective operation of a public policy contemplating that [commodity] exchanges will engage in self-regulation which may well have anticompetitive effects in general and in specific application." *Silver v. New York Stock Exch.*, 373 U.S. 341, 349, 83 S. Ct. 1246, 1252–53, 10 L.Ed.2d 389 (1963).

Under certain circumstances, reconciling antitrust law with a regulatory regime compels the conclusion that Congress intended the latter to oust the former — that is, compels the conclusion that the regulatory regime has impliedly granted antitrust immunity to private parties operating under its rubric. Those circumstances, however, are rare. . . . As with all matters of statutory construction, the intent of Congress governs, but in order to find implied immunity that intent must be clear.

With these precepts in mind, we outline, in some detail, the regulatory environment in which the CBOT adopted, implemented and published the Resolution. As noted, self-regulating contract markets designated under CEA §5 are required to adopt rules "for the prevention of the manipulation of prices and the cornering of any commodity." As a general matter, a market must gain the Commission's approval prior to implementing exchange rules of this nature, and the statute outlines the procedures under which the Commission may approve or disapprove such rules. The statute nonetheless carves an exception for "emergencies" requiring immediate action. Under such circumstances, an exchange, by a two-thirds vote of its governing board, may adopt and immediately implement a temporary emergency rule without prior Commission approval. In lieu of prior approval, the exchange must notify and provide the Commission with a complete explanation of both the emergency and the action it took in response.

Neither the statute nor the applicable regulations explicitly provide for Commission review of temporary emergency rules. Nonetheless, the Commission believes ... [that the CEA] empowers the Commission to overturn, modify or approve a rule after receiving notification from an exchange.

While the Commission has to power to take action ... it need not do so, and oftentimes "simply [chooses] to refrain from acting." ... [If] its Division of Trading and Markets ... determines that a given temporary emergency rule was reasonable and enacted in good faith, the Commission may decide that further or formal action on its part is unnecessary.

That is precisely what happened in this case. ...

Having examined the ... Commission's actions in this case, we return to the principles of implied antitrust immunity. ...

We can dispatch rather quickly with the CBOT's argument — echoing that made by the Commission, as amicus — that the CEA bestows "pervasive" implied immunity upon contract markets. At the outset, it is important to recognize that Congress did not intend the CEA to extend blanket immunity to the exchanges for their adoption and enforcement of exchange rules, emergency or otherwise. The Supreme Court, in 1973, recognized that the CEA did not "confer general antitrust immunity" on the exchanges and their members for conduct taken pursuant to a Commission regulation or exchange rule. ... Shortly thereafter, during deliberations on the 1974 Act, the House Agriculture Committee considered and rejected a provision that would have shielded from antitrust attack any conduct of that nature. ...

Congress' clear rejection of blanket immunity casts serious doubt upon the CBOT's contention that the Commission's regulation of exchange emergency actions ... is so "pervasive" as to demand antitrust immunity. ...

In the absence of a pervasive regulatory scheme, we may imply antitrust immunity in either one of two circumstances: first, where the challenged action was compelled by a statute, regulation, or agency, and, second, where the action was "scrutin[ized] and approv[ed]" by the appropriate agency. Had the Commission ... ordered the CBOT to take emergency action in response to the impending Ferruzzi squeeze, or had it modified the action the CBOT took on its own, there can be no doubt as to the outcome of this case. Exposing the CBOT to potential antitrust liability under such circumstances would subject it to conflicting standards, leading to the inevitable conclusion that Congress intended to grant antitrust immunity. But the Commission did not compel the CBOT to do anything, so implied repealer cannot rest upon this ground.[44]

---

44. [N. 9] Alternatively, the CBOT could argue that its action was compelled by a statute or regulation, namely [the requirement] ... to enforce rules to ensure fair trading and [that] ...

We must determine, then, whether the Commission's performance after receiving notification from the CBOT constitutes "scrutiny and approval" sufficient to warrant antitrust immunity. . . .

The fact that an agency let stand a practice voluntarily initiated by a regulated entity — even when it had the power to review, modify and overturn that practice — is not sufficient, in and of itself, to confer antitrust immunity. . . .

While the issue posed is admittedly a close one, we conclude that the regulatory supervision in this case was not sufficient to cloak the Resolution with similar immunity. . . . [The Commission's] "approval" of the Resolution was not the product of any affirmative action, but rather of acquiescence, or the failure to take action. . . .

Our holding is limited strictly to the issue of implied immunity, and does not in any way portend our view of the legal or factual merits of the . . . antitrust count. To ultimately prevail, the [plaintiffs] will have to demonstrate that the CBOT acted in bad faith. . . .

Even after this ruling, the case took another decade to resolve.[45]

Perhaps due to judicial recognition of the Hobbesian conundrum faced by designated contract markets when responding to market emergencies — historically a rich source of litigation for claims against designated contract markets — we have seen that the bar is high for private claims by traders. There would be no claims at all against the designated contract markets if the CFTC directly ordered emergency action as the Commodity Exchange Act permits.[46] The CFTC has used these powers only four times since its formation, each noted in figure 5.2. Since 1980, the CFTC has not invoked these powers in *de facto* reliance on the designated contract markets themselves taking any emergency actions deemed to be necessary.

---

authorizes it to invoke emergency resolutions to prevent market disruption due to a threatened market cornering. This, however, is the essence of the suit: was the CBOT action taken pursuant to the statute and regulations, making it unassailable . . . or was the emergency resolution adopted in bad faith, not to prevent market disruption but to further private interests, and therefore outside the statutory authority and open to Sherman Act liability? . . . This issue was not addressed by the district court and remains open on remand.

45. The court's ruling resulted in the case being remanded to district court. The court again granted the Chicago Board of Trade's motion to dismiss the antitrust claims. *American Agriculture Movement, Inc. v. Board of Trade of City of Chicago*, 868 F. Supp. 814 (N.D. Ill. 1994). On appeal the Seventh Circuit remanded the case again to the district court with respect to one remaining category of plaintiffs, farmers who sold soybeans at allegedly artificially low prices. *Sanner v. Board of Trade of City of Chicago*, 62 F.3d 918, 930 (7th Cir. 1995). This time the district court judge denied the Chicago Board of Trade's motion to dismiss. *Sanner v. Board of Trade of City of Chicago*, 1996 WL 539110 (N.D. Ill. Sept. 20, 1996). After judgment was ultimately granted by the district court as a matter of law, the Seventh Circuit affirmed this decision in 2004 finally putting the matter to rest. *Zimmerman v. Chicago Board of Trade*, 360 F.3d 612 (7th Cir. 2004).

46. Commodity Exchange Act § 8a(9).

Figure 5.2 The CFTC's Emergency Authority

Date	Commodity	Contract Market	Action
November 1976	Maine potatoes	New York Mercantile Exchange	100% margining and only liquidation of positions permitted
December 1977	Coffee	New York Coffee and Sugar Exchange	Phased orderly liquidation
March 1979	Wheat	Chicago Board of Trade	Suspension of trading and mandatory settlement of positions
January 1980	Wheat, corn, oats, soybeans, soybean meal, and soybean oil	All designated contract markets with contracts referencing the commodities subject to the emergency order	Two-day suspension

4. Listing of Contracts

a. Contracts Generally

The normal means for a designated contract market to offer new futures or commodity options contracts for trading is self-certification with a process similar to that for the designated contract market rulemaking process. By the open of business on the business day before the product is proposed to be listed, the CFTC must receive from the designated contract market, among others, the rules that will govern the contract, the listing date, a description of the product, and a certification that it complies with the Commodity Exchange Act and CFTC rules.[47] A notice of the pending certification also must be posted on the designated contract market's website.[48]

In the interim, the CFTC may request additional information to show that the proposed contract complies with the Commodity Exchange Act and CFTC rules or issue a stay on the listing of the contract if the CFTC determines that the self-certification is incorrect or to use its authority to amend the terms of the contract. Because of specific issues raised in the context of contracts involving virtual currency, the CFTC has issued specific guidance on listing such contracts.[49]

As with the rulemaking process, there are a few exceptions to the self-certification process described above. The first is that the designated contract market may voluntarily request CFTC approval of a new product.[50] To do so, it would provide the same information as with the self-certification method and, additionally, post

---

47. 17 C.F.R. § 40.2(a).

48. 17 C.F.R. § 40.2(a)(vi).

49. CFTC, *Staff Advisory No. 18-14*, https://www.cftc.gov/sites/default/files/idc/groups/public/%40lrlettergeneral/documents/letter/2018-05/18-14_0.pdf (May 21, 2018).

50. 17 C.F.R. § 40.3(a).

details of the request on its website.[51] In such circumstances, the CFTC has forty-five days to review the proposal with an extension for an additional forty-five days if the CFTC determines that it raises novel or complex issues, is of "major economic significance," or the submission is incomplete or inadequately explained.[52]

The second exception is for "event contracts," discussed below.

b. Event Contracts

Event contracts have a special approval procedure. An event contract is "a derivative contract whose payoff is based on a specified event, occurrence, or value such as the value of a macroeconomic indicator, corporate earnings, level of snowfall, or dollar value of damages caused by a hurricane."[53] CFTC rules prohibit event contracts involving terrorism, assassination, war, gaming, unlawful activities, or something similar determined by the CFTC to be "contrary to the public interest."[54] This is a sterner stance than that in the Commodity Exchange Act, where event contracts involving terrorism, assassination, war, gaming, or an unlawful activity are only prohibited if determined by the CFTC to not be in the public interest.[55]

If the CFTC believes a futures contract may be an event contract prohibited by CFTC rule, it can suspend the listing of the product for ninety days while it conducts a review.[56] In 2011, the CFTC took the position that options contracts proposed by the North American Derivatives Exchange based on political events involved gaming and could not be listed.

CFTC, *In the Matter of the Self-Certification by North American Derivatives Exchange, Inc. of Political Event Derivatives Contracts*

https://www.cftc.gov/sites/default/files/idc/groups/public/@rulesandproducts
/documents/ifdocs/nadexorder040212.pdf (Apr. 2, 2012)

By a submission dated and received by the Commodity Futures Trading Commission ("Commission") on December 19, 2011, the North American Derivatives Exchange ("Nadex" or "Exchange") self-certified, pursuant to Section 5c(c)(1) of the Commodity Exchange Act ("CEA") and Commission Regulations 40.2(a) and 40.6(a), new contracts: a Democratic Majority in the U.S. House of Representatives Binary Contract; a Republican Majority in the U.S. House of Representatives Binary Contract; a Democratic Majority in the U.S. Senate Binary Contract; a Republican

---

51. *Id*. There are additional certifications required if the contract in question is a security futures product. *See* 17 C.F.R. § 41.22.

52. 17 C.F.R. §§ 40.3(c) and (d).

53. *See* CFTC, *Contracts and Products*, https://www.cftc.gov/IndustryOversight/Contracts Products/index.htm.

54. 17 C.F.R. § 40.11(a).

55. Commodity Exchange Act §§ 5c(c)(5)(C)(i) and (ii).

56. 17 C.F.R. § 40.11(c).

Majority in the U.S. Senate Binary Contract; and ten 10 U.S. Presidency Binary Contracts (collectively, the "Political Event Contracts") and related rule amendments. The Political Event Contracts are each binary option contracts that payout based upon the results of the various United States federal elections in 2012. Having reviewed the complete record in this matter, including Nadex's submission, public comments and a Nadex supplementary submission, the Commission makes the following findings and rulings:

WHEREAS, under CEA Section 5c(c)(5)(C)(i), the Commission may determine that a contract in certain excluded commodities, as defined in CEA Section 1(a)(19), is contrary to the public interest if the contract involves: (1) activity that is unlawful under any Federal or State law, (2) terrorism, (3) assassination, (4) war, (5) gaming, or (6) other similar activity determined by the Commission, by rule or regulation, to be contrary to the public interest;

WHEREAS, the legislative history of CEA Section 5c(c)(5)(C) indicates that the relevant question for the Commission in determining whether a contract involves one of the activities enumerated in CEA Section 5c(c)(5)(C)(i) is whether the contract, considered as a whole, involves one of those activities;

WHEREAS, CEA Section 5c(c)(5)(C)(ii) mandates that no "contract ... determined by the Commission to be contrary to the public interest under Section 5c(c)(5)(C)(i) may be listed or made available for clearing or trading on or through a registered entity";

WHEREAS, Commission Regulation 40.11(a)(1) provides that registered entities, as defined in CEA Section 1(a)(40) and inclusive of designated contract markets such as Nadex, shall not list for trading any contract based upon an excluded commodity, as defined in CEA Section 1(a)(19), that "involves, relates to, or references terrorism, assassination, war, gaming, or an activity that is unlawful under any State or Federal law";

WHEREAS, several state statutes, on their face, link the terms gaming or gambling (which are used interchangeably in common usage, dictionary definitions and several state statutes) to betting on elections, and state gambling definitions of "wager" and "bet" are analogous to the act of taking a position in the Political Event Contracts;

WHEREAS, a federal statute defines the term "bet or wager" as "the staking or risking by any person of something of value upon the outcome of a contest of others. . . ."[57] and taking a position in a Political Event Contract fits the plain meaning of a person staking "something of value upon a contest of others," as the Political Event Contracts are all premised either directly (in the case of the presidential Political Event Contracts) or indirectly (in the cases of the House and Senate majority

---

57. [N. 3] 31 U.S.C. §§ 5361–5367 (2006).

control Political Event Contracts) on the outcome of a contest between electoral candidates;

WHEREAS, the legislative history of CEA Section 5c(c)(5)(C) indicates Congress's intent to restore, for the purposes of that provision, the economic purpose test that was used by the Commission to determine whether a contract was contrary to the public interest pursuant to CEA Section 5(g) prior to its deletion by the Commodity Futures Modernization Act of 2000;

WHEREAS, the restored economic purpose test calls for an evaluation of an event contract's utility for hedging and price basing purposes;

WHEREAS, the unpredictability of the specific economic consequences of an election means that the Political Event Contracts cannot reasonably be expected to be used for hedging purposes;

WHEREAS, there is no situation in which the Political Event Contracts' prices could form the basis for the pricing of a commercial transaction involving a physical commodity, financial asset or service, which demonstrates that the Political Event Contracts have no price basing utility;

WHEREAS, the Commission has the discretion to consider other factors in addition to the economic purpose test in determining whether an event contract is contrary to the public interest;

WHEREAS, the Political Event Contracts can potentially be used in ways that would have an adverse effect on the integrity of elections, for example by creating monetary incentives to vote for particular candidates even when such a vote may be contrary to the voter's political views of such candidates;

The Commission FINDS that the Political Event Contracts involve gaming as contemplated by CEA Section 5c(c)(5)(C)(i)(V) and Commission Regulation 40.11(a)(l);

The Commission FURTHER FINDS that the Political Event Contracts are contrary to the public interest as contemplated by CEA Section 5c(c)(5)(C);

Therefore:

IT IS HEREBY ORDERED that, pursuant to CEA Section 5c(c)(5)(C)(ii) and Commission Regulation 40.11(a)(1), the Political Event Contracts shall not be listed or made available for clearing or trading on the Exchange.

———————

In the case of the North American Derivatives Exchange, the rejection by the CFTC was public. In a recent application related to an events contract based on NFL football, it was voluntarily withdrawn after, apparently, facing an unlikely prospect of approval. This drew a strong rebuke from one of the CFTC's commissioners. Throughout the below there are references to the "Order." These references are to the proposed order that the CFTC was prepared to issue and then withdrew upon the voluntary withdrawal of the petition.

CFTC, *Statement of Commissioner Brian D. Quintenz on ErisX RSBIX NFL Contracts and Certain Event Contracts: Any Given Sunday in the Futures Market*

https://www.cftc.gov/PressRoom/SpeechesTestimony/quintenzstatement032521
(Mar. 25, 2021)[58]

In December 2020, ErisX filed a self-certification that their RSBIX NFL futures contracts involving the moneyline, point spread, and total points on NFL football games meet the requirements of the CEA for a contract listed by a registered Designated Contract Market (DCM). Prior to 2018, sports gaming was limited by a federal law which only allowed it to legally occur in Nevada. After *Murphy v. NCAA*[59] struck down that law, multiple states have legalized sports gambling and thereby allowed legitimate business activity in that area. Since the derivative markets' historical use is the hedging of commodity price risk associated with economic activity, contracts relating to the outcome of sporting events could now have a legitimate economic and hedging purpose for businesses in these states. Such was the intent of ErisX's contracts.

On December 23, the Commission issued a 90-day stay of the self-certification pursuant to rule 40.11, which subjects any event contract which may involve gaming to a special disapproval process. During those 90 days, the Commission reviewed ErisX's contracts to determine if they were prohibited by statute or Commission regulations. The Commission also requested public feedback on six questions, and received twenty-five responses. Subsequently, Commission staff proposed an Order that found the ErisX NFL contracts involved gaming, were prohibited by regulation, and were also contrary to the public interest. This proposed Order (which for simplicity's sake I will refer to just as the Order) was circulated to the Commission for a vote. . . . Just hours before this voting process could conclude, and likely in anticipation of the Order's approval by the Commission, ErisX decided to withdraw their certification, preventing the Order from being fully and formally considered by the Commission and publicly issued.

Withdrawing the certification had the same functional effect on the ErisX NFL contracts that the Order would have had; the contracts will not be listed. However, the withdrawal also meant that the Commission's Order will never be public. The staff's analysis and working law that was applied to the ErisX NFL contracts may well be the same that Commission staff will apply in current or future direct discussions with exchanges to similar contracts, and outside of the purview of the Commissioners or the public. But the legal analysis and interpretations will remain secret until forced into the open by another, bolder exchange's decision to see a self-certification process through to a conclusion.

---

58. Some italics removed.
59. [N. 1] 138 S.Ct. 1461 (2018).

Secret agency law is anathema in our democracy, and should only be tolerated where absolutely necessary.[60] The government can try to hide behind FOIA exemptions, deliberative process, or prohibitions on disclosing "confidential information," but it shouldn't be able to take the ball home in the middle of the fourth quarter when leading by a field goal.

I would have dissented from the Order prohibiting the ErisX NFL contracts due to significant concerns around the statute's constitutionality, the regulation's validity, and the order's arbitrariness. Customarily, my dissent would be made moot by virtue of ErisX's withdrawal, and my ability to comment on the Order therefore nullified. But, because of the severity of these concerns and their implication for any future event contract filing, I feel compelled to release this statement to bring transparency to this debate and process. So . . . are you ready for some football? . . .

When we think of commodities, we think of tangible things. Oil, corn, gold. There are intangible commodities too, most of which have a connection to the financial system, like a broad stock index (S&P 500) or a borrowing rate (LIBOR). But what about an event? An election? Whether the Summer Olympics will occur in Japan? A . . . football game? Those, too, are commodities!

The statutory definition of a commodity includes ". . . an occurrence, extent of an occurrence, or contingency . . . that is 1) beyond the control of the relevant parties to the contract . . . and 2) associated with a financial, commercial, or economic consequence."[61] Since practically any event has at least a minimal financial, commercial, or economic consequence, all events are commodities. Because of this definition, any contract on the outcome of a future event would be considered a commodity futures contract, and, pursuant to the Commodity Exchange Act (CEA), is required to be traded on a registered Designated Contract Market (DCM).

The Dodd Frank Act inserted a new section into the CEA regarding certain event contracts, which said the Commission "may determine that [event] agreements, contracts, or transactions are contrary to the public interest if the agreements, contracts, or transactions involve — (I) activity that is unlawful under any Federal or State Law; (II) terrorism; (III) assassination; (IV) war; (V) gaming; or (VI) other similar activity determined by the Commission, by rule or regulation, to be contrary to the public interest." If the Commission determines that any such "enumerated" event contracts are contrary to the public interest, the statute then prohibits them from being traded on a registered exchange.

Got that? All events are commodities, which means all contracts on future events are commodity futures contracts, which means all future event contracts need to be traded on a regulated and registered futures exchange. But if the Commission

---

60. [N .2] See generally N.L.R.B. v. Sears, Roebuck & Co., 421 U.S. 132, 153 (1975). For a compelling viewpoint on the perfidy of secret law and financial regulators, see SEC Commissioner Hester Pierce's remarks, SECret Garden, available at https://www.sec.gov/news/speech/peirce-secret-garden-sec-speaks-040819.

61. [N. 4] Section 1a(19)(iv) of the CEA.

deems any event contract that involves one of the enumerated activities to be contrary to the public interest, that contract is banned from trading on any registered futures exchange. The contract cannot trade anywhere else either since it is still a commodity futures contract and, if traded off of an exchange would be illegal.

Now, we may all say to ourselves that this is a good thing. Shouldn't these so-called "event" contracts, that are by nature more "probabilistic" than traditional physical commodity contracts, be more akin to "gaming" or "gambling?" Certainly, they are, generally speaking, less related to traditional economic goods. Before we get into the specifics around ErisX's NFL contracts and the Constitutional and administrative issues with the statute, regulation, and the Commission's proposed Order, let me take a minute to dispel two notions: that taking an economic position on an event's outcome is legally equivalent to a gaming/gambling activity, and that there is no fundamental or qualitative difference between gambling and speculating. Understanding these points may help to better define what our markets are truly meant to do and why participants in them, regardless of their motives, are vital to it.

First, it is not the case that trading an event contract with a binary outcome is automatically considered a bet, wager, or gamble from a regulatory perspective. The statute's language proves that. If the statute assumed that participating in any event contract involved making a wager or gamble, there would have been no need for Congress to individually enumerate "gaming" as a distinct category of event contracts upon which the Commission could make a public interest determination. (This is an important federal statutory point that conflicts with many state laws, to which we will return at the end).

Secondly, speaking in broad policy terms and putting aside the voluminous technical and legal nuances, there are qualitative and logical distinctions between speculation and betting. Whereas bettors participate in games of pure chance, whose sole purpose is to completely reward the winner and punish the loser for an outcome that would otherwise provide no economic utility (think roulette), speculators in the derivatives market participate in non-chance driven outcomes that have price forming impacts upon which legitimate businesses can hedge their activities and cash flows.

There are plenty of events that have a discernable and legitimate economic impact and whose probabilistic outcomes can be estimated through an analysis of relevant factors. That could now be just as true for sporting events as it is for oil, corn, or gold production. Try telling a professional sports team's general manager (or even die-hard fantasy footballers) that their outcomes are purely chance driven. . . . The other factor which makes speculation different than pure-chance gambling is the price forming impact it has on markets which allow businesses to hedge their risk. Post *Murphy*, it is at least logically possible that sport books would qualify for that economic justification.

If you are unconvinced, think more broadly about how a market probability of other potential events could provide an economic good and is different than betting on a true game of chance. How valuable would it have been to restaurants across

California and New York during the pandemic lockdowns to have had an event contract in place for hedging that asked in March 2020 whether indoor dinning would be allowed within one year? From a probabilistic perspective, if you think that the outcome is purely a political decision, you would be right. But if you think that there are no discernable, influential, or acute facts that would go into predicting any decision on that outcome, you are wrong. From an economic perspective, the value of that market derived probability could have provided crucial hedging utility for small businesses, many of which are now gone. Unfortunately, such contacts have yet to come to market. . . .

As described above, [section 5c(c)(5)(C)] . . . provides, among other things, a "special rule" for the disapproval of certain enumerated event contracts, specifically those that "involve" activity that is: unlawful under any Federal or State law, terrorism, assassination, war, gaming, or other similar activity that is determined by the Commission by rule or regulation to be contrary to the public interest. . . . The presumption of the statute's special rule for these enumerated event contracts, perhaps surprisingly, is not that they are prohibited. . . . An enumerated event contract is only prohibited if the contract is determined by the Commission to be contrary to the public interest. . . .

In 2012, the Commission promulgated Regulation 40.11 implementing this section of the statute. This regulation states that, "pursuant to" CEA section 5c(c)(5)(C), the Commission is prohibiting all event contracts that involve the enumerated activities above. The regulation also allows for a 90-day review period of contracts to allow the Commission to determine whether the contract is an enumerated event contract. If the contract is found to be an enumerated event contract, then it is subject to the per se prohibition in the regulation. . . .

The Order that would have been issued by the Commission on March 23rd would have prohibited ErisX's NFL contracts under both the statute and the regulation. The Order first found that the ErisX NFL contracts are enumerated event contracts because they involve gaming. . . . The Order concluded that the "record in this matter does not establish that the ErisX NFL event contracts have a hedging utility," and the contracts "do not form the basis for the pricing of a commercial transaction involving a physical commodity, financial asset or service." In addition to the economic purpose test, the Order asserted that the Commission can also consider other factors in determining that the contracts are contrary to the public interest. The Order listed one such factor, that "the ErisX NFL event contracts could potentially promote sports gambling," which, the order found, also makes the contracts contrary to the public interest. . . .

You might have noticed there is a conflict between the statutory framework and regulatory framework. As I discuss in length below, the statute's default is to allow the enumerated event contracts unless there is a determination by the Commission that an enumerated event contract is contrary to the public interest. The regulation simply announces a blanket prohibition on all enumerated event contracts in accordance with its interpretation of the statute's intent.

You also might have noticed from the description of the Order that it made two conflicting official rulings. On the one hand, the Order found that the ErisX NFL contracts involve gaming and are therefore enumerated event contracts. Under Regulation 40.11, that means game over — the ErisX NFL contracts are prohibited. However, the Order also made specific findings that the ErisX NFL contracts are contrary to the public interest, while then claiming that future enumerated event contracts that are not found to be contrary to the public interest will be allowed, directly contradicting the blanket prohibition in Regulation 40.11.

The confusion within the Order is not surprising when you consider the fundamental problems with the statute and the regulation that the Order attempted to incorporate. As explained below, the statute is unconstitutional, and, arguendo, even if it were constitutional, the regulation would still be invalid. . . .

The statute is an impermissible and non-constitutional delegation of legislative power to the agency because 1) it gives the Commission complete discretion on whether to allow or effectively ban any given enumerated contract by arbitrarily undertaking (or abstaining from) a public interest determination process, and 2) that public interest determination is not bounded by any set of guiding principles or limiting circumstances around which the Commission should apply its expertise to any associated fact-finding. . . .

While the Supreme Court was divided in the outcome of the recent case of *Gundy v. United States*,[62] the justices unanimously agreed that a statutory delegation to an agency is generally not constitutional if Congress fails to "lay[] down by legislative act an intelligible principle to which the person or body authorized to [exercise the delegated authority] is directed to conform."[63] Congress could have simply withheld listing events as commodities. Congress could also just as easily have declared that any contract referencing war, terrorism, assassination, or gaming is illegal, and required the Commission to play the role of fact finder to identify which contracts crossed that threshold. But it did not. It punted on the policy making, instead giving the Commission the sole ability and with complete and unbounded discretion, to decide when to conduct an analysis to determine if the contracts referencing the certain enumerated activities were "not in the public interest," and thereby banning them from trading. . . .

The delegation in CEA section 5c(c)(5)(C) presents the same issue that was presented almost 100 years ago in *Panama Refining Co. v. Ryan*,[64] where the Supreme

---

62. [N. 5] 139 S.Ct. 2116 (2019).

63. [N. 6] *Id.* at 2123 (plurality opinion of Justice Kagan); *id.* at 2145 (dissenting opinion of Justice Gorsuch). Justice Gorsuch takes the more stringent view on what Congress may delegate. The Justice may find an unconstitutional delegation even if Congress provided "an intelligible principle." Justice Kagan may adopt a broader view of what Congress is allowed to delegate. Relevant here is that even according to Justice Kagan's lenient view, and a fortiori under Justice Gorsuch's strict view, a delegation such as here, where Congress failed to provide "an intelligible principle" is unconstitutional.

64. [N. 9] 293 U.S. 388 (1935).

Court held that Congress unconstitutionally delegated its legislative power to the executive branch. Here, like there, the statute provides "no requirement, no definition of circumstances and conditions in which" the Executive Branch should take action.[65] In this statute, Congress failed to set forth any indication of what it intended the Commission to do, let alone a standard, "sufficiently definite and precise to enable Congress, the courts, and the public to ascertain" whether Congress's intentions were followed.[66] If confronted with the statute at issue here, the Court should find an unconstitutional delegation of legislative authority. This is what the Court did in *Panama Refining Co.*, and would have done in *Gundy* if the statute there was as clearly devoid of intelligible principles as the one here. . . .

Independent of the problem with the statute completely submitting to the Commission's discretion of *when* to make a determination, is the problematic use of the sole phrase "public interest" as to *how* to make a determination. In his book *Go East, Young Man*, Justice Douglas opined, "I also realized that Congress defaulted when it left it up to an agency to do what the 'public interest' indicated should be done. 'Public interest' is too vague a standard to be left to free-wheeling administrators. They should be more closely confined to specific ends or goals."[67] . . . The "public interest" could be a moral consideration. It could be an interest based on financial stability, the integrity of sporting events, enhancing the regulatory apparatus around sports betting, or even, perhaps, increasing fair access to gaming. And there can be competing interests amongst the public. To the public that enjoys sports betting, a contract that makes their interest easier, safer, or cheaper, is in the public interest. However, that same contract is contrary to the interest of the public that is opposed to sports betting. . . . Identifying the interests, and balancing the competing interests, is a job for Congress, not the Commission. . . .

And what about Congress's estimation of the public interest? Did Congress have an idea in mind of what the public interest is? We don't know, because in adopting such a vague standard, Congress took a knee. In this statute, did Congress provide us a standard we should use that is "sufficiently definite and precise to enable Congress, the courts, and the public to ascertain" whether Congress's intentions were followed? Absolutely not. There are literally no requirements, guidance, criteria, tests, or parameters listed in the statute to consider in making such a determination. . . . The Order itself referenced none. It simply stated that the "the legislative history of CEA Section 5c(c)(5)(C) indicates Congress's intent to restore, for the purposes of that provision, the economic purpose test that the Commission used to determine whether a contract was contrary to the public interest pursuant to CEA Section 5(g) prior to the deletion of CEA Section 5(g) by the Commodity Futures Modernization Act of 2000." . . .

---

65. [N. 10] *Id.* at 430. . . .

66. [N. 11] *Gundy*, 139 S.Ct. at 2142. . . .

67. [N. 12] W. Douglas, Go East, Young Man 216–217 (1974) cited in *Gundy*, 139 S. Ct. at 2140 fn 63.

As to the "legislative history" interpretation on which the Order so heavily relied, I suspect that the reference is to a simple colloquy between Senator Lincoln and Senator Feinstein, which stated that the Commission "needs the power to, and should, prevent derivatives contracts that are contrary to the public interest because they exist predominantly to enable gambling through supposed event contracts."[68] . . .

When left to its own devices, the Commission is not a good substitute for Congress. It is a phenomenal body for ensuring the safety, security, and functioning of the markets it regulates. It possesses vast knowledge and expertise in financial regulation relevant to its mandate. The Commission enjoys the benefit of a talented and dedicated staff that includes some of the foremost experts in their fields. But the Commission is not a moral arbiter. It is not expert in determining what the is in the public's interest, and it is certainly not equipped to tell the public what its interest *should* be. . . .

The Commission is also not a transparent arbitrator of debate. Consider the very convenient example of the Order. ErisX submitted its contracts, and the agency got into a huddle. There were inside discussions, meetings, draft Orders and revisions to those draft, none of which were presented in a public forum as would a Congressional Committee hearing or floor vote with amendments and debate. While the Commission eventually determined to open a comment period to allow the public to give input that ostensibly would assist the Commission in its public interest analysis, you wouldn't even know that comments were submitted because the Order discussed none. . . . There is not even a normal public disclosure of which specific Commissioners voted for an Order, and which against. Should the lack of the NFL contracts have massive negative ramifications for legitimate businesses, no one would know whom to blame or for what reasoning.

The Commission's Order would have been akin to the referees overruling a game winning touchdown upon further review, but without allowing anyone else to see the replay. And who would have enforced the prohibition? You got it, the Commission. And let's just suppose that ErisX is not the only one interested in listing similar event contracts. Who will decide whether to review those other contracts, or to just play spectator, do nothing, and allow them? Once again, the Commission. . . .

The statute that provides the special rule for event contracts has a default position, that contracts referencing the enumerated events are allowed. . . .

The regulation is so unrelated to the statute, it cannot even be called its opposite. The regulation simply ignores the default rule and the requirement for the Commission to make a determination that an enumerated event contract is contrary to the public interest. Instead, the regulation adopts a per se rule that all enumerated event contracts are prohibited regardless of their utility or benefit. The regulation does not even offer any potential for an enumerated event contract to be allowed, regardless of any contrarian or even unanimous outside view as to their public

---

68. [N. 19] Congressional Record — Senate, S5906 (July 15, 2010).

utility or propriety. This is not only out of bounds from what the statute authorized, it is completely contrary to the statute's rule that even enumerated event contracts are by default allowed. . . .

The only explanation given in the adopting release for prohibiting all enumerated event contracts is, "Pursuant to Section 745(b) of the Dodd-Frank Act, the Commission proposed § 40.11(a)(1) to prohibit the listing of certain contracts involving terrorism, assassination, war, gaming, or activities that are unlawful under any State or Federal law."[69] . . .

The regulation clearly did not make a public interest determination, it made a prohibition through misstating a statutory declaration. Because of this misinterpretation, there is a complete absence of reasoning in Regulation 40.11 to support its declared prohibition. Why did the Commission propose and adopt a blanket rule? We don't know, because the regulation fails to say. . . .

[E]ven if, for arguments sake, the statute was constitutional, and the regulation valid, the Order . . . incorrectly placed the burden on ErisX to show that the contracts are in the public interest, failed to give ErisX its due process, arbitrarily defined gaming, and used insufficiently justified and arbitrarily selected tests to support its findings. . . .

The Order prohibited the ErisX NFL contracts in part because it found that the "record in this matter does not establish that the ErisX NFL event contracts have a hedging utility." This portion of the Order was a very deliberately and carefully worded hedge. The Order did not say that the ErisX NFL contracts do not have a hedging utility. Instead, it equivocated in the worst way; by shifting the burden, and the blame, to ErisX. This flips where the plain meaning of the statute places that burden. . . .

It is the Commission's burden to overcome the default presumption of statute — that all event contracts including the enumerated ones are in the public interest. . . . It is not the private sector's burden to prove in the negative. Yet, that is exactly what the Commission did in the Order: the Order contained no determination that the ErisX NFL contracts do not have a hedging utility, only a "finding" that ErisX hasn't successfully proved it. Yet, the Commission itself failed to meet any burden of proof in Regulation 40.11, and, instead of providing that proof here in the Order, the Commission shifted the burden to the exchange to disprove the Commission's previously unsubstantiated declaration. . . .

Even if the burden was upon the private petitioner to prove a contract was affirmatively in the public interest, and even if the economic purpose test was a Congressionally directed principle to determine the public interest, the Order's finding that "the record in this matter does not establish that the ErisX NFL event contracts have a hedging utility" is hard to reconcile with the only truly valid part of

---

69. [N. 29] Provisions Common to Registered Entities, 76 FR 44776, 44785 (July 27, 2011).

this process—the comment file. The Commission requested public comments and received twenty-five comment letters. At least thirteen of these commented that the NFL contracts have hedging utility, and many described how. ErisX's own submission substantively discussed this very point. If the Order actually declared that the contracts lack hedging utility, at least the Commission would have shown, cursorily, that it gave the comments enough consideration to disagree with them. However, the Order's hedge to blame the "record" for failing to establish a hedging utility ignored the comments completely. If the Commission truly did consider the comments, the Order gave no indication why they were summarily dismissed as insufficient to meet an unknown and undisclosed threshold of proof.

Similarly, and confusingly, the Order suggested that future submissions may "include new data" (data that ErisX or commenters assumingly failed to include) which could alter the Commission's view of enumerated event contracts. If this phrase was to be read seriously, then the Commission acknowledged that some type or kind of future data may prove that these contracts can be used for hedging purposes. Given the comment file's demonstration of this fact already, the Commission must have some standard of proof in mind, which it did not disclose, perhaps because it would be unattainable. If the Commission knew what kind of information or data could have changed its view, it should have more thoroughly sought such information through this process or it should have at least described what information could have been more persuasive. Otherwise, we are left with an arbitrary dismissal of current facts viewed as insufficient to an unknown provision of future facts. . . .

After concluding that the contracts fail the economic purpose test, the Order separately concluded that the ErisX NFL contracts are contrary to the public interest because they "could potentially promote sports gambling through the derivatives markets." . . . [T]he question of whether or not gambling should be promoted has nothing to do with the Commission's expertise or mandate. This is a question that should be answered by Congress, not by the Commission. . . .

In November 2020, KalshiEX LLC received designation as a contract market.[70] It allows for direct trading, with no intermediation of a broker (we discuss the role of intermediaries in chapter 6), in event contracts. These contracts are phrased as simple "yes" or "no" questions. For example, some of the trades are "Will US greenhouse gas emissions increase this year?" and "Will the Consumer Price Index increase this month?"[71]

---

70. CFTC, *In the Matter of the Application of KalshiEX LLC for Designation as a Contract Market*, https://www.cftc.gov/sites/default/files/filings/documents/2020/orgkexkalshidesignation201103.pdf (Nov. 3, 2020).

71. https://kalshi.com.

D. Derivatives Clearing Organizations

Designated contract markets are associated with clearing firms that clear trades on behalf of the markets. Whereas the designated contract market is where trades actually occur, the derivatives clearing organization, commonly known as the "DCO" or "clearinghouse" is the actual central counterparty for the two parties entering into the trade. In chapter 6, section A.1, we describe the operation of the market and the role of clearinghouses and in chapter 10, section B, we visit derivatives clearing organizations in the context of swaps.

Although derivatives clearing organizations have an essential role in the operation of the marketplace, they were not regulated separate and apart from their associated designated contract market until passage of the Commodity Futures Modernization Act of 2000. The Commodity Futures Modernization Act created a new registration category, derivatives clearing organizations.

Note in the below CFTC release accompanying a proposed rules framework for derivatives clearing organizations how, as with designated contract markets, derivatives clearing organizations are self-regulatory organizations governed by high-level "core principles."

CFTC, *A New Regulatory Framework for Clearing Organizations*

66 Fed. Reg. 24308-01 (May 14, 2001)

. . . Congress on December 15, 2000, passed, and the President on December 21, 2000, signed into law, the . . . [Commodity Future Modernization Act "CFMA"], which substantially amended the Commodity Exchange Act ("Act"). New Section 5b(a) of the Act, added by the CFMA, requires that contracts of sale of a commodity for future delivery, options on such contracts, and options on a commodity be cleared only by a derivatives clearing organization ("DCO") registered with the Commission. . . .

To be registered as a DCO, an applicant must demonstrate that it complies with fourteen[72] core principles set forth in the CFMA. . . .

If certain conditions were met, an organization would be deemed to be registered with the Commission as a DCO under part 39 . . . sixty days after receipt by the Commission of an application for registration, unless notified otherwise. This would include submission of the applicant's rules, a demonstration that the applicant satisfies the core principles of the Act, submission of any agreements with third parties that enable the applicant to meet one or more of the core principles, and descriptions of any system test procedures and results.

Appendix A to part 39 would provide guidance that applicants could use to meet the core principles. The CFMA provides that an applicant shall have reasonable

---

72. Now eighteen. *See* Commodity Exchange Act § 5b(c)(2).

discretion in establishing the manner in which it complies with the core principles. The guidance in proposed Appendix A is intended merely to illustrate the manner in which a clearing organization may meet a core principle and is not intended to be a mandatory checklist. . . .

An applicant may request that the Commission approve any of its rules . . . at the time it makes its initial application or thereafter.

New section 5b(d) of the Act provides that existing DCOs shall be deemed to be registered with the Commission to the extent that the DCO clears agreements, contracts, or transactions for a board of trade that has been designated by the Commission as a contract market for such agreements, contracts, or transactions prior to enactment of the CFMA. This provision captures all futures clearing organizations regulated by the Commission that have ever cleared any futures contracts for designated contract markets prior to December 21, 2000, the effective date of the CFMA. This language does not capture any organization approved to clear futures in connection with a pre-CFMA contract market designation which has not yet cleared any contracts. . . .

[Under] part 39, a DCO and the clearing of transactions on a DCO are exempt from all Commission regulations except for . . . certain select regulations relating to, for example, the segregation of customer funds and recordkeeping. To maintain registration as a DCO, part 39 would require DCOs to remain in compliance at all times with the core principles. . . .

[Part 39] . . . also contains an antifraud provision. This provision would be specifically limited to prohibit fraudulent actions by persons in or in connection with the clearing of transactions on a DCO. . . .

[Part 39] provides that a contract or transaction cleared pursuant to the rules of a DCO shall not be void, voidable, subject to rescission, or otherwise invalidated or rendered unenforceable as a result of a violation by the DCO. . . .

———————

These rules were finalized in substantially similar form in August 2001.[73]

E. Foreign Boards of Trade

We discuss cross-border issues in chapter 17. Of immediate relevance in the context of designated contract markets is the regulatory status of a foreign futures market that provides trading access to persons in the United States. Evaluated in light of the Commodity Exchange Act alone, such foreign futures market, which we will refer to as a "foreign board of trade," commonly known as an "FBOT" (pronounced,

———————

73. *See* CFTC, *A New Regulatory Framework for Clearing Organizations*, 66 Fed. Reg. 45604-02 (Aug. 29, 2001).

f-bot), would be required to register as a designated contract market. Instead of requiring registration, though, historically the CFTC staff provided no-action letters on an individual basis to foreign boards of trade wishing to offer access to persons in the United States.[74] A no-action letter, discussed in detail in chapter 4, section B.2.b, is a statement by the staff of a division of the CFTC that the staff will not recommend an enforcement action to the commission for a violation of the Commodity Exchange Act or CFTC regulations so long as the conduct is consistent with the terms of the no-action letter.

Though the staff's position is not binding on the commission, it is highly unlikely in such circumstances that the commission will not honor the position taken by the staff. A no-action letter is not precedential and theoretically may be relied upon only by those to whom it is directly addressed. In the case of the no-action letters provided to some foreign boards of trade offering access to persons in the United States, CFTC staff agreed not to require registration as a designated contract market provided that the foreign board of trade met specified criteria.

In 2011, dissatisfied with this piecemeal approach and with the Dodd-Frank Act providing a regulatory framework for the establishment of rules for the approval of foreign boards of trade, the CFTC revoked the various no-action letters and established formal registration requirements for foreign boards of trade wishing to provide access to persons in the United States.

CFTC, *Registration of Foreign Boards of Trade*
76 Fed. Reg. 80674 (Dec. 23, 2011)

. . . Section 738 of the Dodd-Frank Act amended CEA section 4(b) to provide that the Commission may adopt rules and regulations requiring FBOTs that wish to provide their members or other participants located in the United States with direct access to the FBOT's electronic trading and order matching system to register with the Commission. Direct access is defined in the statute as an explicit grant of authority by an FBOT to an identified member or other participant located in the U.S. to enter trades directly into the FBOT's trade matching system.[75] CEA section 4(b) also authorizes the Commission to promulgate rules and regulations prescribing procedures and requirements applicable to the registration of such FBOTs.

Accordingly, on November 19, 2010, the Commission published a notice of proposed rulemaking that set forth proposed regulations that would establish a registration requirement and related registration procedures and conditions applicable to FBOTs that wish to provide their members or other participants located in the United States with direct access to their electronic trading and order matching

---

74. Some also operated as exempt commercial markets, a now defunct category of CFTC registrant.

75. [N. 4] Direct access is defined in CEA section 4(b)(1)(A).

system (NPRM).... [T]he Commission has determined to issue these final rules which are substantially the same as those proposed...

Since 1996, FBOT requests to provide members and other participants that are located in the U.S. with direct access to their electronic trading and order matching systems have been addressed by Commission staff in accordance with the no-action process set forth in Commission regulation 140.99.[76] Specifically, such FBOTs seeking to provide direct access to members and participants located in the U.S. have requested, and, where appropriate, received from the relevant division of the Commission, a no-action letter in which division staff represents that, provided the FBOT satisfies the conditions set forth therein, the division will not recommend that the Commission institute enforcement action against the FBOT for failure to register as a designated contract market (DCM).... Since 1996, Commission staff has issued 24 direct access no-action relief letters (formerly referred to as foreign terminal no-action relief letters) to FBOTs, 20 of which remain active....

While the no-action process has served a useful purpose, the Commission, given the new authority provided by Congress in the Dodd-Frank Act to promulgate registration requirements applicable to FBOTs that provide direct access, has determined to replace the staff no-action process with generally applicable Commission regulations....

In determining to adopt formal registration rules for FBOTs, the Commission has also considered that the no-action process is generally better suited for discrete, unique factual circumstances and for situations where neither the CEA nor the Commission's regulations address the issue presented. The Commission has determined that, where the same type of relief is being granted on a regular and recurring basis, as it has been with respect to permitting FBOTs to provide direct access to their trading systems to specified members and other participants that are located in the U.S., it is no longer appropriate to handle requests for the relief through the no-action process. Rather, such matters should be addressed in generally applicable registration regulations.

By implementing uniform application procedures and registration requirements and conditions, the process by which FBOTs are permitted to provide members and other participants located in the United States with direct access to their trading systems will become more standardized and more transparent to both registration applicants and the general public and will promote fair and consistent treatment of all applicants. Further, generally applicable regulations will provide greater legal certainty for FBOTs providing direct access than the no-action relief process

---

76. [N. 6] *See, e.g.,* CFTC Letter No. 96-28 (February 29, 1996). Commission regulation 140.99 defines the term "no-action letter" as a written statement issued by the staff of a Division of the Commission or of the Office of the General Counsel that it will not recommend enforcement action to the Commission for failure to comply with a specific provision of the Act or of a Commission rule, regulation or order if a proposed transaction is completed or a proposed activity is conducted by the beneficiary.

because no-action letters are issued by the staff and are not binding on the Commission. The Commission also notes that an FBOT registration regime will be more consistent with the statutory authority pursuant to which other countries, including the United Kingdom, Australia, Singapore, Japan and Germany, among others, permit U.S.-based DCMs to provide direct access internationally.

Accordingly, for the reasons noted above and pursuant to the new authority provided by amended CEA section 4(b), the Commission has determined to adopt FBOT registration regulations. The final rules will replace the existing policy of accepting and reviewing requests for no-action relief to permit an FBOT to provide for direct access to its trading system with a requirement that an FBOT seeking to provide such access must apply for and be granted registration with the Commission. . . .

———————

Questions and Comments

1. What are the pros and cons of the Commodity Exchange Act's requirement that commodity futures be traded exclusively on designated contract markets?

2. Contrast "core principles" with the regulatory construct applicable in other fields, such as securities law. Do "core principles" provide more or less latitude to a regulator such as the CFTC? Do they make it easier or more difficult for an entity subject to regulation to identify legal requirements?

3. What conflicts might exist for a self-regulatory organization? What are some potential ways to mitigate conflicts?

4. In section A.2 there is a reference to the Dodd-Frank Act's removal of the exempt commercial market registration category. What are the benefits, if any, of a low regulation alternative to designated contract markets? If such an alternative existed again, should retail investors be able to access it? Which of the designated contract market "core principles" should apply?

5. As the court in *American Agricultural Movements, Inc.* noted, immunity from antitrust claims is likely available to a designated contract market acting with the CFTC's explicit approval.[77] Moreover, acting with the CFTC's informal approval is an indicium of good faith. Should the CFTC be more prescriptive? How much involvement by the CFTC is appropriate in this context?

6. Event contracts raise the question of the difference between hedging and speculation. Should all types of event contracts be permitted? If some should be permitted and some prohibited, why?

7. What might the public policy rationale be for permitting foreign boards of trade to offer access to persons in the United States (and, similarly, for non-U.S.

———————

77. *American Agricultural Movements, Inc. v. Board of Trade of City of Chicago*, 977 F.2d 1147 (7th Cir. 1992).

jurisdictions to allow designated contract markets in the United States to give their residents access)?

8. What are the comparative advantages and disadvantages in the context of foreign boards of trade of the CFTC issuing *ad hoc* no-action relief compared to a single rule applicable to all?

Chapter 6

Futures and Options Market Intermediaries

A. Background

In the previous chapter we examined the CFTC's direct regulation of the trading markets for commodity futures and options. In addition to regulating the trading markets, the CFTC requires the registration of intermediaries in these markets as either futures commission merchants, introducing brokers, or floor brokers.

Market intermediaries act on behalf of third party customers. Though at least some of their activities are on behalf of third party customers, market intermediaries can also trade on their own accounts for their own profits. This is known as proprietary trading. A continuing question is how best to address the possibility of conflicts of interest between an intermediary's customer and proprietary accounts.

Futures commission merchants, introducing brokers, and floor brokers are akin to what are, in the securities markets, broker-dealers. Before we examine these categories of CFTC registrant in detail, there are some preliminary items that need, at this point, to be fully addressed, some of which overlap with previous chapters.

1. Operation of the Marketplace

The designated contract markets we discussed in chapter 5 have members. These members are bound to follow the rules of the designated contract market and accept the jurisdiction of the designated contract market as a self-regulatory organization with the ability to monitor and enforce rules. In return, members have the privilege to place trades directly on the designated contract market.

Trades on designated contract markets are "cleared," which means that a central counterparty, known as a clearinghouse, agrees to be the counterparty to each of the parties who initially agreed to the trade. In other words, instead of facing each other for performance of the agreed upon trade, each party faces the central clearinghouse. These clearinghouses are required to register with the CFTC as derivatives clearing organizations.

Some members of designated contract markets are also members of the associated clearinghouse. These members are required to post initial and variation margin to collateralize positions with the clearinghouse. If a member of a designated contract market or derivatives clearing organization is trading on its own behalf, it is considered a trader in the marketplace. It is subject to the market manipulation prohibitions and position limits we discuss in chapter 15. However, there is no CFTC registration obligation unless it is physically trading on the floor of the exchange, in which case it would be required to register as a floor trader.

CFTC (and as we will see, National Futures Association) registration obligations are triggered when a party acts as an intermediary. For example, a party will be required to register as an intermediary if the party provides a non-member of a designated contract market or derivatives clearing organization access to a designated contract market or derivatives clearing organization. This most commonly arises with retail traders who have no direct access to the market. It is also a common occurrence that a professional trader is a member of a designated contract market and not a member of the associated derivatives clearing organization and, therefore, needs an intermediary so that its trades can clear on the clearinghouse. The criteria to receive trading privileges as a member of a designated contract market are less strict than the criteria for clearing membership of a derivatives clearing organization.

There are three categories of intermediaries we examine in this chapter: futures commission merchants, introducing brokers, and floor brokers. It is typical for a futures commission merchant or introducing broker to be simultaneously a member of one or more exchange, and subject to each exchange's self-regulatory authority, while also being a member of the National Futures Association and subject to its self-regulatory authority.

To avoid duplication of requirements in such cases, the two or more self-regulatory organizations can agree that one of them will be the "designated self-regulatory organization" (sometimes known as "DSRO") with primary self-regulatory responsibility over the member.[1]

2. Role of the National Futures Association

The Commodity Futures Trading Commission Act of 1974, in addition to providing for the creation of the CFTC, provided a framework for the formation of industrywide "registered futures associations" that would operate as self-regulatory organizations for members of the futures industry. However, no such registered futures association for the futures industry was formed until the passage of the Futures Trading Act of 1978 granted the CFTC the authority to require registrants to be members of a registered futures association. The only registered futures association, the National Futures Association — commonly known as the "NFA" — was designated a registered futures association in 1981 and began operations in 1982.[2]

---

1. 17 C.F.R. § 1.52(d). A retail foreign exchange dealer is also eligible for this. 17 C.F.R. § 1.52(d)(1).
2. https://www.nfa.futures.org/about/nfa-history.html.

The CFTC has used the authority granted by the Futures Trading Act of 1978 to require that, in addition to registering with the CFTC, futures commission merchants and introducing brokers be members of a "registered futures organization."[3] Since, as noted above, there is only one such organization, the National Futures Association, they must by default become National Futures Association members. Floor brokers are not required to be a member of a registered futures organization. However, they receive similar oversight from the exchanges to which they are associated as floor brokers since each futures exchange is a self-regulatory organization. Commodity pool operators and most commodity trading advisors, discussed in chapters 7 and 8, swap dealers and major swap participants, both discussed in chapter 11, and retail foreign exchange dealers and leverage transaction merchants, both discussed in chapter 14, must also be members of a registered futures association, by default the National Futures Association.[4]

We saw in chapter 5, sections C.1 and 2 and D that, when performing a legal analysis with respect to designated contract markets, we must look at the intersection of the Commodity Exchange Act, CFTC rules, and the rules of the relevant designated contract market and derivatives clearing organization. Similarly, for futures and options market intermediaries, it is necessary to look to the Commodity Exchange Act, CFTC rules, National Futures Association rules, and, in some cases, the rules of the designated contract market and derivatives clearing organization.

Although the National Futures Association has the authority to promulgate rules binding on its members,[5] in some instances the CTFC reserves the right to abrogate a rule,[6] require the National Futures Association to change an existing rule, or require the National Futures Association to implement a new rule.[7]

The sanctions the National Futures Association can impose for a rule violation can be stiff. They range from suspension or even expulsion from membership to a monetary fine of up to $500,000 per violation.[8] Since many categories of CFTC registrant are required to be National Futures Association members, expulsion could mean the end of a business enterprise or, if an individual, a career and means of financial sustenance.

The CFTC has delegated the processing of registration applications to the National Futures Association with respect to futures commission merchants,

---

3. 17 C.F.R. §§ 170.15 and 170.17. There is an exception for futures commission merchants registered as securities broker-dealers and whose only futures activity is securities futures. 17 C.F.R. § 170.15(b).

4. 17 C.F.R. §§ 5.22, 31.27, 170.16, and 170.17.

5. 17 C.F.R. § 21(p).

6. 17 C.F.R. § 21(k)(1).

7. 17 C.F.R. §§ 21(j) and 21(k)(2).

8. National Futures Association Rule 3-14(a).

introducing brokers, floor brokers, and floor traders; retail foreign exchange dealers, and leverage transaction merchants (both discussed in chapter 14); commodity pool operators and commodity trading advisors (discussed in chapters 7 and 8); and swap dealers and major swap participants (both discussed in chapter 11).[9]

3. Associated Persons and Principals

a. Function of Associated Persons

In this chapter, we will be examining futures commission merchants, introducing brokers and floor brokers. In chapters 7 and 8, we will examine commodity pool operators and commodity trading advisors; in chapter 11, swap dealers and major swap participants; and chapter 14, retail foreign exchange dealers and leverage transaction merchants. All of these are categories of market participants that require registration with the CFTC and, except for floor brokers (which have to be registered with the designated contract market at which they are engaged in floor brokerage activities) and, in rare circumstances, commodity trading advisors, membership of the National Futures Association.[10]

Additionally, other than with respect to floor brokers, each of their "associated persons" have registration obligations.[11] An associated person is, in essence, a natural person, such as a partner, officer, or employee, whose function involves soliciting customer orders, funds, property, or discretionary account management, or supervising anyone in such role.[12] Associated persons are subject to oversight, fingerprinting, background checks, and can be "statutorily disqualified" from eligibility for registration as an associated person if, among others, the applicant has committed certain criminal offenses, been denied as an applicant in the preceding five years, or been previously suspended by the CFTC or National Futures Association.[13] Competency examinations or, for associated persons of swaps dealers, swaps proficiency requirements, are required by the National Futures Association.[14] Just as the principals with which they are associated, associated persons are subject to the rules

---

9. 17 C.F.R. §§ 3.2, 3.10, and 3.11.

10. The circumstances in which a commodity trading advisor is not required to be a member of the National Futures Association is if it is voluntarily registered with the CFTC and, nonetheless, is eligible for an exemption because it does not direct accounts or provide tailored advice. *See* 17 C.F.R. §§ 170.17 and 4.14(a)(9).

11. 17 C.F.R. § 3.12. In the case of swap dealers and major swap participants, the associated persons technically do not need to register with the CFTC or National Futures Association. However, the swap dealer or major swap participant, as applicable, is responsible for vetting its associated persons to make sure they are not subject to a "statutory disqualification." *See* Commodity Exchange Act § 4s(b)(6) and 17 C.F.R. § 23.22(b).

12. 17 C.F.R. § 1.3 (definition of associated person).

13. Commodity Exchange Act §§ 8a(2) and (3).

14. *See* http://www.nfa.futures.org/NFA-registration/proficiency-requirements.HTML.

and discipline of the National Futures Association or other CFTC self-regulatory organization with which their employer is associated.

b. Disqualification as an Associated Person

In some circumstances, individuals are disqualified by statute from being associated persons or CFTC registrants via CFTC notice and without a hearing. For example, a person who: (1) is currently suspended from registration, had a CFTC registration revoked, or is subject to a CFTC order suspending or barring registration with a designated contract market or other CFTC-regulated self-regulatory organization or membership of the National Futures Association; (2) was refused, within five years beforehand, registration as an associated person by the CFTC; (3) is enjoined by a court or regulatory order from acting in any registered capacity with the CFTC or the SEC; (4) has been convicted, within ten years beforehand, of a variety of felonies involving the derivatives or securities businesses or involving embezzlement, fraud, theft, bribery or misappropriation of funds; (5) has violated or aided and abetted violation, as reflected in the results of a proceeding or a settlement, within ten years beforehand, a provision of the Commodity Exchange Act or various other statutes where such violation involves embezzlement, fraud, theft, bribery or misappropriation of funds; or (6) has made a materially false statement or omission on these matters in an application or update to an application.[15] With respect to item (5) in the above list and settlements generally, the CFTC has clarified via interpretative statement that it will not exercise its authority if a party has entered into an agreement or settlement that specifically restricts the use of the order or findings in subsequent collateral proceedings.[16] The reason is because the CFTC does not wish to impede the common practice of negotiating settlements for CFTC rule violations that state that the settlement "will not form the sole basis for the denial, suspension or revocation of such person's registration with the Commission."[17]

Without providing a hearing, the CFTC has the authority to refuse, suspend, or revoke a registration on the bases described above. With a hearing, the CFTC has broad authority to refuse, suspend, or revoke the registration of a person for a much broader variety of wrongdoings. These include: (1) felony convictions generally; (2) misdemeanor convictions involving the derivatives or securities businesses or involving embezzlement, fraud, theft, bribery or misappropriation of funds; (3) violating, or aiding and abetting violation of, a CFTC rule or order or a securities law or Foreign Corrupt Practices Act rule or order; (4) a failure to supervise a person committing a violation of the Commodity Exchange Act or CFTC rule; and (5) "other good cause."[18] Although the below case was decided before the current incarnation

---

15. Commodity Exchange Act § 8a(2). *See also* 17 C.F.R. § 3.60.
16. 17 C.F.R. Pt. 3, App. A.
17. *Id.*
18. Commodity Exchange Act § 8a(3). *See also* 17 C.F.R. § 3.60.

of the standards for disqualification, it demonstrates the deference granted to the CFTC's actions in refusing, suspending, or revoking a registration.

Silverman v. CFTC

562 F.2d 432 (7th Cir. 1977)

CUMMINGS, Circuit Judge.

Petitioner Jeffrey L. Silverman is an account executive employed by a commodity futures commission merchant in Chicago, Illinois. Petitioner presently appeals from the revocation of his registration as an "associated person" licensed to do business on commodity futures markets pursuant to the regulatory authority of the Commodity Futures Trading Commission (Commission) as empowered by the Commodity Futures Trading Commission Act of 1974. . . .

On February 16, 1977, in Silverman v. Commodity Futures Trading Commission, 549 F.2d 28 (7th Cir. 1977), this Court affirmed a two-year suspension of petitioner's trading privileges on commodity futures markets as a result of certain unauthorized and fraudulent trades on behalf of five customers' accounts in 1970 and 1971.[19] The nature of petitioner's improvident trades was the subject matter of a disciplinary petition dated March 13, 1973. . . . At issue there was Silverman's allegedly fraudulent placement of 23 futures transactions in eggs, hogs, and pork bellies, with respect to five customers' accounts during September and October 1970 and in March 1972. . . . [W]e fully concurred in the Commission's finding that petitioner had wilfully violated the anti-fraud provision of the [Commodity Exchange Act] . . . and held that the suspension of his trading privileges was justified by the record. . . .

[P]etitioner on March 31, 1975, applied for registration as an "associated person" with the Commission. . . . The completed application form . . . [disclosed] that Silverman was currently involved in administrative proceedings before the Commission. . . . Nonetheless, on July 18, 1975, the Commission granted petitioner's application for registration as an "associated person." . . . Thereafter, on February 28, 1977, during the pendency of this controversy, petitioner's registration was renewed for another two years as a matter of course. . . .

Events subsequent thereto before the Commission have resulted in petitioner's revocation of registration as an "associated person," in accordance with the Commission's regulatory authority as an independent federal agency entrusted with the safeguarding of the nation's commodity futures industry. The revocation of registration[20] was to be effective 15 days from the date of the Commission's final order of

---

19. [N. 1] The two-year suspension of trading privileges went into effect on May 25, 1976, and would, therefore, continue in full force until May 25, 1978. The record does not disclose nor do the parties make mention in their briefs of any stay of enforcement of the sanction.

20. [N. 4] Even though petitioner is precluded by virtue of the suspension of trading privileges order from trading on his own account or for the account of any other person for two years, as an

March 14, 1977, which would have been March 29, 1977. However, due to the serious effect of this unreviewed sanction, this Court on March 29, 1977, granted Silverman's emergency motion to stay enforcement of the Commission's order pending our decision in this matter and ordered that the appeal be expedited. This appeal arises on a petition to review the revocation of petitioner's registration. . . .

On October 23, 1974, Congress enacted the Commodity Futures Trading Commission Act of 1974 which extensively amended the Commodity Exchange Act of 1936, its predecessor. The legislative aim of the 1974 Act was to further the purpose of the previous Act in "ensuring fair practice and honest dealing on the commodity exchanges and providing a measure of control over those forms of speculative activity which often demoralizes the markets to the injury of producers, and consumers, and the exchanges themselves." See Senate Report No. 93-1131, 93rd Cong., 2nd Sess. (1974), reported in 3 U.S.Code Cong. & Admin.News (1974), pp. 5843, 5856.

An integral part of the 1974 Act was the creation of a new independent fedcral regulatory agency to be known as the Commodity Futures Trading Commission. . . .

The 1974 Act also added a new category known as the "associated person" to the list of those persons required to be registered with the Commission in order to conduct business.

In relevant part, 7 U.S.C.A. Sup. s 6k regulates an "associated person" as follows:

"(1) It shall be unlawful for any person to be associated with any futures commission merchant . . . as a partner, officer, or employee . . . in any capacity which involves (i) the solicitation or acceptance of customer's orders . . . or (ii) the supervision of any person or persons so engaged, unless such person shall have registered . . . with the Commission." . . .

Critical to the present controversy is the Commission's discretionary power to revoke the registration of an "associated person." . . . [T]he Commission may upon reasonable belief of wrongdoing serve an "associated person" with a complaint and order to show cause why his registration should not be suspended or revoked. . . .

On May 27, 1976, an order to show cause was issued by the Commission. . . . Therein petitioner was ordered to appear before an Administrative Law Judge (ALJ) . . . for the purpose of attending a public hearing to determine whether Silverman's registration as an "associated person" should be revoked.

The order to show cause, inter alia, contained the following allegations:

"A. Jeffrey L. Silverman willfully violated Section 4b of the Act (7 U.S.C. s 6b) in that, while employed as a solicitor and account executive for two registered futures commission merchants in 1970 and 1972, Jeffrey L. Silverman cheated and defrauded five customers of such registered futures

---

"associated person" registered with the Commission, he could, nevertheless, solicit or accept customers' orders and supervise others so engaged unless his registration was revoked.

commission merchants by executing trades for the accounts of such customers without their knowledge, consent or prior authorization.

"B. On May 5, 1976, the Commission issued a Final Order, in CFTC Docket No. 75-6, prohibiting Jeffrey L. Silverman from trading on or subject to the rules of any contract market for a period of two years and ordering that all contract markets should refuse him all trading privileges during said period. It was further ordered that Jeffrey L. Silverman permanently cease and desist from placing, or causing to be placed, in any customer's account, any contracts of sale of any commodity for future delivery, without the prior knowledge, consent or authorization of such customer or otherwise to cheat or defraud, or attempt to cheat or defraud, any person in connection with any order to make, or the making of, any contract of sale of any commodity for future delivery on or subject to the rules of any contract market for, or on behalf of, any person.

"C. By reason of the willful violations of the Act as alleged in paragraph A above and the sanctions imposed as described in paragraph B above, the registration of Jeffrey L. Silverman as an associated person as described in Section 4k of the Act (7 U.S.C. s 6k) should be revoked." . . .

On June 24, 1976, the hearing was commenced in this case before an ALJ. . . . The cause was prosecuted by the Commission's Department of Enforcement (DE). . . .

At the conclusion of the DE's case, petitioner moved for a directed verdict on the grounds that the Commission had failed to meet its "high" burden of proof as to his unfitness and that the official documents previously introduced into evidence were insufficient to satisfy this burden. Petitioner argued that "the Government must actually show that a licensee is truly unfit, that he is morally degenerate, that he cannot be trusted with customer's funds, that he is thoroughly a bad guy and does not deserve to act in the industry or earn his livelihood to support his family in and around the commodities markets." . . .

Thereafter petitioner presented his defense of mitigation and rehabilitation. The evidence consisted entirely of testimony garnered from 15 witnesses personally acquainted with him. All of the witnesses, with the exception of one, were intimately involved with the commodity futures markets and in varying professional capacities had dealt with petitioner.

Fairly summarized, the evidence consisted of testimony as to their opinion of petitioner's honesty and integrity since the filing of the March 13, 1972, complaint (CFTC Docket No. 75-6); testimony as to his expertise as an associated person in the commodities markets; and the probable financial, as well as personal, consequences the revocation of registration would have on his career. To a limited extent the witnesses were cross-examined by the DE.

On August 24, 1976, the ALJ entered an initial decision in this matter concluding that the evidence did not warrant revocation of petitioner's registration and ordering the proceeding dismissed. . . .

On August 27, 1976, the DE filed a timely notice of appeal with the Commission seeking review of the ALJ's adverse ruling. . . . [T]he five-member Commission unanimously reversed the ALJ and ordered petitioner's registration revoked, stating:

"(W)e have carefully reviewed respondent's (Silverman's) evidence of extenuation and rehabilitation, but conclude that it is insufficient in view of the serious nature of his violations. While revocation is a severe sanction the public cannot be adequately protected, or the requisite deterrent effects achieved, if a person who has intentionally cheated and defrauded customers . . . is allowed to continue to handle customer accounts or to supervise others so engaged." (Final Opinion and Order, CFTC Docket No. 76-18, R. 231.)

The Commission accordingly ordered petitioner's registration revoked effective fifteen days hence. . . .

[It is] clear to us that the Commission has been entrusted by Congress with the special mission of enforcing fair practice and honest dealing on the commodity futures markets. As was made clear in Savage v. Commodity Futures Trading Commission, 548 F.2d 192, 197 (7th Cir. 1977):

". . . we must be mindful of a Congressional purpose, clearly evidenced at least since 1933, to protect the American investing and speculating public not only from fraud and fraudulent practices, but from those whose past actions indicate that they might be tempted to engage in such practices. . . . Congress cannot specify licensing requirements for each particular applicant but, of necessity, must within reason adopt somewhat general standards and authorize some agency to apply them." (Citations and footnote omitted).

Contrary to petitioner's arguments, the DE did not have to shoulder a special burden of proof here and need only have established a prima facie case in order for the Commission to revoke petitioner's registration. . . . [O]nce the DE proved Silverman's willful violation of the anti-fraud provisions of Section 4b of the 1936 Act (7 U.S.C. s 6b), it became his burden to go forward to persuade the Commission to exercise its discretion to permit his continued registration.

The Commission's final opinion in this matter articulated a rational connection between the petitioner's willful violations of Section 4b of the 1936 Act . . . and its considered choice to revoke his registration. . . . As the Commission explained, otherwise the public could not be adequately protected and deterrent effects would not be achieved. The Commission also exercised its expert discretion by balancing the evidence of extenuation and rehabilitation against the seriousness of the offense and the need to insure the highest fiduciary standards for persons registered under the 1974 Act. . . .

Petitioner was unable to convince the Commission that he presents no further danger to the investing public. . . . While there is a surface inconsistency between the suspension imposed in the prior proceeding and the revocation imposed here, Commission counsel has pointed out that Congress had not required registration of associated persons nor provided for revocation of such registration at the time of the 1973 disciplinary proceeding.

The revocation of petitioner's registration was a permissible administrative sanction addressed to the sound discretion of the Commission. Congress invested the Commission with revocation power to safeguard the public interest in the well being of the nation's commodity futures markets. Petitioner may reapply for registration at any time. On this record, we cannot say that the penalty imposed was an abuse of discretion.

The Commission's order is affirmed.

———

A more recent case affirms that, even with a presidential pardon for conduct underlying a registration revocation, the CFTC's authority to disqualify a person from registration in broad. That case, *Hirschberg v. CFTC*,[21] involved a floor broker, not an associated person. Its findings should apply *mutatis mutandis* to an associated person. It is discussed below in section D.

c. Principals

In addition to associated persons, principals are required to be identified to the CFTC and any applicable self-regulatory organization. They are generally subject to the same fingerprinting and background checks as associated persons, even though they are not registered with the CFTC. In effect, they are subject to the same disqualification standards as associated persons because they do need to be approved by the National Futures Association. Their functions differ from that of associated persons. Instead of being in a solicitation or similar role, as is the case for associated persons, principals are in a managerial, control, or ownership role. For example, a futures commission merchant's president, chief executive officer, chief financial officer, chief operating officer, chief compliance officer, anyone in charge of a business unit, and owners owning ten percent or more of voting shares are all among those principals required to be registered.[22]

B. Futures Commission Merchants

1. Generally

a. Role in Futures Trading

Futures Commission Merchants, commonly known as "FCMs," are central to the architecture of futures trading. To trade on a futures exchange, a party needs to be able to place a trade on the designated contract market and then to have the trade cleared by the associated derivatives clearing organization. A party has the right to

---

21. 414 F.3d 679 (7th Cir. 2005).
22. 17 C.F.R. § 3.1(a).

do both by being a member of the designated contract market and the associated derivatives clearing organization.

Oftentimes, the party wishing to trade is not a member of the designated contract market and associated derivatives clearing organization. In such circumstances, an affiliate who is a member can provide access.

Most commonly, though, a third party provides access. That third party will fall into either of two of the three registration categories that are the subject of this chapter, i.e., futures commission merchant or introducing broker. As we will see, either a futures commission merchant or an introducing broker can provide a trader access to the designated contract market. *Only* a futures commission merchant can provide a trader access to the derivatives clearing organization — though, sometimes, an introducing broker will intermediate between the trader and the futures commission merchant.

The futures commission merchant agrees to take economic and legal responsibility with the designated contract market or derivatives clearing organization for its customer's trades. To ensure its customer's ability to perform, it holds its customer's initial margin, an amount specified as a minimum by the designated contract market for each futures contract, and variation margin, an amount largely reflecting the positive or negative value of the contract. Holding customer margin in association with a futures or options trade is primarily what requires registration with the CFTC as a futures commission merchant.

b. Example

Suppose that Manhattan Poultry Feed Corporation produces poultry feed from, among other ingredients, corn. It expects to need, in a year's time, fifty thousand bushels of corn. Each corn contract on the Chicago Board of Trade, a designated contract market, is for five thousand bushels of corn. Therefore, it wishes to buy ten such contracts for delivery in a year. How exactly does it go about doing that?

If its management shows up at the Chicago Board of Trade in person, they will be turned away by security. Instead, the Manhattan Poultry Feed Corporation will need to establish an account, including a customer agreement, with a Chicago Board of Trade member.

Provided there is sufficient margin in its account, the Manhattan Poultry Feed Corporation will be able to place the corn futures trade on the Chicago Board of Trade. The member will either: (1) enter a bid or accept an offer for ten corn contracts on the Chicago Board of Trade on behalf of the Manhattan Poultry Feed Corporation; or (2) as is more common today, provide the Manhattan Poultry Feed Corporation electronic access to the current bids and offers on the designated contract market so that the Manhattan Poultry Feed Corporation can make bids and accept offers on its own.

If the member, in addition to being a member of the Chicago Board of Trade, is a clearing member of its associated derivatives clearing organization, it can also provide clearing services to the Manhattan Poultry Feed Corporation. To do so, it must, of course, be registered with the CFTC as a futures commission merchant. If it is not a clearing member, it will ordinarily have a relationship with a futures commission merchant that is a clearing member. In such a case, it could be registered as a futures commission merchant or as an introducing broker, discussed in section C below.

The trades will be cleared by CME Clearing (a division of Chicago Mercantile Exchange, Inc.[23]), and the clearing member must post collateral to CME Clearing for all of its exposures, including the positions cleared on behalf of the Manhattan Poultry Feed Corporation.

The minimum initial margin that the Manhattan Poultry Feed Corporation must post for the corn contract is established by the Chicago Board of Trade and normally remains the same through the life of the trade. Over time, the amount of variation margin required will fluctuate as the market price of the corn contracts purchased by the Manhattan Poultry Feed Corporation changes.

In figure 6.1 next page, the Manhattan Poultry Feed Corporation is in the role of one of the customers, able to access the designated contract market through a futures commission merchant who is a member of the designated contract market and the derivatives clearing organization.

c. The Business of Futures Commission Merchants

Futures commission merchants obtain income by charging trade commissions, reinvesting customers' margin, and through proprietary trading in "house" accounts, i.e., making speculative trades or investments with its own money.

Regarding commissions, the most entertaining explanation is found in the movie *Trading Places* (1983), where Eddie Murphy's character Billy Ray offers the following analysis to the movie's antagonists, Mortimer and Randolph Duke, principles of Duke & Duke,[24] as they seek to explain the role of commodities brokers:

> Randolph Duke: . . . Now, some of our clients are speculating that the price of gold will rise in the future. And we have other clients who are speculating that the price of gold will fall. They place their orders with us, and we buy or sell their gold for them.
>
> Mortimer Duke: Tell him the good part.
>
> Randolph Duke: The good part, William, is that, no matter whether our clients make money or lose money, Duke & Duke get the commissions.

---

23. CME Clearing has provided clearing services for the Chicago Board of Trade since 2003. In 2007, the Chicago Board of Trade and the Chicago Mercantile Exchange, which operated CME Clearing, merged to form the CME Group Inc. *See* CME Group, *Timeline of CME Achievements*, http://www.cmegroup.com/company/history/timeline-of-achievements.html.

24. In the context of the movie, it is not clear whether Duke & Duke is a futures commission merchant or an introducing broker, discussed in section C below. In either case, they do have floor brokers. We discuss floor brokers in section D below.

Figure 6.1 Trading Futures with a Futures Commission Merchant as Intermediary

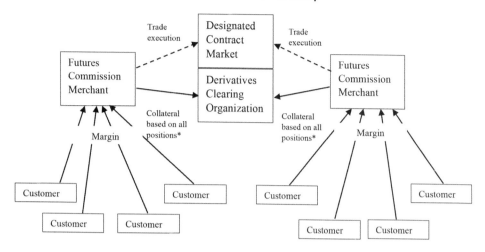

* Customer and proprietary

Mortimer Duke: Well? What do you think . . . ?

Billy Ray: Sounds to me like you guys a couple of bookies.[25]

The reinvestment of customer margin has been controversial in recent years due to the failure of MF Global, discussed below in subsection 3. Although in *MF Global*, customer margin was not directly invested in risky investments, it was effectively exposed to them. As a result, what appeared to be a shortfall in customer accounts occurred. As we will see, in reaction to this event, the CFTC has adjusted what investments a futures commission merchant can make with customer margin. However, that a futures commission merchant is entitled to reinvest customer funds at its own risk for its own benefit is discussed in the following case.

Marchese v. Shearson Hayden Stone, Inc.

644 F. Supp. 1381 (C.D. Cal. 1986)

Wm. Matthew Byrne, Jr., District Judge.

Plaintiff, Dominic Marchese, filed this action against Shearson Hayden Stone, Inc. (Shearson), a securities broker and futures commission merchant, seeking a declaratory judgment that "interest and increment" on margin funds maintained pursuant to . . . the Commodities [*sic*] Exchange Act (CEA) may not be retained by Shearson in excess of its lawful commission. The action is brought on behalf of a class consisting of all persons, who, within the relevant limitations period, gave money, securities, or property to Shearson to margin, guarantee or secure trades or contracts. . . .

---

25. *Trading Places*, Motion Picture (Paramount Pictures 1983).

The central issue presented by this motion is whether under section 4d of the CEA and its attendant regulations the interest and increment earned on margin funds is the property of the futures commission merchant. This Court finds that the futures commission merchant is entitled to retain all interest and increment on margin funds, and the motion to dismiss is granted. . . .

Investors enter into contracts of purchase or sale of commodities for future delivery as a means of speculating on the price changes in various commodities. The investors do not ordinarily anticipate taking delivery of the commodity, rather, they seek to enter into "offsetting" contracts prior to the delivery date, liquidate their obligations, and reap a profit should the market price move favorably. H.R. Rep. No. 93-975, 93rd Cong., 2d Sess. 1, 149, *reprinted in* 1974 U.S. Code Cong. & Ad. News 5843 (House Report) (only 3% of all futures contracts culminate in delivery). . . .

Futures trading occurs on exchanges designated as contract markets by the Commodities [*sic*] Futures Trading Commission (CFTC). Generally, an investor makes his futures trades through a Futures Commodities [*sic*] Merchant (FCM), who may be viewed as the commodities counterpart to a securities broker. In addition to the FCM's role in the exchange, each contract market has an affiliated clearing organization which is substituted as the buyer to every seller, and as the seller to every buyer. This substitution occurs at the end of each trading day; thereafter the contracting parties are obligated only to the clearing organization.

An investor must deposit a specified amount of money with the FCM when he enters into a futures transaction. This deposit, called "initial margin money" or "original margin" insures that the contract will be performed. The FCM, in turn, is required to deposit margin with the clearing organization to secure the investor's futures position.

Contract markets determine the minimum initial margin which must be deposited by the investor, as well as what form the margin may take (cash, Treasury bills or securities). The margin not only varies with each contract market, but with the underlying commodity itself. As the price of the futures contracts fluctuate, the investor may be required to make adjustments to the margin account. If the price moves adversely to the investor's position, his margin will be viewed as declining, and he will be required to deposit additional funds. This "margin call" is necessary to restore the margin account to the initial margin level. On the other hand, if the price moves favorably, the investor may be permitted to withdraw funds from the margin account. . . .

Prior to 1936, brokers commingled customer monies with their own, used customer monies as part of their own working capital, lent customer deposits to other customers, and used customer monies for their own speculative purposes. Similarly, banks holding customer funds commingled and used these funds as their own. And, in the event of the bankruptcy of a broker or bank, the customers ranked only as general creditors, and suffered considerable losses.

Congress responded by enacting the Commodities [*sic*] Exchange Act. . . . Significant among the new requirements was . . . that FCMs treat funds and property received by them "to margin, guarantee, or secure" trades or contracts or accruing "as the result of such trades or contracts" as belonging to the customer [and] . . . that customer funds and property be separately accounted for; FCMs were prohibited from commingling customer funds with their own funds, or using customer funds to margin the trades of other customers. . . . [The CEA] authorized FCMs to continue investing customer monies, but carefully circumscribed the class of permissible investments. . . .

The statutory language does not express any intention by Congress that interest and increment gained on margin funds is the property of the customer. In fact, if any inference can be drawn from the text, it is that Congress intended that such interest and increment need not be treated as belonging to the customer. By its terms . . . [the CEA] provides that only two categories of funds, securities or property, be treated as belonging to the customer — those received by the FCM to margin, guarantee or secure trades or contracts, and those accruing to such customer as a result of trades or contracts. . . . [The CEA] specifically allows FCM's to invest margin funds in certain securities. If Congress intended that income gained as a result of the FCM's investment of the margin was to be treated as belonging to the customer, it could have included this. . . .

While Congress has been silent or ambiguous in its statutory language on this issue, the regulatory body charged with implementing the statute has expressed itself clearly. Regulations 1.25 through 1.29, originally promulgated in 1937, deal specifically with the investment of customer funds, and the rights to resulting increment and interest.[26] Regulation 1.25 sets out those investments permitted . . . and requires that such investments be made through customer accounts, and that proceeds from the sale of the obligations be redeposited in such accounts. Regulation 1.29 specifically allows the FCM to retain the increment or interest resulting from investment of customer funds. . . .

Prior to the enactment of the CEA . . . futures commission merchants commingled customer funds with their own funds and used customer funds for their own business purposes. As a result, when commission firms went bankrupt customer funds were lost.[27] The House version . . . attacked these abuses by prohibiting any

---

26. [N. 13] Regulations 1.25–1.29, 2 Fed. Reg. 1223–28 (1937), currently, 17 C.F.R. sections 1.25–1.29 (1984).

27. [N. 17] During the Senate debate . . . Senator Pope summarized the problem. He stated that customer margin deposits: "[h]ave been intermingled with the funds of these futures commission merchants, and have been used by them in the conduct of their own business. They have not been held intact for the benefit of the traders. It further appears that certain favored dealers have not been required actually to put up the money for margins, and have been extended credit in that respect. This gives these favored dealers an advantage. In some instances, large commission firms have become bankrupt and the funds placed with them by a large number of dealers were lost." 80 Cong. Rec. S6162 (1936).

investment of customer funds by the FCM. This blanket prohibition was rejected by the Senate, which felt that FCMs should be able to invest customer funds in trustworthy securities. The Senate therefore introduced an amendment . . . which would allow FCMs to use margin funds for certain investments. The amendment accommodated the twin aims of the section, "to protect properly the margin of the customers and to provide some limitation under which the commission men may use that money to invest." 80 Cong. Rec. S7911 (1936) (Remarks of Senator Norris). The House later approved the bill as amended, and it was signed into law as the Commodity Exchange Act. Ch. 545, 49 Stat. 1491 (1936).

This legislative history illustrates that Congress could have completely prohibited FCMs from investing customer funds. Instead, it chose to curb the previous abuses by limiting the category of permissible investments, thereby allowing merchants to continue benefitting from the use of customer funds. The inference that Congress intended the FCMs to profit from investment of customer margin is strengthened by the fact that the FCMs are given discretion as to whether they will make such investments. FCMs would have little incentive to exercise their discretion to invest margin funds if they were unable to retain the interest and increment.[28] . . .

Congress intended that futures commission merchants be entitled to retain any and all interest on their investment of customer margin funds. The motion to dismiss is granted.

Shrinking Industry?

The number of registered futures commission merchants has been in significant decline. Whereas, in 2008 there were 154,[a] by March 2021 there were only 63.[b] Whatever this trend indicates, it does not correlate with a decline in the volume of futures transactions. In approximately the same period, the volume of futures and options contracts traded on North American exchanges increased from 7 billion[c] to 10.27 billion.[d]

[a] CFTC, *Selected FCM Financial Data as of December 31, 2007*, http://www.cftc.gov/files/tm/fcm/fcmdata1207.pdf.

[b] CFTC, *Selected FCM Financial Data as of March 31, 2021*, https://www.cftc.gov/sites/default/files/2021-03/01-%20FCM%20Webpage%20Update%20-%20March%202021.pdf.

[c] Galen Burghardt and Will Acworth, Futures Industry Association, *Annual Survey 2008*, https://www.fia.org/sites/default/files/2019-05/March-Volume.pdf.

[d] Will Acworth, Futures Industry Association, *2019 Market Data — Derivatives Volume Grows BRIC by BRIC*, https://www.fia.org/marketvoice/articles/2019-market-data-derivatives-volume-grows-bric-bric (Mar. 3, 2020).

---

28. [N. 21] This is particularly true in light of the regulatory history of the section. The FCM must put his own funds in the customer account if the value of the investment declines. The FCM would have little reason to take this risk without the prospect of realizing a profit on the investment.

2. Regulatory Requirements

a. Generally

Futures commission merchants are subject to at least two overlapping regulatory regimes. The first is the CFTC's regulations. The second are the rules resulting from membership in the National Futures Association. There are also frequently rules imposed by self-regulatory organizations, such as designated contracts markets, of which a futures commission merchant might be a member.

Many futures commission merchants are "dually registered" with the SEC as securities broker-dealers. This is unsurprising, since the functional role of a futures commission merchant is somewhat similar to that of a securities broker-dealer. For a comparison of the two registration categories, see chapter 13, section A.1. A registered securities broker-dealer is required to be a member of a self-regulatory organization, the Financial Industry Regulatory Authority, commonly known as "FINRA." The Financial Industry Regulatory Authority has a role in the securities industry analogous to that of the National Futures Association. If the futures commission merchant, as a registered broker-dealer, is a member of any securities exchanges, it will also be subject to their authority, although, in practice, by agreements with the Financial Industry Regulatory Authority, overlap between the exchanges' regulations and that of the Financial Industry Regulatory Authority is greatly reduced. To add another analytical layer, a failed securities broker-dealer is subject to a Securities Investor Protection Corporation proceeding.[29] This means that a failed futures commission merchant, if it is dually-registered as a broker-dealer, would go through wind-down via a Securities Investor Protection Corporation proceeding, not the bankruptcy process.

The focus here will solely be on the regulations imposed by the CFTC on futures commission merchants. The public policy objective of these regulations is generally to protect the customers of the futures commission merchant and the self-regulatory organizations of which it is a member.

b. Risk Management Program

Futures Commission Merchants are required to establish a risk management program, i.e., risk management policies and procedures designed to manage, among others, market, credit, liquidity, foreign currency, legal, operational, and settlement, segregation of customer funds from the futures commission merchant's own funds, technological, and capital risks.[30] The risk management program must include regu-

---

29. There is an exception if the broker-dealer's principal business is outside of the United Sates or it exclusively distributes mutual funds, variable annuities, or insurance. *See* SEC, *Guide to Broker-Dealer Registration* sec. 3.3, https://www.sec.gov/reportspubs/investor-publications/divisionsmarketregbdguidehtm.html (Apr. 2008).

30. 17 C.F.R. §1.11. There is also a requirement for policies addressing conflicts of interest. *See* 17 C.F.R. §1.71. The National Futures Association requires an information systems security

lar monitoring and risk tolerance limits. The risk management function must be staffed by a risk management unit independent of the business function.

A strong focus for futures commission merchants is customer fund segregation. We discuss customer funds and the importance of segregation of customer funds in subsection 3 below.

Quarterly reports on the above risks, including recommended changes and the status of items previously recommended but not yet acted upon, must be provided to management and the CFTC. The risk management policies and procedures must be internally examined and tested at least once a year.

c. Capital

A futures commission merchant must maintain "adjusted net capital" of the greater of: (1) at least $1 million though, in many circumstances, this amount is higher; and (2) eight percent of the sum of all margin for non-proprietary futures, options on futures, and cleared swaps.[31] To calculate adjusted net capital, a futures commission merchant must subtract liabilities from assets. However, much of what would normally count as an "asset" for accounting purposes is excluded.[32] For example, many unsecured balances, receivables, or loans are excluded, as is much working inventory. That calculation of assets minus liabilities leads to a "net capital" number.

To get from the "net capital" number to "adjusted net capital," there must be additional deductions for what are known as "charges against net capital."[33] The term "charges against net capital" is the sum of various percentage decreases in the assumed value of assets. These charges are intended to be based on the risk that the assets will not perform. For example, longer-term or unsecured assets generally have a higher "risk charge" than assets that will be repaid soon or are fully secured. Assets and liabilities of affiliates must be consolidated with the futures commission merchant for the purposes of calculation of adjusted net capital where the futures commission merchant has guaranteed the obligations of an affiliate.[34]

For futures commission merchants dually registered as securities broker-dealers with the SEC, it is possible to elect to apply the SEC's capital rules.[35] These capital rules are based on similar principles as those of the CFTC.

So now we see that the $1 million adjusted net capital amount is, in reality, much higher than merely having $1 million set aside. The form in which the "capital" must

---

program to protect customer data and a business continuity and disaster recovery plan. National Futures Association Rules 2-9, 2-36, 2-38, and 2-49.

31. 17 C.F.R. §§ 1.17(a)(1)(i) and (ii) and NFA Financial Requirements § 1(a).

32. 17 C.F.R. § 1.17(c)(2).

33. 17 C.F.R. § 1.17(c)(5).

34. 17 C.F.R. § 1.17(f). There is also a process for voluntarily obtaining consolidated treatment. Id.

35. 17 C.F.R. § 1.17(c)(6).

be held is determined by calculating the value of the equity in the futures commission merchant plus some types of subordinated debt. As demonstrated in the table in figure 6.2, the amount of adjusted net capital is the excess of the assets adjusted by charges against net capital minus the liabilities. It is held in the form of equity and some types of eligible subordinated debt.[36] Note that, when calculating adjusted net capital, both sides of the table in figure 6.2 are always equal to one another. For those with an accounting background, in this respect, it is similar in nature to a balance sheet.

Figure 6.2 Adjusted Net Capital

Assets Adjusted by Charges Against Net Capital	Liabilities
	Equity and Eligible Subordinated Debt

d. Reporting, Disclosures, and Recordkeeping

A futures commission report must make monthly financial reports to the CFTC.[37] They need not be audited. Annually, an audited financial report must be filed with the CFTC.[38] A daily report must also be sent to the CFTC and the applicable designated self-regulatory organization (see section A.1 above for a reminder on what is a "designated self-regulatory organization") of the amount of segregated customer funds held in futures trading accounts.[39] A futures commission merchant may deposit customer funds with banks and other similar entities and, twice a month, must provide a list to the CFTC and the designated self-regulatory organization of all the third-party entities holding such funds.[40]

Before opening an account, a customer must receive and acknowledge a disclosure on trading risks written by the CFTC.[41] Additionally, the futures commission merchant must make specific disclosures to the customer about its "business, operations, risk profile, and affiliates, that would be material to the customer's decision to entrust such funds to and otherwise do business with the futures commission merchant and that is otherwise necessary for full and fair disclosure" with at least annual updates.[42] Each customer must also receive a monthly statement showing all transactions and the account balance.[43] Within a business day of every trade, a confirmation of the transaction must be sent to the customer.[44]

---

36. 17 C.F.R. §§ 1.17(d) and (e).
37. 17 C.F.R. § 1.10(b).
38. *Id.*
39. 17 C.F.R. §§ 1.32(a)–(e).
40. 17 C.F.R. § 1.32(f).
41. 17 C.F.R. § 1.55(a) and (b).
42. 17 C.F.R. §§ 1.55(i) and (k).
43. 17 C.F.R. § 1.33(a).
44. 17 C.F.R. § 1.33(b).

Detailed records must be kept by futures commission merchants including customer details, transactions with dates and times, pre-trade communications, recordings of oral communications leading to a trade, and customer financial records.[45] They must be stored for five years. If stored in paper form, they must be readily accessible for productions to the CFTC or the National Futures Association for the preceding two years and, if stored electronically, they must be readily accessible for the entire five year period.[46] Voice recordings are subject to a shorter retention period of one year.[47] Advertising and marketing materials designed to reach the public via mass media, such as television or radio, must be pre-approved by the National Futures Association.[48]

e. Chief Compliance Officer

Futures commission merchants must designate a listed principal of the firm (see section A.3.c above for what is a "principal") to serve as the "chief compliance officer." The chief compliance officer, in addition to overseeing the monitoring and supervision of the futures commission merchant's activities must provide an annual report to the CFTC.

This annual report must identify existing policies and disclose material noncompliance that occurred during the year and what action was taken.[49] We further discuss the chief compliance officer role and related issues in chapter 11, section D.3.

f. Impact of Not Being Registered

Regardless of whether registered or not, a person or entity that "is engaged in soliciting or in accepting orders for the purchase or sale of any commodity for future delivery [or] a commodity option authorized under [CEA] section 4c of the Act . . . and in connection with any of these activities accepts any money, securities, or property (or extends credit in lieu thereof) to margin, guarantee, or secure any trades or contracts that result or may result therefrom" is a futures commission merchant.[50] An important exception exists for entities that have only proprietary accounts, i.e., accounts of related entities, such as affiliates.[51]

Therefore, a person or entity meeting the definition of a futures commission merchant and not exempt from registration will be held to the same requirements as a futures commission merchant, regardless of whether registered or not. Of special interest in the following case is that both the parties had the same common owner, the People's Republic of China.

---

45. 17 C.F.R. §§ 1.31–1.37
46. 17 C.F.R. § 1.31(b).
47. 17 C.F.R. § 1.31(b)(2).
48. National Futures Association Rule 2-29(h).
49. 17 C.F.R. § 3.3.
50. 17 C.F.R. § 1.3 (definition of futures commission merchant).
51. *See* 17 C.F.R. § 3.10(c)(1) and 1.7 C.F.R. § 1.3 (definition of proprietary account).

Ping He (Hai Nam) Co. Ltd. v. NonFerrous Metals (U.S.A.) Inc.

22 F. Supp. 2d 94 (S.D.N.Y. 1998)

Sotomayor, District Judge. . . .

The two instant actions arise from a dispute between plaintiff Ping He (Hai Nam) Company Limited ("Ping He") and defendant NonFerrous Metals (U.S.A.) Inc. ("NFM") over a commodity futures trading account opened by Ping He with NFM in 1993. Ping He moves for summary judgment . . . seeking the return of $350,000 it deposited into the account, on the grounds that NFM defrauded Ping He into opening the account, engaged in unauthorized trading, falsified an invoice, and misappropriated Ping He's funds. . . . In opposing the motion, NFM claims that Ping He owes it more than $650,000 in trading losses. . . .

The following facts are undisputed. Ping He and NFM are both entities owned by the People's Republic of China. Ping He is a foreign corporation with its principal place of business in China. NFM, although owned by the Chinese government, is a New York corporation with its principal place of business in Manhattan. NFM holds itself out as being in the business of soliciting orders for the purchase and sale of commodity futures. Once an order is placed with NFM, NFM arranges for the order to be executed on American and foreign markets through registered floor brokers. NFM, however, is not and has never been registered with the Commodity Future Trading Commission ("CFTC"), or with any federal or state regulatory body in the United States, in any capacity.

In or about April 1993, Ping He agreed to open a futures trading account with NFM. . . . [A]ll trades were to be non-discretionary, meaning that NFM was only authorized to execute trades for Ping He upon the express instructions of Ping He or Ping He's designated agent. Toward that end, by letter dated April 27, 1993, Ping He advised NFM that it was authorizing Mr. Li Zheng of China National Metal Products Co. ("China Metals") to act as Ping He's agent in all matters relating to its futures trading account. . . .

Unfortunately, nearly all facts concerning what actually happened to Ping He's trading account after it was opened are in dispute, including: whether NFM conducted any trading for Ping He; when such trading began and ended; whether trades on Ping He's account were authorized or unauthorized; and whether trades conducted for Ping He resulted in profits or losses. The parties additionally dispute whether Ping He knew when it opened the account that NFM was not registered with the CFTC. . . .

China Metals sent NFM a fax suspending the account. The letter stated:

> We are very pleased to see that we have made a little profits [sic] through those deals done with your brokerage. . . . As a result of our internal arrangements, we would like to inform you that we have suspended our future trading account with your brokerage effective from today. . . .

China Metals' . . . letter also requested that NFM provide it with a list of all trades executed on the account, together with a list of all commissions charged.

Soon afterwards, NFM sent China Metals an account invoice . . . [which] stated that $344,893 was due on Ping He's account. . . . That figure consisted of $104,500 in alleged trading losses and $240,393 in commissions and interest, for trading activity. . . . Several months later . . . Ping He wired NFM the sum of $300,000. . . .

Ping He brought the instant suit . . . claiming that NFM defrauded it at every step of their dealings. First, Ping He claims, NFM misrepresented itself as a registered commodity broker in order to induce Ping He to open an account with NFM. Ping He further claims that, after the account opened, neither it nor China Metals ever authorized NFM to execute trades on its behalf, but that NFM nevertheless improperly charged it for large trading losses. According to Ping He, NFM either engaged in unauthorized trading on Ping He's account, charged Ping He for fictitious trades, or fraudulently allocated to Ping He's account losing trades that had been undertaken for other customers. Whichever was the case, Ping He contends that NFM's fraudulent conduct is evinced by the fact that NFM has been unable to produce any records reflecting trades ordered by Ping He or China Metals, or showing that the losing trades charged to Ping He were in fact made for Ping He's account. . . .

NFM maintains that all of the trades it conducted for Ping He were authorized by NonFerrous B.M. Corp. ("B.M. Corp."), a private New Jersey corporation (unrelated to NFM and Ping He) that China Metals allegedly retained to give trading instructions for Ping He's account. In effect, NFM claims that a two-tiered agency structure existed: Ping He authorized China Metals to act as its agent, which in turn authorized B.M. Corp. to act as *its* agent. . . . Furthermore, NFM maintains that Ping He knew from the outset that NFM was not registered with the CFTC. According to NFM, it had no reason to misrepresent its registration status because it was at all times legally exempt from registration. . . .

Central to the regulatory scheme [of the Commodity Exchange Act (the "CEA")] . . . are its registration requirements. . . .

Because of their critical importance, the CEA's registration requirements apply to nearly every class of professionals who deal in commodities. Thus, under the Act, anyone who acts as a broker and executes sales of commodities on the trading floor of a contract market must be registered as a broker. . . . Futures commission merchants ("FCMs"), who do not trade themselves on the floor, but who, like NFM, solicit transactions which are then executed through brokers, must also register.[52] . . . Those who either fail to register or who misrepresent their registration status can be criminally prosecuted. . . .

---

52. [N. 2] It is evident that, at all relevant times, NFM operated as an FCM. By its own account, NFM solicited and accepted customer orders for futures trades, which it then placed through floor brokers. This squarely meets the CFTC's definition of an FCM. . . .

[A] key purpose of the CEA is to protect customers against fraudulent and abusive trading practices by FCMs and other market participants. . . .

Also, . . . [the CEA] requires FCMs to maintain intelligible daily trading records for each customer, and to report to customers on their transactions, in the manner prescribed by the CFTC. In that regard, the CFTC has promulgated Rules 1.33 and 1.35, setting forth strict record-keeping and reporting requirements. . . .

Ping He seeks to recover $350,000 on the basis that NFM failed to register as an FCM. . . . However, Ping He offers no evidence or basis for believing that it incurred damages simply by dealing with an unregistered FCM. . . .

If Ping He can assert any damages claim based upon NFM's unregistered status, it is . . . on the grounds that NFM fraudulently induced it to open a futures trading account by misrepresenting or concealing its unregistered status. Cast as a fraudulent inducement claim, there is a causal link between NFM's alleged violation of the statute and Ping He's out-of-pocket losses because, the argument goes, "but for" NFM's misrepresentation or concealment of its unregistered status, a material fact, Ping He would not have opened the account with NFM and would not have incurred any losses. . . .

Rule 1.33 requires FCMs to send customers monthly statements setting forth, among other things, the profits or losses realized upon trades and all financial charges assessed a customer during the monthly reporting period. Here, there is no question that NFM violated Rule 1.33. NFM has not produced copies of any monthly reports it prepared for Ping He's account, nor does NFM maintain that it ever prepared such reports for Ping He, or Ping He's agent. . . . Nevertheless, Ping He's damages claim under Rule 1.33 must be dismissed because Ping He has never contended that NFM's failure to issue it monthly reports . . . is what caused its loss of $350,000. . . .

Ping He has, however, made a case for actual injury by NFM's violation of Rule 1.35. . . . Rule 1.35 imposes numerous record-keeping requirements upon FCMs. The requirements are intended to ensure the complete segregation of customer accounts, the correct attribution of trades to the customers who ordered them, and the maintenance of detailed records for every transaction relating to each customer account. Here, Ping He claims that NFM failed so miserably to comply with any of Rule 1.35's requirements, that any demand by NFM for the payment of trading losses was guaranteed to be false because NFM had no way of itself knowing or checking what trades had been done for Ping He, and whether those trades had produced profits or losses. Indeed, Ping He claims that NFM's violations of Rule 1.35 were so pervasive, as to suggest strongly the commission of fraud. . . .

Rule 1.55 prohibits any FCM from opening a commodity futures account for any customer unless the FCM has first provided the customer with a risk disclosure statement containing . . . prescribed language. . . . It is undisputed that NFM did not provide Ping He, or any agent of Ping He, with the required risk disclosure statement. . . .

[T]he CFTC has held in reparations proceedings that Rule 1.55 is so critical to protecting customers that, when an FCM violates the rule, a causal link between the customer's damages and the Rule 1.55 violation will be presumed. . . .

The Court now must turn to the factual record in this case, to determine whether Ping He is entitled to summary judgment for NFM's alleged unauthorized trading, invoice falsification, and record-keeping violations. . . .

Even a cursory review . . . makes it painfully obvious that the losses reported in the . . . invoice were entirely falsified, and, furthermore, that NFM could not possibly have prepared an accurate invoice for any loss amount because NFM maintained no records indicating what trades were made on Ping He's behalf, and whether such trades resulted in profits or losses. . . .

Given the record in this case, there is no question that Ping He is entitled to summary judgment based upon [these] claims. . . . No rational juror could possibly find NFM innocent of violations under these statutory provisions. . . .

———————

The result of acting as a futures commission merchant without being so registered is dramatic. Being held to every prescriptive requirement applicable to futures commission merchants can have drastic consequences.

3. Failure of Futures Commission Merchants

The balance between protecting customers' margin funds and ensuring that futures commission merchants have incentives to hold customer accounts is a challenge. If, for example, reinvestment of customer margins were prohibited, futures commission merchants would be forced to significantly increase the commissions they charge. If, on the other hand, futures commission merchants had no restrictions on possible investments, customers may be deterred from keeping margin at risk in the account.

In addition to the permissible investment limitations, other methods that the Commodity Exchange Act and CFTC rules use to mitigate customer risk are, as noted above, minimum capital, disclosure, and recordkeeping requirements. After the failure of a large futures commission merchant, MF Global, the CFTC sought to balance these risks and reviewed the current risk management and compliance requirements, including the recent changes made to it.

CFTC, *Enhancing Protections Afforded Customers and Customer Funds Held by Futures Commission Merchants and Derivatives Clearing Organizations*
78 Fed. Reg. 68506 (Nov. 13, 2013)

. . . The protection of customers — and the safeguarding of money, securities or other property deposited by customers with an FCM — is a fundamental component of the Commission's disclosure and financial responsibility framework. Section 4d(a)(2) of the Commodity Exchange Act ("the Act" or "the CEA") requires each FCM to segregate from its own assets all money, securities, and other property deposited by futures customers to margin, secure, or guarantee futures contracts and options on futures contracts traded on designated contract markets. Section 4d(a)(2) further requires an FCM to treat and deal with futures customer funds as belonging to the futures customer, and prohibits an FCM from using the funds deposited by a futures customer to margin or extend credit to any person other than the futures customer that deposited the funds....

[CFTC] Regulation 1.20 requires each FCM and DCO to separately account for and to segregate from its own proprietary funds all money, securities, or other property deposited by futures customers for trading on designated contract markets. In addition, all futures customer funds must be separately accounted for, and may not be commingled with the money, securities or property of an FCM or of any other person, or be used to secure or guarantee the trades, contracts or commodity options, or to secure or extend the credit, of any person other than the one for whom the same are held. Regulation 1.20 also provides that an FCM or DCO may deposit futures customer funds only with a bank or trust company, and for FCMs only, a DCO or another FCM. The funds must be deposited under an account name that clearly identifies the funds as belonging to the futures customers of the FCM or DCO and further shows that the funds are segregated as required....

FCMs and DCOs also are restricted in their use of futures customer funds. Regulation 1.22 prohibits an FCM from using, or permitting the use of, the futures customer funds of one futures customer to purchase, margin, or settle the trades, contracts, or commodity options of, or to secure or extend the credit of, any person other than such futures customer. In addition, § 1.22 provides that futures customer funds may not be used to carry trades or positions of the same futures customer other than in commodities or commodity options traded through the facilities of a contract market. Under § 1.20, an FCM or DCO may, however, for convenience, commingle and hold funds deposited as margin by multiple futures customers in the same account or accounts with one of the recognized depositories. An FCM or DCO also may invest futures customer funds in certain permitted investments under § 1.25....

FCMs also are subject to minimum net capital and financial reporting requirements that are intended to ensure that such firms meet their financial obligations in a regulated marketplace, including their financial obligations to customers and DCOs. Each FCM is required to maintain a minimum level of "adjusted net capital," which is generally defined under § 1.17 as the firm's net equity as computed under generally accepted accounting principles, less all of the firm's liabilities (except for certain qualifying subordinated debt) and further excluding all assets that are not liquid or readily marketable. Regulation 1.17(c)(5) further requires an FCM to impose capital charges (i.e., deductions) on certain of its liquid assets to protect against possible market risks in such assets.

FCMs also are subject to financial recordkeeping and reporting requirements. FCMs that carry customer accounts are required under § 1.32 to prepare a schedule each business day demonstrating their compliance with the segregation and secured amount requirements. Regulation 1.32 requires the calculation to be performed by noon each business day, reflecting the account balances and open positions as of the close of business on the previous business day.

Each FCM also is required by § 1.10 to file with the Commission and with its designated self-regulatory organization ("DSRO") monthly unaudited financial statements and an annual audited financial report.[53] Regulation 1.12 requires an FCM to file a notice with the Commission and with the firm's DSRO whenever, among other things, the firm: (1) Fails to maintain compliance with the Commission's capital requirements; (2) fails to hold sufficient funds in segregated or secured amount accounts to meet its regulatory requirements; (3) fails to maintain current books and records; or (4) experiences a significant reduction in capital from the previous month-end. . . .

The statutory mandate to segregate customer funds — to treat them as belonging to the customer and not use the funds inappropriately — takes on greater meaning in light of the devastating events experienced over the last two years. Those events, which are discussed in greater detail below, demonstrate that the risks of misfeasance and malfeasance, and the risks of an FCM failing to maintain sufficient excess funds in segregation: (i) Put customer funds at risk; and (ii) are exacerbated by stresses on the business of the FCM. . . .

The recent insolvencies of two FCMs demonstrate the need for revisions to the Commission's customer protection regime. On October 31, 2011, MF Global, Inc. ("MFGI"), which was dually-registered as an FCM with the Commission and as a securities broker-dealer ("BD") with the U.S. Securities and Exchange Commission ("SEC"), was placed into a liquidation proceeding under the Securities Investor Protection Act by the Securities Investor Protection Corporation ("SIPC").

The trustee appointed to oversee the liquidation of MFGI reported a potential $900 million shortfall of funds necessary to repay the account balances due to customers trading futures on designated contract markets, and an approximately $700 million shortfall in funds immediately available to repay the account balances of customers trading on foreign futures markets.[54] The shortfall in customer segregated accounts was attributed by the MFGI Trustee to significant transfers of funds out of the customer accounts that were used by MFGI for various purposes other than to meet obligations to or on behalf of customers.

---

53. [N. 9] The term "self-regulatory organization" is defined by § 1.3 to mean a contract market, a swap execution facility, or a registered futures association [i.e., the National Futures Association]. A DSRO is the SRO that is appointed to be primarily responsible for conducting ongoing financial surveillance of an FCM that is a member of two or more SROs under a joint audit agreement submitted to and approved by the Commission under § 1.52.

54. [N. 10] *See* Report of the Trustee's Investigation and Recommendations, In re MF Global Inc., No. 11-2790 (MG) SIPA (Bankr. S.D.N.Y. June 4, 2012). [Note that customers ultimately received full restitution. *See Customers of MF Global Inc. to Begin Receiving Final Restitution Payments from MF Global*, CFTC Press Release PR6904-14, http://www.cftc.gov/PressRoom/PressReleases/pr6904 -14 (Apr. 3, 2014).]

In addition, the Commission filed a civil injunctive complaint in federal district court on July 10, 2012, against Peregrine Financial Group, Inc. ("PFGI"), a registered FCM and its Chief Executive Officer ("CEO") and sole owner, Russell R. Wasendorf, Sr., alleging that PFGI and Wasendorf, Sr., committed fraud by misappropriating customer funds, violated customer fund segregation laws, and made false statements regarding the amount of funds in customer segregated accounts in financial statements filed with the Commission. The complaint states that in July 2012 during an NFA examination PFGI falsely represented that it held in excess of $220 million of customer funds when in fact it held approximately $5.1 million.[55] ...

These recent incidents highlighted weaknesses in the customer protection regime prescribed in the Commission's regulations and through the self-regulatory system. ...

In December 2011, the Commission adopted final rule amendments revising the types of investments that an FCM or DCO can make with customer funds under § 1.25, for the purpose of affording greater protection for such funds.[56] Among other changes to §§ 1.25 and 30.7, the final rule amendments removed from the list of permitted investments: (1) Corporate debt obligations not guaranteed by the U.S. Government; (2) foreign sovereign debt; and (3) in-house and affiliate transactions.

In adopting the amendments to § 1.25, the Commission was mindful that customer segregated funds must be invested by FCMs and DCOs in a manner that minimizes their exposure to credit, liquidity, and market risks both to preserve their availability to customers and DCOs, and to enable investments to be quickly converted to cash at a predictable value in order to avoid systemic risk. The amendments are consistent with the general prudential standard contained in § 1.25, which provides that all permitted investments must be "consistent with the objectives of preserving principal and maintaining liquidity." ...

The Commission also included customer protection enhancements in a final rulemaking for designated contract markets issued in June 2012. These enhancements codify into regulations staff guidance on minimum requirements for SROs regarding their financial surveillance of FCMs. The regulations require a DCM to have arrangements and resources for effective rule enforcement and trade and financial surveillance programs, including the authority to collect information and examine books and records of members and market participants. The regulations also establish minimum financial standards for both member FCMs and IBs and non-intermediated market participants. ...

––––––––––

There is no analogue to the Federal Deposit Insurance Corporation or the Securities Investor Protection Corporation for the futures markets. This is the case even where

––––––––––

55. [N. 11] Complaint, *U.S. CFTC v. Peregrine Financial Group, Inc., and Russell R. Wasendorf, Sr.*, No. 12-cv-5383 (N.D. Ill. July 10, 2012). A copy of the Commission's complaint has been posted to the Commission's Web site.

56. [N. 14] *See* Investment of Customer Funds and Funds Held in an Account for Foreign Futures and Foreign Options Transactions, 76 FR 78776 (Dec. 19, 2011).

an entity is registered as both a broker-dealer and a futures commission merchant because the Securities Investor Protection Corporation regime only protects securities and cash held to purchase securities. In other words, to the extent that a futures commission merchant fails there is no guarantee insurance fund to make the customers whole.

Moreover, notwithstanding the regulatory safeguards imposed on futures commission merchants, numerous futures commission merchants have failed since the passage of the Commodity Futures Trading Commission Act of 1974 including, most significantly: (1) Chicago Discount Commodity Broker in 1980; (2) Incomco in 1980; (3) Volume Investors in 1985 (the subject of the litigation in *Westheimer v. Commodity Exchange, Inc.* in chapter 4 and *Comex Clearing Association, Inc. v. Flo-Arb Partners* excerpted below); (4) Refco, Inc., in 2005; (5) Lehman Brothers, Inc., in 2008; (6) MF Global in 2011; and (7) Peregrine Financial Group in 2012 (Peregrine's failure spurred *Prestwick Capital Management, Ltd. v. Peregrine Financial Group, Inc.*, excerpted in section C.2 below, and the criminal complaint in *United States v. Wasendorf*, excerpted in chapter 13).[57] As noted above in section B.1.d, the failure of MF Global and Peregrine Financial Group triggered renewed scrutiny of the protection of customer funds held by futures commission merchants. Futures trading operates such that, as a practical matter, customer funds are at risk in the case of a so-called double default, i.e., where a large customer defaults in making a margin payment and its futures commission merchant, still contractually committed to the clearinghouse, is unable to make up for the shortfall:

> Under the traditional futures model, DCOs hold an FCM's futures customers' funds on an omnibus basis in a futures customer account. In the event of a double default, which is a situation where a futures customer defaults on its obligation to its clearing FCM and the loss is so great that the clearing FCM defaults on its obligation to the DCO, the DCO is permitted to use the funds held in the [defaulting FCM's] futures customers' omnibus account to cover the loss of the defaulting futures customer before applying its own capital or the guaranty fund contributions of non-defaulting FCM members.[58]

As we will see in chapter 10, section B.1, and chapter 18, section C, a different regime applies for swaps clearing where non-defaulting customers are protected against the "fellow customer" risk that arises in a double default scenario.

A "double default" occurred in the gold futures and options market in 1985 when a futures commission merchant, Volume Investors, failed. Shortfalls to the

---

57. For a detailed analysis of futures commission merchant failures and their potential regulatory causes, *see* Compass Lexecon, *Customer Asset Protection Insurance for U.S. Futures Market Customers* 13-14 (Nov. 15, 2013) available at https://www.nfa.futures.org/news/insurance-study-files /Customer_Asset_Protection_Insurance_Study.pdf. For a comprehensive list of futures commission merchant defaults occurring before 1986, *see* National Futures Association, *Customer Account Protection Study* 16–36 (Nov. 20, 1986).

58. *Enhancing Protections Afforded Customers and Customer Funds Held by Futures Commission Merchants and Derivatives Clearing Organizations,* 78 Fed. Reg. 685061, 68510 (Nov. 13, 2013).

clearinghouse were apportioned among all of the account balances of Volume's customers. Innocent, non-defaulting customers of Volume saw their accounts debited *pro rata* to pay the shortfalls owed by it to the clearinghouse.

Comex Clearing Association, Inc. v. Flo-Arb Partners
711 F. Supp. 1169 (S.D.N.Y. 1989)

Kevin Thomas Duffy, District Judge . . .

This opinion will, I hope, conclude the story of the financial collapse of Volume Investors Corporation ("Volume"). At all pertinent times, Volume was a member of the Commodities Exchange, Inc. ("COMEX"), and the Comex Clearing Association ("CCA"). Volume was also a futures commission merchant ("FCM") registered with the Commodities [*sic*] Futures Trading Commission ("CFTC"). . . . In its position as an FCM and as a member of COMEX and CCA, Volume handled accounts for members of the public and for other FCMs. . . .

Flo-Arb Partners ("Flo-Arb") was also an FCM duly registered and, through one of its partners, a member of COMEX. To clear its trades through CCA, Flo-Arb put all of its accounts with Volume and was permitted to act as a floor broker on the Commodities Exchange by reason of a guarantee issued by Volume. Flo-Arb is made up of two general partners: Ronny Apfel and Abraham Goldstein. . . . [B]oth Apfel and Goldstein were quite knowledgeable about the futures market. . . .

On March 21, 1985, prior to the commencement of trading on COMEX, Frank H. Wohl was appointed Temporary Receiver of Volume. The appointment was made pursuant to an order of a judge of this court, on application of CFTC and on consent of Volume. At the same time Volume was suspended as a member of COMEX and of CCA. The Temporary Receiver undertook to liquidate the positions of Volume in an orderly manner and pursuant to the rules of CCA as approved by CFTC. Wohl effectively secured the records and property of Volume and worked out arrangements for the initial liquidation of the Volume account at CCA.

Shortly thereafter, I appointed John F. X. Peloso as the Receiver of the Estate of Volume. Peloso undertook the wind-up of the estate, including sales of property, renegotiation of leases, and payments to public customers of Volume. The claims of Flo-Arb against Volume and its successors, and the claims of Volume and the receivers against Flo-Arb are now the main barrier to completion of the wind-up. These claims were held aside to be resolved after all of the public was out of the picture and all of the din appurtenant thereto had quieted.

During the pendency of these actions, CCA paid out the purely public customer accounts, i.e., the non-members of COMEX, and became the successor to the receiver of Volume.[59] . . .

---

59. [N. 2] The matters presently before the court involve only the claims between Flo-Arb Partners, Ronny Apfel and Abraham Goldstein, on the one hand and Volume Investors, Inc. and its successors in interest on the other hand.

Once before, in a dispute related to this matter, I set forth my views on the risks involved in trading on certain commodities and futures markets. I nonetheless believe it necessary to reiterate what I have said because much of it has apparently fallen on deaf ears.

Trading in gold options is a highly volatile market where fortunes can be made and lost in one day. This case should stand as a reminder that the fallout from an explosive day in the gold market can affect not only the traders in that market but can also have a detrimental effect on the market place, including the organized exchanges dealing in gold, the exchange clearing house, the members of the exchange, and the innocent public customers of member firms, which customers may not even be involved in the trading of gold or gold options. . . .

Apfel and Goldstein, were not "hedging" by their activities in the futures markets. They were pure speculators seeking to make money at the expense of others in the marketplace. . . .

Both Goldstein and Apfel were aware that the CCA viewed all of Volume's accounts (whether house accounts or for customers like Flo-Arb) as the accounts of one member. The CCA does not differentiate between the types of accounts held by any member, and Goldstein and Apfel had to be aware that there was a risk clearing through another FCM. Specifically, if the clearing FCM went broke, the accounts held would be netted by CCA with the possible result that the customers would lose everything. . . .

Volume permitted other customers, the Westheimers, and their agent to have a large number of gold futures contracts. Following a dramatic change in gold prices the Westheimers were caught short and were unable to come up with the amounts required to maintain their margin accounts. The amounts necessary were so enormous that Volume was also unable to meet the margin demands of CCA, which had netted all of the Volume accounts, including those of the Westheimers. Because of the Westheimers, Volume was broke and CCA sold out all the Volume accounts. In effect, everyone connected with Volume lost and the problem became how to spread the loss equitably among all of the victims. By this point this court was involved both directly and through its receiver. While there was no precedent on point that could guide me in this task, I decided that it would be most appropriate and fair to analogize this situation to the rule of "general average" found in the law of Admiralty.

"General average" is perhaps the oldest, still extant, doctrine of the law of Admiralty. It is used when a ship loses some of its cargo due to the perils of the sea. In that situation the remaining cargo is liquidated and each of the cargo owners, regardless of whose cargo was lost, and the ship owner share the monetary loss. Throughout history, beginning at least with the Greeks and the Phoenicians, this has been considered a fair and equitable method of resolving the problem. The liquidation and distribution of Volume was effected according to this time-honored principle and each step was taken with the approval of this court. . . .

No one has suggested that the collapse of Volume was caused by Flo-Arb. Indeed, it is irrelevant. Volume's accounts were not liquidated because of some fault on the part of Flo-Arb or its partners. Rather, they were liquidated because Volume could not meet the CCA's margin requirements. Flo-Arb in first entering its arrangements with Volume assumed that risk along with the sundry other risks that the futures markets entail. In speculating in the market, Flo-Arb accepted the risk of losing its money. If Flo-Arb's trading resulted in this loss, the loss would be assessed without regard to blame. So also, here, it is totally unnecessary to assess blame and the absence of "fault" (in that sense) is irrelevant. . . .

Flo-Arb has successfully delayed paying what it owes to the estate of Volume for redistribution to the truly innocent public customers. To obviate any bad public relations, CCA has already put up the money owed to public customers under the rule of general average. This permitted the public to be paid without delay arising from the arguments of Flo-Arb. By making the payment to the public customers, CCA has succeeded to their interests and now can collect from Flo-Arb through the estate of Volume. . . .

Ultimately, due to two Volume Investors executives paying a combined $4.1 million to customers, non-defaulting customers were made whole.[60] However, the event resulted in much government and industry introspection regarding customer risk.

More recently, another "near miss" for customer losses occurred when a much larger futures commission merchant, MF Global, failed. The facts are somewhat complicated. MF Global, under a new chief executive, began focusing more on "investment banking" activities, including trading securities for its proprietary accounts. Many of these trades were on margin and, due to market events and a perceived credit deterioration of MF Global, significant margin was demanded at the same time that many customers began closing their MF Global securities and futures accounts.

MF Global, despite technically having assets, lacked liquidity, i.e., immediately available cash to accommodate these short-term demands. In an ultimately unsuccessful effort to maintain its liquidity, during the trading day MF Global used amounts in futures commission merchant customer accounts that arguably were in excess of CFTC requirements, returning the funds to customer accounts by the close of business. As its position deteriorated, MF Global begin using the funds for longer periods and, when it failed, there was a shortfall in customer funds. It is notable that these events occurred just three years after MF Global was nearly felled

---

60. Michael A. Hiltzik, *Comex, Failed Trading Firm Settle: Volume Investors' Owners to Pay Customers $4.1 Million*, Los Angeles Times (July 17, 1985), available at http://articles.latimes.com /1985-07-17/business/fi-8003_1_trading-firm. The CFTC references a $1.3 million payment by the chief executive of Volume Investors. *See* CFTC, *Release 2586-86*, Docket 85-25 (Jul. 29, 1986) available at http://www.nfa.futures.org/BasicNet/Case.aspx?entityid=0002121&case=85-25&contrib =CFTC.

in 2008 by a rogue trader accruing $141 million in losses in one night trading from his home on behalf of MF Global.[61]

MF Global was registered as both a futures commission merchant with the CFTC and a securities broker-dealer with the SEC. As a result, it was subject to a Securities Investor Protection Corporation insolvency proceeding, pursuant to which a trustee was appointed to manage MF Global and facilitate customer recoveries.

Report of the Trustee's Investigation and Recommendation, In re MF Global Inc.

http://www.cftc.gov/idc/groups/public/@newsroom/documents/file /mfglobaliinvestreport060412.pdf (Bankr. S.D.N.Y. June 4, 2012) (No. 11-2790 (MG) SIPA, available on PACER)

James W. Giddens (the "Trustee"), as Trustee for the liquidation of MF Global Inc. ("MFGI" or the "Firm"), respectfully submits this Report of the Trustee's Investigation and Recommendations (the "Report.") . . .

This Report reflects the Trustee's initial findings regarding the failure of MFGI, whose parent, MF Global Holdings, Ltd. ("Holdings") . . . filed for reorganization under Chapter 11 of the Bankruptcy Code on the morning of October 31, 2011 (the "Filing Date"), following which the Securities Investor Protection Corporation ("SIPC") commenced a proceeding to liquidate MFGI under [the Securities Investor Protection Act ("SIPA")]. . . . Holdings, together with MFGI and other MF Global subsidiaries and affiliates, is referred to collectively as "MF Global." The focus of the Report is on the underlying reasons for and the consequences of the collapse of MF Global, including the shortfall of segregated customer property that MFGI publicly announced early on the morning of October 31, 2011. . . .

Jon Corzine became CEO and Chairman of the Board of Holdings in March 2010, at a time when MF Global had reported losses for five straight quarters. He quickly moved to try to transform what had been a longstanding FCM combined with a . . . [securities broker-dealer] conducting a relatively modest customer and proprietary securities business into a full-service global investment bank. With Mr. Corzine at the helm, dramatic changes ensued, including changes in personnel, lines of business, and markets into which MF Global expanded its business.

Historically, MFGI had generated revenue by earning interest on customer margin deposits, commissions on customer securities and future transactions, proprietary trading activities, and interest revenues from its matched repo book.[62] In

---

61. Peter Elkind with Doris Burke, *The Last Days of MF Global*, Fortune (June 4, 2012), available at http://fortune.com/2012/06/04/the-last-days-of-mf-global.

62. [N. 6] A repurchase agreement (repo) is a financing transaction involving what is in form a sale of securities together with an agreement for the seller to buy back the securities at a later date. http://www.cftc.gov/ConsumerProtection/EducationCenter/CFTCGlossary. . . .

the face of declining interest rate revenues,[63] MF Global's proprietary investment strategy shifted from short-term, low-yield investments to longer-term high-yield and highly-leveraged investments. As part of the shift in its proprietary investment strategy to generate greater streams of apparent or realized income, MF Global also developed and launched a number of new lines of business, all of which increased the daily demands for liquidity. With these changes, a significant percentage of the MF Global workforce was terminated and replaced with new employees.

Notwithstanding the increased demands on global money management and liquidity, the Firm's Treasury Department, which was involved in implementing the transfers of funds, did not expand or modernize. Likewise, the technology for recording and tracking transactions and liquidity did not materially change. These critical functions remained essentially as they had been prior to Mr. Corzine's arrival, with the Firm often tracking liquidity and ability to transfer funds by informal means that were derived from a number of different reports, both computerized and oral.

While Mr. Corzine acted as CEO of the entire MF Global enterprise, he also traded actively on its behalf through a specially designated account. Among the lines of business that Mr. Corzine built up to attempt to improve profitability at MF Global was the trading of a portfolio of European sovereign debt securities. These trades provided paper profits booked at the time of the trades, but presented substantial liquidity risks including significant margin demands that put further stress on MF Global's daily cash needs. . . .

[T]he sovereign debt portfolio consisted of sovereign bonds issued primarily by European nations experiencing severe financial distress (Ireland, Italy, Portugal and Spain). . . . MF Global's investment in sovereign debt peaked at nearly $7 billion (net) in October 2011, and still stood at nearly $6 billion as of the Filing Date. As early as May 2010, the Chief Risk Officer at the time, Michael Roseman, began expressing concerns regarding liquidity risk . . . which reportedly led to his termination in January of 2011. As the Board and management were aware, the exposure from this portfolio was the equivalent of 14% of MF Global's assets as of September 30, 2011, and was more than four-and-a-half times MF Global's total equity, a level that was orders of magnitude greater than the relative exposure at other, larger financial institutions. . . .

In August of 2011, because of concerns about MF Global's exposure to sovereign debt, the Financial Industry Regulatory Authority ("FINRA") [the self-regulatory

---

63. [N. 7] Although the Federal Funds interest rate had been gradually declining since 2007, the Federal Reserve cut the rate to essentially zero following the financial crisis in the fall of 2008. MF Global had historically generated a substantial portion of its income from interest generated from repurchase agreements, government securities in inventory or held for commodities customers, and failed transaction fees. The drop in the Fed Funds rate caused a dramatic decline in MF Global's interest income; Holdings' interest income decreased nearly 90% from 2007 to the Filing Date and MFGI's interest income decreased by more than 80% over the same period. . . . As interest rates decreased sharply in recent years, MF Global's net interest income earned on the cash sitting in the Customer Accounts plummeted, from $4.01 billion in 2007, to $517 million in 2011. . . .

organization for securities broker-dealers] required MFGI to record additional capital charges to reflect risks associated with the European sovereign debt portfolio. The increased capital charges meant that, in FINRA's view, MFGI had a net capital deficiency as of July 31, 2011, and MFGI had to re-state its financial results. . . . As a result, MFGI underwent a $183 million capital infusion. . . .

Regardless of whether Mr. Corzine's bet on European sovereign debt would ultimately have been profitable, in the short term, MF Global became increasingly vulnerable to the developments that ensued in the fall of 2011. Risk and perception of risk quickly turned MF Global's longstanding liquidity problems into a crisis for which it had neither the tools nor the emergency resources to withstand.

One of the sources of liquidity that MF Global considered tapping to help satisfy ever-increasing liquidity demands of the proprietary securities business was the perceived "excess" funds in customer accounts at the FCM. While an FCM must segregate customer funds from proprietary funds, some confusion and differences of opinion existed within MF Global regarding the extent to which excess funds might be available to meet liquidity needs across the MF Global enterprise. The Commodity Futures Trading Commission ("CFTC") requires that customer funds be kept in "Customer Segregated" or "Foreign Secured" accounts (collectively "Customer Accounts"). CFTC regulations provide for Customer Segregated accounts or "4d accounts" to hold the property of customers trading on domestic exchanges, and for Foreign Secured accounts, or "30.7 accounts," to hold customer property of customers trading on foreign exchanges. The regulated customer funds in the Customer Accounts were not to be used for other purposes. . . .

[T]he regulations for Customer Segregated accounts require a daily accounting of the net liquidation value of the customer funds in the account (the "Net Liquidating Method"). CFTC regulations, however, did not require that all customer funds necessarily be maintained on a dollar-by-dollar basis in the Foreign Secured accounts. Instead, unlike Customer Segregated accounts (for trades on domestic exchanges), the CFTC regulations allowed an "Alternative Method" for calculating whether Foreign Secured accounts were in regulatory compliance even though less than all customer funds deposited for trading on foreign exchanges might actually be deposited in Foreign Secured accounts. MFGI used this "Alternative Method," and during the month of October 2011, the amount of "Regulatory Excess"—the average amount of customer funds in excess of the regulatory requirement under the Alternative Method (but not the Net Liquidating Method)—was approximately $1 billion. Some at MF Global considered the Regulatory Excess to be a potential source of funds for intraday, or even overnight, transfers to fund the non-FCM activities of MF Global, although others were of the view that the Regulatory Excess would still have to be "locked up" for the benefit of customers. Finally, since the CFTC required that the calculations be done "as of the close of business each day," questions existed as to whether funds needed to be "locked up" for the benefit of customers intraday as well.

CFTC regulations allow an FCM to deposit its own funds in the Customer Accounts as the FCM deems necessary to prevent Customer Accounts from becoming under-segregated, and, conversely, to withdraw its own funds for proprietary use. MFGI referred to Firm funds kept in Customer Accounts, including funds that were swept in each night, as the "Firm Invested in Excess." This excess had the beneficial result of acting as a cushion to prevent shortfalls in customer funds owing to changing margin requirements resulting from daily market movements. The benefit of having such funds as a cushion would be achieved, however, only as long as funds removed from those accounts for proprietary activity were limited to the Firm Invested in Excess, the amount above the level that was needed to satisfy obligations to customers on a net basis.

As MF Global's liquidity needs intensified, senior management looked increasingly to the FCM as a source of liquidity for the non-FCM business. . . . Firm Invested in Excess funds were . . . allowed to be used to fund MF Global's proprietary activities both overnight and during the day, and it appears that part of the Regulatory Excess was, at times, also used for intraday funding of the non-FCM business. When MF Global's proprietary trading gave rise to a need for additional liquidity, Operations in New York would request what they referred to colloquially as an intraday "loan" — actually, not a true loan but simply a transfer of funds — from the Treasury Department in Chicago.[64] The Customer Segregated or Foreign Secured accounts at the FCM were at times tapped to fund these transfers. Because compliance with the CFTC regulations was computed as of the close of business, as long as the transfers were returned before the end of each day, some MFGI employees did not consider the transfers to have any regulatory implications, although the CFTC has stated that FCMs must be in regulatory compliance at all times. By the summer of 2011, however, what had previously been relatively small, intermittent intraday transfers from the FCM to New York, became nearly a daily event in increasingly greater amounts. In addition, transfers from the FCM to Operations in New York were kept overnight or longer, presumably with the intention that any overnight transfers would be limited to the Firm Invested in Excess. . . .

Although MF Global disclosed the net capital deficit and the $183 million capital infusion required by FINRA on September 1, this event did not garner much national attention until an October 17 report in *The Wall Street Journal*, after which events rapidly came to a head. On October 24, Moody's Investors Service downgraded MF Global's credit rating to near-junk status. Then, on October 25 . . . S&P put MF Global on "Credit Watch Negative," and on October 27, Moody's cut MF Global to junk status. Together with the downgrades of MF Global's credit rating and growing concerns about the large sovereign debt portfolio, this news contributed to a major loss of market confidence.[65]

---

64. [N. 8] These intraday "loans" were not loans at all since they were simply temporary transfers within the same consolidated entity. There were no repayment terms or interest, but simply an expectation that the funds would be returned each day.

65. [N. 9] MF Global's results for the second quarter of fiscal year 2012 showed a decline in financial strength. . . .

A classic run on the bank ensued as customers sought to withdraw their property from their MFGI accounts, while counterparties and exchanges demanded increased collateral or margin. At the same time, other counterparties declined to do business with MF Global altogether, leaving it with illiquid securities. . . . It was, in the words of one former MF Global executive, a "liquidity asphyxiation." . . .

These events during the final week of MF Global's operations increased the demands to use FCM funds to meet liquidity needs elsewhere in the enterprise. Most significantly, on October 26, there was an unprecedented intraday transfer of $615 million from the FCM to fund proprietary securities trading, an amount that was not returned to the FCM before the close of business. . . . Although some of this transfer was ultimately repaid, MFGI was out of regulatory compliance with respect to Customer Segregated funds on October 26, and remained so through October 31. At the same time, MFGI was advising customers that it was "hold[ing] all customer cash and collateral in CFTC Rule 1.25 and Rule 30.7 — Customer Segregation [accounts]," implying that 30.7 funds were subject to the same segregation requirements as 4d funds. To make matters worse, on October 28, MF Global personnel made a $175 million transfer from FCM customer funds to MFGUK, to clear an overdraft balance at JPMorgan Chase ("JPM") in London.

Before a transfer was made on the morning of October 31 — when certain funds that had been locked up for securities customers pursuant to SEC Rule 15c3-3 were transferred to the FCM — the shortfall resulting from transfers from the FCM amounted to approximately $900 million. Contrary to some public reports, the shortfall of customer property at MFGI was not caused by direct investment of customer funds in sovereign debt or even by losses on proprietary investments such as the sovereign debt. Rather, as detailed below, the actions of management and other employees, along with lack of sufficient monitoring and systems, resulted in FCM customer property being used during the liquidity crisis to fund the extraordinary liquidity drains elsewhere in the business, including margin calls on the European sovereign debt positions.

Immediately after MF Global's failure, customers found their MF Global accounts frozen.[66] Not until over two years later would the final distributions occur to MF Global customers.[67] The customers received a full recovery.[68]

---

66. David Sheppard and Jeanine Prezioso, *Anger Mounts as MF Global Clients See $3 Billion Still Stuck*, Reuters, http://www.reuters.com/article/us-mfglobal-customers-funds-idUSTRE7AJ 0PW20111121 (Nov. 20, 2011).

67. CFTC, *Customers of MF Global Inc. to Begin Receiving Final Restitution Payments from MF Global to Satisfy More Than $1 Billion in Customer Losses as Order by Federal Court in CFTC Action*, Release PR6904-14, https://www.cftc.gov/PressRoom/PressReleases/6904-14 (Apr. 3, 2014).

68. *Id.*

The CFTC brought an enforcement action for failure to supervise against the chief executive of MF Global at the time of its failure, Jon Corzine, former chief executive of Goldman Sachs, U.S. senator, and governor of New Jersey. He settled for $5 million and a permanent ban from being associated with a futures commission merchant.[69]

Insurance Fund?

A perennial question has been whether there should be a mandatory insurance regime for the futures industry similar to the Federal Deposit Insurance Corporation for bank customers and the Securities Investor Protection Corporation for broker-dealer customers.

The CFTC studied the question in 1976, shortly after its establishment, and again in 1985, after the failure of a futures commission merchant. The National Futures Association issued a landmark report study in 1986. The study concluded that "there are currently substantial and wide ranging customer account protections in place" in the futures industry and that, as a result, there is a "historically low incidence of loss. . . ."[a]

In keeping with the tradition of inquiring into customer insurance after a highly publicized futures commission merchant failure, after the failure of MF Global, various industry participants and the National Futures Association jointly commissioned a report published in 2013 that concluded that a government mandated insurer would be impractical.[b] But the debate continues with numerous calls for a mandatory insurance fund for the futures industry.[c]

  [a] National Futures Association, *Customer Account Protection Study* 16–36 (Nov. 20, 1986).

  [b] Compass Lexecon, *Customer Asset Protection Insurance for U.S. Futures Market Customers* vii (Nov. 15, 2013) available at https://www.nfa.futures.org/news/insurance-study-files/Customer_Asset_Protection_Insurance_Study.pdf (accessed Apr. 23, 2017).

  [c] *See, e.g.*, Christian Chamorro-Courtland, *Collateral Damage: The Legal and Regulatory Protections for Customer Margin in the U.S. Derivatives Markets*, 7 Wm. & Mary Bus. L. Rev. 609 (Apr. 2016), and Anita K. Krug, *Uncertain Futures in Evolving Financial Markets*, 93 Wash. U. L. Rev. 1209 (2016).

---

69. Consent Order for Permanent Injunction, Civil Monetary Penalty and Other Equitable Relief Against Defendant Jon S. Corzine, *CFTC v. MF Global Holdings Ltd.*, http://www.cftc.gov/idc/groups/public/@lrenforcementactions/documents/legalpleading/enfcorzineorder010517.pdf (S.D.N.Y. Jan. 4, 2017) (No. 11-cv-7866, available on PACER).

C. Introducing Brokers

1. Generally

Introducing broker is a category of registration created by the Futures Trading Act of 1982 and is, therefore, newer than the futures commission merchant or floor broker categories of registration discussed in section B above and D below. Previously, a regulatory gap was perceived for an entity soliciting or placing orders on behalf of customers through a futures commission merchant with which the entity had an agency relationship. These entities had no obligation to register as futures commission merchants because they never took custody of customer assets.

The House of Representatives Committee on Agriculture, in reporting on the bill that was to become the Futures Trading Act of 1982, described the quandary it intended to address as follows:

> Although agents may perform the same functions as branch officers of futures commission merchants, agents generally are separately owned and run. Futures commission merchants frequently disavow any responsibility for sales abuses or other violations committed by these agents. The Committee believes that the best way to protect the public is to create a new and separate registration category for "agents" (e.g., as introducing brokers). Many of these "agents" are individuals or very small businesses. Activities of agents and those of commodity trading advisors or associated persons of futures commission merchants may be virtually identical, yet commodity trading advisors and such associated persons are registered and regulated under the Act while many agents are not.

> The new registration category of "introducing broker" would encompass persons who solicit or accept futures orders but who do not handle customer funds, and in the case of individuals, who elect to be registered as introducing brokers rather than associated persons [of a futures commission merchant]. The current ambiguity and the resulting uncertainties of the regulatory status of agents would thus be eliminated.[70]

By creating a new class of registrant, Congress took a path between, on the one hand, leaving these entities unregulated and, on the other hand, placing responsibility for their acts on the futures commission merchants for which they acted as agent.

The hallmark of an introducing broker is that it is engaged in "soliciting or in accepting" orders.[71] What constitutes an order solicitation, however, is not always clear as illustrated in the following case.

---

70. House Report 97-565, 48 (May 17, 1982).
71. Commodity Exchange Act § 1a(31).

CFTC v. Mass Media Marketing, Inc.

156 F. Supp. 2d 1323 (S.D. Fla. 2001)

Graham, District Judge. . . .

Mass Media Marketing, Inc. ("Mass Media") and Commodity Referral Service, Inc. ("CRS") (collectively "Defendants") are Florida advertising, marketing, video production and syndication companies whose marketing services range from advertising Ginsu knives and exercise equipment to promoting culinary schools and private universities. Rolando Nanasca ("Nanasca") is the President of both companies.

In 1995, Defendants added commodity futures to their marketing curriculum. Commodity futures involve the purchase of an option to buy or sell a particular commodity, such as unleaded gasoline, at a predetermined price on or before a given date.[72] Defendants' marketing services entailed producing, directing and arranging for the broadcast of 60-second commercials and 30-minute long infomercials ("advertisements") touting the benefits of commodity futures investments. Each advertisement urged viewers, who had at least $5,000 to invest, to call a toll-free number featured in the advertisement to obtain information on how to profit from investments in commodity options. Once a viewer placed a call to the toll-free number, the answering service operator would ask what product or service the viewer was calling about. If the viewer was calling in reference to a commodities advertisement, the answering service operator would give the caller a short description of the product or service being offered and would try to obtain the callers [sic] name, address and telephone number in order to create a "lead."

Defendants marketed two forms of advertisements, sponsored and non-sponsored. Sponsored advertisements were advertisements that Defendants created and broadcasted on behalf of a commodity broker registered with the Commodity Futures Trading Commission ("CFTC"). A registered commodity broker, also known as an Introducing Broker, essentially operates as a brokerage firm that solicits potential investors to place orders on commodity options. An Introducing Broker would seek the marketing services of Defendants to produce an advertisement approved by the Introducing Broker and featuring the Introducing Broker's name. Defendants would agreed [sic] to sell a specified number of leads generated by the advertisement to the sponsoring Introducing Broker. Any excess leads would be sold to other Introducing Brokers whose names did not appear in the advertisement.

Non-sponsored ("blind") advertisements were not approved by an Introducing Broker and did not include the name of an Introducing Broker in the advertisement. The leads generated from blind advertisements were sold on a random basis to any interested Introducing Broker. The contents of blind advertisements were ultimately approved by Nanasca who is not registered as a commodity broker.

---

72. This is not correct—an option to buy or sell a commodity in the future is a commodity option not a commodity future. This misstatement does not impact the rest of the opinion.

Sponsored and blind advertisements essentially claimed that existing supply and demand factors in the cash market for a particular product, such as unleaded gasoline or soy beans, make options on that product's futures contracts "predictable" and "logical" and an investor had a "legitimate chance of doubling, tripling, or even quadrupling" his money. One advertisement described the manner in which commodities trading function as follows:

> We're discussing some common-sense approaches for investing in the commodities futures market and how to know when to invest.

> One of the most direct approaches in determining your investment in commodities options is what is known as trends. If you analyze and act upon a sound trend, then the profits can be astounding.

> There are many reasons that trends develop in commodities, but one of the more common reasons are of the cyclical nature, commodities such as unleaded gasoline and heating oil, for example.

> There's a much larger demand for heating oil in the winter, for obvious reasons. And for unleaded gasoline, the demand increases in the summer when people drive the most. These are seasonal trends, where the movement in price becomes predictable.

The advertisements assured viewers that although investment in commodities "[is] not for everybody, and it does involve risk," such "risks are, in fact, predetermined" and "known."

Nanasca wrote most of the scripts for the advertisements produced by Defendants or had otherwise the "final say-so on the scripts." Nanasca never "really researched" the background of commodities trading or the "way that commodities markets actually work" prior to writing the scripts and airing the advertisements. Instead, Nanasca based the advertisements' contents primarily on radio advertisements which he thought "sounded exciting," though he never took any steps to verify the accuracy of such information. . . .

The marketing and advertising services provided by Defendants never required Defendants to enlist callers to become Introducing Brokers' customers or to collect any money from callers. Rather, any discussions with callers about commodity investments occurred once the Introducing Broker purchased the leads from Defendants and contacted the prospective customers.

The National Futures Association ("NFA") is the commodity futures and options industry's self-regulatory organization. In the early 1990's, the NFA determined that some Introducing Brokers provided prospective investors with misleading information about the seasonality trends of commodities when soliciting their orders. Most of these Introducing Brokers received severe monetary penalties or were otherwise subjected to disciplinary action. To remedy this situation . . . the NFA issued a notice stating that seasonality claims were a violation of its rules. In early 1997, Nanasca discovered that the NFA "frowned upon" blind advertisements because "someone's got to be responsible for the contents of those advertisements." Consequently, Nanasca voluntarily ceased to broadcast blind advertisements. . . .

Introducing Brokers form a category of commodity futures market participants created by Congress in 1982. Prior to 1982, Introducing Brokers acted as independently affiliated "agents" of Futures Commission Merchants ("FCM").[73] The main function of such agents was to procure business for FCMs. These unregistered agents operated free from regulation due to a gap in the Act's registration requirement which precluded jurisdiction by the CFTC over such agents. In 1982, the CFTC advised Congress that the number of agents had increased significantly, and that FCMs who used their services "have often disavowed any responsibility for violations of the Act by these 'agents.'" To remedy the ambiguity and the resulting uncertainties of the agents' regulatory status, the CFTC proposed that "each 'agent' of a futures commission merchant be required to register as an associated person of that futures commission merchant."

Congress, however, opted to resolve the problem by amending the Act to require all persons who solicit or accept customer orders for FCMs to register either as "associated persons" of the FCMs, or as part of a new class of registrants called Introducing Brokers.[74] Unlike associated persons of a FCM, Congress viewed Introducing Brokers as independent entities that solicited and accepted customer orders, but used the services of FCMs for clearing, record keeping and retaining customer funds. . . .

[T]he Act defines an Introducing Broker as:

> any person (except an individual who elects to be and is registered as an associated person of a futures commission merchant) . . . engaged in soliciting or in accepting orders for the purchase or sale of any commodity for future delivery [who] does not accept any money, securities or property (or extend credit in lieu thereof) to margin, guarantee, or secure any trades or contracts that result or may result therefrom.

In the instant case, the CFTC claims that by soliciting and referring prospective investors to Introducing Brokers, Defendants have themselves acted as unregistered Introducing Brokers in violation of the Act. The CFTC interprets the phrase "soliciting or in accepting orders" contained in the definition of an Introducing Broker as covering a whole range of conduct, including Defendants' solicitation to the public through television advertisements. In contrast, Defendants assert that the plain language of the Introducing Broker registration requirement excludes them from registration because they are advertising production companies that neither solicit

---

73. [N. 1] FCMs function as the commodity market's equivalent of a securities brokerage house, soliciting and accepting orders and funds for futures contracts and extending credit in connection therewith.

74. [N. 2] Like Introducing Brokers, Associated Persons of an FCM solicit futures orders and deal directly with the public, but do so under the supervision and control of the FCM that clear their orders.

orders, nor accept orders from customers. Defendants posit that the phrase "soliciting or in accepting orders" cannot conceivably cover general solicitation to the public through television advertisements, which neither invite nor accept the placement of an order. . . .

Giving the words used in the Act their ordinary meaning, the Court finds that the phrase "engaged in soliciting or in accepting orders" contained within the definition of an Introducing Broker is subject to several interpretations. The Court cannot naturally discern whether Congress intended the term "soliciting" to modify the term "order" or if Congress intended the term "soliciting" to remain open-ended. The Act does not define the term "soliciting" nor does it explain its application. Even assuming the Court were to accept either party's interpretation of the phrase, the Court is still unable to determine whether the definition applies to advertisers. Accordingly, the Court finds the phrase to be ambiguous. . . .

The CFTC interprets the phrase "engaged in soliciting or accepting orders" as covering customer "solicitation[ ] for compensated referral to other registrants so that a trading relationship can be initiated and the customer's orders executed." Based on this interpretation, the CFTC concludes that Defendants' activities fall within the Act because:

> Mass Media produces and arranges for the broadcast of its advertisements and infomercials for the sole purpose of obtaining the names, phone numbers and addresses of individuals who may be interested in purchasing options. Mass Media's entire activities are tied to the number of leads that they generate. It is compensated on a per-lead basis by the IBs to which the leads are sold and it pays, in some cases, for television air time on a per-lead basis as well. It also licenses these leads to IBs and attempts to relicense these leads to other IBs after a period of time. . . .

[T]he Court cannot conclude that the CFTC's interpretation of the phrase "engaged in soliciting or in accepting orders" is a permissible interpretation of the Act.

First, Defendant advertisers' primary goal is to obtain leads, not orders for commodity futures. The CFTC's expert opines that Defendants' "entire activities are tied to the number of leads that they generate" and Defendants conduct their advertisements "for the sole purpose of obtaining the names, phone numbers and addresses of individuals who may be interested in purchasing options." Defendants never collected any money from viewers of the advertisements and never received compensation for the number of callers who subsequently opened accounts through an Introducing Broker. Accordingly, the Court finds that Defendants' main objective in broadcasting the advertisements was to facilitate the collection of leads, not to facilitate the purchases of orders for futures contracts.

Second, Defendants have a "good reason" to conduct their advertising activities that is not entirely ancillary to requesting purchases. Through their advertisements, Defendants find individuals who may become prospective commodity customers. As such, Defendants' activities are better characterized as those of a customer finder rather than an Introducing Broker. The Act, however, does not require a person who acts as a customer finder to register as an Introducing Broker. Moreover, unlike Introducing Brokers, whose compensation is commensurate with the orders obtained, Defendants receive compensation for the leads regardless of the Introducing Broker's success in soliciting, accepting or introducing an order to an FCM. Hence, Defendants have a "good reason" for conducting their solicitation activities that is not ancillary to requesting purchases. Accordingly, the Court finds that Defendants' activities . . . do not amount to "solicitation of orders."

Other factors similarly fail to support the CFTC's interpretation of the Introducing Broker registration requirement. First, the CFTC's prior understanding of the objective behind the 1982 Introducing Broker registration requirement cannot be reconciled with the CFTC's current interpretation. In its Rules and Regulations, passed shortly after the 1982 amendments, the CFTC expressed its understanding of Congress' intent "to require registration as Introducing Brokers those persons who were formerly agents of FCMs" or who "performed the types of activities traditionally engaged in by agents." . . . The CFTC expressed no concern about advertisers or entities who simply generate and sell leads to Introducing Brokers. The Court finds this factor to be specifically relevant because[,] based on the CFTC's prior interpretation of the Introducing Broker requirement, Defendants would not be required to register under the Act.

Second, the Act's legislative history, which delineates the underlying purpose of the Introducing Broker registration requirement, makes not a single reference to advertisers or an intent by Congress to regulate as Introducing Brokers entities who neither invite, nor accept the placement of an order. . . .

[I]n the instant case, Defendants never introduced an account to an FCM or any registered entity. Defendants' general solicitation through their advertisements never involved the making of an offer to enter into a commodity transaction or assisting customers in carrying out such transactions. . . .

[T]he CFTC has introduced no evidence to establish that Defendants' advertisements have caused commodity investors the type of harm Congress intended to prevent by enacting the Introducing Broker registration requirement. On the contrary, the record shows that the CFTC is effectively protecting the public by imposing strict solicitation guidelines on Introducing Brokers. The CFTC's expert confirms that the NFA has taken "several disciplinary actions against Members [Introducing Brokers] for the foregoing promotional practices." Moreover, Introducing Brokers are subject to serious monetary penalties, including customer restitution, if they fail to fully disclose to prospective investors the risks involved in commodity investments, especially when the investor's interest in commodities stems from television advertisements. *See Scheufler v. Stuart,* 1997 WL 599871 (C.F.T.C.) (Introducing Broker held liable for failure to fully disclose realistic profit and risk information to infomercial viewer). Hence, the evidence before the Court supports the view that the "simple act of referral does not directly jeopardize the interests of the investing public." After examining these relevant factors . . . the Court finds no permissible basis that would justify the CFTC's expansive interpretation of the Act's Introducing Broker registration requirement.

Congress has ample authority to expand the Act's registration requirement to include advertisers, such as Defendants. Congress, however, has not done so. . . .

Whereas the placement of general advertisements regarding commodity futures trading may not be enough to trigger a requirement to register as an introducing broker, sharing in trading commissions or other fee-based compensation probably is likely sufficient to trigger a registration obligation.[75] Mere referrals or acting as a "finder" is not enough.[76]

2. Regulatory Requirements

The regulatory requirements applying to introducing brokers are largely similar or identical to those applying to futures commission merchants, including with respect to National Futures Association membership. There are a few major differences, though.

First, there is no risk management program requirement.[77]

Second, the capital requirement is much lower. Instead of $1,000,000 in adjusted net capital, introducing brokers need only have $50,000.[78] Moreover, as discussed below in subsection 3, if an introducing broker's obligations are guaranteed by a futures commission merchant, it does not have a capital obligation.[79] Otherwise, the capital regime is largely the same as that for futures commission merchants.

Third, instead of monthly unaudited financial reports, introducing brokers are required to provide them biannually, and introducing brokers guaranteed by a futures commission merchant are not required to produce them to the CFTC at all. The requirements to segregate customer funds, report on customer funds, send daily confirmations, and send monthly statements do not apply. This is because introducing brokers do not hold customer funds.

---

75. *Carr v. Phoenix Futures, Inc.*, 1991 WL 121184 *2–3 (E.D.N.Y. June 24, 1991).

76. *Id.*

77. They are, however, subject to National Futures Association requirements to have an information systems security program in place to protect customer data and a business continuity and disaster recovery plan. National Futures Association Rules 2-9, 2-36, 2-38, and 2-49.

78. Technically, it is $45,000 by CFTC rule, but the National Futures Association, of which the introducing broker must be a member, expects members to have $50,000 minimum so that there is a cushion. *See* 17 C.F.R. §1.17(a)(1)(iii) and National Futures Association, *Compliance Requirements for Introducing Broker (IB) Applicants*, https://www.nfa.futures.org/registration-membership/who-has-to-register/ib-applicants-compliance-requirements.html.

79. 17 C.F.R. §1.17(a)(2)(ii).

Fourth, an introducing broker with $5 million or less in revenue is not required to record oral communications leading to a trade.[80]

Last, an introducing broker is not required to designate a chief compliance officer.

3. Guaranteed Introducing Brokers

As we can see from the above, there is a significant lessening of regulatory burdens for introducing brokers guaranteed by a futures commission merchant. The creation of the introducing broker registration was partially intended to put to rest the question of whether a futures commission merchant is liable for the acts of an introducing broker with which it has a relationship. It clarified that futures commission merchants are not ordinarily liable for the acts of an introducing broker with which it transacts and established an introducing broker registration regime intended to provide some safeguards for the public.

The CFTC, however, leaves open the possibility of a futures commission merchant voluntarily guaranteeing the obligations of an introducing broker and allows for, in such circumstances, relief from some regulatory responsibilities otherwise applicable to such introducing broker.

To the extent a futures commission merchant can revoke such a guarantee at will, it might allow the introducing broker and futures commission merchant to "have their cake and eat it too," since the futures commission merchant could reduce its exposure to the introducing broker by revoking the guarantee at will, and—until such revocation—the introducing broker would have reduced regulatory responsibilities. The customer of the formerly guaranteed introducing broker may not be aware that the introducing broker is no longer guaranteed and that the customer no longer has the protections originally in place. This, indeed, was the fact-pattern in the below case, the facts of which we revisit in chapter 15, section B.

Prestwick Capital Management, Ltd. v. Peregrine Financial Group, Inc.

727 F.3d 646 (7th Cir. 2013)

Barker, District Judge. . . .

[T]he instant lawsuit requires us to clarify the scope of a futures trading "guarantee gone wrong." . . .

In 2009, Prestwick Capital Management Ltd., Prestwick Capital Management 2 Ltd., and Prestwick Capital Management 3 Ltd. (collectively, "Prestwick") sued Peregrine Financial Group, Inc. ("PFG"), Acuvest Inc., Acuvest Brokers, LLC, and two of Acuvest's principals (John Caiazzo and Philip Grey), alleging violations of the Commodity Exchange Act ("CEA"). Prestwick asserted . . . a guarantor liability

---

80. 17 C.F.R. § 5(a).

claim against PFG. After the district court awarded summary judgment to PFG in August 2011, Prestwick moved to dismiss the remaining defendants with prejudice in order to pursue its appeal of right against PFG. . . .

This commodities fraud lawsuit presents a corporation's attempt to recoup investments allegedly depleted during commerce involving an underfunded trading pool. . . .

In August 1983, the CFTC promulgated a final rule setting forth minimum financial benchmarks for [introducing brokers, hereafter "IBs"]. . . . The current requisite minimum adjusted net capital is $45,000 or "[t]he amount of adjusted net capital required by a registered futures association of which [an IB] is a member." . . . However, an IB "shall be deemed to meet the adjusted net capital requirement" if it is a party to a binding guarantee agreement [with an FCM]. . . . According to the CFTC, this dispensation is appropriate because "the guarantee agreement provides that the FCM . . . will guarantee performance by the [IB] of its obligations under the Act and the rules, regulations, and order thereunder . . . [and] is an alternative means for an [IB] to satisfy the [CFTC's] standards of financial responsibility." . . .

In the case before us, the plaintiff, Prestwick, is a conglomerate of Canadian investment companies. . . . The defendant, PFG, is an Iowa corporation with its principal place of business in Chicago, Illinois; it also conducts business in New York as an active foreign corporation. Importantly, PFG is registered with the CFTC as an FCM that guarantees compliance with the CEA by certain registered IBs, including two of the Acuvest defendants (Acuvest Inc. and Acuvest Brokers, LLC). . . .

In 2004, pursuant to the CFTC regulations discussed *supra*, Acuvest and PFG executed a guarantee agreement ("the 2004 Guarantee Agreement"). The portion of their 2004 Guarantee Agreement that is the focus of this lawsuit provided, in relevant part, as follows:

> PFG guarantees performance by [Acuvest] . . . of, and shall be jointly and severally liable for, all obligations of the IB . . . with respect to the solicitation of and transactions involving all commodity customer, option customer, foreign futures customer, and foreign options customer accounts of the IB entered into on or after the effective date of this Agreement.

Thus, the arrangement between PFG and Acuvest contemplated (1) Acuvest's solicitation of customers and subsequent engagement with customers for business dealings, and (2) PFG's willingness to assure Acuvest's customers that Acuvest would conform its conduct to the mandates of the CEA. Further, as the district court noted, this provision made PFG responsible for any fraudulent conduct engaged in by Acuvest.

Two years later, PFG's compliance director, Susan O'Meara, sent a memorandum to the NFA to inform the NFA of a change in PFG's relationship with Acuvest. This correspondence, titled "Guaranteed IB Termination," was dated August 25, 2006 and advised, "As of August 24, 2006, [PFG] will terminate its guarantee agreement with Acuvest. . . . This termination has been done by mutual consent."

Acuvest and PFG executed an agreement of a slightly different nature the very same month — a "Clearing Agreement for Independent Introducing Broker" ("the 2006 IIB Agreement"). . . . [T]he 2006 IIB Agreement stated that this contract "supersede[d] and replace[d] any and all previous agreements between [Acuvest] and PFG." Under the new arrangement, PFG agreed to "execute[,] buy [,] and sell orders and perform settlement and accounting services for and on behalf of [c]ustomers introduced by [Acuvest]." . . . Acuvest, by contrast, assumed significantly more responsibilities to PFG and its customers. Notably, Acuvest's signature on the 2006 IIB Agreement evinced its consent to:

> comply with the rules and regulations of all relevant regulatory entities, exchanges[,] and self-regulatory organizations related to the purchase and sale of [f]utures [i]nvestments. . . .

This adjustment was consistent with the CFTC's official differentiation between guaranteed and independent IBs: "By entering into the agreement, the [guaranteed IB] is relieved from the necessity of raising its own capital to satisfy minimum financial requirements. In contrast, an independent [IB] must raise its own capital to meet minimum financial requirements."[81] Here, Acuvest was accountable for all customer losses, charges, and deficiencies. . . . Acuvest also accepted absolute financial responsibility for its own actions and pledged to indemnify PFG from any harm resulting therefrom. Perhaps the most salient feature of the 2006 IIB Agreement was its treatment of guarantees. As an independent IB, Acuvest was bound by a new indemnification provision: "[Acuvest] guarantees all the financial obligations of the [c]ustomer accounts of [c]ustomers serviced by [Acuvest] and/or carried on the equity run reports produced by PFG for [Acuvest]."

PFG and Acuvest . . . [entered] into yet another agreement ("the 2008 Guarantee Agreement"). As was true of the 2006 IIB Agreement, this contract superseded all previous agreements between Acuvest and PFG. However, the new arrangement restored Acuvest to its prior status as a guaranteed IB. . . . Acuvest's role as an IB eventually intersected with Prestwick. The Acuvest-Prestwick business relationship arose when Acuvest advised Prestwick to become a limited partner in Maxie Partners L.P. ("Maxie"), a New York commodity trading pool. . . . For purposes of the instant litigation, Acuvest was the IB for all of Maxie's accounts. Prestwick elected to join the Maxie trading pool and invested approximately $7,000,000 in that fund. . . . During this time period, the Acuvest defendants assumed full responsibility for Maxie's management and investment decisions regarding the account holding Prestwick's funds and maintained open lines of communication with Prestwick.

In April 2007, Prestwick informed Grey (one of Acuvest's executive vice presidents) of its intent to redeem Prestwick's limited partnership interest in Maxie. . . . Believing that Maxie's assets were valued at approximately $20,000,000, Prestwick

---

81. [N. 5] U.S. Commodity Futures Trading Comm'n, CFTC Glossary. . . .

was understandably alarmed to learn . . . that much of its $7,000,000 investment in Maxie was unavailable. . . .

Ultimately, Prestwick's notice of redemption did not generate the anticipated payout. Prestwick claims to have received only two disbursements of its original investment in the pool — one in August 2007, and the other in October 2007 — totaling approximately $3,000,000. . . . Prestwick's efforts to collect the remaining balance since October 2007 have been wholly unsuccessful. . . .

Prestwick raises . . . for our review . . . whether termination of PFG's guarantee of Acuvest's obligations under the CEA also terminated such protection "for existing accounts opened during the term of the guarantee," a result Prestwick vehemently repudiates. . . .

Prestwick's challenge to the district court's decision regarding the temporal scope of the 2004 Guarantee Agreement is threefold. First . . . Prestwick's suggested construction of the 2004 Guarantee Agreement would render PFG liable for Acuvest's obligations concerning any account opened with PFG "during the term of" that agreement — no matter when any subsequent wrongdoing related to such account occurred. Second . . . [a]ccording to Prestwick, the parties did not intend the 2006 IIB Agreement to end PFG's guarantee of Acuvest's obligations for accounts predating its execution. Third, Prestwick argues that the district court's ruling contravenes significant consumer protection policies underlying the CFTC's regulatory scheme for guaranteed IBs. . . .

The CFTC explicitly addressed the contours of termination in its final rule on "Registration and Other Regulatory Requirements" for IBs, dated August 3, 1983, as follows:

> If [a] guarantee agreement does not expire or is not terminated in accordance with the provisions of § 1.10(j) . . . it shall remain in effect indefinitely. The [CFTC] wishes to make clear that the termination of a guarantee agreement by an FCM or by an introducing broker, or the expiration of such an agreement, does not relieve any party from any liability or obligation arising from acts or omissions which occurred during the term of the agreement.

48 Fed. Reg. 35,248, 35,265 (citation omitted). This rule corresponds to Title 17, Section 1.10(j) of the Code of Federal Regulations, which provides the protocol for ending a guaranteed IB relationship. Termination of a guarantee agreement may take place at any time during its effective term. . . .

[T]he 2006 agreement unequivocally states: "[t]his Agreement supersedes and replaces any and all previous agreements between IB [Acuvest] and PFG." It is difficult to imagine a clearer way in which the parties could have terminated the 2004 agreement. . . .

[R]ecords of the NFA — the organization vested with IB registration authority — verify PFG's status as Acuvest's designated guarantor from June 26, 2004 until August 24, 2006. The same records demonstrate that between August 24, 2006 and

July 8, 2008 (one day prior to the "start date" of the 2008 Guarantee Agreement), Acuvest was not a party to any guarantee agreement with a FCM. Without a legally binding agreement establishing such a relationship, Acuvest was not a guaranteed IB from August 24, 2006 until July 9, 2008. The corollary to this historical recitation must be, and is, that in July 2007, when the misconduct of which Prestwick complains allegedly occurred, Acuvest was not a guaranteed IB.

Nonetheless, according to Prestwick, the foregoing records have no bearing on PFG's contractual duties to Acuvest. . . .

[W]e . . . find Prestwick's position perplexing. Nothing within the governing regulations or the "four corners of the contract" remotely indicates that . . . [the 2004 Guarantee Agreement] was to continue in full force with respect to "existing accounts." That Prestwick asks us to impute this intent into the 2004 Guarantee Agreement (or, for that matter, any of the operative documents) is contrary to time-honored principles of contract interpretation. . . . Despite Prestwick's ardent pronouncements that it does not consider the 2004 Guarantee Agreement a perpetual guarantee, we fail to see how else to credit Prestwick's interpretation. . . .

Equally untenable is Prestwick's argument that . . . the 2004 Guarantee Agreement was not terminated. . . . Prestwick asserts that the parties did not intend the 2006 IIB Agreement to end PFG's guarantee of Acuvest's obligations regarding Prestwick's Maxie account because the contract (1) defines "customer" as an entity that opens a "new" account with PFG or transfers an existing account from another FCM to PFG, and (2) "does not mention existing accounts." . . . The fact that the 2006 IIB Agreement covered new accounts does not prompt the inference that the 2004 Guarantee Agreement was not terminated. . . .

Prestwick's third argument regarding termination of the 2004 Guarantee Agreement implicates our understanding of public policy in the area of consumer protection. Prestwick apparently believes that CFTC regulations—and guarantee agreements executed thereunder—have different meanings based on brokers' actions after such agreements are terminated. It is unclear to us why Prestwick would consider this fair or sound policy. . . . [Congress has] expressly disapproved of "impos[ing] vicarious liability on a futures commission merchant for the actions of an in-dependent [broker]." S.Rep. No. 97-384, at 41. . . .

According to PFG, [NFA rules] give FCMs "the responsibility, and hence the authority, to supervise" the guaranteed IB, but "[o]nce the guarantee agreement has been terminated, the FCM no longer has the authority to force this independent legal entity to conform its conduct to the FCM's requirements." Prestwick's most compelling rejoinder is that this argument undercuts a major goal of the CEA and its attendant rules: protecting IBs' customers. . . . We are, of course, sympathetic to the plight of investors, like Prestwick, who may have no idea when a guarantee relationship is severed. Although some due diligence must be expected, we understand that a few weeks may elapse after guarantee termination wherein investors cannot protect themselves from the actions of unguaranteed brokers. This can certainly be an unfortunate result, but it does not authorize us — or even permit us — to require FCMs to close all accounts opened during the term of a severed guarantee agreement with an IB and then reopen those accounts if a new guarantee arises. There is simply no evidence that Congress, through the CEA, intended to place such a burden on FCMs. Thus, despite our sense that the well-being of investors ought to be considered in some fashion in these cases, perhaps by recognizing a right to notice of the end of the guarantee agreement (which would enable the investor to take appropriate self-protective steps), the courts are not the proper place to impose new regulatory requirements.

No policy arguments can overcome the simple fact that the contracts at issue in this lawsuit are definitive. . . . Fairness aside, we are unwilling to resolve a legislative issue through a ruling that would contravene the CEA and established common-law contract rules. Guarantee agreements would simply make no sense if they required parties to look back in time for some FCM that might well be insolvent or no longer in existence. Prestwick's policy arguments, therefore, are untenable in our current legislative and regulatory atmosphere. Although Prestwick may have legitimate grounds to challenge this framework, the place to do so is not before the courts. . . .

The decision was, of course, a hard outcome for the Prestwick plaintiffs who were unaware and never put on notice of Acuvest's unguaranteed status. It is difficult to see by what mechanism a customer could be made aware that a guaranteed introducing broker has ceased to be guaranteed other than, perhaps, a covenant in the customer's agreement with the introducing broker requiring the introducing broker to notify the customer. A more common practice is to have the introducing broker not be guaranteed, i.e., a so-called "independent" introducing broker, or for the futures commission merchant to hire the individuals as associated persons.

Of course, if an introducing broker is no longer guaranteed, the introducing broker is required to have capital in reserves for, among other things, the benefit of customers.

D. Floor Brokers

Floor traders have privileges to place trades as principal on the trading floor of a designated contract market. Floor brokers, on the other hand, have privileges to place trades directly on the trading floor of a designated contract market as agent for third party customers. As with floor traders, floor brokers are almost non-existent due to the replacement of physical trading floors with electronic trading. However, it is helpful to consider some of the benefits and detriments of having a physical trading floor. On the one hand, a physical trading floor may be more robust in the event of a serious computer problem and provide continuity during times of market illiquidity. On the other hand, the practical limitations on the size of a trading floor and the ability of parties to trade face-to-face with sufficient volume and frequency to accommodate market needs militates against a physical trading floor.

As can be seen from the below case, whereas electronic trading potentially faces the risk of hacking, a physical trading floor also has security risks.

United States v. Sanders

688 F. Supp. 367 (N.D. Ill. 1988)

Aspen, District Judge:

Currently before this Court is defendant Thompson Sanders' motion to dismiss the indictment. For the reasons stated below, that motion is denied. . . .

The indictment sets forth a scheme in which Sanders and his three co-defendants engaged in fraudulent trading on the Chicago Board of Trade ("CBT"). . . . Sanders and his co-defendants devised a scheme wherein . . . utilizing stolen, bogus and counterfeit CBT trading jackets and identification credentials and with the help of wigs and make-up, the conspirators made risk-free trades on the floor of the CBT. . . .

Proper commodity trading on the floor of the CBT proceeds in the following manner. In order to enter into a trading contract, one must open and maintain a margin account with a Futures Commission Merchant ("FCM"). A FCM is a corporation which accepts orders for the purchase of commodities for future delivery. Margin is money or other property of value which a customer is required to deposit into a commodity trading account as earnest money to demonstrate their good faith that they will pay any losses incurred as a result of entering into commodity futures trades and to ensure future performance on commodity futures trades by customers.

All commodity trading at the CBT is done in a restricted trading area which is closed to the public.[82] Access to this area is restricted by CBT rules to authorized CBT members and employees. Trading on the floor of the CBT is conducted by floor brokers who execute trades on behalf of their customers.

When a floor broker enters into a contract to buy or sell a particular commodity with another floor broker, the brokers must record the transaction on a trading card or endorse an order listing certain information material to the trade such as the commodity traded, the trading price, the time of the trade, the name of the opposite broker and his member firm. After the brokers fill out the trading cards, the cards are delivered to the brokerage firms employing the respective brokers.

After receiving the trading cards, the information listed by the floor brokers on the cards is entered into the computer records of the clearing house for the CBT. At the end of the trading day, the clearing house for the CBT matches up various buy and sell commodity trades for that day based upon the information initially listed

---

82. Today, there is electronic trading with cryptographic access restrictions.

by the floor brokers on the trading cards and subsequently entered into the computer records of the clearing house.

After the clearing house has finished matching up trades, the brokerage firms receive from the clearing house a record of that day's trading activity involving that firm. Based upon this record, the brokerage firm will determine whether to issue a margin call to a customer, that is, a request that the customer deposit additional money into the margin account due to trading losses sustained or trading positions assumed by the customer during that trading day. . . .

It is charged in sum that beginning in May 1986, Sanders and his three co-defendants hatched a plan to fraudulently engage in "risk-free" trading on the CBT. Defendants Sanders and David Pelleu did "steal, obtain and create false, bogus and counterfeit" CBT trading jackets and identification credentials. These items were used by defendants Daniel Dewey and Daniel Kolton to enter restricted CBT trading areas. Dewey would also wear wigs and cosmetic make-up to alter his physical appearance. Dewey would enter the trading area in disguise with bogus identification and trading jackets and would then place orders to buy or sell Treasury Bond commodities with various floor brokers. Dewey would then transfer the trading cards for the trades to Sanders.

Sanders and the others would then determine whether the trades had been profitable or whether there had been a loss. If the trades placed by Dewey turned out to be profitable, the defendants would claim the trade and take the profits. But if the trades lost money, the defendants would not claim the trade. Because these trades had been executed with bogus credentials and while in disguises, the losing commodity trades placed by this conspiracy could not be traced. Thus, the government charges that defendants created a way to engage in truly risk-free trading, only at the expense of the other floor broker's customers. . . .

[The Commodity Exchange Act] makes it a felony for any person to misrepresent himself as a member of a contract market in "handling" or "soliciting" a futures contract order. 7 U.S.C. § 6h states . . .

> It shall be unlawful for any person falsely to represent such person to be a member of a contract market[83] or the representative or agent of such member, or to be a registrant under this chapter or the representative or agent of any registrant, in soliciting or handling any order or contract for the purchase or sale of any commodity in interstate commerce or for future delivery, or falsely to represent in connection with the handling of any such order or contract that the same is to be or has been executed on, or by or through a member of, any contract market.

Sanders contends that this section, *unambiguously*, makes it only unlawful to defraud *public customers* in the "solicitation" and "handling" of their futures

---

83. Now this provision applies to all "registered entities," i.e., contract markets, derivatives clearing organizations, swap data repositories, and swap execution facilities.

contract orders and not the defrauding of commodity traders and brokers as is alleged in the indictment. The government agrees that the statute is unambiguous, but finds Sanders' interpretation "narrow and misguided." The government fails to read any limitation . . . to prohibit misrepresentations only to public customers. We agree with the government. . . .

[E]ven if there were such a limitation, it would be satisfied in this case. The misrepresentation charged in the indictment occurred when Daniel Dewey, falsely dressed and bearing identification as a floor broker, executed trades on the floor of the CBT with a legitimate floor broker who was led to believe the disguised Dewey was also a legitimate floor broker. . . . [A] floor broker is merely a conduit for a customer. Therefore, when Dewey falsely pretended to be a legitimate floor broker, he was in essence falsely representing himself to the customer upon whose behalf the duped floor broker made the trade.

Accordingly, even if we found that § 6h was limited to a situation where the false representation is made to a *"customer,"* we would conclude that the indictment makes such an allegation. . . .

Accordingly, Sanders' motion to dismiss the indictment is denied. It is so ordered.

In the late 1980s the Chicago Board of Trade was rocked by another scandal. An agricultural services company, Archer Daniels Midland, complained about fraud at the Chicago Board of Trade and cooperated with the FBI.[84] At least four FBI agents infiltrated the Chicago Board of Trade, pretending to be floor traders or floor brokers and renting apartments in a glitzy Chicago neighborhood, one agent going so far as to wear a gold Rolex and drive a Mercedes-Benz.[85]

Ultimately, a 534-count indictment was brought against nineteen defendants.[86] One court described the wrongdoing:

> The defendants consist of two types of floor traders: "locals," who trade on their own accounts [i.e., floor traders], and brokers who execute orders from customers who may be CBOT members, but usually are members of the public trading through brokerage firms [i.e., floor brokers]. The defendants, as well as numerous other traders, both indicted and unindicted, traded contracts for soybeans futures. . . .

> At trial, the government presented hundreds of allegedly fraudulent trades executed by the various defendants. The core of the charged crimes involved brokers surreptitiously avoiding [competitively executing trades and, instead, arranging them directly with floor traders, i.e.,] . . . locals at selected

----

84. Mark Dobrzycki, *F.B.I. Commodities 'Sting': Fast Money, Secret Lives*, N.Y. Times A1 (Jan. 30, 1989).
85. *Id.*
86. *U.S. v. Dempsey*, 724 F. Supp. 573, 575 (N.D. Ill. 1989).

prices. These arranged trades, determined without the usual open . . . bid or offer in the market, guaranteed profits to the local [at the expense of the floor broker's customer]. The local would then do one of three things (or some combination) with these profits: he might keep the profits as repayment . . . [to set-off a debt] with the broker; he might hold the profits from the arranged trade as a credit against future . . . [debts]; or he might pass the profits back to the broker who had arranged the trade in the first place (i.e., a kickback) or to another trader to whom the broker owed money. . . .[87]

As with the other categories of registrants, the CFTC has broad discretion as to whether a party may be registered as a floor broker. In fact, the conclusion of the court that a presidential pardon does not prevent the CFTC from considering a criminal conviction in deciding upon a registration application, can be applied to any registrant, not just floor brokers.

Hirschberg v. CFTC

414 F.3d 679 (7th Cir. 2005)

Kanne, Circuit Judge.

Judd Hirschberg's floor broker registration was revoked after he was convicted of mail fraud in 1991. In 2000, he received a presidential pardon for that conviction, but the Commodity Futures Trading Commission ("CFTC") nevertheless denied his post-pardon application for floor broker registration. Because a pardon does not eliminate the legal determination that Hirschberg was guilty of the crime of which he was convicted, and the crime was properly considered in the CFTC's application process, we affirm the decision of the CFTC and deny Hirschberg's petition for review. . . .

Hirschberg became a registered floor broker in 1985. According to the Commodities [sic] Exchange Act, floor brokers buy and sell futures contracts for others on an exchange floor such as that of the Chicago Mercantile Exchange ("CME"), where Hirschberg worked. Floor brokers commonly act as fiduciaries in conducting transactions. They are required to register with the CFTC, which has delegated most of the registration process to the National Futures Association ("NFA"). The CFTC also has the power to revoke registration from floor brokers who violate CFTC or NFA rules.

The CFTC initiated revocation proceedings against Hirschberg in 1991, alleging disqualification under Sections 8(a)(2) (conviction of a felony involving fraud) and 8(a)(3) (for good cause) of the Commodities [sic] Exchange Act. Hirschberg had indeed been convicted in federal court on four felony counts of mail fraud and two felony counts of tampering with vehicle identification numbers. These 1991 convictions stemmed from an insurance fraud scheme that took place in 1984,

---

87. *United States v. Ashman*, 979 F.2d 469, 475–477 (7th Cir. 1992).

when Hirschberg reported that his car had been stolen and then collected $43,300 from his insurance company. Several years later, evidence was discovered suggesting that Hirschberg had voluntarily transferred the car to a friend and altered its vehicle identification number to hide the crime. On appeal, this court found insufficient evidence to uphold the conviction for identification number tampering, but affirmed the conviction for mail fraud. Hirschberg was ordered to serve three years of probation and pay $40,000 in restitution.

The CFTC proceedings ultimately led to revocation of Hirschberg's registration in 1994. The Administrative Law Judge ("ALJ") presiding over the hearing did not find sufficient evidence of mitigation or rehabilitation to justify Hirschberg keeping his registration. Weighing against Hirschberg was evidence of disciplinary proceedings brought against him by the CME—several years after the 1984 insurance fraud, Hirschberg was disciplined for engaging in pre-arranged trading in violation of CME rules. Hirschberg has made his living since 1994 (earning substantially less than he did as a floor broker) by consulting for trading houses and training young traders.

In 1998, Hirschberg applied for a presidential pardon of his mail fraud conviction, which was granted by President Clinton in 2000. Pardon in hand, he applied to the NFA for registration as a floor broker in July 2001. After a designated subcommittee conducted a hearing, the NFA denied Hirschberg's application. The subcommittee found that Hirschberg's conviction and subsequent revocation of registration subjected him to a Section 8a(2)(A) disqualification based on his prior revocation. Although this merely created a rebuttable presumption that he was unfit for registration, the subcommittee did not find that Hirschberg presented enough mitigating evidence to rebut the presumption of unfitness. The CFTC affirmed the denial of registration in 2004. Hirschberg appeals the denial on the grounds that the CFTC's decision violates the Pardon Clause, due process, and his statutory rights under the Commodities [*sic*] Exchange Act. . . .

[T]he legal effect of a presidential pardon is to preclude further punishment for the crime, but not to wipe out the fact of conviction. The CFTC did not violate the pardon clause by considering the conduct underlying Hirschberg's conviction in determining whether he was qualified to do business as a floor trader, because its decision was grounded in protection of the public rather than in punishing Hirschberg as a convicted felon. Hirschberg's due process and statutory rights arguments also do not justify reversal of the decision to deny his application for registration. . . .

The CFTC denied Hirschberg's 2001 application for registration based on Section 8a(2)(A) of the Commodities [*sic*] Exchange Act, which . . . allows the CFTC to revoke or deny registration of any person "if a prior registration of such person in any capacity has been suspended . . . or has been revoked[.]" The revocation underlying this statutory disqualification was, of course, based on Hirschberg's 1991 conviction for mail fraud. Hirschberg asserts that, because he received a full and unconditional pardon for that conviction, the CFTC's denial unconstitutionally interferes with the presidential pardon power. . . .

The Constitution gives the President "Power to grant Reprieves and Pardons for Offences against the United States, except in cases of impeachment." U.S. Const. art. II § 2. . . .

A pardon in no way reverses the legal conclusion of the courts. . . . The effect of a pardon is not to prohibit all *consequences* of a pardoned conviction, but rather to preclude future *punishment* for the conviction. The question we must answer, then, is whether the CFTC's denial of Hirschberg's registration is impermissible punitive action or simply a consequence of the conduct underlying the conviction that the pardon could not erase.

The answer turns on whether the conduct for which Hirschberg was convicted has any bearing on his ability to work as a floor broker. Government licensing agencies may consider conduct underlying a pardoned conviction — without improperly "punishing" the pardoned individual — so long as that conduct is relevant to an individual's qualifications for the licensed position. . . . In cases where governmental action has been held to violate the pardon clause, on the other hand, the pardoned individual is stripped of his rights based not on the conduct underlying the conviction, but on the fact of conviction alone. . . .

The statutory disqualification scheme under which Hirschberg's registration was revoked in 1994 and then denied in 2004 was enacted with the Futures Trading Act of 1982. It was designed to "streamline and simplify the [former] registration procedures to enable the [CFTC] to register fit persons more expeditiously and to remove unfit persons from the industry more promptly." H.R. Rep. No. 97-565, pt. 1, at 50 (1982). Given the fiduciary nature of most of the transactions engaged in by a floor broker, there can be no serious doubt that honesty and integrity are legitimate qualifications for the job. Engaging in fraudulent behavior (such as an insurance scam) demonstrates a serious lack of these qualities. In revoking Hirschberg's original registration, the CFTC was allowed to use the conviction as an authoritative source on whether the fraudulent conduct occurred, theoretically improving efficiency and "freeing resources for the performance of its other important regulatory and oversight functions." That revocation served as presumptive evidence that Hirschberg was unfit to be a floor broker when he reapplied for registration, again eliminating the need for the CFTC to spend time and money determining whether Hirschberg had engaged in fraudulent conduct. Convictions for fraud play into the CFTC's registration process because the conduct underlying such convictions is relevant to the business of floor trading, not because the CFTC is interested in further punishing convicted felons. This enables the CFTC to protect the public from unfit floor brokers and to register fit applicants more efficiently.

Further evidence of the CFTC's non-punitive purpose in denying Hirschberg's application is the fact that the conduct underlying Hirschberg's mail fraud conviction would be cause for denial even if he had not been criminally convicted for it. Fraud can be grounds for statutory disqualification when it is the subject of an injunction or of a civil court or administrative ruling in a case to which a government agency is a party. CFTC may also revoke registration "for good cause" . . .

which includes any conduct demonstrating moral turpitude, lack of honesty, or financial irresponsibility, with no prior formal proceedings. Hirschberg's registration in 1991 was not revoked because he was a convict per se, but because he engaged in fraudulent conduct that demonstrated the lack of qualities necessary to be a floor broker. He would have met with the same consequences (the 1994 revocation and the 2004 denial of registration) had the fraudulent conduct been proven independent of a criminal conviction.

One further element convinces us that the CFTC was not impermissibly punishing Hirschberg for his pardoned conviction: Hirschberg was given a chance to rebut the presumption that he was unfit to be a floor broker. Hirschberg would have obtained registration in 2004 if he had been able to demonstrate that he would not pose a significant risk to the public. Unfortunately, Hirschberg did not offer enough evidence in mitigation or of rehabilitation to overcome the presumption that he was unfit for floor broker registration — to the contrary, the evidence of CME disciplinary action bolstered the presumption. The fact that the CFTC's procedural scheme provides an applicant with the opportunity to rebut a presumption of unfitness shows that the relevant consideration is not the conviction itself, but the conduct underlying it.

Given the fiduciary nature of transactions made by a floor trader, the CFTC's reasons for denying Hirschberg's application were both prudent and within the law of presidential pardon. The decision was based on concern for protecting the public in an efficient manner rather than on the desire to punish Hirschberg for his criminal conviction. The denial of floor broker registration based on fraudulent conduct underlying a pardoned criminal conviction does not constitute a violation of the pardon clause. . . .

The CFTC's denial of Hirschberg's registration was based on Section 8a(2)(A) of the Commodities [sic] Exchange Act, which states: "[T]he Commission is authorized . . . to refuse to register . . . any person and with such a hearing as may be appropriate to revoke the registration of any person — if a prior registration of such person in any capacity has been suspended . . . or has been revoked[.]" . . . [T]he plain language of this provision does not contain a time limit for underlying suspensions or revocations. Hirschberg argues that the ten-year time limit from Section 8a(2)(D),[88] the provision on which his 1994 revocation was based, should be incorporated into Section 8a(2)(A). Because he was convicted in 1991, more than ten years prior to filing his current application, this incorporated time limit would make Section 8a(2)(A) inapplicable to Hirschberg. . . .

Limitations periods are favored in connection with lawsuits to encourage prompt resolution of claims and to prevent a party from being prosecuted or sued after witnesses have become incapacitated due to faded memory or death. Neither these

---

88. [N. 1] This provision . . . allows the CFTC to revoke or deny registration to a person who "has been convicted *within ten years* preceding the filing of the application for registration or at any time thereafter of any felony that . . . (iv) involves the violation of section [1341] . . . of Title 18 [mail fraud]." (emphasis added).

policy reasons nor the tradition of inferring a time limitation are present in the context of disciplinary actions.

Looking at Section 8a as a whole reinforces the notion that a time limitation should not be inferred in Section 8a(2)(A). While the plain language of that provision contains no time limit, some of the other twenty-two subsections laying out grounds for disqualification in Sections 8a(2) and 8a(3) do. This suggests a conscious choice by Congress to require that a person who has lost his registration once must affirmatively show rehabilitation before again obtaining registration, regardless of when the conduct underlying the revocation occurred. . . .

The CFTC violated neither the pardon clause nor principles of due process, because it did not seek to punish Hirschberg for his pardoned federal conviction. The CFTC permissibly and rationally considered the conduct underlying Hirschberg's conviction in ascertaining whether he would be fit to act as a floor broker. Also, we are not compelled to infer a time limitation on the statutory disqualification relied upon by the CFTC. We therefore AFFIRM the decision of the CFTC and deny Hirschberg's petition.

* * *

Questions and Comments

1. Although typically seen as a useful auxiliary to CFTC regulation, some have expressed concern that "too much deference to [self-regulatory organizations] can lead to the very harms the [Commodity Exchange Act] was designed to prevent—for example, market manipulation, because of the dangers associated with allowing those who must follow the rules to make and enforce said rules."[89] Why might industry participants have incentives to impose self-regulation and in what circumstances might they not?

2. Many of the registrant categories discussed in this chapter are required to be members of the National Futures Association. What questions arise in mandating membership and association with a private organization as a predicate to registration?

3. What would be the ramifications of the CFTC removing all restrictions on futures commission merchants' investment of customer margin funds? Would it increase the care customers take in selecting a futures commission merchant? Would customers impose contractual restrictions on investments that can be made by their futures commission merchant with their margin funds? What might a smaller customer who might not have the leverage to bargain for customized terms with a futures commission merchant do?

4. In the wake of the failure of MF Global, the CFTC enacted rules adding further restrictions on the use of customer funds by futures commission merchants.

---

89. Derek Fischer, *Dodd-Frank's Failure to Address CFTC Oversight of Self-Regulatory Organization Rulemaking*, 115 Colum. L. Rev. 69, 78 (Jan. 2015) (footnotes omitted).

Do you think these efforts will be successful? Would they have prevented the MF Global debacle? How, on the other hand, if at all, can outright fraud be addressed by regulators?

5. Customers of securities broker-dealers may be able to avail of Securities Investor Protection Corporation protection and customers of banks may be able to avail of Federal Deposit Insurance Corporation protection. Should a similar regime exist with respect to customer funds held by futures commission merchants?

6. The decision in *Prestwick v. Peregrine* appears to allow for cancellation of a guarantee of an introducing broker by a futures commission merchant without notice to customers of the introducing broker. What are ways of allowing futures commission merchants the freedom to cancel contractual relationships while protecting customers of introducing brokers who may not be aware that a guarantee has been cancelled?

7. The court in *Prestwick v. Peregrine* notes that "Although Prestwick may have legitimate grounds to challenge this framework, the place to do so is not before the courts." What might the court be suggesting?

8. In *United States v. Sanders*, the commodity trading floor at the Chicago Board of Trade was infiltrated by brazen fraudsters armed with wigs and stolen jackets. Is electronic trading more or less susceptible to fraud?

9. Are there any advantages to open outcry floor trading over electronic trading?

Chapter 7

Commodity Pool Operators

A. Background

1. General

As we have seen in the preceding chapters, the CFTC regulates the markets on which commodity futures and options trade and the primary intermediaries that operate in those markets. In chapters ahead, we will examine the other markets regulated by the CFTC, i.e., the swap market, foreign exchange market, and retail commodity markets.

The backdrop for this chapter and the next is the investment industry. Core activities of the investment industry generally include managing money of third parties, advising third parties regarding trading, and the formation of collective investment vehicles such as mutual funds, hedge funds, private equity funds, and commodity pools.

The CFTC regulates the derivatives investment and advisory industry, including by requiring the registration of commodity pool operators and commodity trading advisors. Commodity pool operators are the subject of this chapter, and commodity trading advisors are the subject of the following chapter. We will also look at the many exemptions from registration or from some of the requirements associated with registration. These exemptions are particularly important for the private fund industry (e.g., hedge funds).

2. Relation to Securities Law

While the CFTC generally regulates these activities where they involve derivatives, the SEC also regulates significant aspects of this industry. Any investment interest offered by a collective investment vehicle, for example, is a security subject to the securities laws for which the SEC is the regulator. States also have an important role in regulating securities offerings through their "blue sky" laws.

For those with an exposure to securities law, it is natural to seek parallels between the SEC's securities investment industry regulatory regime and the CFTC's derivatives investment industry regulatory regime. In fact, one category of SEC securities investment registrants, investment advisers, is largely analogous to a CFTC registrant, commodity trading advisor. It is not uncommon to see a "dual registrant," i.e., an entity simultaneously registered with the SEC as an investment adviser and with the CFTC as a commodity trading advisor. This is similar to futures commission merchants, many of which, as we discussed in chapter 6, section A, are also dually registered as securities broker-dealers.

On the other hand, the securities law term "investment company," a collective investment vehicle commonly referred to as a "mutual fund," does not have a direct analogue in "commodity pool operator." As we will see in more detail below, whereas the SEC regulates the collective investment vehicle itself, the CFTC regulates the "operator" of the collective investment vehicle, treating the vehicle itself largely like any other trader in the marketplace.

Those who have an exposure to securities law will benefit in some ways from analogizing the two fields, most notably with the regulation of investment advice. On the other hand, care must be taken, especially with derivatives investment vehicles, to look at derivatives regulations apart from pre-existing understandings of the regulation of securities investment vehicles. Even fundamental terminology differs in that parties are often said to "invest" in securities and "trade" derivatives.

B. Commodity Pools and Commodity Pool Operators

As noted above, unlike investment companies, the closest counterpart to commodity pools under the securities laws, commodity pools do not have a registration obligation. The registration and regulatory burdens are, instead, placed on the operators of commodity pools. The Commodity Exchange Act defines a commodity pool operator as a person "engaged in a business that is of the nature of a commodity pool, investment trust, syndicate, or similar form of enterprise, and who, in connection therewith, solicits, accepts, or receives from others, funds, securities, or property, either directly or through capital contributions, the sale of stock or other forms of securities, or otherwise, for the purpose of trading in commodity interests. . . ."[1] To understand whether a person is a "commodity pool operator," one must first understand the meaning of a "commodity pool."

1. Commodity Pools

a. What Is a Commodity Pool?

The Commodity Exchange Act defines a commodity pool as "any investment trust, syndicate, or similar form of enterprise operated for the purpose of trading in commodity interests, *including*" a futures contract, security futures contract, commodity option, swap, and certain retail foreign exchange and commodity transactions.[2]

---

1. Commodity Exchange Act § 1a(11).
2. Commodity Exchange Act § 1a(10) (emphasis added).

The definition is apparently duplicative, since "commodity interests" already is defined by the CFTC to include the products over which the CFTC has jurisdiction. Namely, these are the same as those enumerated in the definition of "commodity pool."[3] A more colloquial way to define a commodity pool might be as a collective investment enterprise operated for the purpose of trading futures, commodity options, swaps, or certain retail foreign exchange and retail commodity transactions.

Two questions that remain are what activities are "enterprises" and what does it mean for a collective investment enterprise to be operated for the "purpose of trading" these products?

b. What Is an "Enterprise"?

The term "enterprise" implies the existence of a common venture, a concept consistent with the ordinary meaning of "commodity pool." The word "pool" is referring to a pooling of assets, i.e., assets being put together.

What level of commonality is needed? The case below analyzed this question and the resulting four-part test for a commodity pool has been broadly adopted by courts.

Lopez v. Dean Witter Reynolds, Inc.

805 F.2d 880 (9th Cir. 1986)

Nelson, Circuit Judge:

Alfred D. Lopez ("Lopez") and Jeanie Reitzell ("Reitzell") appeal the district court dismissal of their claims for violations of the Securities Act of 1933 and the Commodity Exchange Act against Dean Witter Reynolds Inc. ("Dean Witter").

They argue that the district court erred in dismissing these claims because the account in which Reitzell invested was one in which commodities futures contracts were purchased and sold, and therefore constituted both a commodity pool and a security. . . .

This action arose as a result of losses sustained by Lopez and Reitzell in investments which they made through Dean Witter. . . .

[A]ppellants . . . [claimed] that churning[4] by Dean Witter of their investment accounts, constituted a violation of the Securities and Exchange Act of 1934 and Rule 10b-5 promulgated thereunder. In addition, Lopez and Reitzell charged Dean Witter with violating Section 10(b) and Rule 10b-5 by entering into transactions unsuitable to their investment accounts, and they also raised several common law and constructive fraud claims and breach of contract claims.

---

3. 17 C.F.R. § 1.3 (definition of commodity interest).

4. [N. 1] Churning is defined to occur "when a broker, exercising control over the volume and frequency of trades, abuses his customer's confidence for personal gain by initiating transactions that are excessive in view of the character of account and the customer's objectives as expressed to the broker."

Reitzell, individually, charged Dean Witter with violating the Commodity Exchange Act by inducing her to invest in its Commodity Guided Account Program ("CGAP").[5] She also alleged that Dean Witter engaged in mishandling of her CGAP account in violation of the Securities Act of 1933. It is these claims which are the subject of this appeal....

The two issues presented for our review are:

(1) Whether the district court erred in dismissing appellant's claim alleging a violation of the Commodity Exchange Act, finding that the program in which appellant had invested was not a commodity pool subject to the provisions of the Act; and

(2) Whether the district court erred in dismissing appellant's claim alleging a violation of the Securities Act of 1933, finding that the program in which appellant had invested was not a security subject to the provisions of the Act....

In order to determine whether the commodity accounts which Appellants held with Dean Witter were subject to the provisions of the ... [Commodity Exchange Act], our first inquiry must be whether Dean Witter was running a commodity pool subject to the requirements of the Commodity Exchange Act. A commodity pool operator ("CPO") ... is one who is engaged in a business "of the nature of investment trust, syndicate, or *similar* form of enterprise." (emphasis supplied). The Commodity Futures Trading Commission ("CFTC") regulations track the statute. However, no authority binding on us has spelled out the definition more precisely....

Dean Witter argues that in order to constitute a commodity pool, there must be a pro rata sharing by the participants of profits and losses, and since here, there was no such sharing, there was no pool.

Appellants on the other hand, argue that at the crucial moment when a trade was executed, it was executed for the combined account, not for any individual customer. Thereafter, the contracts were allocated to individual accounts, and this allocation of contracts performed a function similar, although not identical, to a pro rata division of the profits and losses.

Those courts which have raised the issue require the following factors to be present in a commodity pool: (1) an investment organization in which the funds of various investors are solicited and combined into a single account for the purpose of investing in commodity futures contracts; (2) common funds used to execute transactions on behalf of the entire account; (3) participants share pro rata in accrued

---

5. [N. 2] The CGAP in which Reitzell invested ... was a program in which ... twenty percent [of a customer's deposit was] placed in an account, along with funds from other participants in the CGAP. It was from these combined funds that commodities futures contracts were purchased and sold. However, each investor had separate accounts to which individual account numbers were assigned, and an individual's ability to engage in any purchases or trades of a particular commodity was dependent upon the minimum equity level in that individual's account. Thus, not all accounts traded the same contracts....

profits or losses from the commodity futures trading; and (4) the transactions are traded by a commodity pool operator in the name of the pool rather than in the name of any individual investor. . . .

Applying the above requirements to Dean Witter's CGAP, we find that the program did not have the necessary characteristics to constitute a pool. There was a disparity in investment in the individual accounts, and because of the equity level required to engage in certain purchases and trades, not all accounts traded the same contracts. Therefore, not all accounts shared a pro rata profit or loss.

Although the CGAP possessed some of the requirements which have been deemed necessary to constitute a commodity pool . . . the CGAP's characteristics are sufficient to distinguish it from a commodity pool.

Furthermore, while we recognize that the speculative commodities market requires strict regulation, we do not find the CGAP to be the type of account which Congress intended to constitute a commodity pool subject to the registration, [*sic*] reporting requirements of the Commodity Futures Exchange Act.

We hold, therefore, that because the CGAP was not a commodity pool, the district court was correct in its finding and grant of summary judgment on this claim. . . .

Reitzell argues that the CGAP constitutes an investment contract and is therefore a security subject to the registration requirement of section 5 of the Securities Act of 1933. . . .

We have previously held that a discretionary commodities trading account, such as the CGAP, is not an investment contract. . . .

While we recognize a need for added investor protection, under current case law and the law of this circuit, the district court properly granted summary judgment in favor of Dean Witter. . . .

The court in *Lopez* laid out a four-part test for identifying a commodity pool, stating that a commodity pool is:

(1) an investment organization in which the funds of various investors are solicited and combined into a single account for the purpose of investing in commodity futures contracts [or, we would add, commodity options, swaps, or certain retail foreign exchange and commodity transactions];

(2) common funds used to execute transactions on behalf of the entire account;

(3) participants share pro rata in accrued profits or losses from the commodity futures trading; and

(4) the transactions are traded by a commodity pool operator in the name of the pool rather than in the name of any individual investor.[6]

---

6. *Lopez v. Dean Witter Reynolds, Inc.*, 805 F.2d 880, 884 (9th Cir. 1986).

The *Lopez* test implies that a prerequisite to commodity pool status is the existence of actual commodity futures trades when it requires "common funds used to execute transactions."[7] Subsequent courts took up the question of whether, for a commodity pool to exist, actual trading in commodity futures must occur or whether the mere solicitation of funds for that purpose is sufficient. This is an important question for determining the CFTC's enforcement authority with respect to frauds where customer funds are solicited for an ostensible "commodity pool" and, instead, personally appropriated by the party making the solicitation. We look at one of the cases addressing this question, *CFTC v. Perkins*, below.

Also, the *Lopez* court was focused on the requirement that a commodity pool operator "solicit" funds. However, that finding is specific to *Lopez*. The actual definition of commodity pool operator includes one who "solicits, accepts, or receives" funds.[8]

c. *"Purpose of Trading"*

As noted immediately above, courts have grappled with the question of what level of activity demonstrates that a collective investment enterprise is operated for the purpose of trading one of the products over which the CFTC has jurisdiction. Where trading activities have been extensively undertaken, the question is easily answered. But what if funds are solicited from third parties ostensibly for a trading venture and no trading activities are undertaken? Or what if the funds are on-forwarded to an investment operated by someone other than the person soliciting the funds? This typically comes up in the context of fraud where a fraudster solicits funds intending to embezzle them while claiming to the victims, for example, that the funds will be used to trade commodity futures. The CFTC in such cases frequently charges the perpetrator of the fraud with failure to register as a commodity pool operator and with violating many of the requirements that apply to commodity pool operators.

In such cases, can the fraudster claim that, since the funds were not solicited for the purposes of trading, there was accordingly no commodity pool, and that, in the absence of a commodity pool, the fraudster cannot be deemed an unregistered commodity pool operator? For these reasons, the extent to which a collective investment enterprise must engage in actual trading activities before being deemed a commodity pool has been a source of controversy that courts, including the court in the following case, have struggled to resolve.

---

7. These references to commodity futures should be deemed to also include the other products over which the CFTC has jurisdiction.

8. Commodity Exchange Act § 1a(11)(A)(1) (emphasis added). *See also CFTC v. Amerman*, 645 Fed. Appx. 938 n. 4 (11th Cir. 2016).

What Happens If the CFTC Cannot Act?

Fraud cases present unique challenges to judges when there is clearly out-and-out fraud and, nonetheless, there is a claim that the activity is outside of the CFTC's jurisdiction. Arguably, some judges feel a pull to find a basis for the CFTC's jurisdiction so that the perpetrator of the fraud does not get away with it.

However, what are the consequences of the CFTC not having jurisdiction? Does it mean that there is no remedy for the fraud? Even if there is not another federal regulator with jurisdiction, what about state regulators or attorneys general? Is financial fraud of such a complexity and scale that state regulators cannot adequately police it in the absence of a federal regulator?

CFTC v. Williams D. Perkins

385 Fed. Appx. 251 (3d Cir. 2010)

Barry, Circuit Judge.

This is the second of two actions brought by the Commodity Futures Trading Commission ("CFTC") in response to a multi-million dollar investment fraud scheme involving commodity futures trading. In the first case, we affirmed the judgment entered against the manager of an investment vehicle called Shasta Capital Associates ("Shasta"), holding that Shasta's manager, Equity Financial Group LLC ("Equity Group"), was a "commodity pool operator" ("CPO") for purposes of the Commodity Exchange Act even though Shasta did not actually execute any futures trades and instead forwarded money to another fund — Tech Traders — which executed trades. *Commodity Futures Trading Comm'n v. Equity Fin. Group LLC*, 572 F.3d 150 (3d Cir.2009) ("*Equity*"), cert. denied, *Shimer v. Commodity Futures Trading Comm'n*, 559 U.S. 991, 130 S. Ct. 1737, 176 L.Ed.2d 212 (2010). We consider here whether appellant William Perkins ("Perkins"), the manager of another investment vehicle, Universe Capital Appreciation, LLC ("Universe"), which also did not execute futures trades, and instead forwarded investment funds to Shasta (which in turn forwarded the funds to Tech Traders), was a CPO.

The issue before us is essentially identical to the one we considered in *Equity*, and we respectfully decline Perkins's emphatic invitation to revisit our recently-established precedent. The District Court determined that Perkins acted as a CPO. We agree, and will affirm. . . .

Perkins argues that he was not acting as a CPO because Universe did not participate in "the actual trading itself . . . in the name of the pool entity from a commodity futures trading account that has been opened at a futures commission merchant . . . in the name of the pool." That argument is unavailing in light of our opinion in Equity, in which we explained that

> the statute does not require a commodity pool operator to execute commodity futures transactions. The language of the definition lacks an explicit

trading requirement, and the remedial purposes of the statute would be thwarted if the operator of a fund could avoid the regulatory scheme simply by investing in another pool rather than trading. If an entity is engaged in a business in the nature of an investment trust, syndicate, or similar form of enterprise, and it solicits, accepts, or receives funds for the purpose of trading, it is a commodity pool operator. The actual trading of commodity futures is not required.

572 F.3d at 158.

Perkins offers numerous reasons why he believes we should revisit *Equity* and follow *Lopez v. Dean Witter Reynolds, Inc.*, 805 F. 2d 880 (9th Cir. 1986), which he insists imposes a trading requirement. In *Equity*, we quoted *Lopez's* four-part test (for determining whether an entity is a commodity pool) and wrote that "[t]he *Lopez* court confronted . . . a different legal question" and "did not address whether a commodity pool operator must itself execute commodity futures transactions." 572 F.3d at 158. Thus, we have already considered the specific arguments Perkins raises, and rejected them.

Perkins nevertheless suggests that we might benefit from "a competent analysis of the legislative history of the . . . [Commodity Exchange Act (the "CEA")] and the expectation of Congress about the direct involvement in commodity futures trading activity by CPO's [sic]." We think our legislative history analysis in Equity was more than satisfactory. There, we determined that "[t]he absence of a trading requirement is consistent with the purposes of the" CEA, explaining that "when Congress defined commodity pool operator, it sought to regulate the solicitation of funds from customers and potential customers. And it intended to protect them from harmful conduct, especially fraudulent solicitation. The statute would be undermined if one entity could escape regulation merely by having another execute its trades." *Equity*, 572 F.3d at 157.

Perkins posits that the District Court's analysis of *Lopez* is "a stunning example of why appellate review is . . . necessary," arguing that Universe could not have been a commodity pool because the Universe funds did not remain "combined" in "a single account," but were instead "periodically transferred from time to time over a period of more than two years to . . . Shasta which, in turn, periodically wired the funds . . . to . . . Tech [Traders]." (emphasis omitted.) This argument is without merit. Similar fund transfers took place in Equity, and we made clear that such transfers do not offend the definition of "commodity pool." Allowing an investment manager to circumvent regulation merely by transferring funds from one account to another does not comport with Congress's aim of protecting investors.

In his reply brief, Perkins cites thirty-eight provisions of the CFTC regulations and argues that our holding in *Equity* is "in direct conflict with all thirty-eight!"[9] The cited provisions unsurprisingly require CPOs to provide commodity pool participants with

---

9. [N. 2] For example, Perkins quotes regulations requiring that CPOs provide pool participants with certain information which only the trader is likely to know, like the "commodity interest

extensive information about the commodity futures trades involving their money. Perkins reads those provisions as signaling that the CFTC itself interprets the terms "commodity pool" and "CPO" more narrowly than we did in *Equity*. However, as we pointed out in *Equity*, other CFTC regulations suggest just the opposite. 572 F.3d at 157 n. 13. The conflicting language of those regulations does not change our conclusion that Congress intended broad definitions of "commodity pool" and "CPO."

Perkins also contends that Universe is distinguishable from Equity Group in that Universe was further from the actual trading (twice removed, instead of just once), and so did not have the character of a commodity pool. Our holding in *Equity* makes clear that the proximity to trading is not an important factor. If the pool is established with the purpose of trading in commodity futures, then the pool is a commodity pool for CEA purposes. *See Equity*, 572 F.3d at 158.

We reject the other arguments made by Perkins and the Tax Accounting Office, Inc., without further discussion. We will affirm the judgment of the District Court.

If the *Lopez* four-part test is adopted verbatim it would mean, as one court noted, the exemption of "pool operators who receive investors' money 'for the purpose of trading in any commodity for future delivery,' but simply misappropriate the entire fund without trading in any commodities futures at all."[10] This is not likely an outcome the *Lopez* court intended. Moreover, it is difficult to reconcile an actual trading requirement with the statutory language defining a commodity pool as "any investment trust, syndicate, or similar form of enterprise *operated for the purpose of trading in* commodity interests. . . ."[11] It does not contain an actual trading requirement.

But let us look at another possible fact pattern. In *CFTC v. Perkins*, Perkins was deemed to be a commodity pool operator when he solicited funds for the purpose of commodity investments and then forwarded the investors' funds to a third entity which itself forwarded the investors' funds to yet another entity. Since Perkins was deemed to be a commodity pool operator all of the obligations of commodity pool operators applied to him despite his protestations that he was unable to comply with some, such as the provision to investors of investment information, because he did not hold the investors' funds.

Even in a legitimate enterprise, a person soliciting funds from investors and placing the funds with a third party would not be able to comply with the CFTC's regulations on commodity pool operators. The solicitor would not know all the trading activity of the commodity pool and all its customers. Of course, it is doubtful that the CFTC would assert that such a person is an unregistered commodity pool

---

positions liquidated," "unrealized gain or loss in which the pool engaged," and the "total amount of all brokerage commissions during the reporting period." (emphasis omitted.)

10. *CFTC v. Vision Capital Corp.*, 2007 WL 4246302 (D. Utah Nov. 28, 2007), at *3 (emphasis added).

11. Commodity Exchange Act § 1a(10).

operator in a non-fraud situation. So what changes when it is a situation with an allegation of fraud such as that in *CFTC v. Perkins*?

Accordingly, another way to look at the *Lopez/CFTC v. Perkins* circuit split is as a narrow versus broad construction of the Commodity Exchange Act's grant of jurisdiction to the CFTC over pooled investments. In the context of fraud, a court might feel compelled to take a broad view of CFTC jurisdiction so that the fraud is addressed. However, it is important to remember that the CFTC is not the only means to address fraud. For example, state prosecutors often have the option of pursuing common law fraud claims.

2. Commodity Pool Operators

Once a commodity pool is found to exist, it is necessary to determine who is the commodity pool operator. The commodity pool operator is generally the party that sponsors or controls the activities of the commodity pool. For example, the commodity pool operator would normally be the general partner of a commodity pool formed as a limited partnership, the managing member of a commodity pool formed as a limited liability company, or the trustee of a commodity pool formed as a trust. As with other categories of registrant, this question is often examined in situations where the CFTC asserts that an entity was obligated to register and did not.

In the following case related to *CFTC v. Perkins*, the court, building on a finding by a trial court that the trading pool at issue was a commodity pool (ultimately upheld by the Third Circuit[12]), examined the question of whether parties were commodity pool operators or, alternatively, "associated persons" of a commodity pool operator (for a discussion on associated persons generally, see chapter 6, section A.3.a) and, therefore, liable for either failure to register as a commodity pool operator or as associated persons of a commodity pool operator. Additionally — in what should be a salutary caution to lawyers — an attorney was charged with aiding and abetting the failure to register by the operators of the commodity pool.

CFTC v. Equity Financial Group, LLC
2006 WL 3751911 (D.N.J. Dec. 18, 2006)

Kugler, United States District Judge.

Before the Court is a motion by Plaintiff Commodity Futures Trading Commission for partial summary judgment against Defendants Equity Financial Group, Robert W. Shimer and Vincent J. Firth with respect to charges that they violated . . . the Commodities [sic] Exchange Act. . . . In addition, Plaintiff moves for summary judgment with respect to the charge that Defendant Shimer aided and abetted [Commodity Exchange Act violations]. . . . For the reasons provided below, Plaintiff's motion will be granted in part and denied in part. . . .

---

12. *See CFTC v. Equity Financial Group LLC*, 572 F.3d 150 (3d Cir. 2009).

The motions presently before the Court relate to the role of Robert W. Shimer ("Shimer"), Vincent J. Firth ("Firth") and Equity Financial Group, LLC ("Equity"), (collectively "Equity Defendants"), in a multi-million dollar commodity fraud operated by Defendants Tech Traders and its president Coyt Murray ("Murray"). Between June 2001 and April 2004, Tech Traders allegedly solicited over $47 million in investments by claiming to employ a portfolio trading system that guaranteed significant annual returns. While Tech Traders and its supposedly independent certified public accountant ("CPA"), Defendant Vernon Abernethy ("Abernethy"), reported substantial monthly and quarterly gains, Tech Traders was actually hemorrhaging money at a remarkable rate, resulting in losses in excess of $20 million. Tech Traders lost at least $7 million in trading commodity futures contracts, and unlawfully appropriated investors' funds to pay salaries, expenses, and make disbursements under the guise of profit.

The Equity Defendants' liability arises from their control and operation of a related investment group, Shasta Capital Associates, LLC ("Shasta"), which was essentially a feeder fund for Tech Traders. The Commodity Futures Trading Commission ("CFTC" or "Plaintiff") alleges that the Equity Defendants solicited approximately $15 million from 74 investors between June 2001 and March 2004, for the purpose of investing in Tech Traders. . . . Upon receipt, investor funds were deposited into Shimer's attorney escrow account and then transmitted to Tech Traders. . . .

Plaintiff CFTC alleges that because Equity failed to register with CFTC as a Commodity Pool Operator ("CPO"), Equity violated 7 U.S.C. § 6m(1) when it allegedly used instrumentalities of interstate commerce, such as the telephone and the mail, in connection with its business as a CPO. Equity Defendants do not directly address this count in their opposition papers. Rather, they continue to insist that Shasta is not a "commodity pool," the threshold issue for bringing this action under the jurisdiction of the CFTC. . . .

This Court previously held that Shasta constituted a commodity pool. *See Commodity Futures Trading Comm'n v. Equity Fin. Group*, No. 04-1512, 2006 WL 3359418 (D.N.J. Nov. 16, 2006); *see also Commodity Futures Trading Comm'n v. Equity Fin. Group*, No. 04-1512, 2005 WL 2864784 (D.N.J. Oct. 4, 2005). Likewise, the Court concludes that Equity is the CPO for Shasta, because Equity solicited funds from investors, pooled those funds, and invested them in futures trading through Tech Traders. . . .

The question now before the Court is whether Equity used the mails and other instrumentalities of interstate commerce in connection with its business as a CPO. . . .

The evidence demonstrates that Equity, acting as an unregistered CPO, used instrumentalities of interstate commerce, i.e., the telephone, in connection with its business. Therefore, the Court . . . grants Plaintiff's motion for summary judgment with regard to this count. . . .

Plaintiff also moves for summary judgment on the charge that Defendant Shimer aided and abetted Equity's failure to register as a CPO.

The Act provides that:

> Any person who commits, or who willfully aids, abets, counsels, commands, induces, or procures the commission of, a violation of any of the provisions of this chapter, or any of the rules, regulations, or orders issued pursuant to this chapter, or who acts in combination or concert with any other person in any such violation, or who willfully causes an act to be done or omitted which if directly performed or omitted by him or another would be a violation of the provisions of this chapter or any of such rules, regulations, or orders may be held responsible for such violation as a principal.

7 U.S.C. §13c(a).

Plaintiff asserts that Defendant Shimer "had the requisite knowledge that Equity was a CPO ... because he was a lawyer ... and [had] been registered as an [Associated Person ("AP")] of a CPO before." Although the evidence supports Plaintiff's assertions regarding Shimer's status as a lawyer and as a registered Associated Person of another CPO, the evidence does not conclusively establish that Defendant Shimer acted willfully. In his deposition testimony, Defendant Firth stated that Defendant Shimer researched whether Shasta, Equity, or any individuals needed to register with CFTC. Firth further testified that Shimer concluded that registration was not required, and his findings were subsequently verified by a "firm." Given this evidence, there is a genuine issue of material fact as to whether Defendant Shimer willfully violated the Act by failing to register Equity as a CPO. Therefore, Plaintiff's motion for summary judgment on the aiding abetting count associated with 7 U.S.C. §6m(1) is denied....

Plaintiff CFTC [also] alleges that Defendants Firth and Shimer violated 7 U.S.C. §6k(2) of the Act by failing to register as Associated Persons ("APs") of the CPO....

The question now before the Court is whether Defendants Shimer and Firth are APs under the Act, and if so, whether they registered with CFTC. Courts define an AP as someone who "engage[s] in the solicitation of customers' orders." *Miller v. Commodities* [sic] *Future Trading Comm'n*, 197 F.3d 1227, 1229 (9th Cir. 1999); see also *Commodities* [sic] *Future Trading Comm'n v. Sidoti*, 178 F.3d 1132, 1134 (11th Cir. 1999) (defining APs as "salespeople" for the brokerage house).

The record demonstrates that Shimer and Firth acted as APs for Equity.... [T]he deposition testimony of Defendant Firth, as well as Nicholas Stevenson, referenced telephone conversations during which Defendant Firth solicited prospective investors. Stevenson further elaborated that his understanding was that Defendant Firth was the "marketing sales guy" for the CPO, and that Defendant Shimer was not only the "legal representative" for Shasta, but that he also played a "meaningful role getting investors" because he was an attorney, and his credentials made potential investors more comfortable because the investors assumed that Shimer, as member of the bar, performed the proper due diligence. In addition, the record demonstrates that Defendant Shimer personally referred potential investors to Shasta.

Finally, the record demonstrates that neither Defendant Firth, nor Defendant Shimer, were registered as APs for Equity. . . .

This Court previously held that Defendant Shimer acted as an AP for Shasta, a CPO. . . . [T]he next inquiry is whether Shimer used the "mails or any means or instrumentality of interstate commerce" to "engage[ ] in any transaction, practice or course of business which operate[d] as a fraud or deceit on any client or participant or prospective client or participant."

CFTC offers uncontroverted evidence that Shimer drafted the [private placement memorandum] which touted the Tech Traders' system and performance . . .

In addition, there were signs throughout the relationship with Murray and Tech Traders that there was a problem. . . .

Because Shimer, who had a fiduciary relationship to Shasta's investors, intentionally ignored the numerous and varied warning signs regarding Tech Traders and Murray, his lack of action had the effect of perpetrating a fraud on Shasta's investors. In addition, Shimer used the internet to post . . . [the private placement memorandum] on the Shasta website, and he communicated with the CPAs, potential investors, and Murray via e-mail. . . .

––––––––––––

Note that in *CFTC v. Equity Financial Group*, at issue were additional allegations that Equity failed to register as a commodity trading advisor, a category of registration that is the subject of chapter 8. The court ruled in favor of the defendants and then, on a subsequent motion for reconsideration filed by the CFTC, found a violation of a failure to register as a commodity trading advisor by Tech Trader, Inc., and aiding and abetting liability for the attorney, Robert Shimer.[13] The Third Circuit subsequently affirmed the district court's rulings.[14]

3. Regulatory Requirements

a. Generally

Commodity pool operators are required to be registered with the CFTC and to be members of the National Futures Association. As discussed in section A.2 above, there are also overlaps with securities law. Unlike with respect to futures commission merchants, there is no requirement for a commodity pool operator to establish a risk management program,[15] maintain capital, or appoint a chief compliance officer and submit annual compliance reports. While the futures commission merchant

––––––––––––

13. *CFTC v. Equity Financial Group, LLC*, 2007 WL 1038754 (D.N.J. Mar. 30, 2007). After additional factual findings, the court ruled in favor of the CFTC on additional claims. *See CFTC v. Equity Financial Group LLC*, 537 F. Supp. 2d 677 (D.N.J. 2008).

14. *CFTC v. Equity Financial Group LLC*, 572 F.3d 150 (3d Cir. 2009).

15. Commodity pool operators are, however, subject to National Futures Association requirements to have an information systems security program in place to protect customer data and a

regulatory regime described in chapter 6 is mostly focused on protecting customers' funds, the regulatory regime for commodity pool operators is largely focused on disclosure to potential investors.

As with futures commission merchants and introducing brokers, associated persons and principals of commodity pool operators must pass proficiency exams administered by the National Futures Association, be fingerprinted, and not be disqualified.

b. Disclosure Documents

Before a participant in a pool invests, the commodity pool operator must send a highly detailed disclosure document accepted by the National Futures Association.[16] The disclosure document is required to contain specific text mandated by CFTC rule and all "material information."[17] Among other details, "material information" includes details of principals, their business backgrounds, risk factors, trading strategy, fees and expenses, conflicts of interest, and material litigation.[18] National Futures Association rules require it to be in "plain English."[19] Historical performance data, where available, must also be provided.[20]

Incorrect statements in the disclosure document that the commodity pool operator "knows or should know" are materially inaccurate or incomplete must be corrected within twenty-one days of such time.[21]

What Is "Plain English"?

National Futures Association Rule 2-35 requires commodity pool disclosure documents to be "as clear and concise as possible, using plain English principles." This leads to the question, what does "plain English" mean?

The National Futures Association provides guidance that disclosure documents ought to be written:

- In the active voice;

- Using short sentences and paragraphs;

---

business continuity and disaster recovery plan. National Futures Association Rules 2-9, 2-36, 2-38, and 2-49.

16. 17 C.F.R. § 4.21. *See also* National Futures Association, *Disclosure Documents: A Guide for CPOs*, https://www.nfa.futures.org/members/member-resources/files/cpo-disclosure-documents.pdf (Fed. 2020).

17. 17 C.F.R. §§ 4.24(a), (b), and (w).

18. 17 C.F.R. § 4.24.

19. National Futures Association Rule 2-35(a)(1).

20. 17 C.F.R. § 4.25.

21. 17 C.F.R. § 4.26(c)(1)(i).

- Breaking up the document into short sections, using titles and sub-titles that specifically describe the contents of each section;

- Using words that are definite, concrete, and part of everyday language;

- Avoiding legal jargon and highly technical terms;

- Using glossaries to define technical terms that cannot be avoided;

- Avoiding multiple negatives;

- Saying something once where it is most important rather than repeating information;

- Using tables and bullet lists, where appropriate.[a]

[a] National Futures Association Interpretative Notice 9035 (Apr. 30, 1999).

c. Financial Statements

Within 30 days of the end of each month,[22] commodity pool operators must prepare two types of financial statements for commodity pool participants. The first is a "Statement of Operations." This show the gains and losses on the commodity pool's positions in the preceding month along with fees, commissions, and expenses paid.[23] The second is a "Statement of Changes in Net Assets." This shows the commodity pool's net asset value, i.e., assets minus liabilities, withdrawals and redemptions by participants, and the addition of funds from new participants.[24]

Commodity pool operators also must distribute an audited financial report to commodity pool participants and the National Futures Association.[25]

d. Reporting and Recordkeeping

On a quarterly basis, commodity pool operators must provide the National Futures Association information about itself and the commodity pools it operates.[26] Commodity pool property cannot be commingled with other property, such as the assets of other commodity pools.[27]

Records that must be kept by commodity pool operators include commodity pool transactions, financial records, participant details, trade confirmations, all marketing materials including their dates, and records regarding proprietary trading activities of the commodity pool operator.[28] As is the case for futures commis-

---

22. If a commodity pool's assets are $500,000 or less, this is only a quarterly requirement. 17 C.F.R. § 4.22(b).

23. 17 C.F.R. § 4.22(a)(1).

24. 17 C.F.R. § 4.22(a)(2).

25. 17 C.F.R. § 4.22(c).

26. National Futures Association Rule 2-46.

27. 17 C.F.R. § 4.20(c).

28. 17 C.F.R. § 4.23.

sion merchants and introducing brokers, they must be stored for five years. If stored in paper form, they must be readily accessible for productions to the CFTC or the National Futures Association for the preceding two years and, if stored electronically, they must be readily accessible for the entire five-year period.[29] Voice recordings are subject to a shorter retention period of one year.[30]

e. Advertising and Marketing Restrictions

Advertisements and marketing materials, regardless of the medium, are subject to a general prohibition on fraud and deceit.[31] There are also required disclaimers for simulated or hypothetical performances and testimonials.[32] At no point can there be an implication that the commodity pool operator is endorsed, sponsored, recommended, or approved by the CFTC, the federal government, or its agencies.[33]

Advertising and marketing materials designed to reach the public via mass media, such as television or radio, must be pre-approved by the National Futures Association.[34]

C. Private Funds and Exemptions to Registration as Commodity Pool Operators and Commodity Trading Advisors

1. Private Funds

In general, a private fund is an investment vehicle that operates within a variety of regulatory exemptions from the rules that would apply to an investment vehicle offered to the general public. Examples of such a fund might be a so-called hedge fund or private equity fund.

Many private funds invest only in securities and, therefore, need only be concerned with the relevant securities law regulations and exemptions. A large portion of private funds invest in both commodities and securities and, therefore, may need to be mindful of both regulatory regimes. Others invest exclusively in commodities. Any investment in "commodity interests," i.e., a product subject to CFTC jurisdiction, could subject an investment vehicle's management or principals to the requirement to register as a commodity pool operator or commodity trading advisor.

Other than for security-based swaps, discussed in chapter 13, or perhaps futures commission merchants dually-registered as securities broker-dealers, no other

---

29. 17 C.F.R. § 1.31(b).

30. 17 C.F.R. § 1.31(b)(2).

31. 17 C.F.R. § 4.41(a).

32. 17 C.F.R. §§ 4.41(a)(3) and (b) and National Futures Association Rule 2-29(c).

33. Commodity Exchange Act § 4o and 17 C.F.R. § 4.16.

34. National Futures Association Rule 2-29(h).

area of derivatives law has as great an intersection with securities law. Therefore, to understand the nature of private funds and whether their sponsors and advisors are subject to the CFTC regulatory regime or are eligible for exemption from some or most of the requirements applicable to commodity pool operators, it is necessary to understand their nature, structure, and treatment under securities laws.[35]

SEC, *Implications of the Growth of Hedge Funds*

Staff Report (Sept. 2003), available at https://www.sec.gov/files/implications
-growth-hedge-funds-09292003.pdf (some footnotes omitted)

. . . II. Legal Structure and Benefits of Hedge Funds

A. What is a Hedge Fund

Although there is no universally accepted definition of the term "hedge fund," the term generally is used to refer to an entity that holds a pool of securities and perhaps other assets, whose interests are not sold in a registered public offering and which is not registered as an investment company under the Investment Company Act. Alfred Winslow Jones is credited with establishing one of the first hedge funds as a private partnership in 1949. That hedge fund invested in equities and used leverage and short selling to "hedge" the portfolio's exposure to movements of the corporate equity markets.[36] Over time, hedge funds began to diversify their investment portfolios to include other financial instruments and engage in a wider variety of investment strategies. Today, in addition to trading equities, hedge funds may trade fixed income securities, convertible securities, currencies, exchange-traded futures, over-the-counter derivatives, . . . commodity options and other non-securities investments.

Furthermore, hedge funds today may or may not utilize the hedging and arbitrage strategies that hedge funds historically employed, and many engage in relatively traditional, long-only equity strategies.

B. Market Benefits of Hedge Funds

Hedge funds seek to achieve positive investment returns, often with less volatility than traditional asset classes such as stocks and bonds. Hedge funds engage in a wide variety of investment strategies, such as investing in distressed securities, illiquid securities, securities of companies in emerging markets and derivatives, as well as pursue arbitrage opportunities, such as those arising from possible mergers or acquisitions. They typically are managed by entrepreneurs who employ more complicated, flexible investment strategies than advisers at mutual funds [and brokerage firms]. . . .

---

35. In all cases, they remain subject to the Commodity Exchange Act's anti-fraud provisions. *See* 17 C.F.R. § 4.15.

36. [N. 10] Carol Loomis, *Hard Times Come to Hedge Funds* ("Loomis"), Fortune 100, 101 (Jan. 1970).

Hedge funds can provide benefits to financial markets by contributing to market efficiency and enhancing liquidity. Many hedge fund advisers take speculative trading positions on behalf of their managed hedge funds based on extensive research about the true value or future value of a security. They may also use short-term trading strategies to exploit perceived mispricings of securities. Because securities markets are dynamic, the result of such trading is that market prices of securities will move toward their true value. Trading on behalf of hedge funds can thus bring price information to the securities markets, which can translate into market price efficiencies.[37] Hedge funds also provide liquidity to the capital markets by participating in the market.

Hedge funds play an important role in a financial system where various risks are distributed across a variety of innovative financial instruments. They often assume risks by serving as ready counterparties to entities that wish to hedge risk. For example, hedge funds are buyers and sellers of certain derivatives. . . .

Hedge funds also can serve as an important risk management tool for investors by providing valuable portfolio diversification. Hedge fund investment strategies are typically designed to protect investment principal. Hedge funds frequently use financial instruments (e.g., derivatives) and techniques (e.g., short selling) to hedge against market risk and construct a conservative investment portfolio — one designed to preserve wealth. In addition, hedge fund investment performance can exhibit low correlation to that of traditional investments in the equity and fixed-income markets.[38] Institutional investors have used hedge funds to diversify their investments based on this historic low correlation with overall market activity.

C. Pooled Investment Vehicles that Are Not Hedge Funds

Hedge funds are often compared to registered investment companies. In addition, unregistered investment pools, such as venture capital funds, [and] private equity funds . . . , are sometimes referred to as hedge funds. Although all of these investment vehicles are similar in that they accept investors' money and generally invest it on a collective basis,[39] they also have characteristics that distinguish them from hedge funds.

---

37. [N. 11] "[M]any of the things which [hedge funds] do . . . tend to refine the pricing system in the United States and elsewhere. And it is that really exceptionally and increasingly sophisticated pricing system which is one of the reasons why the use of capital in this country is so efficient . . . there is an economic value here which we should not merely dismiss. . . . I do think it is important to remember that [hedge funds] . . . , by what they do, they do make a contribution to this country." Testimony of Alan Greenspan, Chairman of the Board of Governors of the Federal Reserve, Before the House Committee on Banking and Financial Services (Oct. 1, 1998).

38. [N. 12] *See, e.g.,* Mark J.P. Anson, *Handbook of Alternative Assets* 37–40 (2002) ("*Handbook of Alternative Assets*").

39. [N. 13] But for certain exclusions set forth in the Investment Company Act, all of these vehicles would meet the definition of investment company in Section 3(a) of the Investment Company Act. . . .

1. Registered Investment Companies

As a practical matter, hedge funds are similar to registered investment companies in a number of respects. Both are entities that issue securities to investors and hold pools of securities and perhaps other assets through which investors can obtain, among other things, investment diversification and professional asset management by an investment adviser who typically organizes the pool. Hedge funds and registered investment companies may invest in similar types of securities and may even share similar investment strategies.

Registered investment companies, however, . . . are registered with the [Securities and Exchange Commission, ("the Commission")] and are subject to the provisions of the Investment Company Act. . . .

[R]egistered investment companies are subject to extensive operational restrictions designed to prevent the potential for abuse that exists when an investment adviser has control of the assets of other persons who do not actively oversee the management of those assets. For example, registered investment companies are subject to regulations concerning the computation of the fund's net asset value, as well as regulations designed to protect against conflicts of interest and limit leverage (and consequently certain trading strategies). They also are subject to regulations requiring shareholder reports.

2. Private Equity Funds

A private equity fund, like a hedge fund, is an . . . investment vehicle in which investors pool money to invest in securities. Private equity funds concentrate their investments in unregistered (and typically illiquid) securities. Both private equity funds and domestic hedge funds are typically organized as limited partnerships. . . . The investors in private equity funds and hedge funds typically include high net worth individuals and families, pension funds, endowments, banks and insurance companies. Like hedge funds, many private equity funds establish offshore "mirror" funds that are typically managed by the general partner of the companion U.S. fund and have similar investments.

Private equity funds, however, differ from hedge funds in a number of significant ways. Private equity investors typically commit to invest a certain amount of money with the fund over the life of the fund, and make their contributions in response to "capital calls" from the fund's general partner. Because private equity funds typically do not retain a pool of uninvested capital, their general partners make a capital call when they have identified or expect to identify a portfolio company in which the private equity fund will invest.[40] Private equity funds are long-term investments, provide for liquidation at the end of the term specified in the fund's governing documents, and offer little, if any, opportunity for investors to redeem their

---

40. [N. 21] A hedge fund investor, by contrast, generally can decide when and how much to invest in the fund.

investments.[41] A private equity fund, however, may distribute cash to its investors when it sells its portfolio investment, or it may distribute the securities of a portfolio company (assuming the portfolio company has complied with the registration requirements of the . . . [Securities Act of 1933 (the "Securities Act")] in connection with the distribution) to its investors.

3. Venture Capital Funds

Venture capital funds are . . . investment vehicles, which are structurally similar to hedge funds and attract similar types of investors. Venture capital pools are generally organized, however, to invest in the start-up or early stages of a company.

Venture capital funds have the same features that distinguish private equity funds generally from hedge funds, such as mandatory capital contributions over the life of the fund and the long-term nature of the investment. In addition, unlike hedge fund advisers, general partners of venture capital funds often play an active role in the companies in which the funds invest, either by sitting on the board of directors or becoming involved in the day-to-day management of these companies. In contrast to a hedge fund, which may hold an investment in a portfolio security for an indefinite period based on market events and conditions, a venture capital fund typically seeks to liquidate its investment once the value of the company increases above the value of the investments. . . .

D. Domestic and Offshore Hedge Funds

The corporate structure of a hedge fund depends primarily on whether the fund is organized under U.S. law ("domestic hedge fund") or under foreign law and located outside of the United States ("offshore hedge fund"). The investment adviser of a domestic hedge fund often operates a related offshore hedge fund, either as a separate hedge fund or often by employing a "master-feeder" structure that allows for the unified management of multiple pools of assets for investors in different taxable categories.[42]

1. Domestic Hedge Funds

Domestic hedge funds are usually organized as limited partnerships to accommodate investors that are subject to U.S. income taxation. The fund's sponsor typically is the general partner and investment adviser. The sponsor also typically handles marketing and investor services. . . . Domestic hedge funds typically do not

---

41. [N. 22] There is typically no formal secondary market for shares in a private equity fund, although there may be a small informal secondary market comprised of private equity funds that buy interests in other established private equity funds. . . .

42. [N. 26] The master fund is usually organized as a corporation, such as an international business company, under non-U.S. law. It offers shares to one or more domestic feeder funds and one or more offshore corporate feeder funds, all of which share common investment strategies and objectives. *See* Gerald T. Lins ("Lins"), *Hedge Fund Organization*, in *Hedge Fund Strategies: A Global Outlook* 98, 100–101 (Brian R. Bruce, ed., 2002).

have a board of directors or any oversight body analogous to the board of directors of a registered investment company.

2. Offshore Hedge Funds

Offshore hedge funds are typically organized as corporations in countries such as the Cayman Islands, British Virgin Islands, the Bahamas, Panama, the Netherlands Antilles or Bermuda. Offshore funds generally attract investment of U.S. tax-exempt entities, such as pension funds, charitable trusts, foundations and endowments, as well as non-U.S. residents.

U.S. tax-exempt investors favor investments in offshore hedge funds because they may be subject to taxation if they invest in domestic limited partnership hedge funds.[43] Offshore hedge funds may be organized by foreign financial institutions or by U.S. financial institutions or their affiliates.[44] Sales of interests in the United States in offshore hedge funds are subject to the registration and antifraud provisions of the federal securities laws.

Offshore hedge funds typically contract with an investment adviser, which may employ a U.S. entity to serve as subadviser. An offshore hedge fund often has an independent fund administrator, also located offshore, that may assist the hedge fund's adviser to value securities and calculate the fund's net asset value, maintain fund records, process investor transactions, handle fund accounting and perform other services. An offshore hedge fund sponsor typically appoints a board of directors to provide oversight activities for the fund. . . .

III. The Regulation of Hedge Funds and Their Advisers

A. Hedge Funds and the Investment Company Act of 1940

Most hedge funds have substantial investments in securities that would cause them to fall within the definition of investment company under the Investment Company Act.[45] Hedge funds, however, typically rely on one of two statutory exclusions from the definition of investment company, which enables them to avoid the regulatory provisions of that Act. . . .

---

43. [N. 29] Under U.S. income tax laws, a tax-exempt organization . . . engaging in an investment strategy that involves borrowing money is liable for a tax on "unrelated business taxable income" ("UBTI"), notwithstanding its tax-exempt status. The UBTI tax can be avoided by the tax-exempt entity by investing in non-U.S. corporate structures (i.e., offshore hedge funds). . . .

44. Or, of course, standalone managers.

45. [N. 32] Section 3(a)(1)(A) of the Investment Company Act defines an investment company as an issuer which is or holds itself out as being engaged primarily, or proposes to engage primarily, in the business of investing, reinvesting or trading in securities. Section 3(a)(1)(C) of that Act defines an investment company as an issuer that is engaged or proposes to engage in the business of investing, reinvesting, owning, holding or trading in securities, and owns or proposes to acquire investment securities having a value exceeding 40 percent of the value of its total assets (exclusive of government securities and cash items) on an unconsolidated basis. Many hedge funds meet both of these definitions.

Section 3(c)(1)

Section 3(c)(1) of the Investment Company Act excludes from the definition of investment company any issuer whose outstanding securities (other than short-term paper) are beneficially owned by not more than 100 investors. . . . In general, ownership by a corporate investor is counted as one investor in testing compliance with the 100-investor limitation of Section 3(c)(1). Section 3(c)(1) reflects Congress's view that . . . investment companies owned by a limited number of investors do not rise to the level of federal interest under the Investment Company Act. . . .

Section 3(c)(7)

Section 3(c)(7) of the Investment Company Act excludes from the definition of investment company any issuer whose outstanding securities are owned exclusively by persons who, at the time of acquisition of such securities, are "qualified purchasers,"[46] and which is not making and does not at that time propose to make a public offering of its securities. This exclusion reflects Congress's view that certain highly sophisticated investors do not need the protections of the Investment Company Act because those investors are in a position to appreciate the risks associated with pooled investment vehicles.

A hedge fund relying on Section 3(c)(7) may accept an unlimited number of qualified purchasers for investment in the fund.[[47]] . . . A Section 3(c)(7) fund is only required to look through any company (investment company or otherwise) that invests in its shares to determine whether that company's investors are qualified purchasers if the company was "formed for the purpose" of investing in the Section 3(c)(7) fund.

B. Hedge Funds and the Securities Act of 1933

One of the Securities Act's primary objectives is to provide full and fair disclosure in securities transactions. To accomplish this objective, Section 5 of the Securities Act mandates the registration with the Commission of public securities offerings and the delivery to purchasers of a prospectus containing specified categories of information about the issuer and the securities being offered, unless there is an available exemption from the registration requirements. Since limited partnership, LLC and other interests offered to investors in the case of a typical hedge fund fall within the definition of the term "securities" for purposes of the federal securities

---

46. [N. 37] Section 2(a)(51) of the Investment Company Act generally defines "qualified purchaser" to be [among others] . . . any natural person who owns not less than $5 million in investments . . . [and] any person acting for its own account or the accounts of other qualified purchasers, that owns and invests on a discretionary basis not less than $25 million in investments. . . . The staff of the Division of Investment Management takes the position that a hedge fund that is incorporated offshore but relies on Section 3(c)(7) to offer its securities privately in the United States is not subject to the qualified purchaser requirements with respect to its investors who are non-U.S. residents. . . .

47. As a practical matter, funds relying on Section 3(c)(7) typically have no more than 1,999 investors in order to avoid registration and reporting requirements of section 12(g) of the Securities Exchange Act of 1934. *See* 17 CFR 240.12g-1.

laws, the hedge funds must either register the offer and sale of the securities or rely on an exemption from registration. Offerings of hedge fund securities in the United States generally rely on the private offering exemption . . . of the Securities Act[48] or Rule 506 promulgated under that Section to avoid the registration and prospectus delivery requirements of Section 5. . . .

Section . . . [4(a)(2)] of the Securities Act exempts from the registration and prospectus delivery requirements of Section 5 any "transactions by an issuer not involving any public offering." . . . [This] exemption, commonly known as the "private offering" or "private placement" exemption, requires no notice or other filing or regulatory approval as a prerequisite for its availability. . . .

The Supreme Court in *Ralston Purina* stated that a private offering is an "offering to those who are shown to be able to fend for themselves" and that the availability of the exemption "turns on the knowledge of the offerees" and is limited to situations where the offerees have access to the kind of information afforded by registration under Section 5 of the Securities Act.[49] . . .

Rule 506 of Regulation D under the Securities Act is a set of requirements promulgated by the Commission to govern private offerings. Although compliance with the Rule 506 requirements is not required to establish the availability of a private offering exemption, . . . Rule 506 establishes "safe harbor" criteria for the private offering exemption. . . . [M]any hedge funds tailor their offering and sale procedures to the criteria specified in Rule 506. . . .

The safe harbor protection most often relied upon by hedge funds under Rule 506 exempts offerings that are made exclusively to "accredited investors."[50] Issuers are permitted under these provisions to sell securities to an unlimited number of "accredited investors." In addition, if the offering is made only to accredited investors, no specific information is required to be provided to prospective investors.

The term "accredited investors" is defined to include:

> Individuals who have a net worth, or joint worth with their spouse, above $1,000,000 [excluding the value of one's primary residence], or have income above $200,000 in the last two years (or joint income with their spouse above $300,000) and a reasonable expectation of reaching the same income level in the year of investment; or are directors, officers or general partners of the hedge fund or its general partner; and

> Certain institutional investors, including: banks; savings and loan associations; registered brokers, dealers and investment companies; licensed

---

48. Securities Act § 4(a)(2).

49. [N. 42] *SEC v. Ralston Purina Co.*, 346 U.S. 119, 125, 126–27 (1953).

50. [N. 43] While Rule 506(b)(2)(i) limits the number of purchasers in a Rule 506 transaction to 35, this numerical limitation becomes irrelevant if the offering is made only to "accredited investors" because Rule 501(e)(1)(iv) provides that "accredited investors" are not counted for purposes of determining whether the issuer has exceeded the 35-purchaser limit.

small business investment companies; corporations, partnerships, limited liability companies and business trusts with more than $5,000,000 in assets; and many, if not most, employee benefit plans and trusts with more than $5,000,000 in assets.[51] . . .

C. Hedge Funds and the Securities Exchange Act of 1934. . . .

The beneficial ownership reporting rules under Sections 13(d) and 13(g) of the Exchange Act generally require that any person who, after acquiring beneficial ownership of any equity securities registered under Section 12 of the Exchange Act, beneficially owns greater than five percent of the class of equity securities, file a beneficial ownership statement. . . . Due to the power a hedge fund's adviser may exercise over the equity securities held by the fund, both the hedge fund and its adviser generally will be deemed to beneficially own any equity securities owned by the hedge fund. . . .

In addition, hedge fund advisers also may be subject to the quarterly reporting obligations of Section 13(f) of the Exchange Act, which apply to any "institutional investment manager" exercising investment discretion with respect to accounts having an aggregate fair market value of at least $100 million in equity securities. . . .

Section 16 applies to every person who is the beneficial owner of more than ten percent of any class of equity security registered under Section 12 of the Exchange Act and each officer and director of the issuer of the security (collectively, "reporting persons" or "insiders"). Upon becoming a reporting person, a person is required by Section 16(a) to file an initial report with the Commission disclosing the amount of his or her beneficial ownership of all equity securities of the issuer. Section 16(a) also requires reporting persons to keep this information current by reporting to the Commission changes in ownership of these equity securities, or the purchase or sale of security-based swap agreements involving these securities. . . .

D. Hedge Fund Advisers and the Investment Advisers Act of 1940

Virtually all hedge fund advisers meet the definition of "investment adviser" under the Advisers Act.[52] Under the Advisers Act, investment advisers must register with the Commission and comply with the provisions of that Act and Commission rules. Registered investment advisers must keep current a Form ADV that is filed with the Commission and provide a disclosure statement that includes the information disclosed on Part II of Form ADV to clients. These disclosures provide

---

51. [N. 45] *See* Rule 501 under the Securities Act.

52. [N. 64] Section 202(a)(11) of the Advisers Act generally defines an investment adviser as "any person who, for compensation, engages in the business of advising others, either directly or through publications or writings, as to the value of securities or as to the advisability of investing in, purchasing, or selling securities, or who, for compensation and as part of a regular business, issues or promulgates analyses or reports concerning securities." The Advisers Act contains certain limited exceptions from this definition for banks, certain professionals, including lawyers and accountants, broker-dealers, publishers and persons giving advice only about U.S. government securities.

both the Commission and investors with current information about the adviser's business practices and disciplinary history, among other things. Registered advisers must maintain required books and records and submit to periodic examinations by the Commission's staff. Advisers registered with the Commission also must comply with other requirements, including those relating to safeguarding client assets that are in the adviser's custody and requiring that clients be told of an adviser's adverse financial condition....

The remainder of this chapter is focused on Commodity Exchange Act provisions that exclude certain entities completely from the scope of provisions of the Commodity Exchange Act otherwise applicable to commodity pool operators, known as "exclusions," and those that provide relief from some of those requirements, known as "exemptions." As a general matter, private funds are structured so as to benefit from Commodity Exchange Act exclusions or exemptions of the provisions in the Act applicable to commodity pool operators (and commodity trading advisors). Some of these exclusions and exemptions have criteria that make it possible for private funds to benefit while others provide relief to other categories of market participants.

2. CFTC Rule 4.5

Formally, CFTC Rule 4.5[53] is an exclusion not an exemption since entities that fall within its parameters are excluded from the definition of commodity pool operator and its application.

Rule 4.5 is based on the Commodity Exchange Act's definition of commodity pool operator that allows for the CFTC to provide for exclusions consistent with "effectuat[ing] the purposes of the statute."[54] The CFTC has accordingly provided relief for investment companies registered under the Investment Company Act of 1940, business development companies, insurance companies, banks, and pension funds, requiring only a self-executing notice filing with the National Futures Association.[55] Before 2003, the CFTC also required that all trading of interests in products subject to the CFTC's jurisdiction be for bona fide hedging purposes save for a *de minimis* amount of up to five percent in margin amount of the investment vehicle's liquidation value that could be for speculative purposes.[56]

In 2003, the CFTC eliminated this requirement[57] but then restored it in 2012 solely for registered investment companies (leaving insurance companies, banks,

---

53. 17 C.F.R. § 4.5.

54. Commodity Exchange Act § 1a(11)(B).

55. *See* 17 C.F.R. §§ 4.5(a)(1)–(4) and 4.5(c).

56. 17 C.F.R. § 4.5 (2002).

57. CFTC, *Additional Registration and Other Regulatory Relief for Commodity Pool Operators and Commodity Trading Advisors*, 68 Fed. Reg. 47221 (Aug. 8, 2003).

and pension funds free to engage in an unlimited amount of speculative commodity interest trading).[58] The impact of reinstating the five percent limitation was enhanced because, whereas in 2003 only commodity futures and options products counted toward the five percent test, changes to the Commodity Exchange Act by the Dodd-Frank Act, resulted in swaps, commonly traded by registered investment companies, now being included.

This change in regulatory treatment led the primary industry association for investment companies to challenge the rule. The following case illustrates the leeway that an agency has in promulgating rules and amending them.

Investment Company Institute v. CFTC

720 F.3d 370 (D.C. Cir. 2013)

Sentelle, Senior Circuit Judge:

The Investment Company Institute and the Chamber of Commerce of the United States brought this action against the Commodity Futures Trading Commission (CFTC), seeking a declaratory judgment that recently adopted regulations of the Commission regarding derivatives trading were unlawfully adopted and invalid, and seeking to vacate and set aside those regulations and to enjoin their enforcement. . . .

Under . . . [the Commodity Exchange Act ("CEA" or "Act")], the Commission has regulatory jurisdiction over a wide variety of markets in futures and derivatives. . . . [T]he CEA also directly imposes certain duties on regulated entities. As relevant here, the Act requires that Commodity Pool Operators (CPOs) register with CFTC and adhere to regulatory requirements related to such issues as investor disclosures, recordkeeping, and reporting. . . . The CEA, however, empowers CFTC to exclude an entity from regulation as a CPO if CFTC determines that the exclusion "will effectuate the purposes of" the statute.

Since 1985, the Commission has exercised its authority to exclude "otherwise regulated" entities through § 4.5 of its regulations. *See* Commodity Pool Operators, 50 Fed. Reg. 15,868 (Apr. 23, 1985) (codified at 17 C.F.R. § 4.5). Under the version of § 4.5 that applied before amendments of 2003, otherwise regulated entities could claim exclusion by meeting certain regulatory conditions. These conditions included that the entity:

> (i) Will use commodity futures or commodity options contracts solely for bona fide hedging purposes . . . [;] (ii) Will not enter into commodity futures and commodity options contracts for which the aggregate initial margin and premiums exceed 5 percent of the fair market value of the entity's assets . . . [;]

---

58. CFTC, *Commodity Pool Operators and Commodity Trading Advisors: Compliance Obligations*, 77 Fed. Reg. 11252 (Feb. 24, 2012). Note that due to "numerous errors," this was amended by a subsequent release, CFTC, *Commodity Pool Operators and Commodity Trading Advisors: Compliance Obligations*, 77 Fed. Reg. 17328 (Mar. 26, 2012).

(iii) Will not be, and has not been, marketing participations to the public as or in a commodity pool or otherwise as or in a vehicle for trading in the commodity futures or commodity options markets; [and,] (iv) Will disclose in writing to each prospective participant the purpose of and the limitations on the scope of the commodity futures and commodity options trading in which the entity intends to engage[.]

These conditions were amended slightly in 1993, when CFTC promulgated a rule removing the bona fide hedging requirement and excluding bona fide hedging from the trading threshold. Commodity Pool Operators, 58 Fed. Reg. 6,371, 6,372 (Jan. 28, 1993). Under these conditions, there was no automatic exclusion for registered investment companies, or "RICs," regulated by the Securities and Exchange Commission pursuant to the Investment Company Act of 1940. Therefore, a commodity pool operator that was also a registered investment company was included within CFTC's regulatory definition of CPOs unless it met all of the § 4.5 requirements for exclusion. . . .

[T]he Commission [subsequently] amended its requirements for exclusion to eliminate the five percent ceiling. See Additional Registration and Other Regulatory Relief for Commodity Pool Operators and Commodity Trading Advisors, 68 Fed. Reg. 47,221, 47,224 (Aug. 8, 2003). These 2003 amendments "effectively excluded RICs from the CPO definition," freeing registered investment companies from most CFTC CPO regulations. . . .

In 2010, the Commission began shifting back to a more stringent regulatory framework. This shift came in the wake of the 2007–2008 financial crisis. . . . As relevant here, Dodd-Frank repealed several statutory provisions that had excluded certain commodities transactions from CFTC oversight. Dodd-Frank also gave CFTC regulatory authority over swaps, and amended the statutory definition of commodity pool operators to include entities that trade swaps.

Dodd-Frank, however, did not affect CFTC's authority to set exclusion requirements for CPOs. . . .

After Congress passed Dodd-Frank, the National Futures Association (NFA), to which all CPOs must belong, filed a petition of rulemaking with CFTC requesting that CFTC amend § 4.5 to limit the scope of its exclusion for registered investment companies. See Petition of the National Futures Association, 75 Fed. Reg. 56,997 (Sept. 17, 2010). In NFA's view, mutual funds were using the relaxed § 4.5 standards to evade CFTC oversight of their derivative operations, reducing transparency and potentially harming the public because no other regulator had rules equivalent to CFTC's. . . . In essence, NFA sought a return to the pre-2003 regulatory framework, but only for registered investment companies.

On February 11, 2011, CFTC proposed new regulations that would amend § 4.5 "to reinstate the pre-2003 operating criteria" for all registered investment companies. Commodity Pool Operators and Commodity Trading Advisors: Amendments to Compliance Obligations, 76 Fed. Reg. 7,976, 7,984 (Feb. 11, 2011). One notable difference from the 2003 framework is that because of Dodd-Frank's extension of CFTC authority to swaps, the regulations proposed that swaps be included in the trading thresholds. *See id.* at 7,989.... CFTC provided four explanations for these proposed regulations: First, the regulations would align CFTC's regulatory framework "with the stated purposes of the Dodd-Frank Act." Second, they would "encourage more congruent and consistent regulation of similarly situated entities among Federal financial regulatory agencies." Third, they would "improve accountability and increase transparency of the activities of CPOs" and commodity pools. Fourth, they would make it easier to collect data for the Financial Stability Oversight Council ("FSOC"), a new body created by Dodd-Frank charged with "identify[ing] risks to the financial stability of the United States."...

CFTC promulgated a Final Rule amending § 4.5 ... largely as proposed. *See* Commodity Pool Operators and Commodity Trading Advisors: Compliance Obligations, 77 Fed. Reg. 11,252 (Feb. 24, 2012), as corrected due to Fed. Reg. errors in its original publication, 77 Fed. Reg. 17,328 (Mar. 26, 2012)....

In its Final Rule, CFTC justified its decision to return to the pre-2003 regulatory framework on the basis of "changed circumstances [that] warrant revisions to these rules." According to CFTC, the 2003 "system of exemptions was appropriate because [registered investment companies] engaged in relatively little derivatives trading." Since the 2003 amendments, however, such companies have engaged in "increased derivatives trading activities" and "now offer[ ] services substantially identical to those of registered entities [that] are not subject to the same regulatory oversight." Given this changed circumstance, and Dodd-Frank's "more robust mandate to manage systemic risk and to ensure safe trading practices by entities involved in the derivatives markets," CFTC considered it necessary to narrow the exclusions from its derivatives regulation. Following this rule change, RICs that do not satisfy the exclusion requirements must register with CFTC per § 4.5....

Appellants contend that CFTC violated the [Administrative Procedures Act (the "APA")] ... in its rulemaking by: (1) failing to address its own 2003 rationales for broadening CPO exemptions; (2) failing to comply with the Commodity Exchange Act and offering an inadequate evaluation of the rule's costs and benefits; (3) including swaps in the trading threshold, restricting its definition of bona fide hedging, and failing to justify the five percent threshold; and, (4) failing to provide an adequate opportunity for notice and comment. We address each contention in turn....

The appellants first contend that CFTC failed to explain why it changed from its more generous exemption requirements that had existed since 2003 to the more stringent requirements contained in the Final Rule. Though it is true that the Final Rule stated that investment companies are increasing their participation in derivatives markets, the 2003 rule was explicitly designed to promote liquidity in the commodities markets by making it easier for registered investment companies to participate in derivatives markets. CFTC, according to the appellants, completely failed to address the liquidity issue, and therefore its change in position was arbitrary and capricious.

We disagree. An agency changing course "need not demonstrate to a court's satisfaction that the reasons for the new policy are better than the reasons for the old one; it suffices that the new policy is permissible under the statute, that there are good reasons for it, and that the agency believes it to be better." . . . So long as CFTC provided a reasoned explanation for its regulation, and the reviewing court can "reasonably . . . discern[ ]" the agency's path, we must uphold the regulation, even if the agency's decision has "less than ideal clarity."

CFTC's regulation clears this low bar. CFTC explicitly acknowledged that it was changing its position from its 2003 rulemaking. The Final Rule detailed the changed circumstances that prompted CFTC to amend the rule, including increased derivatives trading by investment companies (an issue inherently tied to liquidity) and a perceived lack of market transparency that could lead to a buildup of systemic risk. It is clear that the Commission, in adopting the changes and the rule, was attempting to respond to those changed circumstances by adding registration and reporting requirements. . . . Such reasoned decisionmaking is an acceptable way to change CFTC's past rules the appellants' policy disagreements with CFTC notwithstanding. . . .

Appellants next contend that CFTC failed to adequately consider the costs and benefits of the rule. The Commodity Exchange Act requires that CFTC "consider the costs and benefits" of its actions and "evaluate[ ]" those costs and benefits "in light of" five factors: "(A) considerations of protection of market participants and the public; (B) considerations of the efficiency, competitiveness, and financial integrity of futures markets; (C) considerations of price discovery; (D) considerations of sound risk management practices; and (E) other public interest considerations." . . .

Appellants point to two recent cases in which we vacated SEC regulations because SEC had failed to address existing regulatory requirements to determine whether sufficient protections were already present. *See Business Roundtable v. SEC*, 647 F.3d 1144, 1154 (D.C.Cir.2011); *American Equity Inv. Life Ins. Co. v. SEC*, 613 F.3d 166, 179 (D.C.Cir.2010). According to the appellants, CFTC similarly failed to consider whether existing regulations made its proposed regulation unnecessary.

We are unconvinced. In its Final Rule, CFTC explicitly discussed SEC's oversight in the derivatives markets. . . . We hold that CFTC's consideration and evaluation of the rule's costs and benefits was not arbitrary or capricious. . . .

The appellants challenge three particular aspects of the Final Rule. The first is CFTC's decision to include swap transactions in the registration threshold, which has the effect of requiring more investment companies to register pursuant to §4.5. The appellants claim that this decision was arbitrary and capricious because Dodd-Frank implemented a separate reporting framework with regard to swaps. . . .

CFTC gave sufficient . . . explanations for including swap trades in the §4.5 trading threshold that we can "reasonably . . . discern[ ]" its rationale. . . .

The second aspect of the rule challenged by the appellants is its definition of bona fide hedging transactions, a definition that the appellants claim is too narrow and should encompass risk management strategies in financial markets. This argument amounts to nothing more than another policy disagreement with CFTC, so we must reject it....

The third and final particular aspect of the rule challenged by the appellants is the five percent registration threshold for § 4.5, which the appellants argue is too low.... We defer to CFTC's judgment and hold that adopting the five percent threshold was neither arbitrary nor capricious....

Finally, appellants contend that CFTC failed to provide adequate opportunity for notice and comment.... We disagree. The APA requires "reference to the legal authority under which the rule is proposed" and "either the terms or substance of the proposed rule or a description of the subjects and issues involved." 5 U.S.C. § 553(b). The proposed rule included a separate section entitled "Cost-Benefit Analysis" that gave adequate notice of CFTC's approach to the cost-benefit analysis by setting forth the factors that CFTC would consider and summarizing expected costs and benefits....

For the foregoing reasons, the decision of the district court is Affirmed.

---

3. CFTC Rule 4.7

a. Generally

CFTC Rule 4.7[59] provides relief from a variety of compliance requirements, particularly regarding disclosure, which would otherwise be imposed on registered commodity pool operators. It works in parallel with and specifically references four securities law offering exceptions. It was adopted in 1992 in response to industry requests for a rule that would operate similarly to existing securities law exceptions. The most commonly used of these securities law exemptions is SEC Regulation D.[60] To understand the role of the Rule 4.7 exception, an overview of SEC Regulation D is, accordingly, helpful.

Regulation D provides assurance that a securities offering will not be treated as "public," and subject to the most stringent securities regulation standards, if it meets the "safe harbor" criteria in the regulation. Among the benefits of the reduced regulatory burden is that disclosure requirements are much less prescriptive and detailed. To qualify for Regulation D, the number of purchasers must be limited to thirty-five purchasers who either personally or through a representative have or are reasonably believed to have sufficient "knowledge and experience in financial and business matters" to evaluate the "merits and risks of the prospective investment."[61] However, if a purchaser is an "accredited investor," it does not count toward this

---

59. 17 C.F.R. § 4.7.
60. 17 C.F.R. § 230.501 *et seq.*
61. 17 C.F.R. § 230.506(b)(2)(i).

thirty-five purchaser limit.[62] In other words, up to thirty-five non-accredited investors and unlimited accredited investors can be purchasers of an offering and the
offering will potentially qualify for Regulation D. There are additional requirements, including a prohibition on "general solicitation" (unless all the purchasers
are "accredited investors"[63]), resale limitations, and "bad actor" disqualifications
from using the safe harbor of Regulation D if a principal falls into one of the enumerated "bad actor" categories.[64] These "bad actor" categories are similar to the disqualification categories discussed in chapter 6, section A.3.b.

While the definition of "accredited investor" is more nuanced and has additional
categories not enumerated here, a rule of thumb is that an accredit investor is: (1)
a natural person with $200,000 in annual income for each of last two years (or
$300,000 if married and filing jointly) or over $1,000,000 in assets excluding primary residence; (2) specified financial entities such as banks, insurance companies,
mutual funds, and securities broker-dealers; or (3) an entity with over $5,000,000 in
assets.[65]

b. Rule 4.7 Qualification

Rule 4.7 may be relied upon by registered commodity pool operators of commodity pools offered solely to "qualified eligible persons," commonly known as "QEPs."
To build on the shorthand definition of "accredited investor" used above, a qualified
eligible person is effectively an accredited investor satisfying a "portfolio requirement" by having $2 million invested in securities, $200,000 on margin for futures
and options trading with a futures commission merchant, or a combination thereof,
such as $1 million in securities and $100,000 on margin for futures and options trading.[66] Specified entities such as futures commission merchants, securities broker-
dealers, swap dealers, commodity pool operators operating pools with assets over
$5,000,000, commodity trading advisors or investment advisers managing accounts
over $5 million, and non-U.S. persons, among others, do not have to satisfy this
portfolio requirement.[67]

Fundamentally, the offering must be eligible for one of four securities law offering
exceptions. The first is Regulation D, discussed above. The second relates to offers
to non-U.S. persons and is known as SEC Regulation S.[68] The third is for a type of
securities offering by banks pursuant to section 3(a)(2) of the Securities Act of 1933.
The fourth, SEC Rule 144A, provides relief from some resale restrictions that are
otherwise imposed in private securities offerings so long as the parties are "qualified

---

62. *See* 17 C.F.R. § 230.501(e)(1)(iv).
63. 17 C.F.R. § 230.506(c).
64. *See* 17 C.F.R. §§ 230.502 and 23.506(d).
65. 17 C.F.R. § 230.501(a).
66. 17 C.F.R. § 4.7(a)(1)(v).
67. 17 C.F.R. § 4.7(a)(2).
68. 17 C.F.R. § 230.901 *et seq.*

institutional buyers," an umbrella term for large financial institutions with at least $100 million in discretionary securities investments.[69]

The exemption requires a filing with the National Futures Association.[70]

c. Rule 4.7 Relief

The relief granted by Rule 4.7 is dependent on the method by which the commodity pool is offered pursuant to securities law. If it is a Regulation D offering *and* all of the purchasers are "accredited investors," then the CFTC rule mirrors SEC Regulation D in allowing general solicitation, referred to by Rule 4.7 as "marketing to the public."[71] In all other cases, marketing to the public by a commodity pool operator relying on Rule 4.7 is prohibited. Moreover, while ordinarily there are resale restrictions for a Rule 4.7 offering, to the extent resale is permitted pursuant to SEC Rule 144A, it is also permissible pursuant to Rule 4.7.[72]

The most significant relief provided by Rule 4.7 is from the detailed disclosure requirements that otherwise apply to commodity pool offerings. In lieu of the prescriptive requirements otherwise imposed, a CFTC-specified paragraph explaining that the offering is exempt must be provided along with "material" past performance disclosure and enough information in an offering memorandum to make the information "not misleading."[73]

Rule 4.7 provides relief from the financial statement requirements otherwise applying. Instead, a quarterly report must be distributed to pool participants with net asset value information along with annual financials to the participants and the National Futures Association. The financials need not be audited.[74] Recordkeeping is also greatly simplified, limited to the offering documents, quarterly reports, and "all books and records prepared in connection with" being a commodity pool operator of the exempt pool.[75]

4. CFTC Rule 4.12

a. Generally

CFTC Rule 4.12[76] provides relief similar to Rule 4.7 for three categories of commodity pool operators. The first category is for commodity pools with a *de minimis* portion of assets that are futures, commodity options, swaps, retail foreign exchange,

---

69. 17 C.F.R. § 230.144A. There are some exceptions to the requirement to have $100 million in discretionary securities investments. *See* 17 C.F.R. §§ 230.144A(a)(1)(ii)–(iv).

70. *See* 17 C.F.R. § 4.7(d).

71. 17 C.F.R. § 4.7(b)(1)(i)(A).

72. 17 C.F.R. § 4.7(b)(1)(ii).

73. 17 C.F.R. § 4.7(b)(2).

74. 17 C.F.R. § 4.7(b)(3) and (4).

75. 17 C.F.R. § 4.7(b)(5).

76. 17 C.F.R. § 4.12.

or leverage contracts. The second is for SEC-registered public pool offerings, i.e., typically exchange-traded funds, and the third is for SEC-registered mutual fund offerings. The third is known as the "substituted compliance" exemption because it operates on the assumption that the pre-existing SEC regulation is sufficient for many purposes.

In all three cases, a filing is required with the National Futures Association.[77]

b. Rule 4.12(b)

To satisfy the requirements of Rule 4.12(b), i.e., the *de minimis* pool exemption, the relevant commodity pool must be: (1) publicly registered with the SEC or offered pursuant to an exemption such as SEC Regulation D; (2) the initial margins, value, premiums, and deposits on all futures, commodity options, swaps, retail foreign exchange, and leverage contracts must not exceed ten percent of the commodity pool's fair market value; and (3) these restrictions must be disclosed to pool participants.[78]

The relief is primarily regarding the disclosure document requirements. The disclosure document must still contain all "material information," including details of principals, their business backgrounds, risk factors, trading strategy, fees and expenses, conflicts of interest, and material litigation. However, it is not required, among others, to include the specific text otherwise mandated by CFTC rule and historical performance data.[79]

Also, the financial reporting requirements are laxer, requiring quarterly statements of net asset value with less detail for distribution to participants and simplified annual audited financial statements for delivery to participants and the National Futures Association.[80]

c. Rule 4.12(c)(1)(i)

To satisfy the requirements of Rule 4.12(c)(1)(i), the relevant commodity pool must be a pool offering publicly registered with the SEC.[81]

This circumstance typically arises with exchange-traded funds. Before adding the exemption via rule in 2011, the CFTC had issued ad hoc no-action letters to address the reality that the commodity pool operator may not have contact information for each of the investors in an exchange-traded fund.[82] Commodity pool operators relying on this exemption can satisfy disclosure document delivery and

---

77. 17 C.F.R. § 4.12(d).
78. 17 C.F.R. § 4.12(b)(1).
79. 17 C.F.R. § 4.12(b)(2)(i).
80. 17 C.F.R. § 4.12(b)(2)(ii) and (3).
81. 17 C.F.R. § 4.12(c)(1)(i).
82. CFTC, *Commodity Pool Operators: Relief from Compliance with Certain Disclosure, Reporting and Recordkeeping Keeping Requirements*, 76 Fed. Reg. 28641, 28641 (May 18, 2011).

acknowledgment requirements and financial reporting requirements by posting the documents on the Internet.[83]

d. Rule 4.12(c)(1)(ii)

To satisfy the requirements of Rule 4.12(c)(1)(ii), i.e., the "substituted compliance" exemption, the relevant commodity pool must be a mutual fund publicly registered with the SEC.[84] It was promulgated in 2013 to accommodate some commodity pool operators managing commodity pools registered as mutual funds and no longer eligible for relief under CFTC Rule 4.5.[85]

So long as compliant with applicable securities law, disclosure and financial reporting obligations for such exempt commodity pools are limited to making current net asset information available to participants and, where there is a less than three year operating history, disclosing the performance of accounts and pool managed by the commodity pool operator that have "investment objectives, policies, and strategies substantially similar" to those of the relevant commodity pool.[86] The SEC has provided guidance for 4.12(c)(1)(ii) exempt pools in complying with applicable securities law requirements.[87]

5. CFTC Rule 4.13

While the relief in CFTC Rules 4.7 and 4.12 is available only to registered commodity pool operators, CFTC Rule 4.13, provides an exemption from registration for a commodity pool operator that offers small or family pools or pools that trade a *de minimis* amount of commodity interests. Other than with respect to the family office exemption described below, the commodity pool operator must file a notification with the National Futures Association, certify that the commodity pool operator and its principals would not be subject to statutory disqualification were registration required, and notify potential participants of its registration exemption.[88]

a. Single Pool Exemption

The single pool exemption requires that the commodity pool operator receives no compensation except reimbursement for ordinary administrative expenses, only operates one pool at a time, is not otherwise required to register with the CFTC (or

---

83. 17 C.F.R. § 4.12(c)(2).

84. 17 C.F.R. § 4.12(c)(1)(ii).

85. *See* CFTC, *Harmonization of Compliance Obligations for Registered Investment Companies Required to Register as Commodity Pool Operators*, 78 Fed. Reg. 52308, 52308 (Aug. 22, 2013).

86. 17 C.F.R. § 4.12(c)(3).

87. SEC, *Disclosure and Compliance Matters for Investment Company Registrants That Invest in Commodity Interests*, https://www.sec.gov/divisions/investment/guidance/im-guidance-2013-05 .pdf (Aug. 2013).

88. 17 C.F.R. §§ 4.13(b) and 4.13(a)(7).

affiliated with someone who does), and does no advertising in connection with the commodity pool.[89]

b. Small Pools Exemption

The small pools exemption requires the commodity pool operator to only operate pools with no more than fifteen participants at any time and limit total gross capital contributions for participation in the pools to $400,000, excluding principals and near relatives.[90]

c. De Minimis Exemption

The *de minimis* exemption applies if: (1) the interests in the commodity pool are exempt from registration as securities; (2) the commodity pool is offered and sold without marketing to the public in the United States (unless offered exclusively to accredited investors in reliance on SEC Rule 506(c) or subject to the requirements of SEC Rule 144A so long as they are not marketed as a means of trading in the futures or commodity options markets); and (3) all participants in the commodity pool are accredited investors or qualified eligible persons.[91]

Additionally, the commodity pool cannot exceed a *de minimis* amount of: (1) trading with margining of more than 5% of its liquidation value in futures, commodity options, swaps, retail foreign exchange, and leverage commodity transactions; or (2) notional amounts from such activities equal to 100% of its liquidation value.[92]

The *de minimis* exemption is the exemption typically relied upon by private funds, such as hedge funds, especially after one of the primary exemptions historically relied upon by private funds, the Rule 4.13(a)(4) exemption, was repealed by the CFTC in 2012.[93] The Rule 4.13(a)(4) exemption had allowed unlimited trading in derivatives provided that all participants were qualified eligible persons; it did not limit derivatives trading to five percent of liquidation value as does the Rule 4.13(a)(3) *de minimis* exemption.

Initially, as will be seen in the CFTC proposal immediately below, the CFTC had considered repealing both the Rule 4.13(a)(3) and the Rule 4.13(a)(4) exemptions.[94] The CFTC decided against repealing the Rule 4.13(a)(3) exemptions after receiving

---

89. 17 C.F.R. § 4.13(a)(1).

90. 17 C.F.R. § 4.13(a)(2).

91. 17 C.F.R. § 4.13(a)(3).

92. *Id.*

93. It was adopted in 2003 at the same time as CFTC Rule 4.13(a)(3). *See* CFTC, *Commodity Pool Operators and Commodity Trading Advisors: Compliance Obligations*, 77 Fed. Reg. 11252 (Feb. 24, 2012), and the corrections in CFTC, *Commodity Pool Operators and Commodity Trading Advisors: Compliance Obligations*, 77 Fed. Reg. 17328 (Mar. 26, 2012).

94. *See* CFTC, *Commodity Pool Operators and Commodity Trading Advisors: Amendments to Compliance Obligations*, 76 Fed. Reg. 7976, 7985–7987 (Feb. 11, 2011).

mostly critical comments and due to concerns about CFTC and National Futures Association resources. Only the Rule 4.13(a)(4) exemption was ultimately repealed.

CFTC, *Commodity Pool Operators and Commodity Trading Advisors: Amendments to Compliance Obligations*
76 Fed. Reg. 7976 (Feb. 11, 2011)

. . . On July 21, 2010, President Obama signed the Dodd-Frank Wall Street Reform and Consumer Protection Act ("Dodd-Frank Act"). The legislation was enacted to reduce risk, increase transparency, and promote market integrity within the financial system by, inter alia, enhancing the Commodity Futures Trading Commission's (the "Commission" or "CFTC") rulemaking and enforcement authorities with respect to all registered entities and intermediaries subject to the Commission's oversight. . . .

The Commodity Exchange Act ("CEA") empowers the Commission with the authority to register Commodity Pool Operators ("CPOs") and Commodity Trading Advisors ("CTAs"), exclude any entity from registration as a CPO or CTA,[95] and to require "[e]very commodity trading advisor and commodity pool operator registered under [the CEA to] maintain books and records and file such reports in such form and manner as may be prescribed by the Commission."[96]

The Commission also has the power to "make and promulgate such rules and regulations as, in the judgment of the Commission, are reasonably necessary to effectuate the provisions or to accomplish any of the purposes of [the CEA]."[97] The Commission's discretionary power to exclude or exempt persons from registration was intended to be exercised "to exempt from registration those persons who otherwise meet the criteria for registration . . . if, in the opinion of the Commission, there is no substantial public interest to be served by the registration."[98] It is pursuant to this authority that the Commission has promulgated the various exemptions from registration as a CPO that are enumerated in § 4.13 of its regulations as well as the exclusions from the definition of CPO that are delineated in § 4.5.

Following the recent economic turmoil, and consistent with the tenor of the provisions of the Dodd-Frank Act, the Commission has reconsidered the level of regulation that it believes is appropriate with respect to entities participating in the commodity futures and derivatives markets. The Commission believes that it is necessary to rescind or modify several of its exemptions and exclusions to more effectively oversee its market participants and manage the risks that such participants pose to the markets. . . .

---

95. [N. 5] 7 U.S.C. 1a(11) and 1a(12).

96. [N. 6] 7 U.S.C. 6n(3)(A). Under part 4 of the Commission's regulations, entities registered as CPOs have reporting obligations with respect to their operated pools. *See* 17 C.F.R. 4.22. Although CTAs have recordkeeping obligations under part 4, the Commission has not required reporting by CTAs, *See* [sic] *generally*, 17 C.F.R. part 4.

97. [N. 7] 7 U.S.C. 12a(5).

98. [N. 8] *See* H.R. Rep. No. 93-975, 93d Cong., 2d Sess. (1974), p. 20.

Title IV of the Dodd-Frank Act requires advisers to large private funds[99] to register with the SEC.[100] Through this registration requirement, Congress sought to make available to the SEC "information regarding [the] size, strategies and positions" of large private funds, which Congress believed "could be crucial to regulatory attempts to deal with a future crisis." In section 404 of the Dodd-Frank Act, Congress amended section 204(b) of the Investment Advisers Act to direct the SEC to require private fund advisers registered solely with the SEC[101] to file reports containing such information as is deemed necessary and appropriate in the public interest and for investor protection or for the assessment of systemic risk. These reports and records must include a description of certain prescribed information, such as the amount of assets under management, use of leverage, counterparty credit risk exposure, and trading and investment positions for each private fund advised by the adviser. . . .

In order to ensure that the Commission can adequately oversee the commodities and derivatives markets and assess market risk associated with pooled investment vehicles under its jurisdiction, the Commission is re-evaluating its regulation of CPOs and CTAs. Additionally, the Commission does not want its registration and reporting regime for pooled investment vehicles and their operators and/or advisors to be incongruent with the registration and reporting regimes of other regulators, such as that of the SEC for investment advisers under the Dodd-Frank Act. . . .

The Commission's proposed amendments are designed to (1) bring the Commission's CPO and CTA regulatory structure into alignment with the stated purposes of the Dodd-Frank Act; (2) encourage more congruent and consistent regulation of similarly situated entities among Federal financial regulatory agencies; (3) improve accountability and increase transparency of the activities of CPOs, CTAs, and the commodity pools that they operate or advise; and (4) facilitate a collection of data that will assist the FSOC [the Financial Stability Oversight Council established by the Dodd-Frank Act], acting within the scope of its jurisdiction, in the event that the FSOC requests and the Commission provides such data. The proposed amendments

---

99. [N. 14] Section 202(a)(29) of the Investment Advisers Act of 1940 ("Investment Advisers Act") defines the term "private fund" as "an issuer that would be an investment company, as defined in section 3 of the Investment Company Act of 1940 (15 U.S.C. 80a-3), but for section 3(c)(1) or 3(c)(7) of that Act." 15 U.S.C. 80a-3(c)(1), 80a-3(c)(7). . . .

100. [N. 15] The Dodd-Frank Act requires private fund adviser registration by amending section 203(b)(3) of the Advisers Act to repeal the exemption from registration for any adviser that during the course of the preceding 12 months had fewer than 15 clients and neither held itself out to the public as an investment adviser nor advised any registered investment company or business development company. See section 403 of the Dodd-Frank Act. There are exemptions from this registration requirement for advisers to venture capital funds and advisers to private funds with less than $150 million in assets under management in the United States. There also is an exemption for foreign advisers with less than $25 million in assets under management from the United States and fewer than 15 U.S. clients and private fund investors. See sections 402, 407 and 408 of the Dodd-Frank Act.

101. [N. 17] In this release, the term "private fund adviser" means any investment adviser that is (i) registered or required to be registered with the SEC (including any investment adviser that is also registered or required to be registered with the CFTC as a CPO or CTA) and (ii) advises one or more private funds (including any commodity pools that satisfy the definition of "private fund").

will also allow the Commission to more effectively oversee its market participants and manage the risks posed by the commodities and derivatives markets. To those ends, the [proposed] amendments [, among other things,] rescind the exemptions from registration under §§ 4.13(a)(3) and (a)(4). . . .

Section 4.13(a)(3) of the Commission's regulations currently provides that a person is exempt from registration as a CPO if the interests in the pool are exempt from registration under the Securities Act of 1933 and offered only to QEPs, accredited investors, or knowledgeable employees, and the pool's aggregate initial margin and premiums attributable to commodity interests do not exceed five percent of the liquidation value of the pool's portfolio. Section 4.13(a)(4) of the Commission's regulations provides that a person is exempt from registration as a CPO if the interests in the pool are exempt from registration under the Securities Act of 1933 and the operator reasonably believes that the participants are all QEPs.

As a result of the creation of exemptions from registration as a CPO under §§ 4.13(a)(3) and (a)(4), a large group of market participants have fallen outside of the oversight of regulators (i.e., there is very little if any transparency or accountability over the activities of these participants). The Commission has concluded that continuing to grant an exemption from registration and reporting obligations for these market participants is outweighed by the Commission's concerns of regulatory arbitrage.

Indeed, the Commission believes that it is possible for a commodity pool to have a portfolio that is sizeable enough that even if just five percent of the pool's portfolio were committed to margin for futures, the pool's portfolio could be so significant that the commodity pool would constitute a major participant in the futures market.

In addition, the Commission proposes to eliminate the exemption in § 4.13(a)(4) because there are no limits on the amount of commodity interest trading in which pools operating under this regulation can engage. That is, it is possible that a commodity pool that is exempted from registration under § 4.13(a)(4) could be invested solely in commodities. . . .

The Commission's proposal seeks to eliminate the exemptions under §§ 4.13(a)(3) and (4) for operators of pools that are similarly situated to private funds that previously relied on the exemptions under §§ 3(c)(1) and (7) of the Investment Company Act and § 203(b)(3) of the Investment Advisers Act. It is the Commission's view that the operators of these pools should be subject to similar regulatory obligations . . . in order to provide improved transparency and increased accountability with respect to these pools. The Commission has determined that it is appropriate to limit regulatory arbitrage . . . so that operators of such pools will not be able to avoid oversight by either the Commission or the SEC through claims of exemption under the Commission's regulations. . . .

As noted above, the CFTC ultimately decided to retain the Rule 4.13(a)(3) exemption reasoning that maintaining a *de minimis* exemption was preferable because "overseeing entities with less than five percent exposure to commodity interests is not the best use of the Commission's limited resources."[102] The lack of a *de minimis* limit underlay the CFTC's elimination of the Rule 4.13(a)(4) exemption:

> [A]s stated in the proposal, there are no limits on the amount of commodity interest trading in which pools operating under this regulation can engage. That is, it is possible that a commodity pool that is exempted from registration under § 4.13(a)(4) could be invested solely in commodities, which, in the Commission's view, necessitates Commission oversight to ensure adequate customer protection and market oversight. Therefore, the Commission adopts the rescission of § 4.13(a)(4) as proposed.[103]

d. Family Office Exemption

In 2019, the CFTC codified various ad hoc no-action letters related to family offices.[104] The family office exemption applies where the commodity pool offerings are not publicly registered with the SEC and the commodity pool operator is eligible for the "family office" exemption from registration as an SEC investment adviser.[105] This requires that it be owned exclusively by family members, former family members, key employees, former key employees, or various legal entities closely associated with the family members or key employees.[106] Control over the commodity pool operator must be held by family members or entities closely associated with family members.

The failure of a large vehicle operating as a family office, Archegos Capital Management, led to renewed calls to reduce the scope of the CFTC family office exemption.

CFTC, *Statement of Commissioner Dan M. Berkovitz: CFTC Oversight of Family Offices Must Be Strengthened*

https://www.cftc.gov/PressRoom/SpeechesTestimony/
berkovitzstatement040121 (Apr. 1, 2021)

The collapse of Archegos Capital Management[107] and the billions of dollars in losses to investors and other market participants is a vivid demonstration of the havoc that errant large investment vehicles called "family offices" can wreak on our financial markets.[108] Family offices can be active in both securities and commodities

---

102. *See* CFTC, *Commodity Pool Operators and Commodity Trading Advisors: Compliance Obligations*, 77 Fed. Reg. 11252, 11261 (Feb. 24, 2012).

103. *Id.* at 1265.

104. CFTC, *Registration and Compliance Requirements for Commodity Pool Operators and Commodity Trading Advisors: Family Offices and Exempt CPOs*, 84 Fed. Reg. 67355 (Dec. 10, 2019).

105. *See* 17 C.F.R. § 4.13(a)(6) and 17 C.F.R. § 275.202(a)(11)(G)-1.

106. *Id.*

107. [N. 1] Archegos is widely reported to be a "family office." *See, e.g.,* Linkedin, Archegos Capital Management, LP, available at https://www.linkedin.com/company/archegos-capital -management-lp/about/; and Wikipedia, Archegos Capital Management, available at https://en .wikipedia.org/wiki/Archegos_Capital_Management.

108. [N. 2] The forced de-levering of risky positions of Archegos is now estimated to have caused $5 billion to $10 billion in losses to prime brokers and significant losses to investors in the related

markets. Unfortunately, in the last two years the CFTC has loosened its oversight of family offices. In 2019, and again in 2020, the Commodity Futures Trading Commission (CFTC) approved rules that exempted family offices from some of our most basic requirements. I objected to these exemptions at the time, warning in 2019 that "[t]he approval of [these rules] without any checks and balances on exempt family office CPOs [commodity pool operators] will increase risks to our markets and market participants."[109] The Archegos failure highlights the importance of strengthening the CFTC's oversight of these large funds and preventing bad actors from trading in our markets.

A "family office" has nothing to do with ordinary families. Rather, it is an investment vehicle used by centimillionaires and billionaires to grow their wealth, reduce their taxes, and plan their estates.[110] According to a 2019 report, the average wealth of family offices surveyed in North America was $1.3 billion, with $852 million in assets under management.[111] As we have just seen, the failure of a large family office can cause significant harm to our financial markets.

Because family offices do not solicit investments from the public, they are generally exempt from certain CFTC regulations that relate to investor protection. But the CFTC strayed far beyond this rationale when it also exempted multimillionaire and billionaire family offices from basic requirements related to market protection and integrity.

In November 2019, the Commission exempted family offices operating in CFTC regulated markets from providing notice that they are exempt from CFTC registration requirements.[112] All other entities claiming similar exemptions must provide notice. The information required would fit on a post-it note, and the CFTC

---

stocks. Jan-Patrick Barnert and Marion Halftermeyer, *JPMorgan Says Banks' Archegos Hit May Be Up to $10 Billion*, Bloomberg, Mar. 30, 2021, https://www.bloomberg.com/news/articles/2021-03-30/banks-may-take-up-to-10-billion-hit-on-archegos-loss-jpmorgan-kmw5xjkh.

109. [N. 3] Statement of Dan M Berkovitz, *Rulemaking to Provide Exemptive Relief for Family Office CPOs: Customer Protection Should be More Important than Relief for Billionaires*, (Nov. 25, 2019), https://www.cftc.gov/PressRoom/SpeechesTestimony/berkovitzstatement112519; Statement of Dan M. Berkovitz, *Prohibiting Exemptions from Commodity Pool Operator Registration for Persons Subject to Certain Statutory Disqualifications*, (June 4, 2020) (2020 Statement), https://www.cftc.gov/PressRoom/SpeechesTestimony/berkovitzstatement060402b. A CPO is a person who accepts funds from others for the purpose of trading contracts for future delivery or swaps in commodities. Commodity Exchange Act § 1a(11).

110. [N. 4] Securities and Exchange Commission (SEC), *SEC Adopts Rule Under Dodd-Frank Defining "Family Offices"* (June 22, 2011), https://www.sec.gov/news/press/2011/2011-134.htm; *see also* Kirby Rosplock, The Complete Family Office Handbook, *A Guide for Affluent Families and the Advisors Who Serve Them* (Bloomberg Press, 2014).

111. [N. 5] Campden Research and UBS, *The Global Family Office Report 2019*, at 11, available at https://www.ubs.com/global/en/wealth-management/uhnw/global-family-office-report/global-family-office-report-2019.html.

112. [N. 6] Registration and Compliance Requirements for Commodity Pool Operators (CPOs) and Commodity Trading Advisors: Family Offices and Exempt CPOs, 84 FR 67355 (Dec. 10, 2019).

estimated the annual cost of the filing to be merely $28.50. There is no rational justification for exempting large family offices with billions of dollars under management from minimal notice requirements with relatively trivial costs. Without a notice filing, the Commission remains generally unaware of the very existence of these large commodity pools, is hampered in its ability to oversee their activities, and does not even know whom to contact should issues arise.

In July 2020, the Commission exempted persons in family offices from a new CFTC rule designed to foreclose bad actors from acting as CPOs if they are subject to statutory disqualification. In other words, even if a family office operator or one of its principals has been barred from CFTC markets, committed a felony involving commodity or securities laws, or has been found to have violated specified statutes involving embezzlement, theft, extortion, forgery, and fraud, they can remain exempt from CFTC registration.[113] Thus, convicted felons, market manipulators, and other financial market miscreants can operate freely within the confines of a family office, unbeknownst to the CFTC. In my view, there is no reasonable justification for such a policy.

As I previously stated, disqualification should mean disqualification. In response to the 2020 rulemaking I stated:

> [U]nder this set of new rules completed today, CPOs of family offices are exempt from registration, exempt from providing notice that they are using an exemption, and exempt from the statutory disqualifications that generally apply to all other CPOs. This triad of exemptions for CPOs of family offices leaves the Commission uniquely unaware of the activities and integrity of these entities.

To protect the integrity of the commodity markets, the Commission must be aware of and able to monitor the activities of large family offices. In order to do this the Commission should have basic information about family offices that are operating commodity pools. The qualifications of persons operating family offices should be no less than for persons operating other exempt and non-exempt pools. I urge the Commission to revisit these issues soon.

The multi-billion dollar losses some large banks had in relation to Archegos Capital Management began when Archegos defaulted on margin due in relation to total

---

113. [N. 7] Registration and Compliance Requirements for Commodity Pool Operators and Commodity Trading Advisors: Prohibiting Exemptions on Behalf of Persons Subject to Certain Statutory Disqualifications, 85 FR 40877 (July 8, 2020). The new rule prohibits persons who are subject to a statutory disqualification under section 8a(2) of the Commodity Exchange Act from claiming an exemption from CPO registration under Regulation 4.13, and thus closed a loophole that enabled persons who were disqualified from registration to nonetheless operate as a CPO for a pool that is exempt from registration. The loophole remains open, however, with respect to operators of family offices.

return swaps. The total return swaps had allowed Archegos to obtain a synthetic exposure to various share prices, including in ViacomCBS Inc. When ViacomCBS Inc.'s stock price dropped due to an announcement that it was issuing more shares, the margin payable to the banks was untenable for Archegos. The banks were forced to sell the ViacomCBS stock they held to hedge the total return swaps. This drove the price of the stock even lower as ViacomCBS shares flooded the market.[114]

It is not clear how a filing to the National Futures Association stating that Archegos Capital Management was relying on the family office exemption from commodity pool operator registration would have had an impact on the above events. For one thing, it is not clear that Archegos needed to use the CFTC's family office exemption in the first place. Second, the total return swaps were most likely security-based swaps regulated exclusively by the SEC and the shares the banks sold at losses are solely under the SEC's jurisdiction. Therefore, what intersection would there be with the CFTC even if there were a National Futures Association filing requirement?

Regarding whether statutory disqualification should be applied to commodity pool operators using the family office exemption, it raises interesting public policy questions as to whether wrongdoers should still be able to invest their and their family's money.

Questions and Comments

1. Why regulate commodity pool operators instead of the commodity pools themselves?

2. What is the public policy underlying the regulation of private funds that limit investors to ultra-high net worth entities and individuals? Surely not investor protection, along with market manipulation, one of the original impetuses for the regulation of the securities and commodities investment industries. What, today, might be additional drivers for the regulation of investment industries?

3. In section D.1 above, we look at the many ways funds are potentially subject to regulation under the securities laws. Why are there so many categories of regulation? Is it possible to have a simpler framework achieving the same objectives?

4. Are the activities of funds trading in the derivatives market so distinct from funds trading in the securities market that a separate funds regulatory regime is merited?

5. As discussed in section D.2 above, exemptions added to CFTC Rule 4.5 in 2003 were rescinded in 2012. When implementing a regulatory reversal of this nature,

---

114. Alexander Osipovich and David Benoit, *Archegos Blowup Puts Spotlight on Gaps in Swap Regulation*, Wall St. J. (Apr. 1, 2021), available at https://www.wsj.com/articles/archegos-blowup-puts-spotlight-on-gaps-in-swap-regulation-11617280278, and Gregory Zuckerman, Juliet Chung, and Maureen Farrell, *Inside Archego's Epic Meltdown*, Wall St. J. (Apr. 1, 2020), available at https://www.wsj.com/articles/inside-archegoss-epic-meltdown-11617323530.

what are some of the factors for which a regulator should account? How do such policy changes impact market participants relying on the previous regime? Are there ways, such as long transition periods or grandfathering (i.e., allowing entities relying on the old regime to continue to do so), to soften the transition?

6. What regulations would have avoided the market disruption unleashed by the losses of Archegos Capital Management? Are any regulations that would have prevented it be able to be universally applied without causing their own market disruptions?

Chapter 8

Commodity Trading Advisors

A. Background

As noted in chapter 7, there are many similarities with respect to the SEC's regulatory regime for investment advisers and the CFTC's regulatory regime for commodity trading advisors. As a result, it is very common for entities to be dually-registered as an investment adviser and a commodity trading adviser.

Commodity trading advisors occupy a critical role in the investment industry. Just as with commodity pool operators, the exclusions and exemptions applicable to the commodity trading advisory regulatory regime are of great importance to the private investment industry.

B. Definition of Commodity Trading Advisor

The Commodity Exchange Act defines as a commodity trading advisor any person who "for compensation or profit, engages in the business of advising others, either directly or through publications, writings, or electronic media, as to the value of or the advisability of trading in [among others] any contract of sale of a commodity for future delivery [or] for compensation or profit, and as part of a regular business, issues or promulgates analyses or reports concerning [among others] any contract of sale of a commodity for future delivery."[1]

To fully understand the definition of commodity trading advisor, we also need to see what it excludes. We look at exclusions and exemptions in detail below in section E. For the purposes of the immediate discussion, it is important to know that the following are excluded from the definition of commodity trading advisor so long as "the furnishing of such services . . . is solely incidental to the conduct of their business or profession":

   i. any bank or trust company or any person acting as an employee thereof;

   ii. any news reporter, news columnist, or news editor of the print or electronic media, or any lawyer, accountant, or teacher;

   iii. any floor broker or futures commission merchant;

---

1. Commodity Exchange Act § 1a(12)(A).

   iv. the publisher or producer of any print or electronic data of general and regular dissemination, including its employees;

   v. the fiduciary of any defined benefit plan that is subject to the Employee Retirement Income Security Act of 1974 (29 U.S.C. 1001 et seq.); [and]

   vi. any contract market. . . .[2]

Without these exclusions, any news report on the subject of, for example, commodity futures or swaps, could be deemed to be advice for "compensation or profit" thereby triggering a commodity trading advisor registration obligation. Without the exclusion for a teacher, even a law professor teaching or writing on the subject could theoretically have a registration obligation if, in doing so, he or she incidentally offered commodity trading advice!

C. Constitutional Issues

The provision of advice, whether "directly or through publications, writings, or electronic media" or otherwise, is a speech activity. The requirement to register as a commodity trading advisor restricts speech, thereby potentially conflicting with the First Amendment's imperative that "Congress shall make no law respecting an establishment of religion, or prohibiting the free exercise thereof; or abridging the freedom of speech, or of the press. . . ."[3] Moreover, commodity trading advisors have risk disclosure requirements to customers that arguably are compelled speech.[4] The Supreme Court has visited this question in the context of the SEC's regulation of securities investment advisors. Though the Supreme Court ultimately decided the case on narrower grounds without the need to address the constitutional issues, the obiter analysis is instructive, as is the separate opinion of Justice White (with Chief Justice Rehnquist's concurrence), which is grounded in the First Amendment.

The free speech questions stemming from the regulation of financial advisory activities are nearly identical whether applied to securities or derivatives, despite the otherwise distinct regimes for regulating securities investment advisors and commodity trading advisors. Therefore, it is appropriate to treat the reasoning in the precedent below as wholly applicable to the regulatory regime for commodity trading advisors.

---

2. Commodity Exchange Act §§ 1a(12)(B) and (C).

3. U.S. Const. amend. I.

4. *See, e.g.,* 17 C.F.R. §§ 4.7, 4.31, 4.34, and 4.35.

Lowe v. SEC

472 U.S. 181 (1985) (White, J., concurring in result)

Justice Stevens delivered the opinion of the Court.

The question is whether petitioners may be permanently enjoined from publishing nonpersonalized investment advice and commentary in securities newsletters because they are not registered as investment advisers under . . . the Investment Advisers Act of 1940 (Act).

Christopher Lowe is the president and principal shareholder of Lowe Management Corporation. From 1974 until 1981, the corporation was registered as an investment adviser under the Act. During that period Lowe was convicted of misappropriating funds of an investment client, of engaging in business as an investment adviser without filing a registration application with New York's Department of Law, of tampering with evidence to cover up fraud of an investment client, and of stealing from a bank. Consequently, on May 11, 1981, the Securities and Exchange Commission (Commission), after a full hearing before an Administrative Law Judge, entered an order revoking the registration of the Lowe Management Corporation, and ordering Lowe not to associate thereafter with any investment adviser.

In fashioning its remedy, the Commission took into account the fact that petitioners "are now solely engaged in the business of publishing advisory publications." The Commission noted that unless the registration was revoked, petitioners would be "free to engage in all aspects of the advisory business" and that even their publishing activities afforded them "opportunities for dishonesty and self-dealing."

A little over a year later, the Commission commenced this action by filing a complaint in the United States District Court for the Eastern District of New York, alleging that Lowe, the Lowe Management Corporation, and two other [related] corporations, were violating the Act, and that Lowe was violating the Commission's order. The principal charge in the complaint was that Lowe and the three corporations (petitioners) were publishing two investment newsletters and soliciting subscriptions for a stock-chart service. The complaint alleged that, through those publications, the petitioners were engaged in the business of advising others. . . .

Although three publications are involved in this litigation, only one need be described. A typical issue of the Lowe Investment and Financial Letter contained general commentary about the securities and bullion markets, reviews of market indicators and investment strategies, and specific recommendations for buying, selling, or holding stocks and bullion. The newsletter advertised a "telephone hotline" over which subscribers could call to get current information. The number of subscribers to the newsletter ranged from 3,000 to 19,000. It was advertised as a semimonthly publication, but only eight issues were published in the 15 months after the entry of the 1981 order.

Subscribers who testified at the trial criticized the lack of regularity of publication, but no adverse evidence concerning the quality of the publications was offered. There was no evidence that Lowe's criminal convictions were related to the publications; no evidence that Lowe had engaged in any trading activity in any securities that were the subject of advice or comment in the publications; and no contention that any of the information published in the advisory services had been false or materially misleading. . . .

A splintered panel of the Court of Appeals for the Second Circuit . . . held that petitioners were engaged in business as "investment advisers" within the meaning of the Act. It concluded that the Act does not distinguish between person-to-person advice and impersonal advice given in printed publications. . . .

[T]he Court of Appeals rejected petitioners' constitutional claim, reasoning that this case involves "precisely the kind of regulation of commercial activity permissible under the First Amendment."

In order to evaluate the parties' constitutional arguments, it is obviously necessary first to understand, as precisely as possible, the extent to which the Act was intended to regulate the publication of investment advice. . . .

Moreover, in view of the fact that we should "not decide a constitutional question if there is some other ground upon which to dispose of the case," and the further fact that the District Court and the dissenting judge in the Court of Appeals both believed that the case should be decided on statutory grounds, a careful study of the statute may either eliminate, or narrowly limit, the constitutional question that we must confront. . . .

One of the statutory exclusions [in the Act] is for "the publisher of any bona fide newspaper, news magazine or business or financial publication of general and regular circulation."[5] Although neither the text of the Act nor its legislative history defines the precise scope of this exclusion, two points seem tolerably clear. Congress did not intend to exclude publications that are distributed by investment advisers as a normal part of the business of servicing their clients. . . . Congress, plainly sensitive to First Amendment concerns, wanted to make clear that it did not seek to regulate the press through the licensing of nonpersonalized publishing activities. . . .

The exclusion itself uses extremely broad language that encompasses any newspaper, business publication, or financial publication provided that two conditions are met. The publication must be "bona fide," and it must be "of regular and general circulation." Neither of these conditions is defined, but the two qualifications precisely differentiate "hit and run tipsters" and "touts" from genuine publishers. Presumably a "bona fide" publication would be genuine in the sense that it would contain disinterested commentary and analysis as opposed to promotional material disseminated by a "tout." Moreover, publications with a "general and regular"

---

5. Note that there is a similar exclusion in the Commodity Exchange Act's definition of commodity trading advisor. *See* Commodity Exchange Act § 1a(12)(b)(iv).

circulation would not include "people who send out bulletins from time to time on the advisability of buying and selling stocks" or "hit and run tipsters." Because the content of petitioners' newsletters was completely disinterested, and because they were offered to the general public on a regular schedule, they are described by the plain language of the exclusion. . . .

The Act was designed to apply to those persons engaged in the investment-advisory profession — those who provide personalized advice attuned to a client's concerns, whether by written or verbal communication. The mere fact that a publication contains advice and comment about specific securities does not give it the personalized character that identifies a professional investment adviser. Thus, petitioners' publications do not fit within the central purpose of the Act because they do not offer individualized advice attuned to any specific portfolio or to any client's particular needs. On the contrary, they circulate for sale to the public at large in a free, open market — a public forum in which typically anyone may express his views.

The language of the exclusion, read literally, seems to describe petitioners' newsletters. Petitioners are "publishers of any bona fide newspaper, news magazine or business or financial publication." The only modifier that might arguably disqualify the newsletters are the words "bona fide." Notably, however, those words describe the publication rather than the character of the publisher; hence Lowe's unsavory history does not prevent his newsletters from being "bona fide." . . . Moreover, there is no suggestion that they contained any false or misleading information, or that they were designed to tout any security in which petitioners had an interest. Further, petitioners' publications are "of general and regular circulation." Although the publications have not been "regular" in the sense of consistent circulation, the publications have been "regular" in the sense important to the securities market: there is no indication that they have been timed to specific market activity, or to events affecting or having the ability to affect the securities industry. . . .

We therefore conclude that petitioners' publications fall within the statutory exclusion for bona fide publications and that none of the petitioners is an "investment adviser" as defined in the Act. It follows that neither their unregistered status, nor the Commission order barring Lowe from associating with an investment adviser, provides a justification for restraining the future publication of their newsletters. It also follows that we need not specifically address the constitutional question we granted certiorari to decide. . . .

Justice White, with whom the Chief Justice and Justice Rehnquist join, concurring in the result.

The issue in this case is whether the Securities and Exchange Commission may invoke the injunctive remedies of the Investment Advisers Act to prevent an unregistered adviser from publishing newsletters containing investment advice that is not specifically tailored to the needs of individual clients. The Court holds that it may not because the activities of petitioner Lowe (hereafter petitioner) do not make him an investment adviser covered by the Act. For the reasons that follow, I disagree with this improvident construction of the statute. In my view, petitioner is an investment adviser subject to regulation and sanction under the Act. I concur in the judgment, however, because to prevent petitioner from publishing at all is inconsistent with the First Amendment. . . .

[O]ur duty to avoid constitutional questions through statutory construction is not unlimited: it is subject to the condition that the construction adopted be "fairly possible." As Chief Justice Taft warned, "amendment may not be substituted for construction, and . . . a court may not exercise legislative functions to save the law from conflict with constitutional limitation." *Yu Cong Eng v. Trinidad*, 271 U.S. 500, 518, 46 S. Ct. 619, 623, 70 L. Ed. 1059 (1926). . . .

When the choice facing a court is between finding a particular application of a statute unconstitutional and adopting a construction of the statute that avoids the difficulty but at the same time materially deviates from the legislative plan and frustrates permissible applications, the choice of constitutional adjudication may well be preferable. . . .

Although petitioner does not offer his subscribers investment advice specifically tailored to their individual needs and engages in no direct communications with them, he undeniably "engages in the business of advising others . . . through publications . . . as to the value of securities" and "issues or promulgates analyses or reports concerning securities." Thus, he falls outside the definition of an "investment adviser" only if each of his publications qualifies as a "bona fide newspaper, news magazine or business or financial publication of general and regular circulation." The question is whether the "bona fide publications" exception is to be construed so broadly as to exclude from the definition all persons whose advisory activities are carried out solely through publications offering impersonal investment advice to their subscribers. . . .

If the [bona fide publications] exception is expanded to include more than just publications that are not primarily vehicles for distributing investment advice, it is difficult to imagine any workable definition that does not sweep in all publications that are not personally tailored to individual clients. . . .

The aim of the Act is the protection of the investing public against fraud or manipulation on the part of advisers. Viewed in light of this purpose, a publication that is no more than a vehicle for investment advice is an obvious target for regulatory measures: it makes sense to treat the entire publication as an adviser and to impose liability on the publication itself in the case of fraud or manipulation. On the other hand, the publisher of a publication that presents diverse forms of information and is not narrowly focused on the provision of investment advice is not so likely to engage in abusive practices. . . .

Nothing in the legislative history of the statute supports a construction of "investment adviser" that would exclude persons who offer investment advice only through such publications as newsletters and reports. . . .

The question is whether the First Amendment permits the Federal Government so to prohibit petitioner's publication of investment advice. . . .

This issue involves a collision between the power of government to license and regulate those who would pursue a profession or vocation and the rights of freedom of speech and of the press guaranteed by the First Amendment. . . .

Regulations on entry into a profession, as a general matter, are constitutional if they "have a rational connection with the applicant's fitness or capacity to practice" the profession. *Schware v. Board of Bar Examiners*, 353 U.S. 232, 239, 77 S. Ct. 752, 756, 1 L.Ed.2d 796 (1957).

The power of government to regulate the professions is not lost whenever the practice of a profession entails speech. . . .

Perhaps the most obvious example of a "speaking profession" that is subject to governmental licensing is the legal profession. Although a lawyer's work is almost entirely devoted to the sort of communicative acts that, viewed in isolation, fall within the First Amendment's protection, we have never doubted that "[a] State can require high standards of qualification, such as good moral character or proficiency in its law, before it admits an applicant to the bar. . . ." *Schware v. Board of Bar Examiners*, *supra*, 353 U.S. at 239, 77 S. Ct., at 756. . . .

The Government's position is that these same principles support the legitimacy of its regulation of the investment advisory profession, whether conducted through publications or through personal client-adviser relationships. . . .

But the principle that the government may restrict entry into professions and vocations through licensing schemes has never been extended to encompass the licensing of speech per se or of the press. At some point, a measure is no longer a regulation of a profession but a regulation of speech or of the press. . . .

One who takes the affairs of a client personally in hand and purports to exercise judgment on behalf of the client in the light of the client's individual needs and circumstances is properly viewed as engaging in the practice of a profession. . . . Where the personal nexus between professional and client does not exist, and a speaker does not purport to be exercising judgment on behalf of any particular individual with whose circumstances he is directly acquainted, government regulation ceases to function as legitimate regulation of professional practice with only incidental impact on speech; it becomes regulation of speaking or publishing as such, subject to the First Amendment's command that "Congress shall make no law . . . abridging the freedom of speech, or of the press." . . .

The application of the Act's enforcement provisions to prevent unregistered persons from engaging in the business of publishing investment advice for the benefit of any who would purchase their publications, however, is a direct restraint on freedom of speech and of the press. . . .

Not all restrictions on speech are impermissible. . . . Under the commercial speech doctrine, restrictions on commercial speech that directly advance a substantial governmental interest may be upheld. . . .

I do not believe it is necessary to the resolution of this case to determine whether petitioner's newsletters contain fully protected speech or commercial speech. The

Act purports to make it unlawful for petitioner to publish newsletters containing investment advice and to authorize an injunction against such publication. The ban extends as well to legitimate, disinterested advice as to advice that is fraudulent, deceptive, or manipulative. Such a flat prohibition or prior restraint on speech is, as applied to fully protected speech, presumptively invalid and may be sustained only under the most extraordinary circumstances. . . .

But even where mere "commercial speech" is concerned, the First Amendment permits restraints on speech only when they are narrowly tailored to advance a legitimate governmental interest. The interest here is certainly legitimate: the Government wants to prevent investors from falling into the hands of scoundrels and swindlers. The means chosen, however, is extreme. . . . Accordingly, I would hold that the Act, as applied to prevent petitioner from publishing investment advice altogether, is too blunt an instrument to survive even the reduced level of scrutiny called for by restrictions on commercial speech. . . .

For many years, the CFTC's commodity trading advisor regime had a broader scope than the SEC's investment adviser regime. The SEC regime had an exemption from registration as an investment adviser for "generalized advice," and the CFTC did not add a comparable exemption from registration as a commodity trading advisor until 2000. The CFTC's addition of the exemption came about due, in part, to a decision of the Fifth Circuit, *R&W Technical Services Ltd. v. CFTC*.[6] While the court in that case ruled in the CFTC's favor on other grounds, the decision cast doubt on the viability of the commodity trading advisor registration requirement in circumstances where only generalized commodity advice was provided.[7]

The final straw for the CFTC, though, was a pending decision of the District of Columbia Circuit in a First Amendment challenge to the CFTC's commodity trading advisor regime.[8] The case was settled before the decision could be rendered, and the CFTC adopted Rule 4.14(a)(9) to address the "uncertainty" caused by the litigation at the time.[9] Rule 4.14(a)(9) provides a broad exemption, similar to the SEC's exemption for investment advisers, for providers of general advice not directing client accounts. To rely on the CFTC's exemption, though, in addition to not directing accounts, the commodity trading advice may not be based on, or tailored to, the commodity interest or cash market positions or other circumstances or characteristics of particular

---

6. 205 F.3d 165 (5th Cir. 2000).

7. *Id.* at 176.

8. The United States District Court for the District of Columbia found that *Lowe* was not distinguishable and that Commodity Exchange Act section 4m(1), as implemented by the CFTC, operated as an unconstitutional prior restraint. *See Taucher v. Born*, 53 F. Supp. 2d 464 (D.D.C. 1999). It was settled before appeals were heard by the Court of Appeals for the District of Columbia. *See Taucher v. Rainier*, 2000 WL 516081 (D.C. Cir. Mar. 28, 2000).

9. *See* CFTC, *Exemption from Registration as a Commodity Trading Advisor*, 65 Fed. Reg. 12938, 12939 (Mar. 10, 2000).

clients. The adoption of Rule 4.14(a)(9) further insulated the CFTC's commodity trading advisor regime from a successful First Amendment challenge.[10]

The Second Circuit case below was decided before the adoption of Rule 4.14(a)(9). It examines First Amendment questions arising from the CFTC's commodity trading advisor regime. The context in the case is a computerized trading program that provided direct instructions as to when to trade futures. The court ruled in favor of the CFTC that defendant AVCO Financial Corp. was an unregistered commodity trading advisor. The court also struck down a broad injunction prohibiting the defendants from engaging in any activities requiring registration as a commodity trading advisor since it would operate as a prior restraint on some protected speech activities. Reviewing the *CFTC v. Vartuli* decision, a question to ask is what would a court decide about a similar injunction today now that the scope of speech activity that requires registration as a commodity trading advisor has narrowed?

CFTC v. Vartuli

228 F.3d 94 (2d Cir. 2000)

Sack, Circuit Judge:

The Commodity Futures Trading Commission (the "Commission" or the "CFTC"), an independent federal regulatory agency charged with the administration and enforcement of the Commodity Exchange Act (the "CEA"), and the regulations promulgated thereunder brought a civil enforcement action ... against defendants AVCO Financial Corp., Anthony Vartuli and J. Michael Gent. In its complaint, the Commission claimed that the defendants had violated the CEA by manufacturing, selling and advertising a computer program called "Recurrence," which the defendants fraudulently claimed provided profitable trading opportunities for its purchasers and users in the market for currency futures. . . .

The district court . . . conducted a bench trial [and] entered judgment against AVCO and Vartuli. . . . *See CFTC v. Avco Fin. Corp.*, 28 F.Supp.2d 104, 122 (S.D.N.Y.1998) ("*Avco II*"). The complaint against Gent was dismissed in its entirety. The court issued a permanent injunction against AVCO and Vartuli and ordered the disgorgement of the profits that they had garnered from the sale of Recurrence. . . .

Because we agree that AVCO and Vartuli violated the CEA, we affirm the district court's holding to that effect, although on somewhat different grounds. Because the conduct enjoined by the district court included the dissemination of Recurrence as speech and the district court did not first engage in prior restraint analysis, however, we conclude that the injunctive relief granted by the district court is in part unconstitutional, and to that extent we reverse and remand for the injunction to be modified. . . .

---

10. For example, the Seventh Circuit ruled that a First Amendment challenge to the commodity trading advisor regime was moot after promulgation of Rule 4.14(a)(9). *See Commodity Trend Service, Inc. v. CFTC*, 233 F.3d 981, 991 (7th Cir. 2000).

In 1989 AVCO, of which Vartuli was the sole shareholder, began marketing a set of materials called the "Recurrence" system, which Vartuli had developed with defendant Gent. Five versions of Recurrence were eventually produced (Recurrence I–V), the first two in book form and the latter three as computer software on disk. In this appeal, we are concerned principally with the computerized versions.

AVCO told its customers to obtain a market reporting service to feed current market prices for Swiss franc future contracts (or, for Recurrence V, Japanese yen future contracts) into a computer loaded with the Recurrence program. Recurrence would then analyze the transactions taking place in the futures market and give the user instantaneous "buy" or "sell" signals. AVCO claimed that following these signals would enable Recurrence users to trade futures contracts profitably. . . .

In addition to selling the system, AVCO gave occasional supplemental advice to Recurrence users by telephone. It also provided customers with a list of "authorized brokers" who were willing to trade for the account of an AVCO customer using the Recurrence system if the purchaser of the system did not want to order each specific transaction him or herself. . . .

The advertising made clear that Recurrence was being sold as a system for trading commodities futures, and that for the system to function properly its commands were to be followed explicitly. . . .

AVCO advertised that "Recurrence III makes money automatically," [and that] "the system turned a $10,000 trading account into a $544,704 fortune — a return of 833% per year." . . . But AVCO's claims were based on computer-generated hypothetical use of the system rather than actual trades. . . .

The results of actual trading using the Recurrence system did not live up to AVCO's promotional claims. The district court found that trading as directed by the Recurrence system, whether conducted by individuals or "authorized broker[s]," resulted in substantial losses. . . .

[T]he [district] court found that AVCO's representations about the Recurrence system's level of risk and past performance were material, false, misleading, and made with scienter[,] . . . that AVCO was in fact a CTA even though it had never registered as one, and that AVCO's actions were therefore subject to the regulations governing CTA conduct. . . .

Because the district court concluded that AVCO was a CTA and AVCO concededly never registered with the Commission, the district court held that AVCO was liable . . . [for] failure to register as a CTA. . . .

[T]he court permanently enjoined AVCO and Vartuli from acting as CTAs, trading in commodities, and soliciting customers for commodities trading. . . .

On appeal, Vartuli argues that . . . a software publisher such as AVCO does not fall within the statutory definition of a CTA; that if software publishers are CTAs then the CEA licensing scheme violates the First Amendment; [and] that AVCO's customers were not "clients." . . .

We conclude that AVCO meets the statutory definition of a CTA and affirm the district court's holding that AVCO violated the fraud provisions applicable to CTAs. Those provisions apply to CTAs irrespective of whether they are "exempt from registration under the Act," so the question of whether the CEA's registration requirement would be unconstitutional as applied to AVCO is independent from the question of whether AVCO is a CTA for purposes of the remainder of the Act. . . .

[T]he term "commodity trading advisor" [as defined by the CEA] means any person who—

(i) for compensation or profit, engages in the business of advising others, either directly or through publications, writings, or electronic media, as to the value of or the advisability of trading in—

(ii) any contract of sale of a commodity for future delivery made or to be made on or subject to the rules of a contract market; . . . or

(iii) for compensation or profit, and as part of a regular business, issues or promulgates analyses or reports concerning any of the activities referred to in clause (i).

[The definition of commodity trading advisor excludes] certain classes of people and entities from this definition, however. Relevant for our purposes, they exclude both "any news reporter, news columnist, or news editor of the print or electronic media," and "the publisher or producer of any print or electronic data of general and regular dissemination, including its employees," provided that "the furnishing of such [advisory services as described] . . . is solely incidental to the conduct of their business or profession."

There is no dispute that as the district court found, AVCO advised others through the electronic media, for profit, as to "the value or the advisability of trading in" futures contracts for Swiss francs and Japanese yen. . . .

The question thus becomes whether AVCO fits within the relevant CEA exclusions from the definition of CTA. Based upon the plain language of the statute it does not. The electronic data it produced were not "general[ly] and regular[ly] disseminat[ed]." And the information about the currency futures markets provided by Recurrence was not "solely incidental" to the conduct of AVCO's business; it was AVCO's business.

Vartuli relies on *Lowe v. SEC*, 472 U.S. 181, 105 S. Ct. 2557, 86 L.Ed.2d 130 (1985), to argue that one of the exclusions must nonetheless apply.

Because the Lowe court, in order to avoid the First Amendment issue, read the Investment Advisers Act's registration provision to apply only to personalized communications, Vartuli would have us read Lowe to state, by implication, that we must construe the CEA's general definition of CTA to include only those who engage in personalized communications. To do otherwise, he argues, would render the CEA, or at least its registration provision . . . , unconstitutional.

But *Lowe* was decided on the basis of the language and history of the Investment Advisers Act. The *Lowe* court . . . refused to reach the constitutional question. Thus *Lowe* provides us with neither a binding interpretation of the CEA, which was not the subject of the litigation before the Court, nor a constitutional analysis of the Investment Advisers Act.

We are thus left where we began, with the statutory language of the CEA. First, to fit within the exclusion, AVCO's data had to be "of general and regular dissemination." . . . [As] the Supreme Court reasoned when analyzing the identical phrase in the Investment Advisers Act, regular dissemination requires that there be " . . . no indication that [dissemination] ha[s] been timed to specific market activity." In this case, the petitioners' recommendations were provided by software that was programmed to "speak" only when certain market conditions were met. Thus, the petitioners' recommendations were timed to particular market activity and not "regularly" disseminated.

Second, whereas the Investment Advisers Act excluded from its registration requirement "the publisher of any bona fide newspaper, news magazine or business or financial publication of general and regular circulation," the CEA exclusion from its definition of a CTA applies to publishers and disseminators of information only if "the furnishing of such services . . . is solely incidental to the conduct of their business or profession." The publishing of Recurrence was AVCO's primary business. The exclusion therefore does not cover AVCO, and for purposes of . . . the complaint AVCO was a CTA. . . .

[Vartuli] argues, however, that AVCO did not violate the . . . [Commodity Exchange Act and CFTC rules] because those provisions apply only to frauds committed by a CTA upon a "client or participant or prospective client or participant." . . .

One would not ordinarily think of a purchaser of software as a "client" of the seller of the software, even if the purpose of the software was to tell the purchaser when to buy and sell futures contracts or other securities. . . .

The Commission has suggested to us that [this] issue was not raised in the district court, and Vartuli has not established that it was. . . .

The district court was right to ignore the issue if it was not litigated before the court. . . . We therefore decline to reach this question, at least at this time. . . .

The district court concluded that treating AVCO as a CTA, and therefore enjoining and sanctioning the defendants . . . for the fraud in which the defendants engaged, avoided constitutional infirmity because Recurrence "constituted personalized investment advice." *AVCO II*, 28 F.Supp.2d at 119. The emphasis on "personal" advice comes from *Lowe*. 472 U.S. at 191–96, 105 S. Ct. 2557. *Lowe's* holding was based on the Investment Advisers Act, not the Constitution. It therefore does not provide a framework for analysis of the constitutional issues raised on this appeal.

We are also not as certain as was the district court that AVCO provided "personalized investment advice." The advice was not personal in the sense that the defendants learned about the needs, resources and sophistication of individual clients and gave individualized advice based upon that information. . . .

But we agree with the district court nonetheless that there are no constitutional impediments to the court's judgment in this respect. . . . [T]he district court found, and we agree, that the defendants "made false and misleading representations to customers regarding the past profitability and track record of Recurrence in an effort to induce customers to purchase the program and follow Recurrence's recommendations." *Avco II*, 28 F. Supp. 2d at 119. It has long been understood that such "[f]rauds may be denounced as offenses and punished by law."

Moreover, . . . [the speech at issue is] not statements made by Recurrence, but those made in the advertisements for Recurrence. These communications about Recurrence did "no more than propose a commercial transaction," between AVCO and its prospective customers. They were, therefore, commercial speech. . . . It has long been firmly established that "[f]or commercial speech to come within [the protection of the First Amendment], it at least must . . . not be misleading." The misleading statements that were the subject of the CFTC's attack . . . were therefore not protected by the First Amendment. . . .

[W]e agree with the district court that AVCO acted as a CTA. By the terms of the statute, it was therefore required to register as one. But the CEA's registration requirements insofar as they are a prerequisite for constitutionally protected speech are a quintessential form of prior restraint. . . .

We note in this connection that the electronic form in which Recurrence supplies information does not affect the constitutional analysis. *Leaves of Grass* is protected speech irrespective of whether it is communicated by print on leather-bound pages or by electrons translated to words and read from a cathode-ray tube. A prior restraint against speech is no less suspect because the speech is conveyed electronically. . . .

The First Amendment issues arise, however, only if AVCO is being sanctioned for having engaged in or is being prevented from freely engaging in constitutionally protected speech. The First Amendment prohibits governmental abridgement of "the freedom of speech." We do not think that Recurrence in the form it was sold and marketed by the defendants was "speech" of the sort thus protected.

AVCO sold Recurrence not as a learning program, or an editorial, or an informational newsletter, but as a "system" and "trading program." "The system [was] automatic," with "NO complicated rules to follow. NO calculations to make. NO fundamentals to analyze. And NOTHING to interpret." Users were told they must "follow the signals with no second-guessing." When Recurrence displayed a "sell" signal, the customer was supposed to sell; when it flashed "buy" the customer was supposed to buy. He or she was expected to make no decision of his or her own. The system was advertised and marketed on the basis that it was to be trusted implicitly and followed explicitly. The customer or "client" was to be an automaton, mechanically following Recurrence's commands. . . .

In selling Recurrence in the manner in which it was sold, as an automatic trading system, AVCO acted as a CTA without engaging in constitutionally protected speech. For that it could, consistent with the First Amendment, be required to register, and its failure to do so can constitutionally be punished. The defendants are of course entitled to constitutional protection, but the applicable protection is that which would protect AVCO, Vartuli and their non-speech behavior from overreaching by the government, under the Due Process Clause of the Fifth Amendment, for example, not that which would protect their speech under the First Amendment. . . .

As part of the relief granted to the Commission, however, the district court permanently enjoined AVCO and Vartuli from "[a]cting as [] commodity trading advisor[s] . . . and from using the mails or any means or instrumentality of interstate commerce in connection with activity as [] CTA[s] unless registered with the Commodity Futures Trading Commission." . . . [I]t is clear that publishing Recurrence alone—i.e., not as an automatic trading system—would qualify as "acting as a commodity trading advisor." The district court enjoined the defendants from acting as such unless they registered with the CFTC. Under the injunction as it currently stands, therefore, the defendants would be required to register with the Commission to publish Recurrence even if it were being used solely as speech, if for example it were being advertised, sold and used as an academic commentary on the commodities markets. Thus formulated, the injunction together with the registration requirement may act as a prior restraint on constitutionally protected speech for which the district court did not perform any constitutional analysis. We therefore remand for the district court to limit the injunction to the dissemination of systems for the automatic trading of futures contracts. . . .

D. Regulatory Requirements

1. Generally

Commodity trading advisors are required to be registered with the CFTC and to be members of the National Futures Association. There is a significant overlap with securities law, and many commodity trading advisors are also registered as investment advisers with the SEC. Unlike with commodity pool operators, there is no requirement for the establishment of a risk management program,[11] to maintain capital, or appoint a chief compliance officer and submit annual compliance reports. Commodity trading advisors never hold customer funds, even though a customer

---

11. Commodity trading advisors are, however, subject to National Futures Association requirements to have an information systems security program in place to protect customer data and a business continuity and disaster recovery plan. National Futures Association Rules 2-9, 2-36, 2-38, and 2-49.

may give a commodity trading advisor authority to direct accounts held in the customer's name.[12]

Associated persons and principals of commodity trading advisors must pass proficiency exams administered by the National Futures Association, be fingerprinted, and not be statutorily disqualified.

2. Disclosure Documents

Before a commodity trading advisor may direct a client's account or guide its trading by some type of "systematic program that recommends specific transactions," highly detailed disclosure documents must be provided to the customer.[13] The disclosure documents are required to contain specific text mandated by CFTC rule and all "material information."[14] Among other details, "material information" includes information on principals, their business backgrounds, risk factors, trading strategy, fees and expenses, conflicts of interest, and material litigation.[15] National Futures Association rules require it to be in "plain English."[16] Historical performance data, where available, must also be provided.[17]

Incorrect statements in the disclosure document that the commodity trading advisor "knows or should know" is materially inaccurate or incomplete must be corrected within twenty-one days of such time.[18]

3. Reporting and Recordkeeping

Commodity trading advisors must file quarterly reports with the National Futures Association.[19] These reports provide general information about the commodity trading advisor, its key relationships, and its trading programs.

Records that must be kept by commodity trading advisors include client information, documents authorizing the commodity trading advisor to direct a client's account, agreements between the commodity trading advisor and its clients, all transactions for the account of clients and copies of their confirmations, all marketing materials including their dates, and records regarding proprietary trading activities of the commodity trading advisor.[20] The retention timing is the same as for commodity pool operators, discussed in chapter 7, section B.3.d.

---

12. 17 C.F.R. § 4.30(a).
13. 17 C.F.R. § 4.31.
14. 17 C.F.R. §§ 4.34(a), (b), and (o).
15. 17 C.F.R. § 4.34.
16. National Futures Association Rule 2-35(a)(1).
17. 17 C.F.R. § 4.35.
18. 17 C.F.R. § 4.36(c)(1)(i).
19. National Futures Association Rule 2-46.
20. 17 C.F.R. § 4.33.

4. Advertising and Marketing Restrictions

Advertising and marketing limitations are identical to those for commodity pool operators. See chapter 7, section B.3.e.

5. Failure to Register as a Commodity Trading Advisor

The Commodity Exchange Act provides a private right of action, the subject of chapter 16.[21] This private right of action gives a party the means in some circumstances to sue another party for its violation of the Commodity Exchange Act. For the immediate purposes of this chapter, it is important to know that, in the context of trading advice, the necessary prerequisites to a successful private right of action are the provision of such advice for a fee and a violation of the Commodity Exchange Act.[22] However, these two elements are not sufficient to succeed in a claim. As the decision below demonstrates, a causal relationship between the Commodity Exchange Act violation and the actual harm needs to be proven.

In the case below, the motion the court was ruling on was a motion for summary judgment. When a party makes a motion for summary judgement, the judge evaluates all of the other party's factual allegations in the most favorable light possible. If there is still no prospect for success of the other party as a matter of law, the judge will grant the motion.

In this case, the defendant, Farms.com, Inc., made a motion for summary judgement. One of the allegations of the plaintiff was that Farms.com, Inc. had an obligation to register with the CFTC as a commodity trading advisor and had failed to do so. Since the motion made by Farms.com was for summary judgement, the judge effectively assumed the truth of some of the plaintiff's allegations, including that Farms.com was required to register with the CFTC and was not so registered.

S & A Farms, Inc. v. Farms.com, Inc.

862 F. Supp. 2d 898 (S.D. Iowa 2011)
(citations to trial documents omitted),
aff'd, 678 F.3d 949 (8th Cir. 2012)

Robert W. Pratt, Chief Judge.

Before the Court is a Motion for Summary Judgment, filed on March 11, 2011 by Farms.com Risk Management, Ltd. ("Defendant"). S & A Farms, Inc. ("Plaintiff") filed a resistance to the Motion on April 1, 2011.

I. Factual Background

Plaintiff is an Iowa corporation that is in the business of producing corn and both producing and selling soybeans and hogs. It was formed in 1992 by Scott Renaud

---

21. Commodity Exchange Act § 22.
22. Commodity Exchange Act § 22(a)(1).

("Renaud") and Abbie Renaud (collectively "the Renauds"), who are its sole officers, directors, and shareholders. Renaud is the Plaintiff's sole employee. Renaud did not attend college, other than two eight-week programs for farmers. He did not have any formal training in hedging or risk management techniques, but had been involved in — and had prior experience with — commodities trading with three different brokers in years prior to 2007.

At some point in time, Howard Vroom ("Vroom"), a local feed salesman, introduced Renaud to Victor Aideyan ("Aideyan"),[23] the Senior Consultant/Manager for Defendant. In a brochure, Defendant stated that it was "an agricultural commodity marketing and price risk management service provider for farmers, producers and agribusiness across North America." In marketing materials, Aideyan was listed as a "Senior Risk Management Consultant" on Defendant's "Risk Management Team," with "over 14 years experience in commodity trading and marketing."

In September 2007, Vroom arranged a meeting at Defendant's Ames, Iowa office between Renaud, Aideyan, and Jack Ticky ("Ticky"), another employee of Defendant. In attending this meeting, Renaud advised Aideyan that Plaintiff was increasing the size of its hog production and needed risk management advice. Renaud wanted Aideyan and Ticky to explain how Defendant could help provide risk management services in relation to the corn he purchased to feed Plaintiff's hogs.[24] On September 17, 2007, Aideyan and Renaud executed a Price Risk Management Service Letter (hereinafter the "Contract"), wherein Defendant agreed to provide, and Plaintiff agreed to purchase, consulting services related to the corn inputs and hog outputs involved in Plaintiff's operation. . . .

Shortly after the September 2007 meeting between Renaud, Aideyan, and Ticky, Renaud established and opened a commodities trading account with MF Global, Inc. ("MF Global").[25] Only Renaud was authorized to make trades in the MF Global account. Thus, after discussing potential trades and positions with Aideyan, Renaud would call MF Global and execute trades. On occasion, Aideyan would either contact MF Global in advance, or participate in the calls to MF Global to ensure that Renaud accurately communicated Plaintiff's desired trade. In September 2008,

---

23. [N. 2] Aideyan has a master's degree in business administration and a derivative market specialist designation from the Canadian Securities Institute. He is a certified member of the Canadian Association of Farm Advisors. *Id.*

24. [N. 3] Plaintiff contends that during the September 2007 meeting, Aideyan described himself as an expert in the use of futures and options for risk management purposes and assured Renaud that he would leave speculation to gamblers. Defendant denies this assertion.

25. [N. 5] Plaintiff contends that Aideyan recommended that Plaintiff open a commodity trading account with MF Global. Defendant, however, avers that Aideyan recommended several potential brokerages to Renaud, and that Renaud chose MF Global because he already had an account open with that firm. . . .

Aideyan left his employment with Defendant. Thereafter, Maurizo Agostino ("Agostino") provided services to Plaintiff.[26]

Renaud, at times, provided copies of Plaintiff's MF Global account statements so that Aideyan could monitor the trades made on the account. Aideyan acknowledged in his deposition that he regularly discussed trades with Renaud and that the trading strategy reflected in the MF Global account was the strategy developed by Defendant.[27] All of the trades reflected in Plaintiff's MF Global account, save for one cotton trade on October 21, 2008, were recommended to Renaud by either Aideyan or Agostino.[28]

On February 24, 2009, Plaintiff unilaterally liquidated its positions and stopped obtaining and relying on advice from Defendant. Between September 20, 2007 and February 24, 2009, Plaintiff's account with MF Global incurred a net loss of $1,040,958.75.

On December 8, 2009, Plaintiff filed a Complaint in this Court alleging that Defendant is liable to Plaintiff for violating the Commodity Exchange Act ("CEA"), 7 U.S.C. §1 et seq. Specifically, Plaintiff claims that Defendant failed to disclose that it was required to register with the Commodity Futures Trading Commission ("CFTC"), but had not so registered, and additionally failed to disclose its trading experience and other material information required by the CFTC regulations.[29] According to Plaintiff, had it known that Defendant was operating in violation of the CEA, it never would have done business with Defendant. . . .

II. Standard for Summary Judgement. . . .

Summary judgment is appropriately granted when the record, viewed in the light most favorable to the nonmoving party and giving that party the benefit of all reasonable inferences, shows that there is no genuine issue of material fact, and that the moving party is therefore entitled to judgment as a matter of law. . . . The Court does not weigh the evidence, nor does it make credibility determinations. . . .

---

26. [N. 6] Agostino was identified in Defendant's marketing materials as a "Senior Risk Management Consultant" who has "obtained his U.S. Series 3 Futures and Options License Course."

27. [N. 7] Defendant's trading advice and recommendations were intended as hedges for risk management purposes.

28. [N. 8] According to Defendant, Agostino rendered little "advice" to Plaintiff because Agostino only spoke to Renaud a few times. Defendant contends that in their second or third conversation, Renaud advised Agostino that he was going to sue Defendant and Agostino. Agostino, thereafter, refused to give advice to Renaud regarding Plaintiff's account with MF Global.

29. [N. 9] Defendant does not dispute that it has never been registered with CFTC or the National Futures Association ("NFA"), and never consulted an attorney to determine whether it was required to register as a commodity trading advisor. Defendant also does not dispute that neither Aideyan nor Agostino have ever been registered in any capacity in the United States, or that Defendant advised more than 15 persons in its Elite Service Hog Program. While Defendant admits that it did not advise Plaintiff of its lack of registration with the CFTC, it denies that it was required to be registered with the CFTC in the first instance.

III. Law and Analysis . . .

The CEA provides, in pertinent part:

(1) Any person (other than a registered entity or registered futures association) who violates this chapter or who willfully aids, abets, counsels,
induces, or procures the commission of a violation of this chapter shall be
liable for actual damages resulting from one or more of the transactions
referred to in subparagraphs (A) through (D) of this paragraph and caused
by such violation to any other person —

(A) who received trading advice from such person for a fee.

7 U.S.C. § 25(a)(1). Thus, to prevail on its claim against Defendant for a CEA violation, Plaintiff must demonstrate, among other things, that Defendant violated a provision of the CEA and that Plaintiff sustained "actual damages" that were "caused by
such violation" when it received trading advice from Defendant for a fee.

According to Count I of Plaintiff's Complaint, Defendant violated the CEA by
failing to register with the CFTC as a commodity trading advisor ("CTA"). . . .
Specifically, Plaintiff alleges that "[Defendant] violated Section 4o(1) of the CEA,
7 U.S.C. § 6o(1) . . . which prohibits fraud by a commodity trading advisor. [Plain-
tiff] received trading advice from [Defendant] for a fee and incurred actual damages
from receiving that trading advice." Though Defendant denies that it was required
to register as a CTA, its Motion for Summary Judgment does not focus on the legal
requirement of registration. Rather, Defendant argues that, "[r]egardless of whether
Plaintiff would be able to establish that Defendant violated the CEA by failing to
register as a CTA with the CFTC, Plaintiff will not be able to provide that such violation caused it 'actual damages.'" . . .

[T]he Court finds summary judgment in favor of Defendant appropriate. To
prove a case for fraudulent inducement, Plaintiff must prove that Defendant: 1) acted
with scienter;[30] 2) made a misrepresentation of material[31] fact; 3) Plaintiff reasonably

---

30. [N. 17] Plaintiff's Complaint does not allege that Defendant acted with scienter; it merely
alleges failure to disclose. . . . In fact, the Court cannot find any allegation anywhere in the record
that Defendant knowingly or intentionally sought to "induce" Plaintiff into transacting business
with it by not disclosing its registration status. This constitutes a separate basis upon which Plaintiff's CEA claim is inadequate as a matter of law.

31. [N. 18] . . . Renaud's deposition testimony admitting that he does not know anything about
the CEA (and presumably the significance of registration thereunder) undercuts the presumption
to at least some extent:

Q. Did you ask if [Defendant] was registered as a commodity trading advisor in that
meeting?
A. No.
Q. Did you even know what the Commodity Exchange Act was at that time?
A. I'm sure I didn't.
Q. When did you first learn about a thing called the Commodity Exchange Act?
A. I have no idea.
Q. Do you even know what that is today?

relied on the misrepresentation; and 4) the misrepresentation proximately caused Plaintiff's injury. *See Beck v. Jonasson*, CFTC No. 08-R027, Comm. Fut. L. Rep. P 31313, 2009 WL 290970, at *3 (C.F.T.C. Feb. 4, 2009).

Proximate causation generally requires evidence that a defendant's conduct was not only the "but for" cause of a plaintiff's damages, but was also a "substantial factor" in bringing about such damages.... While Plaintiff has arguably demonstrated "but for" causation by alleging that it would not have contracted with Defendant had it known Defendant was not registered as a CTA, it has failed to demonstrate that Defendant's failure to register was a "substantial factor" in bringing about the Plaintiff's loss. That is, even assuming that Plaintiff would not have relied on Defendant to advise it in regard to commodity trading "but for" Defendant's failure to advise of its non-registered status, Plaintiff has presented no evidence that Defendant's lack of CTA registration made it reasonably probable that Plaintiff would sustain losses by relying on Defendant's advice....

[In cases] where risks of commodities trading remain undisclosed or are misrepresented, it is easy to see how an unsuspecting investor could foreseeably sustain losses far beyond those reasonably expected absent the misrepresentations or omissions. Without diminishing the importance of registration under the CEA, however, the same cannot be said of a registration violation, i.e., the mere fact that an advisor is required to be registered, but is not, does not naturally, proximately, and foreseeably support a belief that an investor will be financially damaged by relying on the unregistered advisor's advice. To accept Plaintiff's arguments of causation in this case would transform the failure to register into a strict liability tort.[32] That is, whenever an investor experiences losses in commodities trades, it can hold its advisor liable for any and all losses merely by discovering a registration violation and claiming that it would not have transacted business with the advisor had it known

---

A. No.

Q. Did the Commodity Exchange Act have any bearing on your decision to use [Defendant's services]?...

A. I don't know what he's talking about.

Q. You don't know what that act is?

A. No. Maybe if you said it and then I could put it together. But, no, I cannot tell you what that act is.

32. [N. 20] The Court finds it worthy of note, in regard to the causation analysis, that Plaintiff has never stated it would not have engaged in trading commodities at all were it aware of Defendant's non-registered status, merely that it would not have "done business with Defendant []." This emphasizes the "strict liability" nature of Plaintiff's asserted CEA claim, i.e., if Defendant had been registered and rendered precisely the same trading advice, with precisely the same outcome to Plaintiff's bottom line, Defendant would not be subject to liability for Plaintiff's claimed losses. However, merely due to the lack of registration, Defendant is arguably "on the hook" for whatever loss Plaintiff claims, even though the mere fact of registration cannot assure the propriety or reliability of an advisor's trading advice.

of the violation. Such a result does not, in this Court's view, comport with tradi-tional principles of proximate causation or fairness.[33]

The requirement of more than "but for" causation in the context of Plaintiff's fraud claim in this case is further supported by the statutory language that creates the CEA cause of action. In *Hudson v. Wilhelm*, the Court emphasized the fact that recovery under the CEA can only be had pursuant to 7 U.S.C. § 25, which provides that a person who violates the CEA shall be liable "for actual damages . . . *caused by such violation*." 651 F.Supp. 1062, 1067 (D.Colo.1987) (emphasis added). The *Hudson* court determined that the "caused by such violation" language of 7 U.S.C. § 25 "clearly indicates the violation must cause the actual damages alleged." *Id.* at 1067. Accordingly, the court rejected causation in circumstances similar to those here:

> Plaintiff contends causation is "clearly present, since plaintiff would have never permitted the defendants to illegally trade on her account if she had known that the defendants were not properly registered in commodities futures." Plaintiff seems to be arguing a "but for" type of causation in this sentence. Had she known of the registration deficiencies, she would not have allowed defendants to trade on her account. This argument, however, tacitly concedes plaintiff's monetary losses are not themselves the direct result of defendants' registration improprieties. Instead, plaintiff argues she never would have incurred the losses in the first place because, had she known of the registration problem, she would not have permitted defendants to handle her money at all. The legal import of this argument is to transform the eighth claim for relief into a claim for misrepresentation. Plaintiff is not alleging her monetary losses were caused by defendants' failure to register properly. Rather, she is contending her pecuniary damages were occasioned by defendants' concealment of possible registration problems.

Id. at 1068; *see also Biedron v. Futures*, No. 87C8425, 1989 WL 134796, at *4 (N.D.Ill.1989) ("Biedron does not say how the fact that Dorsey was not registered served to cause him, Biedron, to suffer financial loss. Even if Biedron intended . . . to say that had he known that Dorsey was not registered he would never have con-sented to having his account traded by him, it still would not suffice to state a claim under the CEA. That line of argument suggests that Dorsey's failure to be registered serves as a *but for* cause of Biedron's losses, not a proximate cause.").

Since Plaintiff may only recover actual damages *caused by* the Defendant's failure to register, there must be some evidence beyond "but for" causation linking Plain-tiff's damages to the Defendant's registration requirements. No such evidence exists in this case. Indeed, Renaud has testified that, to this day, he does not even know what the CEA is. . . .

---

33. [N. 21] At least one court has found that the "mere failure to register does not amount to fraud, deceit or misrepresentation sufficient to justify rescission." *Hofmayer v. Dean Witter & Co. Inc.*, 459 F.Supp. 733, 739 (N.D.Cal.1978).

IV. Conclusion

The Court does not take away a party's right to a jury trial lightly, and it is extremely cognizant of the harsh result its ruling imposes on Plaintiff in this matter. Nonetheless, after carefully reviewing the record in the light most favorable to Plaintiff, the Court is convinced that Plaintiff has failed to generate a genuine issue of material fact on several essential elements of its claims. Indeed, an equally harsh result would be imposed on the Defendant were the case permitted to proceed to trial when evidence of matters so fundamental as scienter, duty, breach, and proximate causation are insufficiently supported by the record. Accordingly, for the reasons stated herein, Defendant's Motion for Summary Judgment is GRANTED. The Clerk of Court shall enter judgment in favor of Defendant on all claims.

The CFTC did not take an action against Farms.com, Inc. for failing to register as a commodity trading advisor. Since Farms.com, Inc.'s activities, as described in the decision, appear to be consistent with a commodity trading advisor, it is possible that Farms.com, Inc. was eligible for an exemption from registration. We now examine the exemptions from registration for commodity trading advisors.

E. Commodity Trading Advisor Exemptions and Exclusions

1. Commodity Exchange Act §§ 1a(12)(B) and (C)

There is a statutory exclusion from the definition of commodity trading advisor for the following entities so long as "the furnishing of such services . . . is solely incidental to the conduct of their business or profession":

i. any bank or trust company or any person acting as an employee thereof;

ii. any news reporter, news columnist, or news editor of the print or electronic media, or any lawyer, accountant, or teacher;

iii. any floor broker or futures commission merchant;

iv. the publisher or producer of any print or electronic data of general and regular dissemination, including its employees;

v. the fiduciary of any defined benefit plan that is subject to the Employee Retirement Income Security Act of 1974 (29 U.S.C. 1001 et seq.); [and]

vi. any contract market. . . .[34]

----

34. Commodity Exchange Act § 1a(B) and (C).

2. CFTC Rule 4.6

Rule 4.6 is an exclusion from the definition of commodity trading advisor. It operates for the benefit of insurance companies and their affiliates, a person relying on the Rule 4.5 exclusion from the definition of "commodity pool operator," and swap dealers.[35] In all cases, the commodity trading advisory activities must be "incidental" to the overall activities of the entity claiming the exclusion.[36]

3. CFTC Rule 4.7

Rule 4.7 may be relied upon by a registered commodity trading advisor advising a qualified eligible person.[37] In lieu of the prescriptive disclosure document requirements otherwise imposed, the commodity trading advisor relying on a Rule 4.7 exemption must provide a CFTC-specified paragraph explaining that the offering is exempt, past performance disclosure only to the extent it is "material" to that account, and enough information in a brochure or other disclosure statement to make the information "not misleading."[38] Recordkeeping is limited to books and records relating to activities as a commodity trading advisor of qualified eligible persons.[39] The exemption requires a filing with the National Futures Association.[40]

4. CFTC Rule 4.14

CFTC Rule 4.14 is a catch-all provision, exempting from registration entities that are not intended to be captured by the commodity trading advisor registration requirements. Among the entities exempted are:

- *Cash market transactions*: A "dealer, processor, broker, or seller in cash market transactions of any commodity (or product thereof)" where the person's commodity trading advice "is solely incidental" to the conduct of its cash market business.

- *Not-for-profit*: A "non-profit, voluntary membership, trade association or farm organization" where the person's commodity trading advice is "solely incidental" to the conduct of its business.

- *Associated person*: Associated persons whose commodity trading advice is "solely in connection" with their employment as an associated person.

---

35. 17 C.F.R. § 4.6.
36. *Id.*
37. 17 C.F.R. § 4.7(c).
38. 17 C.F.R. § 4.7(c)(1).
39. 17 C.F.R. § 4.7(c)(2).
40. *See* 17 C.F.R. § 4.7(d).

- *Commodity pool operator*: A commodity pool operator either registered with the CFTC or exempt from registration with the CFTC where its commodity trading advice is solely for the relevant commodity pools.

- *Introducing broker, leverage transaction merchant, or retail foreign exchange dealer*: An introducing broker, leverage transaction merchant, or retail foreign exchange dealer registered as such with the CFTC where its commodity trading advice is solely in connection with the applicable activities.

- *Registered investment adviser*: (1) Must be registered with the SEC as an investment adviser or benefiting from a number of exclusions the definition similar to those in Commodity Exchange Act section 1a(12)(B); (2) commodity trading advice must be directed to and solely incidental to activities related to any of an insurance company, mutual fund, some types of trusts, pension plan, non-U.S. commodity pool, or a commodity pool using the *de minimis* exemption described above in chapter 7, section D.5.c; (3) notice must be filed with the National Futures Association, affirmed annually; and (4) related books and records must be kept for five years.

- *Generalized advice*: Someone who is not directing any client accounts as a commodity trading advisor or providing commodity trading advice based on or tailored to the commodity positions or other circumstances of particular clients.

- *De minimis activities*: Anyone who in the preceding year has provided commodity trading advice to fifteen or fewer persons and does not publicly hold him- or herself out as a commodity trading advisor.[41]

- *Family office*: If the advice is solely for family, former family, key employees, former key employees, and specified entities closely related to the foregoing.[42]

Questions and Comments

1. In light of *Lowe v. SEC*, was the Commodity Exchange Act's definition of commodity trading advisor, as implemented by the CFTC, unconstitutionally overbroad before it added the exemption contained in Rule 4.14(a)(9)[43] and discussed in section C above?

2. What about after the addition of Rule 4.14(a)(9)? Could a claim be made that the commodity trading advisor regime violates the First Amendment? In what circumstances might an argument be raised that the commodity trading advisor regime conflicts with the First Amendment?

---

41. A similar private adviser exemption for securities investment advisers, exempting investment advisers with fourteen or fewer clients, was repealed by section 403 of the Dodd-Frank Act.

42. 17 C.F.R. § 4.14.

43. 17 C.F.R. § 4.14(a)(9).

3. In *S & A Farms, Inc. v. Farms.com, Inc.*, the judge states that the court "is extremely cognizant of the harsh result its ruling imposes on Plaintiff in this matter."[44] Should the court have protected the plaintiff in some way? If so, how, and what would be the consequences of doing so?

4. What is the purpose of regulating commodity advice? What would happen if it were not regulated at all?

5. Evaluating the exemptions in CFTC Rule 4.14, is there anything missing that should be included?

---

44. *S & A Farms, Inc. v. Farms.com, Inc.*, 862 F. Supp. 2d 898, 918 (S.D. Iowa 2011), *aff'd*, 678 F.3d 949 (8th Cir. 2012).

Chapter 9

Introduction to the Regulation of Swaps and Prohibited Derivatives Transactions

A. Introductory Note

We are now making a significant transition from the CFTC's well-established regime for the regulation of futures and exchange-traded commodity options to its ongoing establishment of a regulatory regime for swaps. The Dodd-Frank Act imposed a new regulatory regime for the swaps market and its participants, which has been jointly summarized by the CFTC and SEC as:

> a statutory framework to reduce risk, increase transparency, and promote market integrity within the financial system by, among other things: (i) providing for the registration and regulation of swap dealers and major swap participants; (ii) imposing clearing and trade execution requirements on standardized derivative products; (iii) creating recordkeeping and real-time reporting regimes; and (iv) enhancing the [CFTC's and SEC's] rulemaking and enforcement authorities with respect to all registered entities and intermediaries subject to [their] oversight.[1]

In this chapter and chapters 10, 11, and 12, we examine the CFTC's regime for the regulation of swaps. At this point it may be helpful to revisit the economic description of a swap in chapter 1, sections B.3.e and B.3.f, and the descriptions of swap products in chapter 1, section D.2.

It is important to recognize the novelty of this regulatory regime for swaps. It originates solely from the 2010 passage of the Dodd-Frank Act.[2] Immediately before passage of the Dodd-Frank Act, swaps were unregulated unless traded with "retail" counterparties, i.e., consumers of ordinary economic means, though federal and state remedies were available for actual fraud. The regulation of swaps through the Dodd-Frank Act was an occasion as momentous to financial regulation as was federal regulation of the securities markets through the Securities Act of 1933 and the

---

1. *Further Definition of "Swap Dealer," "Security-Based Swap Dealer," "Major Swap Participant," "Major Security-Based Swap Participant" and "Eligible Contract Participant"*, 77 Fed. Reg. 30596, 30596 (May 23, 2012).

2. Pub. L. 111-203.

Securities Exchange Act of 1934 or the commodity futures markets through the Commodity Exchange Act of 1936.

A major difference between the genesis of federal regulation of the securities and commodity futures markets, on the one hand, and swaps, on the other hand, is that the acts regulating the securities and futures markets were passed with bipartisan support. The Securities Act of 1933 was passed by voice vote and the Securities Act of 1934 was passed 281 to 84 in the House and 62 to 13 in the Senate.[3] The Commodity Exchange Act was passed by voice vote in the House of Representatives and 62 to 16 in the Senate.[4]

By contrast, the Dodd-Frank Act passed 237 to 192 in the House with only three Republicans voting in favor and nineteen Democrats voting against and 60 to 39 in the Senate with only three Republicans voting in favor and one Democrat voting against.[5] Therefore, it is important to keep this background in mind to understand the continuing disagreements over the propriety and scope of the derivatives regulation mandated by the Dodd-Frank Act.

The Dodd-Frank Act also charged the SEC with the establishment of a regulatory regime for security-based swaps (see chapter 13). The SEC has finalized the last of the rules required to implement this regime, and it is newly effective in November 2021. Since we specifically discuss it in chapter 13, it is not covered in this chapter.

The historical antecedents to the CFTC's swaps regulatory regime and the impetus for its establishment provided by the Financial Crisis beginning in 2007 were discussed in chapter 2, section E.2 and are further discussed in section B below.

Since the swaps regulatory regime is a new one, instituted by the Dodd-Frank Act in 2010 and rolled out incrementally over the following years, caselaw is less available as a resource for understanding the law. We are forced to rely more on regulatory releases, analogy to other better-established areas of law, such as for the regulation of commodity futures, and ancillary materials, such as congressional reports. The one area where significant caselaw related to swaps has developed is with respect to interpretation of Bankruptcy Code provisions specific to swaps. In chapter 18, we examine those cases.

What Is a "Retail" Market?

We use the term "retail" in this chapter to distinguish the "retail" market from the "wholesale" market. We discuss the legal definition of non-retail swap market participants, known as "eligible contract participants" in section E below. In the meantime, a good rule of thumb is to think of a retail market as one

---

3. 77 Cong. Rec. 8116 (1933) and 78 Cong. Rec. 8713 (1934).

4. 80 Cong. Rec. 8293 (1936).

5. *See* http://clerk.house.gov/evs/2010/roll413.xml.

> with the participation of consumers of ordinary economic means, including especially natural persons other than high net worth individuals. The wholesale market, on the other hand, has mostly dealers, other large corporations and partnerships, and governments as participants.

B. Impetus for the Dodd-Frank Act's Regulation of Swaps

1. Background

In chapter 2, section E.2 we listed significant financial institution failures and "fire sale" acquisitions occurring during the peak of the Financial Crisis. What at the time were household names — venerable institutions such as Wachovia Bank, Bear Stearns, Lehman Brothers, and Washington Mutual — seemingly disappeared overnight.

The Congressional Oversight Panel was an office within the Department of the Treasury's Office of Financial Stability. The Panel was created in 2008 to "review the current state of the financial markets and the regulatory system" in light of the Financial Crisis and submit various reports to Congress.[6] It was bipartisan, constituted by five appointees selected by congressional leadership.[7] The Congressional Oversight Panel was terminated in April 2011. In its March Oversight Report — its final report — it described the extent of government-assistance provided to the finance and auto industries and to one insurance company, the largest in the world at the time.[8] The unprecedented scale of this government intervention is important for understanding the backdrop in which the Dodd-Frank Act was enacted.

Congressional Oversight Panel, *March Oversight Report*

(Govt. Printing Off. 2011), available at http://www.gpo.gov/fdsys/pkg /CHRG-112shrg64832/pdf/CHRG-112shrg64832.pdf

... The first tremors of the impending financial crisis and the severe recession that followed were seen in the American housing market.... The rapid appreciation in home prices ... helped fuel housing speculation and a boom in mortgage refinancing and home equity loans. ...

In late 2006, home prices began to decline and delinquencies on home mortgages ... began to rise. ...

---

6. Emergency Economic Stabilization Act of 2008, Pub. L. No 110-343 (2008), §125(b).

7. *Id*. at §125(c).

8. According to 12 U.S.C. §5233, the Congressional Oversight Panel was required to terminate by December 31, 2009. However, an exclusion in 12 U.S.C. §5211(a)(3) allowed for an extension.

Bear Stearns closed two mortgage-backed securities (MBS) focused hedge funds, and two of the largest subprime mortgage originators and securitizers — New Century Financial and American Home Mortgage — filed for bankruptcy. On August 9, 2007, BNP Paribas, the largest bank in France, suspended redemptions in three investment funds due to their exposure to the U.S. subprime mortgage market....

As housing fundamentals continued to weaken and financial fear spread, some of the nation's largest financial firms began to teeter on the edge of failure. On January 11, 2008, Bank of America announced its purchase of a major mortgage originator, Countrywide Financial. Then on March 14, the Federal Reserve intervened to rescue Bear Stearns by helping to arrange for and assisting with its purchase by JPMorgan.... The nation's gross domestic product . . . contracted for four consecutive quarters through June 2009.... [U]nemployment rose sharply in 2008 and early 2009....

As the effects of the crisis spread to the wider market . . . IndyMac Bank, one of the nation's largest savings and loans and the second largest mortgage lender in the country, came under pressure as fear spread about its potential insolvency. Over an eleven-day period, depositors withdrew over $1.3 billion of the $19 billion it held in deposits and the institution was subsequently taken over by the Federal Deposit Insurance Corporation (FDIC)....

In September, the housing bubble, the liquidity crunch, and the financial crisis culminated in a string of unprecedented events and government interventions that took place over a 19-day stretch. During this period, Fannie Mae and Freddie Mac were placed into conservatorship, Lehman Brothers filed for bankruptcy, the Federal Reserve initiated an $85 billion government rescue of American International Group (AIG) [an insurance company], Treasury announced a temporary guarantee of the $3.7 trillion money market funds (MMFs), and the FDIC steered Washington Mutual through the largest bank failure in U.S. history. By the beginning of October 2008, the value of the stock market had declined by nearly 20 percent from its level in January of that year, losing 10 percent in September alone....

As a result of these events . . . Chairman of the Board of Governors of the Federal Reserve System Ben S. Bernanke and Secretary of the Treasury Henry M. Paulson, Jr. concluded . . . that their only realistic option to contain the rapidly spreading financial crisis was to convince Congress to authorize an overwhelming fiscal response by the federal government....

[Congress] authorized the Treasury Secretary to purchase not only mortgage-related securities under the [troubled asset relief program, commonly known as "TARP," a Federal program allowing for purchases of mortgage-related securities from financial institutions,] but also "any other financial instrument" the purchase of which the Secretary determined to be "necessary to promote financial market stability." . . . Although the federal government has intervened to rescue financial institutions . . . on several previous occasions in U.S. history, the scale and breadth of the financial rescue . . . was unprecedented. . . .

On October 14, 2008, Secretary Paulson met with the heads of the nine largest U.S. banks . . . and told them that Treasury would . . . make direct capital injections into each of their institutions [instead of purchasing troubled assets directly].

The nine institutions . . . included the four largest U.S. commercial banks (JPMorgan, Bank of America, Citigroup, and Wells Fargo), the three largest investment banks (Goldman Sachs, Morgan Stanley, and Merrill Lynch), and the two largest custodian banks (State Street and BNY Mellon). At that time, these banks held $10.3 trillion in assets, representing more than 75 percent of all the assets in the American banking system. . . .

In addition to the initial capital investments made in the nation's largest banks, Treasury undertook additional steps to ensure the stability of Citigroup and Bank of America in November and December 2008 by purchasing an additional $20 billion of preferred shares from both institutions. . . .

Furthermore, in November, Treasury, in conjunction with the Federal Reserve and the FDIC, put together a hastily crafted $301 billion guarantee of Citigroup assets. . . .

Also in November, the federal government supplemented the original $85 billion loan to AIG and initiated a second round of assistance to AIG in which the TARP purchased $40 billion of preferred equity and the Federal Reserve provided $44 billion to create two special purpose vehicles (SPVs) to take ownership of certain AIG financial assets. Treasury also made its first investments in the automotive industry in late 2008 with loans and preferred stock purchases for General Motors, GMAC, Chrysler, and Chrysler Financial. By the end of January 2009, TARP assistance outstanding amounted to $301 billion with over 75 percent having been provided to only a few firms: the nation's biggest banks, the automotive industry, and AIG. . . .

By providing a complete bailout that called for no shared sacrifice among AIG and its creditors, FRBNY and Treasury fundamentally changed the rules of America's financial marketplace.

U.S. policy has long drawn a distinction between two different types of investments. The first type is safe products, such as checking accounts, which are highly regulated and are intended to be accessible and relatively risk free to even unsophisticated investors. Banks that offer checking accounts must accept a substantial degree of regulatory scrutiny, offer standardized features, and pay for FDIC insurance on their deposits. In return, the bank and its customers benefit from an explicit government guarantee: within certain limitations, no checking account in the United States will be allowed to lose even a penny of value.

By contrast, risky products, which are more loosely regulated, are aimed at more sophisticated players. These products often offer much higher profit margins for banks and much higher potential returns to investors, but they have never benefited from any government guarantee.

Before the AIG bailout, the derivatives market appeared to fall cleanly in the second category. Yet by bailing out AIG and its counterparties, the federal government signaled that the entire derivatives market — which had been explicitly and completely deregulated by Congress through the Commodities [*sic*] Futures Modernization Act — would now benefit from the same government safety net provided to fully regulated financial products. In essence, the government distorted the marketplace by transforming highly risky derivative bets into fully guaranteed transactions, with the American taxpayer standing as guarantor.

The Panel believes that the moral hazard problem unleashed by making whole AIG's counterparties in unregulated, unguaranteed transactions undermined the credibility of specific efforts at addressing the financial crisis that followed, including the entirety of the TARP, as well as America's system of financial regulation. . . .

Figure 9.1 FDIC-Insured Bank Failures, 2000–2021*

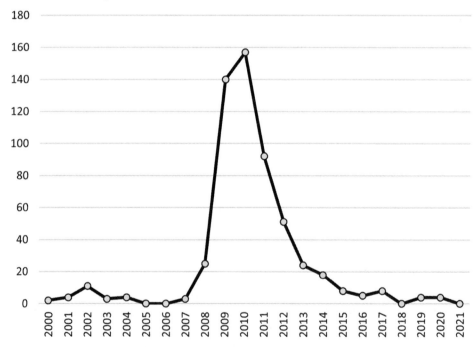

* Data sourced from Federal Deposit Insurance Corporation, Failed Bank List, available at https://www.fdic.gov/resources/resolutions/bank-failures/failed-bank-list.

Whereas Federal Reserve provision of assistance to bank depository institutions has historically been tolerated, support of this nature going to American International Group, a non-bank, with respect to its derivatives exposures and to the auto industry was unprecedented. As the Congressional Oversight Committee noted with respect to American International Group in particular, its bailout "undermined the credibility of . . . America's system of financial regulation."[9]

Derivatives exposures were the proximate cause of failure of American International Group. However, it was not derivatives exposures that caused the auto companies or banks insured by the Federal Deposit Insurance Corporation referenced in figure 9.1 to fail in the aftermath of the Financial Crisis.[10] Instead, for many of these institutions, it was primarily a result of excessive exposures to real estate, which saw increasing borrower defaults amidst declining values:

> While the vulnerabilities that created the potential for crisis were years in the making, it was the collapse of the housing bubble — fueled by low interest rates, easy and available credit, scant regulation, and toxic mortgages — that was the spark that ignited a string of events, which led to a full-blown crisis in the fall of 2008. Trillions of dollars in risky mortgages had become embedded throughout the financial system, as mortgage-related securities were packaged, repackaged, and sold to investors around the world. When the bubble burst, hundreds of billions of dollars in losses in mortgages and mortgage-related securities shook markets as well as financial institutions that had significant exposures to those mortgages and had borrowed heavily against them.[11]

With, as noted above, only one major financial entity, an insurance company, felled primarily by exposure to derivatives, the extent to which derivatives indirectly contributed to the Financial Crisis is a point of controversy. In the immediate aftermath of the Financial Crisis, Congress established an ostensibly bipartisan commission, the Financial Crisis Inquiry Commission, to investigate its causes. The Commission, reflecting the political divisions in Congress at the time of its establishment in 2009, had six Democrat members and four Republican members. Its final report was intended to be the definitive and authoritative account of the causes of the Financial Crisis similar to the Pecora Commission whose report helped trigger federal regulation of the securities markets in the midst of the Great Depression.[12] However, it failed in this regard due to a partisan split between the majority Democrat

---

9. Congressional Oversight Panel, *March Oversight Report* 114 (Govt. Printing Off. 2011), available at https://journalistsresource.org/wp-content/uploads/2011/07/CHRG-112shrg64832.pdf.

10. Although the number of failures of insured banks in the aftermath of the Financial Crisis was unprecedented in recent decades, a crisis among savings and loan banks in the late 1980s resulted, in 1989 alone, 531 failures, greatly exceeding the peak of 157 failures in 2010. *See* https://www.fdic.gov/resources/resolutions/bank-failures/failed-bank-list *select* Bank Failures and Assistance Data.

11. Financial Crisis Inquiry Commission, *The Financial Crisis Inquiry Report* xvi (Govt. Printing Off. 2011), available at https://www.gpo.gov/fdsys/pkg/GPO-FCIC/pdf/GPO-FCIC.pdf.

12. *Stock Exchange Practices: Report of the Committee on Banking and Currency*, Sen. Rpt. 1455 (Oct. 23, 1934), available at https://www.senate.gov/about/resources/pdf/pecora-final-report.pdf. In recognition of the efforts of the chief counsel who ultimately led the investigation and wrote the report, it has become commonly known as the "Pecora Report."

members and minority Republican members. This split resulted in an official report supported only by Democrat members (it should be noted that one of the Democrat members was Brooksley Born who, we will recall from chapter 2, section D.4, had sought to regulate the swap market a decade beforehand) and dissents supported only by Republican members. The report written by the Democrats emphasized a significant contribution of derivatives to the Financial Crisis whereas the Republican dissents disputed this.

Financial Crisis Inquiry Commission, *The Financial Crisis Inquiry Report*

(Govt. Printing Off. 2011), available at https://www.gpo.gov/fdsys /pkg/GPO-FCIC/pdf/GPO-FCIC.pdf

... We conclude over-the-counter derivatives contributed significantly to this crisis. The enactment of legislation in 2000 to ban the regulation by both the federal and state governments of over-the-counter (OTC) derivatives was a key turning point in the march toward the financial crisis.

From financial firms to corporations, to farmers, and to investors, derivatives have been used to hedge against, or speculate on, changes in prices, rates, or indices or even on events such as the potential defaults on debts. Yet, without any oversight, OTC derivatives rapidly spiraled out of control and out of sight, growing to $673 trillion in notional amount. This report explains the uncontrolled leverage; lack of transparency, capital, and collateral requirements; speculation; interconnections among firms; and concentrations of risk in this market.

OTC derivatives contributed to the crisis in three significant ways. First, one type of derivative — credit default swaps (CDS) — fueled the mortgage securitization pipeline. CDS were sold to investors to protect against the default or decline in value of mortgage-related securities backed by risky loans. Companies sold protection — to the tune of $79 billion, in AIG's case — to investors in these newfangled mortgage securities, helping to launch and expand the market and, in turn, to further fuel the housing bubble.

Second, CDS were essential to the creation of synthetic CDOs. These synthetic CDOs were merely bets on the performance of real mortgage-related securities. They amplified the losses from the collapse of the housing bubble by allowing multiple bets on the same securities and helped spread them throughout the financial system. Goldman Sachs alone packaged and sold $73 billion in synthetic CDOs from July 1, 2004 to May 31, 2007. Synthetic CDOs created by Goldman referenced more than 3,400 mortgage securities, and 610 of them were referenced at least twice. This is apart from how many times these securities may have been referenced in synthetic CDOs created by other firms.

Finally, when the housing bubble popped and crisis followed, derivatives were in the center of the storm. AIG, which had not been required to put aside capital reserves as a cushion for the protection it was selling, was bailed out when it could not meet its obligations. The government ultimately committed more than $180 billion because of concerns that AIG's collapse would trigger cascading losses throughout the global financial system. In addition, the existence of millions of derivatives contracts of all types between systemically important financial institutions — unseen and unknown in this unregulated market — added to uncertainty and escalated panic, helping to precipitate government assistance to those institutions. . . .

However, as noted above, this position of the Democratic majority did not reflect the position of the Republican members of the Financial Crisis Inquiry Commission. Illustrating this difference, two Republican commission members retorted:

> Despite a diligent search, the FCIC never uncovered evidence that unregulated derivatives, and particularly credit default swaps (CDS), was a significant contributor to the financial crisis through "interconnections." The only company known to have failed because of its CDS obligations was AIG, and that firm appears to have been an outlier. Blaming CDS for the financial crisis because one company did not manage its risks properly is like blaming lending generally when a bank fails. Like everything else, derivatives can be misused, but there is no evidence that the "interconnections" among financial institutions alleged to have caused the crisis were significantly enhanced by CDS or derivatives generally. For example, Lehman Brothers was a major player in the derivatives market, but the Commission found no indication that Lehman's failure to meet its CDS and other derivatives obligations caused significant losses to any other firm, including those that had written CDS on Lehman itself.[13]

If the Financial Crisis was the result of the collapse of a real estate bubble, why then were off-exchange swaps heavily regulated subsequent to the Financial Crisis? It is impossible to parse out every motivation for regulating the industry. For example, as we saw in chapter 2, section D.4, efforts to regulate the industry, such as that spurred by former CFTC Chairman Brooksley Born, preceded the Financial Crisis by a decade. It could have been that the moment was right for those who were already in favor of derivatives regulation to get broad congressional support.

On the other hand, it could have been the unprecedented nature of a Federal Reserve bailout for an insurance company with enormous swaps exposures. Its bailout resulted in counterparties to these swaps not suffering losses. It is one thing for retail depositors at banks to get protection on their deposits for which, indirectly, they pay for Federal Deposit Insurance Corporation protection, and another for sophisticated financial counterparties to be protected against losses in arms-length, negotiated transactions due to failure of their counterparty. Indeed, whatever the true motivation for each proponent of the regulation of off-exchange derivatives,

---

13. Financial Crisis Inquiry Commission, *The Financial Crisis Inquiry Report* 447 (Govt. Printing Off. 2011), available at https://www.gpo.gov/fdsys/pkg/GPO-FCIC/pdf/GPO-FCIC.pdf.

the match that lit the fire was certainly the taxpayer-funded bailout of American International Group.

Definitively answering the question of whether and to what extent swaps contributed to the Financial Crisis is beyond the scope of this book. However, in the following section we look at the types of swaps and related instruments that resulted in the government bailout of American International Group, once the largest insurance company in the world, and that some policymakers claim significantly contributed to the Financial Crisis.

2. Derivatives and the Financial Crisis

Whereas subsequent to the Financial Crisis there was a substantial chorus criticizing the unregulated nature of derivatives generally, the bulk of the focused critique was on credit default swaps. Particularly noted was a perceived link between the mortgage products that contributed to the grievous losses in the financial sector — namely "residential mortgage backed securities" and "collateralized debt obligations" — and credit default swaps. In the below report, these links are explained in detail. Note that American International Group's financial implosion was caused primarily by its subsidiary AIG Financial Products Corporation "selling" credit protection on some of these mortgage instruments through credit default swaps.[14] This means that AIG Financial Products Corporation was economically exposed to a decline in the residential mortgage market — exactly what happened at the onset of the Financial Crisis.

Senate Permanent Subcommittee on Investigations, *Wall Street and the Financial Crisis: Anatomy of a Financial Collapse*

S. Hrg. 112-675, Vol. 5, Part. I (Apr. 13, 2011), available at http://www.hsgac .senate.gov/download/report-psi-staff-report-wall-street-and-the -financial-crisis-anatomy-of-a-financial-collapse

A key factor in the recent financial crisis was the role played by complex financial instruments, often referred to as structured finance products, such as residential mortgage backed securities (RMBS), collateralized debt obligations (CDOs), and credit default swaps (CDS), including CDS contracts linked to the ABX Index [discussed below]. These financial products were envisioned, engineered, sold, and traded by major U.S. investment banks.

---

14. *See* Senate Permanent Subcommittee on Investigations, *Wall Street and the Financial Crisis: Anatomy of a Financial Collapse*, S. Hrg. 112-675, Vol. 5, Part. I at 343–344 (Apr. 13, 2011), available at http://www.hsgac.senate.gov/download/report-psi-staff-report-wall-street-and-the-financial-crisis -anatomy-of-a-financial-collapse and John Carney, *Here's the Untold Story of How AIG Destroyed Itself*, Business Insider (Mar. 3, 2010), available at https://www.businessinsider.com/heres-the-untold -story-of-how-aig-destroyed-itself-2010-3.

From 2004 to 2008, U.S. financial institutions issued nearly $2.5 trillion in RMBS securities and over $1.4 trillion in CDOs securitizing primarily mortgage related products.[15] Investment banks charged fees ranging from $1 to $8 million to act as the underwriter of an RMBS securitization,[16] and from $5 to $10 million to act as the placement agent for a CDO securitization.[17] Those fees contributed substantial revenues to the investment banks which set up structured finance groups, and a variety of RMBS and CDO origination and trading desks within those groups, to handle mortgage related securitizations. Investment banks placed these securities with investors around the world, and helped develop a secondary market where private RMBS and CDO securities could be bought and sold. The investment banks' trading desks participated in those secondary markets, buying and selling RMBS and CDO securities either for their customers or for themselves.

Some of these financial products allowed investors to profit, not only from the success of an RMBS or CDO securitization, but also from its failure. CDS contracts, for example, allowed counterparties to wager on the rise or fall in the value of a specific RMBS security or on a collection of RMBS and other assets contained or referenced in a CDO. Major investment banks also developed standardized CDS contracts that could be traded on a secondary market. In addition, they established the ABX Index which allowed counterparties to wager on the rise or fall in the value of a basket of subprime RMBS securities, and which could be used to reflect the state of the subprime mortgage market as a whole.

Investment banks sometimes matched up parties who wanted to take opposite sides in a structured finance transaction, and other times took one or the other side of a transaction to accommodate a client. At still other times, investment banks used these financial instruments to make their own proprietary wagers. In extreme cases, some investments banks set up structured finance transactions which enabled them to profit at the expense of their clients. . . .

[I]nvestment banks engaged in high intensity sales efforts to market new CDOs in 2007, even as U.S. mortgage delinquencies climbed, RMBS securities incurred losses, the U.S. mortgage market as a whole deteriorated, and investors lost confidence. . . . [T]hese investment banks benefitted from structured finance fees, and had little

---

15. [N. 1237] 3/4/2011 "U.S. Mortgage-Related Securities Issuance" and 1/1/2011 "Global CDO Issuance," charts prepared by Securities Industry and Financial Markets Association, www.sifma .org/research/statistics.aspx. The RMBS total does not include about $6.6 trillion in RMBS securities issued by government sponsored enterprises like Fannie Mae and Freddie Mac.

16. [N. 1238] See, e.g., 2/2011 chart, "Goldman Sachs Expected Profit from RMBS Securitizations," prepared by the U.S. Senate Permanent Subcommittee on Investigations using Goldman-produced documents for securitizations from 2005–2007 (underlying documents retained in Subcommittee file). . . .

17. [N. 1239] See "Banks' Self-Dealing Super-Charged Financial Crisis," ProPublica (8/ 26/ 2010), http://www.propublica.org/article/banks-self-dealing-super-charged-financial-crisis ("A typical CDO could net the bank that created it between $5 million and $10 million — about half of which usually ended up as employee bonuses. Indeed, Wall Street awarded record bonuses in 2006, a hefty chunk of which came from the CDO business."). . . .

incentive to stop producing and selling high risk, poor quality structured finance products. . . . [T]he development of complex structured finance products, such as synthetic CDOs and naked credit default swaps, amplified market risk by allowing investors with no ownership interest in the "reference obligations" to place unlimited side bets on their performance. . . .

Investment banks were a major driving force behind the structured finance products that provided a steady stream of funding for lenders to originate high risk, poor quality loans and that magnified risk throughout the U.S. financial system. The investment banks that engineered, sold, traded, and profited from mortgage related structured finance products were a major cause of the financial crisis. . . .

Over time, investment banks have devised, marketed, and sold increasingly complex financial instruments to investors, often referred to as "structured finance" products. These products include residential mortgage backed securities (RMBS), collateralized debt obligations (CDOs), and credit default swaps (CDS), including CDS contracts linked to the ABX Index, all of which played a central role in the financial crisis.

RMBS and CDO Securities. RMBS and CDO securities are two common types of structured finance products. RMBS securities contain pools of mortgage loans, while CDOs contain or reference pools of RMBS securities and other assets. RMBS concentrate risk by including thousands of subprime and other high risk home loans, with similar characteristics and risks, in a single financial instrument. Mortgage related CDOs concentrate risk even more by including hundreds or thousands of RMBS securities, with similar characteristics and risks, in a single financial instrument. In addition, while some CDOs included only AAA rated RMBS securities, others known as "mezzanine" CDOs contained RMBS securities that carried the riskier BBB, BBB-, and even BB credit ratings and were more susceptible to losses if the underlying mortgages began to incur delinquencies or defaults.

Some investment banks went a step farther and assembled CDO securities into pools and resecuritized them as so-called "CDO squared" instruments, which further concentrated the risk in the underlying CDOs.[18] Some investment banks also assembled "synthetic CDOs," which did not contain any actual RMBS securities or other assets, but merely referenced them. Some devised "hybrid CDOs," which contained a mix of cash and synthetic assets.

The securitization process generated billions of dollars in funds that allowed investment banks to supply financing to lenders to issue still more high risk mortgages and securities, which investment banks and others then sold or securitized in exchange for still more fees. This cycle was repeated again and again, introducing more and more risk to a wider and wider range of investors.

---

18. [N. 1252] CDO squared transactions will generally be referred to in this Report as "CDO2." Some Goldman materials also use the term "CDO^2."

Credit Default Swaps. Some investment banks modified still another structured finance product, a derivative known as a credit default swap (CDS), for use in the mortgage market. Much like an insurance contract, a CDS is a contract between two parties in which one party guarantees payment to the other if the assets referenced in the contract lose value or experience a negative credit event. The party selling the insurance is referred to as the "long" party, since it profits if the referenced asset performs well. The party buying the insurance protection is referred to as the "short" party, because it profits if the referenced asset performs poorly.

The short party, or CDS buyer, typically pays periodic premiums, similar to insurance premiums, to the long party or CDS seller, who has guaranteed the referenced assets against a loss in value or a negative credit event such as a credit rating downgrade, default, or bankruptcy. If the loss or negative credit event occurs, the CDS seller is required to pay an agreed upon amount to the CDS buyer. Many CDS contracts also tracked the changing value of the referenced assets over time, and required the long and short parties to post cash collateral with each other to secure payment of their respective contractual obligations.

CDS contracts that reference a single, specific security or bond for protection against a loss in value or negative credit event have become known as "single name" CDS contracts. Other CDS contracts have been designed to protect a broader basket of securities, bonds, or other assets.

By 2005, investment banks had standardized CDS contracts that referred to a "single name" RMBS or CDO security. Some investment banks and investors, which held large inventories of RMBS and CDO securities, purchased those single name CDS contracts as a hedge against possible losses in the value of their holdings. Other investors, including investment banks, began to purchase single name CDS contracts, not as a hedge to offset losses from the RMBS or CDO securities they owned, but as a way to profit from particular RMBS or CDO securities they predicted would lose value or fail. CDS contracts that paid off on securities that were not owned by the CDS buyer became known as "naked credit default swaps." Naked CDS contracts enabled investors to bet against mortgage related assets, using the minimal capital needed to make the periodic premium payments and collateral calls required by a CDS contract.

The key significance of the CDS product for the mortgage market was that it offered an alternative to investing in RMBS and CDO securities that would perform well. Single name CDS contracts instead enabled investors to place their dollars in financial instruments that would pay off if specific RMBS or CDO securities lost value or failed.

ABX Index. In January 2006, a consortium of investment banks, led by Goldman Sachs and Deutsche Bank, launched still another type of structured finance product, linked to a newly created "ABX Index," to enable investors to bet on multiple subprime RMBS securities at once. The ABX Index was administered by a private company called the Markit Group and consisted of five separate indices, each of which tracked the performance of a different basket of 20 designated subprime RMBS securities.[19] The values of the securities in each basket were aggregated into a single composite value that rose and fell over time. Investors could then arrange, through a broker-dealer, to enter into a CDS contract with another party using the ABX basket of subprime RMBS securities as the "reference obligation" and the relevant ABX Index value as the agreed upon value of that basket. For a fee, investors could take either the "long" position, betting on the rise of the index, or the "short" position, betting on the fall of the index, without having to physically purchase or hold any of the referenced securities or raise the capital needed to pay for the full face value of those referenced securities. The index also used standardized CDS contracts that remained in effect for a standard period of time, making it easier for investors to participate in the market, and buy and sell ABX-linked CDS contracts.

The ABX Index allowed investors to place unlimited bets on the performance of one or more of the subprime RMBS baskets. It also made it easier and cheaper for investors, including some investment banks, to short the subprime mortgage market in bulk.[20] Investment banks not only helped establish the ABX Index, they encouraged their clients to enter into CDS contracts based upon the ABX Index, and used it themselves to bet on the mortgage market as a whole. The ABX Index expanded the risks inherent in the subprime mortgage market by providing investors with a way to make unlimited investments in RMBS securities.

Synthetic CDOs. By mid-2006, there was a large demand for RMBS and CDO securities as well as a growing demand for CDS contracts to short the mortgage market. To meet this demand, investment banks and others began to make greater use of synthetic CDOs, which could be assembled more quickly, since they did not require the CDO arranger to find and purchase actual RMBS securities or other assets. The increasing use of synthetic CDOs injected even greater risk into the mortgage market by enabling investors to make unlimited wagers on various groups of mortgage related assets and, if those assets performed poorly, expanding the number of investors who would realize losses.

Synthetic CDOs did not depend upon actual RMBS securities or other assets to bring in cash to pay investors. Instead, the CDO simply developed a list of existing RMBS or CDO securities or other assets that would be used as its "reference

---

19. [N. 1253] Each of the five indices tracked a different basket of subprime RMBS securities. One index tracked a basket of 20 AAA rated RMBS securities; the second a basket of AA rated RMBS securities; and the remaining indices tracked baskets of A, BBB, and BBB-rated RMBS securities. Every six months, a new set of RMBS securities was selected for each index. See 3/2008 Federal Reserve Bank of New York Staff Report No. 318, "Understanding the Securitization of Subprime Mortgage Credit," at 26. Markit Group Ltd. administered the ABX Index which issued indices in 2006 and 2007, but has not issued any new indices since then.

20. [N. 1254] Subcommittee Interview of Joshua Birnbaum (4/22/2010); Subcommittee Interview of Rajiv Kamilla (10/12/2010).

obligations." The parties to the CDO were not required to possess an ownership interest in any of those reference obligations; the CDO simply tracked their performance over time. The performance of the underlying reference obligations, in the aggregate, determined the performance of the synthetic CDO.

The synthetic CDO made or lost money for its investors by establishing a contractual agreement that they would make payments to each other, based upon the aggregate performance of the underlying referenced assets, using CDS contracts. The "short" party essentially agreed to make periodic payments, similar to insurance premiums, to the other party in exchange for an agreement that the "long" party would pay the full face value of the synthetic CDO if the underlying assets lost value or experienced a defined credit event such as a ratings downgrade. In essence, then, the synthetic CDO set up a wager in which the short party bet that its underlying assets would perform poorly, while the long party bet that they would perform well.

Synthetic CDOs provided still another vehicle for investors looking to short the mortgage market in bulk. The synthetic CDO typically referenced a variety of RMBS securities. One or more investors could then take the "short" position and wager that the referenced securities as a whole would fall in value or otherwise perform poorly. Synthetic CDOs became a way for investors to short multiple specific RMBS securities that they expected to incur delinquencies, defaults, and losses.

Synthetic CDOs magnified the risk in the mortgage market because arrangers had no limit on the number of synthetic CDOs they could create. In addition, multiple synthetic CDOs could reference the same RMBS and CDO securities in various combinations, and sell financial instruments dependent upon the same sets of high risk, poor quality loans over and over again to various investors. Since every synthetic CDO had to have a "short" party betting on the failure of the referenced assets, at least some poor quality RMBS and CDO securities could be included in each transaction to attract those investors. When some of the high risk, poor quality loans later incurred delinquencies or defaults, they caused losses, not in a single RMBS, but in multiple cash, synthetic, and hybrid CDOs whose securities had been sold to a wide circle of investors.[21]

Conflicts of Interest. Investment banks that designed, obtained credit ratings for, underwrote, sold, managed, and serviced CDO securities, made money from the fees they charged for these and other services. Investment banks reportedly netted from $5 to $10 million in fees per CDO.[22] Some also constructed CDOs to transfer

---

21. [N. 1255] See, e.g., "Senate's Goldman Probe Shows Toxic Magnification," Wall Street Journal (5/2/2010) (showing how a single $38 million subprime RMBS, created in June 2006, was included in 30 CDOs and, by 2008, had caused $280 million in losses to investors).

22. [N. 1256] See "Banks' Self-Dealing Super-Charged Financial Crisis," ProPublica (8/ 26/ 2010), http://www.propublica.org/article/banks-self-dealing-super-charged-financial-crisis ("A typical CDO could net the bank that created it between $5 million and $10 million — about half of

the financial risk of poorly performing RMBS and CDO securities from their own holdings to the investors they were soliciting to buy the CDO securities. . . . By selling the CDO securities to investors, the investment banks profited not only from the CDO sales, but also eliminated possible losses from the assets removed from their warehouse accounts. In some instances, unbeknownst to the customers and investors, the investment banks that sold them CDO securities bet against those instruments by taking short positions through single name CDS contracts. Some even took the short side of the CDO they constructed, and profited when the referenced assets lost value, and the investors to whom they had sold the long side of the CDO were required to make substantial payments to the CDO. . . .

The above-described credit default swaps were those that were central to American International Group's financial distress. At the same time, before generalizing that derivatives were an underlying cause of the Financial Crisis, it should be noted that Lehman Brothers, an investment bank that failed during the Financial Crisis due to a loss of short-term liquidity unrelated to derivatives, held an estimated five percent of global swap positions at the time of its failure, slightly less than a staggering one million contracts, most of which settled in an organized fashion.[23]

In the following two sections, C and D, we evaluate Dodd-Frank Act section 619 (the Volcker Rule) and Dodd-Frank Act section 716 (the rule prohibiting FDIC-insured banks from entering into the types of swaps entered into by AIG Financial Products Corporation).

C. The Volcker Rule

The Dodd-Frank Act also prohibited "insured depository institutions" *or* their affiliates from engaging in "proprietary trading." We will go into more detail on what "proprietary trading" is below. In the meantime, a rough working definition would be "short-term speculative trading" in, among other financial products, commodity futures, options, swaps, and security-based swaps. It also prohibited such entities, with some exceptions, from investments in "covered funds," i.e., investments in hedge funds, private equity funds, and similar vehicles. This "covered fund" prohibition is outside of the field of derivatives law and better covered within a banking or securities law framework. Therefore, our discussion herein does not focus on the ban on banking entities investing in covered funds.

---

which usually ended up as employee bonuses. Indeed, Wall Street awarded record bonuses in 2006, a hefty chunk of which came from the CDO business."). . . .

23. Michael J. Fleming and Asani Sarkar, *The Failure Resolution of Lehman Brothers*, New York Federal Reserve Economic Policy Review, vol. 20 no. 2, 182 and 184 at Table 2 (Dec. 2014), available at https://www.newyorkfed.org/medialibrary/media/research/epr/2014/1412flem.pdf.

The prohibition on proprietary trading only applies to "banking entities" which is, essentially, "insured depository institutions," some non-U.S. banks operating in the United States, and the affiliates of both. The term "insured depository institution" is a technical one in banking. It means a bank — this includes a savings and loan association and excludes a credit union — that accepts retail deposits, i.e., those insured by the Federal Deposit Insurance Corporation.[24] In common usage, an insured depository institution is often referred to as a "commercial bank" to distinguish it from an "investment bank." A commercial bank is a deposit-taking bank, and an investment bank is normally a securities broker-dealer underwriting securities offerings and facilitating mergers and acquisitions.

In the context of the Volcker Rule discussed herein, "banking entity" sometimes also includes U.S. branches or agencies of non-U.S. banks, even though such entities do not take deposits insured by the Federal Deposit Insurance Corporation.[25] For the purposes of this discussion, though, we look at the application of the Volcker Rule only to an insured depository institution that is a U.S. bank or its affiliate.

Since the Volcker Rule operates as a limitation on futures and options in addition to swaps, it's a subject that could be discussed in multiple chapters. It is discussed in this chapter because it originates with the Dodd-Frank Act.

The section of the Dodd-Frank Act commonly known as the "Volcker Rule" is section 619. It is named after Paul Volcker, former chairman of the Federal Reserve Board. The concept was originally publicized before the July 21, 2010 enactment of the Dodd-Frank Act by President Obama who, in a press conference on January 21, 2010, coined the section's colloquial name:

> I'm proposing a simple and common-sense reform, which we're calling the "Volcker Rule." . . . Banks will no longer be allowed to own, invest, or sponsor hedge funds, private equity funds, or proprietary trading operations for their own profit, unrelated to serving their customers. If financial firms want to trade for profit, that's something they're free to do. Indeed, doing so — responsibly — is a good thing for the markets and the economy. But these firms should not be allowed to run these hedge funds and private equities [sic] funds while running a bank backed by the American people.[26]

Paul Volcker's own first public remarks on the proposal bearing his name were in a *New York Times* op-ed piece[27] just over a week later, followed by his testimony to the Senate in which he explained the public policy basis for the Volcker Rule.

---

24. 12 U.S.C. § 1813(c)(2).

25. 12 U.S.C. § 1851(h).

26. President Obama, *Remarks by the President on Financial Reform* (Jan. 21, 2010), https://obamawhitehouse.archives.gov/the-press-office/remarks-president-financial-reform.

27. Paul Volcker, *How to Reform Our Financial System*, N.Y. Times WK11 (Jan. 31, 2010).

Hearing before the Committee on Banking, Housing and Urban Affairs, *Prohibiting Certain High-Risk Investment Activities by Banks and Bank Holding Companies: Statement of Paul Volcker*

S. Hrg. 11-771 (Feb. 2, 2010)

Mr. Chairman, Members of the Banking Committee ...

I appreciate the opportunity today to discuss with you one key element in the reform effort that President Obama set out so forcibly a few days ago.

That proposal, if enacted, would restrict commercial banking organizations from certain proprietary and more speculative activities.... It is particularly designed to help deal with the problem of "too big to fail" and the related moral hazard that looms so large as an aftermath of the emergency rescues of financial institutions, bank and non-bank, in the midst of crises....

The basic point is that there has been, and remains, a strong public interest in providing a "safety net" — in particular, deposit insurance and the provision of liquidity in emergencies — for commercial banks carrying out essential services. There is not, however, a similar rationale for public funds — taxpayer funds — protecting and supporting essentially proprietary and speculative activities.

Hedge funds, private equity funds, and trading activities unrelated to customer needs and continuing banking relationships should stand on their own, without the subsidies implied by public support for depository institutions....

A number of the most prominent of [investment banks], each heavily engaged in trading and other proprietary activity, failed or were forced into publicly-assisted mergers under the pressure of the crisis. It also became necessary to provide public support via the Federal Reserve, The Federal Deposit Insurance Corporation, or the Treasury to the largest remaining American investment banks[, Goldman Sachs and Morgan Stanley[28]], both of which assumed the cloak of a banking license to facili-

---

28. Each of Morgan Stanley, Morgan Stanley Capital Management LLC, Morgan Stanley Domestic Holdings, Inc., Goldman Sachs Group, Inc., and Goldman Sachs Bank USA Holdings LLC were simultaneously approved as bank holding companies. *See* Federal Reserve Board, *Order Approving Formation of Bank Holding Companies* (Morgan Stanley, Morgan Stanley Capital Management LLC, and Morgan Stanley Domestic Holdings, Inc.) (Sept. 21, 2008), and Federal Reserve Board, *Order Approving Formation of Bank Holding Companies* (Goldman Sachs Group, Inc. and Goldman Sachs Bank USA Holdings LLC) (Sept. 21, 2008). Before this, each did not own subsidiaries engaged in commercial banking. Their focus was primarily "investment banking" activities, i.e., activities such as securities underwritings, and they owned no regulated banks other than industrial loan companies. Since industrial loan companies do not meet the definition of "bank" in Bank Holding Company Act § 2(c)(1) (they either have less than $100 million in assets or take no demand deposits — *see* Bank Holding Company Act § 2(c)(2)(h)), their ownership did not result in Morgan Stanley or Goldman Sachs being subject to the strict regulatory regime applicable to bank holding companies. The industrial loan companies, however, were ineligible for federal assistance from the Federal Reserve, and these orders made possible the conversion of the industrial loan companies to banks that were eligible for federal assistance.

tate the assistance. The world's largest insurance company[, American International Group], caught up in a huge portfolio of credit default swaps quite apart from its basic business, was rescued only by the injection of many tens of billions of dollars of public loans and equity capital. . . .

It is critically important that those institutions . . . do not assume a public rescue will be forthcoming in time of pressure. . . .

[E]very banker I speak with knows very well what "proprietary trading" means and implies. My understanding is that only a handful of large commercial banks — maybe four or five in the United States and perhaps a couple of dozen world-wide — are now engaged in this activity in volume. In the past, they have sometimes explicitly labeled a trading affiliate or division as "proprietary," with the connota-tion that the activity is, or should be, insulated from customer relations.

Most of those institutions and many others are engaged in meeting customer needs to buy or sell . . . stocks or bonds, derivatives, various commodities or other investments. Those activities may involve taking temporary positions. In the process, there will be temptations to speculate by aggressive, highly remunerated traders. . . .

[P]atterns of exceptionally large gains and losses over a period of time in the "trad-ing book" should raise [a bank] examiner's eyebrows. Persisting over time, the result should be not just raised eyebrows but substantially raised capital requirements. . . .

I [also] want to note the strong conflicts of interest inherent in the participation of commercial banking organizations in proprietary or private investment activ-ity. . . . When the bank itself is a "customer," i.e., it is trading for its own account, it will almost inevitably find itself, consciously or inadvertently, acting at cross pur-poses to the interests of an unrelated commercial customer of a bank. . . . More gen-erally, proprietary trading activity should not be able to profit from knowledge of customer trades. . . .

What we can do, what we should do, is recognize that curbing the proprietary interests of commercial banks is in the interest of fair and open competition as well as protecting the provision of essential financial services. . . .

By appropriately defining the business of commercial banks . . . we can go a long way toward promoting the combination of competition, innovation, and underlying stability that we seek.

The Volcker Rule ultimately embodied in section 619 of the Dodd-Frank Act required regulatory rulemaking for its implementation because, despite being named the "Volcker Rule," it is actually a statutory provision, not a rule. Five agen-cies were charged with implementing the Volcker Rule for the entities they regulate, the Office of the Comptroller of the Currency, the Federal Reserve Board, the Fed-eral Deposit Insurance Corporation, the SEC, and the CFTC. On December 10, 2013, four of the five agencies, the Federal Reserve Board, the Federal Deposit Insurance Corporation, the Office of the Comptroller of the Currency, and the SEC, issued the final rulemaking with the CFTC's nearly identical release occurring simultaneously.[29] Illustrating the complexity and scope of the subject matter underlying the final rule, the release accompanying it contains 2,826 footnotes (2,833 in the CFTC version).[30] This rule was subsequently amended in July and November 2019 and July 2020.[31] The release accompanying the two amendments pertaining to the ban on proprietary trading contained 1,221 footnotes, and 790 footnotes.[32] As even a governor of the Federal Reserve stated in 2017, "[S]everal years of experience have convinced me that there is merit in the contention of many firms that, as it has been drafted and implemented, the Volcker rule is too complicated."[33]

The Volcker Rule prohibition on banking entities engaging in short-term speculative trading may seem straightforward at first. However, it is replete with many exceptions that, in the aggregate, make the Volcker Rule especially complex. The following extract is from the final rulemaking in which the regulators describe the comments they received and the extent to which their original proposal will be implemented in the final rules.

Note that, in the below, there is reference to a rebuttable presumption that proprietary trading in positions held for fewer than sixty days are "short term." Originally, the regulators noted that they "are not providing a safe harbor or a reverse presumption (i.e., a presumption for positions that are outside of the trading account), as suggested by some commenters, in recognition that some proprietary trading could occur outside of the 60 day period."[34] This was modified in 2019 to replace the rebuttable presumption that proprietary trading positions held for fewer than sixty days

---

29. Office of the Comptroller of the Currency, Federal Reserve Board, et al., *Prohibitions and Restrictions on Proprietary Trading and Certain Interests in, and Relationships With, Hedge Funds and Private Equity Funds*, 79 Fed. Reg. 5535 (Jan. 31, 2014), and CFTC, *Prohibitions and Restrictions on Proprietary Trading and Certain Interests in, and Relationships With, Hedge Funds and Private Equity Funds*, 79 Fed. Reg. 5807 (Jan. 31, 2014).

30. *Id.*

31. *See* Office of the Comptroller of the Currency, Federal Reserve Board, et al., *Revisions to Prohibitions and Restrictions on Proprietary Trading and Certain Interests in, and Relationships With, Hedge Funds and Private Equity Funds*, 84 Fed. Reg. 35008 (July 22, 2019), and Office of the Comptroller of the Currency, Federal Reserve Board, et al., *Prohibitions and Restrictions on Proprietary Trading and Certain Interests in, and Relationships With, Hedge Funds and Private Equity Funds*, 84 Fed. Reg. 61974 (Nov. 14, 2019), and Office of the Comptroller of the Currency, Federal Reserve Board, et al., *Prohibitions and Restrictions on Proprietary Trading and Certain Interests in, and Relationships With, Hedge Funds and Private Equity Funds*, 85 Fed. Reg. 46422 (July 31, 2020).

32. *See* Office of the Comptroller of the Currency, Federal Reserve Board, et al., *Prohibitions and Restrictions on Proprietary Trading and Certain Interests in, and Relationships With, Hedge Funds and Private Equity Funds*, 84 Fed. Reg. 61974 (Nov. 14, 2019), and Office of the Comptroller of the Currency, Federal Reserve Board, et al., *Prohibitions and Restrictions on Proprietary Trading and Certain Interests in, and Relationships With, Hedge Funds and Private Equity Funds*, 85 Fed. Reg. 46422 (July 31, 2020).

33. Daniel K. Tarullo, Speech, *Departing Thoughts* (Princeton, N.J. Apr. 4, 2017) (transcript available at https://www.federalreserve.gov/newsevents/speech/tarullo20170404a.htm).

34. Office of the Comptroller of the Currency, Board of Governors of the Federal Reserve System, Federal Deposit Insurance Corporation, and the SEC, *Prohibitions and Restrictions on*

are short term with a rebuttable presumption that those held for sixty days or longer are *not* short term.[35]

Office of the Comptroller of the Currency, Board of Governors of the Federal Reserve System, Federal Deposit Insurance Corporation, and the SEC, *Prohibitions and Restrictions on Proprietary Trading and Certain Interests in, and Relationships with, Hedge Funds and Private Equity Funds*
79 Fed. Reg. 5536 (Jan. 31, 2014)[36]

. . . Section 13(a)(1)(A) of the . . . [Bank Holding Company Act ("BHC Act")] prohibits a banking entity from engaging in proprietary trading unless otherwise permitted in section 13. . . . Section 13(h)(4) of the BHC Act defines proprietary trading, in relevant part, as engaging as principal for the trading account of the banking entity in any transaction to purchase or sell, or otherwise acquire or dispose of, a security, derivative, contract of sale of a commodity for future delivery, or other financial instrument that the Agencies include by rule. . . .

Section 13(h)(6) of the BHC Act defines trading account as any account used for acquiring or taking positions in financial instruments principally for the purpose of selling in the near-term (or otherwise with the intent to resell in order to profit from short-term price movements). . . .

[T]he proposed rule provided that an account would be presumed to be a short-term trading account if it was used to acquire or take a covered financial position that the banking entity held for a period of 60 days or less. . . .

Based on their supervisory experience, the Agencies find that 60 days is an appropriate cut off for a regulatory presumption [of short-term trading]. . . .

Definition of "Financial Instrument"

Under the final rule, a financial instrument is defined [with some exclusions, such as for loans and purchases or sales of physical commodities] as:

> (i) a security, including an option on a security; (ii) a derivative, including an option on a derivative; or (iii) a contract of sale of a commodity for future delivery, or option on a contract of sale of a commodity for future delivery. . . .

Proprietary Trading and Certain Interests in, and Relationships with, Hedge Funds and Private Equity Funds, 79 Fed. Reg. 5536, 5549–5550 (Jan. 31, 2014).

35. Office of the Comptroller of the Currency, Federal Reserve Board, et al., *Prohibitions and Restrictions on Proprietary Trading and Certain Interests in, and Relationships With, Hedge Funds and Private Equity Funds*, 84 Fed. Reg. 61974, 61976 (Nov. 14, 2019).

36. The CFTC issued a substantially identical release on the same day at 79 Fed. Reg. 5807 (Jan. 31, 2014).

[T]he final rule provides exclusions [1] ... [for] repurchase and reverse repurchase agreements and securities lending agreements; [2] for bona fide liquidity management purposes; [3] [for trades] by ... clearing agencies, derivatives clearing organizations in connection with clearing activities; [4] [for trades] by a member of a clearing agency, derivatives clearing organization, or designated financial market utility engaged in excluded clearing activities; [5] to satisfy existing delivery obligations; [6] to satisfy an obligation of the banking entity in connection with a judicial, administrative, self-regulatory organization, or arbitration proceeding; [7] [for acting] solely as broker, agent, or custodian; [8] [trades] through a deferred compensation or similar plan; and [9] to satisfy a debt previously contracted. ...

Section 75.4(b): Market-Making Exemption. ...

Section 13(d)(1)(B) of the BHC Act provides an exemption from the prohibition on proprietary trading for the purchase, sale, acquisition, or disposition of securities, derivatives, contracts of sale of a commodity for future delivery, and options on any of the foregoing in connection with market making-related activities. ...

[T]he final rule focuses on providing a framework for assessing whether trading activities are consistent with market making. ... [W]hile a bright-line or safe harbor based approach would generally provide a high degree of certainty about whether an activity qualifies for the market-making exemption, it would also provide less flexibility ... [and] would be more likely to be subject to gaming and avoidance as new products and types of trading activities are developed. ...

[T]he final rule has been crafted around the overall market making-related activities of individual trading desks, with various requirements that these activities be demonstrably related to satisfying reasonably expected near term customer demands and other market-making activities. ... Thus, banking entities will be able to continue to engage in market making-related activities across markets and asset classes. ...

Section 75.5: Permitted Risk-Mitigating Hedging Activities. ...

Section 13(d)(1)(C) [of the BHC Act] provides an exemption for risk-mitigating hedging activities [(the "hedging exemption")]. ...

The final rule provides a multi-faceted approach ... intended to permit hedging activities that are risk-mitigating and to limit potential abuse of the hedging exemption. ...

[T]he final hedging exemption ... permits risk-mitigating hedging activities ... while requiring a robust compliance program and other internal controls to help ensure that only genuine risk-mitigating hedges can be used in reliance on the exemption. ...

[T]he final rule requires that the hedging activity at inception of the hedging activity, including, without limitation, any adjustments to the hedging activity, be designed to reduce or otherwise significantly mitigate ... one or more specific, identifiable risks, including market risk, counterparty or other credit risk, currency or foreign exchange risk, interest rate risk, commodity price risk, basis risk, or similar risks, arising in connection with and related to identified individual or aggregated positions, contracts, or other holdings of the banking entity. . . .

[T]he final rule [requires] that the compensation arrangements of persons performing risk-mitigating hedging activities be designed not to reward prohibited proprietary trading. The final rule [makes] clear that rewarding or incentivizing profit making from prohibited proprietary trading is not permitted. . . .

Section 75.6(a)–(b): Permitted Trading in Certain Government and Municipal Obligations. . . .

Section 13(d)(1)(A) permits [proprietary] trading in various U.S. government, U.S. agency and municipal securities. . . .

The final rule [does not] permit a banking entity to engage in proprietary trading of derivatives on U.S. government and agency obligations. . . .

[T]he Agencies have determined not to provide an exemption for proprietary trading in municipal securities, beyond the underwriting, market-making, hedging and other exemptions provided generally in the rule. . . .

Section 75.6(c): Permitted Trading on Behalf of Customers

Section 13(d)(1)(D) of the BHC Act provides an exemption from the prohibition on proprietary trading for the purchase, sale, acquisition, or disposition of financial instruments on behalf of customers. . . .

Section 75.7: Limitations on Permitted Trading Activities

. . . [S]ection 13(d)(2) of the BHC Act . . . provides that a banking entity may not engage in certain exempt activities (e.g., permitted market making-related activities, risk-mitigating hedging, etc.) if the activity [1] would involve or result in a material conflict of interest between the banking entity and its clients, customers, or counterparties; [2] result, directly or indirectly, in a material exposure by the banking entity to a high-risk asset or a high-risk trading strategy; [3] or pose a threat to the safety and soundness of the banking entity or U.S. financial stability. . . .

———————

The Volcker Rule, as can be seen from the above, is extremely complicated due to, among others, the breadth and number of its exceptions, and presents a substantial departure from pre-existing market practices. At one time, the costs of the Volcker Rule had been estimated by the Office of the Comptroller of the Currency, primary regulator of many of the affected banks, as between $412 million and $4.3 billion upon implementation and up to $550 million in annual compliance costs thereafter.[37]

———————

37. Office of the Comptroller of the Currency, *Analysis of 12 CFR Part 44* at 1, available at https://www.databoiler.com/index_htm_files/OCC%20Analysis%20of%2012%20CFR%20Part%2044.pdf.

Volcker Rule's First Casualty

Deutsche Bank, a large international bank, was fined $19.71 million when the Federal Reserve Board determined that its compliance program was inadequate.[a] The Volcker Rule requires banking entities with assets greater than $20 billion (it was $10 billion at the time of Deutsche Bank's violation) to establish a compliance program specifically for monitoring the entity's compliance with the Volcker Rule.

[a] Federal Reserve Board, *In the Matter of: Deutsche Bank AG*, Docket Nos. 17-009-B-FB; 17-009-CMP-FB (Apr. 20, 2017), available at https://www.federalreserve.gov/newsevents/pressreleases/files/enf20170420a2.pdf.

D. Asset-Backed Swap Push-Out

The perceived excesses within the credit default swap market led to a specific passage of the Dodd-Frank Act that, when initially enacted, required financial institutions, with some exceptions, to forgo federal assistance, including deposit insurance from the Federal Deposit Insurance Corporation, if they entered into many types of swaps. For commercial banks whose core funding source is retail bank deposits insured by the Federal Deposit Insurance Corporation, the requirement was, in effect, a prohibition, since such banks could not countenance losing the insurance from the Federal Deposit Insurance Corporation and the ability to take retail bank deposits. However, their affiliates could enter into such swaps and, therefore, it was termed "swap push-out" since it pushed many swap types out from the commercial bank to its affiliates.

Recognizing the potentially harmful effects this might have on the health of the financial system, it was subsequently rolled back to merely "push out" swaps on asset-backed securities, such as the residential mortgage backed securities and collateralized debt obligations discussed in section B.2 above.

Gary E. Kalbaugh and Alexander F. L. Sand, *Cutting Back: Revisions to Dodd-Frank Derivatives Rules*

35 No. 5 Futures & Derivatives L. Rep. No. 1 (June 2015)

... Section 716 of the Dodd-Frank Act (known as the "Swap Push-Out Rule"), as originally passed, prohibited entities engaged in many swaps activities from receiving federal assistance, effectively requiring swap trading operations to be pushed out from bank entities into non-bank affiliates. Specifically, banks significantly engaged in swaps activity would be unable to offer Federal Deposit Insurance Corporation ("FDIC") insurance[38] to their depositors or to access the Federal Reserve Discount

---

38. [N. 5] FDIC insurance is the guarantee to any retail depositor that up to $250,000 of a depositor's funds will be guaranteed against the insolvency of the bank. FDIC insurance has

Window.[39] Significant exceptions were provided for insured depository institutions engaged in interest rate and foreign exchange swaps, credit default swaps referencing an asset national banks were permitted to invest in, and any other swap entered into as a hedge against risk.[40] Nonetheless, the law had the effect of requiring non-bank affiliates of banks to engage in many swaps transactions in which the bank would otherwise engage. Among other consequences, this "split the book" so that a bank customer engaging in a broad array of swaps activities would have two risk exposures, one to the bank and one to the bank's non-bank affiliate, instead of a sole net exposure to one entity.

The underlying premise of these prohibitions was that a bank's ability to offer FDIC insurance and to access the Federal Reserve Discount Window is a form of public assistance.[41] Based on this premise, the argument is that the same banks should not be able to engage in speculative derivatives activities while, simultaneously, enjoying the benefits of public assistance not available to non-bank dealers. . . .

Even when proposed, however, significant questions were raised as to the wisdom of Dodd-Frank Act section 716. Writing in opposition to the provision, the Chairman of the FDIC Sheila Bair wrote:

> I would like to share some concerns with respect to section 716. . . . If enacted, this provision would require that some $294 trillion in notional amounts be moved outside of banks or from bank holding companies that owned insured depository institutions, presumably to nonbank financial firms, such as hedge funds and futures commission merchants. . . .

---

remedied the retail panics that, before the passage of the Banking Act of 1933, Pub. L. 73-66, and the implementation of the FDIC's retail insurance deposit regime, recurred periodically throughout history, including during the Great Depression. One cost of retail deposit insurance is arguably moral hazard: it reduces the incentives of depositors to select their bank based on perceived solvency.

39. [N. 6] The Federal Reserve Discount Window is a means by which bank members of the Federal Reserve (and, in some emergency situations, non-members) can obtain short-term collateralized loans from the Federal Reserve. . . .

40. [N. 7] Dodd-Frank Act, Pub. Law 111-203 § 716. There was some controversy as to whether, in this context, the term included foreign banks operating U.S. branches or agencies. Federal Reserve Regulation KK resolved this issue by expressly including "foreign banking organizations" within the definition of the term "insured depository institutions" for the purposes of section 716 of the Dodd-Frank Act.

41. [N. 8] This is despite the requirement that banks pay the FDIC an insurance premium based on balances held and that the rate that Federal Reserve members are required to pay to access the Federal Reserve Discount Window is intended to be high enough to deter accessing Federal Reserve credit in lieu of commercially available options. *See* 12 C.F.R. Part 327; 67 Fed. Reg. 67777, 67780, *available at* http://www.federalreserve.gov/boarddocs/press/bcreg/2002/200210312/attachment .pdf. On the other hand, such lending would presumably be occurring in circumstances where no such loan is available in the marketplace.

> I urge you to carefully consider the underlying premise of this provision —
> that the best way to protect the deposit insurance fund is to push higher risk
> activities into the so-called shadow sector.[42]

Also opposing the inclusion of section 716 in the Dodd-Frank Act, then Chairman
of the Federal Reserve Ben Bernanke wrote:

> I am concerned, however, that section 716 is counter-productive to achiev-
> ing these goals.
>
> In particular, section 716 would essentially prohibit all insured depository
> institutions from acting as a swap dealer or a major swap participant — even
> when the institution acts in these capacities to serve the commercial and
> hedging needs of its customers or to hedge the institution's own financial
> risks. Forcing these activities out of insured depository institutions would
> weaken both financial stability and strong prudential regulation of deriva-
> tive activities.[43]

While this critical commentary did not prevent section 716 from being included
in the final version of Dodd-Frank, these critical sentiments never faded and, on
December 16, 2014, section 716 was "revised." . . .[44] The new version requires only
swaps referencing asset-backed securities or indices comprised primarily of asset-
backed securities to be pushed out.[45] This is likely due to the perception, bolstered
by the conclusions of the Financial Crisis Inquiry Commission,[46] that asset-backed
securities and, in particular, mortgage-backed securities, were significant contributors to the Financial Crisis of 2008. . . .

---

42. [N. 10] Letter from Sheila Bair, President, Federal Deposit Insurance Company, to Senators
Lincoln and Dodd, 156 Cong. Rec. S3069 (daily ed. May 4, 2010).

43. [N. 11] WSJ.com, *Bernanke Letter to Lawmakers on Swaps Spin Off*, *available at* http://blogs
.wsj.com/economics/2010/05/13/bernanke-letter-to-lawmakers-on-swaps-spin-off/.

44. [N. 12] *See* The Dodd-Frank Act, Pub. L. 111-203, §716, as amended by Pub.L. 113-235, Div.
E, Title VI, §630.

45. [N. 13] Nationallawreview.com, *Swap Push-Out Rule Narrowed*, Dec. 19, 2014, *available at*
http://www.natlawreview.com/article/swap-push-out-rule-narrowed. Asset-backed securities are
securities collateralized by a pool of assets held by the issuer of the security. Before the Financial
Crisis, a popular category of asset-backed securities were asset-backed securities collateralized by
mortgages, also known as mortgage-backed securities.

46. [N. 14] The Financial Crisis Inquiry Commission was established by Congress via section 5
of the Fraud Enforcement and Recovery Act, Public Law 111-21 (2009). It was comprised of three
commissioners selected by the Speaker of the House, three commissioners selected by the Senate
majority leader, and two commissioners by each of the House and Senate minority leaders. *Id.*,
§5(b)(1). The primary function of the Financial Crisis Inquiry Commission was to "examine the
causes of the current financial and economic crisis in the United States . . . [and] the causes of the
collapse of each major financial institution that failed (including institutions that were acquired to
prevent their failure) or was likely to have failed if not for the receipt of exceptional Government
assistance from the Secretary of the Treasury during the period beginning in August 2007 through
April 2009. . . ." *Id.*, §5(c)(1) & (2).

In addition to limiting the application of section 716 to investments in asset-backed securities, the revised section 716 clarified another issue that had previously caused controversy. Specifically, the revised section 716 clarified whether the exceptions available to U.S. banks are equally available to non-U.S. banks operating a branch or agency in the U.S. by noting that non-U.S. banks operating a branch or agency in the U.S. could avail themselves of the same exemptions to section 716 as U.S. banks.[47] . . .

E. Retail Swaps Prohibition

The final transactional prohibition imposed by the Dodd-Frank Act is a prohibition on retail swaps, other than if traded on designated contract markets. As we know from chapter 5, designated contract markets are the futures exchanges historically regulated by the CFTC where all commodity futures contracts are required to be traded.

The Dodd-Frank Act added a new section to the Commodity Exchange Act requiring swaps traded on other than a designated contract market to be between "eligible contract participants."[48] As we will see, the eligible contract participant definition, due to the high minimum net worth test, excludes retail, i.e., ordinary consumer, counterparties.

1. Historical Function of Eligible Contract Participant Definition

The definition of "eligible contract participant" first appeared in the Commodity Futures Modernization Act (though its predecessor, "eligible swap participant," first appeared in CFTC regulations in 1993[49]). Its purpose after passage of the Commodity Futures Modernization Act in 2000 was to denote categories of derivatives transactions for which the CFTC's and SEC's oversight was limited to fraud prevention.[50] If swap transactions were between eligible contract participants and met other criteria, the CFTC and SEC only had jurisdiction for fraud. If swap transactions were not between eligible contract participants the CFTC or SEC could, conceivably, assert jurisdiction. As a practical matter, there was no legal framework for retail swaps and no established market for them.

---

47. [N. 17] *See* 15 U.S.C. § 8305.

48. Commodity Exchange Act § 2(e) (as amended by Dodd-Frank Act § 723(a)(2)).

49. *See* CFTC, *Exemption for Certain Swap* Agreements, 58 Fed. Reg. 5587, 5589 (Jan. 22, 1993).

50. For more on its predecessor, the "eligible swap participant" definition, *see* chapter 2, section D.1.

The Federal Reserve Board, Department of the Treasury, CFTC, and SEC jointly evaluated the question of whether there was demand for retail swaps.

Board of Governors of the Federal Reserve System, Department of the Treasury, CFTC, and SEC, *Joint Report on Retail Swaps*

https://www.treasury.gov/press-center/press-releases/Documents/rssfinal.pdf
(Dec. 26, 2001)

The Commodity Futures Modernization Act of 2000 ("CFMA") requires the Board of Governors of the Federal Reserve System ("Board"), the Secretary of the Treasury ("Treasury"), the Commodity Futures Trading Commission ("CFTC"), and the Securities and Exchange Commission ("SEC") to conduct a study of issues involving the offering of swap agreements to persons other than eligible contract participants. . . .

A primary purpose of the CFMA was to create a clear legal foundation and regulatory framework for many types of over-the-counter ("OTC") derivatives transactions entered on a principal- to-principal basis between "eligible contract participants" ("ECPs") as defined in . . . the Commodity Exchange Act ("CEA"). Parties that do not qualify as ECPs include individuals who do not have total assets in excess of $10 million (or $5 million if they enter swap agreements for risk management) and non-financial entities that do not have total assets in excess of $10 million (or net worth in excess of $1 million if they enter swap agreements in the ordinary conduct of business or for risk management). For purposes of this study, non-ECPs are "retail customers," and swaps offered to them are "retail swaps." . . .

The CFMA did not address the legal or regulatory status of swap agreements with retail customers. . . .

[T]he CFMA posed the following topics for the agencies to investigate in the study:

1. The potential uses of swap agreements by persons other than eligible contract participants.

2. The extent to which financial institutions are willing to offer swap agreements to persons other than eligible contract participants. . . .

To investigate these topics, the agencies interviewed representatives of derivatives dealers (including commercial and investment banks and a non-financial firm), a derivatives trading system, and a trade association on August 1 and 2, 2001, in New York. . . .

Among the potential uses for swap agreements by non-ECPs that the interviewees identified in the course of the study are the following.

1. Equities

The interviewees generally observed that equity derivatives may be used for two purposes: to hedge an existing position in an individual equity security or to create synthetic exposure to one or more individual securities or security indices.

Hedging. OTC equity derivatives are frequently used to hedge exposure to adverse price movements in a security, typically when the counterparty has a concentrated position in the security that it does not wish to liquidate, perhaps due to tax consequences, or when the counterparty is unable to liquidate a position in a security due to transfer restrictions under federal securities laws. . . .

Several of the interviewees noted, however, that firms generally do not recommend the use of swap agreements to hedge positions in individual equity securities because of tax considerations. . . . Consequently, the commercial and investment banks interviewed indicated that they typically advise persons seeking to hedge partially or reduce exposure to an equity position to enter into OTC options contracts, based on their view that the use of such contracts may not always trigger a taxable event. They also indicated that this strategy does not raise CEA issues, since options on securities are considered "securities" under the federal securities laws and are not subject to the CEA.

Synthetic Exposure. The interviewees also noted that OTC equity derivatives could be used to gain exposure to a security in lieu of purchasing or selling the security directly. It might be advantageous to use an equity derivative for this purpose, in their view, if greater leverage could be obtained (as compared to a traditional margin account), or if the cost of executing, clearing or settling trades in the underlying security or securities were comparatively expensive, as in the case of the component stocks of a security index or securities in certain non-U.S. markets.

Several interviewees questioned, however, whether retail investors would be able to use retail swaps for these purposes. Some interviewees expressed the view that swap dealers were unlikely to permit retail investors to obtain significantly greater leverage using a swap agreement than by purchasing or selling the underlying security or a standardized derivative instrument in a traditional margin account, largely because of credit concerns. For example, some of the commercial and investment banks interviewed indicated that they typically require their customers to collateralize the derivative contract with the securities they are seeking to hedge.

Some interviewees opined that, in light of the relative cost of negotiating and entering into swap agreements, individually-tailored swap agreements might not be cost effective for all but the highest net worth individuals and institutional investors as a means of establishing a synthetic exposure. The commercial and investment banks interviewed also generally noted that retail investors currently have access to a wide variety of securities and derivatives products to gain exposure to equity securities, including equity-linked notes, warrants, exchange-traded funds, mutual funds, [and] exchange-traded options. . . .

2. Interest Rate Products

Several interviewees noted that there was very little demand for interest-rate swap agreements at present except among institutions and high net worth individuals that already qualify as ECPs. For example, one firm remarked that, to the best of its representatives' recollections, it had never entered into fixed income swaps with an entity that owned or had under management less than $100 million in assets.

Some interviewees said that non-ECPs could potentially use interest-rate swap agreements to obtain the benefit of more favorable interest rates on household or small business expenses, such as mortgage or consumer debt, separately from the underlying loan. These interviewees added, however, that at the present time, it is convenient for non-ECPs to refinance a mortgage or transfer consumer debt, and the ability to enter into an "unbundled" swap agreement would not appear to offer retail customers a cost-effective or convenient alternative.

3. Energy

Several interviewees stated that non-ECPs may have an interest in swap agreements on energy products, such as electricity, natural gas, and heating oil, as a tool to assist small businesses and households in controlling energy costs. One firm further indicated an interest in offering such contracts as a third party — *i.e.*, to provide risk management transactions for such commodities without also supplying the underlying commodity.

This firm noted that, as a result of the deregulation of the energy markets in certain states, households and businesses have entered into forward contracts for full or partial energy requirements with competing energy providers at fixed or capped prices. It was further noted that, in localities where physical delivery of energy products may be restricted because of regulatory or operational constraints, cash-settled swap agreements have in some cases been available for ECPs in order to provide them a means to hedge their exposure to price fluctuations. Accordingly, small businesses and, to some extent, households that are not ECPs may similarly desire to enter into swap agreements in order to control their energy costs when forward delivery contracts are not available; in this firm's view, current uncertainty about the status of such contracts under the CEA has hindered their development.

Some interviewees, however, opined that the current tax treatment of gains and losses on swap agreements entered into by individuals (and outside the context of conducting a trade or business) to hedge energy costs may make such agreements less attractive. They indicated that while gains on energy swap agreements would be fully taxable, losses on these swaps either would not be deductible or would qualify as a miscellaneous deduction, which are only deductible to [a limited extent]. . . .

According to most of the interviewees, derivatives market participants are not generally planning to offer swap agreements to retail customers at present, apart from the interest there may be in offering retail swaps with respect to energy products. In general, the interviewees noted that firms currently have no commercial interest in offering swaps to retail customers because there is no demonstrable demand for them. Lack of demand is apparently sufficient to preclude any desire on the part of these institutions to explore issuance of these instruments, thus obviating the need to analyze legal issues. . . .

The agencies do not believe it is necessary at this time to recommend legislative action for swap agreements offered to persons other than ECPs.

According to the interviewees, persons who are not ECPs seem at this time to have sufficient instruments at their disposal to meet their risk management and investment needs, and there is currently a lack of interest among most major market participants in offering swaps to retail customers. As noted in this report, energy swaps are a possible exception to both findings. . . .

Although the study was two decades ago, it is not clear that its conclusions would be different were the question evaluated today. Moreover, the Dodd-Frank Act changed the function of the definition dramatically from its pre-Dodd-Frank function to outright ban swaps with retail counterparties unless traded on a futures exchange.

2. Eligible Contract Participants

Swaps post-Dodd-Frank Act are not only heavily regulated, as we will see in the forthcoming chapters, they are also illegal *unless* between eligible contract participants or traded on a designated contract market. This reflects a substantial retreat from deregulation of transactions between sophisticated counterparties and potential CFTC and SEC regulation of all others. Its effect is that swaps involving a retail counterparty are illegal unless traded on a futures exchange.

The prohibition on retail swaps operates by way of amendment to the Commodity Exchange Act made by the Dodd-Frank Act:

> It shall be unlawful for any person, other than an eligible contract participant, to enter into a swap unless the swap is entered into on . . . a board of trade designated as a contract market. . . .[51]

The definition of eligible contract participant, since it determines who may participate in the non-retail swaps market, is of critical importance. Although the definition has multi-faceted tests applying to some entities, the definition is straightforward for the preponderance of potential parties to a swap. Parties that are corporations have a $10 million net worth test (or $1 million if the swap relates to its business or is for risk hedging) and parties that are natural persons must have $10 million for investment on a discretionary basis (or $5 million if the swap is for risk hedging).[52]

----

51. Commodity Exchange Act § 2(e) (as amended by Dodd-Frank Act § 723(a)(2)).

52. Commodity Exchange Act § 1a(18). The CFTC, by rulemaking, has made minor additions to the list of entities qualifying as eligible contract participants. *See* CFTC, *Further Definition of "Swap Dealer," "Security-Based Swap Dealer," "Major Swap Participant," "Major Security-Based Swap Participant," and "Eligible Contract Participant"*, 77 Fed. Reg. 30596 (May 23, 2012).

In the Matter of Absa Bank, Ltd.

CFTC Docket No. 20-23 (Jul. 13, 2020)

The Commodity Futures Trading Commission ("Commission") has reason to believe that from in or about December 2017 to October 2019 (the "Relevant Period"), Plutus Financial, Inc. doing business as Abra ("Abra"), and Plutus Technologies Philippines Corporation doing business as Abra International ("Plutus Tech") (collectively, "Respondents") violated Sections 2(e) and 4d(a)(1) of the Commodity Exchange Act ("Act"), 7 U.S.C. §§ 2(e), 6d(a)(1) (2018). Therefore, the Commission deems it appropriate and in the public interest that public administrative proceedings be, and hereby are, instituted to determine whether Respondents engaged in the violations set forth herein and to determine whether any order should be issued imposing remedial sanctions.

In anticipation of the institution of an administrative proceeding, Respondents have submitted an Offer of Settlement ("Offer"), which the Commission has determined to accept. Without admitting or denying any of the findings or conclusions herein, Respondents consent to the entry of this Order Instituting Proceedings Pursuant to Section 6(c) and (d) of the Commodity Exchange Act, Making Findings, and Imposing Remedial Sanctions ("Order"), and acknowledge service of this Order. . . .

The Commission finds the following:

During the Relevant Period, Respondents violated Section 2(e) of the Act, 7 U.S.C. § 2(e)(2018), by illegally entering into off-exchange swaps with U.S. and overseas customers. Respondents also operated as unregistered futures commission merchants ("FCMs") in violation of Sections 4d(a)(1) of the Act, 7 U.S.C. § 6d(a)(1) (2018). . . .

During the Relevant Period, Abra developed, owned, and operated a mobile phone application that enabled users to enter into financial transactions, with Abra or Plutus Tech acting as the counterparty, to gain exposure to price movements of over seventy-five virtual and foreign currencies, among other assets. Via this app, Respondents accepted orders for and entered into thousands of virtual currency and foreign currency-based contracts, which constituted swaps under the Act, with U.S. and overseas individuals. At times during the Relevant Period, Respondents and their customers were not eligible contract participants ("ECPs"). The swaps were not entered into on, or subject to the rules of, a designated contract market as required under the Act, and neither Abra nor Plutus Tech has ever been registered with the Commission.

Abra's product offerings evolved over time, but the basic structure of the financial transactions and contracts remained the same. First, customers would set up an Abra wallet and then fund their wallet via bank transfer, credit card, or virtual currency deposit. Abra would then convert those customer funds to Bitcoin, which were accounted for on the Bitcoin blockchain. When a customer decided to gain price exposure to one of the available assets (referred to as reference assets), the customer selected the reference asset, posted collateral (in Bitcoin) equal to the amount of exposure they wanted, and entered into a Bitcoin blockchain-settled "smart contract" with Abra as the counterparty.[53] At the end of the contract term, settlement occurred on the Bitcoin blockchain. If the market price for the reference asset had increased, then the customer would receive the collateral plus a payment (in Bitcoin) equivalent to the increase. If the market price had fallen, then the customer's collateral would be reduced by an equivalent amount.[54] Because Abra was the counterparty to each contract, the customer was exposed to the risk that Abra would not have sufficient funds to cover any increases in price. To eliminate this exposure, Abra borrowed Bitcoin and then exchanged that bitcoin for whatever asset it needed to hedge against on a one-to-one basis. . . .

After being contacted by the Commission and the Securities and Exchange Commission in early 2019 and cooperating with their investigations, Abra voluntarily ceased offering its virtual currency and foreign currency-based swaps to U.S. customers and undertook measures to ensure that these swaps were only offered to non-US customers through Plutus Tech. Although Plutus Tech was the counterparty to these swaps with overseas customers, Abra played a significant role in the swaps. For example, Abra employees in California designed the swap contract, including setting the contract's price and establishing the hedging mechanism. Those same Abra employees also drafted marketing materials relating to the swaps and conducted limited managerial functions, including providing technical support and accounting.

Respondents promoted all of these contracts to U.S. and overseas customers via websites, social media, and various other marketing channels. Respondents did not set any requirements that customers own any specific amount of assets to enter into the swaps and did not require customers to provide any financial information other than their bank account number or credit card number to fund their wallet. That is, Respondents did not take steps to determine whether customers were ECPs as defined by the Act. In July 2019, Abra stopped all offers and sales of swaps in the United States. Plutus Tech has ceased offering swaps to overseas customers. . . .

Section 2(e) of the Act, 7 U.S.C. § 2(e) (2018), makes it unlawful for any person, other than an ECP, to enter into a swap unless the swap is entered into on, or subject to the rules of, a board of trade designated as a contract market.

The contracts that Respondents entered into were swaps as defined by the Act because the contracts (1) provided on an executory basis for the exchange, on a fixed

---

53. [No. 2] Plutus Tech served as the counterparty for some transactions involving overseas customers.

54. [No. 3] The contract operated like a contract for difference ("CFD"), which the Commission has described as "an agreement to exchange the difference in value of an underlying asset between the time at which a CFD position is established and the time at which it is terminated." *See* Joint SEC-CFTC Final Rule Further Definition of "Swap," "Security-Based Swap," and "Security-Based Swap Agreement"; Mixed Swaps; Security-Based Swap Agreement Recordkeeping, 77 Fed. Reg. 48,208, 48,259 (Aug. 13, 2012) (Joint Statement on Swaps).

or contingent basis, of one or more payments based on the value or level of one or more commodities, currencies, economic interests, or property of any kind; and (2) transferred the financial risk associated with the future change in value without also conveying an ownership interest. *See* Section 1a(47)(A)(iii) of the Act, 7 U.S.C. § 1a(47)(A)(iii) (2018).[55]

As described above, Respondents unlawfully entered into swaps with U.S. and overseas customers that were not entered into on or subject to the rules of a board of trade designated as a contract market. Therefore, Respondents violated Section 2(e) of the Act. . . .

In addition to the outright prohibitions on swap activities enacted by Dodd-Frank Act sections 619 and 716 and added by the Dodd-Frank Act to the Commodity Exchange Act related to retail swaps,[56] the Dodd-Frank Act also instituted a comprehensive regulatory regime that, though influenced by the existing regulatory regime for commodity futures and options, was nonetheless new. This regulatory regime is the subject of chapters 10 through 13.

Questions and Comments

1. Why was the bailout of American International Group such a dramatic event? What is the difference in public policy concerns, if any, between the bailout of an insured depository bank and an entity such as American International Group?

2. How did the Financial Crisis affect you, if at all? What were your views at the time, and have they changed?

3. It is noted in section A that the Dodd-Frank Act passed with a split largely along party lines. Are there benefits to obtaining bipartisan support for financial legislation? If so, what are they?

4. Enumerate some of the functions of derivatives (chapter 1, section E provides some refreshment on this topic). To the extent the swap push-out rule displaces traditional bank participants in the derivatives area, how should the gap be filled?

5. Could products that were heavily criticized in the wake of the Financial Crisis, such as credit default obligations (i.e., "CDOs"), have societal benefits? If so, what are they?

6. The Volcker Rule has been criticized for its complexity. Much of the complexity, however, lies in its exemptions. If you were charged with implementing the policy goals of the Volcker Rule (i.e., limiting commercial deposit banks to their traditional lending-focused activities), how would you implement them?

---

55. [No. 4] In addition, as CFDs, the contracts constitute swaps under the Act. See Joint Statement on Swaps, 77 Fed. Reg. at 48,260 ("CFDs, unless otherwise excluded, fall within the scope of the swap . . . definition[.]"); *supra* note 3.

56. Commodity Exchange Act § 2(e) (as amended by Dodd-Frank Act § 723(a)(2)).

7. The prohibition on non-eligible contract participants trading swaps is motivated, to a large extent, by a view that non-eligible contract participants lack the economic sophistication and financial risk-taking means to trade swaps. This is similar to the rationale underlying, among others, the securities "accredited investor" regime that allows broad participation in private securities offerings only by "accredited investors." Is it appropriate for government to allow only some (wealthier) persons to participate in these activities? Should a *caveat emptor* approach apply, just as it does with most other economic sectors?

Chapter 10

Swaps Markets

A. Background

1. Historical Notes

Organized markets in the United States for trading swaps have only been permitted since passage of the Commodity Futures Modernization Act in December 2000. Before the passage of the Commodity Futures Modernization Act, trading a swap on an organized market (other than, theoretically, a designated contract market) would have incurred significant legal risk. The swap risked characterization as a futures contract (illegal to trade other than on a designated contract market), the market itself could be liable for its failure to register as a designated contract market with the CFTC, and, depending on the circumstances, one or both of the parties to the trade could be deemed unregistered futures commission merchants. For the pre-Commodity Futures Modernization Act uncertainty as to whether swaps could be deemed illegal off-exchange futures, see chapter 2, section D.1; for the registration requirements applying to futures markets, see chapter 5.

The Commodity Futures Modernization Act provided legal certainty for most types of "over-the-counter" swaps, i.e., swaps traded bilaterally without use of a trading facility, by prohibiting the CFTC and the SEC from exercising jurisdiction over them other than for fraud. It also permitted them to be cleared and trade on three alternative facilities to designated contract markets. These alternatives were exempt commercial markets, exempt boards of trade, and derivatives transaction execution facilities. All three were abolished by the Dodd-Frank Act.[1] Their successor in spirit is the "swap execution facility" created by the Dodd-Frank Act and discussed below in section C.[2]

2. Impact of the Dodd-Frank Act

The focus of this chapter is on the impact to swap trading facilities of the Dodd-Frank Act. Whereas the Commodity Futures Modernization Act permitted most swap categories to be cleared and traded on trading facilities, the Dodd-Frank Act

---

1. Dodd-Frank Act §§ 723 and 734. *See also* CFTC, *Repeal of the Exempt Commercial Market and Exempt Board of Trade Exemptions*, 80 Fed. Reg. 59575 (Oct. 2, 2015) and CFTC, *Adaptation of Regulations to Incorporate Swaps*, 77 Fed. Reg. 66288, 66301 (Nov. 2, 2012).

2. *See* Walter Lukken, CLE Paper, *Regulation of Futures and Derivatives* 7–8 (Naples, Fl. Jan. 30, 2010) (on file with author).

amended the Commodity Exchange Act to *require* some categories of swaps to be both cleared by a derivatives clearing organization and traded on either a designated contract market or on a new category of registrant created by the Dodd-Frank Act, a swap execution facility. Reporting obligations are imposed on both facilities. Many of these reporting obligations are undertaken by reporting trade details to another category of registrant newly created by the Dodd-Frank Act, a swap data repository.

However, even where a clearing and on-facility trading requirement applies to a category of swaps, exemptions are available for certain counterparty types. These counterparty types have the option of not having their swaps cleared.[3] In such cases, neither mandatory clearing nor mandatory on-facility trading apply.

In this chapter we will examine clearing and on-facility trading requirements, the exemptions to both, and the registration requirements and obligations of swap execution facilities, and swap data repositories. We will also discuss derivatives clearing organizations, a category of registrant we encountered in chapter 5, section D.

B. Derivatives Clearing Organizations and the Clearing Requirement

1. Derivatives Clearing Organizations

As discussed in chapter 5, derivatives clearing organizations are a creation of the Commodity Futures Modernization Act of 2000. Entities must be registered as derivatives clearing organizations to clear swaps.[4] Swaps clear similarly — albeit not identically — to futures and it may be a good time to review chapter 6, sections B.1.a and b, for refreshment on clearing generally.

In the context of swap clearing, let us assume that two parties are each customers of futures commission merchants. (In reality, instead of being a customer of a futures commission merchant, either or both could instead themselves be a registered futures commission merchant or, even if unregistered, be a "self-clearing" member of a derivatives clearing organization.) Just as with futures clearing. the derivatives clearing organization would step between the two parties and be counterparty to each, with futures commission merchants that are members of the derivatives clearing organization guaranteeing each of their customer's positions to the derivatives clearing organization. Each party would post a per contract initial margin to its futures commission merchant. In the event the value of the position changes significantly, the party impacted will either see an account credit if the market movement is favorable to them or be subject to a "margin call" by its futures commission merchant for an amount equivalent to the adverse market movement. This is known as variation margin.

---

3. Commodity Exchange Act § 2(h)(7).
4. Commodity Exchange Act § 2(h)(1)(A).

Unlike futures, though, not all categories of swaps are required to be traded on a trading facility and cleared. Many categories of swaps may, and usually are, traded off-facility. Sometimes parties voluntarily use a swap execution facility to execute a swap trade. Or execute a swap bilaterally off-facility and then voluntarily submit it for clearing with a derivatives clearing organization. You may also recall that futures are traded on an exchange and then cleared by a derivatives clearing organization integrated with the exchange. With swaps traded on a facility, the derivatives clearing organization is not an integrated affiliate of the trading facility.

To further this separation of the roles of trading facility and clearinghouse, derivatives clearing organizations are required to abide by "open access" requirements. These requirements "provide for non-discriminatory clearing of a swap . . . executed bilaterally or on or through the rules of an unaffiliated designated contract market or swap execution facility."[5] In cases where a swap is traded off-facility, i.e., executed bilaterally, and then given up to a derivatives clearing organization, the choice of derivatives clearing organization is, technically, made by the end user if the other party is a swap dealer or major swap participant (we discuss these two entities in the following chapter).[6] If the swap is traded on a swap execution facility and given up for clearing by a derivatives clearing organization, the terms of the swap will include the relevant derivatives clearing organization.

A second distinction relates to the "double default" or "fellow customer" risk we discussed in chapter 6, section B.3. As a reminder, "double default" risk arises when a large customer or customers of a futures commission merchant incur significant adverse movements on positions and default on a margin payment that is so large it results in the insolvency of the futures commission merchant and a shortfall on what it owes to the clearinghouse. With futures, such a circumstance — which actually occurred in the late 1980s — results in non-defaulting customers' funds held by the futures commission merchant being reduced *pro rata* to pay the shortfall owed to the clearinghouse.

With swaps, this cannot occur. Cleared swaps, as will also be discussed in chapter 18, are "legally segregated and operationally commingled." This means that default of a fellow swaps customer resulting in failure of the futures commission merchant and a shortfall to the clearinghouse will not result in the non-defaulting customers' accounts being reduced as necessary to make up the shortfall. This is because swaps clearing customer accounts are "legally segregated," i.e., treated as legally separate from the assets of the futures commission merchant available to satisfy third party liabilities.

On the other hand, the futures commission merchant does have the ability to "operationally commingle" different customer swaps accounts for the purpose of investing the cash and generating income. An MF Global situation (see chapter 6, section

---

5. Commodity Exchange Act § 2(h)(1)(B). *See also* 17 C.F.R. § 39.12(b).
6. 17 C.F.R. § 23.432.

B.3), where poorly performing investments indirectly resulted in what at one point appeared to be a shortfall in customer accounts, is still possible with cleared swaps.

2. Clearing Requirement

The Dodd-Frank Act added a new section to the Commodity Exchange Act that makes it "unlawful for any person to engage in a swap unless that person submits such swap for clearing to a derivatives clearing organization . . . if the swap is required to be cleared."[7] However, all swaps are not required to be cleared. Instead, categories of swaps are required to be cleared only through two designation mechanisms. One is by designation of the CFTC itself and the other is by designation of a derivatives clearing organization.[8]

The first is initiated by the CFTC if the CFTC determines, after allowing for at least a thirty-day public comment period, that a category of swaps should be cleared.[9] The second is initiated by any derivatives clearing organization that intends to clear a category of swap.[10] The CFTC must review the submission of the derivatives clearing organization and provide a thirty-day public comment period before the clearing determination is deemed final.[11]

In both cases, the analysis for the final determination is the same. The CFTC must consider:

   i. The existence of significant outstanding notional exposures, trading liquidity, and adequate pricing data.

   ii. The availability of [a] rule framework, capacity, operational expertise and resources, and credit support infrastructure to clear the contract on terms that are consistent with the material terms and trading conventions on which the contract is then traded.

   iii. The effect on the mitigation of systemic risk, considering the size of the market for such contract and the resources of the derivatives clearing organization available to clear the contract.

   iv. The effect on competition, including appropriate fees and charges applied to clearing.

   v. The existence of reasonable legal certainty in the event of the insolvency of the relevant derivatives clearing organization or 1 or more of its clearing members with regard to the treatment of customer and swap counterparty positions, funds, and property.[12]

---

  7. Commodity Exchange Act § 2(h).

  8. Commodity Exchange Act §§ 2(h)(2)(A) & (B).

  9. Commodity Exchange Act § 2(h)(2)(A).

 10. Commodity Exchange Act § 2(h)(2)(B).

 11. Commodity Exchange Act § 2(h)(2)(B)(iii).

 12. Commodity Exchange Act § 2(h)(2)(D)(ii).

The first four statutory factors that must be accounted for are specific to the relevant category of swaps subject to the determination. The fifth applies to derivatives clearing organizations and their futures commission merchant members generally. The CFTC, in its first clearing determination, discussed further below in subsection a below, concluded that the fifth statutory factor is satisfied as a matter of law for U.S. derivatives clearing organizations (for one non-U.S. derivatives clearing organization, the CFTC relied on an opinion of external counsel), noting that:

> [N]either a clearing member's bankruptcy nor any order of a bankruptcy court could prevent [a U.S. derivatives clearing organization] from closing out/liquidating [swap] positions. . . . [C]ustomers of clearing members would have priority over all other claimants with respect to customer funds that had been held by the defaulting clearing member to margin swaps. . . .

> Similarly, [the Bankruptcy Code and CFTC rules] would govern the bankruptcy of a [derivatives clearing organization] . . . providing for the termination of outstanding contracts and/or return of remaining clearing member and customer property to clearing members.[13]

We examine bankruptcy issues generally in chapter 18.

The definitive questions are: (1) whether a swap is required to be cleared; and (2) if so, whether the counterparty in question benefits from an exemption from clearing. Question (1) we examine now and question (2) we examine below in section 3.

Why Aren't All Swaps Cleared?

Even assuming clearing is desirable from a public policy perspective (more on that below in subsection 4), there is not a cleared swaps market for every swap category. What makes a derivatives clearing organization offer clearing for one category of swap and not another?

A study by Deutsche Bank focusing on the credit default swap market cites two factors, liquidity and volatility. Higher liquidity and lower volatility results in a greater likelihood that a swap category will be accepted for clearing, and lower liquidity and higher volatility results in a lesser likelihood that a swap category will be accepted for clearing.

[a] Orçun Kaya, *Liquidity is Key for the Central Clearing of Derivatives*, Deutsche Bank Research Briefing (Mar. 12, 2015), available at https://www.dbresearch.com/PROD/RPS_EN -PROD/PROD0000000000455140/Research_Briefing%3A_Liquidity_is_key_for_the_centra .pdf.

---

13. CFTC, *Clearing Requirement Determination Under Section 2(h) of the CEA*, 77 Fed. Reg. 74284-01, 74299 (Dec. 13, 2012).

a. CFTC Initiated Clearing Determinations

The Commodity Exchange Act requires the CFTC to "on an ongoing basis" decide as to whether any category of swaps should be cleared.[14] If the CFTC concludes that a clearing determination may be merited, it must provide at least a thirty-day comment period.[15]

To date, the CFTC has issued two clearing determinations.[16] Together, they require the clearing of nearly all interest rate swaps denominated in the most commonly traded currencies other than, in essence, interest rate options, interest swaps with more than one currency, interest rates where the notional changes over time, or interest rate swaps with other esoteric features.[17] Also required to be cleared are specific credit default swaps referencing commonly used indices.[18]

b. Derivatives Clearing Organization Initiated Clearing Determinations

A derivatives clearing organization can submit to the CFTC notice of any category of swaps it intends to accept for clearing.[19] The CFTC is required to review this submission, release it for a minimum thirty-day comment period, and has ninety days to make its determination.[20]

To date, no submissions have been made using this method.

3. Clearing Exemptions

a. Generally

Swaps that are required to be cleared are also required to be traded on a designated contract market or swap execution facility, if "made available to trade."[21] Below, in section C, we will examine this process. In many cases, swaps that are required to be cleared are coterminous with swaps that are required to be traded on a facility, i.e., traded on a designated contract market or swap execution facility. It is sufficient for now to know that only swaps required to be cleared may be required to be traded on a trading facility. In other words, if a swap is exempt from mandatory clearing, it will also be exempt from any requirement to trade on a trading facility.

---

14. Commodity Exchange Act § 2(h)(2)(A)(i).

15. Commodity Exchange Act § 2(h)(2)(A)(ii).

16. CFTC, *Clearing Requirement Determination Under Section 2(h) of the CEA*, 77 Fed. Reg. 74284 (Dec. 13, 2012) and CFTC. *Clearing Requirement Determination Under Section 2(h) of the Commodity Exchange Act for Interest Rate Swaps*, 81 Fed. Reg. 71202 (Oct. 14, 2016).

17. *See* 17 C.F.R. § 50.4.

18. *Id.*

19. Commodity Exchange Act § 2(h)(2)(B).

20. Commodity Exchange Act §§ 2(h)(2)(B) and (C).

21. Commodity Exchange Act § 2(h)(8).

b. What Is a Financial Entity?

In chapter 1, section C, we distinguished dealers from hedgers and speculators, both of which we can term end users. End users can be further subdivided into financial entities and non-financial entities. As we will see below in subsection c, the term "financial entity" is crucial to understanding whether an exemption applies.

A financial entity is any of:

- *Certain CFTC or SEC Registrants*: A swap dealer, security-based swap dealer, major swap participant, major security-based swap participant, or commodity pool.[22]

- *Certain Funds*: A hedge fund, private equity fund, or pension plan.[23]

- *Banks*: An entity engaged in the "business of banking."[24]

- *An Entity Primarily Engaged in Activities "Financial in Nature"*: "Financial in nature" includes lending, investing for others, safeguarding money or securities, insurance activities, financial advisory activities, issuing interests in certain assets, underwriting, dealing or market making in securities, merchant banking activities and acting as a "finder" in securities transactions.[25]

c. Non-Financial Entity and Other Exemptions

As noted above, even if a category of swaps is subject to clearing, there are exemptions. These exemptions provide certain types of entities the option of whether to have their trades cleared or not so long as the swap is for hedging purposes. Seven categories of entities are exempt from mandatory clearing for swaps entered into for hedging purposes:

- *Non-Financial Entity* (also known as the "commercial end user" exemption): A non-financial entity is exempt so long as it reports certain information related to its use of the clearing exemption, such as how it generally meets its obligations in association with uncleared swaps, to a swap data repository or the CFTC.[26] We will discuss below in more detail what constitutes a "non-financial entity."

- *Cooperative:* A cooperative whose members are all non-financial entities or eligible for the small bank exemption is exempt from clearing, even if the cooperative itself is a financial entity, so long as the swap for which the exemption from clearing is sought is in connection with loans to members.[27] Such an entity is subject to the same reporting requirements as a non-financial entity.

---

22. Commodity Exchange Act § 2(h)(7)(C)(i).

23. *Id.*

24. *Id.*

25. *See* U.S.C. § 1243(k) and 12 C.F.R. § 225.86(d).

26. Commodity Exchange Act § 2(h)(7)(A) and 17 C.F.R. §§ 50.50(a)(1)(iii) and 50.50(c).

27. 17 C.F.R. § 50.51 via the CFTC's statutory exemptive authority in Commodity Exchange Act § 4(c).

- *Inter-Affiliate:* Two entities affiliated with one another (i.e., one owns the other, directly or indirectly, or both are commonly controlled) that report their financial statements on a consolidated basis are exempt from clearing requirements if the trades are documented and subject to a centralized risk management program.[28] There are special rules applicable that require both affiliates' swaps with third parties to be subject to the U.S. rules applicable to clearing or a comparable regime.[29] One of the entities must report to a swap data repository or the CFTC information similar to that required for a non-financial entity.[30]

- *Small Bank:* A bank, bank holding company,[31] savings association, savings and loan holding company,[32] credit union, or member of the farm credit system with $10 billion or less in assets has been deemed by the CFTC to be a "non-financial entity" for the purposes of the clearing exemption even though its activities are financial in nature.[33] Such an entity is subject to the same reporting requirements as a non-financial entity.

- *Captive Finance Company:* Also deemed to be a "non-financial entity," this is an entity the primary business of which is to finance products, ninety percent or more of which are manufactured by an affiliate, using derivatives solely to hedge interest rate and foreign exchange risks, ninety percent or more of which stem from financing related to the purchase or lease of its products.[34] It is subject to the same requirements as any other non-financial entity.

- *Affiliate of Non-Financial Entity:* An affiliate of a non-financial entity is exempt so long as it is hedging commercial risk for its non-financial entity affiliate. The affiliate cannot be a swap dealer, security-based swap dealer, major swap participant, major security-based swap participant, commodity pool, hedge fund or private equity fund, bank holding company, non-banking entity owned by a bank holding company, pension fund, bank or similar entity, or insurance company, and neither of the entities can be affiliated with a swap dealer,

---

28. 17 C.F.R. § 50.52 via the CFTC's statutory exemptive authority in Commodity Exchange Act § 4(c).

29. 17 C.F.R. § 50.52(b)(4).

30. *See* 17 C.F.R. §§ 50.52(c) and (d).

31. *See* 17 C.F.R. § 50.78 via the CFTC's statutory exemptive authority in Commodity Exchange Act § 4(c).

32. *See* 17 C.F.R. § 50.79 via the CFTC's statutory exemptive authority in Commodity Exchange Act § 4(c).

33. 17 C.F.R. § 50.53. Commodity Exchange Act section 2(h)(7)(C)(ii) required the CFTC to consider exempting small banks, savings associations, credit unions, and members of the farm credit system. They are all deemed to be part of the "small bank" exemption, even though not all are banks.

34. Commodity Exchange Act § 2(h)(7)(C)(iii). *See also* CFTC No-Action Letter No. 15-27 (May 4, 2015) including a securitization special purpose vehicle wholly owned by a non-financial entity as a captive finance company.

security-based swap dealer, major swap participant, or major security-based swap participant.[35] The ultimate owner of the non-financial entities affiliate cannot be a financial entity.[36]

- *Community Development Financial Institution:* A community development financial institution is a type of bank, savings bank, holding company of a bank or savings bank, or credit union, with the "primary mission of promoting community development."[37] Such an entity is exempt from clearing requirements so long as the swap is an interest rate swap or forward rate agreement and the total notional of all swaps it has entered into over the prior year does not exceed $200 million comprised of no more than ten swaps.[38] A community development financial institution is subject to the same reporting requirements as a non-financial entity.

Additionally, swaps are exempt from clearing, regardless of whether the swap is for the purpose of hedging, if one of the parties is: (1) a central bank or government (including governmental agencies);[39] or (2) one of a list of specified international financial institutions, such as the European Bank for Reconstruction and Development or the Inter-American Development Bank.[40] These exemptions are summarized in the table in figure 10.1.

In addition to non-financial entities being able to avail of the non-financial entity exemptions from clearing, non-financial entities generally have a right to require clearing when trading with counterparties registered with the CFTC as swap dealers or major swap participants (both discussed in chapter 11), even if the swap is not in a category subject to a mandatory clearing requirement.[41]

---

35. Commodity Exchange Act § 2(h)(7)(D)(i). Initially, there was a statutory limitation requiring the affiliate to act solely as agent of the non-financial entity and not, as was more commonly done, principal to a third party with an internal mechanism then in place to reflect the transfer of the hedge to its non-financial entity affiliate whose risk was being hedged. The CFTC rectified this with CFTC No-Action Letter No. 14-144 (Nov. 6, 2014) superseding CFTC No-Action Letter No. 13-22 (June 4, 2013). Ultimately, Congress provided a statutory fix. *See* Consolidated Appropriations Act, 2016 § 705, Pub. L. 114-113 (Dec. 18, 2015).
36. Commodity Exchange Act §§ 2(h)(7)(D)(i)(III) and (IV).
37. 12 C.F.R. § 1805.201.
38. 17 C.F.R. § 50.77(b) via the CFTC's statutory exemptive authority in Commodity Exchange Act § 4(c).
39. 17 C.F.R. § 50.75 via the CFTC's statutory exemptive authority in Commodity Exchange Act § 4(c).
40. 17 C.F.R. § 50.76 via the CFTC's statutory exemptive authority in Commodity Exchange Act § 4(c).
41. Commodity Exchange Act § 2(h)(7)(E)(ii).

Figure 10.1 Clearing Exemptions

Exemption	Legal Basis
Non-Financial Entity	Commodity Exchange Act § 2(h)(7)(A) & 17 C.F.R. § 50.50
Small Bank	Commodity Exchange Act § 2(h)(7)(C)(ii) & 17 C.F.R. § 50.50(d)
Captive Finance Company	Commodity Exchange Act § 2(h)(7)(C)(iii)
Affiliate of Non-Financial Entity	Commodity Exchange Act § 2(h)(7)(D)(i)
Cooperative	17 C.F.R. § 50.51
Inter-affiliate	17 C.F.R. § 50.52

d. Application of the Clearing Exemption

Let us evaluate the non-financial entity exemption in light of the following three examples.

Example One: The Ocean Waves Baking Company is borrower under a loan facility where the interest rate is "floating" and, therefore, changes from month-to-month. The Ocean Waves Baking Company approaches Mega Bank to enter into an interest rate swap to hedge its loan exposure. The interest rate swap is subject to a clearing determination, requiring it to be cleared, unless there is an exemption to clearing. The Ocean Waves Baking Company informs Mega Bank that it would like the swap to be uncleared.

Result: This is permissible because the Ocean Waves Baking Company is a non-financial entity hedging risk and has elected to use the clearing exemptions. Either the Ocean Waves Baking Company or Mega Bank will have to report required information to the CFTC related to the Ocean Waves Baking Company's status as a non-financial entity.

Example Two: Suppose the same facts as in Example One except that the Ocean Waves Baking Company expresses no view on whether it would like the swap to be cleared or uncleared. Instead, the swap trader from Mega Bank informs her counterpart at the Ocean Waves Baking Company that Mega Bank will trade the swap without clearing it.

Result: This violates the Commodity Exchange Act and CFTC rules because the non-financial entity exemption is only available if elected by the non-financial entity.

Example Three: A trader from the Ocean Waves Baking Company decides that entering into an interest rate swap that takes the position that interest rates will increase would be a good idea in the current economic climate and that, though speculative in nature, it has a good chance of being profitable for the Ocean Waves Baking Company. He calls his colleague at Mega Bank and says that he elects to not clear the swap since Ocean Waves Baking Company is a non-financial entity.

Result: This violates the Commodity Exchange Act and CFTC rules because the non-financial entity, Ocean Waves Baking Company, would not be entering into the swap to hedge risk.

In order to determine whether a counterparty claiming eligibility to use an exemption from clearing is indeed eligible, swap dealers and major swap participants rely on direct representations from the non-financial entity counterparty, usually in questionnaire form. These can be exchanged directly or, more commonly, are exchanged automatically through an online system operated by IHS Markit (a financial information platform) known as "ISDA Amend."[42] We discuss this in chapter 12, section F.

4. Public Policy Motivations

Clearing is a double-edged sword. Clearing reduces the risk of credit default inherent in a bilateral transaction. Instead of two parties to a swap facing each other and each bearing the risk that the other will not perform, in a cleared swap each party faces the clearinghouse, a highly creditworthy central counterparty with an extremely low probability of default. Clearinghouses are capitalized, their obligations are guaranteed by their members, and their members are required to collateralize exposures the derivatives clearing organization has to them.

On the other hand, clearinghouses concentrate risk in a handful of clearinghouses. A default or failure of a clearinghouse, due to the high concentration of risks therein, could be catastrophic.

Ben S. Bernanke, *Clearinghouses, Financial Stability, and Financial Reform*

2011 Financial Markets Conference, Stone Mountain, Georgia (Apr. 4, 2011)
available at http://www.federalreserve.gov/newsevents/speech
/bernanke20110404a.htm

I am pleased to speak once again at the Federal Reserve Bank of Atlanta's Financial Markets Conference. . . .

Tonight I would like to discuss post-crisis reform as it relates to a prominent part of our financial market infrastructure — namely, clearinghouses for payments, securities, and derivatives transactions. . . .

[V]irtually all clearinghouses perform certain basic functions. Notably, by centralizing and standardizing specific classes of financial transactions, clearinghouses reduce the costs and operational risks of clearing and settlement among multiple market participants. In many cases they also act as a guarantor of transactions — the

---

42. *See* IHS Markit, *Counterparty Manager*, https://ihsmarkit.com/products/counterparty-manager.html.

counterparty to every trade—thereby helping to reduce counterparty credit and liquidity risks. However, the flip side of the centralization of clearing and settlement activities in clearinghouses is the concentration of substantial financial and operational risk in a small number of organizations, a development with potentially important systemic implications. Because the failure of, or loss of confidence in, a major clearinghouse would create enormous uncertainty about the status of initiated transactions and, consequently, about the financial positions of clearinghouse participants and their customers, strong risk management at these organizations as well as effective prudential oversight is essential. . . .

The first important clearinghouse in the United States . . . was founded by New York City's commercial banks in 1853 to streamline the clearing and settling of checks. . . .

In the case of exchange-traded derivatives, the significant benefits of clearinghouses . . . became apparent over time. The Chicago Board of Trade (CBOT), now part of the CME Group, was established in 1848. After various experiments to manage the paperwork associated with growing trading volumes, the CBOT established a clearinghouse in 1883. Although the role of the clearinghouse was initially limited, it significantly reduced back-office work and the amount of funds and credit needed by its members.[43] In 1925, the members of the CBOT set up a full-fledged and independent central counterparty—The Board of Trade Clearing Corporation, now called The Clearing Corporation—to provide the guarantee and settlement functions that are familiar today. . . .

As clearinghouses developed, their resilience—in particular, their ability to manage their liquidity and ensure the integrity of transactions under stressed conditions—was tested by financial shocks and crises. . . . [T]hese episodes warn us to remain vigilant and to guard against complacency; complexity and change in the financial system will continue to present new challenges to stability, as they have in the past. . . .

Overall, the historical record shows that clearinghouse arrangements have generally withstood even severe crises. This solid performance reflects good planning and sound institutional structures but also some degree of good luck. . . . Clearly, if we do not want to put all our trust in continued good fortune, we will have to continue to be proactive in identifying and remedying weaknesses in these critical infrastructures. . . .

Broadly speaking, the recent financial reform legislation bears on the future structure and role of clearinghouses in two different ways. First, it aims to increase the resilience of these critical institutions against severe financial shocks, the issue that I have emphasized thus far. Second, it also encourages the greater development and use of clearinghouses to address weaknesses identified in other parts of the

---

43. [N. 7] *See* The Clearing Corporation (2011), *A History: Trusting, Growing, Leading, Clearing* (Chicago: Board of Trade Clearing Corporation).

financial system. Of course, increased reliance on clearinghouses to address problems in other parts of the system increases further the need to ensure the safety of clearinghouses themselves. As Mark Twain's character Pudd'nhead Wilson once opined, if you put all your eggs in one basket, you better watch that basket.

The theme of expanded use of clearinghouses as a tool to address other problems in the system is perhaps best illustrated by the derivatives provisions of the Dodd-Frank Act. Prior to the crisis, some of the same economic forces that had led to the development of clearinghouses for other instruments were already pushing industry participants toward greater use of clearinghouses for OTC derivatives transactions. For example, as one response to the growth of the market for interest rate swaps in the early 1990s, a clearinghouse was created in London in 1999 that, by the onset of the financial crisis, was handling a major portion of interdealer activity in those swaps. Also, in the years leading up to the crisis, the Federal Reserve Bank of New York initiated joint efforts with other regulators and market participants to improve clearing arrangements for credit default swaps. However, for several reasons, the willingness of market participants to move all derivatives transactions to clearinghouses was limited. Notably, many believed that the standardization of derivatives contracts that is needed for multilateral clearing imposed too high a cost on end users with needs for customized arrangements. Market participants also were concerned that the establishment of clearinghouse guarantees might require implicit subsidies from clearinghouse members with stronger credit to those with weaker credit.

These calculations, however, were substantially changed by the galvanizing events of 2008, notably the development of large and uncertain counterparty credit risks in many bilateral derivatives agreements. On the heels of the crisis, the Group of Twenty countries endorsed a policy of mandatory central clearing for standardized OTC derivatives. The aim was to reduce systemic risk in the financial system more broadly as well as to improve the transparency of the OTC derivatives markets. In the United States, title 7 of the Dodd-Frank Act incorporated a mandatory clearing policy for standardized derivatives. Other major countries are following suit. In the spirit of keeping a close eye on the basket, as dependence on clearinghouses grows, private-sector participants and regulators will need to review risk-management and member-default procedures for financial market utilities to ensure that they meet high standards of safety. . . .

What was once a landscape of numerous, separate clearinghouses that operated largely independently from one another has now become dominated by fewer and larger clearinghouses supporting more integrated markets and consolidated, global financial firms. Moreover, the same globally active banks participate in all of the major clearinghouses, and the major clearinghouses often rely on similar sets of banks for payment services, funding, settlement, and emergency liquidity. In such a world, problems at one clearinghouse could have significant effects on others, even in the absence of explicit operational links. The need for strong risk management and oversight will only increase as we go forward. . . .

Given the growing interdependencies among clearinghouses, along with the new mandates for central clearing, now is a good time to reflect on the lessons of the recent crisis and consider whether further improvements are possible.

For more than a century, financial stability has depended on the resilience under stress of clearinghouses and other parts of the financial infrastructure. As we rely even more heavily on these institutions in the United States and around the world, we must do all that we can to ensure their resilience, even as our financial system continues to evolve rapidly and in ways that we cannot fully predict. In short, I think Pudd'nhead Wilson would agree that that is one important basket.

Why Is Clearing Mandatory?

If clearing is inherently risk-reducing, one might be tempted to wonder why it has been made compulsory for many swap transactions instead of being practiced voluntarily by market participants.

Indeed, research by Darrell Duffie and Haoxiang Zhu[a] indicates that clearing may increase risk if different clearinghouses are used to clear different categories of derivatives. This is because of close-out netting, a concept we discuss in chapter 12, section E.1. Close-out netting reduces overall exposures by combining exposures across a broad set of transactions to benefit from offsets. If clearing is fragmented, this netting benefit is substantially reduced, thereby increasing exposures.

Also, to the extent more swaps are required to be mandatorily cleared, the remaining swaps an entity has that are uncleared have a diminishing pool of transactions to net. The exposure for those remaining uncleared swaps increases compared to their exposures before due to the smaller pool of transactions against which offsets can be made.

[a] Darrell Duffie and Haoxiang Zhu, *Does a Central Counterparty Reduce Counterparty Risk?*, Review of Asset Pricing Studies, v. 1, no. 1, p. 74 (2011).

C. Swap Execution Facilities and the On-Facility Trading Requirement

The Commodity Exchange Act requires that all swaps required to be cleared also be transacted on a designated contract market or swap execution facility *unless* neither facility "makes the swap available to trade. . . ."[44] Swap execution facilities, therefore, like designated contract markets, are an essential part of the derivatives market.

---

44. Commodity Exchange Act § 2(h)(8).

Further below we assess how it is determined whether a swap is made available to trade. Immediately below we examine swap execution facilities themselves.

1. Swap Execution Facilities Generally

The on-facility trading requirement for swaps in the Commodity Exchange Act is satisfied if a swap is traded on a designated contract market or a swap execution facility. We are familiar with designated contract markets from chapter 5. Swap execution facilities are a creation of the Dodd-Frank Act. The Dodd-Frank created the swap execution facility registration category while simultaneously abolishing its precursors. Its precursors were the first efforts to have trading facilities for swaps, derivatives transaction execution facilities, exempt commercial markets, and exempt boards of trade.[45]

a. Public Policy Motivation

As with much of the Dodd-Frank swaps regulatory regime, a paramount principle of the on-facility trading requirement is to obtain greater market transparency. As we will see below, the requirement to trade specified swap categories on a facility is paired with public reporting requirements.

Gary Gensler, *Remarks of Chairman Gary Gensler at Swap Execution Facility Conference: Bringing Transparency and Access to Markets*

available at http://www.cftc.gov/pressroom/speechestestimony/opagensler-152

... For the first time, all swaps market participants have access to compete. For the first time, all — and that means dealers and non-dealers alike — benefit from transparency.

Since the time of Adam Smith and The Wealth of Nations, economists have consistently written that transparency and open access to markets benefits the broad public and the overall economy.

When markets are open and transparent, markets are more efficient, competitive, and liquid, and costs are lowered for companies and their customers.

President Roosevelt understood this when he asked Congress during the Great Depression to bring transparency, access and competition to the commodities and securities markets. ...

---

45. They were abolished by sections 723 and 734 of the Dodd-Frank Act. *See also* CFTC, *Repeal of the Exempt Commercial Market and Exempt Board of Trade Exemptions*, 80 Fed. Reg. 59575 (Oct. 2, 2015) and CFTC, *Adaptation of Regulations to Incorporate Swaps*, 77 Fed. Reg. 66288, 66301 (Nov. 2, 2012).

The swaps market emerged nearly 50 years later, but remained dark and closed until just last year. Lacking transparency and common-sense rules of the road, the swaps market contributed to the 2008 crisis. . . .

Bright lights now are shining on the swaps market. Transparency is shining both prior to and after a trade. . . .

The playing field has been leveled through transparency, impartial access, central clearing and straight-through processing. Asset managers, pension funds, insurance companies, community banks and all market participants are gaining benefits that until recently only swap dealers had. . . .

Congress said that [swap execution facilities ("SEFs")] . . . are to provide market participants with impartial access to the market.

Consistent with Congress' direction, the Commission's final SEF rules . . . are clear. Impartial access is about allowing market participants to "compete on a level playing field." . . .

[T]he Commission's regulations require SEFs to provide all its market participants — dealers and non-dealers alike — with the ability to fully interact on order books or request-for-quote (RFQ) systems.

SEFs are required to provide dealers and non-dealers alike the ability to view, place or respond to all indicative or firm bids and offers, as well as to place, receive, and respond to RFQs. . . .

Further, SEFs must provide to all eligible contract participants (ECPs) market services, including quote screens and similar pricing data displays. . . .

Dodd-Frank reforms truly are about bringing greater access to these markets. Reforms really are about allowing multiple market participants to meet and transact with multiple market participants. . . .

Congress was also clear that transparency must shine on the swaps market both before and after a trade.

When light shines on a market, the economy and public benefit. . . .

The price and volume of each swap transaction can be seen as it occurs. This post-trade transparency spans the entire market, regardless of product, counterparty, or whether it's a standardized or customized transaction.

This information is available, free of charge, to everyone in the public. The data is listed in real time — like a modern-day tickertape — on the websites of each of the three swap data repositories.

Regulators also gained transparency into the details on each of the 1.8 million transactions and positions now in data repositories. The data repositories, swap dealers and SEFs, though, need to do more to ensure that the data flowing into the data repositories is accurate; consistent; and able to be readily sorted, filtered, and aggregated. . . .

To benefit the public, broaden competition, and promote transparency, Congress required that certain standardized swaps must be executed on a SEF or designated contract market (DCM). The trade execution requirement covers all swaps that are subject to mandatory clearing and made available to trade. . . .

Requiring trading platforms to be registered and overseen by regulators was central to the swaps market reform President Obama and Congress included in the Dodd-Frank Act. They expressly repealed exemptions, such as the so-called "Enron Loophole," for unregistered, multilateral swap trading platforms. . . .

––––––––––

The reference to the "Enron loophole" is to exempt boards of trade and exempt commercial markets, one of which was operated by Enron, an energy trading firm that infamously went bankrupt in 2001.[46] The "Enron loophole" was discussed in chapter 2, section E.1.b.

b. Definition

A swap execution facility is defined in the Commodity Exchange Act as a "trading system or platform in which multiple participants have the ability to execute or trade swaps by accepting bids and offers made by multiple participants in the facility or system. . . ."[47] The central feature, then, is the "multiple-to-multiple" nature of the facility. We discussed this concept in chapter 5, section B.1 in the context of what constitutes a trading facility generally. We revisit it here with some new examples.

> *Example One*: The Ocean Waves Baking Company sends out a request-for-quotes using an online system that shows selected dealers the swaps in which the Ocean Waves Baking Company would like bids.
>
> *Result*: This is not a "multiple-to-multiple" facility because, even though it is available to multiple offerors, the dealers, it only has one offeree, the Ocean Waves Baking Company.
>
> *Example Two*: Mega Bank decides to give its customers access to an online system whereby they can see what Mega Bank's bids or offers are for particular swaps.
>
> *Result*: This is not a "multiple-to-multiple" facility because, even though it has multiple offerees, the customers, it has only one offeror, Mega Bank.
>
> *Example Three*: Mega Bank and Wonder Bank decide that their customers will be better served if they jointly develop a platform to provide access to customers where the parties can see bids and offers.

––––––––––

46. They were abolished by sections 723 and 734 of the Dodd-Frank Act. *See also* CFTC, *Repeal of the Exempt Commercial Market and Exempt Board of Trade Exemptions*, 80 Fed. Reg. 59575 (Oct. 2, 2015).

47. Commodity Exchange Act § 1a(50).

Result: Although this may indeed better serve their customers, Mega Bank and Wonder Bank would be required to register their platform as a swap execution facility. This is because there are two offerors, Mega Bank and Wonder Bank, using the platform to potentially enter into swaps with multiple offerees, their combined customers.

The essence, then, of a swap execution facility is the provision of a multiple-to-multiple platform for trading swaps. Note that, such a platform can be, among others, electronic, telephonic, or in person.

2. Swap Execution Facilities as Self-Regulatory Organizations

a. Core Principles

Just as designated contract markets must comply with the "core principles" outlined in chapter 5, so must swap execution facilities. The core principles are similar in many respects. One major difference worth highlighting, though, relates to access to swap execution facilities. Though, just as with designated contract markets, there is a requirement to provide "impartial access,"[48] with swap execution facilities such access must be limited to "eligible contract participants," a definitional category we discussed in chapter 9, section E.[49]

Core Principles for Swap Execution Facilities
Commodity Exchange Act § 5h(f)

(1) . . . To be registered, and maintain registration, as a swap execution facility, the swap execution facility shall comply with . . . core principles described [herein,] . . . any requirement that the Commission may impose by rule or regulation. . . . [and] shall have reasonable discretion in establishing the manner in which the swap execution facility complies with the core principles. . . .

(2) . . . A swap execution facility shall . . . establish and enforce compliance with any rule of the swap execution facility . . . [and] establish and enforce trading, trade processing, and participation rules that will deter abuses and have the capacity to detect, investigate, and enforce those rules, including . . . to provide market participants with impartial access to the market. . . .

(3) . . . The swap execution facility shall permit trading only in swaps that are not readily susceptible to manipulation.

---

48. For impartial access requirements of designated contract markets, *see* 17 C.F.R. § 38.151(b) and, for swap execution facilities, *see* Commodity Exchange Act § 5b-3(f)(2)(B)(i) and 17 C.F.R. § 37.202(a).

49. Commodity Exchange Act § 2(e) and 17 C.F.R. § 37.702(a).

(4) . . . The swap execution facility shall . . . establish and enforce rules or terms and conditions defining, or specifications detailing . . . trading procedures [and processing and] . . . monitor trading in swaps to prevent manipulation, price distortion, and disruptions of the delivery or cash settlement process through surveillance, compliance, and disciplinary practices and procedures. . . .

(5) . . . The swap execution facility shall . . . establish and enforce rules that will allow the facility to obtain any necessary information to perform any of the functions described [herein and] . . . provide the information to the Commission on request. . . .

(6) . . . To reduce the potential threat of market manipulation or congestion, especially during trading in the delivery month, a swap execution facility . . . shall adopt for each of the contracts . . . position limitations or position accountability for speculators. . . .

(7) . . . The swap execution facility shall establish and enforce rules and procedures for ensuring the financial integrity of swaps entered on or through [its facilities]. . . .

(8) . . . The swap execution facility shall adopt rules to provide for the exercise of emergency authority, . . . including the authority to liquidate or transfer open positions in any swap or to suspend or curtail trading in a swap.

(9) . . . The swap execution facility shall make public timely information on price, trading volume, and other trading data on swaps to the extent prescribed by the Commission. . . .

(10) . . . A swap execution facility shall . . . maintain records of all activities . . . , including a complete audit trail, in a form and manner acceptable to the Commission for a period of 5 years. . . .

(11) . . . Unless necessary or appropriate to achieve the purposes of this chapter, the swap execution facility shall not . . . adopt any rules or taking [*sic*] any actions that result in any unreasonable restraint of trade . . . [or] impose any material anticompetitive burden on trading or clearing.

(12) . . . The swap execution facility shall . . . (A) establish and enforce rules to minimize conflicts of interest in its decision-making process; and (B) establish a process for resolving the conflicts of interest.

(13) . . . The swap execution facility shall have adequate financial, operational, and managerial resources to discharge each responsibility of the swap execution facility. . . . The financial resources of a swap execution facility shall be considered to be adequate if the value of the financial resources exceeds the total amount that would enable the swap execution facility to cover the operating costs of the swap execution facility for a 1-year period, as calculated on a rolling basis.

(14) . . . The swap execution facility shall

(A) establish and maintain a program of risk analysis and oversight to identify and minimize sources of operational risk, through the development of appropriate controls and procedures, and automated systems, that . . . are reliable and secure . . . [and] have adequate scalable capacity;

(B) establish and maintain emergency procedures, backup facilities, and a plan for disaster recovery . . . ; and

(C) periodically conduct tests to verify that the backup resources of the swap execution facility are sufficient to ensure continued —

(i) order processing and trade matching;

(ii) price reporting;

(iii) market surveillance[;] and

(iv) maintenance of a comprehensive and accurate audit trail.

(15) . . . Each swap execution facility shall designate an individual to serve as a chief compliance officer . . . [and the] the chief compliance officer shall . . .

(i) report directly to the board or to the senior officer of the facility;

(ii) review compliance with the core principles in this subsection;

(iii) in consultation with the board of the facility, a body performing a function similar to that of a board, or the senior officer of the facility, resolve any conflicts of interest that may arise;

(iv) be responsible for establishing and administering . . . policies and procedures . . . ;

(v) ensure compliance with [statutory and regulatory requirements applying to swap execution facilities] . . . ; and

(vi) establish procedures for the remediation of noncompliance issues found during compliance office reviews, look backs, internal or external audit findings, self-reported errors, or through validated complaints. . . .

In accordance with rules prescribed by the Commission, the chief compliance officer shall annually prepare and sign a [certified] report that contains a description of . . . the compliance of the swap execution facility with this chapter . . . [and] the policies and procedures, including the code of ethics and conflict of interest policies, of the swap execution facility. . . .

----

b. Rulemaking and Disciplinary Actions

A comparison to the core principles for designated contract markets discussed in chapter 5 will demonstrate that the core principles for swap execution facilities are very similar. This is not the only similarity. The CFTC's part 40 rules apply uniformly to all CFTC self-regulatory organization registrants, known as "registered entities."[50]

----

50. 17 C.F.R. pt. 40.

These are designated contract markets, derivatives clearing organizations, swap execution facilities, and swap data repositories.[51] The CFTC's part 40 rules govern rulemaking by registered entities and, for designated contract markets and swap execution facilities, the listing of products for trading. For a refresher on this, see chapter 5, sections C.2.a and C.4.a. And, just like any of the registered entities, as a self-regulatory organization, swap execution facilities can bring disciplinary actions against members and those trading on it.

3. On-Facility Trading Requirement

Whereas the CFTC or a derivatives clearing organization can initiate a mandatory clearing requirement, only a designated contract market or swap execution facility can initiate a determination that a swap that is subject to mandatory clearing is also "available to trade" and, therefore, pursuant to the Commodity Exchange Act,[52] must trade on a designated contract market or swap execution facility.[53] The factors that must be considered are designed with similar objectives—namely that there is a liquid available market—to those that must be considered before making a determination that a category of swaps is required to be cleared. The factors are:

1. Whether there are ready and willing buyers and sellers;
2. The frequency or size of transactions;
3. The trading volume;
4. The number and types of market participants;
5. The bid/ask spread; or
6. The usual number of resting (i.e., outstanding and available to be matched) firm or indicative bids and offers.[54]

There are two methods for a designated contract market or swap execution facility to make an "available to trade" determination. They are identical to the rulemaking process described in more detail in chapter 5, section C.2.a, and applicable to all registered entities.

The first is to self-certify that a category of swaps are available to trade. If preconditions are met, such as having already vetted the proposal to market participants, the self-certification is effective ten business days after submission to the CFTC unless the CFTC issues a ninety-day stay to solicit comments from the public.[55]

---

51. 17 C.F.R. § 1.3 (definition of registered entity).
52. Commodity Exchange Act § 2(h)(8).
53. 17 C.F.R. §§ 37.10(a)(1) and 38.12(a)(1).
54. 17 C.F.R. §§ 37.10(b) and 38.12(b).
55. 17 C.F.R. §§ 40.6(a) and (c).

The second is to submit the proposal to the CFTC without certifying that the proposal has already been vetted with market participants. The CFTC has forty-five days to review it, extendable in some circumstances for an additional forty-five days.[56]

Regardless of the method chosen, once the submission is approved, the determination is effective thirty days later.[57]

Swaps that are required to be traded on a facility are by definition a sub-set of swaps that are required to be mandatorily cleared since the on-facility trading requirement only applies to swaps that already must be cleared.[58] Therefore, a counterparty exempt from clearing is also exempt from on-facility trading requirements.

Currently, the only categories of swaps required to be traded on a designated contract market or swap execution facility are most fixed-to-floating USD interest swaps, some denominated in pound sterling or euros, and two credit default swaps referencing a commonly used index.[59]

There are three possible ways for swaps to trade on swap execution facilities:

Order Book: With an order book system all participants in the system can make bids and offers and see and accept other participants' bids and offers.[60]

Request for Quote: With a request for quote system a request can be sent from one requestor providing at least three parties the ability to bid.[61]

Block Trade: Trades meeting minimum size requirements can be privately negotiated.[62]

There is an exemption for "package transactions," i.e., two or more transactions where one of the transactions is a swap otherwise required to be traded on a facility and the transactions as a whole are contingent on one another and priced or quoted as one economic unit with nearly simultaneous execution.[63] Such transactions are not limited to these three methods of execution and can use any offered by the swap execution facility so long as one of the transactions in the package is: (1) a swap not required to be cleared; (2) a primary market bond issuance;[64] or (3) a swap subject to CFTC and SEC jurisdiction.[65] Additionally, all of the transactions, other than the

---

56. 17 C.F.R. § 40.5.

57. 17 C.F.R. §§ 37.12(a)(2) and 38.11(a)(2).

58. Commodity Exchange Act § 2(h)(8) and 17 C.F.R. § 36.1(b).

59. CFTC, *Swaps Made Available to Trade*, http://www.cftc.gov/idc/groups/public/@otherif /documents/file/swapsmadeavailablechart.pdf (Feb. 18, 2014).

60. 17 C.F.R. § 37.3(a)(3).

61. 17 C.F.R. § 37.9(a)(3).

62. 17 C.F.R. §§ 37.9(a)(2)(i) and 43.2.

63. 17 C.F.R. § 37.9(d)(1).

64. 17 C.F.R. § 36.1.

65. 17 C.F.R. § 37.9(d)(2)–(4). It is assumed that the references in this rule to "exclusive jurisdiction" of the CFTC are intended to solely refer to the CFTC's jurisdiction qua the SEC. The CFTC does not have exclusive jurisdiction over swaps not traded on a registered entity and, apparently unintentionally, this could lead to a broader interpretation of what is a "package transaction" than the CFTC perhaps intended.

swap otherwise required to be traded on a facility, cannot be: (1) U.S. Treasury securities; (2) future contracts; or (3) agency mortgage-backed securities.[66]

4. Operation of Market

The following case is useful for background on the operation of the swap execution facility market. Note that, as it is a motion to dismiss, the facts in the plaintiff's complaint are deemed true.

Tera Group, Inc. v. Citigroup, Inc.

2019 WL 3457242 (S.D.N.Y. July 30, 2019) (citations to briefs omitted)

RICHARD J. SULLIVAN, United States Circuit Judge Sitting by Designation

Plaintiffs Tera Group, Inc., Tera Advanced Technologies, LLC, and TeraExchange, LLC (collectively, "Tera") bring this action against twelve financial institutions (collectively, "Defendants"), alleging that Defendants conspired to "block [Tera's] electronic [credit default swap] trading platform . . . from successfully entering the market" in violation of the Sherman Act and state antitrust law. Tera also brings claims for unjust enrichment and tortious interference with business relations. Now before the Court is Defendants' joint motion to dismiss all claims. For the reasons stated below, the motion to dismiss Tera's Sherman Act claim and Donnelly Act claim is granted as to HSBC, Deutsche Bank, Goldman Sachs, Morgan Stanley, and Bank of America and denied with respect to the remaining Defendants, while the motion to dismiss Tera's unjust enrichment and tortious interference with business relations claims is granted as to all Defendants. . . .

A credit default swap ("CDS") is a widely-traded financial instrument that functions like a tradable insurance contract, deriving its value from the risk associated with a specified credit event. A CDS can be either single-name (based on a single debt instrument issued by one underlying reference entity) or a CDS index (referencing a basket of underlying single-name reference-entities). Together, Defendants control approximately ninety-five percent of the CDS market, with JP Morgan, Bank of America, and Citigroup together comprising forty percent of all CDS dealing in the United States. Defendants generate significant profit by creating and selling CDS contracts to the "buy-side," which includes mutual funds, insurance companies, hedge funds, and other investors.

As the exclusive market-makers for CDS, Defendants dictated the structure of the CDS market, establishing two distinct tiers. Defendants traded CDS among themselves using anonymous inter-dealer platforms and maintained exclusive access to the price at which CDS was trading. The buy-side, meanwhile, was relegated to trading exclusively through a "Request for Quote" ("RFQ") system — an opaque, over-the-counter protocol that kept information about CDS pricing solely in the hands

---

66. 17 C.F.R. § 37.9(d)(3)(i)–(iii).

of Defendants. Under the inefficient RFQ protocol, a customer who wanted to buy a CDS had to contact a Defendant directly, disclose their identity, specify the terms of the CDS they wanted, and then receive a price quote from that Defendant. According to Tera, this cumbersome procedure empowered Defendants to set CDS prices and create grossly inflated "bid/ask" spreads that generated massive profits. . . .

[The] Dodd-Frank [Act] sought to end the RFQ-only model by requiring CDS and other swaps to be traded on a regulated electronic exchange called a Swap Execution Facility ("SEF"), which would allow market participants to make bids and offers on CDS in the same manner that they would trade common stock. . . . Because customers could choose which swaps they wanted to buy or sell based on available competitive bids and offers prior to entering a transaction, the new system would promote pre-trade price transparency relative to the RFQ-only model. Dodd-Frank's other reforms to the swaps market included creating "post-trade" price transparency by requiring that (1) market participants promptly report the details of their transactions to a centralized recordkeeping entity known as a Swap Data Repository ("SDR"), (2) swap values be reported continuously for the duration of the trade, and (3) swap transactions be cleared through a central Derivatives Clearing Organization ("DCO"), which removed the risk of a counterparty defaulting. . . .

Under Dodd-Frank, regulation of the CDS market was divided, with the CFTC maintaining authority over CDS indices while the SEC regulates single-name CDS. The CFTC's SEF execution mandate went into effect on February 26, 2014 for CDS indices, which made up seventy-six percent of total CDS transaction volume in the first half of 2014. The SEC, meanwhile, "has yet to mandate SEF execution and central clearing" for single-name CDS. Nevertheless, a significant volume of single-name CDS have been executed on SEFs and centrally cleared through clearinghouses since 2013. . . .

Seeking to capitalize on the opportunity presented by Dodd-Frank's reforms, a group of experienced former Wall Street traders founded TeraExchange. Tera secured millions of dollars from outside investors and spent several years developing a CDS trading platform that used a central limit order book ("CLOB") to enable anonymous electronic trading among all market participants ("all-to-all trading"). Tera maintains that it was "the first SEF to offer an anonymous all-to-all CLOB to the CDS market." . . .

After the CFTC finalized its SEF registration rules, TeraExchange devoted resources to making its platform compliant and received a temporary SEF certification on September 9, 2013. . . .

Tera thereafter developed an "aggressive marketing plan," seeking liquidity from Defendants and other market participants such as inter-dealer brokers ("IDBs") and hedge funds, and garnering "overwhelming" market response. An April 2014 survey by IPC Systems Inc. reported that fifty percent of market participants surveyed stated that they had already connected or planned to connect to the TeraExchange platform, while *The Wall Street Letter* nominated TeraExchange for three of its 2013

Institutional Trading Awards. IDBs, banks, and large buy-side CDS trading firms were among the market participants that signed up to use TeraExchange, while the top CDS clearinghouses agreed to clear CDS and other derivatives executed on the platform. Many of Tera's prospective customers had signed end-user license agreements and were in "simulation" with the platform, meaning that "they were in the process of testing and integrating TeraExchange with their own systems." . . .

By late 2013, investors increased their estimate of TeraExchange's valuation to exceed $50 million, even before a single trade had taken place on the platform.

On June 13, 2014, the world's first anonymous swap transaction on any all-to-all CLOB was executed on TeraExchange.

Immediately afterward, according to Tera, Defendants "began working together to shut down TeraExchange." . . .

The next business day, June 16, 2014 — despite the fact that the trade had never been publicly announced — BNP Paribas, Citi, JP Morgan, and UBS "almost simultaneously called and told TeraExchange that they would not clear any trades executed on TeraExchange until they conducted an 'audit' of TeraExchange's Rulebook." Although many Defendants had previously expressed interest in trading on or providing liquidity to the platform, they too blocked trading on the platform pending a rulebook "audit," even though some had already been reviewing the document for lengthy periods. None of these audits were ever completed, and the rulebook, which was largely standardized and mirrored those of other SEFs, had already been reviewed by the CFTC, which granted TeraExchange a temporary certification. Other rationales given by Defendants for delaying or refusing to conduct business with TeraExchange included the need to review the end-user license agreement and other core documents. But while Tera promptly provided the requested documents, Defendants never completed their reviews and consistently refused to direct any of their CDS business to the platform or allow their buy-side customers to trade on TeraExchange. . . .

Tera also alleges that Defendants controlled the CDS clearing business in their capacity as owners of ICE Clear, the largest clearinghouse for CDS, and in their roles as the dominant clearing members at ICE Clear, CME, and LCH.Clearnet. As clearing members of CDS clearinghouses, Defendants were gatekeepers to the clearinghouse and also controlled the pre-trade mechanisms of clearing by providing pre-trade credit checks. Defendants allegedly leveraged this control over CDS clearing and took advantage of Dodd-Frank's central clearing requirement to carry out their boycott of TeraExchange by (1) using their internal clearing divisions, known as FCMs, to block buy-side customers from using the platform by refusing to participate in the pre-trade credit check process or clear trades for transactions executed on TeraExchange, and (2) quoting TeraExchange customers "obscenely high clearing fees" while simultaneously offering to clear similar trades for lower fees or for free if they traded on other SEFs that adhered to the RFQ protocol. . . . As a result, market participants began to "waver in their support for TeraExchange's platform" and were unable to find FCMs to clear their trades because of the alleged coordination between Defendants. . . .

Tera alleges that Defendants jointly used a variety of techniques to enforce their boycott and maintain the status quo in the CDS market. First, Defendants agreed to collectively insist on the practice of "name give-up," or post-trade name disclosure, as a means of surveilling who was conducting trades on all-to-all SEFs. Although name give-up was necessary in the pre-central clearing era to enable parties to manage counterparty risk, it no longer serves a practical purpose in the post-Dodd-Frank era. Whereas anonymous trading would have opened up the CDS market and encouraged competition, enforcing name give-up discouraged the use of all-to-all CLOBs and contributed to an information asymmetry, as buy-side customers were forced to reveal their trading positions, and thus elements of their trading strategies, to Defendants and other customers.[67]

Recognizing the importance of preserving name give-up, Defendants allegedly agreed to "keep the practice in place by making their provision of liquidity to a trading platform conditional on the use of the practice" and boycotting any platform that refused to require it. They also ensured name give-up by insisting on the use of a service known as MarkitWIRE, operated by MarkitSERV. . . . MarkitWIRE is a trade processing service that offers counterparties a "last look" at a trade, revealing their identities and permitting an opportunity to terminate the transaction. Buy-side firms expressed opposition to the use of MarkitWIRE because it is inefficient relative to straight-through processing and enables Defendants to control information flow and preserve the traditional market structure. Nevertheless, Tera alleges that numerous SEFs, including all the largest inderdealer SEFs, caved to this "collective pressure" from Defendants to adhere to name give-up, resulting in "no meaningful volume on the few order-book platforms built by SEFs to date." . . .

Though Tera had obtained commitments from numerous non-traditional liquidity providers and stood ready to inject increased price competition into the CDS market, the alleged collective boycott and pressure placed on IDBs, the buy-side, and other market participants starved the platform of the liquidity it needed to survive. No further trading occurred on TeraExchange after its initial trade on June 13, 2014. . . .

Section 1 of the Sherman Antitrust Act prohibits "[e]very contract, combination . . . , or conspiracy, in restraint of trade or commerce among the several States." 15 U.S.C. § 1. To plead a violation of Section 1, a plaintiff must allege facts showing (1) "a combination or some form of concerted action between at least two legally distinct economic entities," and (2) "that the agreement constituted an unreasonable restraint of [interstate] trade." *Capital Imaging Assocs., P.C. v. Mohawk Valley Med. Assocs., Inc.*, 996 F.2d 537, 542 (2d Cir. 1993). . . .

---

67. Note that post-trade name give-up in these circumstances is now prohibited. *See* 17 C.F.R. § 37.9(f).

To plausibly allege a conspiracy under Section 1, plaintiffs must set forth "enough factual matter (taken as true) to suggest that an [illegal] agreement was made." [*Bell Al Corp. v. Twombly*, 550 U.S. 544, 556 (2007).] . . . Thus, while there is no "probability requirement at the pleading stage," plaintiffs must plead "enough fact to raise a reasonable expectation that discovery will reveal evidence of illegal agreement." *Id.* . . .

Direct evidence of a conspiracy is not required. Plaintiffs may rely on "indirect or circumstantial evidence, that is, 'inferences that may fairly be drawn from the behavior of the alleged conspirators.'" *In re IRS*, 261 F. Supp. 3d 432, 461 (S.D.N.Y. 2017) (quoting *Anderson News, LLC v. Am. Media, Inc.*, 680 F.3d 162, 183 (2d Cir. 2012)). Typically, a "horizontal agreement among competitors, the sort of pact alleged here, is . . . based on claims of parallel conduct by the alleged co-conspirators." *Id.* at 461–62. "Examples of parallel conduct allegations that might be sufficient under *Twombly*'s standard include parallel behavior that would probably not result from chance, coincidence, independent responses to common stimuli, or mere interdependence unaided by an advance understanding among the parties." [*Mayor & City Council of Balt. v.*] *Citigroup*, 709 F.3d at 137 (internal quotation marks and citation omitted).

Yet, "as the Supreme Court held in *Twombly*, 'alleging parallel conduct alone is insufficient, even at the pleading stage.'" *In re IRS*, 261 F. Supp. 3d at 462 (quoting *Citigroup*, 709 F.3d at 136). Rather, to withstand a motion to dismiss, plaintiffs must also place the allegations "in a context that raises a suggestion of a preceding agreement, not merely parallel conduct that could just as well be independent action." *Twombly*, 550 U.S. at 557. Courts have interpreted this additional obligation as a requirement that plaintiffs plead "plus factors" or other circumstantial evidence that, combined with parallel conduct, demonstrate "circumstances under which . . . the inference of rational independent choice [is] less attractive than that of concerted action." *In re IRS*, 261 F. Supp. 3d at 463 (quoting *In re Ins. Brokerage Antitrust Litig.*, 618 F.3d 300, 323 (3d Cir. 2010)). . . .

Before turning to the parallel conduct and plus factors alleged by Tera, the Court considers three of Defendants' threshold arguments in favor of dismissing the Complaint: first, that the complaint constitutes impermissible "claim splitting;" next, that the conspiracy alleged by Tera is facially implausible; and, finally, that the Complaint engages in improper group pleading. . . .

As an initial matter, Defendants contend that Tera's claims should be dismissed in their entirety for violating a prohibition against "claim splitting." (Mem. at 38–43.) Defendants argue that because "plaintiffs have no right to maintain two actions on the same subject in the court, against the same defendant at the same time" (Mem. at 38 (quoting *Curtis v. Citibank, N.A.*, 226 F.3d 133, 140 (2d Cir. 2000))), the Complaint must be dismissed in light of its "striking overlap" with Tera's earlier complaint in *In re IRS* (*id.* at 43). The Court is unpersuaded. . . .

[T]he Court finds that no impermissible claim splitting has taken place here. While this case and *In re IRS* arise from substantially the same events, encompass many of the same defendants, and involve sometimes identical allegations in the pleadings . . . there are also key differences between the two cases. . . .

Defendants also argue that the conspiracy alleged by Tera is facially implausible, meaning it fails to "make . . . economic sense," *United Magazine Co. v. Murdoch Magazines Distrib., Inc.* 146 F. Supp. 2d 385, 401 (S.D.N.Y. 2001), or accord with "common economic experience," *Twombly*, 550 U.S. at 565. (*See* Mem. at 17.) But "[s]uch an argument presents a high hurdle in the context of a motion to dismiss, and a hurdle that is not crossed here," *Iowa Pub. Emps. Ret. Sys. v. Merrill Lynch, Pierce, Fenner & Smith, Inc.* ("*IPERS*"), 340 F. Supp. 3d 285, 312 (S.D.N.Y. 2018).

First, Defendants point out that Tera failed to allege that the Defendants boycotted four other CDS platforms, rendering the alleged conspiracy economically nonsensical. Yet Tera readily accounts for Defendants' decision to target its platform specifically by alleging that it was the first SEF to offer an anonymous all-to-all CLOB for CDS and that it was the only independent CLOB. . . . Thus, the failure to plead that Defendants boycotted *all* CDS platforms does not doom the Complaint at this stage. *See In re IRS*, 261 F. Supp. 3d at 472 (denying a motion to dismiss where complaint alleged Defendants boycotted three out of five platforms for all-to-all IRS trading).

Next, Defendants argue that the conspiracy is facially implausible because the alleged conduct is fully consistent with unilateral and independent decision-making. Defendants argue that Tera had too little trading volume to be attractive to Defendants, and that refraining from supporting Tera was consistent with the individual business goals of each Defendant because helping Tera become successful would have strengthened a threat to their own individual business profits. (*Id.*) But these arguments fall short of the "high hurdle" for establishing facial implausibility. . . .

Defendants next argue that Tera's allegations fail because they rely excessively on "group-pleading allegations directed at 'the Dealer Defendants' as an undifferentiated whole." Indeed, the Complaint is rife with homogenous group allegations. Of the seventy-four paragraphs in the Complaint that set forth factual allegations about Defendants' conduct, forty consist of allegations that are directed solely at the Defendants as a group without providing any examples or otherwise specifying a Defendant who engaged in the alleged acts.

Notably, as Judge Engelmayer recognized in *In re IRS*, not all group allegations are improper. . . .

Nevertheless, the Complaint's pervasive reliance on group allegations impacts the viability of Tera's claims because it results in a paucity of details linking certain of the Defendants to the alleged conspiracy. It is Tera's burden to set forth sufficient facts to establish that each Defendant, "in their individual capacities, consciously committed themselves to a common scheme designed to achieve an unlawful objective." *AD/SAT, a Div. of Skylight Inc. v. Associated Press*, 181 F.3d 216, 234 (2d Cir. 1999). At the pleading stage, Tera must provide each Defendant with "'fair notice of what the claim is and the grounds on which it rests,' including the factual connection of that defendant to the scheme and the identity of its alleged co-conspirators." *In re IRS*, 261 F.

Supp. 3d at 478 (first quoting *Anderson News*, 680 F.3d at 182; then citing *In re Foreign Exch. Benchmark Rates Antitrust Litig.*, 74 F. Supp. 3d 581, 594 (S.D.N.Y. 2015)). . . .

Yet the Court's duty to consider the Complaint as a whole in making the overall determination of whether Tera has plausibly pleaded a conspiracy does not supplant Tera's basic obligation to set forth facts connecting each individual Defendant to the conspiracy. . . . Accordingly, the Court will now consider each remaining Defendant in turn to determine whether Tera has alleged sufficient facts to establish the requisite connection to the alleged conspiracy. . . .

[After dismissing the claims against some of the defendants for insufficiently specific allegations, as] to Barclays, Credit Suisse, JP Morgan, BNP Paribas, UBS, and Citi, the Court will now analyze the parallel conduct and plus factors set forth in the Complaint to determine the viability of Tera's Section 1 claim. "Unanimity of action" among all the remaining Defendants "is not required;" rather, "[a]t the pleading stage, the issue is whether the inference of conspiracy, viewing the well-pled allegations holistically, is plausible." *In re IRS*, 261 F. Supp. 3d at 479. For the reasons stated below, the Court finds that Tera has adequately alleged parallel conduct and plus factors to survive Defendants' motion to dismiss. . . .

Tera argues that a conspiracy to boycott the TeraExchange platform can be inferred from parallel conduct by Defendants, in addition to circumstantial evidence and "plus factors" that indicate a prior agreement rather than mere parallelism. . . .

The Court finds that, viewed holistically, the Complaint adequately pleads parallel conduct that makes the inference of a conspiracy among the six remaining Defendants plausible.

Of the three "plus factors" previously recognized by the Second Circuit, the Court finds that one — a common motive to conspire — lends strong support to the inference of a prior agreement, and another — a high degree of interfirm communications — lends moderate support. Tera also pleads circumstantial evidence that gives further credence to the conspiracy claim. Tera has therefore adequately pleaded plus factors "which, when combined with parallel behavior, might permit a jury to infer the existence of an [illegal] agreement." *Citigroup*, 709 F.3d at 136 n.6. . . .

Viewed holistically, the Court finds that Tera has pleaded sufficient parallel conduct and plus factors to state a plausible Section 1 claim with respect to Barclays, Credit Suisse, JP Morgan, BNP Paribas, UBS, and Citi. The Defendants' motion to dismiss is therefore DENIED with respect to those Defendants. The Court now turns to the Defendants' motion to dismiss Tera's state-law claims. . . .

New York's Donnelly Act . . . was "modelled on" the Sherman Act and therefore "should generally be construed in light of Federal precedent. . . .

Because Tera's Donnelly Act claim therefore rises and falls with the Section 1 claim, the motion to dismiss is GRANTED with respect to HSBC, Deutsche Bank, Goldman Sachs, Morgan Stanley, and Bank of America, and DENIED with respect to Barclays, Credit Suisse, JP Morgan, BNP Paribas, UBS, and Citi. . . .

The Court next turns to Tera's unjust enrichment claim. . . .

Tera's unjust enrichment theory is too attenuated to state a claim. . . .

Finally, the Court turns to Tera's claim for tortious interference with business relations. Here, too, the Complaint asserts merely three boilerplate sentences and fails to identify the applicable state law. . . .

The Court agrees that the Complaint fails to state a claim for tortious interference with business relations. . . .

Accordingly, the motion to dismiss Tera's claim for tortious interference with business relations is GRANTED as to all Defendants.

D. Treatment of Swaps Compared to Treatment of Futures

1. Futurization

With the Dodd-Frank Act's swaps regulatory regime largely influenced by the existing regulatory regime for futures, questions have arisen as to what extent the CFTC is seeking to "futurize" swaps, i.e., have swaps trade as futures or in circumstances where a substantially similar regulatory structure and trading methodology exists to that operating in the futures market. Some market participants have alleged that the CFTC's swap execution facility rules were crafted in such a way as to create incentives for parties to trade on designated contract markets instead.

The main objection, the subject of the below litigation, is that CFTC rules effectively require derivatives clearing organizations to demand higher margin amounts for swaps executed on a swap execution facility than for a series of futures executed on a designated contract market that economically replicate the swap. This differential in margin incentivizes parties to trade on a designated contract market instead of a swap execution facility.

Bloomberg L.P. v. CFTC

949 F. Supp. 2d 91 (D.D.C. 2013)

Beryl A. Howell, District Judge.

This is a challenge to a regulation [by the CFTC] . . . which sets minimum liquidation times for swaps and futures contracts. The plaintiff Bloomberg L.P. ("Bloomberg") . . . alleges that, unless immediately enjoined, the Commission's regulation prescribing minimum liquidation times, when combined with other regulatory and market forces, will encourage the plaintiff's subscribers to migrate permanently to competitors' trading venues. . . . [A]s discussed below, the Court denies the plaintiff's application for preliminary injunctive relief and dismisses this case for lack of standing. . . .

This case is about how the CFTC regulates the trading of derivatives. . . .

Although derivatives can come in many forms, there are two categories of derivatives implicated in this lawsuit: "swaps" and "futures." . . .

[The Commodity Exchange Act (the "CEA") requires] futures to be traded on centralized exchanges known as "designated contract markets" ("DCMs") which are subject to a variety of regulatory requirements that ensure transparency and prudent risk management. For example, a DCM is required to "make public daily information on settlement prices, volume, open interest, and opening and closing ranges for actively traded contracts on the contract market." 7 U.S.C. § 7(d)(8). Specifically, DCMs are required to make information on prices, trading volume, and other trading information "readily available to the news media and the general public without charge, in a format that readily enables the consideration of such data, no later than the business day following the day to which the information pertains." 17 C.F.R. §§ 16.01(e), 38.451.

Additionally, every transaction executed on a DCM must be "cleared" through an entity called a "derivatives clearing organization" ("DCO"). . . .

[The] Dodd-Frank [Act] generally requires that all cleared swaps be traded on either a DCM or a new entity called a "swap execution facility" ("SEF"). Since the CFTC's rules regarding mandatory clearing and SEFs are still being phased in, however, large swaths of swaps continue to be traded [over-the-counter]. . . .

A transaction is "cleared" when a member of a DCO uses a novation to interpose itself between the two original counterparties to the derivatives contract, thereby assuming the credit risk of both counterparties. . . .

DCO members are generally large financial institutions who "invest capital that the clearinghouse can use to cover default losses," and in this way a DCO is "analogous to a mutual insurance company." Unlike a mutual insurance company, however, which charges premiums to the customers it insures, DCOs require their members to post a "margin" or a "performance bond," which acts as collateral against the possibility of default. When a trade is first cleared, the DCO collects an initial margin payment based on the amount of default risk assumed by the DCO, and then periodically (usually twice per day), the DCO will "mark positions to market" to ensure that "collateral reflects current market conditions." For example, if the price of a commodity goes down during the trading day, the buyer of a futures contract would be required to post additional margin "to offset the risk that a buyer might walk away from a futures contract in which the agreed-upon price now seems too high." . . .

Pursuant to . . . the rulemaking authority delegated by Congress in the CEA, the Commission published a Notice of Proposed Rulemaking ("NPRM"). . . .

The NPRM . . . proposed requiring DCOs to use liquidation times for this margin model that were: (1) "a minimum of five business days for cleared swaps that are not executed on a DCM," and (2) "a minimum of one business day for all other products that it clears." . . .

After considering this diverse array of public comments, the Commission published its final rule regarding minimum liquidation times. . . . *See* Derivatives Clearing Organization General Provisions and Core Principles ("Final Rule"), 76 Fed. Reg. 69,334 (Nov. 8, 2011) (codified at 17 C.F.R. pt. 39). This Final Rule [requires] . . . that a DCO must use (A) "[a] minimum liquidation time that is one day for futures and options," (B) "[a] minimum liquidation time that is one day for swaps on agricultural commodities, energy commodities, and metals," (C) "[a] minimum liquidation time that is five days for all other swaps," or (D) "[s]uch longer liquidation time as is appropriate based on the specific characteristics of a particular product or portfolio." . . .

As to the benefits of the Final Rule with regard to protection of market participants and the public, the Commission stated that the five-day and one-day minimum liquidation times were "consistent with existing requirements" and "reflect the risk assessments DCOs have made." In the Commission's opinion, the DCOs' determination that "these are the appropriate standards for these instruments" was "a reasonable and prudent judgment." At the same time, however, the Commission stated that "[a] minimum standard is designed to prevent DCOs from competing by offering lower margin requirements than other DCOs and, as a result, taking on more risk than is prudent." Related to this concern about a "race to the bottom," the Commission was also "concerned that a DCO may misjudge the appropriate liquidation time frame because of limited experience with clearing and managing the risks of financial swaps" in particular. In sum, prescribing minimum liquidation times was intended to "prevent DCOs from taking on too much risk." . . .

The Commission's Final Rule regarding minimum liquidation times went into effect on January 9, 2012. . . . On December 13, 2012, the Commission published a final rule regarding the categories of swaps that would be required to be cleared. . . .

A month and a half after this clearing requirement was published—and over fourteen months after the minimum-liquidation-time rule was published—the plaintiff sent a letter to the Commission, which raised "a serious concern . . . with the [Final Rule], and more specifically, with regulation 39.13(g)(2)(ii) [sic] which sets out the minimum liquidation time for financial futures and financial swaps." The plaintiff was interested in the Final Rule because it "operates the Bloomberg Professional® service, a leading privately held electronic service that, among other things, facilitates the trading and processing of swaps [OTC]." Bloomberg generates revenue from its swap trading platform by charging a monthly fee to those who subscribe to its Bloomberg Professional® service (also known as "Bloomberg terminals"), and thus Bloomberg does not generate revenue on a per-trade basis. In addition, Bloomberg "intends to operate a SEF in order to facilitate trading in the swaps market" and, to that end, "has already created a subsidiary that will operate the SEF, has drafted a rulebook for that SEF . . . , and has taken substantial steps toward creating the technological infrastructure for operating the SEF."

In its January 30, 2013 letter to the Commission, Bloomberg raised a number of objections to the minimum-liquidation-time rule, most of which focused on the so-called "futurization of swaps." Futurization, according to the plaintiff, refers to "a phenomenon by which futures products are designed to mimic the essential characteristics of a swap." More specifically, a swap can be "futurized" by "preassembling strips of futures contracts with aggregate cash flows that resemble swaps with the same size, tenor, and reset characteristics." The resulting financial product is often referred to as a "swap future." Bloomberg contended in its January 30, 2013 letter that the Commission's minimum-liquidation-time rule "on its face will be the strongest driver of the forced 'futurization' of economically equivalent financial swaps."

A major premise of this concern was that so-called "swap futures" have "the same risk characteristics as a swap," and thus, by the plaintiff's logic "[e]ither the swap executed on a SEF or futures exchange is being 'over-margined' by a factor of five, or the futures contract executed on a futures exchange is being 'under-margined' by a factor of five." The plaintiff was concerned that this scenario "could lead to clearinghouses absorbing more risk than they otherwise would have if they were permitted to margin cleared financial products that are economically equivalent using an appropriate risk-based metric regardless of the formal label given to the product." . . . Since Bloomberg believed "futurization" generally was "exactly the type of situation the Commission had in mind when it approved this language," Bloomberg "formally request[ed] that the Commission adopt an order that requires DCOs to impose the same margin requirements for financial swaps as they impose on financial futures that are economically equivalent and have a comparable risk profile."

On March 11, 2013, Bloomberg sent a second letter to the Commission — this time through counsel — which laid out its objections to the minimum-liquidation-time rule in more detail and stated for the first time that the Final Rule "threatens significant adverse effects for Bloomberg" that would be "irreversible." In its March 11, 2013 letter Bloomberg also sought more far-reaching relief from the Commission, requesting "that the Commission promptly take all steps necessary to stay the five-day minimum liquidation period for financial swaps, so that the same one-day minimum period applies to all cleared swaps and futures." Two days later, on March 13, 2013, Ananda Radhakrishnan, the Commission's Director of the Division of Clearing and Risk, responded by letter to Bloomberg. In that letter, Mr. Radhakrishnan stated that Bloomberg's January and March 2013 letters "have been referred to the Division of Clearing and Risk for consideration." After explaining the Commission's rationale for adopting the minimum-liquidation-time rule, Mr. Radhakrishnan concluded that Bloomberg's requests "will be given prompt and careful consideration," though "[t]o assist the Commission staff in considering them," Mr. Radhakrishnan requested that Bloomberg "provide any data, studies, or other supporting information" by March 29, 2013.

In response to the Commission's request, Bloomberg sent a third letter, through counsel, to the Commission on March 29, 2013, which attached "two sets of data for each trading day in February 2013." . . . Bloomberg concluded by stating that, since it had not received a response to its March 11, 2013 letter by March 19, 2013, as requested, it had "proceeded with preparing a federal court complaint, which [it] expect[ed] to file shortly."

Bloomberg filed its Complaint in the instant action eighteen days later on April 16, 2013. . . .

[O]n April 25, 2013, the Commission sent a letter responding to the data submitted by Bloomberg in its March 29 letter. In that letter, Mr. Radhakrishnan stated that the Division of Clearing and Risk had "identified a number of questions which require further data and analysis" before the Commission could come to a conclusion regarding Bloomberg's request to stay the five-day minimum liquidation rule. . . .

To summarize, the plaintiff's chain of injury goes as follows: (1) at least some DCOs will set lower liquidation times for financial swap futures than for financial swaps; (2) this lower liquidation time will result in lower margin requirements for financial swap futures than for financial swaps; (3) . . . entities will trade financial swap futures on DCMs rather than trading financial swaps on Bloomberg's trading platform; and, thus (4) at least some . . . [entities] will stop subscribing to Bloomberg's trading platform, causing Bloomberg to lose revenue. The actualization of this chain of events, however, depends on several assumptions about the behavior of third parties who are not before the Court. Most fundamentally, Bloomberg's injury rises or falls with the behavior of third-party DCOs, who are the entities actually regulated by the minimum-liquidation-time rule and are the ones who actually decide what liquidation times to set and how much margin to collect. Yet, inexplicably, Bloomberg has not put forth a single factual allegation that any DCO has set or intends to set liquidation times for financial swap futures at a level lower than that set for financial swaps.

Instead, Bloomberg . . . simply assume the worst-case scenario — DCOs will set liquidation times for financial swap futures at the minimum of one day, and will set liquidation times for financial swaps at the minimum of five days — without grounding their assumption in the actual behavior of DCOs. . . .

Due to the absence of any factual allegation that DCOs are setting or are imminently likely to set liquidation times for financial swap futures at a level lower than that for financial swaps, the plaintiff cannot establish a "'substantial probability' of injury as a result of the rule." . . .

[T]he Court concludes that the plaintiff lacks standing to assert its claims. . . .

There is some evidence that Bloomberg's central allegation that different regulatory treatment of futures and swaps incentivizes parties to choose futures over swaps has been shown to be correct. Using the open interest of futures and market value of interest rate and foreign exchange swaps as proxies for the relative sizes of the markets, the ratio of total market value of all such swaps to the open interest of all such futures was .77 by year-end 2013, dropped to .57 by year end 2016, and was down to .33 by year end 2019.[68] This means that, relative to futures transactions, off-

---

68. *See* Bank for International Settlements, *Exchange-Traded Futures and Options, by Location of Exchange,* http://stats.bis.org/statx/srs/table/d1, and Bank for International Settlements, *Global OTC Derivatives Market,* http://stats.bis.org/statx/srs/table/d5.1.

exchange swap transactions significantly decreased. What is not fully understood is to what extent exchange-traded swaps — as opposed to futures replacing what were formally traded as swaps — are responsible for the relative decline of off-exchange swaps compared to exchange-traded futures.[69]

2. Derivatives Clearing Organization Selection

In the futures trading model, as noted in chapter 6, the clearing function is embedded in the designated contract market because clearing is provided via either a division of the designated contract market or an affiliate of the designated contract market. With the regulatory model for swaps, the relevant swap being traded on a swap execution facility will have, as one of its terms, the derivatives clearing organization with which it will be cleared. The derivatives clearing organization is unrelated to the swap execution facility.

3. Processing of Trades

The clearing and on-facility trading requirements necessitate trade processing infrastructure. Trade processing infrastructure is the information technology and other systems that ensure a seamless process from entry into a trade through to the trade being cleared and reported.

truEX, LLC v. MarkitSERV Ltd.

266 F. Supp. 3d 705
(S.D.N.Y. July 18, 2017) (citations to court filings omitted)

Lewis A. Kaplan, District Judge.

This matter is before the Court on trueEX's and truePTS's (collectively, "plaintiffs") motion for a preliminary injunction to prevent MarkitSERV Limited and MarkitSERV, LLC (collectively, "MarkitSERV") from barring plaintiffs' access to certain of MarkitSERV's technology and software. . . .

This case centers around a business relationship between two entities operating in the world of interest rate swaps ("IRS"), a type of financial derivative. . . .

Until the enactment of the Dodd-Frank Wall Street Reform and Consumer Protection Act of 2010 ("Dodd-Frank"), IRS traded in unregulated over-the-counter ("OTC") markets. Most IRS were traded on a bilateral, principal-to-principal basis with the ultimate counterparty being the entity with which the trade was executed. . . . Dodd-Frank, however, introduced new regulatory requirements with the goal of increasing transparency in the OTC derivatives markets. . . .

---

69. Also, the comparison is based on statistics for the global market, not just the United States. It is difficult to obtain accurate historical data for the off-exchange derivatives market on a national basis due to its global nature and the absence, until recently, of trade reporting requirements.

In Dodd-Frank, Congress mandated that certain IRS trade only on platforms called swap execution facilities ("SEFs"). In response, many trade execution platforms sought to and did register as SEFs in order to fill the new role created by Dodd-Frank. An SEF is a trading platform regulated by the Commodity Futures Trading Commission that provides pre-trade information (*i.e.*, bids and offers) and an execution mechanism for swap transactions. A buy-side participant can use an SEF to transmit to multiple dealers on the platform requests for quotes of offers to sell IRS having particular terms. If the buy-side participant finds a willing dealer, the SEF provides a mechanism for the parties to execute their trade. There are three major SEFs that deal in IRS: TradeWeb, Bloomberg, and trueEX.

Dodd-Frank requires that IRS that *must* be traded on SEFs be "cleared," *i.e.*, "submitted to a central counterparty clearinghouse that functions as an intermediary between buyer and seller to reconcile transactions and reduce risk." In a cleared transaction, a clearinghouse steps between the counterparties — effectively becoming the buyer to the original seller and the seller to the original buyer. It processes the transaction, guarantees completion, and remains a part of the trade throughout its life cycle. In the United States, the major clearinghouses are CME Group and London Clearing House.

Dodd-Frank requires also that SEFs report trade pricing and volume information to swap data repositories ("SDRs"), which provide central facilities for swap data reporting and recordkeeping. SDRs enable market participants to see trading data for all executed trades, which promotes transparency in the market. The largest SDR in the United States is the Depository Trust and Clearing Corporation ("DTCC").…

After two counterparties agree upon an IRS trade that is required to be cleared, details about that trade must be reported to four entities [:] … the clearinghouse that clears the trade, the two counterparties to the trade, and the SDR. Completion of that reporting is a key aspect of a process known as trade processing. In addition to reporting IRS trades to clearinghouses and SDRs, trade processing encompasses such tasks as "matching … buyer and seller records, confirming the terms of trades, allocating aggregated trades among a client's different subaccounts, and managing other life-cycle events such as trade amendments, assignments, and payments." The large majority of IRS post-trade processing is handled by MarkitSERV.…

MarkitSERV is an electronic trade confirmation network for OTC derivatives. It provides trade processing for "OTC derivative transactions across all major asset classes, including credit, equity, foreign exchange and interest rates products, including [IRS]." MarkitSERV does not, however, offer trade execution services. Rather, parties execute OTC derivative trades on other platforms, such as SEFs, and those platforms in turn send the transaction details to MarkitSERV for trade processing. MarkitSERV's clients include "asset managers, hedge funds, pension funds, fund administrators, dealers and inter-dealer brokers, prime brokers and futures commissions merchants [*sic*]," as well as clearinghouses, six reporting agencies, and thirteen SEFs. . . .

MarkitSERV is the sole provider of IRS trade processing for (1) IRS transactions between dealers, (2) cleared, direct trades that are not required to be traded on SEFs, and (3) uncleared swaps (a limited category of IRS that need not be cleared). Together, those three categories "make up approximately 92% of the overall IRS market, based on the notional values of trades." . . .

The only transactions for which MarkitSERV does not control every step of post-trade processing are trades between dealers and buy-side customers that are executed on the SEFs operated by Bloomberg, TradeWeb, and trueEX. Even for trades executed on SEFs, however, most market participants rely on MarkitSERV's trade processing method (discussed below) to ensure that their books and records are accurate and up-to-date. . . .

When customers choose MarkitSERV to perform trade processing, MarkitSERV "will simultaneously submit the trade to the clearinghouse for intermediation, to the two counterparties[,] and to the SDR using an automated workflow called 'straight-through-processing' [("STP")]." In order to process trades using STP, MarkitSERV has established direct communication lines to and application program interfaces ("APIs")[70] with its customers to facilitate "real-time updates of market participants' books and records." STP ensures that market participants' books and records "reflect current financial and risk exposures." For that reason, "STP facilitation is vital to dealers and buy-side clients." Over the fourteen years MarkitSERV has existed, it has set up some manner of direct connection to "hundreds of dealers and close to 2,000 buy side customers."

In addition to its own trade-processing services, MarkitSERV facilitates SEFs' trade processing through a "drop copy" workflow. For example, if a customer executes a trade on an SEF, it in some circumstances may elect to have the SEF process that trade too. When the customer chooses to use the SEF for trade processing, the SEF "delivers the trade details directly to the clearinghouse and SDR, and simultaneously gives (or 'drops') a copy of the trade to MarkitSERV, which then uses its network to redistribute the trade confirmation to the counterparties." Utilizing MarkitSERV's drop-copy service allows the SEF to process trades executed on its platform using STP without having to invest in its own direct communication lines — at least with respect to customers that already are connected to Markit-SERV's network. . . .

---

70. [N. 29] APIs "allow a programmer writing an application to instruct an operating system or another program to carry out specific tasks. In essence, [APIs] act as building blocks. When programmers have the [APIs], they can create software to complete tasks through the program providing the interfaces by putting the interfaces together. If programmers do not have the [APIs] they must completely recreate instructions for the tasks with original code." *Lantec, Inc. v. Novell, Inc.*, 306 F.3d 1003, 1008 n.3 (10th Cir. 2002) (citations omitted).

As discussed above, trueEX is an SEF for IRS trades that has been active since April 2014. In addition to trade execution, trueEX provides certain post-trade processing services to its clients. Like the other IRS SEFs, however, trueEX does not have direct communication lines to all of the entities that trade on its platform. Thus, in order to process trades using STP for clients with which it does not have a direct connection, trueEX requires electronic access to those clients' books and records through other means.

trueEX approached MarkitSERV to solve this STP connectivity problem. In due course, the parties entered into a contract, referred to as the Broker Terms Agreement ("BTA"), in which MarkitSERV agreed, among other things, to provide drop-copy service to trueEX. trueEX utilizes MarkitSERV's drop-copy workflow in a similar manner to the other SEFs, TradeWeb and Bloomberg — when two counterparties execute a trade on trueEX, trueEX submits the trade details directly to the clearinghouse and SDR and simultaneously drops a copy of the trade to Markit-SERV for redistribution to the counterparties. Unlike TradeWeb and Bloomberg, however, trueEX does not give its customers a choice in terms of trade processing. In other words, any customer that uses trueEX to execute its IRS trades also must use trueEX to process those trades.

In cases where trueEX has built a communication pipeline to and has an API with a trader, trueEX does not need to rely on MarkitSERV's network for STP. "Only if there is no pipeline to the trader does [t]rueEX rely on MarkitSERV's network to fill that gap and provide a 'drop copy' to the customer." . . .

In December 2015, trueEX announced that it was working on a new IRS trade processing business. trueEX's chief executive officer, Sunil Hirani, launched this new venture — truePTS — in June 2016. truePTS "seeks to process trades other than, or in addition to, trades executed on the [t]rueEX SEF." . . . According to Mr. Hirani, "truePTS will offer the same IRS trade processing services as MarkitSERV, but at a substantially lower rate and with faster and more innovative technology." Between August 2016 and April 2017, truePTS met with thirty-five different participants in IRS trading to discuss truePTS's purpose, functionality, and competitive advantage over MarkitSERV.

truePTS now "is still in the developmental stage." . . . According to plaintiffs, "truePTS can and will develop its own network [for STP facilitation]." But truePTS would have to rely on MarkitSERV's drop-copy workflow to process its customers' trades until it does. Accordingly, truePTS sought to enter into an agreement with MarkitSERV for STP facilitation on similar terms as trueEX. In January 2017, truePTS sent MarkitSERV a proposal outlining what such a relationship might look like. For the next two months, truePTS repeatedly inquired as to the status of the proposal. Although MarkitSERV informed truePTS that it was reviewing the request internally, MarkitSERV never provided a definitive response. . . .

Meanwhile, MarkitSERV concluded that trueEX "was seeking a fundamental shift in the nature of [their] relationship in order to facilitate the development of its new business," truePTS. In MarkitSERV's view, trueEX "sought to create a situation in which [t]ruePTS, acting through [t]rueEX's relationship with MarkitSERV, could use MarkitSERV's processing network to offer its own, competing trade processing service" — without making the financial and technical expenditures MarkitSERV did. MarkitSERV feared that truePTS thus could undercut MarkitSERV's pricing and appeal to customers by offering a lower price point. To prevent trueEX from "leverag[ing] its relationship with MarkitSERV for the benefit of its new competing business" — and, in turn, to thwart the competitive threat posed by truePTS — MarkitSERV notified trueEX that it was terminating the BTA effective May 14, 2017.

Needless to say, plaintiffs dispute MarkitSERV's characterization of the events leading to the termination of the BTA. In their view, MarkitSERV's termination was "a transparent effort to choke off . . . competition and preserve its monopoly." In any event, the parties negotiated over the next several weeks the future of their business relationship. . . .

After the parties were unable to reach a new agreement, MarkitSERV, on May 8, 2017, "advised approximately 19 customers that [it was] terminating [its] relationship with [t]rueEX as of May 15" — which, according to Mr. Hirani, "sow[ed] confusion and uncertainty" among trueEX's clients about the possible loss of STP connectivity. . . .

trueEX asserts that it "cannot survive as a business without connectivity to MarkitSERV's network." It claims that any dealer or buy-side client that uses MarkitSERV for STP will leave the trueEX platform if trueEX loses the ability to send drop-copy reports to MarkitSERV. Moreover, it contends, "the loss of drop-copy would . . . cause the dealers that provide liquidity to the trueEX platform to abandon trueEX. . . . An exodus of dealers would drain all liquidity from trueEX. And without that liquidity, trueEX simply could not function as a trading platform." . . .

The threat to truePTS is far simpler. . . . If trueEX shuts down, truePTS will fail as well because it "relies on trueEX for all of its staffing, support, and funding." . . .

Plaintiffs filed this action in response to MarkitSERV's May 8 announcement. trueEX and truePTS each assert claims for monopolization and attempted monopolization under Section 2 of the Sherman Act, while trueEX alone asserts also a claim for promissory estoppel under New York law. The Court has set an expedited schedule for the matter, with a trial on the merits to take place in March 2018.

Pursuant to a standstill agreement the parties entered into on May 10, 2017, the effective date of the BTA is tolled until July 24, 2017. Once the agreement is terminated, however, MarkitSERV will be free to cut off trueEX's access to its STP network. Plaintiffs have moved the Court for a preliminary injunction that would preserve the status quo — i.e., the BTA would remain in effect until trial. Plaintiffs contend that, without the Court's intervention, trueEX will go out of business before it has its day in court, a harm for which it could not adequately be compensated.

And without trueEX's support, truePTS "will die on the vine before it can become a viable business." . . .

For a preliminary injunction to issue [in this circumstance], the movant must establish "(1) 'irreparable harm'; (2) 'either (a) a likelihood of success on the merits, or (b) sufficiently serious questions going to the merits of its claims to make them fair ground for litigation, plus a balance of the hardships tipping decidedly in favor of the moving party'; and (3) 'that a preliminary injunction is in the public interest.'"[71] . . .

The historic purpose of a preliminary injunction is to maintain the *status quo* pending a full trial where all facts and arguments may be considered with adequate preparation and in their complete context. . . . [T]his is a case in which full and expanded consideration is essential. At a minimum, there are serious questions going to the merits. In the circumstances, the balance of hardships tips decidedly in trueEX's favor. . . . [P]laintiffs' motion for a preliminary injunction . . . is granted with respect to trueEX. It is denied, however, with respect to truePTS, principally because truePTS has not shown any likelihood of success . . . [because it has no pre-established business relationship with MarkitSERV, an important factor in its antitrust claims].

It is important to recognize that the Court is dealing here only with a preliminary injunction the purpose of which is to preserve the status quo pending trial. The Court already has raised with the parties the question whether trueEX, were it to prevail, would be entitled to a permanent injunction requiring MarkitSERV to continue to deal with it in perpetuity in the manner it did prior to the termination notice, which would be a very different matter. . . .

In all the circumstances, defendants MarkitSERV Limited and MarkitSERV, LLC be and they hereby are enjoined and restrained, pending hearing and determination of the action, from directly or indirectly terminating the BTA or discontinuing the provision of drop-copy service to plaintiff trueEX, LLC.

No bond is required because the Court finds that there is no likelihood of harm to defendants. . . .

This case demonstrates the importance of technology in modern trading. Due to the complexity of swap processing and the importance of having a critical mass of onboarded customers, it also demonstrates the challenges of maintaining a competitive framework for the provision of these services.

---

71. [N. 84] *N.Y. ex rel. Schneiderman v. Actavis PLC*, 787 F.3d 638, 650 (2d Cir.) . . .

E. Reporting Requirements and Swap Data Repositories

1. Reporting Requirements

There are regulatory and public reporting requirements for swaps cleared and traded on swap execution facilities.[72] The objective of these reporting requirements is "to enhance transparency and price discovery."[73] Below we analyze the reporting requirements for swaps that are cleared and traded on a swap execution facility. In chapter 12, we evaluate reporting requirements for such swaps when not traded on a swap execution facility.

a. Real-Time Public Reporting

Swap execution facilities are required to report swap transaction and pricing data to a swap data repository for dissemination to the public "as soon as technologically practicable."[74] The public reports contain the pricing and volume of each trade and exclude the identities of the parties, so that parties may maintain anonymity.[75] It is required to be in a format using sixty-four standardized reporting fields, some of which only apply to specific categories of swaps.[76] For block trades and large notional off-facility swaps, reporting delays ranging from fifteen minutes to twenty-four hours are permitted, depending on the counterparties and product.[77] These delays are intended to provide enough time, assuming one of the parties may seek to hedge the large trade it entered into, to obtain hedges without other market participants having advance knowledge of upcoming hedging needs and trading on such knowledge.

b. Regulatory Reporting Requirements

There is other information that, though not publicly reportable, the CFTC is able to access in its role as regulator. As with the real-time public reporting requirements, parties are required to report this information to a swap data repository, which then holds the data to which the CFTC has access.

---

72. Or, theoretically, a designated contract market. Since no swaps currently trade on designated contract markets, we will proceed exclusively referencing swap execution facilities.

73. 17 C.F.R. § 43.1(a).

74. 17 C.F.R. § 43.3(b)(1). In the rare circumstance that a swap is given up for clearing and has not already been reported by one of the parties, if traded off-facility, or a designated contract market or swap execution facility, if traded on-facility, the derivatives clearing organization has the reporting requirement. *See* 17 C.F.R. § 43.3(a)(5).

75. 17 C.F.R. § 43.4(c). *See also* Commodity Exchange Act § 2(a)(13)(E)(i).

76. 17 C.F.R. pt. 43 app. A.

77. 17 C.F.R. §§ 43.5 and 43.6.

Two categories of data must be reported:

Creation Data: These are all of the relevant terms agreed by the parties. It includes the sixty-four fields previously reported for the real-time public reporting and, in total, uses 128 standardized reporting fields, some of which, as was the case with real-time reporting, only apply to specific categories of swaps.[78] It must be reported by the swap execution facility to a swap data repository of its choosing[79] by the end of the business day following the date on which the trade was executed.[80] The accuracy of data must be periodically verified by comparing existing reported trade details with the swap data repositories' records.[81]

Continuation Data: Continuation data requires reporting of life cycle events, i.e., changes to the previously reported swap data. For cleared swaps, the life cycle events are required to be reported to a swap data repository by the derivatives clearing organization.[82] For uncleared swaps, whether traded on a swap execution facility or not, such responsibility will fall to the parties to the transaction.[83]

c. Large Trader Reporting for Physical Commodity Swaps

Derivatives clearing organizations must periodically report to the CFTC information on some swaps referencing physical commodities.[84] Swaps within the scope of reporting are those settled in full or in part on the price of a specified list of forty-six physical commodity futures contracts traded on futures exchanges (or some commodity indices) or the price of a commodity for physical delivery in the location specified in the relevant futures contract. The report must be grouped by clearing members' proprietary accounts and each of their customer accounts.

2. Swap Data Repositories

Swap data repositories are a category of registrant created by the Dodd-Frank Act. Perhaps an oddity of swap reporting is that different parties report different sets of data to a swap data repository. A dispute arose over whether such swap data repository should, regardless of the reporting party, be whichever swap data repository the swaps were originally reported to or whether each reporting party should be able to choose the swap data repository to which it reports required data. Originally the CFTC had taken the position that each reporting party should be able

---

78. 17 C.F.R. pt. 45 app. 1.

79. 17 C.F.R. § 45.3(f)(1).

80. 17 C.F.R. § 45.3(a).

81. 17 C.F.R. § 45.14(b).

82. 17 C.F.R. § 45.4(b).

83. 17 C.F.R. § 45.4(c).

84. 17 C.F.R. § 20.3.

to choose the swap data repository — this changed after the Chicago Mercantile Exchange filed a lawsuit.[85] The CFTC reversed its position, the Chicago Mercantile Exchange dropped its lawsuit,[86] and The Depository Trust & Clearing Corporation sued the CFTC.

DTCC Data Repository (U.S.) LLC v. CFTC

25 F. Supp. 3d 9 (D.D.C. 2014)

Amy Berman Jackson, United States District Judge. . . .

Plaintiffs, The Depository Trust & Clearing Corporation ("DTCC") and DTCC Data Repository (U.S.) LLC ("DDR"), challenge three separate but interrelated actions taken by the Commission, all of which relate to the Commission's new requirements for swaps. Defendants have moved to dismiss all but one count of the amended complaint. . . .

[The] Dodd-Frank [Act] requires that most swaps be "cleared" by a derivatives clearing organization ("DCO"). DCOs are regulated by the Commission. In the clearing process, a DCO substitutes its own credit for the credit of the original parties to a swap, thereby reducing risk and assuring the financial integrity of a swap transaction. To that end, the Commission requires DCOs to maintain significant financial resources. The Commission also oversees DCOs in a variety of other ways, including by requiring them to submit changes to their internal rules for review.

Dodd-Frank also requires that data about swaps be reported to new entities called "registered swap data repositories" ("SDRs"), which are also regulated by the Commission. This reporting requirement is intended to increase transparency by providing data both to the public and to regulators. The data to be reported includes data about the creation and confirmation of swaps. It also includes "continuation" data, which encompasses any changes made to the terms of a swap over its lifetime, including clearance by a DCO. . . .

According to the amended complaint, plaintiff DDR is the only SDR that is not affiliated with a derivatives clearing organization, or DCO.

This litigation centers on the question of whether it is lawful for the Commission to permit DCOs to require that cleared swap data be reported to their affiliated, or "captive," SDRs. Plaintiffs believe that the Commission has violated the letter and spirit of Dodd-Frank and its own regulations by failing to prohibit what they characterize as "anticompetitive tying arrangements" between DCOs and their captive SDRs. Plaintiffs allege that these arrangements elbow any independent SDRs (that is, plaintiff DDR) out of the marketplace and reduce market participant choice.

---

85. Compl., *Chicago Mercantile Exchange Inc. v. CFTC*, No. 1:12-cv-01820 (D.D.C. Nov. 8, 2012). The Depository Trust & Clearing Corporation intervened on the CFTC's behalf. *See* Mot. to Intervene as a Def., *Chicago Mercantile Exchange Inc. v. CFTC*, No. 1:12-cv-01820 (D.D.C. Nov. 12, 2012).

86. Notice of Voluntary Dismissal, *Chicago Mercantile Exchange Inc. v. CFTC*, No. 1:12-cv-01820 (D.D.C. Nov. 29, 2012).

Plaintiffs also claim that permitting DCOs to require that cleared swap data be reported to their affiliated SDRs injures the public interest by imposing increased costs on market participants and by causing "duplication and fragmentation of swap data" that "[has] the potential to create significant systemic risk to the market as a whole." Finally, plaintiffs allege that the Commission has unlawfully reversed course, and that until November 2012, it had clearly expressed that it would not permit DCOs to require that cleared swap data be reported to their captive SDRs.

Plaintiffs allege that the CFTC violated the Administrative Procedure Act ("APA") and the Commodity Exchange Act in three separate ways in connection with its regulation of swaps. First, in Count I, plaintiffs challenge the revisions of the Commission's published answers to Frequently Asked Questions ("FAQs") that originally indicated that DCOs would be prohibited from requiring that cleared swaps data be reported to their captive SDRs. The three FAQs in question were withdrawn on November 28, 2012.[87] Plaintiffs claim that the withdrawal of the FAQs was the first step in the Commission's reversal of its position regarding the relationship between DCOs and SDRs.

Second, in Counts II and III, plaintiffs object to the Commission's approval of a new rule submitted by a DCO, the Chicago Mercantile Exchange, Inc. ("CME"), that would require that cleared swaps be reported to CME's captive SDR. CME is a wholly-owned subsidiary of the CME Group, a prominent derivatives marketplace....

Third, in Counts IV and V, plaintiffs challenge the self-certification of a substantially similar rule by ICE Clear Credit ("ICE"), another DCO.... Like [the CME Rule the ICE Rule] ... provides that all swaps cleared by ICE must be reported to ICE's SDR....

The Commission's withdrawal of three Frequently Asked Questions six weeks after issuing them is not a reviewable final agency action. At the outset, it is not clear that the withdrawal of the FAQs constitutes "agency action" at all, since "[a]n agency action is not final if it is only 'the ruling of a subordinate official.'" The FAQs plainly state that they reflect the views of Commission staff, not of the Commission itself. And the Commission asserts that its staff, not the Commission, made the decision to withdraw the FAQs at issue here. But the Court need not decide this issue because even if the withdrawal of FAQs could be considered an "agency action," it was not a "final" action, and therefore it is not reviewable.

To be final, an agency action must not be "tentative or interlocutory," and must "be [an action] from which 'rights or obligations have been determined' or from which 'legal consequences will flow.'" The withdrawal of the FAQs did not determine any rights or obligations, nor was it the culmination of a Commission decision-making process. Rather, the Commission or its staff withdrew the advice it had been posting online about a particular question, leaving that question open for later decision

---

87. [N. 1] Plaintiffs characterize the withdrawal of the FAQs as an action of the Commission itself, but the Commission insists that the withdrawal was a decision made by its staff.

by the Commission.[88] Indeed, the Commission's subsequent approval of [the] CME Rule . . . , which, as plaintiffs point out, expressly "supersede[d]" any prior conflicting guidance, underscores the fact that the withdrawal of the FAQs was not a final agency action. The withdrawal of the FAQs was merely "tentative or interlocutory," and is therefore not final agency action subject to APA review. . . .

Counts IV and V challenge the Commission's tacit approval of [the] ICE Rule . . . [b]ut that rule was approved by operation of law, and therefore the Court finds that Counts IV and V do not present any agency action or "failure to act" that would be subject to review under the APA. If Congress has "spelled out the legal effect" of agency inaction without articulating any limiting principle, that inaction is typically unreviewable. . . .

[T]he Court finds that since Congress has not articulated a limitation on the approval by operation of law of a rule like [the] ICE Rule . . . , there is no "discrete" agency action to review, and the self-certification . . . is not a reviewable "failure to act." . . .

The Court will grant defendant's motion to dismiss Counts I, IV, and V for failure to state a claim because plaintiffs have failed to allege any final agency action that would be reviewable under the APA. The Court will deny defendant's motion to dismiss Count III because it advances a unique legal theory and is not duplicative of Count II. Defendants do not challenge Count II in this motion, and so Counts II and III will remain in this case.

The Depository Trust & Clearing Corporation subsequently dropped its lawsuit challenging the CFTC's approval of the Chicago Mercantile Exchange's rule requiring swaps cleared by its associated clearinghouse to be reported to its captive swap data repository and the rule remained intact.[89]

Questions and Comments

1. Is centralized clearing a public good and does it reduce risk? What risks might it reduce and to what risks might the economic system be exposed by centralized clearing?

2. Examining the exemptions from clearing, what might be the public policy motivations for providing them? If clearing is a public good and reduces risk, why is it not applied to all counterparties?

---

88. [N. 2] Plaintiffs assert that until the withdrawal of the FAQs, the Commission had "repeatedly affirmed" that it would not allow a DCO to require that data be reported to its captive SDR. Even if true, this would not transform the withdrawal of the FAQs into a final agency action, because the withdrawal, on its own, was not a repudiation of the Commission's alleged prior statements.

89. *See* Jt. Stip. to Voluntary Dismissal, *DTCC Data Repository (U.S.) LLC v. CFTC*, 2014 WL 6669527 (D.D.C. Oct. 29, 2014) and Chicago Mercantile Exchange Rule 1001, available at http://www.cmegroup.com/rulebook/CME/I/10.pdf.

3. If clearing is beneficial and risk-reducing, why did lawmakers and regulators make it mandatory? Why wouldn't market participants act on existing incentives to clear trades?

4. Trades on designated contract markets are cleared using a derivatives clearing organization associated with the designated contract market. Trades on swap execution facilities use a different model in which the derivatives clearing organization is selected by the parties to the trade. Why might the Dodd-Frank Act have implemented this model instead of the pre-existing "captive" model used by designated contract markets?

5. Does the Dodd-Frank Act tend to incentivize futures trading on designated contract markets over trading on swap execution facilities as alleged in *Bloomberg v. CFTC*?

6. How can futurization be empirically demonstrated or disproven? What are available sources? In the absence of hard empirical data, what about anecdotal sources. For example, if you know someone in the derivatives industry, what about asking him or her for thoughts on futurization?

7. Swap processing has unique challenges because it requires the provider of swap processing services to have a relationship with both parties to the trade. This tends to lead to parties selecting an established service provider with many on-boarded relationships over a new startup without established customers. Moreover, due to its complexity, swap processing requires a significant upfront investment by a new entrant. In such an environment, in what ways can competition be fostered? Is a competitive framework the correct one? Is it better to have a single processor for each major category of swaps? Or even a regulated utility exempt from the antitrust laws? Consider not just what is best for now but also what is best for encouraging future technological innovation and fostering efficiency.

8. What are the public policy benefits to having the swap data repository where a trade was initially reported continue to be the swap data repository throughout such trade's life? What are the benefits to ensuring that swap data is "portable" among swap data repositories?

9. As a general matter, what are some of the pros and cons of publicly available swap trading data?

Chapter 11

Swap Entity Registrants

A. Background

1. Newly Created CFTC Registration Categories

In the immediately preceding chapters we have focused on elements of the new swap regulatory regime established by the Dodd-Frank Act, jointly summarized by the CFTC and SEC as:

a statutory framework to reduce risk, increase transparency, and promote market integrity within the financial system by, among other things: (i) providing for the registration and regulation of swap dealers and major swap participants; (ii) imposing clearing and trade execution requirements on standardized derivative products; (iii) creating recordkeeping and real-time reporting regimes; and (iv) enhancing the [CFTC's and SEC's] rulemaking and enforcement authorities with respect to all registered entities and intermediaries subject to [their] oversight.[1]

This chapter focuses on the first item enumerated in the above list, i.e., the two main categories of swap market registrants required to register with the CFTC, swap dealers and major swap participants, and the regulatory requirements that apply to them. The Dodd-Frank also created other new categories of registrants. Two of them, swap execution facilities and swap data repositories, we discussed in chapter 10. The others we will discuss in chapter 13 when we examine the security-based swap regulatory regime.

Before we discuss swap dealers and major swap participants, however, we will assess how the Dodd-Frank Act impacted the pre-existing registration categories of futures commission merchants, introducing brokers, commodity pool operators, and commodity trading advisors.

2. Treatment of Existing CFTC Registration Categories

As we recall from chapters 6, 7, and 8, the CFTC bears primary responsibility (shared with the National Futures Association) for the registration and regulation of futures commission merchants, introducing brokers, commodity pool operators,

---

1. CFTC, *Further Definition of "Swap Dealer," "Security-Based Swap Dealer," "Major Swap Participant," "Major Security-Based Swap Participant" and "Eligible Contract Participant"*, 77 Fed. Reg. 30596, 30596 (May 23, 2012).

and commodity trading advisors. The Dodd-Frank Act expanded this regime in two particularly significant ways discussed immediately below.

a. Swaps Trigger Registration

Before the Dodd-Frank Act, as a general matter, some engagement in the commodity futures or options market was necessary to require registration as a futures commission merchant, introducing broker, commodity pool operator, or commodity trading advisor. This could take the form of, for example, trading, intermediating, or advising. Swaps activities, in most cases, were not activities that could trigger registration as a futures commission merchant, introducing broker, commodity pool operator, or commodity trading advisor. This was primarily due to the Commodity Futures Modernization Act of 2000 which, as we recall from chapter 2, section D.5, prohibited regulation of most swaps activities.

After the Dodd-Frank Act, engagement in the commodity futures or options market *or the swaps market* could require registration as a futures commission merchant, introducing broker, commodity pool operator, or commodity trading advisor. (Foreign exchange and retail commodities require a separate regulatory analysis, discussed in chapter 14.)

Example One: Hot Swap Trades, LLC, accepts money from a broad base of investors, which it will pool in an entity it manages titled Swaps Only Return Pool and seek to obtain a return for the investors solely by entering into swaps.

Result Before the Dodd-Frank Act: Swaps Only Return Pool would not meet the definition of commodity pool (for a discussion on commodity pools, commodity pool operators, and commodity trading advisors generally, see chapter 6) because the money was not pooled for the purposes of trading commodity futures or option transactions. Instead, the money was pooled for the purpose of trading swaps. Activities of any nature in the swaps markets could not, in most cases, trigger registration as a futures commission merchant, introducing broker, commodity pool operator, or commodity trading advisor. Without Swaps Only Return Pool meeting the definition of commodity pool, Hot Swap Trades, LLC, would not have an obligation to register with the CFTC as a commodity pool operator.

Result After the Dodd-Frank Act: Swap trading activities are now included as one of the activities of a pool that would cause it to be deemed a commodity pool. With Swaps Only Return Pool meeting the definition of "commodity pool," Hot Swap Trades, LLC, subject to the exceptions discussed in chapter 7, section D, would be required to register with the CFTC as a commodity pool operator.

Example Two: The Cutting Edge Swap Advisory Company has a business where, for a percentage of market returns, it will provide customized advice to customers as to how to make money in the swap markets. The business is very successful, with over thirty customers.

Result Before the Dodd-Frank Act: The Cutting Edge Swap Advisory Company would not have an obligation to register as a commodity trading advisor with the CFTC because its advisory role did not relate to commodity futures or options transactions. Activities of any nature in the swaps markets could not, in most cases, trigger registration as a futures commission merchant, introducing broker, commodity pool operator, or commodity trading advisor.

Result After the Dodd-Frank Act: The Cutting Edge Swap Advisory Company would now, subject to the exceptions discussed in chapter 8, section E, be required to register with the CFTC as a commodity trading advisory because swap advisory activities are among the advisory activities that trigger registration as a commodity trading advisor.

Example Three: Swap Brokerage Services Inc. provides a service where, for a fee, when one party is looking to execute a particular type of swap, it will find a counterparty willing to take the other side of the trade.

Result Before the Dodd-Frank Act: Swap Brokerage Services Inc. would not have an obligation to register as an introducing broker with the CFTC because its brokerage role relates to swaps, not commodity futures or options. Activities of any nature in the swap markets did not, in most cases, trigger registration as a futures commission merchant, introducing broker, commodity pool operator, or commodity trading advisor.

Result After the Dodd-Frank Act: Swap Brokerage Services Inc. would now be required to register with the CFTC as an introducing broker due to its brokerage activities with respect to swaps.

b. CFTC Oversight of Swap Activities of Registrants

In addition to swap activities potentially triggering registration as a futures commission merchant, introducing broker, commodity pool operator, or commodity trading advisor, the CFTC now has explicit oversight of the swaps activities of existing futures commission merchant, introducing broker, commodity pool operator, and commodity trading advisor registrants.

3. Comparison to Historical Market Practices

In chapter 1, section C, we described the three main way traders interact with the market, i.e., as dealers (also known as marketmakers), hedgers, and speculators. These categories are useful to understand the framework that the Dodd-Frank imposes on swap traders.

Swap Dealers: The Dodd-Frank Act imposes an obligation on some parties engaged in swaps dealing or marketmaking activities to register as swap dealers.

Hedgers: Hedgers are largely treated as mere traders in the market, i.e., with no registration requirement. Any trader in the market, even if not required to be registered in some capacity with the CFTC, is subject to market regulations and prohibitions such as those against market manipulation discussed in chapter 15.

Speculators: The Dodd-Frank Act imposes an obligation on some parties engaged in speculative swaps trading with significant exposures to register as major swap participants.

The below case describes the roles of these participants in the off-exchange swap market. Note that it does not distinguish between "hedgers" and "speculators," treating them generically as "end users." Although the case describes the framework before the Dodd-Frank Act, swaps which are uncleared today trade largely as described with the addition of the registration and other requirements, such as trade reporting, discussed in this chapter and the following chapter.

Bank One Corporation v. Commissioner of Internal Revenue
120 T.C. 174 (Tax 2003)

... Those who use financial derivatives in general can identify, isolate, and manage separately the fundamental risks and other characteristics which are bound together in traditional financial instruments. In addition to increasing the range of financial products available, financial derivatives have fostered more precise ways of understanding, quantifying, and managing financial risk. Most institutional borrowers and investors ... use financial derivatives. Many of these entities also act as intermediaries dealing in those financial products. ...

Interest rate swaps generally require that the parties thereto negotiate and agree upon several economic terms. These terms generally include (1) a notional amount, (2) a fixed interest rate, (3) a floating interest rate index, (4) a duration (term or tenor) of the contract, (5) an effective date of the contract, and (6) a payment schedule. The parties to an interest rate swap also must negotiate a particular country's currency (or countries' currencies) in which a swap is denominated. ...

The main participants in the interest rate swaps market are end users, dealers, and brokers. ...

End users are typically major corporations, government or governmental-related entities, investment funds, or other financial institutions. These end users typically use ... swaps to combat interest rate movements, express market preferences through position taking, and/or reduce their cost of funding. ...

Since at least 1992, the swaps market has been almost entirely intermediated by institutions acting as dealers. Swaps dealers are generally major financial institutions (e.g., securities firms and banks . . .) which hold themselves out as market-makers; i.e., entities ready and willing to take either side of a swap transaction for the purpose of earning a profit by originating new swaps. On some occasions, these institutions enter into swaps in their capacity as swaps dealers. On other occasions, these institutions enter into swaps in their capacity as end users to manage the overall structure of their portfolios to minimize the net exposure to interest rate movements. Swaps dealers trade with both end users and other dealers. . . .

Swaps dealers maintain a portfolio of swaps on their books and usually attempt to maintain a neutral, hedged position in the market. Swaps dealers attempt to maintain a neutral, hedged position either by: (1) Serving as a counterparty to opposite sides of two matching swaps or (2) managing the overall structure of the portfolio so as to minimize the net exposure to interest rate movements. . . .

When the swaps market first began, every swap generally was facilitated by a dealer. The dealer was not a party to the transaction but, generally for a fee, arranged the swap by introducing the counterparties to each other and helping them to effect the mechanics of the transaction. With the evolution of the market, dealers became parties to each swap. In the early years of the market's evolution, a dealer would effect a swap transaction by warehousing the swap (i.e., entering into the swap without having entered into a matching swap but with the expectation of hedging the entered-into swap either through a matching swap or a portfolio of swaps or temporarily in the cash, securities, or futures market) until the dealer could arrange an offsetting swap with another counterparty (i.e., match a book). In the later years of the market's evolution, the dealer would simply accept a position opposite the counterparty without expecting to locate another counterparty transaction to match the first transaction. . . .

Swap brokers do not take a position or act as a principal in a swap transaction, and they do not maintain any exposure with respect to a swap. Swap brokers simply arrange for dealers to enter into interdealer swaps by matching dealers who want to effect a particular swap with other dealers who want to effect a similar swap. . . . A swap broker is paid a standard fee for its services based on a percentage of the notional principal amount. . . .

Note the references to swap dealers and swap brokers. An entity acting as a swap dealer is, with some exceptions, now required to register as such and an entity acting in a swap broker capacity is now required to register as an introducing broker or futures commission merchant.

Bank One also references end users that use swaps to "express market preference." This is another way to describe speculation. Today a speculator exceeding established exposure thresholds is required to register as a major swap participant even though, as we will see, no entity is currently registered as one.

4. Role of National Futures Association

Although swap dealers and major swap participants must register with the CFTC, the actual function of receiving, vetting, and deciding upon their registration application has been delegated to the National Futures Association.[2] Every swap dealer or major swap participant applicant must file a National Futures Association Form 7-R.[3] Swap dealers and major swap participants are also required to be members of the National Futures Association which, as a self-regulatory organizations, has its own set of rules that swap dealers and major swap participants must comply with in addition to the CFTC's rules.[4]

Principals of swap dealers and major swap participants also must register with the CFTC through filing a Form 8-R with the National Futures Association. Principal means, generally, senior officers and owners of ten percent or more.[5] Principals must not be "statutorily disqualified." A "statutory disqualification" includes matters such as "felony convictions, commodities or securities law violations, and bars or other adverse actions taken by financial regulators."[6]

Persons engaged in soliciting or accepting swaps or supervising someone in that role, known as "associated persons,"[7] are not required to register with the CFTC or the National Futures Association. They are required to pass an NFA proficiency exam.[8] As discussed in chapter 5, section A.3, corresponding roles with other CFTC registrants in many cases trigger a registration requirement.

However, swap dealers and major swap participants may not have a person in such a role if the swap dealer or major swap participant knows or in the exercise of reasonable care should know that such person is statutorily disqualified.[9]

---

2. 17 C.F.R. § 3.2(c)(3).

3. 17 C.F.R. § 3.10(a). This is the same form as is used for the registration applications of futures commission merchants, retail foreign exchange dealers and leverage transaction merchants (both discussed in chapter 12), introducing brokers, commodity pool operators, and commodity trading advisors.

4. 17 C.F.R. § 170.16.

5. 17 C.F.R. § 3.1(a).

6. CFTC, *Registration of Swap Dealers and Major Swap Participants*, 75 Fed. Reg. 71379, 71380 at n. 13 (Nov. 23, 2010).

7. Commodity Exchange Act § 1a(4) and 17 C.F.R.§ 1.3 (definition of associated person § 6).

8. National Futures Association Bylaw 301(l) and Rule 2-24(a). There is also a swap proficiency requirement for associated persons of futures commission merchants, introducing brokers, commodity pool operators, and commodity trading advisors engaged in swaps activities. *Id.*

9. Commodity Exchange Act § 4s(b)(6) and 17 C.F.R. § 23.22(b).

B. Swap Dealers

Swap dealers, functionally described in *Bank One*, now are legally defined by the Commodity Exchange Act and CFTC regulation. As discussed above, they are required to register with the CFTC and to be members of the National Futures Association. The Commodity Exchange Act defines a swap dealer as any person who:

   i. holds itself out as a dealer in swaps;

   ii. makes a market in swaps;

   iii. regularly enters into swaps with counterparties as an ordinary course of business for its own account; or

   iv. engages in any activity causing the person to be commonly known in the trade as a dealer or market maker in swaps, provided however, in no event shall an insured depository institution be considered to be a swap dealer to the extent it offers to enter into a swap with a customer in connection with originating a loan with that customer.[10]

The CFTC and SEC were tasked by Congress to jointly formulate rules further defining "swap dealer."[11] Their jointly agreed rules largely reflect the statutory definition. They also excluded from what is deemed swap dealing activity swaps between affiliates, swaps between cooperatives and their members, and swaps entered into for hedging a physical commodity (as opposed to a financial commodity).[12]

A broad exception is provided for *de minimis* swap dealing activities.[13] Swap dealer registration is not required if the sum of the notional of all the swaps entered into through swap dealing activities over any preceding twelve-month period for the party and its affiliates (i.e., entities "controlling, controlled by or under common control"[14]) is below $8 billion. A lower limit of $25 million applies to "special entities" other than municipally-owned utilities.[15] We will discuss special entities in more detail in chapter 12, section C.2; in essence, they are municipalities and pension funds.

However, the release accompanying issuance of the final rules further defining "swap dealer" also contained detailed interpretative guidance. This guidance is necessary to understand the agencies' approach in applying the definitions. Of particular note, is the deference to the body of law and administrative materials regarding securities dealing as being highly influential in identifying swap dealing activities.

---

10. Commodity Exchange Act § 1a(49).
11. *See* Dodd-Frank Act §§ 712(d)(1) and (3).
12. 17 C.F.R. § 1.3 (definition of swap dealer § 6).
13. *See* 17 C.F.R. § 1.3 (definition of swap dealer § 4(i)(A)).
14. *Id.*
15. *Id.*

This relates to how to distinguish a mere trader in the market from a dealer and is known as the "dealer-trader distinction."

A question to ask, as you read through the below excerpt, how would you advise a client as to whether it is required to register as a swap dealer? What are the activities a client might engage in that would be clearly hedging (i.e., not swap dealing) and what are the activities a client might engage in that would be clearly dealing? What types of activities would you be unsure as to whether they would be characterized as swap dealing?

CFTC and SEC, *Further Definition of "Swap Dealer," "Security-Based Swap Dealer," "Major Swap Participant," "Major Security-Based Swap Participant" and "Eligible Contract Participant"*
77 Fed. Reg. 30596 (May 23, 2012)

... [W]e are adopting a final rule [that] ... defines the term "swap dealer" using terms from the four statutory tests....

This guidance separately addresses the following: application of the dealer-trader framework; the "holding out" and "commonly known" criteria; market making; [and] the not part of "a regular business" exception....

Use of the Dealer-Trader Distinction

We believe that the dealer-trader distinction—which already forms a basis for identifying which persons fall within the longstanding [Securities Exchange Act of 1934] definition of "dealer"—in general provides an appropriate framework for interpreting the statutory definition of the term "swap dealer." While there are differences in the structure of those two statutory definitions,[16] we believe that their parallels—particularly their exclusions for activities that are "not part of a regular business"—warrant analogous interpretive approaches for distinguishing dealers from non-dealers. Thus, the dealer-trader distinction forms the basis for a framework that appropriately distinguishes between persons who should be regulated as swap dealers and those who should not. We also believe that the distinction affords an appropriate degree of flexibility to the analysis, and that it would not be appropriate to seek to codify the distinction in rule text.

The Commissions recognize that the dealer-trader distinction needs to be adapted to apply to swap activities in light of the special characteristics of swaps and the differences between the "dealer" definition, on the one hand, and the "swap

---

16. [N. 174] For example, while the "dealer" definition encompasses certain persons in the business of "buying and selling" securities, the "swap dealer" definition does not address either "buying" or "selling." We also note that the "dealer" definition requires the conjunctive "buying and selling"—which connotes a degree of offsetting two-sided activity. In contrast, the swap dealer definition (particularly the "regularly enters into" swaps language of the definition's third prong) lacks that conjunctive terminology.

dealer" definition, on the other. Relevant differences between the swap market and the markets for securities (other than security-based swaps) include:

> Level of activity — Swap markets are marked by less activity than markets involving certain types of securities. . . . [I]n the swap context, concepts of "regularity" should account for a participant's level of activity in the market relative to the total size of the market.

> No separate issuer — Each counterparty to a swap in essence is the "issuer" of that instrument; in contrast, dealers in cash market securities generally transact in securities issued by another party. This distinction suggests that the concept of maintaining an "inventory" of securities is inapposite in the context of swaps. . . .

> Predominance of over-the-counter and non-standardized instruments — Swaps . . . thus far are not significantly traded on exchanges or other trading systems. . . .

> Mutuality of obligations and significance to "customer" relationship — In contrast to a . . . [securities] purchase or sale transaction . . . , the parties to a swap often will have an ongoing obligation to exchange cash flows over the life of the agreement. . . .

[T]he following activities are indicative that a person is acting as a swap dealer: (i) Providing liquidity by accommodating demand for or facilitating interest in . . . [a swap,] holding oneself out as willing to enter into swaps . . . or being known in the industry as being available to accommodate demand for swaps; (ii) advising a counterparty as to how to use swaps to meet the counterparty's hedging goals, or structuring swaps on behalf of a counterparty; (iii) having a regular clientele and actively advertising or soliciting clients in connection with swaps; (iv) acting in a market maker capacity on an organized exchange or trading system for swaps; and (v) helping to set the prices offered in the market (such as by acting as a market maker) rather than taking those prices. . . .

The Commissions further note that the following . . . [elements apply to the] swap dealer definition . . . : (i) A willingness to enter into swaps on either side of the market is not a prerequisite to swap dealer status; (ii) the swap dealer analysis does not turn on whether a person's swap dealing activity constitutes that person's sole or predominant business; (iii) a customer relationship is not a prerequisite to swap dealer status; and (iv) in general, entering into a swap for the purpose of hedging, absent other activity, is unlikely to be indicative of dealing. . . .

Prior interpretations and future developments in the law . . . regarding securities . . . may inform the interpretation of the swap dealer definition, but will not be dispositive in identifying dealers in the swap markets.[17]

---

17. [N. 185] In interpreting the term "swap dealer," we intend to consider, but do not formally adopt, the body of court decisions, SEC releases, and SEC staff no-action letters that have interpreted the dealer-trader distinction.

Indicia of Holding Oneself Out as a Dealer in Swaps or Being Commonly Known in the Trade as a Dealer in Swaps. . . .

[T]he term [swap dealer] includes a person that is holding itself out as a dealer in swaps or is engaging in any activity causing it to be commonly known in the trade as a dealer or market maker in swaps. . . . [A] number of factors . . . [are] indicia of "hold[ing] itself out as a dealer in swaps" and "engag[ing] in any activity causing [itself] to be commonly known in the trade as a dealer or market maker in swaps."[18] . . .

Because of the flexibility—including the consideration of applicable facts and circumstances—needed for such an analysis, we do not believe that it is appropriate to codify this guidance in rule text. . . .

Market Making. . . .

The final rule defining "swap dealer" includes the provision from the proposed rule which incorporates the statutory requirement that this term include a person that "makes a market in swaps." . . .

[W]e clarify that making a market in swaps is appropriately described as routinely standing ready to enter into swaps at the request or demand of a counterparty. In this regard, "routinely" means that the person must do so more frequently than occasionally, but there is no requirement that the person do so continuously. . . .

Such activities include routinely: (i) quoting bid or offer prices, rates or other financial terms for swaps on an exchange; (ii) responding to requests made directly, or indirectly through an interdealer broker, by potential counterparties for bid or offer prices, rates or other similar terms for bilaterally negotiated swaps; (iii) placing limit orders for swaps; or (iv) receiving compensation for acting in a market maker capacity on an organized exchange or trading system for swaps. . . .

In determining whether a person's routine presence in the market constitutes market making under these four factors, the dealer-trader interpretative framework may be usefully applied. . . .

Exception for Activities Not Part of "a Regular Business"

The final rule includes the provisions . . . of the statutory definition regarding activities that are not part of "a regular business" of entering into swaps. One provision states that the term "swap dealer" includes a person that "regularly enters into swaps with counterparties as an ordinary course of business for its own account"; the other provision states that the term "swap dealer" does not include a person that

---

18. [N. 187] . . . [The relevant] factors are as follows: Contacting potential counterparties to solicit interest; developing new types of swaps . . . and informing potential counterparties of their availability and of the person's willingness to enter into the swap . . . ; membership in a swap association [such as the International Swaps and Derivatives Association, also known as "ISDA"] in a category reserved for dealers; providing marketing materials describing the type of swaps . . . the party is willing to enter into; and generally expressing a willingness to offer or provide a range of products or services that include swaps. . . .

"enters into swaps for such person's own account, either individually or in a fiduciary capacity, but not as a part of a regular business." . . .

[A]ny one of the following activities would generally constitute both entering into swaps "as an ordinary course of business" and "as a part of a regular business": (i) Entering into swaps with the purpose of satisfying the business or risk management needs of the counterparty (as opposed to entering into swaps to accommodate one's own demand or desire to participate in a particular market); (ii) maintaining a separate profit and loss statement reflecting the results of swap activity or treating swap activity as a separate profit center; or (iii) having staff and resources allocated to dealer-type activities with counterparties, including activities relating to credit analysis, customer onboarding, document negotiation, confirmation generation, requests for novations and amendments, exposure monitoring and collateral calls, covenant monitoring, and reconciliation. . . .

As of the time of writing, 130 swap dealers have provisionally registered with the CFTC and are members of the National Futures Association, and twenty-one of those are in the process of withdrawing their registration.[19] The analysis of whether or not a party is a swap dealer is conducted by category of swaps (rates, credit, equity, and other commodity swaps[20]) so that, theoretically, a swap dealer could apply to be a swap dealer for one category of swaps and not for another. Only two swap dealers have done so; the rest are swap dealers with respect to all swap categories.[21]

C. Major Swap Participants

1. Regulatory Motivation

Whereas significant numbers of swap market participants have registered with the CFTC as swap dealers, only two have ever registered as major swap participants. Both withdrew their registrations.[22] No entity has sought to register as a major swap participant since March 31, 2013.

The "major swap participant" category was intended to encompass hedge funds and other non-dealers acquiring significant exposures to swaps on a speculative

---

19. CFTC, *Provisionally Registered Swap Dealers*, available at http://www.cftc.gov/LawRegulation/DoddFrankAct/registerswapdealer. *See also* National Futures Association, *SD/MSP Registry*, available at https://www.nfa.futures.org/NFA-swaps-information/SD_MSP_Registry2.csv.

20. 17 C.F.R. § 1.3 (definition of category of swaps; major swap category).

21. *See* National Futures Association, *SD/MSP Registry*, available at https://www.nfa.futures.org/NFA-swaps information/SD_MSP_Registry2.csv.

22. These are Cournot Financial Products LLC and MBIA Insurance Corporation. *See* National Futures Association, *Membership and Directories*, available at https://www.nfa.futures.org/registration-membership/membership-and-directories.html.

basis. The bailout of American International Group, discussed in chapter 9, section B, provided the primary motivation for the creation of this category of registrant.

Unlike the term "swap dealer," which existed prior to the swap dealer registrant category, the term "major swap participant" is an invention of the Dodd-Frank Act. In the following Senate hearing, during a discussion on a proposal by the Department of the Treasury that formed the backbone of the bill later enacted as the Dodd-Frank Act, the new term "major swap participant" was discussed. The participants are the former chair of the Senate Agriculture Committee, Senator Blanche Lincoln, and Gary Gensler, an ardent proponent of the Dodd-Frank Act and, at the time, chairman of the CFTC. The reference to a "substantial net position" test for determining whether an entity is a major swap participant is a reference to a test, discussed in more detail below, based on overall unhedged, uncollateralized swaps exposures. The references to "AIG" are to "American International Group," an insurance company, at the time the largest in the world, that needed emergency government assistance during the Financial Crisis due to swap exposures. It is an understatement to note that the events related to American International Group provided the primary motivation for the major swap participant registration category. The following discussion illustrates the centrality of American International Group in the creation of the major swap participant category.

Senate Committee on Agriculture, Nutrition and Forestry, *Reforming U.S. Financial Market Regulation*
S. Hrg. 11-799 (Nov. 18, 2009)

. . . Chairman LINCOLN: A major swap participant is defined in the Treasury proposal as a non-dealer who maintains substantial net positions in outstanding swaps. For the purpose other than to create and maintain an effective hedge. . . . I understand that some of the players want a limited . . . definition of the MSP so that, not to kind of get pulled into that category. . . .

Are you comfortable with the Treasury's definition of major swap participants? . . . Is a substantial net position standard workable and is it going to capture all the institutions that pave the kind of systemic risk that we're trying to get at?

Mr. GENSLER: What we're trying to do in the legislation is ensure that there's two complementary regimes: that the dealers are regulated, they have to register and be regulated, have capital and business conduct [standards]; and then that the markets themselves have these clearing and trading requirements.

"Major swap participant" is a term that nine months ago none of us knew.

It was just created in the legislative language. But what it's really trying to address is the next AIG or the near-dealers, something that is not quite a financial institution, but it holds itself out to the public as a substantial net swaps business. There are many counterparties that would be at risk if it failed.

And I don't know it's [a] broad category. It's not meant to pick up the thousands of end-users or even the hundreds of end-users. It's supposed to — I believe it should be a category that is included, that we not just bring this regulation to the five or six large financial institutions. There are some, sort of, the next AIG or the next swap dealer category. . . .

Mr. GENSLER [speaking to Senator Stabenow of Michigan]: I think that every manufacturer in your state and all of the states suffered greatly when AIG went asunder and $180 billion of our taxpayer money. I mean roughly $3.5 billion per state. . . . And so, that's the risk we're trying to protect against [with, among others, the major swap participant registration category] — that large financial institutions aren't so interconnected with the economy at large. . . .

Senator CONRAD: I remember, very well, Senator [Lincoln], several years ago Warren Buffett called derivatives a "nuclear time bomb." And we saw the bomb go off.

I will never forget, as long as I live, being called after one of our group of 10 meetings, Senator Chambliss, being called to the leader's office and I got there and there were the leaders, Republican and Democrat of Congress, and the chairman of the Federal Reserve and the secretary of treasury, and they were telling us they were taking over AIG the next day. They weren't there to ask us. They were there to inform us. And they told us, in no uncertain terms they believed if it was not done, there would be a global financial collapse. Now that's about as stark as anything can be.

So, already just on the AIG debacle, we've seen taxpayers saddled with $180 billion of debt. We must act to prevent that from ever happening again. . . .

Senator CHAMBLISS: If we have had had total transparency, if AIG had been required to report to . . . [the CFTC] the details of all of their transactions, would not that have put not only CFTC in a better position, but the potential buyers of AIG products or investors in AIG products in a much better position to look at them and say: Wow, they've got all these transactions out there, and all these obligations out there, but they don't [have] the capital. And aren't these sophisticated traders just that. They are so sophisticated that they would have known that AIG was not capable of delivering on the products that they were selling or that their capital was so low that there was no way they could meet those commitments, and they wouldn't have made the investment if there had been total transparency at that time. . . .

Senator CONRAD: . . . [I]n that meeting when I described where we were told the government was going to take over AIG because there would be a global financial collapse if it was not done, what became clear is that AIG had written insurance contracts and they didn't have the capital to back up the commitment. And somehow, we have got an absolute obligation to make sure that can't happen again. . . . It would be unthinkable if we were to permit that same circumstance to occur again. . . .

What strikes me about this conversation is transparency as I see it is necessary, but not sufficient. In the case of AIG, as my memory serves me, one of the big financial houses wanted to go from 10-to-one leverage to 30-to-one leverage. They knew there was inherent risk in moving to that kind of leverage. If everything is going well, you make a lot more money. If things are not going well, you lose a lot more money.

And so they recognized the need for an insurance product and they went to AIG and convinced them to write such insurance products, and AIG saw a gift horse and said, "Oh, yes, we can make a lot of money on this deal." What they forgot about is having the resources to cover against the downside risk of these transactions. And when the downside risk occurred, here we go. Taxpayers were the ultimate funder of the liability. That we cannot permit to happen again. . . .

———————

Understanding the motivation for policymakers at the time to create a category of CFTC registrant for entities with large uncollateralized speculative swap positions, we now turn to the question of what activities require registration as a major swap participant.

2. Definition

a. Generally

A major swap participant is defined as any entity that is not a swap dealer and either: (1) maintains a "substantial position" in swaps that are not for hedging purposes (i.e., are speculative in nature) (the "Substantial Position Test"); (2) whose swaps exposure to counterparties "could have serious adverse effects on the financial stability of the United States banking system or financial markets," (the "Serious Adverse Affects Test"); or (3) is a financial entity that maintain a "substantial position" in swaps, *including swaps for hedging purposes*, and is "highly leveraged relative to the amount of capital such entity holds and that is not subject to capital requirements established by" a federal banking agency (the "High Leverage Test").[23] The term "highly leveraged" is defined as a ratio of liabilities to equity exceeding twelve to one.[24]

The analysis of whether or not a party is a major swap participant is conducted by category of swaps (rates, credit, equity, and other commodity swaps[25]) so that, as with swap dealers, theoretically, a major swap participant could apply to be a major swap participant for one category of swaps and not for another.[26]

It could be that no parties are currently choosing to be registered as major swap participants because the compliance obligations, discussed below in E, are so similar to those applying to swap dealers and swap dealers have the additional benefit of being permitted to engage in swap dealing activities. Nonetheless, it is important to have a foundational understanding of what activities can trigger major swap participant registration to avoid inadvertently triggering registration.

———————

23. 17 C.F.R. §1.3 (definition of major swap participant §1(ii)).
24. 17 C.F.R. §1.3 (definition of financial entity; highly leveraged §2).
25. 17 C.F.R. §1.3 (definition of category of swaps; major swap category).
26. 17 C.F.R. §1.3 (definition of major swap participant §2).

b. Substantial Position Test and the Serious Adverse Affects Test

We now examine the Substantial Position Test and the Serious Adverse Affects Test. "Substantial Position" is defined as positions meeting *either* Test #1 or Test #2 in the table in figure 11.1.[27] Test #1 uses the phrase "Daily Average Aggregate Uncollateralized Mark-to-Market Exposure." Though the actual calculations involved are as complicated as the phrase sounds, for the purposes hereof it is best to treat is a reference to the aggregate of the economic exposures a party's counterparties have to it averaged daily over a quarter from swaps that are neither collateralized nor for hedging purposes. Test #2 uses an equally daunting phrase, "Daily Average Aggregate Outward Exposure." This can be conceptualized as an estimation as to how much a party's collateralized or uncollateralized exposure, averaged daily over a quarter, can increase over time. Exposures from hedging are, again, excluded. An entity meeting either test for a category of swaps is required to register as a major swap participant though, as noted above, it can seek to have its registration limited to the relevant category of swaps.

The Serious Adverse Affects Test is summarized in the final row.[28] When calculating the Serious Adverse Affects Test hedging swaps are *not* excluded as they are when calculating the Substantial Position Test.

Figure 11.1 "Substantial Position Test" and "Serious Adverse Affects Test"
(Rates, Credit, Equity, and Other Commodity Rows Reflect
"Substantial Position Test" and the All Swaps Row Reflects
the "Serious Adverse Effects Test")

Category of Swaps	Test #1: Daily Average Aggregate Uncollateralized Mark-to-Market Exposure Equals or Exceeds	Test #2: Amount in Test #1 Plus Daily Average Aggregate Outward Exposure
Rates (Substantial Position Test)	$3 billion	$6 billion
Credit (Substantial Position Test)	$1 billion	$2 billion
Equity (Substantial Position Test)	$1 billion	$2 billion
Other Commodity (Substantial Position Test)	$1 billion	$2 billion
All Swaps (Serious Adverse Affects Test)	$5 billion	$8 billion

c. High Leverage Test

The High Leverage Test only applies to financial entities that are not already subject to capital requirements from a banking regulator. Such an entity is required to register as a major swap participant if it: (1) meets the Substantial Position Test

---

27. 17 C.F.R. §1.3 (definition of substantial position).
28. 17 C.F.R. §1.3 (definition of substantial counterparty exposure).

including swaps for hedging; and (2) has a ratio of liabilities to equities exceeding twelve to one.

d. Major Swap Participant De Minimis *Exception*

As with swap dealers, there is a *de minimis* exception.[29] The exception, however, is comparatively complicated. It exempts any entity that meets both of Required Element #1 and Required Element #2 for either Test #1, Test #2, Test #3, or Test #4 as described in figure 11.2.

Figure 11.2 De Minimis Exception for Major Swap Participants

Relevant test is satisfied if each of Required Element #1 and Required Element #2 are Satisfied		
	Required Element #1	**Required Element #2**
Test #1[a]	Total uncollateralized exposure to all counterparties does not exceed $100 million due to express terms of all agreements	No more than: (1) $2 billion in total notional in any category of swaps; or (2) $4 billion notional in all categories
Test #2[b]	Total uncollateralized exposure to all counterparties cannot exceed $200 million due to express terms of all agreements	Monthly calculations applying Substantial Position Test and Serious Adverse Affects Test have results less than or equal to: (1) $1 billion in Aggregate Uncollateralized Mark-to-Market Exposure plus Daily Average Aggregate Outward Exposure in any swap category (including all hedging swaps otherwise excluded if it meets the High Leverage Test); or (2) $2 billion in Aggregate Uncollateralized Mark-to-Market Exposure plus Daily Average Aggregate Outward Exposure of all swap categories combined
Test #3[c]	Monthly calculations applying Substantial Position Test have results less than or equal to $1.5 billion with respect to the interest rate swap category and less than $500 million with respect to each other category	The amount calculated pursuant to the Substantial Position Test plus the aggregate notional amounts of swaps in the relevant category multiplied by multipliers provided in a table in the regulations[d] is less than $3 billion with respect to rate swaps and $1 billion with respect to any other category of swaps
Test #4[e]	Monthly calculations applying Substantial Position Test have results less than or equal to $500 million for all swap categories	The amount calculated pursuant to the Substantial Position Test plus the aggregate notional amounts of swaps in all swap categories multiplied by 0.15 is less than $1 billion

[a] 17 C.F.R. §1.3(hhh)(6)(i).
[b] 17 C.F.R. §1.3(hhh)(6)(ii).
[c] 17 C.F.R. §1.3(hhh)(6)(iii)(A).
[d] 17 C.F.R. §1.3(jjj)(3)(ii)(1).
[e] 17 C.F.R. §1.3(hhh)(6)(iii)(B).

---

29. 17 C.F.R. §1.3 (definition of major swap participant §6).

D. Entity Level Obligations of Registrants

1. Introduction

The requirements applicable to swap dealers and major swap participants can be divided into "entity level" requirements and "transaction level requirements." Entity level requirements are requirements pertaining to management of the enterprise as a whole. They are capital adequacy, chief compliance officer, risk management, and recordkeeping requirements. Transaction level requirements are requirements that pertain to actual swap transactions. They are clearing and on-facility trade execution requirements, margin for uncleared swaps, swap trading relationship documentation, portfolio reconciliation and compression, swap trade reporting, trade confirmation, and external business conduct requirements.[30] Transaction level requirements often differ depending on whether a swap is centrally cleared or not. In this section we will examine entity level requirements for swap dealers and major swap participants and, in chapter 12, we will examine transaction level requirements.

2. Capital

a. Jurisdictional Split

Whereas the CFTC's jurisdiction is nearly plenary with respect to most aspects of swap regulation, capital (and, we will see in chapter 12, margin) presents an exception. A swap dealer or major swap participant regulated by a "prudential regulator," i.e., the Federal Reserve Board, Office of the Comptroller of the Currency, Federal Deposit Insurance Corporation, Farm Credit Administration, or Federal Housing Finance Agency,[31] is required to follow their regulator's capital requirements instead of the CFTC's capital requirements.[32] Although the technical legal definition of "bank" is more nuanced, in the vernacular, these entities can be thought of as "banks." Though the Federal Reserve Board regulates non-bank subsidiaries of bank holding companies (i.e., entities that own banks), such non-bank subsidiaries are subject to CFTC capital rules.[33]

---

30. Though the CFTC categorizes the general requirement to report uncleared swaps to a swap data repository, discussed in chapter 12, and large swaps trader reporting requirements as entity level and only real-time public reporting requirements as transaction level, all reporting is treated herein as transaction level. *See* CFTC, *Interpretative Guidance and Policy Statement Regarding Compliance with Certain Swap Regulations*, 78 Fed. Reg. 45292, 45337–45339 (July 26, 2013).

31. Commodity Exchange Act § 1a(39).

32. Commodity Exchange Act § 4s(e).

33. *See* CFTC, *Capital Requirements of Swap Dealers and Major Swap Participants*, 81 Fed. Reg. 91252, 91253 (Dec. 16, 2016) and Department of the Treasury, Federal Reserve Board, et al., *Margin and Capital Requirements for Covered Swap Entities*, 76 Fed. Reg. 27564, 27566 at n. 4 (May 11, 2011).

b. Calculation Methods for Futures Commission Merchants

The CFTC rules apply to non-banks. That is a broad category with a variety of entity types. For non-banks which are futures commission merchants, the capital rules apply in largely the same way as those applying to futures commission merchants, discussed in chapter six, section B.2.c. The major difference is that, instead of maintaining $1 million in net capital, swap dealers must maintain the greater of: (1) $20 million in net capital; or (2) eight percent of the sum of all margin for non-proprietary futures, options on futures, and cleared swaps plus two percent of all the initial margin that would be required to be collected if initial margin requirements applied to all uncleared swaps.[34] Alternatively, a futures commission merchant registered as a swap dealer can use an internal model if net capital is $100 million or more or adjusted net capital is $20 million or more. In other words, if an approved internal model is used to calculate credit and market risks, $100 million of net assets is calculated by subtracting liabilities from the allowed assets. There is no additional reduction of the value of the assets by taking "charges against net capital" as is done when calculating "adjusted" net capital. Finally, if a futures commission merchant is registered as a swap dealer and as a securities broker-dealer, the securities broker-dealer capital requirements apply since they are, ordinarily, higher.

c. Calculation Methods for All Other Non-Banks

CFTC rules allow entities other than futures commission merchants to select one of three capital calculation methodologies: (1) net liquid assets capital approach; (2) bank-based capital approach; or (3) tangible net worth capital approach. The net liquid assets approach is largely intended to provide a consistent framework for an SEC-registered broker-dealer and security-based swap dealer. We discuss security-based swap dealers in chapter 13.

The bank-based capital approach is intended to be consistent with the capital requirements applying to bank swap dealers so that, for example, if a bank is registered as a swap dealer and its affiliate is also registered as a swap dealer, a consistent capital framework applies.[35] Specifically, the CFTC requires that a swap dealer using the bank-based capital approach maintain: (1) a type of equity bank capital known as "tier 1 capital" in excess of $20 million; (2) tier 1 capital in excess of 6.5 percent of risk-weighted assets (and, with a type of capital known as tier 2 capital, 8 percent), and (3) tier 1 and tier 2 capital in excess of 8 percent of all the initial margin that would be required to be collected if initial margin requirements applied to all uncleared swaps.[36] The calculation of "risk weighted assets" is similar in theory to the calcula-

---

34. 17 C.F.R. § 1.17(a)(1)(i) and NFA Financial Requirements § 1(a). In reality, as seen in chapter 12, section D.1.b, initial margin does not apply to all counterparty relationships and transactions.

35. CFTC, *Capital Requirements of Swap Dealers and Major Swap Participants*, 85 Fed. Reg. 57462, 57467 (Sept. 15, 2020).

36. 17 C.F.R. § 23.101(a)(1)(i).

tion of "risk charges" discussed in chapter 6, section B.2.c. It can be calculated using an approved model or via standardized deductions based on assets types.[37]

The tangible net worth capital requirement applies to enterprises which are deemed predominantly non-financial entities. An example might be a large commodities exploration and extraction firm with a very actively trading swap dealer subsidiary. To be eligible to use this model, less than fifteen percent of the swap dealer's revenue and assets must be derived from financial activities.[38] If it is a wholly owned subsidiary consolidated for accounting purposes with its parent, the parent's revenue and assets can be used for this calculation. Such entities must maintain a net worth, pursuant to accounting standards with minor exclusions and market value of all swaps and security-based swaps, of the greater of: (1) $20 million (plus additional charges to reflect credit and markets risks); and (2) eight percent of all the initial margin that would be required to be collected if initial margin requirements applied to all uncleared swaps.[39]

d. Calculation Method for Banks

The prudential regulators already have capital frameworks for banks that account for swap exposures. Therefore, bank swap dealers or major swap participants have no additional capital requirements beyond those already applying to them as banks.[40]

e. Major Swap Participants

Under CFTC rules, a major swap participant must merely maintain positive tangible net worth.[41]

3. Chief Compliance Officer

In addition to other compliance and oversight roles, the chief compliance officer of a swap dealer or major swap participant is required to submit an annual report to the CFTC describing internal policies and procedures, provide an assessment on the effectiveness of the policies, including what can be improved, and disclose any material noncompliance and any action taken in association therewith.[42] It is the same as the requirement applying to chief compliance officers of futures commission merchants which we discussed in chapter 6, section B.2.e.

---

37. *Id. See also* 12 C.F.R. § 217.20.

38. 17 C.F.R. § 23.101(a)(2). For what is deemed financial, *see* 12 C.F.R. § 242.3(d) and pt. 242, app. A.

39. 17 C.F.R. § 23.101(a)(2)(ii).

40. Department of the Treasury, Federal Reserve Board, et al., *Margin and Capital Requirements for Covered Swap Entities*, 80 Fed. Reg. 74840, 74847–74848 (Nov. 30, 2015).

41. 17 C.F.R. § 23.101(b).

42. 17 C.F.R. § 3.1(e).

It puts the chief compliance officer in the difficult role of affirmatively disclosing to the CFTC every material violation of the Commodity Exchange Act or CFTC rules. It also raises ethical questions for any lawyer appointed as a chief compliance officer who as an attorney is bound to preserve client confidences if the client swap dealer or major swap participant does not agree to disclosure, and, yet, is simultaneously mandated to affirmatively disclose to the CFTC noncompliance with applicable law or regulation.

In other compelled disclosure contexts, such as with a lawyer representing a natural person, such conflicts and questions would not arise to the same extent due to the application of the client's Fifth Amendment right against self-incrimination.[43] However, the Fifth Amendment has been found not to apply to corporations. Moreover, questions arise as to in what form an assertion of the right against self-incrimination could be asserted by a chief compliance officer *in personam* and what impact such an assertion would have on the required annual report.

In the following Supreme Court case, two natural persons sought to claim that interrogatories compelled from a corporation in a civil case and then used against the individuals in a criminal case violated their right against self-incrimination. The Court clarified that no right against self-incrimination applies to a corporation. If a natural person responding to the interrogatory on behalf of the corporation was at risk of self-incrimination, the Court ruled, such person could claim the right. The corporation, however, would then be required to provide someone who would either be unable or unwilling to assert a right against self-incrimination to provide the interrogatory responses on behalf of the corporation.

United States v. Kordel
397 U.S. 1 (1970)

Mr. Justice Stewart delivered the opinion of the Court.

The respondents are the president and vice president, respectively, of Detroit Vital Foods, Inc. They were convicted . . . along with [Detroit Vital Foods, Inc.] for violations of the Federal Food, Drug, and Cosmetic Act. The Court of Appeals for the Sixth Circuit reversed the respondent's convictions on the ground that the Government's use of interrogatories to obtain evidence from the respondents in a nearly contemporaneous civil condemnation proceeding operated to violate their Fifth Amendment privilege against compulsory self-incrimination. . . .

[T]he . . . Food and Drug Administration (hereafter FDA) instructed the agency's Detroit office to investigate the respondents' possible violations of the Food, Drug, and Cosmetic Act. . . . [C]ivil seizure of two of the respondents' products . . . was recommended. . . . The [FDA's] General Counsel requested . . . [commencement of] an *in rem* action against these products of the corporation, and the United States

---

43. U.S. Const. amend. V.

Attorney filed a libel three days later. The corporation, appearing as the claimant answered the libel. . . . An FDA official . . . prepared extensive interrogatories to be served on the corporation. . . .

[T]he FDA serve[d] upon the corporation and the respondents a notice that the agency contemplated a criminal proceeding against them with respect to the transactions that were the subject of the civil action. . . .

[T]he corporation . . . moved to stay further proceedings in the civil action or, in the alternative, to extend the time to answer the interrogatories until after disposition of the criminal proceeding. . . . The moving papers urged the District Court to act "in the interest of substantial justice." . . . Permitting the Government to obtain proof of violations of the Act by resort to civil discovery procedures, the movant urged, would be "improper" and would "work a grave injustice against the claimant." . . . Counsel expressly disavowed any "issue of a self-incrimination privilege in favor of the claimant corporation." And nowhere in the moving papers did counsel raise a claim of the Fifth Amendment privilege against compulsory self-incrimination with respect to the respondents.

[T]he District Court denied the motion. . . . The court reasoned that the . . . notice did not conclusively indicate the Government would institute a criminal proceeding, that six to 12 months could elapse from the service of the statutory notice to initiation of a criminal prosecution, and that the Government could obtain data for a prosecution from the testimony in the civil action or by subpoenaing the books and records of the corporation. Accordingly, the court concluded, the interests of justice did not require that the Government be denied the information it wanted simply because it had sought it by way of civil discovery procedures. . . . [I]n compliance with the court's directive, the corporation, through the respondent Feldten, answered the Government's interrogatories. . . .

The civil case, still pending in the District Court, proceeded to settlement by way of a consent decree . . . and eight months later the Government obtained the indictment underlying the present judgments of conviction. . . .

[W]e assume that the information Feldten supplied the Government in his answers to the interrogatories . . . provided evidence or leads useful to the Government. However, the record amply supports . . . that the Government did not act in bad faith in filing the interrogatories. . . .

The Court of Appeals thought the answers to the interrogatories were involuntarily given. The District Judge's order denying the corporation's motion to defer the answers to the interrogatories, reasoned the court, left the respondents with three choices: they could have refused to answer, thereby forfeiting the corporation's property that was the subject of the libel; they could have given false answers to the interrogatories, thereby subjecting themselves to the risk of a prosecution for perjury; or they could have done just what they did — disclose the requested information, thereby supplying the Government with evidence and leads helpful in securing their indictment and conviction. . . .

[W]e think the Court of Appeals erred. For Feldten need not have answered the interrogatories. Without question he could have invoked his Fifth Amendment privilege against compulsory self-incrimination. Surely Feldten was not barred from asserting his privilege simply because the corporation had no privilege of its own,[44] or because the proceeding in which the Government sought information was civil rather than criminal in character.

To be sure, service of the interrogatories obliged the corporation to "appoint an agent who could, without fear of self-incrimination, furnish such requested information as was available to the corporation." The corporation could not satisfy its obligation ... by pointing to an agent about to invoke his constitutional privilege. "It would indeed be incongruous to permit a corporation to select an individual to verify the corporation's answers, who because he fears self-incrimination may thus secure for the corporation the benefits of a privilege it does not have." Such a result would effectively permit the corporation to assert on its own behalf the personal privilege of its individual agents.

The respondents press upon us the situation where no one can answer the interrogatories addressed to the corporation without subjecting himself to a "real and appreciable" risk of self-incrimination. For present purposes we may assume that in such a case the appropriate remedy would be a protective order ... postponing civil discovery until termination of the criminal action. But we need not decide this troublesome question. For the record before us makes clear that even though the respondents had the burden of showing that the Government's interrogatories were improper, they never even asserted ... that there was no authorized person who could answer the interrogatories without the possibility of compulsory self-incrimination. To the contrary, the record shows that nobody associated with the corporation asserted his privilege at all. ... His failure at any time to assert the constitutional privilege leaves him in no position to complain now that he was compelled to give testimony against himself. ...

It would seem that, based on *United States v. Kordel*, a chief compliance officer at risk of self-incrimination in supplying the annual chief compliance officer report, would have to either decide to waive Fifth Amendment rights or resign due to an incapability to acquit the role. A resignation would not act as a barrier to the swap dealer or major swap participant's obligation to produce the report. Instead, the swap dealer or major swap participant would need to appoint another chief compliance officer to undertake the role or face sanction for not complying with the CFTC rule.

What about a lawyer acting as a chief compliance officer? Suppose the lawyer's client, the swap dealer or major swap participant, refused to waive attorney-client

---

44. [N. 9] That the corporation has no privilege is of course long established, and not disputed here.

privilege? How does a lawyer navigate, if it is possible at all, between the obligation to maintain attorney-client privilege and the obligation to affirmatively disclose regulatory violations to the CFTC?

The chief compliance officer's annual report imposes substantial obligations of affirmative disclosure. As can be seen from the below matter, where there is actual knowledge of an adverse compliance finding, it is perilous not to disclose it in the chief compliance officer annual report. Note the references to "Large Trader Reports." We discuss this swap dealer requirement in chapter 12, section D.2.b.

In the Matter of Commerzbank AG

CFTC Docket No. 19-03 (Nov. 8, 2018)

... The Commodity Futures Trading Commission ("Commission") has reason to believe that from December 31, 2012 until at least 2018 (the "Relevant Period"), Commerzbank AG ("Commerzbank," "Respondent," or the "Bank") violated ... the Commodity Exchange Act (the "Act") ... [and] the Commission's Regulations ("Regulations") promulgated thereunder. ...

In anticipation of the institution of an administrative proceeding, Respondent has submitted an Offer of Settlement ("Offer"), which the Commission has determined to accept. Without admitting or denying any of the findings or conclusions herein, Respondent consents to the entry of this Order. ...

From December 31, 2012, when Commerzbank provisionally registered with the Commission as a swap dealer ("SD"), until at least 2018, Commerzbank management routinely failed to supervise its SD's activities. ... Commerzbank's failure to supervise the operations of its SD resulted in thousands of violations of the Act. Even after Commerzbank management became aware of the Commission's investigation of its SD, it did not effectively address many of the SD's compliance issues. In June 2018, a Commerzbank internal audit report concluded that the Bank's processes for swap reporting were still "not satisfactory" due to "a number of deficiencies across the risk and control management framework."

During the Relevant Period, Commerzbank was not transparent with the Commission regarding the compliance inadequacies at the SD. In 2015 and 2016, Commerzbank filed misleading reports with the Commission that omitted material facts regarding the state of compliance at the SD. ...

As a result of Commerzbank management's failure to adequately supervise the SD, during the Relevant Period, Commerzbank violated numerous provisions of the Act and accompanying Regulations. These violations included failure to implement policies reasonably designed to determine whether swap transactions with certain non-U.S. swap counterparties were subject to the requirements of the Dodd-Frank Wall Street Reform and Consumer Protection Act of 2010 ("Dodd-Frank") ...; failure to report swap transactions to swap data repositories ("SDRs") ...; failure to submit Large Trader Reports to the Commission ...; and failure to execute swaps on swap execution facilities ("SEFs"). ...

Personnel in Commerzbank's New York office were tasked with overseeing SD compliance, but did not have the authority, the funding, or the necessary information to effectively implement bank-wide policies and controls for swap transactions. . . .

SDs provisionally registered with the Commission normally submit an annual Chief Compliance Officer report ("CCO report") discussing the SD's operations and compliance with the Act in the preceding calendar year.

Commerzbank submitted a CCO report for the 2014 calendar year on or about April 29, 2015 (the "2014 Report") and a CCO report for the 2015 calendar year on or about April 28, 2016 (the "2015 Report," together with 2014 Report, the "CCO Reports").[45] The CCO Reports did not adequately disclose to the Commission the numerous deficiencies in Commerzbank's systems and controls for SD compliance. Specifically, the CCO Reports, both of which were signed by a senior Commerzbank compliance officer, falsely imply that Commerzbank had sufficient systems and controls to generally ensure effective compliance with the Act and accompanying regulations. This depiction of the state of affairs at the Commerzbank SD was generally misleading regarding the overall state of compliance at the Commerzbank SD.

Moreover, not only were the CCO Reports generally misleading, but they also contained specific statements of material fact that were misleading, and omitted material facts regarding compliance issues that were known internally at Commerzbank before the reports were submitted to the Commission (which, in turn, made other statements in the reports misleading). Senior Commerzbank compliance personnel knew about these compliance issues, but decided not to discuss them in the CCO Reports. Commerzbank's misleading statements and omissions violated Section 6(c)(2) of the Act, 7 U.S.C. § 9(2) (2012). . . .

In 2014, Commerzbank hired a "Big Four" accounting firm to conduct an eight-week long review of Dodd-Frank compliance at the Commerzbank SD. This external compliance consultant's findings were memorialized in May 2014, and circulated contemporaneously within Commerzbank.

The external compliance consultant found fifty regulatory gaps and twenty-two business gaps in the SD's policies and processes for Dodd-Frank compliance. The external compliance consultant concluded that thirty-six of these gaps were "high impact," meaning that they had a significant impact leading to non-compliance with the applicable Dodd-Frank requirement. Another thirty-five gaps were deemed "medium impact," meaning that they could potentially lead to non-compliance with Dodd-Frank. . . .

In early 2015, Commerzbank drafted its CCO report to the Commission for the 2014 calendar year. During the drafting process, Commerzbank personnel discussed

---

45. [N. 3] These CCO reports to the Commission contained material specific to the swap dealer's Dodd-Frank compliance and were submitted along with an overarching bank-wide report on compliance. The misleading statements and material omissions discussed in this order relate to the material that was specific to the swap dealer's Dodd-Frank compliance.

whether to include the external compliance consultant's findings in the 2014 Report. A Commerzbank employee in Frankfurt initially recommended disclosing the external compliance consultant's findings. However, Commerzbank compliance personnel in New York argued against this, and their view prevailed.

Accordingly, on or about April 29, 2015, Commerzbank submitted the 2014 Report to the Commission. Without mentioning the external compliance consultant, the 2014 Report stated that between March and May of 2014 Commerzbank had conducted an eight-week long review of SD Dodd-Frank compliance. The 2014 Report did not disclose the external compliance consultant's findings regarding seventy-two compliance gaps at the SD. This omission was material and, by submitting the 2014 Report to the Commission without disclosing these findings, Commerzbank omitted material facts that were necessary to make the 2014 Report's discussion of the external compliance consultant's SD review, as well as other statements in the 2014 Report, not misleading in material respects.

Additionally, Commerzbank made specific statements in the 2014 Report that were misleading in light of the external compliance consultant's findings. For instance, Commerzbank stated that its policies and procedures for Regulation 43.3, 17 C.F.R. § 43.3 (2018), which govern reporting to SDRs, were "effective," and specifically asserted that the firm had adequate written policies and procedures to ensure that swap transactions and pricing data were reported in real-time. The external compliance consultant, however, found in May 2014 that Commerzbank's Regulation 43.3 reporting infrastructure lacked controls to verify the accuracy of data submitted to SDRs, and also lacked controls to verify that the data was submitted within the timeframe required by the Commission. Commerzbank did not include these findings in its 2014 Report. These omissions were both material and misleading.

Commerzbank also stated in the 2014 Report that its written policies and procedures for compliance with Regulation 45.2, 17 C.F.R. § 45.2 (2018), the Commission rule pertaining to SD recordkeeping, were "effective." The external compliance consultant, however, had reached the opposite conclusion, finding that, in total, there were four high-impact gaps and one medium- impact gap in Commerzbank's procedures for Regulation 45.2 compliance. According to the external compliance consultant, Commerzbank did not have detailed procedures for record retention and retrieval as required by Regulation 45.2. The external compliance consultant also found that Commerzbank lacked system capabilities to perform storage and archiving per Commission requirements, did not have controls in place to verify data entered when swap counterparties were onboarded, and lacked ownership of and controls over the recordkeeping process. Commerzbank did not disclose any of these findings in the 2014 Report. These omissions were material, and Commerzbank's statement to the Commission regarding the supposed effectiveness of its policies and procedures for Regulation 45.2 compliance was, at best, misleading.

Moreover, Commerzbank's 2014 Report stated that its written policies and procedures were effective to prevent evasion of the Commission's mandatory clearing requirements. The external compliance consultant, however, had reached a different conclusion, finding multiple gaps in Commerzbank's controls to ensure mandatory clearing. Commerzbank did not disclose these findings in its 2014 Report and, instead, stated inaccurately that its written policies and procedures for ensuring compliance with clearing requirements were "effective." This statement was material and misleading. . . .

In March 2015, a Commerzbank computer specialist flagged internally several problems with Commerzbank's Part 20 Large Trader reporting to the Commission. In an email chain that was circulated widely throughout Commerzbank, including to senior SD compliance personnel, the computer specialist stated that for a period of 327 days from 2013 to 2014, Commerzbank had made Part 20 submissions that did not comply with Commission requirements. After self- identifying this issue, Commerzbank corrected the reporting problem going forward. The computer specialist also flagged two other Part 20 reporting problems. Specifically, he stated that on two days, April 23, 2013, and April 1, 2014, Commerzbank did not make any Part 20 submissions whatsoever, and that, since 2013, Commerzbank had not aggregated its Part 20 submissions consistent with Commission requirements. The computer specialist further observed that he had repeatedly flagged the aggregation problem previously. In March 2015, Commerzbank resubmitted 325 days of data to the Commission to correct the first of these problems, but it did not even attempt to remediate the other two problems until well after the Division began to investigate the Commerzbank SD.

All three of these Part 20 reporting problems (the one that was remediated in 2015 and the two that were not remediated until much later) were omitted from the 2014 Report that Commerzbank filed with the Commission on April 29, 2015, even though SD compliance personnel, including personnel responsible for drafting the 2014 Report, were notified of these problems in March 2015.

In early 2016, these Part 20 reporting violations were again brought to the attention of SD compliance personnel. A new hire in the SD's compliance department, who had started working at Commerzbank in February 2016 as a Markets Compliance officer, found the computer specialist's email chain in the course of preparing the 2015 Report to the Commission. She promptly emailed her supervisor, a senior compliance officer in New York, and recommended in April 2016 that the Bank disclose these Part 20 violations to the Commission. Despite this recommendation, Commerzbank did not disclose these Part 20 violations in the 2015 Report, which was submitted to the Commission on or about April 28, 2016.

The non-disclosure of Part 20 Large Trader reporting violations in the CCO Reports were material omissions that had the effect of misleading the Commission. The 2014 Report included a discussion of one issue of material non-compliance, involving confirmation reports incorrectly submitted to an SDR, and any reader of this Report would have reasonably (but incorrectly) concluded that this was Commerzbank's only instance of material non-compliance during 2014. By omitting the Part 20 reporting failures from the 2014 Report, Commerzbank omitted material facts that were necessary to make the 2014 Report's discussion of Commerzbank's ostensibly singular issue of material non-compliance, as well as other statements in the 2014 Report, not misleading in material respects.

The 2015 Report likewise did not discuss the Part 20 reporting issues that had previously been omitted from the 2014 Report. Commerzbank personnel, including senior compliance personnel, knew about these Part 20 violations, and discussed them internally, but decided to omit them from the 2015 Report. A senior compliance officer for Commerzbank in New York specifically considered whether to include these Part 20 violations in the 2015 Report prior to its submission, but decided not to include them — even though the compliance officer primarily responsible for drafting the 2015 Report recommended disclosing them. Moreover, the 2015 Report discussed in some detail two different Part 20 reporting issues that were, if anything, less serious than the omitted Part 20 violations. A reader of the CCO Reports could reasonably, but incorrectly, conclude that these were Commerzbank's only Part 20 reporting violations during 2014 and 2015. By omitting the other Part 20 reporting violations, even though a Commerzbank compliance officer had recommended disclosing them, Commerzbank omitted material facts that were necessary to make the 2015 Report's statements regarding Part 20 reporting issues, as well as other statements in the 2015 Report, not misleading in material respects. Accordingly, Commerzbank violated Section 6(c)(2) of the Act....

Section 4s(h)(1)(B) of the Act, 7 U.S.C. §6s(h)(1)(B) (2012), requires "diligent supervision of the business of the registered swap dealer." Regulation 23.602, 17 C.F.R. §23.602 (2018), requires that SDs and major swap participants "establish and maintain a system to supervise, and shall diligently supervise, all activities relating to its business performed by its partners, members, officers, employees, and agents (or persons occupying a similar status or performing a similar function)."

The operative language of Regulation 23.602 (governing SDs and major swap participants), is similar to the language of the Commission's longstanding supervision regulation for futures and options, Regulation 166.3, 17 C.F.R. §166.3 (2018). Under Regulation 166.3, when a registrant's supervisory system is generally inadequate, or the registrant fails to perform its supervisory duties diligently, that fact alone is sufficient to establish a violation of the supervision requirement....

Commerzbank management failed to diligently supervise the SD. The failure was systemic and occurred over a long period of time. Management's failure to supervise the SD directly resulted in violations of other provisions of the Act and accompanying Regulations....

Section 6(c)(2) of the Act, 7 U.S.C. §9(2) (2012), prohibits making "any false or misleading statement of a material fact to the Commission, including ... information relating to a swap, ... or to omit to state in any such statement any material fact that is necessary to make any statement of a material fact made not misleading in any material respect."

As detailed above, in its 2014 Report to the Commission, which was submitted to the Commission on or about April 29, 2015, Commerzbank made misleading statements of material fact relating to SD compliance. In the same report, Commerzbank omitted material facts that were necessary to make other statements of material fact in the 2014 Report not misleading in material respects. In its 2015 Report, which was submitted on or about April 28, 2016, Commerzbank likewise omitted material facts that were necessary to make other statements of material fact in the 2015 Report not misleading in material respects. . . .

Section 2(a)(1)(B) of the Act, 7 U.S.C. § 2(a)(1)(B) (2012), and Regulation 1.2, 17 C.F.R. § 1.2 (2018), provide that the act, omission, or failure of any official, agent, or other person acting for any individual, association, partnership, corporation, or trust within the scope of his employment or office shall be deemed the act, omission, or failure of such individual, association, partnership, corporation, or trust. Pursuant to Section 2(a)(1)(B) of the Act and Regulation 1.2, strict liability is imposed on principals for the actions of their agents. *See, e.g., Rosenthal & Co. v. CFTC*, 802 F.2d 963, 966 (7th Cir. 1986); *Dohmen-Ramirez & Wellington Advisory, Inc. v. CFTC*, 837 F.2d 847, 857–58 (9th Cir. 1988).

The foregoing acts, omissions, and failures of Commerzbank's employees occurred within the scope of their employment, office, or agency with Commerzbank; therefore, pursuant to Section 2(a)(1)(B) of the Act, and Regulation 1.2, Commerzbank is liable for those acts, omissions, and failures in violation of the Act and Regulations. . . .

———————

Commerzbank was fined $12 million and had additional oversight requirements imposed. One of these was retention of an external consultant for up to three years to review Commerzbank's swap dealer's compliance with the Commodity Exchange Act and CFTC regulations. The consultant's yearly report, including recommendations, was required to be sent to the CFTC.

Whistleblowers

The Dodd-Frank Act gave the CFTC the authority to grant awards to "whistleblowers," i.e., persons providing information related to a violation of the Commodity Exchange Act or CFTC rules that leads to at least $1 million in monetary sanctions.[a] The whistleblower is eligible for ten to thirty percent of the total award.[b]

However, attorneys should not rejoice. Individuals acting as attorneys generally cannot act as whistleblowers due to their relevant bar association's prohibition on disclosure of information subject to the attorney-client privilege.[c]

Currently, due to a potential payment of more than $100 million and a critical depletion of funds available — by law, it can only be replenished by enforcement awards when it falls below $100 million — the whistleblower program is in peril. Legislative efforts are underway to resolve this conundrum.[d]

[a] 17 C.F.R. § 165.8.

[b] *Id.*

[c] 17 C.F.R. § 165.2(g)(2).

[d] Alexandra Berzon, *CFTC Whistleblower Program in Peril Over Potential $100 Million-Plus Payout,* https://www.wsj.com/articles/cftc-whistleblower-program-in-peril-over-potential-100-million-plus-payout-11620732600 (May 11, 2021).

4. Risk Management

Swap dealers and major swap participants are required to establish a risk management program, accounting for, among others, market, credit, liquidity, foreign currency, legal, operational, and settlement risks.[46] The risk management program must include regular monitoring and trading limits. The risk management function must be staffed by a risk management unit independent of the trading function. New products require a special risk assessment and a business continuity/disaster recovery plan needs to be in place to ensure continued operation of critical functions in adverse conditions.

Quarterly reports on the above risks, including recommended changes and the status of items previously recommended but not yet acted upon, must be provided to management and the CFTC. The risk management policies and procedures must be internally examined and tested at least once a year.

5. Recordkeeping

All categories of records of a swap dealer or major swap participant that are required to be retained are open to inspection by the CFTC, Department of Justice, or any "prudential regulator."[47] Records generally need to be kept for five years and be "readily accessible" for two.

Swaps and related transactions, however, must be kept for five years *after* the transaction ends and be "readily accessible" for the first two. An exception exists for "records of oral communications," which may be kept for one year only.

The categories of records required to be maintained are:

- Transaction and position records of all swaps "including, but not limited to, records of all orders (filled, unfilled, or cancelled); correspondence; journals; memoranda; ledgers; confirmations; risk disclosure documents; statements of

---

46. 17 C.F.R. § 23.600(b).
47. Commodity Exchange Act § 1a(39).

purchase and sale; contracts; invoices; warehouse receipts; [and] documents of title . . ." and records of every position identified as "long" or "short" and whether or not it is cleared.

- Business records such as governance documents, organizational charts, biographies, and job descriptions of senior personnel, audit reports, financial records, customer complaints, including the resolution thereof, and marketing and sales materials.

- Daily trading records such as original records of transactions, swap trade information sufficient to allow a "comprehensive and accurate trade reconstruction," searchable by transaction and counterparty, pre-trade communications, and post-trade events.[48]

6. Supervision

A swap dealer or major swap participant will also be held responsible for proper supervision of its associated persons.

In the Matter of INTL FCStone Markets, LLC

CFTC Docket No. 15-27 (Aug. 19, 2015)

The Commodity Futures Trading Commission ("Commission") has reason to believe that since at least January 2013 through July 21, 2013 (the "Relevant Period"), INTL FCStone Markets, LLC ("IFCS" or "Respondent") violated Commission Regulation ("Regulation") 23.602, 17 C.F.R. § 23.602 (2014). Therefore, the Commission deems it appropriate and in the public interest that public administrative proceedings be, and hereby are, instituted to determine whether Respondent engaged in the violations as set forth herein and to determine whether any order should be issued imposing remedial sanctions. . . .

In anticipation of the institution of this administrative proceeding, Respondent has submitted an Offer of Settlement ("Offer"), which the Commission has determined to accept. Without admitting or denying any of the findings or conclusions herein, Respondent consents to the entry of this Order. . . .

The Commission finds [that] . . . Respondent violated Regulation 23.602, 17 C.F.R. § 23.602 (2014), when it failed to diligently supervise limited purpose traders ("LPTs")[49] in its Kansas City Energy Group (the "KCEG"), failed to implement existing policies and procedures regarding discretionary trading, and failed to enforce its own policies regarding the application of mark-ups to customer transactions. . . .

---

48. 17 C.F.R.§§ 23.201 and 23.202.

49. [N. 2] An "LPT" is a broker who performs both sales and trade execution functions, i.e. in limited instances swaps traders were permitted to execute trades in IFCS's name, and also hedge those transactions with futures trades.

Respondent is registered with the Commission (NFA ID 0449652) as a swap dealer (provisionally, effective December 31, 2012). Respondent is a subsidiary of INTL FCStone Inc., which is a financial services company incorporated in Delaware and headquartered in New York. INTL FCStone Inc. is a publicly held company traded on the NASDAQ. . . .

During the Relevant Period, Gregory Evans ("Evans"), then employed in Respondent's KCEG as an . . . [associated person ("AP")], entered into energy swap agreements on behalf of IFCS with its customers. He also entered into futures trades on behalf of IFCS to hedge the risk from these swap agreements. He handled both discretionary accounts, an arrangement where a broker has power of attorney, usually a written agreement to buy and sell without prior approval, and non-discretionary accounts, an arrangement where a broker has to obtain prior approval to buy and sell a particular contract.

Evans engaged in thirty (30) unauthorized trades in a non-discretionary customer account during the Relevant Period. Evans also applied large "reverse mark-ups" to bilateral swap agreement transactions in order to disguise these unauthorized trades.

"Reverse mark-ups" reference the price of a hedge contract entered into by IFCS, in which it provided the customer with better prices than the actual prices at which Respondent entered into the underlying hedge transactions. A reverse mark-up resulted in gains for customers and corresponding losses for Respondent. This practice assisted Evans in disguising his unauthorized trading and increasing his own compensation.

Respondent failed to diligently supervise Evans and the other LPTs in the KCEG as it (i) provided inadequate oversight of Evans and the other LPTs; (ii) lacked adequate policies and procedures to ensure that discretionary trading of customer accounts was appropriate and properly controlled; and (iii) failed to implement policies and procedures already in place.

For example, LPTs often obtained verbal authorization to enter into discretionary trades, although IFCS's written compliance procedures required written authorization if an LPT exercised discretion over customer trades. Moreover, IFCS did not have sufficient procedures or controls in place to monitor discretionary trading during the Relevant Period. Although IFCS's policies and procedures provided for an individual with supervisory duties to work on the KCEG "Swaps Sales desk," LPTs' trading activities were not closely or regularly monitored by supervisors. Finally, Respondent failed to adequately monitor compliance with, and enforce, its own procedures, which purported to require that mark-ups and reverse mark-ups applied to customers be within a predetermined range.

Respondent's lack of supervision contributed to Evans engaging in unauthorized trading for a period of several months without detection. Ultimately, however, the losses and resultant pressure on Evans mounted, culminating with his July 21, 2013 resignation from IFCS.

Respondent has been cooperative with DSIO throughout the course of its review and is finalizing implementation of DSIO's recommendations. Respondent reimbursed its customers more than $1.2 million for the identified losses in their accounts. IFCS also suffered losses from the reverse mark-ups Evans applied to customer accounts. . . .

Regulation 23.602(a) requires that swap dealers and major swap participants

> establish and maintain a system to supervise, and shall diligently supervise, all activities relating to its business performed by its partners, members, officers, employees, and agents (or persons occupying a similar status or performing a similar function). Such system shall be reasonably designed to achieve compliance with the requirements of the Commodity Exchange Act and Commission regulations. . . .

Regulation 23.602(b) defines a "supervisory system" as one that, at a minimum, provides

for:

> (1) [t]he designation, where applicable, of at least one person with authority to carry out the supervisory responsibilities of the swap dealer or major swap participant for all activities relating to its business as a swap dealer or major swap participant.
>
> (2) [t]he use of reasonable efforts to determine that all supervisors are qualified and meet such standards of training, experience, competence, and such other qualification standards as the Commission finds necessary or appropriate. . . .

Respondent failed to diligently supervise the activities of its swap dealer business in violation of Regulation 23.602. Specifically, there was inadequate supervision of the junior LPTs and trading activity of the KCEG. Although Respondent had some written procedures regarding discretionary accounts and mark-ups, IFCS failed to enforce those policies, and thus failed to perform its supervisory duties diligently. Evidence of violations that "should be detected by a diligent system of supervision, either because of the nature of the violations or because the violations have occurred repeatedly" is probative of a failure to supervise. . . .

Similarly, Respondent lacked a system to monitor mark-ups and reverse mark-ups on trades, or compliance with the procedures it purportedly adopted in May 2013 regarding minimum and maximum mark-ups. . . .

Based on the foregoing, the Commission finds that, during the Relevant Period, Respondent failed to supervise its employees and agents diligently by establishing, implementing, and executing an adequate supervisory structure and compliance programs in violation of Regulation 23.602, 17 C.F.R. § 23.602 (2014). . . .

Respondent has submitted the Offer in which it, without admitting or denying the findings and conclusions herein . . . [and, among others,] orders Respondent to cease and desist from violating Regulation 23.602, 17 C.F.R. § 23.602 (2014) . . . [and] orders Respondent to pay a civil monetary penalty in the amount of two hundred thousand dollars ($200,000), plus post-judgment interest. . . .

———————

In addition to demonstrating the importance of adequate supervision and risk controls, this CFTC order emphasizes the importance of CFTC registrants, including swap dealers and major swap participants, having policies and procedures covering every applicable Commodity Exchange Act provision and CFTC rule. And as important as having policies and procedures is, of course, ensuring they are followed.

Questions and Comments

1. In *Bank One Corporation*, the swaps market is described as historically having operated as follows:

> When the swaps market first began, every swap generally was facilitated by a dealer. The dealer was not a party to the transaction but, generally for a fee, arranged the swap by introducing the counterparties to each other and helping them to effect the mechanics of the transaction. With the evolution of the market, dealers became parties to each swap. In the early years of the market's evolution, a dealer would effect a swap transaction by warehousing the swap (i.e., entering into the swap without having entered into a matching swap but with the expectation of hedging the entered-into swap either through a matching swap or a portfolio of swaps or temporarily in the cash, securities, or futures market) until the dealer could arrange an offsetting swap with another counterparty (i.e., match a book). In the later years of the market's evolution, the dealer would simply accept a position opposite the counterparty without expecting to locate another counterparty transaction to match the first transaction.[50]

Evaluate the potential benefits and shortcomings of each of these paradigms: one in which the swap dealer facilitates a transaction between two parties transacting with each other, and one in which the swap dealer acts as counterparty with one of those parties. Now contrast these with a model in which there is a central intermediary, such as with commodity futures and as has been mandated for some categories of swaps (see chapters 5 and 10).

2. What are the policy objectives of requiring the registration of some market participants?

3. The release accompanying the final definition of swap dealer, jointly agreed by the CFTC and the SEC, states: "We also believe that the [trader/dealer] distinction affords an appropriate degree of flexibility to the analysis, and that it would not be

---

50. *Bank One Corporation v. Commissioner of Internal Revenue*, 120 T.C. 174, 196 (Tax 2003).

appropriate to seek to codify the distinction in rule text."[51] What are the positives associated with the regulators retaining "flexibility" in how a term such as "swap dealer" will be defined? What are the downsides? What impact does this have on market participants seeking to prospectively plan?

4. Was the creation of the "major swap participant" category of registration driven too singularly by one event, the bailout of American International Group? Or was that the "shot across the bow" that the regulators addressed before it could reoccur?

5. What purposes might a registration category that has no registrants have?

6. Should corporations be able to assert Fifth Amendment rights? How would that change enforcement efforts?

7. Can an attorney act as chief compliance officer? If so, what safeguards, if any, might be appropriate?

---

51. *See* CFTC and SEC, *Further Definition of "Swap Dealer," "Security-Based Swap Dealer," "Major Swap Participant," "Major Security-Based Swap Participant," and "Eligible Contract Partici-pant"*, 77 Fed. Reg. 30596, 30607 (May 23, 2012).

Chapter 12

Uncleared Swaps

A. Background

The subject of chapter 10 was cleared swaps. With a cleared swap the two parties entering into the swap each face a central clearinghouse for performance of the swap obligations instead of each other. Frequently, cleared swaps are entered into using a facility, most commonly a swap execution facility, that matches bids and offers. In this way, cleared swaps trade with some similarity to futures. As we discussed in chapter 10, the Dodd-Frank Act and CFTC regulation requires clearing for some categories of swap transactions.

Two general subjects form the core of this chapter. The first is the regulatory regime applying to swaps that are not cleared. When swaps are traded off-facility and without being cleared, swap dealers and major swap participants have enhanced regulatory obligations.[1] The largest category of such obligations are "external business conduct" requirements, i.e., requirements applying to swap-related interactions with third parties. There are also requirements relating to: (1) initial and variation margin; (2) reporting; (3) portfolio reconciliation and compression; and (4) documentation, all of which we examine. Some of these requirements are only applicable when a swap dealer or major swap participant is trading with a counterparty that is not a swap dealer or major swap participant. For the sake of simplicity, we will use the term "end user" to describe such non-swap dealer, non-major swap participant counterparties.

We will see that, to simplify compliance with many of these regulations, a standardized multilateral system known as ISDA Amend has been developed whereby parties can comply with many of the uncleared swap regulatory obligations and exchange relevant information. We discuss this in section F.

The second major subject of this chapter is how uncleared swaps are documented. Focusing on the documentation of uncleared swaps is especially important because, whereas cleared swaps are usually largely standardized, uncleared swaps are individually negotiated.

---

1. Swaps can be — and are — traded on facilities without subsequently being cleared or traded bilaterally and subsequently cleared. In some of these circumstances, there is relief from the full set of requirements otherwise applying to uncleared swaps. *See, inter alia*, 17 C.F.R. § 23.430(e), CFTC Letter No. 13-70 (Nov. 15, 2013), and CFTC Letter No. 18-03 (Feb. 20, 2018).

B. External Business Conduct Requirements

External business conduct requirements are the requirements that apply when a swap dealer or major swap participant interacts with a third party regarding an uncleared swap transaction.[2] There are two standards of external business conduct requirements. One is the basic level of external business requirements that a swap dealer or major swap participant must apply to all counterparties. We discuss these in this section. The second are stricter additional requirements applicable to "special entities," i.e., pension funds and municipalities. These are discussed in section C.

1. Verification of Counterparty Status

A swap is illegal unless both parties are eligible contract participants or it is traded on a futures exchange.[3] Uncleared swaps by their nature are not traded on futures exchanges. Therefore, no uncleared swap may be traded by anyone who is not an eligible contract participant. (For a discussion of eligible contract participants, see chapter 9, section E.)

Swap dealers and major swap participants have the additional obligation of affirmatively verifying that their counterparties are eligible contract participants.[4] Notwithstanding this regulatory requirement, such verification is, of course, salutary to avoid entering into a swap with a party that is not an eligible contract participant and, thereby, violating the Commodity Exchange Act.

Swap dealers and major swap participants must also ascertain whether a counterparty is a "special entity." As discussed in section C below, swap dealers and major swap participants are subject to heightened external business conduct requirements for interactions with special entities.

Both in ascertaining whether or not a counterparty is an eligible contract participant or a special entity, CFTC rules allow swap dealers to rely on a written representation from the counterparty.[5]

2. Disclosures and Communications to Counterparties

a. Disclosure Requirements

With respect to any particular swap, swap dealers and major swap participants must disclose to any end user counterparty the material risks (such as market, credit, liquidity, foreign currency, legal, and operational risks), characteristics, and any incentives or conflicts of interest the swap dealer or major swap participant might have and that the counterparty has a right to clear the swap at a derivatives clearing

---

2. Even, in some cases, if it is ultimately cleared. *See* CFTC Letter No. 13-70 (Nov. 15, 2013).

3. Commodity Exchange Act § 2(e).

4. 17 C.F.R. § 23.430.

5. 17 C.F.R. § 23.430(d).

organization of its choosing.[6] Part of a disclosure of "incentives" is informing the end user what the "mid-market" is of the proposed swap.[7] The mid-market shows the price of the swap without the additional amounts that the end user counterparty is paying as a spread to the swap dealer or major swap participant, thereby allowing the end user counterparty to see the swap dealer's or major swap participant's potential profits. After the parties enter into a swap, the mid-market amount must thereafter be provided each business day along with associated disclosures on the methodology and limitations of this daily mid-market amount.[8]

Moreover, on the request of any end user counterparty, a swap dealer or major swap participant is required, before entering into a swap, to collaborate with the end user counterparty in preparing a "a scenario analysis to allow the counterparty to assess its potential exposure in connection with the swap. . . ."[9]

Both of these requirements only apply when a swap dealer or major swap participant is entering into a swap with an end user counterparty. In a swap where both parties are swap dealers or major swap participants these requirements do not apply.

Adhering to an appropriate mid-market calculation methodology — and adequately disclosing it to customers — is an essential component of the requirement.

In the Matter of Cargill, Inc.

CFTC Docket No. 18-03 (Nov. 6, 2017)

The Commodity Futures Trading Commission ("Commission") has reason to believe that from at least in or about 2013 to the present (the "Relevant Period"), Cargill, Inc. ("Respondent") violated Section 4s(h)(1) of the Commodity Exchange Act ("Act"), 7 U.S.C. § 6s(h)(1) (2012), and Commission Regulations ("Regulations") 23.431(a) and (d), 45.4(d)(2), and 166.3, 17 C.F.R. §§ 23.431(a), (d), 45.4(d)(2), 166.3 (2017). . . .

In anticipation of the institution of an administrative proceeding, Respondent has submitted an Offer of Settlement ("Offer"), which the Commission has determined to accept. . . .

Beginning in early 2013, when it provisionally registered as a swap dealer, and continuing through the present, Cargill, through its Cargill Risk Management business ("CRM") has provided its counterparties to certain complex swaps with mid-market marks ("marks") that failed to comply with the Act and Regulations.

Swap dealers such as Cargill are required to comply with certain external business conduct requirements. These include disclosing to potential counterparties, prior to the transaction, the swap dealer's material incentives and conflicts of interest related to the swap, including the mid-market mark of the swap. The requirements also

---

6. 17 C.F.R. §§ 23.431(a) and 23.432.
7. 17 C.F.R. § 23.431(a)(i).
8. 17 C.F.R. § 23.431(d).
9. 17 C.F.R. § 23.431(b).

include daily disclosure to counterparties, during the life of each swap, of the mid-market mark of that swap. Regulations prohibit the mark, either pre-trade or during the life of the swap, from including any amount for profit, credit reserve, hedging, funding, liquidity, or any other costs or adjustments.

In 2012 and 2013, as it prepared to register as a swap dealer, Cargill identified the mid- market mark provisions of the Act and the Commission's external business conduct regulations as potentially problematic for Cargill's business because the provisions would require Cargill to disclose its full mark up on swaps to its counterparties. In particular, Cargill was reluctant to disclose its mark up on certain complex swaps because of a concern that such transparency might ultimately reduce its revenue. As a result of this concern, Cargill chose to provide a mark that was based on a termination or "unwind" value that included a portion of Cargill's estimated revenue during the first sixty calendar days of the swap, and also credited the counterparty with a portion of its estimated revenue if the counterparty terminated the swap during that same period. This method had the effect of concealing from the counterparty the full revenue that Cargill expected to make from the swap transaction. Cargill took this approach despite concerns that its contemplated mid-market mark methodology did not meet the requirements of the Commission's regulations concerning mid-market marks, either pre-trade or during the first sixty calendar days of the swap. As a result of this conduct, Cargill violated the mid-market mark disclosure requirements and swap reporting rules, and failed to supervise its employees. . . .

Cargill, Inc. is a global agricultural, commodity, and financial services business headquartered in Minnesota. Cargill has been provisionally registered as a swap dealer since February 28, 2013; its application to be designated as a limited purpose swap dealer[10] was approved by the Commission on October 29, 2013. Cargill is also listed as a principal for certain of its affiliates that are registered with the Commission. . . .

Section 4s(h) of the Act, 7 U.S.C. § 6s(h), sets forth certain business conduct standards for swap dealers.[11] These include requirements that swap dealers disclose to counterparties (1) information about the material characteristics of the swap, (2) the swap dealer's material incentives and conflicts of interest related to the swap, and (3) a daily mark of each uncleared swap transaction.

---

10. [N. 2] A "limited purpose" swap dealer is an entity that the Commission designates as a swap dealer for one type, class, or category of swap or activities without the entity being considered a swap dealer for other types, classes, categories, or activities. *Further Definition of "Swap Dealer," "Security-Based Swap Dealer," "Major Swap Participant," "Major Security-based Swap Participant" and "Eligible Contract Participant,"* 77 Fed. Reg. 30,596, 30,643 (May 23, 2012). Cargill's swap dealer activity is conducted exclusively by its CRM business unit. *In the Matter of the Request of Cargill, Incorporated for Limited Purpose Swap Dealer Designations Under Section 1(a)(49)(B) of the Commodity Exchange Act* (CFTC Oct. 29, 2013).

11. [N. 3] Section 4s(h), 7 U.S.C. § 6s(h), also sets forth business conduct standards for major swap participants. Because Cargill is a swap dealer, the remainder of this Order will discuss the Act and Regulations only as they relate to swap dealers.

Regulation 23.431, 17 C.F.R. § 23.431, implements, among other provisions, the disclosure requirements of Section 4s(h), 7 U.S.C. § 6s(h). Pursuant to Regulation 23.431, swap dealers must disclose to counterparties,[12] among other things, "[a]t a reasonably sufficient time prior to entering into a swap," (1) the material characteristics of the particular swap, "which shall include the material economic terms of the swap, the terms relating to the operation of the swap, and the rights and obligations of the parties during the term of the swap," and (2) the material incentives and conflicts of interest the swap dealer may have in connection with the swap, which shall include "[w]ith respect to disclosure of the price of the swap, the price of the swap and the mid-market mark of the swap."[13]

Regulation 23.431 also requires that swap dealers disclose to counterparties the mid- market mark of uncleared swaps daily during the term of the swap, as well as "[t]he methodology and assumptions used to prepare the daily mark" and "[a]dditional information concerning the daily mark to ensure a fair and balanced communication."[14] In requiring that swap dealers disclose their methodology and assumptions, the Commission noted that "[t]he statutory daily mark requirement is meaningless unless the counterparty knows the methodology and assumptions that were used to calculate the mark. To make its own assessment of the value of the swap for its own purposes, the counterparty has to have information from the swap dealer . . . about how the mid-market mark was calculated."[15] The Commission further noted that for swaps in illiquid markets, the mid-market mark could be calculated using a model;[16] Regulation 23.431 itself provides that a swap dealer is "not required to disclose to the counterparty confidential, proprietary information about any model it may use to prepare the daily mark."[17]

---

12. [N. 4] Both Section 4s(h) and Regulation 23.431 limit the disclosure requirements discussed in this Order to counterparties who are not swap dealers, major swap participants, security-based swap dealers, or major security-based swap participants. Section 4s(h)(3)(B), 7 U.S.C. § 6s(h)(3)(B); Regulation 23.431(a), (d), 17 C.F.R. § 23.431(a), (d). The remainder of this Order will use the more general term "counterparties" to refer to the requirements of the Act and Regulation.

13. [N. 5] 17 C.F.R. § 23.431(a).

14. [N. 6] 17 C.F.R. § 23.431(d). Communicating in a fair and balanced manner with counterparties is independently required by the Regulations. Regulation 23.433, 17 C.F.R. § 23.433 (2017) ("With respect to any communication between a swap dealer . . . and any counterparty, the swap dealer . . . shall communicate in a fair and balanced manner based on principles of fair dealing and good faith.").

> Regulation 23.431 provides three examples of additional information that could be "appropriate" to disclose to ensure a fair and balanced communication: (a) that the mark may not be a price at which the swap could be terminated or unwound; (b) that the mark may not be a basis for margin calls; and (c) that the mark may not be the same as the value of the swap on the swap dealer's books. 17 C.F.R. § 23.431(d)(3)(ii).

15. [N. 7] *Business Conduct Standards for Swap Dealers and Major Swap Participants With Counterparties* ("Final Rule Release"), 77 Fed. Reg. 9,734, 9,768 (Feb. 17, 2012).

16. [N. 8] *Id.*

17. [N. 9] Regulation 23.431(d)(3)(i), 17 C.F.R. § 23.431(d)(3)(i).

Regulation 23.431 instructs swap dealers that both the pre-trade and daily mid-market marks the swap dealer discloses "shall not include amounts for profit, credit reserve, hedging, funding, liquidity, or any other costs or adjustments."[18] In adopting the rule, the Commission noted that the term mid-market "has been used by many industry participants since at least 1994,"[19] and characterized the mid-market mark as an "objective"[20] and "transparent"[21] value. The intention of the mid-market mark standard in the rule was "to achieve a degree of consistency in the calculation of the daily mark across swap dealers and major swap participants."[22] However, because the mid-market mark requirement was a "principal based" rule the Commission declined to "endorse any particular methodology" of calculating the mark.[23]

As part of the comprehensive regulatory regime for swaps, Regulation 23.402(a)(1), 17 C.F.R. § 23.402(a)(1) (2017), requires that swap dealers have written policies and procedures reasonably designed to ensure compliance with swap dealer business conduct standards, including Regulation 23.431, 17 C.F.R. § 23.431. In adopting Regulation 23.431, 17 C.F.R. § 23.431, the Commission noted that "the Commission will consider good faith compliance" with those policies and procedures as "a mitigating factor when exercising its prosecutorial discretion for violation of the rules."[24] . . .

Pre-dating its registration as a swap dealer, Cargill, through its CRM business unit, has offered various swaps to its customers, primarily to allow its customers to manage commodity risk. Cargill offers a range of swaps from more standardized, or "vanilla," swaps to highly complex, customized swaps tailored to customers' specific needs or preferences. Most of the customers of Cargill's swaps business are commodity producers and commercial end users.

For a number of years prior to its registration as a swap dealer, the most complex swaps Cargill offered were managed by a division of CRM known as Hedging Products, or "HP." These swaps could contain features to embed volatility or optionality

---

18. [N. 10] 17 C.F.R. § 23.431(d)(2). The Commission considered, but ultimately did not require, swap dealers to disclose their profit separately. *Business Conduct Standards for Swap Dealers and Major Swap Participants with Counterparties* ("Proposed Rule Release"), 75 Fed. Reg. 80,638, 80,645 (Dec. 22, 2010).

19. [N. 11] Final Rule Release, 77 Fed. Reg. at 9,768.

20. [N. 12] *Id.*

21. [N. 13] Proposed Rule Release, 75 Fed. Reg. at 80,646.

22. [N. 14] Final Rule Release, 77 Fed. Reg. at 9,811.

23. [N. 15] *Id.* at 9,768.

24. [N. 16] *Id.* at 9,744; see also *id.* at 9,766, 9,768 (noting specifically that good faith compliance would be relevant to violations of the mid-market mark requirements). The Commission further stated:

> To be considered good faith compliance, the Commission will consider, among other things, whether the swap dealer . . . made reasonable inquiry and took appropriate action where the swap dealer . . . had information that would cause a reasonable person to believe that any person acting for or on behalf of the swap dealer . . . was violating the CEA or the Commission's Regulations in connection with the swaps related business of the swap dealer. . . .
>
> *Id.* at 9,746.

into the transaction, such as caps, collars, floors, knock-in or knock-out rights, or various accrual or accumulation features.

From at least 2007 to 2012, Cargill's Hedging Products division provided swap counterparties with statements that contained a "market value" of the swap. For certain complex swaps, Cargill's policy was to report to counterparties a "market value" of the swap that amortized Cargill's expected revenue[25] on the swap equally over the first sixty calendar days of the swap. If—as occasionally happened—a counterparty sought to terminate a swap early, CRM would terminate the swap at or near the reported market value, and thus counterparties who terminated early would not be charged Cargill's full expected revenue.[26] One purpose of this policy was to amortize Cargill's mark up over the first sixty calendar days of the swap instead of showing the entire mark up to the counterparty on day one. . . .

Shortly after the Commission made public the final form of Regulation 23.431, 17 C.F.R. § 23.431, Cargill employees identified the mid-market mark requirements as meaning that Cargill would "have to show [its] mark up on swap trades."

From the beginning, this requirement concerned Cargill, particularly as it related to the Hedging Products division of CRM, which had previously been amortizing its revenue over sixty days for purposes of customer reporting. One CRM senior executive ("Cargill Executive") described the mid-market mark requirements as the number one concern about Cargill's impending registration as a swap dealer. The leadership group of Cargill's swaps business, which included a senior member of the compliance team and business executives, held at least one meeting to discuss "the implications" to Hedging Products, if Cargill had to register as a swap dealer, "of the requirement that they provide a mid-market mark price along with the execution price on each trade." In relation to that meeting, a senior member of the compliance team went on to say "Providing the mid-market mark price is concerning to HP and the impact it could have on earnings." In another email, this senior member of the compliance team described concern that "the transparency of the mid-market mark . . . could result in lower margins" for Hedging Products.

In light of its concerns about the effect of the mid-market mark requirements on its earnings and margins, Cargill explored various other options for calculating and providing mid-market marks. During this process, certain Cargill employees identified an opportunity to raise questions about the mid-market mark requirement with the Commission, but ultimately decided not to raise the topic because it

---

25. [N. 17] As used in this Order, the term "expected revenue" means the revenue Cargill expected to realize over the life of the swap.

26. [N. 18] Cargill calculated market value using a sophisticated propriety model that would value the various components of the complex swap using a common valuation methodology that accounted for past and present market conditions, the underlying price of the commodity or commodities, volatility, and prevailing interest rates, among other factors. Changes in the market value reported to customers over the life of the swap would be affected not only by the amortization of expected revenue, but also by changes in these model inputs, such as changes to the price of the underlying commodity and other market conditions.

was "too sensitive" and asking questions might "tip [Cargill's] hand" and result in an answer from the Commission that Cargill did not like.

Ultimately, Cargill decided to continue to use its prior practice of amortizing its expected revenue over sixty days for certain complex swaps, including complex swaps offered by Hedging Products, and providing an "unwind" or "termination" value as the mid-market mark. As a result, instead of showing the entire mark up on day one, after registration as a swap dealer Cargill reported a mid-market mark that did not reveal the unamortized revenue, both pre-trade and during the first sixty days of the swap.

Cargill, however, made one modification to its previous practice. Rather than amortizing all of its expected revenue over the first sixty days—which resulted in a "market value" of the swap on the date of the transaction that closely matched the price the customer had paid for the swap—Cargill decided to "recognize" ten percent of its expected revenue on the day of the swap and amortize the remaining ninety percent over the next sixty calendar days. One consideration in recognizing ten percent of expected revenue on the day of the swap was to create a mid-market mark that, pre-trade and shortly after the trade, was sufficiently different than the price the counterparty had paid that it would be believable to counterparties as Cargill's mark up.[27] Multiple Cargill employees, including the Cargill Executive, discussed whether ten percent would be a believable number to counterparties, and concluded that it would be.

The result of Cargill's amortization methodology for complex swaps was that, pre-trade and on the transaction date, Cargill provided mid-market marks to counterparties that concealed ninety percent of Cargill's expected revenue, including Cargill's expected profits and all other costs and adjustments Cargill used when setting the price it would charge to its counterparty. Cargill then reduced the mark over the next sixty days as it amortized the remaining revenue equally each day.

From its registration as a swap dealer until June 2016, Cargill did not disclose to its counterparties that it used an amortization methodology in connection with its complex swaps. In June 2016, after it learned of the Division of Enforcement's investigation, Cargill began disclosing that it employed a "revenue recognition policy" for complex swaps that "factored" ten percent of Cargill's revenue on the trade date and the remaining ninety percent equally over the next sixty calendar days, and disclosed elsewhere that it would calculate a daily mid-market mark "in accordance with [its] revenue recognition policy." Even after June 2016, Cargill did not directly disclose that, because the mid-market mark was calculated based on unamortized revenue, the mark failed to reveal all of Cargill's mark up.

---

27. [N. 19] Another consideration was Cargill's view that recognizing ten percent of expected revenue at the inception of a trade, even if the counterparty immediately unwound the transaction, was a reasonable amount to compensate Cargill for the upfront costs associated with structuring and selling complex swaps to its counterparties.

Certain employees expressed concern within Cargill about Cargill's use of the amortization methodology, both before and after Cargill's registration as a swap dealer. Among the concerns expressed was that the methodology masked the actual value of the swap from counterparties and did not comport with the requirements of the rule.[28] These concerns were expressed to employees at the highest level within Cargill's swap business, including to business leaders of Cargill's CRM division and CRM's compliance leadership. Nevertheless, despite the fact that certain Cargill employees identified issues with Cargill's mark methodology and raised their concerns with CRM leadership, Cargill has used the amortization methodology to calculate its mid-market marks on certain complex swaps from its provisional registration as a swap dealer until the date of this Order.

All swap dealers are subject to the mid-market mark requirements in Section 4s(h)(1), 7 U.S.C. § 6s(h)(1), and Regulation 23.431, 17 C.F.R. § 23.431. While the swaps for which Cargill uses its amortization methodology are complex and tailored to particular customers, certain other swap dealers offer similar products. By providing counterparties with mid-market marks that had the effect of concealing up to ninety percent of Cargill's estimated revenue, Cargill potentially advantaged itself over other swap dealers and may have prevented customers from making fully informed decisions about their options for hedging.

Since its registration as a swap dealer, Cargill has provided hundreds of customers with mid-market marks that amortized estimated revenue, in thousands of swap transactions. . . .

As discussed above, both Section 4s(h)(1), 7 U.S.C. § 6s(h)(1), and Regulation 23.431, 17 C.F.R. § 23.431, require swap dealers to disclose to counterparties (1) information about the material characteristics of the swap, (2) the swap dealer's material incentives and conflicts of interest related to the swap, and (3) a daily mark of each uncleared swap transaction. The Regulation additionally requires, as part of the disclosure of material incentives and conflicts of interest, disclosure of a pre-trade mark. 17 C.F.R. § 23.431. Regulation 23.431 requires that both the daily mark and the pre-trade mark "shall not include amounts for profit, credit reserve, hedging, funding, liquidity, or any other costs or adjustments." *Id.* Finally, the Regulation requires the swap dealer to disclose the "methodology and assumptions used to prepare the daily mark" and any additional information about the mark necessary to "ensure a fair and balanced communication." *Id.* In adopting Regulation 23.431, 17 C.F.R. § 23.431, the Commission stated that it would "consider good faith compliance with policies and procedures reasonably designed to comply with the business conduct standards rules as a mitigating factor when exercising its prosecutorial discretion for violation of the rules." Final Rule Release, 77 Fed. Reg. at 9,744.

---

28. [N. 20] Cargill employees, including the Cargill Executive, also recognized that Cargill's marks included anticipated profit, and that Regulation 23.431, 17 C.F.R. § 23.431, did not allow profit to be included in the marks. A compliance employee explained to the Cargill Executive that Cargill was choosing not to follow that portion of the Regulation.

Cargill, a swap dealer, provided counterparties with both pre-trade and daily mid-market marks that had the effect of concealing Cargill's full mark-up from counterparties, in that they were calculated based on amortizing Cargill's estimated revenue. Cargill further did not disclose to counterparties that it was employing this methodology for its marks until June 2016; as a result, Cargill's communications with counterparties prior to June 2016 were not "fair and balanced." Cargill also did not disclose to counterparties prior to June 2016 that counterparties who terminated complex swaps within the first sixty calendar days would not be charged Cargill's full estimated revenue, and therefore failed to disclose information about a material characteristic of its complex swaps. Cargill therefore violated Section 4s(h)(1), 7 U.S.C. § 6s(h)(1), and Regulation 23.431(a) and (d), 17 C.F.R. § 23.431(a), (d).

Moreover, in engaging in these violations, Cargill did not act in "good faith compliance with policies and procedures reasonably designed to comply with the business conduct standards rules." Final Rule Release, 77 Fed. Reg. at 9,744. Various Cargill employees expressed concerns that Cargill's marks for certain complex swaps did not accurately reflect the mid-market mark of the swaps during the first sixty calendar days of the trade. Further, Cargill employees chose not to seek Commission guidance on Cargill's mid-market mark methodology for these swaps out of concern that the Commission would disagree with Cargill's methodology. In light of these facts, Cargill does not meet the requirements of the Commission's policy statement regarding mitigation.

––––––––––

Cargill was fine $10 million as a result of these and other related violations.

b. Communications

In all communications to counterparties (whether end users or not), swap dealers and major swap participants must "communicate in a fair and balanced manner based on principles of fair dealing and good faith."[29]

There is precedent for "fair dealing" requirements in the rules of the National Futures Association. CFTC rules require the National Futures Association to adopt "rules to protect customers and ... to promote fair dealing with the public."[30] The National Futures Association has, among others, adopted rules requiring "high standards of commercial honor and just and equitable principles of trade" and prohibiting misleading or deceitful communications with the public.[31]

These rules were originally adopted for application to retail-facing entities such as futures commission merchants. One might ask what in the context of the swaps market constitutes "fair dealing"? The CFTC has offered little guidance other than to note that it is intentionally an open-ended concept to provide the CFTC flexibility.

––––––––––

29. 17 C.F.R. § 23.433.
30. 17 C.F.R. § 170.5.
31. *See* National Futures Association Rule Nos. 2-4 and 2-29.

CFTC, *Business Conduct Standards for Swap Dealers and Major Swap Participants with Counterparties*
77 Fed. Reg. 9734 (Feb. 17, 2012)

... [T]he Commission is providing the following guidance regarding the ... fair dealing rule.... [T]he fair dealing rule works ... to ensure that counterparties receive material information that is balanced and fair at all times. The Commission intends [the rule to address] ... concerns raised ... regarding transactions ... [involving] structured CDOs, [that] were problematic because they were designed to fail and the disclosures omitted and/or misrepresented the material risks, characteristics, incentives and conflicts of interest.... [T]he Commission's fair dealing rule ... operate[s] as an independent basis for enforcement proceedings.

The fair dealing rule ... is principles based and applies flexibly based on the facts and circumstances of a particular swap. For example, when addressing the risks and characteristics of a swap with features ... that increase its complexity, the fair dealing rule requires the swap dealer or major swap participant to provide a sound basis for the counterparty to assess how those features would impact the value of the swap under various market conditions during the life of the swap. In a complex swap, where the risks and characteristics associated with an underlying asset are not readily discoverable by the counterparty upon the exercise of reasonable diligence, the swap dealer or major swap participant is expected, under both the disclosure rule and fair dealing rule, to provide a sound basis for the counterparty to assess the swap by providing information about the risks and characteristics of the underlying asset. The fair dealing rule also will supplement requirements to inform counterparties of material incentives and conflicts of interest that would tend to be adverse to the interests of a counterparty in connection with a swap.... In this regard, a swap dealer or major swap participant will have to follow policies and procedures reasonably designed to ensure that the content and context of its disclosures are fair and complete to allow the counterparty to protect itself and make an informed decision.

In addition ... the Commission is confirming that it will look to [National Futures Association] guidance when interpreting [this requirement] and, as appropriate, will consider providing further guidance, if necessary.... The Commission concludes that the futures and securities industry familiarity with these precedents considerably mitigates concerns about legal certainty as a result of the principles based rule. Also, in the absence of fraud, the Commission will consider good faith compliance with policies and procedures reasonably designed to comply with the business conduct standards rules as a mitigating factor when exercising its prosecutorial discretion in connection with a violation of the rules....

––––––––––

As with other CFTC requirements, note the importance of "good faith compliance with policies and procedures" referenced in the final sentence. This implies CFTC recognition of interpretational latitude on the part of swap dealers and major swap participants. It may be more important to have a solid policy and procedure (and internal enforcement and monitoring thereof) than it is to perfectly ascertain the scope of the CFTC's fair dealing rule.

3. Recommendations and Suitability

Normally, the provision of recommendations regarding swaps would potentially subject the party making the recommendation to registration as a commodity trading advisor. However, there is an exemption for swap dealers so long as its advisory activities are incidental to its swap dealing activities.[32] This exemption is only applicable to swap dealers; a major swap participant would be required to register as a commodity trading advisor even if its advisory activities were merely incidental to its major swap participant activities.

> *Example One*: Washington Adams Bank is registered with the CFTC as a swap dealer. Its sales people frequently make presentations to potential customers about possible swaps hedging strategies in which it will act as counterparty.

> *Result*: The provision of swaps hedging strategies combined with the potential to act as a swap counterparty to its customers almost certainly meets the definition of commodity trading advisor since it constitutes advising "for compensation or profit." Nonetheless, Washington Adams Bank is not required to register as a commodity trading advisor because the relevant activities are incidental to its swap dealing activities.

> *Example Two*: Jefferson Madison Bank is registered with the CFTC as a swap dealer. Recognizing new business opportunities, it begins to offer a service where, for a monthly fee, it provides advice on hedging using the futures market. It proves to be very popular and more than fifty customers subscribe.

> *Result*: Jefferson Madison Bank meets the definition of commodity trading advisor by provide advice on the futures market for a fee. These activities are not incidental to its swap dealing activities and, therefore, it is required to register as a commodity trading advisor.

Swap dealers making recommendations to end users must: (1) "[u]ndertake reasonable diligence to understand the potential risks and rewards associated with the recommended swap"; and (2) "[h]ave a reasonable basis to believe that the recommended swap . . . is suitable for the counterparty."[33] This requirement does not apply to major swap participants. This is likely because swap dealers are exempt from commodity trading advisor registration for swap advice and major swap participants are not. A major swap participant making swap recommendations for profit would have to register as a commodity trading advisor unless it were eligible for an exemption.

---

32. 17 C.F.R. § 4.6(a)(3).
33. 17 C.F.R. § 23.434(a).

CFTC rules deem the second portion of the recommendation rule satisfied if the swap dealer determines that the end user, either by itself or with an advisor, is capable of independently evaluating the swap[34] and the end user represents in writing that it (or, if applicable, its advisor) is exercising independent judgement.[35] The swap dealer must in turn disclose in writing that it is acting as a counterparty and is not assessing the suitability of the swap for the end user.[36]

C. External Business Conduct Requirements with "Special Entities"

1. Background

Additional external business conduct requirements apply to swap dealers and major swap participants interacting with special entities. These are based on a perception that special entities require additional protections. Special entities are defined as, essentially, federal agencies, states and state agencies, municipalities and other political subdivisions, certain employee benefit plans, and charities.[37]

The perception that special entities need additional protection is partially grounded in a number of derivatives losses associated with special entities occurring over the last twenty-five years.[38] Before the Dodd-Frank Act and CFTC rules applied additional requirements for swap activities with special entities, courts were largely unwilling to treat them differently than other market counterparties.[39]

Another possible factor underlying the heightened requirements for special entities is the allegation of widespread bid-rigging in the municipal derivatives market. Investigations begun in 2008 by state attorneys general resulted in more than $400 million in settlements.[40]

---

34. For this purpose, a swap dealer may reasonably rely on a representation in writing that "the counterparty has complied in good faith with written policies and procedures that are reasonably designed to ensure that the persons responsible for evaluating the recommendation and making trading decisions on behalf of the counterparty are capable of doing so." 17 C.F.R. § 23.434(c)(1).

35. 17 C.F.R. § 23.434(b)(1) and (2).

36. 17 C.F.R. § 23.434(b)(3).

37. 17 C.F.R. § 23.401(c).

38. For a list of the derivatives losses receiving the most significant media attention, see Edward S. Adams and David E. Runkle, *The Easy Case for Derivatives Use; Advocating a Corporate Fiduciary Duty to Use Derivatives*, 41 William & Mary L. Rev. 595 (2000). For a more recent example of a municipal derivatives loss, albeit one attracting less media attention, see *Hinds County, Miss. v. Wachovia Bank N.A.*, 708 F. Supp. 2d 348 (S.D.N.Y. 2010).

39. *See, e.g.*, *Power & Telephone Supply Company v. SunTrust Banks*, 447 F.3d 923 (6th Cir. 2006), and *St. Matthew's Baptist Church v. Wachovia Bank National Association*, 2005 WL 1199045 (D.N.J. May 18, 2005).

40. Anne Steele, *Natixis, Société Générale Settle Municipal Bond Fraud Charges*, W.S.J. (Feb. 24, 2016).

2. Requirements When Acting as Counterparty to a Special Entity

a. Representative Requirements

The Dodd-Frank Act and CFTC regulations prohibit swap dealers or major participants from entering into a swap with a special entity unless the special entity has an independent representative. The swap dealer or major swap participant must reasonably believe that the representative is acting as a fiduciary to the special entity[41] and has "sufficient knowledge to evaluate the transaction and risks," acts in the best interest of the special entity, "[m]akes appropriate and timely disclosures" to the special entity, and evaluates "fair pricing and the appropriateness of the swap."[42]

The requirement that the representative be "independent," is multi-faceted. It precludes any transaction between a special entity and a swap dealer or major swap participant if the representative of the special entity:

- Has in the preceding year worked for the swap dealer or major swap participant in anything other than a clerical or ministerial function;

- Is directly or indirectly affiliated with the swap dealer or major swap participant;

- Was recommended or introduced to the special entity during the past year by the swap dealer or major swap participant; or

- Has not disclosed to the special entity all material conflicts of interest which could affect its independence or has not complied with policies and procedures designed to mitigate such conflicts.[43]

Note that the first three items are within the knowledge of a swap dealer or major swap participant and, therefore, easily determined by the swap dealer or major swap participant. The fourth, whether or not the special entity's representative has made the required disclosures to the special entity, is likely not known to the swap dealer or major swap participant. This reaffirms the importance of written disclosures and representations by the special entity or its representative as a means to satisfy many of these requirements. The CFTC deems the fourth requirement satisfied if a swap dealer gets written representations stipulating conformity with these provisions from the special entity and its advisor.[44]

In addition to the requirements pertaining to a special entity's representative, swap dealers and major swap participants must disclose the capacity in which they are acting with respect to the swap and, if they are acting in more than one

---

41. 17 C.F.R. § 23.450(b)(2).
42. 17 C.F.R. § 23.450(b)(1).
43. 17 C.F.R. § 23.450(c).
44. 17 C.F.R. § 23.450(d).

capacity (for example, arranging a competitive bid for the swap and acting as a competitor), they must disclose those capacities and the material differences between them.[45]

b. Limitation on Political Contributions

Swap dealers may not offer to enter into a swap with a governmental special entity, i.e., a state or state agency, municipality or other political subdivision, or certain government employee benefit plans,[46] if the swap dealer, its senior management, its employees who solicit swaps with governmental special entities, or the supervisors of such employees have made any contribution to an official of such special entity within the last two years.[47] The purpose of this prohibition is to combat "pay-to-play," i.e., a quid pro quo where, in return for political campaign contributions, an elected official will direct lucrative business to the employer of the contributor.

There is an exception for an up to $350 limit per official per election for management or employees who are entitled to vote for the official or $150 limit per official per election for management or employees not entitled to vote for the official. Contributions made by management or employees, other than those soliciting swaps with governmental entities, more than six months before being employed by the swap dealer are also excluded.[48] The CFTC provides a process for petitioning the CFTC for relief from the two-year ban in individual cases.[49]

The political contribution limitations do not apply to major swap participants. At the time the rule was issued, the CFTC reasoned:

> [T]he Commission decided to exclude major swap participants from the pay-to-play prohibition [i.e., the limitations on political contributions] because major swap participants, as defined, do not "solicit" swap transaction business within the meaning of the final rule and, as such, the Commission does not expect that major swap participants will assume a dealer-type role in the swap market.[50]

Limitations on political contributions raise First Amendment questions since they restrict a political speech activity. Similar limitations were upheld in the context of a rule issued by the Municipal Securities Rulemaking Board in relation to securities activities such as bond issuances with a municipality as issuer.

---

45. 17 C.F.R. § 23.450(g).

46. 17 C.F.R. § 23.451(a)(3).

47. 17 C.F.R. § 23.451(b)(1).

48. 17 C.F.R. § 23.451(b)(2). There is also relief in 17 C.F.R. § 23.451(e) that does not appear to differ in practical effect from relief already provided by 17 C.F.R. § 23.451(b)(2)(i).

49. 17 C.F.R. § 23.451(d).

50. CFTC, *Business Conduct Standards for Swap Dealers and Major Swap Participants with Counterparties*, 77 Fed. Reg. 9734, 9800 (Feb. 17, 2012).

Blount v. SEC

61 F.3d 938 (D.C. Cir. 1995)

Stephen F. Williams, Circuit Judge:

In late 1993, regulators of the municipal securities markets began to investigate reports that brokers and dealers were engaging in a variety of ethically questionable practices in order to secure underwriting contracts. These practices, often lumped together under the label "pay to play", include as a paradigmatic example the making of political contributions to state and local officials who may influence the choice of underwriter. Concerned that such practices were becoming more prevalent and were undermining the integrity of the $250 billion municipal securities market, the Municipal Securities Rulemaking Board ("MSRB" or "Board") drafted several new rules, which were then approved by the Securities and Exchange Commission. Among these was Rule G-37, the rule challenged in this case.

The two principal sections of Rule G-37, (b) and (c), together restrict the ability of municipal securities professionals to contribute and to solicit contributions to the political campaigns of state officials from whom they obtain business. Section (d) serves as a loophole-closer, prohibiting indirect violations of the restrictions in (b) or (c). . . .

The petitioner, William B. Blount, is the chairman of the Alabama Democratic Party and a registered broker and dealer of municipal securities. He challenges the SEC's order approving Rule G-37, claiming that each of the three sections of the rule we have described impermissibly infringes his First Amendment rights; that section (d) is, in addition, unconstitutionally vague; and that the rule as a whole violates the Tenth Amendment. The SEC rebuts each of these claims, and the MSRB, as intervenor, raises two defenses not urged by the SEC: that Blount does not have standing under the Exchange Act to pursue his claim and that the rule is not the product of government action and thus cannot violate either the First or Tenth Amendments. We find that Blount has standing to sue and that Rule G-37 is government action. We therefore meet all of Blount's arguments on the merits, though ultimately we reject them and deny the petition for review. . . .

We turn now to the central issue in this case, petitioner's claim that Rule G-37 violates his First Amendment rights to free speech and free association. . . .

All three sections of Rule G-37 at issue here infringe speech. Giving money is one method of indicating one's devotion to a cause; hence the familiar challenge, "Put your money where your mouth is." The Supreme Court has characterized the campaign contribution as a "symbolic act" that "serves as a general expression of support for the candidate and his views", though noting at the same time that the contribution does not indicate the basis for the support and that a limit on contributions does not "infringe the contributor's freedom to discuss candidates and issues." *Buckley v. Valeo*, 424 U.S. 1, 21, 96 S. Ct. 612, 636, 46 L.Ed.2d 659 (1976) (*per curiam*). Solicitation of campaign funds, the target of sections (c) and (d), is close to the core of protected speech, as it is "characteristically intertwined" with both information and advocacy and essential to the continued flow of both. . . .

The intensity with which we scrutinize Rule G-37 depends on whether the rule is content-based, eliciting "strict" scrutiny, or content-neutral, eliciting only "intermediate" scrutiny. The proper categorization of Rule G-37 is not clear-cut. As petitioner points out, under the everyday meaning of the word "content", the rule appears to be content-based, as it restricts only messages that concern one "topic", specifically, financial contributions to political campaigns. But the Supreme Court does not regard a rule's use of subject-based categories as automatically establishing it as content-based. The critical issue is whether the state's justification for the distinction is the "content" of the speech itself or some other concern. . . .

If the rule can withstand strict scrutiny there is no need to decide the issue. Accordingly we turn to applying such scrutiny and ask . . . whether the rule is narrowly tailored to serve a compelling government interest. . . .

The Commission claims that Rule G-37 supports two interests . . . : (1) protecting investors in municipal bonds from fraud and (2) protecting underwriters of municipal bonds from unfair, corrupt market practices. Both of these interests are not only substantial . . . but, we think, compelling. . . .

[P]etitioner claims there is no support for the Commission's finding that pay-to-play practices are prevalent in the negotiated municipal bond business, because the record contains no evidence of specific instances of *quid pro quos.* But underwriters' campaign contributions self-evidently create a conflict of interest in state and local officials who have power over municipal securities contracts and a risk that they will award the contracts on the basis of benefit to their campaign chests rather than to the governmental entity. Petitioner himself remarked on national radio that "most likely [state and local officials] are gonna call somebody who has been a political contributor" and, at least in close cases, award contracts to "friends" who have contributed. Morning Edition (National Public Radio, June 1, 1994), available in LEXIS, News Library, Transcript No. 1358-9. While the risk of corruption is obvious and substantial, actors in this field are presumably shrewd enough to structure their relations rather indirectly — indeed, the phrase "pay to play" suggests that a contribution brings the donor merely a chance to be seriously considered, not the assurance of a contract. . . . Although the record contains only allegations, no smoking gun is needed where, as here, the conflict of interest is apparent, the likelihood of stealth great, and the legislative purpose prophylactic. . . .

Even assuming the prevalence of *quid pro quos,* Blount maintains, the Commission has not demonstrated that eliminating such activity advances the asserted interests in protecting investors and promoting just and equitable principles of trade. As to the harm to investors, we tend to share the petitioner's skepticism. . . .

On the other hand, the link between eliminating pay-to-play practices and the Commission's goals of "perfecting the mechanism of a free and open market" and promoting "just and equitable principles of trade" is self-evident. . . .

Blount asserts that Rule G-37 is too broad, arguing that the Commission could have achieved its goal with less restrictive means. . . .

[T]he regulation is "closely drawn" and thus "avoid[s] unnecessary abridgement" of First Amendment rights, *Buckley v. Valeo*, 424 U.S. at 25, 96 S. Ct. at 638. Rule G-37 constrains relations only between the two potential parties to a *quid pro quo*: the underwriters and their municipal finance employees on the one hand, and officials who might influence the award of negotiated municipal bond underwriting contracts on the other. Even then, the rule restricts a narrow range of their activities for a relatively short period of time. The underwriter is barred from engaging in business with the particular issuer for only two years after it makes a contribution, and it is barred from soliciting contributions only during the time that it is engaged in or seeking business with the issuer associated with the donee. A municipal finance professional may contribute [a limited amount] per election to each official for whom he or she is entitled to vote, without triggering the business bar. Furthermore, as the Commission interprets the rule, municipal finance professionals are not in any way restricted from engaging in the vast majority of political activities, including making direct expenditures for the expression of their views, giving speeches, soliciting votes, writing books, or appearing at fundraising events. . . .

Because Rule G-37 withstands all of Blount's challenges, the petition for review is Denied.

———————

Blount was decided before the Supreme Court ruled, in *Citizens United v. FEC*[51] that the First Amendment applies to some corporations. The SEC has subsequently issued Rule 206(4)-5,[52] which limits political contributions by SEC-regulated investment advisers in a similar fashion to MSRB Rule G-37's limitations on securities broker-dealers and the CFTC's limitations on swap dealers. The SEC sought to distinguish *Citizens United* by arguing that "*Citizens United* deals with certain independent expenditures (rather than contributions to candidates), which are not implicated by our rule."[53] The SEC also approved a rule by the Financial Industry Regulatory Authority, a self-regulatory organization for the securities industry analogous to the Futures Industry Association, applying similar political contribution limitations to placement agents used by some investment advisers to obtain investment adviser customers.[54]

Subsequently, the Supreme Court abolished individual campaign contribution limits in *McCutcheon v. Federal Election Commission*.[55] However, in the context

———————

51. 558 U.S. 310 (2010).

52. 17 C.F.R. § 275.206(4)-5.

53. SEC, *Political Contributions by Certain Investment Advisers*, 75 Fed. Reg. 41018-01, 41023 at n. 68 (July 14, 2010).

54. Financial Industry Regulatory Authority Rule 2030. We discuss the role of the Financial Industry Regulatory Authority in chapter 16.

55. 572 U.S. 185 (2014).

of the Financial Industry Regulatory Authority's new rule, the Circuit Court for the District of Columbia upheld the rule and distinguished the facts from those in *McCutcheon*.[56] Due to the similarity of the CFTC's limitations on swap dealers, the decision should provide even more certainty to the likelihood of the CFTC's limits on political contributions by swap dealers being upheld in court.

3. Requirements When Acting as Advisor to a Special Entity

Additional requirements are imposed on a swap dealer acting as an advisor to a special entity in relation to swaps. As noted in section B.3 above, for swap dealers such advisory activities do not trigger a requirement to register as a commodity trading advisor so long as the advisory activities are incidental to its swap dealer activities.[57]

These requirements do not apply to a major swap participant. This is possibly the case because a major swap participant providing swap advisory services for compensation would be required to register as a commodity trading advisor and be subject to that regulatory scheme.[58]

A swap dealer is deemed to be acting as an advisor if it recommends a swap trading strategy tailored for the special entity.[59] The general duty imposed on swap dealers is to make a "reasonable determination" that any recommended swap is in the "best interests" of the special entity.[60] The CFTC has affirmed that, despite this standard bearing similarity to a fiduciary's duty of care, these requirements do not impose a fiduciary relationship between a swap dealer and a special entity.

CFTC, *Business Conduct Standards for Swap Dealers and Major Swap Participants with Counterparties*
77 Fed. Reg. 9734 (Feb. 17, 2012)

. . . The Commission has determined not to define the term "best interests," but rather to provide further guidance as to the meaning of the term and the scope of the duty.

The Commission has considered commenters' views and the legislative history in regard to whether [Commodity Exchange Act] Section 4s(h)(4) [the statutory provision on which the rule is based] imposes a fiduciary duty. The Commission has determined that the "best interests" duty under Section 4s(h)(4) is not a fiduciary

---

56. *N.Y. Republican State Committee v. SEC*, 927 F.3d 499, 511 (D.C. Cir. 2019).

57. 17 C.F.R. § 4.6(a)(3).

58. Whereas Commodity Exchange Act section 4s(h)(5), the statutory basis for the regime on trading swaps as principal with special entities, incudes swap dealers and major swap participants, Commodity Exchange Act section 4s(h)(4), the statutory basis for the regime on acting as an advisor to a special entity with respect to swaps, applies only to swap dealers.

59. 17 C.F.R. § 23.440(a).

60. 17 C.F.R. § 23.440(c).

duty. Additionally, the Commission does not view the business conduct standards statutory provisions or rules . . . [as imposing] a fiduciary duty on a swap dealer with respect to any other party.

Whether a recommended swap is in the "best interests" of the Special Entity will turn on the facts and circumstances of the particular recommendation and particular Special Entity. However, the Commission will consider a swap dealer that "acts as an advisor to a Special Entity" to have complied with its duty . . . where the swap dealer (1) . . . [makes] a reasonable effort to obtain necessary information [for making a recommendation], (2) acts in good faith and makes full and fair disclosure of all material facts and conflicts of interest with respect to the recommended swap, and (3) employs reasonable care that any recommendation made to a Special Entity is designed to further the Special Entity's stated objectives.

For a recommendation of a swap to be in the best interests of the Special Entity, the swap does not need to be the "best" of all possible alternatives that might hypothetically exist, but should be assessed in comparison to other swaps, such as swaps offered by the swap dealer or "made available for trading" on a SEF or DCM. To be in the best interests of a Special Entity, the recommended bespoke swap would have to further the Special Entity's hedging, investing or other stated objectives. Additionally, whether a recommended swap is in the best interests of the Special Entity will be analyzed based on information known to the swap dealer (after it has employed its reasonable efforts [as] required . . .) at the time the recommendation is made. The "best interests" duty does not prohibit a swap dealer from negotiating swap terms in its own interests, nor does it prohibit a swap dealer from making a reasonable profit from a recommended transaction. Depending on the facts and circumstances, the "best interests" duty also does not require an ongoing obligation to act in the best interests of the Special Entity. For example, a swap dealer would be able to exercise its rights under the terms and conditions of the swap when determining whether to make additional collateral calls in response to the Special Entity's deteriorating credit rating, whether or not such collateral calls would be, from the Special Entity's perspective, in the Special Entity's "best interests." . . .

———————

CFTC rules also provide that a swap dealer will not be deemed an advisor if, with respect to special entities that are employee benefit plans, the special entity represents in writing that it has a fiduciary advisor and the advisor represents that it will evaluate any swap recommendations.[61] Similar relief is available to swap dealers with respect to all other special entities so long as the swap dealer, on the one hand, does not express an opinion as to whether the special entity should enter into a swap and discloses that it is not acting in the special entity's best interest, and, on the

———————

61. 17 C.F.R. § 23.440(b)(1).

other hand, the special entity represents in writing that it will not rely on the swap dealer's advice and that it has an independent representative.[62]

D. Other Regulations Applying to Uncleared Swaps

1. Variation Margin and Initial Margin

Swap dealers and major swap participants entering into uncleared swaps are in many circumstances required to exchange variation margin. Some very large market participants are also required to exchange initial margin. We examined both of these concepts in the context of futures trading in chapter 6, section B.1. As we will see, even though with uncleared swaps variation margin and initial margin are not always exchanged, when they are exchanged, they operate similarly to variation margin and initial margin in futures trading.

As is also the case with capital requirements, discussed in chapter 11, responsibility for issuing margin rules and overseeing margin regulation is divided between the CFTC and the "prudential regulators." The prudential regulators are the Federal Reserve Board, Office of the Comptroller of the Currency, Federal Deposit Insurance Corporation, Farm Credit Administration, and Federal Housing Finance Agency.[63] Entities regulated by one of the prudential regulators must follow the prudential regulators' margin rules.[64]

Unlike capital, there are minimal differences between the CFTC's and the prudential regulators' rules. The largest difference is that the prudential regulators' rules apply to swaps and security-based swaps, while the CFTC's apply only to swaps, and SEC rules apply to security-based swaps (see chapter 13). Due to the similarities, the CFTC rules will be used as the model for our discussions herein on initial margin and variation margin requirements.

The impetus for the requirements, like most of the Dodd-Frank initiated regulations, stems from the Financial Crisis.

CFTC, *Margin Requirements for Uncleared Swaps for Swap Dealers and Major Swap Participants*
76 Fed. Reg. 23732 (Apr. 28, 2011)

... During the recent financial crisis, derivatives clearing organizations ("DCOs") met all their obligations without any financial infusions from the government. By contrast, significant sums were expended as the result of losses incurred in

---

62. 17 C.F.R. § 23.440(b)(2).
63. Commodity Exchange Act § 1a(39).
64. Commodity Exchange Act § 4s(e).

connection with uncleared swaps, most notably at AIG. A key reason for this difference is that DCOs all use variation margin and initial margin as the centerpiece of their risk management programs while these tools were often not used in connection with uncleared swaps. Consequently, in designing the proposed margin rules for uncleared swaps, the Commission has built upon the sound practices for risk management employed by central counterparties for decades.

Variation margin entails marking open positions to their current market value each day and transferring funds between the parties to reflect any change in value since the previous time the positions were marked. This process prevents losses from accumulating over time and thereby reduces both the chance of default and the size of any default should one occur.

Initial margin serves as a performance bond against potential future losses. If a party fails to meet its obligation to pay variation margin, resulting in a default, the other party may use initial margin to cover most or all of any loss based on the need to replace the open position.

With the notable exception of AIG, before the onset of margin rules, some parties to uncleared swaps did exchange initial margin and many exchanged variation margin. However, there were occasional disputes as to the calculation of the margin, some resolved by dialogue and some resolved in court. The following case provides a typical example of such a dispute and provides a backdrop to the context in which mandatory margining of many uncleared swaps was imposed. As we progress through the margin regulations further below, a question to consider is to what extent the existence of margin regulations affects the occurrence of disputes.

Note that the below case refers to "independent amount." This is another term for initial margin.

VCG Special Opportunities Master Fund v. Citibank, N.A.

594 F. Supp. 2d 334 (S.D.N.Y. 2008), *aff'd*, 355 Fed. Appx. 507
(2d Cir. 2009) (citations to pleadings omitted)

Barbara S. Jones, District Judge. . . .

Citibank, N.A. ("Citibank") moves this Court for judgment . . . dismissing the complaint of . . . VCG Special Opportunities Master Fund Limited ("VCG"). . . . For the reasons that follow, Citibank's motion is GRANTED. . . .

This action arises from a credit default swap (or "CDS") transaction between VCG and Citibank, by which VCG sold Citibank credit protection against the risk of a credit default by a collateralized debt obligation (or "CDO"). In a typical CDS transaction of this kind, the "protection buyer" makes regular payments to a "protection seller," with "reference" to a specific credit obligation. The credit obligation is generally referred to as the "reference obligation," and the issuer of that obligation is generally referred to as the "reference entity." In return for receiving the protection buyer's payments, the protection seller agrees to undertake the credit exposure of the underlying reference obligation. . . .

The primary contract documents governing the parties' rights and obligations under the CDS transaction are the 2002 version of the Master Agreement of the International Swap Dealers Association ("ISDA"), dated September 1, 2006 (the "ISDA Master Agreement"); the Schedule to the ISDA Master Agreement, dated September 1, 2006 (the "Schedule"); the 1994 ISDA Credit Support Annex, dated September 1, 2006 (the "Credit Support Annex"); and the Confirmation Letter by Citibank, dated July 5, 2007 (the "Confirmation Letter"). . . .

Pursuant to these documents (collectively, the "CDS Contract"), Citibank acted as the protection buyer in the parties' transaction. Citibank agreed to make . . . periodic "Fixed Payments" to VCG based on a fixed percentage of 5.50% per annum on an "Initial Face Amount" of the reference obligation, Class B Notes. The Class B Notes were issued by the reference entity, the Millstone III CDO Ltd. III-A (the "Millstone III CDO"). . . .

VCG acted as the protection seller for the CDS transaction. As protection seller, VCG undertook the default risk of the reference obligation; that is, VCG agreed to pay Citibank a "Floating Payment" if certain credit events (or "Floating Amount Events") took place during the term of the CDS Contract. VCG also agreed to deposit collateral at the time of the execution of the CDS Contract to secure Citibank against the risk that VCG would not be in a position to make the Floating Payments. This collateral is called the "Independent Amount," the amount of which was specified in the Confirmation Letter. . . .

Apart from the Independent Amount, some CDS transactions allow the protection buyer to demand additional collateral (or "variation margin") based upon a downward movement in the daily "mark-to-market value" of the underlying reference obligation.[65] The parties disagree on whether the CDS Contract allowed Citibank to demand variation margin from VCG. The record reflects, however, that on August 1, 2007, Citibank demanded additional collateral from VCG. Citibank demanded additional collateral from VCG three more times over the weeks that followed. VCG alleges that while it delivered the sums requested, it nonetheless questioned Citibank's evaluation of the credit risk of the Class B Notes. Further, VCG maintains that it delivered the sums out of fear that Citibank might seize upon VCG's refusal to post variation margin as a reason to declare a technical default and seize VCG's collateral. . . .

The gravamen of VCG's complaint is that Citibank improperly demanded from VCG additional collateral beyond the Independent Amount. . . .

---

65. [N. 4] "Mark-to-market" is a term of art in the financial and accounting industries. When an institution marks an asset to market, it assesses and records on its books a change in the asset's value since the last time a valuation took place, whether the gain (or loss) is realized or not.

VCG argues that Citibank's requests for additional collateral were inconsistent with the terms set forth in the Confirmation Letter that the parties signed as part of the CDS Contract. The Court disagrees. The Credit Support Annex allowed for Citibank to request additional collateral from VCG depending upon Citibank's calculation of its "Exposure," or the amount of loss Citibank would incur (or gains it would realize) in replacing the CDS transaction with an economically equivalent transaction at the time of calculation. In turn, the Confirmation Letter states clearly that "[t]his Transaction shall be subject to the Credit Support Annex . . . between Citibank and [VCG]." The Court finds nothing in the Confirmation Letter that modifies VCG's obligation to transfer additional collateral as set forth in the Credit Support Annex.

Further, whether or not any inconsistency exists, VCG's challenge is waived in light of its continued agreement to post additional collateral. "It is well-established that where a party to an agreement has actual knowledge of another party's breach and continues to perform under and accepts the benefits of the contract, such continuing performance constitutes a waiver of the breach." *Nat'l Westminster Bank, U.S.A. v. Ross*, 130 B.R. 656, 675 (S.D.N.Y.1991), *aff'd sub nom., Yaeger v. Nat'l Westminster*, 962 F.2d 1 (2d Cir.1992). Although VCG maintains that it "believed it was not obligated to pay the sums demanded by Citibank," it nonetheless continued to post the sums requested "because it was concerned that Citibank might seize upon [VCG's] refusal to post variation margin as an excuse to declare a technical default and seize [its] collateral." Given VCG's actual posting of the disputed credit support, and its receipt of Citibank's regular payments during this time, VCG cannot now claim that Citibank breached the CDS Contract by wrongly demanding additional collateral.

The Court also notes that the Credit Support Annex contains a Dispute Resolution provision as a mechanism to challenge Citibank's Exposure determinations or demands for additional collateral. VCG concedes that it did not invoke this Dispute Resolution provision. It argues that doing so would have been meaningless, as the parties had not yet finished discussing the issue of variation margin before Citibank declared that a Floating Amount Event had occurred. This position suggests that the Dispute Resolution process was optional instead of mandatory. New York public policy, however, favors alternative dispute resolution mechanisms that reflect the informed negotiation and endorsement of the parties. . . . As VCG was aware of the expedited Dispute Resolution clause set forth in the CDS Contract, VCG cannot now challenge Citibank's request for additional collateral without having first vetted this claim in the manner agreed upon in the CDS Contract. *See Acme Supply Co., Ltd. v. City of New York*, 39 A.D.3d 331, 834 N.Y.S.2d 142, 143 (2007) (construing clauses providing for alternative dispute resolution mechanisms as mandatory is supported by the long-standing principle under New York law that contracts are to be interpreted in a manner that would give full effect to all provisions). VCG's claim that Citibank wrongly demanded variation margin therefore fails. . . .

VCG alleges in the alternative claims of rescission . . . [and] breach of the implied covenant of good faith and fair dealing. . . . For the following reasons, these claims are without merit. . . .

VCG claims that it believed it was agreeing "to sell credit protection on a credit default swap" and "not to take the risk of daily mark-to-market movement in the value of the reference obligation." . . . Under New York law, rescission of a contract on the basis of a unilateral mistake may be had if a party establishes that "(i) he entered into a contract based upon a mistake as to a material fact, and that (ii) the other contracting party either knew or should have known that such a mistake was being made." *NCR Corp. v. Lemelson Medical, Educ. and Research Foundation*, No. 99 Civ. 3017(KNF), 2001 WL 1911024, at *7 (S.D.N.Y.2001), *aff'd,* 33 Fed.Appx. 7 (2d Cir.2002). Furthermore, "[a] contract may be voided on the ground of unilateral mistake of fact only where the enforcement of the contract would be unconscionable, the mistake is material and made despite the exercise of ordinary care by the party in error." *William E. McClain Realty, Inc. v. Rivers*, 144 A.D.2d 216, 534 N.Y.S.2d 530, 531 (1988); *see Morey v. Sings*, 174 A.D.2d 870, 570 N.Y.S.2d 864, 867 (1991). But rescission of a contract is not appropriate where a unilateral mistake is the product of negligence. *See NCR Corp.*, 2001 WL 1911024, at *7.

VCG's claim of entitlement to rescission based upon unilateral mistake is not supportable here. First, the language of the Credit Support Annex makes clear that Citibank may request additional collateral from VCG depending on the current value of the CDS Contract at the time of Citibank's calculation of its Exposure. Second, VCG is a sophisticated hedge fund. No claim has been made by VCG that it was limited in its ability to review drafts of the agreement or to discuss the provisions of the CDS Contract before it was executed. Notwithstanding VCG's assertions to the contrary, it appears that the instant case presents a circumstance where VCG, a sophisticated hedge fund, simply failed to review carefully the terms of the parties' agreement. If VCG was negligent in this regard, this does not justify rescission. . . .

VCG next contends that Citibank breached the implied covenant of good faith and fair dealing by "making oppressive [variation] margin demands without justification." . . . With regard to VCG's allegation of a breach of the implied covenant on the basis of variation margin . . . this claim is waived in light of VCG's continued posting of the demanded collateral and acceptance of the benefits of the CDS Contract. . . .

For reasons discussed above, Citibank's motion for judgment on the pleadings is GRANTED. . . .

––––––––––

In *VCG Special Opportunities Fund*, the initial margin (termed "independent amount") and variation margin requirements were exclusively by contract. Much discretion in calculating the variation margin amount was granted to Citibank. Many swap arrangements still operate as described in *VCG Special Opportunities Fund*. As we will see, just as there are exemptions for clearing if, among other requirements, one of the parties to a swap is not a swap dealer, major swap participant, or "financial entity," there are almost coterminous exemptions from margin requirements if, among other requirements, one of the parties is not a swap dealer, major swap participant, or what is termed a "financial end user." For such swap trading relationships there are no margin requirements and, if the parties wish to exchange margin, it will operate largely as described in *VCG Special Opportunities Fund*—albeit one hopes without the dispute in that case.[66]

The Dodd-Frank Act, in addition to mandating the exchange of variation and initial margin in some uncleared swap relationships, required that mandatory initial margin must be segregated, i.e., held by third-party custodians. Variation margin is not subject to this requirement. Additionally, swap dealers or major swap participants trading with end users must, if initial margin is voluntarily exchanged, notify the end user beforehand that it has a right for it to be held by a third-party custodian.[67] There is no such segregation right for variation margin.

a. Variation Margin

Variation margin requirements apply to all swaps trades (other than physically-settled foreign exchange swaps and forwards) between, on the one hand, swap dealers or major swap participants and, on the other hand, swap dealers, major swap participants, or financial end users. Although the definition of financial end user differs in some respects from the definition of financial entity, a general rule of thumb is that if a party can claim a clearing exemption it can also claim an exemption from margin requirements. (As a reminder, "financial entity" is the category used to determine whether or not an end user party to a swap can claim an exemption from a swap that is otherwise required to be cleared; see chapter 10, section B.3.) There are exceptions for inter-affiliate swaps, bank holding companies, savings and loan holding companies, and community development financial institutions.[68] Swaps with these entities are exempt from clearing but, if the swap is with a swap dealer or major swap participant, these entities would not be exempt from variation margin requirements.

The regulations require that the parties have a written agreement providing for the framework for exchange of variation margin.[69] The most typical such agreement used, the ISDA Credit Support Annex, is briefly discussed below in section E.

---

66. Note that collection and posting of independent amount is less common than the collection and posting of variation margin.

67. 17 C.F.R. § 23.701.

68. *See* CFTC, *Swap Clearing Requirement Exemptions*, 85 Fed. Reg. 76428, 76441 (Nov. 30, 2020). There is also a difference in that there is an exemption from clearing for a list of twenty-two "international financial institutions" (17 C.F.R. § 50.76) and an exemption from variation margin for a list of one named entity and thirteen "multilateral development banks" (17 C.F.R. § 23.151). The gap of eight entities may be accounted for because both sections have a catch-all for "any other entity that provides financing for national or regional development in which the U.S. government is a shareholder or contributing member. . . ."

69. 17 C.F.R. § 23.158.

The agreement must provide for the variation margin amount to be calculated on each business day that there is a swap trade outstanding between parties. The variation margin amount is calculated by determining what the overall amount one party would owe to the other if all of the swap trades between the parties were unwound.[70] This is known as the "mark-to-market" value and it changes frequently requiring the parties to readjust the level of variation margin.

If the relationship is between a swap dealer or major swap participant and a financial end user, the variation margin that is provided can take the form of cash as well as government securities, bonds, equities, and gold.[71] For non-cash margin, the value of the margin is discounted (termed a "haircut") based on its perceived volatility.[72] Swap dealers and major swap participants trading among themselves may only provide cash for variation margin.

> *Example*: Monroe Adams Bank and Jackson Polk Fund have a swap trading relationship. Monroe Adams Bank is a swap dealer and Jackson Polk Fund is a financial end user. The calculation of the exposure of all of their swaps together (including or excluding physically-settled foreign exchange swaps and forwards at their option) results in Jackson Polk Fund having an exposure to Monroe Adams Bank of $5 million if the swaps were unwound today. Monroe Adams Bank posts $5 million in cash as collateral to Jackson Polk Fund.
>
> The next day the exposure is calculated again. This time Jackson Polk Fund only has an exposure to Monroe Adams Bank of $4.5 million due to market movements. Jackson Polk Fund must return $500,000 of the cash collateral provided the day before by Monroe Adams Bank.
>
> The next day the exposure is calculated once more. This time Jackson Polk Fund has an exposure to Monroe Adams Bank of $5.5 million. Monroe Adams Bank, therefore, must provide more collateral. It could provide $1 million in cash. Instead, it decides to provide corporate debt maturing in four years. CFTC rules provide that such debt needs to be discounted, i.e., "haircut," by 4% when assessing its value as collateral for variation margin. To meet its variation margin obligation Monroe Adams Bank must provide $1,041,667 in face amount of the corporate debt. (In case it is of interest, this result can be calculated by dividing $1,000,000 by 96%; $41,667 is 4% of $1,041,667.)

If in the above example we had, instead, two swap dealers, the swap dealers would have been restricted solely to using cash for variation margin purposes.[73] Although in this example, Monroe Adams Bank owed variation margin to the Jackson Polk

---

70. 17 C.F.R. § 23.151.

71. 17 C.F.R. § 23.156(b)(1)(2).

72. *See* 17 C.F.R. § 23.156(b)(2). There are also "haircuts" potentially applied to the cash depending on the currency in which it is denominated. *Id.*

73. 17 C.F.R. § 23.156(b)(1)(i).

Fund, the example could just as easily reversed these as the party who owes variation margin depends on the mark-to-market value of their swaps.

To avoid frequent transfers of small amounts of margin, CFTC rules allow the parties to exchange margin only once the amount to be transferred is in excess of $500,000.[74] This is known as a "minimum transfer amount." If the parties also are required to exchange initial margin (see below), this $500,000 minimum transfer amount must be divided between variation and initial margin in whatever way the parties negotiate. For example, it might be $250,000 minimum transfer amount for variation margin and $250,000 minimum transfer amount for initial margin or $500,000 minimum transfer amount for variation margin and zero minimum transfer amount for initial margin.

b. Initial Margin

Initial margin has a narrower applicability. It only applies to parties already subject to variation margin with the additional requirement that both parties have "material swaps exposure." Although it is being progressively implemented beginning with much higher thresholds for what constitutes a "material swaps exposure,"[75] once fully implemented in September 2022 "material swaps exposure" is similar to the *de minimis* threshold we discussed in chapter 11 in which an entity engaged in swap dealing activities is not required to register as a swap dealer if its activities are below the *de minimis* threshold. Both are defined at $8 billion notional calculated over a year including all swaps among affiliated entities. For example, if Parent Co. owns more than fifty percent of the shares of Sub Co. their total swap notional amounts are combined.[76] When calculated for initial margin, the main difference from the *de minimis* calculation is that foreign exchange swaps and forwards, most security-based swaps, and swaps entered into for hedging purposes are included in the material swaps exposure calculation for initial margin and excluded from the calculation of swaps to assess the *de minimis* threshold.[77]

Initial margin is calculated on a per trade basis and it is intended to provide a buffer for changes to mark-to-market values that may occur between a close-out of positions and establishment of new ones thereby providing protection to a party who is owed variation margin that goes unpaid. It can be calculated using a standard reference table showing the amount that needs to be provided as initial margin for each category and size of trade or by use of a model approved by the relevant regulators.[78] The latter is the only method currently in use.

---

74. 17 C.F.R. § 23.152(c).

75. 17 C.F.R. § 23.161(a).

76. 17 C.F.R. §§ 23.151. The standard is, strictly speaking, whether the entities would be or are consolidated for accounting purposes with each other or a common third entity.

77. *Id.*

78. 17 C.F.R. § 23.154.

Initial margin may be in the form of cash, government securities, bonds, equities, or gold.[79] Just as with variation margin collateral, for non-cash margin the value of the margin is discounted based on its perceived volatility.[80]

Parties subject to the initial margin requirement only must post initial margin when the amount of initial margin owed exceeds a threshold of $50 million.[81] This threshold is applied on a group-to-group basis. For example, if Mega Bank and its fully-owned subsidiary, Mega Bank Sub, each have swap trading relationships with Swap Bank, the $50 million threshold must be allocated between Mega Bank and Mega Bank Sub. It can be done as the parties desire. For example, it could be $25 million and $25 million or one of the Mega Bank entities could use the whole $50 million for its swap trading relationship with Swap Bank and the other would have a zero threshold in its trading relationship with Swap Bank.

Initial margin collected or posted pursuant to the initial margin rules must be segregated with a third-party custodian.[82] As with variation margin, the regulations require that the parties have a written agreement providing for the framework for exchange of initial margin.[83] The most typical such agreement used is a special form of the ISDA Credit Support Annex. In addition, documentation must be agreed with the third-party custodians for each of the parties. Due to the complexities of negotiating this suite of agreements, the CFTC has clarified that the documentation only must be in place once the $50 million initial margin threshold is exceeded.[84] As a practical matter, this requires parties to regularly calculate initial margin to see if the level of trading activity and market movements is resulting in it approaching $50 million.

How Much Does It Cost?

It is a difficult exercise to prospectively quantify the costs that regulations will impose. The CFTC's efforts to do so with respect to margin requirements for uncleared swaps were criticized by the CFTC's Office of the Inspector General as insufficient in numerous ways and the CFTC was said to "lack an institutional commitment to robust cost-benefit considerations."[a]

The Office of the Comptroller of the Currency estimated costs for the eighty percent of swap dealers for which it oversees compliance with margin rules (it is one of the "prudential regulators"; see section D.1). The costs it estimated for

---

79. 17 C.F.R. § 23.156(a)(1).
80. 17 C.F.R. § 23.156(a)(3).
81. 17 C.F.R. 23.154(a)(3).
82. 17 C.F.R. § 23.157. If it is voluntarily exchanged without a regulatory requirement, then it only must be segregated if requested by an end user counterparty. 17 C.F.R. § 23.701.
83. 17 C.F.R. § 23.158.
84. CFTC Letter No. 19-16 (July 9, 2019).

> the prudential regulators' margin rule (substantially similar for these purposes
> to that adopted) were between \$2.8 billion and \$5.2 billion.[b] Remember, nearly
> all regulations impose a cost.
>
> [a] CFTC, Office of the Inspector General, *A Review of the Cost-Benefit Consideration for the Margin Rule for Uncleared Swaps* pp. i and ii (June 5, 2017), available at http://www.cftc.gov/idc/groups/public/@aboutcftc/documents/file/oig_rcbcmrus060517.pdf.
>
> [b] Office of the Comptroller of the Currency, *Economic Impact Analysis for Swaps Margin Proposed Rule* 1 (Aug. 28, 2014).

2. Reporting

a. Trade Reporting

We examined swap reporting requirements for cleared swaps in chapter 10. The reporting categories are the same as for uncleared swaps. What is different is the party with the reporting responsibility. Whereas with cleared swaps that responsibility largely falls on the derivatives clearing organization or the swap execution facility, with uncleared swaps one of the parties to the trade has the reporting obligation.

We will not revisit the content of the reports since the content is the same as for cleared swaps. Instead, we will identify who the reporting party is for uncleared swaps.

If a swap is traded on a facility, i.e., a designated contract market or swap execution facility, real-time public reporting must be done by the facility "as soon as technologically practicable" and creation data must be reported by the end of the next business day.[85] Continuation data, however, must be reported by whichever party is identified in the table in figure 12.1.[86]

If a swap is not traded on a facility, the reporting party is as identified in figure 12.1. Only one party to a trade must report the trade. The relevant party is determined by a "reporting hierarchy" that specifies which party is required to report a particular trade. The reporting hierarchy differs depending on whether the trade reporting is the real-time or regulatory reporting. Figure 12.1 provides a summary.

The reporting hierarchy is dependent somewhat on the location of the party with U.S. entities having the reporting obligation in trades with non-U.S. entities of the same registration category. Note that, if both parties are non-U.S. persons trading outside the United States, CFTC jurisdiction normally would not apply and, therefore, there would be no CFTC reporting requirements.

---

85. 17 C.F.R. §§ 43.3(a)(2) and 45.3(a).
86. 17 C.F.R. §§ 45.4(c) and 45.8.

Figure 12.1 Reporting Hierarchy for Real-Time and Regulatory Trade Reporting

Real-Time Trade Reporting[a]	Regulatory Trade Reporting (i.e., primary economic terms, confirmation data, and continuation data)[b]
If a swap dealer is a party to the trade, the swap dealer is always required to be the reporting party (if both parties are swap dealers, they must agree as to which is the reporting party)	Same as for real-time reporting
If no swap dealer is a party to the transaction, a major swap participant is required to be the reporting party (if both parties are major swap participants, they must agree as to which is the reporting party)	Same as for real-time reporting
If no swap dealer or major swap participant is a party to the transaction then the parties must agree on the reporting party	If no swap dealer or major swap participant is a party to the transaction, the end user that is a U.S. person is required to be the reporting party
Not applicable	If both end users are U.S. persons, the end user that is a financial entity is the reporting party (if both parties are financial entities, they must agree as to which is the reporting party)
Not applicable	If both end users are not financial entities they must agree as to which is the reporting party

[a] 17 C.F.R. § 43.3(a)(3). [b] 17 C.F.R. § 45.8(a)-(f).

The costs of reporting errors are high. Reporting failures resulted in a CFTC investigation and consent order imposing a $2.5 million fine on a swap dealer, Deutsche Bank.[87] This was followed by a CFTC enforcement action against Deutsche Bank for reporting problems that continued thereafter.

CFTC v. Deutsche Bank AG

2016 WL 6135664 (S.D.N.Y. Oct. 20, 2016)

William H. Pauley III, District Judge

The U.S. Commodity Futures Trading Commission ("CFTC") brings this enforcement action against Deutsche Bank AG ("Deutsche Bank") alleging a chronic failure to comply with swap data reporting regulations under the Dodd-Frank Act. On August 18, 2016, simultaneous with the filing of its Complaint, the CFTC submitted a Proposed Consent Order of Preliminary Injunction and Other Equitable Relief against Deutsche Bank (the "Proposed Consent Order"). Among other things, the Proposed Consent Order provides for the appointment of an independent monitor. . . .

---

87. *In the Matter of Deutsche Bank AG*, CFTC Docket No. 15-40 (Sept. 30, 2015).

The Dodd-Frank Act introduced sweeping reforms in the financial markets. One such reform centered on making the derivatives markets — which originally operated with scant oversight — more transparent. Dodd-Frank empowered the CFTC to promulgate rules and regulations requiring swap dealers, like Deutsche Bank, to comply with certain disclosure, recordkeeping, and reporting requirements concerning swaps transactions. *See* 17 C.F.R. §§ 43, 45 (2014).

More than one year ago, in September 2015, the CFTC issued an order commencing administrative proceedings against Deutsche Bank and imposing remedial sanctions (the "CFTC Order"). The CFTC Order recounts that as early as January 2013, Deutsche Bank failed to report cancellations of swap transactions, resulting in hundreds of thousands of reporting violations, errors, and omissions in its reporting. (CFTC Order at 4.) According to the CFTC Order, Deutsche Bank struggled to investigate the various messages it received from the swap data repository in a timely manner, and experienced technology-related failures concerning its reporting system. (CFTC Order at 4–5.)

Deutsche Bank retained a consultant and implemented changes designed to improve the accuracy and effectiveness of its reporting. . . . In its negotiated settlement with the CFTC last year, Deutsche Bank also agreed to pay a $2.5 million fine, undertake a number of remediation efforts, and submit periodic reports updating the CFTC on its compliance efforts every six months. (CFTC Order at 9–10.)

But the reporting problems at Deutsche Bank continued, compelling the CFTC to initiate this enforcement action. According to the Complaint, Deutsche Bank's swap data reporting system crashed in April 2016, preventing the bank from reporting any swap data for approximately five days. . . . Deutsche Bank's efforts to fix the outage only exacerbated the reporting problems and exposed other deficiencies. . . . For example, Deutsche Bank discovered that its Business Continuity and Disaster Recovery Plan failed to prevent a system outage. The system then failed to re-boot, inhibiting Deutsche Bank's swap data reporting functions. Moreover, it appears that Deutsche Bank has struggled to report real-time data for foreign exchange (FX) swaps and submit accurate swap data information in a timely manner. . . .

The consequences are significant. Inaccurate and untimely reporting of swaps data undermines the integrity of the markets, and impedes the CFTC's mission to protect swaps customers. This is particularly true because Deutsche Bank reportedly commands one of the largest derivatives portfolios in the world, valued at approximately €42 trillion.[88] . . .

The CFTC argues that because the scope of Deutsche Bank's reporting problems are unknown and of a recurring nature, an independent monitor should be appointed to identify and evaluate those problems, and then oversee "implementation of

---

88. [N. 1] Jack Ewing, *Deutsche Bank, Facing Criticism, Surveys Limited Options*, The N.Y. Times, July 27, 2016, available at: http://www.nytimes.com/2016/07/28/business/dealbook/deutsche-bank-q2-earnings.html.

appropriate measures for the generation of accurate, complete, and timely swap data reports by Deutsche Bank, as required by the Act and Regulations." (Proposed Consent Order ¶ 4; CFTC Memo of Law at 9–10.) The CFTC also contends that entry of the Proposed Consent Order is in the public interest because it will "ensure a fair and transparent marketplace" for both market participants and the CFTC. . . .

This Court agrees that the appointment of an independent monitor is warranted. . . .

SO ORDERED.

———————

Ultimately, after the conclusion of the court-appointed monitor in 2019 and implementation of all its recommendations, Deutsche Bank settled with the CFTC by payment of a $9 million fine. Other swap dealers received fines of $450,000, $2.5 million, and $5 million for the failure to accurately report swap trades to a swap data repository.[89]

b. Large Trader Reporting for Physical Commodity Swaps

Swap dealers and members of clearinghouses must periodically report to the CFTC information on some swaps referencing physical commodities.[90] Swaps in scope are swaps settled in full or in part on the price of a specified list of forty-six physical commodity futures contracts traded on futures exchanges (or some commodity indices) or the price of a commodity for physical delivery in the location specified in the relevant futures contract. However, the position only becomes reportable if the position exceeds fifty or more "futures equivalent" swaps, i.e., if the swaps, once converted using a CFTC-supplied methodology, exceed fifty futures contracts.[91]

3. Portfolio Reconciliation and Compression

As a risk management function, swap dealers and major swap participants are required to periodically ensure agreement with counterparties on their relevant positions, including the market value of those positions, and to engage in exercises to reduce duplicative exposures.[92] If there are material discrepancies in each party's

———————

89. *In the Matter of Société Générale SA*, CFTC Docket No. 47-01 (Dec. 7, 2016), *In the Matter of Société Générale International Limited*, CFTC Docket No. 19-38 (Sept. 30, 2019), and *In the Matter of Morgan Stanley Capital Services LLC*, CFTC Docket No. 20-78 (Sept. 30, 2020). Société Générale International Limited was originally Newedge UK Financial Ltd., part of a joint venture with Calyon Financial that Société Générale acquired full ownership of in May 2014. *See* Daniel P. Collins, *New Day for Newedge, or Should we Say SocGen?*, http://www.futuresmag.com/2014/07/11/new-day-newedge-or-should-we-say-socgen (July 11, 2014).

90. 17 C.F.R. § 20.4. Technically, cleared and uncleared swaps are included. We discuss the swap dealer's obligations in this chapter because most of the physical commodity swaps market is uncleared.

91. 17 C.F.R. Pt. 20, App. A.

92. 17 C.F.R. §§ 23.502 and 503.

view of the market value of their positions, such discrepancies must be resolved or reported to the CFTC. Figure 12.2 summarizes the requirements.

Figure 12.2 Portfolio Reconciliation Obligations for Swap Dealers and Major Swap Participants

Counterparty Type	Size of Swap Portfolio	Frequency	Time Period for Resolving Material Difference in Terms Applying to Swap	Time Period for Resolving Material Difference (10% or more) in Portfolio Valuation	Timing of Report to CFTC of Valuation Dispute in Excess of $20 MM
Swap dealer or major swap participant	>500	Daily	Immediate	5 business days	3 business days
Swap dealer or major swap participant	>50 < 500	Weekly	Immediate	5 business days	3 business days
Swap dealer or major swap participant	≤ 50	Quarterly	Immediate	5 business days	3 business days
All other types	>100	Quarterly	"timely fashion"	"timely fashion"	5 business days
All other types	≤ 100	Annually	"timely fashion"	"timely fashion"	5 business days

4. Swap Trading Relationship Documentation

Swap trading relationship documentation are the agreements governing swap transactions between parties. The CFTC has implemented rules with highly prescriptive requirements for what such documentation must contain in circumstances where at least one of the parties is a swap dealer or major swap participant. Swap documentation must be in writing and minimally contain, among others:

> [A]ll terms governing the trading relationship ... including, without limitation, terms addressing payment obligations, netting of payments, events of default or other termination events, calculation and netting of obligations upon termination, transfer of rights and obligations, governing law, valuation, and dispute resolution. ... [A]ll confirmations of swap transactions. ... [C]redit support arrangements, which shall contain, in accordance with applicable requirements under Commission regulations or regulations adopted by prudential regulators ... [i]nitial and variation margin requirements, if any ... assets that may be used as margin and asset valuation haircuts, if any ... [i]nvestment and rehypothecation terms for assets used as margin for uncleared swaps, if any [and] [c]ustodial arrangements for

margin assets, including whether margin assets are to be segregated with an independent third party . . . [and upon request by a non-financial end user and automatically with respect to all other parties] . . . written documentation in which the parties agree on the process, which may include any agreed upon methods, procedures, rules, and inputs, for determining the value of each swap at any time from execution to the termination, maturity, or expiration of such swap for the purposes of complying with . . . margin requirements . . . [and] risk management requirements. . . .[93]

Most of these requirements are already met by the industry-standard documentation used to agree to swap transactions, the ISDA Master Agreement (it has a 1992 and a 2002 version), prepared by the primary industry association for the swaps industry, the International Swaps and Derivatives Association, more commonly referred to as "ISDA" (*iz-da*) and, where the swaps between the parties are collateralized, the 1994 Credit Support Annex, 2016 Phase One Credit Support Annex for Initial Margin, or the 2016 Credit Support Annex for Variation Margin, each also prepared by the International Swaps and Derivatives Association. The CFTC, while recognizing that the ISDA Master Agreement and Credit Support Annex together satisfy many of the documentation requirements, also noted shortfalls at the time it released the swap trading relationship documentation rule.

CFTC, *Confirmation, Portfolio Reconciliation, Portfolio Compression, and Swap Trading Relationship Documentation Requirements for Swap Dealers and Major Swap Participants*
77 Fed. Reg. 55904 (Sept. 11, 2012)

. . . Several commenters requested that the Commission clarify the standing under the rules of the ISDA Master Agreement and Credit Support Annex (the ISDA Agreements), which are prevalent in the swaps market [and] . . . requested that the Commission acknowledge the general adequacy of the ISDA Agreements for purposes of the rule. . . . Similarly, . . . [a commentator] argued that many end users have already negotiated existing documentation under the ISDA architecture and thus requested that the Commission make clear that: (1) ISDA Agreements or any substantially similar master agreements satisfy the documentation requirements of the final rules; (2) in accordance with the ISDA Agreements and applicable state law, swaps are binding when made orally; and (3) long-form confirmations that contain all requisite legal terms to establish a binding agreement also satisfy the requirements of the rules. . . . [Another commentator] also recommended that the Commission expressly state that the ISDA Agreements satisfy the documentation requirements of the final rules or state how the ISDA Agreements are deficient to

---

93. 17 C.F.R. § 23.504(b).

eliminate any confusion. Finally, the Coalition for Derivatives End-Users argued that, given that the ISDA Agreements are used by nearly all end users and that such documentation substantially complies with the proposed rules, the Commission should expressly state that the ISDA Agreements satisfy the documentation requirements of the rules.

On the other hand, the Committee on the Investment of Employee Benefit Assets (CIEBA) anticipates that ISDA may initiate a uniform protocol to conform existing ISDA Agreements to the requirements of the rules. In this regard, CIEBA stated that ISDA protocols, which in the past have typically been developed by dealer-dominated ISDA committees, are not form documents that can be revised by the parties. Rather, CIEBA argues, end users may only adopt these protocols on a "take it or leave it" basis, which may not be in their best interests.

Accordingly, CIEBA recommended that the Commission not, either explicitly or implicitly, require market participants to consent to ISDA protocols in order to comply with the Dodd-Frank Act or the Commission's regulations.

The Commission notes that many comments received with respect to this and other rulemakings stated that swaps are privately negotiated bilateral contracts. Although the Commission recognizes that the ISDA Agreements in their pre-printed form as published by ISDA are capable of compliance with the rules, such agreements are subject to customization by counterparties. In addition, the Commission notes that while the pre-printed form of the ISDA Master Agreement is capable of addressing the requirements . . . it is not possible to determine if the pre-printed form of the ISDA Credit Support Annex will comply . . . because . . . [the documentation rule] requires that the documentation include credit support arrangements that comply with the Commission's rules regarding initial and variation margin and custodial arrangements. . . . Further, the Commission does not believe that the standard ISDA Agreements address the swap valuation requirements . . . [or] orderly liquidation termination provisions. . . . Given the foregoing, the Commission declines to endorse the ISDA Agreements as meeting the requirements of the rules in all instances.

Whereas the ISDA Master Agreement and Credit Support Annex may not fully satisfy the CFTC's documentation rules, they satisfy most of the requirements. Where there are shortfalls ISDA has established a process, known as the "Dodd-Frank Protocols." The Dodd-Frank Protocols are described further below in section F. They are intended to plug the gaps between the standardized ISDA Master Agreements in near universal use and swap trading relationship documentation requirements by facilitating necessary amendments to ISDA Master Agreements already in place between parties. The Dodd-Frank Protocols have the additional benefit of satisfying many of the other regulatory requirements pertaining to uncleared swaps.

E. Documentation of Uncleared Swaps

1. ISDA Documentation and the Negotiation Thereof

Because of their prevalence, it is important to have a basic understanding of the ISDA Master Agreement, including of its negotiation. It will help, in going through this section, if you can obtain access to a 2002 ISDA Master Agreement.

Gary E. Kalbaugh and Richard A. Miller, *Master Agreements for OTC Derivatives*

In *Commercial Contracts: Strategies for Drafting and Negotiation* (Vladimir R. Rossman and Morton Moskin, eds., 2d ed., Aspen Publishers 2014)

. . . Frequently, a dealer or "end-user" of derivatives may enter into many derivatives of different types contemporaneously. To avoid individually negotiating the legal terms to apply to each such transaction, and to ensure that each transaction can be viewed as forming one single agreement,[94] widely used "master agreements" have been created for documenting derivatives transactions.

This chapter describes the . . . 2002 Master Agreement published by the International Swaps and Derivatives Association, Inc. (ISDA)[95] and discusses the most important terms that are negotiated in connection with this agreement. Consideration is also given to the reasons for choosing among the pre-listed elections made available under the master agreement and to the special provisions that are most commonly added to ISDA master agreements to customize coverage to the special circumstances of the parties. . . .

[T]he form used most commonly for documenting OTC derivatives is the form entitled "2002 ISDA Master Agreement" which was released in 2002[96] (hereinafter referred to as the "ISDA Master," or the "Master"). Documentation for OTC transactions of types that can be covered by an ISDA Master generally consists of the Master Agreement, a Schedule to the ISDA Master and one or more Confirmations memorializing particular transactions.

The ISDA Master comprises 28 pages and 14 paragraphs that are never altered by interlineation or physical mark-up. All elections under, or modifications to, the Master are included in the Schedule or, in some cases, one or more Confirmations.

---

94. [N. 5] *See* Netting at *infra* [A].

95. [N. 6] . . . Also commonly used for over-the-counter derivatives transactions is the Multi-currency-Cross Border version of the 1992 Master Agreement. Due to the similarity of the 1992 and 2002 agreements, much of the discussion herein with respect to the 2002 agreement applies equally to the 1992 agreement. Where there are significant divergences between the two, they are noted.

96. [N. 46] The earliest official version of the ISDA Master Agreement was entitled the 1987 Interest Rate & Currency Exchange Agreement. It was superseded by the 1992 ISDA Master Agreement. The 2002 ISDA Master Agreement, based on the structure of the 1992 ISDA, is now generally the market standard though the 1992 ISDA Master Agreement is still in circulation.

The ISDA Master by its terms provides that provisions in the Schedule supersede any inconsistent provisions in the Master, and any provisions in Confirmations supersede any inconsistent provisions in the Schedule. The Master covers the broad, substantive terms of the parties' agreement and its operation. The Master has a well-recognized status as an agreement that can provide for netting of payments on an ongoing basis (payment netting) and upon termination of the Master (close-out netting) that is considered enforceable in accordance with its terms in a great many jurisdictions.[97]

The Master, Schedule, and Confirmation should be read in conjunction with a number of other ISDA-published documents which are incorporated either by specific reference or by industry practice. Which documents are relevant will depend upon the type of transaction involved[98] but, at a minimum, the 2006 ISDA Definitions and the User's Guide to the 2002 ISDA Master Agreement are generally relevant. Very broadly speaking, the ISDA Master includes:

(a) Representations made by each party to the other, some of which have been the subject of dispute and litigation in the past, including regarding a party's power to enter into derivative transactions and the resulting enforceability of derivative agreements.[99]

(b) Conditions precedent to each party's payment to the other. . . .

(c) Agreements by the parties to furnish certain information to each other.

(d) Events that would constitute "Events of Default," giving the nondefaulting party the right to close out all (but not less than all) of the transactions entered into under the ISDA Master. Such Events of Default include failure to make a payment, failure to comply with or perform an obligation under the ISDA Master, misrepresentations, Default under Specified Transactions (*see infra* [C][4]), Cross-Default (*see infra* [C][5]), bankruptcy, and merger of a party with another entity where the resulting entity fails to assume the obligations of the party under the ISDA Master.

(e) "Termination Events," which are "no-fault" events which give one or both parties (depending on the applicable Termination Event)[100] the right to close

---

97. [N. 48] ISDA has obtained opinions of counsel or memoranda in many jurisdictions analyzing the application of bankruptcy laws to transactions documented under ISDA Master Agreements. . . .

98. [N. 49] For example, there are ISDA-specified definitions and user's guides for foreign currency transactions, equity derivatives, credit derivatives, and commodity transactions. In each instance, the definitions are an effort to incorporate market-standard practices that will provide conformity and certainty to the parties' dealings. These definitions and guides are available from ISDA.

99. [N. 52] *See, e.g., Lehman Bros. Commercial Corp. v. Minmetals Int'l Non-Ferrous Metal Trading Co.*, 2001 WL 423031 (S.D.N.Y. Apr. 25, 2001) and *Borough of Hammersmith & Fulham v. Hazell* 2 A.C.1 (1992).

100. [N. 55] Somewhat confusingly, this could be the "Non-affected party" in a Credit Event Upon Merger, the "Burdened Party" in the case of a Tax Event Upon Merger and the "Affected Party" in case of any of the other Termination Events.

out all "affected" transactions under the ISDA Master, but which (unlike Events of Default) provide, in the case of some Termination Events, some time for the other party to cure the Termination Event by transferring transactions to an Affiliate, and also provide, when there are two "Affected Parties," for pricing closed-out transactions based on the average of each parties' estimate, ensuring that neither party is disadvantaged as they might be in circumstances where one party makes the sole determination of the payment due or owed as a result of termination.[101] The ISDA Master's standard Termination Events include changes in law that make a previously lawful transaction unlawful, force majeure,[102] tax events (including as the result of a merger), and Credit Event Upon Merger (*see infra* [C][6]).

(f) Rights and procedures to terminate transactions upon an Event of Default or Termination Event, including methodologies for calculating amounts due from one party to the other on a net basis (*see infra* [B]).

In addition, one or both of the parties may require "up-front" or "mark-to-market" collateral to be posted to support a party's exposure from transactions under the Master. ISDA has issued a form of collateral agreement, called the Credit Support Annex that sets forth standard terms for the posting of collateral and, like the Schedule to an ISDA Master, permits the parties to make various elections, in this case about their collateral arrangements.[103] . . .

A party to an agreement or transaction is sometimes referred to herein as a "Party" or "Counterparty."

[A] Netting

Derivatives frequently represent a bilateral commitment between the parties to exchange payments based upon the price movement of the underlying interest rate, currency, security, commodity or other reference. For example, in a typical interest rate swap, one party will agree to pay to its counterparty an amount equal to a quarterly fixed percentage (e.g., 5.75 percent) of a "notional" sum (e.g., 100 million dollars) on a periodic basis, for a designated period of time. In return, the counterparty agrees to pay the first party an amount equal to a variable percentage (e.g., the prevailing U.S. Treasury bill yield plus 25 basis points (i.e., 0.25 percent)) on the agreed-upon payment dates. Only the amounts calculated by multiplying the

---

101. [N. 56] . . . The 1992 ISDA had different calculation methodologies. Notwithstanding, it was also structured to provide a calculation methodology which limits disadvantage to a particular party in the event of their being two "Affected Parties."

102. [N. 57] The 2002 ISDA Master Agreement is the first to contain a force majeure event. All preceding ISDA Master Agreements, including the 1992 ISDA Master Agreement, did not contain such a clause though such clauses were sometimes negotiated by the parties.

103. [N. 58] The current Credit Support Annex most commonly in use in New York law transactions dates from 1994. On June 7, 2013 ISDA issued a new Credit Support Annex, known as the 2013 Standard Credit Support Annex. *See* "ISDA Publishes 2013 Standard Credit Support Annex (SCSA)," ISDA News Release (June 7, 2013) [and in 2016 issued a 2016 Credit Support Annex for Variation Margin]. An analysis of the CSA is outside the scope of this chapter.

percentage rate by the notional amount are exchanged. The notional amounts them-selves are not exchanged or paid. Thus, the parties are "swapping" fixed versus float-ing obligations and will calculate the payments required by their agreement on each payment date. However, instead of making two separate payments (one fixed and one floating), the Master permits the parties to net their obligations so that the party with the greater payment obligation will pay the net difference between the gross payment calculations to the other party. The Master also permits the parties to elect, in the Schedule, to net obligations across different transactions entered into under the Master.

Similarly, the Master provides that if one party elects to terminate the Master, and all transactions outstanding that were entered into under the Master, early (because, for example, an Event of Default or Termination Event — both of which are discussed below — has occurred with respect to the other party), the parties' obligations will be closed out and netted, even when one of the parties is bankrupt. Because swap transactions are so integral to the ebb and flow of finance, inter-national regulators and legislators have enacted laws and regulations consistent with this close-out and netting regime. In the United States, these initiatives have included . . . Bankruptcy Code provisions . . . , federal banking laws, and the New York State banking law.

ISDA has obtained numerous memorandum opinions supporting the view that the termination and close-out netting provisions of an ISDA Master will be enforced under the laws of a variety of jurisdictions. . . .

[B] Termination and Calculation Methodology

The 1992 ISDA Master permitted the parties to elect among calculation method-ologies for determining amounts due or owed as a result of a termination of an ISDA Master.[104] The 2002 ISDA uses one calculation methodology, comprised of the sum of (a) the present value of future payments under the transactions underlying the agreement, known as "Close-out Amount"; and (b) the aggregate of payments due, payable and unpaid, known as "Unpaid Amounts."

---

104. [N. 62] Under the 1992 ISDA Master, the Parties were required to decide between "Market Quotation" or "Loss" as the means of measuring the value of the Terminated Transactions as of the Early Termination Date. Market Quotation provided that the value of the Transactions would be set by obtaining price quotations from leading dealers in the relevant derivatives. The Market Quo-tation would be for the replacement cost of the particular Terminated Transaction(s). However, if fewer than three quotations were obtained — for example, because of chaotic market conditions or because there were few dealers who deal in particular types of illiquid transactions — or if a Market Quotation would not (in the reasonable belief of the Party making the determination) produce a commercially reasonable result, the 1992 ISDA Master's form language stated that Loss would apply in respect of the relevant Terminated Transaction(s). "Loss," the alternative in the 1992 ISDA Master to Market Quotation, was a general indemnification provision and the 1992 ISDA Master defined it as a payment measure by which a party reasonably determines in good faith its total losses and gains in connection with the Terminated Transactions. Although a party could deter-mine its Loss based upon quotations obtained from third parties, there was no requirement that the determining party obtain such quotations. . . .

It is important to note that, pursuant to the 2002 ISDA, even if this calculation results in an amount payable to the defaulting party, the nondefaulting party is obligated to pay such amount, even though the defaulting party's default is the cause of the termination.[105]

Close-out Amount is calculated, when termination is triggered by an Event of Default, by the nondefaulting party or, depending on the trigger for the Termination Event, one or both parties. The party calculating the Close-out Amount is known as the "Determining Party." If there are two Affected Parties, both parties make a calculation of close-out amount which is then averaged.

The Determining Party is required to calculate the present "economic equivalent" of the transactions documented under the ISDA Master and state this net amount as a loss (*i.e.* a negative amount, signaling an amount owed to it by the other party) or a gain (*i.e.* a positive amount signaling an amount it owes to the other party). The amount must be calculated in "good faith" using "commercially reasonable procedures in order to produce a commercially reasonable result." Further limiting the discretion of the Determining Party is the requirement that, unless reasonably believing in good faith that market quotations from third parties or other market data are not readily available or would not provide for a commercially reasonable result, the Determining Party must consider such sources in calculating Close-out Amount.

The ISDA Master also provides that a nondefaulting party or the party not affected by the termination event may set-off amounts that it owes to the other party against any amounts due from the other party under any other agreements.[106] When these amounts are denominated in different currencies, the party exercising the set-off may convert the other currency using "the rate of exchange at which such party would be able, in good faith and using commercially reasonable procedures, to purchase the relevant amount of such currency."

[C] Negotiating an ISDA Schedule

As noted above, modifications and alterations to an ISDA Master Agreement are documented in an attached Schedule. The preprinted Schedule includes a number of provisions that require an election to be made (or, in some cases, if an election is not made, a standard term of the ISDA Master will apply) and allows the parties to

---

105. [N. 63] This was not necessarily the case under the 1992 ISDA Master where the parties could choose between a "First Method" and "Second Method." The "First Method," sometimes referred to as a "walkaway" or "walk away" provision, provided that if the party that has defaulted is owed money, the nondefaulting out-of-the-money party is allowed to "walk away" from its payment obligation because of the default. This clause triggered significant regulatory opposition [and litigation] . . . [F]ar more common in 1992 ISDA Master's is the election of the Second Method which operates so that a Party receives any Termination Amount it is owed, even if it is the Defaulting Party.

106. [N. 66] The 1992 ISDA did not have a built-in set-off provision. However, parties frequently included one in the schedule based on the User's Guide to the ISDA 1992 Master Agreement.

make further additions. In the following sections we will review the elections that are in the preprinted Schedule and touch upon others that may be, and often are, added. Readers may also consult the above-referenced ISDA user's guides, particularly the User's Guide to the 2002 ISDA Master Agreements.

[1] Choosing an "as of" Date. . . .

The "as of" date will normally, but is not required to be, the date of execution.

[2] Naming the Parties

Customarily, the party drafting the Schedule and generating confirmations, which is frequently a derivatives dealer, will designate itself as "Party A." The other party will be "Party B." Each party will thereinafter be referred to as a "Party" or "Counterparty," as applicable. In accordance with market practice, and (if agreed upon) unless there is an event of default or potential event of default with respect to Party A, Party A is typically also the party selected to act as "Calculation Agent," calculating the amounts due to it or Party B, as the case may be, on the designated payment dates.[107] . . .

[3] Choice of a "Specified Entity"

Part 1 of the Schedule allows each party to name one or more entities as a "Specified Entity" with respect to four substantive provisions of the Master. These provisions govern Default under Specified Transactions (Section 5(a)(v) of the Master; *see infra* [C][4]), Cross-Default (Section 5(a)(vi) of the Master; *see infra* [C][5]), Bankruptcy (Section 5(a)(vii) of the Master) and Credit Event Upon Merger (Section 5(b)(v) of the Master;[108] *see infra* [C][6]), all of which are capable of triggering a default or being deemed a Termination Event, as the case may be, under the Master.

If no "Specified Entity" is named, the four provisions listed above will apply only to the named parties to the Master. By naming, for example, the parent of a party as a "Specified Entity" with respect to any or all of such provisions, an adverse event that affects the parent of a party may also trigger a default or termination under such party's Master. Similarly, other of the party's "Affiliates" may be included as "Specified Entities" of the party. If a party anticipates that credit weakness in its counterparty's corporate family could endanger the counterparty's ability to perform on transactions under the Master, "Affiliates" is often an election in the Schedule defining what are "Specified Entities" for this purpose.

[4] Defining a "Specified Transaction"

The Master includes a definition of "Specified Transaction" that incorporates a broad array of derivatives, repurchase and similar transactions when entered into between the parties to the Master. Under the Master, a default by a party (or a Specified Entity of the party) under any Specified Transaction with the counterparty (or a Specified Entity of the counterparty) will trigger an Event of Default under the

---

107. [N. 68] For the role of Calculation Agent, *see infra* [C][16].
108. [N. 69] Section 5(b)(iv) under the 1992 ISDA Master Agreement.

Master. Whether the pre-printed definition of a "Specified Transaction" is too broad will depend upon the types of transactions between the parties. The definition in the Master of "Specified Transaction" may be fine-tuned in the Schedule if the parties want to exclude certain types of transactions.[109]

It is also common for parties to modify the Master by providing that a default caused by administrative circumstances, such as communications break-downs and clerical errors, will not constitute a default with respect to a Specified Transaction, provided the funds necessary to performance were available at the time of the "default" and the administrative default is promptly cured.[110]

[5] "Cross-Default," "Specified Indebtedness," and "Threshold Amount"

As discussed above, a party's default with respect to "Specified Transactions" with a third party can trigger an Event of Default under the subject Master if the parties elect to include third-party transactions. Similarly, if the appropriate elections are made in the Schedule, a party's default with respect to any indebtedness (to any person, not just the counterparty) may also trigger an Event of Default. For it to do so, a party will require that "Cross-Default" (as defined in the Master) shall apply to that counterparty. Under the Master, a Cross-Default is triggered by a party's default, event of default or other similar conditions or events with respect to Specified Indebtedness, where the sum in default is not less than a specified Threshold Amount for that party. Specified Indebtedness is defined as any "obligation . . . in respect of borrowed money." However, there are other transactions that are similar to "obligations in respect of borrowed money" that might also be included by modification in the Schedule. These could include, for example, collateral payments under margining agreements and capital leases. Again, however, the parties may wish to excuse mere administrative and clerical defaults if timely cured.

The Threshold Amount may be specified in the Schedule and is often expressed as a percentage of shareholders' equity, in the case of large public companies, or in absolute dollar terms for smaller entities.[111] Parties sometimes specify a "zero" threshold with respect to indebtedness between the immediate parties and their Affiliates. What is appropriate for particular counterparties will depend upon their respective financial circumstances and relative creditworthiness.

---

109. [N. 71] Under the 1992 ISDA Master, however, credit derivatives are not specifically included, although the phrase "any other similar transaction" in the Master's standard definition may be construed to include such transactions. Forward contracts (other than forward rate agreements), repurchase agreements and securities lending agreements are also not included in the standard definition in the 1992 ISDA Master.

110. [N. 72] This is also a commonly negotiated change to Section 5(a)(i) (the "Failure to Pay" Event of Default) itself.

111. [N. 73] The 1992 ISDA Master is similar except that payment defaults and other events of default are not aggregated for the purposes of determining whether the default in question exceeds the threshold.

The Cross-Default provision, unmodified, applies to defaults which in the aggregate, if made due and payable immediately or, if capable of being made due and payable immediately, will exceed the threshold. However, it is common to modify the provision by removing the words ", or becoming capable at such time of being declared," so that, with respect to non-payment defaults, only an actual amount being due and payable as a result of the default in question will apply to the threshold. This is known, in industry parlance, as a replacement of the "cross-default" provision with a "cross-acceleration" clause.

[6] "Credit Event Upon Merger"

The parties may elect to have "Credit Event Upon Merger" (as defined in Section 5(b)(v) of the Master) apply to one or both parties. If elected, a merger of a party, comparable asset transfer by a party or change of control or substantial change in capital structure of a party will be a Termination Event (rather than an Event of Default) if the creditworthiness of the resulting, surviving, or transferee entity is materially weaker than that of such party prior to the occurrence of the event.[112] This provision, like the other credit-sensitive provisions included in the Schedule, may also be made to apply to a party's Credit Support Provider (as that term is specified in the Schedule) and/or its Specified Entities. Parties may wish to define "materially weaker" for purposes of this provision, and often substitute external credit rating criteria for this general term.

[7] "Automatic Early Termination"

Ordinarily, a Master Agreement, and all Transactions thereunder, will terminate after the occurrence of an Event of Default or Termination Event and upon the non-defaulting party providing the requisite notice to the Defaulting Party designating an Early Termination Date. Alternatively, the parties may elect to have Automatic Early Termination (AET) apply.

When AET applies, the Master should be construed to read that the Master, and all Transactions thereunder, constructively terminate immediately prior to certain bankruptcy or insolvency events. In jurisdictions where the insolvency laws are less favorable to netting agreements than, for example the United States, AET may be an appropriate election.[113] However, it should be noted that its primary disadvantage is that an AET would, as its definition says, occur automatically. This may happen without the knowledge of the non-defaulting party, and before the nondefaulting party becomes aware of the termination, the relevant market could have moved significantly. In these circumstances, the nondefaulting party may be out-of-pocket

---

112. [N. 74] The 1992 ISDA Master has a more limited scope, covering only a merger or comparable asset transfer.

113. [N. 75] ... [P]arties do not typically elect to have Automatic Early Termination apply in Masters where both parties are domiciled in the United States and are subject to the Bankruptcy Code. On the other hand, AET remains a useful alternative for cross-border swaps, where one or more of the parties is domiciled in a jurisdiction that has not endorsed the enforceability of netting agreements. ...

on its hedge positions. For these reasons, the User's Guide advises practitioners to exercise caution when deciding to elect AET.

[8] Choice of "Termination Currency"

The parties may choose a "Termination Currency" in the Schedule. If so specified and provided, all Terminated Transactions will be converted to the selected currency. If no election is made, or if the elected currency is not freely available, U.S. dollars are selected by operation of the Schedule.[114]

[9] Specification of "Additional Termination Events"

The parties may provide for Additional Termination Events at Part 1(g) of the Schedule. Examples of Additional Termination Events include, where cross-default might not be applicable, a narrower cross-default applying only to a specified loan facility, a ratings downgrade below a specified level, the death, disability, or end of association with a party of an important individual or material officer, or the failure to maintain a certain specified level of capitalization or assets.

[10] "Tax Representations"

As stated above, the Master Agreement and Schedule include representations that each party makes to the other. Specifically, the Schedule allows each party to make certain tax representations to the other party consisting of "Payer Tax Representations" and "Payee Tax Representations." The tax representations are ongoing until termination of the Master Agreement and, in general, enable each party to determine whether any withholding taxes should be imposed with respect to any payments made under a Transaction, and whether information reporting may be required.

Each party should make the Payer Tax Representations. Under the Payer Tax Representations, each party typically represents that it is not required, under current law, to make any deduction or withholding for any taxes of the "Relevant Jurisdiction"[115] from any payment made by it to the counterparty (excluding certain payments of interest made under the Agreement). In addition, the Payer Tax Representations generally specify that the party making the Payer Tax Representations may rely on (i) the Payee Tax Representations made by the counterparty, (ii) the delivery by the counterparty of properly completed tax forms and documents as specified in the Schedule,[116] and (iii) the counterparty's agreement to give timely notification that a Payee Tax Representation is not accurate and true.

Each party should request that the counterparty make certain Payee Tax Representations. The Payee Tax Representations generally relate to a counterparty's

---

114. [N. 78] Or Euro if the agreement is subject to English Law.

115. [N. 79] With respect to a "Payer," a relevant jurisdiction is generally a jurisdiction (i) where the Payer is incorporated, organized, managed or controlled, (ii) where the office through which the Payer is acting for purposes of the Master Agreement is located, (iii) where the Party executes the agreements; and (iv) from or through which the Payer makes such payment.

116. [N. 80] An exception to this requirement is with respect to certain documents that might materially prejudice the delivering party's "legal or commercial position."

tax status with respect to a specific tax jurisdiction and often establish whether the counterparty is eligible for an exemption from any withholding taxes or reporting requirements imposed by the specific tax jurisdiction. In addition, as noted above, the Payee Tax Representations interact with the Payer Tax Representations. For example, if the counterparty is a U.S. corporation, for U.S. withholding tax and information reporting purposes, the counterparty may be requested to represent that (i) it is a corporation and (ii) it is a U.S. person for U.S. federal tax purposes.

If the counterparty is a foreign corporation and has no connection with the U.S., for U.S. withholding tax and information reporting purposes, the counterparty may be requested to represent that (i) it is a foreign person for U.S. federal tax purposes, (ii) it is a corporation, and (iii) no part of any payment received or to be received by it is attributable to a trade or business carried on by it in the United States. Alternatively, if the counterparty is a foreign corporation and may act through a U.S. branch or a non-U.S. branch, for U.S. withholding tax and information reporting purposes, the counterparty may be requested to represent that (i) it is a foreign person for U.S. federal tax purposes, (ii) it is a corporation, (iii) for each payment received by its U.S. branch, the payment will be effectively connected with its conduct of a trade or business in the United States, and (iv) for each payment it receives that is not attributable to its U.S. branch, the payment will be attributable to a foreign person or a non-U.S. branch of a foreign person. In addition, if benefits are available under an income tax treaty, a counterparty that is a foreign corporation may be requested to represent that it is eligible to receive benefits under the treaty.

[11] Agreement to Deliver Documents

The parties may specify in the Schedule various forms, documents or certificates to be delivered. Such forms often include requisite tax forms (e.g., U.S. IRS Form W-8BEN, Form W-8ECI or Form W-9), incumbency certificates, formation and operative documents and annual or quarterly audited or unaudited financial reports. A party may sometimes request a legal opinion from the counterparty's counsel as to the corporate power of the counterparty to enter into the Master, Schedule and/or a Confirmation, the enforceability of such agreements or other matters.

[12] Addresses for Notices

This provides for the address at which notices should be delivered to a party. Notices pursuant to the termination provisions of the ISDA Master, *i.e.*, Sections 5 and 6 thereof, may not be sent by e-mail or by electronic messaging system, despite the Schedule having line items for e-mail and electronic messaging system. Other notices under the agreement, such as change of account information, can be sent by e-mail or electronic messaging system.

[13] Process Agent

If a party is not located in the jurisdiction in which the agreement is to be enforced it is advisable to have the party appoint a process agent so that, to the extent there is a dispute and service of process is required, process can be served on such party.

[14] Offices

The parties can elect to have Section 10(a) of the ISDA Master apply or not apply. Section 10(a) provides that all obligations of a branch or office entering into the transaction will be deemed to be obligations of the head or home office.[117] It is common to have this election apply and, because serious economic consequences may result from not receiving such a representation and then having recourse to only a local branch or office, in the authors' experience disapplication of this clause is extremely uncommon.

[15] Multibranch Party

The Schedule allows bank counterparties to indicate whether they intend to enter into transactions through specific branches (as opposed to just their head office or the branch which is signing the ISDA Master) and, if so, to specify which branches.

[16] Calculation Agent

The term "Calculation Agent" is defined in the 2006 ISDA Definitions. It is the party responsible for calculating ordinary payments. The Schedule allows the parties to select which party will be the Calculation Agent though, in cases where one party is a dealer counterparty and the other is not, it is usually the dealer counterparty.

[17] Credit Support Document

The parties should insert into this section clear and identifiable descriptions of any guarantees or other types of credit support (including a Credit Support Annex which, without being defined as a Credit Support Document only receives a portion of the protections the ISDA Master provides to Credit Support Documents). By doing so, among others, the representations and other agreements made in the ISDA Master apply, in addition to the ISDA Master, to the Credit Support Document. Moreover, it allows for application of a unique Event of Default, Section 5(a)(iii) of the ISDA Master, "Credit Support Default".

[18] Credit Support Provider

For the same reasons applying to Credit Support Document . . . the parties should insert into this section clear and identifiable descriptions of any guarantor or provider of credit support in order to assure the application of certain representations and other agreements made in the ISDA Master to the Credit Support Provider and to benefit from the entirety of the protections in-built into Section 5(a)(iii) of the ISDA Master, "Credit Support Default".

[19] Governing Law

The Schedule is structured to provide for English or New York law.[118] The choice of law election also determines the applicable jurisdiction, i.e. the exclusive or

---

117. [N. 82] Banks often act through local branches or representative offices.

118. [N. 84] Though the scope of this . . . is limited to analysis of New York law, since this is an explicit Schedule election, we have included its analysis herein.

non-exclusive jurisdiction of the English courts[119] or the non-exclusive jurisdiction of the courts of the State of New York and the United States District Court located in Manhattan.

[20] Netting of Payments

The general standard in Section 2(c) of the ISDA Master is that payments between parties denominated in the same currency and due on the same date with respect to the same transaction should be netted. However, the Schedule provides the opportunity to the parties to apply "Multiple Transaction Payment Netting" which would net all transactions subject to the ISDA Master between the parties, or a specified group of such transactions, so long as they are denominated in the same currency and due on the same day.

[21] Affiliate

The Schedule provides the parties a line item for re-defining the term "Affiliate," otherwise defined in Section 14 of the ISDA Master. It is important to emphasize that Part 5 of the Schedule provides the opportunity to the parties to amend any provisions of the ISDA Master which they wish to amend. Therefore, though the Schedule explicitly contemplates amendment of the "Affiliate" definition, it is not intended to exclude other possible definitional amendments.

[22] Absence of Litigation

One of the representations made by the parties and their Credit Support Providers is that there is no pending or actual litigation or similar proceedings "likely to affect the legality, validity or enforceability" of the ISDA Master or any Credit Support Document or obligations under either. The parties can also elect to include "Specified Entities" in the Schedule with respect to which the relevant party will also be deemed to make this representation.[120]

[23] No Agency

Each party represents, pursuant to Section 3(g) of the ISDA Master that "It is entering into this Agreement, including each Transaction, as principal and not as agent of any person or entity."[121] The Schedule explicitly provides the option of applying or disapplying this representation if, for example, one of the parties is acting as agent for a third-party.

---

119. [N. 85] Whether it is the exclusive or non-exclusive jurisdiction of the English courts depends on whether the matter involves a "Convention Court" in which case the jurisdiction of the English courts is exclusive. A "Convention Court" is defined in Section 14 of the ISDA Master as "any court which is bound to apply to the Proceedings either Article 17 of the 1968 Brussels Convention on Jurisdiction and the Enforcement of Judgments in Civil and Commercial Matters or Article 17 of the 1988 Lugano Convention on Jurisdiction and the Enforcement of Judgments in Civil and Commercial Matters." Note that, under the 1992 ISDA, a selection of English governing law resulted in the exclusive jurisdiction of the English courts.

120. [N. 88] The 1992 ISDA automatically included all "Affiliates" in the representation.

121. [N. 89] The 1992 ISDA did not have this representation, though many parties included a similar one via the Schedule.

[24] Additional Representations

In addition to the standard representations built into Section 3 of the ISDA Master, the Schedule contains an election to include three additional representations, namely that each party has made an independent decision to enter into the transaction without reliance on the other party for a recommendation or investment advice, that it is capable of understanding and assuming the risks of each transaction and it is not acting as a fiduciary for or advisor to the other party.[122] It is uncommon for these representations not to be made.

[25] Recording of Conversations

New York State's General Obligations Law, in § 5-701 thereof, provides that certain categories of agreements, including those which by their terms are "not to be performed within one year from the making thereof . . ." are void "unless it or some note or memorandum thereof be in writing, and subscribed the party to be charged therewith, or by his lawful agent. . . ."

An exception, however, is provided for a "qualified financial contract" a definition capturing most, if not all, commonly traded over-the-counter derivatives so long as there is "sufficient evidence to indicate that a contract has been made . . ." One of the categories defined as "sufficient evidence" is "evidence of electronic communication (including without limitation, the *recording of a telephone call* or the tangible written text produced by computer retrieval), admissible in evidence under the laws of this state, sufficient to indicate that in such communication a contract was made between the parties." (Emphasis added.)

Since recorded calls . . . [are] a common method by which over-the-counter derivatives trade (to be subsequently documented by a Confirmation signed by the parties), the Schedule provides elective language providing for the consent of each party to the recording of calls,[123] the agreement to provide personnel appropriate notices or to obtain appropriate personnel consents and the agreement that, to the extent permitted by law, recordings may be submitted in evidence in any dispute.

---

122. [N. 90] Though these representations were not in the 1992 ISDA or form of Schedule, they are commonly included by parties using a 1992 ISDA. Such representations became common following *Procter & Gamble Co. v. Bankers Trust Co. & BT Sec. Corp.*, 925 F. Supp. 1270 (S.D. Ohio 1996) in which ultimately unsuccessful claims were made that the bank defendant, although a counterparty to an ISDA Master with a corporation, also acted as an advisor to the corporation on complex derivative transactions for purposes of federal securities and commodities laws and acted inappropriately in that capacity.

123. [N. 91] It is also a requirement for swap dealer's and major swap participant's registered with the Commission. *See* 17 C.F.R. § 23.202(a)(1). Under the laws of some states, the recording of a call without the consent of the other party may be deemed a wiretapping offence. "Currently . . . California, Connecticut, Florida, Illinois, Maryland, Massachusetts, Michigan, Montana, Nevada, New Hampshire, Pennsylvania and Washington require the consent of both, or all, parties to a conversation." Jasmine McNealy, *Balancing Statutory Privacy and the Public Interest: A Review of State Wiretap Laws as Applied to the Press*, Law Tech., First Quarter 2011, Vol. 44, at 1, 2. *See also* Charles H. Kennedy and Peter P. Swire, *State Wiretaps and Electronic Surveillance After September 11*, 54 Hastings L.J. 971 (Apr. 2003).

[26] Other Provisions . . .

[T]he parties may choose to add any other provisions to the Master in the Schedule. The following are some common additional provisions that parties may put in the Schedule:

[a] "Eligible Contract Participant"

In light of the basic requirement that parties to a swap not traded on a Designated Contract Market must be Eligible Contract Participants, it is industry practice to include mutual representations to this effect.

[b] Set-off

The standard set-off provision in the ISDA Master does not include set-off of amounts due or from affiliates of either party. Consideration should be paid as to whether, via the Schedule, to modify the standard set-off provision to provide for such rights.[124]

[c] ERISA Representations

A party may request additional representations to be made by the other party relating to compliance with applicable law. For example, particular representations related to ERISA, as amended, may be required of a party that is a "plan" under ERISA, so that the transactions contemplated by the Master are not considered "prohibited transactions" under ERISA.

[d] Dodd-Frank Provisions

The Dodd-Frank Act and Commission regulations, known as the "external business conduct" requirements, impose disclosure and communications obligations on swap dealers and major swap participants, an obligation to "know your counterparty" and an obligation to verify its Eligible Contract Participant status. Moreover, any recommendations must meet a suitability standard. The Dodd-Frank Act and Commission regulations also impose swap trading relationship documentation, portfolio reconciliation and confirmation process requirements.

To facilitate compliance with . . . [the Dodd-Frank requirements], ISDA has prepared two "DF Protocols" by which parties can augment their contractual documentation to implement representations and covenants that assist with complying with the Dodd-Frank Act and Commission rules and the exchange of questionnaires satisfying the aforementioned requirements.

---

124. [N. 98] However, note that there is caselaw indicating that such "triangular" set-off rights are not enforceable in bankruptcy. See *In re Lehman Bros. Inc.*, 2011 WL 4553015 (Bankr. S.D.N.Y. 2011) and *In re SemCrude, L.P.*, 399 B.R. 388 (Bankr. D. Del. 2009), aff'd, 428 B.R. 590 (D. Del. 2010).

2. Confirmations

The ISDA Master Agreement is the most common method of documenting derivatives agreements between parties for trades that will be uncleared and not traded on a facility, such as a swap execution facility. However, the ISDA Master Agreement is a framework agreement the parties put in place before trading. It does not contain the specific economics of a particular swap transaction.

To reflect the economic terms of each swap entered into by the parties, one of the parties will issue a trade confirmation to the other, reflecting in writing the specific terms of a swap trade that the parties have already recently transacted.

The CFTC has imposed timing requirements for confirmations to be executed by both parties to a trade where one of the parties is a swap dealer or major swap participant.[125] These are summarized in figure 12.3 below with "t" representing the time of trade and the number following the "+" symbol representing the number of business days remaining in which the confirmation must be fully executed by both parties.

You will note a reference below to "acknowledgement" and then to an "executed confirmation." An acknowledgement is, in effect, a draft confirmation or one that is only signed by the swap dealer or major swap participant who sent it out. An executed confirmation is a confirmation signed by both parties.

The motivation for these rules was a concern that, before passage of the Dodd-Frank Act, parties had substantial swap trading positions and a backlog of confirmations definitively documenting the trades.[126]

Figure 12.3 Confirmation Obligations for Swap Dealers and Major Swap Participants

Counterparty Type	Type of Swap	Latest Permitted Timing
Another swap dealer or major swap participant	Interest rate and credit default swaps	Executed confirmation t + 1
Another swap dealer or major swap participant	Equity, foreign exchange and commodity swaps	Executed confirmation t + 1
Financial entity	Interest rate and credit default swaps	Acknowledgment t + 1, policies and procedures designed to ensure executed confirmation t + 1
Financial entity	Equity, foreign exchange and commodity swaps	Acknowledgment t + 1, policies and procedures designed to ensure executed confirmation t + 1

---

125. 17 C.F.R. § 23.501(c).

126. *See* CFTC, *Confirmation, Portfolio Reconciliation, Portfolio Compression, and Swap Trading Relationship Documentation Requirements for Swap Dealers and Major Swap Participants*, 77 Fed. Reg. 55904, 5597 (Sept. 11, 2012).

**Figure 12.3 Confirmation Obligations for Swap Dealers and
Major Swap Participants (*continued*)**

Counterparty Type	Type of Swap	Latest Permitted Timing
Non-financial entity	Interest rate and credit default swaps	Acknowledgment t + 1, policies and procedures designed to ensure executed confirmation t + 2
Non-financial entity	Equity, foreign exchange and commodity swaps	Acknowledgment t + 1, policies and procedures designed to ensure executed confirmation t + 2

F. Dodd-Frank Protocols

The Dodd-Frank Protocols provide a means by which parties can make required amendments to their ISDA Master Agreements to conform the documentation to CFTC swap trading relationship documentation requirements; exchange questionnaires containing representations that satisfy many of the CFTC requirements such as those relating to eligible contract participant verification, status of the "representative" of a special entity, and eligibility of a counterparty for a clearing exception; and for swap dealers and major swap participants to provide required disclosure documentation.[127] The amendments are effected by each party adhering to an adherence letter to the International Swaps and Derivatives Association and paying a fee. This is a more convenient way to amend existing documentation than multiple bilateral exchanges organized by each counterparty pair.

Moreover, instead of bilaterally exchanging questionnaires, parties can do so *en mass* using an online service, known as Counterparty Manager, provided jointly by the International Swaps and Derivatives Association and IHS Markit (a financial information platform) where parties post their questionnaires, agree to "match," and automatically exchange questionnaires.[128]

Questions and Comments

1. The fair dealing rule is described by the CFTC as "principles based and ... applied flexibly based on the facts and circumstances of a particular swap."[129] Does the CFTC thereby grant itself too much discretion? Should the rule's parameters be more clearly delineated at the expense of the CFTC's flexibility? Or would more prescriptive rules be unwieldy and ill-adapted to the facts and circumstances of individual cases?

---

127. *See* https://www2.isda.org/functional-areas/protocol-management/faq/8 and https://www2.isda.org/functional-areas/protocol-management/faq/12.

128. *See* https://ihsmarkit.com/products/counterparty-manager.html.

129. CFTC, *Business Conduct Standards for Swap Dealers and Major Swap Participants with Counterparties*, 77 Fed. Reg. 9734, 9769 (Feb. 17, 2012).

2. Could heightened regulatory requirements applicable to special entities have unintended consequences? For example, do they incentivize some swap dealers and major swap participants to not transact with special entities? Might those who continue to transact with special entities charge more as compensation for the increased risk and obligations?

3. The public policy rationale underlying the enhanced regulatory regime applying to swaps transactions with special entities is spurred by a perception that mistakes regarding derivatives transactions have historically been a significant source of problems to municipalities. Even accepting this view uncritically, if the enhanced regulation causes costs to increase for all special entities, well-managed or otherwise, does this operate as a subsidy from well-managed special entities that do not need the increased protections of the special entity rules to the handful that do? Does the fact that many special entities, such as municipalities, are funded by taxpayers make this more or less palatable?

4. Initial and variation margin requirements ostensibly protect each party to a trade from non-performance of the other party. If such protection is deemed valuable, why wouldn't parties arrange for it voluntarily?

5. The historic focus of the regulation of securities and commodity futures and options has been protecting market participants perceived as the least sophisticated. Why is it that initial margin requirements—a protection against counterparty default—only applies to the largest market participants?

6. Evaluate the advantages and disadvantages of standardized documentation such as the ISDA Master Agreement.

Chapter 13

Security-Based Swaps

A. Conceptual Framework

1. The SEC and CFTC Regimes Compared

As we discuss more in chapter 17, section B.2, only the United States and Japan have different regulators for derivatives and securities markets. The United States is alone in, for regulatory purposes, dividing swaps and security-based swaps and using different regulators for each.

After a decade in gestation, a security-based swaps regulatory framework has been implemented by the SEC. It is comprised of elements of the long established securities regulatory regime and the newly established swaps regulatory regime. The swaps regulatory regime, of course, is itself heavily influenced by the pre-existing commodity futures regulatory regime. Before focusing on the developing regulatory regime for security-based swaps, it is important to recognize some differences between the conceptual framework for the regulation of securities and the conceptual framework for the regulation of commodity futures.

A few preliminary items to keep in mind. Whereas the CFTC-regulated sphere has futures commission merchants and introducing brokers, the analogous roles in the securities markets are filled by broker-dealers. The CFTC has registered commodity trading advisors and the SEC has registered investment advisors. Designated contract markets and derivatives clearing organizations have an analogue on the securities side in national securities exchanges and clearing agencies.

A major difference between the two is in the treatment of investment vehicles. As discussed in chapter 7, the SEC regulates the actual vehicle, known as an "investment company." The CFTC, on the other hand, regulates the operator of the vehicle, known as a "commodity pool operator" and the vehicle itself is treated as any other trader in the marketplace.

These comparisons are summarized in figure 13.1.

Specific to derivatives regulation, the Dodd-Frank Act created completely parallel categories of registration. Swaps have the registration categories of swap dealers, major swap participants, swap execution facilities, and swap data repositories. Security-based swaps have the registration categories of security-based swap dealers, major security-based swap participants, security-based swap execution facilities, and security-based swap data repositories. These are summarized in figure 13.2.

Figure 13.1 Comparison of CFTC and SEC Major Categories of Registrant

Role with respect to commodity futures and swaps or securities and security-based swaps, as applicable	CFTC Registrant Category	SEC Analogue
Trading intermediary, entity holding customer funds, member of clearinghouse	Futures commission merchant	Broker-dealer
Trading intermediary, business of referring trades or brokering trades	Introducing broker	Broker-dealer
Provision of advice	Commodity trading advisor	Investment adviser
Retail market	Designated contract market	National securities exchange
Clearinghouse	Derivatives clearing organization	Clearing Agency
Operator of investment vehicle	Commodity pool operator	N/A
Investment vehicle	N/A	Investment company

Figure 13.2 Comparison of CFTC and SEC Categories of Swap-Specific Registrants

Role with respect to commodity futures and swaps or securities and security-based swaps, as applicable	CFTC Registrant Category	SEC Analogue
Dealer or marketmaker	Swap dealer	Security-based swap dealer
Speculator or investor with very large exposures to derivatives	Major swap participant	Major security-based swap participant
Non-retail exchange for derivatives	Swap execution facility	Security-based swap execution facility
Entity to which required trade reporting can be made	Swap data repository	Security-based swap data repository

This is not to suppose that the SEC and CFTC regulatory regimes are largely interchangeable. Far from it. Though outside of the scope of this work, a practical understanding of the securities regulatory framework requires its own independent study. What we will seek to establish in this chapter is a broad understanding of the different underpinnings of the SEC's and CFTC's regimes and what are some of their substantial differences.

To do so, it is helpful to assess foundational differences in their frameworks. While some convergence has occurred (namely with the CFTC using its anti-manipulation authority to take some "insider trading" claims alleging misappropriation and trading in CFTC-regulated markets on non-public information), there are still significant theoretical differences in their approaches to fraud and market manipulation.

CFTC and SEC, *A Joint Report of the SEC and the CFTC on Harmonization of Regulation*

http://www.cftc.gov/idc/groups/public/@otherif/documents/ifdocs
/opacftc-secfinaljointreport101.pdf (Oct. 16. 2009)

... Since the 1930s, securities and futures have been subject to separate regulatory regimes. While both regimes seek to promote market integrity and transparency, securities markets are concerned with capital formation, which futures markets are not. The primary purpose of futures markets is to facilitate the management and transfer of risk, and involve management of positions in underlying assets of limited supply. Certain securities markets, such as securities options and other securities derivatives markets, also facilitate the transfer of risk. The unique capital formation role of certain securities markets has informed the manner in which the two regulatory regimes have developed and, in part, explain differences between the regulatory structures of the CFTC and the SEC.

Because of the role of certain securities markets in capital formation, securities regulation is concerned with disclosure — including accounting standards related to such disclosure, while commodities regulation is not. For example, because futures markets for physical commodities concern regulation of instruments which reference a limited supply of an underlying asset, regulation permits imposition of position limits. Position limits in the securities markets is important for different reasons, namely to mitigate the potential for derivatives to be used to manipulate the market for underlying securities. ...

Oversight of New Products. The CFTC and the SEC are governed by different approaches to reviewing and approving products. Specifically, the securities laws are premised on the notion of high quality disclosure of material information about an issuer's securities. An issuer that seeks to list on an exchange must also satisfy that exchange's listing standards, which are filed with the SEC. The SEC has the authority to ensure that listing standards are consistent with the purposes of the Securities Exchange Act of 1934 ("Securities Exchange Act"), such as market integrity, public interest, and investor protection. The CFTC, however, does not have the authority to disapprove of a product listing unless it makes an affirmative finding that a product "would violate" the Commodity Exchange Act ("CEA"). .... Moreover, under the CEA, exchanges are permitted to provide "self-certification" that a product meets the requirements of the statute and CFTC regulations, which allows the product to be immediately listed. ...

Markets and Clearing Systems. ... Identical, fungible securities are traded on multiple markets in the United States as part of the "national market system." ...

Under this model, exchanges compete for trading and execution services, and clearing is done through one central clearinghouse for each product type. This structure differs from the futures markets, where individual futures contracts generally are traded on the exchange that creates the contract. Each futures exchange then "directs" clearing, that is, it selects the clearinghouse for the instruments it lists. Often, there is vertical integration where the exchange and the clearinghouse to which it directs trades have common ownership. [Note that this is not the case for swaps where the swap execution facility and derivatives clearing organization are not integrated.] ... Although product offerings in futures exchanges may be similar in terms and their functions, they are not fungible across markets and clearing organizations. ...

Obligations to Customers. On the question of what duties are owed by the financial professional to the customer, the two statutory and regulatory schemes are varied. Under the SEC's regime, investment advisers are considered fiduciaries, but [broker-dealers ("BDs")] ... are not as such. While the statutes and regulations do not uniformly impose fiduciary obligations on a BD, a BD may have a fiduciary duty under certain circumstances, [or] at times under state common law, which varies by state. Generally, BDs that exercise discretion or control over customer assets, ... have a relationship of trust and confidence with their customers, [or that advise regarding retirement plans,] are found to owe customers a fiduciary duty similar to that of investment advisers. ...

As with BDs, there are no explicitly defined fiduciary duties under the CEA or the CFTC's regulations for financial professionals such as futures commission merchants [("FCMs")], commodity trading advisors ("CTAs"), or commodity pool operators ("CPOs"). State common law imposes fiduciary duties upon persons who make decisions regarding the assets of others. This law generally holds that a futures professional owes a fiduciary duty to a customer if it is offering personal financial advice. ...

Prevention of Fraud and Manipulation. ... The SEC Division of Enforcement investigates possible violations of the federal securities laws, recommends SEC action when appropriate, either in a federal court or before an administrative law judge, prosecutes those actions, negotiates and recommends settlements, and administers the distribution of funds to harmed investors. The four primary statutes the Enforcement Division enforces are the Securities Act,[1] the Securities Exchange Act,[2] the Investment Company Act of 1940 (Investment Company Act),[3] and the Investment Advisers Act of 1940 (Advisers Act).[4]

Investigations and enforcement actions undertaken by the Enforcement Division include fraud by any person or entity, whether or not such actor is otherwise

---

1. [N. 174] 15 U.S.C. 77a *et seq.*
2. [N. 175] 15 U.S.C. 78a *et seq.*
3. [N. 176] 15 U.S.C. 80a-1 *et seq.*
4. [N. 177] 15 U.S.C. 80b-1 *et seq.*

regulated by the SEC, where the violation is in connection with the offer, purchase, or sale of securities or security-based swap agreements. Areas of fraud enforcement include: financial fraud and disclosure violations by public issuers, fraud involving broker-dealers or associated persons, fraud involving mutual funds and investment advisers, fraud involving municipal securities, securities offering frauds (including Ponzi schemes), market abuse and manipulation, and insider trading. In addition to fraud, the Enforcement Division also investigates and prosecutes regulatory misconduct, including registration, reporting, and recordkeeping violations relating to issuers, broker-dealers, municipal securities dealers, investment advisers, investment companies, and transfer agents.

Rule 10b-5 under the Securities Exchange Act makes it unlawful for any person, directly or indirectly: (1) to employ any device, scheme, or artifice to defraud; (2) to make any untrue statements of material fact or to omit to state a material fact necessary in order to make the statements made, in light of the circumstances under which they were made, not misleading; or (3) to engage in any act, practice, or course of business which operates or would operate as a fraud or deceit upon any person, "in connection with the purchase or sale" of any security.[5] Rule 10b-5 implements Section 10(b) of the Securities Exchange Act[6] prohibiting any person, in connection with a purchase or sale of any security or any security-based swap agreement, from using or employing any manipulative or deceptive device or contrivance in contravention of the SEC's rules and regulations. Similarly, Section 17 of the Securities Act makes it unlawful for any person, directly or indirectly: (1) to employ any device, scheme, or artifice to defraud; (2) to obtain money or property by means of any untrue statement of material fact or any omission to state a material fact necessary in order to make the statements made, in light of the circumstances under which they were made, not misleading; or (3) to engage in any transaction, practice, or course of business which operates or would operate as a fraud or deceit upon the purchaser, "in the offer or sale" of any security or any security-based swap agreement.[7] . . .

Manipulation, in the context of the federal securities laws, is conduct designed to deceive or defraud investors by controlling or artificially affecting the price of securities. Manipulation cases brought by the SEC generally fall into two broad, sometimes overlapping categories: pump and dump cases and manipulative trading cases.

A pump-and-dump case generally involves the use of false disclosures to cause the price of a stock to go up — i.e., the price of a stock is "pumped" by the issuance of false or misleading press releases, spam emails, message board postings, or other promotional materials. In addition, a pump and dump scheme may include some of the classic manipulative trading techniques described below.

---

5. [N. 178] 17 CFR 240.10b-5.

6. [N. 179] 15 U.S.C. 78j(b).

7. [N. 180] 15 U.S.C. 78q.

In manipulative trading cases, a stock's price is artificially affected not by false disclosures, but by artificial or deceptive trading conduct. Examples of manipulative trading practices include effecting wash sales (transactions in which there is no change in beneficial ownership) or matched trades (pre-arranged transactions to artificially maintain or otherwise affect a stock's price), painting the tape (buying activity among nominee accounts at increasingly higher prices or causing fictitious transactions reports to appear on the ticker tape), and marking the close (placing orders at or near the close of the market in order to inflate the reported closing price).

Both pump-and-dump and manipulation trading cases can be brought under the general antifraud provisions described above. In a case brought under Section 10(b) and Rule 10b-5, the SEC is required to establish that the violator acted with scienter, a mental state that the courts have held is satisfied by knowing or reckless conduct. . . .

Insider trading is prosecuted as a type of fraud under the federal securities laws. In general, insider trading refers to buying or selling securities on the basis of material, nonpublic information in breach of a duty. The prohibitions against insider trading have been developed largely by SEC and court decisions arising under the general antifraud provision of Section 10(b) of the Securities Exchange Act . . . and Rule 10b-5 thereunder. . . .

The courts have recognized two different "theories" of insider trading. Under what is known as the "traditional" or "classical theory" of insider trading, it is a violation of Section 10(b) and Rule 10b-5 for corporate insiders — a category that includes officers, directors, and employees of a corporation, as well as certain outside advisers or consultants who temporarily become fiduciaries of the corporation — to trade in the securities of their corporation on the basis of material, nonpublic information.[8] Under the classical theory, trading on such information is fraudulent because the insider, who has a relationship of trust and confidence with the corporation's shareholders, is under a duty to disclose the material information that is not known to the shareholders if the insider decides to trade.[9] This is to prevent the insider from taking unfair advantage of uninformed shareholders. . . .

The second theory of insider trading is the "misappropriation theory." Under the misappropriation theory, a person violates Section 10(b) and Rule 10b-5 "when he misappropriates confidential information for securities trading purposes, in breach of a duty owed to the source of the information." . . .

In addition, Section 16(b) of the Securities Exchange Act imposes liability for short-swing profits in the issuer's stock upon all persons required to file reports under Section 16(a) of the Securities Exchange Act (officers, directors and beneficial owners of

---

8. [N. 190] *United States v. O'Hagan*, 521 U.S. 642 (1997).

9. [N. 191] *Chiarella v. United States*, 445 U.S. 222, 228 (1980).

more than ten percent of any class of equity security). These statutory insiders must disgorge to the issuer any profit realized as a result of a purchase and sale or sale and purchase of covered equity securities occurring within a six-month period.

In order to prevent insiders and misappropriators of information from indirectly exploiting material nonpublic information, the courts have also held that Section 10(b) and Rule 10b-5 prohibit "tipping" — that is, the improper disclosure of material nonpublic information to another person who engages in trading. Further, in a tipping case, trading by the recipients of the information — the "tippees" — will also violate Section 10(b) and Rule 10b-5 when the insider's disclosure has been in breach of a duty and the tippee knows or should know that there has been a breach.[10] . . .

Trading on material non-public information is prohibited under the CEA, but only with respect to three general categories of persons. First, the statute prohibits CFTC Commissioners, employees and agents from trading on non-public information.[11] The statute similarly prohibits Commissioners and CFTC employees from delivering non-public information to third parties with the intent to assist them in conducting trades; the CEA also forbids individuals who receive this information from trading on it.[12] Finally, the CEA prohibits employees and board/committee members of a board of trade, registered entity, or registered futures association, from willfully and knowingly trading for their own or on behalf of any other account, futures or options contracts on the basis of any material non-public information obtained through special access related to the performance of their duties.[13] These felony violations are punishable by fines of up to $500,000, plus the amount of any profits realized from the trading. In the case of criminal prosecutions, there is a maximum sentence of five (5) years. . . .

Manipulation is unlawful under both the securities and futures laws. While there is some overlap in the concepts of manipulation as they relate to the securities and futures markets, panelists observed that the fact patterns of manipulation cases often differ between the two markets. In securities markets, for example, attempts to "corner" a market in a particular stock (or to "squeeze" the shorts) are relatively rare; the more common manipulation case in the securities field is the "pump and dump" scheme, which involves dissemination of false information to raise the price of a stock.

In futures markets, corners, squeezes, and the use of manipulative trading practices are of primary concern. As a result, some panelists noted that the standards that would satisfy a finding of scienter in the making of a false statement under the

---

10. [N. 196] *Dirks v. SEC*, 463 U.S. 646, 660 (1983).
11. [N. 215] CEA Section 9(c), 7 U.S.C. 13(c).
12. [N. 216] CEA Section 9(d), 7 U.S.C. 13(d).
13. [N. 217] CEA Section 9(e), 7 U.S.C. 13(e).

securities laws (e.g., "recklessness" under Rule 10b-5) may not fit precisely with all varieties of manipulation in the futures markets. . . .

[T]he approaches of the securities laws and the futures laws diverge on the issue of insider trading. . . . One of the cornerstones of the market integrity provisions of the securities laws is the prohibition on insider trading.

The CEA generally contains no such ban (except for the categories of persons enumerated above). The difference between the statutes is attributable in part to the historical functions of the futures markets to permit hedgers to protect themselves against risks to their commodity positions based on their own knowledge of those positions.

Thus, unlike securities cases brought under the classical theory of insider trading, where trading while in possession of material nonpublic company information by management insiders is in breach of a fiduciary obligation to shareholders, use of inside information by a company to hedge its risks is integral to futures markets and does not give rise to similar concerns. . . .

In other words, a hedger on the commodity futures market may be expected to have inside information. For example, supposing the hedger is a farm operation, by knowledge of its actual harvest conditions or, for a hedger that is an oil producer, by knowledge of the potential of an oil field. An insider of a company with material nonpublic information may not, however, use that information to trade on the securities market.

However, subsequent to the CFTC and SEC's joint report, the CFTC has taken the position that the Commodity Exchange Act's anti-manipulation provisions prohibit an insider from trading in a product subject to the CFTC's jurisdiction on the basis of "misappropriated" information. The CFTC has noted that CFTC Rule 180.1 prohibits: "trading on the basis of material nonpublic information in breach of a pre-existing duty (established by another law or rule, or agreement, understanding, or some other source), or by trading on the basis of material nonpublic information that was obtained through fraud or deception."[14]

2. Definition of Security-Based Swap

a. Definition Generally

As we discussed in chapter 4, section C.1.b, security-based swaps are, first, swaps. In addition to meeting the definition of "swap," they must be based on:

I. an index that is a narrow-based security index, including any interest therein or on the value thereof;

---

14. CFTC, *Prohibition on the Employment, or Attempted Employment, of Manipulative and Deceptive Devices and Prohibition on Price Manipulation*, 76 Fed. Reg. 41398, 41403 (July 14, 2011).

II. a single security or loan, including any interest therein or on the value thereof; or

III. the occurrence, nonoccurrence, or extent of the occurrence of an event relating to a single issuer of a security or the issuers of securities in a narrow-based security index, provided that such event directly affects the financial statements, financial condition, or financial obligations of the issuer.[15]

Distilling this definition to its essence, the only categories of swaps that can come within the definition of security-based swap are those that reference securities or loans. Security-based swaps can only be swaps in the category of equity swaps or credit default swaps. If such swaps reference a single security or loan, they are clearly security-based swaps. If referencing more than one security or loan, we need to examine the definition of "narrow-based security index."[16]

The test for a narrow-based index is complicated. As discussed in chapter 4, section C.1.a, a general rule of thumb is that an index comprised of nine or fewer securities is a narrow-based security index (with some additional tests if there are exactly nine securities). However, because there are further exceptions based on the weighting and trading volume of the index's constituent securities, each equity swap or credit default swap referencing more than one security or loan must be evaluated independently.

Some swaps have characteristics of swaps and security-based swaps. For example, an equity swap referencing one security that also has a foreign exchange option. Such products, known as "mixed swaps," are regulated by both the CFTC and the SEC.[17]

b. Relationship to Definition of "Security"

Before passage of the Dodd-Frank Act, the SEC had anti-fraud jurisdiction over security-based swaps. Otherwise, SEC jurisdiction over security-based swaps was prohibited by the Commodity Futures Modernization Act and security-based swaps were not defined as "securities," the instruments over which the SEC primarily asserts jurisdiction. Since 1982, securities options are the exception to this — they have been and remain defined as securities.[18]

The Dodd-Frank Act redefined "security" under the Securities Act of 1933 and the Securities Exchange Act of 1934 to include security-based swaps.[19] This had a profound impact — including some unanticipated consequences. As a result, the

---

15. Securities Exchange Act of 1934 § 3(a)(68).

16. *See* Securities Exchange Act of 1934 § 3(a)(55)(B)–(F) and Commodity Exchange Act § 1a(35).

17. *See* Dodd-Frank Act § 712(a)(8), Securities Exchange Act of 1934 § 3(a)(68)(D), and Commodity Exchange Act § 1a(47)(D).

18. *See* Securities Act of 1933 § 2(a)(1), Securities Exchange Act of 1934 § 3(a)(10), and Commodity Exchange Act § 1a(47)(B)(iii).

19. Securities Act of 1933 § 2(a)(1) and Securities Exchange Act of 1934 § 3(a)(10).

SEC has provided relief for participants in the security-based swaps market from some of the otherwise applicable securities regulatory regime.[20]

B. Security-Based Swap Entities

By November 2021, it is expected that the Dodd-Frank Act-mandated security-based swap regulatory regime will be fully operative. Until then, the only effective portion of the SEC's regulatory regime has been the anti-fraud provisions in operation before the Dodd-Frank Act.

The security-based swap regulatory regime has the same overall framework as the swap regulatory regime. Rules can be divided into internal and external business conduct rules. The relevant sub-categories of those rules are also the same.

1. Definition and Registration of Security-Based Swap Entity Registrants

The SEC and CFTC were required by the Dodd-Frank Act to promulgate joint rules for the definition of swap, security-based swap, mixed swap, eligible contract participant, swap dealer, security-based swap dealer, major swap participant, and major security-based swap participant.[21] They did so[22] and security-based swap dealer was defined as any person holding itself out as a dealer in security-based swaps, making a market in security-based swaps, regularly entering into security-based swaps as an ordinary course of business, or engaging in an activity causing it be commonly known as a dealer or market-maker in security-based swaps.[23]

Just as with swap dealers, there is a *de minimis* exception. In the case of security-based swap dealers, it is set at $8 billion notional for security-based swaps that are credit default swaps and $400 million notional for all others calculated over any twelve month period.[24] For security-based swaps with "special entities" (see chapter 11, section C), the *de minimis* threshold is a miniscule $25 million meaning that

---

20. SEC, *Order Granting Exemptions from Sections 8 and 15(a)(1) of the Securities Exchange Act of 1934 and Rules 3b-13(b)(2), 8c-1, 10b-10, 15a-1(c), 15a-1(d) and 15c2-1*, Release No. 34-90308 (Nov. 2, 2020).

21. Dodd-Frank Act § 712(d)(1).

22. *See* CFTC and SEC, *Further Definition of "Swap," "Security-Based Swap," and "Security-Based Swap Agreement"; Mixed Swaps; Security-Based Swap Agreement Recordkeeping*, 77 Fed. Reg. 48208 (Aug. 13, 2012) and CFTC and SEC, *Further Definition of "Swap Dealer," "Security-Based Swap Dealer," "Major Swap Participant," "Major Security-Based Swap Participant" and "Eligible Contract Participant,"* 77 Fed. Reg. 30796 (May 23, 2012) as corrected by CFTC and SEC, *Further Definition of "Swap Dealer," "Security-Based Swap Dealer," "Major Swap Participant," "Major Security-Based Swap Participant" and "Eligible Contract Participant"; Correction*, 77 Fed. Reg. 39626 (July 5, 2012).

23. 17 C.F.R. § 240.3a71-1(a).

24. 17 C.F.R. § 240.3a71-2. In theory, the $8 billion and $400 million are phase-in levels with the levels at some indeterminate time being reduced to $3 billion and $150 million. *Id.*

nearly any security-based swap dealing activity with a special entity is sufficient to trigger registration.[25]

The definition for major security-based swap participant is similarly modeled on the definition of major swap participant discussed in chapter 12, section C.[26]

Security-based swap dealers and major security-based swap participants are required to register with the SEC.[27] No membership of a self-regulatory organization, such as the Financial Industry Regulatory Authority (known as "FINRA"), is required.

2. Reporting and Verification of Trades

There are two reporting requirements for security-based swap transactions, the primary trade information and the secondary trade information.[28] Each must be reported within twenty-four hours of a trade to a security-based swap data repository (the analogue to the swap data repository for swap reporting).[29] The content of the reports is largely similar to the content of swap trade reporting and there is also a requirement to report "life cycle events," i.e. significant changes to the parties or the trade.[30]

For security-based swaps traded on an exchange or security-based swap execution facility and cleared, all reporting obligations are the responsibility of the exchange or security-based swap execution facility, as applicable.[31] If a security-based swap is not traded on such a trading platform but is cleared, the clearing agency is required to undertake reporting obligations.[32] In all other cases, the reporting hierarchy is as described in figure 13.3.

There is also a requirement that uncleared security-based swap trades be verified promptly and no later than the business day after which they are transacted.[33] This requirement is analogous to the swap confirmation requirements discussed in chapter 12, section E.2. The party required to provide the verification is the security-based swap dealer unless the other party is also a security-based swap dealer. In such a case, the parties mutually agree on which party provides the verification. For the entire hierarchy, see figure 13.4.

---

25. 17 C.F.R. § 240.3a71-2(a)(1)(iii).

26. 17 C.F.R. § 240.3a67-1.

27. *See* Securities Exchange Act of 1934 § 15F and SEC, *Registration Process for Security-Based Swap Dealers and Major Security-Based Swap Participants*, 80 Fed. Reg. 48964, 48964 (Aug. 14, 2015).

28. 17 C.F.R. §§ 242.901(c) and (d).

29. 17 C.F.R. §§ 242.901(a)(2) and (j).

30. 17 C.F.R. §§ 242.901(e).

31. 17 C.F.R. § 242.901(a)(1).

32. 17 C.F.R. § 242.901(a)(2)(i).

33. 17 C.F.R. § 240.15Fi-2(b).

Figure 13.3 Reporting Hierarchy for Uncleared Security-Based Swaps*

Party A	Party B	Party with Reporting Obligation?
Security-based swap dealer	Security-based swap dealer	Parties decide
Security-based swap dealer	Any other type of counterparty	Party A
Major security-based swap participant	Major security-based swap participant	Parties decide
Major security-based swap participant	Party other than a security-based swap dealer or a major security-based swap participant	Party A
U.S. person that is not a security-based swap dealer or major security-based swap participant	U.S. person that is not a security-based swap dealer or major security-based swap participant	Parties decide
Entity that is not a security-based swap dealer or major security-based swap participant and either: (1) a U.S. person; or (2) a non-U.S. person having used personnel in a U.S. branch or office (or agent in either) to arrange, negotiate, or execute the security-based swap	Entity that is not a security-based swap dealer or major security-based swap participant and a non-U.S. person having used personnel in a U.S. branch or office (or agent in either) to arrange, negotiate, or execute the security-based swap	Parties decide
Entity that is not a security-based swap dealer or major security-based swap participant and either: (1) a U.S. person; or (2) a non-U.S. person having used personnel in a U.S. branch or office (or agent in either) to arrange, negotiate, or execute the security-based swap	Entity that is not a security-based swap dealer or major security-based swap participant and a non-U.S. person *that did not use* personnel in a U.S. branch or office (or agent in either) to arrange, negotiate, or execute the security-based swap	Party A

* 17 C.F.R. § 242.901(a)(2)(ii). Though not indicated in the table, if both parties are non-U.S. person operating outside of the United States and use a U.S. broker-dealer, the broker-dealer has a reporting obligation. 17 C.F.R. § 242.901(a)(2)(E)(4).

3. Registration and Regulatory Framework for Security-Based Swap Data Repositories

As noted above, security-based swap trades will need to be reported to a security-based swap data repository. The SEC has finalized the rules and framework for security-based swap data repositories. These rules establish the means of registration, core principles, recordkeeping requirements, chief compliance officer duties, and other obligations pertaining to security-based swap data repositories.[34]

---

34. 17 C.F.R. §§ 240.13n-1 through 12.

Figure 13.4 Trade Verification Responsibility for Uncleared Security-Based Swaps*

Party A	Party B	Party with Reporting Obligation?
Security-based swap dealer	Security-based swap dealer	Parties decide
Security-based swap dealer	Any other type of counterparty	Party A
Major security-based swap participant	Major security-based swap participant	Parties decide
Major security-based swap participant	Party other than a security-based swap dealer or a major security-based swap participant	Party A
Not a security-based swap dealer or major security-based swap participant	Not a security-based swap dealer or major security-based swap participant	No obligation

* 17 C.F.R. § 240.15Fi-2(a).

4. Business Conduct

Security-based swap dealers and major security-based swap dealers have business conduct requirements that directly parallel those applying to swap dealers and major swap participants.[35] These were discussed in chapter 11, sections B and C. Namely, there are requirements to, among others:

- Verify that a counterparty is an eligible contract participant;[36]

- Disclose material risks reasonably before transacting a security-based swap with an entity other than a security-based swap dealer, major security-based swap participant, swap dealer, or major swap participant.[37]

- Provide a daily mark showing the mid-point between the bid price and the offer price for each security-based swap with parties other than security-based swap dealers, major security-based swap participants, swap dealers, or major swap participants.[38]

- For security-based swap dealers only, satisfy enhanced obligations if making a recommendation unless making a recommendation to a security-based swap dealer, major security-based swap participant, swap dealer, or major swap participant.[39]

- Communicate in a "fair and balanced" manner with all counterparties.[40]

---

35. Securities Exchange Act of 1934 § 15F(h) and 17 C.F.R. § 240.15Fh-3.
36. 17 C.F.R. § 240.15Fh-3(a).
37. 17 C.F.R. § 240.15Fh-3(b).
38. 17 C.F.R. § 240.15Fh-3(c).
39. 17 C.F.R. § 240.15Fh-3(f).
40. 17 C.F.R. § 240.15Fh-3(g).

As with swap dealers and major swap participants, security-based swap dealers and major security-based swap participants have enhanced obligations to "special entities."[41] For a review of what constitutes a "special entity," see chapter 12, section C.

5. Chief Compliance Officer

As with swap dealers and major swap participants, security-based swap dealers and major security-based swap participants are required to appoint a chief compliance officer.[42] The chief compliance officer's obligations are largely commensurate with those we discussed in chapter 11, section D.3, including an annual report requirement detailing "material non-compliance" with applicable laws or regulations.[43]

6. Cross-Border

The SEC has specified how the application of the security-based swap regulatory regime will operate across borders.[44] In doing so, the SEC has defined U.S. person and the scope of activities that bring an entity into the SEC's security-based swap jurisdiction.

In a related matter, the SEC has finalized the process for determining that a non-U.S. regime has "comparable" regulations thereby allowing non-U.S. SEC-registered security-based swap dealer or major security-based swap participants subject to such regimes to comply with local requirements in some circumstances in lieu of SEC requirements.[45]

7. Clearing

Although there is a process for designating security-based swaps that must be mandatorily cleared,[46] no category of security-based swap has been accordingly designated.

8. Portfolio Reconciliation, Portfolio Compression, and Security-Based Swap Trading Relationship Documentation

These rules are largely commensurate with the equivalent CFTC rules discussed in chapter 12, section D.3. As the SEC has noted:

---

41. Securities Exchange Act of 1934 § 15F(h)(4) and (5) and 17 C.F.R. §§ 240.15Fh-4 through 6.
42. 17 C.F.R. § 240.15Fk-1.
43. 17 C.F.R. § 240.15Fk-1(c)(2)(i)(D).
44. 17 C.F.R. § 240.3a71-3.
45. 17 C.F.R. § 240.3a71-6.
46. 17 C.F.R. §§ 240.3Ca-1 and 2.

[T]he Commission continues to recognize that the CFTC rules pertaining to portfolio reconciliation, portfolio compression, and written trading relationship documentation have been in effect since 2012, and that any SBS Entity that also is registered with the CFTC as a Swap Entity will already have incurred systems and compliance costs in connection with the corresponding CFTC requirements. Accordingly, we have endeavored throughout this rulemaking to harmonize the final rules with the existing CFTC rules wherever possible. There are, however, a very limited number of provisions where we continue to believe it is appropriate to diverge from a particular aspect of the CFTC rules. Each of those differences is described below, along with an explanation of the Commission's reasons for adopting the different approach. To the extent that no such substantive difference is described, it is because we have not identified any such differences or identified only technical differences.[47]

The types of differences are largely unavoidable, such as that the terms reconciled by parties are different. Under the security-based swap regime, the terms that are required to be reconciled are those reported to a security-based swap dealer.

9. Capital and Margin

a. Capital

Note that, as with the CFTC, the SEC has limited authority over capital and margin rules. To the extent a security-based swap dealer or major security-based swap participant is a bank or similar entity directly regulated by one of the "prudential regulators," it is not subject to the SEC's capital or margin rules. Moreover, the SEC has implemented an "alternative compliance mechanism" allowing for CFTC-registered swap dealers that are dually-registering with the SEC as security-based swap dealers to apply CFTC capital and margin rules to security-based swaps so long as the notional of security-based swaps activities are below the lesser of 10% of the notional of all swap and security-based swaps and $250 billion (slated to drop to $50 billion by October 2024 without SEC intervention).[48]

The security-based swap dealer registrants not subject to the prudential regulators' or the CFTC's rules would be subject to the SEC's existing securities broker-dealer capital regime, if already registered as securities broker-dealers, or a similar regime otherwise.[49]

---

47. SEC, *Risk Mitigation Techniques for Uncleared Security-Based Swaps*, 85 Fed. Reg. 6359, 6362 (Feb. 4, 2020).

48. 17 C.F.R. § 240.18a-10.

49. For securities broker-dealers, see 17 C.F.R. § 240.15c3-1, and for all others, see 17 C.F.R. § 18a-1.

b. Margin

Security-based swap dealers are required to collect initial margin, and security-based swap dealers and major security-based swap participants are required to collect and post variation margin, except as described in figure 13.5.[50] There is no requirement for a security-based swap dealer to post initial margin. The collateral types allowed for exchange of variation margin are broader than with swap dealers.[51]

Figure 13.5 Security-Based Swap Dealer Margin Requirements

Exception	Status of Exceptions to Collecting Margin		Status of Exceptions to Delivering VM
	Variation Margin	Initial Margin	
Commercial End User	Need Not Collect	Need Not Collect	Need Not Deliver
BIS or European Stability Mechanism	Need Not Collect	Need Not Collect	Need Not Deliver
Multilateral Development Bank	Need Not Collect	Need Not Collect	Need Not Deliver
Financial Market Intermediary	Must Collect	Need Not Collect	Must Deliver
Affiliate	Must Collect	Need Not Collect	Must Deliver
Sovereign with Minimal Credit Risk	Must Collect	Need Not Collect	Must Deliver
Legacy Account	Need Not Collect	Need Not Collect	Need Not Deliver
IM Below $50 Million Threshold	Must Collect	Need Not Collect	Must Deliver
Minimum Transfer Amount	Need Not Collect	Need Not Collect	Need Not Deliver

Source: SEC, *SEC Adopts Capital, Margin, and Segregation Requirements for Security-Based Swap Dealers and Major Security-Based Swap Participants and Amends the Capital and Segregation Requirements for Broker-Dealers*, Press Rel. 2019-105 (June 21, 2019), available at https://www.sec .gov/news/press-release/2019-105.

C. Current Application of SEC Regulatory Regime to Security-Based Swaps

1. Fraud Jurisdiction

Even before passage of the Dodd-Frank Act, the SEC had authority to police fraud with respect to security-based swaps. This includes the application of prohibitions on insider trading to security-based swaps.

---

50. 17 C.F.R. § 240.18a-3(c).

51. 17 C.F.R. § 240.18a-3(c)(4).

Although the SEC lost the below case on the facts, it provides an example of a security-based swap to which — had the facts supported the SEC's allegations — insider trading prohibitions would apply.

SEC v. Rorech

720 F. Supp. 2d 367 (S.D.N.Y. 2010)

. . . This is a case about alleged insider trading in credit derivatives. The Securities and Exchange Commission (the "SEC") alleges that the defendants, Jon-Paul Rorech and Renato Negrin, engaged in insider trading in credit-default swaps ("CDSs").

While there are different types of CDSs, the CDSs that are at issue in this case are contracts that provide protection against the credit risk of a particular company. The seller of a CDS agrees to pay the buyer a specific sum of money, called the notional amount, if a credit event, such as bankruptcy, occurs in the referenced company. If a credit event occurs, the buyer generally must provide to the seller any of certain debt instruments that are deliverable pursuant to the CDS contract. In exchange for this risk protection from the CDS-seller, the CDS-buyer agrees to make periodic premium payments during the course of the contract. The CDS-buyer can use the CDS to provide protection, like insurance, against the possibility that the debt instruments the buyer holds will seriously deteriorate in value because of a credit event in the referenced company. The CDS-buyer could also buy the CDS without owning the underlying referenced security, a "naked CDS," in the expectation that it would increase in value based on any one of a number of factors including the likelihood that a credit event will occur in the referenced company.

The CDSs at issue in this case provided for payment if certain credit events occurred at VNU N.V. ("VNU"), a Dutch media holding company. The CDSs referenced a specific VNU security that would have to be delivered in return for the notional amount, although it was possible to deliver certain other securities instead.

In July 2006, Deutsche Bank Securities Inc. ("Deutsche Bank") served as the lead underwriter for a bond offering by two of VNU's subsidiaries. During its efforts to sell the bonds, Deutsche Bank learned that there was demand in the market for bonds issued by the holding company, VNU, rather than by its subsidiaries. This demand existed because the bonds to be issued by VNU's subsidiaries would not be deliverable instruments under the terms of VNU CDSs then in the market. Because VNU was also planning on retiring its then-outstanding deliverable bonds, CDS-holders would be left with only a limited number of bonds that would be deliverable under the CDS contracts. Holders of VNU CDSs, and prospective purchasers, preferred that VNU modify the bond offering to issue at least some bonds at the holding company level.

The SEC alleges that Mr. Rorech, a high-yield bond salesperson at Deutsche Bank, passed confidential information to Mr. Negrin, a portfolio manager for the hedge fund Millennium Partners, L.P. ("Millennium"), regarding plans to modify the VNU bond offering. The SEC alleges that Mr. Rorech told Mr. Negrin during two unrecorded cellular telephone calls on July 14 and July 17, 2006, (1) that Deutsche Bank would recommend to VNU's financial sponsors that VNU issue the holding company bonds and (2) that at least one of Mr. Rorech's customers already had placed an order for $100 million of the holding company bonds.

Mr. Negrin bought two VNU CDSs on behalf of Millennium on July 17 and July 18, 2006. After the July 24, 2006, announcement that VNU's bond offering would be amended to include bonds issued by the holding company, the price of VNU CDSs increased substantially. Mr. Negrin subsequently sold the VNU CDSs for a profit to Millennium of approximately $1.2 million.

The Court conducted a non-jury trial in this case from April 7, 2010, to April 28, 2010. Despite the SEC's allegations of the information passed by Mr. Rorech to Mr. Negrin during the two cellular phone calls, there is no evidence of what was actually said on those calls and neither Mr. Rorech nor Mr. Negrin could recall the substance of the calls. While the SEC attempts to attribute nefarious content to those calls through circumstantial evidence, there is, in fact, no evidence to support this inference and ample evidence that undercuts the SEC's theory that the defendants engaged in insider trading.

First, the SEC produced no evidence that Deutsche Bank had actually decided to recommend that the sponsors issue a holding company tranche at the time of Mr. Rorech's cellular phone calls with Mr. Negrin, and there is no evidence that any such decision was conveyed to Mr. Rorech before the phone calls. Having set forth no evidence that Mr. Rorech either received or shared with Mr. Negrin any allegedly confidential information concerning Deutsche Bank's recommendation, the SEC's allegation of insider trading based on that information fails.

Second, the SEC has failed to prove that either piece of alleged information was material. Immediately after the bond deal was announced, there was widespread discussion in the market regarding investor demand for a restructuring of the VNU bond offering to include deliverable bonds. Even the SEC's own expert, David Barcus, admits that it was publicly known—particularly to sophisticated high yield bond buyers—that, with such strong market demand, Deutsche Bank would be speaking to the sponsors and working with them to try to find a way to issue additional deliverable bonds. Because any information that Mr. Rorech possessed on July 17, 2006 . . . about Deutsche Bank's alleged intention to recommend a holding company issuance was based on information in the market and was completely speculative in any event, any information Mr. Rorech shared with Mr. Negrin cannot be considered material. Likewise, information regarding Mr. Rorech's customer's indication of interest was not material because the demand for deliverable bonds was known in the market. The fact that Jeremy Barnum, a portfolio manager at the hedge fund Blue Mountain Capital Management LLC ("Blue Mountain") who placed the initial $100 million indication of interest, subsequently sold VNU CDSs after having actually learned of Deutsche Bank's intent to recommend the holding company tranche and after having placed his own indication of interest is substantial evidence that these two pieces of information were not considered material to reasonable investors in VNU CDSs.

Third, the evidence also confirms that the information that Mr. Rorech could have shared with Mr. Negrin was not confidential and that Mr. Rorech did not breach any duty to Deutsche Bank. Pursuant to Deutsche Bank's written policy on the use of confidential information, as well as testimony from Deutsche Bank's compliance officer, information is deemed confidential only when there is an expectation or contractual agreement that it will be kept confidential. The evidence does not show that Mr. Rorech possessed any information about Deutsche Bank's decision to recommend that VNU issue the holding company bonds. Any information that he did share with Mr. Negrin, therefore, would have been speculative and his own opinion. If Mr. Rorech shared such information, that would not amount to a breach of his duty of confidentiality to Deutsche Bank. Similarly, Mr. Rorech's customer's indication of interest in holding company bonds was not confidential, because, among other things, Mr. Barnum at Blue Mountain, who submitted the order for holding company bonds, testified unequivocally that he had no expectation of confidentiality in his proposed order. To the contrary, Mr. Barnum, like other customers, expected that Deutsche Bank would discuss his order with other potential investors to generate additional demand for a holding company issuance of bonds. Because Mr. Barnum had no expectation that the information would be confidential, Deutsche Bank did not consider the information confidential and Mr. Rorech did not breach any duty to Deutsche Bank....

Fourth, deceit — or the unauthorized theft of confidential information — is the cornerstone of the misappropriation theory of insider trading liability, on which the SEC's case relies. *United States v. O'Hagan*, 521 U.S. 642, 652–55, 117 S.Ct. 2199, 138 L.Ed.2d 724 (1997). The SEC has not established that there was any deception in this case. Mr. Rorech disclosed to his supervisors on the sales desk and in capital markets that he was, in fact, sharing information about the potential holding company issuance with his customers, including Mr. Negrin's hedge fund, Millennium. Mr. Rorech was never told to stop sharing such information nor cautioned as to its allegedly confidential nature.

Similarly, Mr. Rorech lacked the requisite intent to be held liable for insider trading. Mr. Rorech believed that, in discussing the information about VNU with prospective investors, he was doing his job as a high yield salesperson. This belief comported with both the custom and practice in the industry as well as the actions of capital markets officers and other Deutsche Bank salespeople on the high yield desk, including Mr. Rorech's direct supervisor, Wight Martindale. It is farfetched to think that Mr. Rorech could believe that the very information shared with outsiders by his supervisor and the head of high yield capital markets would somehow not be appropriate for him to share.

The SEC also has failed to present any evidence that Mr. Rorech had any motive to provide "inside" information to Mr. Negrin, who was neither a personal friend nor his most significant account. This is not a case where a securities firm employee receives undisclosed benefits for his "tips." The only benefit Mr. Rorech allegedly received was any increase in compensation that he received from doing his job of selling securities. The SEC did not even present any evidence as to the significance of Mr. Negrin's CDS order on Mr. Rorech's overall compensation. Mr. Negrin's CDS order of a $10 million VNU CDS from Deutsche Bank appears relatively small compared to the $200 million in VNU bond orders that Mr. Rorech obtained during the same period. In light of all of the evidence that shows that Mr. Rorech believed his conduct was entirely appropriate, the fact that Mr. Rorech and Mr. Negrin had two cellular phone calls during the marketing period of the VNU bond offering is insufficient to establish scienter. . . .

The single claim in this case alleges insider trading in CDSs in violation of section 10(b) of the Securities Exchange Act of 1934, 15 U.S.C. § 78j(b), and Rule 10b-5, 17 C.F.R. § 240.10b-5, promulgated thereunder. . . . The SEC brings this action under the misappropriation theory of insider trading. . . .

To establish liability as to Mr. Rorech, the SEC must prove that Mr. Rorech, in connection with the purchase or sale of a security or "securities-based swap agreement," misappropriated material nonpublic information in breach of a fiduciary duty to Deutsche Bank, and that Mr. Rorech acted with scienter. . . .

Under the misappropriation theory, an individual violates section 10(b) and Rule 10b-5 "when he misappropriates confidential information for securities trading purposes, in breach of a duty owed to the source of the information." *O'Hagan*, 521 U.S. at 652, 117 S.Ct. 2199. . . .

Scienter is a necessary element of every section 10(b) and Rule 10b-5 claim. . . . Scienter encompasses "a mental state embracing intent to deceive, manipulate, or defraud." *Ernst & Ernst v. Hochfelder*, 425 U.S. 185, 193 n. 12, 96 S.Ct. 1375, 47 L. Ed.2d 668 (1976). . . .

The SEC has failed to prove by a preponderance of the credible evidence that Mr. Rorech . . . intended to deceive, manipulate, or defraud by sharing the allegedly "inside" information. . . .

For the reasons explained above, the defendants are entitled to a Judgment dismissing the plaintiff's complaint. The Clerk is directed to enter Judgment in favor of the defendants and closing this case.

––––––––––

One can see how, if insider trading prohibitions applied to securities and not security-based swaps, security-based swaps would be a means to obtain the same economic outcome while evading the prohibition on insider trading of securities.

For example, suppose the CEO of the Arctic Lumber Company knows that the company will be filing for bankruptcy in two months. She cannot "short" the Arctic Lumber Company's stock, i.e., borrow some shares, sell them today at a high price, and then, after they drop precipitously in value due to the bankruptcy filing, buy them low and return them to the party that lent the shares. That would run afoul of prohibitions on insider trading.

Applying the insider trading prohibitions to security-based swaps is necessary because, otherwise, the CEO could obtain a similar economic outcome as in the previous example by buying a credit default swap. In the event of a default by the Arctic Lumber Company, a credit default swap could be designed to allow her to obtain a cash settlement from the seller of protection equal to the face amount of a selected Artic Lumber Company bond minus its actual market value. Since she knows that, upon the forthcoming bankruptcy filing, the market value of Artic Lumber Company bonds will plummet, she is assured of a return well exceeding what she initially paid for the credit default swap's protection.

2. Extent of Extraterritorial Jurisdiction

In chapter 17, we examine a statutory demarcation of the extraterritorial application of the CFTC's swap regulatory authority added by the Dodd-Frank Act.[52] Hence a different treatment for the CFTC's extraterritorial jurisdiction over swaps than *Morrison*, which we will examine in chapter 17, would otherwise demand.[53]

The Dodd-Frank Act did not add a similar provision that would modify the application of *Morrison* with respect to the SEC's authority over security-based swaps. It did, however, add a new provision providing the SEC jurisdiction over securities transactions solely involving non-U.S. persons so long as there is a "foreseeable substantial effect" on the United States.[54] The extent to which this provision partially obviates the ruling in *Morrison* remains to be seen with one court ruling that it does[55] and another asserting, *obiter*, that it does not.[56] Since a security-based swap has been redefined by the Dodd-Frank Act as a type of security, this new provision applies equally to a security-based swap.

The court in the below case decided, based on the pre-Dodd-Frank securities acts, that, in obedience to the Supreme Court's *Morrison* decision, there was no jurisdiction with respect to a security-based swap in the absence of a U.S. person purchaser or seller. This decision should still hold even after the aforementioned amendments providing the SEC extraterritorial jurisdiction over securities where there is a "foreseeable substantial effect" on the United States because the amendments only provided the SEC or the United States jurisdiction to bring a proceeding. It does not apply to a private right of action such as the action in the case below.

---

52. Commodity Exchange Act § 2(i).

53. *Morrison v. National Australia Bank, Ltd.*, 561 U.S. 247 (2010. If unfamiliar with *Morrison*, it is recommended to read chapter 17, section B, for background on *Morrison* and related cases.

54. Dodd-Frank Act § 929P(b)(1)–(3) adding Securities Act of 1933 § 22(c), Securities Exchange Act of 1934 § 27(b), and Investment Advisers Act of 1940 § 214(b).

55. *SEC v. Traffic Monsoon, LLC*, 245 F. Supp. 3d 1275, 1285–1295 (D. Utah, Mar. 28, 2017), appeal filed, Notice of App., *SEC v. Traffic Monsoon, LLC* (D. Utah, Apr. 17, 2017) (2:16-CV-00832-JNP, available on PACER).

56. *Parkcentral Global Hub Limited v. Porsche Automobile Holdings SE*, 763 F.3d 198, 211 at n. 11 (2d Cir. 2014).

Parkcentral Global Hub Limited v. Porsche
Automobile Holdings SE
763 F.3d 198 (2d Cir. 2014)

. . . In *Morrison v. National Australia Bank Ltd.*, 561 U.S. 247, 130 S.Ct. 2869, 177 L. Ed.2d 535 (2010), the Supreme Court established that, by virtue of the presumption against extraterritorial application of U.S. statutes, § 10(b) of the Securities Exchange Act of 1934, the basic antifraud provision of the U.S. securities laws, has no extra- territorial application, and no civil suit under that section may be brought unless predicated on a purchase or sale of a security listed on a domestic exchange or on a domestic purchase or sale of another security. . . . In *Absolute Activist Value Master Fund Ltd. v. Ficeto*, 677 F.3d 60 (2d Cir.2012), this Court set forth the means to be used to determine when a transaction in securities is "domestic" such that it may furnish the basis for a suit under that section. We concluded that in order for such a transaction to qualify as domestic, "the parties [must] incur irrevocable liability to carry out the transaction within the United States or . . . title [to the securities must be] passed within the United States." *Id.* at 69.

In this case, the securities transactions upon which the plaintiffs brought suit were so-called "securities-based swap agreements" relating to the stock of Volkswa- gen AG ("VW"), a German corporation; the amount of gain and loss in the transac- tions depended on prices of VW stock recorded on foreign exchanges. The parties accused of fraud are Porsche Automobil Holding SE ("Porsche"), also a major Ger- man corporation, and its executives. Their allegedly fraudulent statements con- sisted of assertions about Porsche's intentions with respect to the stock of VW; their statements were made primarily in Germany, but were also accessible in the United States and were repeated here by the defendants. The thorny issue presented by this appeal is how to apply the rules established by the *Morrison* and *Absolute Activist* decisions to this case.

The plaintiffs, more than thirty international hedge funds, employed securities- based swap agreements pegged to the price of VW shares, which trade on European stock exchanges, to bet that VW stock would decline in value. The positions they took through their swap agreements were roughly economically equivalent to short positions in VW stock, in that they would gain to the extent VW stock declined in value and would lose to the extent it rose. Plaintiffs allege that, in 2008, defen- dants made various fraudulent statements and took various manipulative actions to deny and conceal Porsche's intention to take over VW. The plaintiffs allege that they relied on defendants' fraudulent denial of Porsche's intention to take over VW in making their swap agreements. When, in October 2008, Porsche made its true intentions public, the price of VW shares rose dramatically, causing the plaintiffs to suffer large losses.

The plaintiffs brought the instant complaints in the United States District Court for the Southern District of New York against Porsche and two of its corporate officers alleging, among other things, that the defendants' fraudulent statements and manipulative actions violated U.S. securities laws. Following the Supreme Court's decision in *Morrison,* the defendants moved to dismiss the complaint because the plaintiffs' swap agreements referenced securities trading on foreign exchanges. The district court (Harold Baer, Jr., Judge) granted the defendants' motion, concluding that the swaps were essentially transactions in securities on foreign exchanges.

We affirm the judgment, although on the basis of different reasoning. In our view, the imposition of liability under § 10(b) on these foreign defendants with no alleged involvement in plaintiffs' transactions, on the basis of the defendants' largely foreign conduct, for losses incurred by the plaintiffs in securities-based swap agreements based on the price movements of foreign securities would constitute an impermissibly extraterritorial extension of the statute. Our ultimate conclusion that this suit seeks impermissibly to extend § 10(b) extraterritorially depends in some part on the particular character of the unusual security at issue. For reasons explained below, we express no view whether we would have reached the same result if the suit were based on different transactions. . . .

Porsche, the well-known German automobile manufacturer, is also an active investor in various securities and derivatives. Indeed, in the fiscal year ending July 31, 2008, the company . . . derived eighty-eight percent of its total profits from its investments and twelve percent of its total profits from selling motor vehicles.

From late 2005 through 2007, Porsche gradually increased its investment in VW, another well-known German automobile manufacturer, whose shares trade primarily on European exchanges. At the time, a German statute known as the "VW Law" limited any one VW shareholder's voting rights to twenty percent of the total voting rights, regardless of how many VW shares the shareholder actually owned. In the face of public speculation that the European Court of Justice would soon invalidate the VW Law, Porsche claimed publicly that its acquisition of these shares was intended to prevent a hostile takeover of VW, with which it had important business relationships. Porsche also disavowed any intention to obtain a controlling interest in VW — then defined by the VW Law as eighty percent of the company's outstanding shares, or seventy-five percent of the shares in the event that other stakeholders agreed to vote in favor of a "domination agreement."[57] By the end of 2007, Porsche had become VW's largest shareholder, owning thirty-one percent of the company.

The plaintiffs allege that in spite of its public assurances to the contrary, at least as early as February 2008, Porsche had developed a secret plan to acquire the minimum

---

57. [N. 1] Under German law, "[a] domination agreement between an acquiring firm and a target firm allows the acquiring firm to control the target firm's decisions." Third Amended Complaint ¶ 6, *Elliot Assocs., L.P. v. Porsche Automobil Holding SE,* 10 Civ. 532 (S.D.N.Y. July 21, 2010) (the "Elliott Compl.").

seventy-five percent interest needed to gain control of VW.[58] Porsche's problem was that VW's stock was held in large part by parties who either did not want to, or could not for political or other reasons, sell it. As a result, VW's "float"—the amount of shares available to the public for trading—was insufficient to allow Porsche to acquire a seventy-five percent stake outright. But if those shareholders unwilling to sell could nevertheless be induced to *lend* their shares to third parties engaged in short sales of VW stock, the shares would temporarily enter the market, giving Porsche the opportunity to buy them.... This became the core of Porsche's strategy.

The plaintiffs allege that Porsche induced them to bet on a decline in the price of VW shares ... principally by "express[ly] den[ying] that it would take over VW in the near future," and thus making VW's shares "appear [ ] increasingly overvalued relative to the shares of other publicly traded automobile companies."... The plaintiffs allege that, by concealing its intention to acquire control of VW, Porsche led them to conclude erroneously that the demand for VW stock was lower than it actually was. For these and other reasons, the plaintiffs then entered into various short-sale transactions involving VW stock and into securities-based swap agreements economically equivalent to short sales of VW stock—standing to gain if VW share price fell, and to lose if it rose.

To tap into the market for VW shares offered by short-sellers such as the plaintiffs, Porsche purchased call options. These gave Porsche the right to buy VW shares at a specified future date and price.... To hedge against Porsche's exercise of its option rights, its call option counterparties bought and held the VW shares that short-sellers had sold into the market. The plaintiffs allege that Porsche took various steps to conceal its acquisition of call rights, including buying a sufficiently small number of call options from each of many counterparties so that no one counterparty would acquire enough VW stock for hedging purposes as to trigger legal disclosure requirements.

Throughout this period, Porsche made repeated public statements disclaiming any intention to acquire a controlling share of VW, and denying that it was trying to obtain a seventy-five percent stake. The plaintiffs' investment managers—located in New York City and elsewhere in the United States—concluded, based on the publicly available information, that Porsche was unable or unwilling to acquire control of VW. Because Porsche's strategy had avoided triggering counterparty disclosures, the investment managers remained unaware that Porsche could at any moment exercise rights to purchase large numbers of VW shares....

Porsche financed its purchase of call options by selling put options on VW stock. These options obligated Porsche to pay its counterparties the difference between a pre-set "strike" price and the actual price of VW stock if the actual price fell below the strike price.... While revenue from its sale of put options allowed Porsche to

---

58. [N. 2] According to German press accounts published nearly a year after the fact, representatives of Porsche met with officials from the State of Lower Saxony—which held approximately twenty percent of VW's stock—in February 2008, and informed them of this plan.

covertly fund its purchase of call options, the strategy also carried risks. If the price of VW stock fell, the difference between the share price and the strike price would increase, exposing Porsche to potentially massive liability. Indeed, Porsche had entered into so many of these contracts that it risked insolvency in the event VW stock price fell precipitously.

Through the first three quarters of 2008, VW's share price continued to rise and Porsche's strategy proceeded as planned. As the global financial crisis became increasingly serious in late October 2008, however, VW's stock price began a sharp decline. By October 24, 2008, the price had fallen thirty-nine percent from its average closing price between October 1 and October 17, 2008. As a result, Porsche's liability to its put option counterparties grew dramatically. The plaintiffs allege that, in a bid to shore up VW's share price and avert disaster, Porsche finally decided to disclose its theretofore secret plan to the public. On Sunday, October 26, 2008, the company issued a press release entitled "Porsche Heads for Domination Agreement," revealing that Porsche had acquired 74.1 percent of VW through a combination of direct holdings and call options.... The release explained that Porsche hoped to "increase [its VW stake] to 75% in 2009, paving the way to a domination agreement." ... And it stated that the disclosure of the actual extent of Porsche's ownership of VW "should give so called short sellers ... the opportunity to settle their relevant positions without rush and without facing major risks." ...

The irony of that statement may have been unintentional, but on the following day, "all hell broke loose." ... With Porsche holding 74.1 percent of VW's shares, and the German State of Lower Saxony holding another twenty percent, just 5.9% of the company's outstanding shares remained theoretically available for purchase. Short-sellers obligated to acquire and return nearly thirteen percent of VW's outstanding shares to the parties from whom they had borrowed them found themselves facing a severe shortage. Compounding the problem, a substantial proportion of the 5.9 percent in the float was held by index funds that would not or could not sell some or all of their shares.

As the market absorbed the news of Porsche's takeover plan, the price of VW stock began to skyrocket, leaving short-sellers scrambling to purchase the shares they needed to unwind their short sales and limit their losses. That flurry of activity caused the price of VW stock to rise even more rapidly, further increasing the short-sellers' losses and increasing their desperation to buy shares. This vicious cycle — a "short squeeze" — led the price of VW stock to nearly quintuple from its price during the preceding week. Indeed, for several hours, VW became the most valuable corporation in the world measured by market capitalization. To satisfy some of this demand, Porsche agreed to release five percent of its holdings, obtaining a huge windfall as a result.

When the dust had settled, parties with short positions in VW had lost an estimated total of $38.1 billion, and VW's share price had fallen back to roughly 2007 levels. German authorities later investigated Porsche and its executives ... in connection with these events....

The transactions in which plaintiffs incurred the losses that are the subject of this suit were synthetic investments, known as securities-based swap agreements.[59] These investments were economically equivalent to short sales referencing VW shares. . . .

Securities-based swap agreements are designed to roughly replicate the economic effect of owning the referenced share of stock for one counterparty, and shorting the referenced share of stock for the other counterparty, without either party taking an actual ownership interest in the reference security. The plaintiffs allege that because they took the "short" side of these synthetic investments, "the swap agreement[s] [would] generate[ ] gains as the price of VW shares declined and [would] generate[ ] losses as the price of VW shares rose, achieving an economic result similar to a short sale." . . .

Inasmuch as this appeal involves the applicability of the securities laws to claims involving foreign elements, the location of certain key events, entities, and instruments is essential to our analysis.

The plaintiffs have, to varying degrees, alleged that they entered into the swap agreements referencing VW shares in the United States. . . . The plaintiffs do not allege, however, that Porsche was a party to any securities-based swap agreements referencing VW stock, or that it participated in the market for such swaps in any way.

Although the securities-based swap agreements in this case may have been concluded domestically, the VW shares they referenced appear to trade only on foreign exchanges. VW shares trade on the Frankfurt Stock Exchange and "international stock exchanges in Switzerland, Luxembourg, and the UK." . . . The plaintiffs do not allege that they are traded on any United States exchange. . . .

Porsche's allegedly deceptive conduct occurred primarily in Germany, although the plaintiffs allege that some of Porsche's statements denying any intention to acquire control of VW were made into the United States or were available here. . . .

Morrison and *Absolute Activist Value Master Fund Ltd. v. Ficeto*, 677 F.3d 60 (2d Cir.2012) ("*Absolute Activist* "), comprise the principal case authority in this Circuit governing the application of § 10(b) and Rule 10b-5 to claims involving extraterritorial conduct. . . .

We are of course [therefore] bound by *Morrison* and *Absolute Activist* in determining whether § 10(b), and Rule 10b-5 promulgated by the Securities and Exchange Commission pursuant thereto, applies to the defendants' alleged conduct. We must proceed cautiously in applying teachings the *Morrison* Court developed in a case involving conventional purchases and sales of stock to derivative securities, like securities-based swap agreements, that vest parties with rights to payments based on changes in the value of a stock.

---

59. [N. 6] The securities laws use the term "security-based swap agreement" in 15 U.S.C. § 78c, but use the term "securities-based swap agreement" in 15 U.S.C. § 78j(b). Because this opinion focuses on § 10(b), we use the latter term throughout this opinion.

A question of potentially determinative importance for this case is whether, under *Morrison,* a domestic transaction in a security (or a transaction in a domestically listed security) — in addition to being a *necessary* element of a domestic § 10(b) claim — is also *sufficient* to make a particular invocation of § 10(b) appropriately domestic. If a domestic transaction in a security is not only necessary but also sufficient to justify the application of § 10(b) to otherwise foreign facts, and the plaintiffs' securities-based swap agreements (which we assume for these purposes were executed and performed in the United States) are deemed domestic transactions under *Absolute Activist,* then all other questions would drop away. The mere fact that the plaintiffs based their suit on a domestic transaction would make § 10(b) applicable to allegedly fraudulent conduct anywhere in the world. In such a case, these complaints would properly invoke a domestic application of § 10(b).

Morrison established two important rules about the applicability of § 10(b). First, *Morrison* held that, because Congress did not indicate an intention that § 10(b) should apply extraterritorially, the presumption against extraterritoriality dictates that § 10(b) has no extraterritorial application. *Morrison,* 561 U.S. at 265, 130 S.Ct. 2869. Second, *Morrison* ruled that § 10(b) does not apply unless the suit is predicated on either a domestic securities transaction or a transaction in a domestically listed security. *Id.* at 267, 130 S.Ct. 2869. Because neither was present in the case before it, the Court held that the invocation of § 10(b) was impermissibly extraterritorial, and the complaint failed to state a valid claim.

On careful consideration of *Morrison* 's words and arguments as applied to the facts of this case, we conclude that, while that case unmistakably made a domestic securities transaction (or transaction in a domestically listed security) necessary to a properly domestic invocation of § 10(b), such a transaction is not alone sufficient to state a properly domestic claim under the statute. We reach this conclusion for several reasons.

First, and most important, the Court did not *say* that such a transaction was sufficient to make the statute applicable. The language the Court used was consistent with the description of necessary elements rather than sufficient conditions. *See id.* at 267 ("And it is in our view *only* transactions in securities listed on domestic exchanges, and domestic transactions in other securities, to which § 10(b) applies." (emphasis added)). The Court never said that an application of § 10(b) *will* be deemed domestic *whenever* such a transaction is present.

Second, a rule making the statute applicable whenever the plaintiff's suit is predicated on a domestic transaction, regardless of the foreignness of the facts constituting the defendant's alleged violation, would seriously undermine *Morrison* 's insistence that § 10(b) has no extraterritorial application. It would require courts to apply the statute to wholly foreign activity clearly subject to regulation by foreign authorities solely because a plaintiff in the United States made a domestic transaction, even if the foreign defendants were completely unaware of it. Such a rule would inevitably place § 10(b) in conflict with the regulatory laws of other nations.

The principal reason that the Court "reject[ed] the notion that the Exchange Act reaches conduct in this country affecting exchanges or transactions abroad," *id.* at 269, 130 S.Ct. 2869, was not that Congress lacked the power to do so. Indeed, the Court implied the contrary. *See id.* at 255, 130 S.Ct. 2869 (explaining that the presumption is not a "limit upon Congress's power to legislate"). But "[t]he probability of incompatibility with the applicable laws of other countries [in the case of transfers of shares of common stock] is so obvious that if Congress intended such foreign application it would have addressed the subject of conflicts with foreign laws and procedures" in the statute. *Id.* at 269, 130 S.Ct. 2869 (citation and internal quotation marks omitted). The Court apparently thought that, if an extraterritorial application of federal law would likely be incompatible with foreign law, and that application was intended by Congress, Congress would have addressed the conflict. The corollary of that proposition is that if an application of the law would obviously be incompatible with foreign regulation, and Congress has *not* addressed that conflict, the application is one which Congress did not intend.

Applying that axiom to this case illustrates the problem with treating the location of a transaction as the definitive factor in the extraterritoriality inquiry. If the domestic execution of the plaintiffs' agreements could alone suffice to invoke § 10(b) liability with respect to the defendants' alleged conduct *in this case,* then it would subject to U.S. securities laws conduct that occurred in a foreign country, concerning securities in a foreign company, traded entirely on foreign exchanges, in the absence of any congressional provision addressing the incompatibility of U.S. and foreign law nearly certain to arise. That is a result *Morrison* plainly did not contemplate and that the Court's reasoning does not, we think, permit. . . .

We therefore affirm the district court's dismissal of the complaints. . . .

As noted by the court in *Parkcentral, Morrison* identified the occurrence of a purchase or sale of a security in the United States as a necessary element of U.S. jurisdiction for a securities law claim under Security Exchange Act section 10(b). It did not address a more complicated situation where one securities transaction occurs in the United States (since security-based swap is defined as a type of security) in relation to a second security issued by a non-U.S. issuer and listed on non-U.S. securities exchanges. Since the claim related to alleged fraud with respect to the second security, not the first, it was determined to be precluded by *Morrison* because, otherwise, it would apply section 10(b) extraterritorially.

3. Prohibition of Retail Security-Based Swaps

As with swaps, it is illegal for a party that is not an eligible contract participant to enter into a security-based swap. The same definition of "eligible contract participant" is used for security-based swaps as is used for swaps. We discussed this definition in chapter 9, section E.

There is an exception allowing a non-eligible contract participant to enter into a security-based swap if the security-based swap is: (1) registered with the SEC using the same process used for the registration of securities offered to the public; and (2) traded on a securities exchange. In the below case, a company developed a phone application that allowed participants to pay an entry fee and then compete against one another for a cash prize by successfully ranking ten pre-selected stocks by best performance to worst performance over a specified time period. Although the company that developed the phone application, Forcerank LLC, retained a percentage of the entry fees, it also intended to resell the data it obtained related to the competitors' behavior and predictive abilities.

In the Matter of Forcerank LLC

Securities Act Rel. No. 10232 (Oct. 13, 2016)

The Securities and Exchange Commission ("Commission") deems it appropriate that cease-and-desist proceedings be, and hereby are, instituted pursuant to Section 8A of the Securities Act of 1933 ("Securities Act") and Section 21C of the Securities Exchange Act of 1934 ("Exchange Act") against Forcerank LLC ("Respondent").

In anticipation of the institution of these proceedings, Respondent has submitted an Offer of Settlement (the "Offer") which the Commission has determined to accept. . . . Respondent consents to the entry of [the below Order]. . . .

The Dodd-Frank Wall Street Reform and Consumer Protection Act of 2010 ("Dodd-Frank") was enacted to address many of the abuses that contributed to the 2008 financial crisis, including certain abuses associated with the over-the-counter derivatives market, through the establishment of a comprehensive regulatory framework for swaps and security-based swaps. As a general matter, these products include any agreement, contract or transaction whose value is based upon — or "derivative" of — the value of something else, e.g., interest rates, currencies, commodities, or securities, or that provides for a payment that is dependent on the occurrence, or the extent of the occurrence, or the extent of the occurrence, of an event or contingency associated with a potential financial, economic, or commercial consequence.

Among other reforms, Dodd-Frank sought to limit the sale of security-based swaps to persons who are not "eligible contract participants."[60] For example, Dodd-Frank modified Section 5 of the Securities Act to make offers and sales of security-based swaps to such persons unlawful without an effective registration statement covering the offering. This requirement was intended to ensure that persons who

---

60. [N. 1] The definition of "eligible contract participant" includes several categories of persons and, in certain cases, contains monetary thresholds that vary depending on the particular type of person or entity involved. For example, individuals need to have at least $5 million and often $10 million invested on a discretionary basis to qualify as eligible contract participants. *See* 7 U.S.C. § 1a(18).

are not eligible contract participants receive financial and other significant information to allow them to properly evaluate a transaction involving security-based swaps. In addition, Section 6 of the Exchange Act was amended to require that all transactions in security-based swaps involving persons who are not eligible contract participants be effected only on a national securities exchange. This requirement was enacted in order to help ensure that these types of transactions occur only on exchanges subject to the highest level of regulation, which in turn helps ensure that such security-based swaps are cleared on registered clearing agencies. For products such as these, exchange trading and central clearing benefit those investors by providing public price discovery mechanisms, access to relevant trading information, appropriate monitoring of trading activity, and regulated counterparty credit risk management.

Forcerank LLC ran mobile phone games where players predicted the order in which 10 securities would perform relative to each other. In each week-long game, players won points for each instrument based on the accuracy of their prediction, and players with the most aggregate points received cash prizes at the end of the competition. Forcerank LLC kept 10% of the entry fees and obtained a data set about market expectations that it hoped to sell to hedge funds and other investors.

Forcerank LLC's agreements with players were security-based swaps because they provided for a payment that was dependent on the occurrence, or the extent of the occurrence, of an event or contingency that was "associated with" a potential financial, economic, or commercial consequence and because they were "based on" the value of individual securities. From February to June 2016, Forcerank LLC violated Section 5(e) of the Securities Act and Section 6(l) of the Exchange Act when it offered and sold those security-based swaps to persons who were not eligible contract participants. . . .

Starting in mid-2015, the people behind Forcerank LLC developed the software and structure for a platform — which they called "Forcerank" — to operate contests in which players would rank a group of stocks or exchange traded funds ("ETFs") based on expected performance over the upcoming week. They envisioned using the information obtained from those Forcerank games — especially changes in players' rankings over time — to create data sets about market expectations that could eventually be sold to hedge funds. . . .

In 2016, Forcerank LLC released applications for iOS and Android phones to let users participate in Forcerank contests. As discussed in detail below, Forcerank LLC created multiple contests each week. For each contest, it provided participants with a list of 10 stocks or ETFs. Players paid an entry fee, ranked the stocks or ETFs based on expected performance in the upcoming week, and then received points based on the accuracy of each ranking. The players whose predictions earned the most points received cash payments. . . .

Players signed up for accounts with Forcerank LLC using the mobile phone applications. They deposited money into their account using a credit card, and Forcerank

LLC kept the money in its bank account. When players wanted to withdraw money, Forcerank LLC credited their credit card or issued checks, depending on the amount of the withdrawal. At the start of each contest, Forcerank LLC deducted the contest's entry fee from the players' accounts. At the end of the contest, it credited the accounts of players who had scored the most points in the game. . . .

On or about March 10, 2016, Forcerank LLC began publicizing the contests and put the applications into on-line stores where anyone could download them. Forcerank LLC sought to attract users through press releases, podcasts, social media posts, and other means. Much of the initial publicity about the Forcerank contests focused on its similarities to daily fantasy sports competitions. For example, Estimize issued a press release announcing the official launch of the Forcerank contests that was titled "Get Involved in the Competition CNBC Dubbed 'Fantasy Sports for Stocks' — Estimize Introduces Forcerank." . . .

No one at Forcerank LLC confirmed the identity or financial resources of players when they signed up for accounts or entered Forcerank games. Players voluntarily provided some information, but Forcerank LLC set no requirements that players own any specific amount of assets. . . .

Forcerank executives recognized that players might be concerned that the Forcerank contests violated laws, including those related to the purchase and sale of swaps and security-based swaps. The Forcerank LLC website said:

> Given that the Forcerank contest is not a security or security based swap, and is a skill based contest, it is not currently regulated by the federal government, any state government, or financial regulatory authority. Forcerank has been in close contact with various financial regulatory authorities both before and after launching Forcerank contests. . . .

No regulatory authority had cleared the Forcerank contests as not involving swaps or security-based swaps. . . .

No registration statements were in effect for the Forcerank contests. None of the contests were effected on a national securities exchange. . . .

Two provisions added by Dodd-Frank apply to the transactions entered by Forcerank LLC:

- Under what is currently Section 5(e) of the Securities Act, it is unlawful for any person to offer to sell, offer to buy, or purchase or sell a security-based swap to any person who is not an eligible contract participant without an effective registration statement. 15 U.S.C. § 77e(e).

- Under Section 6(l) of the Exchange Act, it is unlawful for any person to effect a transaction in a security-based swap with or for a person that is not an eligible contract participant, unless such transaction is effected on a national securities exchange. 15 U.S.C. § 78f(l). . . .

[E]ach Forcerank entry was a swap because each participant paid to enter into an agreement with Forcerank LLC that provided for the payment of points and, in certain cases, cash. Those payments were dependent upon the occurrence, or the extent of the occurrence, of an event or contingency (i.e., the player's predictions about the price performance of individual securities being compared to actual performance and the player's aggregate points being compared to other players). Such event or contingency was "associated with a potential financial, economic or commercial consequence" because it was calculated by measuring the change in the market price of an individual security over a period of time and comparing that change to an identical metric based on the market price of other individual securities. . . .

Second, each swap was a security-based swap because it was based on the value of single securities. The term "based on" does not require an exclusive relationship between the payment and the movement of a security. In the Forcerank contests, players received points based on the change in the market price of a single security relative to the change in the market price of other securities. . . . For example, a player would receive 100 points if the player correctly predicted a security to finish first in a contest and it outperformed each of the other securities. In addition, a player could receive cash based on several factors, including 1) that player's score, which was calculated by aggregating the points derived from the change in the market price of each single security in the contest relative to the change in the market price of other securities and 2) a comparison of that score to other players' aggregate points derived from equivalent calculations. For example, a player would receive cash as the first place finisher if the player made predictions precise enough to receive points such that his or her score was higher than the other players' scores. . . .

Thus, Forcerank LLC violated Section 5(e) of the Securities Act and Section 6(l) of the Exchange Act when it entered into contracts with Forcerank game players who were not eligible contract participants because no registration statements were in effect for the offer and sale of the contracts and the contracts were not effected on a national securities exchange. . . .

Accordingly, it is hereby ORDERED that: . . . Respondent Forcerank LLC cease and desist from committing or causing any violations and any future violations of Section 5(e) of the Securities Act and of Section 6(l) of the Exchange Act [and] . . . pay a civil money penalty in the amount of $50,000. . . .

––––––––––

The process for registering a security with the SEC and then listing it on an exchange is laborious, time-consuming, and expensive. Since a security-based swap available to counterparties that do not qualify as eligible contract participants must be registered and listed on an exchange, it deters phone applications similar to that developed by Forcerank.

D. Documentation of Security-Based Swaps

Security-based swaps almost uniformly use the same ISDA Master Agreements and Schedules we discussed in chapter 12, section E.1. The close-out netting provisions of this agreement applies to all transactions entered into pursuant to the agreement. This means that swaps and security-based swaps alike are terminated and netted together for a close-out net amount.

Questions and Comments

1. Is the boundary between a swap and security-based swap clear enough? Are there circumstances where parties might not know which regulator and set of regulations apply?

2. Should insider trading prohibitions apply, as they do now, to security-based swaps? How do they currently apply to security-based swaps?

3. The SEC made significant efforts to model the security-based swap regulatory regime on the existing CFTC swap regulatory regime. What is the benefit of doing so?

4. Why have two different regimes at all? What are the differences between swaps and security-based swaps that might make two regulatory regimes appropriate?

5. The SEC took nearly ten years longer than the CFTC to initiate a security-based swap regulatory regime. Part of this was a difference in approach. Whereas the CFTC finalized and implemented portions of the swap regulatory regime piecemeal, the SEC only made it effective after finalizing all the applicable rules. Which approach do you prefer and why?

6. Was Forcerank LLC's phone application mere gambling, defined for these purposes as speculation without socially-redeeming value? Or did it confer some sort of societal benefit? If so, what? Should such smaller ventures be legally accommodated without imposing SEC registration and exchange-listing requirements?

Chapter 14

Foreign Exchange Transactions, Retail Commodities, Virtual Currency, and Commodity Options

A. Background

In this chapter, we evaluate product and transaction categories that do not squarely fit into the same regulatory category as futures, swaps, or security-based swaps. These are product categories that require their own analysis. In some cases, their regulatory treatment is totally distinct from that for futures, swaps, and security-based swaps generally; in other cases, it overlaps.

Retail foreign exchange transactions and retail commodities have their own regulatory regimes. Foreign exchange transactions other than spot transactions are, with a few important exceptions we discuss in this chapter, treated identically to futures, swaps, or commodity options.

We address virtual currency separately due to its novelty and the regulatory question it begs: Is virtual currency a commodity or a currency? The answer is not intuitive. Despite being termed "virtual currency," the CFTC treats virtual currency as a commodity for regulatory purposes and not as a currency.

Finally, we examine commodity options — today effectively regulated as futures if traded on a futures exchange and swaps if traded otherwise — because of their distinct regulatory pedigree and history.

Note that some of the products we will discuss in this chapter are not derivatives. We include these non-derivatives because of the CFTC's jurisdiction over them.

B. Foreign Exchange Transactions

Foreign exchange transactions can be divided into the following economic classifications: (1) spot transactions, i.e., an exchange of currencies settled on a market basis that, except for exotic currencies, means settlement within two days after the exchange is agreed; (2) forwards, i.e., an agreement to exchange physical currencies at a pre-agreed fixed price at the later of two days after the agreement or the customary spot settlement period for that currency; (3) futures, i.e., an agreement, traded on a futures exchange, to exchange currency (either by physical exchanges of the currencies or by cash settlement denominated in one of the currency pairs) at a pre-agreed fixed price at the later of two days after agreement or the customary settlement period for that currency; (4) options, i.e., agreements by which one party grants the other the right, though not the obligation, to exchange currency at a specified price on a specified date or dates; and (5) swaps, i.e., pre-agreed multiple exchanges of currencies (either by physical exchanges of the currencies or by cash settlement denominated in one of the currency pairs) at specified dates in the future. Currency swaps are sometimes combined with other swaps. For example, see the discussion of cross-currency swaps in chapter 1, section D.2.b.

Foreign exchange forwards and swaps are treated in many, though not all, contexts as swaps. The few differences are discussed in subsection 3 below. We have already discussed the regulatory regime for commodity futures in chapters 5 and 6. Foreign exchange futures are treated identically and do not need to be separately addressed here. Foreign exchange options are discussed below in subsection 3. Spot transactions of foreign exchange are, in ordinary cases, unregulated except that participants in the business of making spot foreign exchanges are minimally regulated at the federal level for anti-money laundering purposes and in most states.

Where leveraged or financed, however, spot foreign exchange is subject to a CFTC regulatory regime for "retail foreign exchange dealers."

1. Evolution of Regulation of Foreign Exchange Transactions

a. The Treasury Amendment

The history of foreign exchange transaction regulation was discussed in chapter 2. As discussed therein, the Commodity Futures Trading Commission Act of 1974 explicitly excluded "transactions in foreign currencies" from the otherwise broad jurisdiction over commodities provided to the CFTC unless they were traded on a board of trade.[1] This occurred via an amendment to the predecessor bill that today is referred to as the "Treasury Amendment" due to the Department of the Treasury's advocacy for the exclusion.[2]

The Treasury Amendment excluded all "transactions in foreign currencies" from the CFTC's jurisdiction. Despite the CFTC's efforts to argue that foreign currency options were not part of this exclusion and that the CFTC could regulate them, the Supreme Court interpreted the Treasury Amendment robustly.

---

1. *See* 7 U.S.C. § 2(ii) (1994). Or, relying on at least one district court, an entity required to register as a board of trade. *See CFTC v. Noble Wealth Data*, 90 F. Supp. 2d 676, 687–692 (D. Md. 2000).

2. For the Department of the Treasury's advocacy for an exclusion for foreign exchange transactions, see *Letter from Donald L.E. Richter, Acting General Counsel, Department of the Treasury*, S. Rep. 93-1311, 1974 U.S.C.C.A.N. 5843, 5587–5890.

Dunn v. CFTC

519 U.S. 465 (1997)

Justice Stevens delivered the opinion of the Court.

The question presented is whether Congress has authorized the Commodity Futures Trading Commission (CFTC or Commission) to regulate "off-exchange" trading in options to buy or sell foreign currency.

The CFTC brought this action in 1994, alleging that, beginning in 1992, petitioners solicited investments in and operated a fraudulent scheme in violation of the Commodity Exchange Act (CEA) and CFTC regulations.[3] The CFTC's complaint, affidavits, and declarations . . . indicate that customers were told their funds would be invested using complex strategies involving options to purchase or sell various foreign currencies. Petitioners apparently did in fact engage in many such transactions. To do so, they contracted directly with international banks and others without making use of any regulated exchange or board of trade. In the parlance of the business, petitioners traded in the "off-exchange" or "over-the-counter" (OTC) market. No options were ever sold directly to petitioners' customers. However, their positions were tracked through internal accounts, and investors were provided weekly reports showing the putative status of their holdings. Petitioners and their customers suffered heavy losses. Subsequently, the CFTC commenced these proceedings. . . .

The outcome of this case is dictated by the so-called "Treasury Amendment" to the CEA. . . . As a part of the 1974 amendments that created the CFTC and dramatically expanded the coverage of the statute to include nonagricultural commodities "in which contracts for future delivery are presently or in the future dealt in," Congress enacted the . . . exemption, which has come to be known as the "Treasury Amendment." . . .

The CFTC argues . . . that an option is not itself a transaction "in" foreign currency, but rather is just a contract right to engage in such a transaction at a future date. Hence, the Commission submits that the term "transactions in foreign currency" includes only the "actual exercise of an option (i.e., the actual purchase or sale of foreign currency)" but not the purchase or sale of an option itself. That reading of the text seems quite unnatural to us, and we decline to adopt it. . . .

---

3. [N. 2] . . . [T]he CFTC calls our attention to statements in the legislative history of a 1982 amendment to the CEA indicating that the drafters of that amendment believed that the CFTC had the authority to regulate foreign currency options "when they are traded other than on a national securities exchange." *See* S.Rep. No. 97-384, p. 22 (1982). Those statements, at best, might be described as "legislative *dicta*" because the 1982 amendment itself merely resolved a conflict between the Securities Exchange Commission and the CFTC concerning their respective authority to regulate transactions on an exchange. The amendment made no change in the law applicable to off-exchange trading. Although these "*dicta*" are consistent with the position that the CFTC advocates, they shed no light on the intent of the authors of the Treasury Amendment that had been adopted eight years earlier.

We think it ... plain as a matter of ordinary meaning that ... [a foreign exchange] option is a transaction "in" foreign currency for purposes of the Treasury Amendment.

Indeed, adopting the Commission's reading would deprive the exemption of the principal effect Congress intended. The CFTC acknowledges that futures contracts fall squarely within the Treasury Amendment's exemption, and there is no question that the exemption of off-exchange foreign currency futures from CFTC regulation was one of Congress' primary goals. Yet on the CFTC's reasoning the exemption's application to futures contracts could not be sustained.

A futures contract is no more a transaction "in" foreign currency as the Commission understands the term than an option. The Commission argues that because a futures contract creates a legal obligation to purchase or sell currency on a particular date, it is somehow more clearly a transaction "in" the underlying currencies than an option, which generates only the right to engage in a transaction. This reasoning is wholly unpersuasive. No currency changes hands at the time a futures contract is made. And, the existence of a futures contract does not guarantee that currency will actually be exchanged. Indeed, the Commission concedes that, in most cases, futures contracts are "extinguished before delivery by entry into an offsetting futures contract." Adopting the CFTC's reading would therefore place both futures and options outside the exemption, in clear contravention of Congress' intent.

Furthermore, this interpretation would leave the Treasury Amendment's exemption for "transactions in foreign currency" without any significant effect at all, because it would limit the scope of the exemption to "forward contracts" (agreements that anticipate the actual delivery of a commodity on a specified future date) and "spot transactions" (agreements for purchase and sale of commodities that anticipate near-term delivery). Both are transactions "in" a commodity as the CFTC would have us understand the term. But neither type of transaction for any commodity was subject to intensive regulation under the CEA at the time of the Treasury Amendment's passage. Our reading of the exemption is therefore also consonant with the doctrine that legislative enactments should not be construed to render their provisions mere surplusage.

Finally, including options in the exemption is consistent with Congress' purpose in enacting the Treasury Amendment. Although at the time the Treasury Amendment was drafted a thriving off-exchange market in foreign currency futures was in place, the closely related options market at issue here had not yet developed. The CFTC therefore suggests that Congress could not have intended to exempt foreign currency options from the CEA's coverage. The legislative history strongly suggests to the contrary that Congress' broad purpose in enacting the Treasury Amendment was to provide a general exemption from CFTC regulation for sophisticated off-exchange foreign currency trading, which had previously developed entirely free from supervision under the commodities laws. ...

Although the OTC market for foreign currency options had not yet developed in 1974, the reasons underlying the Treasury Department's express desire at that time to exempt off-exchange commodity futures trading from CFTC regulation apply with equal force to options today.

The judgment of the Court of Appeals is reversed, and the case is remanded for further proceedings consistent with this opinion. . . .

———————

Note that the Treasury Amendment's exclusion did not extend to transactions traded on a board of trade. Such transactions could be regulated by the CFTC pursuant to its authority to regulate contract markets. Similarly, foreign exchange transactions carried out on a securities exchange were within the SEC's jurisdiction.

b. Limited Authority over Retail Foreign Exchange

The CFTC obtained expanded authority over retail foreign exchange futures and options as a result of the Commodity Futures Modernization Act of 2000. Unless traded through a financial institution,[4] any such foreign exchange transactions with a retail counterparty (a retail counterparty being any party that was not an "eligible contract participant" — see chapter 9, section E) was subject to CFTC regulation.[5]

A dispute arose as to the extent of the CFTC's new jurisdiction with respect to "rolling" cash-settled foreign exchange spot transactions, i.e., transactions that, though nominally settled within two days of being agreed, are habitually renewed for another two days just before settlement would otherwise have been required and usually are ultimately cash-settled.

CFTC v. Zelener

373 F.3d 861 (7th Cir. 2004)

Easterbrook, Circuit Judge.

This appeal presents the question whether speculative transactions in foreign currency are "contracts of sale of a commodity for future delivery" regulated by the Commodity Futures Trading Commission. Until recently almost all trading related to foreign currency was outside the CFTC's remit . . . [b]ut Congress modified the Treasury Amendment as part of the Commodity Futures Modernization Act of 2000, and today the . . . [CFTC has jurisdiction] unless the parties to the contract are "eligible contract participants". "Eligible contract participants" under the Commodity Exchange Act are the equivalent of "accredited investors" in securities markets: . . . persons who can look out for themselves . . . Defendants, which sold foreign currency to casual speculators rather than "eligible contract participants," are not protected by the Treasury Amendment except to the extent that it permits them to deal over-the-counter. . . .

———————

4. *See* 7 U.S.C. § 2(c)(2)(B) (2002) and 7 U.S.C. § 2(d)(1) (2002).
5. 7 U.S.C. § 2(c)(2)(A) (2002).

[The CFTC] believes that some of the defendants deceived some of their customers.... This allegation (whose accuracy has not been tested) makes it vital to know whether the contracts are within the CFTC's regulatory authority.

AlaronFX deals in foreign currency. Two corporations doing business as "British Capital Group" or BCG solicited customers' orders for foreign currency. (Michael Zelener, the first-named defendant, is the principal owner and manager of these two firms.) Each customer opened an account with BCG and another with AlaronFX; the documents made it clear that AlaronFX would be the source of all currency bought or sold through BCG in this program, and that AlaronFX would act as a principal. A customer could purchase (go long) or sell (short) any currency.... The customer specified the desired quantity, with a minimum order size of $5,000; the contract called for settlement within 48 hours. It is agreed, however, that few of BCG's customers paid in full within that time, and that none took delivery. AlaronFX could have reversed the transactions and charged (or credited) customers with the difference in price across those two days. Instead, however, AlaronFX rolled the transactions forward two days at a time — as the AlaronFX contract permits, and as BCG told the customers would occur. Successive extensions meant that a customer had an open position in foreign currency. If the dollar appreciated relative to that currency, the customer could close the position and reap the profit in one of two ways: take delivery of the currency... or sell an equal amount of currency back to AlaronFX. If, however, the dollar fell relative to the other currency, then the client suffered a loss when the position was closed by selling currency back to AlaronFX.

The CFTC believes that three principal features make these arrangements "contracts of sale of a commodity for future delivery": first, the positions were held open indefinitely, so that the customers' gains and losses depended on price movements in the future; second, the customers were amateurs who did not need foreign currency for business endeavors; third, none of the customers took delivery of any currency, so the sales could not be called forward contracts, which are exempt from regulation....

These transactions could not be futures contracts... because the customer buys foreign currency immediately rather than as of a defined future date ... and because the deals lack standard terms. AlaronFX buys and sells as a principal; transactions differ in size, price, and settlement date. The contracts are not fungible and thus could not be traded on an exchange. The CFTC replies that because AlaronFX rolls forward the settlement times, the transactions are for future delivery in practice even though not in form; and the [CFTC] ... insists that fixed expiration dates and fungibility are irrelevant. It favors a multi-factor inquiry with heavy weight on whether the customer is financially sophisticated, able to bear risk, and intended to take or make delivery of the commodity....

In organized futures markets, people buy and sell contracts, not commodities. Terms are standardized, and each party's obligation runs to an intermediary, the clearing corporation. Clearing houses eliminate counterparty credit risk. Standard terms and an absence of counterparty-specific risk make the contracts fungible, which in turn makes it possible to close a position by buying an offsetting contract. All contracts that expire in a given month are identical; each calls for delivery of the same commodity in the same place at the same time. Forward and spot contracts, by contrast, call for sale of the commodity; no one deals "in the contract"; it is not possible to close a position by buying a traded offset, because promises are not fungible; delivery is idiosyncratic rather than centralized. . . .

It is essential to know beforehand whether a contract is a future or a forward. The answer determines who, if anyone, may enter into such a contract, and where trading may occur. Contracts allocate price risk, and they fail in that office if it can't be known until years after the fact whether a given contract was lawful. Nothing is worse than an approach that asks what the parties "intended" or that scrutinizes the percentage of contracts that led to delivery ex post. What sense would it make — either business sense, or statutory-interpretation sense — to say that the same contract is either a future or not depending on whether the person obliged to deliver keeps his promise? That would leave people adrift and make it difficult, if not impossible, for dealers (technically, futures commission merchants) to know their legal duties in advance. . . .

These transactions were, in form, spot sales for delivery within 48 hours. Rollover, and the magnification of gain or loss over a longer period, does not turn sales into futures contracts. . . .

The *Zelener* court viewed the form of the contract as the primary means of determining whether the transaction was a spot foreign exchange transaction. Because the transaction allowed for physical delivery within forty-eight hours, it was deemed a spot transaction regardless of the parties' actual behavior in usually agreeing to "roll" the transaction without closing it out by physical delivery.

2. Regulation of Retail Foreign Exchange Transactions

The *Zelener* decision was perceived by some, including the CFTC, as creating a regulatory gap in the retail foreign exchange market.

Written Testimony of CFTC Acting Chairman Walter Lukken

U.S. House of Representatives Committee on Agriculture (October 24, 2007), available at http://www.cftc.gov/ucm/groups/public/@newsroom /documents/speechandtestimony/opalukken-29.pdf

Good afternoon Chairman Etheridge, Ranking Member Moran and Members of the Subcommittee. I am pleased to appear on behalf of the Commodity Futures Trading Commission (Commission or CFTC) to discuss the important issues surrounding the reauthorization of the Commodity Exchange Act (CEA), the Commission's governing statute. . . .

In our commitment to protecting market participants and market integrity, I want to turn to the issue of retail fraud in foreign currency trading. In 2004, the Seventh Circuit Court of Appeals curtailed the Commission's ability to combat retail off-exchange foreign currency (forex) fraud. In the *Zelener* case, the court held that the contracts at issue were not futures contracts, but rather a type of spot contract that could not be the basis for a CFTC fraud action. This has provided a potential road map to scam artists as to how to deceive innocent retail customers while evading enforcement by the CFTC.

The CFTC believes that the *Zelener* case and others that have followed it were incorrectly decided and that the contracts at issue are futures contracts. Rather than continue to expend scarce Commission resources litigating this issue, however, we present to Congress the opportunity to restore legal certainty by clarifying the CFTC's jurisdiction in this area. . . .

[B]ecause of the *Zelener* decision and its progeny, the Commission has lost some key forex cases and now finds it is more difficult to prosecute forex actions. Unless Congress clarifies the Commission's jurisdiction over off-exchange forex transactions, a large sector of retail fraud will remain effectively outside of the prosecutorial authority of the CFTC. . . .

Congress heeded CFTC Acting Chairman Lukken's call by enacting the CFTC Reauthorization Act of 2008,[6] which amended the Commodity Exchange Act to grant the CFTC jurisdiction for off-exchange foreign exchange or commodity transactions sold to retail investors on a leveraged or margined basis or financed by the offeror, the counterparty, or someone working with either. A new category of registrant was created, "retail foreign exchange dealers."[7]

CFTC, *Regulation of Off-Exchange Retail Foreign Exchange Transactions and Intermediaries*
75 Fed. Reg. 3282 (Jan. 20, 2010)

. . . The Commodity Futures Trading Commission Reauthorization Act of 2008 [the "CRA"] . . . was intended, among other things, to further clarify the Commission's jurisdiction in the area of retail forex, particularly in light of the proliferation of look-alike forex transactions such as those in [*Zelener*] . . . , and to give the Commission additional authority to regulate retail forex transactions and to register persons involved in intermediating these products with members of the public. To remedy the large number of fraud cases where jurisdiction had been questioned, the CRA gave the Commission jurisdiction over certain leveraged retail foreign exchange contracts without regard to whether it could prove the contracts were

----

6. Pub. L. No. 110-246, Title XIII (2008).
7. See Commodity Exchange Act § 2(c)(2)(B).

off-exchange futures contracts. The CRA thus grants the Commission anti-fraud authority in leveraged retail forex transactions even if the transactions at issue are not futures or options. This allows the Commission to protect the public from fraud and provides a workable solution to the split in the decisions in the Federal appellate courts regarding when a so-called "spot" contract is a futures contract.

The CRA also created a new category of registrant, the retail foreign exchange dealer, or "RFED," and gave the Commission rulemaking authority over, and required registration of, intermediaries engaging in retail forex. The CRA provided that RFEDs and these other intermediaries must be NFA members and must register with the Commission subject to such terms as the Commission may prescribe. Among other requirements, the CRA established a $20 million minimum capital requirement for RFEDs and FCMs that offer retail forex.

The grant of authority over look-alike forex contracts is very broad and is intended to encompass transactions that do not result in actual delivery, or for which no legitimate business purpose exists for the customer to enter into the transaction. It is not intended to interfere with the large, sophisticated interbank market or to place additional requirements on businesses with a need to engage in forex transactions in connection with their legitimate business activities.

The CRA further provides that look-alike forex contracts are subject to the CFTC's authority if they are offered on a leveraged or margined basis, or financed by the offeror, counterparty, or someone acting with the offeror or counterparty. The Commission's authority, however, does not extend to securities, or to contracts that result in actual delivery within two days or that create an enforceable obligation to deliver between buyer and seller that have the ability to deliver or accept delivery in connection with their line of business. Thus, the CRA charges the Commission with regulating speculative forms of retail forex trading, but excludes from the Commission's purview true spot transactions that have a legitimate business purpose or that result in actual delivery. . . .

In the nine years since the passage of the [Commodity Futures Modernization Act], the Commission has observed a number of improper practices that have raised concern, among them solicitation fraud, a lack of transparency in the pricing and execution of transactions, unresponsiveness to customer complaints, and the targeting of unsophisticated, elderly, low net worth and other vulnerable individuals.[8]

In addition to the regulations explicitly mandated by the CRA — including new registration requirements and enhanced financial requirements — the proposed regulations will require forex registrants to maintain records of customer complaints;

---

8. [N. 44] Between December 2000 and September 2009, the Commission has filed 114 forex-related enforcement actions on behalf of more than 26,000 customers. Those efforts have thus far resulted in the award of approximately $476 million in restitution and disgorgement, and $576 million in civil monetary penalties. An overwhelming majority of these cases have involved solicitation fraud.

require forex counterparties to guarantee the performance of all persons who introduce accounts to the counterparty; require counterparties to disclose, with the Risk Disclosure Statement, the percentage of profitable nondiscretionary forex customer accounts; and require forex counterparties to designate a chief compliance officer to be responsible for development and implementation of customer protection policies and procedures.

As noted above, the Commission believes that these additional requirements are militated both by the essential differences between on-exchange transactions and off-exchange retail forex transactions, and the history of fraudulent practices in this sector of the forex market. . . .

———————

The CFTC ultimately finalized regulations reflecting the outline in their proposal.[9] Exempted from registration as retail foreign exchange dealers are futures commission merchants, banks and bank holding companies, and insurance companies.[10] Retail foreign exchange dealers have a $20 million net capital requirement, the same as for futures commission merchants, and must be National Futures Association members.[11] Only four retail foreign exchange dealers are registered with the CFTC.[12]

Outside of the scope of CFTC regulation completely are spot foreign exchange transactions that do not use leverage or margin and are not financed by the offeror, the counterparty, or someone working with either, regardless of whether they are transacted in the retail market. What would be an example of such a transaction? An example would include an exchange of currency at, for example, an airport kiosk. The retail buyer or seller of currency does not maintain an account with the kiosk merchant and the kiosk merchant does not extend credit to the customer.

These transactions are not derivatives in an economic sense, either. They are not futures, options, or swaps. Though these transactions are outside the subject of this book, it should be noted that those commercially engaged in the activity are

———————

9. CFTC, *Regulation of Off-Exchange Retail Foreign Exchange Transactions and Intermediaries*, 75 Fed. Reg. 55410 (Sept. 10, 2010).

10. Commodity Exchange Act § 2(c)(2)(E)(ii)(1) requires the regulators of such entities to enact enabling rules, which has been the case for: (1) the SEC (SEC, *Retail Foreign Exchange Transactions*, 78 Fed. Reg. 42439 (July 16, 2013)), (2) the Federal Deposit Insurance Corporation (Federal Deposito Insurance Corporation, *Retail Foreign Exchange Transactions*, 76 Fed. Reg. 40779 (July 12, 2011)), (3) Office of the Comptroller of the Currency (Office of the Comptroller of the Currency, *Retail Foreign Exchange Transactions*, 76 Fed. Reg. 41375 (July 14, 2011)) and (4) Federal Reserve Board (Federal Reserve Board, *Retail Foreign Exchange Transactions (Regulation NN)*, 78 Fed. Reg. 21019 (April 9, 2013)). The SEC rule, allowing for non-registration of broker-dealers as retail foreign exchange dealers, lapsed. *See* Rita M. Molesworth and Michael A. DeNiro, *SEC Allows Rule Permitting Broker-Dealers to Engage in Retail Forex Transaction to Expire*, 36 No. 7 Futures & Derivatives L. Rep. 15 (July/Aug. 2016).

11. National Futures Association Financial Requirements § 11(a), available at https://www.nfa.futures.org/rulebook/rules.aspx?Section=7&RuleID=SECTION%2011.

12. National Futures Association, *Membership and Directories*, https://www.nfa.futures.org/registration-membership/membership-and-directories.html (April 30, 2021).

generally subject to the anti-money laundering framework established by the Financial Crimes Enforcement Network (commonly known as "FinCEN"), a bureau of the Department of the Treasury responsible for combatting money laundering. There are also often applicable state law requirements.

3. Non-Retail Foreign Exchange Transactions

Before passage of the Dodd-Frank Act in 2010, off-exchange foreign exchange transactions between eligible contract participants were not subject to CFTC or SEC regulation. The Dodd-Frank Act, however, brought any transaction falling within the CFTC's definition of swap within the CFTC's jurisdiction. Included in the Dodd-Frank Act's definition of "a swap" were currency options,[13] currency swaps,[14] foreign exchange forwards,[15] and foreign exchange swaps.[16]

However, the secretary of the treasury was vested with (and as we will see, exercised) the authority to limit the CFTC's jurisdiction with respect to physically-settled foreign exchange swaps and forwards by limiting their treatment as swaps solely to swaps reporting requirements other than real-time reporting and, for swap dealers or major swap participants, business conduct standards.[17] In other words, if the secretary of the treasury determined that foreign exchange swaps and forwards were not swaps, then neither would contribute to an assessment of whether registration as a swap dealer or major swap participant is required nor be subject to clearing, margin, and on-facility trading requirements.

A "foreign exchange swap" is defined as a transaction "that solely involves . . . an exchange of 2 different currencies on a specific date at a fixed rate that is agreed upon on the inception of the contract covering the exchange . . . [and] a reverse exchange of [those two currencies] at a later date and at a fixed rate that is agreed upon on the inception of the contract covering the exchange."[18] A "foreign exchange forward" is defined as: "[A] transaction that solely involves the exchange of 2 different currencies on a specific future date at a fixed rate agreed upon on the inception of the contract covering the exchange."[19]

What foreign exchange transactions are not foreign exchange swaps or foreign exchange forwards? Namely, currency or foreign exchange options; interest rate swaps with two currencies, known as "cross-currency swaps"; and cash-settled foreign exchange transactions, known as "non-deliverable forwards or "NDFs." All of these transaction types are identical to swaps in their regulatory treatment.

---

13. Commodity Exchange Act § 1a(47)(A)(i).
14. Commodity Exchange Act § 1a(47)(A)(iii)(VII).
15. Commodity Exchange Act § 1a(47)(E)(i).
16. Commodity Exchange Act § 1a(47)(A)(iii)(VIII).
17. Commodity Exchange Act § 1a(47)(E).
18. Commodity Exchange Act § 1a(25).
19. Commodity Exchange Act § 1a(24).

On November 20, 2012, Secretary of the Treasury Timothy Geithner determined to exempt foreign exchange swaps and forwards as authorized by the Dodd-Frank Act.

Department of the Treasury, *Determination of Foreign Exchange Swaps and Foreign Exchange Forwards under the Commodity Exchange Act*
77 Fed. Reg. 69694 (Nov. 20, 2012)

. . . In general, swaps, including foreign exchange derivatives, carry three types of risks: (i) Counterparty credit risk prior to settlement; (ii) market risk; and (iii) settlement risk. Counterparty credit risk prior to settlement is the risk that a party to the transaction potentially could default prior to the settlement date, which could result in the non-defaulting party suffering an economic loss associated with having to replace the defaulted contract with another transaction at the then-current terms. Market risk is the risk that the value of the contract changes over the term of the transaction. In this context, market risk is intertwined with counterparty credit risk prior to settlement because the non-defaulting party (who thus bears the credit risk) also bears the risk that the value of the prior contract might have declined when that party seeks to replace the defaulted contract with another transaction. Settlement risk, particularly in the context of a foreign exchange swap or forward transaction, is the risk that the contract will not be settled in accordance with the initial terms, including when one party to the transaction delivers the currency it owes the counterparty, but does not receive the other currency from that counterparty. . . .

Settlement of most types of swaps and derivatives involves only payments of net amounts that are based on the changes in the value of the variables underlying the derivatives contracts. Given the features of most swaps and derivatives, including some types of foreign exchange derivatives, the clearing and exchange-trading requirements under the CEA, where applicable, would mitigate the relevant risks, notably counterparty credit risks prior to settlement.

By contrast, foreign exchange swap and forward participants know their own and their counterparties' payment obligations and the full extent of their exposures at settlement throughout the life of the contract. Thus, while the mark-to-market value of a position in a foreign exchange swap or forward may vary based on changes in the exchange rate or interest rates, the actual settlement amounts do not.

Under the regulatory regime enacted by the Dodd-Frank Act, foreign exchange swaps and forwards generally are subject to the requirements of the CEA and, in particular, would be subject to central clearing and exchange trading, unless the Secretary determines that foreign exchange swaps and forwards "(I) should not be regulated as swaps under [the CEA]; and (II) are not structured to evade [the Dodd-Frank Act] in violation of any rules promulgated by the [CFTC] pursuant to section 721(c) of the [Dodd-Frank Act]." . . .

The Secretary's authority to issue a determination is limited to foreign exchange swaps and forwards and does not extend to other foreign exchange derivatives. Foreign exchange options, currency swaps, and [non-deliverable forwards (NDFs)] . . . may not be exempted from the CEA's definition of "swap" because they do not satisfy the statutory definitions of a foreign exchange swap or forward. . . .

[T]he Secretary is issuing this determination to exempt foreign exchange swaps and forwards because of the distinctive characteristics of these instruments. Unlike most other swaps, foreign exchange swaps and forwards have fixed payment obligations, are settled by the exchange of actual currency, and are predominantly short-term instruments.

Counterparty credit risk prior to settlement is significantly reduced by the structure of a foreign exchange swap or forward transaction, particularly because the term for each type of transaction generally is very short. For the vast majority of foreign exchange swap or forward contracts, the risk profile is centered on settlement risk. Settlement risk often is addressed in foreign exchange swaps and forwards through the use of payment-versus-payment ("PVP") settlement arrangements,[20] particularly with large financial institutions.

Treasury believes . . . that requiring central clearing and trading under the CEA on foreign exchange swaps and forwards would potentially introduce operational risks and challenges to the current settlement process. If central clearing were to be required, the central clearing facility would be effectively guaranteeing both settlement and market exposure to replacement cost. As a result, combining clearing and settlement in a market that involves settlement of the full principal amounts of the contracts would require capital backing, in a very large number of currencies, well in excess of what will be required for swaps that are settled on a "net" basis. Treasury believes that requiring foreign exchange swaps and forwards to be cleared and settled through the use of new systems and technologies could introduce new, unforeseen risks in this market. . . .

The Secretary's determination that foreign exchange swaps and forwards should not be regulated as "swaps" under the CEA does not affect the application of relevant provisions of the CEA that are designed to prevent evasion and improve market transparency. . . . [A]ll foreign exchange transactions would remain subject to the CFTC's new trade-reporting (but not the real-time reporting) requirements, enhanced anti-evasion authority, and [business-conduct standards]. . . .

Unlike other types of swaps, foreign exchange swaps and forwards are distinct because, as defined by the CEA, these transactions must (1) involve the exchange of the principal amounts of the two currencies exchanged, as opposed to a set of

---

20. [N. 12] PVP settlement arrangements permit the final transfer of one currency to take place only if the final transfer of the other currency also takes place, thereby virtually eliminating settlement risk.

cash flows based upon some floating reference rate, and (2) be settled on a physical basis.[21]

A "swap" regulated under the CEA, such as a currency swap, interest rate swap, or other derivative, generally involves a periodic exchange of a floating amount of cash flows between the counterparties based on the value of the underlying variable(s) on which the derivative contract is based. In contrast, a foreign exchange swap (which will be exempt from the definition of "swap" under this determination) involves a simple exchange of principal at one point in time and a reversal of that exchange at some later date. For example, a user of a currency swap could seek funding advantages by obtaining financing in a foreign currency and swapping those cash flows back to the user's locally denominated currency. This would then entail paying or receiving a series of floating interest rate payments (i.e., based on prevailing interest rates) over the life of the transaction. This ability to receive periodic payments during the term of a transaction is a significant feature of "swaps" that will be regulated under the CEA, which is absent from a foreign exchange swap or foreign exchange forward. . . .

Though foreign exchange spot transactions are unregulated by the CFTC, the CFTC has expressed concerns about efforts to evade application of the swaps regulatory regime to non-spot foreign exchange transactions. The CFTC, spurred in part by its experiences in *Zelener*, has caveated that it will be on guard against any effort to avoid foreign exchange regulatory requirements by labelling as spot "transactions that regularly settle after the relevant foreign exchange spot market settlement deadline, or with respect to which the parties intentionally delay settlement, both of which would be properly categorized as foreign exchange forwards. . . ."[22]

C. Leverage and Retail Commodity Transactions

1. Background

Commodity transactions can generally be divided into: (1) spot transactions, i.e., a payment for a commodity actually delivered within twenty-eight days;[23] (2) forwards, i.e., transactions for cash commodities for deferred shipment or delivery;[24] (3) futures, i.e., a contract of sale of a commodity for future delivery (either physically or by cash settlement); (4) options, i.e., agreements by which one party grants

---

21. [N. 74] In this regard, Treasury notes that, in other swaps transactions, the parties may, by agreement, physically settle their obligations.

22. CFTC and SEC, *Further Definition of "Swap," "Security-Based Swap," and "Security-Based Swap Agreement"; Mixed Swaps; Security-Based Swap Agreement Recordkeeping*, 77 Fed. Reg. 48208, 48257 (Aug. 13, 2012).

23. Commodity Exchange Act § 2(c)(2)(D)(ii)(III).

24. Commodity Exchange Act § 1a(27).

the other the right, though not the obligation, to purchase or sell a commodity at a specified price on a specified date or dates; and (5) swaps, i.e., pre-agreed multiple purchases or sales of a commodity (with either physical delivery of the commodity or settlement of the cash equivalent) at specified dates in the future.

In the preceding chapters, we have already discussed commodity forwards, swaps, and futures and we do not revisit them in detail here. Options on commodities are discussed further below in section E. Spot transactions of commodities are, in ordinary cases, unregulated. Where leveraged or financed, however, commodity transactions are prohibited unless traded on a futures exchange, treated as a swap, settled by delivery within twenty-eight days, or eligible for the very narrowly tailored "leverage transaction" regime involving a registered "leverage transaction merchant."

2. Leverage Transactions

The Commodity Futures Trading Commission Act of 1974 conferred jurisdiction to the CFTC over "leverage" or "margin" transactions solely with respect to silver or gold.[25] In 1978, Congress prohibited leverage or margin transactions with respect to specified agricultural commodities and granted the CFTC jurisdiction over leveraged margin transactions with respect to all commodities.[26] In 1986, Congress expanded the prohibition on leverage or margin transactions to all commodities other than silver, gold, or platinum.[27]

CFTC rule has defined leverage contracts as contracts with terms of ten years or more to purchase or sell silver, gold, or platinum, to or from a CFTC-registered leverage transaction merchant.[28] It requires periodic payments by the customer and provision of initial and variation margin. The pricing is determined by the leverage transaction merchant. Ultimately, the actual silver, gold, or platinum must be delivered to the customer.[29]

Leverage transaction merchants are required to be National Futures Association members and have minimum $20 million adjusted net capital.[30] There have been no registered leverage transaction merchants since 1991.[31]

---

25. Commodity Futures Trading Commission Act of 1974, Pub. L. 94-463, § 217, 88 Stat. 1389 (1974).

26. Futures Trading Act of 1978, Pub. L. 95-405, § 23, 92 Stat 865 (1978).

27. Futures Trading Act of 1986, Pub. L. 99-641, § 109, 100 Stat 3556 (1986) amending Commodity Exchange Act § 19.

28. Leverage Transaction Merchants are also required to be National Futures Association members. There are currently no registered leverage transaction merchants.

29. 17 C.F.R. § 31.4(w).

30. National Futures Association Financial Requirements § 6(a), available at https://www.nfa .futures.org/rulebook/rules.aspx?RuleID=SECTION%206&Section=7.

31. National Futures Association, Monex International Ltd., https://www.nfa.futures.org/basic net/Details.aspx?entityid=oHBfiH%2fgQ9E%3d&rn=N.

Without the leverage transaction definition category, most such transactions would likely be deemed illegal off-exchange futures transactions (see chapter 5, section A) and the dealer party accepting margin an unregistered futures commission merchant. For example, in a Ninth Circuit case, the court noted that because there was "some basis" in ordinary trade usage for the CFTC's definition of "leverage contracts" as having a minimum ten year duration, "there can be no such thing as a leverage contract with a duration of less than ten years."[32] The court ultimately decided that the leveraged precious metal contracts in the case "were not a subset of leverage contracts left unregulated by the Commission, but futures contracts" that were illegal off-exchange contracts.[33]

Or, if both parties to the transaction were eligible contract participants, such transactions likely would be able to be treated as swaps. Therefore, the leverage transaction regime should be seen as a very narrowly tailored carveout from the prevailing regulatory regime for commodity futures and swaps created to accommodate a type of retail transaction (there is no requirement that the parties be "eligible contract participants" or have a similar non-retail status) that pre-existed the Commodity Futures Trading Commission Act of 1974's expansion of CFTC authority beyond agricultural commodities.

The nature of leveraged or margined commodity transactions, as described in the below case, arguably are akin to gambling without the socially redeeming benefits of providing market liquidity for hedgers. Historically, it appears that, unlike the other derivatives markets discussed herein in which hedgers participate, only speculators and dealers operated in these markets.

Purdy v. CFTC
968 F.2d 510 (5th Cir. 1992)

John R. Brown, Circuit Judge:

This dispute arose from a complaint to the Commodity Futures Trading Commission ("CFTC" or "Commission") by an elderly investor who lost a fortune investing (one might say gambling) in precious metal leverage contracts. After a judgment for the broker house by an Administrative Law Judge ("ALJ"), and subsequent summary affirmation by the Commission, the investor appeals to this court. . . . [W]e affirm the decision of the Commission.

The Road to Las Vegas

Theodore Purdy Sr. . . . sold his fifty-year-old auto parts business and retired in 1983. At the time of his retirement, Purdy's business grossed $1.5 million annually, and he paid himself approximately $150,000 a year. Both he and his son, Theodore

---

32. *CFTC v. P.I.E.*, 853 F.2d 721, 724 (9th Cir. 1988).

33. *Id.*

Purdy, Jr., have high school educations and, prior to their first dealings with Monex International ("Monex"), had no investing experience.

In 1972, Purdy started buying Krugerrands from Monex with cash, and stored the coins under his kitchen sink. By 1980, he had purchased over 1,100 Krugerrands and some silver bars, all stored under the sink. At this time John Mullins, one of Monex' account representatives, informed Purdy about precious metal leverage accounts.

The Rules of the Game

Leverage contracts arrived in the late 1960s and early 1970s as a way for individual investors to purchase precious metal coins or bars from coin dealers on a credit basis.[34] An investor paid down 20–30 percent of the full purchase price plus sales commissions, and signed a credit agreement for the balance, which stipulated interest rates and the possibility of margin calls if the commodity price dropped. . . .

The Casino

Monex is a registered leverage transaction merchant ("LTM"). . . . John Albrecht is a registered associated person ("AP") of Monex. . . . Monex has actively bought and sold leverage contracts on precious metals since 1967. Monex operates like a typical LTM as regulated by the Act. It buys and sells precious metals for individuals, either on a credit or cash basis. Monex acts as a principal, not broker, for these transactions, and bases its prices on world market conditions. If a buyer pays full price, then Monex delivers the actual precious metals to the customer. If, however, the buyer elects a credit plan, then Monex establishes a ten year purchase contract; financing the balance while the buyer pays periodic interest charges. Monex covers its physical delivery obligations by maintaining inventory, and trading in the futures market. . . .

The Play

In 1980, Purdy began leveraged investing with Monex. At that time, John Mullins handled Purdy's accounts. For each leveraged transaction made, Purdy received a Commodity Account Agreement, which he signed and returned to Monex, and an Offering Statement (essentially a risk disclosure statement). He bought silver bars on the margin, and within two months, he lost about $14,000. He closed out these accounts, but continued to buy metals from Monex at full price. In 1982, John Albrecht began handling Purdy's accounts for Monex.

Purdy sold his business in 1983, and decided to use all or some of the proceeds to purchase leverage contracts from Monex again, although this time on a much larger scale. . . . His strategy was to use some precious metals stored under the sink . . . as starting capital. He then could invest in as much gold and silver as possible by trading on the margin, thus maximizing profits. The money saved by leveraging, and the proceeds thereof, would support his living expenses, he contemplated. . . .

---

34. [N. 2] *See Hearings on S. 2485, S. 2837, and H.R. 13113 Before the Senate Comm. on Agriculture, Nutrition, and Forestry,* 93d Cong.2d Sess., pt 3 at 748 (1974) (Statement of M. Martin Rom, Chairman, International Precious Metals Corporation).

Early in 1983, he suffered huge losses in three days when the price of silver dropped by fifty percent overnight.[35] Rather than cut his losses, Purdy continued to invest heavily; delving deeper into his metals stored at home under the sink and obtaining loans from Monex on other, more profitable, accounts. Purdy testified that he believed "the metal market will come back," and he felt that "[i]f I get something I believe in I will stay with it." Throughout 1983 and 1984, Purdy continued to lose money.

When 1985 began, losses in Purdy's accounts exceeded $1,250,000. Purdy asked Albrecht what could be done to stop the financial hemorrhage. Albrecht suggested hedging long investments with short investments, but tempered his advice with the caveat that although short postures would stop losses, they would prevent gains as well.[36] Purdy then bought some short contracts.

In March of 1985, news wire services reported the possibility of Brazil's default on foreign bank loans. Albrecht called Purdy and stressed to him that Brazil's default could increase the price of silver. Albrecht explained that Purdy's short positions would inhibit profits should the price of silver rise due to Brazil's default. Purdy authorized Albrecht to sell most of the short contracts, but when Brazil did not default, Purdy did not immediately reinstate his short hedges. Purdy bought short again in July 1985, but then closed all accounts with Monex in September 1985.

In sum, from 1980 through 1985 Purdy sent $1,313,323 to Monex, but he withdrew $675,614 in the form of precious metal or funds. Monex charged him $217,934 in interest for the leverage accounts he maintained at Monex.

Almost a year after closing his accounts Purdy filed a reparation complaint with the Commission. After two failed attempts to file a complaint that alleged a specific violation and actual damages suffered, Purdy obtained new counsel through the assistance of the Commission. The second amended complaint charged Monex with bucketing, fraud, and numerous violations of the CEA and the Rules of the CFTC.

After Herculean discovery efforts by both sides, a hearing was held before an ALJ in Houston, Texas, in December 1987. Counsel represented both sides; presenting evidence and cross-examining witnesses. The ALJ issued his Initial Decision ("ID") on June 29, 1988,[37] concluding that Purdy failed to establish by a preponderance of the evidence any actual violations by Monex. . . .

---

35. [N. 16] The record conflicts as to the exact amount of these losses, but they were at least as high as $75,000 and may have been in excess of $290,000.

36. [N. 17] Prior to 1985, Purdy purchased long leverage contracts. In layperson's terms, "long" means the investor speculates that the price will go up over time. The investor hopes to buy low now, and sell high later, although not necessarily ten years later as is the term for a standard leverage contract at Monex. "Short" means the investor wants the price to go down over time. The investor then "sells" a leverage contract to Monex, and "buys" it back at a lower price later, thus making a profit (assuming the price did actually decrease over time).

37. [N. 18] *Purdy v. Monex Int'l, Ltd.*, CFTC Docket No. 86-R244, 1988 WL 228733 (June 29, 1988).

Purdy filed a proper and timely notice of appeal with the Commission in July of 1988. On May 20, 1991 the Commission affirmed the ID without opinion. . . . Purdy then filed a timely petition for review with this court. . . .

A court of appeals does not re-evaluate the evidence, but . . . determine[s] if the Commission's (or its designee, the ALJ's) conclusions based on the facts were justified. . . .

We view our task here as a search for substantial evidence in the record that would reasonably uphold the factual findings of the ALJ.

Proximate Cause. . . .

The ALJ was the designated fact finder for Purdy's reparation proceeding. Thus, under the substantial evidence standard of review, if the ALJ found Purdy sustained no injuries caused in fact by the respondent-intervenor's alleged CEA violations, then we must find substantial evidence to support the ALJ's findings as to proximate cause.

The ALJ based much of his decision on weighing the conflicting testimony given by both Monex and the Purdys. As finder of fact, he sat in the best position to evaluate the credibility of the witnesses, their demeanor, and their testimony. After hearing all the oral statements, and reviewing a "huge record," the ALJ came to a crucial core conclusion which permeates this entire case: "Complainant's losses were not caused by any wrongdoing on the part of Respondents. Rather, those losses resulted from Complainant's intractable belief that precious metals prices would increase in the 1980's." . . .

Purdy had been speculating in precious metals since 1972, had read at least two treatises on investing by a recognized financial author, and read related periodicals at least once a week. . . . [T]he ALJ, based on Purdy's 650+ page deposition (and earlier pleadings), found him to be well versed in the nuances of margin and leverage contracts: the risk involved, and the extent of his exposure to that risk.

Conclusion

While we sympathize with Mr. Purdy's extensive losses so late in his life, the evidence here compels us to agree with the Commission's acceptance of the ALJ's actions and findings. To do otherwise might encourage other market bulls to seek refuge in the courts for judicial licking of their wounds after suffering at the claws of a bear market. We therefore hold the order of the CFTC was correct. AFFIRMED.

———————

Monex International withdrew its leverage transaction merchant registration in 1991.[38] Today there are no registered leverage transaction merchants.[39] This is

———————

38. *See* National Futures Association, *Monex International Ltd.*, https://www.nfa.futures.org /basicnet/Details.aspx?entityid=oHBfiH%2fgQ9E%3d&rn=N.

39. National Futures Association, *Membership and Directories*, https://www.nfa.futures.org /registration-membership/membership-and-directories.html (May 29, 2021).

unsurprising considering the narrow scope of permissible leveraged or margined transactions. Additionally, leverage transaction merchants have, when compared to the limited scope of potential transactions types, a prohibitive minimum net capital requirement of $20 million.[40]

A regulatory gap was perceived to exist. On the one hand, *Zelener* and its progeny (discussed above in section B.1.b) held that the terms of the contract predominate over parties' actual practices. Therefore, even if leveraged or margined, a foreign exchange (and, by extension in this context) or commodity transaction that provided for physical delivery within the ordinary spot settlement time period was not an off-exchange futures contract. Per *Zelener*, this was the case even if the parties' actual practice was to habitually "roll" the transaction continuously, pushing the delivery date forward indefinitely. On the other hand, the CFTC's claim that its authority over leverage transactions allowed it to prohibit leveraged commodity transactions with contractual durations less than ten years had been unsuccessful in court.

CFTC v. American Precious Metals

845 F. Supp. 2d 1279 (S.D. Fl. 2011)

William J. Zloch, District Judge.

Plaintiff Commodity Futures Trading Commission (hereinafter "the CFTC") initiated the above-styled cause [alleging] . . . that Defendants violated Section 19 of the Commodities Exchange Act (hereinafter "the CEA"), 7 U.S.C. § 23, and Rule 31.3 thereunder, 17 C.F.R. § 31.3, by making fraudulent misrepresentations to customers while marketing precious metals. In Count II, the CFTC alleges that Defendants violated Section 19(b) of the CEA, 7 U.S.C. § 23(b), by engaging in transactions involving palladium. . . . [T]he Parties dispute whether the CFTC has regulatory jurisdiction under Section 19 of the CEA. . . .

Defendant American Precious Metals, LLC (hereinafter "APM") is a telemarketing firm purporting to sell physical gold, silver, platinum and palladium to customers through what it describes as its "leverage program." Since at least July of 2007, APM has allegedly elicited more than $37 million from its customers. Defendant Harry Robert Tanner, Jr. is the Managing Member of APM, and together with Defendant Sammy J. Goldman, controls the daily operations of the firm.

Acting at the direction of Defendants Tanner and Goldman, APM's agents and employees solicited customers through telephone, mail, and APM's web-sites. These APM representatives told customers that:

---

40. National Futures Association Financial Requirements § 6(a), available at https://www.nfa .futures.org/rulebook/rules.aspx?Section=7&RuleID=SECTION%206.

(1) APM sells physical precious metals to customers on a leveraged basis; (2) APM arranges for a loan to the customer through a second company named Global Asset Management (hereinafter "GAM"), which purportedly lends up to 80% of the funds for the purchase of physical precious metals; (3) customers' physical precious metals are stored in an independent depository; and (4) interest accrues on funds lent to the customer by GAM. . . .

However, the CFTC alleges that:

In fact, APM [did] not buy, sell, or store physical precious metals . . . and no actual financing [was] ever provided. Instead, APM record[ed] each customer's transaction on paper, [took] a hefty commission of 40% of the customer's funds, [pooled] the customer's remaining funds together with funds received from its other customers, and periodically [sent] those pooled funds to GAM. In turn, GAM pooled the funds received from APM with funds received from similar boiler rooms, and [sent] a portion of those funds to accounts in GAM's name with three London-based firms, where it [held] positions on margin in off-exchange metals derivatives. In the meantime, APM actively conceal[ed] its fraud, in part by creating and sending customers false trade confirmation statements that reflect[ed] the purchase of actual, physical precious metals. . . .

APM customers signed agreements with GAM to supposedly invest in precious metals. The GAM agreements provided for initial five year terms, followed by automatic renewals of successive five year terms. . . .

By this conduct, the CFTC alleges, *inter alia,* that Defendants committed fraud in violation of Section 19 of the CEA, 7 U.S.C. § 23, and Rule 31.3 thereunder, 17 C.F.R. § 31.3. . . . Defendants argue that the transactions at issue do not fall within the CFTC's regulatory jurisdiction under Section 19 because they last fewer than ten years, and therefore are not "leverage contracts" as defined by the CFTC's Rule 31.4z(w) [*sic*], 17 C.F.R. § 31.4(w). In response, the CFTC argues, *inter alia,* that Rule 31.4(w) only applies to a subset of a broader class of "Section 19 transactions." . . . Thus, the CFTC asserts that it still has jurisdiction over contracts it determines are the functional equivalent of leverage contracts, as well as contracts it determines are marketed or managed in substantially the same manner as leverage contracts. . . .

When an agency construes a jurisdictional provision of a statute it is responsible for administering, courts have regularly resolved the dispute by applying the framework established in *Chevron, U.S.A., Inc. v. Natural Res. Def. Council, Inc.,* 467 U.S. 837, 843, 104 S.Ct. 2778, 81 L.Ed.2d 694 (1984). *See, e.g., Coeur Alaska, Inc. v. Southeast Alaska Conservation Council,* 557 U.S. 261, 129 S.Ct. 2458, 2469, 174 L.Ed.2d 193 (2009). . . . *Chevron* established a principle of judicial deference to an agency's construction of a statute it is responsible for administering. . . . The Court thus turns to examine whether judicial deference to the CFTC's construction of the CEA is warranted here. . . .

Here, the language of Section 19 of the CEA demonstrates that Congress did not directly speak to the precise question of how a "standardized contract" is defined.[41] Section 19(a) provides that:

> Except as authorized under subsection (b) of this section, no person shall offer to enter into, enter into, or confirm the execution of, any transaction for the delivery of any commodity under a standardized contract commonly known to the trade as a margin account, margin contract, leverage account, or leverage contract, or under any contract, account, arrangement, scheme, or device that the Commission determines serves the same function or functions as such a standardized contract, or is marketed or managed in substantially the same manner as such a standardized contract.

7 U.S.C. § 23(a). In turn, Section 19(b) states:

> Subject to paragraph (2), no person shall offer to enter into, enter into, or confirm the execution of, any transaction for the delivery of silver bullion, gold bullion, bulk silver coins, bulk gold coins, or platinum under a standardized contract described in subsection (a) of this section, contrary to the terms of any rule, regulation, or order that the Commission shall prescribe, which may include terms designed to ensure the financial solvency of the transaction or prevent manipulation or fraud.

7 U.S.C. § 23(b)(1). Thus, Congress left a gap — or ambiguity — for the CFTC to fill in the exercise of its own discretion.

Here, the Court must examine whether the CFTC has reasonably resolved the ambiguity Congress created by not defining the term "standardized contract" in Section 19. To do so, the Court looks first to the relevant agency regulation, Rule 31.4(w)....

Congress's decision not to define the term "standardized contract" (more commonly known as a "leverage contract" or "leverage agreement") in Section 19 of the CEA caused confusion in the financial industry. *See, e.g., First Nat'l Monetary Corp. v. Commodity Futures Trading Comm'n*, 860 F.2d 654, 658 (6th Cir.1988) ("The problem of differentiating between a futures contract and a leverage agreement has plagued both Congress and the CFTC for years.") (internal citation omitted). The problem was that "a section 19 leverage contract 'look[ed] strikingly like a futures contract traded off a designated contract market'." *Id.*

To clear up this confusion, Congress passed legislation in 1982 requiring the CFTC to regulate leverage contracts "as an entirely separate class of transactions." *Purdy v. Commodity Futures Trading Comm'n*, 968 F.2d 510, 514–515 (5th Cir.1992) (*citing* the Futures Trading Act of 1982, Pub.L. No. 97-444, § 234, 96 Stat. 2294 (*codified as amended* at 7 U.S.C.A. § 23 (West Supp 1992))). What Congress wanted to

---

41. [N. 1] The CFTC's Section 19 jurisdiction flows from Section 2 of the CEA, which grants the CFTC exclusive jurisdiction over "transactions subject to regulation by the Commission pursuant to section 23 of this title." 7 U.S.C. § 2(a)(1)(A).

know was "whether a leverage transaction is really a different type of contract, or merely a species of futures contracts." *First Nat'l Monetary Corp., supra.*

In 1984, the CFTC responded by promulgating, among others, Rule 31.4(w) which defined the term "leverage contract" as a contract lasting ten years or more. . . .

Any contract lasting fewer than ten years was therefore not a leverage contract under Rule 31.4(w). *See, e.g., First National Monetary Corp., supra* (holding that the ten year threshold in Rule 31.4(w) was in fact a "durational requirement"); *accord Commodity Futures Trading Comm'n v. P.I.E., Inc.,* 853 F.2d 721 (9th Cir.1988); *Galvin v. First Nat. Monetary Corp.,* 624 F. Supp. 154, 156 (E.D.N.Y.1985). In the instant case, the Parties do not dispute the fact that Defendants' transactions lasted for terms of only five years and thus are not leverage contracts. . . .

Instead, the Parties' central dispute in this litigation is whether Rule 31.4(w) limited the CFTC's Section 19 jurisdiction to leverage contracts alone. If it did, then the CFTC would lack regulatory jurisdiction over Defendants' contracts under Section 19, and this matter would have to be dismissed.

Under the *Chevron* framework, the Court must resolve this dispute by looking first to Rule 31.4(w) to determine whether it reasonably resolves the ambiguity in question. *See Coeur Alaska, Inc.,* 129 S.Ct. at 2469. The text of Rule 31.4(w) clearly docs not address the question at issuer [*sic*] whether the scope of the CFTC's Section 19 jurisdiction is broader than leverage contracts alone. Instead, the text merely defines the term "leverage contract," without any indication that this definition constitutes the entirety of the CFTC's Section 19 jurisdiction. Reading the Rule's text alone, therefore, it is plausible to conclude that the CFTC's Section 19 jurisdiction extends more broadly. For instance, the CFTC argues that Rule 31.4(w) leverage contracts were just one subset of a broader class of Section 19 "standardized transactions." Further, the CFTC asserts that Rule 31.4(w) did nothing to truncate its Section 19 jurisdiction over transactions that are the "functional equivalent" of leverage contracts, or over transactions that are "marketed or managed in substantially the same manner as" leverage contracts. *See* 7 U.S.C. § 23(a).

Since Rule 31.4(w)'s text is ambiguous, the Court must resolve the ambiguity by looking to the agency's interpretation of the Rule. . . .

The Court now turns to examine three sources in which the CFTC has interpreted Rule 31.4(w).

First, the preamble to the interim final version of Rule 31.4(w) clearly stated that "leverage contracts" and "standardized contracts" are one and the same:

> Through its definition . . . of a leverage contract, the Commission is exercising its exclusive regulatory jurisdiction over transactions that fall within the scope of Section 19 of the Act. In adopting that definition, the Commission has exercised its authority to specify the standardized contracts that Congress expected to be regulated under Section 19 of the Act. *As a result . . . those transactions that do not meet the Commission's definition of*

a leverage contract are not within the Commission's regulatory jurisdiction under Section 19 of the Act and are not subject to Commission registration and regulation pursuant to Part 31. This "bright line" distinction between transactions subject to exclusive Commission jurisdiction under Section 19 and those not subject to Commission regulation thereunder is one of the salutary effects of the comprehensive definition adopted by the Commission. Those transactions not subject to exclusive Commission jurisdiction under Section 19 are open to regulation and enforcement by the states.

Fed.Reg. 5498-01, 5499–5500 (1984) (emphasis added). Thus, at the time Rule 31.4(w) was taking effect, the CFTC's position was that its Section 19 jurisdiction only included leverage contracts.

Second, Defendants point to a statutory and regulatory interpretation letter issued by CFTC General Counsel Kenneth M. Raisler on March 25, 1985, less than a year after Rule 31.4(w) took effect (hereinafter "the letter" or "the General Counsel's letter"). Quoting the preamble to the interim final rule, the letter confirmed that: "[T]ransactions that do not meet the Commission's leverage contract definition in Rule 31.4(w) are not subject to regulation under Section 19." However, the letter explained that such transactions may still be subject to CFTC jurisdiction under Section 4(a) of the CEA:

While the terms and conditions of any particular transaction must be examined on a case-by-case basis, the Commission's Office of General Counsel is of the view that many off-exchange future delivery type transactions, whether or not "masquerading" as leverage contracts, are in fact commodity futures contracts and are per se unlawful under section 4(a) of the Commodity Exchange Act.

50 Fed.Reg. 11656-01. Thus, the General Counsel's letter confirmed that Rule 31.4(w) did in fact limit the CFTC's Section 19 jurisdiction to leverage contracts alone. In addition, it explained how Rule 31.4(w) and Section 19 fit into the larger statutory framework of the CEA. Under that framework, the CFTC could regulate leverage contracts under Section 19, and futures contracts under Section 4. Transactions that looked like leverage contracts but did not meet Rule 31.4(w)'s criteria could still be regulated under Section 4, on a case-by-base basis.

Third, Defendants highlight Interpretive Letter 85-2, issued by the CFTC on August 6, 1985, entitled *Bank Activities Involving the Sale of Precious Metals.*, 22,673, Commodity Futures Trading Commission. . . . In Interpretive Letter 85-2, the CFTC fielded a request for an interpretation of the applicability of the CEA to certain precious metals transactions. The Letter is significant because it concluded that the transactions at issue were "not leverage contracts within the meaning of Commission Rule 31.4(w) and. . . . thus not subject to Commission regulation as such." *Id.* at p. 3. Thus, the agency once again interpreted Rule 31.4(w)'s leverage contract definition as clearly demarcating its Section 19 jurisdictional boundaries.

The Court finds that these three interpretations of Rule 31.4(w) are entitled to judicial deference for two reasons. First, they are not plainly erroneous or inconsistent with the Rule. *See Auer* [*v. Robbins*, 519 U.S. 452 (1997)], *supra.* On the contrary, they are perfectly consistent with Congress's intent that the CFTC distinguish between leverage contracts and futures contracts by regulating leverage contracts "as an entirely separate class of transactions." *Purdy v. Commodity Futures Trading Comm'n*, 968 F.2d 510, 514–515 (5th Cir.1992) (*citing* the Futures Trading Act of 1982, Pub.L. No. 97-444, §234, 96 Stat. 2294 (*codified as amended at* 7 U.S.C.A. §23 (West Supp.1992))). . . . Second, the preamble to the interim final rule and the General Counsel's letter both "interpret the agency's regulatory scheme" by explaining how Rule 31.4(w) and Section 19 fit into the CEA's statutory framework. *Coeur Alaska, supra.* Under *Coeur Alaska,* this fact "entitl[es] [them] to a measure of deference." *Id.; accord Sottera, Inc. v. Food & Drug Administration,* 627 F.3d 891, 903 at fn. 4 (D.C.Cir.2011).

Nevertheless, the CFTC objects that these sources represent a narrow jurisdictional view that the agency no longer holds. Instead, it urges the Court to adopt the broader jurisdictional view the agency advances in this litigation. . . .

Here, the CFTC has not demonstrated that it has consistently interpreted Section 19 in the broad manner it now advances in this action. *See Bradberry* [*v. Dir., Office of Worker's Comp. Programs*, 117 F. 3d 1361 (11th Cir. 1997)], *supra.* Moreover, the CFTC's current position is not a written interpretation. *See id.* While the CFTC's current position may not be a mere litigating position, there is no evidence that it embodies the agency's "longstanding policy" on the subject. *Id.* For all these reasons, the Court finds that the CFTC's current position is not entitled to deference.

Instead, the Court will defer to the CFTC's prior position embodied in the interim final version of Rule 31.4(w), the General Counsel's letter, and Interpretive Letter 85-2. Accordingly, the Court finds that the CFTC's regulatory jurisdiction under Section 19 of the CEA only extends to leverage contracts as defined in Rule 31.4(w). Thus, in the instant case, the CFTC lacks Section 19 regulatory jurisdiction because Defendants' transactions are not leverage contracts under Rule 31.4(w). Therefore, the Court must dismiss the Complaint. . . .

In making this finding, the Court notes that several federal courts have reached the same conclusion. *See Commodity Futures Trading Comm'n v. P.I.E., Inc.,* 853 F.2d 721 (9th Cir.1988) (holding that Rule 31.4(w) drew a "bright line" between leverage contracts and future contracts, and no third category or Section 19 transactions exists); *accord In re Bybee,* 945 F.2d 309 (9th Cir.1991); *Commodity Futures Trading Comm'n v. 20/20 Trading Co., et al.,* 2011 WL 2221177 (C.D.Cal. June 7, 2011) (holding that "leverage contracts" are the sole type of transaction over which the CFTC has jurisdiction under Section 19). By contrast, the CFTC has proven unable to cite a single case in which a court has adopted the broad view of Section 19 espoused by the agency in this litigation.

In addition, the CFTC has cited no precedent for its assertion of Section 19 jurisdiction in Count II of the Complaint . . . over Defendants' palladium transactions. . . . Thus, the Court finds that the CFTC has not met its burden of establishing that these transactions fall under the CFTC's Section 19 jurisdiction. *See 20/20 Trading, supra,* at *7, fn. 4 (finding that the CFTC lacked jurisdiction under Section 19 over the defendants' palladium transactions because they were not leverage contracts). Thus, the Court will also dismiss Count II of the Complaint. . . .

———

Partially patching this perceived regulatory gap were amendments to the Commodity Exchange Act providing additional CFTC enforcement authority over retail commodity transactions. We discuss this in the following section.

3. Retail Commodities

The Dodd-Frank Act modified the Commodity Exchange Act to additionally mandate that any leveraged or margined commodity transaction be traded on a futures exchange[42] with an exception for: (1) securities; (2) banking products; (3) if both parties to the transaction are eligible contract participants;[43] (4) if the transaction is a contract resulting in "actual delivery" within twenty-eight days; or (5) if the transaction "creates an enforceable obligation to deliver between a seller and a buyer that have the ability to deliver and accept delivery, respectively, in connection with the line of business of the seller and buyer."[44]

The question of what constitutes "actual delivery" is the subject of the following case. Note that the decision is a denial of a motion to dismiss filed by the defendant and not a final decision on the merits of the CFTC's claim.

CFTC v. Monex Credit Company
931 F.3d 966 (9th Cir. 2019)

Siler, Circuit Judge: . . .

Congress, acting shortly after the economy began to stabilize from the financial crisis that began a decade earlier, passed the Dodd-Frank Wall Street Reform and Consumer Protection Act, Pub. L. No. 111-203, 124 Stat. 1376 (2010), which amended the Commodity Exchange Act (CEA) to expand the Commodity Future Trading Commission's (CFTC) enforcement authority. This case is about the extent of those powers.

Monex Credit Company, one of the defendants and appellees, argues that the CFTC went too far when it filed this $290 million lawsuit for alleged fraud in precious

———

42. Dodd-Frank Act § 742 (2010).

43. Or in a similar non-retail category, eligible commercial entity. *See* Commodity Exchange Act §§ 1a(17) and 2(c)(2)(D)(iv).

44. Commodity Exchange Act § 2(c)(2)(D)(ii).

metals sales. According to Monex, Dodd-Frank extended the CFTC's power only to fraud-based manipulation claims, so stand-alone fraud claims — without allegations of manipulation — fail as a matter of law.

Not only that, Monex argues, but Dodd-Frank also immunizes Monex from the CFTC's claims that it ran an unregistered, off-exchange trading platform. The CEA's registration provisions do not apply to retail commodities dealers who "actual[ly] deliver[]" the commodities to customers within twenty-eight days. *See* 7 U.S.C. § 2(c)(2)(D)(ii)(III)(aa). Monex insists that it falls within this exception.

On both fronts, the district court agreed with Monex and dismissed the CFTC's complaint for failure to state a claim under Civil Rule 12(b)(6). We REVERSE and REMAND. . . .

California-based Monex has been a major player in the precious metal markets for decades. It sells gold, silver, platinum, and palladium to investors who have a variety of buying options, but here we focus on what Monex calls its "Atlas Program." Through Atlas, investors can purchase commodities on "margin." Also known as "leverage," the concept is simple: A customer buys precious metals by paying only a portion of the full price. The remaining amount is financed through Monex.

Once a customer opens an account, she may take open positions in precious metals. But the trading occurs "off exchange" — that is, it does not happen on a regulated exchange or board of trade. Instead, Monex controls the platform, acts as the counterparty to every transaction, and sets the price for every trade.

Since mid-2011, Monex has made more than 140,000 trades for more than 12,000 Atlas accounts, each of which requires margin of 22–25% of the account's total value. A customer who deposits $25,000 in Atlas as margin can open positions valued at $100,000; she owes the additional $75,000 to Monex. Over time, the account's value changes — it goes up and down — as markets do. The difference between the account's total value and the amount the customer still owes to Monex is the account's "equity." And if that difference falls below a certain threshold, Monex can issue a "margin call" — it can require customers to immediately deposit more money into the accounts to increase the equity. Monex can do so at any time, and it can change margin requirements whenever it wants.

Monex also retains sole discretion to liquidate trading positions without notice to the customer if equity drops too low, and it controls the price for every trade. Price spreads — the difference between the bid price and ask price — are 3% and generate much of the program's revenue. Commissions and fees make up the rest, and that money comes directly out of customer accounts' equity. Over the last eight years, Monex has made margin calls in more than 3,000 Atlas accounts and has force-liquidated at least 1,850.

Atlas investors can make either "short" or "long" trades. Short trades bet on metal prices going down, and long up. Monex allows investors to place "stop" or "limit" orders to manage their trading positions. About a quarter of trading positions in leveraged Atlas accounts open and close within two weeks.

Customers must sign the Atlas account agreement, which gives Monex control over the metals. Monex does not hand over any metals, and customers never possess or control any physical commodity. Instead, Monex stores the metals in depositories with which Monex has contractual relationships. Monex retains exclusive authority to direct the depository on how to handle the metals; investors and the depositories have no contractual relationship with each other. Customers can get their hands on the metals only by making full payment, requesting specific delivery of metals, and having the metals shipped to themselves, a pick-up location, or an agent.

This structure applies to both long and short positions. For a long position, Monex retains the right to close out the position at any time in its sole discretion and at a price Monex chooses. Metal remains in the depository, but Monex claims to transfer ownership of the metals to the customer. The same is true for short positions, except that instead of transferring ownership, Monex loans the customer metals that the customer immediately sells back to Monex. According to the CFTC, Monex simply makes a "book entry" when customers make trades — nothing more. . . .

The CFTC regulates commodity futures markets under the CEA. *See* 7 U.S.C. §§ 1 *et seq.* Part of the CEA's purpose is "to protect all market participants from fraudulent or other abusive sales practices and misuses of customer assets." *Id.* § 5(b). The CEA requires that futures be traded on regulated exchanges. *Id.* § 6(a)(1). Brokers must register with the CFTC. *Id.* § 6d(a)(1). The CEA further protects against conflicts of interest and market abuse. *Id.* §§ 6d(c), 7(d). And the statute prohibits fraud. *Id.* § 6b(a)(2).

Originally, the CEA did not apply to retail commodity transactions because they were not futures contracts. *See CFTC v. Zelener,* 373 F.3d 861 (7th Cir. 2004). As *Zelener* recognized, the CEA applied only to futures contracts, even though other types of sales — such as leveraged retail commodity sales — can have similar economic effects. *Id.* at 866–67.

This changed in 2010 when Congress, acting in the wake of financial turmoil, passed Dodd-Frank — part of which amended the CEA. *See* Dodd-Frank Wall Street Reform and Consumer Protection Act of 2010, Pub. L. No. 111-203, 124 Stat. 1376 (2010). Congress extended the CEA to commodity transactions offered "on a leveraged or margined basis, or financed by the offeror" "as if" they were futures trades. *See* 7 U.S.C. § 2(c)(2)(D)(iii). But Congress carved out an exception: The CEA would not apply to leveraged retail commodity sales that resulted "in actual delivery within 28 days." *Id.* § 2(c)(2)(D)(ii)(III)(aa). . . .

The CFTC contends that Atlas is a scheme that has violated the CEA since at least July 2011. Monex tells its customers that leveraged precious metals trading is "a safe, secure and profitable way for retail customers to invest" when, in fact, the program requires that many customers lose money. What's more, the CFTC alleges, Atlas is designed so that when customers lose, Monex gains: Because Monex is the counterparty for each Atlas transaction, Monex benefits from large price spreads at the customer's expense. Sales representatives, too, have an incentive to push the program:

Monex pays salespeople with "commissions and bonuses tied directly to the number of Atlas accounts they open" and the number of transactions completed; account performance is not a factor in compensation. So Monex engages in "high-pressure sales tactics," cajoling potential customers into buying leveraged precious metals while it "misrepresent[s] the likelihood of profit" and "systematically downplay[s] the risks" to ensure customers invest in Atlas, inevitably leading to customer losses.

The complaint alleges deep and broad losses to about 90% of all leveraged Atlas accounts — totaling some $290 million. In some cases, individual losses were extreme: some customers lost hundreds of thousands of dollars, and many others suffered five-figure losses. New investors never learned about those losses because Monex never told them. Instead, Monex promised that precious metals are safe and "will always have value," so a customer cannot lose her investment.

The CFTC filed this lawsuit seeking an injunction and restitution against Monex Deposit Company, Monex Credit Company, Newport Services Corporation, Louis Carabini, and Michael Carabini (Monex). The CFTC contends that Atlas is an illegal and unregistered leveraged retail commodity transaction market. . . .

Under CEA §§ 2(c)(2)(D)(i) and (iii), any "agreement, contract, or transaction in any commodity that is entered into . . . on a leveraged or margined basis" is subject to "sections 6(a), 6(b), and 6b" of the CEA "as if the agreement, contract or transaction was a contract of sale of a commodity for future delivery." 7 U.S.C. §§ 2(c)(2)(D) (i) and (iii). But not all sales; the adjacent section excludes "a contract of sale that results in actual delivery within 28 days." *Id.* § 2(c)(2)(D)(ii)(III)(aa).

The statute does not define "actual delivery," and undefined terms receive their ordinary meaning. *See Taniguchi v. Kan Pac. Saipan, Ltd*, 566 U.S. 560, 566, 132 S. Ct. 1997, 182 L.Ed.2d 903 (2012). "Delivery" means "[t]he formal act of voluntarily transferring something; esp. the act of bringing goods, letters, etc. to a particular person or place." Black's Law Dictionary (9th ed. 2009). Black's defines "actual" as "[e]xisting in fact; real." *Id.* "Actual delivery" is the "act of giving real and immediate possession to the buyer or the buyer's agent." *Id.* By contrast, "constructive delivery" denotes "[a]n act that amounts to transfer of title by operation of law when actual transfer is impractical or impossible." *Id.*

The Eleventh Circuit adopted these definitions in *CFTC v. Hunter Wise Commodities, LLC*, 749 F.3d 967 (11th Cir. 2014), where it held that a seller failed to actually deliver commodities when it "did not possess or control an inventory of metal from which it could deliver to retail customers." *Id.* at 980. The court did "not define the precise boundaries of 'actual delivery,'" but it held that "[d]elivery must be *actual*." *Id.* at 979 (emphasis in original). "If 'actual delivery' means anything, it means something other than simply 'delivery,' for we must attach meaning to Congress's use of the modifier 'actual.'" *Id.* The defendant in *Hunter Wise* could not actually deliver anything because it did not have the commodities.

According to Monex, *Hunter Wise* tells us that the actual delivery exception applies only when the commodities do not in fact exist. Monex argues that it makes actual delivery "because the metals exist in fact and, upon sale, are voluntarily delivered to independent depositories for the buyer's benefit." . . . Monex, unlike the defendant in *Hunter Wise*, has the underlying commodities—they actually exist. So, Monex argues, *Hunter Wise* does not apply, and Atlas fits the exception.

Hunter Wise is not so limited. That court first held that "actual delivery" means giving "real and immediate possession to the buyer or buyer's agent." *Hunter Wise*, 749 F.3d at 979 (quoting Black's Law Dictionary 494 (9th ed. 2009)). The seller in *Hunter Wise* did not give the buyer possession of the commodities because it did not possess any in the first instance. *Id.* Without inventory, the seller could not *actually* deliver anything. *Id.* But "actual" in the statute modifies *delivery*, not existence. *See id.* Of course, as *Hunter Wise* recognizes, existence is a prerequisite to delivery— one cannot deliver that which does not exist. But the fact that the commodity's existence is *necessary* to comply with the exception does not mean existence is *sufficient* to fit the exception. If Congress wanted only to ensure enough inventory it could have said so. It did not; it required "actual delivery."

Thus, the plain language tells us that actual delivery requires at least some meaningful degree of possession or control by the customer. It is possible for this exception to be satisfied when the commodity sits in a third-party depository, but not when, as here, metals are in the broker's chosen depository, never exchange hands, and are subject to the broker's exclusive control, and customers have no substantial, non-contingent interests.

This interpretation is confirmed by the broader statutory context. *See Abramski v. United States*, 573 U.S. 169, 179, 134 S.Ct. 2259, 189 L.Ed.2d 262 (2014). Dodd-Frank expanded the CEA to close the so-called *Zelener* loophole, which allowed companies to offer commodity sales on margin without regulation, because these transactions mimic conventional futures trades long regulated by the CFTC. *See Zelener*, 373 F.3d at 866. On the other hand, sales where customers obtain meaningful control or possession of commodities, i.e., when actual delivery occurs, do *not* mimic futures trading and are therefore exempt from registration and related CEA requirements.

Monex argues that in the context of a provision regulating leveraged commodity sales, it would make little sense for "actual delivery" to turn on possession or control, because such a reading would clash with "margin," which means "[c]ash or collateral required to be paid to a securities broker by an investor to protect the broker against losses from securities bought on credit." Black's Law Dictionary (9th ed. 2009). Because the very meaning of the word "margin" requires that the buyer deposit *collateral* with the seller, actual delivery must mean something other than transferring possession or control to the buyer. Otherwise, Monex argues, margin would mean nothing.

Yet, even if the commodity serves as collateral, there is no reason why the buyer cannot control it. In many financing contexts, some degree of buyer possession or control is commonplace. While permitting customers to obtain significant control over or possession of metals might be practically difficult here, that fact does not displace the statute's plain meaning.

If we had any lingering doubt about the statute's plain meaning, resort to conventional canons of interpretation would further support our conclusion. First, the CEA uses "delivery" in § 1a(27), which we have said "cannot be satisfied by the simple device of a transfer of title." *CFTC v. Noble Metals Int'l, Inc.*, 67 F.3d 766, 773 (9th Cir. 1995). And because we assume that "Congress means the same words in the same statute to mean the same thing," *actual* delivery must require more than simple title transfer. *Texas Dept. of Housing & Cmty. Affairs v. Inclusive Cmtys. Project, Inc.*, —— U.S. ——, 135 S. Ct. 2507, 2535, 192 L.Ed.2d 514 (2015). Second, our interpretation presents no ineffectiveness or surplusage problems because it does not, as the district court believed, mean that "every financed transaction would violate Dodd-Frank," thus "eliminat[ing] the Actual Delivery Exception from the CEA." 311 F. Supp. 3d 1173, 1181 (C.D. Cal. 2018) (quoting *CFTC v. Worth Grp., Inc.*, No. 13-80796-CIV, 2014 WL 11350233, at *2 (S.D. Fla. Oct. 27, 2014)). The CFTC does not present a bare-bones complaint. It includes detailed and specific factual allegations. All we say today is that those allegations, taken as true, do not establish actual delivery.

Finally, even if the statute were ambiguous, we would find the CFTC's interpretive guidance persuasive. *Retail Commodity Transactions Under CEA*, 78 Fed. Reg. 52,426 (Aug. 23, 2013); *see Skidmore v. Swift & Co.*, 323 U.S. 134, 65 S.Ct. 161, 89 L. Ed. 124 (1944). There, the CFTC stated it would employ a "functional approach" that considers "[o]wnership, possession, title, and physical location of the commodity purchased or sold." 78 Fed. Reg. at 52,428. Other factors included "the nature of the relationship between the buyer, seller, and possessor of the commodity," and the "manner in which the purchase or sale is recorded and completed." *Id.*

Monex insists that Atlas matches the second illustrative example of actual delivery set forth in the guidance: physical transfer of all purchased commodities into an independent depository plus transfer of title to the buyer. *Id.* However, these steps constitute actual delivery only if they are "not simply a sham." *Id.* The CFTC engages in a "careful consideration" of the relevant functional factors (listed above) to determine if the exception is indeed applicable. Here, customers have no contractual rights to the metal; Monex, not customers, has a relationship with depositories; Monex maintains total control over accounts and can liquidate at any time in its own discretion; and the entire transaction is merely a book entry. This amounts to sham delivery, not actual delivery.

To recap, "actual delivery" unambiguously requires the transfer of some degree of possession or control. Other interpretive tools, including the CFTC's guidance, reinforce this conclusion. . . .

Although Monex contends that no fraud occurred, we must, at this point, accept as true the CFTC's well-pleaded complaint to the contrary. And because the CFTC's claims are plausible, this lawsuit should continue.

Note that third-party custodians are the norm in precious metal trading. These custodians are expected to have the secure physical facilities appropriate to storing precious metals. Therefore, it is appropriate that the CFTC does not assert that actual physical possession is required to satisfy the "actual delivery" requirement. The *Monex* court, recognizing that actual delivery can be to a third-party custodian so long as the customer has "some degree of possession or control," leaves open the question of what level of possession or control is sufficient.

Raising even more novel questions is what constitutes actual delivery with respect to virtual currency. As we discuss below in Section D, virtual currency is a commodity under the Commodity Exchange Act and CFTC rules and, therefore, subject to the retail commodity regime.

D. Virtual Currency

Increasing media and regulatory attention has been given to virtual currency. Despite being termed in the vernacular as "currency," virtual currency is not treated as such by the CFTC for regulatory purposes. Instead, as upheld by numerous courts, it is treated identically to any other commodity.

Since virtual currency is a commodity, it is subject to the CFTC's retail commodity authority discussed above in section C.3. However, the "actual delivery" requirement for the exception for retail commodities actually delivered within twenty-eight days raises novel issues in the context of virtual currency. The CFTC provided interpretative guidance as to the meaning of "actual delivery" in this context. In doing so, the CFTC also outlined the regulatory treatment of virtual currency.

CFTC, *Retail Commodity Transactions Involving Certain Digital Assets*
85 Fed. Reg. 37734 (June 24, 2020)

. . . With certain exceptions, the CFTC has been granted exclusive jurisdiction over commodity futures, options, and all other derivatives that fall within the definition of a swap.[45] Further, the Commission has been granted general anti-fraud and anti-manipulation authority over any swap, or a contract of sale of any commodity in interstate commerce, or for future delivery on or subject to the rules of any registered entity.[46] The Commission's mission is to promote the integrity, resilience, and vibrancy of the U.S. derivatives markets through sound regulation; it does so, in part, by protecting the American public from fraudulent schemes and abusive practices in those markets and products over which it has been granted jurisdiction.

---

45. [N. 1] 7 U.S.C. 2(a)(1)(A). The CFTC shares its swap jurisdiction in certain aspects with the Securities and Exchange Commission ("SEC"). *See* 7 U.S.C. 2(a)(1)(C).

46. [N. 2] 7 U.S.C. 9(1).

The Commission has long held that certain speculative commodity transactions involving leverage or margin are futures contracts subject to Commission oversight.[47] However, certain judicial decisions called that view into question with respect to certain leveraged retail transactions primarily in foreign currencies.[48] In 2008, Congress addressed this judicial uncertainty by providing that certain enumerated provisions of the CEA apply to certain retail foreign currency transactions pursuant to CEA section 2(c)(2)(C)(iv). . . . This new statutory provision is subject to an exception for retail foreign currency transactions that result in "actual delivery" within two days.[49] Two years later, in the Dodd-Frank Act, Congress similarly extended certain provisions of the CEA to apply to all other "retail commodity transactions" pursuant to CEA section 2(c)(2)(D)(iii).[50]

Specifically, CEA section 2(c)(2)(D) applies to any agreement, contract, or transaction in any commodity that is (i) entered into with, or offered to (even if not entered into with), a person that is neither an eligible contract participant . . . nor an eligible commercial entity . . . ("retail"), (ii) on a leveraged or margined basis, or financed by the offeror, the counterparty, or a person acting in concert with the offeror or counterparty on a similar basis. . . . CEA section 2(c)(2)(D) provides that such an agreement, contract, or transaction is subject to [critical provisions of the CEA] . . ."as if the agreement, contract, or transaction was a contract of sale of a commodity for future delivery" (i.e., a futures contract).[51] The statute, however, excepts certain transactions from its application. In particular, CEA section 2(c)(2)(D)(ii)(III)(aa) . . . excepts a contract of sale that "results in actual delivery within 28 days or such other longer period as the Commission may determine by rule or regulation based upon the typical commercial practice in cash or spot markets for the commodity involved."[52] . . .

---

47. [N. 3] *See In re Stovall*, CFTC Docket No. 75-7 [1977–1980 Transfer Binder] Comm. Fut. L. Rep. (CCH) paragraph 20,941, at 23,777 (CFTC Dec. 6, 1979) (applying traditional elements of a futures contract to a purported cash transaction).

48. [N. 4] *See, e.g., CFTC v. Zelener*, 373 F.3d 861 (7th Cir. 2004); *CFTC v. Erskine*, 512 F.3d 309 (6th Cir. 2008)

49. [N. 6] 7 U.S.C. 2(c)(2)(C)(i)(II)(bb)(AA).

50. [N. 7] *See* Sec. 742 of the Dodd-Frank Wall Street Reform and Consumer Protection Act of 2010, Public Law 111-203, 124 Stat. 1376 (2010); *see also Hearing to Review Implications of the CFTC v. Zelener Case Before the Subcomm. on General Farm Commodities and Risk Management of the H. Comm. on Agriculture*, 111th Cong. 52–664 (2009) (statement of Rep. Marshall, Member, H. Comm. on Agriculture) ("If in substance it is a futures contract, it is going to be regulated. It doesn't matter how clever your draftsmanship is."); 156 Cong. Rec. S5, 924 (daily ed. July 15, 2010) (statement of Sen. Lincoln) ("Section 742 corrects [any regulatory uncertainty] by extending the Farm Bill's 'Zelener fraud fix' to retail off-exchange transactions in *all* commodities.") (emphasis added).

51. [N. 14] 7 U.S.C. 2(c)(2)(D)(iii). In addition, retail commodity transactions fall within the definition of "commodity interest," which also includes futures, options, and swaps. 17 CFR 1.3 (defining "commodity interest").

52. [N. 16] The Commission has not adopted any regulations permitting a longer actual delivery period for any commodity pursuant to this statute. Accordingly, the 28-day actual delivery period remains applicable to all commodities, while retail foreign currency transactions remain subject to

[T]he Commission [has] determined that virtual currency is a commodity as that term is defined by CEA section 1a(9).[53] Subsequently, the Commission brought its first enforcement action against a platform that offered virtual currency transactions to retail customers on a leveraged, margined, or financed basis without registering with the Commission.[54] In the *Bitfinex* settlement order, the Commission found that the virtual currency platform violated CEA sections 4(a) and 4d because the unregistered entity "did not actually deliver bitcoins purchased from them." . . . Rather, the entity "held the purchased bitcoins in bitcoin deposit wallets that it owned and controlled." . . .

[W]hile the CEA addresses several different types of transactions, this final interpretive guidance specifically concerns the "actual delivery" exception in CEA section 2(c)(2)(D) as it applies to digital assets that serve as a medium of exchange. Notably, CEA section 2(c)(2)(D) and its exceptions remain separate and distinct from application of the swap definition in CEA section 1a(47).[55]

The Commission notes that this interpretive guidance is intended to provide an efficient and flexible way to communicate the agency's current views on how the actual delivery exception in Section 2(c)(2)(D) may apply in various situations. Given the complex and dynamic nature of these markets, the Commission believes it is appropriate to take an adaptable approach while it continues to follow developments in this space and evaluate business activity on a case-by-case basis. . . .

[T]he Commission considers virtual currency to be a commodity as defined under Section 1a(9) of the Act,[56] like many other intangible commodities that the Commission has previously recognized (e.g., renewable energy credits and emission allowances, certain indices, and certain debt instruments, among others). . . .

---

a 2-day actual delivery period pursuant to CEA section 2(c)(2)(C). In addition, certain commercial transactions and securities are excepted pursuant to CEA section 2(c)(2)(D)(ii).

53. [N. 32] *In re Coinflip, Inc., d/b/a Derivabit, and Francisco Riordan*, CFTC Docket No. 15-29, 2015 WL 5535736, [Current Transfer Binder] Comm. Fut. L. Rep. (CCH) paragraph 33,538 (CFTC Sept. 17, 2015) (consent order); *In re TeraExchange LLC*, CFTC Docket No. 15-33, 2015 WL 5658082, [Current Transfer Binder] Comm. Fut. L. Rep. (CCH) paragraph 33,546 (CFTC Sept. 24, 2015) (consent order).

54. [N. 33] *In re BFXNA INC. d/b/a BITFINEX*, CFTC Docket No. 16-19 (June 2, 2016) (consent order) (hereinafter, *Bitfinex*).

55. [N. 40] 7 U.S.C. 1a(47). For example, certain retail transactions that may involve leverage, such as contracts for difference ("CFDs"), are swaps. See Joint Final Rule, Further Definition of "Swap," "Security-Based Swap," and "Security-Based Swap Agreement"; Mixed Swaps; Security-Based Swap Agreement Recordkeeping, 77 FR 48208 at 48259 (Aug. 13, 2012). Pursuant to CEA section 2(e), U.S. retail persons are prohibited from entering into such swaps unless they are offered on a designated contract market ("DCM").

56. [N. 144] 82 FR at 60337-38; *In re Coinflip, Inc., d/b/a Derivabit, and Francisco Riordan*, CFTC Docket No. 15-29, 2015 WL 5535736, [Current Transfer Binder] Comm. Fut. L. Rep. (CCH) paragraph 33,538 (CFTC Sept. 17, 2015) (consent order); *In re TeraExchange LLC*, CFTC Docket No. 15-33, 2015 WL 5658082, [Current Transfer Binder] Comm. Fut. L. Rep. (CCH) paragraph 33,546 (CFTC Sept. 24, 2015) (consent order); *see also In re BFXNA Inc.*, CFTC No. 16-19, 2016 WL 3137612, at *5 (June 2, 2016) (consent order).

In addition, multiple federal courts have held that virtual currencies fall within the CEA's commodity definition.[57] As a commodity, virtual currency is subject to applicable provisions of the CEA and Commission regulations, including CEA section 2(c)(2)(D).

The Commission continues to interpret the term "virtual currency" broadly. In the context of this interpretation, virtual currency:[58] Is a digital asset that encompasses any digital representation of value or unit of account that is or can be used as a form of currency (i.e., transferred from one party to another as a medium of exchange); may be manifested through units, tokens, or coins, among other things; and may be distributed by way of digital "smart contracts," among other structures. However, the Commission notes that it does not intend to create a bright line definition given the evolving nature of the commodity and, in some instances, its underlying public distributed ledger technology ("DLT" or "blockchain"). . . .

The Commission continues to recognize that certain virtual currencies and their underlying blockchain technologies have the potential to yield notable advancements in applications of financial technology ("FinTech"). . . .

Moreover, since virtual currency may serve as an underlying component of derivatives transactions, the Commission maintains a close interest in the development of the virtual currency marketplace generally. . . . [S]everal listed derivatives contracts based on virtual currency have been self-certified to be listed on CFTC registered entities . . . in accordance with the CEA and Commission regulations.

In addition, the Commission continues to closely follow the evolution of the cash or "spot" market for virtual currencies, including related execution venues, especially since such markets may inform and affect the listed derivatives markets. Many cash market execution venues offer services to retail customers that wish to speculate on the price movements of a virtual currency against other currencies. For example, a speculator may purchase virtual currency using borrowed money in the hopes of covering any outstanding balance owed through profits from favorable price movements in the future. Among other scenarios, . . . this interpretation is meant to address the Commission's concern with such "retail commodity transactions," whereby an entity, platform or execution venue: (i) Offers margin trading

---

57. [N. 147] *See CFTC v. McDonnell*, 287 F. Supp. 3d 213, 217 (E.D.N.Y. 2018) ("Virtual currencies can be regulated by CFTC as a commodity. . . . They fall well-within the common definition of 'commodity' as well as the [Act's] definition of 'commodities' as 'all other goods and articles . . . in which contracts for future delivery are presently or in the future dealt in.'"); *McDonnell*, 332 F. Supp. 3d at 650–51 (entering judgment against defendant following bench trial); *CFTC v. My Big Coin Pay, Inc.*, 334 F. Supp. 3d 492, 495–98 (D. Mass. 2018) (denying motion to dismiss; applying a categorical approach to interpreting "commodity" under the Act and determining that a non-bitcoin virtual currency is a "commodity" under the Act).

58. [N. 148] . . . [T]he term "virtual currency" for purposes of this interpretive guidance is meant to be viewed as synonymous with "digital currency" and "cryptocurrency" as well as any other digital asset or digital commodity that satisfies the scope of "virtual currency" described herein.

or otherwise facilitates[59] the use of margin, leverage, or financing arrangements for their retail market participants; (ii) typically to enable such participants to speculate or capitalize on price movements of the commodity — two hallmarks of a regulated futures marketplace. . . .

Despite this concern, the Commission has sought to take a deliberative and measured approach in this area . . . as the Commission does not wish to stifle nascent technological innovation. . . . .

The Commission, in interpreting the term "actual delivery" for the purposes of CEA section 2(c)(2)(D)(ii)(III)(aa), will . . . [follow] and "employ a functional approach and examine how the agreement, contract, or transaction is marketed, managed, and performed, instead of relying solely on language used by the parties in the agreement, contract, or transaction."[60] . . .

More specifically, in the Commission's view, "actual delivery" has occurred within the context of virtual currency when: . . .

(1) A customer secures:[61] (i) Possession and control of the entire quantity of the commodity, whether it was purchased on margin, or using leverage, or any other financing arrangement, and (ii) the ability to use the entire quantity of the commodity freely in commerce (away from any particular execution venue) no later than 28 days from the date of the transaction and at all times thereafter; and

(2) The offeror[62] and counterparty seller (including any of their respective affiliates or other persons acting in concert with the offeror or counterparty seller on a similar basis) . . . do not retain any interest in, legal right, or control over any of the commodity purchased on margin, leverage, or other financing arrangement at the expiration of 28 days from the date of the transaction.[63] . . .

[A] sham delivery is not consistent with the Commission's interpretation of the term "actual delivery." As noted above, the Commission believes that actual delivery occurs when the offeror and counterparty seller, including their agents, cease

---

59. [N. 152] As noted earlier, CEA section 2(c)(2)(D)(i) captures any such retail transaction entered into, or offered on a leveraged or margined basis, or financed by the offeror, the counterparty, or a person acting in concert with the offeror or counterparty on a similar basis. The Commission views any financing arrangements facilitated, arranged, or otherwise endorsed by the offeror or counterparty to satisfy this statutory definition for purposes of this interpretive guidance.

60. [N. 159] 78 FR at 52428.

61. [N. 163] While this interpretation speaks to the customer, the burden of proof would always rest on the party that relies on this exception from the Commission's jurisdiction in CEA section 2(c)(2)(D). *See CFTC v. Monex Credit Company, et al.*, 931 F.3d 966, 973 (9th Cir. 2019).

62. [N. 164] The Commission views the term "offeror" broadly in this interpretation to encompass any persons that present, solicit, or otherwise facilitate a retail commodity transaction under the Act. As noted, an offeror may include those with operational control of a particular blockchain protocol. . . .

63. [N. 166] Among other things, the Commission may look at whether the offeror or seller retain any ability to access or withdraw any quantity of the commodity purchased from the purchaser's account or wallet.

to retain any interest, legal right, or control whatsoever . . . in the virtual currency acquired by the purchaser at the expiration of 28 days from the date of entering into the transaction or at any time prior to expiration of the 28-day period once "actual delivery" occurs. Indeed, in its simplest form, actual delivery of virtual currency connotes the ability of a purchaser to utilize the virtual currency purchased "on the spot" as a medium of exchange in commerce or within the entirety of its relevant blockchain ecosystem.

The Commission believes that, in the context of an "actual delivery" determination in virtual currency, physical settlement involving the entire amount of purchased commodity must occur. A cash settlement or offset mechanism, as described in Example 5 below, is not consistent with the Commission's interpretation. The distinction between physical settlement and cash settlement in this context is akin to settlement of a spot foreign currency transaction at a commercial bank or hotel in a foreign nation — the customer receives physical foreign currency, not U.S. dollars. As mentioned, actual delivery occurs if such physical settlement occurs within 28 days from the date on which the "agreement, contract, or transaction is entered into." . . .

While the preponderance of authority supports that virtual currency is a commodity, in some circumstances, it is a security. As a security, it is subject to the jurisdiction of the SEC, not the CFTC.

SEC v. NAC Foundation, LLC

2021 WL 76736 (N.D. Cal. Jan. 8, 2021)

Richard Seeborg, United States District Judge . . .

In successfully raising millions through an "initial coin offering" ("ICO"), the NAC Foundation (a blockchain development company), along with its CEO, Marcus Rowland Andrade (collectively, "defendants"), also raised a few governmental eyebrows. Two enforcement actions followed: a criminal indictment against Andrade for wire fraud and money laundering, and this civil suit, brought by the Securities and Exchange Commission ("SEC"), alleging the fraudulent and unregistered sale of digital securities in violation of the 1933 Securities Act and 1934 Securities Exchange Act. Apparently keen to punch back, defendants now move to dismiss, insisting the SEC's complaint is legally deficient, factually erroneous, and borderline malicious. The SEC counters that it has stated plausible claims for relief. For the reasons set forth herein, the motion is denied. . . .

Into the sometimes uncertain world of cryptocurrency transactions, defendants sought to introduce AML BitCoin: a regulatorily compliant digital asset. Expounding their project around the time of its ICO fundraising event, defendants produced an October 2017 publication entitled "White Paper of AML BitCoin (AMLBit) and its Business Model" (the "White Paper"). There, defendants stated "AML BitCoin rests on a privately regulated public blockchain that facilitates . . . anti-money laundering [and] 'know your customer' [] compliance and identifies criminals associated with illicit transactions, while maintaining and strengthening the privacy protections for legitimate users." "[A]s a result," the White Paper went on, AML BitCoin "is compliant with a host of laws," including those of the United States.

Beyond promoting these novel features, the White Paper—which was posted to the NAC Foundation website—made three additional pertinent points about AML BitCoin. First, it explained that because certain aspects of the "privately regulated public blockchain" upon which AML BitCoin would operate were still under development, ICO participants would not be issued actual AML BitCoin tokens, but rather stand-in "ABTC tokens." These latter tokens could be exchanged on a one-for-one basis with AML BitCoin once AML BitCoin (or, more accurately, its complementary blockchain) was completed; otherwise, ABTC tokens lacked any practical use. Second, the White Paper clarified that both ABTC and its successor would be subject to "trade, [sale] and purchase . . . on participating exchanges and trading websites," and that AML BitCoin "can appreciate in value through speculative trading. . . ." Third, it took considerable pains to disclaim any theory by which the ICO might interact with U.S. securities law. This final effort accounted for a substantial portion of the White Paper. Plucking legal standards directly from the Supreme Court, defendants forcefully and repeatedly advised that ICO participation did not result in "investment contracts."

The ICO ran from October 2017 to February 2018, . . . with participants exchanging either fiat currency or other digital assets (e.g. Bitcoin) for ABTC tokens. Hoping to spur the buying along, defendants ran a parallel marketing campaign comprising press releases, social media posts, and other forms of AML BitCoin-friendly online content. Most colorfully, these efforts—which portrayed AML BitCoin's core anti-money laundering and know-your-customer features as fully functional and market-ready—included the assertion that defendants had nearly aired a Super Bowl commercial, only to be rebuffed at the last minute by the NFL and NBC.

Per the White Paper, defendants intended to distribute 76 million ABTC tokens to the public, retain 115 million tokens for internal use, and raise $100 million in the process. Ultimately, though, only $5.6 million was raised, attributable principally to purchases from some 2,400 retail U.S. participants. These proceeds were pooled in the NAC Foundation's bank accounts and digital asset wallets, for use in connection with future business activities. Although defendants took steps to ensure that ABTC tokens were available for online trading, and the tokens did indeed trade on numerous such platforms, at no time was any effort made to register ABTC (or AML BitCoin) as a security with the SEC. Accordingly, after determining that ABTC had been offered as an investment, and that defendants had made materially false statements in connection with that offering, the SEC brought suit in June 2020, seeking disgorgement of the ICO proceeds, monetary penalties, and enjoinment of the defendants from further securities-related activity. . . . Defendants now move to dismiss the action in its entirety, contending that the SEC has failed to establish, with sufficient particularity, that ABTC tokens are "securities" within the meaning of federal law. . . .

Defendants' motion stumbles on two levels. First, it improperly relies upon evidence drawn from beyond the four corners of the complaint. Second, it falls well short of demonstrating that the SEC's characterization of ABTC as a "security" is implausible for pleading purposes. . . .

[D]efendants' motion distills down to a straightforward application of the *Howey* test.[64] "To establish a claim for violation of federal securities law, it is necessary to show that the violation involved a 'security,'" which federal securities law in turn defines as, "among other things, an 'investment contract.'" *SEC v. Rubera*, 350 F.3d 1084, 1089–90 (9th Cir. 2003) (citations omitted). "Under the *Howey* test, 'an investment contract . . . means a contract, transaction, or scheme whereby a person invests his money in a common enterprise and is led to expect profits solely from the efforts of the promoter or a third party.'" *Warfield v. Alaniz*, 569 F.3d 1015, 1020 (9th Cir. 2009) (quoting *SEC v. W.J. Howey Co.*, 328 U.S. 293, 298–99, 66 S.Ct. 1100, 90 L.Ed. 1244 (1946)).

The Ninth Circuit has "distilled *Howey*'s definition into a three-part test requiring (1) an investment of money (2) in a common enterprise (3) with an expectation of profits produced by the efforts of others." *Id.* (internal quotation marks and citation omitted). Here, only the second and third *Howey* prongs are in dispute. Bearing in mind "the Supreme Court's repeated rejection of a narrow and literal reading of the definition of securities," both prongs are pled sufficiently in the SEC's complaint. *Warfield*, 569 F.3d at 1020; *see also Tcherepnin v. Knight*, 389 U.S. 332, 336, 88 S.Ct. 548, 19 L.Ed.2d 564 (1967) ("[I]n searching for the meaning and scope of the word 'security' . . . form should be disregarded for substance and the emphasis should be on economic reality.") . . .

In the Ninth Circuit, a common enterprise exists where the investment scheme involves either "horizontal commonality" or "strict vertical commonality." *Hocking v. Dubois*, 885 F.2d 1449, 1459 (9th Cir. 1989). "Horizontal commonality describes the relationship shared by two or more investors who pool their investments together and split the net profits and losses in accordance with their pro rata investments." *Hocking v. Dubois*, 839 F.2d 560, 566 (9th Cir. 1988), *aff'd in relevant part*, 885 F.2d 1449, 1459 (9th Cir. 1989). By contrast, "vertical commonality may be established by

---

64. [N. 5] Or at least, the remainder of the *serious* aspects of defendants' motion so distills. After lodging an earnest (if unpersuasive) argument that ABTC is not a security under *Howey*, defendants spill ink on two plainly spurious propositions: that the ICO resulted in "forward contracts"—as in, contracts akin to those an oil trader might make, for deferred delivery of a cash commodity—outside the SEC's jurisdiction, and that the SEC's lawsuit is rooted in a malicious intent, and characterized by ongoing misconduct. The first of these propositions is legally mistaken; the latter, both legally mistaken *and* strategically misguided. Neither is supported by applicable fact and law.

showing that the fortunes of the investors are linked with those of the promoters." *SEC v. R.G. Reynolds Enterprises, Inc.*, 952 F.2d 1125, 1130 (9th Cir. 1991) (internal quotation marks and citation omitted).

On the facts as the SEC has alleged them, it is quite plausible—and indeed, probable—that there is strict vertical commonality between the defendants and the ICO participants. Per the complaint, retail U.S. investors exchanged capital for ABTC tokens, which could, at the time of the exchange, be put to no use aside from online trading. Simultaneously, defendants retained a healthy share of ABTC tokens for their personal and corporate coffers. The ICO proceeds would fund the development of the AML BitCoin ecosystem, and each ABTC token could (eventually) be redeemed for an AML BitCoin. Thus, the "fortunes" of ICO participants—as measured by either the trading value of their ABTC tokens *or* the future trading value of AML BitCoin—were "linked" to the "fortunes" of defendants—as measured by the trading value of their ABTC tokens, the future trading value of AML BitCoin, *or* the general success of their enterprise (which would, as a matter of efficient market theory, drive the price of both digital assets). *Howey's* second prong is therefore satisfied.[65] . . .

The third *Howey* prong, "requiring an expectation of profits produced by the efforts of others, involves two distinct concepts: whether a transaction involves any expectation of profit and whether the profits are a product of the efforts of a person other than the investor." *Warfield*, 569 F.3d at 1020 (internal quotation marks omitted); *see also id.* at 1020 n.6 (observing that other circuits "have identified *Howey's* test as a four-part test"). . . .

Here, the SEC has averred ample facts to meet both components of *Howey's* final prong. With the White Paper, ICO participants were "led to expect" that both ABTC tokens and AML BitCoins would be tradeable on stock market-like exchanges, and that the latter (and, implicitly, the former) could "appreciate in value through speculative trading." *Id.*; *see also SEC v. Hui Feng*, 935 F.3d 721, 730–31 (9th Cir. 2019) (explaining that an "expectation of profit" under *Howey* does not require the investor to be motivated solely by profit). Tellingly, even as the White Paper made all this clear, it failed to apprise participants of *any* practical ABTC token use: while they could be redeemed for AML BitCoin at some future point, they were, at the time of the transaction, solely objects for trading. Nor, given the totality of circumstances,

---

65. [N. 6] This finding comports with that made by another district court, outside this circuit, scrutinizing a similar ICO-based fact pattern. In *SEC v. Telegram Group, Inc.*, the court found that "the SEC ha[d] made a substantial showing of strict vertical commonality" where each ICO participant's "anticipated profits were directly dependent on [defendants'] success in developing and launching" the underlying blockchain project. 448 F.Supp.3d 352, 370 (S.D.N.Y. 2020). So too here. Moreover, whereas the *Telegram* defendants had pledged eventually to relinquish control of all tokens they had retained during the ICO process, no such pledge has been made here. *Id.* In this respect, defendants' "financial fortunes" are, in this case, more closely tied to that of ICO participants than were the fortunes of the *Telegram* defendants.

can defendants brush away the inference that an objectively reasonable ABTC purchaser likely viewed his or her prospective trading success as a function of the defendants' efforts: after all, the demand for ABTC or AML BitCoin, as reflected in those assets' pricing, would rely almost exclusively on market perception of defendants' work product.[66] Proceeding with a mind toward "economic reality," the complaint therefore meets the final *Howey* prong. *Tcherepnin*, 389 U.S. at 336, 88 S.Ct. 548. All told, then — and over defendants' strenuous protestations — the SEC adequately has pled the defendants' sale of an unregistered security. . . .

Consistent with the foregoing, the motion to dismiss is denied.

———————

Often a security is self-identified by, for example, being certificated as such, seeking registration as a security with the SEC, or being issued under an exemption from registration with the SEC as a security. "Investment contracts" differ in this regard because, while having sufficient attributes of securities, they do not necessarily have the exterior indicia. The *Howey* test, as applied by *SEC v. NAC Foundation* is a necessary analytical component with respect to any virtual currency offering. It is hard to imagine a virtual currency that does not involve "investment of money" by the purchaser in a "common enterprise." Therefore, whether there is an "expectation of profits produced by the efforts of others" would seem to be the critical element.

E. Commodity Options

Commodity options (including foreign exchange options) generally have the same regulatory treatment as swaps, with an exception for "trade options," discussed below, or if traded on a designated contract market. When traded on a designated contract market, typically as options on commodity futures contracts, commodity options are treated identically to commodity futures.[67]

Trade options are in some cases exempt from the entirety of the swaps regulatory regime. Their evolution to get to that point has been unique and irregular.

———————

66. [N. 7] Put differently, ICO participants "recognized that an investment in [ABTC tokens] was a bet that [defendants] could successfully encourage the mass adoption of [AML BitCoin], thereby enabling a high potential return" on either the "resale of [ABTC tokens]" or the future sale of AML BitCoin, for which ABTC tokens could be redeemed. *Telegram*, 448 F.Supp.3d 352, 377 (citations omitted); *see also SEC v. Kik Interactive, Inc.*,——F.Supp.3d——, —— , 2020 WL 5819770, at *7 (S.D.N.Y. Sep. 30, 2020) (citations omitted) (explaining, on analogous facts, that "the value of" an ICO investment relies heavily on the developers "entrepreneurial and managerial efforts"; without the developers' "promised digital ecosystem," a cryptocurrency token "would be worthless").

67. Technically, the CFTC's jurisdiction for an option on a commodity futures contract is based on Commodity Exchange Act § 2(a)(1), while for an option on a commodity it is based on Commodity Exchange Act § 4c(b).

Gary E. Kalbaugh, *The Erratic Journey of U.S. Commodity Options Regulation*

33 No. 10 Futures & Derivatives L. Rep. 1 (Nov. 2013)

... The regulatory history of commodity options has been ... circuitous. It includes moments of prohibition; forays into regulated exchange-traded and off-exchange commodity options; retrenchments into prohibitions; differing treatments for agricultural commodity options, options for physical delivery of non-agricultural products and options on non-agricultural futures; the inclusion of options for physical delivery of non-agricultural products and options on non-agricultural futures in the same framework for regulation of other derivatives; and, little more than a year ago, the convergence of treatment of options on agricultural commodities with other derivatives along with an exemption for commercial interests. ...

The General Prohibition on Commodity Options

Prior to Federal regulation of commodity options, their status frequently varied. The Chicago Board of Trade prohibited them in 1865, before permitting them in 1869.[68] Ruling in a bankruptcy case in 1874, a Federal court concluded that cash-settled options were prohibited under Illinois law as contracts which "partake of all of the characteristics of a wager" the effect of which "is to beget wild speculations, to derange prices, to make prices artificially high or low ... thereby tending to destroy healthy business and unsettle legitimate commerce. ..." That same year the Illinois legislature banned grain options. ... From 1906–1913 the Chicago Board of Trade permitted "indemnities" which, although economically identical to options, were characterized as being akin to insurance.[69] In 1913, the Illinois legislature amended the 1874 legislation to narrow the prohibition on options only to those that were intended to be cash-settled. ...

By 1932, the House of Representatives Committee on Agriculture had reported a bill prohibiting options on grain and additional commodities[70] as "gambling transactions ... objectionable also because they burden interstate commerce in that they lend themselves to improper uses by professional speculators and short sellers." ...

[T]he Commodity Exchange Act of 1936 simply prohibited outright any options on the commodities subject to the statute. ...

The commodities subject to the Commodity Exchange Act were broader than the grains defined in the Grain Futures Act and ultimately included "wheat, cotton, rice, corn, oats, barley, rye, flaxseed, grain sorghums, mill feeds, butter, eggs, Solanum tuberosum (Irish potatoes), wool, wool tops, fats and oils (including lard,

---

68. [N. 5] *See* Report of the Federal Trade Commission on the Grain Trade, Vol. II, Terminal Grain Markets and Exchanges, September 15, 1920, Federal Trade Commission, Washington, Government Printing Office (1920), 113.

69. [N. 10] Report of the Federal Trade Commission on the Grain Trade, Vol. II, Terminal Grain Markets and Exchanges, 118.

70. [N. 22] 72 H.R. 12287.

tallow, cottonseed oil, peanut oil, soybean oil and all other fats and oils), cotton-seed meal, cottonseed, peanuts, soybeans, soybean meal, livestock, livestock products, and frozen concentrated orange juice."[71] These commodities will be referred to herein as the "Enumerated Commodities" since, as a category, they continued until recently to have significant regulatory relevance.

Fraud in Options on Non-Enumerated Commodities

Although options on Enumerated Commodities were forbidden, the statutory prohibition did not apply to options on non-Enumerated Commodities. . . . [T]hey seemingly fell into a regulatory lacuna between the Securities and Exchange Commission and the Commodity Exchange Commission, the body established by the Commodity Exchange Act to administer the act. . . . Numerous commodity option firm failures occurred, in many cases amidst allegations of fraud. The most notorious one, Goldstein, Samuelson, Inc., parlayed $800 in capital into an investment empire selling $88 million in options and that eventually resulted in $70 million in customer losses.[72]

Divided Statutory Treatment for Agricultural and non-Agricultural Commodities

To remedy the unregulated status of non-Enumerated Commodity futures and options, the Commodity Futures Trading Commission Act of 1974 . . . expanded [the definition of commodity"] to include, in addition to the Enumerated Commodities, "all other goods and articles . . . and all services, rights, and interests in which contracts for future delivery are presently or in the future dealt in. . . ." The Commodity Futures Trading Commission Act . . . maintained the Commodity Exchange Act's prohibition on options trading in Enumerated Commodities . . . [and] prohibited any options on non-Enumerated Commodities unless explicitly permitted under regulations of the newly formed Commodity Futures Trading Commission. . . .

The First Attempt to Regulate Off-Exchange Options. . . .

[A]fter evaluating the possible prohibition of options on non-Enumerated Commodities to parallel the one in place via statute with respect to Enumerated Commodities,[73] the CFTC instead proposed a regulatory plan for options on non-Enumerated Commodities comprised of two phases. . . . The regulatory framework for the first phase was . . . comprised of a general prohibition on all trading of options on Enumerated Commodities combined with two exemptions which, in recognizable forms, survive in some way to the present. . . .

---

71. [N. 31] Commodity Exchange Act, Section 2(a). . . .

72. [N. 35] Joseph B. Dial, Commissioner, Commodity Futures Trading Commission, Status Report on Regulatory and Self-Regulatory Responses to the Barings Bankruptcy, 18th Annual Commodities Law Institute and 4th Annual Financial Services Law Institute," October 19, 1995, available at http://www.cftc.gov/opa/speeches/opachic95s.htm (accessed on August 17, 2013).

73. [N. 43] *See* Commodity Options: Temporary Regulations, 40 FR 49360 (October 22, 1975), 49360–49361. . . .

The first exemption was an exemption which required any person "soliciting or accepting orders for the purchase or sale of commodity options," or supervising any such person, to register as an associated person of a futures commission merchant. . . . Futures commission merchants engaged in commodity option transactions were required to have more capital than futures commission merchants who limited their business to futures transactions. . . . This exemption existed to accommodate participation by speculators and non-speculator alike in the retail market in so-called "London options," i.e. options bought and sold on well-established options exchanges in London on precious metals and "world commodities" such as coffee and cocoa, and options on precious metals offered directly by domestic dealers. . . .

The other exemption was the so-called "trade option" exemption which allowed a commodity option to be offered without the dealer option requirements outlined above so long as the offeree had "a reasonable basis to believe that the option is offered to a producer, processor, or commercial user of, or a merchant handling, the commodity which is the subject of the commodity option transaction" and that the offeree entered "into the commodity option transaction solely for purposes related to its business as such."[74] This exemption existed to accommodate commercial interests trading in commodity options for non-speculative purposes, such as hedging. . . .

[C]iting "fraudulent and other unlawful and unsound practices" in commodity options sales activities "[d]espite implementation and enforcement of the Commission's interim commodity option regulations" the CFTC . . . [declared a suspension of] all commodity option trading, including dealer options, other than option sales relying on the trade option exemption . . . effective [June 1, 1978]. . . . Motivation for the ban was provided by the continuation of commodity option fraud on a par with that which existed before the Commodity Futures Trading Commission Act established CFTC jurisdiction.[75] In one particularly egregious fraud, Alan Abrahams, an escaped convict going by the name of James A. Carr, established Lloyd Carr & Co. in July 1976 just one month after a spree of wrongdoing including an escape from a New Jersey prison farm in 1974, an arrest in Montreal and a disappearance before his deportation hearing, another arrest in Nassau where he apparently convinced the U.S. Consul to front his bail before fleeing, and a third arrest in California after floating a bad check to buy a used car.[76] Annual sales at Lloyd Carr & Co. peaked at $50 million, despite operating in an environment where "some salesmen regularly made trips to the lavatory to smoke marijuana." . . .

---

74. [N. 54] [Regulation and Fraud in Connection with Commodity and Commodity Option Transactions,] 41 FR 51808, 51815 [(November 24, 1976)].

75. [N. 61] *See* "Futures Trading Act of 1982," S.Rep. 97-384, 16.

76. [N. 62] *See* Outlaw's Legacy: How a Flim-Flam Man Causes a Big Shake-up in Commodity Options, Wall Street Journal, February 14, 1978. The Lloyd Carr & Co. scandal also resulted in Dun & Bradstreet Inc.'s payment of a $2.6 million settlement in relation to a list of prospective customers allegedly sold to Lloyd Carr & Co. *See* Dun & Bradstreet Inc. to Pay $2.6 Million to Settle Fraud Case, Wall Street Journal, March 30, 1983.

On May 11, 1978, innocents expected to be harmed by the approaching ban petitioned the CFTC to disapply the ban to parties currently utilizing the dealer exemption and otherwise in good standing. . . . The CFTC relented and, just before the June 1 deadline for the effective date of the ban, provided that the dealer exemption would remain available for entities which, on May 1, 1978, were "both in the business of granting options on a physical commodity and in the business of buying, selling, producing, or otherwise utilizing that commodity" so long as net worth and other criteria aimed at customer protection were met. . . .

[T]he Futures Trading Act of 1978 codified many of the CFTC's recent actions with respect to commodity options. . . .

Following passage of the Futures Trading Act, the CFTC implemented a final rule restating much of the dealer option exemption regime . . . [without a] notice of proposed rulemaking. . . .

[T]he rule was withdrawn and re-proposed in substantially similar form one month later. The rule was re-re-proposed in a substantially modified form again over two years later in April 1981 presumably spurred by an industry campaign to roll-back the options prohibition to allow non-grandfathered entities to trade dealer options[77] and then was the subject of an advanced notice of a proposed rulemaking in March 1985.[78] It was never finalized, leaving the prohibition on off- exchange options trading intact until the passage of the Commodity Futures Modernization Act . . . save for grandfathered dealers relying on the dealer option exemption as of May 1, 1978 and for parties relying on the trade option exemption. . . .

A Renewed Effort for Exchange-Traded Commodity Options

The early 1980s saw a renewed drive to establish exchange-traded commodity options trading. . . .

Congress' passage of the Futures Trading Act of 1982 allowed for the possibility, with CFTC assent, of trading options on Enumerated Commodities. . . .

[B]y January 1987, the exchange trading of commodity options — without further distinction between options on non-Enumerated Commodity futures, non-Enumerated Commodity physicals or Enumerated Commodities — was permanently established. . . .

Commodity Futures Modernization Act of 2000

The impact of the Commodity Futures Modernization Act was as sweeping with respect to commodity options as it was for other derivatives. Other than with regard to "agricultural commodities" and fraud, the CFTC's jurisdiction over off-exchange derivatives transactions between "eligible contract participants," i.e. high net worth

---

77. [N. 79] *See* H.J. Maidenberg, Commodities; Key Topics at Industry Convention, New York Times, March 9, 1981.

78. [N. 80] *See* Regulations Permitting the Grant, Offer and Sale of Options on Physical Commodities (Dealer and Trade Options), 50 FR 10786-01 (March 18, 1985).

entities or persons,[79] was eviscerated.[80] In a way, the clock was wound back to 1975. Just like in 1975, the CFTC had anti-fraud jurisdiction over all commodity options. The primary differences were that now: (1) exchange-traded options were permissible; and (2) instead of off-exchange options on Enumerated Commodities being prohibited, the CFTC's regulations now only applied to the "agricultural commodities," a category comprised of, at a minimum, the Enumerated Commodities.[81]

The Dodd-Frank Act

The interlude of deregulation of most commodity options — and most derivatives for that matter — was to last less than a decade. In 2010, the Dodd-Frank Wall Street Reform and Consumer Protection Act, known as the Dodd-Frank Act, granted the CFTC jurisdiction over nearly all swaps . . . [defined as including] all commodity options other than exchange-traded options on futures over which the CFTC maintained its pre-Dodd-Frank Act jurisdiction.[82] The Dodd-Frank Act also imposed an intricate regulatory apparatus with respect to swaps activities. . . .

Options on "agricultural commodities," having remained subject to CFTC regulation even after the passage of the . . . [Commodity Futures Modernization Act] continued to be subject to CFTC regulation (along with agricultural swaps).[83] To harmonize the nascent regulatory regime for swaps with that for options on "agricultural commodities" and agricultural swaps, the CFTC proposed merging the preexisting regulatory regime for agricultural options and swaps into Dodd-Frank's regulatory regime for all other swaps.[84] The final rules provide for this absorption of the agricultural swaps and options regime into the Dodd-Frank regulatory regime

---

79. [N. 98] *See* Commodity Futures Modernization Act, Section 101(4) adding Commodity Exchange Act, Section 1a(12) (now Section 1a(18)).

80. [N. 99] *See* Commodity Futures Modernization Act, Sections 103, 105(b) and 106 adding Commodity Exchange Act, Sections 2(d), 2(g) and 2(h). Note, however, that the CFTC did not modify its Part 32 rules relating to commodity options (17 CFR Part 32 (2000)) despite their scope as theoretically regulating options on Enumerated Commodities and non-Enumerated Commodities. Moreover, despite apparently contradictory sections in the Commodity Futures Modernization Act (*see* Commodity Futures Modernization Act Sections 103, 105(b) and 106 adding Commodity Exchange Act, Sections 2(d), 2(g) and 2(h) and Section 301 defining "swap agreement," albeit not explicitly in relation to the Commodity Exchange Act), the CFTC continued to claim "plenary authority over [commodity] options . . . ," not just retail commodity options. *See* Agricultural Swaps, 75 FR 59666-01 (September 28, 2010), 59667–59668 and 76 FR 6095-01, 6098.

81. [N. 100] Until the Dodd-Frank Act mandated otherwise, the term "agricultural commodity" was left undefined by statute or the CFTC. However, "agricultural commodities" were viewed by the CFTC as having a broader scope than the Enumerated Commodities. *See* 75 FR 59666-01 (September 28, 2010), 59667.

82. [N. 102] *See* Dodd-Frank Act, Section 721(a)(21) adding Commodity Exchange Act, Section 1a(47).

83. [N. 104] *See* Commodity Futures Modernization Act, Sections 103, 105(b) and 106 adding Commodity Exchange Act, Sections 2(d), 2(g) and 2(h).

84. [N. 105] The CFTC did this in a number of proposals while, in parallel, finalizing the definition of "agricultural commodity". *See* Agricultural Commodity Definitions, 75 FR 65586-01 (October 26, 2010) and Agricultural Commodity Definitions, 76 FR 41048-01 (July 13, 2011) for the final rules defining "agricultural commodity" in 17 CFR § 1.3(zz) and 75 FR 59666-01 and 76 FR 6095 for

for swaps while reinstating a trade option exemption covering non-financial commodities (including agricultural options).

The trade option exemption itself requires that the offeree be a "producer, processor, or commercial user of, or a merchant handling the commodity that is the subject of the commodity option transaction, or the products or by-products thereof, and such offeree is offered or entering into the commodity option transaction solely for purposes related to its business as such"[85] and that the offeror either meet the preceding criteria or be an eligible contract participant.[86] Additionally, the offeror must have a "reasonable basis to believe" that the offeree meets the trade option criteria . . . [and] an intent to physically deliver the commodity underlying the option.[87] Trade options are generally exempt "from the rules otherwise applicable to other swaps (i.e., the Dodd-Frank swaps regime)." . . . CFTC-registered swap dealers and major swap participants must comply with risk management, capital and margin requirements in addition to recordkeeping and reporting requirements.[88]

Options on agricultural commodities had evolved from being prohibited outright to being, in the context of trade options, the least regulated derivative under the CFTC's jurisdiction. . . .

After a long regulatory journey of prohibitions, deregulation, and everything in-between, today, options are treated identically to futures if traded on a futures exchange (although, ordinarily, they are traded as options on commodity futures subject to Commodity Exchange Act section 2(a)(1)) and, otherwise, as swaps. The main exception — the trade option exception — applies to physically delivered options purchased by commercial entities. For commercial entities, these are exempt from all swap requirements.

The offeree must be a "producer, processor, or commercial user of, or a merchant handling" the relevant commodity or a by-product of the commodity and it must be for purposes related to its commercial activities.[89] The offeror must meet the same criteria or be an eligible contract participant.[90]

In the immediate aftermath of the Dodd-Frank Act, commercial entities availing themselves of the exemption had some reporting and other obligations. The CFTC

----

the proposals to merge the agricultural option and swap regimes with the Dodd-Frank mandated swap regime.

85. [N. 106] 17 CFR § 32.3(a)(2).

86. [N. 107] 17 CFR § 32.3(a)(1).

87. [N. 109] *See* Agricultural Swaps, 76 FR 49291-01 (August 10, 2011), Commodity Options, 77 FR 25320 (April 27, 2012) and 17 CFR § 32.3(a)(3). The trade option exemption can apply to all commodity options save for those on "excluded commodities" which are generally defined as financial commodities. *See* Commodity Exchange Act, Section 1a(19).

88. [N. 112] *See* 76 FR 25320, 25328 for the specific compliance obligations applying to trade option counterparties which are registered with the CFTC as swap dealers or major swap participants.

89. 17 C.F.R. § 32.3(a)(2).

90. 17 C.F.R. § 32.3(a)(1).

has disapplied all requirements other than that, when trading with a swap dealer or major swap participant, the commercial entity must obtain a "legal entity identifier" so that the swap dealer or major swap participant can comply with its swap trade reporting obligations.[91]

Figure 14.1 Comparison of CFTC's Jurisdiction Over Foreign Exchange and Commodities in General

CFTC Jurisdiction Over:	Foreign Exchange	Commodities in General
Futures	Yes	Yes
Exchange-Traded Options	Yes, unless traded on securities exchange	Yes
Off-exchange Options	Yes, treated as swaps and with additional CFTC jurisdictional basis if traded with a retail customer (i.e., a person that is not an "eligible contract participant") and an entity that is not regulated by a "Federal regulatory agency" other than the SEC	Yes, unless qualifying as a "trade option"
Forwards	Yes but, if physically settled, it will not be treated as a swap for calculation of swap dealer *de minimis* and CFTC regulations regarding clearing, margin, and on-facility trading	Yes, (1) if not settled by actual delivery within 28 days and if entered into with or offered to a retail counterparty on a leveraged or margined basis, or financed by the offeror, the counterparty, or a person acting in concert with the offeror or counterparty on a similar basis; or (2) with respect to manipulation and fraud
Swaps	Yes but, if physically settled, it will not be treated as a swap for calculation of swap dealer *de minimis* and CFTC regulations regarding clearing, margin, and on-facility trading	Yes
Spot	Yes, if entered into with or offered to a retail counterparty by an entity that is not regulated by a "Federal regulatory agency" on a leveraged or margined basis, or financed by the offeror, the counterparty, or a person acting in concert with the offeror or counterparty on a similar basis (if not physically settled within 2 days or customary spot settlement period for the currency — *see* "Forwards" *supra*)	Yes, with respect to manipulation and fraud (if not settled by actual delivery within 28 days — *see* "Forwards" *supra*)

---

91. *See, generally,* CFTC, *Trade Options,* 81 Fed. Reg. 14966 (Mar. 21, 2016).

Questions and Comments

1. What may have been some of the motivations underlying the Department of the Treasury's lobbying for the "Treasury Amendment" in the time period immediately preceding passage of the Commodity Futures Trading Commission Act of 1974?

2. Why did the Dodd-Frank Act, with respect to foreign exchange swaps and foreign exchange forwards, maintain the regulatory tradition of treating foreign exchange transactions distinctly?

3. Consider why Congress in passing the Dodd-Frank Act only allowed limited foreign exchange exemptions from the Dodd-Frank Act and only with respect to physically-settled foreign exchange swaps and foreign exchange forwards. In what ways do these merit distinct regulatory treatment from, say, a cross-currency swap, currency option, or non-deliverable foreign exchange forward?

4. Historically, the CFTC has struggled to regulate commodity options, even resorting to nearly entirely prohibiting them. Is there a reason options might raise public policy concerns not arising with futures? If they do, assess whether prohibition is the best remedy.

5. There are no registered leverage transaction merchants. Why might that be the case? Is making regulatory requirements so burdensome as to dissuade anyone to register tantamount to prohibiting the activity? If prohibition is the policy, why would Congress not have simply prohibited engaging in leverage transaction merchant activities by statute?

6. Do you see a future for virtual currency? If so, what role do you see it playing? In what ways might it impact society at large?

7. Consider the difficult role of a regulator that seeks to maintain an existing prescriptive regulatory regime while maintaining flexibility to accommodate innovation in the marketplace. What are some strategies for simultaneously achieving these goals? Is it possible to do so?

Chapter 15

Fraud and Market Manipulation

A. Background

In previous chapters, we covered the CFTC's and self-regulatory organizations' authority over registrants, including for rule violations. This chapter focuses on prohibitions in the Commodity Exchange Act and CFTC rules against fraudulent or manipulative marketplace conduct. These prohibitions are applicable to any trader in the marketplace and can be enforced by the CFTC in a civil enforcement action or the Department of Justice in a criminal case. This chapter also provides an overview of disciplinary actions by self-regulatory organizations such as exchanges or the National Futures Association.

The Dodd-Frank Act greatly expanded the CFTC's enforcement authority by broadening the scope of conduct that could result in CFTC enforcement actions. It also included swaps within the scope of the entire range of the CFTC's enforcement authority, instead of just its anti-fraud authority. We will examine the CFTC's authority, as expanded. Though some of the cases we look at are pre-Dodd-Frank Act, these represent the baseline for the CFTC's authority since they occurred before it was expanded.

The expansion of the CFTC's authority tracks a similar expansion in CFTC enforcement awards, shown in figure 15.1 below, with a peak at the height of the LIBOR rates benchmark scandal. As can be seen by figure 15.2, while the total size of enforcement actions has since dropped from its peak in 2014 and 2015, the cumulative total of awards is at a record high.

In addition to the enforcement powers granted to the CFTC, the Commodity Exchange Act and CFTC rules directly or indirectly provide various means for private enforcement of the Act through court proceedings or in reparations proceedings before the CFTC. We examine these in chapter 16.

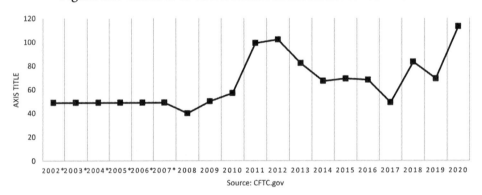

Figure 15.1 CFTC Civil Penalties and Restitution Payments (in Millions): 2002–2020

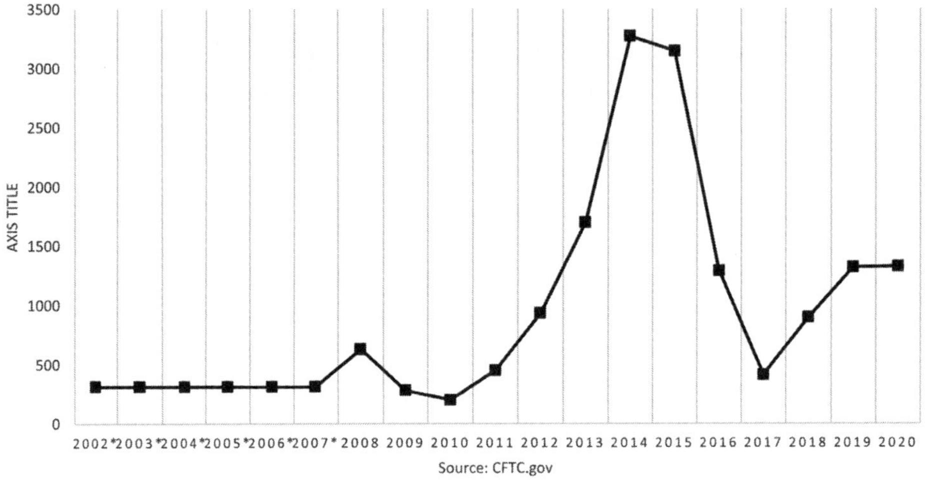

Source: CFTC.gov

Figure 15.2 Number of CFTC Enforcement Actions: 2002–2020

Source: CFTC.gov

B. General Fraud Prohibition

It has been noted that "[f]raud is as varied as the ingenuity of man."[1] A large motivation for the regulation of marketplaces is the prevention of fraud. Fraud has many guises. It spans from something as straightforward as embezzlement to scams as elaborate and intricate as so-called Ponzi schemes.[2]

---

1. *All Service Life Ins. Corp. v. Catling,* 171 F. Supp. 686 (S.D. Cal. 1959).

2. A Ponzi scheme is where a fraudster solicits money from investors. The first to invest are given large returns based on money solicited from newer investors. These returns encourage more investment. Pay-offs continue until there are not enough new investors to pay the false returns to existing investors. The scheme is named after Charles Ponzi, a perpetrator of such a fraud in the early twentieth century. *See Cunningham v. Brown,* 265 U.S. 1 (1924).

We usually think of fraud as an intentional act done by a fraudster or con artist to victimize someone else. As we will discuss below, in the post-Dodd-Frank era, the CFTC by rule has enacted prohibitions against "reckless" fraud (and manipulation). The question of how this comports with the common understanding of what is "fraud" is one we will revisit.

1. Civil Proceedings

a. Prohibitions

The Commodity Exchange Act makes it unlawful in connection with a commodity future or swap:

> . . . (A) to cheat or defraud or attempt to cheat or defraud the other [party to the transaction or potential transaction]; (B) willfully to make or cause to be made to the other person any false report[,] . . . statement or . . . record; [or] (C) willfully to deceive or attempt to deceive the other person by any means whatsoever in regard to any order or contract. . . .[3]

With respect to swaps particularly, the Commodity Exchange Act imposes an additional potential basis for liability. A party is prohibited from entering "into a swap knowing, or acting in reckless disregard of the fact, that its counterparty will use the swap as part of a device, scheme, or artifice to defraud any third party. . . ."[4]

This swap-specific provision exists because many categories of swaps are bilaterally negotiated, making substantive transaction-related discussions and coordination between the parties possible. This is less of a possibility in a futures trade executed on a designated contract market since the contracts there are standardized and each party normally does not know with whom they traded due to the use of anonymous order books.

Finally, the CFTC by rule imposes a recklessness standard by making it unlawful:

> in connection with any swap, or contract of sale of any commodity in interstate commerce, or contract for future delivery on or subject to the rules of any [designated contract market, swap execution facility, derivatives clearing organization, or swap data repository], to intentionally or recklessly:
>
> (1) Use or employ, or attempt to use or employ, any manipulative device, scheme, or artifice to defraud;
>
> (2) Make, or attempt to make, any untrue or misleading statement of a material fact or to omit to state a material fact necessary in order to make the statements made not untrue or misleading; [or]
>
> (3) Engage, or attempt to engage, in any act, practice, or course of business, which operates or would operate as a fraud or deceit upon any person. . . .[5]

---

3. Commodity Exchange Act § 4b(a).
4. Commodity Exchange Act § 4c(a)(7).
5. 17 C.F.R. § 180.1.

We will discuss how a "reckless" standard is applied to fraud or market manipulation in more detail below in section C.1.

b. Sanctions and Statute of Limitation

The CFTC has the authority to initiate and conduct an administrative enforcement hearing for violation of the Commodity Exchange Act or any CFTC rule[6] and may impose:

- A prohibition on trading on a designated contract market or swap execution facility;[7]
- Suspension of the registration of any CFTC registrant;[8]
- Penalties of up to the greater of $170,129 per violation in a CFTC enforcement action, $187,432 if in federal district court, $1,227,202 million for certain market manipulation offenses, or triple the monetary gain from the violation;[9] and
- Restitution for any customer losses caused by the violation.[10]

However, in applying any of these remedies it is subject to a federal five-year statute of limitation on any "fine, penalty, or forfeiture."[11] The CFTC has in the past successfully argued that equitable remedies such as disgorgement or restitution are not fines, penalties, or forfeitures subject to the five-year statute of limitation.[12] Supreme Court precedent with respect to a similar enforcement tactic by the SEC raises the question of whether the CFTC's use of similar tactics will be upheld going forward.

Kokesh v. SEC

137 S. Ct. 1635 (2017)

Justice Sotomayor delivered the opinion of the Court.

A 5-year statute of limitations applies to any "action, suit or proceeding for the enforcement of any civil fine, penalty, or forfeiture, pecuniary or otherwise." 28 U.S.C. § 2462. This case presents the question whether § 2462 applies to claims for disgorgement imposed as a sanction for violating a federal securities law. The Court holds that it does. Disgorgement in the securities-enforcement context is a "penalty" within the meaning of § 2462, and so disgorgement actions must be commenced within five years of the date the claim accrues. . . .

---

6. Commodity Exchange Act § 6(c)(4).

7. Commodity Exchange Act § 6(c)(4)(C)(ii)(I).

8. Commodity Exchange Act § 6(c)(4)(C)(ii)(II).

9. Commodity Exchange Act § 6(c)(10)(C). The amounts frequently change because they are indexed to inflation. *See, e.g.,* CFTC, *Annual Adjustment of Civil Monetary Penalties to Reflect Inflation-2021,* 86 Fed. Reg. 7802 (Feb. 2, 2021).

10. Commodity Exchange Act § 6(c)(10)(D).

11. 28 U.S.C. § 2462.

12. *See, e.g., CFTC v. Reisinger,* 2013 WL 3791691 *7-10 (N.D. Ill. July 18, 2013).

This Court has already held that the 5-year statute of limitations set forth in 28 U.S.C. § 2462 applies when the [Securities and Exchange Commission (the "Commission" or "SEC")] . . . seeks statutory monetary penalties. *See Gabelli v. SEC*, 568 U.S. 442, 454, 133 S.Ct. 1216, 185 L.Ed.2d 297 (2013). The question here is whether § 2462, which applies to any "action, suit or proceeding for the enforcement of any civil fine, penalty, or forfeiture, pecuniary or otherwise," also applies when the SEC seeks disgorgement. . . .

Charles Kokesh owned two investment-adviser firms that provided investment advice to business-development companies. In late 2009, the Commission commenced an enforcement action in Federal District Court alleging that between 1995 and 2009, Kokesh, through his firms, misappropriated $34.9 million from four of those development companies. The Commission further alleged that, in order to conceal the misappropriation, Kokesh caused the filing of false and misleading SEC reports and proxy statements. The Commission sought civil monetary penalties, disgorgement, and an injunction barring Kokesh from violating securities laws in the future.

After a 5-day trial, a jury found that Kokesh's actions violated the Investment Company Act of 1940, . . . the Investment Advisers Act of 1940, . . . and the Securities Exchange Act of 1934. . . . The District Court then turned to the task of imposing penalties sought by the Commission. As to the civil monetary penalties, the District Court determined that § 2462's 5-year limitations period precluded any penalties for misappropriation occurring prior to October 27, 2004 — that is, five years prior to the date the Commission filed the complaint. . . . The court ordered Kokesh to pay a civil penalty of $2,354,593, which represented "the amount of funds that [Kokesh] himself received during the limitations period." Regarding the Commission's request for a $34.9 million disgorgement judgment — $29.9 million of which resulted from violations outside the limitations period — the court agreed with the Commission that because disgorgement is not a "penalty" within the meaning of § 2462, no limitations period applied. The court therefore entered a disgorgement judgment in the amount of $34.9 million and ordered Kokesh to pay an additional $18.1 million in prejudgment interest.

The Court of Appeals for the Tenth Circuit affirmed. 834 F.3d 1158 (2016). It agreed with the District Court that disgorgement is not a penalty, and further found that disgorgement is not a forfeiture. . . .

Statutes of limitations "se[t] a fixed date when exposure to the specified Government enforcement efforts en[d]." *Gabelli*, 568 U.S., at 448, 133 S.Ct. 1216. Such limits are "'vital to the welfare of society'" and rest on the principle that "'even wrongdoers are entitled to assume that their sins may be forgotten.'" *Id.*, at 449, 133 S.Ct. 1216. The statute of limitations at issue here — 28 U.S.C. § 2462 — finds its roots in a law enacted nearly two centuries ago. 568 U.S., at 445, 133 S.Ct. 1216. In its current form, § 2462 establishes a 5-year limitations period for "an action, suit or proceeding for the enforcement of any civil fine, penalty, or forfeiture." This limitations period applies here if SEC disgorgement qualifies as either a fine, penalty, or forfeiture. We hold that SEC disgorgement constitutes a penalty.[13] . . .

SEC disgorgement is imposed by the courts as a consequence for violating . . . public laws. The violation for which the remedy is sought is committed against the United States rather than an aggrieved individual — this is why, for example, a securities-enforcement action may proceed even if victims do not support or are not parties to the prosecution. As the Government concedes, "[w]hen the SEC seeks disgorgement, it acts in the public interest, to remedy harm to the public at large, rather than standing in the shoes of particular injured parties." Brief for United States 22. . . .

Second, SEC disgorgement is imposed for punitive purposes. In *Texas Gulf* — one of the first cases requiring disgorgement in SEC proceedings — the court emphasized the need "to deprive the defendants of their profits in order to . . . protect the investing public by providing an effective deterrent to future violations." 312 F. Supp., at 92. In the years since, it has become clear that deterrence is not simply an incidental effect of disgorgement. Rather, courts have consistently held that "[t]he primary purpose of disgorgement orders is to deter violations of the securities laws by depriving violators of their ill-gotten gains." *SEC v. Fischbach Corp.*, 133 F.3d 170, 175 (C.A.2 1997). . . .

Finally, in many cases, SEC disgorgement is not compensatory. As courts and the Government have employed the remedy, disgorged profits are paid to the district court, and it is "within the court's discretion to determine how and to whom the money will be distributed." *Fischbach Corp.*, 133 F.3d, at 175. Courts have required disgorgement "regardless of whether the disgorged funds will be paid to such investors as restitution." *Id.*, at 176. . . . Some disgorged funds are paid to victims; other funds are dispersed to the United States Treasury. . . . Even though district courts may distribute the funds to the victims, they have not identified any statutory command that they do so. When an individual is made to pay a noncompensatory sanction to the Government as a consequence of a legal violation, the payment operates as a penalty. . . .

SEC disgorgement thus bears all the hallmarks of a penalty: It is imposed as a consequence of violating a public law and it is intended to deter, not to compensate. The 5-year statute of limitations in § 2462 therefore applies when the SEC seeks disgorgement. . . .

———————

It is worth noting that the Supreme Court declined to express a view on whether disgorgement is available to the SEC as a remedy at all.[14] If the authority of courts to

———————

13. [N. 3] Nothing in this opinion should be interpreted as an opinion on whether courts possess authority to order disgorgement in SEC enforcement proceedings or on whether courts have properly applied disgorgement principles in this context. The sole question presented in this case is whether disgorgement, as applied in SEC enforcement actions, is subject to § 2462's limitations period.

14. *Kokesh v. SEC*, 137 S. Ct. 1635, 1642 at n. 3 (2017).

provide such remedies in the context of securities proceedings was uncontroversial, such a caveat would probably not be necessary. However, the SEC's disgorgement authority was not based in statute, while the CFTC's is statutory.[15] This makes it likely that, whatever weakness the SEC's disgorgement authority has, the CFTC's authority will likely be upheld.[16]

Therefore, the primary question for the CFTC remains whether the five-year statute of limitation applies to disgorgement. At least one court has ruled that it does, while another declined to address the question.[17] It is difficult to find a basis to distinguish the CFTC from the SEC in terms of whether the five-year limitation should apply to the CFTC's disgorgement authority.[18] It seems likely that it does.

2. Criminal Proceedings

If a violation of the Commodity Exchange Act or a CFTC rule is willful, then such violation is a felony, punishable by a $1 million fine plus costs of prosecution and imprisonment of up to ten years (with an exception, solely for imprisonment, which provides that a person cannot be imprisoned if the person proves no "knowledge of such rule or regulation. . . .")[19]

It is also a felony knowingly:

> [T]o make, or cause to be made, any statement in any application, report, or document required to be filed under [the Commodity Exchange Act] . . . or any [CFTC] rule . . . which statement was false or misleading with respect to any material fact, or knowingly to omit any material fact required to be stated therein or necessary to make the statements therein not misleading . . . [or to willfully] falsify, conceal, or cover up by any trick, scheme, or artifice a material fact, make any false, fictitious, or fraudulent statements or representations, or make or use any false writing or document knowing the same to contain any false, fictitious, or fraudulent statement or entry to . . . [a board of trade, a swap execution facility, a derivatives clearing organization, a swap data repository, or the National Futures Association].[20]

The CFTC has broad scope to bring civil enforcement actions. It does not have the authority to bring a criminal complaint and is dependent upon the Department of Justice to prosecute criminal violations. In practice, the criminal prosecution of a

---

15. Commodity Exchange Act § 6c(d)(3).

16. *See CFTC v. Reisinger*, 2017 WL 4164197 *3–6 (N.D. Ill. Sept. 19, 2017).

17. *See CFTC v. Gramalegui*, 2018 WL 4610953 *30 (D. Colo. Sept. 26, 2018) (applying the five-year limitation to the CFTC's claims), and *CFTC v. Reisinger*, 2017 WL 4164197 *6 (N.D. Ill. Sept. 19, 2017).

18. *See, e.g.*, Daniel Mullen, Charles Mills, and Shaun Boedicker, *SEC Disgorgement Limits Should Apply to FERC and CFTC*, Law360 (June 9, 2017), available at https://www.steptoe.com/images/content/6/2/v4/6280/SEC-Disgorgement-Limits-Should-Apply-To-FERC-And-CFTC.pdf.

19. Commodity Exchange Act § 9(a)(5).

20. Commodity Exchange Act §§ 9(a)(3) and (4).

common fraud committed in the commodity context is nearly always based on the federal mail and wire fraud statutes, which prohibit fraud generally, and *not* on the Commodity Exchange Act.[21]

This practice was unsuccessfully challenged shortly after passage of the Commodity Futures Trading Commission Act of 1974.

United States v. Abrahams
493 F. Supp. 296 (S.D.N.Y. 1980)

Conner, District Judge:

Defendant Alan Herbert Abrahams ("Abrahams") is charged with one count of violating the conspiracy statute and forty-nine counts of violating the mail fraud and wire fraud statutes, 18 U.S.C. ss 1341 and 1343, respectively. The charges arise out of his operation, between July 1, 1976 and January 15, 1978, of Lloyd, Carr & Company, which was in the business of offering to the public options to purchase or sell futures contracts on commodities traded on markets in London, England.... [T]he Government charges that Abrahams knowingly engaged in a conspiracy to obtain money by means of a scheme to defraud investors by employing such techniques as ... representing to customers that Lloyd, Carr & Company would purchase options for them when in fact such options were never purchased; disseminating false and misleading recommendations respecting commodity options to the public; and employing unskilled salespersons who were encouraged to use high pressure techniques to sell options to the public.... [The Government] charge[s] defendant with mail fraud or wire fraud:[22] the Government alleges that having devised the scheme to defraud the public ... defendant then utilized the mails and the wires to send confirmations of purchases of options to customers and to place orders for the purchase of options for Lloyd, Carr & Company customers.

Abrahams moves to dismiss the indictment on several grounds [including]: that he is being prosecuted under the wrong criminal statute....

Abrahams contends that for federal prosecutions for mail and wire fraud involving commodity options, the exclusive vehicle is the [Commodity Exchange Act ("the Act")] ... ; that by its enactment Congress intended that commodity options would be regulated solely under the Act; and that Congress implicitly repealed those provisions of other, more general statutes, including the mail and wire fraud statutes, imposing penalties for conduct now proscribed as criminal under the Act....

Abrahams further contends that ... [the section] of the Act ... which prohibits the use of the United States mails or any means of interstate commerce to perpetuate fraudulent schemes involving commodity options, was intended by Congress to

---

21. *See* 18 U.S.C. §§ 1341 and 1343.

22. [N. 4] The wire fraud statute, 18 U.S.C. s 1343, is modeled after the mail fraud statute, 18 U.S.C. s 1341. The Court will discuss them collectively as the mail fraud statute.

be the sole means by which fraudulent conduct in the commodities field, including such conduct as is alleged in the instant indictment, should be prosecuted, even if that conduct violates the mail fraud statute as well.

The Government argues that neither the express wording of the Act nor its legislative history offers any support for defendant's theory that the Government is prohibited from prosecuting fraudulent schemes involving commodity options under the general criminal antifraud statutes, such as the mail fraud statute. The Government's position is that the mail fraud statute serves as a useful supplement to the criminal antifraud sanctions provided by Congress in the Act and that the two statutes . . . work in harmony in attempting to prevent fraud and misrepresentation in the commodities field. For the reasons that follow, this Court shares the Government's view. . . .

Defendant contends that by enacting the . . . [Commodity Futures Trading Commission Act of 1974,] a comprehensive statutory scheme to regulate trading in futures[,] Congress intended to repeal, by implication, the more general mail fraud statute insofar as it relates to schemes to defraud involving futures.

Whether the passage of a specific law precludes prosecution under a more general law covering the same offense is a question of legislative intent. The law is well settled, however, that repeal by implication is not favored and that it follows only where the later act is clearly intended to be in substitution for the earlier act.

In order to determine whether the Act's specific antifraud provision should be deemed to have repealed the mail fraud statute, this Court must first examine the legislative history of the Act to determine whether Congress expressed an intent partially to repeal the mail fraud statute and, second, must examine the two statutes to determine whether there is a repugnancy in the subject matter of the two statutes which would justify an implication of repeal. . . .

A review of the legislative history of the Act establishes that Congress intended to vest the Commodity Futures Trading Commission ("the Commission") with exclusive jurisdiction over the regulation of commodity futures; however, the legislative history does not support defendant's view that Congress, by the "exclusive jurisdiction" language, intended that prosecutions for fraudulent schemes involving commodity options would lie solely under the Act.

Prior to the enactment of the 1974 Act . . . a regulatory gap . . . existed and some forms of futures went unregulated. . . . [Accordingly,] Congress created a single federal agency equipped with broad authority to regulate futures trading and exchange activities. . . .

In addition to broad rule-making authority, the Commission was equipped with significant enforcement powers, including the authority to conduct investigations; to issue cease and desist orders; to obtain court-ordered injunctions; and to punish specified fraudulent conduct with fines . . . or imprisonment. . . .

The legislative history makes clear that Congress intended the Commission to exercise sole jurisdiction over the regulation of futures contracts. . . .

Although Congress equipped the Commission with the power to prosecute violations of the Act by including civil and criminal sanctions in the Act, there is no indication in the legislative history of a Congressional intent to make the criminal sanction provisions of the Act the sole vehicle for prosecuting fraud in the sale of futures. . . .

The little evidence relevant to this issue in the legislative history supports the Government's view that Congress contemplated that both the Act and the general criminal antifraud statutes would be utilized to punish fraud in futures markets. . . .

[I]n introducing the 1974 Act to the Senate for consideration, Senator Talmadge, Chairman of the Senate Committee on Agriculture and Forestry, stated:

> "In establishing this Commission, it is the committee's intent to give it exclusive jurisdiction over those areas delineated in the act. This will assure that the affected entities-exchanges, traders, customers, et cetera will not be subject to conflicting agency rulings. However, it is not the intent of the committee to exempt persons in the futures trading industry from existing laws or regulations such as the antitrust laws. . . ." 120 Cong. Rec. S. 30459 (Sept. 9, 1974).

In summary, there is no indication in the legislative history that, with the passage of the Act, Congress intended to repeal the general federal criminal antifraud statutes insofar as they relate to commodity futures. The Court must next determine whether there is a repugnancy in the subject matter of the two statutes which would justify an implication of repeal. . . .

The language of the mail fraud statute is broad: it condemns any scheme to defraud in which the mails are employed. . . . [E]ven where Congress has enacted comprehensive legislation, including criminal sanctions, to govern conduct in a particular field, the courts have very often held that the mail fraud statute continues in force. . . .

Despite the pervasive Government regulation of the drug industry, postal fraud statutes still play an important role in controlling the solicitation of mail-order purchases by drug distributors based upon fraudulent misrepresentations. . . .

The mail fraud statute and the criminal provisions of the Act are not in conflict; instead, they complement each other. The Court concludes that there is no conflict between the two statutory provisions which would justify an implication of repeal.

For the foregoing reasons, the Court concludes that the mail fraud statute has not been implicitly repealed by . . . the Act. Defendant's motion to dismiss on the ground that the exclusive jurisdiction for prosecuting defendant lies under the Act is denied. . . .

A person making a materially false statement to the federal government could have criminal liability.[23] This has the potential to arise with persons registered with the

---

23. 18 U.S.C. § 1001(a).

CFTC if, for example, reports to the CFTC are falsified. This, and the process by which a fraud is addressed by federal authorities, is illustrated by the prosecution of the decades-long customer fraud that occurred at Peregrine Financial Group, Inc., formerly a CFTC-registered futures commission merchant. Note that, as with *Abrahams*, the criminal violation charged was based on a general federal statute prohibiting fraud. However, in the below case there were also felony charges for violation of the Commodity Exchange Act.

United States v. Wasendorf

2012 WL 4052834 (N.D. Iowa Sept. 13, 2012)

Jon Stuart Scoles, United States Chief Magistrate Judge. . . .

On the 11th day of September 2012, this matter came on for hearing to determine whether Defendant Russell R. Wasendorf, Sr. should be detained pending further proceedings. . . .

On July 11, 2012, Defendant was charged by criminal complaint with making and using false statements in a matter within the jurisdiction of the Government of the United States, in violation of 18 U.S.C. § 1001(a)(1) and (3).

On August 13, 2012, Defendant was charged in the instant action with 31 counts of making and using false documents in violation of 18 U.S.C. § 1001(a)(3). Defendant was arraigned on August 17, and trial was scheduled for October 15. On September 7, the Court was advised that Defendant was asking for a detention hearing. The hearing was . . . scheduled for September 11. . . .

On Monday, July 9, 2012, Black Hawk County sheriff's deputies responded to a call of a suspicious vehicle outside the offices of Peregrine Financial Group, Inc. in Cedar Falls, Iowa. Deputies found Defendant unconscious inside the vehicle, with a hose connected to the exhaust pipe cut into the convertible roof. A bottle of vodka was found in the car and authorities later learned that Defendant had taken sleeping pills which he had "stockpiled" during the previous two months. Defendant was transported to the University of Iowa Hospitals in Iowa City, where he remained until he was arrested four days later. . . .

Defendant is the chairman and CEO of Peregrine Financial Group, Inc. ("PFG"). Found in the car was a four-page typed note in which Defendant admits committing fraud in connection with the business.

> Through a scheme of using false bank statements I have been able to embezzle millions of dollars from customer accounts at Peregrine Financial Group, Inc. The forgeries started nearly twenty years ago and have gone undetected until now.

Note of Russell R. Wasendorf, Sr.

According to Defendant's note, "[m]ost of the misappropriated funds went to maintain the increasing levels of Regulatory Capital to keep PFG in business and to pay business loses [*sic*], with a portion being used to build the office building at One

Peregrine Way." In his note, Defendant states that "I am ready to die. I guess this is the only way out of a business I hate so much."

At the hearing, Special Agent William Langdon of the Federal Bureau of Investigation provided details regarding Defendant's criminal activity. Briefly stated, Defendant diverted funds from a bank account, which was intended to hold segregated customer funds, to his own uses. For example, customer funds were used to support a restaurant ("My Verona") owned by Defendant in Cedar Falls, and a construction and development company in Romania, partially owned by Defendant.

Defendant concealed his illegal activity by falsifying bank statements. For example, a fake bank statement prepared by Defendant for the period ending May 31, 2012 shows a balance in the customer's segregated account of $224,830,835.85. The true balance in the account at that time was $5,446,891,086 [*sic*; presumably, $5,446,891.86 is intended]. . . . Defendant also filed false statements with the Commodity Futures Trading Commission ("CFTC"). . . .

The parties have entered into a plea agreement, which was signed by Defendant and his attorney on September 7 and by the prosecutors on September 11. According to the agreement, Defendant will waive indictment and plead guilty to a four-count Information charging him with mail fraud, embezzlement of customer funds by a person registered under the Commodity Exchange Act, making false statements to the Commodity Futures Trading Commission, and making false statements to a futures association registered under the Commodity Exchange Act. Collectively, the charges carry a maximum prison term of 50 years.

In the plea agreement, Defendant stipulates to facts supporting the charges. Specifically, Defendant admits that beginning in the early 1990s, he "fraudulently obtained and misappropriated for his own use customer funds that were supposed to be maintained by PFG for the benefit of and use by such customers to margin, guarantee, or secure commodities futures and options trades." The full amount of the loss is undetermined, but Defendant admits that he "embezzled and otherwise misappropriated in excess of $100,000,000 in PFG customer funds." Defendant also admits making false reports to the CFTC and the National Futures Association ("NFA"), a not-for-profit industry membership corporation operated under the supervision of the CFTC.

Special Agent Langdon testified that Defendant has been cooperative with law enforcement authorities, and with a court appointed receiver, in attempting to locate and recover assets. On July 27 — just two weeks after he was arrested — Defendant met for approximately six hours with two FBI agents, two assistant United States attorneys, the receiver from Chicago, and the receiver's attorney. One month later, on August 27, Defendant met again for approximately six hours with an FBI agent, an assistant United States attorney, a postal inspector, the bankruptcy trustee, the receiver, and two or three CFTC attorneys. Langdon acknowledged that one of the CFTC attorneys was "aggressive" in his questioning, including raising his voice, but

Defendant continued to cooperate and did not "lose his cool." According to Langdon, Defendant attempted to answer all of the questions put to him, and is willing to cooperate further. Letters from AUSA Deegan to Defendant's counsel confirm that Defendant "has not requested a proffer agreement or any other protection" with regard to the interviews....

On July 10, 2012 — the day after Defendant's attempted suicide — the CFTC filed an action against PFG and Defendant in the United States District Court for the Northern District of Illinois. As part of that action, a receiver was appointed to "[t]ake exclusive custody, control, and possession of all funds, property, and other assets in the possession, ownership, or control" of Defendant and any of his businesses, wherever situated, including property held jointly by Defendant and others. Also on July 10, PFG filed a Chapter 7 bankruptcy petition in the United States Bankruptcy Court for the Northern District of Illinois. Special Agent Langdon testified at the instant hearing that either the receiver, the bankruptcy trustee, or the FBI have taken possession of, or restrained, all of Defendant's known assets, with the exception of those in Romania....

On September 10 . . . the receiver filed a 29-page First Report . . . [which] describes Defendant's assets.

- My Verona, the restaurant owned by Defendant in Cedar Falls, "never generated a profit" and has ceased operating.

- Wasendorf & Associates, Inc. is a publishing business which includes an online bookstore and an online magazine geared toward futures trading. The receiver . . . is attempting to sell the assets.

- Wasendorf Construction, LLC . . . owns several buildings used by Defendant's other businesses, including the PFG corporate headquarters in Cedar Falls.

- Wasendorf Air, LLC . . . [owns] a Hawker Beechcraft model 400A. . . .

- Rhombus Asset Management, Inc. is a company owned by Defendant and others to invest in Romanian real estate and related ventures. . . .

- Peregrine Charities is a 501(c)(3) corporation founded by Defendant and organized for charitable purposes. . . .

- The receiver also identified and has preserved various bank accounts held by Defendant or his businesses.

- Defendant owns his personal residence in Cedar Falls, another home in Cedar Falls used by PFG as a "corporate residence" for visiting staff and corporate guests, and a condominium in Chicago. . . .

- The receiver has surrendered a life insurance policy which had a cash surrender value of $1,287,339.55. . . .

- The receiver is making arrangements to sell Defendant's personal property, including a wine collection, motor vehicles, and boats. . . .

Wasendorf's final plea included guilty pleas to three felony provisions in the Commodity Exchange Act.[24] He received a fifty-year sentence.[25]

In an additional ironic twist, just months before the Peregrine fraud was uncovered, Peregrine had commissioned a white paper on protecting customer funds entitled *Commodity Customer Protections and Regulations: History and Potential Solutions for the Future 1938–2012* for the Commodity Customer Coalition, a not-for-profit group formed in the wake of the MF Global failure.[26]

A Case Study in Manipulation: The Onion Corner[a]

In 1955, Vince Kosuga, an onion farmer and commodity trader, and Sam Siegel successfully cornered the onion market. They did this by buying all of the onions they could and storing them. Then they bought a large number of onion futures contracts.

When the delivery date of the onion futures arrived, onions were artificially scarce due to Kosuga and Siegel's warehousing of onions. Therefore, the price of onions skyrocketed and Kosuga and Siegel, holding futures contracts requiring delivery of the onions, greatly profited.

Then they sold futures contracts for forthcoming delivery months. Right after they sold these futures contracts at high prices they began releasing the onions they had warehoused into the market, depressing onion prices. Once more, they profited greatly.

In 1958, in direct response to the onion corner, onion futures were abolished. Did the prohibition of onion futures help onion farmers? In 1965, one economist concluded that it had not and that "futures trading in onions had . . . a desirable effect"[b] in managing seasonal price variations for farmer.

[a] Source: Keith Romer, *The Great Onion Corner and the Futures Market*, http://www.npr.org/2015/10/22/450769853/the-great-onion-corner-and-the-futures-market (Oct. 22, 2015).

[b] Roger W. Gray, *Onions Revisited*, 45 No. 2 J. of Farm Economics 273, 276 (May 1963).

---

24. Commodity Exchange Act §§ 9(a)(1), (3), and (4).

25. U.S. Attorney's Office for the Northern District of Iowa, *Peregrine Financial Group CEO Sentenced to 50 Years for Fraud, Embezzlement, and Lying to Regulators* (Jan. 31, 2013), available at https://www.justice.gov/usao-ndia/pr/peregrine-financial-group-ceo-sentenced-50-years-fraud-embezzlement-and-lying.

26. Susan Abbott Gidel, *White Paper: Commodity Customer Protections and Regulations History and Potential Solutions for the Future 1938–2012* (Feb. 14, 2012), available at https://web.archive.org/web/20120226210735/http://www.pfgbest.com/common/docs/WHITE%20PAPER%20on%20Customer%20Protections%202012.pdf. For MF Global, *see* chapter 6, section B.3.

C. Market Manipulation Generally

Fraud of the Peregrine variant, where funds of third parties are embezzled, can be found in many contexts, including outside of the derivatives markets. Market manipulation is a specific type of fraud in which, instead of directly stealing customer funds (as, for example, occurred with Peregrine), the integrity of the market is compromised for the benefit of the perpetrator of the manipulation. This type of wrongdoing requires the existence of an established market, such as the derivatives or securities markets.

The Commodity Exchange Act has a number of provisions specific to market manipulation. Some ban market manipulation generically and others ban particular types of market manipulation. We will examine the generic statutory prohibitions here. The statutory provisions focusing on particular types of manipulation are examined below in section D under the heading for each such type of manipulation.

Whereas fraud is generally commonly understood, defining market manipulation is more challenging. Throughout, consider what activities constitute market manipulation. Historically, the following four factors needed to be present for a market manipulation under the Commodity Exchange Act: (1) the manipulator could influence prices; (2) an artificial price existed; (3) the manipulator caused this price; and (4) the manipulator intended to cause the artificial price.[27] However, other courts have emphasized the importance of flexibility, essentially restating the argument that the "methods and techniques of manipulation are limited only by the ingenuity of man."[28]

Even assuming application of the four-factor test as a foundation, is it evolving? Its foundation was laid by the CFTC itself in its *Indiana Farm Bureau* decision in 1982.[29] In recent years, the CFTC has argued that an "intent to affect" prices in the market is equivalent to intent to cause artificial prices.[30] Courts have been unsympathetic to this approach. As one court noted, that the theory "is simply an attempt to read out the artificial price element . . . by collapsing it into the subjective intent requirement."[31] Of course, the existence of an artificial price is not a required element for an *attempted* manipulation.[32]

Finally, note that the fourth factor is no longer required for a finding of a civil violation since, in some cases, recklessness is now sufficient. We discuss this below.

---

27. *CFTC v. Kraft*, 195 F. Supp. 3d 996, 1005–1006 (N.D. Ill. 2016).
28. *Cargill, Inc. v. Hardin*, 452 F.2d 1154, 1163 (8th Cir.1971).
29. *In re Indiana Farm Bureau*, CFTC Docket No. 75-14 (Dec. 17, 1982).
30. *CFTC v. Wilson*, 2018 WL 6322024 *14 (S.D.N.Y. Nov. 30, 2018).
31. *See, e.g., CFTC v. Wilson*, 2018 WL 6322024 *15 (S.D.N.Y. Nov. 30, 2018).
32. *CFTC v. Kraft*, 195 F. Supp. 3d 996, 1008 (N.D. Ill. 2016).

1. Civil Prohibitions on Market Manipulation

Commodity Exchange Act § 6(c)

... (1) Prohibition against manipulation

It shall be unlawful for any person ... to use or employ, or attempt to use or employ, in connection with any swap, or a contract of sale of any commodity in interstate commerce, or for future delivery on or subject to the rules of any registered entity, any manipulative or deceptive device or contrivance. ...

(A) Special provision for manipulation by false reporting

Unlawful manipulation for purposes of this paragraph shall include, but not be limited to, delivering, or causing to be delivered ... a false or misleading or inaccurate report concerning crop or market information or conditions that affect or tend to affect the price of any commodity in interstate commerce, knowing, or acting in reckless disregard of the fact that such report is false, misleading or inaccurate. ...

(C) Good faith mistakes

Mistakenly transmitting, in good faith, false or misleading or inaccurate information to a price reporting service would not be sufficient to violate paragraph (1)(A). ...

(3) Other manipulation. ...

[I]t shall be unlawful for any person, directly or indirectly, to manipulate or attempt to manipulate the price of any swap, or of any commodity in interstate commerce, or for future delivery on or subject to the rules of any ... [designated contract market, swap execution facility, derivatives clearing organization, or swap data repository].

Above, in section B, we examined the civil and criminal general anti-fraud provisions of the Commodity Exchange Act. The civil sanctions for market manipulation are the same, save that the potential civil penalty is up to the greater of $1,227,202 (instead of $170,129 or $187,432 for violations of the Commodity Exchange Act and CFTC rules generally depending on whether the penalty is imposed by the CFTC or a federal district court) or triple the monetary gain from the violation.

To give a sense of how large civil penalties for market manipulation can rise, in 2012, JPMorgan suffered a more than $6 billion loss due to the trading activities of a London-based trader taking very large positions in the credit default swap market who was known to the marketplace as the "London Whale." It was fined $100 million for what the CFTC deemed "reckless" manipulation.

The enforcement action against JPMorgan was the CFTC's first use of its new authority making it unlawful to intentionally or recklessly "[u]se or employ, or attempt to use or employ, any manipulative device, scheme, or artifice to defraud."[33]

In the Matter of JPMorgan Chase Bank, N.A.

CFTC Docket No. 14-01 (Oct. 16, 2013)

. . . The Commodity Futures Trading Commission ("Commission") has reason to believe that JPMorgan Chase Bank, N.A. ("JPMorgan") violated the Commodity Exchange Act ("Act") and Commission Regulations ("Regulations"). Therefore, the Commission deems it appropriate and in the public interest that public administrative proceedings be, and hereby are, instituted to determine whether JPMorgan has engaged in the violations as set forth herein and to determine whether any order should be issued imposing remedial sanctions. . . .

In anticipation of the institution of this administrative proceeding, JPMorgan has submitted an Offer of Settlement ("Offer"), which the Commission has determined to accept. . . .

The credit default swap ("CDS") market comprises globally traded credit derivatives used by various market participants to speculate on and hedge against credit defaults, and, as a result of the Dodd-Frank Wall Street Reform and Consumer Protection Act of 2010 ("Dodd-Frank Act"), the market for CDS that reference broad-based credit indices is subject to the Commission's jurisdiction. Tens of trillions of dollars in notional value of CDS instruments are traded and held by market participants seeking to transfer risk of credit defaults by companies in the United States and around the world. As such, the CDS market is an important aspect of the global economy. Market participants are entitled to rely on the notion that CDS prices are established based on legitimate forces of supply and demand. However, on February 29, 2012, JPMorgan traders acted recklessly with respect to this fundamental precept by employing an aggressive trading strategy concerning a particular type of CDS known as "CDX."

From approximately 2007 through 2011, a JPMorgan unit, the Chief Investment Office ("CIO"), operating through a trading desk in a JPMorgan branch in London, purchased and sold default protection in a portfolio of CDX and other credit default indices. As of the end of 2011, the CIO held a substantial position in CDX and other credit default indices, with a net notional value of more than $51 billion, including $217 billion in long risk positions and $166 billion in short risk positions. At the end of each trading day, traders in the CIO "marked" the positions in this swaps portfolio "to market," assigning a value to the portfolio's positions using various measures including market prices for the credit default index positions. The traders' marks were used to calculate profits and losses ("P&L").

---

33. 17 C.F.R. § 180.1(a)(1).

Although previously quite profitable, as early as late January 2012 the portfolio's value had taken a serious turn for the worse. In February 2012, daily losses were large and growing, and by February 29 the traders believed the portfolio's situation was grave. Just ahead of critical February month-end internal portfolio valuations that would be distributed widely within JPMorgan through the P&L statement, the traders in the CIO, who wanted to reduce mark-to-market losses, recklessly employed an aggressive trading strategy on February 29 in connection with one particular CDX, the CDX.NA.IG.9 10 year index ("IG9 10Y"). In particular, as the value of the portfolio stood to benefit as the IG9 10Y market price dropped, on February 29, the CIO sold on net more than $7 billion of IG9 10Y, a staggering, record-setting, volume, $4.6 billion of which was sold during a three hour period as that day drew to a close. The February 29 trading followed sales of protection of more than $3 billion of this index in the previous two days. To put the quantity sold by the CIO into perspective, the net volume sold by the CIO over those three days amounted to roughly one-third of the volume traded for the entire month of February by all other market participants. During this same period at month-end, the market price on IG9 10Y dropped substantially and the CIO was selling at generally declining prices. The value of the position that the CIO held benefited on a mark-to-market basis from the declining market prices.[34]

JPMorgan's controls and supervision over the CIO did not prevent the CIO from first accumulating the massive portfolio of positions in certain CDX and other credit default indices, and then from taking the steps to conceal the losses. In July 2012, JPMorgan's parent company disclosed that it had lost confidence in the integrity of the traders' marks and acknowledged that it ultimately lost more than $6 billion in 2012 in connection with the CIO's CDS index trading. . . .

The Act, as modified by the Dodd-Frank Act, provides the Commission with exclusive jurisdiction over accounts, agreements and transactions involving swaps, except to the extent otherwise provided by the Dodd-Frank Act. . . .

Section 6(c)(1) of the Act provides, among other things, that it is unlawful for any person "to employ, or attempt to use or employ, in connection with any swap . . . any manipulative or deceptive device or contrivance, in contravention of [Commission rules and regulations]." Commission Regulation 180.1(a), 17 C.F.R. § 180.1

---

34. [N. 3] Two now former JPMorgan traders have been accused of concealing trading losses from others at JPMorgan by using deceptive practices in how they marked the portfolio to market. These two traders' alleged deceptive practices are the subject of criminal charges brought against them by the United States Attorney for the Southern District of New York. . . . *See U.S. v. Martin-Artajo*, No. 1:13-MJ-1975 (S.D.N.Y., filed Aug. 9, 2013) . . . [and] *U.S. v. Grout*, No. 1:13-MJ-1976 (S.D.N.Y., filed Aug. 9, 2013). . . . The facts alleged in these two sets of fraud charges also provide a basis for the Commission to charge the two traders with violations of Section 6(c)(1) of the Act and Regulation 180.1, 17 C.F.R. § 180.1 (2012), which prohibit, among other things, "any act, practice, or course of business, which operates or would operate as a fraud or deceit upon any person" "in connection with any swap." Nevertheless, . . . based on the facts and circumstances presented here as well as resource constraints faced by the Commission, the Division of Enforcement has determined not to recommend . . . virtually identical U.S. fraud charges against these two individuals at this time.

(2012), which became effective on August 15, 2011, in relevant part, makes it unlawful for any person:

> in connection with any swap . . . to intentionally or recklessly: (1) Use or employ, or attempt to use or employ, any manipulative device, scheme, or artifice to defraud; (2) Make, or attempt to make, any untrue or misleading statement of a material fact or to omit to state a material fact necessary in order to make the statements made not untrue or misleading; (3) Engage, or attempt to engage, in any act, practice, or course of business, which operates or would operate as a fraud or deceit upon any person. . . .

By way of background, under long-standing Commission precedent, manipulation was historically described as

> any and every operation or transaction or practice, the purpose of which is not primarily to facilitate the movement of the commodity at prices freely responsive to the forces of supply and demand; but, on the contrary, is calculated to produce a price distortion of any kind in any market either in itself or in its relation to other markets. If a firm is engaged in manipulation it will be found using devices by which the prices of contracts for some one month in some one market may be higher than they would be if only the forces of supply and demand were operative. . . . Any and every operation, transaction, device, employed to produce those abnormalities of price relationship in the futures markets, is manipulation.

. . . Under this standard, any device intentionally employed to distort pricing relationships may be manipulative. . . .

Section 6(c)(1) and Commission Regulation 180.1, because of their relatively recent enactment, have not been interpreted in this context by any court. Precedent applying very similar provisions in the SEC regime, however, provides guidance: "The language of CEA section 6(c)(1), particularly the operative phrase 'manipulative or deceptive device or contrivance,' is virtually identical to the terms used in section 10(b) of the Securities Exchange Act of 1934 ('Exchange Act')." Indeed, when the Commission promulgated Rule 180.1, the Commission observed that "[g]iven the similarities between CEA section 6(c)(1) and Exchange Act section 10(b), the Commission deems it appropriate and in the public interest to model final Rule 180.1 on SEC Rule 10b-5." . . . Accordingly, case law developed under Section 10(b) of the Exchange Act and SEC Rule 10b-5 is instructive in construing CEA Section 6(c)(1) and Commission Regulation 180.1(a).

It is well-settled that prohibitions on manipulative devices are designed to protect the market from devices that could interfere with legitimate pricing forces. . . .

In a properly functioning market, prices reflect the competing judgments of buyers and sellers as to the fair price of a commodity or, in this instance, swaps. Here, acting on behalf of JPMorgan, the . . . traders' activities . . . constituted a manipulative device in connection with swaps because they sold enormous volumes of the IG9 10Y in a very short period of time. . . .

Consistent with long-standing precedent under the commodities and securities laws, the Commission defines recklessness as an act or omission that "departs so far from the standards of ordinary care that it is very difficult to believe the actor was not aware of what he or she was doing." *Drexel Burnham Lambert Inc. v. CFTC,* 850 F.2d 742, 748 (D.C. Cir. 1988). Under this standard, the Commission need not prove that the defendant's motive or primary motive was to interfere with the forces of supply and demand. For example, even if a trader were motivated by a desire to obtain compensation rather than by a desire to affect a market price, if the trader recklessly effected the manipulative trades, he will be held liable.

The ... traders here acted recklessly. Operating out of desperation to avoid further losses, they developed a resolve to "defend the position" ..., i.e., protect its value ... predicated, at least in part, on the market price. Recognizing that the sheer size of the ... position in IG9 10Y had the potential to affect or influence the market, they recklessly sold massive amounts of protection on the IG9 10Y during a concentrated period. ...

Such activity designed to "defend" the position or "fight" other market participants, whether through concentrated month-end trading or otherwise, falls squarely within the prohibitions of Section 6(c)(1) of the Act and Commission Regulation 180.1(a). ...

JPMorgan has submitted the Offer in which it ... [c]onsents, solely on the basis of the Offer, to the Commission's entry of this Order that:

1. makes findings by the Commission that JPMorgan violated Section 6(c)(1) of the Act and Regulation 180.1, 17 C.F.R. § 180.1 (2012), when it recklessly used or employed manipulative devices and contrivances in connection with swaps;

2. orders JPMorgan to cease and desist from violating Section 6(c)(1) of the Act and Regulation 180.1, 17 C.F.R. § 180.1 (2012); [and]

3. orders JPMorgan to pay a civil monetary penalty in the amount of one hundred million dollars ($100,000,000) within ten (10) days of the date of entry of this Order, plus post-judgment interest. ...

One of the CFTC commissioners, Scott D. O'Malia dissented from the CFTC's decision, stating:

Because the settlement Order does not allege that JPMorgan engaged in manipulative or fraudulent conduct, I believe the Commission needs to do a better job of explaining why the company's aggressive trading strategy constitutes a "manipulative device."

Regrettably, neither the CEA nor Commission regulations define a "manipulative device." This lack of a legal standard makes it even more difficult to determine whether JPMorgan engaged in a reckless behavior that put the company at risk or whether such behavior constitutes a "manipulative device."

Although, some case law supports the Commission's conclusion that any device that is intentionally employed to distort a pricing relationship may be manipulative, the Commission has failed to produce data or conduct a more careful evaluation of the actual price to determine whether JPMorgan's conduct distorted the price of certain CDX indices. This problem is compounded even more by the fact that the allegations in the settlement Order center on bilateral or over-the-counter trading. Given this trading environment, I am not clear how the Commission can distinguish between "real" and "distorted" prices if the trades were executed through bilateral negotiations.[35]

The concept of "reckless" manipulation leaves many questions to be answered. Since all trades impact supply and demand and, therefore, pricing, what is the dividing line between "manipulation" and ordinary trading activities? With a willful or intentional mens rea the dividing line is determined by motivation, i.e., was it a bona fide trade or was the objective of the trade to somehow distort the marketplace? This dividing line is unavailable when the mens rea is recklessness.

2. Criminal Prohibitions on Market Manipulation

Similar to the willful violations of the Commodity Exchange Act or CFTC rules we discussed above in subsection 1, a criminal manipulation is a felony punishable by up to ten years in prison and a $1 million fine, plus costs of prosecution. But unlike the civil burden of proof for proving market manipulations, the standard for proving a criminal charge requires intention, not mere recklessness.

The below case is the first successful prosecution for a violation of the Commodity Exchange Act's criminal prohibitions on market manipulation.[36]

United States v. Reliant Energy
420 F. Supp. 2d 1043 (N.D. Cal. 2006)

Walker, Chief Judge.

The United States has filed criminal charges against Reliant Energy Services, Inc. ("Reliant") and four Reliant employees: Jackie Thomas, Reginald Howard, Lisa Flowers and Kevin Frankeny (collectively "defendants"). The indictment charges each defendant with one count of commodities price manipulation in violation of §9(a)(2) of the Commodity Exchange Act (CEA), four counts of wire fraud in violation of 18 U.S.C. §1343 and one count of conspiracy in violation of 18 U.S.C. §371. Defendants jointly moved to dismiss the original indictment on vagueness and other grounds. . . .

---

35. Scott D. O'Malia, *Statement of Commissioner Scott D. O'Malia Regarding JPMorgan's Use of Manipulative Device* (Oct. 15, 2013), available at http://www.cftc.gov/PressRoom/PressReleases/omaliastatement101613.

36. Commodity Exchange Act §9(a)(2).

This case arises from California's electricity "crisis" in summer 2000. In 1996, California created two new non-governmental entities to orchestrate the transmission and sale of electricity: the California Independent System Operator ("CAISO") and the California Power Exchange ("CalPX"). . . . CalPX was a crucial hub of the electricity generation market, overseeing an auction system for the sale and purchase of electricity. . . . CalPX would determine, on an hourly basis, a single "market clearing price" which all electricity wholesalers would be paid based on short-term supply and demand bids submitted by all CalPX participants ("spot market"). In addition, CalPX operated a block forward market by matching supply and demand bids for long-term electricity contracts ("term market").

Responsibility for the efficient functioning of the high-voltage transmission grid fell to CAISO and, to that end, it ran the spot market for electricity. During the time period in question in this case, if consumer demands were not met by scheduled supplies into CalPX or other sources, CAISO was required to procure additional electricity to serve consumers' requirements and maintain the stability of the grid. To facilitate this, CAISO purchased reserve capacity from wholesalers. . . . The CAISO-operated market was called the "real time" or "imbalance" market. . . .

Reliant, based in Houston, Texas, owns five generation plants in southern California. According to the indictment, in early June 2000, defendant Flowers (on behalf of Reliant) entered into long-term trading contracts for electricity delivery for the third quarter of 2000 and 2001, expecting that electricity prices would increase. On June 19, 2000, however, the spot market price for electricity unexpectedly fell. Based upon the trading contracts entered into by Flowers and the sharply decreased market price, defendants determined that Reliant was facing a multi-million dollar loss. To avoid this loss, the indictment alleges that defendants conspired to manipulate (and did manipulate) the California electricity market to increase the price of electricity.

Specifically, the government asserts that defendants manipulated the market by creating a false and misleading appearance of an electricity supply shortage to CalPX, CAISO and other market participants. Defendants were able to create this illusion of a supply shortage by (1) shutting down some of Reliant's generation plants, (2) physically withholding electricity from the spot market, (3) submitting supply bids at inflated prices to ensure that the bids were not accepted and (4) disseminating false and misleading rumors and information to CAISO, brokers and other traders regarding the availability and maintenance status of, and environmental limitations on, Reliant's southern California generation plants.

The government asserts that defendants' scheme was successful; by June 21, 2000, the purported electricity supply shortage had caused the spot market price of electricity to soar. The indictment alleges that defendants took advantage of the artificial price they had created by selling large amounts of electricity at this inflated price. Ultimately, the government alleges, instead of suffering a loss, Reliant made millions in profits and that California electricity purchasers overpaid by as much as $32 million.

Based upon defendants' alleged conspiracy, scheme to defraud and manipulation ... the government filed the criminal charges at issue here ... (hereinafter the "criminal manipulation provision"). ...

It is appropriate to address first defendants' ... [allegation] that the criminal manipulation provision is unconstitutionally vague on its face and as applied to the case at hand. ...

Defendants make much of the fact that, "[i]n the 68 years since commodity 'manipulation' was made a crime, there has never been a reported criminal prosecution" — until now. Yet, as Judge Selya stated when presented with this argument by a criminal defendant: "There is a first time for everything." *United States v. Nippon Paper Industries Co., Ltd.*, 109 F.3d 1, 6 (1st Cir.1997). There had to be a first time a defendant was prosecuted for price fixing under the Sherman Act. There had to be a first time a defendant was charged with illegal dumping under the Clean Water Act. The fact that this might be the government's premiere criminal prosecution under the criminal manipulation provision does not itself answer the court's inquiry whether the statute is unconstitutionally vague.

To be sure, a gap of two generations between enactment of a statute and prosecution under that statute is certainly a surprise. If commodities price manipulation were sufficiently harmful to society to require a criminal prohibition, it seems strange that it would take the government this long to get around to enforcing the statute. Surely, if there is such a thing as criminal market manipulation, the California energy crisis in the early 21st century cannot be the first instance of such conduct. Perhaps, the government has been able to deal with market manipulation through other criminal laws. If so, one wonders what a prosecution under the CEA adds to the government's law enforcement arsenal? But the absence of prior prosecutions is not enough to support dismissal of the indictment. ...

Next, defendants argue that the CEA's criminal manipulation provision is void for vagueness on its face. ...

Defendants argue that the criminal manipulation provision is unconstitutionally vague as applied for three reasons: (1) the term "manipulate" has no ordinary or plain meaning, (2) judicial explication has not remedied the term's ambiguity and (3) the legislative history of the CEA fails to evidence a sufficient definition of the term. ...

As mentioned above, when a term lacks a statutory definition, the court will normally construe the term in accord with its ordinary meaning. This canon of construction begins by examining the term's dictionary definition.

As pertinent here, one modern dictionary defines "manipulate" as "to control, manage or play upon by artful, unfair or insidious means[;] esp. to one's own advantage." Webster's Third New Int'l Dictionary 1376 (1981); *see also* The Oxford American Dictionary and Language Guide 604 (1999) (defining manipulate as to "manage (a person, situation, *etc.*) to one's own advantage, esp. unfairly or unscrupulously"). Based on this definition, a person who "manages, controls or plays upon" the price of a commodity in interstate commerce by "artful, unfair or unscrupulous means" may be liable for criminal price manipulation under the CEA. Defendants characterize this ordinary meaning as full of "vague and subjective concepts." The court shares defendants' concern to some extent. Terms such as "unfairly," "unscrupulously" and the like are too subjective to afford a determinable legal standard by which criminal liability may be imposed.

Because a term's ordinary meaning should be assessed as of the time Congress enacted the provision at issue, dictionary definitions contemporaneous with enactment are most useful. Congress enacted § 9(a)(2) in 1936. At that time, Webster defined "manipulate" as "to manage or treat artfully or fraudulently." To the extent § 9(a)(2) of the CEA makes it a crime to "manage" the price of a commodity in interstate commerce by "fraudulent" means, the court is less inclined to agree that the term "manipulate" provides too vague a standard. . . .

Any uncertainty surrounding the term "manipulation" has been to an extent clarified by judicial explication. As defendants observe, the term "manipulation," like any term left to judicial interpretation, did not have a fixed meaning at the CEA's incipiency or during its adolescence.

In more recent times, . . . the courts and the CFTC have adopted four necessary elements an accuser must prove to prevail on a manipulation claim: (1) the defendants possessed the ability to influence prices, (2) an artificial price existed, (3) the defendant caused the artificial price and (4) the defendant specifically intended to cause the artificial price. . . .

Perhaps realizing that the judicial explication of the term "manipulate" is in line with the term's ordinary meaning, defendants' reply memorandum singles out a different term — "artificial price" — and attempts to demonstrate why this term's proposed definition is unconstitutionally vague. . . .

[D]efendants posit that criminalizing conduct undertaken with the intent to create a price that does not reflect the basic forces of supply and demand would "require businesses to guess what the 'reasonable' or 'real' value of a good was in order to conform their conduct to the law." In other words, defendants argue that the criminal manipulation provision requires them first to guess what the price of a commodity would be if the forces of supply and demand were uninhibited (i.e., guess what the "reasonable" or "real" price would be) and then avoid conduct that would cause the price of the commodity to deviate from this reasonable price. . . .

To avoid liability, defendants are not required to guess what the reasonable price of electricity is and then conform their conduct so as to create this price or sell at this price. The criminal manipulation provision does not criminalize the selling of a product at an unreasonable price. Rather, the criminal manipulation provision prohibits defendants from engaging in intentional conduct aimed at preventing the basic forces of supply and demand from operating properly. Thus, the criminal manipulation provision is concerned less with the price itself than it is with the process by which the price is set. . . .

The dissemination of false information into a commodities market has long been recognized as a form of price manipulation.

This is as it should be. Fraud and deceit are not legitimate market forces. Fundamentally, markets are information processing systems. The market price is only as "real" as the data that inform the process of price discovery. By the same token, the market price is "artificial" when the market is misinformed. Just as price artificiality implies misinformation, a specific intent to create an artificial price implies fraud or deceit. . . .

Putting aside the theoretical question whether a person of ordinary intelligence would understand that defendants' conduct was prohibited, it is sufficiently clear that defendants themselves knew their conduct was prohibited. Because all parties are familiar with them and in the interest of protecting the confidentiality of these criminal proceedings, the court will not recite portions of the taped telephone conversations offered by the government. It should suffice to say that one defendant actually uses the phrase "market manipulation" to explain why one of Reliant's generating facilities was idle. . . .

While the court does not afford much, if any, weight to these calls in addressing defendants' vagueness challenge, these telephone calls certainly do not add credibility to defendants' claims that they were unaware that their conduct in June 2000 was illegal.

Accordingly, defendants' motion to dismiss [the CEA market manipulation] count . . . of the indictment on vagueness grounds is DENIED. . . .

[D]efendants [also] argue that the "alleged conduct is not 'manipulation' as a matter of law." Specifically, defendants contend that unilateral supply decisions cannot constitute commodities price manipulation. As the court has already explained, if [the indictment] . . . were predicated solely upon defendants' unilateral supply decisions, "this would be a very different motion." But the indictment alleges that artificial prices were effected through the illusion of a supply shortage, which was created by the interplay between defendants' supply and bidding practices and the false and misleading rumors and information they allegedly disseminated into the market. . . .

Although *United States v. Reliant* established the viability of a criminal prosecution for market manipulation under the Commodity Exchange Act, it resulted in a settlement in which the defendants consented to a two-year deferred prosecution agreement (i.e., if, after two years, the defendants engaged in no unlawful behavior, the charges would be dropped) and a $22.2 million fine with no admission of wrongdoing by the defendants.[37]

---

37. *Reliant Energy Services Resolves Pending Indictment Through Deferred Prosecution Agreement; To Pay $22.2 Mln Penalty—Update*, RTT News (Mar. 6, 2007) available at http://www
.rttnews.com/251607/reliant-energy-services-resolves-pending-indictment-through-deferred
-prosecution-agreement-to-pay-22-2-mln-penalty-update.aspx?Arch=1.

D. Types of Market Abuse and Manipulation

1. Introduction

The types of market manipulation are varied and will always evolve as the markets evolve. Just as was noted above with respect to fraud generally, one court has noted "[w]e think the test of manipulation must largely be a practical one if the purposes of the Commodity Exchange Act are to be accomplished [because the] methods and techniques of manipulation are limited only by the ingenuity of man."[38]

Therefore, in addition to the more general prohibitions of market manipulation described above in section C, specific types of market manipulation have been identified and prohibited by the Commodity Exchange Act and CFTC rules.

2. Wash Sales, Fictitious Trades, and Order Bucketing

The Commodity Exchange Act makes it unlawful to:

> (i) . . . bucket an order if the order is either represented by the person as an order to be executed, or is required to be executed, on or subject to the rules of a designated contract market; or (ii) to fill an order by offset against the order or orders of any other person, or willfully and knowingly and without the prior consent of the other person to become the buyer in respect to any selling order of the other person, or become the seller in respect to any buying order of the other person, if the order is either represented by the person as an order to be executed, or is required to be executed, on or subject to the rules of a designated contract market unless the order is executed in accordance with the rules of the designated contract market. . . .[39]

The Commodity Exchange Act also prohibits:

> a transaction that [is] . . . or is commonly known to the trade as, a "wash sale" or "accommodation trade"; or . . . is a fictitious sale; or . . . is used to cause any price to be reported, registered, or recorded that is not a true and bona fide price. . . .[40]

a. Wash Sales

"Wash sales" are prohibited by the CFTC. The classical wash sale is where two parties trade offsetting trades with one another, often with the objective of creating inflated trade volume. For example, in one case, an exchange offered an incentive

---

38. *Cargill, Inc. v. Hardin*, 452 F.2d 1154, 1163 (8th Cir.1971).

39. Commodity Exchange Act § 4b(a)(2)(D). There is an exception for floor brokers and future commission merchants matching customer orders so long as they are executed at market price and in public on the floor of the exchange.

40. Commodity Exchange Act § 4c(a)(2).

program rebating trading fees if participants in the program traded sufficient volume in an otherwise lightly-traded futures contract.[41] To meet these volume targets and qualify for the rebate, a manager directed two traders at the same firm to trade offsetting positions with one another. It resulted in a $200,000 fine.[42]

Similarly, a party controlling two accounts who entered offsetting orders on their behalf was found to have engaged in fictitious wash sale trading despite arguing that the orders were an expeditious way to close out positions in each account.

CFTC v. Moncada

31 F. Supp. 3d 614 (S.D.N.Y. July 15, 2014)

Memorandum Order Granting In Part And Denying In Part Plaintiff's Motion For Summary Judgment And Scheduling Case For Trial

McMahon, J. . . .

The Commodity Futures Trading Commission (CFTC) . . . moves for summary judgment, arguing that . . . the undisputed facts admit of but one inference — defendant intended to manipulate the market in CBOT December 2009 Wheat Futures. . . .

I agree with the CFTC that virtually no material facts are in dispute — the trading records are the only material facts and they show what they show about the defendant Eric Moncada's trading history. I also agree with the CFTC that the most compelling inference one might draw from the trading records is that Moncada was indeed trying to manipulate the market. . . .

[T]he Court finds the following as a matter of fact:

On Oct. 6, 2009, at 10:20:09.476 am, Moncada placed a buy order in the Serdika account for 80 lots at a price of 466 cents. At 10:20:10.943 am, approximately 1.5 seconds later, Moncada placed an offsetting sell order in the BES account for 80 lots also at a price of 466 cents. The entire BES sell order filled at the price of 466 cents within 0.001 seconds. The majority of the Serdika buy order, 58 lots, was filled at the price of 466 cents. The majority of the BES sell order and Serdika buy order filled against each other. . . .

Moncada testified that he was trying to match the two orders against each other. . . .

On October 12, 2009, at 11:27:56.161 am, Moncada placed a sell order in the BES account for 116 lots at a price of 483 ½ cents. At 11:27:57:793, approximately 1.6 seconds later, Moncada placed on offsetting buy order in the Serdika account for 116 lots at a price of 483 ½ cents. Both orders immediately filled at the price of 483 ½

---

41. *In re Lorenzen*, CFTC Docket No. 13-16 (Feb. 8, 2013).
42. *Id.*

cents. The majority of the BES sell orders and Serdika buy orders filled against each other. . . .

Moncada testified that he was trying to match the orders against each other. . . .

On October 15, 2009, at 10:34:54.801 am, Moncada placed an order in the BES account to sell 271 lots at a price of 499 cents. At 10:34:55.516, approximately 0.7 seconds later, Moncada placed an offsetting buy order in the Serdika account for 271 lots at a price of 499 cents). Both orders were completely filled at a price of 499 cents. The majority of the BES sell orders and Serdika buy orders filled against each other. . . .

Moncada testified that he was trying to match the orders against each other. . . .

Finally, on October 29, 2009, at 12:08:59.899, Moncada placed an order in the Serdika account to sell 154 lots at a price of 508 cents. At 12:09:17.266, approximately 17.3 seconds later, Moncada placed an offsetting buy order in the BES account for 154 lots at a price of 508 ¼ cents, thereby bidding to buy at a price one tick higher than the Serdika sell order. Both orders were immediately and completely filled at a price of 508 cents. The offsetting trade on October 29 was the only transaction that Moncada made in the BES account on that day. But orders at prices above the best offer price will first fill against any orders at the best offer price, which means an order to buy at a price of 508 ¼ cents would first be filled against a sell order at a price of 508. Not surprisingly, the entirety of the BES buy orders and Serdika sell orders filled against each other. . . .

Moncada testified that he was trying to match the orders against each other. . . .

Moncada argues that the trades at issue were not fictitious because they placed the parties at risk; were intended only to "close out" positions in the relevant lots in one of the two accounts for which he traded; and were filled in part by other traders, not by each other.

A "wash" sale or a fictitious sale in violation of Section 4c(a) of the Commodity Exchange Act, 7 U.S.C. § 6c(a) and Reg. 1.38 thereunder, is one that has the appearance of submitting trades to the open market while negating the risk of price competition incident to such a market. *Stoller v. CFTC*, 834 F.2d 262 (2d Cir.1987). Prearranged trading is a form of fictitious sale because, "By determining trade information such as price and quantity outside the pit, then using the market mechanism to shield the private nature of the bargain from public scrutiny, both price competition and market risk are eliminated." *Harold Collins*, [1986–87 Transfer Binder] Comm. Fut. L. Rep. (CCH), ¶ 22,982 at 31,903 (C.F.T.C. April 4, 1986), *rev'd on other grounds sub nom. Stoller v. CFTC, supra.*

Reg. 1.38 requires that all purchases and sales of commodity futures be executed "openly and competitively." Conduct that violates Section 4c(a) also violates Reg. 1.38. Such non-competitive transactions include orders placed by a trader with the intent that those orders trade against each other — transactions that, while giving the appearance of submitting trades to the open market, actually negate the market risk of the trade. *Lorenzen,* [2012–13 Transfer Binder] Comm. Fut. L. Rep. (CCH) ¶ 32,535 . . . ; *Harold Collins, supra,* [1986–87 Transfer Binder] at 31, 903, n. 23.

To prove such a claim, the CFTC must establish that there was:

1. A purchase and sale of any commodity for future delivery

2. Of the same delivery month of the same futures contract

3. At the same or similar price

4. With the intent of not making a bona fide trading transaction.

Wilson v. CFTC, 322 F.3d 555, 559–60 (8th Cir.2003); *Reddy v. CFTC,* 191 F.3d 109, 119 (2d Cir.1999).

Items 1–3 are established by virtue of facts the parties agree are undisputed. The question, again, is intent.

Here, there is no need for any trial, for there can be absolutely no dispute about Mr. Moncada's intent: he admitted it at his deposition. He testified that he intended to match the opposing orders from the two accounts he controlled. Game over. That he was doing so for the "benign" purpose of "closing out" his position in one of the two accounts is of no moment. Similarly, that others who happened to be in the market at the precise moment when three of the trades were made "caught" some portion of his orders and executed them, so that they did not trade entirely against each other, is of no moment; serendipity does not negate what Moncada was trying to do, because the orders would have traded against one another if no one else had been in the market at that moment. By placing the orders for the same commodity future at the identical or near-identical price and so close in time, Moncada eliminated the risk that the sell orders would not execute at a particular price. The sales qualify as fictitious sales.

This constitutes the decision and order of the Court.

A more nuanced question arose in the case below. The backdrop was a manipulation of the potato market that occurred in 1976 and resulted in a large default on delivery obligations required by parties holding a short position in the May 1976 Maine potato futures contracts.[43] Being among the last to receive delivery was considered advantageous since, assuming delivery would be impossible at that point, it would provide leverage for the buyer to insist on a high financial settlement. The question before the court was whether it was an illegal wash sale to enter into offsetting and otherwise identical trades that had the effect of modifying the date by which the underlying commodity would be delivered.

---

43. It was the subject of one of the CFTC's uses of its emergency authority described in chapter 5, sections C.3.b and c.

Stoller v. CFTC

834 F.2d 262 (2d Cir. 1987)

Pierce, Circuit Judge:

Manning Stoller ("Stoller"), a registered account executive with a commodities brokerage firm, petitions for review of a decision and order entered in an administrative enforcement proceeding before the Commodity Futures Trading Commission (the "Commission"). The administrative complaint charged Stoller and others with engaging in "wash sales" in violation of section 4c(a)(A) of the Commodity Exchange Act (the "Act"). The Commission found that Stoller had engaged in prohibited transactions. . . . For the reasons stated below, we grant Stoller's petition and reverse the Commission's order. . . .

This case concerns trading practices on the New York Mercantile Exchange (the "NYMEX") relating to May 1976 Maine potato futures contracts (the "Contracts"). . . .

[T]he market price of potato futures was being artificially depressed . . . by an illegal conspiracy. The conspirators planned to reap large profits when the May potato crop proved to be less plentiful than they were leading the market to believe, thereby causing the price of the futures contracts to rise. In the end, holders of many Contracts failed to deliver potatoes on the specified dates, "resulting in the largest default in the history of commodities futures trading in this country." . . .

In early May 1976, however, the details of this fraudulent scheme were still unknown. It apparently is clear that Stoller sensed that artificial forces were being brought to bear upon the market and recognized that the market price of the Contracts was below the level that would otherwise be indicated by an anticipated short supply of potatoes. Further, it appears that Stoller consequently believed that the artificial depression of the market would cease, either through official intervention or by investors' realization that the potato crop would be small. Futures prices would then rise, thereby creating a profit for those holding fixed-price "long" contracts to receive delivery of potatoes in May 1976.

NYMEX regulations specified that commodity deliveries were to be made first to those who had held their futures contracts the longest, with holders of the most recently acquired contracts receiving their deliveries last. Thus, when the price of the cash crop is expected to rise during the period when deliveries are made, it likely would be profitable to acquire long contracts very shortly before the close of trading in order to "get behind [i.e., get at the end of] the delivery line." Those like Stoller who already owned Contracts, and who therefore expected to have to take early delivery of potatoes, probably in mid-May, would likely prefer to sell their existing Contracts and to acquire newer ones, which would entitle them to take delivery instead in late May or early June, when the value of the commodity was expected to be higher. Stoller claims that this "rollover" or "roll forward" was a commonly-used practice in Maine potato futures.

On May 5 and 6, 1976, Stoller placed orders with floor brokers to sell existing Contracts, which carried early delivery dates because of the length of time for which they had been held, and to replace them one-for-one with other Contracts at a price as near as possible to the price for which the old ones were sold. . . .

The Commission brought a three count enforcement proceeding against Stoller in June 1977, alleging, inter alia, that these virtually simultaneous sale and repurchase transactions at substantially the same price constituted "wash sales" within the prohibitory language of section 4c(a)(A) of the Act. . . .

In August 1979, the administrative law judge ("ALJ") granted summary disposition in favor of Stoller on the ground that he had demonstrated a legitimate market purpose to the transactions, thereby excluding them from the intended scope of the "wash sales" prohibition. . . . [T]he Division of Enforcement appealed to the Commission from the ALJ's order with respect to the wash sale allegations, and in April 1986, almost ten years after the trades in question were executed, the Commission reversed the ALJ's decision and entered judgment against Stoller. In its decision, it said, "We infer from his conduct that [Stoller] initiated transactions with the intent to create the appearance of genuine purchases and sales while avoiding any *bona fide* market transaction."

The Chicago Mercantile Exchange requested a clarification of this decision on the ground that [it] . . . seemed to prohibit transactions in which the parties seek to minimize market risk. The Commission modified its holding and explained that it only sought to prohibit transactions that did not expose the principals to any risk of market price fluctuation. Nevertheless, it reaffirmed its decision that Stoller had violated this prohibition. This case never progressed beyond the stage of summary disposition; and no factual hearing was ever held at which Stoller would have had the opportunity to establish his defense that he did not have the requisite intent to avoid a bona fide market transaction. . . .

Stoller's . . . claims that the Commission did not provide adequate prior notice to the commodities industry and the public that the conduct in question would be considered to constitute prohibited "wash sales." . . .

The term "wash sale" is not defined in the Act itself, in any applicable regulations, or in any interpretive releases. The Commodity Exchange Authority (the "CEA"), the predecessor organization to the Commission, had advised commodities merchants and floor brokers by memorandum in 1948 that it considered trading to "get behind the delivery line" to constitute a "wash sale." However, this document was not published as an interpretive release. . . . In 1959, in another unpublished memorandum to the brokers, the CEA repeated this position. The CEA took the same position with respect to "roll forward" trading in an internal 1955 memorandum and in a 1971 letter to the Chicago Mercantile Exchange. However, we do not consider these documents to be sufficient to apprise the public at large of the rule interpretation, particularly when the policy apparently remained unenforced for years and the allegedly proscribed conduct apparently remained commonplace, as is asserted in this case.

An agency is free, of course, to interpret its governing statute case by case through adjudicatory proceedings rather than by rulemaking. However, if the Commission suddenly changes its view, as we discuss below, with respect to what transactions are "*bona fide* trading transactions," it may not charge a knowing violation of that revised standard and thereby cause undue prejudice to a litigant who may have relied on the agency's prior policy or interpretation.

Like the ALJ, we are unaware of any prior instances in which the Commission had sought sanctions against anyone who engaged in futures trading that accomplished only a modification of the delivery date of the commodity. The 1948 and 1959 memoranda from the CEA to floor brokers and the 1955 internal CEA memorandum were not generally available to the public; nor does the Commission assert that they were well-known to the commodity futures community. The 1971 letter to the Chicago Mercantile Exchange was sent to an exchange other than the one on which Stoller's alleged trading violations occurred. None of these documents was formally promulgated as an administrative interpretation or incorporated in adjudicative decisions. Thus, even if Stoller had investigated the Commission's view of "roll forward" trading, it seems unlikely that he would have been able to tell from that inquiry alone that such action was impermissible....

The various prior decisions on the subject of "wash sales" had concerned transactions that were virtually risk-free, often prearranged, and intentionally designed to mislead or to serve other illicit purposes. The transactions in this case, by contrast, are claimed to have been designed only to minimize risk and to fulfill a purpose generally considered legitimate in the industry....

At oral argument before this Court, counsel for the Commission conceded that a market sale followed by instructions to repurchase the same quantity at the closest possible price would not constitute a "wash sale" because the individual would be exposed to the risk of market fluctuation between the trades.... The Commission contends, however, that the preceding scenario is inapplicable to this case because Stoller's ... instruction somehow operated to negate the risk entirely....

The Commission first held that all "transactions which give the appearance of a *bona fide* purchase and sale, while avoiding any actual change in ownership" are illegal. It then revised its interpretation, claiming that the statute only prohibits transactions that negate market risk. The fact that the Commission abruptly changed its own interpretation in the middle of the proceedings in our judgment further demonstrates the need both for a clearer and more explicit interpretation and for appropriate notice thereof to the public as to what conduct is permissible. Because we find that the public was not adequately apprised that the Commission views "roll forward" trading to be encompassed within the "wash sale" prohibition, we conclude that Stoller may not be held liable under that interpretation for his alleged violations with respect to the Contracts at issue herein.

The petition for review is granted and the Commission's order is reversed.

Based on the Second Circuit's decision, if the trades have a *bona fide* benefit, such as changing the delivery timing, it follows that they are less likely to be deemed "wash sales." Another factor was that the technique was "commonly used."

As the following CFTC enforcement action illustrates, what the CFTC deems a "wash sale" is broad. Moreover, a non-party to the wash sale can bear responsibility.

In the Matter of TeraExchange LLC

CFTC Docket No. 15-33 (Sept. 24, 2015)

The Commodity Futures Trading Commission ("Commission") has reason to believe that TeraExchange, LLC ("Tera"), a provisionally registered swap execution facility ("SEF"), has violated Section 5h(f)(2) of the Commodity Exchange Act ("Act"), 7 U.S.C. §7b-3(f)(2) (2012), and Commission Regulation ("Regulation") 37.203, 17 C.F.R. §37.203 (2014). . . .

In anticipation of the institution of an administrative proceeding, Tera has submitted an Offer of Settlement ("Offer"), which the Commission has determined to accept. . . .

On October 8, 2014, two traders executed a transaction in a non-deliverable forward contract based on the relative value of the U.S. Dollar and Bitcoin, a virtual currency (the "Bitcoin swap"). Six minutes later, the two traders executed a fully offsetting transaction in the Bitcoin swap for the same price and notional amount. As a result, the two transactions (the "October 8 transactions") constitute both wash trading and prearranged trading in violation of Section 4c(a) of the Act, 7 U.S.C. §6c(a) (2012).

Tera arranged the two transactions with the understanding that the parties, who did not know of each other's identities, would execute "a round-trip trade with the same price in, same price out (i.e. no P/L [profit/loss] consequences)[.]" Tera employees were on Skype calls with the two traders as they executed the transactions. The two traders involved were the only market participants on Tera's SEF who had completed the membership process and had received trading privileges on the SEF.

On October 9, 2014, Tera issued a press release, stating that "TeraExchange announced today the first bitcoin derivative transaction to be executed on a regulated exchange." Tera intended for its press release and a related statement by its then-president to create the impression of actual trading interest in the Bitcoin swap.

Section 5h(f)(2)(B) of the Act, 7 U.S.C. §7b-3(f)(1) (2012) and Regulation 37.203(a), 17 C.F.R. §37.203(a) (2014), obligate Tera to establish and enforce rules prohibiting wash trading and prearranged trading on the SEF. Instead, Tera actively arranged for the two traders to enter into prearranged wash trades. . . .

Tera began offering the Bitcoin swap for trading on September 12, 2014. Valuations of the Bitcoin swap are determined by reference to an index of bids, offers, and executed transactions on a number of Bitcoin exchanges (the "Tera Bitcoin index").

As of October 8, 2014, only two market participants ("Firm A" and "Firm B") had completed the onboarding processes to trade on the Tera SEF.

On October 7, 2014, an employee of Tera sent an email to an authorized trader for Firm B ("Trader B"), which had recently completed the onboarding process. The Tera employee stated that Tera had "a counterparty [Firm A] who would like to do a trade." The Tera employee said "we would like to test the pipes by doing a round-trip trade with the same price in, same price out, (i.e. no P/L [profit/loss] consequences) no custodian required." On a call that afternoon with the Tera employee, Trader B agreed to the trade, scheduled for the following day.

On the morning of October 8, 2014, Tera employees initiated Skype calls with both Trader A and Trader B to walk them through the trade. At 9:22 a.m., Trader A initiated a transaction to buy a Bitcoin swap with a notional amount of $500,000 at a defined price, which Trader B accepted. Six minutes later, Trader A initiated a transaction to sell a Bitcoin swap with a notional amount of $500,000 and at the same defined price, which Trader B also accepted.

The two transactions on October 8 canceled each other out. The transactions were offsetting, were intended to negate, and did negate, any market risk and achieved a "wash" result. The transactions did not create any bona fide position in the Bitcoin swap. Further, Tera did not charge a transaction fee or commission to either party, meaning that there were no transaction costs associated with the two transactions.

On October 8, 2014, the National Futures Association ("NFA") (which provides regulatory services for Tera) and the CFTC's Division of Market Oversight ("DMO") separately contacted Tera regarding the two offsetting transactions. Tera told DMO and the NFA that the purpose of the transactions was to "test the pipes."

Nevertheless, on October 9, 2014, Tera issued a press release, stating that "Tera-Exchange announced today the first bitcoin derivative transaction to be executed on a regulated exchange." . . . Also on October 9, 2014, Tera's then-president appeared at a meeting of the Commission's Global Markets Advisory Committee ("GMAC"), where he stated that trades had occurred in the Bitcoin swap the day before.

The October 8 transactions were the only transactions in the Bitcoin swap executed on the Tera SEF as of the date of this Order and provided an opportunity for Tera to state publicly that trading in the Bitcoin swap had occurred. Tera intended for its press release and statements at the GMAC to create the impression of actual trading interest in the Bitcoin swap. As a result, neither Tera's press release nor the statements at the GMAC indicated that the October 8 transactions were pre-arranged wash sales executed solely for the purpose of testing Tera's systems.

These facts should be distinguished from a situation where a SEF or other designated contract market runs pre-operational test trades to confirm that its systems are technically capable of executing transactions and, to the extent that these simulated transactions become publicly known, makes it clear to the public that the trades do not represent actual liquidity in the subject market. . . .

By failing to enforce its rules against wash trading, and in fact actively arranging a wash trade, Tera failed to comply with its obligations under SEF Core Principle 2 and Regulation 37.203(a), 17 C.F.R § 37.203(a) (2014). Further, as a result of the wash trading and prearranged trading, Tera's trading platform submitted reports of the two transactions to a swap data repository which made the reports public. The reports of the two transactions created a misleading impression of trading volume in the Bitcoin swap. . . .

———————

Tera received no fine and, effectively, no sanction other than the public's knowledge of the CFTC enforcement action. One commissioner dissented, noting "Tera Exchange facilitated wash trading and prearranged trading in violation of the Commodity Exchange Act [and] . . . I fundamentally disagree with the notion that they deserve no penalty."[44]

b. Fictitious Trades

Wash sales are one type of fictitious trade. Other types include pre-arranged trades and any trade giving the appearance of a bona fide trade executed on the market when nothing of economic value occurred.

In the Matter of Absa Bank, Ltd.

CFTC Docket No. 14-30 (Sept. 25, 2014)

The Commodity Futures Trading Commission ("Commission") has reason to believe that Respondent Absa Bank, Ltd. ("Absa") violated Section 4c(a)(1) of the Commodity Exchange Act ("the Act"), 7 U.S.C. § 6c(a)(1) (2012),[45] and Commission Regulation ("Regulation") 1.38(a), 17 C.F.R. § 1.38(a) (2013). . . .

In anticipation of the institution of an administrative proceeding, Absa has submitted an Offer of Settlement ("Offer"), which the Commission has determined to accept. Without admitting or denying any of the findings or conclusions herein, Absa consents to the entry of this Order Instituting Proceedings Pursuant to Sections 6(c) and 6(d) of the Act, Making Findings, and Imposing Remedial Sanctions ("Order") and acknowledges service of this Order. . . .

On several occasions, from June 2009 to August 2011, Absa and FirstRand Bank, Ltd. ("FirstRand"), both South African companies, prearranged noncompetitive corn and soybean futures trades on the Chicago Board of Trade ("CBOT"), a

———————

44. Sharon Y. Bowen, *Dissenting Statement by Commissioner Sharon Y. Bowen Regarding TeraExchange LLC* (Sept. 24, 2015), https://www.cftc.gov/PressRoom/SpeechesTestimony/bowenstatement092415.

45. [N. 1] Although Section 4c(a)(1) was amended as part of the Dodd-Frank Wall Street Reform and Consumer Protection Act, Pub. L. No. 111-203, 124 Stat. 1376 (2010) (codified as amended in scattered sections of 7, 12, and 15 U.S.C.), that amendment did not affect the operative language for the violations described in this Order.

designated contract market of the CME Group.[46] Before these trades were entered on the CBOT, employees of Absa and FirstRand had telephonic conversations with each other during which they agreed upon the product, quantity, price, direction, and timing of those trades. These prearranged trades negated market risk and price competition and constituted fictitious sales, in violation of Section 4c(a)(l) of the Act. Further, by entering prearranged trades for corn and soybean futures contracts, Absa also engaged in noncompetitive transactions in violation of Regulation l.38(a). . . .

Regarding the timing, one party would initiate a countdown so that each party could electronically enter their respective bid and offer at as close to the same time as possible in order to increase the likelihood that their orders would cross.

Absa maintains that it participated in these prearranged trades as part of its strategy to hedge its position on related futures contracts traded on the Johannesburg Stock Exchange's ("JSE") SAFEX Commodity Derivatives Market (formerly the Agricultural Products Division). Those JSE futures contracts were inward listed products that were traded in the local currency (South African Rand) but referred to commodity futures contracts traded on CME exchanges. Absa asserts that because the JSE permits prearranged trades between market makers in these inward listed JSE futures contracts, Absa mistakenly believed that such prearranged trades were permissible on the CME as well. Upon being alerted to concerns about its prearranged trading on the CME, Absa immediately ceased such trading, and it has cooperated fully during this investigation. . . .

Section 4c(a)(l) and (2) of the Act makes it unlawful "for any person to offer to enter into, enter into, or confirm the execution of a transaction that is . . . a fictitious sale." The Act does not define what a "fictitious sale" is, but that term includes wash sales, accommodation trades, and prearranged trades. *In re Harold Collins*, [1986–1987 Transfer Binder] Comm. Fut. L. Rep. (CCH) ¶ 22,982 at 31,902–03 (CFTC Apr. 4, 1986). "[T]he central characteristic of . . . fictitious sales[ ] is the use of trading techniques that give the appearance of submitting trades to the open market while negating the risk or price competition incident to such a market." *Id.* at 31,902; *see also In re Fisher*, [2003–2004 Transfer Binder] Comm. Fut. L. Rep. (CCH) ¶ 29,725 at 56,052 n.11 (CFTC Mar. 24, 2004). A prearranged trade is a textbook example of a fictitious sale. "By determining trade information such as price and quantity outside the pit, then using the market mechanism to shield the private nature of the bargain from public scrutiny, both price competition and market risk are eliminated." *In re Harold Collins*, Comm. Fut. L. Rep. (CCH) at 31,903.

Congress's intent in enacting Section 4c(a) was to "ensure that all trades are focused in the centralized marketplace to participate in the competitive determination of

---

46. [N. 3] On August 27, 2014, the Commission issued an Order Instituting Proceedings Pursuant to Sections 6(c) and 6(d) of the Commodity Exchange Act, Making Findings, and Imposing Remedial Sanctions against FirstRand with regard to the transactions that are the subject of this Order. *See In re FirstRand Bank, Ltd.*, CFTC Docket No. 14-23 (CFTC filed August 27, 2014).

the price of the futures contracts." *In re Thomas Collins*, [1996–1998 Transfer Binder] Comm. Fut. L. Rep. (CCH) ¶ 27,194 at 45,742 (CFTC Dec. 10, 1997) (quoting S. Rep. No. 93-1131, 93d Cong., 2d Sess. at 16–17 (1974)). In other words, Section 4c(a) was meant "to prevent collusive trades conducted away from the trading pits," *Merrill Lynch Futures, Inc. v. Kelly*, 585 F. Supp. 1245, 1251 n.3 (S.D.N.Y. 1984), and "to outlaw insofar as possible all schemes of trading that are artificial and not the result of arms-length trading on the basis of supply and demand factors," *In re Goldwurm*, 7 Agric. Dec. 265, 276 (1948). Consistent with Section 4c(a)'s purpose, in order to establish a violation, the Commission must demonstrate that a person knowingly participated in a transaction initiated with an intent to avoid a bona fide market position. . . .

In this case, Absa engaged in pre-trade discussions with a counterparty (FirstRand) in order to agree to enter into virtually simultaneous trades against each other in the same market, for the same product, and at the same quantity and price. By entering orders for these prearranged trades on the CBOT, Absa donned the appearance of submitting trades to the open market when, in fact, it was negating the risk and price competition incident to such a market. Consequently, by entering orders for prearranged trades, Absa violated Section 4c(a)(1) of the Act, which makes it unlawful to offer to enter into, or to enter into, any commodity futures transaction that is a fictitious sale.

[Additionally,] Regulation 1.38(a) requires that all purchases and sales of commodity futures be executed "openly and competitively." The purpose of this requirement is to ensure that all trades are executed at competitive prices and that all trades are directed into a centralized marketplace to participate in the competitive determination of the price of futures contracts. Noncompetitive trades are generally transacted in accordance with express or implied agreements or understandings between and among the traders. . . . Noncompetitive trades are also a type of fictitious sales because they negate the risk incidental to an open and competitive market. . . .

By knowingly structuring and entering into prearranged noncompetitive trades, employees of Absa violated Commission Regulation 1.38(a). . . .

Absa was required, by the terms of the settlement, to pay a $150,000 fine and stipulate to specified enhanced policies and procedures.

c. Bucketing

As discussed in chapter 2, section A.4, order bucketing was one of the impetuses for the initial federal regulation of derivatives. In short, bucketing is where a customer order, instead of being put onto the exchange so that it might be filled by anyone, is filled by the customer's broker or someone affiliated with the customer's broker. The following case centers on allegations of order bucketing and wash sales.

Reddy v. CFTC

191 F.3d 109 (2d Cir. 1999)

Winter, Chief Judge:

Steven F. Reddy and John W. Sorkvist petition for review of an order of the Commodity Futures Trading Commission which found them guilty of several violations of the Commodity Exchange Act ("CEA"). . . . Solomon Mayer ("SMayer"), Barry Mayer ("BMayer"), SHB Commodities, Inc. ("SHB"), Maye Commodities Corp. ("MCC"), and Steven Gelbstein petition for review of a similar order. Because of the similarity of issues, we heard these petitions together. . . .

In April 1992, the Enforcement Division of the Commission ("Division") filed an eight-count complaint against petitioners Reddy and Sorkvist, along with two other traders, accusing them of multiple violations of the CEA and the Commission's Rules in connection with their trading activities in the sugar pit of the Coffee, Sugar & Cocoa Exchange ("CSCE"). The complaint alleged that from June 29 through October 31, 1988, and during March 1989, Reddy and Sorkvist—both "dual traders"[47]—had engaged in fraudulent executions of customer orders and had accommodated each other in such transactions. Specifically, the complaint alleged that Reddy had engaged in 35 trade-practice violations, including indirect "bucketing" of customers' orders and "wash trades." The complaint also alleged that Sorkvist had engaged in 19 trade-practice violations, primarily "accommodation" trades.

A broker buckets a customer's order by trading opposite the order for the broker's own account or for an account in which the broker has an interest. "Indirect bucketing" occurs when a broker, aided by an accommodating trader, trades opposite his own customer while appearing to trade opposite the accommodator.[48] For example, if a customer directs a broker to buy five contracts, the broker can trade against the customer by buying the five contracts for the customer from a trader while selling five identical contracts from the broker's personal account to the same trader. A broker can profit from bucketing by obtaining a better price than available through open outcry or by trading ahead of the customer and reaping the difference between the price of the early trade and the predetermined price for the customer.

A wash trade is a transaction made without an intent to take a genuine, *bona fide* position in the market, such as a simultaneous purchase and sale designed to negate each other so that there is no change in financial position. Wash trades may be used, *inter alia*, to avoid margin requirements, to rearrange gains and loss for tax purposes, or to manipulate prices.

---

47. [N. 2] "Dual traders" are "floor brokers" who trade for customers and for their own accounts. . . .

48. [N. 3] An "accommodator" is a trader who enters into noncompetitive trading to assist others with illegal trades.

On November 2, 1995, the Administrative Law Judge ("ALJ") found Reddy liable for CEA violations in 35 trade sequences and Sorkvist liable in 16 trade sequences. Based on these findings, the ALJ imposed the following sanctions: cease and desist orders against both petitioners; revocation of their floor broker registrations; imposition of a ten-year trading ban on Reddy and a five-year trading ban on Sorkvist; and a $300,000 civil penalty on Reddy and a $150,000 penalty on Sorkvist. On February 4, 1998, the Commission affirmed both the ALJ's liability findings and the imposition of sanctions. . . .

In April 1992, petitioners SMayer, BMayer, SHB, MCC, and Gelbstein were, along with other traders, charged in a 23-count complaint of multiple recordkeeping and trade practice violations in connection with futures trading in the heating oil pit of the New York Mercantile Exchange ("NYMEX") from 1987 through mid-1989. With respect to the trade practice violations, the complaint alleged that: (i) SMayer, BMayer, SHB, and MCC knowingly engaged in noncompetitive trades to achieve wash results by trading the SHB and MCC accounts opposite each other . . . ; (ii) SMayer, SHB, and MCC knowingly engaged in noncompetitive trades and Gelbstein accommodated them . . . ; (iii) SMayer bucketed his customers' orders and Gelbstein accommodated him . . . ; and (iv) SMayer bucketed his customers' orders and Gelbstein accommodated him. . . .

On May 15, 1996, the ALJ found petitioners liable on 22 of the 23 counts alleged in the complaint and imposed sanctions. SMayer, BMayer, SHB, MCC, and Gelbstein were ordered to cease and desist from violating the CEA and the Commission's Rules; the registrations of SMayer, BMayer, and SHB were revoked; SMayer, BMayer, and SHB were prohibited from trading on, or subject to the rules of, any contract market for five years; Gelbstein was prohibited from doing the same for 30 days; and a civil monetary penalty of $200,000 was assessed against SMayer, $100,000 each against BMayer, SHB, and MCC, and $25,000 against Gelbstein.

Petitioners appealed the ALJ's decision to the Commission. . . .

[The Commission] affirmed the ALJ's imposition of cease and desist orders against all petitioners and affirmed the revocation of SMayer's, BMayer's, and SHB's registrations. Instead of the five-year trading ban imposed by the ALJ on SMayer and SHB, however, the Commission permanently banned them from trading. It also ordered a permanent trading ban against MCC, although the ALJ had imposed no ban. And, instead of the five-year trading ban imposed by the ALJ on BMayer and the thirty-day ban imposed upon Gelbstein, the Commission imposed ten-year bans upon each of them. . . .

The Commission's liability findings are conclusive if supported by the weight — or preponderance — of the evidence. However, our role in reviewing the Commission finding of preponderance is narrow. We will not "mechanically reweigh[ ] the evidence to ascertain in which direction it preponderates. . . ." Rather, we review the record only for the "purpose of determining whether the finder of [ ] fact was *justified, i.e., acted* reasonably, in concluding that the evidence, including the demeanor of the witnesses, the reasonable inferences drawn therefrom and other pertinent circumstances, supported [its] findings." . . .

With regard to Reddy and Sorkvist, the evidence was as follows. The Division's expert, Martha Kozlowski, examined thousands of trading cards and identified transactions in which a broker had simultaneously bought and sold identical sugar futures contracts in identical, or nearly so, quantities at or about the same price opposite the same trader. In the transactions pertinent to Reddy and Sorkvist, the broker's trades were both for a customer and for the broker's personal account. The accommodating trader bought and sold only for his personal account.

Kozlowski testified that trading with those characteristics — principally simultaneous trades of the same contracts, at the same price, in the same quantity, and between the same broker and trader — is unlikely to occur in a competitive open outcry. In her view, such trades exhibited the characteristics of indirect bucketing.

Petitioners countered this evidence with expert and other testimony that such trading configurations can just as plausibly involve lawful dual trading, in particular a practice known as "scalping." Scalping involves the buying and selling of the same contracts within a very short period of time on small market fluctuations, and sometimes, if the attempt to profit fails, buying and selling at the same price. Based on the existence of lawful practices that might result in similar trading configurations, petitioners argue that the evidence against them is no better than in equipoise and cannot as a matter of law support a more-probably-than-not finding of a violation. We disagree.

The Commission had a not unreasonable skepticism about viewing the transactions in question as lawful. . . . The Commission noted that the transactions occurred when the market was unusually volatile and the immediate turn-arounds prevented any hope of gain as well as avoiding any loss . . . [and] found such risk-adverseness implausible. The Commission also noted that some of the trades occurred early in the day and were therefore not designed to end the day without margin fees. . . .

Moreover . . . Petitioners were required to record the terms and times of trades on trading cards . . . [and the] cards reflecting the trades described above showed [irregularities]. . . . Given the evidence, we cannot overturn the Commission's finding of liability. . . .

Sorkvist, whose only proven roles were as a money-passer or accommodating trader, argues that the Division failed to establish that he had a motive to participate in noncompetitive trading and thereby failed to prove scienter. He correctly argues that proof of participation in noncompetitive trades alone is not a sufficient basis for inferring knowing participation in trades. However, Sorkvist confuses intent with motive.

It is true that the Division must prove intent to establish a violation of either Section 4b or 4c of the CEA. *See CFTC v. Savage*, 611 F.2d at 284 ("One cannot have an 'accommodation' sale or a 'fictitious' transaction if one in fact believes he is bargaining faithfully and intends to effect a *bona fide* trade."). However, scienter may be inferred from . . . evidence other than motive. . . .

In addition to the evidence of a recurring pattern of noncompetitive trading, the audit trail irregularities suggested artificial trading in every trade sequence for which charges were brought. These irregularities, in conjunction with the suspicious pattern of trading, are highly probative evidence that Sorkvist knowingly assisted others in illegal transactions. . . .

SMayer, BMayer, SHB, and MCC claim that the Commission erred as a matter of law by finding that . . . [their] trades constituted illegal wash sales. These trades were between various accounts alleged by the division to be controlled jointly by SMayer and BMayer, and, if so, all gains were offset by all losses among the same parties. Petitioners argue that there is legally insufficient evidence of either common control of the accounts or identity of control of the trading. We disagree.

Although SMayer denied any ownership interest in MCC, he reported capital gains from MCC in an amount equal to that of his mother, the avowed owner, and the Commission quite plausibly found that he had such an interest. It further found that: SMayer, who together with BMayer owned two-thirds of SHB, "managed and controlled the operations of SHB"; "[f]unds were transferred between [MCC and SHB] without documentation of any underlying obligation"; "witnesses were unable to explain the reasons for various transfers"; and "all family members had authority to withdraw funds from the accounts at their own discretion." . . .

Petitioners claim that even if the trades were wash sales, there was legally insufficient evidence that their participation in such transactions was knowing. This claim is entirely meritless. . . .

The Commission based its finding on several compelling factors. SMayer was in the heating oil pit daily while BMayer entered the heating oil pit only rarely and sometimes only long enough to execute a single trade. For example, . . . [evidence] shows that on more than one occasion, BMayer executed trades in both the heating oil pit and the platinum and palladium pit during the same minute. It is also highly significant that although BMayer rarely executed heating oil trades, a substantial percentage of those trades were with SMayer on the other side. . . .

[W]e note that the transgressions here are extremely serious. Artificial trades, such as wash transactions or bucketing, have no purpose save to avoid some legal, statutory, regulatory, or contractual obligation or to manipulate the market. They are used, for example, to avoid margin requirements, or taxes, to defraud customers, or to manipulate prices. That is reason enough to impose meaningful sanctions. But artificial trading also strikes at the core purpose of exchanges — efficiently establishing accurate prices for futures contracts. More is at stake, therefore, than loss of revenue to the government or faithlessness to contractual or fiduciary obligations to customers.

We also note that, while artificial trading can over time be profitable, it is also difficult to detect. Because the gains available from artificial trading can be great and

634   15 · FRAUD AND MARKET MANIPULATION

the danger of detection may seem low, the temptation to engage in such practices may be great. If deterrence is to be achieved, substantial penalties may be necessary. . . .

The petitions for review are therefore denied.

---

3. Disruptive Practices

The Commodity Exchange Act prohibits "disruptive practices," i.e.:

> [engaging] in any trading, practice, or conduct on or subject to the rules of a designated contract market or swap execution facility that — (A) violates bids or offers; (B) demonstrates intentional or reckless disregard for the orderly execution of transactions during the closing period [known as "banging the close"]; or (C) is, is of the character of, or is commonly known to the trade as, "spoofing" (bidding or offering with the intent to cancel the bid or offer before execution). . . .[49]

This is a new authority, granted to the CFTC by amendments to the Commodity Exchange Act by way of the Dodd-Frank Act.

CFTC, *Antidisruptive Practices Authority*
78 Fed. Reg. 31890 (May 28, 2013)

. . . Section 747 of the Dodd-Frank Act amends section 4c(a) of the [Commodity Exchange Act (the "CEA") ("Prohibited Transactions")] to add a new section entitled "Disruptive Practices." . . .

Dodd-Frank Act section 747 also amends section 4c(a) of the CEA by granting the Commission authority under new section 4c(a)(6) of the CEA to promulgate such "rules and regulations as, in the judgment of the Commission, are reasonably necessary to prohibit the trading practices" enumerated therein "and any other trading practice that is disruptive of fair and equitable trading."

The Commission is issuing this interpretive guidance and policy statement ("interpretive statement") to provide market participants and the public with guidance on the manner in which it intends to apply the [three new] statutory prohibitions set forth in section 4c(a)(5) of the CEA [i.e., prohibitions on violating bids and offers, "banging the close," and spoofing]. . . .

Violating Bids and Offers. . . .

The Commission declines requests to interpret CEA section 4c(a)(5)(A) as applying only where a person intends to disrupt fair and equitable trading. The Commission interprets CEA section 4c(a)(5)(A) as a *per se* offense. Congress did not

---

49. Commodity Exchange Act § 4c(a)(5).

include an intent requirement in CEA section 4c(a)(5)(A) as it did in both CEA sections 4c(a)(5)(B) and 4c(a)(5)(C). Therefore, the Commission does not interpret CEA section 4c(a)(5)(A) as requiring the Commission to show that a person acted with scienter in violating bids and offers (e.g., that a person acted with either the intent to disrupt fair and equitable trading or with the intent to violate bids and offers). . . . While the Commission's determination of whether to bring an enforcement action depends on facts and circumstances, the Commission does not, for example, intend to exercise its discretion to bring an enforcement action against an individual who, purely by accident, makes a one-off trade in violation of CEA section 4c(a)(5)(A). . . .

The Commission agrees with commenters that parties trading non-cleared swaps may take into consideration factors other than price, such as counterparty risk, when determining how to best execute their trades. Therefore, the Commission interprets CEA section 4c(a)(5)(A) as not applying to non-cleared swap transactions, even if they are transacted on or through a registered entity. In such swap transactions, the credit considerations of the counterparties are important components of choosing which bid or offer to accept. . . .

Therefore, the Commission interprets CEA section 4(c)(a)(5)(A) as prohibiting a person from buying a contract on a registered entity at a price that is higher than the lowest available price offered for such contract or selling a contract on a registered entity at a price that is lower than the highest available price bid for such contract subject to the situations described above. Such conduct, regardless of intent, disrupts fair and equitable trading by damaging the price discovery function of CFTC-regulated markets. By adopting a policy that market participants cannot execute trades at prices that do not accurately reflect the best price for such contracts, this interpretive statement furthers the CEA's purpose of ensuring the integrity of the price discovery process by helping ensure that the prices disseminated to market users and the public reflect *bona fide* prices that accurately reflect the normal forces of supply and demand. . . .

Disregard for the Orderly Execution of Transactions During the Closing Period. . . .

The Commission interprets Congress's inclusion of a scienter requirement in CEA section 4c(a)(5)(B) as meaning that accidental, or even negligent, trading, practices, or conduct will not be a sufficient basis for the Commission to claim a violation under CEA section 4c(a)(5)(B). The Commission interprets CEA section 4c(a)(5)(B) as requiring a market participant to at least act recklessly to violate CEA section 4c(a)(5)(B). The Commission declines to interpret CEA section 4c(a)(5)(B) to include either an extreme recklessness standard or a manipulative intent requirement because this modification would alter the scienter standard mandated by the statute, which prohibits conduct that demonstrates "intentional or reckless disregard for the orderly execution of transactions during the closing period." Recklessness is a well-established scienter standard, which has consistently been defined as conduct that "departs so far from the standards of ordinary care that it is very difficult to believe the actor was not aware of what he or she was doing." Consistent with long-standing precedent under commodities and securities law, the Commission intends to apply this commonly-known definition of recklessness to CEA section 4c(a)(5)(B). A person with manipulative intent, such as one attempting to "bang" or "mark the close" may also intend to disrupt the orderly execution of transactions during the closing period, but the finding of a manipulative intent is not a prerequisite for a finding of a violation of CEA section 4c(a)(5)(B).

The Commission interprets the prohibition in CEA section 4c(a)(5)(B) to apply to any trading, conduct, or practices occurring within the closing period that demonstrates an intentional or reckless disregard for the orderly execution of transactions during the closing period. The Commission interprets the closing period to be defined generally as the period in the contract or trade when the settlement price is determined under the rules of a trading facility such as a DCM or SEF. . . . Additionally, the Commission's policy is that conduct outside the closing period may also disrupt the orderly execution of transactions during the closing period and may thus form the basis of a violation under CEA section 4c(a)(5)(B) and any other applicable CEA sections. . . .

The Commission interprets CEA section 4c(a)(5)(B) violations as including not only executed orders by market participants that disrupt the orderly execution of transactions during the closing period, but also any bids and offers submitted by market participants that disrupt the orderly execution of transactions during the closing period. . . .

"Spoofing". . . .

The Commission interprets a CEA section 4c(a)(5)(C) violation as requiring a market participant to act with some degree of intent, or scienter, beyond recklessness to engage in the "spoofing" trading practices prohibited by CEA section 4c(a)(5)(C). Because CEA section 4c(a)(5)(C) requires that a person intend to cancel a bid or offer before execution, the Commission does not interpret reckless trading, practices, or conduct as constituting a "spoofing" violation. Additionally, the Commission interprets that a spoofing violation will not occur when the person's intent when cancelling a bid or offer before execution was to cancel such bid or offer as part of a legitimate, good-faith attempt to consummate a trade. Thus, the Commission interprets the statute to mean that a legitimate, good-faith cancellation or modification of orders (e.g., partially filled orders or properly placed stop-loss orders) would not violate section CEA 4c(a)(5)(C). However, the Commission does not interpret a partial fill as automatically exempt from being classified as "spoofing" and violating CEA section 4c(a)(5)(C).

When distinguishing between legitimate trading (such as trading involving partial executions) and "spoofing," the Commission intends to evaluate the market context, the person's pattern of trading activity (including fill characteristics), and other relevant facts and circumstances. For example, if a person's intent when placing a bid or offer was to cancel the entire bid or offer prior to execution and not attempt to consummate a legitimate trade, regardless of whether such bid or offer was subsequently partially filled, that conduct may violate CEA section 4c(a)(5)(C). . . .

---

a. "Banging the Close"

Before the Dodd-Frank Act's enhancement of the CFTC's enforcement authority, the CFTC's position was that "banging the close," also known as "slamming the close," was a violation of the Commodity Exchange Act's general anti-manipulation provisions. For example, a former portfolio manager for Moore Capital Management, LP, a registered commodity trading advisor, was found by the CFTC to have engaged in "banging the close" by having:

> Caused to be entered market-on-close . . . buy orders that were executed in the last ten seconds of the closing period for . . . [palladium and platinum futures] contracts in an attempt to exert upward pressure on the settlement prices of the futures contracts.[50]

An incentive to bang the close potentially arises from swaps contracts priced based on futures daily settlement prices. A trader might seek to put many buy or sell orders in just before the short period in which futures trades are volume averaged to determine the daily settlement price (this is typically just before the market close) just to obtain a high or low settlement price in a way that benefits the party on much larger swaps positions it has. These facts are the subject of *In re Amaranth Natural Gas Commodities Litigation*,[51] discussed below in subsection 4. One court noted a variety of similar ways to express the concept of banging the close:

> . . . [T]he parties largely agree on what it means to "bang the close." According to [Defendant] Wilson, banging the close occurs where a party makes a bid in which "they think they're going to lose a little bit of money on the transaction but the movement of the price would still help some other position." [Defense expert] Harris agreed that "banging the close" involves "someone putting in a disproportionate number of trades to push the price up or down to affect the closing price, typically in a noneconomic fashion, to benefit a position that they held elsewhere." . . . Citing the CFTC's own glossary of terms, [CFTC expert] MacLaverty more circularly defined "banging the close" to be a "manipulative or disruptive trading practice whereby a trader buys or sells a large number of futures contracts during the closing period of a futures contract (that is, the period during which the futures settlement price is determined) in order to benefit an even larger position in an option, swap, or other derivative that is cash settled based on the futures settlement price on that day." . . .[52]

---

50. *In the Matter of: Moore Capital Management, LP*, CFTC Docket No. 10-09 at p. 2 (Apr. 29, 2010).
51. 730 F.3d 170 (2d Cir. 2013).
52. *CFTC v. Wilson*, 2018 WL 6322024 *17 (S.D.N.Y. Nov. 30, 2018).

b. "Spoofing"

When trading was in-person in trading pits, spoofing was self-regulating. If a trader were to make various bad faith bids and offers to create an exaggerated sense of interest in a market while avoiding actually entering into trades, the other traders would eschew him or her. One would expect it would ultimately be self-correcting, since whatever perceived benefits obtained from spoofing once would be outweighed by the long-term detriment of ostracization. With the advent of electronic trading, social sanction is no longer an effective means of disincentivizing such conduct, and the CFTC and Department of Justice have aggressively pursued spoofing cases.

In the below case, a defendant's conviction and thirty-six-month sentence for violating the new Commodity Exchange Act prohibitions on spoofing, the Commodity Exchange Act's market manipulation prohibitions, and federal criminal provisions related to fraud was upheld by the Seventh Circuit.

United States v. Michael Coscia

866 F.3d 782 (7th Cir. Aug. 7, 2017)

Ripple, Circuit Judge.

Today most commodities trading takes place on digital markets where the participants utilize computers to execute hyper-fast trading strategies at speeds, and in volumes, that far surpass those common in the past. This case involves allegations of spoofing[53] and commodities fraud in this new trading environment. The Government alleged that Michael Coscia commissioned and utilized a computer program designed to place small and large orders simultaneously on opposite sides of the commodities market in order to create illusory supply and demand and, consequently, to induce artificial market movement. Mr. Coscia was charged with violating the anti-spoofing provision of the Commodity Exchange Act, 7 U.S.C. §§ 6c(a) (5)(C) and 13(a)(2), and with commodities fraud, 18 U.S.C. § 1348(1). He was convicted by a jury and later sentenced to thirty-six months' imprisonment. . . .

Mr. Coscia now appeals. . . . He submits that the anti-spoofing statute is void for vagueness and, in any event, that the evidence on that count did not support conviction. With respect to the commodities fraud violations, he submits that the Government produced insufficient evidence. . . .

We cannot accept these submissions. The anti-spoofing provision provides clear notice and does not allow for arbitrary enforcement. Consequently, it is not unconstitutionally vague. Moreover, Mr. Coscia's spoofing conviction is supported by sufficient evidence. With respect to the commodities fraud violation, there was more than sufficient evidence to support the jury's verdict, and the district court was on solid ground with respect to its instruction to the jury on materiality. . . .

---

53. [N. 1] The term "spoofing," as will be explained in greater detail below, is defined as "bidding or offering with the intent to cancel the bid or offer before execution." 7 U.S.C. § 6c(a)(5)(C).

The charges against Mr. Coscia are based on his use of preprogrammed algorithms to execute commodities trades in high-frequency trading.[54] This sort of
trading "is a mechanism for making large volumes of trades in securities and commodities based on trading decisions effected in fractions of a second."[55] Before
proceeding with the particular facts of this case, we pause to describe the trading
environment in which these actions took place.

The basic process at the core of high-frequency trading is fairly straightforward:
trading firms use computer software to execute, at very high speed, large volumes of
trades. A number of *legitimate* trading strategies can make this practice very profitable. The simplest approaches take advantage of the minor discrepancies in the
price of a security or commodity that often emerge across national exchanges. These
price discrepancies allow traders to arbitrage between exchanges by buying low on
one and selling high on another. Because any such price fluctuations are often very
small, significant profit can be made only on a high volume of transactions. Moreover, the discrepancies often last a very short period of time (i.e., fractions of a second); speed in execution is therefore an essential attribute for firms engaged in this
business.[56]

Although high-frequency trading has legal applications, it also has increased
market susceptibility to certain forms of criminal conduct. Most notably, it has
opened the door to spoofing, which Congress criminalized in 2010 as part of the
Dodd-Frank Wall Street Reform and Consumer Protection Act, Pub. L. No. 111-
203, 124 Stat. 1376 (2010). The relevant provision proscribes "any trading, practice,
or conduct that . . . is, is of the character of, or is commonly known to the trade
as, 'spoofing' (bidding or offering with the intent to cancel the bid or offer before

---

54. [N. 4] Mr. Coscia's opening brief conflates algorithmic trading and high-frequency trading. . . . High-frequency trading, or HFT, is perhaps better conceptualized as "a subset of algorithmic trading." Tara E. Levens, Comment, *Too Fast, Too Frequent? High-Frequency Trading and
Securities Class Actions*, 82 U. Chi. L. Rev. 1511, 1527 (2015).

55. [N. 5] *United States v. Aleynikov*, 676 F.3d 71, 73 (2d Cir. 2012); *see also United States v.
Aleynikov*, 737 F.Supp.2d 173, 175 (S.D.N.Y. 2010) (explaining that HFT "involves the rapid execution
of high volumes of trades in which trading decisions are made by sophisticated computer programs
that use complex mathematical formulae known as algorithms"); *United States v. Pu*, 814 F.3d 818,
821 (7th Cir. 2016) (defining HFT as "the rapid buying and selling of publicly traded stocks").

56. [N. 6] The Southern District of New York has noted that "[s]ome commentators and, at
points, the SEC, have stated that HFT firms have a positive effect on the market by creating significant amounts of liquidity, thereby permitting the national stock market to operate more efficiently
and benefitting ordinary investors." *In re Barclays Liquidity Cross & High Frequency Trading Litig.*,
126 F.Supp.3d 342, 350 (S.D.N.Y. 2015).
Nonetheless, HFT is not unambiguously good. Rather, some have sharply criticized the HFT firms'
trading practices. Chief among their criticisms . . . is that the HFT firms use the speed at which
they are capable of trading to identify the trading strategies being pursued by ordinary investors
and react in a manner that forces ordinary investors to trade at a less advantageous price, with
the HFT firm taking as profit a portion of the "delta" — that is, the difference between the price at
which the ordinary investor would have traded and the price at which it actually traded as a result
of the HFT firm's actions. *Id.*

execution)." 7 U.S.C. § 6c(a)(5).[57] For present purposes, a bid is an order to buy and an offer is an order to sell.

In practice, spoofing, like legitimate high-frequency trading, utilizes extremely fast trading strategies. It differs from legitimate trading, however, in that it can be employed to *artificially move* the market price of a stock or commodity up and down, instead of taking advantage of natural market events (as in the price arbitrage strategy discussed above). This artificial movement is accomplished in a number of ways, although it is most simply realized by placing large and small orders on opposite sides of the market. The small order is placed at a desired price, which is either above or below the current market price, depending on whether the trader wants to buy or sell. If the trader wants to buy, the price on the small batch will be lower than the market price; if the trader wants to sell, the price on the small batch will be higher. Large orders are then placed on the opposite side of the market at prices designed to shift the market toward the price at which the small order was listed.

For example, consider an unscrupulous trader who wants to *buy* corn futures at $3.00 per bushel in a market where the current price is $3.05 per bushel. Under the basic laws of supply and demand, this trader can drive the price downward by placing *sell* orders for large numbers of corn futures on the market at incrementally decreasing prices (e.g., $3.04, then $3.03, etc.), until the market appears to be saturated with individuals wishing to sell, the price decreases, and, ultimately, the desired purchase price is reached. In short, the trader shifts the market downward through the illusion of downward market movement resulting from a surplus of supply. Importantly, the large, market-shifting orders that he places to create this illusion are ones that he never intends to execute; if they were executed, our unscrupulous trader would risk extremely large amounts of money by selling at suboptimal prices. Instead, within milliseconds of achieving the desired downward market effect, he cancels the large orders.

Once our unscrupulous trader has acquired the commodity or stock at the desired price, he can then *sell* it at a higher price than that at which he purchased it by operating the same scheme in reverse. Specifically, he will place a small sell order at the desired price and then place large buy orders at increasingly high prices until the market appears flooded with demand, the price rises, and the desired value is hit. Returning to the previous example, if our unscrupulous trader wants to sell his corn futures (recently purchased at $3.00 per bushel) for $3.10 per bushel, he will place large buy orders beginning at the market rate ($3.00), quickly increasing that dollar value (e.g., $3.01, then $3.02, then $3.03, etc.), creating an appearance of exceedingly high demand for corn futures, which raises the price, until the desired price is hit. Again, the large orders will be on the market for incredibly short periods

---

57. [N. 7] The provision has almost no legislative history. The only meaningful reference reads as follows: "The CFTC requested, and received, enforcement authority with respect to insider trading, restitution authority, and *disruptive trading practices*." 156 Cong. Rec. S5992 (daily ed. July 15, 2010) (statement of Sen. Lincoln) (emphasis added).

of time (fractions of a second), although they will often occupy a large portion of the market in order to efficiently shift the price. . . .

On October 1, 2014, a grand jury indicted Mr. Coscia for spoofing and commodities fraud based on his 2011 trading activity. Prior to trial, he moved to dismiss the indictment, arguing that the anti-spoofing provision was unconstitutionally vague. He further argued that he did not commit commodities fraud as a matter of law. The district court rejected both arguments.

Trial began on October 26, 2015, and lasted seven days. The testimony presented at trial explained that the relevant conduct began in August of 2011, lasted about ten weeks, and followed a very particular pattern. When he wanted to purchase, Mr. Coscia would begin by placing a small order requesting to trade at a price below the current market price. He then would place large-volume orders, known as "quote orders," . . . on the other side of the market. A small order could be as small as five futures contracts, whereas a large order would represent as many as fifty or more futures contracts. At times, his large orders risked up to $50 million. . . . The large orders were generally placed in increments that quickly approached the price of the small orders.

Mr. Coscia's specific activity in trading copper futures helps to clarify this dynamic. During one round of trading, Mr. Coscia placed a small sell order at a price of 32755,[58] which was, at that time, higher than the current market price. . . . Large orders were then placed on the opposite side of the market (the buy side) at steadily growing prices, which started at 32740, then increased to 32745, and increased again to 32750. . . . These buy orders created the illusion of market movement, swelling the perceived value of any given futures contract (by fostering the illusion of demand) and allowing Mr. Coscia to sell his current contracts at the desired price of 32755 — a price equilibrium that he created.

Having *sold* the five contracts for 32755, Mr. Coscia now needed to *buy* the contracts at a lower price in order to make a profit. Accordingly, he first placed an order to buy five copper futures contracts for 32750, which was below the price that he had just created. . . . Second, he placed large-volume orders on the opposite side of the market (the sell side), which totaled 184 contracts. These contracts were priced at 32770, and then 32765, which created downward momentum on the price of copper futures by fostering the appearance of abundant supply at incrementally decreasing prices. The desired devaluation of the contracts was almost immediately achieved, allowing Mr. Coscia to buy his small orders at the artificially deflated price of 32750. The large orders were then immediately cancelled. . . . The whole process outlined above took place in approximately two-thirds of a second, and was repeated tens of thousands of times, resulting in over 450,000 large orders, and earning Mr. Coscia

---

58. [N. 10] As explained at trial: The tick size for copper futures is one-half of one-thousandth of a cent. So for purposes of the way these prices are here, the tick size is an increment of five. . . . In other words, increments of five represent (at least for copper futures) one-half of one-thousandth of a cent.

$1.4 million. All told, the trial evidence suggested that this process allowed Mr. Coscia to buy low and sell high in a market artificially distorted by his actions.

The Government also introduced evidence regarding Mr. Coscia's intent to cancel the large orders prior to their execution. The primary items of evidence in support of this allegation were the two programs that Mr. Coscia had commissioned to facilitate his trading scheme: Flash Trader and Quote Trader. The designer of the programs, Jeremiah Park, testified that Mr. Coscia asked that the programs act "[l]ike a decoy," which would be "[u]sed to pump [the] market." [Park] . . . noted that the large-volume orders were designed specifically to avoid being filled and accordingly would be canceled in three particular circumstances: (1) based on the passage of time (usually measured in milliseconds); (2) the partial filling of the large orders; or (3) complete filling of the small orders. . . .

A great deal of testimony was presented at trial to support the contention that Mr. Coscia's programs functioned within their intended parameters. . . .

The jury convicted Mr. Coscia on all counts. Mr. Coscia then filed a motion for acquittal. The district court denied the motion in a memorandum opinion and order issued on April 6, 2016. The district court determined that the evidence was sufficient to prove that Mr. Coscia committed commodities fraud and that his deception was material. Moreover, with respect to the spoofing charge, the court held that the statute was not void for vagueness. Finally, the court denied a challenge to the definition of materiality provided in the commodities fraud jury instructions.

Thereafter, the district court, applying a fourteen-point enhancement for the estimated loss attributable to the illegal actions, sentenced Mr. Coscia to thirty-six months' imprisonment to be followed by two years' supervised release. . . .

For the convenience of the reader, we set forth the statutory provision in its entirety: . . .

> It shall be unlawful for any person to engage in any trading, practice, or conduct on or subject to the rules of a registered entity that . . .
>
> is, is of the character of, or is commonly known to the trade as, "spoofing" (bidding or offering with the intent to cancel the bid or offer before execution). . . .

Mr. Coscia first submits that the statute gives inadequate notice of the proscribed conduct. He submits that Congress did not intend the parenthetical included in the statute to define spoofing. . . . Mr. Coscia contends that, by "placing 'spoofing' in quotation marks and referring to a 'commonly known' definition in the trade, Congress clearly signaled its (mistaken) belief that the definition of 'spoofing' had been established in the industry as a term of art." . . . We cannot accept this argument; it overlooks that the anti-spoofing provision . . . contains a parenthetical definition, rendering any reference to an industry definition irrelevant. . . .

Mr. Coscia contends that the lack of a Commodity Futures Trading Commission regulation defining the contours of spoofing adds to his lack of notice. Nonetheless, the Supreme Court has explained that "the touchstone [of a fair warning inquiry] is whether the statute, either standing alone or as construed, made it reasonably clear at the relevant time that the defendant's conduct was criminal." *United States v. Lanier*, 520 U.S. 259, 267, 117 S.Ct. 1219, 137 L.Ed.2d 432 (1997). Consequently, because the statute clearly defines "spoofing" in the parenthetical, Mr. Coscia had adequate notice of the prohibited conduct.

Mr. Coscia also makes a broader notice argument. He contends, in effect, that the absence of *any* guidance external to the statutory language — no legislative history, no recognized industry definition, no Commodity Futures Trading Commission rule — leaves a person of ordinary intelligence to speculate about the definition Congress intended when it placed "spoofing" in quotation marks. . . .

Congress enacted the anti-spoofing provision specifically to stop spoofing — a term it defined in the statute. Accordingly, any agency inaction . . . is irrelevant; Congress provided the necessary definition and, in doing so, put the trading community on notice. . . .

Mr. Coscia next contends that, even if the statute gives adequate notice, the parenthetical definition encourages arbitrary enforcement. He specifically notes that high-frequency traders cancel 98% of orders before execution and that there are simply no "tangible parameters to distinguish [Mr.] Coscia's purported intent from that of the other traders." . . .

This argument does not help Mr. Coscia. The Supreme Court has made clear that "[a] plaintiff who engages in some conduct that is clearly proscribed cannot complain of the vagueness of the law as applied to the conduct of others." *Holder v. Humanitarian Law Project*, 561 U.S. 1, 18–19, 130 S.Ct. 2705, 177 L.Ed.2d 355 (2010) (alteration in original). . . . Rather, the defendant must prove that *his* prosecution arose from arbitrary enforcement. . . .

Mr. Coscia cannot claim that an impermissibly vague statute has resulted in arbitrary enforcement because his conduct falls well within the provision's prohibited conduct: he commissioned a program designed to pump or deflate the market through the use of large orders that were *specifically designed* to be cancelled if they ever risked actually being filled. His program would cancel the large orders (1) after the passage of time, (2) if the small orders were filled, or (3) if a single large order was filled. Read together, these parameters clearly indicate an intent to cancel, which was further supported by his actual trading record. Accordingly, because Mr. Coscia's behavior clearly falls within the confines of the conduct prohibited by the statute, he cannot challenge any allegedly arbitrary enforcement that could hypothetically be suffered by a theoretical legitimate trader. . . .

[T]he anti-spoofing statute's intent requirement renders spoofing meaningfully different from legal trades such as "stop-loss orders" ("an order to sell a security once it reaches a certain price") . . . or "fill-or-kill orders" ("an order that must be executed in full immediately, or the entire order is cancelled") . . . because those orders are designed to be executed upon the arrival of *certain subsequent events*.

Spoofing, on the other hand, requires, an intent to cancel the order *at the time it was placed*. . . . The fundamental difference is that legal trades are cancelled only following a condition subsequent to placing the order, whereas orders placed in a spoofing scheme are never intended to be filled at all. . . .

Having determined that the anti-spoofing provision is not void for vagueness, we next address Mr. Coscia's contention that the evidence of record does not support his spoofing conviction. . . .

[A] conviction for spoofing requires that the prosecution prove beyond a reasonable doubt that Mr. Coscia knowingly entered bids or offers with the present intent to cancel the bid or offer prior to execution. Mr. Coscia's trading history clearly indicates that he cancelled the vast majority of his large orders. Accordingly, the only issue is whether a rational trier of fact could have found that Mr. Coscia possessed an intent to cancel the large orders at the time he placed them.

A review of the trial evidence reveals the following. First, Mr. Coscia's cancellations represented 96% of all Brent futures cancellations on the Intercontinental Exchange during the two-month period in which he employed his software. . . . Second, on the Chicago Mercantile Exchange, 35.61% of his small orders were filled, whereas only 0.08% of his large orders were filled . . . [and] only 0.5% of his large orders were filled on the Intercontinental Exchange. . . . Mathew Evans, the senior vice president of NERA Economic Consulting, testified that Coscia's order-to-trade ratio was 1,592%, whereas the order-to-trade ratio for other market participants ranged from 91% to 264%. . . . As explained at trial, these figures "mean[ ] that Michael Coscia's average order [was] much larger than his average trade" — i.e., it further suggests that the large orders were placed, not with the intent to actually consummate the transaction, but rather to shift the market toward the artificial price at which the small orders were ultimately traded.

We believe that, given this evidence, a rational trier of fact easily could have found that, at the time he placed his orders, Mr. Coscia had the "intent to cancel before execution." As in all cases based upon circumstantial evidence, no single piece of evidence necessarily establishes spoofing. Nonetheless, when evaluated in its totality, the cumulative evidence certainly allowed a rational trier of fact to determine that Mr. Coscia entered his orders with the intent to cancel them before their execution. . . .

Mr. Coscia also challenges his conviction for commodities fraud. . . .

Mr. Coscia contends that the jury could not reasonably have found that he had a fraudulent intent because his conduct was not fraudulent as a matter of law. He also contends that the court applied an incorrect materiality standard. . . .

Mr. Coscia contends that because "his orders were fully executable and subject to legitimate market risk," they were not, as a matter of law, fraudulent. . . .

We cannot accept this argument. At bottom, Mr. Coscia "confuses *illusory* orders with an *illusion* of market movement." The evidence of record supports the conclusion that Mr. Coscia designed a scheme to pump and deflate the market through the placement of large orders. His scheme was deceitful because, at the time he placed the large orders, he intended to cancel the orders. . . .

Mr. Coscia engaged in ten weeks of trading during which he placed orders with the clear intent to cancel those orders prior to execution. As a result, Mr. Coscia violated the plain wording of the Dodd-Frank Act's anti-spoofing provision. Mr. Coscia engaged in this behavior in order to inflate or deflate the price of certain commodities. His trading accordingly also constituted commodities fraud. . . . Mr. Coscia's conviction is affirmed. . . .

———————

Some recent criminal spoofing cases do not charge the defendant with a Commodity Exchange Act violation. Instead, the charge is for violation of the federal mail and wire fraud statute. As one court noted, referring to *United States v. Coscia*:

> In the face of the Seventh Circuit's unequivocal holding that futures orders placed with an undisclosed intent to cancel them before they are filled can be fraudulent, the defendants acknowledge that "there is some precedent" that spoofing violates subsection (1) of the commodities fraud statute and therefore assume "for the sake of argument" that a scheme to place orders that one intends not to fill constitutes a species of commodities fraud. . . . But, they urge, the failure to disclose such intent is not fraudulent in the context of this case because "mere failure to disclose, absent something more, does not constitute fraud under the mail and wire fraud statutes." . . .
>
> In seeking to limit *Coscia*'s import to commodities fraud charges, the defendants' acknowledgment of the Seventh Circuit's holding is far too grudging. *Coscia* plainly held that a spoofing scheme can constitute a "scheme to defraud." 866 F.3d at 796-97. That holding is controlling authority, binding on this Court, and must be confronted head on: A spoofing scheme like the one the defendants are alleged to have engaged in is a scheme to defraud under the commodities fraud statute. The wire fraud statute, like the commodities fraud statute at issue in *Coscia*, requires proof of a scheme to defraud. Per force, unless a "scheme to defraud" under the commodities fraud statute means something different than a "scheme to defraud" under the wire fraud statute, a spoofing scheme that employs interstate wire communications constitutes wire fraud as well. . . .
>
> Given that the Seventh Circuit borrowed the definition of a "scheme to defraud" from the mail and wire fraud instructions, the defendants' contention that *Coscia*'s holding that a spoofing scheme constitutes a scheme to defraud is "irrelevant" to an assessment of the wire fraud charge in this case is plainly wrong. If spoofing can be a scheme to defraud under §1348(1) — and it can, the Seventh Circuit has held — it can be a scheme to defraud under the wire fraud statute as well. . . .[59]

———————

59. *United States v. Vorley*, 420 F. Supp. 3d 784, 791-795 (N.D. Ill. 2019).

On the other hand, one can ask whether the criminal prohibitions on spoofing and the more generic federal wire fraud prohibition operate with the extensive similarly described by the court in *Vorley*. If they do, then how does the Department of Justice determine whether to charge a party with one or the other?[60]

Possibly providing a setback to the CFTC's expansive inference of spoofing intent was the district court in *CFTC v. Wilson*. The CFTC's action related to events predating the Commodity Exchange Act's specific spoofing prohibition. Therefore, it was predicated on the Commodity Exchange Act's general anti-fraud and anti-market manipulation provisions. Since the central allegation was spoofing, it could provide some insight into future skepticism that an expansive assertion by the CFTC of what conduct falls within the spoofing prohibition might receive in court.

In *Wilson*, Donald Wilson and his firm DRW Investments, LLC identified what was believed to be a mispricing in the market. It bid, during the settlement period, on a contract called the "IDEX USD Three-Month Interest Rate Swap Futures Contract" traded on a futures exchange and cleared by a clearinghouse. The settlement price of the contract was determined by the clearinghouse considering, among others, bids and offers placed during a fifteen-minute settlement window. The variation margin posted or received depended on the settlement price. The existence of variation margin made it economically different than an otherwise identical uncleared swap where the parties did not exchange margin. To influence the pricing of the contract to what DRW thought it should be, it placed bids during the settlement period that were seemingly off-market and only matched once (and, due to a clearing delay caused by a snowstorm, the other party refused to honor the trade and it ended up settling as a pre-litigation dispute).

The court noted:

> First, there is no evidence that DRW ever made a bid that it thought might be unprofitable. . . .
>
> Second, there is no credible evidence that DRW ever made a bid that it thought could not be accepted by a counterparty. . . .
>
> Third, the CFTC provided no credible evidence as to what the fair value of the contract actually was at the time DRW was making its bids. . . .
>
> Fourth, there is no credible evidence that DRW's bidding practices ever scared off would-be market participants. . . .
>
> And finally, there is no evidence that DRW ever made a bid that violated any rule of the exchange — a fact the CFTC conceded in its closing argument. . . .[61]

---

60. *See, e.g., United States v. Bases*, 2020 WL 2557342 (N.D. Ill. May 20, 2020), where the parties were charged with violating the Commodity Exchange Act's prohibition on spoofing, the federal criminal prohibition on fraud in commodity futures or options, and the wire fraud statute.

61. *CFTC v. Wilson*, 2018 WL 6322024 *11 (S.D.N.Y. Nov. 30, 2018).

More pointedly, the court concluded that:

> It is not illegal to be smarter than your counterparties in a swap transaction, nor is it improper to understand a financial product better than the people who invented that product. In the summer and fall of 2010, Don Wilson believed that he comprehended the true value of the Three-Month Contract better than anyone else. . . . He developed a trading strategy based on that conviction, and put his firm's money at risk to test it. He didn't need to manipulate the market to capitalize on that superior knowledge, and there is absolutely no evidence to suggest that he ever did so in the months that followed.
>
> By August 2011, virtually every market participant . . . came to acknowledge that Wilson was right, that the Three-Month Contract was not the economic equivalent of an OTC swap, and that it was in fact significantly more valuable. . . . It is only the CFTC's Enforcement Division that has persisted in its cry of market manipulation, based on little more than an "earth is flat"-style conviction that such manipulation must have happened because the market remained illiquid. Clearly, that is not enough to prove market manipulation or attempted market manipulation, and the CFTC has simply failed to meet its burden on any cause of action. . . .[62]

Therefore, it seems that a good faith bid or offer that is unlikely to be matched may not be sufficient indicia of spoofing, regardless of how frequently the bids and offers are made. This results in an enforcement challenge for the CFTC—how does one distinguish between a good faith market perspective and purposeful distortion? Perhaps it does not matter, because the CFTC's new specific anti-spoofing authority has a lower legal standard, simply prohibiting what "is, is of the character of, or is commonly known to the trade as, 'spoofing' (bidding or offering with the intent to cancel the bid or offer before execution)"?[63]

The Benefits of Cooperation

The CFTC settled numerous spoofing claims in 2017 related to activities at Citigroup. For the first time in the CFTC's history, it also entered into non-prosecution agreements with three individuals. The CFTC noted the individuals' "timely and substantial cooperation, immediate willingness to accept responsibility for their misconduct, material assistance to the CFTC's investigation of Citigroup, and the absence of a history of prior misconduct."[a]

[a] CFTC, *CFTC Enters into Non-Prosecution Agreements with Former Citigroup Global Markets Inc. Traders Jeremy Lao, Daniel Liao, and Shlomo Salant*, CFTC Release pr7581-17 (June 29, 2017), available at https://www.cftc.gov/PressRoom/PressReleases/7581-17.

---

62. *CFTC v. Wilson*, 2018 WL 6322024 *21 (S.D.N.Y. Nov. 30, 2018).
63. Commodity Exchange Act § 4c(a)(5).

4. Position Limits and Cornering

The Commodity Exchange Act in addition to criminalizing manipulation generally as described in section C above, also prohibits "cornering" by making it a felony for anyone to "corner or attempt to corner any . . . commodity or knowingly to deliver or cause to be delivered . . . false or misleading or knowingly inaccurate reports concerning crop or market information or conditions that affect or tend to affect the price of any commodity. . . ."[64] For physical commodities, in addition to the prohibition on cornering, a method of combating cornering is through position limits. Both the CFTC and designated contract markets have position limit rules.

a. CFTC Position Limits

CFTC rules impose position limits on commodity futures or options (algebraically converted into a "futures equivalent") on corn, soybeans, wheat, soybean oil, and soybean meal traded on the Chicago Board of Trade, hard red spring wheat traded on the Minneapolis Grain Exchange, cotton traded on ICE Futures, and hard winter wheat traded on the Kansas City Board of Trade.[65] There is a general exemption for any *bona fide* hedging position.[66]

Note that, for the commodities for which the CFTC has not established position limits directly, the Commodity Exchange Act and the CFTC require designated contract markets to establish position limits or "accountability levels," both discussed below in subsection b.[67] During the "spot month," i.e., the month in which a contract matures and physical delivery will be required, position limits are typically stricter.

Note also that these particular position limits do not apply to swaps. For a discussion of position limits and swaps, see subsection c below.

In re AG Processing Inc A Cooperative

CFTC Docket No. 21-02 (Jan. 26, 2021)

. . . The Commodity Futures Trading Commission ("Commission") has reason to believe that from in or about December 2017 to at least July 2019 ("Relevant Period"), Ag Processing Inc a cooperative ("AGP") violated Section 4a(b)(2) of the Commodity Exchange Act ("Act"), 7 U.S.C. § 6a(b)(2) (2018), and Regulation 150.2, 17 C.F.R. § 150.2 (2019), of the Commission Regulations ("Regulations") promulgated thereunder. Therefore, the Commission deems it appropriate and in the public interest that public administrative proceedings be, and hereby are, instituted to determine

---

64. Commodity Exchange Act § 9(a)(2).
65. 17 C.F.R. § 150.2.
66. 17 C.F.R. § 150.3(a)(1).
67. *See* Commodity Exchange Act § 5(d)(5) and 17 C.F.R. § 150.5.

whether AGP engaged in the violations set forth herein and to determine whether any order should be issued imposing remedial sanctions.

In anticipation of the institution of an administrative proceeding, AGP has submitted an Offer of Settlement ("Offer"), which the Commission has determined to accept. . . .

On multiple occasions during the Relevant Period, AGP held a position in Chicago Board of Trade ("CBOT") Soybean Meal futures contracts that exceeded the all-months speculative position limit for that contract set forth in Regulation 150.2, 17 C.F.R. §150.2 (2019). In exceeding the position limits for these futures contracts during the Relevant Period, AGP violated Section 4a(b)(2) of the Act, 7 U.S.C. §6a(b) (2) (2018), and Regulation 150.2. . . .

Regulation 150.2, 17 C.F.R. §150.2 (2019), sets forth the speculative position limit levels for soybean meal futures contracts, including the position limit for the spot month and all-months. Regulation 150.1(a), 17 C.F.R. §150.1(a) (2019), defines "spot month" as "the futures contract next to expire during that period of time beginning at the close of trading on the trading day preceding the first day on which delivery notices can be issued to the clearing organization of a contract market." Regulation 150.1(c) defines "all-months" as "the sum of all futures trading months including the spot month future." Regulation 150.2 provides that the all-months limit for the soybean meal futures contract is 6500.

"Bona fide hedging transactions," as defined in Regulation 1.3, 17 C.F.R. §1.3 (2010), are exempt from the Commission's position limits. *See* Regulation 150.3, 17 C.F.R. §150.3 (2019). Persons holding or controlling futures positions that are "reportable[,] . . . any part of which constitute bona fide hedging positions[,]" must file a Form 204 with the Commission. *See* Regulation 19.00(a)(1), 17 C.F.R. §19.00(a) (1) (2019). A "reportable position" includes any combined futures contract position in any one month or in all months combined, either net long or net short in any commodity on any one reporting market, which at the close of the market on the last business day of the week exceeds the position limit for that commodity as set forth in Regulation 150.2. *See* Regulation 15.00(p)(2), 17 C.F.R. §15.00(p)(2) (2019). The Form 204 must show "the composition of the fixed price cash position of each commodity hedged." *See* Regulation 19.01(a), 17 C.F.R. §19.01(a) (2019).

During the Relevant Period, AGP purchased large volumes of local soybeans, which it processed into soybean meal and crude soybean oil through a process known as crushing. In order to hedge its risk as a soybean crusher, AGP, among other things, took positions in the CBOT Soybean Meal futures contract that exceeded the Commission's speculative position limit and its fixed price cash positions for such contracts, as reflected in its Form 204s filed with the Commission. AGP applied for and received exemptions from the CME Group, Inc. ("CME") that permitted AGP to exceed CME's position limits as set forth in Rule 559 of the CBOT Rulebook. AGP filed timely Forms 204 with the Commission and traded within its CME-granted exemptions, but at no point during the Relevant Period did AGP either seek or receive authorization from the Commission to exceed its position limits set forth in Regulation 150.2.[68] As a result, on multiple occasions during the Relevant Period, AGP violated the Commission's all-months position limit for the soybean meal futures contract because its cash positions, as reflected in its Form 204s, were insufficient to offset its futures positions. During these numerous violations, AGP was over the all-months position limit by between 63 and 1357 futures positions. These futures positions represented overages of anywhere between 1% and 20.9%. AGP has since filed its submission with the Commission and received approval for its anticipated unfilled hedge exemption. AGP also cooperated with the Commission during its investigation. . . .

The Commission is not required to establish scienter to prove a violation of the Commission's speculative position limit provisions. That is, the Commission does not need to prove that AGP intended to exceed a position limit. *Saberi v. CFTC,* 488 F.3d 1207, 1212 (9th Cir. 2007); *CFTC v. Hunt,* 591 F.2d 1211, 1218 (7th Cir. 1979). The Act "unambiguously imposes liability" for violations of position limits. *Saberi,* 488 F.3d at 1212 n.4 (rejecting a trader's contention that the Division was required to prove that he intended to violate the speculative position limits) (citing *Hunt,* 591 F.2d at 1218).

Because AGP held positions in the CBOT Soybean Meal futures contract that exceeded the all-months speculative position limit for that contract on multiple occasions during the Relevant Period, it violated Section 4a(b) of the Act and Regulation 150.2. . . .

————

The CFTC fined AG Processing Inc $400,000 for the violations. Note the CFTC's position that there is no scienter requirement for a position limits violation.

For the purposes of calculating whether a person has exceeded position limits, positions in separate accounts are aggregated when they are commonly controlled or when "two or more persons [are] acting pursuant to an expressed or implied agreement or understanding. . . ."[69]

————

68. [N. 2] The CME's exemption approval letters to AGP specifically state that "the Commodity Futures Trading Commission has separate rules regarding position limits in agricultural futures and options contracts with which the holder of this exemption must also comply." Moreover, CBOT Rule 559 states that an applicant for a CME exemption must "[a]ffirm that the requested exemption complies with any applicable CFTC requirements and, for those contracts with Federal limits, that the exemption request has been approved by the CFTC." Nevertheless, AGP mistakenly believed that its exchange-granted exemptions also applied to federal position limits.

69. Commodity Exchange Act § 4a(a)(1).

CFTC v. Hunt

591 F.2d 1211 (7th Cir. 1979)

Swygert, Circuit Judge.

This case presents several issues arising out of a complaint brought by the Commodity Futures Trading Commission, pursuant to the Commodity Exchange Act, against seven members of the Hunt family and an affiliated company. The complaint was instituted by the Commission . . . to compel the defendants to comply with limits established by the Commission on the speculative position that any individual or group may have in soybean futures contracts.

The Commission's complaint alleges that from at least January 17, 1977 and continuing to the commencement of the court action, two brothers, Nelson Bunker Hunt and William Herbert Hunt, five of their children, and a corporation they control, had been exceeding collectively the limit of three million bushels that had been set for soybean futures contracts. . . .

[T]he district court . . . concluded that the Hunts . . . had acquired soybean futures in excess of the three million bushel limit prescribed by regulation. . . .

The Hunts . . . [seek] to overturn the district court's declaratory judgment that the Hunts had violated the speculative limit. . . .

[T]he Commodity Exchange Act . . . authorizes the Commodity Futures Trading Commission to set commodity trading limits. Congress concluded that excessive speculation in commodity contracts for future delivery can cause adverse fluctuations in the price of a commodity, and authorized the Commission to restrict the positions held or trading done by any individual person or by certain groups of people acting in concert. . . .

[The Commodity Exchange Act] provides for the aggregation of commodity positions for purposes of determining whether the speculative limit has been exceeded, when one person "directly or indirectly" controls the trading of another, or when two persons are acting "pursuant to an express or implied agreement or understanding. . . ." Thus, even though two persons acting in concert might each individually have a commodity position below the limit, if their combined position exceeds the limit they have violated the statute. Further, contrary to the arguments advanced by the Hunts, there is nothing in either the statutory language or legislative history which suggests that intent either to affect market prices or specific intent to exceed the speculative limits is a necessary element of a violation. . . . A violation occurs simply when an individual or several individuals acting in concert exceed the commodity position limits set pursuant to the statute. . . .

Nelson Bunker Hunt and William Herbert Hunt were the principal family figures in these transactions. They are brothers, and the chief officers of the Hunt Energy Corporation. In mid-1976 N. B. and W. H. Hunt entered the soybean market. By

August 1 each brother consistently held a long position at the three million bushel limit, usually for the closest delivery month. Through a series of purchases the date, timing, and size of which were virtually identical each brother, by January 1977, held a three million bushel position in March 1977 soybeans. Over the next six weeks each of the Hunt brothers entered into eight transactions on the same days, using the same broker, involving virtually identical quantities and prices. Throughout this time an employee of the Hunt Energy Corporation, Charles Mercer, prepared commodity position statements for the brothers reflecting their combined holdings and unrealized profits and losses.

On February 25, with both N. B. and W. H. Hunt at the personal position limit, N. B. Hunt ordered a purchase, through one of his brokers, of 750,000 bushels of May soybeans in the name of his son, Houston Hunt. On March 3 he ordered the purchase of 750,000 May bushels to be allocated equally among accounts he had opened on behalf of his three daughters. And, although the bank accounts of the various children lacked the funds to cover these purchases, the transactions were made possible by a short-term transfer of interest-free funds from their father's account. N. B. Hunt's children did not participate in these initial soybean transactions made in their names: they had nothing to do with opening the accounts, placing the first order, or arranging financing for their purchases. And once these family members had entered the soybean market, their transactions were added to the composite report sent to N. B. Hunt.

A similar relationship existed between W. H. Hunt and his son, Douglas. On March 1 W. H. Hunt and his wife transferred their interests in Hunt Holdings, Inc. to their three sons. Less than a week later Douglas Hunt personally and through Hunt Holdings, whose trading he controlled, began purchasing July soybeans. These purchases were financed in part by money advanced by his father. . . .

As of April 14, 1977 the Hunt family's collective position involved over twenty-three million bushels of old crop soybeans: over 10.8 million in May futures, 7.7 million in July futures, and 5.2 million in August futures. . . . [T]he evidence presented in the district court clearly indicates that the individual positions of the family members should be aggregated. Thus, the Hunt family soybean transactions constituted a violation of the Commodity Exchange Act. . . .

———————

b. Position Limits Imposed by Designated Contract Markets

In addition to the position limits imposed directly by the CFTC, the Commodity Exchange Act and CFTC rules require designated contract markets to impose their own position limits or, alternatively, with CFTC approval, accountability reporting requirements that, instead of imposing a hard limit on the number of contracts that may be traded by any common enterprise, require notifications to the exchange once specified thresholds are exceeded and provide the exchange the opportunity to prohibit the acquisition of further positions.[70] As with the CFTC's position limits, there is a *bona fide* hedging exemption.[71]

In the following case, the question arose as to the extent of aiding and abetting liability for a futures commission merchant whose customer has exceeded position and accountability limits as well as engaged in "slamming the close" market manipulation. (As noted in section D.3.a above, "slamming the close" is another phrase for "banging the close.") We examined a related case, *Hunter v. FERC* in chapter 4, section C.3, in the context of evaluating a jurisdictional dispute that arose between the CFTC and the Federal Energy Regulatory Commission.

In re Amaranth Natural Gas Commodities Litigation
730 F.3d 170 (2d Cir. 2013)

Debra Ann Livingston, Circuit Judge:

In the fall of 2006, Amaranth Advisors LLC ("Amaranth"), a hedge fund that had heavily invested in natural gas futures, collapsed. A Senate investigation would later conclude that Amaranth, in the months leading up to its demise, had taken positions in natural gas futures and swaps so massive that its trading directly affected domestic natural gas prices and price volatility. Plaintiffs-Appellants, traders who had bought or sold natural gas futures during these same months, filed a complaint in the United States District Court for the Southern District of New York alleging that Amaranth had manipulated the price of natural gas futures in violation of the Commodities [sic] Exchange Act ("CEA"). Plaintiffs-Appellants also alleged that Defendants-Appellees J.P. Morgan Chase & Co., J.P. Morgan Chase Bank, Inc., and J.P. Morgan Futures, Inc. ("J.P. Futures") (collectively, "J.P. Morgan") had aided and abetted Amaranth's manipulation of natural gas futures through J.P. Futures's services as Amaranth's futures commission merchant and clearing broker. The district court ... concluded that both Plaintiffs-Appellants' complaint and amended complaint failed to state claims against J.P. Morgan. ...

We conclude that the district court did not err. ...

NYMEX is a designated contract market, or "DCM." As a DCM, NYMEX may offer options and futures trading for any type of commodity, but is subject to extensive oversight from the Commodity Futures Trading Commission ("CFTC"). ... NYMEX [must] establish position limits and accountability levels for each type of contract that it offers for trading. A "position limit" is a cap on the number of contracts that a trader may hold or control for a particular option or future at a particular time, with exceptions provided for traders engaged in *bona fide* hedging. An "accountability level" provides that once a trader holds or controls a certain

---

70. Commodity Exchange Act § 5(d)(5) and 17 C.F.R. § 150.5(e).
71. 17 C.F.R. § 150.5(d).

number of contracts for a particular option or future she must provide information about that position upon request by the exchange and, if the exchange so orders, stop increasing her position. At the time of the events alleged in the amended complaint, NYMEX had set a position limit of 1,000 contracts, net short or net long, for any natural gas future, applicable during the last three days of trading. NYMEX had also set corresponding accountability limits, which varied in size based on the trader's capitalization and applied at all times the future was traded. . . .

Amaranth . . . began to acquire large "spread" positions in NYMEX natural gas futures.[72] Specifically, Amaranth acquired "calendar" spreads between natural gas futures for different months. Since many homes and businesses use it for indoor heating, natural gas has a highly seasonal price that rises in the colder winter months and falls in the warmer summer months. By taking large spread positions, Amaranth was betting that the difference between these winter and summer prices would increase.

Amaranth started to build up short positions for the March 2006, April 2006, and November 2006 NYMEX natural gas futures, while at the same time acquiring a long position for the January 2007 future. The sizes of these positions were exceptional. Most traders consider control of only a few hundred contracts to be a substantial position; a position of 10,000 NYMEX natural gas futures contracts, meanwhile, will produce $1,000,000 in profit or loss for every cent of price change. Amaranth, however, soon acquired positions of over 40,000 March 2006 and 27,000 April 2006 contracts. These positions also represented a substantial share of the market. By February, Amaranth controlled over half of the open interest on NYMEX November 2006 natural gas futures contracts, and held a similar percentage of January 2007 contracts.

While Amaranth was building its spread positions during the first half of 2006, it also engaged in several unusual transactions, referred to by Plaintiffs-Appellants in their amended complaint as "slamming the close" trades. These trades all followed the same pattern: in the weeks leading up to a NYMEX future's expiration, Amaranth would simultaneously acquire a long position in the future and a short position in the corresponding swap on ICE. Then, during the last half hour of trading on the final trading day—the final settlement period—Amaranth would sell most or all of its long position, thus lowering the future's final settlement price. This would then lower the final settlement price of the corresponding ICE swap, allowing Amaranth to profit from its short position in that swap.

Amaranth engaged in these "slamming the close" trades for the March 2006, April 2006, and May 2006 NYMEX natural gas futures [contracts]. . . . Subsequent investigations would reveal that Amaranth traders discussed "smashing" the settlement price of these NYMEX futures and directed floor brokers not to sell the contracts until the final minutes of trading.

---

72. [N. 6] A spread position is created when a trader takes a long position in one future and a short position in another. The trader seeks to profit from changes in the difference between the two futures' prices, rather than from any absolute changes to the futures' prices themselves.

In conducting these trades, Amaranth violated NYMEX position limits and accountability levels, which prompted investigations from both NYMEX and the CFTC. NYMEX also sought to limit Amaranth's trading for the June 2006 future, even contacting J.P. Futures, Amaranth's clearing broker, in May to remind it that Amaranth needed to remain below applicable position limits. Amaranth failed to heed these warnings, and on June 1 it appeared on a list of traders exceeding applicable accountability levels. Nevertheless, NYMEX's initial response to Amaranth's having again exceeded accountability levels was to recommend their temporary increase. Then in early August, NYMEX informed Amaranth that it should reduce its positions in the September 2006 natural gas future. Amaranth responded by shifting its positions in September and October natural gas futures to the corresponding swaps. . . .

By early September 2006, Amaranth had a total open position in natural gas futures and swaps of 594,455 contracts. The fund's ever-increasing positions kept the spreads between winter and summer natural gas prices artificially high. Indeed, energy traders would subsequently describe the spread between winter and summer prices as "clearly out-of-whack" and "ridiculous." The Senate Permanent Subcommittee on Investigations would later conclude that Amaranth "dominated" the domestic natural gas market in 2006, and "had a direct effect on U.S. natural gas prices and increased price volatility in the natural gas market." This investigation would reveal that Amaranth traders discussed using the fund's large positions to, among other things, "push" and "widen" spreads.

By September 2006, however, the market for natural gas moved in ways that disrupted Amaranth's positions. As the winter months approached, it became clearer that the price of natural gas would not rise considerably; the winter/summer price spreads in which Amaranth had invested consequently began to fall. Amaranth, faced with ballooning margin requirements, struggled to find the capital or credit necessary to continue buying large positions that could prop up prices. On the brink of collapse, the fund entered into negotiations with several investment banks to sell off its natural gas positions. These negotiations fell through, and on September 20, 2006, Amaranth sold most of its natural gas portfolio to J.P. Morgan. J.P. Morgan eventually earned $725 million from the takeover. Amaranth liquidated the remainder of its assets. . . .

As Amaranth's clearing broker, J.P. Futures "marked to market" Amaranth's positions on a daily basis in order to determine if Amaranth needed to deposit additional margin. This, along with J.P. Futures's other roles as a clearing broker, meant that it knew of Amaranth's positions and trading activity. As the clearing broker, J.P. Futures also knew when Amaranth violated NYMEX position limits or exceeded NYMEX accountability levels. Indeed, NYMEX contacted J.P. Futures directly in May 2006 to warn it about Amaranth's position in the June 2006 NYMEX natural gas future. Additionally, J.P. Futures knew of the positions Amaranth took in connection with its "slamming the close" trades. It similarly knew about the NYMEX and CFTC investigations into Amaranth's trading.

Throughout the class period, J.P. Futures continued to service all of Amaranth's trades, including those that put Amaranth's positions above applicable NYMEX position limits and accountability levels. On one occasion in late May 2006, J.P. Futures bypassed its own internal position limits for natural gas futures in order to clear a series of large trading transactions undertaken by Amaranth. During the summer months of 2006, J.P. Futures regularly granted Amaranth credit limit increases to support its positions on ICE. J.P. Futures facilitated Amaranth's transfer of positions from NYMEX natural gas futures to ICE natural gas swaps, which were beyond CFTC and NYMEX scrutiny. This transfer resulted in higher margin requirements for Amaranth, and thus increased fees and interest for J.P. Futures. . . .

[B]oth the CFTC and courts have determined that the standard for aiding and abetting liability under the CEA is the same as that for aiding and abetting under federal criminal law. . . .

As stated earlier, Plaintiffs-Appellants allege that Amaranth manipulated the price of NYMEX natural gas futures in two ways: (1) the accumulation of large open positions that artificially propped up natural gas calendar spreads; and (2) its "slamming the close" trades. Plaintiffs-Appellants allege that J.P. Futures had knowledge of these manipulative schemes because it had information on Amaranth's daily trading activity and open positions on NYMEX and ICE. This information also meant that J.P. Futures knew when Amaranth was in violation of NYMEX position limits or accountability levels. Plaintiffs-Appellants further allege that J.P. Futures performed multiple overt acts to assist Amaranth in its manipulations, including the clearing of trades, the extension of credit, and assistance in moving positions from NYMEX to ICE. According to the amended complaint, J.P. Futures assisted Amaranth because of the large commissions J.P. Futures earned from the fund's trading, as well as fees and interest it earned on the fund's margin deposits.

With respect to Plaintiffs-Appellants' first theory of manipulation — the building of large open positions — the amended complaint alleges, at most, a very weak inference that J.P. Futures actually knew of Amaranth's manipulative intent, much less that it intended to assist in carrying it out. This is for a simple reason: while J.P. Futures may have known about Amaranth's large positions in natural gas futures and swaps, such large positions do not necessarily imply manipulation. A trader may indeed acquire a large position in order to manipulate prices. But a trader may also acquire a large position in the belief that the price of the future will, for reasons other than the trader's own activity, move in a favorable direction. Put differently, large positions can be indicative either of manipulation or of excessive speculation. The amended complaint contains no allegation from which we can draw the conclusion that a clearing broker like J.P. Futures would know which is the goal of any particular large position held by a client.

This remains true even if a trader's positions violate applicable position limits and accountability levels. As the CEA explains, position limits and accountability levels are intended not only to prevent manipulation, but also "to diminish, eliminate, or prevent excessive speculation," "to ensure sufficient market liquidity for bona fide hedgers," and "to ensure that the price discovery function of the underlying market is not disrupted." 7 U.S.C. § 6a(a)(3)(B).[73] This makes sense: excessive speculation, just as much as manipulation, can result in market illiquidity and artificial prices. If the violation of these restrictions does not necessarily entail manipulation, moreover, then neither should their evasion: that a trader shifts contracts from NYMEX to . . . [swaps] in order to maintain a large open position, standing alone, does not reveal why the trader seeks that large position. . . .

The allegations supporting Plaintiffs-Appellants' second theory of manipulation — the "slamming the close" trades — present a closer issue. In contrast to the acquisition of large open positions, J.P. Futures has provided no obvious legitimate economic reason why Amaranth would wait until the final minutes of trading to sell large quantities of a particular future. This type of trading activity, while not dispositive of manipulation, does strongly suggest it. Indeed, the district court found that "the timing of the sales are suspicious in themselves."

Still . . . we must consider J.P. Futures's alleged knowledge and intent regarding Amaranth's "slamming the close" trades in connection with J.P. Futures's alleged actions. The amended complaint does not allege that J.P. Futures did anything more to assist Amaranth in these trades than to provide routine clearing firm services. . . .

Plaintiffs-Appellants argue that the amended complaint also alleges that J.P. Futures performed "non-routine" tasks to assist Amaranth, including helping to transfer positions from NYMEX to ICE, extending credit limits, and bypassing internal position limits. But these acts, even if they are "non-routine," are alleged to have been performed only in connection with Amaranth's accumulation of large open positions. . . .

In sum, Plaintiffs-Appellants have cited no authority establishing that an FCM must at all times monitor its clients' trading in order to prevent manipulation. . . .

For the foregoing reasons, we AFFIRM the judgment of the district court.

———————

Even though the claim that J.P. Futures aided and abetted Amaranth in its manipulative activities was not successful, it is a reminder of the outstanding question before futures commission merchants as to what extent they can be held liable for their customers' activities. We discuss this in more detail in chapter 16, section A.2.a.

c. Position Limits and Swaps

The CFTC had finalized a rule imposing position limits on swap transactions that referenced twenty-eight specified physical commodities. This rule, however, was challenged in court and vacated.[74] Subsequently, the CFTC twice proposed new

---

73. [N. 16] Though . . . [7 U.S.C.] 6a(a)(3)(B) is specifically about position limits set by the CFTC, its description of their purpose applies to position limits and accountability levels generally. Indeed, 7 U.S.C. § 7(d)(5), which relates to position limits and accountability levels set by the exchanges, similarly states that position limits are "[t]o reduce the potential threat of market manipulation or congestion (especially during trading in the delivery month)." . . .

74. *International Swaps and Derivatives Association v. CFTC*, 887 F. Supp. 2d (D.D.C. 2012).

position limits rules applying to swaps, first in 2013 and then in late 2016.[75] Finally, in January 2021, the CFTC finalized a new swap position limits rule that has not been legally challenged.[76]

The final rule limits the size of swap positions that are "economically equivalent" to twenty-five specified futures contracts. It is effective in January 2023. As with the position limits on futures and exchanged-traded options, the CFTC's objective is to prevent manipulation in circumstances where markets require physical delivery and too many parties demanding physical delivery results in delivery problems if the demand nears or exceeds available supply.

To calculate the overall position for a particular commodity, all of a party's long positions of each relevant futures contract (including options on futures) and "economically equivalent" swaps are added and, separately, all the short positions of each relevant futures contract (including options on futures) and "economically equivalent" swaps are added. To be "economically equivalent" to a futures contract, a swap must have "identical material" terms except for: (1) lot size specifications or notional amounts; (2) post-trade risk management arrangements (for example, there is a big difference here between an uncleared swap and a cleared futures contract); and (3) for physically-settled swaps, delivery dates, as long as they do not deviate more than one calendar day (two for natural gas).

A cash-settled swap can only be economically equivalent to a cash-settled futures contract, and a physically-settled swap can only be economically equivalent to a physically-settled futures contract. For example, a swap settling based on a May crude oil futures contract is not economically-equivalent to a futures position in a June crude oil futures contract.

The position limit for sixteen of the twenty-five commodities only apply in the "spot month." The term "spot month" has a technical market meaning. Generally, it is the day before notices demanding physical delivery can begin to be sent. Nine of the futures contracts subject to this rule, those known as the "Legacy Agricultural" futures contracts, have all-month and, in some cases, any single month limits.

There are numerous exceptions to the requirement. The most significant is, as is the case with the position limits applying to commodity futures and exchange-traded options, the "bona fide hedging transaction" exception which, basically, is:

---

75. For the initial proposal, see CFTC, *Position Limits for Derivatives*, 78 Fed. Reg. 75680 (Dec. 12, 2013), as corrected by CFTC, *Position Limits for Derivatives*, 78 Fed. Reg. 76787 (Dec. 19, 2013), and supplemented by CFTC, *Position Limits for Derivatives; Exemptions and Guidance*, 81 Fed. Reg. 38457 (June 13, 2016). For the reproposal, see CFTC, *Position Limits for Derivatives*, 81 Fed. Reg. 96704 (Dec. 30, 2016). The CFTC also finalized a rule on the methodology for aggregating positions. *See* CFTC, *Aggregation of Positions*, 81 Fed. Reg. 91454 (Dec. 16, 2016).

76. CFTC, *Position Limits for Derivatives*, 86 Fed. Reg. 3236 (Jan. 14, 2021).

(1) a position that is a substitute for a transaction done in a "physical marketing channel"; (2) appropriate to reduce price risk related to management of a "commercial enterprise"; and (3) arises from a potential change in assets, liabilities, or services that are to be produced, manufactured, processed, or provided. If a dealer entity trades with a counterparty who credibly represents that it meets the "bona fide hedging criteria," that swap does not count toward the dealer's position limits as long as the dealer hedges the trade with futures, options on futures, or another swap.

The second exemption is for a spread transaction. It is defined as: "an intramarket spread, inter-market spread, intracommodity spread, or inter-commodity spread, including a calendar spread, quality differential spread, processing spread, product or by-product differential spread, or futures-option spread." The third is with explicit CFTC permission; for example, due to an emergency.

d. Cornering

The position limits authority is just one means of preventing market manipulation due to the aggregation of positions. The CFTC also has enforcement authority with respect to attempts to "corner" the market.

In the below matter, Fenchurch Capital Management held large futures positions requiring delivery of U.S. government notes yielding a minimum 8 1/2% interest rate. Fenchurch successfully prevented a substantial portion of outstanding U.S. government notes yielding an 8 1/2% interest rate from being available for delivery. When the delivery date arrived on Fenchurch's futures positions, some counterparties were required to deliver to Fenchurch more valuable U.S. government notes yielding 8 3/4% interest because they were unable to locate any U.S. government notes yielding 8 1/2% interest.

Corners and Squeezes

A corner is where a substantial portion of the cash market of a commodity is owned or controlled at the same time long futures contracts requiring delivery of the commodity are held. When it comes time for delivery, the sellers of the futures contract are unable to obtain adequate supply to make their required deliveries. The cash market prices go up and the perpetrator of the corner can demand higher cash settlement payments as compensation for non-delivery. The perpetrator of the corner can then buy short futures contracts for a forthcoming delivery month and flood the market with the physical commodities it holds to increase the value of its short futures contracts.

A squeeze is where one party has control over the long futures contracts during a known shortage of the physical in the cash market and then demands delivery on all of the contracts.

In the Matter of Fenchurch Capital Management, Ltd.

CFTC No. 96-7 (July 10, 1996)

. . . The Commodity Futures Trading Commission ("Commission") has reason to believe that Fenchurch Capital Management, Ltd. ("Fenchurch") has violated Sections 6(c) and 9(a)(2) of the Commodity Exchange Act, as amended ("Act"). . . .

The Commission finds [that] . . . Fenchurch is, and was at all times relevant to this matter, registered with the Commission as a commodity trading advisor and commodity pool operator. . . . Fenchurch trades extensively in the U.S. government securities cash and futures markets, has held large positions in government securities futures contracts as part of arbitrage positions, and has taken large deliveries on several futures contracts. . . .

In June 1993, Fenchurch stood for delivery on a large futures position on the June 1993 Ten Year U.S. Treasury Note futures contract ("June contract") traded on the Chicago Board of Trade ("CBT"). During the last four business days of the delivery period and after the last trading day on the June contract, Fenchurch intentionally gained and maintained control over a dominant portion of the available supply of the cheapest-to-deliver Treasury notes on the June contract. Fenchurch increased its position in the issue through a series of repurchase ("repo") market transactions at a time when the notes were in tight supply. . . . Fenchurch exacerbated the tightness in the supply of the cheapest-to-deliver notes by increasing its position and intentionally withholding the notes from the market. As a result, shorts on the futures contract were unable to obtain sufficient quantities of the notes and had to deliver a more valuable security without offsetting compensation. . . .

Through its conduct, Fenchurch increased and thus manipulated upward the value of its position on the June contract by cornering the available supply of the cheapest-to-deliver notes in violation of Sections 6(c) and 9(a)(2) of the Act. . . .

On June 21, 1993, the last day of trading on the June contract, Fenchurch stood for delivery on a long futures position of about 12,700 contracts. Fenchurch's position was 76% of the open interest on the June contract. At that time, the total open interest was the third largest to be satisfied by delivery in the history of the CBT 10 Year Note contract. The terms of the June contract allowed shorts to deliver any Treasury security in a basket of notes having certain maturity characteristics. Typically, one note in the basket becomes the cheapest-to-deliver based principally on coupon rates and times to maturity, and the price of the contract converges with the cash market value of the cheapest-to-deliver issue. Throughout the month of June 1993, the cheapest-to-deliver note on the June contract was the 8 1/2% February 15, 2000 United States Treasury Note ("8 1/2% note"). Thus, the settlement price of the June contract at expiration reflected the value of the 8 1/2% note in the cash market.

Shorts on the June contract could make delivery anytime during the delivery month, with the last delivery day being on June 30. Because long term interest rates were higher than short term rates in June 1993, it was most economical for the shorts to delay delivery until the last delivery day, if possible. When the notes are readily available in the market, acquisition and delivery of the notes occurs quickly and easily through use of the Federal wire. If there is no indication that the cheapest-to-deliver note is in tight supply, shorts generally prepare for delivery within a few days prior to the last delivery day. . . .

In June 1993, there were no signs that the cheapest-to-deliver note, the 8 1/2% note, was in short supply until Friday, June 25. . . .

As of June 25, Fenchurch was in a position to benefit from the developing scarcity of the 8 1/2% notes and the increased value of receiving the 8 7/8% notes on delivery. Fenchurch already held a sizable pre-existing position in the 8 1/2% note. In addition to its large futures position, Fenchurch also had entered into several repo transactions using the 8 1/2% note as collateral. . . .

With the developing scarcity of the 8 1/2% notes and the increasing value of receiving the 8 7/8% notes, Fenchurch proceeded to increase its position in the 8 1/2% notes to over $2 billion and withheld the notes from the markets. Fenchurch knew that if it acquired and maintained control over a dominant portion of the available supply of the 8 1/2% notes until delivery on June 30, shorts would have to deliver the more valuable 8 7/8% note on the June contract. Between June 25 and 29, Fenchurch borrowed the notes in the repo market at the increasingly low repo rates for the 8 1/2% notes and entered into overnight repo transactions with several counterparties using the 8 1/2% notes as collateral. . . . In negotiating each repo transaction, Fenchurch's repo trader ensured that the counterparty would not relend the notes to the repo market.

At the same time that Fenchurch was entering into new repo transactions in which it lent the 8 1/2% notes to counterparties who would not relend them to the market, Fenchurch was intentionally "failing" on various repo transactions, i.e., failing to return the notes to counterparties from whom it had borrowed them. By failing to return the notes, Fenchurch gave up the interest it would have received on the transactions. Several of the counterparties on the transactions in which Fenchurch failed to return the security were preparing to make delivery on the June contract. . . .

Fenchurch withheld from the markets a dominant portion of the available supply of the 8 1/2% notes [and] . . . increased substantially the value of its futures position, thus benefitting itself and the two pools it manages. . . .

In pursuing the course of action set forth above, Fenchurch attempted to manipulate and did manipulate upward the value of Fenchurch's long futures position in the June contract by attempting to corner and cornering the available supply of the cheapest-to-deliver notes on the June contract. . . .

Although the conduct here occurred after the expiration of the contract, Fenchurch nonetheless engaged in intentional conduct through which it controlled a dominant portion of the cheapest-to-deliver notes available for delivery on the June Contract and thus restricted the available supply of the cheapest-to-deliver issue. Fenchurch's conduct resulted in the value of the futures contract being artificially altered.

Fenchurch intentionally acquired and maintained its dominant position in the 8 1/2% notes at a time of tight supplies and as a result the shorts had to deliver the more valuable 8 7/8% notes. By receiving the 8 7/8% notes on approximately one third of its futures position, the value of Fenchurch's position became artificially high. The Commission believes that Fenchurch's activities . . . did not have an economic or business rationale but for an intent to restrict the supply of the notes in order to obtain delivery of a more valuable security. . . .

It is the Commission's responsibility to ensure that futures markets remain free of illegitimate forces throughout the trading and delivery periods. If longs are allowed to engage in conduct of the type found in this case, the price discovery function of the futures markets could be jeopardized. . . .

Based on the foregoing, the Commission finds that Fenchurch violated Sections 6(c) and 9(a)(2) of the Act. . . .

The Sumitomo Scandal

In one of the most famous modern-day corners, the head copper trader at Sumitomo had severe losses from copper trades which he obscured from his employer. To reverse these losses, the trader sought to corner the market in copper, at one point owning nearly all the copper interests available at the major exchange, the London Metals Exchange. He also held a large number of long futures contracts on which he demanded delivery. The CFTC, noting market irregularities, initiated an investigation that resulted in the firing of the trader and unwinding of the scheme.

Ultimately, Sumitomo was fined $150 million by the CFTC and was liable for $99 million of a more than $134 million settlement of a related class action case.[a]

[a] For an excellent description of the events, see Benjamin E. Kozinn, *Great Copper Caper: Is Market Manipulation Really a Problem in the Wake of the Sumitomo Debacle*, 69 Fordham L. Rev. 243 (2000).

Questions and Comments

1. The CFTC's Division of Enforcement issues annual reports advertising the size and number of enforcement awards. What impact do larger enforcement awards have? What about number of enforcement actions?

2. Why, at the time *United States v. Reliant Energy* was decided in 2006, had there never been a criminal prosecution based on the Commodity Exchange Act's anti-manipulation provisions? Why have the criminal provisions in the Commodity Exchange Act if the more common practice is to charge defendants with violations of the federal mail and wire fraud statutes?

3. What are some of the reasons the Department of Justice might seek to criminally prosecute a defendant under the federal mail or wire fraud statutes? Familiarity with the statutes, abundant supporting case law, different standards of proof?

4. The "London Whale" lost JPMorgan more than $6 billion in total. In a context where the alleged manipulator absorbs such a significant loss does a CFTC enforcement action alleging market manipulation make sense?

5. As a practical matter, why might the plaintiffs in *In re Amaranth Natural Gas Commodities Litigation* have sought to make a claim against J.P. Morgan Futures, Inc. for aiding and abetting liability instead of focusing on claims against Amaranth itself?

6. Devise a market manipulation. Now evaluate the civil enforcement and criminal prosecution strategies you would employ if you were the CFTC enforcing the civil provisions of the Commodity Exchange Act and the Department of Justice enforcing the criminal provisions.

7. What impact does the unavailability of remedies outside of the five-year federal statute of limitation have on regulators?

Chapter 16

Private Enforcement

A. Private Right of Action

In the preceding chapter, we examined the mechanism for enforcement of the Commodity Exchange Act and CFTC anti-fraud and anti-manipulation rules available to the CFTC and the Department of Justice. Such public enforcement by the government is not the exclusive means to enforce the Commodity Exchange Act. Another means is by a private right of action. A private right of action is the ability of an aggrieved individual to bring a civil claim against another party for violation of a statute or regulation.

1. Before the Futures Trading Act of 1982

Before the Futures Trading Act of 1982, the Commodity Exchange Act contained no explicit private right of action. In the below case, the Supreme Court concluded that Congress nonetheless implicitly intended private parties to have the ability to make a claim for a violation of the Commodity Exchange Act.

The decision occurred during the tail end of a judicial explosion in "discovering" implied private rights of action in statutes.[1] As we will see further below, shortly after the Supreme Court affirmed an implied private right of action in the Commodity Exchange Act, Congress amended the Act to undo the effect of the Court's decision and provide an explicit and limited private right of action.

Merrill Lynch, Pierce, Fenner & Smith, Inc. v. Curran
456 U.S. 353 (1982)

Justice Stevens delivered the opinion of the Court. . . .

The central question presented . . . is whether a private party may maintain an action for damages caused by a violation of the [Commodity Exchange Act (the "CEA")]. . . .

[I]n a broad sense, futures trading has a direct financial impact on three classes of persons. Those who actually are interested in selling or buying the commodity are described as "hedgers"; their primary financial interest is in the profit to be earned from the production or processing of the commodity. Those who seek financial

---

1. For a history of judicial inference of private rights of action, *see* Jonathan A. Marcantel, *Abolishing Implied Private Rights of Action Pursuant to Federal Statutes*, 39 J. of Legislation 251, 255–267 (2012–2013).

gain by taking positions in the futures market generally are called "speculators" or "investors"; without their participation, futures markets "simply would not exist."[2] Finally, there are the futures commission merchants, the floor brokers, and the persons who manage the market; they also are essential participants, and they have an interest in maximizing the activity on the exchange. The petitioners in these cases are members of this third class whereas their adversaries, the respondents, are speculators or investors. . . .

In the four cases before us, the allegations in the complaints filed by respondents are assumed to be true. The first involves a complaint by customers against their broker. The other three arise out of a malfunction of the contract market for futures contracts covering the delivery of Maine potatoes in May 1976, "when the sellers of almost 1,000 contracts failed to deliver approximately 50,000,000 pounds of potatoes, resulting in the largest default in the history of commodities futures trading in this country." . . .

From the enactment of the original federal legislation [regulating commodity futures], Congress primarily has relied upon the exchanges to regulate the contract markets. . . . [T]he exchanges promulgated rules and regulations, but they did not always enforce them. In 1968, Congress attempted to correct this flaw in the self-regulation concept by enacting § 5a(8), which requires the exchanges to enforce their own rules.

The enactment of § 5a(8), coupled with the recognition by the federal courts of an implied private remedy for violations of the CEA, gave rise to a new problem. As representatives of the exchanges complained during the hearings preceding . . . 1974 amendments [to the Commodity Exchange Act], the exchanges were being sued for not enforcing their rules. The complaint was taken seriously because it implicated the self-regulation premise of the CEA. . . .

Congress could have removed this impediment to exchange rulemaking by eliminating the implied private remedy, but it did not follow that course. . . .

---

2. [N. 11] " . . . Speculators . . . embrace all representatives of the general public . . . who seek financial gain by taking positions in volatile markets. The principal role of the speculator in the markets is to take the risks that the hedger is unwilling to accept. The opportunity for profit makes the speculator willing to take those risks. The activity of speculators is essential to the operation of a futures market in that the composite bids and offers of large numbers of individuals tend to broaden a market, thus making possible the execution . . . of the larger trade hedging orders. By increasing the number of bids and offers available at any given price level, the speculator usually helps to minimize price fluctuations rather than to intensify them. Without the trading activity of the speculative fraternity, the liquidity, so badly needed in futures markets, simply would not exist. Trading volume would be restricted materially since, without a host of speculative orders in the trading ring, many larger trade orders at limit prices would simply go unfilled due to the floor broker's inability to find an equally large but opposing hedge order at the same price to complete the match." [H.R.Rep. No. 93-975, p. 1 (1974), U.S.Code Cong. & Admin.News 1974 ("House Report")] . . . , at 138.

Congress in 1974 created new procedures through which traders might seek relief for violations of the CEA, but the legislative evidence indicates that these informal procedures were intended to supplement rather than supplant the implied judicial remedy. These procedures do not substitute for the private remedy either as a means of compensating injured traders or as a means of enforcing compliance with the statute. . . .

As the Solicitor General argues on behalf of the Commission as amicus curiae, the private cause of action enhances the enforcement mechanism fostered by Congress over the course of 60 years. . . .

In addition to their principal argument that no private remedy is available under the CEA, petitioners also contend that respondents, as speculators, may not maintain such an action. . . .

The characterization of persons who invest in futures contracts as "speculators" does not exclude them from the class of persons protected by the CEA. The statutory scheme could not effectively protect the producers and processors who engage in hedging transactions without also protecting the other participants in the market whose transactions over exchanges necessarily must conform to the same trading rules. . . .

The legislative history quite clearly indicates that Congress intended to protect all futures traders from price manipulation and other fraudulent conduct violative of the statute. It is assumed, of course, that federal regulation of futures trading benefits the entire economy; a sound futures market tends to reduce retail prices of the underlying commodities. The immediate beneficiaries of a healthy futures market are the producers and processors of commodities who can minimize the risk of loss from volatile price changes on the cash market by hedging on the futures market.

The judgments of the Courts of Appeals [finding that a private right of action is available] are affirmed. . . .

––––––––––

During the time period in which the Supreme Court jurisprudence spurring *Merrill Lynch v. Curran* occurred, the inference of private rights of action was not without detractors. For example, Justice Powell noted in a dissent in an earlier Supreme Court case on private rights of action that, whereas courts had found at least twenty private rights of action by that time (1979), it "defies reason to believe that in each of these statutes Congress absentmindedly forgot to mention an intended private action."[3] In this case, Congress chose to act within months of the decision.

––––––––––

3. *Cannon v. University of Chicago*, 441 U.S. 677, 741 (1979) (Powell J., dissenting).

2. Futures Trading Act of 1982

In response to the decision in *Merrill Lynch v. Curran*, Congress added an explicit private right of action to the Commodity Exchange Act via the Futures Trading Act of 1982.[4] However, even before the decision was rendered, Congress was considering taking statutory action.

House of Representatives Report on the Futures Trading Act of 1982

H.R. Rept. 97-565 (May 17, 1982)

... At the time the Committee considered the bill, the Supreme Court had not yet resolved the issue of whether a private right of action could be implied under the [Commodity Exchange] Act. The Committee is of the view that the right of an aggrieved person to sue a violator of the Act is critical to protecting the public and fundamental to maintaining the credibility of the futures market.

To that end the Committee added a new section to the bill to provide specific authority for private rights of action for recovery of actual damages against violators of the Act. In order to recover the violation must have arisen from a transaction on the futures market, a regulated option or leverage contract, or participation in a commodity pool.

The Committee also specifically provided for liability for actual damages by a contract market, clearing organization of a contract market, licensed board of trade or registered futures association that failed to enforce a bylaw, rule or regulation made a condition of its designation or license. In addition, a cause of action could be brought against an officer, director, or employee who willfully aided or induced such a violation. The cause of action in these cases would be restricted to cases where the plaintiff had engaged in a regulated commodity transaction and could show that there was bad faith in failing to take the necessary action. Any action by a private litigant under the Act must be brought within two years after the date the cause of action accrued.

The Committee included these restrictions on the causes of action to avoid suits for speculative damages to assets that are affected by fluctuations in prices on the commodity market but which are not the subject of transactions on such market.

The availability of these remedies — reparations, arbitration and private rights of action — supplements, but does not substitute, for the regulatory and enforcement program of the CFTC and self-regulatory agencies. The Committee fully expects that these agencies will vigorously use the tools at its command to protect the investing public so that it does not become necessary to rely on private litigants as a policeman of the Commodity Exchange Act. . . .

---

4. Pub. L. No. 97-444 (Jan. 11, 1983) at § 235.

The above-described provisions were enacted into the Commodity Exchange Act by the Futures Trading Act of 1982. They were amended by the Dodd-Frank Act to include swaps in their scope. There is a two-year statute of limitations for private rights of action under the Commodity Exchange Act.[5]

Claims fall into two categories: (1) claims against market participants; and (2) claims against the National Futures Association and "registered entities," i.e., designated contract markets, derivatives clearing organizations, swap execution facilities, and swap data repositories.

a. Claims against Market Participants

We examine the special regime for claims against registered entities and the National Futures Association below. Claims against all other entities for violation of the Commodity Exchange Act — or for willfully aiding or abetting a violation of the Commodity Exchange Act — are only available if there are one of four relationships between the claimant and the violator of the Commodity Exchange Act. One of the following relationships must exist:

1. The claimant received trading advice for a fee from the Commodity Exchange Act violator;

2. The Commodity Exchange Act violator acted as a futures commission merchant or introducing broker with the claimant as customer;

3. The claimant purchased from, sold to, or placed an order to do so with the Commodity Exchange Act violator in relation to an option, leverage contract, commodity pool participation, or swap; or

4. The claimant purchased or sold a futures contract or swap and the violator violated the Commodity Exchange Act's prohibitions on manipulation.[6]

Actual damages must also be demonstrated along with, of course, causation.[7]

In all other circumstances, the Commodity Exchange Act violator may be held to account by the CFTC or, if violating a self-regulatory organization rule, by a self-regulatory organization.[8] No private action, however, will be available against such a party.

The above limitations on private rights of action for Commodity Exchange Act violations have provided fertile ground for plaintiffs propounding theories seeking to broaden the scope of possible parties against whom such a private right of action is available. One theory, backed by the CFTC and the Seventh Circuit,[9] is that the determination of who is a willful aider or abettor of a Commodity Exchange Act violation is to be broadly construed to include a willful aider or abettor of a violation

---

5. Commodity Exchange Act § 22(c).
6. Commodity Exchange Act § 22(a).
7. Commodity Exchange Act § 22(a)(1).
8. Commodity Exchange Act § 22(a)(2).
9. *Damato v. Hermanson*, 153 F.3d 464 (7th Cir. 1998).

of the Commodity Exchange Act so long as the aiding and abetting is in relation to one of the above four relationships. Another possible interpretation, derived from a strict reading of the statute and discussed but not adopted by any circuit, is that there can only be aider or abettor liability if the aider or abettor, in addition to aiding and abetting a Commodity Exchange Act violation, is one of the parties in the above four relationships.

The below case explores these two competing theories regarding the scope of aider and abettor liability. It also explores a third theory where a claimant does not stand in one of the four required relationships with the Commodity Exchange Act violator. The violator, though, does stand in one of the four required relationships with a third party. Under this theory, the claimant argues that the violator was acting as agent for the claimant with the third party therefore allowing the claimant to claim directly against the third party.

When would a fact pattern arise where this agency theory would be used? Namely in a case where funds are given to a Commodity Exchange Act violator for the purposes of, for example, futures trades. The Commodity Exchange Act violator gains access to the futures exchange through a clearing member registered as a futures commission merchant and places trades on behalf of the claimant. The Commodity Exchange Act violator files for bankruptcy or is otherwise not a probable source of recovery so the claimant argues that the Commodity Exchange Act violator acted as its agent in placing the trades with the futures commission merchant and, therefore, the claimant effectively stands in one of the four required relationships with the futures commission merchant and can make a claim against the futures commission merchant.

Nicholas v. Saul Stone & Co. LLC

224 F.3d 179 (3d Cir. 2000)

Pollak, District Judge.

Appellants seek review of a judgment of the District Court of New Jersey granting defendants' motion to dismiss plaintiffs' amended complaint. . . .

According to the amended complaint, the plaintiffs . . . are persons who . . . were lured into improvident investments in the commodities market by Chuck ("Chuckles") Kohli, Nungambukkam Swamy Ramchandran, and certain corporate pawns of Kohli and Ramchandran known collectively as "Sigma." . . . The investors were told that the funds would be placed in a commodities trading pool and used to invest in commodities futures and options. . . . Plaintiffs further alleged that . . . the bulk of those investments failed. However, . . . investors seeking to withdraw their funds or profits were paid with the funds of later investors, thus creating the aura of success. The plaintiffs' pleadings characterized this structure as a Ponzi scheme. . . .

Kohli has since pled guilty to federal criminal charges stemming out of these events, and Ramchandran has since filed for bankruptcy. As a result, plaintiffs have undertaken to seek recoupment of their losses elsewhere. Plaintiffs brought suit in the District Court for New Jersey against the FCMs used by Kohli, Ramchandran, and Sigma. . . .

Because of the various registration requirements (detailed below) laid down by the Commodities [*sic*] Exchange Act ("CEA") . . . Kohli, Ramchandran, and Sigma were, so plaintiffs alleged, under a duty to register with the Commodities [*sic*] Futures Trading Commission (the "CFTC") . . . ; they were also, plaintiffs alleged, obligated to become members of the NFA. Plaintiffs further alleged that Kohli, Ramchandran, and Sigma, in fact, did not register with the . . . [CFTC] or become members of the NFA, and hence that the various FCMs that accepted their business acted improperly. In particular, plaintiffs alleged that the defendant FCMs and their employees failed to inquire into the source of funds in the Sigma accounts or into the CFTC registration status and NFA membership of Kohli, Ramchandran, and Sigma. . . . Plaintiffs alleged that the FCMs and their employees, by failing to make the necessary investigation, directly violated the CEA, and aided and abetted violations of the CEA. . . .

Appellants have raised numerous issues. Most do not, in our view, require discussion in this opinion because they have been fully and correctly canvassed in the District Court's comprehensive opinion. There are, however, a few issues arising under section 22 of the CEA which, we think, call for additional analysis. . . .

Subsection 22(a)(1) of the CEA creates a private right of action for "actual damages" caused by "[a]ny person . . . who violates this chapter [the CEA] or who willfully aids [or] abets . . . the commission of a violation of this chapter." . . .

A plaintiff may bring a private damage action against "[a]ny person who violates" the CEA when that person stands in one of four relationships with the plaintiff specified in subparagraphs (A) through (D) of subsection 22(a)(1). Each of the required relationships involves the "person" sued having given advice related to the sale of commodities, or having participated in a transaction related to such sales. Subparagraph (A) imposes liability on the "person" sued when a plaintiff "received trading advice from such person for a fee"; subparagraph (B) imposes liability on the "person" sued when the plaintiff "made through *such person*" a contract for futures or options thereon, or when the plaintiff deposited money or other property with "*such person*" in connection with a futures or options contract; subparagraph (C) imposes liability on the "person" sued when the plaintiff purchased from or sold to "*such person*," or placed through "*such person*" an order for, certain specified options or commodities contracts, or "an interest or participation in a commodity pool"; and subparagraph (D) imposes liability on the "person" sued when the plaintiff "purchased or sold a contract referred to in subparagraph (B) if the violation constitutes a manipulation of the price of any such contract or the price of the commodity underlying such contract." (Emphasis added). If the "person" sued has participated in one of the transactions specified in these four subparagraphs, then "such person" can be held liable "for actual damages resulting from one or more of the [specified] transactions . . . and caused by such violation" to the plaintiff. Thus, in order for a plaintiff to sue a defendant for directly violating subsection 22(a)(1), the defendant must (1) have violated the CEA, and (2) stand in an appropriate relationship to the plaintiff with respect to the violative conduct.

Appellants, in their amended complaint, alleged that the FCMs were liable under subsection 22(a)(1) to plaintiffs because of their participation in transactions described in subparagraphs (A), (B), and (C). In particular, appellants alleged that the defendant FCMs gave trading advice to Kohli, who was, so appellants alleged, in some sense, appellants' agent. Similarly, appellants alleged that the FCMs accepted orders of the kind described in subparagraph (B) from Kohli. And finally, appellants contended that the FCMs fell under subparagraph (C) insofar as they permitted Kohli, Ramchandran, and Sigma to sell to appellants interests in commodity pools in violation of the CEA.

Appellants do not contend that the defendant FCMs themselves stood in one of the listed relationships to one or more of the appellants. . . . According to appellants, the conclusion that "Defendant FCMs were dealing directly with Plaintiffs for purposes of violating 7 U.S.C. § 25(a)(1)(A)–(D)" follows from the fact that "Kohli, the acknowledged primary violator was the Plaintiff's [sic] agent." The District Court rejected appellants' theory, stating that "[p]laintiffs have provided no authority for allowing a [subsection 22(a)(1)] relationship to be established through an agency theory and there is no indication in the statute indicating the availability of such relief." Without deciding whether or to what extent an agency relationship can ever appropriately be used to establish a subsection 22(a)(1) relationship, we agree with the District Court that the agency theory invoked by appellants does not fit this case. For, as the District Court stated, "allowing such a theory in the instant case, where Kohli, although technically the agent of the plaintiff[s], was clearly not operating in plaintiffs' interests does not seem appropriate." Accordingly, the FCMs' transactions with Kohli (and/or Ramchandran and/or Sigma) do not suffice to make them liable to appellants under subsection 22(a)(1).

We turn, then, to appellants' alternate subsection 22(a)(1) theory — namely that the defendant FCMs can be found liable to appellants by virtue of having "aided and abetted" Kohli (and/or Ramchandran and/or Sigma) in violating the CEA.

The District Court held that the FCMs could not be liable under subsection 22(a) (1) as aiders and abetters based on its view that, in order to establish aider-and-abetter liability, a defendant must be in one of the four subparagraph-(A)-through-(D) relationships with a plaintiff. The District Court . . . reached this conclusion on the basis of language in subsection 22(a)(1) which appears to treat direct and aider-and-abetter liability in parallel terms. Thus, for example, subsection 22(a)(1) provides, "*Any person* who violates this chapter or who willfully aids [and] abets . . . the commission of a violation of this chapter shall be liable for actual damages resulting from one or more of the [specified] transactions . . . and caused by such violation to any other person — (A) who received trading advice from *such person* for a fee." 7 U.S.C. § 25(a)(1) (emphasis added). Each of the specified transactions in subparagraphs (A), (B), and (C) (the three subparagraphs invoked in the amended complaint) involves activity by "such person" — the antecedent of which appears to be a "person who violates this chapter or who willfully aids [and] abets . . . the commission of a violation."[10] Accordingly, the syntactic structure of the statute seems to contemplate that "any person" who aids and abets can only be held liable if he is also "such person," i.e., a person who performs one of the acts enumerated in (A), (B), and (C). Under this reading of the statute, it would appear that — just as with direct violators of the CEA — a plaintiff can bring private causes of action against aiders and abetters only if they (1) aid and abet a violation of the CEA; and (2) themselves stand in one of the relationships specified in subparagraphs (A), (B), and (C). . . .

In holding that only "such persons" can be liable as aiders and abetters under subsection 22(a)(1) of the CEA, the District Court expressly rejected the position of the Commodities [sic] Futures Trading Commission ("CFTC"), as expressed in an amicus curiae brief, which had been filed by the CFTC in the then-pending appeal to the Seventh Circuit in *Damato v. Hermanson* [153 F.3d 464 (7th Cir. 1998)] . . . and which had been presented to the District Court in the present case by plaintiffs. The CFTC, in that brief, had argued that the reading adopted by the district court in *Damato* would unnecessarily limit aider and abetter liability:

> Indeed, requiring that the aider and abettor be "such person" within the meaning of subparagraphs (A) through (D) renders § 22(a) internally inconsistent and does violence to the clear intent of § 22. As indicated above, § 22(a)(1)(A)–(D) defines the persons who are appropriate plaintiffs under the CEA. It also sets forth the damages that may be recovered in a private right of action. It limits recovery to damages caused by the violation and "resulting from one or more of the transactions referred to in subparagraphs (A) through (D)." If "such person" under subparagraphs (A) through (D) referred to the aider and abettor (i.e., if the aider and abettor were required to have the direct relationship with plaintiff), then the only damages recoverable would be those resulting from the transaction between the aider and abettor and the plaintiff. This is nonsensical, because the plaintiff's damages result not from the act of the aider and abettor in providing trading advice or selling futures, options or pool interests to the plaintiff, but from the violation itself by the primary violator. . . . Thus, for the language of § 22 to make sense, "such person" in subparagraphs (A) through (D) must refer to the primary violator and not the aider and abettor.

Thus, according to the CFTC, "§ 22(a) creates liability for an aider and abettor if (i) he or she assists in a violation of the Act, (ii) the plaintiffs' damages are caused by that underlying violation and (iii) the damages result from one of the transactions

10. [N. 14] Although subparagraph (D) does not expressly refer to "such person," its operative focus is on transactions involving "a contract referred to in subparagraph (B)." We need not, however, address the ingredients of aider-and-abetter liability under subparagraph (D), since as the District Court noted, the amended complaint focused on transactions allegedly falling within subparagraphs (A), (B), and (C).

set forth in subparagraphs (A)–(D). There is no independent requirement that both the primary violator and the aider and abettor deal directly with the plaintiff."

After the District Court handed down its order dismissing the amended complaint . . . the Seventh Circuit . . . adopted the CFTC interpretation of subsection 22(a)(1).

In the instant case, appellants urge this court to follow the Seventh Circuit's adoption . . . of the CFTC approach to subsection 22(a)(1)'s aiding and abetting language. By contrast, appellees argue, *contra Damato*, that this court should look to the plain language of subsection 22(a)(1), and that — because the FCMs and their employees took no action described in subparagraphs 22(a)(1)(A) through (C) — the FCMs should not be liable as aiders and abetters. We find it unnecessary, however, to resolve this issue at this juncture. For even assuming that we were to follow *Damato*'s adoption of the CFTC approach, the defendant FCMs could, in any event, only be held liable if their conduct met the basic requirements of aiding and abetting. But plaintiffs, in their amended complaint, have not alleged such conduct. . . .

The closest that the amended complaint comes to alleging that the FCMs knew of the misconduct of Kohli, Ramchandran, and Sigma are the statements that the FCMs "were aware, or with required minimal due diligence would have discovered" that "Kohli, Chandran and the Sigma Entities were a fiction under the CEA," and that the FCMs "knew or recklessly disregarded facts showing that" Kohli, Ramchandran, and the Sigma Entities were engaged in various activities violative of the CEA. In essence, appellants have alleged, at most, that the FCMs acted recklessly, and that they knew or should have known of the violations by Kohli, Ramchandran, and Sigma of the CEA. But these allegations are a far cry from an allegation that the FCMs not only had knowledge of the intent of Kohli and the others to violate the CEA, but, as the Seventh Circuit put it in *Damato*, "the intent to further that violation." Accordingly, even if we were to assume arguendo the correctness of the CFTC construction of subsection 22(a)(1) . . . which was adopted by the Seventh Circuit in *Damato*, plaintiffs' amended complaint nonetheless falls short. Therefore, we conclude that the District Court acted properly in dismissing appellants' aiding and abetting claims. . . .

———————

The most open-ended of the four relationships allowing for a possible private right of action is that between a person violating the market manipulation prohibitions in the Commodity Exchange Act and a trader in the market aggrieved thereby. In recent years these claims have become common as a result of two scandals affecting the financial markets, the interest rate benchmark rigging scandal and the foreign exchange rate rigging scandal. The scandals have resulted in billions of fines by some of the most prominent banks in the world. The below decision on a motion to dismiss summarizes a typical claim arising out of the rigging of interest rate benchmarks.

Laydon v. Mizuho Bank

2014 WL 1280464 (S.D.N.Y. Mar. 28, 2014) (citations to court filings omitted)

George B. Daniels, District Judge.

This case involves the alleged manipulation of Euroyen TIBOR (the Tokyo Interbank Offered Rate), Yen-LIBOR (the London Interbank Offered Rate for Japanese Yen) and the prices of Euroyen TIBOR futures contracts during the period from January 1, 2006 through December 31, 2010 (the "Class Period") by the Defendants. The Defendants are various banks and financial institutions. Plaintiff brings this action to recover for losses that he suffered when he initiated short positions in Euroyen TIBOR Futures contracts during the Class Period, and on behalf of all those similarly situated, allegedly due to the presence of artificial Euroyen TIBOR future prices proximately caused by Defendants' unlawful manipulation and restraint of trade.... Plaintiff alleges [among others] ... : (1) manipulation in violation of the Commodity Exchange Act, 7 U.S.C. §§ 1, et seq.; (2) principal-agent liability in violation of the Commodity Exchange Act, 7 U.S.C. §§ 1, et seq.; [and] (3) aiding and abetting manipulation in violation of the Commodity Exchange Act, 7 U.S.C. §§ 1, et seq.... Defendants jointly move to dismiss Plaintiff's Second Amended Class Action Complaint.[11] ...

Plaintiff has adequately pled a claim under the Commodity Exchange Act for price manipulation and aiding and abetting against all defendants. Defendants' motion to dismiss those claims is denied....

Euroyen TIBOR is set through the [Japanese Bankers Association ("JBA")] ... by its member banks The JBA designates a minimum of 8 reference banks to provide daily rate quotes for the calculation of Euroyen TIBOR rates.... Euroyen TIBOR is calculated on each business day as of 11:00am Tokyo time. Each Euroyen TIBOR reference bank quotes Euroyen TIBOR rates for 13 maturities (1 week and 1–12 months). In calculating Euroyen TIBOR rates, quotes are discarded from the two highest and two lowest financial institutions and the remaining rates are then averaged. The reference banks quote what they deem to be the prevailing market rates, assuming transactions between prime banks on the Japanese offshore market as of 11:00am, unaffected by their own positions.

Yen-LIBOR is set through the [British Bankers Association ("BBA")] ... by its member banks. Yen-LIBOR is calculated each business day as of 11:00am London

---

11. [N. 1] Defendants that move to dismiss are: The Bank of Tokyo-Mitsubishi UFJ, Ltd.; Mitsubishi UFJ Trust and Banking Corporation; The Bank of Yokohama, Ltd.; Barclays Bank PLC; Citibank, N.A.; Citigroup Inc.; Cooperatieve Centrale Raiffeisen-Boerenleenbank B.A.; Deutsche Bank AG; HSBC Holdings plc; HSBC Bank plc; ICAP plc; JPMorgan Chase & Co.; JPMorgan Chase Bank, N.A.; J.P. Morgan Securities plc; Mizuho Corporate Bank, Ltd.; Mizuho Bank, Ltd.; Mizuho Trust & Banking Co., Ltd.; The Norinchukin Bank; Resona Bank, Ltd.; R.P. Martin Holdings Limited; Shinkin Central Bank; Societe Generale; The Shoko Chukin Bank, Ltd.; Sumitomo Mitsui Banking Corporation; and Sumitomo Mitsui Trust Bank, Ltd; Royal Bank of Scotland Group, plc; Royal Bank of Scotland plc; RBS Securities Japan Limited; UBS AG; UBS Securities Japan Co., Ltd.

time. Each Yen-LIBOR reference bank quotes Yen-LIBOR for 15 maturities. In calculating Yen-LIBOR, contributed rates are ranked in descending order and the arithmetic mean of only the middle two quantities is used to formulate the resulting BBA Yen-LIBOR calculation. The contributor banks respond to the BBA's question: "At what rate could you borrow funds, were you to do so by asking for and then accepting inter-bank offers in a reasonable market size just prior to 11 am?"

A three-month Euroyen TIBOR futures contract is an agreement to buy or sell a Euroyen time deposit having a principal value of 100,0000,000 Japanese Yen with a three-month maturity commencing on a specific future date. Three-month Euroyen TIBOR futures contracts are exchange-listed financial instruments that are traded within the United States on the floor of the CME and electronically on the CME's Globex platform, as well as on boards of trade and exchanges accessible by U.S. investors from within the United States, including the Tokyo Financial Exchange Inc. ("TFX"), Singapore Exchange ("SGX"), and NYSE Euronext LIFFE ("LIFFE"). Three-month Euroyen TIBOR futures contracts are standardized contracts, which are identical to one another except for the trading hours. . . .

The final settlement price of a Three-month Euroyen TIBOR futures contract is defined as cash settlement to 100 minus the Three-month TIBOR rate published by the JBA at 11:00am Tokyo time on the second Tokyo bank business day immediately preceding the third Wednesday of the contract month's named month of delivery.

Plaintiff alleges that Defendants manipulated prices of Euroyen TIBOR futures contracts and other Euroyen derivatives through their deliberate and systematic submission of false Euroyen TIBOR and Yen-LIBOR rates to the JBA and BBA, respectively, throughout the Class Period. In support of this, Plaintiff cites many governmental investigations and settlements.

Defendants move to dismiss Plaintiff's CEA claims (causes of action one through three) on the grounds that: (i) Plaintiff lacks standing to bring claims based on alleged manipulation of Yen-LIBOR or Euroyen TIBOR because these benchmarks are not the commodities underlying the Euroyen TIBOR futures contracts Plaintiff claims to have held; (ii) Plaintiff fails to allege the required proximate causation between Defendants' alleged conduct and supposedly artificial prices in Euroyen TIBOR futures contracts; (ii) Plaintiff cannot plead specific intent to manipulate Euroyen TIBOR futures prices because the only factually allegations to specific intent pertain to Yen-LIBOR; and (iv) Plaintiff fails to plead a plausible claim for aiding and abetting or vicarious liability. . . .

Section 22 of the CEA grants a private plaintiff who purchased or sold a futures contract standing to sue for "manipulation of the price of any such contract . . . or the price of the commodity underlying such contract," among other conditions precedent. 7 U.S.C. § 25(a)(1)(D) (2012). . . .

Plaintiff has standing to sue under the CEA. The CFTC has repeatedly found that Yen-LIBOR and Euroyen TIBOR are each a "commodity" within the meaning of the CEA, and that Defendants' false reporting of same violated Sections 6(c), 6(d), and

9(a)(2) of the CEA, 7 U.S.C. §§ 9, 13b, and 13(a)(2) (2006). *See e.g.,* UBS Order, CFTC Docket No. 13-14 at 41 ("UBS regularly attempted to manipulate the official fixings of and knowingly delivered false, misleading or knowingly inaccurate reports concerning Yen-LIBOR, Swiss Franc LIBOR, Sterling LIBOR, Euro LIBOR, Euribor and Euroyen TIBOR, *which are all commodities in interstate commerce.*") (emphasis added); *see also id.* at 4, 52–53, 56; RBS Order, CFTC Docket No. 13-14 at 31, 33, 36. Furthermore, Section 22(a) of the CEA provides Plaintiff with standing to sue under the CEA not for manipulation of the commodity itself (according to Defendants, an offshore Japanese Yen deposit) but for manipulation of the price of (*i.e.,* interest on) that commodity (deposit), which is none other than Euroyen TIBOR and Yen-LIBOR. As a purchaser of a Euroyen TIBOR futures contract, Plaintiff has shown that he stands in an appropriate relationship to the Defendants with respect to the alleged CEA violation....

Plaintiff adequately alleges a CEA manipulation claim. A CEA Plaintiff must demonstrate a causal relationship between the purportedly manipulative conduct and the alleged market response.... Defendants' argument that Plaintiff does not allege facts to support a finding that any purported artificiality in the price of Euroyen TIBOR futures contracts was proximately caused by alleged manipulation of the separate Yen-LIBOR benchmark fails. Euroyen TIBOR and Yen-LIBOR both represent the rate of interest charged on short-term loans of unsecured funds denominated in Japanese yen between banks in the offshore interbank market. The allegations in the Complaint are sufficient to show that during the Class Period Yen-LIBOR significantly impacted Euroyen TIBOR. Plaintiff alleges that economic analyses show that Yen-LIBOR impacted Euroyen TIBOR prices during the Class Period and that false reporting of Yen-LIBOR caused artificial Euroyen TIBOR rates....

Plaintiff adequately alleges scienter. Plaintiffs may demonstrate scienter "either (a) by alleging facts to show that Defendants had both motive and opportunity to commit fraud, or (b) by alleging facts that constitute strong circumstantial evidence of conscious misbehavior or recklessness." *In re Crude Oil Commodity Litig.,* 2007 WL 1946553, at *8 (quoting *Lerner v. Fleet Bank, N.A.,* 459 F.3d 273, 290–91 (2d Cir.2006)) (internal quotation marks omitted). On motive, the Complaint contains sufficient allegations that Defendants stood to gain tremendous profits from manipulating Euroyen TIBOR and Yen-LIBOR, *i.e.,* hundreds of millions (if not billions) in ill-gotten trading profits from Euroyen derivatives positions held by the Contributor Bank Defendants (translating into hundreds of millions in illegitimate bonus and other compensation paid to the banks' traders and submitters). Additionally, individual traders had the motive to commit fraud because their compensation was tied to success in trading financial products. On opportunity, Defendants' roles as: (i) JBA Euroyen TIBOR and/or BBA Yen-LIBOR Contributor Banks; (ii) members, directly or through their affiliates, of the CME and/or other exchanges upon which Euroyen TIBOR futures contracts actively trade...; and (iii) intermediaries to other Euroyen market participants in the case of both the Broker and Contributor

Bank Defendants gave them the ability to influence Yen-LIBOR, Euroyen TIBOR and the prices of Euroyen TIBOR futures contracts.

The Complaint also includes overwhelming factual content from which this Court could infer manipulative intent, particularly based on direct evidence from certain Defendants' communications. For example, Defendants allegedly permitted traders — whose compensation was directly connected to their success in trading financial derivative products tied to Yen-LIBOR and/or Euroyen TIBOR — to directly or indirectly exercise improper influence over that Defendant's Yen-LIBOR and/or Euroyen TIBOR submissions, thus creating inherent conflicts of interest and an environment ripe for its derivatives traders and trader-submitters to abuse; and Defendants are alleged to have actively concealed their violations of law from regulators and innocent market participants by, *inter alia:* (i) avoiding discussing the rigging of Yen-LIBOR and/or Euroyen TIBOR in public forums as well as following instructions to curb internal written communications of same; (ii) agreeing to stagger their submission of false reports over successive trading days (e.g., agree that an artificially low rate would be submitted by manipulator A today, by manipulator B tomorrow and manipulator C the next day, etc.) in order to exert greater and longer-lasting manipulative pressure and to mask such false reporting from other market players; (iii) concocting false stories they could give if questioned about their false rate submissions; (iv) lying to attorneys and others during internal investigations of rate manipulation; (v) using cash and derivatives brokers to disseminate false rate information; and (vi) engaging in wash trades and other illicit, non-bona fide trades to surreptitiously pay and facilitate corrupt brokerage payments to broker co-conspirators.

Plaintiff pleads sufficient facts to support a claim of aiding and abetting. . . . The Complaint contains numerous allegations giving rise to an inference that Defendants knew of the other Defendants' unlawful and manipulative conduct and assisted each other in the furtherance of the violation. These allegations include: (i) false reporting of Yen-LIBOR and Euroyen TIBOR was epidemic and done openly during the Class Period; (ii) Defendants are sophisticated market participants who were responsible for the global setting of Yen-LIBOR and Euroyen TIBOR during the Class Period; (iii) Defendants, either directly or through their securities subsidiaries/affiliates, traded Euro yen-based derivatives, including Euroyen TIBOR futures contracts, for profit; (iv) Defendants had a large financial incentive to manipulate Yen-LIBOR, Euroyen TIBOR, and the prices of Euroyen TIBOR futures contracts; (v) Defendants were in continuous communications with each other with respect to Yen-LIBOR and/or Euroyen TIBOR rates; (vi) Defendants worked to report misinformation specifically intended to manipulate Yen-LIBOR, Euroyen TIBOR, and the prices of Euroyen TIBOR futures contracts; (vii) Defendants furthered the manipulation by reporting false Euroyen TIBOR and Yen-LIBOR rates to financially benefit their Euroyen derivatives positions rather than rates reflective of prevailing (true) Euroyen interbank borrowing costs; (viii) Defendants traded Euroyen based derivatives, including Euroyen TIBOR futures contracts, at times when prices were being manipulated; and (ix) Broker Defendants, including ICAP and RP Martin, knowingly facilitated the manipulation of Yen-LIBOR, Euroyen TIBOR, and Euroyen TIBOR futures contract prices during the Class Period. . . .

Plaintiff has adequately pled a claim under the Commodity Exchange Act for price manipulation. . . .

_____

In addition to claims under the Commodity Exchange Act, the plaintiffs also brought antitrust claims. Although the antitrust claims in this case were dismissed, they are a frequent vehicle for seeking damages in relation to alleged derivatives manipulation because, whereas the Commodity Exchange Act only allows for actual damages, successful antitrust claims can receive treble damage and attorneys' fees.[12] Injunctive relief is available.[13] Also, private rights of action under the Commodity Exchange Act have a two-year statute of limitation; for antitrust claims it is four.[14]

As noted above, the rigging of interest rate benchmarks, such as the one in the *Laydon* litigation, was not the only major scandal. Foreign exchange benchmarks — set by reference to foreign exchange trades conducted near the close of the market — were also rigged by major banks.[15]

LIBOR Scandal and the Sunset of LIBOR

Numerous global banks were accused, from approximately 2005–2011, of subverting the process used to establish global benchmark rates. Historically, these benchmark rates, such as the London InterBank Offer Rate, i.e., LIBOR, were established by a process in which established rate-setting banks would each estimate their cost of funds for the benchmark rate. An averaging mechanism would then be applied.

The process was subverted when responsible individuals at some banks provided estimates not truly reflective of circumstances, and instead, intended to accommodate or benefit themselves or other parties. Billions in fines were assessed by the Department of Justice, the CFTC, and regulators from around the world.

LIBOR is intended to reflect the interest rates banks charge each other to lend money in specified currencies and for specified time periods. However, due to the inter-bank lending market no longer being "sufficiently active," it will be

---

12. 15 U.S.C. §15(a).

13. 15 U.S.C. §26.

14. 15 U.S.C. §15b.

15. For a superlative description of the scandals, see Gregory Scopino, *Expanding the Reach of the Commodity Exchange Act's Antitrust Considerations*, 45 Hofstra L. Rev. 573, 573–618 and 663–671, Tables 1 through 12.

> phased out and replaced by year-end 2021 for most currencies and June 30, 2023 for the most common U.S. dollar tenors.[a]
>
> [a] *See* Alternative Reference Rates Committee, *Progress Report: The Transition from U.S. Dollar LIBOR* (March 2021), available at https://www.newyorkfed.org/medialibrary/Microsites/arrc/files/2021/USD-LIBOR-transition-progress-report-mar-21.pdf.

b. Claims Against Registered Entities and the National Futures Association

There are stricter limitations for claims against the National Futures Association and registered entities, i.e., designated contract markets, derivatives clearing organizations, swap execution facilities, and swap data repositories.

A claim may only be made against such entities — or their officers, directors, governors, committee members, or employees — for a failure to enforce their own rules if the failure to enforce was in bad faith.[16] Additionally, in the case of claims against registered entities, the claimant must have traded subject to the rules of the registered entity.[17] For claims against the National Futures Association, the claimant must have entered into one of the four transaction types discussed above in section A.2.a and have had losses resulting from the National Futures Association's failure to enforce its rules.[18] In all cases only actual damages are available.[19]

It is worth noting that the bad faith requirement is such a high barrier that there have been no reported successful Commodity Exchange Act private rights of action against a registered entity or the National Futures Association.

Klein & Co. Futures, Inc. v. Board of Trade of City of New York

464 F.3d 255 (2d Cir. 2006)

B.D. Parker, Jr., Circuit Judge:

Klein & Co. Futures Inc. is a futures commission merchant ("FCM") and a clearing member of New York Clearing Corporation ("NYCC"). Klein appeals the dismissal by the United States District Court for the Southern District of New York . . . for lack of standing to bring claims against Defendant-Appellees the Board of Trade of the City of New York ("NYBOT"), New York Clearing Corporation ("NYCC"), Norman Eisler, and others (collectively "NYBOT Defendants") under Sections 22(a) and (b) of the Commodity Exchange Act (CEA). . . . For the reasons set forth below, we affirm. . . .

---

16. Commodity Exchange Act § 22(b).

17. Commodity Exchange Act § 22(b)(1) and (3).

18. Commodity Exchange Act § 22(b)(2) and (3).

19. Commodity Exchange Act § 22(b).

As a FCM, Klein facilitated the trading and fulfilled certain obligations of its customers who traded through the NYBOT. Prior to May 2000, Defendant Norman Eisler, whose conduct is the focus of Klein's complaint, was the Chairman of the New York Futures Exchange ("NYFE"). The NYFE is a futures and options exchange designated by the Commodity Futures Trading Commission ("CFTC") as a contract market for the trading of commodities futures and options, including P-Tech Futures and Options ("P-Tech contracts"). Eisler was also a member of the NYFE's Settlement Committee for the Pacific Stock Exchange Technology Index Futures Contract & Options (the "Committee"). The Committee's primary responsibility was to calculate the price of P-Tech contracts for the purposes, among other things, of calculating margin requirements in customers' accounts.[20] Eisler was also a customer of Klein and the principal of First West Trading Inc. ("First West"), another Klein customer. Eisler traded in P-Tech contracts for the account of First West. The trades were unsolicited and were made without input or advice from Klein.

Allegedly, Eisler, in his capacity as a member of the Committee, secretly manipulated the settlement prices of P-Tech contracts. This manipulation benefitted Eisler's P-Tech positions but, at the same time, caused Klein to miscalculate the margin requirements for the First West account. Around March 2000, the NYBOT began receiving complaints regarding the P-Tech settlement prices but failed to make proper inquiries or to place Klein or other members of the industry or public on notice of potential irregularities.

In early May 2000, Klein, based on the incorrect settlement prices, computed the required margin in First West's account at $700,000, but Eisler was unable to post that amount. Klein then contacted the NYBOT and expressed concerns regarding the illiquidity of the P-Tech contracts, Eisler's inability to meet First West's margin call, and his inability to liquidate First West's contracts. Klein reported that the First West margin deficit, if not covered, would impair Klein's net capital and cause Eisler significant losses. Klein requested that the NYFE Board halt trading in P-Tech contracts, but no such action occurred.

At that point, the scheme began to unravel. In mid-May, Eisler's NYBOT membership privileges were suspended and he was dropped from the Committee. Once this occurred, the remaining Committee members recalculated the settlement prices and First West's margin deficit ballooned to $4.5 million, an obligation it could not meet. As a result, Klein was required to take an immediate charge against its net capital, forcing it below the minimum required for clearing members of the NYCC and the New York Mercantile Exchange ("NYMEX"). Its membership privileges were suspended and Klein collapsed.

---

20. [N. 1] P-Tech Futures and Options prices are based on a composite index of one hundred technology stocks compiled by the Pacific Stock Exchange. The prices of those stocks and the value of that index may change up to the close of trading. Therefore, the Committee was charged with setting the settlement price after the close of the market.

Klein then sued on various claims. Klein's first claim alleged that NYFE violated § 5b of the CEA by failing to enforce its rules, and sought a declaration that NYFE should be suspended as a contract market. Klein further alleged that the NYBOT Defendants violated the [CEA]. . . .

The NYBOT Defendants moved to dismiss principally on the ground that Klein was not a purchaser or seller of futures contracts or options and, therefore, lacked standing under § 22 of the CEA. They also they moved to dismiss Klein's state law claims with prejudice on the ground that they were preempted by the CEA. The district court agreed and dismissed Klein's claims under the CEA for lack of standing. . . .

The court . . . reasoned that § 22 precluded an action by a plaintiff that "did not suffer its damages in the course of its trading activities on a contract market." . . . This appeal followed. . . .

CEA § 22 enumerates the only circumstances under which a private litigant may assert a private right of action for violations of the CEA. Section 22 includes two types of claims. Section 22(a) relates to claims against persons other than registered entities and registered futures associations. Section 22(b) deals with claims against those entities and their officers, directors, governors, committee members and employees. . . .

Specifically, the remedies afforded by CEA § 22(b) are available only to a private litigant "who engaged in . . . transaction[s] on or subject to the rules of" a contract market. The section contains another important limitation. Subsection 22(b)(5) provides that the private rights of action against the exchanges enumerated in § 22(b) "shall be the exclusive remedy . . . available to any person who sustains a loss as a result of" a violation of the CEA or an exchange rule by a contract market or one of its officers or employees.

Klein does not fall within any of the required subdivisions of § 22(a)(1)(A)–(D). To fit under one of the four, Klein must essentially either have (1) received trading advice from Eisler or First West for a fee; (2) traded through Eisler or First West or deposited money in connection with a trade; (3) purchased from or sold to Eisler or First West or placed an order for the purchase or sale through them; or (4) . . . [been the victim of] certain market manipulation activities in connection with the purchase or sale of a commodity contract.

Here, Klein was a FCM and a clearing member of the NYCC that cleared First West's trades through NYCC. Klein does not contend that it purchased or sold P-Tech contracts. Klein was not a trader of P-Tech contracts; nor did it own the P-Tech contracts at issue. To the contrary, Klein's complaint admits that it had no financial interest in the First West account and that all the trades in question were unsolicited by First West. Klein's losses were not the result of its purchases or sales in the commodities market. Klein functioned merely as a broker or agent that earned commissions for handling its customers [sic] trades. As a clearing member, Klein cleared their trades and was obligated to post margins for them as required. Under

NYCC Rules governing clearing members, Klein was liable for its own failure to post the required margin on its customers' positions, whether or not Klein collected that margin from defaulting customers such as First West. In view of the provisions of sections 22(a) and (b) expressly limiting the categories of persons that can seek remedies under the statute we conclude, as did the court below, that a plaintiff such as Klein who falls outside those categories lacks standing. . . .

Klein contends that it has standing under CEA to challenge the NYBOT Defendants as a "forced" purchaser and seller of securities. Klein contends that the Supreme Court in *Blue Chip Stamps v. Manor Drug Stores*, 421 U.S. 723, 95 S. Ct. 1917, 44 L. Ed.2d 539 (1975), after confirming that the federal securities laws confer an implied private right of action, granted standing under § 10(b) of the Securities Act of 1934 to securities brokers as "forced" purchasers or sellers, in situations where they, as clearing members, suffered damages arising from obligations to guarantee their customers' trades. Klein argues that as a FCM and clearing member, it was subject to federal statutes as well as the rules and by-laws of NYBOT, NYFE, and NYCC that required Klein to maintain funds guaranteeing its customers' transactions on the contract market. In his brief on appeal, Klein asserts that it assumed "a very real investment risk that the commodity contracts its customers traded would maintain or increase in value, a risk that is identical to that taken by any purchaser or seller of a commodity contract who is granted standing under the CEA." In sum, Klein argues that it has standing because it faced essentially the same risks as a purchaser or seller of commodities contracts. We disagree. . . .

[R]egardless of whether the First West trading position rose or declined in value, Klein had no interest in any of the resulting profits or investments losses. . . . Thus, Klein's loss was a credit loss, not a trading loss. . . .

For the reasons discussed, the judgment of the district court is affirmed.

––––––––––

Note the court's declination to apply the "forced purchaser" theory under which Klein, as a futures commission merchant guaranteeing its customers trades to the clearinghouse, would have been treated as standing in its defaulting customer's shoes. In other words, under this theory, Klein would have been a trader in the market and, therefore, able to potentially avail itself of the private right of action.

This would not have helped Klein in asserting a claim under Commodity Exchange Act section 22(a) as that section does not allow for a claim against a registered entity, i.e., the designated contract markets, derivatives clearing organization, and related personnel Klein was suing. It would have opened the door to a claim under section 22(b) — section 22(b) requires a showing of bad faith on the part of a registered entity or its relevant personnel. Although proving bad faith is a difficult hurdle to overcome, in the facts of this case it may not have been insuperable.

In the below case, the plaintiff lost on the facts because the court found that the National Futures Association did not fail to enforce its own rules. The case demonstrates how difficult a claim against the National Futures Association is in practice since, even if a failure to enforce its own rules were demonstrated, the plaintiff would still have to demonstrate bad faith and causation.

Troyer v. National Futures Association

981 F.3d 612 (7th Cir. 2020)

Flaum, Circuit Judge.

Plaintiff-appellant Dennis Troyer brought this claim against the National Futures Association ("NFA") under Section 25(b) of the Commodities Exchange Act. 7 U.S.C. § 25(b). On appeal, he challenges the district court's findings on each element of the action under § 25(b): failure to enforce a required bylaw, bad faith, and causation. Because this Court agrees that NFA Bylaw 301 is not applicable in this case, we affirm the district court's denial of Troyer's motion for summary judgment and grant of NFA's cross-motion for summary judgment. . . .

The Commodity Futures Trading Commission ("CFTC") promotes the integrity of the U.S. derivatives markets through regulation. Through the Commodity Exchange Act ("CEA"), Congress authorized the CFTC to establish futures associations with authority to regulate the practices of its Members. As the sole CFTC-approved registered futures association under the CEA since September 1981, the NFA is charged with processing registrations for futures commission merchants, swap dealers, commodity pool operators, commodity trading advisors, introducing brokers, retail foreign exchange dealers, and relevant associated persons ("APs"). Subject to limited exceptions, entities and accompanying APs registered with the CFTC in these enumerated capacities are both required to be NFA "Members" (or "Associate Members") and are subjected to NFA requirements.

One such requirement—Bylaw 301(a)(ii)(D)—was adopted by the NFA to track the language of 7 U.S.C. § 21(b)(3)(C). This bylaw governs NFA membership eligibility, stating, in relevant part:

> [N]o person shall be eligible to become or remain a Member or associated with a Member who[,] . . . [w]hether before or after becoming a Member or associated with a Member, was, by the person's conduct while associated with a Member, a cause of any suspension, expulsion or order[.]

NFA Bylaw 301(a)(ii)(D).

The NFA has two primary spheres of responsibility within the regulatory space: registration and discipline. Through CFTC delegation, the NFA is authorized to conduct proceedings to deny, condition, suspend, restrict, or revoke CFTC registration of any person, or entity AP, applying for registration as a covered actor. The NFA is empowered to initiate disciplinary action against any Member, or Associate Member, for violating NFA compliance rules, financial requirements, or by-laws. Disciplinary actions are resolved via settlement or evidentiary hearing followed by a written panel decision.

At the center of this dispute are the interactions between two longtime players in the NFA's regulatory space. Between 1983 and 2015, Thomas Heneghan was an AP of fourteen different NFA-Member firms. Dennis Troyer, an investor in financial products since the 1990s, invested hundreds of thousands of dollars in financial derivatives through NFA Members and their associates. Although Troyer chronicled a history of misconduct by Heneghan, dating as far back as 1985, the first interaction between Troyer and Heneghan was not until October 2008. After receiving an unsolicited phone call from Heneghan, Troyer invested more than $160,000 between October 2008 and March 2011 under Heneghan's advisement. From 2007 to 2010, Heneghan was an associate of Statewide FX, Inc. ("Statewide") before transitioning to Atlantis Trading Corp. ("ATC") from 2010 to 2012. Despite the changes in Heneghan's entity affiliation, the terms of his working relationship with Troyer remained constant. Although Troyer did not know every detail of his investment, Heneghan placed only trades authorized by Troyer and provided regular communication to Troyer — including investment statements — about the trades made on his behalf.

During Troyer's initial investment period, Heneghan came under NFA scrutiny. In 2009, the NFA received an unauthorized trade complaint implicating Heneghan. After failing to determine who placed the trades at issue, the NFA closed the matter. The following year, on June 7, 2010, the NFA began an examination of Statewide. The examination process encompassed corporate record review, customer and employer interviews, and evaluation of many Statewide APs, including Heneghan. As the examination progressed, the NFA's Compliance Department recommended that the NFA's Business Conduct Committee initiate a disciplinary action against Statewide, its principals, and three APs. Notably, Heneghan was not one of the three named APs. On December 9, 2010, the NFA's Business Conduct Committee initiated a disciplinary action against Statewide, but at the time of initiation, a voluntary NFA membership withdrawal was already in process by Statewide.

Amid the Statewide investigation, Heneghan transferred his registration to ATC. Tracking the personnel movement from Statewide to ATC, the NFA took note that several APs, including Heneghan, had previously worked for disciplined firms. As part of the NFA's inquiry, Troyer gave feedback that "overall his experience with Heneghan had been very good, even though his account was down in value." This 2011 examination culminated in NFA findings that, while 95% of ATC customers lost money in 2010, there had been significant improvement in investment outcomes and commission-to-equity and break-even ratios between 2010 and 2011. This examination and related findings resulted in the NFA's decision to place ATC on investigative monitoring.

By July 28, 2011, a settlement was reached in the Statewide NFA complaint. The settlement order called for Statewide "never to reapply for NFA membership or act as a principal of an NFA Member, effective immediately." Because Heneghan was not named in the NFA's 2010 disciplinary action, this settlement had no impact on his membership personally.

Although the NFA's Compliance Department did impose an approval hold on Heneghan beginning June 15, 2012, this hold was lifted only four months later. Heneghan was again approved to operate as an AP, this time with Portfolio Managers, Inc. ("PMI").

While Heneghan was registered as an associate of PMI, Troyer began sending money to Heneghan personally in April 2013, allegedly to take advantage of trading firm employee discounts. Between April 2013 and April 2015, these back-channel investments written to Heneghan personally (and delivered to his home) totaled approximately $82,000. In contrast to the monthly account statements he received during his first investment period, Troyer neither received nor asked for any investment documentation during his second investment period.

Again, NFA scrutiny followed Heneghan to his new role at PMI. On November 10, 2014 and September 8, 2015, the NFA's Compliance Department initiated examinations of PMI. Despite Troyer's alleged substantial investment, no accounts were listed with PMI for either Troyer or Heneghan at that time. On December 21, 2015, the NFA issued a complaint against PMI, Heneghan, and others, alleging routine use of high-pressure sales tactics and materially misleading and deceptive statements during customer sales solicitations.

Although Troyer was comfortable during his initial investment period not knowing every detail of his investments with Heneghan, his comfort waned toward the end of his second investment period. During the summer of 2015, Heneghan boasted to Troyer the account had increased to about $525,000. When Troyer directed Heneghan to cash out the fund and return the increased investment to him, "all hell broke loose."

By February 26, 2016, the NFA resolved the PMI complaint by issuing a decision to permanently bar Heneghan from NFA membership, associate membership, and from acting as a principal of an NFA Member. On May 8, 2016, in the wake of the collapse of Troyer and Heneghan's relationship, Troyer filed a four-count complaint in the Northern District of Indiana against several parties seeking accountability for Heneghan's allegedly fraudulent solicitation of funds from Troyer for the purpose of purchasing commodities futures. . . . On appeal, the NFA is the sole remaining defendant. . . .

Following the district court's denial of his motion for relief from judgement under FRCP 60(b)(3), Troyer now appeals the district court's grant of summary judgment to the NFA and corresponding denial of summary judgment for Troyer on his claim arising under 7 U.S.C. § 25(b) for failure to enforce NFA Bylaw 301. . . .

At this stage in Troyer's litigation, the only surviving claim for appeal centers on the NFA's alleged violation of the CEA through its failure to enforce its own bylaws, specifically NFA Bylaw 301(a)(ii)(D). To hold a party liable under the CEA for actual damages sustained by one engaged in futures transactions, three elements must be shown: failure to enforce a required bylaw, bad faith, and causation. 7 U.S.C § 25(b)(2), (4). First, the NFA must have "fail[ed] to enforce [a] bylaw or rule that is required under section 21 of [the CEA]." *Id.* § 25(b)(2). Second, the NFA must have "acted in bad faith in failing to take action or in taking such action as was taken." *Id.* § 25(b)(4). Third, the NFA's "failure or action [must have] caused the loss." *Id.* Troyer appeals the district court's findings on each prong.

Our analysis begins and ends with prong one: whether the NFA failed to enforce NFA Bylaw 301(a)(ii)(D) by not disqualifying Heneghan from continued registration as an NFA Associate Member and as an AP of any NFA-Member firm. Bylaw 301(a)(ii)(D) bars persons from becoming or remaining NFA Members or Associated Members if their conduct was the cause of NFA expulsion. If "expulsion" excludes voluntary withdrawal under a settlement, the bylaw is inapplicable, and Troyer's CEA violation claim fails at the outset.

Alleging Heneghan was "a cause of" the "expulsion" of Statewide, Troyer claims that the NFA was required to immediately terminate Heneghan's membership as of July 28, 2011, the date of the Statewide settlement. Troyer thus contests the district court's and the CFTC's position that Statewide's agreement not to reapply represented a distinct sanction from expulsion, one that does not trigger Bylaw 301(a)(ii)(D). To support his argument that the definition of expulsion encompasses an agreement not to reapply, Troyer attempts to distinguish the CFTC ruling in *Peterson v. National Futures Association*, CFTC No. CRAA-91-1, 1992 WL 289773 (Oct. 7, 1992) [hereinafter *Peterson*]. . . .

In *Peterson*, the NFA denied Leslie Peterson's application for CFTC registration as an AP on account of a past settlement agreement to withdraw and never reapply to the New York Mercantile Exchange, an exchange and self-regulatory organization. 1992 WL 289773, at *1. The CFTC vacated the NFA's decision and remanded for further proceedings. . . . Through this holding, the CFTC clarified that a withdrawal combined with agreement never to reapply is not an order of expulsion, nor does it, standing alone, constitute other good cause for statutory disqualification. *Id.* at *3. . . .

We therefore affirm the district court's holding that the NFA did not fail to enforce Bylaw 301(a)(ii)(D) because the NFA did not "expel" Statewide. Through *Peterson*, the CFTC firmly established that an "agreement not to reapply" is not an "expulsion." 1992 WL 289773. Because Bylaw 301(a)(ii)(D) is triggered only by a suspension, expulsion, or order, Troyer's claim that factual contents within the order accepting Statewide's settlement offer almost certainly establish good cause is irrelevant. . . .

A successful claim under Section 25(b) of the CEA requires failure to enforce a required bylaw, bad faith, *and* causation. 7 U.S.C. § 25(b). In sum, because Troyer cannot satisfy even the first prong of a claim under § 25(b) of the CEA, his claim fails, and our analysis appropriately ends here. . . .

For the reasons explained above, we AFFIRM the district court's grant of the NFA's motion for summary judgment and dismissal of Troyer's motion for summary judgment.

B. Reparation Proceedings and Arbitration

1. Reparation Proceedings

The CFTC has broad powers to award reparations in the form of actual damages to parties harmed by a violation of the Commodity Exchange Act by an entity registered with the CFTC.[21] As with private rights of action, there is a two-year limit for bringing a claim.[22] Also, futures commission merchants can require customers who are eligible contract participants (i.e., non-retail) to contractually waive their right to seek reparation proceedings.[23]

Although a Commodity Exchange Act violation needs to underlie any claim coming before the CFTC in a reparation proceeding, the CFTC has the authority to adjudicate related common law and state law claims, even if not grounded in the Commodity Exchange Act.

CFTC v. Schor
478 U.S. 833 (1986)

Justice O'Connor delivered the opinion of the Court.

The question presented is whether the Commodity Exchange Act (CEA or Act) empowers the Commodity Futures Trading Commission (CFTC or Commission) to entertain state law counterclaims in reparation proceedings. . . .

The CEA broadly prohibits fraudulent and manipulative conduct in connection with commodity futures transactions. . . .

Among the duties assigned to the CFTC . . . [is] the administration of a reparations procedure through which disgruntled customers of professional commodity brokers . . . [can] seek redress for the brokers' violations of the Act or CFTC regulations. Thus, § 14 of the CEA provides that any person injured by such violations may apply to the Commission for an order directing the offender to pay reparations to the complainant and may enforce that order in federal district court. Congress intended this administrative procedure to be an "inexpensive and expeditious" alternative to existing fora available to aggrieved customers, namely, the courts and arbitration. . . .

The instant dispute arose in February 1980, when respondents Schor and Mortgage Services of America, Inc., invoked the CFTC's reparations jurisdiction by filing complaints against petitioner ContiCommodity Services, Inc. (Conti), a commodity futures broker, and Richard L. Sandor, a Conti employee. Schor had an account with Conti which contained a debit balance because Schor's net futures trading losses and expenses, such as commissions, exceeded the funds deposited in the account.

---

21. Commodity Exchange Act § 14(a).
22. Commodity Exchange Act § 14(a)(1).
23. Commodity Exchange Act § 14(g).

Schor alleged that this debit balance was the result of Conti's numerous violations of the CEA.

Before receiving notice that Schor had commenced the reparations proceeding, Conti had filed a diversity action in Federal District Court to recover the debit balance. Schor counterclaimed in this action, reiterating his charges that the debit balance was due to Conti's violations of the CEA. Schor also moved on two separate occasions to dismiss or stay the District Court action, arguing that the continuation of the federal action would be a waste of judicial resources and an undue burden on the litigants in view of the fact that "[t]he reparations proceedings . . . will fully . . . resolve and adjudicate all the rights of the parties to this action with respect to the transactions which are the subject matter of this action."

Although the District Court declined to stay or dismiss the suit, Conti voluntarily dismissed the federal court action and presented its debit balance claim by way of a counterclaim in the CFTC reparations proceeding. Conti denied violating the CEA and instead insisted that the debit balance resulted from Schor's trading, and was therefore a simple debt owed by Schor.

After discovery, briefing, and a hearing, the Administrative Law Judge (ALJ) in Schor's reparations proceeding ruled in Conti's favor on both Schor's claims and Conti's counterclaims. After this ruling, Schor for the first time challenged the CFTC's statutory authority to adjudicate Conti's counterclaim. . . . Schor filed a petition for review with the Court of Appeals for the District of Columbia Circuit. Prior to oral argument, the Court of Appeals, *sua sponte*, raised the question whether CFTC could constitutionally adjudicate Conti's counterclaims. . . .

[T]he Court of Appeals . . . ordered the dismissal of Conti's counterclaims on the ground that "the CFTC lacks authority (subject matter competence) to adjudicate" common law counterclaims. . . .

Our examination of the CEA and its legislative history and purpose reveals that Congress plainly intended the CFTC to decide counterclaims asserted by respondents in reparations proceedings, and just as plainly delegated to the CFTC the authority to fashion its counterclaim jurisdiction in the manner the CFTC determined necessary to further the purposes of the reparations program. . . .

Reference to the instant controversy illustrates the crippling effect that the Court of Appeals' restrictive reading of the CFTC's counterclaim jurisdiction would have on the efficacy of the reparations remedy. The dispute between Schor and Conti is typical of the disputes adjudicated in reparations proceedings: a customer and a professional commodities broker agree that there is a debit balance in the customer's account, but the customer attributes the deficit to the broker's alleged CEA violations and the broker attributes it to the customer's lack of success in the market. The customer brings a reparations claim; the broker counterclaims for the amount of the debit balance. In the usual case, then, the counterclaim "arises out of precisely the same course of events" as the principal claim and requires resolution of many of the same disputed factual issues.

Under the Court of Appeals' approach, the entire dispute may not be resolved in the administrative forum. Consequently, the entire dispute will typically end up in court, for when the broker files suit to recover the debit balance, the customer will normally be compelled either by compulsory counterclaim rules or by the expense and inconvenience of litigating the same issues in two fora to forgo his reparations remedy and to litigate his claim in court. In sum, as Schor himself aptly summarized, to require a bifurcated examination of the single dispute "would be to emasculate if not destroy the purposes of the Commodity Exchange Act to provide an efficient and relatively inexpensive forum for the resolution of disputes in futures trading." . . .

As our discussion makes manifest, the CFTC's long-held position that it has the power to take jurisdiction over counterclaims such as Conti's is eminently reasonable and well within the scope of its delegated authority. . . .

We therefore are squarely faced with the question whether the CFTC's assumption of jurisdiction over common law counterclaims violates Article III of the Constitution. . . .

Article III, § 1, directs that the "judicial Power of the United States shall be vested in one supreme Court and in such inferior Courts as the Congress may from time to time ordain and establish," and provides that these federal courts shall be staffed by judges who hold office during good behavior, and whose compensation shall not be diminished during tenure in office. Schor claims that these provisions prohibit Congress from authorizing the initial adjudication of common law counterclaims by the CFTC, an administrative agency whose adjudicatory officers do not enjoy the tenure and salary protections embodied in Article III. . . .

In the instant cases, Schor indisputably waived any right he may have possessed to the full trial of Conti's counterclaim before an Article III court. Schor expressly demanded that Conti proceed on its counterclaim in the reparations proceeding rather than before the District Court and was content to have the entire dispute settled in the forum he had selected until the ALJ ruled against him on all counts; it was only after the ALJ rendered a decision to which he objected that Schor raised any challenge to the CFTC's consideration of Conti's counterclaim.

Even were there no evidence of an express waiver here, Schor's election to forgo his right to proceed in state or federal court on his claim and his decision to seek relief instead in a CFTC reparations proceeding constituted an effective waiver. . . .

An examination of the relative allocation of powers between the CFTC and Article III courts in light of the considerations given prominence in our precedents demonstrates that the congressional scheme does not impermissibly intrude on the province of the judiciary. The CFTC's adjudicatory powers depart from the traditional agency model in just one respect: the CFTC's jurisdiction over common law counterclaims. . . .

It is clear that Congress has not attempted to "withdraw from judicial cognizance" the determination of Conti's right to the sum represented by the debit balance in Schor's account. Congress gave the CFTC the authority to adjudicate such matters, but the decision to invoke this forum is left entirely to the parties and the power of the federal judiciary to take jurisdiction of these matters is unaffected. In such circumstances, separation of powers concerns are diminished, for it seems self-evident that just as Congress may encourage parties to settle a dispute out of court or resort to arbitration without impermissible incursions on the separation of powers, Congress may make available a quasi-judicial mechanism through which willing parties may, at their option, elect to resolve their differences. This is not to say, of course, that if Congress created a phalanx of non-Article III tribunals equipped to handle the entire business of the Article III courts without any Article III supervision or control and without evidence of valid and specific legislative necessities, the fact that the parties had the election to proceed in their forum of choice would necessarily save the scheme from constitutional attack. But this case obviously bears no resemblance to such a scenario, given the degree of judicial control saved to the federal courts as well as the congressional purpose behind the jurisdictional delegation, the demonstrated need for the delegation, and the limited nature of the delegation.

When Congress authorized the CFTC to adjudicate counterclaims, its primary focus was on making effective a specific and limited federal regulatory scheme, not on allocating jurisdiction among federal tribunals. Congress intended to create an inexpensive and expeditious alternative forum through which customers could enforce the provisions of the CEA against professional brokers. . . .

It also bears emphasis that the CFTC's assertion of counterclaim jurisdiction is limited to [what is] . . . incidental to, and completely dependent upon, adjudication of reparations claims created by federal law, and in actual fact is limited to claims arising out of the same transaction or occurrence as the reparations claim. . . .

The judgment of the Court of Appeals for the District of Columbia Circuit is reversed, and the cases remanded for further proceedings consistent with this opinion. . . .

Reparation decisions are appealable to federal courts of appeal.[24] However, the appellant is liable for the appellee's attorneys' fees if the appellee wins.[25]

2. Arbitration

Another mechanism for the private resolution of disputes is arbitration. CFTC rules provide the framework for where CFTC registrants may use arbitration agreements.[26] National Futures Association rules allow customers of futures commis-

---

24. Commodity Exchange Act § 14(e).
25. *Id.*
26. 17 C.F.R. § 166.5. 9 U.S.C. § 4 provides for the generally federally enforceability of arbitration agreements.

sion merchants, retail foreign exchange dealers, introducing brokers, commodity pool operators, commodity trading advisors, and leverage transaction merchants to compel arbitration of disputes with the entities or their employees.[27] As with private rights of action under the Commodity Exchange Act, there is a two-year period for filing a claim.[28] Other self-regulatory organizations have similar arbitration proceedings available to aggrieved customers of members.[29]

In the following case, a futures commission merchant dually-registered with the SEC as a securities broker-dealer was a member of the National Futures Association and the Financial Industry Regulatory Authority (commonly known as "FINRA"). Its customer sought to compel FINRA arbitration for losses in natural gas futures trading. However, what was critical was whether it was a "customer" with respect to the defendant's futures commission merchant activities or securities broker-dealer activities.

INTL FCStone Financial v. Jacobson

2019 WL 2356989 (N.D. Ill. June 4, 2019)

Joan H. Lefkow, U.S. District Judge

INTL FCStone Financial Inc. has sued several defendants to enjoin them from further pursuing their pending arbitration at the Financial Industry Regulatory Authority (FINRA), which FCStone claims is the wrong arbitral forum. FCStone also asks the court to compel defendants to arbitrate their claims before the National Futures Association (NFA). Defendants have moved to dismiss the complaint and for sanctions against FCStone for pursuing its claim for injunctive relief.

Construing the parties' arbitration agreements and FINRA's rules, the court concludes that the parties agreed to arbitrate their disputes before the NFA, not FINRA, and enters declaratory judgment to that effect, as detailed below. . . .

FCStone is a global financial services firm. Among its services is a futures commission merchant division that helps execute and clear exchange-traded futures, commodities, and options transactions. Separate from that division, FCStone also engages in securities-related business and is therefore a member of FINRA, a self-regulatory organization for the securities and investment banking industry. FINRA members agree to arbitrate before FINRA any disputes with their "customers" that "arise[] in connection with the business activities of the member" on the customer's request. FINRA Rule 12200. . . .

Between October 2016 and July 2018, defendants opened trading accounts with FCStone's futures commission merchant division. Their account agreements did not permit them to trade any securities. . . . All defendants except William and Cynthia

---

27. National Futures Association, *Code of Arbitration* § 2(a)(1)(i)(C).
28. National Futures Association, *Code of Arbitration* § 5.
29. *See, e.g.*, CME Rulebook, ch. 6.

Motley also signed arbitration agreements with FCStone, agreeing, among other things, that

> [a]ny controversy o[r] claim arising out of or relating to your accounts shall be settled by arbitration, either (1) under the Code of Arbitration of the National Futures Association, or (2) upon the contract market on which the disputed transaction was executed or could have been executed. . . . At the time you notify . . . the FCM Division of INTL FCStone Financial Inc. ("FCM") . . . of your intent to submit a claim to arbitration, . . . you will have an opportunity to elect a qualified forum for conducting the proceedings, and will be supplied with a list of qualified organizations. You are required to send notice of your intent to arbitrate by certified mail to the FCM and/ or the Introducing Broker at their respective addresses, and the Secretary of the National Futures Association. . . .

The defendants experienced significant losses in their accounts in November 2018 based on volatility in the natural gas market — so significant that defendants owed balances to FCStone. On December 3, 2018, defendants to the original complaint — the Jacobsons, Musial, the Slanecs, the Schweigers, the Holcombs, the Rogerses, the Greaveses, and Pradko (and their related trusts) ("Original Defendants") — initiated arbitration against FCStone before FINRA, alleging among other things that FCStone violated § 13(a) of the Commodity Exchange Act, 7 U.S.C. § 13c(a).

Taking this as notice of a dispute under the arbitration agreements, FCStone emailed defense counsel on December 13, 2018 offering arbitration at any of three forums: (1) the NFA; (2) the Chicago Mercantile Exchange; or (3) the American Arbitration Association (AAA). (Dkt. 32-7 at 1.) Defense counsel responded that the arbitration agreement was unenforceable because it did not comply with 17 C.F.R. § 166.5 — the Commodity Futures Trading Commission's (CFTC) regulation governing arbitration agreements between Commission registrants like FCStone and their customers — and insisted on arbitration before FINRA. (*Id.*) In February 2019, more than forty-five days after offering its slate of arbitral options, FCStone initiated arbitration before the NFA to collect the original defendants' balances due. . . .

On January 29, 2019, more than forty-five days after FCStone's December 13 email, defense counsel notified FCStone that all his clients — including most of the defendants here — elected to arbitrate before the AAA. . . . In February 2019, the AAA found that FCStone had not agreed to arbitrate defendants' disputes before the AAA. (Dkt. 65-2.)

In February 2019, FCStone filed this action for injunctive and declaratory relief, arguing that FINRA lacks jurisdiction over the underlying disputes. After failing to secure arbitration before the AAA, many customers filed statements of claim before FINRA in March 2019. In April, FCStone amended its complaint to add these customers as new defendants, along with a new count under § 4 of the Federal Arbitration Act, 9 U.S.C. § 4, to compel defendants (except the Motleys) to arbitrate their disputes before the NFA. . . .

FCStone has moved to compel defendants (other than the Motleys) to arbitrate their disputes before the NFA. Under §4 of the Federal Arbitration Act, "[a] party aggrieved by the alleged failure, neglect, or refusal of another to arbitrate under a written agreement may petition any United States district court ... for an order directing that such arbitration proceed in the manner provided for in such agreement." 9 U.S.C. §4. Federal courts "will compel arbitration under the Federal Arbitration Act 'if three elements are present: (1) an enforceable written agreement to arbitrate, (2) a dispute within the scope of the arbitration agreement, and (3) a refusal to arbitrate.'" *A.D. v. Credit One Bank, N.A.*, 885 F.3d 1054, 1060 (7th Cir. 2018) (quoting *Scheurer v. Fromm Family Foods LLC*, 863 F.3d 748, 752 (7th Cir. 2017)).

Under the Federal Arbitration Act, courts presumptively decide whether parties have agreed to arbitrate in the first instance, but arbitrators decide any procedural questions that grow out of the dispute. *Howsam* [*v. Dean Witter Reynolds, Inc.*], 537 U.S. at 84. Absent clear and unmistakable evidence that the parties intended to arbitrate the issue of arbitrability (which neither party argues exists here), the court must determine arbitrability. *First Options of Chicago v. Kaplan*, 514 U.S. 938, 944, 115 S. Ct. 1920 (1995).

Where to arbitrate is a question of arbitrability, not procedure. FCStone asks the court to determine whether it agreed under FINRA Rule 12200 to submit these disputes to FINRA and whether defendants agreed under the arbitration agreements to submit them to the NFA, quintessential decisions for a court under the Federal Arbitration Act. *Howsam*, 537 U.S. at 84 ("[A] disagreement about whether an arbitration clause in a concededly binding contract applies to a particular type of controversy is for the court."). That no party proposes litigation instead of arbitration is irrelevant. Had defendants tried to litigate the dispute and FCStone moved to compel arbitration, the court would have had to review the arbitration agreements to determine whether defendants agreed to arbitrate at the NFA. Had FCStone tried to litigate and defendants moved to compel arbitration before FINRA, the court would have had to determine whether FCStone agreed through Rule 12200 to submit its claims to FINRA. The analytical tasks are the same here as in those cases where the issue is unquestionably committed to the court. *Id.* The court must therefore decide whether (1) defendants agreed to submit these disputes to the NFA; and (2) FCStone agreed to submit these disputes to FINRA.

Defendants urge that even though this case presents an issue of arbitrability for the court, because FINRA arbitration is already underway, the court is powerless to rule on arbitrability until that arbitration ends. ...

Deferring a ruling on arbitrability here would abdicate the court's duty under §4 of the Federal Arbitration Act. FCStone is therefore not required to complete the FINRA arbitration before seeking the court's input on whether it agreed to arbitrate in either FINRA or the NFA. ...

There is no dispute that all defendants but the Motleys signed arbitration agreements. The agreements purport to permit arbitration only at the relevant exchange market or at a futures association. (Dkt. 32-2.) Defendants argue that this makes the agreements unenforceable because they violate CFTC Rule 166.5, which requires FCStone to offer a third option. *See* 17 C.F.R. § 166.5(c)(5)(i). But the arbitration agreements advise that the customers will be given a choice among qualified forums, and FCStone in fact offered the three forums required under Rule 166.5(c)(5)(1). (Dkt. 32-2.) This structure — that the agreement lists only two options, but the email to the customers provided the required third — complies with Rule 166.5, and the arbitration agreements are therefore enforceable. Rule 166.5(c)(4) requires that "[t]he agreement . . . advise the customer that . . . the customer will have the opportunity to elect a qualified forum," 17 C.F.R. § 166.5(c)(4), but does not require that the election-of-forum process be set forth explicitly in the agreement, 17 C.F.R. § 166.5(c)(5) (election-of-forum process lacks "agreement must advise" language). FCStone's agreements thus complied with the requirement to advise that the defendants could choose and then providing an appropriate slate of options, here (1) the NFA; (2) the Chicago Mercantile Exchange; and (3) the AAA. (Dkt. 32-7.) FCStone has therefore satisfied the first element of enforceable agreements to arbitrate.

Defendants concede that these disputes fall within the scope of the arbitration agreements, satisfying the second element. As to the third element, defendants did not arbitrate in accordance with their agreements. After receiving notice of the underlying disputes, FCStone provided defendants a list of three qualified organizations: (1) the NFA; (2) the Chicago Mercantile Exchange; and (3) the AAA. (Dkt. 32-7 at 1.) Defendants did not choose among the three offered forums within forty-five days, which authorized FCStone to pick the NFA. 17 C.F.R. § 166.5(c)(5). Indeed, the Original Defendants went a step further, immediately rejecting all three options in favor of FINRA. (Dkt. 32-7.) FCStone thus chose the NFA in compliance with the arbitration agreements and CFTC Rule 166.5, and defendants' refusal to arbitrate there satisfies the third element. . . .

[C]iting *Belom v. Nat'l Futures Assoc.*, 284 F.3d 795, 797 (7th Cir. 2002), defendants protest that their disputes cannot be arbitrated before the NFA because arbitration there must be "voluntary." It is voluntary. Defendants agreed to arbitrate before the NFA when they signed their arbitration agreements. As the Motleys show, the defendants were not required to sign the agreements to open their commodity futures and options accounts with FCStone.

Thus, under the arbitration agreements and CFTC Rule 166.5(c), defendants signed enforceable agreements to arbitrate their disputes at one of three qualified forums and if they failed to choose within forty-five days, FCStone would choose for them. Having consented to this procedure and failed to choose a qualified option in time, defendants agreed to submit their disputes to the NFA. . . .

Defendants next argue that, notwithstanding the arbitration agreements, FCStone must arbitrate these disputes before FINRA because it is a FINRA member. FCStone is indeed a member of FINRA, and FINRA members agree to arbitrate certain disputes before FINRA. Among eligible disputes are those between members and their customers if the disputes "arise[] in connection with the business activities of the member. . . ." FINRA R. 12200; *UBS Fin. Servs., Inc. v. W. Va. Univ. Hosp., Inc.*, 660 F.3d 643, 649 (2d Cir. 2011) (holding FINRA membership compels members to arbitrate disputes with customers before FINRA).

Specifically, FINRA members must arbitrate a dispute under the FINRA Code[30] if "either: (1) Required by a written agreement, or (2) Requested by the customer;" and if:

- The dispute is between a customer and a member or associated person of a member; and

- The dispute arises in connection with the business activities of the member or the associated person, except disputes involving the insurance business activities of a member that is also an insurance company.

FINRA R. 12200.

FCStone argues that because FINRA regulates only securities and investment banking, defendants (including the Motleys) are not "customers" under FINRA Rule 12200 because they held commodity futures and options accounts and dispute commodity futures and options transactions. Defendants respond that the commodities/securities distinction is only hair splitting. But securities and commodity futures and options are distinct — so distinct that Congress has erected different regulatory regimes and enforcement agencies for the different financial products. *See, e.g., Bd. of Trade of City of Chicago v. S.E.C.*, 187 F.3d 713, 716 (7th Cir. 1999) ("Congress allocated securities and options on securities to exchanges regulated by the SEC, futures and options on futures to boards of trade regulated by the CFTC."). *Amicus* Futures Industry Association helpfully explains these differences and how Congress has given exclusive jurisdiction over commodity-related financial products to the CFTC. (Dkt. 62 at 5 (citing 7 U.S.C. § 2(a)(1)(A)) and *Chicago Mercantile Exch. v. S.E.C.*, 883 F.2d 537, 539 (7th Cir. 1989) ("The CFTC regulates futures and options on futures; the SEC regulates securities and options on securities; jurisdiction never overlaps.").) FINRA, as a self-regulatory organization in the securities market, is overseen by the U.S. Securities and Exchange Commission and has a distinct sphere of influence that Congress has carefully separated from the CFTC's sphere. (*See* dkt. 62 at 5.) The underlying disputes here concern accounts and transactions of commodity futures and options, not securities; indeed, defendants were not even authorized to trade securities through their FCStone accounts. (*See* dkt. 20-1 at 12.) Defendants' relationships and disputes with FCStone do not fall within FINRA's regulatory ambit.

The case thus turns on whether defendants were "customers" under FINRA Rule 12200 even though they did not transact with FCStone's FINRA-regulated business activities. The FINRA Rules define "customer" only by exclusion — that it "shall not include a broker or dealer." FINRA R. 12100(k). But coupling this definition with the broader structure of the FINRA Rules, the circuit courts to have addressed this

---

30. [N. 6] Arbitration under the FINRA Code necessarily means arbitration before FINRA. *Credit Suisse Securities (USA) LLC v. Tracy*, 812 F.3d 249, 254 (2d Cir. 2016).

issue have concluded that FINRA members submit to FINRA arbitration only with customers of their FINRA-regulated business activities, securities and investment banking....

Finally, this interpretation of FINRA rules harmonizes the rules with the carefully hewn balance between SEC and CFTC regulatory authority. *Amicus* highlights the danger of requiring parties to resolve commodity futures and options disputes before FINRA when Congress committed them to the CFTC. The CFTC has exercised its exclusive jurisdiction over the commodity futures and options market, *see* 7 U.S.C. § 2(a)(1)(A), to require its registrants to offer customers three arbitral forums in any arbitration agreement. 17 C.F.R. § 166.5(c). But if the court reads the FINRA rules to require those companies registered with both FINRA and the CFTC to arbitrate all customer disputes before FINRA, Rule 166.5 would have no effect as to some of the largest participants in CFTC-regulated markets....

For all these reasons, the court holds that "customer" under FINRA Rule 12200 means "customer of the member's FINRA-regulated activities." Because commodity futures accountholders do not qualify as "customers," FCStone did not agree to arbitrate the underlying disputes before FINRA. And by signing the arbitration agreements, all defendants except the Motleys agreed to arbitrate their disputes before the NFA. As defendants refuse to arbitrate as agreed, relief is warranted under § 4 of the Federal Arbitration Act.

The motion to compel arbitration is granted. All defendants except the Motleys are ordered to submit their claims to arbitration before the NFA by June 28, 2019....

———————

In the case below, the plaintiff alleged that the CFTC provided insufficient oversight of the National Futures Association in its role as arbitrator. The unfortunate outcome for the plaintiff was a recognition that the CFTC in fact plays no role in overseeing National Futures Association arbitrations other than approving the rule framework as the CFTC does with any self-regulatory organization.

Ikon Global Markets, Inc. v. CFTC

859 F. Supp. 2d 162 (D.D.C. 2012)

Rudolph Contreras, District Judge.

After losing an arbitration to one of its customers, IKON Global Markets, Inc. brought this suit. IKON is a futures commission merchant — essentially, a broker of futures contracts — registered with the National Futures Association ("NFA"), which is regulated by the Commodity Futures Trading Commission ("CFTC"). The arbitration was conducted by an NFA panel. IKON alleges that the panel erred, and asks this court to nullify its decision and ensure that no such error is committed again....

The [Commodity Exchange Act ("CEA")]... requires registered futures associations such as the NFA to "provide a fair, equitable, and expeditious procedure through arbitration or otherwise for the settlement of customers' claims and grievances against any member" of the association. 7 U.S.C. § 21(b)(10). The NFA — a statutorily-authorized self-regulatory organization for the futures industry ... — has accordingly established a code of arbitration and member arbitration rules which, like all NFA rules, are subject to CFTC approval. *See* 7 U.S.C. § 21(j). The code and rules both provide that there is no right of appeal from the decision of an NFA arbitration panel. National Futures Association, NFA Manual, Code of Arbitration, § 10(d); (2012) ("There shall be no right of appeal of the award."); *id.*, Member Arbitration Rules, § 10(d) (same). ... Parties can request that the panel modify its decision on certain limited grounds, but they are explicitly barred from rearguing the merits of the controversy. *Id.*, Code of Arbitration, § 10(c); *id.*, Member Arbitration Rules, § 10(c) (both allowing the modification of an award that is "imperfect in matter of form not affecting the merits of the controversy"). And the CFTC does not review the decisions of NFA arbitration panels. 17 C.F.R. § 171.1(b)(2). Of course, the losing party can challenge the award under the Federal Arbitration Act, but "judicial review of arbitral awards is extremely limited" and does not encompass "claims of factual or legal error by an arbitrator." *Kurke v. Oscar Gruss & Son, Inc.*, 454 F.3d 350, 354 (D.C.Cir.2006) (internal quotation marks omitted).

In 2009, two IKON customers brought claims against the company before NFA arbitrators. Compl. ¶ 11. Both claims involved IKON's decision to close out offsetting currency positions in a customer's foreign exchange account.[31] The NFA had recently adopted a rule forbidding members from maintaining such positions for their customers.[32] IKON prevailed in one arbitration; its customer prevailed in the other. ...

IKON brought this suit against the CFTC. IKON alleges here that it has been subject to inconsistent decisions by NFA arbitration panels, and asks the court to nullify the award against the company and order the CFTC to ensure that the NFA does not allow such arbitral inconsistencies in the future. ...

The CFTC argues that the court lacks subject matter jurisdiction to hear this case because IKON lacks both constitutional and prudential standing and no statute confers jurisdiction. The court will consider each argument in turn. ...

To establish constitutional standing, "a plaintiff must show (1) it has suffered an 'injury in fact' that is (a) concrete and particularized and (b) actual or imminent,

---

31. [N. 2] An offsetting currency position occurs when a customer simultaneously holds a long position — that is, an investment that will return a profit if the currency rises in value — and a short position — which turns a profit if the value of the currency falls — in the same currency in the same amount. Letter of Thomas W. Sexton, Vice President and General Counsel, NFA to David Stawick, Office of the Secretariat, CFTC, Regarding Proposed Adoption of Compliance Rule 2-43 (Dec. 9, 2008), at 6. ...

32. [N. 3] NFA Manual, Rule 2-43(b) (adopted May 15, 2009) ("Forex Dealer Members may not carry offsetting positions in a customer account but must offset them on a first-in, first-out basis."). In 2010, the CFTC promulgated a regulation that established a similar requirement. 17 C.F.R. § 1.46(a)–(b).

not conjectural or hypothetical; (2) the injury is fairly traceable to the challenged action of the defendant; and (3) it is likely, as opposed to merely speculative, that the injury will be redressed by a favorable decision." . . .

IKON alleges that it is being deprived of the benefit of CFTC oversight of NFA arbitration decisions. The company argues that the CFTC must ensure that NFA arbitrators apply and enforce the applicable rules and regulations and that, because the CFTC has not done so, IKON is exposed to the risk of inconsistent arbitration decisions and cannot safely enforce the rules and regulations in question. At bottom, IKON is concerned that if it continues to cancel its customers' offsetting positions, as it understands NFA Rule 2-43 and 17 C.F.R. §1.46 to require it to do, it could lose another arbitration to a customer that objects to the cancellation. Such a hypothetical injury is not sufficient to give IKON standing to prosecute this action. . . .

But IKON also asks the court to order the CFTC to nullify the arbitration decision against it. . . . The arbitration award against IKON is an actual, concrete, and particularized injury that is fairly traceable to the CFTC's alleged action — failing to oversee NFA arbitrations — and that would be redressed by an order requiring the CFTC to nullify the award. Whether the CFTC in fact has an obligation to oversee NFA arbitrations and whether this court has the power to order that it nullify an award are questions of the merits of IKON's case, not the company's standing to bring it.

The question of standing involves not only "constitutional limitations on federal-court jurisdiction," but also "prudential limitations on its exercise." *Bennett v. Spear*, 520 U.S. 154, 162, 117 S.Ct. 1154, 137 L.Ed.2d 281 (1997) (quoting *Warth v. Seldin*, 422 U.S. 490, 498, 95 S.Ct. 2197, 45 L.Ed.2d 343 (1975)). "To establish prudential standing, a party's 'grievance must arguably fall within the zone of interests protected or regulated by the statutory provision or constitutional guarantee invoked in the suit.'" *Nuclear Energy Inst., Inc. v. EPA*, 373 F.3d 1251, 1266 (D.C.Cir.2004) (quoting *Bennett*, 520 U.S. at 162, 117 S.Ct. 1154). When applied to a statute, the zone-of-interests test "is intended to 'exclude only those whose interests are so marginally related to or inconsistent with the purposes implicit in the statute that it cannot reasonably be assumed that Congress intended to permit the suit.'"

The statutory provisions at issue here are 7 U.S.C. §§ 21(b)(10), which requires registered futures associations to "provide a fair, equitable, and expeditious procedure through arbitration or otherwise for the settlement of customers' claims and grievances against any member," and 21(j), which makes NFA rules subject to CFTC approval. These provisions arguably give the members of futures associations a protected interest in the fairness of the arbitration procedures established by such associations — an interest that could allow them to challenge the CFTC's failure to ensure such fairness when it was legally required to do so. (Again, whether the CFTC in fact has such an obligation is a question of the merits of IKON's claims, not its standing to bring them.) The court therefore concludes that IKON has prudential standing to pursue this case. . . .

IKON frames its case as a challenge to the CFTC's failure to act, brought under the Administrative Procedure Act.... The APA provides "a limited cause of action for parties adversely affected by agency action." *Trudeau v. Fed. Trade Comm'n*, 456 F.3d 178, 185 (D.C.Cir.2006). If a party cannot plausibly allege that it has been adversely affected by final agency action, it cannot state a claim upon which relief can be granted—but that inability does not deprive the court of jurisdiction.... The court therefore concludes that this case is within its statutory grant of federal question jurisdiction and goes on to consider whether IKON can state a claim under the APA....

The APA empowers the judiciary to "compel agency action unlawfully withheld or unreasonably delayed." *Id.* § 706(1)....

IKON has not identified any discrete action that the CFTC is required to take. To the contrary, the actions that it would force the Commission to perform are forbidden. IKON asks that this court order the CFTC to ensure that NFA arbitration panels properly enforce NFA and CFTC rules. But under CFTC regulations, "[t]he Commission will not review ... [a] decision in an arbitration action brought pursuant to section 17(b)(10) of the [Commodity Exchange] Act or any rule of the National Futures Association." 17 C.F.R. § 171.1(b)(2). Both that regulation and the NFA Code of Arbitration, which was approved by the CFTC and bars appeal from the decision of an arbitration panel, strike a balance between the desire for efficient resolution of disputes and the need for certain procedural safeguards. The CFTC has made a considered decision not to oversee the outcomes of NFA arbitrations. IKON has not identified any discrete action of oversight that the Commission is legally required to perform. IKON therefore has not stated a failure-to-act claim under section 706(1) of the APA.

Nor can IKON avoid dismissal by invoking 5 U.S.C. § 706(2). That familiar provision empowers the court to "hold unlawful and set aside agency action ... found to be ... arbitrary, capricious, an abuse of discretion, or otherwise not in accordance with law." To be reviewable, "agency action" must be "final agency action" if the APA provides the only cause of action. *Id.* § 704. Because, as discussed above, "agency action" encompasses a "failure to act," *see id.* § 551(13), courts in this district have said that "if a failure to act amounts to 'consummated "agency action" that APA views as final, notwithstanding the fact that the agency "did" nothing,' a party can seek relief under Section 706(2) of the APA." *Hi-Tech Pharmacal Co. v. FDA*, 587 F.Supp.2d 1, 9 (D.D.C.2008) (quoting *Alliance to Save the Mattaponi v. Army Corps of Eng'rs*, 515 F.Supp.2d 1, 10 (D.D.C.2007)). But even if the CFTC's decision not to oversee NFA arbitrations was final enough to provide IKON with a cause of action under the APA, that decision could only be "an abuse of discretion" if it was discretionary. Instead, the Commission is forbidden by regulation from exercising the oversight that IKON would compel here. By the same token, an agency's faithful observance of its own regulations cannot be "arbitrary, capricious ... or otherwise not in accordance with law." Perhaps IKON could have challenged 17 C.F.R. § 171.1(b)(2) when it was promulgated. Having failed to do so, it cannot state a claim challenging the CFTC's decision to obey it. The court will therefore dismiss IKON's complaint. . . .

The NFA has, with the approval of the CFTC, adopted a system of binding arbitration with no right of appeal. Such a system renders fast and final decisions. IKON alleges that it has been injured by an arbitration panel's legal error and may be so injured again. But even if that were so, the risk of such errors is an inevitable cost of arbitration without appeal. IKON has offered this court no legal grounds on which to compel the CFTC to force the NFA to abandon its system for quickly resolving customer disputes. IKON's complaint is therefore dismissed without prejudice for failure to state a claim on which relief can be granted.

————————

The decision in *Ikon* raises interesting questions regarding the CFTC's role. The CFTC used its own regulations as a basis to disclaim responsibility — responsibility conveyed by statute — to exercise some oversight of the National Futures Association. A difficult outcome for Ikon, apparently between a rock and a hard place: required to comply with the National Futures Association rule prohibiting "offsetting" foreign exchange accounts and exposed to customer claims for doing so.

Questions and Comments

1. What are the merits of public versus private enforcement? Which do you believe is more effective?

2. Evaluate the economics of public versus private enforcement. How are each funded? How are awards distributed? Is one fairer than the other? What incentives are relevant with each method of enforcing the Commodity Exchange Act? What incentives do private litigants have? What incentives do public bodies such as the CFTC or Department of Justice or their personnel have?

3. Should Commodity Exchange Act section 22(a)(1) be read to exclude a private claim against a party aiding and abetting one of the four categories of specifically enumerated parties against whom claims can be made?

4. Are the barriers to a private claim by a market intermediary against a designated contract market effectively insuperable? Being mindful of the Second Circuit's decision in *Klein & Co. Futures, Inc. v. Board of Trade of the City of New York*, consider what factual circumstances might lead to a successful claim by a futures commission merchant against a designated contract market?

5. What are the pros and cons of a private right of action pursuant to Commodity Exchange Act section 22 compared to the pros and cons of a reparation proceeding pursuant to Commodity Exchange Act section 14?

6. If you were a customer of a futures commission merchant and legally wronged by the futures commission merchant, in what circumstances would you prefer a private right of action, CFTC reparation proceeding, or NFA arbitration?

Chapter 17

Cross-Border Issues

A. Background

1. Futures and Exchange-Traded Commodity Options

Historically, futures markets were regional, an outgrowth of local agricultural or commodity trading activity. As global markets became more internationalized, futures markets followed suit. New questions arise once a transaction is potentially exposed to more than one legal regime. The purpose of this chapter is to examine these questions.

For futures and exchange-traded options, the Commodity Exchange Act does not have a provision providing for the outer limits of United States jurisdiction. Did Congress intend the Commodity Exchange Act to have extraterritorial effect? The source for discerning these limits, as discussed in section B below, is caselaw. Much of the corpus of caselaw is from decisions on the foundational statutes establishing the U.S. securities regulation regime where there is similar statutory silence on the existence, nature, and extent of extraterritorial jurisdiction.

When it comes to non-U.S. futures exchanges having access to U.S. persons, we come to the topic of foreign boards of trade, sometimes known as "FBOTs," which we discussed in chapter 5, section E. The only way a non-U.S. board of trade can ordinarily access U.S. persons as customers is through registration with the CFTC as a foreign board of trade.

2. Swaps

Swaps, on the other hand, began in a cross-border context in the 1980s. As we saw in chapter 12, section E, the standardized swap documentation prepared by the International Swaps and Derivatives Association assumes that parties from scores of world jurisdictions will choose New York or English law to govern their contract to ensure predictability of outcome. Statutory regimes have been enacted in many jurisdictions explicitly to ensure the enforceability of swaps entered into using International Swaps and Derivatives Association documentation. This worked mostly uneventfully for cross-border transactions during the period in which swaps were largely unregulated.

Subsequent to the Financial Crisis, the United States and other Group of Twenty jurisdictions (see below in section C) enacted new regulatory regimes for swaps.

With a new regulatory framework adopted in these jurisdictions, the potential for conflict between them increased. Moreover, a concern of many financial regulators is now "regulatory arbitrage," i.e., where parties select the jurisdiction with the least burdensome regulations in an effort to avoid a jurisdiction with stricter regulation.

A challenge faced by regulators is how to maintain a global swaps marketplace where parties can seamlessly transact across national boundaries without having the "race to the bottom" inherent in regulatory arbitrage. One remedy that has been attempted is to have international regulators agree to common standards, known as regulatory harmonization. Another is the promulgation of rules, known as anti-evasion rules, intended to prohibit the most egregious regulatory arbitrage. However, the question of whether a seamless global swaps marketplace can cohabitate with heavy regulation has not yet been definitively answered.

The Commodity Exchange Act contains an explicit provision addressing the extraterritorial effect of the swap regulatory regime. The CFTC's initial effort to establish a more detailed blueprint for cross-border regulation was beset by mostly unsuccessful legal challenges. This framework has been replaced with a new one which is expected to provide more certainty and, hopefully, less inhibition of cross-border markets.

B. Extraterritorial Limit of the CFTC's Jurisdiction Generally

Difficult jurisdictional questions arise when transactions or participants are not in the United States. Is there still a sufficient nexus to the United States for the CFTC to assert jurisdiction? We know that the CFTC can exercise its jurisdiction when a transaction and its participants are in the United States. What if portions of the transaction or some of the participants are outside of the United States? To what extent does the CFTC's jurisdiction apply extraterritorially?

The Commodity Exchange Act does not explicitly demarcate the extraterritorial limit of the CFTC's jurisdiction, other than with respect to swaps, discussed below in sections D and E. Therefore, for products over which the CFTC has jurisdiction other than swaps, caselaw is the primary resource.

In this area, Commodity Exchange Act precedents and securities law precedents have historically been treated nearly identically due to the statutes on which they are founded being similarly silent on questions of extraterritoriality.

1. The Historic "Conduct and Effects" Test

Until the decision in *Morrison*, examined below, the applicable test was a "conduct" and "effects" test. This test provided the CFTC broad authority to claim jurisdiction so long as the relevant activities had a nexus to the United States. It is important to understand this test, even though no longer applicable, to understand the context of the new *Morrison* test. It also helps to be aware of it for our discussion below on swaps in section D, since *Morrison* was *sub judice* at the time and provided a motivation for Congress to provide an explicit statutory demarcation of the CFTC's extraterritorial jurisdiction over swaps in the Dodd-Frank Act.

A Seventh Circuit case outlined the background and nature of the conduct and effects test:

> [T]he "conduct" and "effects" tests ... were developed in cases brought under the antifraud provisions of the federal securities laws and have recently been applied in similar cases arising under the Commodity Exchange Act. The conduct test focuses on the foreigner's conduct within the United States as it relates to the alleged scheme to defraud. When the conduct occurring in the United States is material to the successful completion of the alleged scheme, jurisdiction is asserted based on the theory that Congress would not have intended the United States to be used as a base for effectuating the fraudulent conduct of foreign companies. Under the effects test, courts have looked to whether conduct occurring in foreign countries had caused foreseeable and substantial harm to interests in the United States.[1]

In other words, as illustrated in the case below, if United States markets were involved at all with a fraudulent scheme, pre-*Morrison* the CFTC could assert jurisdiction without regard to the location of the parties involved.

Psimenos v. E.F. Hutton & Company, Inc.

722 F.2d 1041 (2d Cir. 1983)

Lumbard, Circuit Judge:

Plaintiff John Psimenos, a citizen and resident of Greece, brought this action under the ... Commodities [*sic*] Exchange Act ("CEA") ... for damages resulting from Hutton's allegedly fraudulent procurement and management of his commodities trading account.

Hutton moved ... to dismiss the federal claims for lack of subject matter jurisdiction. . . . Chief Judge Motley, holding that the alleged fraud was "predominantly foreign" and therefore outside the scope of the Commodities [*sic*] Exchange Act, dismissed the federal claim for lack of subject matter jurisdiction. We disagree with Judge Motley's reading of the jurisdictional limitations of the Act and, accordingly, reverse and remand for further proceedings.[2] . . .

---

1. *Tamari v. Bache & Co. (Lebanon) S.A.L.*, 730 F.2d 1103, 1107–1108 (7th Cir. 1984).

2. [N. 3] At our invitation, the Securities and Exchange Commission and the Commodities Futures Trading Commission each submitted a brief as *amicus curiae* urging us to find that the district court has subject matter jurisdiction to hear Psimenos' claim. The CFTC argues that trading on domestic commodities markets is sufficient to establish jurisdiction both because it involves

In 1975, plaintiff became interested in investing in a commodities trading account with E.F. Hutton. Mathieu Mavridoglou, Hutton's agent and employee in Athens, told Psimenos "that his account would be managed in accordance with Hutton's standard procedures and with rules and regulations of the Commodities [*sic*] Futures Trading Commission." ...

Relying on these statements, Psimenos opened an account with Hutton's Athens office, executing blank forms that granted Hutton discretionary authority to trade in his account. Although Psimenos directed Mavridoglou to seek conservative investments, Hutton's agents often used money in Psimenos' account to participate in unresearched and highly speculative and leveraged transactions.

By 1977, after having incurred heavy losses, Psimenos talked in Athens with Mavridoglou, and in Geneva with Mavridoglou and a Mr. Tome, another Hutton employee. Through these conversations, he was induced to have his account moved to Hutton's Paris office. At some point ... Psimenos ordered trading halted in his account.

In 1981, Mavridoglou convinced Psimenos to move the account back to Athens and to allow trading in his account to resume. Mavridoglou told Psimenos that Hutton would recoup all his losses by assigning a new manager, Marios Michaelides, to the account. Michaelides was represented as a Hutton employee and qualified broker, though in fact he was not a Hutton employee, and was not nor had he ever been registered with the Commodities [*sic*] Futures Trading Commission as a broker. ...

Eventually, Psimenos lost in excess of $200,000. ...

Although most of the fraudulent misrepresentations alleged in the complaint occurred outside the United States, the trading contracts that consummated the transactions were often executed in New York. The issue on appeal is whether that trading in United States commodities markets is sufficient to confer subject matter jurisdiction on a federal district court to hear a claim for damages brought by an alien under the Commodities [*sic*] Exchange Act.

We find that the district court has jurisdiction to hear Psimenos' claim. The trades Hutton executed on American markets constituted the final act in Hutton's alleged fraud on Psimenos, without which Hutton's employees could not have generated commissions for themselves. ...

In construing the reaches of jurisdiction under the CEA, courts have analogized to similar problems under the securities laws which have been more extensively litigated. *See, e.g., Mormels v. Girofinance, S.A.*, 544 F. Supp. 815, 817 n. 8 (S.D.N.Y.1982) ("[s]ecurities cases and principles are used as persuasive aids to interpretation of the CEA").

Several of our decisions have explored the limits of subject matter jurisdiction under the federal securities statutes. Our major consideration concerning

---

substantial conduct in the United States and because it implicates the integrity of the United States markets.

transnational transactions is "whether Congress would have wished the precious resources of United States courts and law enforcement agencies to be devoted to them rather than leave the problem to foreign countries."

Two tests have emerged, the "effects" test and the "conduct" test. Since we find that there is jurisdiction under the latter, we do not need to reach the question whether the effects test provides an independent basis for jurisdiction.

The conduct test does not center its inquiry on whether domestic investors or markets are affected, but on the nature of conduct within the United States as it relates to carrying out the alleged fraudulent scheme, on the theory that Congress did not want "to allow the United States to be used as a base for manufacturing fraudulent security devices for export, even when these are peddled only to foreigners." . . .

We find that under the conduct test, Hutton's activities in the United States in furtherance of the alleged fraud were substantial enough to establish subject matter jurisdiction. . . .

Viewing the conduct test in this light, it is clear that the trading conducted by Hutton on United States exchanges should be weighed in determining this court's jurisdiction. Just as Congress did not want the United States to be used as a base for manufacturing fraudulent securities devices, irrespective of the nationality of the victim, neither did it want United States commodities markets to be used as a base to consummate schemes concocted abroad, particularly when the perpetrators are agents of American corporations. . . .

Trading activities on United States commodities markets were significant acts without which Psimenos' losses could not have occurred, and are sufficient to establish jurisdiction. . . .

―――――――――

The conduct and effects test, in general use until the *Morrison* ruling in 2010, allowed for U.S. jurisdiction if any significant part of the transaction or conduct had a U.S. nexus. This was the case even if the parties were not U.S. persons and most of the relevant actions had no U.S. involvement.

2. Presumption Against Extraterritoriality

a. Presumption Generally

In 2010, the Supreme Court ruled that there is a presumption against a statute applying extraterritorially. In short, for a statute to have extraterritorial application, it needs to explicitly state that it applies extraterritorially.

Although the case in question, *Morrison v. National Australia Bank, Ltd.*, was a securities law case, its findings apply *mutatis mutandis* to the CFTC's jurisdiction over everything other than swaps (which have a distinct statute-based extraterritoriality application discussed in section D below). This is because both the securities laws — with respect to every product other than security-based swaps — and the Commodity

Exchange Act — with respect to every product other than swaps — are silent on extra-territorial application. Also, the historic "conduct and effects" caselaw treated securities and derivatives precedents largely interchangeably for these purposes.

The case contains references to section 10(b) of the Securities Exchange Act of 1934. This section prohibits "any manipulative or deceptive device" in relation to the purchase or sale of a security.[3] This is very similar to section 6(c) of the Commodity Exchange Act which prohibits any manipulative or deceptive device in relation to a swap, commodity, or commodity future.[4] In fact, the Commodity Exchange Act provision, added to the Commodity Exchange Act in 2010 by the Dodd-Frank Act, was modeled after section 10(b) of the Securities Exchange Act. The CFTC similarly promulgated an associated rule, CFTC Rule 180.1, based on SEC Rule 10b-5, the rule implementing section 10(b) of the Securities Exchange Act.[5]

Morrison v. National Australia Bank, Ltd.

561 U.S. 247 (2010)

Justice Scalia delivered the opinion of the Court.

We decide whether § 10(b) of the Securities Exchange Act of 1934 provides a cause of action to foreign plaintiffs suing foreign and American defendants for misconduct in connection with securities traded on foreign exchanges.

Respondent National Australia Bank Limited (National) was . . . the largest bank in Australia. . . . [Its shares are not traded] on any exchange in the United States. There are listed on the New York Stock Exchange, however, National's American Depositary Receipts (ADRs), which represent the right to receive a specified number of National's . . . [shares].

The complaint alleges the following facts. . . . In February 1998, National bought respondent HomeSide Lending, Inc., a mortgage servicing company headquartered in Florida. HomeSide's business was to receive fees for servicing mortgages (essentially the administrative tasks associated with collecting mortgage payments). The rights to receive those fees, so-called mortgage-servicing rights, can provide a valuable income stream. How valuable each of the rights is depends, in part, on the likelihood that the mortgage to which it applies will be fully repaid before it is due, terminating the need for servicing. HomeSide calculated the present value of its mortgage-servicing rights by using valuation models designed to take this likelihood into account. It recorded the value of its assets, and the numbers appeared in National's financial statements.

From 1998 until 2001, National's annual reports and other public documents touted the success of HomeSide's business. . . . But on July 5, 2001, National announced that

---

3. 15 U.S.C. § 78j(b).
4. Commodity Exchange Act § 6(c).
5. *See* 17 C.F.R. § 180.1 and 17 C.F.R. § 240.10b-5.

it was writing down the value of HomeSide's assets . . . The prices of both . . . [the shares] and ADRs slumped. . . .

[P]etitioners Russell Leslie Owen and Brian and Geraldine Silverlock, all Australians, purchased National's . . . [shares] in 2000 and 2001, before the write-downs.[6] They sued National, HomeSide, Cicutto, and . . . three HomeSide executives. . . .

Respondents moved to dismiss for lack of subject-matter jurisdiction. . . . The District Court granted the motion . . . finding no jurisdiction. . . . The Court of Appeals for the Second Circuit affirmed on similar grounds. . . .

It is a "longstanding principle of American law 'that legislation of Congress, unless a contrary intent appears, is meant to apply only within the territorial jurisdiction of the United States.'" This principle represents a canon of construction, or a presumption about a statute's meaning, rather than a limit upon Congress's power to legislate. It rests on the perception that Congress ordinarily legislates with respect to domestic, not foreign matters. Thus, "unless there is the affirmative intention of the Congress clearly expressed" to give a statute extraterritorial effect, "we must presume it is primarily concerned with domestic conditions." . . . When a statute gives no clear indication of an extraterritorial application, it has none.

Despite this principle of interpretation . . . the Second Circuit believed that, because the Exchange Act is silent as to the extraterritorial application of §10(b), it was left to the court to "discern" whether Congress would have wanted the statute to apply. This disregard of the presumption against extraterritoriality did not originate with the Court of Appeals panel in this case. It has been repeated over many decades by various courts of appeals. . . .

[T]he Second Circuit . . . excised the presumption against extraterritoriality . . . and replaced it with the inquiry whether it would be reasonable (and hence what Congress would have wanted) to apply the statute to a given situation. . . .

The Second Circuit had thus established that application of §10(b) could be premised upon either some effect on American securities markets or investors or significant conduct in the United States. It later formalized these two applications into (1) an "effects test," "whether the wrongful conduct had a substantial effect in the United States or upon United States citizens," and (2) a "conduct test," "whether the wrongful conduct occurred in the United States." . . .

Other Circuits embraced the Second Circuit's approach. . . .

Commentators have criticized the unpredictable and inconsistent application of §10(b) to transnational cases. Some have challenged the premise underlying the Courts of Appeals' approach, namely that Congress did not consider the

---

6. [N. 1] Robert Morrison, an American investor in National's ADRs, also brought suit, but his claims were dismissed . . . because he failed to allege damages. . . . Inexplicably, Morrison continued to be listed as a petitioner in the Court of Appeals and here.

extraterritorial application of § 10(b) (thereby leaving it open to the courts, supposedly, to determine what Congress would have wanted).

The criticisms seem to us justified. The results of judicial-speculation-made-law — divining what Congress would have wanted if it had thought of the situation before the court — demonstrate the wisdom of the presumption against extraterritoriality. Rather than guess anew in each case, we apply the presumption in all cases, preserving a stable background against which Congress can legislate with predictable effects.

Rule 10b-5, the regulation under which petitioners have brought suit, was promulgated under § 10(b), and "does not extend beyond conduct encompassed by § 10(b)'s prohibition." Therefore, if § 10(b) is not extraterritorial, neither is Rule 10b-5.

On its face, § 10(b) contains nothing to suggest it applies abroad:

> It shall be unlawful for any person, directly or indirectly, by the use of any means or instrumentality of interstate commerce or of the mails, or of any facility of any national securities exchange . . . [t]o use or employ, in connection with the purchase or sale of any security registered on a national securities exchange or any security not so registered, . . . any manipulative or deceptive device or contrivance in contravention of such rules and regulations as the [Securities and Exchange] Commission may prescribe. . . ."

[T]here is no affirmative indication in the Exchange Act that § 10(b) applies extraterritorially, and we therefore conclude that it does not. . . .

Petitioners argue that the conclusion that § 10(b) does not apply extraterritorially does not resolve this case. They contend that they seek no more than domestic application anyway, since Florida is where HomeSide and its senior executives engaged in the deceptive conduct of manipulating HomeSide's financial models; their complaint also alleged that Race and Hughes made misleading public statements there. . . . [I]t is a rare case of prohibited extraterritorial application that lacks all contact with the territory of the United States. But the presumption against extraterritorial application would be a craven watchdog indeed if it retreated to its kennel whenever some domestic activity is involved in the case. . . .

[W]e think that the focus of the Exchange Act is not upon the place where the deception originated, but upon purchases and sales of securities in the United States. Section 10(b) does not punish deceptive conduct, but only deceptive conduct "in connection with the purchase or sale of any security registered on a national securities exchange or any security not so registered."

Finally, . . . [the] probability of incompatibility with the applicable laws of other countries is so obvious that if Congress intended such foreign application "it would have addressed the subject of conflicts with foreign laws and procedures." Like the United States, foreign countries regulate their domestic securities exchanges and securities transactions occurring within their territorial jurisdiction. And the regulation of other countries often differs from ours as to what constitutes fraud, what disclosures must be made, what damages are recoverable, what discovery is available in litigation, what individual actions may be joined in a single suit, what attorney's fees are recoverable, and many other matters. The Commonwealth of Australia, the United Kingdom of Great Britain and Northern Ireland, and the Republic of France have filed *amicus* briefs in this case. So have (separately or jointly) such international and foreign organizations as the International Chamber of Commerce, the Swiss Bankers Association, the Federation of German Industries, the French Business Confederation, the Institute of International Bankers, the European Banking Federation, the Australian Bankers' Association, and the Association Francaise des Entreprises Privées. They all complain of the interference with foreign securities regulation that application of § 10(b) abroad would produce, and urge the adoption of a clear test that will avoid that consequence. . . .

The Solicitor General points out that the "significant and material conduct" test [an alternative to the "conduct and effects" test that the Solicitor General argued should apply] is in accord with prevailing notions of international comity. If so, that proves that if the United States asserted prescriptive jurisdiction pursuant to the "significant and material conduct" test it would not violate customary international law; but it in no way tends to prove that that is what Congress has done.

Section 10(b) reaches the use of a manipulative or deceptive device or contrivance only in connection with the purchase or sale of a security listed on an American stock exchange, and the purchase or sale of any other security in the United States. . . .

---

b. Presumption Applied to the Commodity Exchange Act

The precedent in *Morrison* regarding Securities Exchange Act of 1934 § 10b has been applied *mutatis mutandis* to the context of claims under the Commodity Exchange Act. In *Prime International Trading*, the claims were based on a private right of action asserting violation of the Commodity Exchange Act's anti-fraud and anti-manipulation provisions. Note that we visit one of the cases heavily relied upon, *Loginovskaya*, immediately below, and we visited *Parkcentral* in chapter 13.

Prime International Trading v. BP P.L.C.

937 F.3d 94 (2d Cir. 2019)

Richard J. Sullivan, Circuit Judge:

This appeal requires us to decide whether alleged misconduct tied to the trading of crude oil extracted from Europe's North Sea constitutes an impermissibly extra-territorial application of the Commodity Exchange Act. For the reasons set forth below, we find that it does. . . .

Plaintiffs-Appellants ("Plaintiffs") are individuals and entities who traded futures and derivatives contracts pegged to North Sea oil — also known as Brent crude — on the Intercontinental Exchange Futures Europe ("ICE Futures Europe") and the New York Mercantile Exchange ("NYMEX") between 2002 and 2015 (the "Class Period").

Defendants-Appellees ("Defendants") are a diverse group of entities involved in various aspects of the production of Brent crude. In addition to producing, refining, and distributing Brent crude, Defendants also purchase and sell Brent crude on the physical market and trade Brent-crude-based futures contracts on global derivatives markets. . . .

Brent crude is extracted from the North Sea of Europe, and refers to oil pulled from four fields in the region: Brent, Forties, Oseberg, and Ekofisk (collectively, "BFOE"). The price of Brent crude serves as the benchmark for two-thirds of the world's internationally-traded crude.

Following extraction, Brent crude is delivered via pipeline to ports in Europe where it is loaded onto ships for delivery. These physical cargoes are bought and sold through private, over-the-counter ("OTC") transactions between producers, refiners, and traders. Because these physical transactions are private and do not occur on an open exchange, the price of Brent crude is not immediately available to the public. Instead, price-reporting agencies collect information about transactions from market participants and report it to the consuming public. . . .

Platts is a prominent London-based price-reporting agency that collects information from market participants regarding their physical Brent crude transactions, analyzes that data to compute benchmark prices, and publishes those prices in real-time price reports as well as various end-of-day price assessments. The price reports track several different submarkets in the Brent crude market, but the "primary pricing benchmark" — widely regarded as the "spot" price for Brent crude — is the "Dated Brent Assessment."

The Dated Brent Assessment tracks physical cargoes of North Sea crude oil that have been assigned specific delivery dates. Rather than averaging the prices of the four grades of Brent crude, the Dated Brent Assessment is based on the lowest price among the four grades, and is calculated each day during the assessment period. Platts uses a Market-on-Close ("MOC") methodology, under which Platts tracks all Brent crude trading activity during the day, but weighs most heavily the bids, offers, and transactions that occur at the end of each trading day, from 4:00 to 4:30 P.M. GMT.

Although Platts relies on market participants to voluntarily self-report their private transactions in order to create and publish the Dated Brent Assessment, they do not just mechanically recite the reported trade activity. Instead, Platts exercises its own discretion to accept or reject transactional data, and makes this assessment based on the reliability, accuracy, and consistency of such data. At the end of the day, Platts' goal in publishing the Dated Brent Assessment is to accurately reflect market prices and to avoid distortion or artificiality. . . .

Plaintiffs focus their claims on Brent-related futures and derivatives contracts ("Brent Futures"), which are primarily traded on two exchanges: NYMEX and ICE Futures Europe. NYMEX is a U.S.-based commodity futures exchange, while ICE Futures Europe is a London-based exchange. Plaintiffs and other market participants trade on both exchanges. The most heavily traded Brent Futures contract is the "ICE Brent Futures Contract," which has a corollary contract on the NYMEX. These contracts stop trading, or "expire," approximately two weeks before the delivery month. If a futures contract is not offset before it expires, the contract is cash-settled. In other words, the in-the-money counterparty receives the cash value of the contract rather than the underlying asset itself.

Brent Futures traded on ICE Futures Europe ("ICE Brent Futures") are cash-settled based on an established benchmark known as the ICE Brent Index. Brent Futures traded on the NYMEX, in turn, settle at expiration to the price of ICE Brent Futures. Unlike the Dated Brent Assessment—which Platts calculates based on prices for the least expensive BFOE grade of Brent cargoes—the ICE Brent Index is calculated based on the *entire* BFOE market of physical Brent cargoes. In addition, the ICE Brent Index incorporates an average of certain designated price-reporting assessments, one of which, Plaintiffs allege, is the Dated Brent Assessment. . . .

Plaintiffs allege that Defendants conspired to manipulate, and did in fact manipulate, the market for physical Brent crude and Brent Futures. . . .

Plaintiffs' claim involves a causal chain that can be summarized as follows: Defendants engaged in artificial trades of physical Brent crude in foreign markets; Defendants systematically reported the artificial trade data to Platts; Platts reviewed and incorporated the fraudulent data into its calculation of the Dated Brent Assessment; ICE Futures Europe in turn incorporated the manipulated Dated Brent Assessment into the ICE Brent Index; the manipulated ICE Brent Index was used to settle Brent Futures that were traded on both the London-based ICE Futures Europe and the U.S.-based NYMEX; as a result, Brent Futures traded and settled at artificial prices, causing economic loss to traders such as Plaintiffs. . . .

This case implicates two antifraud provisions of the [Commodity Exchange Act ("CEA")]. . . . Section 6(c)(1) of the CEA makes it "unlawful for any person . . . to use or employ, . . . in connection with any swap, or a contract of sale of any commodity, . . . any manipulative or deceptive device." 7 U.S.C. § 9(a)(1). . . . Section 9(a)(2) proscribes "manipulat[ing] or attempt[ing] to manipulate the price of any commodity in interstate commerce." 7 U.S.C. § 13(a)(2). Plaintiffs seek to enforce these substantive provisions of the CEA through the Act's private right of action, which permits a party to bring suit against a person whose violation of the CEA "result[s] from one or more of the transactions" listed in the statute. *See* 7 U.S.C. § 25(a)(1). At bottom, this case centers on our interpretation of the CEA—specifically, whether it permits suit against Defendants for alleged manipulative conduct that transpired in Europe.

We interpret the CEA in light of the presumption against extraterritoriality. . . . This reflects the "commonsense notion that Congress generally legislates with domestic concerns in mind," *Smith v. United States*, 507 U.S. 197, 204 n.5, 113 S.Ct. 1178, 122 L.Ed.2d 548 (1993), and acts to "protect against unintended clashes between our laws and those of other nations which could result in international discord," *EEOC v. Arabian Am. Oil Co.*, 499 U.S. 244, 248, 111 S.Ct. 1227, 113 L.Ed.2d 274 (1991).

Generally, courts engage in a "two-step framework for analyzing extraterritoriality issues." *RJR Nabisco* [*v. European Cmty.*], 136 S. Ct. at 2101. First, because there must be an "affirmative intention of the Congress clearly expressed" to give a statute extraterritorial effect, *Morrison v. Nat'l Australia Bank Ltd.*, 561 U.S. 247, 255, 130 S. Ct. 2869, 177 L.Ed.2d 535 (2010) (quoting *Arabian Am. Oil*, 499 U.S. at 248, 111 S.Ct. 1227), courts look to the text of the statute to discern whether there is a "clear indication of extraterritoriality," *id.* at 265, 130 S.Ct. 2869. . . . If the statute lacks such a "clear statement" of extraterritorial effect, the statute does not apply abroad. *Morrison*, 561 U.S. at 265, 130 S.Ct. 2869.

However, a claim may still survive if it properly states a "domestic application" of the statute. *See id.* at 266, 130 S.Ct. 2869. As it is "a rare case . . . that lacks *all* contact with the territory of the United States," *id.* (emphasis in original), many cases present a mixed bag of both domestic and foreign components. Accordingly, at the second step, courts must evaluate whether the domestic activity pleaded is the "focus of congressional concern." *Id.* In other words, because the presumption against extraterritoriality would be a "craven watchdog indeed" if it "retreated to its kennel whenever *some* domestic activity is involved," *id.* (emphasis in original), courts must evaluate whether the domestic activity involved implicates the "focus" of the statute. . . .

As to whether Congress intended Section 22 to apply to conduct abroad, circuit precedent provides the answer. In *Loginovskaya v. Batratchenko*, we held that since Section 22 of the CEA "is silent as to extraterritorial reach," suits funneled through this private right of action "must be based on transactions occurring in the territory of the United States." 764 F.3d 266, 271, 272 (2d Cir. 2014).[7]

The same is also true of Sections 6(c)(1) and 9(a)(2). . . . [O]n its face, Section 6(c)(1) — like Section 22 — "lacks . . . a clear statement of extraterritorial effect." *Morrison*, 561 U.S. at 265, 130 S.Ct. 2869. Section 9(a)(2), which prohibits "manipulat[ing] or attempt[ing] to manipulate the price of any commodity in interstate commerce," 7 U.S.C. §13, likewise contains no affirmative, textual indication that it applies to conduct abroad. . . .

Plaintiffs make a last-ditch effort to establish that extraterritorial application of the CEA is proper by resorting to a separate provision — Section 2(i). Enacted pursuant to the Dodd-Frank Wall Street Reform and Consumer Protection Act, Pub. L. No. 111-203, 124 Stat. 1376 (2010), Section 2(i) of the CEA states:

> The provisions of this Act relating to swaps . . . shall not apply to activities outside the United States unless those activities — (1) have a direct and significant connection with activities in, or effect on, commerce of the United States; or (2) contravene such rules or regulations as the Commission may prescribe . . . to prevent the evasion of any provision of this Act.

---

7. [N. 6] While the Dodd-Frank Wall Street Reform and Consumer Protection Act amended the CEA to apply extraterritorially to certain swap-related activities, *see* 7 U.S.C.A. §2(i), that amendment does not affect our analysis here for reasons separately explained below.

7 U.S.C.A. § 2(i). Unlike Sections 6(c)(1) and 9(a)(2), Section 2(i) contains, on its face, a "clear statement," *Morrison*, 561 U.S. at 265, 130 S.Ct. 2869, of extraterritorial application. If there were any lingering doubts about whether Sections 6(c)(1) and 9(a)(2) independently apply extraterritorially, Section 2(i) forecloses those doubts, because it shows that Congress "knows how to give a statute explicit extraterritorial effect . . . and how to limit that effect to particular applications" within the CEA. *Morrison*, 561 U.S. at 265 n.8, 130 S.Ct. 2869. Therefore, the existence of an enumerated extraterritorial command in Section 2(i) reinforces our conclusion that the lack of any analogous directive in either Section 6(c)(1) or Section 9(a)(2) bars their extraterritorial application here. . . .

Plaintiffs urge that even if the relevant provisions of the CEA do not apply extraterritorially, the district court erred because . . . [they allege] a proper "domestic application of the statute." *RJR Nabisco*, 136 S. Ct. at 2101 ("If the statute is not extraterritorial, then at the second step we determine whether the case involves a domestic application of the statute.").

Whether Plaintiffs' claims constitute a satisfactory domestic application of the CEA requires us to discern the "focus of congressional concern" in enacting the statute. *Morrison*, 561 U.S. at 266, 130 S.Ct. 2869. To divine the CEA's "focus," we consider the "conduct" that the statute "seeks to regulate," as well as "the parties and interests it seeks to protect or vindicate." *WesternGeco* [*LLC v. ION Geophysical Corp.*], 138 S. Ct. at 2137 (quoting *Morrison*, 561 U.S. at 267, 130 S.Ct. 2869). . . .

In *Loginovskaya*, we held that the focus of congressional concern in Section 22 is "clearly transactional," given its emphasis on "domestic conduct [and] domestic transactions." *Id*. Thus, in order for Plaintiffs to state a proper domestic application of Section 22, the suit "must be based on transactions occurring in the territory of the United States." The "domestic transaction test" essentially "decides the territorial reach of [Section] 22."[8] *Id*.

To assess whether Plaintiffs pleaded permissibly domestic transactions under Section 22, typically we would apply a test first announced in *Absolute Activist Value Master Fund Ltd. v. Ficeto*, 677 F.3d 60 (2d Cir. 2012). However, following the course we have taken in securities cases, *see Parkcentral Global Hub Ltd. v. Porsche Automobile Holdings SE*, 763 F.3d 198, 216 (2d Cir. 2014), we need not decide definitively whether Plaintiffs' transactions satisfy *Absolute Activist*, for (as discussed below) their claims are impermissibly extraterritorial even if the transactions are domestic. Thus, we assume without deciding that Plaintiffs' trades on NYMEX and ICE Futures Europe constituted "domestic transactions" under Section 22.

---

8. [N. 8] In evaluating whether Plaintiffs' claims fit within the "focus" of Section 22, we must assess the "*conduct relevant* to the statute's focus." *WesternGeco*, 138 S. Ct. at 2137 (emphasis added) (quoting *RJR Nabisco*, 136 S. Ct. at 2101). Defendants do not dispute that the "relevant conduct" under Section 22 is the purchase and sale of Brent Futures. As such, for the purposes of our Section 22 analysis, we take those commodities transactions to be the relevant conduct.

In *Parkcentral*, investors in equity swaps pegged to the price of Volkswagen stock sued under Section 10(b), alleging that defendants made misleading statements that sought to hide their intentions to take over Volkswagen. 763 F.3d at 201–02. All of defendants' misconduct occurred in Germany, and Volkswagen stock only traded on European stock exchanges. *Id.* We assumed without deciding that the equity swaps at issue there were "domestic transactions" under Section 10(b), but nonetheless dismissed the claims because the facts in that case rendered the suit "predominately foreign." *Id.* at 216. The predicate to our conclusion in *Parkcentral* was the maxim that "a domestic transaction or listing is *necessary*" but "not alone sufficient" to state a claim under Section 10(b). *Id.* at 215–6 (emphasis in original). The question this case presents is whether *Parkcentral*'s rule carries over to the CEA. We hold that it does.

For starters, Section 22 creates no freestanding, substantive legal obligations; instead, it requires the "commission of a violation of this chapter." 7 U.S.C. § 25(a)(1); *see* Doc. No. 242 ("Chamber of Commerce *et al.* Amicus Br.") at 20. And as already discussed above, the conduct-regulating provisions of the CEA — particularly those at issue here — apply only to *domestic* conduct, and not to foreign conduct. . . . Put differently, while a domestic transaction is necessary to invoke Section 22, it is not *sufficient*, for a plaintiff must also allege a domestic violation of one of the CEA's substantive provisions. . . . To hold otherwise would be to divorce the private right afforded in Section 22 from the requirement of a domestic violation of a substantive provision of the CEA. . . . To state a proper claim under Section 22 in this case, Plaintiffs must allege not only a domestic transaction, but also domestic — not extraterritorial — *conduct* by Defendants that is violative of a substantive provision of the CEA, such as Section 6(c)(1) or Section 9(a)(2). . . .

Besides the structure of the CEA and the language of Section 22, the presumption against extraterritoriality also counsels in favor of extending *Parkcentral*'s holding to the instant case. Permitting a suit to go forward any time a domestic transaction is pleaded would turn the presumption against extraterritoriality into a "craven watchdog," *Morrison*, 561 U.S. at 266, 130 S.Ct. 2869, and would fly in the face of the Supreme Court's clear guidance that the presumption against extraterritoriality cannot evaporate any time "*some* domestic activity is involved in the case," *id.* (emphasis in original). . . . Given that courts "have looked to the securities laws" when asked "to interpret similar provisions of the CEA," *Loginovskaya*, 764 F.3d at 272, we do not hesitate in applying *Parkcentral*'s gloss on domestic transactions under Section 10(b) to domestic transactions under Section 22 of the CEA. Therefore, while a domestic transaction as defined by *Absolute Activist* is "necessary" to invoke the private remedy afforded by Section 22, it is not "sufficient."

In order to close the gap between "necessary" and "sufficient," Plaintiffs' claims must not be "so predominately foreign as to be impermissibly extraterritorial." *Parkcentral*, 763 F.3d at 216. Here, the facts are remarkably similar to those in *Parkcentral*, and therefore leave little doubt that Plaintiffs' claims are "predominately foreign."

In both cases, plaintiffs traded derivatives — in *Parkcentral*, equity swaps, and here, futures contracts — which, by their nature, are pegged to the value of another asset. Both underlying assets were foreign: *Parkcentral* involved the price of Volkswagen stock traded on European stock exchanges, and here Plaintiffs' transactions were based on the Dated Brent Assessment, which itself reflects, in part, the value of Brent crude physically traded in Northern Europe. The alleged misconduct in both instances was also entirely foreign. Indeed, *Parkcentral*'s facts are perhaps *less* predominantly foreign than those alleged here, since the misleading statements at issue in *Parkcentral* were "accessible in the United States and were repeated here by the defendants," *Parkcentral*, 763 F.3d at 201, whereas Plaintiffs in this case make no claim that any manipulative oil trading occurred in the United States. Moreover, in *Parkcentral*, the equity swaps traded in the United States were "directly tied to the price of Volkswagen's shares on foreign exchanges." Here, Plaintiffs rely on an even more attenuated "ripple effects" theory whereby (1) the alleged manipulative trading activity taking place in the North Sea (2) affected Brent crude prices — a foreign commodity — which (3) affected a foreign benchmark, the Dated Brent Assessment, which (4) was then disseminated by a foreign price-reporting agency, which (5) was then allegedly used (in part) to price futures contracts traded on exchanges around the world. Nearly every link in Plaintiffs' chain of wrongdoing is entirely foreign — in contrast to *Parkcentral*, where the alleged wrongdoing occurred on American shores at the second causal step, not the fifth. And yet even in *Parkcentral*, we deemed the conduct to be "so predominantly foreign" as to render the claims impermissibly extraterritorial. *Parkcentral*, 763 F.3d at 216. . . . Therefore, we conclude that Plaintiffs have failed to plead a proper domestic application of Section 22 of the CEA. . . .

Plaintiffs have, in any event, also failed to plead a proper domestic application of either Section 6(c)(1) or 9(a)(2). . . .

There is nothing in Section 6(c)(1)'s text suggesting that it is focused on "purchases and sales of securities in the United States," *Morrison*, 561 U.S. at 266, 130 S. Ct. 2869, and other available evidence in the CEA, such as that statute's statement of purpose, suggests that the focus is on rooting out manipulation and ensuring market integrity — not on the geographical coordinates of the transaction. . . . Section 6(c)(1) centers on manipulation in commodities markets. All of the conduct relevant to *that* focus occurred abroad. . . .

Plaintiffs have also failed to plead a domestic application of Section 9(a)(2). . . . The focus of Section 9(a)(2) is preventing manipulation of the price of any commodity. And all of the relevant conduct here relating to *that* focus occurred abroad — Plaintiffs contend that Defendants sought to manipulate the price of Brent crude, and did so by fraudulently transacting in the physical market in Europe. Plaintiffs make no allegation of manipulative conduct or statements made in the United States. . . .

Accordingly, the judgment of the district court is AFFIRMED.

Though private rights of action under section 22 of the Commodity Exchange Act have the same territorial limitations as section 10(b) of the Securities Exchange Act, the CFTC could, in circumstances where a section 22 private right of action would not be possible for a private litigant due to its limited territorial scope, itself decide to directly bring an enforcement action for a violation of section 4o. Alternatively, a party could make a reparations claim for the section 4o violation pursuant to section 18 of the Commodity Exchange Act.

In the context of commodity pool operator and commodity trading advisor fraud, the Second Circuit, *obiter*, left open the possibility of section 4o of the Commodity Exchange Act (which prohibits such fraud) as having a broader extraterritorial effect than section 10(b) of the Securities Exchange Act, the provision at issue in *Morrison*. In understanding why, it is important to note the parallels between section 10(b) of the Securities Exchange Act and the Commodity Exchange Act's private right of action enshrined in section 22 thereof. Section 10(b) requires a purchase or sale of a security and, similarly, section 22 in most circumstances requires an actual transaction.

Commodity Exchange Act section 4o differs from both. The defrauding of a market participant by a commodity trading advisor, commodity pool operator, or an associated person of either is arguably sufficient to alone trigger a violation of section 4o. (For a more detailed discussion on whether fraud, in the absence of an actual trade, is enough, see chapter 7, section B.1.c.)

Because the claim in *Loginovskaya* below was a private right of action, the preconditions to asserting a private right of action in section 22 applied (for refreshment on this, see chapter 16). However, in other circumstances, such as a CFTC enforcement action or reparations proceeding, the possibly broader extraterritorial reach of section 4o has the potential to matter.

Loginovskaya v. Batratchenko
764 F.3d 266 (2d Cir. 2014)

Dennis Jacobs, Circuit Judge:

Ludmila Loginovskaya appeals from a judgment of the United States District Court for the Southern District of New York (Oetken, J.), dismissing . . . her claims under the Commodity Exchange Act ("CEA"). . . . The district court held that the domestic transaction test announced in *Morrison v. National Australia Bank Ltd.*, 561 U.S. 247, 130 S.Ct. 2869, 177 L.Ed.2d 535 (2010), applies to Loginovskaya's CEA claim, and that her Amended Complaint failed to adequately allege a domestic transaction. . . .

Applying the reasoning of *Morrison,* we agree with the district court that a private right of action brought under CEA § 22 is limited to claims alleging a commodities transaction within the United States. Because Loginovskaya fails to allege a domestic commodities transaction, we affirm the district court's judgment. . . .

The Thor Group, an international financial services organization based in New York, manages investment programs, chiefly in commodities futures and real estate....

Defendant Oleg Batratchenko, a U.S. citizen resident in Moscow, is the Group's chief executive officer....

Loginovskaya, a Russian citizen residing in Russia, was solicited by Batratchenko in January 2006 to invest in the Thor programs.... He provided her with brochures, investment memoranda, and other materials, written in Russian, describing the opportunity....

Loginovskaya entered into two investment contracts ... in 2006 and 2007.... Pursuant to the contracts, Loginovskaya transferred a total of $720,000 to Thor United's bank accounts in New York, which were subsequently drawn down to a remaining principal of $590,000.

Loginovskaya's account statements over ensuing years generally showed positive returns. Around May 2009, Loginovskaya sought to realize her gains and withdraw her remaining account funds. No money was forthcoming, and no further monthly account statement was dispatched until the statement dated November 2009, which reported for the first time that her investment had lost more than half its value since May. Loginovskaya again requested the return of her funds, unsuccessfully.

Investors were put off with false assurances that the programs were experiencing a temporary dip in liquidity, that cash would be available shortly, and that the Thor programs would be providing detailed financial statements to the investors. An April 2010 letter from Batratchenko falsely contended that, "due to onerous new regulations in the United States, investors could not withdraw their funds from the investment accounts without providing" burdensome documentation....

Since 2010, Loginovskaya has learned that the Thor programs used investors' funds in a manner inconsistent with the investment contracts. Between 2006 and 2009, Batratchenko caused ... Thor entities to extend $40 million in unsecured loans to Atlant Capital Holdings LLC.... Atlant, which is not an affiliate of the Thor programs, makes equity investments in commercial and residential property in New York.... Atlant was undercapitalized, its real estate investments failed, the unsecured loans were defaulted, and ... [Thor] could not recover Loginovskaya's funds. Batratchenko and Smirnova had personal financial interests in Atlant's real estate activity....

This action was commenced in January 2012; the Amended Complaint, filed in June 2012, alleged that the defendants engaged in fraudulent conduct in violation of CEA § 4o.... The district court granted defendants' motion to dismiss the CEA claim ... on the ground that the CEA claim failed *Morrison*'s domestic transaction test....

The CEA contains several anti-fraud provisions to fulfill this purpose. Among those is § 4o:

(1) It shall be unlawful for a commodity trading advisor, associated person of a commodity trading advisor, commodity pool operator, or associated person of a commodity pool operator, by use of the mails or any means or instrumentality of interstate commerce, directly or indirectly —

(A) to employ any device, scheme, or artifice to defraud any client or participant or prospective client or participant; or

(B) to engage in any transaction, practice, or course of business which operates as a fraud or deceit upon any client or participant or prospective client or participant. . . .

A private right of action is afforded by CEA § 22. . . .

To ascertain the territorial scope of CEA §§ 4o and 22, we consult the Supreme Court's opinion in *Morrison,* which decided whether § 10(b) of the Securities Exchange Act of 1934 ("SEA") applies extraterritorially. . . .

The CEA as a whole — and sections 4o and 22 in particular — is silent as to extraterritorial reach.[9] . . . Given the absence of any "affirmative intention" by Congress to give the CEA extraterritorial effect, we must "presume it is primarily concerned with domestic conditions." *Morrison,* 130 S.Ct. at 2877. . . .

Loginovskaya's suit must satisfy the threshold requirement of CEA § 22 before reaching the merits of her § 4o fraud claim. . . . Given that CEA § 22 limits the private right to suits over transactions, the suits must be based on transactions occurring in the territory of the United States.

"Traditionally, courts have looked to the securities laws when called upon to interpret similar provisions of the CEA." *Saxe v. E.F. Hutton & Co.,* 789 F.2d 105, 109 (2d Cir.1986). Therefore, *Morrison's* domestic transaction test in effect decides the territorial reach of CEA § 22. . . .

[T]o bring a suit under § 22, the transaction at issue — the conduct underlying the suit — must have occurred within the United States. . . .

To summarize, the CEA creates a private right of action for persons anywhere in the world who transact business in the United States, and does not open our courts to people who choose to do business elsewhere. . . .

In the context of SEA § 10(b), we explained that there are two ways to allege a "domestic transaction." *See Absolute Activist,* 677 F.3d at 68. First, "it is sufficient for the plaintiff to allege that title to the [security] was transferred within the United States." *Id.* Second, a plaintiff may allege facts showing "that the parties incurred

---

9. [N. 4] The Dodd-Frank: Wall Street Reform and Consumer Protection Act ("Dodd-Frank"). Pub. L. No. 111-203. 124 Stat. 1376 (2010), amended CEA § 22 to cover swaps, and provided that its "provisions . . . relating to swaps" may, under certain circumstances, "apply to activities outside the United States." 7 U.S.C. § 25(a)(1) (2010); id. § 2(i). The Court takes no view of the effect that the Dodd-Frank amendments may have on the extraterritorial reach of the CEA: no swaps or transactions involving swaps are at issue here.

irrevocable liability within the United States: that is, that the purchaser incurred irrevocable liability within the United States to take and pay for a security, or that the seller incurred irrevocable liability within the United States to deliver a security." *Id.*

Given our holding that *Morrison* applies to a private right of action under CEA § 22 — and the parallels between the CEA and SEA — there is no reason why *Absolute Activist's* formulation should not apply here. Loginovskaya alleges her claim arises from the purchase, sale, or placing an order for the purchase or sale of an interest or participation in a commodity pool. . . . She must therefore demonstrate that the transfer of title or the point of irrevocable liability for such an interest occurred in the United States. . . .

Loginovskaya's complaint . . . fails to allege that Thor . . . incurred irrevocable liability within the United States. At all times, Loginovskaya resided in Russia. Batratchenko solicited her investment while in Russia using investment materials written in Russian. The investment contracts with Thor . . . were negotiated and signed in Russia. True, Thor United [a Thor group entity] is incorporated in New York; but "a party's residency or citizenship is irrelevant to the location of a given transaction." *Absolute Activist*, 677 F.3d at 70.[10] Russia (not the United States) is where Loginovskaya and the defendants reached a "meeting of the minds." . . .

Loginovskaya emphasizes that she was required to wire transfer her funds to Thor's bank account in New York. These transfers, however, were actions needed to carry out the transactions, and not the transactions themselves — which were previously entered into when the contracts were executed in Russia. The direction to wire transfer money to the United States is insufficient to demonstrate a domestic transaction. . . .

Loginovskaya argues that grafting *Morrison*'s domestic transaction test onto CEA § 22 is anomalous because § 4o reaches more broadly. The basis of her argument is that the "focus of congressional concern," *Morrison*, 130 S.Ct. at 2884, in CEA § 4o is on domestic commodities market participants — not domestic transactions. The contention that *Morrison*'s transaction test is inapplicable to § 4o's antifraud protection is not without merit . . . because the wire fraud statute has no requirement that the prohibited conduct be "'in connection with' any particular transaction or event"); *Ebrahimi v. E.F. Hutton & Co.*, 852 F.2d 516, 519 (10th Cir.1988). . . . Nevertheless, we do not have to decide how the presumption against extraterritorial effect defines the reach of § 4o. Our conclusion that *Morrison*'s domestic transaction

---

10. [N. 9] Loginovskaya attempts to distinguish this portion of *Absolute Activist* by pointing out that the residency or citizenship of natural persons is different from corporate entities. . . . She argues that, although natural persons can be physically present in a jurisdiction other than where they are resident, a corporation is only located in the jurisdiction where it exists as a creature of law. Taken to its logical conclusion, any transaction with a United States corporation would constitute a domestic transaction. We reject this argument because it would expand *Morrison*'s transaction test beyond the scope of the "conduct and effects" test with which *Morrison* dispensed.

test applies to CEA § 22 is not anomalous; if § 4o regulates the conduct of domestic commodities market participants in other countries, it would seem Congress has allowed a remedy through the CFTC. *See* 7 U.S.C. § 18. . . .

———————

Loginovskaya raises difficult questions of how to apply *Morrison* to the Commodity Exchange Act. It raises a possible distinction between the extraterritorial jurisdiction that the Commodity Exchange Act permits to be asserted by the CFTC and that which the Commodity Exchange Act permits a party making a claim through the private right of action available under Commodity Exchange Act section 22.

An additional open question is whether *Morrison* imposed a requirement that the trading must occur on a U.S. futures exchange for a private right of action under the Commodity Exchange Act to be available. The court in the below case applies a pre-*Morrison* test assessing where "irrevocable liability" attached instead of where the trading occurred. Although the case is potentially an outlier, it demonstrates that, even within the Second Circuit, there may be much to work out in determining the extent to which the Commodity Exchange Act applies extraterritorially.

Myun-Uk Choi v. Tower Research Capital LLC

890 F.3d 60 (2d Cir. 2018)

John M. Walker, Jr., Circuit Judge:

Plaintiffs, five Korean citizens, transacted on a "night market" of Korea Exchange ("KRX") futures contracts. The KRX is a derivatives and securities exchange headquartered in Busan, South Korea. On the KRX night market, traders enter orders in Korea, when the KRX is closed for business, whereupon their orders are quickly matched with a counterparty by an electronic trading platform ("CME Globex") located in Aurora, Illinois. The trades are then cleared and settled on the KRX when it opens for business the following morning.

Plaintiffs allege that Defendants Tower Research Capital LLC ("Tower"), a New York based high-frequency trading firm, and its founder, Mark Gorton, injured them and others by engaging in manipulative "spoofing" transactions on the KRX night market in violation of the Commodity Exchange Act ("CEA"), 7 U.S.C. §§ 1 *et seq.*, and New York law. The district court dismissed the action principally on the ground that the CEA does not apply extraterritorially as would be required for it to reach Defendants' alleged conduct. Because we conclude Plaintiffs' allegations make it plausible that the trades at issue were "domestic transactions" under our precedent, we do not agree that application of the CEA to Defendants' alleged conduct would be an impermissible extraterritorial application of the act. . . .

The KOSPI 200, a stock index akin to the S&P 500 or the Dow Jones, consists of the weighted averaged [*sic*] of two hundred Korean stocks traded on the KRX. The KRX also includes a KOSPI 200 futures contract in its daytime trading, which allows traders to speculate on the value of the KOSPI 200 index at various future dates. To facilitate after-hours trading of KOSPI 200 futures, the KRX contracted with CME Group, the product of a merger of the Chicago Mercantile Exchange ("CME") and the Chicago Board of Trade, to establish an overnight market for futures trading. Pursuant to that agreement, futures contracts on KRX's "night market" are listed and traded on "CME Globex, an electronic CME platform located in Aurora, Illinois." . . .

A KRX night market trade begins with the placement of a "limit order" on the KRX system in Korea. Within seconds, the trader's order is matched with an anonymous counterparty on CME Globex. . . . Following matching, "settlement of all trades occurs the day after on the KRX." . . .

In 1998, Gorton founded Tower, a high-frequency trading firm. "High frequency trading firms use computers to create and operate algorithms and, by using those algorithms and technology, execute trades faster than anyone else—making pennies on millions and millions of trades executed in milliseconds." . . . In 2012, Tower aggressively brought its algorithm and technology to bear on the KRX night market, executing nearly 4,000,000 trades of futures contracts, approximately 53.8% of all KRX night market trades that year. . . .

Plaintiffs allege that a significant number of these trades were manipulative. . . .

The alleged scheme—which Plaintiffs describe as "spoofing"—operated as follows. Tower's traders would enter large volume buy or sell orders on the KRX night market and then would use Tower's high-frequency technology to immediately cancel their orders or ensure that they themselves were the counterparties on the trades. They would do so because the intent was not to execute the trades but to create a false impression about supply and demand and thereby drive the market price either up or down. Once that was accomplished, the traders would sell contracts at the artificially inflated price or buy contracts at the artificially deflated price, eventually reaping substantial profits either way. In 2012, Plaintiffs allege, Tower's traders used this spoofing practice hundreds of times, earning more than $14,000,000 in illicit profits. . . .

Plaintiffs, for their part, executed more than 1,000 KRX night market trades in 2012. . . . Given the anonymity of CME Globex, Plaintiffs cannot at the moment identify with precision whether they were a counterparty on any of the allegedly manipulative Tower trades, but they allege it to be a near statistical certainty that at least one Tower trader was a direct counterparty with at least one Plaintiff in a KRX night market trade in 2012. . . . In any event, Plaintiffs allege that they traded at artificial prices during and due to Defendants' spoofing waves.

In May 2014, a Korean government regulator, the Financial Services Commission ("FSC"), uncovered Defendants' scheme and referred Tower to Korean prosecutors. FSC publicly stated that "traders of a U.S. based algorithmic trading specialty company accessed the KOSPI 200 Overnight Futures Market and traded with the use of the [sic] proprietary algorithmic trading technique, which manipulated prices to build their buy and sell positions by creating automatically and repeatedly fictitious trades." . . .

In December 2014, Plaintiffs filed a class complaint on behalf of themselves and other individuals or entities that were allegedly harmed by Defendants' spoofing scheme when they traded in futures on the KRX night market in 2012. Plaintiffs alleged that Defendants' conduct violated several sections of the CEA and New York's prohibition on unjust enrichment.

Defendants moved to dismiss and the district court (Kimba M. Wood, J.) granted the motion. Relying on *Morrison v. National Australia Bank Ltd.*, 561 U.S. 247, 130 S. Ct. 2869, 177 L.Ed.2d 535 (2010), the district court concluded that application of the CEA to Defendants' conduct would be an impermissible extraterritorial application of the act. *Myun-Uk Choi v. Tower Research Capital LLC*, 165 F.Supp.3d 42 (S.D.N.Y. 2016). The district court reasoned that, under *Morrison*, Defendants' alleged conduct was within the territorial reach of the CEA only if the contracts at issue were (i) purchased or sold in the United States or (ii) listed on a domestic exchange. *Id.* at 48. The district court determined that the contracts were not purchased or sold in the United States because the orders needed to "first be placed through the KRX trading system [in Korea]," and because any trades matched on CME Globex in Illinois were final only when settled the following morning in Busan. *Id.* at 49. The district court then concluded that although *CME* might be a "domestic exchange," Plaintiffs did not sufficiently plead that the same was true for *CME Globex*. *Id.* at 49–50. Finally, the district court dismissed Plaintiffs' unjust enrichment claim on the ground that Plaintiffs did not allege "any direct dealing or actual, substantive relationship with the Defendants." *Id.* at 51.

Plaintiffs amended their complaint to add allegations about the domesticity of KRX night market transactions, the nature of CME Globex, and the likelihood that they were counterparties with Defendants during the relevant period.

Defendants filed another motion to dismiss, which the district court again granted. *Myun-Uk Choi v. Tower Research Capital LLC*, 232 F.Supp.3d 337 (S.D.N.Y. 2017). The district court concluded that Plaintiffs still failed to sufficiently allege that CME Globex is a "domestic exchange" under *Morrison* because it is not structured like other exchanges, is not registered as an exchange with the Commodity Futures Trading Commission, and is not subject to the rules of a registered exchange. *Id.* at 341–42. The district court also held that the amended allegations did not plausibly show that trades on the KRX night market were "domestic transactions" because, in its view, KRX rules suggest that transactions become final only when they settle on the KRX, not when they match on CME Globex. *Id.* at 342. Finally, the district court again dismissed Plaintiffs' unjust enrichment claim on the ground that Plaintiffs needed "definitive evidence of a direct relationship," yet they "failed to prove that buyers and sellers were direct counterparties under KRX rules." *Id.* at 343. . . .

Plaintiffs contend that the district court erred in dismissing their CEA and unjust enrichment claims. Because we conclude Plaintiffs sufficiently alleged that applying the CEA to Defendants' conduct would not be an extraterritorial application of the act . . . we agree. . . .

Defendants' argument is that, under *Morrison*, KRX night market trades occur outside of the United States and are therefore beyond the CEA's reach.

In *Morrison*, the Supreme Court set out to define the territorial reach of § 10(b) of the Securities Exchange Act, 15 U.S.C. § 78j(b). After discussing the presumption against extraterritoriality, 561 U.S. at 255, 130 S.Ct. 2869, the Court concluded that, given its text, § 10(b) (and Rule 10b-5, promulgated thereunder) has only a domestic reach, and therefore applies only to one of two types of transactions: (i) "transactions in securities listed on domestic exchanges;" and (ii) "domestic transactions in other securities," *id.* at 267, 130 S.Ct. 2869.

Morrison said nothing about the CEA, and we have only once, in *Loginovskaya*, addressed *Morrison*'s effect on that act. There, we concluded that *Morrison*'s "domestic transactions" test applies to the CEA, but, because the plaintiff in *Loginovskaya* did not purchase commodities on an exchange, we had no occasion to address the "domestic exchange" prong. *See Loginovskaya*, 764 F.3d at 272–75. In concluding that *Morrison*'s "domestic transactions" test applies to the CEA, we adopted a rule established in the § 10(b) case of *Absolute Activist Value Master Fund Ltd. v. Ficeto*, 677 F.3d 60 (2d Cir. 2012). *Loginovskaya*, 764 F.3d at 274. In *Absolute Activist*, we concluded that a transaction involving securities is a "domestic transaction" under *Morrison* if "irrevocable liability is incurred or title passes within the United States." 677 F.3d at 67. . . .

Consequently, plausible allegations that parties to a transaction subject to the CEA incurred irrevocable liability in the United States suffice to overcome a motion to dismiss CEA claims on territoriality grounds. We believe in this case that Plaintiffs' allegations make it plausible that parties trading on the KRX night market incur irrevocable liability in the United States. This being a sufficient basis to resolve the extraterritoriality question at this stage, there is no need for us to address whether the CEA has a territorial reach on the basis that the CME Globex is a "domestic exchange." . . .

We have never concluded . . . , as the district court and the parties seemed to assume, that *Morrison*'s "domestic exchange" prong applies to the CEA either to broaden or to narrow its extraterritorial reach. The section of the CEA relevant to a territoriality analysis, *see Loginovskaya*, 764 F.3d at 272–73, does not contain the language similar to the language in § 10(b) that led *Morrison* to craft the "domestic exchange" prong: the "purchase or sale of any security registered *on a national securities exchange*." 15 U.S.C. § 78j(b) (emphasis added). Rather, the CEA speaks only of "registered entit[ies]." 7 U.S.C. § 25(a)(1)(D)(i). . . .

We quickly dispatch Defendants' contention that, under *Morrison*, the CEA cannot apply to a commodity traded on a foreign exchange. Leaving aside whether *Morrison*'s discussion of exchanges is applicable to the CEA, *Morrison* itself refutes Defendants' argument. *Morrison* clearly provided that the "domestic transaction" prong is an independent and sufficient basis for application of the Securities Exchange Act to purportedly foreign conduct. *Morrison* summarized the standard in the disjunctive: "[W]hether the purchase or sale is made in the United States, *or* involves a security listed on a domestic exchange." 561 U.S. at 269–70, 130 S.Ct. 2869 (emphasis added). In applying this standard, *Morrison* assessed the domestic nature of a transaction of securities that were listed on an Australian exchange, *see id.* at 273, 130 S.Ct. 2869, which would have been an unnecessary endeavor under Defendants' view. Similarly, when we applied *Morrison* in *City of Pontiac Policemen's & Firemen's Retirement System v. UBS AG*, 752 F.3d 173 (2d Cir. 2014), we specifically assessed, for trades made on foreign exchanges, whether irrevocable liability attached. *Id.* at 181–82. Plainly the reasoning of *Morrison* does not preclude the application of the CEA to trades made on a foreign exchange when irrevocable liability is incurred in the United States. We therefore turn to whether Plaintiffs sufficiently alleged that the parties incurred irrevocable liability for KRX night market trades in the United States.

The parties do not dispute that the trades at issue were "matched" in the United States on CME Globex and were "cleared and settled" in Korea. The issue is therefore whether the allegations make it plausible that the parties incurred "irrevocable liability" upon matching. Plaintiffs' amended complaint alleges not only that KRX night market trades bind the parties on matching, it also alleges that the express view of CME Group is that "matches [on CME Globex] are essentially binding contracts" and "[m]embers are required to honor all bids or offers which have not been withdrawn from the market." . . . It follows from these allegations that, in the "classic contractual sense," *Absolute Activist*, 677 F.3d at 68, parties incur irrevocable liability on KRX night market trades at the moment of matching. . . .

Plaintiffs' allegations make it plausible that the parties incurred irrevocable liability for their KRX night market trades on CME Globex in Illinois, which is all that is required at this stage of the litigation. Plaintiffs' CEA claims should not have been dismissed on extraterritoriality grounds. . . .

For the reasons stated above, we VACATE the judgment of the district court and REMAND for further proceedings.

One wonders would the case have been decided differently if Tower Research Capital LLC, the defendant, were not U.S.-based? For one thing, there would be questions about personal jurisdiction. Nonetheless, the question remains, would the fact that one operational component of the transaction occurred in the United States of a transaction otherwise entirely in Korea be sufficient to claim that the Commodity Exchange Act applies?

3. Foreign Boards of Trade

Foreign Boards of Trade, commonly known as "FBOTs," are facilities that offer access to U.S. persons to trade commodity futures and options with boards of trade not designated as contract markets in the United States. Whereas, in the past the CFTC has, on an *ad hoc* basis, permitted specific foreign boards of trade to provide U.S. persons access, these arrangements have now been formalized. See chapter 5, section E.

4. Relief for Registrants

With some qualifications, the CFTC explicitly offers relief from registration for futures commission merchants, introducing brokers, commodity trading advisors, and commodity pool operators located outside the United States transacting only with non-U.S. persons or international institutions such as the International Monetary Fund as customers.[11] A major proviso is that, if any trades over which the CFTC has jurisdiction are required to be cleared, they must be cleared by a CFTC-registered futures commission merchant.[12] For a commodity pool operator located outside the United States, the relief can be claimed for non-U.S. commodity pools even if the commodity pool operator operates U.S. pools.[13]

For a commodity pool operator located in the United States, this relief from registration does not apply even if it is operating commodity pools without U.S. customers. However, the CFTC provides relief from some CFTC regulations for CFTC-registered commodity pool operators where the relevant commodity pool: (1) is organized and operated outside of the United States with no meetings or conduct of "administrative activities" in the United States; and (2) has no U.S. shareholders, participants, or U.S.-sourced funds or capital.[14] The commodity pool operator, commodity pool, and any parties affiliated with either also must not engage in marketing that could, or reasonably be expected to, solicit U.S. persons as participants. A filing with the CFTC claiming the exemption is required.

A commodity pool operator qualifying for this relief, is not required to deliver disclosure documents, issue reports to participants, or issue financial statements.[15] For non-U.S. commodity pool operators, there is also some relief related to record-keeping requirements.

This relief is often availed of in the common situation where a CFTC-registered commodity pool operator is operating multiple pools, some for U.S. investors and some for non-U.S. investors. Sometimes this is done through a "master-feeder arrangement" where one or more commodity pools invest their assets in a common "master" fund.[16] That way, one of the pools can be set up for U.S. investors and the other, presumably with lower compliance and regulatory costs and optimized tax structure, for non-U.S. investors. A similar outcome is also achieved by a "parallel pool structure" where two separate pools are operated almost identically in terms of strategy and investments.[17] In both cases, the non-U.S. pool is eligible for relief.

---

11. 17 C.F.R. § 3.10(c)(1)–(4).

12. *Id.*

13. 17 C.F.R. § 3.01(c)(5)(iv).

14. CFTC, *Offshore Commodity Pools: Relief for Certain Registered CPOs*, CFTC Advisory No. 18-96 (Apr. 11, 1996).

15. The specific regulations for which relief is granted are 17 C.F.R. §§ 4.21, 4.22, 4.23(a)(10), and 4.23(a)(11).

16. *See* CFTC, CFTC Form CPO-PQR 6, available at https://www.reginfo.gov/public/do /DownloadDocument?objectID=28356101.

17. *Id.* at 7.

C. Framework for International Swaps Cooperation

1. Group of Twenty

a. Generally

The framework that formed the basis for Title VII of the Dodd-Frank Act, i.e., the portion of the Dodd-Frank Act specifically focused on swaps, resulted from international commitments made after the Financial Crisis. These non-binding commitments were made by representatives of the governments that together comprise the "Group of Twenty," commonly known as the "G-20." The representatives attending the periodic G-20 meetings are generally among the most senior members of government responsible for macroeconomic policy in their nation. The members of the G-20 are intended to represent eighty percent of global gross domestic product.[18] The members of the G-20 are Argentina, Australia, Brazil, Canada, China, European Union, France, Germany, India, Indonesia, Italy, Japan, Mexico, Russia, Saudi Arabia, South Africa, South Korea, Turkey, United Kingdom, and the United States.

In the G-20's 2009 meeting held in Pittsburgh, nearly a year before passage of the Dodd-Frank Act, the broad contours of the forthcoming legislation were outlined.

Group of Twenty, *Leaders' Statement*

Group of Twenty Pittsburgh Summit (Sept. 24–25, 2009), available at https://www.treasury.gov/resource-center/international/g7-g20/Documents/pittsburgh_summit_leaders_statement_250909.pdf

... We meet in the midst of a critical transition from crisis to recovery to turn the page on an era of irresponsibility and to adopt a set of policies, regulations and reforms to meet the needs of the 21st century global economy....

When we last gathered in April, we confronted the greatest challenge to the world economy in our generation....

We [have] assessed the progress we have made together in addressing the global crisis and ... committed to additional steps to ensure strong, sustainable, and balanced growth, to build a stronger international financial system ... and to modernize our architecture for international economic cooperation....

The growth of the global economy and the success of our coordinated effort to respond to the recent crisis have increased the case for more sustained and systematic international cooperation....

Since the onset of the global crisis, we have developed and begun implementing sweeping reforms to tackle the root causes of the crisis and transform the system for global financial regulation. Substantial progress has been made in strengthening prudential oversight, improving risk management, strengthening transparency,

---

18. *See* G-20, *About the G20*, available at https://www.g20.org/about-the-g20.html.

promoting market integrity, establishing supervisory colleges, and reinforcing international cooperation. We have enhanced and expanded the scope of regulation and oversight, with tougher regulation of over-the-counter (OTC) derivatives, securitization markets, credit rating agencies, and hedge funds. . . .

Yet our work is not done. Far more needs to be done. . . .

All standardized OTC derivative contracts should be traded on exchanges or electronic trading platforms, where appropriate, and cleared through central counterparties by end-2012 at the latest. OTC derivative contracts should be reported to trade repositories. Non-centrally cleared contracts should be subject to higher capital requirements. We ask the [Financial Stability Board] and its relevant members to assess regularly implementation and whether it is sufficient to improve transparency in the derivatives markets, mitigate systemic risk, and protect against market abuse. . . .

———————

b. Financial Stability Board

During the Pittsburgh G-20 meeting, the G-20 declared itself "the premier forum for . . . economic cooperation" among its members.[19] It also saw the establishment of the Financial Stability Board as a body to coordinate and monitor the implementation of G-20 commitments.[20] In addition to the G-20 members, the Financial Stability Board includes representatives from Hong Kong, the Netherlands, Singapore, Spain, Switzerland, and various international bodies.[21]

The Financial Stability Board regularly takes stock of the extent to which G-20 commitments have been implemented. In their 2020 report, they noted that implementation of derivatives reform is "well-advanced, though progress since 2019 has been very limited."[22] Out of twenty-four Financial Stability Board member countries, twenty-three have implemented swap reporting requirements, seventeen have implemented swap clearing requirements, sixteen have implemented swap margin requirements, thirteen have implemented mandatory trading on trading platforms, and eight have final capital rules.[23] By market volume, though, nearly all the transactions occur in jurisdictions that have already implemented the reporting, clearing, margining, and on-facility trading requirements.[24]

———————

19. G-20, *Group of Twenty Pittsburgh Summit (Sept. 24–25, 2009)*, available at https://www.treasury.gov/resource-center/international/g7-g20/Documents/pittsburgh_summit_leaders_statement_250909.pdf, p. 3, ¶ 19.

20. *Id.*

21. *See* Financial Stability Board, *Members of the FSB*, available at https://www.fsb.org/about/organisation-and-governance/members-of-the-financial-stability-board/.

22. Financial Stability Board, *Implementation and Effects of the G20 Financial Regulatory Reforms* 12 (Nov. 13, 2020), available at https://www.fsb.org/wp-content/uploads/P131120-1.pdf.

23. Financial Stability Board, *OTC Derivatives Market Reforms* 1-2 (Nov. 25, 2020), available at https://www.fsb.org/wp-content/uploads/P251120.pdf.

24. Financial Stability Board, *Implementation and Effects of the G20 Financial Regulatory Reforms* 12, Graph 3 (Nov. 13, 2020), available at https://www.fsb.org/wp-content/uploads/P131120-1.pdf.

2. International Organization of Securities Commissions

The International Organization of Securities Commissions (commonly known as "IOSCO") is another forum for national securities and futures regulators. In all IOSCO member nations, other than the United States and Japan, one entity is the securities and futures regulator.[25] The U.S. approach of separating the regulation of such products into two regulatory bodies, the SEC and CFTC, is not the norm. Both are IOSCO members.[26]

IOSCO helps to coordinate the development of international standards on issues such as margin requirements and market manipulation.

An Erosion of Sovereignty?

The central role of the G-20 and Financial Stability Board is not without its critics. Although the United States has not in any formal way (such as a treaty) ceded policy authority to the G-20 and the Financial Stability Board, it and the other members of both have *de facto* deferred to its authority in monitoring and guiding the implementation of G-20 commitments made by G-20 members shortly after the Financial Crisis. Critics have contended that this represents a cession of sovereignty without the input of Congress or the public.[a]

[a] *See, e.g.,* Peter J. Wallison and Daniel M. Gallagher, *How Foreigners Became America's Financial Regulators*, W.S.J. (Mar. 19, 2015).

D. Extraterritorial Limit of the CFTC's Jurisdiction Over Swaps

1. Statutory Limit

As noted above, the Commodity Exchange Act does not, as a general matter, explicitly confer extraterritorial jurisdiction to the CFTC over the matters within its purview. However, with respect to swaps specifically, the Commodity Exchange Act expressly addresses extraterritoriality:

> The provisions of this chapter relating to swaps that were enacted by the Wall Street Transparency and Accountability Act of 2010 (including any rule prescribed or regulation promulgated under that Act), shall not apply to activities outside the United States unless those activities —

---

25. Japan has one regulator for securities and many commodity futures products and two other regulators specifically for industrial commodity futures and agricultural commodity futures. *See* Ben McLannahan, *New Push to Ease Japan Commodity Trading Rules*, Financial Times (Nov. 5, 2014), available at https://www.ft.com/content/fe65f912-64db-11e4-ab2d-00144feabdc0.

26. *See* International Organization of Securities Commissioners, *Ordinary Members of IOSCO*, available at https://www.iosco.org/about/?subsection=membership&memid=1.

(1) have a direct and significant connection with activities in, or effect on, commerce of the United States; or

(2) contravene such rules or regulations as the Commission may prescribe or promulgate as are necessary or appropriate to prevent the evasion of any provision of this chapter that was enacted by the Wall Street Transparency and Accountability Act of 2010.[27]

2. History

In 2013, the CFTC issued "interpretative guidance" as to how CFTC staff intended to apply Commodity Exchange Act section 2(i) and related cross-border matters.[28] This "interpretative guidance," though not technically a set of CFTC rules, had many attributes of a set of rules. It was highly prescriptive, detailed, and published in the Federal Register. It led to litigation claiming that, due to its rule-like attributes, the CFTC's "guidance" was a disguised rule. The claimed motivation for issuing a "disguised rule" instead of a real rule was to avoid the more burdensome process rulemaking entails, such as compliance with the Commodity Exchange Act cost-benefit analysis requirements[29] and the Administrative Procedure Act's formalities.[30]

The outcome of the litigation was that the interpretative guidance was upheld as validly issued by the CFTC while confirming that it could not be enforced by the CFTC in the same way a rule could.[31] The CFTC would, in all cases, be required to exclusively ground its extraterritorial application of its swaps regime in the statutory provisions of Commodity Exchange Act section 2(i). The CFTC has also finalized a rule for how it will handle certain conflicts in margin requirements across jurisdictions.[32]

E. Cross-Border Swap Framework

In 2020, the CFTC finalized a cross-border rule superseding the 2013 interpretative guidance.[33] It provided the framework for how the CFTC can be expected to interpret Commodity Exchange Act section 2(i) in the context of swaps. It primarily

---

27. Commodity Exchange Act § 2(i).

28. CFTC, *Interpretative Guidance and Policy Statement Regarding Compliance with Certain Swap Regulations*, 78 Fed. Reg. 45292 (July 26, 2013).

29. Commodity Exchange Act § 15(a).

30. 5 U.S.C. § 553.

31. *Securities Industry and Financial Markets Association v. CFTC*, 67 F. Supp. 3d 373 (D.D.C. 2014).

32. CFTC, *Margin Requirements for Uncleared Swaps for Swap Dealers and Major Swap Participants; Cross-Border Application of the Margin Requirements*, 81 Fed. Reg. 34818 (May 31, 2016).

33. CFTC, *Cross-Border Application of the Registration Thresholds and Certain Requirements Applicable to Swap Dealers and Major Swap Participants*, 85 Fed. Reg. 56924 (Sept. 14, 2020). The CFTC has also finalized a rule for how it will handle certain conflicts in margin requirements across jurisdictions. CFTC, *Margin Requirements for Uncleared Swaps for Swap Dealers and Major Swap Participants; Cross-Border Application of the Margin Requirements*, 81 Fed. Reg. 34818 (May 31, 2016). The CFTC has noted that it "may also consider amending the 'U.S. person' definition" in the margin cross-border

addressed: (1) what is a U.S. person; (2) application of the *de minimis* limit for swap dealers and major swap participants to non-U.S. persons; (3) elements of the CFTC swaps regime that are disapplied in specific cross-border contexts; (4) the framework for substituting compliance with a non-U.S. swap regulatory regime in lieu of the CFTC's regime; and (5) the standards for determining when non-U.S. regulatory regimes are "comparable" to the CFTC's regime and, therefore, can be complied with in lieu of the CFTC's regime. We discuss each of these in turn.

1. U.S. Person

a. Generally

In 2020, the CFTC finalized a cross-border rule superseding the 2013 interpretative guidance. A central element of the cross-border rule is the definition of U.S. person.[34] Whether a counterparty to a swap is a U.S. person is in many cases a prerequisite for, as we discuss below, determining the scope of CFTC swap rules that a swap dealer or major swap participant must apply. It is also necessary for determining whether a party must include swaps in calculating its *de minimis* limits for determining whether swap dealer or major swap participant registration is required.

The cross-border rule's definition of U.S. person is outlined in figure 17.1. Please consult figure 17.1 throughout the below discussion as needed. Note that there is a general exclusion from the U.S. person definition for a variety of international financial institutions, such as the International Monetary Fund or the Inter-American Development Bank.[35]

Although the benefit to doing so is unclear, it is permitted to rely on the otherwise superseded 2013 CFTC interpretative guidance's more extensive definition of "U.S. person" until December 31, 2027, in lieu of the cross-border rule's definition.[36]

Whereas many of the elements of the U.S. person definition outlined in figure 17.1 are commonly understood, deciding U.S. or non-U.S. personhood of a corporation based on its "principal place of business" (see item (B) in figure 17.1) raises challenges. There is no canonical bright line test for understanding what "principal place of business" means in this context. The CFTC has provided significant clarity by defining it as:

> [T]he location from which the officers, partners, or managers of the legal person primarily direct, control, and coordinate the activities of the legal person. With respect to an externally managed investment vehicle, this location is the office from which the manager of the vehicle primarily directs, controls, and coordinates the investment activities of the vehicle.[37]

---

rule. CFTC, *Cross-Border Application of the Registration Thresholds and Certain Requirements Applicable to Swap Dealers and Major Swap Participants*, 85 Fed. Reg. 56924, 56937 (Sept. 14, 2020).

34. 17 C.F.R. § 23.23(a)(23).
35. 17 C.F.R. § 23.23(a)(23)(iii).
36. 17 C.F.R. § 23.23(a)(23)(iv).
37. 17 C.F.R. § 23.23(a)(23)(ii).

In the release accompanying the final cross-border rule, the CFTC provides additional guidance as well as the reasoning for including the provision.

CFTC, *Cross-Border Application of the Registration Thresholds and Certain Requirements Applicable to Swap Dealers and Major Swap Participants*
85 Fed. Reg. 56924 (Sept. 14, 2020)

... § 23.23(a)(23)(ii) provides that the principal place of business means the location from which the officers, partners, or managers of the legal person primarily direct, control, and coordinate the activities of the legal person. With the exception of externally managed entities, as discussed below, the Commission is of the view that for most entities, the location of these officers, partners, or managers generally corresponds to the location of the person's headquarters or main office. However, the Commission believes that a definition that focuses exclusively on whether a legal person is organized, incorporated, or established in the United States could encourage some entities to move their place of incorporation to a non-U.S. jurisdiction to avoid complying with the relevant Dodd-Frank Act requirements, while maintaining their principal place of business — and therefore, risks arising from their swap transactions — in the United States. Moreover, a "U.S. person" definition that does not include a "principal place of business" element could result in certain entities falling outside the scope of the relevant Dodd-Frank Act-related requirements, even though the nature of their legal and financial relationships in the United States is, as a general matter, indistinguishable from that of entities incorporated, organized, or established in the United States. Therefore, the Commission is of the view that it is appropriate to treat such entities as U.S. persons. ...

However, determining the principal place of business of a ... [collective investment vehicle ("CIV")], such as an investment fund or commodity pool, may require consideration of additional factors beyond those applicable to operating companies. ... The Commission interprets that, for an externally managed investment vehicle, this location is the office from which the manager of the vehicle primarily directs, controls, and coordinates the investment activities of the vehicle. ... This interpretation is consistent with the Supreme Court's decision in *Hertz Corp. v. Friend*, which described a corporation's principal place of business, for purposes of diversity jurisdiction, as the "place where the corporation's high level officers direct, control, and coordinate the corporation's activities."[38] In the case of a CIV, the senior personnel that direct, control, and coordinate a CIV's activities are generally not the named directors or officers of the CIV, but rather persons employed by the CIV's investment advisor or promoter, or in the case of a commodity pool, its CPO. Therefore, ... when a primary manager is responsible for directing, controlling, and coordinating the overall activity of a CIV, the CIV's principal place of business under the Final Rule is the location from which the manager carries out those responsibilities. ...

----

38. [N. 150] 559 U.S. 77, 80 (2010). ...

Based on the CFTC's above guidance, an investment vehicle must look at the location of the person making investment decisions to determine whether it is a U.S. person. A common complaint is that the CFTC's position has the potential to incentivize non-U.S. investment vehicles to use non-U.S. managers — lest the "principal place of business" of the non-U.S. investment vehicle be deemed the United States — to lessen their regulatory burden.

Figure 17.1 Definition of U.S. Person

Category	Commentary
"(A) a natural person resident in the United States;"	The reference to a natural person means individuals, not partnerships, corporations or limited liability companies. Residency can be inferred via indicia such as primary residence or "permanent resident," i.e., "green card" status.
"(B) A partnership, corporation, trust, investment vehicle, or other legal person organized, incorporated, or established under the laws of the United States or having its principal place of business in the United States;"	The question of whether a legal entity is organized or incorporated in the United States is simple and objective. However, what constitutes having a "principal place of business in the United States"? This issue is discussed in section E.1.a.
"(C) An account (whether discretionary or non-discretionary) of a U.S. person;"	This covers any private equity fund, hedge fund, commodity pool, or mutual fund (i.e., "investment company") that is not formed in the United States, yet is nonetheless owned mostly by U.S. persons. An exception is provided for such an entity that is publicly offered solely to non-U.S. persons even if it ends up majority-owned by U.S. persons.
"(D) An estate of a decedent who was a resident of the United States at the time of death."	An estate of a decedent is not likely to be a frequent entrant into the swaps market. If a person would have satisfied the U.S. person test in (i) while alive, then their estate will be deemed a U.S. person.
"(vii) any legal entity . . . that is directly or indirectly majority-owned by one or more persons described in . . . (i), (ii), (iii), (iv), or (v) and in which such person(s) bears unlimited responsibility for the obligations and liabilities of the legal entity."	A legal entity formed outside of the U.S., the principal place of business of which is outside the U.S. and that is directly or indirectly owned by U.S. persons bearing unlimited liability for the entity, is considered to be a U.S. person. Though logical to have the U.S. person majority "pass through" the entity since, ultimately, U.S. persons that have unlimited liability bear the responsibility, this category should be uncommon.

b. Treatment of Bank Branches

Another facet of the U.S. person test that benefits from further inquiry is the application of the U.S. person test to bank branches. Banks are unique in that, though one legal entity, the legal entity is comprised of a head office and branches. Branches are similar to offices of an ordinary corporation. They represent physical locations where the relevant legal entity is operating.

Unlike offices, branches — for specific purposes — are treated separately from the head office.[39] However, for the purposes of determining U.S. person status, a branch of a bank is considered to be the same legal entity as the bank, i.e., not a separate legal person, with a few exceptions noted below.

2. Application to *De Minimis* Test

As discussed in chapter 11, section B, an entity is exempt from registering as a swap dealer with the CFTC if it maintains a *de minimis* amount of no more than $8 billion notional in swaps resulting from swap dealing activities calculated over the preceding twelve months. In calculating this amount, aggregation of the positions of all affiliated entities other than those already registered with the CFTC as a swap dealer is required. There is also a *de minimis* level for potential major swap participants, discussed in chapter 11, section C.2.d.

For the purposes of calculating swaps that have the potential to count toward the swap dealer *de minimis* threshold, a non-U.S. entity — so long as its swap obligations are not guaranteed by a U.S. person — need only calculate its swaps with U.S. persons.[40] However, for this purpose only, and to address CFTC concerns as to U.S. persons directly or indirectly having significant swaps exposure to non-registrants, a swap with a non-U.S. entity guaranteed by a U.S. affiliate is deemed to be a swap with a U.S. person unless the U.S. affiliate is itself a swap dealer, affiliated with one, or is a non-financial entity.[41] See chapter 10, section B.3.c, for non-financial entities. Moreover, so long as the identity of the counterparty is unknown, such a non-U.S. entity need not count swaps that are traded on a facility and cleared toward the *de minimis* limit.[42]

Also, even though a non-U.S. branch of a U.S. bank is, for other purposes, treated as a U.S. person since a branch is not a distinct legal entity, solely for the purpose of making this *de minimis* calculation, it is treated as a non-U.S. person so long as it is registered as a swap dealer.[43] Otherwise, a non-U.S. entity might avoid trading with non-U.S. branches of U.S. banks for fear of adding to the swaps counting toward the non-U.S. entity's *de minimis* threshold.

Similar relief applies to major swap participants.[44]

---

39. *See* Geoffrey Sant, *The Rejection of the Separate Entity Rule Validates the Separate Entity Rule*, 65 SMU L. Rev. 813 (Fall 2012).

40. For these purposes, certain large-sized non-U.S. persons with ultimate U.S. parents with more than $50 billion in global assets are deemed U.S. persons. *See* 17 C.F.R. §§ 23.23(b)(1) and 23.23(a)(13) and (14).

41. 17 C.F.R. § 23.23(b)(2).

42. 17 C.F.R. § 23.23(d).

43. 17 C.F.R. § 23.23(b)(2)(i).

44. 17 C.F.R. §§ 23.23(c) and (d).

3. Application of CFTC Swap Regulatory Regime

Depending on the parties to a cross-border swap transaction, some portions of the CFTC swap regulatory regime may be disapplied. Every reference in the below to a "swap dealer" equally applies to a major swap participant. Figure 17.2 defines the Group A, B, and C requirements referenced below.

Figure 17.2 Exemption Categories

Group A Exemptions	Group B Exemptions	Group C Exemptions
Chief compliance officer requirements (17 C.F.R. § 3.3)	Some of the daily trading record requirements (17 C.F.R. § 23.202(a)(2) *et seq.*)	External business conduct requirements (17 C.F.R. § 23.400 *et seq.*)
Recordkeeping and record retention requirements (17 C.F.R. §§ 23.201 and 23.203)	Confirmation requirements (17 C.F.R. § 23.501)	Margin segregation requirements (17 C.F.R. § 17 and C.F.R. § 23.700 *et seq.*)
Risk management program (17 C.F.R. §§ 23.601–.607 and 23.609)	Swap trading relationship documentation requirements (17 C.F.R. § 23.504)	Substituted compliance not available

a. Swap Dealers Outside the United States

Whether a non-U.S. swap dealer or a U.S. swap dealer operating through a non-U.S. branch, there is an exemption from Group B and C requirements if the swap is cleared with an anonymous counterparty. If, on the other hand, the swap is with an entity outside the United States, whether a non-U.S. person or a non-U.S. branch of a U.S. person, the Group C requirements do not apply.[45]

Party Claiming Relief	Counterparty	Exception
(1) Non-U.S. swap dealer, unless operating through a U.S. branch; or (2) U.S. swap dealer, operating through a non-U.S. branch	Anonymous counterparty and cleared swap	Group B and C
(1) Non-U.S. swap dealer, unless operating through a U.S. branch; or (2) U.S. swap dealer, operating through a non-U.S. branch	(1) Non-U.S. person, unless operating through a U.S. branch; or (2) a non-U.S. branch of a U.S. person	Group C

---

45. 17 C.F.R. § 23.23(e)(1).

b. U.S. Branch of Non-U.S. Swap Dealer

If a non-U.S. swap dealer is operating through a U.S. branch it is eligible for relief from the Group C requirements if its counterparty is outside the United States (not operating through a U.S. branch) and the counterparty's swap obligation is not guaranteed by a U.S. person.[46]

Party Claiming Relief	Counterparty	Exception
Non-U.S. swap dealer, operating through a U.S. branch	Non-U.S. person, unless operating through a U.S. branch, whose swap is not guaranteed by a U.S. person	Group C

c. Non-U.S. Swap Dealer Outside the United States with a Non-U.S. Person

A non-U.S. swap dealer is eligible for this exception if it is not: (1) operating through a U.S. branch; (2) a direct or indirect subsidiary of U.S. parent with more than $50 billion in global assets (with some carveouts); or (3) guaranteed by a U.S. person with respect to the swap. Its counterparty must similarly be not: (1) operating through a U.S. branch; (2) a direct or indirect subsidiary of U.S. parent with more than $50 billion in global assets (with some carveouts); or (3) guaranteed by a U.S. person with respect to the swap. If those requirements are met, the Group B requirements do not apply.[47]

Party Claiming Relief	Counterparty	Exception
Non-U.S. swap dealer, unless: (1) operating through a U.S. branch; (2) direct or indirect subsidiary of U.S. parent with more than $50 billion in global assets;[a] or (3) the swap is guaranteed by a U.S. person	Non-U.S. person, unless: (1) operating through a U.S. branch; (2) direct or indirect subsidiary of U.S. parent with more than $50 billion in global assets;[a] or (3) the swap is guaranteed by a U.S. person	Group B

[a] Unless the entity is owned by a bank holding company or subject to capital and margin requirements that the CFTC has found comparable. 17 C.F.R. § 23.23(a)(13).

d. Non-U.S. Branch of U.S. Swap Dealer

A non-U.S. branch of a U.S. swap dealer is relieved from Group B requirements for swaps with non-U.S. persons that are not swap dealers or major swap participants and that are not guaranteed by a U.S. person. A party claiming this relief is

---

46. 17 C.F.R. § 23.23(e)(2).
47. 17 C.F.R. § 23.23(e)(3).

capped in doing so at 5% of all swaps in any quarter, and this relief cannot be used if substituted compliance (see below) is available.[48]

Party Claiming Relief	Counterparty	Exception
Non-U.S. branch of U.S. swap dealer or major swap participant so long as swaps using this exception do not exceed 5% in any quarter of swaps overall and it is not otherwise eligible for substituted compliance	Non-U.S. person that is not a swap dealer or major swap participant and is not guaranteed by a U.S. person	Group B

e. Non-U.S. Person With U.S. Connection

This exception is available for a non-U.S. person not operating through a U.S. branch. In addition, it requires that the non-U.S. person be a direct or indirect subsidiary of a U.S. parent with more than $50 billion in global assets (with some carve-outs) or be guaranteed by a U.S. person with respect to the swap. The counterparty must be a non-U.S. person that is not a swap dealer or major swap participant and that is not guaranteed by a U.S. person. A party claiming this relief is capped in doing so at 5% of all swaps in any quarter, and this relief cannot be used if substituted compliance (see below) is available.[49]

Party Claiming Relief	Counterparty	Exception
Non-U.S. person, unless operating through a U.S. branch, that is: (1) direct or indirect subsidiary of U.S. parent with more than $50 billion in global assets;[a] or (2) the swap is guaranteed by a U.S. person; (3) swaps using this exception do not exceed 5% in any quarter of swaps overall; (4) and it is not otherwise eligible for substituted compliance	Non-U.S. person that is not a swap dealer or major swap participant and is not guaranteed by a U.S. person	Group B

[a] Unless the entity is owned by a bank holding company or subject to capital and margin requirements that the CFTC has found comparable. 17 C.F.R. § 23.23(a)(13).

Some entities may be able to benefit from "substituted compliance," i.e., being able to demonstrate that another jurisdiction's regulations are "comparable." This can help avoid duplicative, overlapping regulations.

4. Substituted Compliance and Comparability Determinations

To claim substituted compliance, a party is required to be able to demonstrate that it is already complying with "comparable" requirements. Whether a regime has comparable requirements is a determination made by the CFTC.

---

48. 17 C.F.R. § 23.23(e)(4).
49. 17 C.F.R. § 23.23(e)(5).

Only non-U.S. swap entities can deem Group A requirements to be satisfied by substituted compliance with a jurisdiction deemed comparable by the CFTC.[50] Non-U.S. swap dealers or non-U.S. branches of U.S. swap dealers trading with non-U.S. persons or non-U.S. branches of U.S. persons can deem Group B requirements to be satisfied by substituted compliance with a jurisdiction deemed comparable by the CFTC.[51] Last, a U.S branch of a U.S. entity trading with a non-U.S. person that is not guaranteed by a U.S. person can deem Group B requirements to be satisfied by substituted compliance with a jurisdiction deemed comparable by the CFTC.[52]

Comparability determinations may be made by the CFTC on application of swap dealers, major swap participants, industry associations for swap dealers or major swap participants, or foreign regulators.[53] It can also be done *sua sponte* by the CFTC.[54] Comparability determinations have been made — to different extents — with respect to the swap regulatory regimes in place in Australia, Canada, the European Union, Hong Kong, Japan, and Switzerland.[55] Finding of comparability among Group of Twenty countries is to be expected due to the commitments on these core areas described in section C.1 above.

There is also statutory authority for exempting a non-U.S. derivatives clearing organization from registration if the regulation of the non-U.S. derivatives clearing organization is found to be comparable to that applying to a CFTC-registered derivatives clearing organization.[56]

---

50. 17 C.F.R. § 23.23(f)(1).

51. 17 C.F.R. § 23.23(f)(2).

52. 17 C.F.R. § 23.23(f)(3).

53. 17 C.F.R. § 23.23(g)(2).

54. 17 C.F.R. § 23.23(g)(1).

55. *See* CFTC, *Australia: Certain Entity-Level Requirements*, 78 Fed. Reg. 78864 (Dec. 27, 2013); CFTC, *Canada: Certain Entity-Level Requirements*, 78 Fed. Reg. 78839 (Dec. 27, 2013); CFTC, *European Union: Certain Entity-Level Requirements* 78 Fed. Reg. 78923 (Dec. 27, 2013); CFTC, *European Union: Certain Transaction-Level Requirements*, 78 Fed. Reg. 78878 (Dec. 27, 2013); CFTC, *Hong Kong: Certain Entity-Level Requirements*, 78 Fed. Reg. 78852 (Dec. 27, 2013); CFTC, *Japan: Certain Entity-Level Requirements*, 78 Fed. Reg. 78910 (Dec. 27, 2013); CFTC, *Japan: Certain Transaction-Level Requirements*, 78 Fed. Reg. 78890 (Dec. 27, 2013); CFTC, *Switzerland: Certain Entity-Level Requirements*, 78 Fed. Reg. 78899 (Dec. 27, 2013); CFTC, *Comparability Determination for Japan: Margin Requirements for Uncleared Swaps for Swap Dealers and Major Swap Participants*, 81 Fed. Reg. 63376 (Sept. 15, 2016); and CFTC, *Comparability Determination for the European Union: Margin Requirements for Uncleared Swaps for Swap Dealers and Major Swap Participants*, 82 Fed. Reg. 48394 (Oct. 13, 2017).

56. Commodity Exchange Act § 5b(h). The CFTC has provided limited exemptions to ASX Clear (Futures) Pty Limited, available at http://www.cftc.gov/idc/groups/public/@otherif/documents/ifdocs/asxclearamdorderdcoexemption.pdf; Japan Securities Clearing Corporation, available at http://www.cftc.gov/idc/groups/public/@otherif/documents/ifdocs/jsccdcoexemptorder10-26-15.pdf; Korea Exchange, Inc., available at http://www.cftc.gov/idc/groups/public/@otherif/documents/ifdocs/krxdcoexemptorder10-26-15.pdf; and OTC Clearing Hong Kong Limited, available at http://www.cftc.gov/idc/groups/public/@otherif/documents/ifdocs/otccleardcoexemptorder12-21-15.pdf.

Questions and Comments

1. In light of *Morrison* and its progeny, how would *Psimenos* be decided today?

2. Is there a reason grounded in statute to apply *Morrison* differently to the Commodity Exchange Act than it has been applied to the Securities Exchange Act?

3. What are the advantages and disadvantages of the "conduct" and "effects" test when compared to the stricter test outlined in *Morrison*? Is there something to be said for a standard intended to not allow the "United States commodities markets to be used as a base to consummate schemes concocted abroad"?[57] If so, is congressional action the right way to achieve such a public policy objective?

4. Why might the plaintiff have sought U.S. subject matter jurisdiction in *Myun-Uk Choi v. Tower Research Capital LLC* even though the nexus to the United States was limited?

5. Evaluate the role of the G-20. Does it raise questions regarding the exercise of national sovereignty or is it a necessary means to harmonize national regulatory regimes?

6. Why does the CFTC put so much weight on where an investment fund is managed in determining whether a fund is a U.S. person for swaps regulatory purposes? Could this have a chilling effect on the selection of U.S. fund managers?

7. Re-read Commodity Exchange Act section 2(i), excerpted in section D.1. Are the CFTC's cross-border rules in 17 C.F.R. § 23.23 and discussed throughout section E reflective of the requirements of Commodity Exchange Act section 2(i)? What approach would you take to identify to what extent cross-border transactions are subject to CFTC jurisdiction in light of Commodity Exchange Act section 2(i)?

8. What is the purpose of substituted compliance? What are its benefits?

---

57. *Psimenos v. E.F. Hutton & Company, Inc.*, 722 F.2d 1041, 1046 (2d Cir. 1983).

Chapter 18

Bankruptcy and Insolvency

A. Background

The true test of documentation is how well it holds up when one of the parties does not perform as expected. While there are myriad potential reasons for non-performance, often it is because a party is unable to make its payments. When a party is unable to make payments, bankruptcy often results. Therefore, it is essential to consider what implications bankruptcy will have on derivatives relationships.

The Bankruptcy Code prohibits the enforcement of some types of contractual provisions in bankruptcy.[1] Bankruptcy judges have broad authority with respect to creditor claims and creditors' conduct in enforcing a contract post-bankruptcy. Accordingly, we particularly examine the extent to which contractual provisions in derivatives agreements will be enforced by a bankruptcy court.

In making this examination, we first assess how the obligations of parties in futures and swaps are generally treated in bankruptcy. Then we will look at the treatment specifically of commodity futures, commodity options, and cleared swaps. Note that commodity futures, commodity options, and cleared swaps are treated the same for Bankruptcy Code purposes and included in the definition of "commodity contracts."[2] As we will see, there are many provisions in the Bankruptcy Code specific to derivatives. Finally, we will look at public policy questions surrounding these Bankruptcy Code provisions.

B. Bankruptcy Code Provisions Applicable to Futures and Swaps

A number of Bankruptcy Code provisions have direct relevance to a claim against a bankrupt debtor related to derivatives. Some of these provisions have direct application to futures and cleared swaps and nearly all of these provisions have direct application to a bankruptcy claim involving an uncleared swap. The provisions in the Bankruptcy Code that benefit derivatives claimants against bankrupt debtors are, in the aggregate, commonly known as the "derivative safe harbors."

---

1. Throughout we use the term "Bankruptcy Code" for the statutory provisions codified in title 11 of the United States Code.

2. *See* Dodd-Frank Act §724(b) amending 11 U.S.C. §761.

Some parties to derivatives transactions are subject to insolvency regimes other than the Bankruptcy Code. For example, a futures commission merchant that is also registered as a securities broker-dealer will be subject to a Securities Investor Protection Corporation proceeding and an insured depository institution (i.e., a bank that takes retail deposits) is subject to a Federal Deposit Insurance Corporation proceeding. However, in most cases, these operate similarly to the mechanisms described in this section.

The below case introduces the safe harbors. It demonstrates their breadth, particularly with respect to the array of transaction types and agreements that fall within its scope under the rubric of "swap agreements." In chapter 1, section B.1 we recognized that the economic definition of "swap" differs from the Commodity Exchange Act's definition we introduced in chapter 3, section C.2. Note that the Bankruptcy Code uses a broader definition for swap than the Commodity Exchange Act definition. The specific Bankruptcy Code provision at issue in the case, the clawback of payments made by a debtor within a specified period before its bankruptcy and the exemption for derivatives from this provision, is discussed in detail below in subsection 3.

In re National Gas Distributors, LLC

556 F.3d 247 (4th Cir. 2009)

Niemeyer, Circuit Judge:

On December 14, 2006, the Trustee in this Chapter 11 bankruptcy of National Gas Distributors, LLC, a distributor of natural gas to industrial, governmental, and other customers, commenced these adversary proceedings ... against three of National Gas' customers by filing complaints to avoid numerous natural gas supply contracts entered into with these customers during the year before the bankruptcy petition was filed. The Trustee alleged that the contracts and transfers of natural gas were fraudulent conveyances because they were made for less than market value and when the debtor was insolvent.

The customers, E.I. du Pont de Nemours and Company, the Smithfield Packing Company, Inc., and Stadler's Country Hams, Inc., ... [claim] that the contracts were "swap agreements," which would provide them with a complete defense to the Trustee's complaints under the Bankruptcy Code. ... Specifically, they claimed that the contracts were "commodity forward agreements," which are included in the definition of "swap agreements." ... They also claimed that they had taken the transfers in good faith, an assertion that the Trustee does not dispute.

The bankruptcy court denied the motions by orders dated May 24, 2007, finding that the contracts in question were not "swap agreements" ... but simply "agreement[s] by a single end-user to purchase a commodity" and therefore were not exempt from avoidance. Relying mostly on legislative history, the court concluded that in exempting "swap agreements," Congress intended to protect financial markets from the destabilizing effects of bankruptcy and that because the natural gas supply contracts in this case were physically settled and not traded in financial markets, exempting them from avoidance proceedings would not serve Congress' purposes. . . .

In this direct interlocutory appeal from the bankruptcy court's orders, we conclude that the grounds given by the bankruptcy court in finding that the contracts in this case were not swap agreements are not supported by the definition of "swap agreement." . . . Accordingly, we reverse and remand for further proceedings, allowing the customers to attempt to demonstrate factually and legally that their natural gas supply contracts were swap agreements. . . .

During the year before National Gas filed its petition, du Pont, Smithfield Packing, and Stadler's Country Hams purchased natural gas for specific facilities under a series of contracts with National Gas. . . . The contracts required National Gas to sell and deliver the gas and the customer to receive and purchase the gas at the specified price, regardless of the market price of natural gas, or to pay the difference between the agreed-upon price and the market price.

In this manner, these natural gas supply contracts provided a hedge against fluctuations in the market price of natural gas and the adverse effects such fluctuations might have on the customers' operations. Although the contracts were not transferred on exchanges, nor did they even involve the use of brokers or middlemen, the customers did use them, along with other forwards and derivatives, to manage their commodity risks. . . .

On January 20, 2006, National Gas filed a voluntary petition for relief under Chapter 11 of the Bankruptcy Code, and shortly thereafter, the bankruptcy court appointed Richard M. Hutson, II, as Trustee. The Trustee thereafter filed complaints against more than 20 former customers of National Gas, including du Pont and Smithfield Packing, seeking to avoid the contracts . . . and to recover the transfers from the customers . . . on the ground that the contracts and transfers were fraudulent. The Trustee alleged that National Gas entered into contracts to sell natural gas to the customers at below market prices and that at the time of the transfers, National Gas was insolvent, thereby resulting in a constructively fraudulent conveyance. *See* 11 U.S.C. § 548(a)(1)(B). In the alternative, the Trustee alleged that the former management of National Gas intentionally used the contracts to "hinder, delay, or defraud" National Gas' creditors, thereby engaging in an actually fraudulent conveyance. *See* 11 U.S.C. § 548(a)(1)(A). The Trustee sought to recover the cash value of the difference between the market prices when the customers took delivery and the prices they paid under the contracts. . . .

The customers, du Pont and Smithfield Packing, filed motions to dismiss the complaints or for summary judgment, contending that the Trustee cannot avoid the contracts and transfers because "each Transfer was made by or to a swap participant under or in connection with a swap agreement" and was thus not avoidable under 11 U.S.C. §§ 546(g) and 548(d)(2)(D). As they asserted, a "swap agreement" is defined in . . . [the Bankruptcy Code] to include a "commodity forward agreement," which they allege covers the natural gas supply contracts in this case. The customers also contended that they received the transfers for value and that, as conceded by the Trustee, they received such transfers "in good faith."

The bankruptcy court denied the customers' motions . . . concluding that the natural gas supply contracts in this case were not "commodity forward agreements." . . . [T]he court ruled that the natural gas supply contracts in this case were insufficiently tied to financial markets to be commodity forward agreements. . . . More particularly, the court found that "commodity forward agreements" must be "regularly the subject of trading" in financial markets and must be settled by financial exchanges of differences in commodity prices, whereas the contracts in this case were directly negotiated between the seller and purchaser and contemplated physical delivery of the commodity to the purchasers. . . .

Since enactment of the 1978 Bankruptcy Code, Congress has provided safe harbors from the destabilizing effects of bankruptcy proceedings for parties to specified commodities and financial contracts in order to protect financial markets. To do this, Congress limited the application to these parties of Bankruptcy Code provisions such as the automatic stay and trustee avoidances of preferences and fraudulent conveyances. It was thought that financial market stabilization would be achieved under the following rationale:

> These exceptions or "safe harbors" are necessary, it is thought, for the protection of financial markets, including over-the-counter ("OTC") markets on which most derivatives contracts are executed. Without these safe harbors, markets might suffer serious shocks — perhaps even a systemic liquidity crisis, causing markets to collapse — when debtors enter bankruptcy. Counterparties to financial contracts would find themselves subject to the automatic stay for extended periods. They would be unable to liquidate volatile contracts and thereby limit their exposure to market movements. Additionally, a debtor in bankruptcy would be free to "cherrypick" multiple contracts with the same party. Instead of netting the contracts — *i.e.,* setting-off losses under some contracts against gains under others *with the same counterparty* — the debtor could dispose of the contracts independently. "In-the-money" contracts could be assumed; "out-of-the-money" contracts could be rejected. In this way, the debtor could lock-in gains on profitable contracts and (due to its insolvency) limit liability for losses under unprofitable ones. The counterparty to these contracts would find itself paying in full on the assumed contracts and receiving only a fraction of its claim on the rejected. Losses from indefinite exposure to market movements and from cherry picking could produce financial distress in the counterparty itself, forcing it to default on its own contracts with other parties. As one distressed party infects another, a domino effect could ensue, undermining the entire financial market.

Edward R. Morrison & Joerg Riegel, *Financial Contracts and the New Bankruptcy Code: Insulating Markets From Bankrupt Debtors and Bankruptcy Judges*, 13 Am. Bankr.Inst. L.Rev. 641, 642 (2005) (footnotes omitted). . . .

With the 2005 Amendments to the Bankruptcy Code, adopted in the Bankruptcy Abuse Prevention and Consumer Protection Act of 2005, Pub.L. No. 109-8, 119 Stat. 23 (2005) ("BAPCPA"), Congress substantially expanded the protections it had given to financial derivatives participants and transactions by expanding the definition of "swap participants" and "swap agreements" that are exempted from the automatic stay and from trustees' avoidance powers. As the House Report attached to the 2005 bill explained,

> As amended, the definition of "swap agreement" will update the statutory definition and achieve contractual netting across economically similar transactions that are the subject of recurring dealings in the swap agreements.

> The definition of "swap agreement" originally was intended to provide sufficient flexibility to avoid the need to amend the definition as the nature and uses of swap transactions matured. To that end, the phrase "or any other similar agreement" was included in the definition.

H.R.Rep. No. 109-31, pt. 1, at 121 (2005), *reprinted in* 2005 U.S.C.C.A.N. 88, 183. The current definition of "swap agreement" is now extremely broad, covering several dozen enumerated contracts and transactions, as well as combinations of them, options on them, and similar contracts or transactions. ... The resulting statutory scheme may be summarized readily, although its application proves more difficult. ... Under the Bankruptcy Code, trustees are authorized to avoid contracts and transfers of debtors' property "made or incurred on or within 2 years before the date of the filing of the petition" when the contract or transfer amounts to a fraudulent contract or transfer, as fraudulent is defined in the Code. 11 U.S.C. § 548(a). The Code, however, exempts from this avoidance authority transfers "made by or to a swap participant or financial participant, under or in connection with any swap agreement." 11 U.S.C. § 546(g); *see also* 11 U.S.C. § 548(d)(2)(D). The term "swap participant" is defined to mean "an entity that ... has an outstanding swap agreement with the debtor." 11 U.S.C. § 101(53C). ...

In this case, National Gas' customers, du Pont and Smithfield Packing, invoked the protections of 11 U.S.C. §§ 546(g) and 548(d)(2)(D), alleging that their natural gas supply contracts with National Gas were "swap agreements" as defined in 11 U.S.C. § 101(53B) in that they were "commodity forward agreements," a class of transactions listed in the definition of "swap agreement." 11 U.S.C. § 101(53B)(A)(i)(VII). "Commodity forward agreement," however, is not itself defined in the Bankruptcy Code, and no case to date has provided a definition. ...

In this case of first impression, we are therefore left to define "commodity forward agreement" without being given any definition by the Bankruptcy Code. ...

In holding in this case that the natural gas supply contracts are not "commodity forward agreements" exempt from the Trustee's avoidance efforts, the bankruptcy court concluded that all of the agreements or transactions listed in ... [the definition of swap agreement] were "financial instruments traded in the swap markets," and therefore, if any agreement was not traded on an exchange or in a financial market, it could not be a "swap agreement." . . .

After concluding that each contract in this case was "simply an agreement by a single end-user to purchase a commodity," which was physically delivered to the purchaser . . . the court explained that a traditional supply contract is not "swept into the realm of swap agreements." . . .

If one were to assume, as the bankruptcy court did, that all swap agreements, including "commodity forward agreements," must be traded on exchanges or in financial markets and that the contracts in this case were simple supply contracts, the court's position is logically sound. The assumptions, however, do not withstand closer scrutiny. . . .

The bankruptcy court also assumed that the contracts in this case were "simple supply contract[s]," which are not within the definition of a swap agreement. . . . But this assumption is an oversimplification. Although the contracts in this case did provide a supply of gas to the customers' facilities, they also were part of a series of contracts by which the customers hedged their risk of future fluctuations in the price of natural gas. Although it is true that these particular contracts were not traded in financial markets — and perhaps were not even assignable — they nonetheless could have an influence on markets in which participants enter into hedging agreements. A business can enter into a forward agreement with a party who then, in reliance on that forward agreement, enters into another contract with yet another market participant, who in turn may enter into even other contracts. And so a simple forward agreement may readily become tied into the broader markets that Congress aimed to protect in BAPCPA. . . .

The bankruptcy court's conclusion that these contracts were simple supply contracts also rested on the fact that the contracts involved the physical delivery of gas, thus distinguishing them from contracts settled financially. The court concluded that a "commodity forward agreement" must have a financial settlement, such as when settlement occurs by the "losing" party transferring cash or financial assets to the "winning" party at the specified time. Thus, supply contracts, contemplating physical delivery of the commodity to purchasers, could not qualify as "commodity forward agreements."

Although the legislative history of BAPCPA does provide support for the notion that traditional supply agreements are not "swap agreements," *see* H.R.Rep. No. 109-31, pt. 1, at 122, *reprinted in* 2005 U.S.C.C.A.N. at 183 (noting that "[t]raditional commercial arrangements, such as supply agreements" cannot be treated as swap agreements under the Bankruptcy Code), the conclusion that the contracts in this case are traditional supply contracts overlooks the fact that the contracts in this case contained real hedging elements. The contracts obliged the customers to buy, and National Gas to sell, gas on a future date at a price fixed at the time of contracting, regardless of fluctuations in the market price. And if either party did not perform, that party was required to pay the difference between the contract price and the market price.

Nothing in the Bankruptcy Code or in its legislative history suggests a requirement that . . . [the agreement] cannot involve the actual delivery of the commodity. . . .

We thus conclude that Congress did not preclude physical delivery in connection with a "commodity forward agreement." . . .

Because the bankruptcy court gave the definition of "commodity forward agreement" a more narrow reading than the statute bears, we reverse . . . and remand for further proceedings consistent with this opinion.

———————

As we will see below in section D, the inclusion of so many transaction types within the scope of the Bankruptcy Code's safe harbor provisions has been the subject of criticism, particularly among bankruptcy practitioners. Now we will examine each of the Bankruptcy Code "safe harbor" exemptions for derivatives.

1. Automatic Stay

a. General Rule and Exemption

The Bankruptcy Code imposes a stay on termination of agreements, collection of liabilities, or any other proceedings against a bankrupt debtor, known as the "automatic stay."[3] This means that, once a party files for bankruptcy, it is protected from creditors terminating agreements or trying to collect on claims. No judicial order is necessary, hence its "automatic" nature.

The idea behind it is that it provides time to organize claims, identify priorities and secured interests, and prevents asymmetric benefits to creditors who are quicker or more aggressive in pursuing claims against the bankrupt debtor. Last, for debtors who are reorganizing, it allows for preservation of value. For example, if a manufacturer plans to continue operations, it would not be possible if creditors with liens on factory equipment gutted the factory.

Exceptions are provided from the automatic stay for: (1) commodity futures, exchanged traded options, and cleared swaps;[4] and (2) all other swaps.[5]

Both exceptions provide that the automatic stay does not apply to "the exercise . . . of any contractual right . . . under any security agreement or arrangement or other credit enhancement forming a part of or related to any [commodity contract, forward contract, securities contract, or swap agreement], or of any contractual right . . . to offset or net out any termination value."[6]

What this means is that, should a counterparty file for bankruptcy, the non-bankrupt party may, if a derivatives contract (e.g., an ISDA Master Agreement) permits,

---

3. 11 U.S.C. § 362(a).

4. 11 U.S.C. § 362(b)(6).

5. 11 U.S.C. § 362(b)(17).

6. 11 U.S.C. §§ 362(b)(6) and (17).

terminate the contract and all transaction entered thereunder and determine a single net amount payable by one party to the other. This process of terminating all of the transactions entered into pursuant to a derivatives contract and determining a single net amount payable by one party to the other is known as close-out netting. Because we will be referring to close-out netting throughout this chapter, it may be a good time to turn to chapter 12, section E and review close-out netting.

b. Mandatory Stay for Receivership Proceeding

Note that Federal Deposit Insurance Corporation receivership proceedings are not subject to the Bankruptcy Code. When a Federal Deposit Insurance Corporation-insured bank has failed and is in receivership, the other party to a swap agreement may not close out positions until the end of the business day following the receivership.[7]

This applies solely to a "direct default" and not a "cross default." A direct default is where the entity that is the counterparty to the non-defaulting party enters receivership, triggering an event of default and associated termination right under a swap agreement. In this context, a cross default is when an affiliate of the counterparty to the non-defaulting party enters receivership (such as the parent of the counterparty) and the receivership triggers an event of default in the swap agreement between the counterparty and the non-defaulting party.

c. Qualified Financial Contract Stay

Banks that have more than $700 billion in assets or that are subsidiaries of entities designated by the Federal Reserve Board as "global systemically important" and their subsidiaries are required to ensure a two business day stay[8] after bankruptcy or a Federal Deposit Insurance Corporation resolution proceeding before counterparties can terminate "qualified financial contracts" with them.[9] Qualified financial contracts are, among others, uncleared swap transactions, commodity options and options on any of the foregoing.[10] The two-day stay requirement applies both when the party subject to the bankruptcy or Federal Deposit Insurance Corporation proceeding directly defaults with the non-defaulting party or when it triggers

---

7. 12 U.S.C. § 1821(e)(10)(B)(i).

8. It is the later of, counting from when the relevant proceeding is initiated: (1) the close of business at the end of the next business day; or (2) forty-eight hours.

9. The rules were promulgated by the three federal bank regulators, the Federal Reserve Board, the Federal Deposit Insurance Corporation, and the Office of the Comptroller of the Currency. *See* 12 C.F.R. Pt. 252, Subpt. I, 12 C.F.R. Pt. 382, and 12 C.F.R. Pt. 47.

10. Futures are technically within the definition. Since they are required to be centrally cleared, they are practically out of scope. For the definition of "qualified financial contract," see 12 U.S.C. § 5390(c)(8)(D)(i). The rule also applies to other types of financial agreements, such as repurchase agreements and securities transactions. For the criteria for a "global systemically important" entity, see 12 C.F.R. §§ 217.402 and 252.87. Also, U.S. branches of non-U.S. banks identified as "global systemically important" are in scope.

a cross-default resulting in one of its affiliates defaulting with the non-defaulting party.

If the agreement is subject to U.S. law (including the law of a U.S. state) and the counterparty is a U.S. entity, the two-day stay will be the case as a matter of operation of law. In all other circumstances, a qualified financial contract providing for a more generous right must be amended to specifically incorporate the two-day stay.

The U.S. requirements were part of a global effort to implement similar rules globally.[11] There are similar requirements implemented in other jurisdictions, such as the European Union.[12]

2. "*Ipso Facto*" Clause

Ipso facto is Latin for "by the fact itself." In the context of bankruptcy it refers to a statutory provision disallowing any termination or modification of a contract due to the mere fact of a party being in bankruptcy.[13]

Here again, the Bankruptcy Code provides an exception for parties to a futures or a swap transaction. The following is the statutory provision applying to swaps (the one applying to futures is substantially similar[14]):

> The exercise of any contractual right of any [party to a] swap . . . to cause the liquidation, termination, or acceleration of one or more swap agreements because of a condition of the kind specified in [11 U.S.C. §] 365(e) (1) . . . or to offset or net out any termination values or payment amounts arising under or in connection with the termination, liquidation, or acceleration of one or more swap agreements shall not be stayed, avoided, or otherwise limited. . . .[15]

In other words, a commodity futures or swap contract providing for "liquidation, termination or acceleration" due to the bankruptcy of one of the agreement's parties, is not a prohibited *ipso facto* provision. The scope of this relief from the *ipso facto* prohibition has been vigorously disputed, especially with respect to swaps.

a. Payment Subordination

Most swap agreements identify a bankruptcy filing as an event of default allowing the non-defaulting party to terminate the agreement and close-out and net all swap transactions. In the recent past, some swap agreements also allowed the non-defaulting party, where close-out netting results in the non-defaulting party owing

---

11. *See* Financial Stability Board, *Key Attributes of Effective Resolution Regimes for Financial Institutions*, https://www.fsb.org/wp-content/uploads/r_141015.pdf (Oct. 15, 2014).

12. *See* Council Directive 2014/59/EU, *Bank Recovery and Resolution* (July 2, 2014).

13. 11 U.S.C. § 365(e)(1).

14. It can be found at 11 U.S.C. § 556.

15. 11 U.S.C. § 560.

a payment to the defaulting party, to "subordinate" the defaulting party. In other words, to only have an obligation to pay the defaulting party after all other creditors are paid. Some swap agreements even allowed the non-defaulting party to be relieved from any payment obligation to the defaulting party. These are known as "walk-away clauses."

In the below case, a district court faced a motion seeking leave to appeal a decision of a bankruptcy court. The underlying questions that were the subject of the litigation were: (1) whether a contractual provision in a swap agreement subordinating a defaulting party in priority of payment as a result of its bankruptcy filing was within the scope of the swap agreement carve-out from the prohibition on *ipso facto* clauses; and (2) whether the *ipso facto* clause prohibition is triggered at all where a swap agreement provides that the *bankruptcy of the parent* of the counterparty allows for subordinating the counterparty based on its parent filing for bankruptcy.

While the decision helps outline the legal controversy, it also acknowledged the uncertain state of the law before granting the leave for appeal. Though the leave to appeal was granted, the actual appeal was never decided because the parties settled out of court.

Lehman Brothers Special Financing Inc. v. BNY Corporate Trustee Services Limited (In re Lehman Brothers Holdings Inc.)

2010 WL 10078354 (S.D.N.Y. Sept. 23, 2010)

McMahon, District Judge. . . .

On September 18, 2008, Lehman Brothers Holdings Inc. ("LBHI"), one of the largest investment banks in the U.S. at the time, filed for chapter 11 bankruptcy protection in the Bankruptcy Court. Eighteen days later, on October 3, 2008 . . . [Lehman Brothers Special Financing Inc. ("LBSF")], an LBHI subsidiary, filed its chapter 11 petition in the Bankruptcy Court.

On May 20, 2009, LBSF initiated this adversary proceeding (the "Adversary Proceeding") against [BNY Corporate Trustee Services Limited "BNY"]. The Adversary Proceeding arises out of a complex series of synthetic collateralized debt obligations ("CDOs") and related credit default swaps. . . .

The Adversary Proceeding involves two series of credit-linked synthetic portfolio notes (the "Notes") that are now held by non-party Perpetual Trustee Company Limited ("Perpetual"), an Australian company. The Notes were secured by various assets and certain secured obligations (the "Collateral"), including credit default swap transactions between LBSF and the issuer of the Notes (a special-purpose vehicle created by Lehman Brothers International (Europe) called Saphir Finance Public Limited Co. ("Saphir")). The Collateral was held by BNY in trust for creditors of Saphir, including LBSF (as swap counterparty) and Perpetual (as the noteholder). LBHI . . . [guaranteed] LBSF's payment obligations under the swap agreements.

Pursuant to the terms of the Transaction Documents, LBSF's interest in the Collateral ordinarily takes priority over Perpetual's interest — this is called "Swap Counterparty Priority." However, in the event of a default by LBSF under a swap agreement, the Transaction Documents provide for a "flip" from Swap Counterparty Priority to "Noteholder Priority," such that Perpetual receives payments before LBSF. Among the events of default under each of the swap agreements are a filing in bankruptcy of any party to the transaction, including LBSF or LBHI.

On December 1, 2008, after LBHI and LBSF had separately filed for bankruptcy, Saphir exercised its right to terminate the swap agreements. . . . The question in this Adversary Proceeding is whether the Swap Counterparty Priority or Noteholder Priority distribution scheme applies — i.e., whether Perpetual or LBSF has priority in the payment of proceeds to satisfy Saphir's obligations. BNY holds the Collateral that is subject to these competing claims. . . .

LBSF initiated the instant Adversary Proceeding against BNY. Count I of LBSF's two-count Complaint seeks a declaratory judgment that the contractual provisions modifying LBSF's payment priority upon an event of default "constitute unenforceable *ipso facto* clauses" that violate the Bankruptcy Code, 11 U.S.C. §§ 365(e)(1) . . . and that, as a result, "LBSF is entitled to payment under Swap Counterparty Priority." Count II seeks a declaratory judgment that any action to enforce such provisions "constitutes a willful violation of the automatic stay under [Bankruptcy Code] section 362(a)(3)." . . .

On January 25, 2010, the Bankruptcy Court issued a "Memorandum Decision Granting Motion for Summary Judgment and Declaring Applicable Payment Priorities." Judge Peck's opinion granted summary judgment to LBSF, holding that "the provisions in the Transaction Documents purporting to modify LBSF's right to a priority distribution solely as a result of a chapter 11 filing constitute unenforceable *ipso facto* clauses" under 11 U.S.C. §§ 365(e)(1) . . . and that "any attempt to enforce such provisions would violate the automatic stay" under § 362(a). . . . [T]he *ipso facto* protections . . . of the Bankruptcy Code . . . prohibit the modification of a debtor's right solely because of a provision in an agreement conditioned on "the commencement of a case under this title."

Relying on his interpretation of the legislative history and "plain meaning" of these *ipso facto* provisions, Judge Peck held that they apply to contract terms conditioned on the commencement of "presumably any [bankruptcy] case that is related in some appropriate manner to the contracting parties." Judge Peck acknowledged that this interpretation was unprecedented, stating that, "No case has ever declared that the operative bankruptcy filing is not limited to the commencement of a bankruptcy case by the debtor-counterparty itself but may be a case filed by a related entity." He further admitted that his interpretation of the Bankruptcy Code's *ipso facto* provisions as applying "to cases filed by debtors other than the counterparty itself has the potential of opening up a proverbial 'can of worms' that may lead to speculation as to the nature and degree of the relationship between debtors that is needed in order to properly apply the provision." Judge Peck then applied his novel statutory interpretation to the circumstances at hand, and concluded that the separate bankruptcy filings of LBHI and its affiliates, including LBSF, constituted "a singular event" for *ipso facto* purposes — but not for purposes of "any other legal determination that may relate to the date of commencement of a case." Accordingly, Judge Peck held that LBHI's petition "entitled LBSF, consistent with the statutory language, fairly read, to claim the protections of the *ipso facto* provisions of the Bankruptcy Code because its ultimate corporate parent and credit support provider, at a time of extraordinary panic in the global markets, had filed a case under the Bankruptcy Code." . . .

Judge Peck entered an Order granting LBSF's motion for summary judgment and ordering that:

> the contractual provisions . . . that purport to modify LBSF's payment priority as a result of its chapter 11 filing and the chapter 11 filing of LBSF's corporate parent, [LBHI], are unenforceable *ipso facto* clauses . . . and any action to enforce such provisions is prohibited by the automatic stay under Bankruptcy Code section 362(a). . . .

Judge Peck's decision resolved a difficult, dispositive legal question of first impression. He forthrightly acknowledged that his unprecedented ruling — which he predicted would be "controversial" — was the "first such interpretation of the *ipso facto* language" in the Bankruptcy Code. He stated that he was not aware of any case that "has ever declared that the operative bankruptcy filing is not limited to the commencement of a bankruptcy case by the debtor-counterparty itself." Indeed, prior cases in this and other circuits appear to assume — albeit in circumstances that are factually distinguishable — that the Bankruptcy Code's *ipso facto* provisions invalidate clauses that condition an event of default on the contracting party's own bankruptcy filing. . . .

Furthermore, BNY has pointed to numerous legal and other commentaries questioning the correctness of Judge Peck's ruling. . . .

LBSF meekly responds, citing a single article, that the commentary on the Bankruptcy Court's decision has, in fact, been "mixed." But even that lone article, which predicts that Judge Peck's decision will be upheld on appeal, supports BNY's position that an interlocutory appeal is warranted — it highlights the "groundbreaking nature" of Judge Peck's ruling, and warns of the possibility that "savvy guarantors will soon begin to use the 'related entity bankruptcy' ploy as a means of invalidating ipso facto cross-corporate default provisions." Dan Schechter, *Debtor's Prepetition Loss of Priority Under Springing Subordination Agreement Triggered by Parent Corporation's Bankruptcy Filing Is Unenforceable Ipso Facto Provision*, 2010 Com. Fin. Newsl. 16 (2010). Moreover, even if LBSF were correct that mainstream views are "mixed," that is consistent with the conclusion that "substantial ground for difference of opinion" exists. . . .

Note the references to the critical commentary the bankruptcy court decision in this case received. A related issue arose in a case in which another ISDA Master

Agreement entered into by Lehman Brothers Special Financing had a provision that ensured that a party who defaulted and was owed a termination payment under an ISDA Master Agreement would be paid after nearly all other creditors of the non-defaulting party were paid.

In that case, *Lehman Brothers Special Financing Inc. v. Ballyrock ABS CDO 2007-1 Limited (In re Lehman Brothers Holdings Inc.)*,[16] the non-defaulting party was a special purpose vehicle and the result of subordinating payment to the defaulting party was to, in effect, not pay the defaulting party to the extent the defaulting party was otherwise owed a termination amount. The special purpose vehicle was a collateralized debt obligation, commonly known as a "CDO." Its income, revenue from asset-backed securities, was finely tuned to bring slightly more revenue each month than its liabilities, generally payments on notes issued by the vehicle.

Because the revenue was finely tuned to the liabilities, rating agencies were concerned about the effect of a sudden liability on the vehicle, such as if Lehman Brothers Special Financing defaulted when the vehicle was out-of-the-money, resulting in a large one-time termination payment payable by the vehicle to Lehman Brothers Special Financing. Therefore, at the time the vehicle was structured, rating agencies required that, if such an event occurred, the termination payment would be deeply subordinated so that it was only payable after the noteholders and other creditors were fully repaid and, in addition, capped at $30,000.

The question before the court was whether such an arrangement hinged on an unenforceable *ipso facto* clause. The court concluded that it was since the provisions subordinating the payments due to its parent Lehman Brothers Holdings "effectively eliminate the right to receive a termination payment. . . ."[17] Unlike in *BNY Corporate Trustee Services Limited*, no leave to appeal was granted by the district court.[18]

Additionally, it is important to note that this structure bears much similarity to a so-called walk away clause that allows a non-defaulting party to a swap to recuse itself from all obligations. Such "walk away" clauses are statutorily unenforceable against most types of financial institutions in the event of such institution's conservatorship or receivership.[19] Since no statutory prohibition in effect at the time applied to Lehman Brothers Special Financing, the question before the court was whether such an arrangement functioned as an unenforceable *ipso facto* clause.[20]

---

16. 452 B.R. 31 (Bankr. S.D.N.Y. 2011)

17. *Id.* at 43.

18. *See Lehman Brothers Special Financing Inc. v. Ballyrock ABS CDO 2007-1 Limited (In re Lehman Brothers Holdings Inc.)*, 2011 WL 9375423 (Bankr. S.D.N.Y. Nov. 3, 2011).

19. *See* 12 U.S.C. §1787(c)(8)(G) (credit unions), 12 U.S.C. 1821(e)(8)(G) (insured depository institutions), 12 U.S.C. 4617(d)(8)(G) (Federal National Mortgage Association, known as "Fannie Mae," the Federal Home Loan Mortgage Corporation, known as "Freddie Mac," and any Federal Home Loan Bank), and 12 U.S.C. §5390(c)(8)(F) (covered financial company as defined in 12 U.S.C. §5381(a)(8)).

20. An advisory committee of the American Bankruptcy Institute Commission to Study the Reform of Chapter 11 has recommended that walk-away clauses be made statutorily unenforceable

Outside of a bankruptcy context, at least two district courts have found that a walk away clause is enforceable. One of the decisions was in 1992 when a district court ruled that a swap agreement allowing for the non-defaulting party to "walk away" from its obligations was "a valid liquidated damages clause and is, therefore, enforceable. . . ."[21] The other was in 2010 and found that a clause allowing one party to walk away from a swap agreement due to the insolvency of the other party was not an unenforceable penalty provision.[22]

Later, the same bankruptcy judge whose decision was the subject of the appeal in *BNY Corporate Trustee Services Limited* and who decided *Ballyrock*, evaluated the breadth of the safe harbor for derivatives providers allowing "termination, liquidation, or acceleration" of a swap agreement even where it is triggered by the bankruptcy of one of the parties. The dispute centered on whether the safe harbor protected a valuation methodology based on quotations from swap dealers indicating the price they would pay to assume the swap (which includes a "bid" or "offer" spread) instead of using "mid-market," which does not include such spreads. The former valuation methodology resulted in a worse economic outcome for the debtor and was triggered only by its bankruptcy.

In many ways, the dispute appeared similar to *BNY Corporate Trustee Services Limited* and *Ballyrock*. Yet, Judge Peck, ruling in a way that was arguably contradictory to each of these cases, sought to distinguish them in the below case.

Michigan State Housing Development Authority v. Lehman Brothers Derivatives Products Inc. (In re Lehman Brothers Holdings Inc.)

502 B.R. 383 (Bankr. S.D.N.Y. 2013)

James M. Peck, United States Bankruptcy Judge

Lehman in its heyday structured and engaged in a dizzying array of sophisticated financial transactions using swaps. . . . As a consequence of that vast and varied prepetition activity in the derivatives markets, these bankruptcy cases have turned out to be a proving ground for interpreting, applying and testing the boundaries of the safe harbor provisions of the United States Bankruptcy Code (the "Bankruptcy Code").

This decision is the latest to consider the scope of the safe harbor for liquidating, terminating and accelerating swap agreements. . . . The question goes to the heart of this safe harbor: if the exercise of a contractual right to cause the liquidation of a

---

if triggered by a bankruptcy of the defaulting party. *See Financial Contracts, Derivatives and Safe Harbors Advisory Committee*, Full Committee Meeting Minutes/Summary 2 (Apr. 2, 2013).

21. *Drexel Burnham Lambert Products Corp. v. Midland Bank PLC*, 1992 WL 12633422 at *2 (S.D.N.Y. Nov. 10, 1992).

22. *Brookfield Asset Management, Inc. v. AIG Financial Products Corp*, 2010 WL 3910590 (S.D.N.Y. Sept. 29, 2010).

swap agreement is protected, are the contractually specified means for conducting that liquidation so connected to the very concept of liquidation that they are also protected?

LBSF says no, arguing that the less favorable procedures triggered by a bankruptcy default are ineffective *ipso facto* alterations of a debtor's rights, and so do not fall within the safe harbor. Michigan State Housing Development Authority ("MSHDA") ... [argues] that the protected right to liquidate cannot be viewed as an isolated right and necessarily includes those contractual provisions that provide needed guidance for liquidating and closing out the swap agreement. ...

As explained in this decision, the Court has concluded that the protected right to liquidate must include a way to execute the liquidation in order to infuse the safe harbored right with meaning. ...

This right of the non-defaulting party to rely upon contractual norms for disposing of collateral is an integrated aspect of what it means to cause the liquidation of a swap agreement and necessarily is protected by the language of Section 560 of the Bankruptcy Code. To rule otherwise ... would strip away the defining characteristics of a contractual right to liquidation that by statute may not be limited in any manner. ...

At an earlier stage in these bankruptcy cases, the Court decided that the safe harbor provisions of Section 560 of the Bankruptcy Code do not extend to a bargained for change in the priority of distributions between LBSF as swap counterparty and certain investors in notes issued by a special purpose vehicle. That dispute dealt with the issue of whether a so-called "flip clause" triggered by a bankruptcy default is an ineffective *ipso facto* provision. ...

Despite the superficial similarity of the issues, the earlier determinations made with respect to impermissible changes to distribution priorities are not controlling. Here the question is more nuanced and closer to the statutory core of Section 560, leading to an examination of whether the methodology for conducting an indisputably exempt liquidation is also exempt. ...

Notwithstanding the argument of LBSF that a liquidation methodology triggered by bankruptcy that generates a smaller termination payment for the defaulting party is comparable to a "flip clause," the Court concludes otherwise. There is a significant difference between the reordering of priorities within a hierarchy of distributions (an *ipso facto* contractual term that is not mentioned in Section 560) and selecting which method to use when disposing and valuing collateral in connection with liquidating a terminated swap agreement. The choice of an accepted and contractually specified method to liquidate, even if it produces a less desirable result from the point of view of the debtor, is consistent with full implementation of the exemption that is codified in Section 560. ...

Accordingly ... the alternative approach to liquidation of collateral used by MSHDA is effective even though it is contained in an *ipso facto* provision because that alternative is protected by the safe harbor of Section 560 and, as a consequence, is not subject to Section 365(e)(1). . . .

What Judge Peck sought to distinguish in *Michigan State Housing Development Authority* is a clause depriving the bankruptcy debtor of a payment for the full market value of swaps transactions due to a change in payment priority triggered by bankruptcy (i.e., the facts at issue in *BNY Corporate Trustee Services* and *Ballyrock*) and a clause depriving the debtor of a payment for the full market value of swaps transactions due to a change in calculation methodology triggered by bankruptcy. This is an area where there remain uncertainties as to how the safe harbor is applied.

Ultimately, the Second Circuit weighed in on these questions and came to conclusions contrary to *BNY Corporate Trustee Services* and *Ballyrock* and largely consistent with *Michigan State Housing Development Authority*. The court also clarified that subordinating a payment is different than a penalty clause.

In re Lehman Brothers Holdings Inc.

970 F.3d 91 (2d Cir. 2020)

Per Curiam:

The Bankruptcy Code generally bars enforcement of "*ipso facto* clauses," which trigger or modify payment obligations when a party seeks relief in bankruptcy. Lehman Brothers Special Financing Inc. ("LBSF") seeks to recover payments made to defendant noteholders (the "Noteholders") in connection with certain synthetic collateralized debt obligations. LBSF argues that "Priority Provisions" that subordinated its interests to those of the Noteholders were unenforceable *ipso facto* clauses because they were triggered as a result of the Chapter 11 bankruptcy of Lehman Brothers Holdings Inc. ("LBHI").[23] The Bankruptcy Court held (and the District Court agreed) that section 560 of the Bankruptcy Code (the "Code"), which creates a safe harbor for the liquidation of swap agreements, allowed the distribution of proceeds according to the Priority Provisions whether or not those provisions are properly characterized as *ipso facto* clauses. For the reasons set forth below, we AFFIRM the judgment of the District Court. . . .

On September 15, 2008, LBHI filed a voluntary petition for relief under Chapter 11. Two weeks later, on October 3, LBSF, an indirect subsidiary of LBHI, began its own Chapter 11 proceeding. About two years later, in September 2010, LBSF initiated an adversary proceeding against 250 defendant noteholders, note issuers, and indenture trustees in connection with 44 synthetic collateralized debt obligations

---

23. [N. 1] The LBHI bankruptcy is considered to be the largest bankruptcy proceeding in U.S. history: When it filed for bankruptcy, LBHI held consolidated assets of $639 billion and liabilities of $613 billion.

("CDOs") that Lehman affiliates structured, negotiated, and marketed (each, a "synthetic CDO transaction"). LBSF sought to recover roughly $1 billion that was distributed to the Noteholders after LBSF defaulted. . . .

In each of the synthetic CDO transactions, LBSF and its affiliates (collectively, "Lehman") established a special purpose vehicle (the "Issuer") through which it marketed and sold notes (the "Notes") to the Noteholders pursuant to an Indenture Agreement. The Issuer then used the proceeds from sale of the Notes to acquire highly rated securities; those valuable securities, in turn, would serve as collateral (the "Collateral"). The Issuer used income generated by the Collateral to make scheduled interest payments to the Noteholders.

The Issuer then entered into a "swap agreement" with LBSF, pursuant to an ISDA Master Agreement and other related contracts, including the Schedule and Confirmation.[24] Under the swap agreement, the Issuer contracted to sell LBSF a credit default swap — credit protection against the potential default of certain "reference entities" or "reference obligations." In exchange, LBSF made regular payments to the Issuer. (LBHI guaranteed LBSF's obligations under the swap.) The Issuer used the flow of payments it received from LBSF to supplement the interest payments it made to the Noteholders.

The swap agreement provided that if the reference entities experienced certain "Credit Events," the Issuer could owe LBSF payment from the Collateral. If, by contrast, the transaction reached its scheduled maturity *without* a Credit Event occurring, then the Noteholders would be repaid the principal amount of their investment from the Collateral. The Trustees — a third party entity — held the Collateral in trust for the benefit of the secured parties — primarily LBSF and the Noteholders.

As described above, the two components of the synthetic CDO transaction — the CDO and the swap — were documented separately, but the swap and indenture agreements (the "Transaction Documents") referenced each other. The Indenture Agreement specified that, upon the occurrence of an "Event of Default," the Trustees were empowered to issue a "Termination Notice," which would accelerate payment due on the Notes and trigger early termination of the swaps. After issuing a Termination Notice, the Trustee could — but was not required to — liquidate the Collateral, and distribute the proceeds according to the stated priority of payments ("Priority Provisions"). Under the Priority Provisions, LBSF enjoyed payment priority over the Noteholders in certain circumstances. But in other circumstances — including in the case of LBSF's default — LBSF's payment was subordinated to that of the Noteholders.

LBHI's bankruptcy filing in 2008 constituted an Event of Default under the ISDA Master Agreement, with LBSF as the defaulting party. LBSF's default triggered the early terminations of the credit default swaps. Those terminations, in turn, led to

---

24. [N. 3] An ISDA Master Agreement is a standard form, published by the International Swaps and Derivatives Association, regularly used to govern over-the-counter derivatives transactions.

the liquidation of the Collateral and to subsequent distributions. Because LBSF defaulted, it dropped in priority and was entitled to receive its portion of the disbursement only after the Noteholders received their portion.

When the early terminations occurred, LBSF was "in the money" — that is, its swap position had value — but because it was also the defaulting party, the Noteholders received payment priority over LBSF. The proceeds from the Collateral were insufficient to make any payment to LBSF after they were drawn from to pay the Noteholders. This precipitous drop in LBSF's priority underlies the dispute between LBSF and defendants in this case. Specifically, at issue is the enforceability in bankruptcy of those contractual provisions — the Priority Provisions — that subordinated LBSF's payment priority upon its default. . . .

In September 2010, LBSF commenced an adversary proceeding in Bankruptcy Court as a putative defendant class action against certain of the Noteholders, the Trustees, and the Issuers. It alleged first that the Priority Provisions are unenforceable *ipso facto* clauses — that is, clauses that modify a debtor's contractual right solely because it petitioned for bankruptcy. *See* 11 U.S.C. § 365(e); *Lehman Bros. Holdings Inc. v. BNY Corp. Tr. Servs. Ltd.*, 422 B.R. 407, 415 (Bankr. S.D.N.Y. 2010) ("*BNY*") ("It is now axiomatic that *ipso facto* clauses are, as a general matter, unenforceable."). It next claimed that the distributions to the Noteholders violated the automatic stay provision in the Bankruptcy Code.[25] Finally, LBSF sought a clawback of the distributions under various other provisions of the Code and asserted several common-law causes of action. Five years later, defendants filed an omnibus motion to dismiss, which the Bankruptcy Court (Chapman, J.) granted. *See Lehman Bros. Special Fin. Inc. v. Bank of Am. Nat'l Ass'n (In re Lehman Bros. Holdings Inc.)*, 553 B.R. 476 (Bankr. S.D.N.Y. 2016) ("*Lehman I*"). . . .

LBSF appealed to the District Court (Schofield, J.), which affirmed. *Lehman Bros. Special Fin. Inc. v. Bank of Am. Nat'l Ass'n (In re Lehman Bros. Holdings Inc.)*, 17 Civ. 1224 (LGS), 2018 WL 1322225 (S.D.N.Y. Mar. 14, 2018) ("*Lehman II*"). Resolving LBSF's bankruptcy-law claims, the court rested its decision entirely on . . . that the Code's safe harbor provision in section 560 permits the enforcement of the Priority Provisions. The District Court also affirmed the dismissal of all of LBSF's state-law claims. LBSF again appeals. . . .

LBSF contends that the Priority Provisions that subordinated its claims and eliminated its priority upon its default are unenforceable *ipso facto* clauses. We disagree. . . .

The Bankruptcy Code generally prohibits enforcement of *ipso facto* clauses — contract clauses that modify or terminate an executory contract due to a debtor's

---

25. [N. 4] Section 362(a) of the Code provides, in relevant part, that the filing of a petition under Chapter 11 "operates as a stay, applicable to all entities, of . . . any act to obtain possession of property of the estate or of property from the estate or to exercise control over property of the estate." 11 U.S.C. § 362(a).

filing of a bankruptcy petition. A number of provisions in the Code effect this prohibition. Section 365(e)(1) of the Code provides:

> [A]n executory contract . . . may not be terminated or modified, and any right or obligation under such contract . . . may not be terminated or modified, at any time after the commencement of the case solely because of a provision in such contract . . . that is conditioned on — (A) the insolvency or financial condition of the debtor at any time before the closing of the case; (B) the commencement of a case under this title; or (C) the appointment of or taking possession by a trustee in a case under this title or a custodian before such commencement.

11 U.S.C. § 365(e)(1). In other words, section 365(e) curtails creditors' ability to modify contracts with a bankrupt party. This general ban helps "deter the race of diligence of creditors to dismember the debtor before bankruptcy and promote equality of distribution." *Merit Mgmt. Grp. v. FTI Consulting, Inc.*, —— U.S. ——, 138 S. Ct. 883, 888, 200 L.Ed.2d 183 (2018) ("*Merit Management*") (internal quotation marks omitted) (discussing an analogous safe harbor provision).

Section 541 of the Code also effects the prohibition of *ipso facto* clauses by providing that a debtor's interest in property

> becomes property of the estate . . . notwithstanding any provision in an agreement, transfer instrument, or applicable nonbankruptcy law . . . that is conditioned on . . . the commencement of a case under this title . . . and that effects or gives an option to effect a forfeiture, modification, or termination of the debtor's interest in property.

11 U.S.C. § 541(c)(1).

Section 363(*l*) further implements the Code's ban on *ipso facto* clauses by preserving the right of the bankruptcy trustee to take certain actions using the property belonging to the bankruptcy estate[26]:

> [T]he trustee may use, sell, or lease property . . . notwithstanding any provision in a contract, a lease, or applicable law that is conditioned on . . . the commencement of a case under this title concerning the debtor . . . and that effects . . . a forfeiture, modification, or termination of the debtor's interest in such property.

11 U.S.C. § 363(*l*). These anti-*ipso facto* provisions strip non-bankrupt counterparties of certain contractual rights they otherwise have and prevent them from collecting debts due from the bankrupt party.

Section 560 carves out an exception, however, and exempts swap agreements from the prohibition of *ipso facto* clauses by protecting a swap participant's contractual

---

26. [N.6] Section 541 of the Code defines the bankruptcy estate to include, *inter alia*, "all legal or equitable interests of the debtor in property as of the commencement of the case." 11 U.S.C. § 541(a)(1)

right to terminate, liquidate, or accelerate a transaction upon a counterparty's bankruptcy:

> The exercise of any contractual right of any swap participant or financial participant to cause the liquidation, termination, or acceleration of one or more swap agreements because of a condition of the kind in section 365(e) (1) of this title [the prohibition on *ipso facto* clauses] or to offset or net out any termination values or payment amounts arising under or in connection with the termination, liquidation, or acceleration of one or more swap agreements shall not be stayed, avoided, or otherwise limited by operation of any provision of this title or by order of a court or administrative agency in any proceeding under this title.

11 U.S.C. § 560. In other words, this safe harbor permits swap participants to modify or terminate an executory contract solely because of the commencement of a bankruptcy case. Originally added to the Code in 1990, section 560 was meant to protect the stability of swap markets and to ensure that swap markets are "not destabilized by uncertainties regarding the treatment of their financial instruments under the Bankruptcy Code." *See* H.R. Rep. No. 101-484, at 1 (1990), *as reprinted in* 1990 U.S.C.C.A.N. 223, 223; *see also* 136 Cong. Rec. S7534-01 (daily ed. June 6, 1990) (statement of Sen. DeConcini) (asserting that the "potential for disruption in the financial markets justified the creation of an exclusion for these contracts from the usual powers of a bankruptcy trustee").

Congress amended section 560 in the Bankruptcy Abuse Prevention and Consumer Protection Act of 2005, Pub. L. No. 109-8, 119 Stat. 23 (2005) (codified in 11 U.S.C.) (the "2005 Act"). Relevant here, the 2005 Act broadened the definition of "swap agreement" to include virtually all derivatives. *See* 11 U.S.C. § 101(53B). The revised section 560 also clarifies that a swap participant's contractual right to liquidate and accelerate a swap agreement—in addition to its right to terminate the swap—are protected under the safe harbor provision. *See* 11 U.S.C. § 560. . . .

LBSF maintains that the Priority Provisions—which define the payment order for distributions of proceeds from the Collateral—are unenforceable *ipso facto* clauses because they modify and downgrade LBSF's right to receive proceeds. Defendants urge that the section 560 safe harbor authorizes enforcement of the Priority Provisions, even if they contain *ipso facto* clauses. The applicability of the safe harbor turns on whether, under section 560, the following conditions apply: (1) the Priority Provisions are "swap agreements"; (2) the distribution of the Collateral constitutes "liquidation"; and (3) the Trustees, in liquidating the Collateral and distributing its proceeds, exercised a "contractual right of a[] swap participant."

Like the District Court, we hold that, even if the Priority Provisions were *ipso facto* clauses, their enforcement was nevertheless permissible under the section 560 safe harbor. . . .

Section 101(53B) of the Bankruptcy Code defines a "swap agreement" to include "any agreement, *including the terms and conditions incorporated by reference in such agreement*, which is" a swap. 11 U.S.C. §101(53B)(A)(i) (emphasis added). . . .

Neither party disputes that the Code's sweeping definition of "swap agreement" includes the ISDA Master Agreement, along with the related schedule and confirmation documents. LBSF contends, however, that the Priority Provisions — laid out in the Indenture Agreement — are not part of the swap agreement, and, therefore, are not protected under the section 560 safe harbor. We disagree: The ISDA Master Agreement incorporates by reference the Priority Provisions, and, therefore, the Priority Provisions, too, are swap agreements under section 560. . . .

Section 560 affords safe harbor from the prohibition on *ipso facto* clauses when a swap participant exercises its contractual right "to cause *the liquidation, termination, or acceleration* of one or more swap agreements." 11 U.S.C. §560 (emphasis added). The question here is whether application of the Priority Provisions — and distribution of the Collateral according to those Priority Provisions — constitutes the "liquidation" of a swap agreement under section 560.

The parties dispute the meaning of the term "liquidation" as used in section 560. Because the Bankruptcy Code does not define the term "liquidation," we interpret the term according to its "ordinary, contemporary, common meaning." *Sandifer v. U.S. Steel Corp.*, 571 U.S. 220, 227, 134 S.Ct. 870, 187 L.Ed.2d 729 (2014) (internal quotation marks omitted). Considered in the abstract, to "liquidate" might plausibly mean "[t]o settle (an obligation) by payment or other adjustment" or "[t]o ascertain the precise amount of (debt, damages, etc.)." *Liquidate*, Black's Law Dictionary (10th ed. 2014). The term thus might refer to the act of ascertaining the precise amount of debt, as LBSF maintains. Alternatively, it could refer to the process of winding down a transaction, as defendants urge. Bearing in mind "the specific context in which that language is used," *Merit Management*, 138 S. Ct. at 892-93, we conclude that the term "liquidation," as used in section 560, must include the disbursement of proceeds from the liquidated Collateral. . . .

Reading section 560's reference to "liquidation" of a swap agreement to include distribution of the Collateral furthers the statutory purpose of protecting swap participants from the risks of a counterparty's bankruptcy filing by permitting parties to quickly unwind the swap. . . .

In a last attempt to avoid the consequences of the section 560 safe harbor, LBSF contends that the Trustees who terminated the swaps and distributed the proceeds of the Collateral were not "swap participants." As a result, LBSF continues, the Trustees' actions fall outside the ambit of section 560's safe harbor, which expressly protects certain contractual rights of "swap participant[s]" only. 11 U.S.C. §560.

Section 101(53C) defines "swap participant" as "an entity that, any time before the filing of the petition, has an outstanding swap agreement with the debtor." Neither party disputes that the Issuers, as parties to the swaps, were "swap participants" under the Bankruptcy Code. The Transaction Documents grant the Issuers the right to terminate the Swaps and liquidate the Collateral, and expressly permit the Trustees to exercise those rights. Section 7.7(c) of the Indenture, for instance, instructs that the "Issuer shall enforce all of its material rights and remedies under the Credit Swaps." App'x 1601. And section 10.1 of the Indenture expressly grants to the Trustee all of the Issuer's rights, title, and interest in the Swap. Specifically, it provides that "[t]he Issuer shall enter into the Credit Swaps . . . and shall Grant its interest therein to the Trustee." *Id.* at 1618. . . .

[T]he mere fact that the Trustees (rather than the Issuers) liquidated the swap does not place the transaction outside the safe harbor. Here, the Transaction Documents enabled the Issuers to grant their right to terminate and liquidate to the Trustees. The Trustees therefore exercised the contractual rights of a swap participant. . . .

[Finally,] LBSF seeks a declaratory judgment that the Priority Provisions constitute unenforceable penalties under New York law by depriving it of payments it was allegedly owed. The penalty doctrine applies to liquidated damages clauses where the "damages [are] grossly disproportionate to the amount of actual damages." *172 Van Duzer Realty Corp. v. Globe Alumni Student Assistance Ass'n,* 24 N.Y.3d 528, 2 N.Y.S.3d 39, 25 N.E.3d 952, 957 (2014) (internal quotation marks omitted). As both the Bankruptcy Court and District Court remarked, however, the Priority Provisions do not fix damages, but rather subordinate LBSF's payment priority. The District and Bankruptcy Courts thus correctly concluded that LBSF is not entitled to declaratory relief. . . .

For the foregoing reasons, the judgment of the District Court is AFFIRMED.

———————

All of the decisions seem to align on one point — that a penalty clause would not be enforceable in this context in bankruptcy. However, the subordination of the termination payment due to Lehman Brothers Special Financing seem to have had the same outcome as a penalty. A future judicial challenge may be distinguishing between a subordination clause and a hidden penalty.

b. Timing Requirements and Payment Suspension

Though the Bankruptcy Code protects the right of a party to a derivatives agreement to terminate the agreement even if triggered by the bankruptcy of the other party to the agreement, it does not explicitly limit the period in which the non-defaulting party can elect to terminate the agreement. The question of whether such a time period should be imputed arose in the following case when a creditor terminated a swap seven weeks after its counterparty had filed for bankruptcy due to unsuccessful interim negotiations with the debtor.

In re Mirant Corporation

314 B.R. 347 (Bankr. N.D. Tex. 2004)

Dennis Michael Lynn, Bankruptcy Judge.

Before the court is Debtors' Motion for the Entry of an Order (i) Enforcing the Automatic Stay Prohibiting MediaNews Group, Inc. ["MNG"] from Terminating its Swap Agreement with the Debtors, (ii) Holding MediaNews in Civil Contempt of the Automatic Stay, (iii) Assessing Sanctions, and (iv) Granting Related Relief (the "Motion"). . . .

Debtors' business is principally the production, purchase, sale and trading of energy products. Debtors conduct their trading and marketing activities through Mirant Americas Energy Marketing, L.P. ("MAEM"). Besides participating in the energy markets, MAEM has from time to time traded for profit various non-energy commodity derivatives including swap agreements.

In the course of that business, on March 17, 1998, MAEM and MNG entered into an International Swap Dealers Association Master Agreement (the "Swap Agreement") by which MAEM and MNG agreed to exchange quarterly cash flows for a period beginning May 1, 1998 and running through April, 2005 based on the pricing of 48.8 gram newsprint. Under the Swap Agreement, MAEM effectively guaranteed MNG a fixed price for newsprint. In other words, if the market price for 48.8 gram newsprint in a given quarter was higher than the price fixed pursuant to the Swap Agreement Schedules, MAEM would be liable to MNG for the difference; if the fixed price exceeded market, MNG would pay MAEM. At all times pertinent to resolution of the Motion, MAEM was "in the money," i.e., the market price of 48.8 gram newsprint was less than the fixed price established by the Swap Agreement.

On July 14, 2003, MAEM filed for relief under chapter 11 of the Bankruptcy Code (the "Code"). . . .

On July 15, 2003, MNG learned of Debtors' chapter 11 cases. . . .

[After negotiations between the parties regarding the Swap Agreement], MNG determined it would exercise its right under section 560 of the Code to terminate the Swap Agreement. On September 4, 2003, . . . [MNG] sent a letter to MAEM advising of the termination, and on September 16, 2003 . . . [MNG] sent a second letter to MAEM . . . [which] advised that MNG had calculated net amounts due to MAEM under the terminated Swap Agreement at $1,135,578. . . .

It is Debtors' position that MNG's termination of the Swap Agreement violated the automatic stay of section 362(a) of the Code. Although sections 362(b)(17) and 560 of the Code exempt from the automatic stay actions taken by a swap participant to terminate or settle a swap agreement, Debtors argue that those provisions are applicable only if the swap participant is terminating and settling the swap agreement in response to a bankruptcy filing. As MNG waited seven weeks after MAEM's case was commenced before terminating the Swap Agreement, Debtors argue MNG was unable to take advantage of sections 362(b)(17) and 560.

Alternatively Debtors insist that MNG "waived" its termination rights by its actions . . . [negotiating with MAEN] between July 15, 2003 and September 4, 2003. . . .

The court does not find merit in either of these arguments. MNG quite reasonably thought it was protected as a Counterparty under [an Interim Order issued by the judge]. . . . Only on September 4, 2003 did MNG learn Debtors contested its right to invoke the Interim Order (and . . . [a] Final Order [subsequently issued]). When MNG learned . . . [this] it determined that it should terminate the Swap Agreement because of Debtors' chapter 11 cases. Debtors urge that MNG's motives were economic: it would be cheaper for MNG to terminate than to continue the Swap Agreement, as MNG was "out of the money." That may be so, but it would be inequitable to allow Debtors now to spring a trap on MNG. Having on July 15, Debtors' first day in chapter 11, given MNG good reason to believe it was covered by the Interim Order and then, on September 4, having refused to acknowledge that coverage, Debtors would be enjoying their cake and yet keeping it whole if the court were to hold that through the passage of time MNG lost its right under Code § 560 to terminate. . . .

It has often been said that the automatic stay of section 362(a) is a shield for a debtor, not a sword to be used offensively. . . . [I]n the case at bar, Debtors appear to be attempting to use the automatic stay and this court's orders in a pincer attack on MNG. Even if MNG had technically violated the automatic stay, the court would not find it equitable to penalize MNG on these facts.

However, MNG did not violate the stay. It was a swap participant that was party to a swap agreement. By reason of MAEM's bankruptcy MNG invoked its rights under Code §§ 362(b)(17) and 560 to terminate the Swap Agreement. It did not waive those rights. Therefore MNG's actions were authorized under section 362(b)(17) and 560 of the Code and the orders entered by this court. . . .

For the foregoing reasons, the Motion must be, and is, DENIED. Any court costs shall be charged to Debtors. Counsel for Debtors shall prepare and submit to the court an order consistent with this opinion.

In *Mirant*, at issue was a seven-week delay that the judge attributed to a large extent to the debtor. In another bankruptcy case, *In re Enron Corporation*, a one-year delay after the bankruptcy of a debtor in terminating a swap agreement was found to result in forfeiture of the safe harbor protections:

> In essence, the Claimant is seeking to achieve, through equity, the statutory protections Congress limited to, among others, a participant in a swap agreement who, based upon the bankruptcy, elects to terminate the swap agreement as provided under section 560 of the Bankruptcy Code. To avail itself of the "safe harbor" provisions of the Bankruptcy Code, however, the swap participant must opt for the early termination of the swap agreement based upon one of the reasons enumerated in section 365(e)(1) of the Bankruptcy Code and if based upon the bankruptcy filing, the election to

terminate must be made fairly contemporaneously with the bankruptcy filing. Here, [Claimant] could not have opted for the safe harbor protection when the rejection notice was provided because it was more than one year after the bankruptcy filing and therefore any termination would not be because of a condition of the kind specified in section 365(e)(1) [of] the Bankruptcy Code. Further, the record supports a finding that the termination was not prompted by the financial condition of the debtor since such condition was present for nearly two years and [Claimant] never took any action to terminate the contract such as, for example, availing itself of the Early Termination provisions.[27]

On the other hand, if the Bankruptcy Code is silent as to any time period, how would the non-bankrupt party be on notice as to what period should apply? In a case, *In re Southern California Edison Company*, evaluating whether a party waived its termination rights after a less than ninety day delay, the court noted:

> [T]he statutory language does not mention the timing of termination. . . . As a result, . . . [the non-bankrupt party] could not have known that it was required to move "quickly" after its counterparty filed bankruptcy to avoid waiver.[28]

Highlighting the conundrum in the context of a swap, in the following case, a party forbore from terminating a swap agreement with a bankrupt debtor to benefit from a provision that allowed it to indefinitely suspend its performance. This was because it was "out-of-the-money" and thus would have had to pay a termination payment if the agreement were terminated. In this case, the party was found to have waived the benefits of the safe harbor provisions.

As background, ISDA Master Agreements contain a clause, section 2(a)(iii) allowing a party to refrain from paying a defaulting counterparty. Metavante Corporation used this clause to suspend payments to Lehman Brothers Special Financing Inc. after the bankruptcy of its guarantor, Lehman Brothers Holdings, Inc., triggered an event of default under the ISDA, while declining to exercise its right to terminate the agreement. If the agreement terminated, Metavante would have owed Lehman Brothers Special Financing a termination payment. By suspending payments using section 2(a)(iii) of the ISDA Master Agreement instead of terminating the agreement, Metavante sought to avoid making this termination payment.

In re Lehman Brothers Holdings, Inc.

No. 08-13555 (JMP) (Bankr. S.D.N.Y Sept. 15, 2009)

. . . [Lehman Brothers Special Financing Inc. ("LBSF")] requests that the Court compel [Metavante Corporation ("Metavante")] . . . to perform its obligations under that certain 1992 ISDA Master Agreement dated as of November 20, 2007, defined

---

27. *In re Enron Corp.*, 2005 WL 3874285 at *4 (Bankr. S.D.N.Y Oct. 5, 2005).
28. *In re Southern California Edison Company*, 2018 WL 949223 at *4 (S.D. Tex. Feb. 15, 2018).

as the "Master Agreement". And that certain trade confirmation dated December 4, 2007, defined as the "Confirmation", and together with the Master Agreement, the "Agreement." . . .

[T]he value of LBSF's position under the Agreement has increased. As of May 2009, under the payment terms of the Agreement, Metavante owed LBSF in excess of 6 million dollars. . . .

Metavante has refused to make any payments to LBSF. In fact, it has refused to perform its obligations under the Agreement. . . . Instead, Metavante claims that LBSF and LBHI, via the filing of their respective Chapter 11 cases, each caused an event of default under the Agreement.

Metavante argues that due to such events of default it has the right, but not the obligation, under the safe harbor provisions of the Bankruptcy Code, to terminate all outstanding derivative transactions under the Agreement. Metavante also maintains that it is not otherwise required to perform under the Agreement. . . .

In the instant case Metavante has refused to perform under the Agreement on account of the event of default that has occurred, and is continuing, on account of the bankruptcies of LBSF and LBHI. Metavante has not, however, attempted to terminate the Agreement. . . .

The safe harbor provisions permit qualifying non-debtor counterparties to derivative contracts to exercise certain limited contractual rights triggered by, among other things, a Chapter 11 filing. They're available, however, only to the extent that a counterparty seeks to one, liquidate, terminate or accelerate its contracts or two, net out its positions. All other uses of *ipso facto* provisions remain unenforceable under the Bankruptcy Code.

Notably, Metavante does not dispute that it has failed to perform under the Agreement. . . . Metavante emphasizes the term, quote, "condition precedent" set forth in Sections [2(a)(i) and (iii)] . . . of the Agreement, which subject payment obligations to the condition precedent that no event of default with respect to the party has occurred and is continuing.

Metavante argues that under New York State contract law a failure of a condition precedent excuses a party's obligation to perform. Metavante states that its unequivocal right to suspend payments until the termination of the Agreement is fundamental to the manner in which swap parties government themselves. . . .

[T]he safe harbor provisions . . . protect a non-defaulting swap counterparty's contractual rights solely to liquidate, terminate or accelerate one or more swap agreements because of a condition of the kind specified in Section 365(e)(1). . . .

In the instant matter Metavante has attempted neither to liquidate, terminate or accelerate the Agreement. . . . Metavante simply is withholding performance, relying on the conditions precedent language in Sections 2(a)(i) and (iii) under the Agreement. . . .

The Court finds that Metavante's window to act promptly under the safe harbor provisions has passed, and while it may not have had the obligation to terminate immediately upon the filing of LBHI or LBSF, its failure to do so, at this juncture, constitutes a waiver of that right at this point. . . .

The court followed up two days later with an order requiring Metavante to perform under the agreement and to pay default interest for the missed payments.[29]

The decision at the time illuminated an apparent split between the U.S. and U.K. approach to the same issue, with the United Kingdom ruling that a party using Section 2(a)(iii) of the ISDA Master Agreement to suspend performance due to the default of a counterparty can do so (though the obligation will revive if the default is cured).[30] However, there is conflict between the decision in *In re Lehman Brothers Holdings, Inc.* and in *In re Southern California Edison Company Decision*, so it is possible that U.S. courts will ultimately rule similar to that of the U.K. courts on this issue. In the meantime, in the face of uncertainty, parties benefit from ensuring documentation reflects the interpretation of Section 2(a)(iii) they desire.

3. Payment Clawbacks

The Bankruptcy Code generally requires that payments made by the bankrupt debtor within ninety days of its bankruptcy be returned to the debtors' estate for distribution to the creditors (i.e., "clawed back") in accordance with the bankruptcy process.[31] This is extended to one year in the case of payments made to insiders of the debtor[32] and two years if there is "intent to hinder, delay, or defraud" or there is "less than a reasonably equivalent value" in exchange for such payment and the debtor at such time was nearly insolvent or insolvent.[33]

The purpose is to prevent a debtor — knowing a bankruptcy filing is a possibility — from transferring its assets away so that they are unavailable to its creditors or to pay off favored creditors.

Futures commission merchants and parties to swaps are exempt from this requirement so long as payments made are pursuant to the relevant agreement.[34]

> *Example A*: The Western Pacific Oil Company enters into an energy swap with the Great Northern Swap Corporation with payments due by the

---

29. *In re Lehman Brothers Holdings Inc.*, 2009 WL 6057286 (Bankr. S.D.N.Y. Sept. 17, 2009).

30. *See Lomas and others v. JFB Firth Rixson Inc and others*, [2012] EWCA Civ 419, ¶¶ 31 and 35. For a similar decision in New South Wales, Australia, see *Sims and Singleton as Liquidators of Enron Australia Pty Limited v TXU Electricity Limited & Anor*, [2005] NSWCA 12.

31. 11 U.S.C. § 547(b)(4).

32. *Id.*

33. 11 U.S.C. § 548(a)(1).

34. *See* 11 U.S.C. §§ 546(e) and (g) and 11 U.S.C. § 548(d)(2).

out-of-the-money party to the in-the-money party on the fifth calendar day of each month. (See chapter 1, sections B.2 and 3 for how "in-the-money" and "out-of-the-money" are determined.) On June 5, July 5, and August 5, the Great Northern Swap Corporation is out-of-the-money and makes the appropriate payments to the Western Pacific Oil Company. On August 10, the Great Northern Swap Corporation acknowledges that it has been insolvent for half a year and files for bankruptcy.

Result: Although generally such payments made by the Great Northern Swap Corporation within ninety days of its bankruptcy would need to be returned, this is not the case here since they were payments made in the ordinary course under the swap agreement between the parties.

Example B: Let us assume the same facts as in Example A except that the Great Northern Swap Corporation doubles the required payments in June, July, and August because the Western Pacific Oil Company "has been a good customer all these years."

Result: These amounts would be required to be "clawed back" and returned to Great Northern Swap Corporation's bankruptcy estate, to the extent they exceed what was provided for in the swap agreement, for distribution to creditors in accordance with the bankruptcy process.

There is a distinction in application of this safe harbor for swaps and other derivatives. For derivatives other than swaps, the payment to be clawed back must be by or to a "commodity broker, forward contract merchant, stockbroker, financial institution, financial participant, or securities clearing agency" to qualify for the safe harbor protection.[35] For swaps, the mere existence of a swap agreement is sufficient.[36]

The question arose as to whether, for securities (and, implicitly, derivatives other than bilateral swaps), it is sufficient to have an intermediary that is a commodity broker, forward contract merchant, stockbroker, financial institution, financial participant, or securities clearing agency, or whether one of the parties to the transaction subject to the potential clawback must be such an entity. Although the following case related to a securities transaction in a merger and acquisition, and not a derivative, the questions it raised apply equally to derivatives other than swaps.

---

35. 11 U.S.C. § 546(e).

36. 11 U.S.C. § 546(g). Though there is a reference to a payment being to or from a "swap participant," the Bankruptcy Code defines a "swap participant" as any party to a swap agreement. 11 U.S.C. § 101(53C).

Merit Management Group v. FTI Consulting

138 S. Ct. 883 (2018)

Justice Sotomayor delivered the opinion of the Court.

To maximize the funds available for, and ensure equity in, the distribution to creditors in a bankruptcy proceeding, the Bankruptcy Code gives a trustee the power to invalidate a limited category of transfers by the debtor or transfers of an interest of the debtor in property. Those powers, referred to as "avoiding powers," are not without limits, however, as the Code sets out a number of exceptions. The operation of one such exception, the securities safe harbor, 11 U.S.C. §546(e), is at issue in this case. Specifically, this Court is asked to determine how the safe harbor operates in the context of a transfer that was executed via one or more transactions, *e.g.*, a transfer from A → D that was executed via B and C as intermediaries, such that the component parts of the transfer include A → B → C → D. If a trustee seeks to avoid the A → D transfer, and the §546(e) safe harbor is invoked as a defense, the question becomes: When determining whether the §546(e) securities safe harbor saves the transfer from avoidance, should courts look to the transfer that the trustee seeks to avoid (*i.e.*, A → D) to determine whether that transfer meets the safe-harbor criteria, or should courts look also to any component parts of the overarching transfer (*i.e.*, A → B → C → D)? The Court concludes that the plain meaning of §546(e) dictates that the only relevant transfer for purposes of the safe harbor is the transfer that the trustee seeks to avoid. . . .

Because the §546(e) safe harbor operates as a limit to the general avoiding powers of a bankruptcy trustee,[37] we begin with a review of those powers. Chapter 5 of the Bankruptcy Code affords bankruptcy trustees the authority to "se[t] aside certain types of transfers . . . and . . . recaptur[e] the value of those avoided transfers for the benefit of the estate." Tabb §6.2, p. 474. These avoiding powers "help implement the core principles of bankruptcy." *Id.*, §6.1, at 468. For example, some "deter the race of diligence of creditors to dismember the debtor before bankruptcy" and promote "equality of distribution." *Union Bank v. Wolas,* 502 U.S. 151, 162, 112 S.Ct. 527, 116 L. Ed.2d 514 (1991) (internal quotation marks omitted); see also Tabb §6.2. Others set aside transfers that "unfairly or improperly deplete . . . assets or . . . dilute the claims against those assets." 5 Collier on Bankruptcy ¶ 548.01, p. 548–10 (16th ed. 2017); see also Tabb §6.2, at 475 (noting that some avoiding powers are designed "to ensure that the debtor deals fairly with its creditors"). . . .

---

37. [N. 1] Avoiding powers may be exercised by debtors, trustees, or creditors' committees, depending on the circumstances of the case. See generally C. Tabb, Law of Bankruptcy §6.1 (4th ed. 2016) (Tabb). Because this case concerns an avoidance action brought by a trustee, we refer throughout to the trustee in discussing the avoiding power and avoidance action. The resolution of this case is not dependent on the identity of the actor exercising the avoiding power.

The particular avoidance provision at issue here is § 548(a), which provides that a "trustee may avoid" certain fraudulent transfers "of an interest of the debtor in property." § 548(a)(1). Section 548(a)(1)(A) addresses so-called "actually" fraudulent transfers, which are "made . . . with actual intent to hinder, delay, or defraud any entity to which the debtor was or became . . . indebted." Section 548(a)(1)(B) addresses "constructively" fraudulent transfers. See *BFP v. Resolution Trust Corporation,* 511 U.S. 531, 535, 114 S.Ct. 1757, 128 L.Ed.2d 556 (1994). As relevant to this case, the statute defines constructive fraud in part as when a debtor:

"(B)(i) received less than a reasonably equivalent value in exchange for such transfer or obligation; and

"(ii)(I) was insolvent on the date that such transfer was made or such obligation was incurred, or became insolvent as a result of such transfer or obligation." 11 U.S.C. § 548(a)(1).

If a transfer is avoided, § 550 identifies the parties from whom the trustee may recover either the transferred property or the value of that property to return to the bankruptcy estate. Section 550(a) provides, in relevant part, that "to the extent that a transfer is avoided . . . the trustee may recover . . . the property transferred, or, if the court so orders, the value of such property" from "the initial transferee of such transfer or the entity for whose benefit such transfer was made," or from "any immediate or mediate transferee of such initial transferee." § 550(a). . . .

The Code sets out a number of limits on the exercise of these avoiding powers. . . . Central to this case is the securities safe harbor set forth in § 546(e), which provides (as presently codified and in full):

"Notwithstanding sections 544, 545, 547, 548(a)(1)(B), and 548(b) of this title, the trustee may not avoid a transfer that is a margin payment, as defined in section 101, 741, or 761 of this title, or settlement payment, as defined in section 101 or 741 of this title, made by or to (or for the benefit of) a commodity broker, forward contract merchant, stockbroker, financial institution, financial participant, or securities clearing agency, or that is a transfer made by or to (or for the benefit of) a commodity broker, forward contract merchant, stockbroker, financial institution, financial participant, or securities clearing agency, in connection with a securities contract, as defined in section 741(7), commodity contract, as defined in section 761(4), or forward contract, that is made before the commencement of the case, except under section 548(a)(1)(A) of this title."

The predecessor to this securities safe harbor, formerly codified at 11 U.S.C. § 764(c), was enacted in 1978 against the backdrop of a district court decision in a case called *Seligson v. New York Produce Exchange,* 394 F.Supp. 125 (S.D.N.Y.1975), which involved a transfer by a bankrupt commodity broker. See S. Rep. No. 95-989, pp. 8, 106 (1978); see also Brubaker, Understanding the Scope of the § 546(e) Securities Safe Harbor Through the Concept of the "Transfer" Sought To Be Avoided, 37 Bkrtcy. L. Letter 11–12 (July 2017). The bankruptcy trustee in *Seligson* filed suit seeking to avoid over $12 million in margin payments made by the commodity broker debtor to a clearing association on the basis that the transfer was constructively fraudulent. The clearing association attempted to defend on the theory that it was a mere "conduit" for the transmission of the margin payments. 394 F.Supp., at 135. The District Court found, however, triable issues of fact on that question and denied summary judgment, leaving the clearing association exposed to the risk of significant liability. See *id.,* at 135–136. Following that decision, Congress enacted the § 764(c) safe harbor, providing that "the trustee may not avoid a transfer that is a margin payment to or deposit with a commodity broker or forward contract merchant or is a settlement payment made by a clearing organization." 92 Stat. 2619, codified at 11 U.S.C. § 764(c) (repealed 1982).

Congress amended the securities safe harbor exception over the years, each time expanding the categories of covered transfers or entities. In 1982, Congress expanded the safe harbor to protect margin and settlement payments "made by or to a commodity broker, forward contract merchant, stockbroker, or securities clearing agency." § 4, 96 Stat. 236, codified at 11 U.S.C. § 546(d). Two years later Congress added "financial institution" to the list of protected entities. . . . In 2005, Congress again expanded the list of protected entities to include a "financial participant" (defined as an entity conducting certain high-value transactions). See § 907(b), 119 Stat. 181–182; 11 U.S.C. § 101(22A). And, in 2006, Congress amended the provision to cover transfers made in connection with securities contracts, commodity contracts, and forward contracts. § 5(b)(1), 120 Stat. 2697–2698. . . .

With this background, we now turn to the facts of this case, which comes to this Court from the world of competitive harness racing (a form of horse racing). Harness racing is a closely regulated industry in Pennsylvania, and the Commonwealth requires a license to operate a racetrack. . . . The number of available licenses is limited, and in 2003 two companies, Valley View Downs, LP, and Bedford Downs Management Corporation, were in competition for the last harness-racing license in Pennsylvania.

Valley View and Bedford Downs needed the harness-racing license to open a . . . racetrack casino. . . . Both companies were stopped before the finish line, because in 2005 the Pennsylvania State Harness Racing Commission denied both applications. The Pennsylvania Supreme Court upheld those denials in 2007, but allowed the companies to reapply for the license. . . .

Instead of continuing to compete for the last available harness-racing license, Valley View and Bedford Downs entered into an agreement to resolve their ongoing feud. Under that agreement, Bedford Downs withdrew as a competitor for the harness-racing license, and Valley View was to purchase all of Bedford Downs' stock for $55 million after Valley View obtained the license. . . .

With Bedford Downs out of the race, the Pennsylvania Harness Racing Commission awarded Valley View the last harness-racing license. Valley View proceeded with the corporate acquisition required by the parties' agreement and arranged for the Cayman Islands branch of Credit Suisse to finance the $55 million purchase price as part of a larger $850 million transaction. Credit Suisse wired the $55 million to Citizens Bank of Pennsylvania, which had agreed to serve as the third-party escrow agent for the transaction. The Bedford Downs shareholders, including petitioner Merit Management Group, LP, deposited their stock certificates into escrow as well. At closing, Valley View received the Bedford Downs stock certificates, and in October 2007 Citizens Bank disbursed $47.5 million to the Bedford Downs shareholders, with $7.5 million remaining in escrow at Citizens Bank under the multiyear indemnification holdback period provided for in the parties' agreement. Citizens Bank disbursed that $7.5 million installment to the Bedford Downs shareholders in October 2010, after the holdback period ended. All told, Merit received approximately $16.5 million from the sale of its Bedford Downs stock to Valley View. Notably, the closing statement for the transaction reflected Valley View as the "Buyer," the Bedford Downs shareholders as the "Sellers," and $55 million as the "Purchase Price." . . .

In the end, Valley View never got to open its racino. Although it had secured the last harness-racing license, it was unable to secure a separate gaming license for the operation of the slot machines in the time set out in its financing package. Valley View and its parent company, Centaur, LLC, thereafter filed for Chapter 11 bankruptcy. The Bankruptcy Court confirmed a reorganization plan and appointed respondent FTI Consulting, Inc., to serve as trustee of the Centaur litigation trust.

FTI filed suit against Merit in the Northern District of Illinois, seeking to avoid the $16.5 million transfer from Valley View to Merit for the sale of Bedford Downs' stock. The complaint alleged that the transfer was constructively fraudulent under § 548(a)(1)(B) of the Code because Valley View was insolvent when it purchased Bedford Downs and "significantly overpaid" for the Bedford Downs stock. . . . Merit moved for judgment on the pleadings under Federal Rule of Civil Procedure 12(c), contending that the § 546(e) safe harbor barred FTI from avoiding the Valley View-to-Merit transfer. According to Merit, the safe harbor applied because the transfer was a "settlement payment . . . made by or to (or for the benefit of)" a covered "financial institution" — here, Credit Suisse and Citizens Bank.

The District Court granted the Rule 12(c) motion, reasoning that the § 546(e) safe harbor applied because the financial institutions transferred or received funds in connection with a "settlement payment" or "securities contract." . . . The Court of Appeals for the Seventh Circuit reversed, holding that the § 546(e) safe harbor did not protect transfers in which financial institutions served as mere conduits. See 830 F.3d 690, 691 (2016). This Court granted certiorari to resolve a conflict among the circuit courts as to the proper application of the § 546(e) safe harbor. . . .

The question before this Court is whether the transfer between Valley View and Merit implicates the safe harbor exception because the transfer was "made by or to (or for the benefit of) a . . . financial institution." § 546(e). The parties and the lower courts dedicate much of their attention to the definition of the words "by or to (or for the benefit of)" as used in § 546(e), and to the question whether there is a requirement that the "financial institution" or other covered entity have a beneficial interest in or dominion and control over the transferred property in order to qualify for safe harbor protection. In our view, those inquiries put the proverbial cart before the horse. Before a court can determine whether a transfer was made by or to or for the benefit of a covered entity, the court must first identify the relevant transfer to test in that inquiry. At bottom, that is the issue the parties dispute in this case.

On one side, Merit posits that the Court should look not only to the Valley View-to-Merit end-to-end transfer, but also to all its component parts. Here, those component parts include one transaction by Credit Suisse to Citizens Bank (*i.e.,* the transmission of the $16.5 million from Credit Suisse to escrow at Citizens Bank), and two transactions by Citizens Bank to Merit (*i.e.,* the transmission of $16.5 million over two installments by Citizens Bank as escrow agent to Merit). Because those component parts include transactions by and to financial institutions, Merit contends that §546(e) bars avoidance.

FTI, by contrast, maintains that the only relevant transfer for purposes of the §546(e) safe-harbor inquiry is the overarching transfer between Valley View and Merit of $16.5 million for purchase of the stock, which is the transfer that the trustee seeks to avoid under §548(a)(1)(B). Because that transfer was not made by, to, or for the benefit of a financial institution, FTI contends that the safe harbor has no application.

The Court agrees with FTI. The language of §546(e), the specific context in which that language is used, and the broader statutory structure all support the conclusion that the relevant transfer for purposes of the §546(e) safe-harbor inquiry is the overarching transfer that the trustee seeks to avoid under one of the substantive avoidance provisions. . . .

Our analysis begins with the text of §546(e), and we look to both "the language itself [and] the specific context in which that language is used. . . ." *Robinson v. Shell Oil Co.,* 519 U.S. 337, 341, 117 S.Ct. 843, 136 L.Ed.2d 808 (1997). The pertinent language provides:

> "Notwithstanding sections 544, 545, 547, 548(a)(1)(B), and 548(b) of this title, the trustee may not avoid a transfer that is a . . . settlement payment . . . made by or to (or for the benefit of) a . . . financial institution . . . or that is a transfer made by or to (or for the benefit of) a . . . financial institution . . . in connection with a securities contract . . . , except under section 548(a)(1) (A) of this title."

The very first clause—"Notwithstanding sections 544, 545, 547, 548(a)(1)(B), and 548(b) of this title"—already begins to answer the question. It indicates that §546(e) operates as an exception to the avoiding powers afforded to the trustee under the substantive avoidance provisions. . . .

Then again in the very last clause—"except under section 548(a)(1)(A) of this title"—the text reminds us that the focus of the inquiry is the transfer that the trustee seeks to avoid. It does so by creating an exception to the exception, providing that "the trustee may not avoid a transfer" that meets the covered transaction and entity criteria of the safe harbor, "except" for an actually fraudulent transfer under §548(a)(1)(A). 11 U.S.C. §546(e). By referring back to a specific type of transfer that falls within the avoiding power, Congress signaled that the exception applies to the overarching transfer that the trustee seeks to avoid, not any component part of that transfer. . . .

The rest of the statutory text confirms what the "notwithstanding" and "except" clauses and the section heading begin to suggest. The safe harbor provides that "the trustee may not avoid" certain transfers. §546(e). Naturally, that text invites scrutiny of the transfers that "the trustee may avoid," the parallel language used in the substantive avoiding powers provisions. See §544(a) (providing that "the trustee . . . may avoid" transfers falling under that provision); §545 (providing that "[t]he trustee may avoid" certain statutory liens); §547(b) (providing that "the trustee may avoid" certain preferential transfers); §548(a)(1) (providing that "[t]he trustee may avoid" certain fraudulent transfers). And if any doubt remained, the language that follows dispels that doubt: The transfer that the "the trustee may not avoid" is specified to be "a transfer that *is*" either a "settlement payment" or made "in connection with a securities contract." §546(e) (emphasis added). Not a transfer that involves. Not a transfer that comprises. But a transfer that is a securities transaction covered under §546(e). The provision explicitly equates the transfer that the trustee may otherwise avoid with the transfer that, under the safe harbor, the trustee may not avoid. In other words, to qualify for protection under the securities safe harbor, §546(e) provides that the otherwise avoidable transfer itself be a transfer that meets the safe-harbor criteria.

Thus, the statutory language and the context in which it is used all point to the transfer that the trustee seeks to avoid as the relevant transfer for consideration of the §546(e) safe-harbor criteria. . . .

Accordingly, after a trustee files an avoidance action identifying the transfer it seeks to set aside, a defendant in that action is free to argue that the trustee failed to properly identify an avoidable transfer under the Code. . . .

In the instant case, FTI identified the purchase of Bedford Downs' stock by Valley View from Merit as the transfer that it sought to avoid. Merit does not contend that FTI improperly identified the Valley View-to-Merit transfer as the transfer to be avoided, focusing instead on whether FTI can "ignore" the component parts at the safe-harbor inquiry. Absent that argument, however, the Credit Suisse and Citizens Bank component parts are simply irrelevant to the analysis under §546(e). The focus must remain on the transfer the trustee sought to avoid. . . .

Reading §546(e) to provide that the relevant transfer for purposes of the safe harbor is the transfer that the trustee seeks to avoid under a substantive avoiding power, the question then becomes whether that transfer was "made by or to (or for the benefit of)" a covered entity, including a securities clearing agency. If the transfer that the trustee seeks to avoid was made "by" or "to" a securities clearing agency (as it was in *Seligson*), then §546(e) will bar avoidance, and it will do so without regard to whether the entity acted only as an intermediary. The safe harbor will, in addition, bar avoidance if the transfer was made "for the benefit of" that securities clearing agency, even if it was not made "by" or "to" that entity. This reading gives full effect to the text of §546(e). . . .

The safe harbor saves from avoidance certain securities transactions "made by or to (or for the benefit of)" covered entities. See §546(e). Transfers "through" a covered entity, conversely, appear nowhere in the statute. And although Merit complains that, absent its reading of the safe harbor, protection will turn "on the identity of the investor and the manner in which it held its investment," that is nothing more than an attack on the text of the statute, which protects only certain transactions "made by or to (or for the benefit of)" certain covered entities.

For these reasons, we need not deviate from the plain meaning of the language used in §546(e). . . .

For the reasons stated, we conclude that the relevant transfer for purposes of the §546(e) safe harbor is the same transfer that the trustee seeks to avoid pursuant to its substantive avoiding powers. Applying that understanding of the safe-harbor provision to this case yields a straightforward result. FTI, the trustee, sought to avoid the $16.5 million Valley View-to-Merit transfer. FTI did not seek to avoid the component transactions by which that overarching transfer was executed. As such, when determining whether the §546(e) safe harbor saves the transfer from avoidance liability, *i.e.,* whether it was "made by or to (or for the benefit of) a . . . financial institution," the Court must look to the overarching transfer from Valley View to Merit to evaluate whether it meets the safe-harbor criteria. Because the parties do not contend that either Valley View or Merit is a "financial institution" or other covered entity, the transfer falls outside of the §546(e) safe harbor. The judgment of the Seventh Circuit is therefore affirmed, and the case is remanded for further proceedings consistent with this opinion. . . .

Ultimately, it was not sufficient to have an entity theoretically benefitting from the safe harbor from payment clawbacks acting as intermediary. To defend against a clawback from the trustee, the relevant transaction had to be "for the benefit" of a commodity broker, forward contract merchant, stockbroker, financial institution, financial participant, or securities clearing agency.

4. Set-Offs

In chapter 12, section E, we saw how a central feature of swap transactions is close-out netting. Close-out netting is where all payments streams that are the subject of a particular agreement are given a present value and netted against each other resulting in one amount due or payable from one party to another.

Set-off differs in that it represents netting an amount due or payable under one agreement with an amount due or payable under another agreement.

Example: At the time the Great Northern Swap Corporation files for bankruptcy, the Western Pacific Oil Company and the Great Northern Swap Corporation have ten swap transactions in place documented under a single ISDA Master Agreement. These transactions are terminated by the Western Pacific Oil Company resulting in a net payment of $500,000 due from the Great Northern Swap Corporation to the Western Pacific Oil Company.

Under a separate agreement, the Great Northern Swap Corporation has lent $700,000 to the Western Pacific Oil Company. Were Western Pacific Oil Company able to legally "set-off" the $500,000 due from the Great Northern Swap Corporation as a result of the close-out netting process under the swap agreement against the $700,000 they owe under the loan, they could reduce their loan obligation to the Great Northern Swap Corporation from $700,000 to $200,000 and the $500,000 owed by the Great Northern Swap Corporation would be deemed paid. Whereas other creditors of the Great Northern Swap Corporation may only receive a portion of what is owed by the Great Northern Swap Corporation, due to the Western Pacific Oil Company's set-off, the Western Pacific Oil Company in effect receives one hundred percent of what was owed to it by the Great Northern Swap Corporation.

Any party with a valid set-off at the time of the bankruptcy filing will be able to claim a set-off as of right in bankruptcy.[38] Whereas the previously examined "safe harbors" only benefit parties to specified transaction types, such as futures or swaps, the Bankruptcy Code's set-off provisions protect any party's valid set-off right. Whether a set-off right is valid or not is a question of applicable state law. Frequently asserted bases for a set-off claim are an explicit contractual provision or common law.

In other words, the Bankruptcy Code merely protects any set-off right a party validly has at the time of the bankruptcy. A creditor cannot claim a set-off right in a bankruptcy proceeding if it did not have a set-off right at the time of the bankruptcy filing.

Additionally, the Bankruptcy Code imposes an obligation of mutuality that case-law has helped delineate, i.e., the parties to all of the obligations to be set-off must be the same.

Though the following case does not involve futures or swaps, the principles are equally applicable. The question that arose in the following case is whether a so-called triangular set-off meets the Bankruptcy Code's mutuality requirement. In this case, Chevron was the creditor and its contracts for the purchase or sale of petroleum products with three related bankrupt debtors represented the obligations that Chevron sought to set-off against one another.

---

38. 11 U.S.C. § 553(a).

In re Semcrude, L.P.

399 B.R. 388 (Bankr. D. Del. 2009)

Brendan Linehan Shannon, Bankruptcy Judge.

Before the Court is the motion (the "Motion") . . . of Chevron Products Company, a division of Chevron USA, Inc. ("Chevron") seeking relief from the automatic stay to effect a "triangular setoff" of certain debts that are owed or owing between it and three separate debtors in these jointly administered cases. For the following reasons, the Court will deny the Motion. . . .

On July 22, 2008 (the "Petition Date"), SemGroup, L.P. ("SemGroup"), and certain direct and indirect subsidiaries (each a "Debtor" and collectively referred to hereinafter as the "Debtors"), including SemCrude, L.P. ("SemCrude"), SemFuel, L.P. ("SemFuel"), and SemStream, L.P. ("SemStream"), each filed a voluntary petition for relief under Chapter 11 of the Bankruptcy Code (the "Code"). The Debtors' Chapter 11 cases have been consolidated for procedural purposes. . . .

In the course of its business, Chevron entered into contracts with three of the Debtors: SemCrude, SemFuel, and SemStream. Chevron contracted with these entities for the sale or purchase of crude oil, regular unleaded gasoline, and/or butane, isobutene and propane, respectively. . . .

Additionally, SemGroup executed a continuing parent guaranty of any indebtedness incurred by SemCrude, SemStream, SemMaterials, L.P., and SemFuel in favor of Chevron (the "Continuing Guaranty.") . . .

Prior to the Debtors' bankruptcy filings, Chevron and the Debtors entered into a number of transactions pursuant to these contracts. As of the Petition Date, these transactions resulted in Chevron owing a balance of $1,405,878.40 to SemCrude. Chevron is owed $10,228,439.34 by SemFuel, however, and is owed an additional $3,302,806.03 by SemStream.

Claiming that the amounts owed under these balances can be setoff against each other pursuant to the contract terms discussed above, Chevron filed the Motion on August 21, 2008 for the purpose of obtaining leave from the automatic stay so that it could effect such a setoff. The Debtors . . . and a host of the Debtors' creditors each filed timely objections . . . [which] took issue with Chevron's argument that the Code allows for parties to contract around the Code's requirement in section 553 that debts be "mutual" in order to be setoff. The objectors contend that triangular setoff is impermissible, even if contemplated by a valid, pre-petition contract. Alternatively, the objectors argue that even if there is such a contract exception to the mutuality requirement, the contracts in the instant case fail to effect such a result. . . .

Chevron asserts that the terms of its contracts with the Debtors permit it to setoff the debt it owes to one corporation, SemCrude, against the debt owed to it by two other corporations, SemFuel and SemStream, thus effecting a "triangular setoff."

The Court does not need to determine whether the specific terms of these various contracts grant SemCrude this right, however. Instead, the Court holds that Chevron is not permitted to effect such a setoff against the Debtors in this case because section 553 of the Code prohibits a triangular setoff of debts against one or more debtors in bankruptcy as a matter of law due to lack of mutuality. . . .

The Code section that governs setoff in bankruptcy, section 553, does not create a right of setoff. . . . Rather, section 553 "preserves for the creditor's benefit any setoff right that it may have under applicable nonbankruptcy law," and "imposes additional restrictions on a creditor seeking setoff" that must be met to impose a setoff against a debtor in bankruptcy. Thus, setoff is appropriate in bankruptcy only when a creditor both enjoys an independent right of setoff under applicable non-bankruptcy law, and meets the further Code-imposed requirements and limitations set forth in section 553. . . .

In order to effect a setoff in bankruptcy, courts construing the Code have long held that the debts to be offset must be mutual, prepetition debts.

The authorities are also clear that debts are considered "mutual" only when "they are due to and from the same persons in the same capacity." . . . [B]ecause each corporation is a separate entity from its sister corporations absent a piercing of the corporate veil, "a subsidiary's debt may not be set off against the credit of a parent or other subsidiary, or vice versa, because no mutuality exists under the circumstances." Allowing a creditor to offset a debt it owes to one corporation against funds owed to it by another corporation — even a wholly-owned subsidiary — would thus constitute an improper triangular setoff under the Code.

Chevron asserts that an exception to the Code's mutuality requirement exists. It contends that a valid, pre-petition contract — executed by a creditor, a debtor, and one or more third parties — either satisfies the mutuality requirement or allows the parties to contract around the mutuality requirement found in section 553(a) if the contract provides that one or more parties to the agreement can elect to setoff any debt it owes to one of the other parties against an amount owed to it by a different party to the agreement. . . .

Chevron's Motion claims that the setoff it seeks is one of "mutual obligations." More specifically, it contends that this "multi-party mutuality is created" by the contracts discussed above. But Chevron also argues that triangular setoffs "are enforceable as an exception to the mutuality requirement" when contemplated by a valid contract. Although Chevron appears to take these positions as part of a single argument, and not as alternative arguments, the Court finds these propositions to be mutually exclusive.[39] If a debt is mutual one, then the rule of mutuality is, by definition, satisfied without the need for an exception to the rule. For a setoff to be enforceable as an "exception" to the mutuality requirement, however, the mutuality requirement itself must not have been satisfied.

---

39. [N. 6] No pun intended.

Therefore, in the complete absence of controlling or persuasive published case-law on the issue, the Court is faced with two distinct questions. First, may debts owing among different parties be considered "mutual" when there are contractual netting provisions governing all parties' business relationship? If the answer is "no," then the second question is whether a "contractual exception" exists to section 553's mutuality requirement. . . .

As is made clear by the express language of the section 553, and the numerous decisions interpreting it, the Code only allows for setoff of "mutual debts" in bankruptcy. No mention is made in the statute of allowing setoff of non-mutual debts, thus a debt must be mutual in order to be setoff under section 553. On this general rule, the courts are in unanimous agreement. . . .

[T]he Court concludes that mutuality cannot be supplied by a multi-party agreement contemplating a triangular setoff. Unlike a guarantee of debt, where the guarantor is liable for making a payment on the debt it has guaranteed payment of, an agreement to setoff funds does not create an indebtedness from one party to another.[40] An agreement to setoff funds, such as the one claimed by Chevron in this case, does not give rise to a debt that is "due to" Chevron and "due from" SemCrude. A party such as SemCrude does not have to actually pay anything to a creditor such as Chevron under a tripartite setoff agreement; rather, it only sees one of its receivables reduced in size or eliminated. SemCrude does not owe anything to Chevron, thus there are no debts in this dispute owed between the "same persons in the same capacity."

Likewise, Chevron does not have a "right to collect" against SemCrude under the agreement in this case. At most, the agreement of the parties would give Chevron a "right to offset" — a right to pay less than it would otherwise have to pay to the extent of the setoff. The agreement does not call for SemCrude to make a payment to Chevron, however. Consequently, the agreement does not call for Chevron to "collect" anything from SemCrude. Chevron is thus without a "right to collect" from SemCrude. At bottom, Chevron may enjoy privity of contract with each of the relevant Debtors, but it lacks the mutuality required by the plain language of section 553. . . .

Accordingly, the Court holds that non-mutual debts cannot be transformed into a "mutual debt" under section 553 simply because a multi-party agreement allows for setoff of non-mutual debts between the parties to the agreement. . . .

Although dictated by the plain language of section 553, the Court's holding also is consistent with the purpose of section 553 and the broader policies of the Code.

---

40. [N. 7] This is not to say that setoff would necessarily be appropriate against SemCrude if it were a guarantor of SemStream or SemFuel's debt, however. The Court notes that a split of authority exists regarding the issue of whether an unpaid guarantee can create mutuality for purposes of section 553. The Court does not reach this issue in this case because the only guarantor in this matter is SemGroup, an entity that is not owed a debt by Chevron.

One of the primary goals — if not the primary goal — of the Code is to ensure that similarly-situated creditors are treated fairly and enjoy an equality of distribution from a debtor absent a compelling reason to depart from this principle. By allowing parties to contract around the mutuality requirement of section 553, one creditor or a handful of creditors could unfairly obtain payment from a debtor at the expense of the debtor's other creditors, thereby upsetting the priority scheme of the Code and reducing the amount available for distribution to all creditors. . . .

For the foregoing reasons, the Court finds that Chevron is not entitled to enact a triangular setoff of the amounts owed between it and the Debtors.

Accordingly, the Court will deny the Motion. . . .

———————

Whereas in *Semcrude* the facts of the triangular set-off involved multiple related bankrupt debtors and one creditor, what if, instead, multiple related creditors sought to exercise a set-off with respect to obligations with a single bankrupt debtor? Such facts occurred in the Lehman bankruptcy where UBS AG held excess collateral that it sought to set-off against amounts owed by Lehman Brothers, Inc., to affiliates of UBS AG.[41] The bankruptcy court, citing *Semcrude*, decided that mutuality did not exist and, therefore, the set-off was impermissible.[42]

The reasoning in *Semcrude* was ratified and expanded upon in a subsequent Third Circuit case. As with *Semcrude*, the claims to be set off against one another were not related to derivatives. However, the decision should apply *mutatis mutandis* to derivatives.

In re Orexigen Therapeutics, Inc.
990 F.3d 748 (3d Cir. 2021)

Jordan, Circuit Judge.

This dispute turns on the meaning of the word "mutual" in the provision of the Bankruptcy Code that allows parties to invoke setoff rights when the debts they owe one another are mutual. *See* 11 U.S.C. § 553.

McKesson Corporation, Inc. ("McKesson") and Orexigen Therapeutics, Inc. ("Orexigen") agreed to a pharmaceutical distribution deal and included a provision in their contract whereby McKesson, as distributor of the drug, could reduce what it owed to Orexigen, the drug manufacturer, by any amount that Orexigen owed to McKesson or any McKesson subsidiary. Shortly thereafter, one of those subsidiaries, McKesson Patient Relationship Solutions ("MPRS"), separately agreed to help Orexigen with a consumer discount program by advancing cash to pharmacies, with Orexigen then obligated to reimburse MPRS. Later, when Orexigen

———————

41. *See In re Lehman Brothers Inc.*, 458 B.R. 134, 138 (Bankr. S.D.N.Y. 2011).

42. *Id.* at 141, 144–145. *See also In re American Home Mortgage, Holdings, Inc.*, 501 B.R. 44 (Bankr. D. Del. 2013).

filed for bankruptcy, it owed MPRS approximately $9 million, and McKesson owed Orexigen approximately $7 million. The Bankruptcy Court and the District Court rejected McKesson's request to set off its debt by the amount Orexigen owed MPRS, which would have reduced MPRS's claim to approximately $2 million and McKesson's debt to zero. Both courts held that what McKesson wanted was a triangular setoff, not a mutual one, and thus was not the kind allowable under § 553 of the Bankruptcy Code. We agree and will affirm. . . .

Orexigen was a publicly traded pharmaceutical company whose only commercial product was a weight management drug called Contrave. On June 9, 2016, Orexigen entered into a "Distribution Agreement" with McKesson, whereby Orexigen sold Contrave to McKesson, and McKesson in turn provided the drug to pharmacies. Included in the Distribution Agreement was a "Setoff Provision" that permitted "each of [McKesson] and its affiliates . . . to set-off, recoup and apply any amounts owed by it to [Orexigen's] affiliates against any [and] all amounts owed by [Orexigen] or its affiliates to any of [McKesson] or its affiliates." . . .

Separate from the Distribution Agreement, MPRS and Orexigen entered into a "Services Agreement" on July 5, 2016. Under the Services Agreement, MPRS managed a customer loyalty program for Orexigen, pursuant to which patients would receive price discounts from pharmacies. MPRS would advance funds to pharmacies selling Contrave, with reimbursement arriving later from Orexigen. The Distribution Agreement and Services Agreement did not reference, incorporate, or integrate one another, and the parties agree that McKesson and MPRS were distinct legal entities.

By the time Orexigen filed its petition for Chapter 11 relief on March 12, 2018 (the "Petition Date"), it owed MPRS approximately $9.1 million under the Services Agreement, and McKesson owed Orexigen some $6.9 million under the Distribution Agreement. Had there been a setoff of those obligations pursuant to the Setoff Provision, Orexigen would have owed MPRS $2.2 million and McKesson would have owed Orexigen nothing.

On March 16, 2018, four days after the Petition Date, Orexigen filed a motion to sell substantially all of its assets for $75 million in cash. McKesson objected to the asset sale, and, following that objection, the parties negotiated for McKesson to pay the approximately $6.9 million receivable it owed to Orexigen, while Orexigen agreed to keep that sum segregated pending resolution of the setoff dispute.[43]

McKesson and MPRS then asked the Bankruptcy Court to decide their rights to the segregated funds under the Setoff Provision in the Distribution Agreement and § 553 of the Code.[44] The Court rejected McKesson's argument for a setoff because,

---

43. [N. 3] The segregated $6.9 million is currently held by Province, Inc., which, as the administrator of the bankruptcy estate, has taken control of Orexigen's remaining assets pursuant to the confirmed liquidation plan.

44. [N. 4] Section 553 reads: "Except as otherwise provided in this section and in sections 362 and 363 of this title, this title does not affect any right of a creditor to offset a mutual debt owing by such creditor to the debtor that arose before the commencement of the case under this title against

while the Setoff Provision constituted an "enforceable contractual right allowing a parent and its subsidiary corporation to [e]ffect a prepetition triangular setoff under state law[,]" that relationship "does not supply the strict mutuality required in bankruptcy." . . .

McKesson appealed the Bankruptcy Court's mutuality decision to the District Court, which affirmed. This timely appeal followed. . . .

Section 553 of the Bankruptcy Code says that, "[e]xcept as otherwise provided . . . , this title does not affect any right of a creditor to offset a *mutual* debt owing by such creditor to the debtor . . . against a claim of such creditor against the debtor[.]" 11 U.S.C. § 553(a) (emphasis added). The meaning of mutuality in that provision is a matter of first impression for us. And while our sister circuits have opined on the importance of mutuality as a distinct limitation of § 553, they have not ruled on whether a contract can create an exception to the requirement of direct mutuality. Our task is to understand what Congress meant in using the term "mutual" in that Code section.

Orexigen asks us to adopt the reasoning of a unanimous line of authority from bankruptcy courts, beginning with *SemCrude*, that requires strict bilateral mutuality for § 553 to apply. McKesson, on the other hand, argues that *SemCrude* and the cases that follow it should be upended because the word "mutual" in § 553 is merely a non-limiting adjective meant to invoke an understanding of how state law set-off rights generally operate. We conclude that the analysis set forth in *SemCrude* is sound and the Bankruptcy Court and District Court here rightly treated mutuality as a distinct statutory requirement under § 553. . . .

The parties agree, as an initial matter, that to assert a setoff exception under § 553, a right to setoff must exist under applicable state law.[45] Their disagreement begins with McKesson's contention that both the general right to enforce a setoff and the requisite mutuality are defined by state law, with § 553 imposing no independent mutuality limitation. In other words, McKesson contends that the term "mutual" is nothing more than a "definitional scope provision that identifies the state-law right that is thereby preserved unaffected in bankruptcy[.]" (Opening Br. at 14.) Orexigen argues in response that the modifier "mutual," as used in § 553, imposes a distinct limitation strictly construed to prohibit enforcement of a setoff agreement involving three or more parties and indirect debt obligations.

---

a claim of such creditor against the debtor that arose before the commencement of the case[.]" 11 U.S.C. § 553(a). Three enumerated exceptions follow. Section 553 uses the terms "offset" and "set-off," while the parties often use the term "setoff." Viewing these as synonyms, we generally use the latter herein, as that is the language used in documents at issue in the case.

45. [N. 8] They are correct. *See United States ex rel. IRS v. Norton*, 717 F.2d 767, 772 (3d Cir. 1983) ("[Section 553] is not an independent source of law governing setoff; it is generally understood as a legislative attempt to preserve the common-law right of setoff arising out of non-bankruptcy law" and "the courts below were correct in looking to state law to determine when a setoff has occurred."); *see also Citizens Bank of Md. v. Strumpf*, 516 U.S. 16, 18, 116 S.Ct. 286, 133 L.Ed.2d 258 (1995).

As the *SemCrude* court noted, a compelling body of precedent, including from this Court, treats mutuality in § 553 as a limiting term, not a redundancy. *See In re SemCrude, L.P.*, 399 B.R. at 393 (collecting cases). . . . McKesson tries to rebut the import of those cases by pointing out that § 553 includes three expressly enumerated federal exceptions to the right to enforce a setoff, and an exception focused on non-mutual debts is not among them.[46] It argues that Congress would have included an enumerated exception bearing on mutuality if it had intended that concept to serve as a limitation under federal law rather than a term simply descriptive of state law.

Orexigen has the better of the argument, however, because McKesson's reading of the statute would render the term "mutual" redundant, as the phrase "any right . . . to offset" provides adequate definitional scope to § 553. To reiterate, the operative language reads "this title does not affect *any right of a creditor to offset a mutual debt*." 11 U.S.C. § 553(a) (emphasis added). Moreover, the text immediately following that language, although not enumerated, provides a limiting effect on the enforceability of § 553 by stating that both the debtor's claim against the creditor and the creditor's claim against the debtor must "ar[i]se before the commencement of the case." *Id.* That requirement is consistently viewed as a distinct limitation on the ability to assert a setoff right, and there is no persuasive reason to treat the requirement of mutuality any differently. . . .

Having determined that mutuality is a distinct and limiting requirement of federal bankruptcy law, we next consider the effect of that limitation. We again agree with and adopt the *SemCrude* court's well-reasoned conclusion that Congress intended for mutuality to mean only debts owing between two parties, specifically those owing from a creditor directly to the debtor and, in turn, owing from the debtor directly to that creditor. Congress did not intend to include within the concept of mutuality any contractual elaboration on that kind of simple, bilateral relationship. . . .

That should end the matter, but McKesson insists that its Setoff Provision in the Distribution Agreement turns the debts between Orexigen and MPRS and between McKesson and Orexigen from a triangular debt arrangement into a mutual debt. The error of that assertion is described in *SemCrude*.[47]

---

46. [N. 10] Those enumerated exceptions are: "(1) the claim of such creditor against the debtor is disallowed; (2) such claim was transferred, by an entity other than the debtor, to such creditor . . . after the commencement of the case; or . . . after 90 days before the date of the filing of the petition; and . . . while the debtor was insolvent . . . or (3) the debt owed to the debtor by such creditor was incurred by such creditor — after 90 days before the date of the filing of the petition; while the debtor was insolvent; and for the purpose of obtaining a right of setoff against the debtor[.]" 11 U.S.C. § 553(a)(1)-(3).

47. [N. 12] *SemCrude* traced the history of attempts to create a contractual exception to strict mutuality, through dicta in various decisions, back to a single case, *In re Berger Steel Co.*, 327 F.2d 401 (7th Cir. 1964), now almost 60 years old. But even *Berger* had not actually authorized such an exception. In *Berger*, a creditor sought a priority interest in a sum of money which the debtor owed to a subsidiary of that creditor, pursuant to an alleged setoff agreement between the three parties.

The reasoning of *SemCrude* has been frequently relied on in other bankruptcy cases, including this one. . . . In embracing the *SemCrude* analysis, the Bankruptcy Court for the Southern District of New York succinctly explained that "mutuality quite literally is tied to the identity of a particular creditor that owes an offsetting debt. The right is personal, and there simply is no ability to get around this language [of § 553]. Parties may freely contract for triangular setoff rights, but not in derogation of these mandates of the Bankruptcy Code." *In re Lehman Bros. Inc.*, 458 B.R. 134, 141 (Bankr. S.D.N.Y. 2011). We agree. . . .

If McKesson wanted mutuality for the debts in question, it should have taken on the customer loyalty support that it instead had its subsidiary MPRS handle for Orexigen. Alternatively, if McKesson wanted MPRS to have a perfected security interest in Orexigen's account receivable due from McKesson, it should have taken steps to arrange that. By perfecting a security interest, MPRS may have obtained a priority right to the same amount McKesson now seeks via setoff, which would have had the added benefit of placing Orexigen's other creditors on advance notice of that priority claim. . . . McKesson's desired outcome, wherein contractual setoff agreements can shoehorn multiparty debts into § 553, would disincentivize public disclosure of prioritized claims, weakening a fundamental purpose of the Code.

In contrast, a rule that excludes nonmutual debts from the setoff privilege of § 553 promotes predictability in credit transactions. . . .

In the alternative, McKesson argues that it actually holds a direct claim against Orexigen under the Setoff Provision of the Distribution Agreement. It tries to frame its requested setoff as effectively being two-sided: on one side, it argues, is the account receivable owed by McKesson to Orexigen, and on the other side is the Setoff Provision of the Distribution Agreement. Again, the *SemCrude* court faced just such an argument and persuasively rejected the attempt to escape triangularity by redefining what constitutes a "claim" under § 553. *See In re SemCrude, L.P.*, 399 B.R. at 397 ("An agreement to setoff funds, such as the one claimed by Chevron in this case, does not give rise to a debt that is 'due to' Chevron and 'due from' Sem-Crude. . . . Likewise, Chevron does not have a 'right to collect' against SemCrude under the agreement in this case."). We follow suit.

McKesson's position is nothing but a recasting of its failed effort to defeat the purpose and meaning of § 553. It focuses on the definition of the term "claim" in isolation and ignores the rest of § 553, which necessarily refines the term's meaning. If McKesson's definition of claim were to be inserted in this context, § 553 would state that "this title does not affect any right of a creditor to offset a mutual debt . . .

See id. at 401–04. The Court did not reach whether such a "tripartite agreement" could be enforced under the predecessor to § 553, instead merely affirming the District Court's ruling that no such contract even existed. *See id.* at 405–06. As explained in *SemCrude*, it "avoided addressing the . . . question of whether a triangular setoff was permissible under the Bankruptcy Act if a contract signed by the parties to the proposed setoff contemplated such a remedy." 399 B.R. at 395. Thus, there is no authority supporting a contractual exception to the mutuality requirement of § 553. *See id.* at 396–99.

against [a setoff right] of such creditor." Trying to offset a debt against a setoff right strikes us as nonsense.[48] Accordingly, we reject McKesson's interpretation of the term "claim" in the context of § 553. . . .

For the foregoing reasons, we will affirm the order of the District Court that affirmed the Bankruptcy Court's ruling.

The mutuality requirement was even more narrowly construed in the following case, where the court concluded that mutuality did not exist between a single creditor seeking to set off obligations accrued before the debtor's bankruptcy petition against obligations incurred after the debtor's bankruptcy petition.

Swedbank AB (PUBL) v. Lehman Brothers Holdings Inc. (In re Lehman Bros. Holdings Inc.)

445 B.R. 130 (S.D.N.Y. 2011)

Naomi Reice Buchwald, District Judge.

Appellant Swedbank AB (publ.) ("Swedbank") appeals from [an order] . . . compelling Swedbank to return post-petition funds to [Lehman Brothers Holdings Inc. ("LBHI")]. . . .

For the reasons stated herein, the decision below is affirmed. . . .

Swedbank and the Lehman Debtors had a multifaceted relationship that long predated the Lehman Debtors' Chapter 11 case. For example, LBHI was a party to an International Swaps and Derivatives Association ("ISDA") Master Agreement between LBHI and Swedbank, dated November 29, 2004 ("LBHI Master Agreement"). Additionally, between 1996 and 2004, Swedbank and certain LBHI affiliates entered into other ISDA Master Agreements. LBHI was a guarantor with respect to this latter set of agreements (together with the LBHI Master Agreement, the "Master Agreements"). Finally, LBHI maintained a general deposit account with Swedbank in Stockholm, Sweden ("Swedbank Account"). . . .

The Master Agreements include certain provisions that are relevant to this dispute. Specifically, the Master Agreements define a voluntary or involuntary bankruptcy filing as an "Event of Default." The Master Agreements further provide that an Event of Default: (1) triggers the early termination of the Master Agreements; and (2) grants the non-defaulting party a right of setoff. . . .

Following . . . [LBHI's] bankruptcy filing, Swedbank placed an administrative freeze on the Swedbank Account. As a result of the freeze, LBHI could not withdraw funds but was able to make deposits or wire transfers into the account. In the days

----

48. [N. 15] The word "setoff" means to subtract, so the term "claim," at least in the context of § 553, must be limited to the types of claims that connote a positive rather than negative value, because when one subtracts a negative one is performing addition.

and weeks to follow, LBHI and others deposited an additional SEK 82,765,466.45 (approximately $11.7 million) into the Swedbank Account.

On November 27, 2008, Swedbank informed LBHI that it intended to setoff LBHI's pre-petition debts, which arose under the Master Agreements, against the funds in the Swedbank Account, including the SEK 82.7 million that was deposited post-petition. Although LBHI contested Swedbank's right to take such action, Swedbank reaffirmed its position in a letter dated January 30, 2009. . . .

The issues presented on appeal are: (1) whether Swedbank's proposed setoff of LBHI's pre-petition obligations against LBHI's post-petition deposits was prohibited by section 553 of the Bankruptcy Code, which permits the offset of "mutual" pre-petition obligations; (2) whether Swedbank's proposed setoff was permissible under sections 560 and 561 of the Bankruptcy Code ("Safe Harbor Provisions"), which govern the right to liquidate, terminate, or accelerate swap agreements and master netting agreements; and (3) whether the Bankruptcy Court correctly ruled that Swedbank violated the automatic stay by placing a freeze on LBHI's post-petition funds. . . .

Swedbank's arguments turn on the relationship among section 553 [a concept in existence for over a century] and the later-enacted Safe Harbor Provisions [i.e. section 560 of the Bankruptcy Code, enacted in 1990 and section 561 of the Bankruptcy Code, enacted in 2005]. . . .

Congress legislates in light of the legal principles in existence at the time. As is relevant to this dispute, the mutuality requirement has existed for more than a century.

When a party argues that Congress has made a fundamental change to a well-settled legal principle, courts often look to legislative history. . . . Thus, if Congress had intended to eliminate the fundamental principle of mutuality, we would expect some discussion of this change in the legislative history. . . .

On appeal, Swedbank concedes that but for the Safe Harbor Provisions, its actions would be unauthorized. Swedbank also admits that the post-petition deposits into the Swedbank Account were made fortuitously and were not required by the terms of the Master Agreements. However, Swedbank contends that sections 560 and 561 specifically authorize the offset of LBHI's pre-petition debts against the post-petition funds in the Swedbank Account. According to Swedbank, the legislative history of the Safe Harbor Provisions demonstrates that Congress intended to grant "special treatment" to swap agreements to prevent disruption to the capital markets. Thus, Swedbank continues, Congress must have intended to permit a creditor to satisfy its claims under a pre-petition swap agreement by offsetting such claims against a debtor's post-petition deposits. . . .

The legislative history of the Safe Harbor Provisions reveals three related themes, all of which focus narrowly on swap transactions and the swap market. First, the legislative history reflects that Congress intended to permit swap participants to terminate swap agreements. According to House Report 101-484:

The new section 560 makes clear that a swap participant may exercise any contractual rights to terminate and net out a swap agreement in the event the other party files a bankruptcy petition, notwithstanding the automatic stay and trustee avoidance provisions of the Bankruptcy Code.... The intent of this provision is to permit either the non-debtor swap participant or the trustee to terminate a swap agreement, so that a swap agreement may continue after the bankruptcy petition is filed only by mutual consent of both the non-debtor swap participant and the trustee.

H.R. Rep. No. 101–484 (1990), reprinted in 1990 U.S.C.C.A.N. 223, 228, available at 1990 WL 92539.

In other words, Congress intended that section 560 would enable parties to swap agreements to terminate those transactions; neither the statute nor the legislative history extends the application of section 560 to the general commercial obligations of parties to swap agreements.

Second, the legislative history reflects a concern for the stability of the often-volatile swap market. Consequently, Congress emphasized that the Safe Harbor Provisions permit immediate termination of swap transactions in order to minimize the non-bankrupt counterparty's exposure to such unpredictability. For example, House Report 101-484 introduces the legislation in the following terms:

U.S. bankruptcy law has long accorded special treatment to transactions involving financial markets, to minimize volatility. Because financial markets can change significantly in a matter of days, or even hours, a non-bankrupt party to ongoing securities and other financial transactions could face heavy losses unless the transactions are resolved promptly and with finality.

H.R. Rep. No. 101-484, 1990 U.S.C.C.A.N. at p. 224....

Third, the legislative history addresses the need for swap participants to be able to close out existing transactions without fear that: (1) closing out swaps would violate the stay; (2) a debtor would opportunistically reject unfavorable swaps and assume favorable ones; or (3) the transactions would be challenged as voidable preferences. According to House Report 101-484:

[u]nder the "avoidance" provisions in current bankruptcy law, if a swap agreement was in effect at the time one of the parties filed a bankruptcy petition, the fund transfer from the debtor to the other party might be "avoidable" by the trustee, while the transfer from the other party to the debtor would not be. Concerns have been raised that under current bankruptcy law, termination and setoff of a swap agreement would be automatically stayed when one of the parties files a bankruptcy petition, whereupon the trustee, after indefinitely postponing termination of the swap agreement, could refuse setoff and unfairly "cherry pick" only the portions of the agreement advantageous to the debtor, while rejecting the portions unfavorable to the debtor.

H.R. Rep. No. 101-484, 1990 U.S.C.C.A.N. at p. 225. . . .

Accordingly, Congress was further motivated by the fairness considerations that support the even-handed netting of favorable transactions against unfavorable ones to determine a single net termination value. . . .

In sum, the legislative history plainly supports the argument that Swedbank was entitled to terminate the Master Agreements and to determine a single net termination value. However, it does not support Swedbank's position that the Safe Harbor Provisions permit setoff against LBHI's post-petition assets, which were fortuitously deposited in the Swedbank Account and which have no connection to the underlying swaps. . . .

For the foregoing reasons, the Bankruptcy Court's decision is affirmed.

––––––––––

Some commentators have argued that tri-party set-off is enforceable in bankruptcy. With *Semcrude* and *Swedbank* in mind, they have argued that the correct arguments were not made or the cases were wrongly decided.[49] However, in light of *Orexigen* and the consistency of decisions on the subject, the weight of precedent is strongly in favor of a strict interpretation of mutuality.

C. Application to Futures and Cleared Swaps

Futures and cleared swaps have similar transactional mechanics. As we discussed in chapters 6 and 10 both use central clearing through futures commission merchants who are members of a derivatives clearing organization. Just as the futures and cleared swaps have some transactional similarities, they also have similarities in treatment under the Bankruptcy Code that are distinct from uncleared swaps due to the intermediation of a futures commission merchant[50] and derivatives clearing organization.

1. Futures

Suppose that a fictional registered futures commission merchant, Midwest Futures, is a member of a fictional registered derivatives clearing organization, the Topeka Clearinghouse. Midwest Futures has dozens of customers who enter

––––––––––

49. *See e.g.*, Martin J. Bienenstock, Chris DiAngelo, Eileen Bannon, and Lee J. Casey, *Are Triangular Setoff Agreements Enforceable in Bankruptcy*, 83 Amer. Bankr. L.J. 425 (2008) and Melvin A. Brosterman, Charles F. Cerria, Harold A. Olsen, Mark A. Speiser, and Claude G. Szyfer, *Multilateral Netting Under Safe Harbor Contracts: The Arguments for Enforceability in Bankruptcy (and for Mandatory Withdrawal of the Issue to District Court)*, Pratt's J. of Bankr. L. 129 (April/May 2015).

50. If a futures commission merchant is dually-registered as a securities broker-dealer, it will be subject to a Securities Investor Protection Corporation proceeding instead of a bankruptcy proceeding.

into trades cleared by the Topeka Clearinghouse due to a guarantee to the Topeka Clearinghouse from Midwest Futures, one of its members. Midwest Futures collateralizes its net positions to the Topeka Clearinghouse and, in turn, requires initial margin for each contract from its customers (which it passes on to the Topeka Clearinghouse *in toto*) and variation margin, which it retains. Initial margin represents a fixed amount of margin that must be provided for each contract and variation margin is correlated to, and varies with, the market value of the customer's position.

The biggest customer of Midwest Futures, Mega Speculator, sees its positions overnight get a lot worse due to market movements. As a result, the next morning, Midwest Futures demands millions of dollars in additional margin. Mega Speculator cannot make the margin call. What happens now?

Regardless of whether Mega Speculator has posted the additional variation margin demanded by Midwest Futures, Midwest Futures ultimately has an obligation to the Topeka Clearinghouse. Midwest Futures will close out Mega Speculator's positions (in case they worsen!) and liquidate whatever margin Mega Speculator has already provided to Midwest Futures. Midwest Futures will then have an obligation to pay any shortfall to the Topeka Clearinghouse due to the guarantee of its customer's payment obligations to the clearinghouse.

To the extent Midwest Futures has insufficient funds to do so, the Topeka Clearinghouse has recourse to the margin of customers of Midwest Futures who are not defaulting. Those customers then, take the risk of a "double default," i.e., a default of their futures commission merchant's customer combined with a default of the futures commission merchant itself.

One real-life example of where such a default occurred is Volume Investors, the subject of the litigation in *Westheimer v. Commodity Exchange, Inc.*, discussed in chapter 5, and *Comex Clearing Association, Inc. v. Flo-Arb Partners*, discussed in chapter 6. In such a "double default" circumstance, non-defaulting customers of the futures commission merchant could have their funds in margin accounts reduced *pro rata* to make up for the loss. More likely, though, is that the position would be transferred. While a double default is rare, futures commission merchants do fail, often without losses to non-defaulting customers. (Some examples of futures commission merchant failures are discussed in chapter 6, section B.3.)

Futures commission merchants re-invest margin posted by customers. Even outside of a so-called double default circumstance, this puts the customers' money at risk to the extent the futures commission is unable to repay the money to the customer when due, whether because of, for example, honest investment losses or fraud by the futures commission merchant. The former event (i.e., investment losses leading to an inability to repay customers) occurred with respect to MF Global in 2011, a subject of discussion in chapter 6, section B.3.

2. Cleared Swaps

The primary difference between the model for cleared swaps and the model for futures is that in the "double default" circumstance described above in subsection 1, the derivatives clearing organization could only use the margin of a defaulting customer to try to recover any shortfalls. Non-defaulting customers would be able to transfer their positions to a solvent futures commission merchant. This model is referred to as "legally segregated with operational commingling" or "LSOC" model.

It is important to note that, though the "legally segregated" aspect of the model protects non-defaulting customers in a "double default" scenario, customer monies are subject to "operational commingling," which means that they can be commingled and aggregated for investment purposes and, to the extent there is an investment loss situation (such as that which occurred in the futures context with respect to MF Global), those losses will be shared *pro rata* across all customers. CFTC rules, discussed in chapter 6, section B, constrain the type of investments that can be lawfully made with customer margin monies to those that are considered minimally risky.

3. Market Impact

The futures model discussed in subsection 1 above indirectly imposes liability on non-defaulting customers of a futures commission merchant for what could be imprudent speculation of defaulting customers of a futures commission merchant. This risk-sharing imposes a potential cost on prudent customers while reducing the derivatives clearing organization's risk since it has recourse to more parties than it has under the "LSOC" model discussed in subsection 2 above. Perhaps the lowered risk to the derivatives clearing organization is reflected in better pricing for all market participants?

On the other hand, the LSOC model results in fewer parties to which a derivatives clearing organization has recourse and, therefore, that risk could be reflected in higher pricing to all parties. (The model is too new to determine this.) On the other hand, a prudent customer benefits from its prudence and is not required to indirectly assume the risk of other customers' failures. In both models, customers are exposed to the risk of fraud or investment losses by a futures commission merchant.

4. Customer Property

Significantly impacting the treatment of the funds of customers of futures commission merchant is in what circumstances the Bankruptcy Code protects them from the claims of other creditors of a bankrupt futures commission merchant. Customer funds cannot be used to pay other creditors. However, in the event there is a shortfall in customer funds, the CFTC has effectively defined all of a futures commission merchant's funds as customer funds. This elevates futures commission merchants' customers above other creditors. The CFTC's authority to do so is unresolved.

In re Griffin Trading Company

245 B.R. 291 (Bankr. N.D. Ill. 2000), *vacated as moot,*
270 B.R. 882 (N.D. Ill. 2001)

Erwin I. Katz, Bankruptcy Judge.

This matter comes before the Court on the motion of the Trustee (the "Trustee") of the Estate of Griffin Trading Company ("Griffin"), a bankrupt commodities broker. . . .

Because there is a shortfall in certain of Griffin's customers' accounts, the Trustee seeks authority to use all estate assets to pay the claims of Griffin's customers (the "Customer Claims") in full, in priority to all other unsecured creditors, pursuant to the [Bankruptcy Code,] . . . the Commodities Exchange Act (the "CEA") . . . and the rules and regulations of the [CFTC]. . . . The CFTC supports the Trustee's position. The Customer Claims all arose through trading activities carried out, if not ordered, in Griffin's London office (the "London Office"). If the Trustee's motion is granted, all estate assets will be used to pay the Customer Claims; there will be no assets available for distribution to Griffin's general creditors.

One general (i.e., non-customer) creditor, MeesPierson N.V. ("MeesPierson"), has objected to the motion . . . [asserting that] the CFTC has exceeded its statutory authority to regulate commodity broker bankruptcies. . . .

Under U.S. law . . . [customers] receive the highest priority, subject only to payment of certain administrative expenses . . . in the distribution of segregated customer accounts and other property that is "customer property," a term defined in the Code, 11 U.S.C. §761(10), and in the CFTC Regulations, 17 C.F.R. §190.08. The CFTC's definition is considerably broader than the Code's definition and the parties disagree about which one should apply. . . .

In the . . . event that there are insufficient funds in customer accounts to pay customer claims in full, the Bankruptcy Code provides that "if a customer is not paid the full amount of such customer's net equity claim from customer property, the unpaid portion of such claim is a claim entitled to distribution under section 726 of this title." 11 U.S.C. §766(j)(2). Section 726 of the Bankruptcy Code sets forth the scheme for distribution of the debtor's assets to unsecured creditors. However, the CFTC has expanded the Code's definition of "customer property." It has provided by regulation that when there is a shortfall in customer property as defined by the Code ("Code Customer Property"), virtually all estate property is to be treated as customer property, thus giving the customers first priority in its distribution, until all customer claims have been paid in full. 17 C.F.R. §190.08(a)(1)(ii)(J). In this case, the shortfall in customer property exceeds the total amount available for distribution. If U.S. law applies, the customers would receive everything and the general unsecured creditors would receive nothing. . . .

MeesPierson argues that the CFTC's definition of "customer property" . . . impermissibly alters and expands the definition of "customer property" provided in the Bankruptcy Code. . . . MeesPierson further argues that the CFTC's definition of "customer property" [(the "Challenged Regulation")] renders meaningless § 766(j) (2) of the Bankruptcy Code, which provides that customer claims not paid out of customer property are claims entitled to distribution only as general unsecured claims. 11 U.S.C. §§ 766(j)(2), 726, 510, 502. . . .

For the reasons expressed in the following opinion, the Court concludes that . . . the CFTC exceeded its statutory grant of rulemaking authority and that the provisions of 17 C.F.R. § 190.08(a)(1)(ii)(J) are invalid. Pursuant to the provisions of Subchapter IV of Chapter 7 of the Bankruptcy Code, any shortfall in customer property as defined in that Subchapter must be treated as a general unsecured claim. . . .

Griffin was a clearing member of and traded on the Chicago Board of Trade ("CBOT") and the Chicago Mercantile Exchange ("CME"). In London, Griffin was a member of the London Clearing House ("LCH") and a clearing member of the London International Financial Futures and Options Exchange ("LIFFE"). . . .

The Customer Claims at issue all arose from a shortfall in the customer accounts of Griffin's London office, where Griffin held customer money to be used for trading on exchanges outside the U.S. . . . Griffin executed all such foreign trades through its London office. This does not mean that all the Customers holding claims were physically present in Griffin's London office or that they had direct contact with the London office.

On December 29, 1998, a breach of . . . [capital requirements in] Griffin's London Office led the [UK authorities to issue an order] . . . prohibiting Griffin from doing business. The actions of one rogue trader, John Ho Park ("Park"), on December 21 and 22, 1998, caused a shortfall in the London Office's segregated customer funds and caused Griffin to be a defaulter. . . . Park, whose funds on deposit with Griffin supported a limit of 900 lots, bought as many as 11,000 lots of German *bund* futures . . . (the "Park Trades"). The Park Trades were a disaster; they lost more than $10,000,000 overnight.

Griffin was unaware that Park had exceeded his limit because, in a manner of speaking, Park slipped the trades through Griffin's back door. Park himself did not execute the trades through Griffin, in which case Griffin would have known that he was so far in excess of his limit, and would, presumably, have acted to halt his trading. Rather, he executed the trades through a third-party broker. . . .

As a result of the Park Trades, Griffin was unable to meet the minimum financial requirements imposed both by the . . . [U.K. Regulators] and the CFTC. The Intervention Order forced Griffin's London office to stop operating as an investment business. Griffin reported to the CFTC that it no longer met, and was unable to meet, minimum financial requirements. On December 30, 1998, Griffin was placed into Chapter 7 proceedings in the U.S. . . .

[I]t is necessary to point out that problems similar to those created by Park have arisen [before]. . . .

On October 22, 1992, two rogue traders at the CBOT vastly exceeded their trading limits and executed trades that forced one clearing firm, Lee B. Stern & Co. of Chicago, to default on an $8.5 million margin call from its clearing house. *U.S. v. Catalfo*, 64 F.3d 1070, 1076 (7th Cir.1995). This loss exceeded the firm's net worth by more than $2 million. *Id.* The company's owner saved it from bankruptcy by paying the debt from his personal funds. Jeffrey Taylor, *Two Are Indicted for a Wild Spree in CBOT Trading*, THE WALL STREET JOURNAL, July 22, 1993, 1993 WL-WSJ 691608. Lee B. Stern & Co. is still in business.

In 1985, a group of three rogue traders exceeded their limits trading gold futures and caused their clearing broker, Volume Investors Corporation ("VIC"), to default to its clearing house on a $14 million margin call. . . .

Congress, recognizing that bankruptcy proceedings for stockbrokers and commodity brokers present "unique problems," S.REP. NO. 95-989, at 3 (1978), *reprinted in* 1978 U.S.C.C.A.N. 5787, 5789 created two special subchapters of Chapter 7, the liquidation chapter of the Bankruptcy Code, to handle those problems. . . . Subchapter III of Chapter 7, 11 U.S.C. §§ 741–752, addresses stockbroker liquidations and Subchapter IV, 11 U.S.C. §§ 761–766, addresses commodity broker liquidations. Congress created the separate subchapters for securities and commodities brokers because it recognized fundamental differences between the two. . . . Congress further recognized that the Bankruptcy Code would apply to stockbroker liquidations only in very rare cases, but would apply to most commodity broker liquidations.

Although the rationale for customer protection in the area of stockbrokers and commodity brokers is identical, there are several differences between the two subchapters. A primary difference derives from the scope of protection afforded. There is no analogue of SIPC to insure commodity brokers' customers. Thus the commodity broker liquidation provisions will apply in the vast majority of commodity broker insolvencies in contradistinction to the rare application of the stockbrokers [*sic*] liquidation provisions. . . .

The CFTC was newly-created . . . when Congress enacted the Bankruptcy Reform Act of 1978. Recognizing that regulation of the industry was in its infancy, Congress avoided drafting statutory sections to cover every possibility, but created instead a framework within which the CFTC could make rules. . . .

Courts uniformly accord deference to regulations issued under express statutory authority. *Bankers Life and Casualty Co. v. U.S.*, 142 F.3d 973, 979 (7th Cir.1998). However, an administrative agency may not determine the extent of its own authority; such a determination rests solely with the courts. *Batterton v. Francis*, 432 U.S. 416, 424 n. 8, 97 S.Ct. 2399, 53 L.Ed.2d 448 (1977) quoting *Social Security Board v. Nierotko*, 327 U.S. 358, 369, 66 S.Ct. 637, 643, 90 L.Ed. 718 (1946). . . .

The Challenged Regulation . . . [has the result that] until customers of a bankrupt commodity broker have been paid in full, they receive first priority not only in the distribution of Code Customer Property, but in the distribution of general estate assets as well. Whether Congress so intended is the precise question at issue. . . .

The plain meaning of § 766(j)(2) is that customers whose claims have not been fully paid from Code Customer Property shall be treated as general unsecured creditors. The section is neither silent nor ambiguous with respect to this issue, but addresses it directly and straightforwardly. While § 766(j)(2) makes reference to other sections of the Code, it is nevertheless simply drafted. It means exactly what it seems to mean: that when customers have not been paid in full from customer property, they will be treated as general unsecured creditors of the estate as to the shortfall. Congressional intent is clear from the text. The CFTC Regulation produces an opposite effect, ensuring that customers, as defined by the Code, 11 U.S.C. § 761(9), will never share *pro rata* with other unsecured creditors in the distribution of the general estate, but will take all that there is to take until they have been fully paid.

This might be the end of the matter because Congressional intent is clear from the text of § 766(j)(2). However, this problem involves not just § 766(j)(2), but 11 U.S.C. § 761(10)(A)(ix) and 7 U.S.C. § 24, as well. The Trustee *et al.* assert that 7 U.S.C. § 24 expressly authorizes the CFTC to change the definition of "customer property" provided in 11 U.S.C. § 761(10). The CFTC argues that "Congress specifically contemplated that the [CFTC] could include or exclude specific property from the definition of 'customer property' in the Bankruptcy Code." . . .

The Court agrees with the CFTC to a certain extent, but not to the extent necessary to validate the regulation. The CFTC can include or exclude *specific*, as it says, or *certain*, as 7 U.S.C. § 24(a) says, property in or from "customer property." The CFTC has done so in other subsections of 17 C.F.R. § 190.08. For instance, § 190.08(a)(1)(i)(E) includes proceeds of letters of credit if the letter of credit was received, acquired, or held to margin, guarantee, secure, purchase, or sell a commodity contract; § 190.08(a)(1)(i)(F) includes customer property hypothecated or pledged to the FCM as security for a loan; § 190.08(a)(1)(ii)(D) includes property that was received, acquired or held to margin, guarantee, secure, purchase or sell a commodity contract, but which has been withdrawn and subsequently is recovered by the avoidance powers of the trustee; and § 190.08(a)(1)(ii)(E) includes recovery of debit balances or other deficits against a customer account. These subsections all refer to property originating in or traceable in some way to a customer's account. However, the authority to include or exclude "certain" or "specific" property is not authority to include any or all property in general. It would have been simple for Congress to grant such authority; substitution of the word "any" or "all" for the word "certain" would have done it. Use of the word "certain" is not a Congressional mistake made in ignorance, or for lack of a better word, but is intended to limit the CFTC's authority to specific items. This intent is made even more apparent by the plain language of 7 U.S.C. § 24(b), which provides that the term "customer property" has the meaning assigned to it in the commodity broker subchapter of the Code. . . .

A review of the [relevant Bankruptcy Code provisions] . . . makes evident that Congress intended that customers should receive first priority in the distribution of "customer property," but should share *pro rata* with other unsecured creditors in the event of a shortfall in "customer property." The CFTC has made a formalistic end-run around this intent by labeling all estate property as "customer property" and bringing it under the provisions of 11 U.S.C. § 766(h), which grants customers first priority to "customer property." In other words, the CFTC has not only altered the Code's definition of "customer property," but has changed the distribution priority scheme set forth in the commodity broker subchapter of the Code. . . .

In light of the Challenged Regulation's failure to harmonize with language, purposes, and origins of the [Bankruptcy Code] . . . the Court holds that the Challenged Regulation is not based on a reasonable interpretation of the statute. It must be stricken. . . .

———————

Note that, despite the apparent ruling partially striking the CFTC's customer funds rule, the decision was vacated on appeal to district court when the parties settled. Nevertheless, the decision has raised questions regarding the enforceability of the provision. Although *Griffin* has been raised in at least one other decision, no court has subsequently resolved the question.[51]

In 2021, the CFTC revised the Part 190 rules at the core of the *Griffin* case.[52] The CFTC, in the proposed rulemaking, addressed *Griffin* by noting:

> The Commission notes that in *In re Griffin Trading Co.* . . . the United States Bankruptcy Court for the Northern District of Illinois ruled that the Commission exceeded its statutory authority. . . . This decision was vacated on appeal pursuant to a settlement reached by the parties. . . . [T]he Commission continues to be of the view that section 20 of the CEA provides it with the authority to include [a provision substantially similar to that which was challenged in *Griffin*]. . . .[53]

Ultimately, the CFTC decided on an approach that achieves the same outcome as the previous approach. Instead of defining all property needed to fill a shortfall in what is owed customers as "customer property," the new rule defines it as what ought to have been segregated according to existing CFTC rules.[54] This amounts to the same thing and is circular — customer property is effectively what ought to have been held by the futures commission merchant for customers. The CFTC's statutory authority is to determine if "certain cash, securities, other property, or commodity contracts" are to be "included in or excluded from" the Bankruptcy Code's

———————

51. *See In re MF Global*, 505 B.R. 623, 630 at n. 5 (S.D.N.Y. 2014).
52. *See* CFTC, *Bankruptcy Regulations*, 86 Fed. Reg. 19324 (Apr. 13, 2021).
53. CFTC, *Bankruptcy Regulations*, 85 Fed. Reg. 36000, 36030 (June 12, 2020).
54. *See* 17 C.F.R. § 190.09(a)(1)(ii)(G).

definition of "customer property."[55] It is not apparent that the CFTC has the authority to invert payment priorities and the statutory treatment of creditors in the Bankruptcy Code to make customers of futures commission merchants supreme in all scenarios.

D. Public Policy

Serious discussion is ongoing regarding the scope of the safe harbor provisions. The safe harbor provisions advantage some creditor parties over others. Therefore, it is an area ripe for reflections on public policy. Although there are references to "qualified financial contracts" below, the study was independent of the later initiative, discussed above in section B.1.c, to modify qualified financial contracts to add an additional stay period.

Board of Governors of the Federal Reserve System,
Study on the Resolution of Financial Companies under the Bankruptcy Code

https://www.federalreserve.gov/publications/other-reports/files/bankruptcy-financial-study-201107.pdf (July 2011)

. . . [Derivatives and other financial contracts "qualified financial contracts" or "QFCs"] receive special treatment under the Bankruptcy Code. The special treatment, called the "safe harbor provisions" of the Bankruptcy Code, exempts these transactions from some of the Bankruptcy Code's principal debtor protections. For example, the safe harbor provisions exempt QFCs from the bankruptcy "automatic stay," the provision of the Bankruptcy Code that automatically prevents creditors and others holding claims against a debtor from taking any action on the claim upon the filing of a voluntary petition. The safe harbor provisions also exempt QFCs from the "trustee avoiding powers," that is, from the provisions of the Bankruptcy Code that allow a trustee (or a debtor-in-possession) to recover certain transfers of the debtor's assets that were made within 90 days of filing the bankruptcy petition ("preferential transfers") or certain "constructive fraudulent conveyances" (or "fraudulent transfers").[56] Because of the safe harbor provisions, the non-defaulting QFC counterparty of the debtor can take actions to exercise its contractual rights to close out, terminate, net, and apply collateral for these transactions.

---

55. Commodity Exchange Act § 20.

56. [N. 108] *See* 11 U.S.C. sections 362(b)(17), (27), 560 (allowing liquidation of collateral in the counterparty's possession notwithstanding automatic stay); 11 U.S.C. sections 546(g), (j) (exempting QFCs from preferential transfer and constructive fraudulent transfer provisions); *see also* 11 U.S.C. sections 553(a), 560 (automatic option to set off); 11 U.S.C. sections 555, 559, 560, 561 (allowing counterparty to terminate, net, and seize collateral).

Congress enacted the safe harbor provisions of the Bankruptcy Code for QFCs because of concerns about systemic risk. Congress was concerned that, without the safe harbor provisions, other market participants who had entered into QFCs with the debtor would be exposed to such a high degree of uncertainty leading to a lack of liquidity that it would pose a potential for systemic risk. Specifically, there was concern that spillover effects from the initial insolvency could be transmitted through QFCs and significantly impair both the debtor's counterparties and the real economy more broadly.[57]

Proposals to Amend the QFC Safe Harbor Provisions of the Bankruptcy Code

Several commentators propose changing or eliminating the safe harbor provisions for QFCs under the Bankruptcy Code. Those proposing partial or total elimination of the safe harbor provisions base their arguments on the principle of treating like transactions similarly,[58] on concerns over moral hazard,[59] and on concerns about systemic risk.[60] These proposals argue that similar types of contracts should be treated under the Bankruptcy Code in a similar manner unless there is a compelling reason not to do so. Under this argument, certain QFCs such as repurchase agreements and some types of swaps are the equivalent of secured loans, and should receive the same treatment as secured loans under the Bankruptcy Code. Also under this argument, derivative contracts are similar to other executory contracts, that is, contracts that have not yet been performed or executed, and therefore should receive the same treatment as other executory contracts under the Bankruptcy Code. In the case of QFCs, some commentators argue that the exemption from the automatic stay coupled with provisions that are triggered upon the debtor's insolvency through ipso facto clauses (which are standard in derivative contracts)

---

57. [N. 109] The treatment of QFCs for banks under the . . . [Federal Deposit Insurance Act ("FDIA")] and for systemic financial companies under [the orderly liquidation authority granted to the Federal Deposit Insurance Corporation ("FDIC") with respect to certain institutions deemed systemically significant ("OLA")] . . . is similar to that under the Bankruptcy Code with one important exception: QFCs are subject to a one business day automatic stay upon the appointment of the FDIC as receiver under both the FDIA and the OLA. During this one-day stay, the FDIC has the power to transfer QFCs to a third party, including a bridge institution. Contracts transferred to a third party, including a bridge institution, may not be considered in default under the ipso facto clauses of the contracts. The FDIC's ability to transfer QFCs to third parties during the one-day stay is only limited by the requirement that all contracts under the same master agreement must receive the same treatment. *See* 12 U.S.C. section 1821(e)(8)–(11).

58. [N. 110] *See, e.g.,* David A. Skeel and Thomas H. Jackson, *Transaction Consistency and the New Finance in Bankruptcy* (U. Penn. Inst. for Law & Econ. Research Paper No. 11-06, 2011); [Thomas H. Jackson, *Bankruptcy Code Chapter 14: A Proposal*, at 29 (Hoover Institution Resolution Task Force, 2011)]. . . .

59. [N. 111] *See Skeel and Jackson, supra* note 110, at 4–5; *see also* Mark J. Roe, *Bankruptcy's Financial Crisis Accelerator: The Derivatives Players' Priorities in Chapter 11* (Harvard Public Law Working Paper No. 10-17, 2010).

60. [N. 112] *See, e.g.,* Roe, *supra* note 111, at 9–12; Brian G. Faubus, Note, "Narrowing the Bankruptcy Safe Harbor for Derivatives to Combat Systemic Risk," 59 Duke L. J. 801–42 (2010); Stephen J. Lubben, "The Bankruptcy Code without Safe Harbors," 84 Am. Bankr. L. J. 123–44 (2010).

elevates the status of QFCs in bankruptcy relative to similar contracts that are not classified as QFCs without a compelling reason for the distinction.[61]

Proposals for changing or eliminating the QFC safe harbor provisions also argue that those provisions have negative impacts on incentives and market discipline. According to these arguments, the exemptions from the automatic stay and trustee avoiding powers change the incentives for QFC counterparties to monitor the debtor prior to bankruptcy. Since QFC counterparties know that they can take action against the debtor on their QFC-related claims at a time when non-QFC creditor claims are stayed, QFC counterparties are likely to reduce their level of monitoring and are less likely to fully price changes in the risk of the debtor. Therefore the safe harbor provisions, according to these commentators, reduce market discipline and lead to increased risk-taking by counterparty firms and to increased risk in the financial system.

Proposals for changing or eliminating the QFC safe harbor provisions also contend that the provisions increase, rather than decrease, systemic risk because of the associated incentive effects. According to these arguments, preferential treatment of QFCs under the Bankruptcy Code changes the incentives for QFC counterparties to monitor and impose discipline on the debtor. Instead, actions that a counterparty might take to contain risk (for example, increased risk premiums, limiting exposure at default) are replaced, in part, by collateral calls as the financial distress of the debtor grows. This behavior can lead to the equivalent of counterparty runs (involving the termination of contracts and the liquidation of collateral) when the debtor files for bankruptcy. Collateral runs, according to these arguments, can both destabilize the debtor and have spillover effects on other creditors, other non-creditor firms and financial markets in general.[62] In effect, according to these arguments, the QFC safe harbor provisions fail to lower systemic risk in the financial system,[63] and simply replace one systemic risk transmission mechanism with another.

Some critics of the QFC safe harbor provisions call for a full repeal.[64] Other critics, however, appear to argue in favor of more narrow amendments. For example, some propose retaining the exemption from the automatic stay for QFCs where the collateral is cash or cash-like assets but imposing a limited automatic stay for other types of QFCs.[65] According to these commentators, exempting QFCs where the underlying collateral consists of cash or cash-like assets is appropriate because the

---

61. [N. 113] *See* Skeel and Jackson, *supra* note 110, at 22.

62. [N. 114] *See* Skeel, *supra* note 35, at 19–39; *see* Skeel and Jackson, *supra* note 110, at 35; *see* Roe, *supra* note 111, at 13–15.

63. [N. 115] For arguments in favor of the special treatment of QFCs in bankruptcy that are not related to systemic risk, *see* Franklin R. Edwards and Edward R. Morrison, "Derivatives and the Bankruptcy Code: Why the Special Treatment?" 22 Yale J. Reg. 91, 110–13 (2005).

64. [N. 116] *See, e.g.*, Stephen J. Lubben, "Repeal the Safe Harbors," 18 Am. Bankr. Inst. L. Rev. 319–36 (2010).

65. [N. 117] *See* Edwards and Morrison, *supra* note 115, at 25 (arguing against imposing the automatic stay where cash or cash-like collateral is involved); Jackson, Chapter 14, *supra* note [110] . . . ;

collateral securing these contracts is not related to the going concern value of the firm. Furthermore, they note that cash and cash-like collateral is liquid, with little controversy over its value. Finally, they argue that, even with the exemption from the automatic stay in place, counterparties in repurchase agreement transactions continued to aggressively monitor borrowers.[66]

Although there appears to be some consensus in proposals to retain the safe harbor provisions for QFCs with cash or cash-like collateral, there appears to be greater diversity among proposals for changing the treatment of other types of QFCs (non-cash QFCs). Some proposals would remove all of the safe harbor provisions for non-cash QFCs,[67] while others would impose an automatic stay of limited duration on non-cash QFCs.[68] Those proposing a limited automatic stay argue that doing so would limit the risk to counterparties associated with market movements that could affect the value of their claim and limit hedge uncertainty. Some also argue that a limited automatic stay would improve transaction consistency by making the Bankruptcy Code treatment of QFCs more consistent with the treatment of QFCs under the FDIA and the OLA. During the limited stay, according to these proposals, the debtor would have the right to net, transfer, affirm, or reject contracts, but would be required to treat all QFCs under the same master agreement identically to eliminate "cherry-picking" (that is, selective assumption and rejection) of QFCs by the debtor. After the limited stay expired, QFC counterparties could exercise all of their contract rights.[69]

Proposals to Retain the QFC Safe Harbor Provisions of the Bankruptcy Code

Supporters of the QFC safe harbor provisions present four general arguments for continuing the special treatment of QFCs in bankruptcy.[70] These proposals are generally framed in terms of opposing the wholesale repeal of the QFC safe harbor provisions, however, and therefore do not address all of the proposals for amendments described above.

Those arguing for retaining the QFC safe harbor provisions claim that the provisions prevent systemic spillover effects associated with tying up collateral in

---

Skeel and Jackson, *supra* note 110, at 26–31 (repurchase agreements, swaps, and other derivatives secured by cash or cash-like assets should be exempt from the automatic stay).

66. [N. 118] *See* Skeel and Jackson, *supra* note 110, at 27–28.

67. [N. 119] *See* . . . [Thomas H. Jackson, "Chapter 11F: A Proposal for the Use of Bankruptcy to Resolve Financial Institutions," in *Ending Government Bailouts As We Know Them* (2010), at 236–237.]

68. [N. 120] *See* Skeel and Jackson, *supra* note 110, at 34; Jackson, Chapter 14, *supra* note [110] . . . , at 22–23. The choice of three days for the automatic stay seems to be an attempt to choose a time period that balances of the costs to non-defaulting QFC counterparties with the benefits to the debtor.

69. [N. 121] *See* Skeel and Jackson, *supra* note 110, at 39–41 (advocating reinstituting a limited form of the avoidance provisions of the Bankruptcy Code for non-cash QFCs).

70. [N. 122] *See* Harold S. Novikoff and Sandeep C. Ramesh, "Special Bankruptcy Code Protections for Derivative and Other Financial Market Transactions," ALI-ABA Bus. L. Course Materials J. (Oct. 2009) at 37–41 (summarizing arguments).

bankruptcy. For QFCs, and especially for repurchase agreements, they argue, subjecting such contracts to the automatic stay could produce spillover effects that might result in financial markets and firms becoming illiquid. They argue that particularly in the case of the market for U.S. Treasury securities, the largest segment of the market for repurchase agreements, freezing of the market could interfere with the U.S. government's ability to manage its debt issuances and with the Federal Reserve's ability to implement monetary policy.

Supporters of the existing QFC safe harbor provisions also contend that the special status of QFCs in bankruptcies has implications for market risk. They argue that the elimination of the QFC safe harbor provisions could increase uncertainty in markets because these financial market transactions, especially derivatives, are critical tools used to manage and hedge financial risks. According to these arguments, dealer banks, relying on derivatives to manage their own risks and to serve as market-makers, enter into positions in order to transfer risks from ultimate buyers to ultimate sellers. Changes in interest rates and other market-risk factors can cause the value of derivatives to fluctuate quite a bit from day to day. If the stay were to be imposed, according to these arguments, the defaulting firm's counterparties might be forced to bear unhedgeable uncertainty — they would not be allowed to terminate their contracts with the defaulting firm, and would not know if or when some, all, or none of the amounts due to them under the contracts would be paid. If market movements caused the value of the contracts to the non-defaulting parties to increase, they continue, the non-defaulting parties would not be allowed to receive any more collateral from the defaulting firm to cover the increase in exposure.

The third principal argument advanced by those supporting the retention of the existing QFC safe harbor provisions asserts that there are only limited benefits associated with eliminating them. The automatic stay, according to these commentators, helps to coordinate creditor negotiations while preserving the going concern value of the debtor in reorganization. According to these arguments, the universe of firms that are large dealers in over-the-counter derivatives and counterparties that might be reorganized under Chapter 11 of the Bankruptcy Code may not be very large. For example, insolvent banks would be resolved under the FDIA. Covered financial companies might under exceptional circumstances be resolved under the OLA, although it is not possible to be certain before the fact which financial companies will be subject to resolution under the OLA because of the extraordinary circumstances and determinations required for its application.[71] Securities broker-dealers and commodities brokers are both prohibited from filing for reorganization under Chapter 11. Insurance companies are resolved under applicable state law, while hedge funds and private investment funds are most often liquidated rather than reorganized. Therefore, according to these arguments, the benefits associated with repealing the QFC safe harbor provisions are unlikely to exceed the costs since the universe of entities to which the repealed provisions might apply is small.

---

71. [N. 123] *See* "Reorganization, Liquidation, Resolution" subsection on pages 3–4.

Finally, supporters of retaining the QFC safe harbor provisions assert that markets should be allowed to protect themselves without undue interference from the Bankruptcy Code. According to these commentators, reinstating the automatic stay and trustee avoidance provisions of the Bankruptcy Code with respect to QFCs interferes with the ability of counterparties to protect themselves through enforcement of ISDA master agreements and contractual rights to seize and liquidate collateral in the event of a counterparty default.[72]

Despite the continuous discussion on the derivative safe harbors, no changes impacting them have been made to the Bankruptcy Code. As the events of the Financial Crisis recede, it is possible that the urgency for evaluating the safe harbors — an event which saw their utilization reach a peak — has decreased.

Questions and Comments

1. Can the different results in *Lehman Brothers Special Financing Inc. v. Ballyrock ABS CDO 2007-1 Limited* and *Michigan State Housing Authority* be reconciled? Both had termination methodologies that changed to the detriment of Lehman Brothers Special Financing due to the bankruptcy of its parent. Were there differences justifying the contradictory outcomes?

2. The Bankruptcy Code does not provide a specific time period for when termination of a swap agreement must be exercised, leading courts to try to devise one. How would you resolve such a claim before you if you were a judge deciding this issue?

3. Why treat claims relating to derivatives differently than other claims in bankruptcy?

4. Why allow parties to reap the benefits of set-off rights related to obligations incurred pre-bankruptcy petition? Should the strict mutuality requirement be weakened to allow for set-off of obligations between one group of affiliated entities and another group of affiliated entities? How would such an approach impact the concept of corporate separateness?

5. The "futures" model and "LSOC" model are each discussed in section C above. Is one model fairer to customers? Is one model an example of better public policy? Why have two different models?

6. In section C.4, the *Griffin Trading* case and the CFTC's definition of "customer property" are discussed. Would the judge in the *Griffin Trading* case rule differently today? What if you were adjudicating a claim by a non-customer creditor of a bankruptcy futures commission merchant challenging the payout of the bankrupt futures commission merchant's assets to customers?

---

72. [N. 124] *See* Novikoff and Ramesh, *supra* note 122, at 40.

Commodity Exchange Act to United States Code Conversion Table

Note that the following sections of the United States Code are contained in the same chapter as the Commodity Exchange without being, formally, a part of the Act: 7 U.S.C. §13-1 (making it a misdemeanor to trade box office receipts or onions on a board of trade), 7 U.S.C. §15b (Cotton Futures Act), 7 U.S.C. §16a (grant of authority to CFTC to collect user fees and commissioning of a National Futures Association report), 7 U.S.C. §§17a and 17b (severability clauses with respect to 1936 and 1968 amendments to the Commodity Exchange Act), and 7 U.S.C. §§27, 27a, 27d and 27f (Legal Certainty for Bank Products Act).

Commodity Exchange Act §	United States Code §
1	1
1a	1a
1b	1b
2	2
3	5
4	6
4a	6a
4b	6b
4b-1	6b-1
4c	6c
4d	6d
4e	6e
4f	6f
4g	6g
4h	6h
4i	6i

Commodity Exchange Act §	United States Code §
4j	6j
4k	6k
4l	6l
4m	6m
4n	6n
4o	6o
4p	6p
4q	6q
4r	6r
4s	6s
4t	6t
5	7
5b	7a-1
5c	7a-2
5e	7b
5f	7b-1
5g	7b-2
5h	7b-3
6(a)	8(a)
6(b)	8(b)
6(c)	9
6(d)	13b
6(e)	9a
6(f)	9b
6(g)	9c
6a	10a
6b	13a
6c	13a-1
6d	13a-2
7	11
8	12
8a	12a
8b	12b

Commodity Exchange Act §	United States Code §
8c	12c
8d	12d
9	13
10	17
12	16
13	13c
14	18
15	19
16	20
17	21
18	22
19	23
20	24
21	24a
22	25
23	26

Glossary

Definitions are based on the usage common in the marketplace. Some of the terms also have special legal or regulatory definitions. Where this is the case, the marketplace definition is provided, followed by a citation to the legal or regulatory definition.

affiliate. An entity that directly or indirectly controls, is controlled by, or is under common control with another entity.

agricultural commodity. Wheat, cotton, corn, butter, eggs, livestock, tobacco, products of horticulture, and anything else that once was or is derived from a living organism, is generally fungible, and is used primarily for food for humans or animals, shelter, or natural fiber. (17 C.F.R. § 1.3 (definition of agricultural commodity))

American option. An option that can be exercised by the holder of the option at any time during the term of the option.

ask. See *offer.*

associated person. A person who is associated with a futures commission merchant, an introducing broker, a commodity pool operator, a commodity trading advisor, leverage transaction merchant, swap dealer, major swap participant, security-based swap dealer, or major security-based swap participant who solicits or accepts orders or such person's supervisor. (Commodity Exchange Act § 1a(3) and 17 C.F.R. § 1.3 [note] (definition of associated person))

at-the-money. Used to describe a derivative with neither positive nor negative market value to either party.

banging the close. Disrupting the orderly execution of trades in the period before the market close. (Commodity Exchange Act § 4c(a)(5)(B))

bid. Price at which a potential buyer is willing to make a purchase.

Bermudan option. An option that can only be exercised by the holder at specified points during the term of the option.

board of trade. A trading facility for futures, commodity options, and some swaps. (Commodity Exchange Act § 1a(6))

bucketing. Becoming a buyer or a seller of a position that was accepted as agent for execution on an organized market. (Commodity Exchange Act § 4b(a)(2)(D))

call option. An option agreement where the holder of the option has the right, but not the obligation, to buy an asset in the future from a seller for a pre-agreed amount.

Capper-Tincher Act. See *Grain Futures Act of 1922*.

cash settlement. A method whereby, in lieu of a physical exchange of assets referenced in a derivatives contract, parties exchange cash equivalents.

cleared swap. A swap for which a derivatives clearing organization has intermediated as counterparty for each of the original parties to the swap.

clearing determination. A determination by the CFTC that a category of swaps must be cleared.

close-out netting. Process by which multiple mutual present and future financial obligations, such as derivatives trades, documented under one instrument, such as an ISDA Master Agreement, are combined at termination of the instrument into one single amount due or payable by one party to the other.

commodity. All goods, articles, services, rights, and interests other than onions and motion picture box office receipts. (Commodity Exchange Act § 1a(9))

Commodity Exchange Act of 1936. Statute amending the pre-existing Grain Futures Act of 1922 and, as amended, the statute that the Commodity Futures Trading Commission administers.

Commodity Futures Trading Commission or *CFTC*. Federal agency created by the Commodity Futures Trading Commission Act of 1974 to administer the Commodity Exchange Act.

commodity pool. A vehicle where funds are collectively pooled for the purpose of trading commodity futures, commodity options, or swaps. (Commodity Exchange Act § 1a(10))

commodity pool operator. A person who solicits or accepts funds on behalf of a commodity pool. (Commodity Exchange Act § 1a(11))

commodity swap. Any swap that is not a credit, equity, or rate swap. See *credit swap*, *equity swap*, and *rate swap*.

commodity trading advisor. A person who for compensation provides investment advice regarding commodity futures, commodity options, or swaps. (Commodity Exchange Act § 1a(12))

confirmation. Means by which parties to a trade documented via an ISDA Master Agreement document memorialize the details of the trade.

cornering. Purchasing available supply of a scarce resource for the purposes of obtaining a dominant market position. (Commodity Exchange Act § 9(a)(2))

credit default swap. See *credit swap*.

credit risk. the risk of a party's non-performance due to a deterioration in creditworthiness.

credit swap. A swap where payments are calculated by reference to specified events related to third-party indebtedness.

derivative. An instrument with a value derived from the value of an underlying asset. See *futures contract*, *option*, and *swap*.

derivatives clearing organization. An entity providing clearing services in relation to commodity futures, commodity options, or swaps. (Commodity Exchange Act § 1a(15))

designated contract market. A board of trade registered with the CFTC as a board of trade designated as a contract market. Designated contract markets are allowed to permit trading in futures and commodity options by retail participants.

designated self-regulatory organization. Self-regulatory organization with primary responsibility for regulating a CFTC-regulated member of more than one self-regulatory organizations. (17 C.F.R. § 1.3 (definition of self-regulatory organization))

Dodd-Frank Act of 2010. Statute providing the CFTC broad authority over swaps and the SEC broad authority over security-based swaps.

eligible contract participant. A person who, based on registration category or amount available for discretionary investment, is deemed to be non-retail and, therefore, permitted to be a swap counterparty. (Commodity Exchange Act § 1a(18))

end user. A party to a swap who is not a swap dealer, security-based swap dealer, major swap participant, or major security-based swap participant.

end user exception. An exception from otherwise applicable clearing requirements available for some end users.

equity swap. A swap where payments are calculated by reference to one or more equity securities.

excluded commodity. Any intangible commodity such as a financial commodity. (Commodity Exchange Act § 1a(19))

exempt commodity. Any commodity other than an agricultural commodity or excluded commodity. For example, metals or oil. (Commodity Exchange Act § 1a(19))

exercise. To require that, at a pre-agreed price, an asset (or, if applicable, its cash equivalent) be sold to the option holder at a pre-agreed price (for a call option) or bought from the option holder (for a put option).

European option. An option that can be exercised only by the holder at the maturity of the option.

event contract. A derivative where a payment is contingent on an event out of the parties' control such as weather events, election outcome, sporting results, or corporate results.

exchange. A central trading marketplace.

exchange-traded derivative. A derivative traded using a trading facility, such as a designated contract market or swap execution facility.

Financial Crisis. A global liquidity crisis that began in 2007 and resulted in the failure of numerous large financial institutions.

financial end user. An end user engaged in one of specified financial activities used to determine whether CFTC uncleared swap margin requirements apply. (17 C.F.R. § 23.151)

financial entity. An end user that is a one of a number of entities engaged in financial activities described in Commodity Exchange Act § 2(h)(7)(C) used to determine whether CFTC mandatory swaps clearing applies.

Financial Stability Board. An international body created by the Group of Twenty as a means of encouraging international economic cooperation.

Financial Stability Oversight Council. An inter-agency body responsible for assessing and responding to threats to U.S. financial stability and vested with, among others, the authority to require that a non-bank financial company submit to a strict supervision regime. (Dodd-Frank Act § 111)

fixed amount or *fixed leg.* An amount required to be paid by a party to a swap and calculated by reference to a constant value.

floating amount or *floating leg.* An amount required to be paid by a party to a swap and calculated by reference to a value that can change on each payment date.

floor broker. A person who places trades directly on the floor of a designated contract market on behalf of customers. (Commodity Exchange Act § 1a(22))

floor trader. A person with the right to place trades directly on the floor of a designated contract market on his or her own behalf. (Commodity Exchange Act § 1a(23))

foreign board of trade. A board of trade established outside of the United States. Foreign boards of trade seeking to offer U.S. persons access are required to register with the CFTC. See *board of trade.* (17 C.F.R. § 1.3 (definition of foreign board of trade))

foreign exchange swap. See *rate swap.*

forward contract. An off-exchange agreement to buy or sell something for future physical delivery.

Future Trading Act of 1921. The first federal statute enacted for broad regulation of commodity futures. Was subsequently invalidated by *Hill v. Wallace*, 259 U.S. 44 (1922), and replaced by the Grain Futures Act of 1922. See **Grain Futures Act of 1922.**

futures commission merchant. A person who solicits or accepts orders for commodity futures, commodity options, or swaps and, in association therewith, accepts money, securities, or property as margin for such transactions. (Commodity Exchange Act § 1a(28))

futures contract. A contract to buy or sell an asset at a pre-agreed price on a future date.

Futures Industry Association. Trade association for futures and exchanged-traded commodity options.

FX swap. See *rate swap.*

governmental special entity. A state, state agency, municipality, or government benefit plan. (17 C.F.R. §23.451(a)(3))

Grain Futures Act of 1922. Statute following invalidation on constitutional grounds of the Future Trading Act of 1921 and the first successful federal effort for broad regulation of commodity futures.

Group of Twenty. Forum for international economic cooperation among the twenty most-developed economies.

hedge fund. A private investment vehicle structured to limit regulatory requirements and oversight.

hedging. Entering into a transaction with the goal of mitigating an existing risk.

initial margin. An amount of collateral calculated on a per contract or trade basis intended to provide a buffer for intra-day changes to mark-to-market values.

interest rate swap. See *rate swap.*

in-the-money. Used to describe a derivative with positive market value from the perspective of the party with the positive exposure.

International Organization of Securities Commissions. An international cooperative forum for national securities and futures regulators.

International Swaps and Derivatives Association. Trade association for derivatives other than futures and exchange-traded commodity options.

introducing broker. A person who solicits or accepts orders for commodity futures, commodity options, or swaps. (Commodity Exchange Act §1a(31))

ISDA. See *International Swaps and Derivatives Association.*

ISDA Master Agreement. Standardized agreement for the documentation of off-exchange derivatives developed by the International Swaps and Derivatives association. Most common variants are the 1992 and the 2002 ISDA Master Agreement.

ISDA Schedule. Part of the ISDA Master Agreement, the Schedule is the means by which parties modify, augment, or complete elections contemplated in the form ISDA Master Agreement.

leverage contract merchant. A legacy category of CFTC registration formerly used by entities offering to enter into commodity transactions with retail customers on a leveraged or margined basis. (17 C.F.R. §1.3 (definition of leverage contract merchant))

LIBOR. See *London InterBank Offer Rate.*

London InterBank Offer Rate. An average of interest rates that select banks estimate they would have to pay if they borrowed from other banks in the London market. It is available in various tenors (i.e., length of time to maturity) and currencies, including the U.S. dollar. It is expected to be phased out by December 31, 2021, for most currencies, and June 30, 2023, for the most commonly-traded U.S. dollar tenors.

made available to trade determination. A determination by the CFTC or a formal declaration by a designated contract market or swap execution facility that a category of swap already subject to mandatory clearing is now available to trade on a trading facility. Has the effect of requiring such swaps to be traded on-facility.

major security-based swap participant. A person, other than a security-based swap dealer, maintaining a substantial speculative position in security-based swaps or whose security-based swaps exposure to counterparties could have serious adverse effects on U.S. financial stability. Additionally, any highly leveraged financial entity that maintains a substantial position in security-based swaps, whether for hedging or speculation, is a major security-based swap participant. (15 U.S.C. § 78c(a)(67))

major swap participant. A person, other than a swap dealer, maintaining a substantial speculative position in swaps or whose swaps exposure to counterparties could have serious adverse effects on U.S. financial stability. Additionally, any highly leveraged financial entity that maintains a substantial position in swaps, whether for hedging or speculation, is a major swap participant. (Commodity Exchange Act § 1a(33))

market risk. the risk of financial exposure due to the fluctuation in value of an asset

mark-to-market. A method of valuing a financial position by assessing what price it would obtain if bought or sold in the marketplace.

mixed swap. A swap subject to CFTC and SEC jurisdiction because it combines elements of swaps subject to CFTC jurisdiction and security-based swaps subject to SEC jurisdiction. (Commodity Exchange Act § 1a(47)(D))

narrow-based security index. Generally, an index with nine or fewer securities or that otherwise is highly concentrated in a few securities. (Commodity Exchange Act § 1a(35))

National Futures Association. Self-regulatory organization for much of the futures industry.

netting. See *close-out netting, payment netting*, and *set-off*.

non-financial end user. An end user that is not a financial end user and, therefore, exempt from CFTC uncleared swap margin requirements. See *financial end user*.

non-financial entity. An end user that is not a financial entity and, therefore, exempt from CFTC mandatory swaps clearing. See *financial entity*.

notional amount. An amount used in swap transactions as a multiplier to calculate swap payments.

offer. Price at which a potential seller is willing to make a sale.

off-exchange derivative. A derivative traded privately off-facility via bilateral agreement.

on-facility derivative. See *exchange-traded derivative*.

option. An agreement whereby one party grants to the other a right, but not an obligation, to take a course of action. (Commodity Exchange Act § 1a(36))

out-of-the-money. Used to describe a derivative with negative market value from the perspective of the party with the negative exposure.

over-the-counter derivative or *OTC derivative.* See *off-exchange derivative.*

payment netting. Process by which, if an amount is owed by X to Y and an amount is simultaneously owed by Y to X, these amounts are combined so that there is only one payment. For example, if X owed Y $100 and Y owed X $75 with payment netting both obligations would be satisfied by X paying Y $25.

physical delivery. A settlement method where one or both parties delivery a physical asset referenced in a derivative.

position limit. A limit on the number of commodity futures and commodity options positions that can be held referencing specified commodities.

premium. The amount paid for an option by the holder of the option.

prudential regulator. The Federal Reserve Board, Office of the Comptroller of the Currency, Federal Deposit Insurance Corporation, Farm Credit Administration, or Federal Housing Finance Agency. (Commodity Exchange Act § 1a(39))

put option. An option agreement where the holder of the option has the right, but not the obligation, to sell an asset in the future to a buyer for a pre-agreed amount.

rate swap. A swap where payments are calculated by reference to a rate, such as an interest rate or foreign exchange rate.

registered entity. A derivatives clearing organization, designated contract market, swap data repository, or swap execution facility. (Commodity Exchange Act § 1a(40))

retail foreign exchange dealer. An entity offering to be a counterparty in certain types of leveraged or margined retail foreign exchange transactions. (17 C.F.R. § 5.1(h)(1))

retail market. A market in which non-eligible contract participants may participate.

secured overnight financing rate. The volume-weighted median of repurchase transactions with U.S. Treasury securities as collateral calculated by the New York Federal Reserve Bank and intended to be a broad measure of the cost of secured borrowing of cash overnight.

Securities and Exchange Commission or *SEC.* Federal agency created by the Securities Exchange Act of 1934 with the authority to regulate securities and security-based swaps.

security-based swap. A swap that references a security or a narrow-based security index. The SEC has jurisdiction over security-based swaps. See *narrow-based security index.* (15 U.S.C. § 78c(a)(68)) *security-based swap data repository.* An SEC registrant that provides a central recordkeeping facility for security-based swap transactions. (15 U.S.C. § 78c(a)(75))

security-based swap dealer. A marketmaker or dealer in security-based swaps. The SEC has jurisdiction over security-based swap dealers. (15 U.S.C. § 78c(a)(71))

security-based swap execution facility. A trading facility for security-based swaps that is limited in participation to eligible contract participants. Security-based swap execution facilities are regulated by the SEC. (15 U.S.C. § 78c(a)(77))

self-regulatory organization. A private member organization that has the authority to make and enforce rules applicable to the members.

set-off. Process by which off-setting obligations between two parties incurred under separate instruments are combined, resulting in one party owing a net amount to the other. For example, if X has borrowed $1,000 from Y and Y owes X $800 under a terminated ISDA Master Agreement, X might exercise a set-off right, if one is legally available, to pay $200 to Y and forgive Y the payment of the $800 under the terminated ISDA Master Agreement in full satisfaction of its obligation to repay the loan.

Shad-Johnson Accord. Agreement between then SEC chair, John Shad, and then CFTC chair, Phillip Johnson, by which the agencies agreed on the jurisdictional dividing line between their agencies. Ratified by Congress via the Futures Trading Act of 1982.

slamming the close. See *banging the close.*

SOFR. See *secured overnight financing rate.*

special entity. A federal agency, a state, state agency, municipality, and certain pension plans and endowments. (Commodity Exchange Act § 4s(h)(2)(C))

speculation. Entering into a transaction that incurs an increased economic exposure in return for a potential economic reward.

spoofing. A form of market manipulation whereby a party places a bid or offer without having an intent to trade. (Commodity Exchange Act § 4c(a)(5)(C))

spread. For exchange-traded derivatives, the difference between the current bid price and the current offer price. For swaps, an amount added to swap payments as the swap dealer's profit and compensation for its exposure to the credit risk of its counterparty.

squeeze. A squeeze is where one party has control over the long futures contracts during a known shortage of the physical in the cash market and then demands delivery on all of the contracts.

strike price. The price, if an option is exercised, that will be paid for the underlying asset or its cash equivalent.

swap. An agreement to exchange payments periodically using predetermined pricing mechanisms. The CFTC has jurisdiction over swaps, except for security-based swaps. See *security-based swap.* (Commodity Exchange Act § 1a(47)) *swap data repository.* A CFTC registrant that provides a central recordkeeping facility for swap transactions. (Commodity Exchange Act § 1a(48))

swap dealer. A marketmaker or dealer in swaps. (Commodity Exchange Act § 1a(49))

swap execution facility. A trading facility for swaps that is limited in participation to eligible contract participants. Swap execution facilities are regulated by the CFTC (Commodity Exchange Act § 1a(50))

tenor. Length of time to maturity.

trading facility. A facility that allows for access by multiple offerors and multiple offerees for the purposes of derivatives trading. (Commodity Exchange Act § 1a(51))

Treasury Amendment. An amendment to the predecessor bill of what became the Commodity Futures Trading Commission Act of 1974, which carved-out, among others, off-exchange foreign exchange transactions from the CFTC's jurisdiction.

variation margin. A calculation of an amount of collateral equal to what the overall amount one party would owe to another in the event specified derivatives exposures were liquidated.

violating a bid or offer. Entering into a trade at a level lower than the highest bid price or higher than the lowest offer price. (Commodity Exchange Act § 4c(a)(5)(A))

virtual currency. A variety of fully digital items providing some or all of the functions currency has traditionally provided such as being a medium of exchange, unit of account, and store of value.

Volcker Rule. A provision of the Dodd-Frank Act named after Paul Volcker, the former chair of the Federal Reserve Board. Requires U.S. banks and non-U.S. banks with branches or agencies in the United States to refrain from proprietary trading or investments in certain hedge funds or private equity funds. (Dodd-Frank Act § 619)

wash sale. A set of trades that completely off-set so that there is no economic impact to either party. (Commodity Exchange Act § 4c(a)(2))

Index